D0138704

Fourth Edition

Career Guidance and Counseling Through the Life Span

Systematic Approaches

Edwin L. Herr
THE PENNSYLVANIA STATE UNIVERSITY

Stanley H. Cramer
STATE UNIVERSITY OF NEW YORK AT BUFFALO

HarperCollins*Publishers*

Dedications

Samuel L. Herr (August 23, 1903–September 7, 1968), weaver, laborer, mechanic, school custodian, whose respect for the dignity of work was exceeded only by his respect for the dignity of people.

Amber, Christopher, and Alicia Herr, whose grandfather would be proud that they have incorporated his legacy and love.

Ruth Kraus Faber, retailer, homemaker, retiree, and world's best mother-in-law.

Liz, Lauren, and Matthew, who inherited all the best from all of their grandparents.

Executive Editor: Christopher Jennison
Full-Service Manager: Michael Weinstein
Production Coordinator: Cindy Funkhouser
Text Design: Publication Services, Inc.
Cover Design: Georgia Parker; Publication Services, Inc.
Cover Illustration: Georgia Parker; Publication Services, Inc.
Production Manager: Priscilla Taguer
Compositor: Publication Services, Inc.
Printer and Binder: R. R. Donnelley & Sons Company
Cover Printer: New England Book Components, Inc.

Career Guidance and Counseling Through the Life Span: Systematic Approaches, Fourth Edition

Library of Congress Cataloging-in-Publication Data

Herr, Edwin L.
Career guidance and counseling through the life span : systematic approaches / Edwin L. Herr, Stanley H. Cramer, – 4th ed.
p. cm.
Includes bibliographical references and index.
ISBN 0-673-52196-6
1. Vocational guidance–United States. I. Cramer, Stanley H. II. Title.
HF5382.5.U5H39 1991
331.702'0973–dc20 91-33619
CIP

93 94 95 9 8 7 6 5 4

Brief Contents

Contents

Preface

Career guidance and career counseling in the United States, and in much of the rest of the world, are in a dynamic state. Maturing theoretical perspectives, transitions to transnational and global economies, dramatic shifts in occupational structures, high unemployment rates among some groups of youths and adults, demands for higher levels of literacy, numeracy, flexibility, and teachability in the labor forces of industrialized nations, concerns about the quality of work life and worker productivity, and changes in the composition of the labor force have combined to change the content, processes, and consumers of career counseling. These factors have increased the national and international significance of career guidance and career counseling and made them more comprehensive in their application to settings and populations across the life span.

In this book we chronicle the evolution of career guidance and counseling from the 1800s to the present. In addition to tracing the roots of professional counseling and counseling psychology in vocational guidance and vocational psychology, we examine the concepts and language systems on which current approaches to interventions in career behavior rest. We also discuss the applications of systematic approaches to career guidance and counseling for children, youths, and adults in various settings: schools, colleges and universities, business and industry, and community agencies.

Several major themes are stressed in this edition. First is the recognition of the effect of career services as instruments of human development and mental health. To understand this effect, it is necessary to probe the history of career guidance, career counseling, and counseling psychology; contemporary shifts in social values and in the meaning of work; international economic competition; change in occupational structures, work, and mental health; and the theoretical approaches that have shaped current views of the career development of persons across the life span. These topics are examined in Chapters 1 through 5.

The second primary theme emphasizes our belief that career guidance and career counseling require developmental rather than solely remedial approaches. This belief mandates that career interventions be thought of as systematic programs or processes designed to effect certain preplanned or practitioner-client agreed-upon behavioral outcomes. To aid in the tailoring of career guidance or career counseling programs to the special characteristics and needs of children, youths, and adults, we consider in Chapter 6 the stages and techniques of systematic planning appropriate to different settings: workplaces, schools and universities, and rehabilitation settings. In Chapters 7 through 11 we examine the rationale for and the developmental characteristics of career intervention techniques particularly important to elementary, middle school, and high school students and to adults in higher education, in the workplace, and in other community settings. Salient features of this fourth edition are the expanded treatment of career guidance and counseling in international contexts and the global economy, among diverse adult populations, and in the workplace. Chapters 12 and 13 give particular attention to special adult career problems of major concern in business and industrial settings.

The third major theme of the book is the identification of particular techniques, assessment devices, materials, and resources that can help career specialists implement theories, planning strategies, and program models with individuals and groups. Although much pertinent information is interspersed throughout the book, Chapters 14 through 16 focus directly on these applications.

The fourth theme accents the research and social issues that must be resolved as the systematic provision of career interventions moves to advanced levels of professional maturity across the life span. In Chapter 17 we address such issues, as well as the growing trend to view quantitative and qualitative research methods as different but complementary ways of studying careers and career interventions.

To enhance the usefulness of this edition, a separate instructor's manual is provided; it includes suggestions for use of the text, learning objectives for each chapter, a large array of learning activities that can be tailored to different student groups, examination items for each chapter, and sample course syllabi from across the country.

This text reflects not only ideas and knowledge that we have gathered over many years but also suggestions made by colleagues. We thank our reviewers—Dr. Spencer Niles of the University of Virginia and Dr. Arnold Spokane of Lehigh University—who read the revised manuscript and offered their helpful criticisms and recommendations. We also wish to express our debt to the many persons cited in this book and to those in particular who gave us permission to quote their work. Just as concepts of career guidance and career counseling have evolved over time, our understanding of these processes have been shaped by many friends, colleagues, associates, and students who have shared their insights with us in person and in the professional literature. We are grateful to the long line of bright and talented people who have influenced our professional lives. We are also indebted to Judy Kauffman, whose word processing and organizational excellence have been major factors in bringing the book to a successful conclusion, and to Mike Redford, whose work in helping to compile the revised bibliography has been of major importance in getting the revised manuscript ready for publication.

Finally, we wish to express our personal debts to Donald E. Super, Professor Emeritus, and to the late Charles Newton Morris, both of the Teachers College of Columbia University. Each man in his unique way has served both of us as an intellectual guide, friend, and mentor. Much of both men lives in this book—in substance and in spirit.

Edwin L. Herr

Stanley H. Cramer

CHAPTER 1

PERSPECTIVES ON CAREER GUIDANCE AND COUNSELING: NEEDS, TRADITIONS, AND EMERGING CHALLENGES

Key Concepts

- Career counseling, career education, and career guidance are not interchangeable in meaning.
- Career guidance is a term that is evolving in response to economic, political, and social changes, and to changes in techniques and content.
- Career guidance encompasses a vocabulary of work, individual development, and interventions in career behavior.
- Career guidance, career education, and career counseling are important to children, youth, and adults in the anticipation, planning, preparation for, and implementation of work.
- Career guidance, career education, and career counseling can be systematically planned and required counselor competencies specified for each.
- Career counseling, education, and guidance are international phenomena. They are becoming major sociopolitical emphases in national development plans concerned with human resource development and the global economy.

As thoughtful observers consider the challenges to career guidance, career counseling, or career education during the 1990s and the early decades of the twenty-first century, they face the overriding reality that as the structure of the the world's economy is transformed from a collection of separate national economies to an interdependent global economy, new demands are placed upon human resources in nation after nation. It is becoming clear in national development plans, in industrial strategic goal setting, in international forums, and in the world's media that the key factor in a nation's ability to compete in the growing global economy is the quality of that nation's work force as defined by the literacy, numeracy, flexibility, teachability, and employability that characterize it.

Many nations in Europe and, particularly, in east Asia have for several decades understood the coming challenge to their human resources. In response, they have set new standards for the unparalleled development of human resources as national priorities and created technological and organizational systems necessary to help maximize the productivity of these human resources (Schlosstein, 1989, p. xv). A major component in these systems of human resource development is the range and deployment of career services—career guidance, career counseling, career education—designed to implement national policies concerned with nurturing human resources as assets to be equipped with the knowledge, skill, and attitudes required to cope with the economic and personal challenges of the future, such as personal flexibility, competence, purpose, and productivity.

Implicit, if not explicit, in this book is that career guidance and counseling are becoming increasingly important sociopolitical processes in national development plans, policies, and legislation concerned with educational, career, and employment issues. As individual nations become increasingly interdependent players in a global economy, they share concerns about

- Ways to develop functionally literate and productive work forces
- Mechanisms to help youth make the transition from school to work and to facilitate the demographic shifts in access to work of emerging work forces—women, minority group members, immigrants
- Procedures to help persons adjust to work effectively and obtain job satisfaction
- Strategies to address high rates of youth unemployment or rapidly aging work forces
- Effective approaches to absorbing immigrant populations into the work force
- Methods by which employers can become increasingly responsive to the needs of employees by viewing them in holistic rather than fragmented ways as assets to be nurtured rather than costs to be reduced, as objects of personnel development not just personnel management
- Paradigms that allow career guidance and counseling to facilitate mental health as well as economic well being.

These issues and related ones are domains in which career guidance and counseling are increasingly the preferred methods of intervention or development.

Although the shape and substance of career guidance and counseling vary among nations that have different levels of industrial development or different human resource concerns, the impact and importance of those who provide career guidance and counseling and the processes they provide are assuming greater visibility in both philosophical and practical terms. One such view is that of Watts, Dartois, and Plant (1988). In a report entitled *Educational and Vocational Guidance Services for the 14–25 Age Group in the European Community,* these authors suggest that "educational and vocational guidance services have a key role to play in any advanced society, both in fostering *efficiency* in the allocation and use of human resources, and in fostering *social equity* in access to educational and vocational opportunities" (p. i). Subsequent parts of this book review American reports that extend these concepts of efficiency and social equity, thereby broadening the notions of career counseling and career guidance as perceived through U.S. lenses. Because perspectives evolve over time, the next sections will deal with the transition in the United States from the term *vocational guidance* to that of *career guidance*.

CAREER GUIDANCE: A TERM IN TRANSITION

Career guidance is both an old and a new term. It is old in the sense that it rests on the heritage yielded by three-quarters of a century of vocational guidance in America. It is old in the role it has played in the origins of counseling in this nation at the beginning of the twentieth century. It is also old in the part it has played in the shaping of counseling psychology as an area of specialization distinct from clinical psychology in the early 1950s (Herr & Cramer, 1987). Career guidance is new because its emphases, conceptual models, and consumer populations tend to go beyond those typically associated with earlier models of vocational guidance and to embrace life-span career concerns. These concerns transcend initial choice of work and initial occupational adjustment to address questions of work and family roles, work and leisure, and work and mental health. Such questions, along with the transition points throughout life when decisions about such matters are implemented, constitute the content of career guidance or career counseling. The evolution of career guidance has represented a series of "paradigm shifts" (Kuhn, 1962) in conceptual models and models of practice throughout this century.

Emerging theoretical perspectives, rapid changes in occupational content, economic realities, legislative mandates, problems of youth and adult unemployment, concerns about the quality of work life and worker productivity, questions about the school-to-work transition, and shifting labor force demographics (such as greater participation by women and minorities) have subtly but inexorably redefined the content, the time spectrum, the technologies, and the consumers of career guidance. Such pressures and forces have increased the comprehensive nature of career guidance and made it a process of international importance (Herr, 1982b; Herr, 1990). During the evolution of such change, it has become obvious to theorists, researchers, and practitioners that career guidance does not operate in a political, economic, and social vacuum. Rather, it is within these contexts that anxieties about achievement and other purposes, information deficits, indecisiveness and role confusion originate and become the content of career guidance.

The use of the term *career guidance* has been tentative for nearly 20 years, having burst into increasingly common usage only since the early 1970s. Career guidance, in its present form, has been stimulated by many phenomena: rapid and diverse social and occupational change, maturation of theoretical perspectives about career behavior, and rising demand in many settings, populated by both youths and adults, for assistance in career planning, job search, and job adjustment skills. Career education, a major educational movement spawned in the 1970s, was also instrumental in reasserting the priority that career guidance needs to have in schools, colleges and universities, and workplaces. Increasingly, human resource systems, employee assistance programs, and the organization of career services in corporations and governmental agencies have further extended the application of career guidance and career counseling to new settings and populations. In this chapter we will examine the evolution from vocational guidance to career guidance during the twentieth century; describe some of the language, issues, and trends associated with this evolution; discuss career counseling as separate from career guidance; and place the support for career guidance into international perspective.

In Chapter 2 we examine contemporary meanings of work and ways to view the characteristics of the workplace and work competencies. In Chapter 3 we discuss the occupational structure, its changing nature, and its classification, and in Chapter 4 we consider the variety of current theoretical and research models essential to understanding career behavior in both *macro* and *micro* terms. In this case macro views attempt to explain the unfolding of career identity, choice, and adjustment across the life span; micro views attempt to explain specific processes of career development, for example, decision making. In Chapter 5 we explore the career problems of specific population groups (for example, women, handicapped, minorities, and so on).

To oversimplify the issue, it is probably useful to suggest that Chapters 2 through 5 describe much of the *content* of career counseling and career guidance: differences in occupational and life alternatives; the influences that shape work values, career identity, and choice-making strategies; and the special circumstances relating to access and adjustment to work associated with gender, social circumstances, disability, and other factors. The remaining 12 chapters of the book tend to describe the multiple *interventions* subsumed by the terms *career guidance, career counseling,* or *career education*. Thus, the descriptions of how work behavior is formed, what influences it, and how it is individually manifested are the objects or targets to which these career interventions are directed. The final chapter discusses research issues related to understanding, extending, and strengthening such interventions.

VOCATIONAL GUIDANCE: A HISTORICAL EVOLUTION

Although it is possible to trace both the philosophies and practices of vocational guidance far into antiquity (Williamson, 1965), our concern here is confined to the rise of vocational guidance in the United States, beginning in the late 1800s.

As the United States was rapidly emerging as a major industrial nation from the 1870s to the early 1900s, fed by immigration to both coasts, and experiencing a large movement of persons from the farms to the cities, considerable attention began to focus on the effects of these events on the American people. Adequate education for children and effective placement of adults into a rapidly growing industrial complex were seen by many prominent spokespersons as social imperatives. Additional concerns of the times were how to effectively distribute immigrants across the spectrum of available occupations; how to bridge the gap between school and the realities of the adult world; how to reduce unnecessary job shifts caused by the large number of workers who moved from job to job because they were not aware of their capabilities or the opportunities available to them; and how to alleviate general job dissatisfaction among workers. (As subsequent parts of this book will attest, most of these concerns have contemporary parallels in this nation and in other industrialized societies.)

These practical considerations were reinforced by the powerful influence of the reform movements of that time. The social reformers, the settlement house workers, and other groups concerned with human rights were making strong efforts to have workers viewed not as chattels of industry but rather as dignified persons with a right to determine their own destinies. Such a philosophy was evident in a document published by the U.S. Bureau of Education (predecessor of the U.S. Office of Education) in 1918, reflecting upon the conditions from which vocational guidance was rising:

> Education in a democracy, both within and without the school, should develop in each individual the knowledge, interests, ideals, habits and powers whereby he will find his place and use that place to shape both himself and society toward ever nobler ends. (Rosengarten, 1936, p. xix)

Influences leading to a rudimentary form of vocational guidance appeared at the turn of this century. Each of the following persons made a significant contribution to the creation of a climate susceptible to the assumptions and procedures upon which vocational guidance could be based: William Rainey Harper, on "The Scientific Study of the Student"; G. Stanley Hall, on child study; Hugo Munsterberg, on occupational choice and worker performance; John Dewey, on the restructuring of education; and Jesse B. Davis and Eli W. Weaver, on educational and career problems of students.

At the beginning of the twentieth century, there was no scientific basis for vocational guidance as we know it today. Alfred Binet had not yet brought his intelligence scales from France. There was no *Dictionary of Occupational Titles* or *Occupational Outlook Handbook*. There were no comprehensive classification systems to describe the American occupational structure. Only an elementary understanding of individual differences and the crudest beginnings of aptitude or performance testing existed. Instead, palmistry, phrenology, and physiognomy were the methods widely used to obtain insights into one's future (Rosengarten, 1936).

Although there were some examples of vocational guidance in the schools in the late 1800s, the more likely sources for these services were philanthropic organizations, settlement houses, the Young Men's Christian Association, and a number of private "vocation bureaus."

Enter Frank Parsons

In 1909 Frank Parsons, a man who is considered the primary architect of vocational guidance in the United States, came on the scene. An engineer by training, Parsons had spent much of his life dealing with various reform movements. During the 1880s and 1890s, he had been highly involved with settlement house activities along the northeastern coast, especially in Boston. Under the general credo that "It is better to choose a vocation than merely to hunt a job," Parsons established the Vocations Bureau in Boston. Parsons worked to provide a scientific basis for assisting immigrants and others in effectively choosing work. He also became an outspoken critic of the Boston public school system.

Parsons contended that in the early education of youth, "We must train our students to full powers of action . . . in the various lines of useful work so far as possible according to their aptitudes as brought out by scientific tests and varied experience" (Stephens, 1970, p. 40). Parsons's posthumously published book, *Choosing a Vocation* (1909), elaborated various techniques that he found useful in helping adolescents identify or diagnose their capabilities and choose jobs with reasonable expecations of success. To accomplish these goals, Parsons advocated a wide variety of means including reading biographies, observing workers in their settings, and examining existing occupational descriptions.

Parsons's most enduring contribution was his outline of the process of vocational guidance or, as he called the procedure, "true reasoning." In his view, vocational guidance consisted of three steps:

> First, a clear understanding of yourself, aptitudes, abilities, interests, resources, limitations, and other qualities. Second, a knowledge of the requirements and conditions of success, advantages and disadvantages, compensation, opportunities, and prospects in different lines of work. Third, true reasoning on the relations of these two groups of facts. (Parsons, 1909, p. 5)

This schema defined the elements of what is now known as an actuarial or trait-and-factor approach to counseling. Such a position assumes that the individual can be described as possessing certain traits (interests, skills, aptitudes, and so on), that different occupations or educational alternatives can be described as requiring differing amounts and configurations of such traits, and that by matching individual traits and occupational requirements through a procedure such as "true reasoning" a choice would occur. More important, Parsons's three-step procedure required better and fuller information about individual differences and methods of assessment (first step), occupations (second step), and the decision-making process itself (third step). Although many other approaches to vocational guidance and counseling have been presented in the ensuing eight decades, much of the history of vocational guidance in this century can be understood in terms of which Parsons's three steps was most dominant in the theoretical positions and practices of a particular decade (Herr, 1977a).

From 1909 until the present, the first two steps, in particular, of Parsons's formulation have spurred research and developmental efforts. The first step has stimulated psychometric efforts to identify and measure individual differences and determine their relationship to occupational satisfaction or success. The second step has stimulated attention to the acquisition and use of occupational information. Together, the use of tests and information with clients has had a continuing effect on vocational guidance practices up to the present. More recently, the third step, true reasoning, has been given considerable research and theoretical attention under the general rubric of decision making.

It is important to note that what is usually described in the professional literature as guidance and counseling or counseling psychology began, in fact, as vocational guidance. The original intent of Parsons and his contemporaries was to provide direct assistance to persons needing to make occupational choices and was not oriented to the range of personal-social adjustments later incorporated into the provinces of counselors and psychologists. Indeed, vocational guidance and vocational education were seen as complementary parts of a comprehensive reform movement, focusing on the rational distribution of persons within a growing reservoir of occupational opportunity.

The First Fifty Years of Vocational Guidance

Stephens has contended that

> To many leaders of the vocational reform movement . . . it was apparent that vocational education was but the first part of a package of needed educational reforms. They argued that a school curriculum and educational goals that mirrored the occupational structure created merely a platform and impetus for launching youth into the world of work. What was clearly needed to consummate the launch were guidance mechanisms that would insure their safe and efficient arrival on the job. Without guidance experts it was argued, other efforts at reform would be aborted. . . . Therefore, in the name of social and economic efficiency, the argument continued, the youth who had been carefully trained would also have to be carefully counseled into a suitable occupational niche. (Stephens, 1970, p. xiv)

Thus, for the first few decades of the twentieth century, guidance and counseling (really vocational guidance) were joined with vocational (industrial) education in response to the social and manpower problems of the day.

Initially, vocational guidance emphasized a "tryout-through-training" approach with emphasis on occupational information. The information available was highly objective, only minimally related to the psychological appraisal of the individual, and delivered through counseling that was essentially directive and advice giving in substance (Miller, 1973). According to E. G. Williamson, vocational educators predominated as vocational guidance practitioners in the early decades of the 1990s. Their confidence in work descriptions as adequate bases for vocational choice and their lack of training in psychology tended to restrict vocational guidance to providing information. Unfortunately, this information was largely of untested validity and did not give commensurate attention to the analysis of the individual (Williamson, 1965). In essence, step one of Parsons's formulation was abandoned in favor of step two. Paterson (1938), speaking about the "genesis of modern guidance," indicated that the vocational guidance movement had become fixed at the level of vocational information. Williamson has argued that this situation existed until at least 1950, when the National Vocational Guidance Association broadened its objectives from the acquisition and proffer of occupational information to a more emphatic concern for the psychological good of the individual.

From 1900 to 1930, three trends prevailed: vocational guidance emphasized the study of occupations rather than the study of individuals; vocational educators predominated as vocational guidance practitioners; and vocational guidance and vocational education were largely seen as complementary components of a total effort to distribute students and others across the proliferating occupational structure.

Two independent approaches to vocational guidance tended to arise in the 1920s and the 1930s: one provided by school counselors (guidance and counseling) and the other provided by vocational educators and specialists employed by the U.S. Department of Labor or by rehabilitation agencies. Except for a few major centers for vocational assistance during the Depression, efforts to rehabilitate the physically handicapped, and the incorporation of vocational guidance procedures into military classification during World War II, vocational guidance, when it existed, was aimed at adolescents and young workers seeking initial employment.

During the 1920s, 1930s, and 1940s, vocational guidance, as practiced by the relatively few school counselors then in existence, became increasingly responsive to several forces. One force was the growing knowledge of individual differences, the awareness of personality dynamics in vocational choice and work adjustment, and the general influence of a psychological approach to vocational guidance. A second force, also psychological, was a growing developmental view of the individual. Reinforced by perspectives such as those of Dewey, Stratemeyer, and the so-called progressives, American education took on "the rhetoric of child-centered pedagogy" (Cremin, 1961). During this period, progressives applied Freudian concepts to child study. Their efforts in the schools focused principally on mental health rather than on skill preparation except for the occupational education sponsored by and largely confined to definitions promulgated by the Smith-Hughes Act of 1917. An even more developmentalist notion was espoused by the advocates of a life adjustment approach to education. This approach advocated that the student learn facts across fields of knowledge relating to specific problems that recur in life, that the artificial barriers between school life and the life of the world beyond the school be minimized, and that the elements of each life situation have a cumulative effect in subsequent life stages and educational experiences. Although using leisure time wisely and earning a living were among the persistent life situations with which students had to cope, life adjustment education related these situations to the affective life of the child and to longitudinal processes rather than to the more narrow definition of acquiring task skills in specific occupations.

A third force that affected perspectives on vocational guidance and counseling challenged information giving as the primary technique and instead advocated therapeutic treatment or psychotherapy as alternatives.

Although the direct effects of the three forces just cited on vocational guidance and counseling practitioners, mainly school counselors, are not easy to document, it is fair to suggest that these forces tended collectively to tie guidance and counseling to an educational mission, to a diagnostic-clinical rather than vocational and information-giving approach to students, and to the psychological or affective rather than performance aspects of individuals. As a consequence, vocational guidance became less than a top priority of school counselors.

On the other hand, the type of vocational guidance practiced primarily by vocational educators and manpower specialists was receiving a somewhat different form of stimulus. The Great Depression of the 1930s had reaffirmed the importance of job training in the various federal programs (Civilian Conservation Corps and others) instituted during that time for the occupationally displaced. Vocational educators were active in developing such programs. More important, perhaps, was the U.S.

Department of Labor publication of the *Dictionary of Occupational Titles* and institution of the *Occupational Outlook Service,* which gave a level of comprehensiveness and credibility to occupational information unavailable prior to that time. The Minnesota Stabilization Research Institute, as well as other similar agencies, undertook studies of vocational choice and adjustment in efforts to identify and demonstrate methods of educational and industrial rehabilitation of workers uprooted by industrial changes. One outcome of this activity was the development of new tests of vocational capabilities (Crites, 1969). Upon the United States' entry into World War II, the application of psychometrics to the selection and classification of personnel assumed massive proportions, and the expertise of vocational educators was instrumental in the development of training programs for an increasingly technical military establishment.

These experiences caused vocational educators to change their perspectives on vocational guidance; they became strongly imbued with a market demand philosophy. Vocational educators viewed vocational guidance as a mechanism for matching individual and job or individual and education curriculum. Such an approach emphasized the importance of individual competency or aptitude for job training or available jobs. This was the criterion to which vocational guidance addressed itself rather than individual preferences, interests, or values—criteria seen as primary in more psychologically based viewpoints.

The Precursors of Career Guidance and Counseling

For most of its first 50 years, whether responding to a market demand philosophy or a more psychologically oriented one, vocational guidance was concerned with predicting occupational choice or occupational success from an individual's test scores prior to entry into the labor market. The primary emphasis was on matching the aptitude for performance from the results of test profiles of those seeking employment to the requirements of available options, always attempting to maximize the compatibility between the two. Vocational guidance was largely confined to one point in the life of the individual, that is, either entry into the labor market or readjustment with an immediate alternative after occupational dislocation. Further, its major reference point was the requirements of the occupational structure rather than individual preferences or values.

Since 1950, this traditional view of vocational guidance has been repeatedly challenged. In that year, Robert Hoppock, president of the National Vocational Guidance Association, announced that the traditional view of vocational guidance was "crumbling" (Hoppock, 1950). In 1951, Donald Super recommended revision of the official National Vocational Guidance Association definition of vocational guidance, one that had stood since 1937: "the process of assisting the individual to choose an occupation, prepare for it, enter upon it, and progress in it" (Super, 1951). The 1951 revision recommended by Super amended this perspective by defining vocational guidance as "the process of helping a person to develop and accept an integrated and adequate picture of himself and of his role in the world of work, to test this concept against reality, and to convert it into a reality, with satisfaction to himself and to society."

This definition did not emphasize the provision of occupational information at a particular time, nor did it emphasize a simple matching of individual to job. Rather, it emphasized the psychological nature of vocational choice. Indeed, Super's definition effectively blended the personal and vocational dimensions of guidance, which previously had been arbitrarily separated, into a unified whole. The resulting base for conceptions of vocational guidance was self-concept oriented. It focused primarily on self-understanding and self-acceptance, to which occupational and educational alternatives available to the individual can be related. It suggested that the earlier rationale for vocational guidance was too limited, its emphasis on occupation alone outmoded, and its techniques applied too mechanically. As Crites has suggested, "More than any other career psychologist, Super has been instrumental in freeing career counseling from the static, single-choice-at-a-point-in-time concept of decision-making drawing attention to the potential contributions of sociology and economics to the field, and placing the study of career behavior in the context of human development" (Crites, 1981, p. 7).

TREATMENT OR STIMULUS?

Perhaps the most important point made by Super's 1951 definition of vocational guidance is that vocational guidance can be construed in at least two different ways: (1) as a treatment condition or (2) as a stimulus variable (Crites, 1969, p. 22). These two conceptions are not mutually exclusive, but they do represent different perceptions of the needs of students, clients, or workers and of the time frame within which vocational guidance operates.

Treatment: A Problem Orientation

If vocational guidance is seen as a treatment condition, it will be seen as problem oriented or, at least, as appropriate primarily at decision points or at other periods of transition when people are most vulnerable to career crises and discontinuity and thus treatment will be restricted in time. In this sense, vocational guidance and counseling will be viewed, either directly or indirectly, as responding to taxonomies of vocational problems or to difficulties in choice by applying certain techniques or knowledge to resolve them. In such a perspective, the vocational guidance practitioner is likely to define the difficulties experienced by persons with whom he or she works in ways similar to those proposed by Williamson, Bordin, Byrne, Robinson, Bordin and Kopplin, Crites, or Campbell and Cellini.

Williamson (1939) has suggested that vocational problems can be described as

1. No choice—Individuals cannot discriminate sufficiently among occupations to select one and commit themselves to it.
2. Uncertain choice—A choice has been made, but the person is uncertain about it.
3. Unwise choice—There is a disagreement between the individual's abilities or interests and the occupation which he selects.
4. Discrepancy between interests and aptitudes—There is disagreement in the type or amount of these two traits as they interact or should interact in defining choice. (p. 428)

Edward S. Bordin (1946, p. 174), commenting on Williamson's problem categories, suggested that "the assignment of the individual's difficulties to one of this set of classes of difficulties does not provide a basis for predictions of the relative success of different treatments." This observation led him to develop five other problem categories more psychologically oriented than those of Williamson:

1. Dependence
2. Lack of information
3. Self-conflict
4. Choice anxiety
5. No problem

Byrne (1958) expressed displeasure at the generalization to high school students from the college samples used by Williamson and Bordin. He suggested that the problems could more adequately be described as

1. Immaturity in situation
2. Lack of problem-solving skill

3. Lack of insight
4. Lack of information
5. Lack of assurance
6. Domination by authority (p. 187)

Robinson (1963) suggested another modification of the Bordin diagnostic constructs into the following categories:

1. Personal maladjustment
2. Conflict with significant others
3. Discussing plans [instead of Bordin's no-problem category]
4. Lack of information about environment
5. Immaturity
6. Skill deficiency (p. 332)

In 1973, Bordin and Kopplin elaborated Bordin's early taxonomy to reflect motivational conflicts that bring clients, particularly college students, to vocational counseling. This scheme involves five basic categories, four of which are divided into subcategories of problem presentation. The categories are ordered to show an approximate structure of lesser to greater disturbance. Somewhat analogous to Tyler's (1961) paradigm of choice-versus-change counseling, discussed elsewhere in this book, Bordin and Kopplin suggest that categories A through C refer to persons who are primarily oriented to decision making, while categories D and E refer to persons who must first make changes in the self before engaging in decision making. The classification in paraphrased form is as follows:

A. Synthetic difficulties—The major problem is difficulty in synthesizing or achieving cognitive clarity for reasons reflected in the following subcategories:
   A_1 diverse interests
   A_2 restricted experience
   A_3 realistic obstacles
B. Identity problems—The major problem is associated with the formation of a viable self-concept or self-percept. Contributing factors might include the following:
   B_1 inappropriate sex model
   B_2 differentiation issues
   B_3 paralysis because of problems of integration of one's roots
   B_4 lack of identity
   B_5 unrealistic identity
   B_6 superimposed identity
   B_7 no model
C. Gratification conflicts—The client is blocked because of approach-avoidance conflicts in gratifications in available work identities.
D. Change orientation—The client is dissatisfied with personal characteristics that a vocational choice might help to change.
   D_1 developmental change with occupational representation
   D_2 therapeutic change in which person attempts to alter stable personality characteristics by adopting an occupational identity that represents desired characteristics
E. Overt pathology—The disturbance is so severe that a vocational focus is not feasible.
   E_1 choice possible
   E_2 choice impossible
F. unclassifiable—motivational conflict.
G. unclassifiable—no motivational conflict.

In modifying Williamson's earlier classification structure, Crites (1981) identified eight vocational problem categories. He used measures of an individual's interests, aptitudes, and occupational choices as the bases for his classification. They include the following three categories and eight problem emphases:

Adjustment
- Adjusted
- Maladjusted

Indecision
- Multipotential
- Undecided
- Uninterested

Unrealism
- Unrealistic
- Unfulfilled
- Coerced

Finally, Campbell and Cellini (1981) proposed a diagnostic classification of adult career problems that is related to developmental theories of career development and adult career problems. Although the full diagnostic taxonomy is provided in Chapter 2, for our purposes here, the four major problem categories and their major subcategories are identified without the presumed causal or etiological factors presumably related to each. The major problem categories and subcategories include

1.0 Problems in career decision making
  - 1.1 Getting started
  - 1.2 Information gathering
  - 1.3 Generating, evaluating, and selecting alternatives
  - 1.4 Formulating plans to implementing decisions

2.0 Problems in implementing career plans
  - 2.1 Characteristics of the individual
  - 2.2 Characteristics external to the individual

3.0 Problems in organization/institutional performance
  - 3.1 Deficiencies in skills, abilities, and knowledge
  - 3.2 Personal factors
  - 3.3 Conditions of the organizational/institutional environment

4.0 Problems in organizational/institutional adaptation
  - 4.1 Initial entry
  - 4.2 Changeover time
  - 4.3 Interpersonal relationships

As their content suggests, these classifications tend to vary according to their acceptance of psychodynamic, developmental, or sociological descriptions of vocational problems. In most cases, an implied deficit of some type in the behavioral repertoire of the individual forms the basis on which the strategies for career counseling or career guidance or a specific treatment approach will be selected. In addition, each of these models assumes that the observed problem is likely to occur at a decision or transition point. Thus, it is further implied that career counseling or guidance will be effective as a post hoc response to a problem that is already present and that impedes the individual's progress to some new phase of life, that is, entry into the labor force, selection of a specific occupation, advancement in an occupation, and so forth.

The weaknesses of these classification systems lie in their descriptive rather than their predictive character. Typically, they tend not to be based on empirical findings about their validity but to evolve from theoretical and anecdotal explanations of career behavior as viewed through specific conceptual lenses. As such, the criteria they use frequently lack reliability from one rater to another, the etiology or specific behavioral anchors lack precision as defining properties of the particular classifications, and the inclusiveness of the vocational problems represented or the populations described varies from one classification to another (Rounds & Tinsley, 1984). Nevertheless, such classifications of vocational problems have enriched the communication or language about the nature of and differences among such problem categories, created a pool of hypotheses useful to counselors in helping clients be more explicit about their concerns and dilemmas, and spurred the construction of psychometric instruments designed to measure the behaviors subsumed in those problem categories. However incomplete or primitive such classifications are, they are steps toward creating a science of vocational or career psychology and a matrix of presenting problem-treatment interactions.

Stimulus: A Developmental Orientation

Conceiving of vocational or career guidance or counseling as a stimulus variable requires a different set of assumptions from viewing it as treatment. As a stimulus variable, career guidance can be more effectively viewed longitudinally and developmentally. The time frame in which it operates depends partly on the setting of the program and partly on the characteristics of the students or adults progressing through the setting.

As a stimulus variable, vocational guidance not only responds to existing problems but also aids in the acquisition of knowledge, attitudes, and skills through which one can develop the behaviors necessary to cope with decision points, to acquire an occupational identity, or to develop career maturity. In the diagnostic categories previously identified, vocational guidance processes or counseling were triggered by the presentation of the problem of the person to be assisted. However, vocational guidance as stimulus is more future oriented and developmental, providing behaviors that anticipate choices and build career maturity rather than reacting to situations in which crises trigger action.

It seems obvious that vocational guidance conceived as a stimulus process fits well within any framework concerned with primary prevention. Indeed, the basic focus of vocational guidance as stimulus is educative, incorporating the philosophy and content of career models. The *raison d'être* of such an approach is the facilitation, indeed the maximization, of growth rather than the repair of deficits.

In this balance between treatment and stimulus, problem remediation or skill development, one can see the difference between clinical and counseling psychology on the one hand and on the other, the difference between the diagnostic/clinical view of traditional forms of vocational guidance and the facilitative and developmental perspective of newer forms of career guidance.

COUNSELING PSYCHOLOGY'S ROOTS IN VOCATIONAL GUIDANCE

To understand this historical and conceptual evolution of career guidance and counseling, it is important to realize that counseling psychology emerged from vocational guidance roots as they were being redefined in the 1950s. Counseling psychology received its major stimulus as an emerging psychological specialty a few years after clinical psychology, in the early and mid-1950s. Its roots were not, like those of clinical psychology, in medical settings and psychiatric disorders but in vocational development, guidance, prevention, and normality.

In a classic distinction between clinical and counseling psychology, Super (1955) offers the following perspectives in an article entitled "Transition: From Vocational Guidance to Counseling Psychology":

> *Clinical psychology* has typically been concerned with diagnosing the nature and extent of *psychopathology,* with the abnormalities of even normal persons, with uncovering adjustment difficulties and maladaptive tendencies, and with the acceptance and understanding of these tendencies so that they may be modified. *Counseling psychology,* on the contrary, concerns itself with *hygiology,* with the normalities of even abnormal persons, with locating and developing personal and social resources and adaptive tendencies so that the individual can be assisted in making more effective use of them. (p. 5)

The emphases on hygiology, on strengthening the use of personal and social resources and adaptive tendencies, are perspectives that have been inherent in counseling psychology and in career guidance and career counseling throughout their common evolution. Specifically, the historical legacy of counseling psychology derived from three distinct movements: (1) vocational guidance, (2) psychological measurement, and (3) personality development (Committee on Definition, 1956). These roots have been reaffirmed by Osipow (1977), who has argued that the core of counseling psychology is direct service, prevention, and vocational development. Other prominent counseling psychologists (Kagan, 1977; Nathan, 1977; Pepinsky, Hill-Frederick, & Epperson, 1978) have agreed with this view.

A major problem in counseling psychology is a blurring of the traditional distinctions between it and clinical psychology. Goldschmidt, Tipton, and Wiggins (1981) have reported that directors of APA-approved counseling psychology programs tend to perceive their programs as focusing more on personal concerns and problems than on vocational concerns and problems. Even so, some observers strongly argue that counseling psychologists should reaffirm their original identity and strengthen their vocational emphases. Such a view prompted Pallone (1977), after a national study of the work settings and functions of various types of psychologists, to indicate that "the educational, vocational, and personal adjustment problems of clients are found to be in the repertoire of counseling psychologists alone, among professional psychologists" (p. 32).

Nathan (1977), a clinical psychologist, echoes Pallone's view when he says:

> The professional contributions counseling psychologists can make are of two distinct kinds, in my judgment. The first, a contribution counseling psychologists can make uniquely, is in the vocational counseling world of work sphere. No other psychologists are trained in vocational counseling techniques; by the same token, no non-psychologist vocational consultant combines this knowledge of the world of work with skills in vocational assessment and competence in psychological counseling techniques. As a result, the counseling psychologist fills a unique role in our society. . . . With a minimum of training and adequate interpersonal skills, many persons can do psychotherapy with some effectiveness; but few professionals have the breadth and the depth of training in vocational assessment and counseling to which the counseling psychologist can lay claim. (p. 37)

Although much more could be written here about the evolution of counseling psychology in the middle 1950s, from a heritage strongly imbued with a vocational guidance emphasis, the strengthening of counseling psychology's distinctiveness in the ensuing decades and the rise of career guidance were clearly related to the shifting of perspective from occupational to career models.

Career Models Emerge

Since Super's redefinition of vocational guidance in 1951, there has been a subtle but important shift from occupational to career models in the vocational guidance literature. The occupational model described several paragraphs ago was the primary emphasis before 1951. Obviously, its influence has been continually significant, but it has competed increasingly with a series of broader perspectives on choice spawned by the career model.

By definition, career embraces a longer time frame than does occupational choice. Indeed, the concept of career embraces prevocational activity such as the effects on students of educational programs and options, as well as the post-vocational activity manifested by the retiree or the pensioner working part-time. Prime considerations in a career model are not the differences among occupations but rather the continuity or discontinuity in the individual's career development, the interactions of educational and occupational choices across time, and the sequence of occupations, jobs, and positions held.

Career models introduce several aspects into the concept of vocational guidance that are not apparent in the occupational model. One concerns developmental career guidance. In such an emphasis, the vocational guidance practitioner is concerned not only with immediate choice of training or job but also with intermediate and long-range goals and the relation of immediate choices to those goals. Thus, personal values, the clarity of the self-concept, personal planfulness, and exploratory behavior vis-à-vis choice options become important variables to be considered in career guidance. In addition, personal behaviors, attitudes, and different kinds of skills are seen as appropriately developed by vocational guidance practitioners if they are not present in the student's or adult's behavioral repertoire.

Such conceptions of vocational guidance are concerned not only with an individual's potential performance on some set of occupational tasks but also with the attitudes and knowledge that facilitate or impede the choosing, learning, and using of such technical skills—what has been described elsewhere as general employability (Herr, 1984). More important, perhaps, a career model reinforces a view of vocational guidance as more than a set of services available at some specific decision point or for persons who, for some reason, are experiencing choice conflicts or work adjustment problems. Career models emphasize the role of career guidance in systematically educating students or adults to the knowledge, attitudes, and skills that will be required of them at future choice points, in planning their educational programs, in selecting and preparing them for work, and in helping them anticipate and prepare for career paths available to them within a workplace. This approach is in contrast to intervention only after it has been clearly established that particular persons have not acquired the necessary skills and behaviors and are now experiencing problems because of these deficits in their behavioral repertoire. (This is what has previously been described as a treatment approach.)

The use of career models in vocational guidance slowly began to elevate the concern for self-understanding to the same level of importance as occupational understanding or task mastery. In this view, the primary objectives of vocational guidance are seen as developing the individual's skills to make a free and informed choice of career and appropriately preparing for that career rather than for the needs of the labor market.

Wrenn (1964) summarized such a perspective well in this observation:

> The planning for which the vocational counselor can be held responsible is planning for work satisfactions from both employed and nonemployed activity. . . . One way to suggest the new emphasis is to say the counselor helps the student to define goals, not merely to inventory capacities. And it is clear that these must be life goals, not occupational goals only. There must be a dove tailing of work in employed and nonemployed settings if life is to be meaningful to the majority of people. . . . It is imperative that vocational counselors accept responsibility for helping students see their work life whole. (p. 41)

In the late 1950s and early 1960s, such perspectives were part of a significant period of growth in school counseling, spurred on by the National Defense Education Act and the constant need to reassess what goals and directions such services should include. This development also touched on the latter part of the dramatic period of change in counseling, spurred on by Carl Rogers's challenges to conventional clinical approaches, resulting in shifts to client-centered, nondirective techniques that deemphasized testing, prediction, and the use of information. Finally, this was the middle stage of the rise of career development theory and its major concern for the role of the person's self-concept as the stimulus for decision making and commitment to various occupational and life goals. Although each of these influences can be examined in great depth, suffice it to say that the interaction of these events and developments continued to be incorporated into the concepts of vocational guidance. With them came a continuing assimilation into perspectives on vocational guidance of those emphases previously seen as the concern only of educational or personal counseling.

Of major concern to the shape of vocational guidance and counseling during the 1960s were discussions of its relationship to the process of decision making and to the therapy process. Tyler (1961) suggested that such counseling concentrates on the individual's willingness to make choices and commitments in accord with a clear sense of ego identity. Moore (1961) argued that counseling, especially at the secondary school level, is concerned primarily with the counselee making choices. Samler (1968) advocated that vocational counseling should be a learning experience in decision making. Brammer and Shostrom (1960) contended that vocational counseling allows counselees to discover facts about themselves and the working world "in a process whereby occupational choice limits are broadened and effective vocational planning really becomes a part of life-planning." Boy and Pine (1963) summarized many of the significant issues of the time as follows:

> The proponents of "vocational guidance" state quite emphatically that the school counselor's first job is vocational counseling and that therapeutic counseling is purely secondary. Yet in the light of the Super, Roe, and Ginzberg theories of vocational development, with their stress on the significant role of the self-concept in the process of vocational development, how can vocational counseling be divorced from therapeutic counseling? If, as Super indicates, the process of vocational development is essentially that of developing and implementing a self-concept, can effective vocational counseling take place just through dispensing and discussing occupational information without considering the psychodynamics of the self-concept? If vocational counseling is a primary task, should not school counselors provide the student with the opportunity to reach new insights, to explore and see his self-concept, to develop and to implement it? (p. 225)

Such broader and longer-term views of the purposes and content of vocational guidance affected not only perspectives on school counseling or counseling psychology but also perspectives on employment counseling as provided by the U.S. Employment Service. During the 1960s and 1970s, a number of observers contended that, whereas employment counseling is generally distinguished from other vocational counseling in that it is typically done with job applicants or employability program enrollees for limited purposes and for a limited time, a more comprehensive and professional role definition of employment counseling was needed in a bureaucratic government agency environment under frequent pressure for case closures, positive termination, and job placements (Darr, 1981). In response to the growing theoretical and process notions that were then moving vocational guidance and counseling toward career guidance and counseling, Sullivan (1970) suggested an enlarged and more developmental approach to employment counseling:

> Through employment counseling, the client is assisted with self-exploration and vocational planning. The Employment Counselor assists the client to discover, evaluate, and synthesize his values, attitudes, and feelings, needs, and desires, motivation forces, self-concept, family and financial pressures, preferences for life style, physical capacities, aptitudes, school achievement, prior work history, skills, and interests. The client is assisted in formulating vocational questions, in exploring vocational alternatives, and in evaluating the possible consequences of various choices or decisions. The Employment Counselor furnishes personal, occupational, and, environmental information to the client, as required, regarding his plans, choices, or problems. The client is encouraged to establish short-term reachable goals related to his interests and to develop concrete steps (supportive services, rehabilitation, education, training, stop-gap work try-outs, and employment) which would readily lead to such goals and result in fast concrete payoffs with respect to the goals. The Employment Counselor then helps the client to develop long-term vocational plans which are broken down into manageable goals, in a time scale that the client believes he can tolerate and at a level of difficulty which the client believes himself capable of accomplishing. (p. 127)

Such a perspective is more than a unidimensional approach to vocational guidance or counseling. It embodies a series of interventions and a developmental perspective consistent with what has come to be viewed as comprehensive career guidance.

COMPREHENSIVE CAREER GUIDANCE

By the late 1960s and early 1970s, the term *career guidance* was appearing in the professional literature almost as frequently as the term *vocational guidance*. The redefinitions and the paradigm shifts associated with the emerging term, *career guidance,* were creating new metaphors. Career guidance was being termed a life-style concept that embodied the need to combine work and leisure counseling (McDaniels, 1978), one that needed to address sex role differentiation and the reduction of sex bias (Hansen & Keierleber, 1978), and one devoted to the holistic development of a career-conscious individual (Gysbers & Moore, 1971, 1981). The implications for the goals of career guidance that emerged from such paradigm shifts were effectively summarized by Hansen (1981) as follows:

1. Career guidance needs to move from a focus strictly on jobs to a focus on life patterns. . . .
2. Career guidance needs to help make clients aware of their own career socialization. . . .
3. Career guidance needs to move from a focus on slotting individuals into what is (matching) to preparing them for the life style choices and options of what might be. . . .
4. Career guidance needs to move from a focus on occupational choice alone to the larger sphere of people's lives and the interface of the vocational and the personal. . . .
5. Career guidance needs to help clients achieve role integration in rapidly changing societies. . . .
6. Career guidance needs to help individuals move beyond the stereotypic choices women and men have made in the past to expanding the range of options they are willing to consider and choose. . . . (p. 28)

Such shifts in goals and terminology were not simply semantic but implied shifts in the role and the purpose of the counselor. Career guidance, as a broadened interpretation of vocational guidance, began forcefully to communicate the importance of an emphasis on the following major organizing themes for career guidance:

1. Efforts to develop decision making—Career guidance is concerned with helping students and adults develop decision-making skills as well as define, get, and use information appropriate to different choices.
2. Concern for the self-concept—Decisions and plans express the self-concept of the chooser. It is necessary that career guidance help the student or adult achieve self-understanding before or as a part of occupational awareness. Thus, information about occupations needs to go beyond the facts of salaries or work content to include their possible relation to aspirations and values or their potential ability to provide satisfaction for psychosocial needs.
3. Concern for life-styles, values, leisure—Education, leisure, occupation, or career all interact to create or influence a life-style. The way the student or adult comes to deal with such an issue is related to the clarity and characteristics of personal values. Career guidance, then, cannot attend to occupational choice without examining the educational or personal/social implications that it holds—its relation to personal values—in both the present and the future.

4. Free choice—Career guidance is directed not to specific subsets of choices (vocational education) alone within a larger category (educational curricula) but to the range of choices available, the personal characteristics and aspirations to which these choices need to relate, and the likely outcomes of specific choices. Vocational education, general education, or college preparation should certainly be seen as options to be considered, but their validity as choices lies in the comparative advantages each has over other possible choices in relation to specific personal criteria. Indeed, the safeguarding of individual integrity argues against any form of prescriptive guidance that coerces the person into pursuing specific careers or other life patterns.
5. Individual differences—Fundamental to a free society is an acknowledgement of differences in individual talents, opportunities by which the range of these talents can be identified and nurtured, and the freedom of each individual to develop and express these talents in a unique way.
6. Flexibility and the ability to cope with change—Career guidance must help persons consider contingency planning, multiple routes to goals, flexibility in goals, and other notions of tentativeness as methods of coping with rapid change in social and occupational conditions.

By the 1980s, these concepts had become almost commonplace attributions to the purposes of career guidance and career counseling. As suggested previously, career guidance was in a dynamic state, adding new concepts, new populations, new techniques. It was becoming increasingly *comprehensive*.

Comprehensive career guidance has come to mean many different things in the professional literature. *Comprehensive* has sometimes been used to mean programmed, preplanned, or systematic. At other times, it has meant longitudinal—articulated over an extended period of time, whether from kindergarten to grade 12 in the public schools, during the four years of college or university, over the six months spent in a halfway house or rehabilitation facility, or across the period of one's tenure within a particular firm, business, or government agency. At still other times, *comprehensive* has referred to a developmental content designed to equip consumers of career guidance with the attitudes, knowledge, and skills by which they can anticipate, plan, and act on a variety of career-related tasks. Finally, *comprehensive* has been used to connote the many ways intervention in career development can occur without confining counselors to a one-to-one framework (Herr, 1982b).

Such notions of comprehensive career guidance have begun to permeate other societal sectors, including federal legislation. For example, Title III, Part D of Public Law 98-524, the Carl D. Perkins Vocational Education Act, (U.S. House of Representatives, October 19, 1984) authorizes grants for "programs (organized and administered by certified counselors) designed to improve, expand, and extend career guidance and counseling programs to meet the career development, vocational education, and employment needs of vocational education students and potential students." The vocational education students referred to in this context are not simply those in secondary schools. Rather, the act includes in its definition adults, single parents, displaced homemakers, ex-offenders, incarcerated persons, the handicapped, the disabled, and the academically and economically disadvantaged. In Section 521(4), the Perkins Act also defines career guidance and counseling:

> Definition: (4) The term "career guidance and counseling" means those programs (A) which pertain to the body of subject matter and related techniques and methods organized for the development in individuals of career awareness, career planning, career decision making, placement

> skills, and knowledge and understanding of local, state, and national occupational, education, and labor market needs, trends, and opportunities, and (B) which assist them in making and implementing informed educational and occupational choices.

In the collective sense, it might be argued that rather than rejecting or being different from vocational guidance in its traditional forms, career guidance has absorbed vocational guidance techniques and expanded them in order to offer a more discriminating repertoire of interventions to a larger number of populations and settings. Within such a perspective, traditional approaches to vocational guidance (for example, matching person and job) have a significant place within the broader perspectives of career guidance, depending on the needs of particular individuals.

Needs for Career Guidance and Counseling: A Life-Span Perspective

A major implication of comprehensive career guidance is its applicability to many kinds of adult populations. As the evolution of vocational guidance to career guidance suggests, the traditional forms of vocational guidance have frequently been focused on adolescents and often been delivered within the school. Increasingly, career guidance programs are being addressed to the total spectrum of adult populations, including retirees. These programs are occurring in community centers, in institutions for postsecondary education, in government agencies, and in business and industry.

Under the impetus of an expanding knowledge of adult development, it has become obvious that in addition to the need to accommodate the special needs of women, racial and ethnic minorities, and handicapped populations, the special requirements of adults *qua* adults must also be responded to within the career guidance delivery system. This perspective does not disparage the significant assistance provided by rehabilitation agencies, employment services, or college career development and placement centers. Rather it suggests that however good these agencies are, they frequently deal only with very visible or very severe problems of occupational choice or adjustment. In many cases their interactions with clients are short-lived and limited to points of crisis rather than to career planning and to helping an individual come to terms with the future. Such agencies often cannot deal with the person who is experiencing job alienation or dissatisfaction in subtle and quietly agonizing ways or the college student who views college as an end in itself rather than as an intermediate vocational decision. Neither can such agencies deal in depth with the woman who has been out of the labor force before her children were in school and now doesn't know where to seek information about starting a career. There are many such persons, but they are often invisible.

As people age, they reassess choices and plot the possibilities of still attaining certain idealized goals, sometimes with anxiety and despair. As opportunities for advancement decrease, persons in their forties and fifties frequently take stock of how their achievements measure up to the self-concepts around which they had organized their self-esteem. If what they believe they have achieved falls significantly below what they expected from life, they may seek to change career patterns if time and circumstances still permit. In other instances, such opportunities may no longer be available to them, and they will have to accept the notion that it is too late for them to accomplish those visions on which their view of personal success rested. In either situation, career guidance or career counseling is needed. In addition to these persons, many other persons will be at a stage of career deceleration as a way of anticipating retirement. Until fairly recently, little attention has been given to the career guidance needs of such persons, for assistance in considering volunteer work, the management of free time, part-time work, continuing education, and self-adjustments in which full-time work is no longer a central focus of identity.

Some observers report that a great many members of the work force are dissatisfied with the work they perform, but they do not know how to extricate themselves from it (O'Toole, 1973, 1975). Such persons need emotional support while they consider acting on their midcareer crises, and they need help to sort out the costs and benefits of executing the changes they are considering. Often such persons have been out of the educational mainstream long enough to have virtually no knowledge of training or career options currently available.

The studies of Northcutt (Knowles, 1977) and others indicate that approximately 40 percent of the American adult population is coping inadequately with typical life problems (for example, getting work and holding a job, buying things, managing economic life, and parenting). Available evidence suggests that such persons need to experience skill-building approaches that are organized around the life crisis they are facing.

Some of the adults who need to be served by career guidance will have multiple problems of substance abuse, marital discord, child abuse, lack of transportation, or inadequate financial or nutrition management skills that need to be treated in multidimensional or "comprehensive" ways. To deal only with such persons' economic needs and to assume that all the other consequences of unemployment will take care of themselves is unrealistic and inappropriate. Therefore, career guidance or counseling programs for such persons will need to interface more effectively with other agency programs in collaborative efforts to give the problems of work and social adaptation simultaneous attention.

Most contemporary adults had little opportunity as adolescents to assess their own characteristics or to plan ways by which their values and goals could be achieved via various alternatives available to them. In line with the rationale of early perspectives on vocational guidance, it was assumed that choosing an occupation or, indeed, a college to enter marked the end of the need for assistance by a counselor. As a result many adults continue throughout life unaware of their potentialities or preferences, often experiencing a vague but gnawing disaffection with what they are now doing or what the future may hold. In many instances, the career choices they made were random and often shallow commitments to those occupations or educational experiences that were available or visible at a time when they had to choose. Having never experienced the use of available exploratory resources, many such persons now experience an information deficit. They simply do not know what options are available, how to access them, or how to identify them.

A variety of national and local surveys report that adults would like to have or to have had more opportunities for career guidance and career counseling than has been available to them. For example, in 1989 a telephone survey of adults was conducted by the Gallup organization for the National Occupational Information Coordinating Committee and the National Career Development Association (National Occupational Information Coordinating Committee, 1990). The survey found that nearly two-thirds of American adults would seek more information about career options if they were starting their careers over again, with blacks (79 percent) and Hispanics (75 percent) showing the greatest interest in additional career data, followed by a majority of whites (63 percent). Only 4 out of 10 working adults followed a definite plan in mapping out their careers, with college graduates (62 percent) more likely than high school graduates (32 percent) to plan a career. Thirty percent got started through a series of chance circumstances (18 percent) or took the only job that was available (12 percent), and (23 percent) were influenced by family and friends.

Twenty-seven percent of African-Americans said they took the only jobs that were available to them, compared to 19 percent of Asians, 17 percent of Hispanics, and 10 percent of whites. Twenty-seven percent of all respondents said that they needed additional assistance in finding information about jobs, with blacks reporting the highest need (44 percent) and whites the least (25 percent) among ethnic groups. Fifty-three percent of the respondents said public high schools are not providing the training in job-seeking skills for students who are not going to college, and 40 percent said high schools are not providing enough help to students to choose careers.

The survey further found that an estimated 12.5 million U.S. adults (7 percent of the adult population) needed help in 1989 in selecting, changing, or getting a job. Nineteen percent of individuals with Asian heritage and 15 percent of African-Americans report they needed assistance in the labor market. For whites the figure was 6 percent, and for Hispanics 8 percent.

Equally important are the results involving relationships between career development and mental health (discussed later in this book). Twenty-five percent of the respondents said job stress or pressure had interfered with their off-the-job relationships; 20 percent said job stress had affected their ability to do their jobs.

The findings for the 1989 Gallup survey essentially parallel those of an earlier survey on career development by the Gallup organization in 1987 (Gallup organization, 1987). However, in the 1987 data somewhat fewer (about 10.8 million employed workers) reported the need for help in selecting, changing, or obtaining a job. About one in three of the respondents (32.7 percent) reported that they had gone to no source for help or advice in career development. Those respondents who did seek help with their career development (41.2 percent), typically sought help through such self-directed activities as library visits, reading classified ads, taking interest inventories, or some combination of these options. Fewer than one in five (17.2 percent) respondents reported that they had sought assistance from school or college counselors and fewer than 9 percent indicated that they had used publicly available job service counselors. About half of all respondents (51.1 percent) believe that most adult Americans do not know how to interpret and use information to make intelligent career decisions. Significantly more college graduates (66.7 percent) believe this than do high school graduates (46 percent).

In summarizing the broad implications of the 1987 Gallup poll data, Lester and Frugoli (1989) suggest that among the many findings important to career guidance practitioners, four were particularly significant:

1. There is a strong need for and interest in career information on the part of both youth and adults.
2. Individuals are extremely interested in career planning.
3. There is a perception that individuals need help in getting career information, and many need help in using such information.
4. There is a need to target career information to the non-college bound. (p. 69)

These observations are supported by findings available from the National Assessment of Educational Progress (Westbrook, 1978) and from other reviews. These sources indicate that a large percentage of adults are weak in basic skills and occupational information, that they have had little opportunity to explore their personal characteristics with a counselor, and that they are unclear about their educational or career needs.

The presence of career education programs and comprehensive career guidance programs today may alleviate some of these problems among tomorrow's adult populations. But because such programs are not universally available and differ in quality, and because the population is mobile, they cannot totally eliminate such needs. Career counselors and other career guidance specialists in the future will need to provide a shifting blend of preplanned and spontaneous on-demand responses to the various consumer groups with whom they will deal. Some, perhaps much, of the activity of these specialists will involve reducing stereotypes and regulatory barriers to opportunity now experienced by the elderly, ex-offenders, minorities, persons of different sexual preferences, women, and the handicapped.

The need for career guidance is not confined to adults. Students in elementary and secondary schools as well as those in colleges give evidence of such needs. Prediger, Roth, and Noeth (1973) studied the student career development of more than 28,000 students in the eighth, ninth, and eleventh grades in 197 schools across the nation. Among their major findings were the following: more than three-fourths of eleventh graders in the sample and nearly as many eighth graders indicated the need for help in career planning; eleventh graders in the sample indicated that making career plans was their major area of need compared to a variety of other academic, personal, or educational choice problems; only 13 percent of the eleventh graders felt that they had received a "lot of help" with career planning; half of the eleventh graders and slightly more eighth graders stated that they received little or no help with career planning; with respect to job preparation, about 40 percent of the eleventh graders were uncertain whether their educational plans were in line with the occupations they were considering, and approximately one-fourth were not sure if they would be able to complete the steps necessary for entering these occupations.

Other national reports suggest that such needs for career guidance among secondary school students remain unmet. For example, the National Commission on Secondary Vocational Education (1985) states:

> Inadequate student knowledge subtly but formidably constrains student access to vocational education. Students and parents need to be accurately informed about what vocational education is, how it relates to their personal and career goals, and how it can be used to help them achieve their goals. One does not choose what one knows little about or is constrained from choosing by unexamined social attitudes. . . . We need comprehensive career guidance programs that will provide this information and remove some of the subtle status distinctions involving vocational education. Comprehensive guidance means counseling that is available to all students, covering all subjects, leading to all occupations. (p. 10)

The need for comprehensive career guidance among secondary school students is not confined to those enrolled in or choosing vocational education. This need spans the spectrum of student subgroups. For example, the College Entrance Examination Board Commission on Pre-College Guidance and Counseling (1986) has stressed the need for strengthened school career guidance programs for economically and socially disadvantaged students who are potentially college bound. The Business Advisory Commission of the Education Commission of the States (1985), in a national report dealing with the growing problem of alienated, disadvantaged, disconnected, and other at-risk youth, recommends "new structures and procedures for effecting the transition from school to work or other productive pursuits. . . . Young people today need more and better guidance than ever before" (p. 26). The report goes on to cite the need for coordinated programs including career counseling, financial assistance, summer jobs, cooperative education options, and role models if such at-risk youth are to be reconnected to schooling and to work. The Research and Policy Committee of the Committee for Economic Development (1985), in a major report dealing with business and the public schools, strongly recommended that schools provide, among other emphases, exploratory programs to assist in career choice, job search, and general employability skills (for example, how to behave in an interview and get to work on time) and employment counseling (p. 31). The National Alliance of Business (1984), in a major analysis of the nation at work, particularly relationships between education and the private sector, has argued for more school-to-work transition programs including job placement assistance, career counseling, cooperative career information activities with business, and counseling about vocational-technical program alternatives to college degree programs (p. 8).

The Commission on Workforce Quality and Labor Market Efficiency supported by the U.S. Department of Labor (1989) was empowered to consider the challenges of what is considered a workforce crisis in the United States as demographic trends, technological change, and increased international competition create shortages of skilled workers and an excess of unskilled workers. Among its strong recommendations was that attention be paid to the dynamics of the school-to-work transition, with state employment security agencies and private industry councils establishing school-based employment services with direct connections to employers. The report encourages employers, both small and large, to provide information on job openings and to consider filling vacancies with recent high school graduates. The intent is that students be provided with evidence that the system works for those who have the necessary skills. Such a recommendation strongly argues that career guidance in schools must not only be active in educating students for choice but be directly involved with concrete steps to help place students in community jobs as an important aspect of their effective transitions from school to work.

The William T. Grant Foundation Commission on Work, Family and Citizenship (1988) in its report, *The Forgotten Half,* has advocated fulfilling the needs of students not bound for college, for whom career guidance and other services are unevenly available throughout the nation. In particular, this report has given strong emphases to school, parent, and community cooperation in ensuring programs necessary for the effective transition of these students to work. Among the specific areas emphasized would be significantly expanded career information and counseling, career information centers, programs to train parents as career educators, and the involvement of community mentors and community-based organizations in supporting efforts to improve counseling and career orientation.

These national commission reports and polls complement and, indeed, validate and extend the findings of a Gallup poll in 1985 that asked a national sample of adults to rate the importance of each of 25 goals of education. After the first- and second-rated goals—developing the ability to read and write correctly (1) and developing standards of right and wrong (2), the goal rated third in importance by this representative sample of adults was "To develop an understanding about different kinds of jobs and careers, including their requirements and rewards." The goal tied for sixth place in importance among the 25 goals evaluated was "To help students make realistic plans for what they will do after graduation" (p. 327). Together, these reports and polls continue to give evidence that certain needs for career guidance and counseling are yet unmet and that both panels of distinguished observers and the public at large want the schools to provide opportunities and services by which the career development of America's youth will be strengthened.

Finally, there are major needs for career guidance in postsecondary education. Studies of graduate and undergraduate students continually indicate that a major problem, and perhaps the most prevalent problem, involves vocational choice and career planning. Research throughout the 1970s and 1980s systematically supports the view that at least one-half of America's college-going population feels a need for assistance with career planning and/or career choice (Kramer, Berger, & Miller, 1974; Snyder, Hill, & Derksen, 1974; Williams et al., 1973; Weissberg et al., 1982; Walters & Saddlemire, 1979).

The following two examples illustrate typical findings of these studies. In the first study 1625 students at the University of Georgia were queried about their academic, career, and personal needs (Weissberg et al., 1982). A greater percentage of students expressed career development needs than either academic or personal needs. For example, over 80 percent of the students wanted to explore job opportunities related to their majors and obtain work experience in a career area, 77 percent wanted to develop job-seeking skills, and 72 percent wanted to learn how to prepare for their careers. Over half said they would very much like to explore their career interests, values, and abilities; obtain information; talk to a career counselor about career plans; and learn how occupations can affect their future life.

The second study (Healy and Reilly, 1989) considered the career needs of 1540 women and 1386 men from 10 community colleges in California. The researchers divided the student sample by age and gender and assessed their career needs across seven categories: (1) knowing more about interests and abilities; (2) understanding/deciding on career goals; (3) becoming more certain of career plans; (4) exploring careers related to interests and abilities; (5) selecting courses relevant to career goals; (6) developing job-finding skills. They found that all age cohorts from 17–19 through 41–50 and both sexes reported at least minor needs in each category, with major needs in each category more likely among younger students. The lowest needs for the older students were in deciding upon career goals, becoming more certain of plans, and obtaining jobs, while their highest needs were in exploring jobs related to talents and interests and selecting courses related to goals. Women of all ages reported more need to become certain about their career plans and men a greater need to obtain a job. Collectively, these studies and the many others available make clear the need for career guidance and counseling services in postsecondary institutions—technical, two-year, and four-year. They also affirm that such needs pertain to younger and older students, to traditional and reentry women, and to virtually every segment of the postsecondary population.

In sum, comprehensive career guidance programs have come to serve all elements of the population—children, youth, and adults—in formal educational settings, in a wide range of community agencies, and in business and industry. As the need for and the responses to career guidance have become more comprehensive, the need for clarity about the meanings of key concepts in career guidance and career counseling has grown. In the next sections some of these concepts will be reviewed.

Career Counseling

Although the terms *vocational* or *career guidance* and *counseling* have been used interchangeably thus far, they do not mean the same thing to all authors. The term *guidance* tends to be used more broadly than *counseling* and is likely to embrace a larger range or series of activities than does the term *counseling*. Indeed, counseling is frequently seen as only one of the functions by which guidance objectives are met. *Guidance* is also a term that has historically been identified with schools rather than with community agencies, private practitioners, or workplaces. As the provision of career services has moved from a primary locus in the schools to noneducational settings with increasing frequency, the use of the term *career counseling* has also been used more commonly than the term *guidance*.

Spokane (1991) has avoided the dichotomy of career guidance or career counseling by using the term *career intervention*. In his view, "Career interventions can be defined broadly as any direct assistance to an individual to promote more effective decision making, or more narrowly focused, intensive counseling to help resolve career difficulties" (p. 22).

As theory and research on career behavior have matured, they have acknowledged both the complexity of influences upon and the psychological characteristics of career choice and adjustment throughout the life span. This development has given credence to career counseling as a therapeutic modality that goes beyond dispensing and discussing information. Crites (1981) has suggested that as insights from client-centered and psychodynamic approaches have been applied to career counseling, choice problems are viewed as essentially personality problems. Therefore, the assumptions that guide the provision of career counseling need to be considered in relation to personal adjustment counseling or psychotherapy.

Crites uses the term *career counseling* to refer specifically to an *interpersonal* process focused upon assisting an individual to make an appropriate career decision: "Ideally, it involves active participation in the decisional process, not simply passive-receptive input of information" (p. 11). For Crites, career counseling is both more and less than personal adjustment counseling or psychotherapy. "Vocational and personal problems are different, but they do interact. Thus, career counseling often embraces personal counseling but it goes beyond this to explore and replicate the client's role in the main area of life—the world of work" (p. 11).

Crites (1981) identifies five propositions to support his perspective that "comprehensive career counseling, synthesized from the best models and methods of career counseling, also incorporates the best from theories of counseling and psychotherapy and goes considerably beyond them" (p. 14). His five propositions are as follows:

1. The need for career counseling is greater than the need for psychotherapy.
2. Career counseling can be therapeutic.
3. Career counseling should follow psychotherapy.
4. Career counseling is more effective than psychotherapy.
5. Career counseling is more difficult than psychotherapy. (pp. 14–15)

Rounds and Tinsley (1984) support Crites's viewpoint in their assumption that "career intervention is simply a form of psychological intervention designed to affect vocationally related feelings, attitudes, cognitions, and behaviors. Thus, it is a form of *psychotherapy* and should be viewed as a method of behavior change and tied to psychotherapy theory. . . . We believe that a conceptual shift in which career interventions are understood as psychological interventions (and career counseling as psychotherapy) would foster advances in the understanding of vocational behavior change processes" (pp. 138–39).

Although these propositions are supported by considerable empirical data as well as interesting conceptualizations, other theorists tend to view career counseling somewhat differently.

Brown (1985) pushes the interaction of career counseling and personal counseling even further than Crites. Brown, who defines career counseling "as the process of helping an individual select, prepare for, enter, and function effectively in an occupation" (p. 197), views career counseling "as a viable intervention with clients that have rather severe emotional problems." In particular, Brown distinguishes between clients who have intrapsychic (cognitive or emotional) problems and those who work in a nonsupportive, stress-producing environment that may cause symptoms that appear to be intrapsychic mental health disorders rather than functions of poor person-work environment fit. Obviously, how the counselor makes such distinctions will determine whether the therapeutic approach focuses upon intrapsychic changes, as in personal counseling and psychotherapy, or on altering the work environment or choosing another work environment through career counseling. Such a view obviously extends both the range of problems likely to be addressed by career counseling and the settings in which career counseling should be offered.

In their 1991 book, Brown and Brooks offer the following definition of career counseling:

> Career counseling is an interpersonal process designed to assist individuals with career development problems. Career development is that process of choosing, entering, adjusting to and advancing in an occupation. It is a lifelong process that interacts dynamically with other life roles. Career problems include, but are not limited to, career indecision and undecidedness, work performance, stress and adjustment, incongruence of the person and work environment, and inadequate or unsatisfactory integration of life roles with other life roles (e.g., parent, friend, citizen). (p. 5)

Central to the view of Brown and Brooks is whether or not individuals possess cognitive clarity, which they define as "the ability to objectively assess one's own strengths and weaknesses and relate the assessment to environmental situations" (p. 5). If career counselors determine that clients are not simply undecided, but rather are experiencing indecisiveness, the equivalent of a deficit in cognitive clarity, Brown and Brooks suggest that "appropriate action may require postponement of consideration of career related matters until cognitive clarity is attained" (p. 6). Thus, moderate mental health problems may require interventions other than career counseling, and temporary crises *as well as* temporary or long-term stress require personal rather than career counseling. In some instances, cognitive clarity concerns can be handled while career development concerns are being addressed; in other cases, the counselor must first concentrate on the factors related to the lack of cognitive clarity or refer the client for personal counseling or what other theorists would define as psychotherapy.

In some contrast to those observers who contend that career counseling is a form of psychotherapy, Spokane (1991) views career counseling as a particular type of career intervention that should be distinguished from psychotherapy. He suggests that there have been misapplications of psychotherapy to career situations. He cites four critical characteristics that distinguish career problems from personal or interpersonal problems:

1. "The social environment forces adjustments in individual career aspirations and impedes sharp changes in choice patterns" (p. 7).
2. "The principle of congruence (person-environment fit) is considered in some way in nearly all theories of career development" (p. 7).
3. "The public has come to expect a special career intervention technology of interest inventories and computer interventions that is independent of most theory positions and results in a more structured and predictable course of intervention than is generally the case in psychotherapy" (pp. 7–8).
4. "Career development proceeds both continuously and discontinuously, and requires certain critical choices at a predictable number of transition points (e.g., high school graduation), as well as the continuous formation of a vocational identity through a series of small but serial choices (Osipow, 1983)" (p. 8).

The sum of Spokane's view suggests that although career counseling overlaps psychotherapy as a dyadic intervention, the extent of overlap is still an open question. Certainly, career counseling is not simply psychotherapy as traditionally practiced, nor are career problems simply personal or interpersonal problems. He further suggests that other career interventions bear little similarity to psychotherapy.

Zunker (1986) tends to take a broader view of the processes included in career counseling than do Crites, Brown, and Brooks or Spokane. In his view career counseling tends to embrace components or strategies that differ for diverse populations. For example, according to Zunker, career counseling for adults in career transition would include seven components or strategies: experience identification, interest identification, skills identification, value and needs identification, education/training planning, occupational planning, and finally the development of a life learning plan (pp. 236–48). Career counseling for women would include such components or strategies as job search skills, working climate, life-style skills, and support and follow-up (pp. 262–68). Within his conception of career counseling, Zunker uses broad terminology that others might define as more guidance than counseling. In fact, he is talking about the broader definition of career intervention as used by Spokane (1991). His attempt to wed the special characteristics of different populations to the treatments or strategies they receive offers a useful perspective.

In 1982, the Board of Directors of the National Vocational Guidance Association (NVGA—now the National Career Development Association) adopted a position statement that outlined the definition of vocational/career counseling and the competency areas required to perform such a role.

In January 1991, the Board of Directors of the National Career Development Association (NCDA) approved a revised document refining the definition of career counseling and the minimum competencies required to perform career counseling. In this document, "career counseling is defined as counseling individuals or groups of individuals about occupations, careers, life/career roles and responsibilities, career decision making, career planning, leisure planning, career pathing, and other career development activities (e.g., resume preparation, interviewing and job search techniques), together with the issues or conflicts that individuals confront regarding their careers" (p. 1).

The 1991 NCDA position paper also revised the minimum competencies necessary for a professional engaged in career counseling. The 10 areas recommended are career development theory, individual and group counseling skills, individual/group assessment, information/resources, program management and implementation, consultation, special populations, supervision, ethical/legal issues, and research/evaluation.

A Vocabulary for Career Counseling and Guidance

As suggested in the previous section, every occupation and profession has its own language system, its own way of using symbols to identify boundaries of domain, time, and space within which its work activities and prerogatives occur. So it is with career counseling and guidance. Key definitions allow the philosophical themes that give career guidance and career counseling a sense of coherence and common cause to be translated to a more operational level.

Some of these key definitions follow:

Career–Various conceptions of career exist, and observers tend to emphasize different aspects of the term. For example, McDaniels (1978) has contended that a career is more than one's job or occupation. It is a "life-style" concept that also involves a sequence of work or leisure activities in which one engages throughout a lifetime. Hansen and Keierleber (1978) have argued for an expanded concept of career that includes helping individuals make choices related to work, education, and family as interrelated phenomena affecting role integration. Gysbers and Moore (1981) have proposed that the term *life career development* be substituted for the term *career* in order to reflect self-development over the life span through the integration of the roles, settings, and events in a person's life. The NCDA defines *career* as the totality of work and leisure one does in a lifetime (Sears, 1982). Raynor and Entin (1982) maintain that

> A career is both a phenomenological concept and a behavioral concept. It is the link between what a person does and how that person sees himself or herself. A career consists of time-linked senses of self that are defined by action and its outcomes. A career defines how one sees oneself in the context of one's social environment—in terms of one's future plans, one's past accomplishments or failures, and one's present competences and attributes (p. 262).

In perhaps the most frequently used concept of career, Super (1976) has defined it as

> the course of events which constitutes a life; the sequence of occupations and other life roles which combine to express one's commitment to work in his or her total pattern of self-development; the series of remunerated and nonremunerated positions occupied by a person from adolescence through retirement, of which occupation is only one; includes work-related roles such as those of student, employee, and pensioner together with complementary avocational, familial, and civic roles. Careers exist only as people pursue them; they are person-centered. It is this last notion of careers, "they exist only as people pursue them," which summarizes much of the rationale for career guidance. (p. 4)

Careers are unique to each person and created by what one chooses or does not choose. They are dynamic and unfold throughout life. They include not only occupations but prevocational and postvocational concerns as well as integration of work with other roles: family, community, leisure.

Career Development–The total constellation of psychological, sociological, educational, physical, economic, and chance factors that combine to shape the career of any given individual over the life span (Sears, 1982); those aspects of an individual's experience that are relevant to personal choice, entry, and progress in educational, vocational, and avocational pursuits; the process by which one develops and refines such characteristics as self- and career identity, planfulness, and career maturity. The lifelong behavioral processes and the influences on them that lead to one's work values, choice of occupation(s), creation of a career pattern, decision-making style, role integration, self- and career identity, educational literacy, and related phenomena. Career development proceeds—smoothly, jaggedly, positively, negatively—whether or not career guidance or career education exists. As such, career development is not an intervention but the object of an intervention.

Career Maturity–The repertoire of behaviors pertinent to identifying, choosing, planning, and executing career goals available to a specific individual as compared with those possessed by an appropriate peer group; being at an average level in career development for one's age (after Super, 1957). Attitudinal and cognitive readiness to cope with the developmental tasks of finding, preparing for, getting established in, pursuing, and retiring from an occupation (Super, 1984b, p. 39).

Career Intervention—"Any activity (treatment or effort) designed to enhance a person's career development or to enable that person to make more effective career decisions" (Spokane, 1991, p. 22).

Technique—"A time-limited application of career intervention principles designed to accomplish a focused goal or to alter a specific vocational behavior. A career life line and a vocational career sort are examples" (Spokane, 1991, p. 22).

Strategy—"A philosophy or plan of action, or a group of techniques intended to change the vocational behavior of an individual, group of individuals or an organization. Career counseling of an individual by a single counselor is an example" (Spokane, 1991, p. 22).

Program—"An organized compilation of techniques or strategies with specific and well-defined objectives that is designed to alter systematically the vocational behavior of a group of individuals in a specific behavior setting (e.g., school, work, or community) over time" (Spokane, 1991, p. 22).

Career Management–The personal state of actively and consciously participating in shaping one's career and accepting responsibility for the activities and choices made toward those ends (Hansen & Tennyson, 1975).

Career Education–The totality of experiences by which persons acquire knowledge and attitudes about self and work and the skills by which to identify, choose, plan, and prepare for work and other life options potentially constituting a career; an effort aimed at refocusing American education and the actions of the broader community in ways that will help individuals acquire and utilize the knowledge, skills, and attitudes necessary for each to make work a meaningful, productive, and satisfying part of his or her way of life (Hoyt, 1978).

Career Guidance–A systematic program of counselor-coordinated information and experiences designed to facilitate individual career development and, more specifically, career management; a major component of career education integrating family, community, and school to facilitate self-direction; a set of multiple processes, techniques, or services designed to assist an individual to understand and to act on self-knowledge and knowledge of opportunities in work, education, and leisure and to develop the decision-making skills by which to create and manage his or her own career development. May include the development of job search, job interview, and job adjustment skills and placement into a chosen occupation. McDaniels (1978) has summarized many of these concepts in his definition of career guidance as an organized program to assist an individual to assimilate and integrate knowledge, experience, and appreciation related to (1) self-understanding; (2) understanding of the work society and those factors that affect its constant change, including worker attitude and discipline; (3) awareness of the part leisure may play in a person's life; (4) understanding of the necessity for many factors to be considered in career planning; and (5) understanding of the information and skills necessary to achieve self-fulfillment in work and leisure (p. 17).

Career Path–A term typically used in business and industry to describe a series of positions available in some occupational or specialized work area, ordinarily connoting possibilities for advancement.

Career Ladder–A term typically used in business and industry to describe opportunities for upward mobility in an occupational area or across occupational areas within a firm. Usually portrays increasing levels of experience and skill. "A succession of jobs available to an individual worker with each job successively offering increased responsibility and wages and more desirable working conditions" (Evans & Herr, 1978, p. 32).

Career Lattice–A term typically used in business and industry to portray all the opportunities in a firm or a subdivision of a firm including those available for upward and horizontal mobility (such as lateral transfer). As such it portrays the opportunities to shift from one career ladder to another (Evans & Herr, 1978, p. 34).

Occupation–A group of similar jobs found in different industries or organizations. Occupations exist in the economy and have existed in history, even when no man, woman, or child is engaged in them. Occupations, trades, and professions exist independently of any person. Careers, on the other hand, only exist when people are pursuing them (Super, 1985b, p. 1).

Job–A group of similar paid positions requiring some similar attributes in a single organization (Super, 1976).

Position–A group of tasks to be performed by one person; in industry, performed for pay. Positions exist whether vacant or occupied; they are task and outcome defined, not person centered (Super, 1976).

Leisure–Time free from required effort or for the free use of abilities and pursuit of interests (Super, 1976). Relatively self-determined activities and experiences that are available due to discretionary income, time, and social behaviors; they may be physical, social, intellectual, volunteer, creative, or some combination of all five (Sears, 1982).

Avocation–An activity pursued systematically and consecutively for its own sake with an objective other than monetary gain, although it may incidentally result in gain (Super, 1976).

Career Awareness–The inventory of knowledge, values, preferences, and self-concepts that an individual draws on in the course of making career-related choices (Wise, Charner, & Randour, 1978).

Work–The systematic pursuit of an objective valued by oneself (even if only for survival) and desired by others; directed and consecutive, it requires the expenditure of effort. It may be compensated (paid work) or uncompensated (volunteer work or an avocation). The objective may be intrinsic enjoyment of the work itself, the structure given to life by the work role, the economic support that work makes possible, or the type of leisure that it facilitates (Super, 1976).

CAREER EDUCATION: CONCEPTS, TECHNIQUES, STATUS

Career education has been defined in the previous section. However, career education is not only a term but a concept that for the past 20 years has been pervasive in education legislation, in federal priorities, and as a stimulus to career guidance and career counseling. Sometimes the term has been used virtually interchangeably with the term *career guidance;* in other instances, it has been used primarily to describe a process of infusing into instructional content and method career development concepts by which the application of academic subject matter of any kind can be related to work or to self-exploration. In either case the presence of career education as a federal priority during the 1970s reestablished the fundamental importance of career guidance for youth and for adults in the throes of planning and choosing among work opportunities. The term also symbolized the need to systematically address a range of conditions that were changing the necessary relationships between education and work, particularly with regard to preparing students to understand the linkages between educational opportunities and the subsequent implications of these in work choice and work adjustment. Although career education was originally introduced in the elementary and secondary schools of the nation, similar concepts were subsequently introduced in colleges and universities as traditional placement services were broadened to include career development activities—decision-making courses, seminars on job search, workshops on the career implications of different academic majors, and the introduction of such college-oriented computer-assisted career guidance systems as SIGI and DISCOVER—planned to address the changing career needs of students from the freshman to the senior years. Further, the notions embraced by career education have also been introduced in business and industry as a part of several different emphases: human resource development, personnel development, employee assistance programs, and training and development.

The concepts embodied by career education strike to the heart of the relationship between education and work and, indeed, the needs of persons attempting to choose and adjust to a work environment that is in dramatic flux. Thus, the values and the substance that career education represents seems to be inherent in modernizing and industrializing societies throughout the world.

Career education, then, is not only a phenomenon of this nation. It took root in many parts of the world almost simultaneously as these nations entered social and occupational phases in their development in which the relationships between education and work were taking on new and independent forms and as they became concerned about the creation of a labor force able to advance individual and national productivity.

Great Britain, France, Canada, the Netherlands, the Scandinavian countries, the Soviet Union, and what was previously East and West Germany among other nations have each embarked on some form of career education since the late 1960s and early 1970s. Like American models, they have developed approaches to the infusion of subject matter with career development concepts, created decision-making courses and experiences, established career resource centers, expanded contacts between schools and the larger community, and strengthened other career-related mechanisms in the schools, in ministries of labor, or in other community sectors. Each of these nations has strengthened its network of "employability" services in which the school may be the centerpiece but in which the employment service, vocational rehabilitation, and many other counseling agencies in the private and public sectors have clearly defined contributions. Many of these countries have developed work-study, career shadowing, apprenticeship schemes, or school-community linkages that are much more comprehensive than our own.

Obviously, the approaches to career education taken by other nations are shaped by their own political belief systems, economic conditions, cultural traditions, and conceptions of free and informed choice. Such models, then, are not necessarily interchangeable or transportable across national boundaries. That is not the point. The point is that nations experiencing particular levels of industrialization, occupational specialization and diversity, and magnitude of information about their work possibility structure must apparently shift their educational content and career guidance processes in order to accommodate these conditions. Career education has tended to symbolize such efforts.

In this nation, career education was introduced as a federal priority by the U.S. commissioner of education, Sidney Marland, on January 23, 1971. In an unfortunately superficial way, many persons view that date as the spontaneous birth of career education. To do so, however, denies the evolutionary character of the concepts involved and their ongoing importance as a stimulus to strengthened programs of career development in schools and community agencies as well as to the fundamental necessity for comprehensive programs of career guidance in a time of social and occupational change.

The Emergence of Career Education

The introduction of the term *career education* is widely attributed to an address entitled "Career Education Now," given by Sidney

Marland on January 23, 1971, before the annual convention of the National Association of Secondary School Principals at Houston, Texas. Although this speech and the many that followed in rapid succession to various professional, civic, and industrial groups gave visibility and credibility to career education, neither the term nor the concepts it embraced were without precedent in American history. Indeed, it is fair to say that Marland's emphasis on career education extended an evolutionary process that had been building rapidly during the 1960s but had antecedents back into the early years of this nation.

In the period from 1960 through 1969 many significant pieces of legislation bearing on employment, educational innovation, and vocational education were passed by the Congress. Several prominent panels of advisors on national education and manpower issues were empowered to make recommendations on needed policy. Both the policy and the legislation that emerged during the period became increasingly sensitive to the career development needs of persons, not just the needs of the occupational structure. Employability was seen as more than simply the acquisition by workers of occupation-task specific skills and needed to include attention to the types of educational, occupational, and personal information required by people choosing among diverse occupational and educational patterns, the effects of work values and attitudes, the ability to plan and choose, the ability to engage in industrial discipline and the affective components of work. Therefore, it became increasingly apparent that one could theoretically train the most competent machinist in the world, but if this person did not value being a machinist, was unwilling to go to work at 8:00 A.M. each day, five days a week, and did not have a commitment to personal productivity, you might just as well not train the person at all. There was a growing move to develop not just competent persons as defined by the needs of the occupational structure but personally competent people defined in broader terms. It was in this context that Commissioner Marland's predecessor, James Allen, actually used the term *career education* a year earlier than Marland when he addressed the National Association of Secondary School Principals Convention in 1970. He said, "It is the renewed awareness of the universality of the basic human and social need for competence that is generating not only increased emphasis today on career education but a whole new concept of its character and its place in the total educational enterprise" (Allen, 1970).

Many persons then, as now, dismissed such observations as nothing more than the periodic rhetoric of the cyclical assaults on education that have occurred since the beginning of the republic. Without overdrawing the matter, however, the issues were deeper and broader than that. The forces that gave rise to career education in the 1970s had been building intensely throughout the 1960s. The United States entered the 1960s in a climate of unemployment. Unemployment in the third recession since the Korean War exceeded 8.1 percent (unadjusted for seasonality in February 1961), causing it to become a key public issue for the first time since the 1930s. The focus of intensive debate was whether the cause of unemployment was slow economic growth and a deficient rate of job creation or inadequate skills among the work force in an economy of abundant but high-level employment opportunities. As the debate ensued through the decade, the U.S. Office of Education formulated a series of 11 conditions that allegedly justified educational reform through the medium of career education. They included the following (Hoyt, 1974):

1. Too many persons leaving our educational system are deficient in the basic academic skills required for adaptability in today's rapidly changing society.

2. Too many students fail to see meaningful relationships between what they are being asked to learn in school and what they will do when they leave the educational system. This is true of both those who remain to graduate and those who drop out of the educational system.
3. American education, as currently structured, best meets the educational needs of that minority of persons who will someday become college graduates. It fails to place equal emphasis on meeting the educational needs of that vast majority of students who will never be college graduates.
4. American education has not kept pace with the rapidity of change in the postindustrial occupational society. As a result, when worker qualifications are compared with job requirements, we find overeducated and undereducated workers are present in large numbers. Both the boredom of the overeducated worker and the frustration of the undereducated worker have contributed to the growing presence of worker alienation in the total occupational society.
5. Too many persons leave our educational system at both the secondary and collegiate levels unequipped with the vocational skills, the self-understanding and career decision-making skills, or the work attitudes that are essential for making a successful transition from school to work.
6. The growing need for and presence of women in the work force has not been reflected adequately in either the educational or the career options typically pictured for girls enrolled in our educational system.
7. The growing needs for continuing and recurrent education on the part of adults are not being met adequately by our current systems of public education.
8. Insufficient attention has been given to learning opportunities which exist outside the structure of formal education and are increasingly needed by both youth and adults in our society.
9. The general public, including parents and the business-industry-labor community, has not been given an adequate role in formulation of educational policy.
10. American education, as currently structured, does not adequately meet the needs of minority or economically disadvantaged persons in our society.
11. Post–high school education has given insufficient emphasis to educational programs at the subbaccalaureate degree level (pp. 3–4).

Although each of these conditions was and is debated, collectively they called attention to conditions in society at large and in the educational structure per se that were seen as reducing the work ethic in America, inadequately providing the information and support to facilitate individual decision making, and permitting a lack of meaningful linkage between education and work.

National Models of Career Education

Immediately following the introduction of career education by Commissioner Marland in 1971, a major effort was begun to translate many of the notions he described into operational models. Such models occurred at both state and national levels. Although these models have now largely been integrated into the school systems or agencies where they were field-tested and their original assumptions have been obscured by adaptations and refinements, it is useful to acknowledge their influence on the implementation of career education both conceptually and operationally.

Space does not permit examination of the state models or the models of private agencies that paralleled or evolved from the original national models. We will limit ourselves here to a consideration of the four federally funded national models that were pioneering prototypes for much that has resulted in the past 20 years. Each of these models was based on somewhat different assumptions, goals, and populations to be served. Each was also changed from its original form as demonstration projects played out. Nevertheless, they remain important reference points from which to understand the current approaches to career education. The four national models were

1. The school-based, or comprehensive career education model
2. The employer-based, or more recently, the experience-based career education model
3. The home/community-based career education model
4. The rural/residential-based career education model

A general overview of the goals and populations served by each of the models is provided in the subsequent sections.

The School-based, Comprehensive Career Education Model. The school-based model originally began as an effort to revitalize education by infusing the curriculum from kindergarten to grade 12 with career education themes. Subsequently, the model was extended from kindergarten to graduate school. Extensive community, industrial, and business involvement; widespread use of cooperative education; and the placement of every student departing the secondary school in either a job or a higher education program have each been stressed as essential to the success of the school-based model.

The original goals of the school-based model were to develop within each student

- A concept of self that is in keeping with a work-oriented society
- Positive attitudes about work, school, and society, and a sense of satisfaction resulting from successful experiences in these areas
- Personal characteristics of self-respect, self-reliance, perseverance, initiative, and resourcefulness
- A realistic understanding of the relationships between the world of work and education
- A comprehensive awareness of career options in the world of work
- The ability to enter employment in an appropriate occupation at a productive level and/or to pursue further education

In 1972, these goals were sharpened and reordered slightly to ensure that students exited school with

- A sense of purpose and direction
- Self-identity and identification with society (and an idea of their relationship)
- Basic skills and knowledge
- A comprehensive awareness of career options and the ability to enter employment and/or further education

The school-based model was designed to reorient the educational system from within by infusing it with ideas, experiences, and skills that, historically, have not been systematically provided to all students. Although the goals of the model have been frequently stated in educational philosophies, they have not been comprehensively carried forth in practice. Specifically, the purposes of the redirection of education as promoted by this model are (1) to acquaint students more intimately with a variety of career opportunities through each of their school experiences; (2) to ensure that every student receives an education that integrates academic skills, social development, and career preparation; and (3) to provide students with a continuing awareness of educational choices for career planning. Weaving throughout the philosophy and practice of this model is an acknowledgement of the need for extensive guidance and counseling activities to help the student develop self-awareness, self-confidence, and mature attitudes, as well as to match his or her interests and abilities with potential careers.

The Employer-based (Experience-based) Model. Career Education Model II, the employer-based model, was designed to meet the individual learning needs of a cross-section of young people, ages 13–18, who need or are seeking a significant alternative to their current educational environments. In contrast to the school-based model, which attempts to redirect the formal educational structure, this model assumes that some students are turned off by the formal educational structure and need a different way to acquire basic academic skills, self-understanding, and career awareness, as well as career preparation. The different way is to consider the community as a learning laboratory capable of providing many opportunities to individualize student experiences with the world of work. More specifically, the model was intended to demonstrate the relevance of the educational process to students through "intimate student involvement in professional and industrial operations." The program emphasizes educational experiences that are available in such settings as scientific and medical laboratories, warehouses, construction and housing projects, parks, museums, banks, insurance companies, hospitals, factories, and prisons. Specifically, employer-based career education begins with identification of learning elements that all students need to acquire and then locates actual work or adult activity situations, managed by employers, in which students can learn these specific elements. Thus, students will experience adult-centered work while they acquire the same education credentials as would be available through the formal educational structure. The original goals of the employer-based model were to

1. Provide an alternative education program for students, ages 13–18, in an employer-based setting
2. Unify the positive elements of academic, general, and vocational curricula into a comprehensive career education program
3. Increase the relevance of the world of education to the world of work
4. Broaden the base of community participation, particularly by involving public and private employers more directly and significantly in education

With respect to student learning, the model was intended to emphasize direct participation by students in learning experiences designed to

1. Review and reinforce students' educational competencies and interests
2. Provide opportunities for a variety of activities with a variety of people other than the limited peer-group and teacher associations available in the public schools
3. Develop a strong self-concept through participation in an individualized and self-directed learning program
4. Provide multiple opportunities for obtaining directly relevant information concerning career opportunities and requirements, and advantages and disadvantages of a variety of career options

The essence of this program is its ability to individualize experience for each student through individual projects, individual contracts, work-study, cooperative education, and other methods. Since the program's success involves a consortium of public and private employers, relatively few constraints are placed on the means by which knowledge, skills, attitudes, motivation, and experiences are imparted to students. In addition, a student is expected to enter and reenter the program freely with options of returning to the traditional school program, getting a job, or moving on to further education.

The guidance system in this model has two functions: (1) to mediate actively between students and their work-education community environments and (2) to assist in mapping an individualized learning program for each student. This active involvement of guidance personnel is critical to the model's success, because student participation is voluntary. More important, each student is expected to participate in the selection of his or her own pattern of work or activity situations from a variety of opportunities, so that learning situations are most relevant to personal interests and needs.

When control of the funding of the four national career education models was transferred from the U.S. Office of Education to the National Institute of education in 1972, the employer-based model was renamed the experience-based model. This name change tended to shift the perspective of the model away from only those students turned off by the formal academic context and to employment/academic opportunities for such students to a greater emphasis on the experiential nature of the involvement of instructional process and a range of community opportunities to accomplish career education goals.

The Home/Community-based Model. The third national career educational model was the first to deal expressly with adult populations, including those who are homebound. Of particular concern in this model are women who have been homebound while raising young children but now wish to reenter the labor market or to advance their education. In this model the home itself is used as a career education center in conjunction with three components: (1) a career-oriented educational television program focused on building motivation in studying for a career, providing information about career opportunities, and some occupational competency instruction; (2) a home and community education system, using television, correspondence programs, and radio and instruction aids; and (3) career classes in the community to provide career guidance and counseling.

The purposes served by the home/community-based model include

1. To develop educational delivery systems in the home and community
2. To provide new career education programs for adults
3. To establish a guidance and career placement system to assist individuals in occupational and related life roles
4. To develop more competent workers for the world of work
5. To enhance the quality of the home as a living center

In essence, the home/community-based model was an effort to enhance the employability and career options of out-of-school adults through the systematic integration of mass media, referral centers, individual counseling, and community resources. Unlike the other models, this one did not attempt to teach skills and attitudes directly. Rather, it was seen as an information clearinghouse and a vehicle by which interested persons could assess their career interests and identify ways by which these interests might be met in the local community.

The changes in this model since its inception are neither philosophical nor related to the clients served but rather focus on the delivery system. As the original objectives suggested, it was expected that cable and public television would be the major vehicles for information delivery. As it turns out, telephone interviews, referrals, and a resource center have emerged as highly important methods for this population. Further, it seems apparent that this project is quite literally an effort to provide career guidance and counseling on an outreach basis from a community level. As such, this model became an important spur to what have emerged as educational brokering centers for adults in many communities as well as to the educational information centers established by Title I of the Education Amendments of 1976 (PL 94-482).

The Rural/Residential-based Model. Career Education Model IV was basically an attempt to test the hypothesis that entire disadvantaged rural families could be helped to improve their economic and social conditions through an intensive program of milieu therapy at a residential center. Therefore, rather than train only the head of a household in occupational skills, this project provided services for the entire family including: day care; elementary and secondary education; career and technical education; parent education; family-living assistance; medical and dental services; welfare services; counseling; and cultural and recreational opportunities for single and married students and their families.

In view of the scope of this model, its original objectives were few:

1. To provide families with employment capabilities suitable to the area
2. To provide leverage on the economic development of the area
3. To improve family living

Only one program, the Mountain-Plains Education and Economic Development Program at Glasgow, Montana, implemented this model. The project focused on chronically underemployed, multiproblem rural families from six north central and northwestern states. Through a total intervention approach, it attempted to influence all significant activities of the family and to make it both economically and socially viable through career counseling, training, homemaking, family development skills, and occupational placement for the parents, as well as remedial education and guidance for the children. At any one time, approximately 210 families were in residence at the model site and remained there for an average of eight to nine months. Programs and services provided by this project included

1. Career guidance, required for both adults in an intact family
2. A career development program for the head-of-household and optionally for the spouse, including foundation education in math skills and communication skills, occupation preparation, and work experience
3. Family and individual counseling for head-of-household and spouse and, based on need, for older children
4. A family core curriculum designed to provide both head-of-household and spouse with home management, health, consumer education, parenting, community organization, and recreation skills
5. Limited basic medical, dental, and optical services through contracted services
6. Financial support of the family while in the program
7. Child development and care for preschool youngsters
8. Placement services
9. Supportive follow-up after placement
10. Research, documentation, and dissemination of the program

Although far more could be said about the beginnings of career education and about the early models designed to make operational the assumptions on which career education rests, it is useful to consider what has been learned from the attempts to implement career education since 1971. The categories of learning are diverse and represent the underlying structure from which projections about the future can be made.

The Changing Definition of Career Education

Among the trends and perspectives associated with the implementation of career education during the past decade has been a changing definition of career education itself.

Although there were many state definitions of career education by 1974 when the first federal definition was provided, that federal definition provides a useful benchmark. It indicated that as a matter of federal policy, "Career Education is the totality of experiences through which one learns about and prepares to engage in work as part of her or his way of life" (Hoyt, 1974). This definition was buttressed by the description of career education found in the Education Amendments of 1974 (Section 406, PL 93-380), which created the Office of Career Education and officially made career education a federal priority. In this legislation, career education was considered to be a process designed to

- Increase the relationship between schools and society as a whole
- Relate the curricula of schools to the needs of persons to function in society
- Provide opportunities for counseling, guidance, and career development for all children
- Extend the concept of the education process beyond the school into employment and the community
- Foster flexibility in attitudes, skills, and knowledge in order to enable persons to cope with accelerating change and obsolescence
- Eliminate any distinction between education for vocational purposes and general or academic education

Since 1974 the federal definition of career education has gone through several iterations, the most recent one being community-based rather than school-based. As such it introduces the concept of collaboration as a major emphasis. It is as follows:

> Career Education is a community effort aimed at helping persons—youth and adults—better prepare themselves for work through acquiring adaptability skills that will enable them to change with change in society in such ways that work—paid and unpaid—will become a more meaningful and more rewarding part of their total lifestyle. (Hoyt, 1979)

This definition goes on to identify the adaptability skills to be imparted through a career education effort:

1. Basic academic skills of reading, oral and written communication, and mathematics
2. Work habits leading to productivity in the workplace
3. A personally meaningful set of work values that lead the person to want to work
4. Basic understandings of the American economic system that will enable the person to respect that system and function effectively within it
5. Career decision-making skills
6. Skills required for self-understanding and understanding of educational/occupational opportunities
7. Job-seeking, job-getting, and job-holding skills
8. Skills required to combat stereotyping as it impinges on full freedom of educational and occupational choice
9. Skills required for the individual to humanize the workplace for himself/herself
10. Skills required to find meaningful work in productive use of leisure time

In deliberating such definitional shifts and emphases and their broader context, readers will find the observations of Hansen (1977), among other theorists, helpful in a comprehensive analysis of the concepts and definitions of career education. Up to that date, Hansen identified dimensions that needed to be incorporated into an expanded view of career education that embraced not only the economic role but other life roles as well. In *paraphrased* form, her perspectives follow.

The expanded career education concept

1. Is person-centered and takes into account the changing nature of both individuals and the environment and the concurrent need for flexible and adaptable human beings

2. Integrates into its basic aims the twin goals of human development and experience
3. Builds on a solid rationale and conceptual framework of the best knowledge available in career development theory and research
4. Identifies a sequential, kindergarten-to-adult set of objectives from the empirical literature in developmental psychology as a basis for exposing all individuals through curriculum, counseling, and community to a wide spectrum of career knowledge, information, skills, and attitudes
5. Provides for a wide range of two-way community involvements, paid and unpaid, including alternative education-to-work linkages, business-industry-labor-government internships and exchanges, parent and worker involvement in schools, and student involvement in community
6. Recognizes the need for individuals to know a great deal about the occupational and educational world in order to manage it; acknowledges that many occupational clustering systems and career information systems can be utilized to assist in acquiring, knowing, and processing information
7. Recognizes the central place of counseling and guidance as part of its delivery system and the unique historical and contemporary contributions of vocational and career guidance to career development of children, youth, and adults
8. Recognizes the importance of role integration—the need for individuals to examine and prepare for work roles in relation to other life roles in family, community, and leisure—and to clarify their values with respect to the meaning of work in their lives
9. Reaffirms the importance of helping individuals in the transition from school to work, school to further education, and school to other alternatives, and of the need for educational institutions and agencies to more adequately fulfill the placement functions in helping individuals take the next step or reach the next stage
10. Stresses the importance of attending to special needs of bypassed and underserved populations, especially women, the handicapped, ethnic minorities, and those in poverty
11. Is seen not only as a response to crisis in education but as a comprehensive, unifying concept of human development that can provide a means for effecting change within individuals (faculty and students) and institutions
12. Is a time-oriented concept that recognizes that it can help individuals not only prepare for the future but see the relationship of the future to the past and to the present (Hansen, 1977, pp. 35–38)

Hoyt and Shylo (1987) have suggested, in updating the ongoing transition of career education, that although the term *career education* is being used less frequently, the concepts it embraces (e.g., to promote the acquisition of general employability skills by students and adults) continue to be viable and supported by a variety of federal and state programs. By 1987, the goals by which career education was being defined by members of the National Career Education Leaders' Communication Network included the following:

- To promote and implement private sector/education system partnerships
- To equip persons with general employability/adaptability/promotability skills
- To help persons in career awareness/exploring/decision making
- To reform education by infusing a "careers" emphasis in classrooms
- To make work a meaningful part of the total life-style
- To relate education and work so that better choices of both can be made
- To reduce bias and stereotyping and thus protect freedom of career choice (pp. 5–6)

Hoyt contends that the total concept of career education embraces the systematic, coordinated implementation of all seven of these components—that implementation of any single component must be regarded as a necessary but not sufficient effort.

Evaluation in Career Education

A further trend during the past 15 years is an emphasis on evaluation in career education. A series of monographs, reports, and published research articles have identified in various forms the outcomes of career education. Space is not available here to do an in-depth analysis of such findings. Herr (1978), Bhaerman (1977), and others have done so, and the reader is referred to them. Suffice it to say here that, in general, career education comes out quite well on most of these findings. As Hoyt (1980) has suggested, evaluation studies clearly demonstrate that a career education approach can, when correctly applied, provide students with general employability/adaptability/promotability skills and increase student academic achievement. Trebilco (1984) has reported similar findings in Australia, where, as a result of data from 38 metropolitan secondary schools, he has concluded that career education programs achieved higher gains in the career maturity of their students between grades 9 and 11 than schools with no career education programs. His findings also demonstrated a strong relationship between the type of program offered, the support of the school for that program, and the gains in career maturity of the students between grades 9 and 11.

In a summative evaluation of 18 studies of career education effects, Baker and Popowicz (1983) used metaanalysis techniques to examine the size and importance of such effects. The results indicated that moderate positive outcomes were present across these studies and that, on average, a person experiencing such career education treatments would be expected to improve on outcome measures by about one-half of a standard deviation above the mean scores in such measures as compared to a person who did not receive such treatment.

The Ingredients of Effective Career Education Models

As a result of the extensive evaluation of career education to the present time, the ingredients of *effective* career education efforts have become increasingly obvious. These have been extracted from major career education programs around the nation that have stood up to various types of evaluation by government agencies (for example, Hoyt, 1980). Although no one model fits every circumstance, setting, or local emphasis, effective models of career education tend to share several ingredients:

1. They have visible and continuing administrative support.
2. The goals of career education are seen as major commitments of a school district, a higher education institution, or a work setting. In this respect, they are seen as central to the institutional mission and to the facilitation of specific behaviors to be attained by graduates or by employees.
3. Career education is a planned, integrative dimension of an education or work setting, not a random add-on or by-product relegated to the responsibility of only one group of specialists. Representatives of all the groups of educators, industrial personnel, and community persons affected by and making a contribution to career education are involved in the planning, and selected advisory groups are used effectively.
4. Resources are provided for planning and for staff development, and these emphases are matters of systematic effort. The planning and the staff development are based on theory and research in career behavior so that

there is concern about not only the how of career education but also the why.

5. Field experiences (whether internships, planned field trips, career shadowing, or something else) are planned to extend and to reinforce curriculum infusion and other career education instruction. They are not independent of the latter. The community is seen as a large learning laboratory that has responsibility to be in partnership with the schools in creating the most effective educational and occupational opportunities available.
6. Career education is not seen as something so different that the school system, teachers, counselors, and others must start from ground zero. Rather it involves the acknowledgment that experiences already in place have career education implications and further career education can be built on them. Organizational changes are planned and developed to facilitate the career education effort, but they are not dramatized as so new as to be threatening to participants.
7. Career education and vocational education are not confused. Career education is seen as being for all children, youth, or adults within the educational level or setting in which it is implemented; it is not confined in its scope to only the development of occupational task specific skills.
8. An evaluation process is built into the planning and implementation of career education so that its results can be examined and advocated as appropriate to policy-making bodies or other decision makers.

The Relationship of Career Education to Career Guidance

The models of career education described in this chapter clearly depend on the presence of career guidance. It is no overstatement to contend that career education has institutionalized, as major aspects of educational and manpower development missions, goals that have long been advanced by career guidance practitioners. Certainly, career education has made visible the complexity of many of these goals. It has reinforced the importance of cooperation between school and community, various networks of persons, and diverse processes and resources, if the goals of career education are to be met.

The Importance of Career Education Personnel. Career education has shown that no one group of persons can accomplish all its goals alone. But it has also made apparent that no other group of specialists is more important to its goals than career guidance personnel (Hoyt, 1984, 1985). Other elements of the school, community, or family may help to lay a broad base of career awareness nor provide specific technical preparation for a chosen career. However, it remains the central task of career guidance to help individuals identify their career options, understand the personal implications of these options, plan the ways by which they can integrate the educational experiences necessary to achieve favored goals, and make decisions wisely when they must be made.

Hoyt (1984) and Hoyt and Shylo (1989) have attempted to clarify the similarities and the differences between career education and career guidance. They are similar in that they

- Are deeply rooted in the career development process and in the theory and research of career development
- Include longitudinal efforts that move developmentally, from career awareness to career exploration to career planning/decision making to implementation
- Are intended to serve the developmental needs of all persons and not limited to any one portion of the general population

- Are committed to protecting and enhancing maximum freedom of career choice for all persons
- Emphasize education/work relationships at all levels of education
- Include efforts that begin at the kindergarten level and continue well into the retirement years
- View the work values of persons as part of their total systems of personal values and so view work as an integral part of their total life-style
- Recognize the importance of both paid and unpaid work
- Recognize, applaud, and seek to facilitate the key role parents play in the career development of their children
- Support career development as an effort extending beyond only the career counselor (that is, the total education system and the broader community have significant roles to play.)

They are different in the following ways:

- Although both are rooted in the career development process, career education is also rooted in the teaching/learning process. Career guidance is not.
- One of the basic reasons for the existence of career education is to serve as a vehicle for educational reform. Educational reform is not part of the basic charter of career guidance.
- Whereas career education is pictured as a total community effort headed by any of several kinds of persons, career guidance efforts are almost always headed by career guidance professionals.
- The most critical aspects of the implementation of career education lies in efforts carried out by classroom teachers. The most crucial aspects of the implementation of career guidance lie in efforts carried out by career guidance specialists.
- Career education places great emphasis and a high priority on bringing a proper and appropriate emphasis to the goal of education as preparation for work among all basic goals of American education. Career guidance has not made this a priority for the movement (Hoyt & Shylo, 1989, pp. 18–19).

Career Education in Settings Other than Schools

Career education has had its major implementation in the elementary and secondary schools of the nation. But it would be wrong to conclude that its effects have been confined to those settings. Colleges and universities and corporate settings have also instituted career education programs, although not always under that title.

It appears that the significant increase in the number of colleges and universities expanding the functions of their placement centers to career development and placement centers is at least an indirect outcome of the influence of career education. Many of the characteristics and purposes of such centers will be described in Chapter 10. Particularly notable are their efforts in providing courses in decision making and career planning within majors, their use of computer-based career guidance systems, and the provision of workshops on job search strategies, interviewing techniques, assertiveness training, and related topics. Most of these centers are developmental and proactive in their emphases. They use both instructional and counseling methodologies to make higher education settings more career relevant.

Career education has also influenced models of career development in business and industry, although this notion is somewhat more diffuse and harder to track than that of career development in higher education. Shifts in work values, the organization of work, employment and unemployment rates, and concerns about work productivity have combined to stimulate new models of personnel *development*, not just personnel *management*. In Chapter 11 we describe many of the models of career guidance in business and industry. As the concepts and practices embodied in these models are closely scrutinized, their resemblance to various career education models is clear, although the language of such implementations is that of business and industry rather than of education. In addition, in comparing career education for youth with that for adults, Rice (1981) has observed that the former has concentrated on the transition from school to work, whereas the latter has focused on the transition from work to school (retraining) or from work to work (midlife career change, moving from a part-time job to a long-term career, and so on). It seems quite likely that the implementation of career education concepts during the past decade has provided the stimulus and the conceptual mortar to bring together a life-span approach to career guidance.

PERSPECTIVES ON COUNSELOR ROLE IN CAREER GUIDANCE

The historical evolution of approaches and definitions pertinent to career guidance has led to considerable speculation about the counselor's role. These perspectives have been captured in various role statements and in a number of articles. Several of the more prominent statements are examined in the following paragraphs.

Among the first statements dealing with the role of guidance specialists in career guidance was that made in a joint position paper of the American Vocational Association, and the National Vocational Guidance Association Commission on Career Guidance and Vocational Education. This paper was officially adopted by the NVGA in May 1973 and by the AVA in July 1973, recommending that the responsibilities of the guidance team (such as counselors and related specialists) include the following efforts to support program leadership and coordination:

1. Coordinate the career guidance program
2. Provide staff with the understanding necessary to assist each student to obtain a full competency-based learning experience
3. Coordinate the acquisition and use of appropriate occupational, educational, and labor market information
4. Help staff understand the process of human growth and development and assess needs of individuals
5. Help staff plan for sequential student learning experiences in career development
6. Coordinate the development and use of a comprehensive, cumulative pupil data system that can be reaidly used by all students
7. Identify and coordinate the use of school and community resources needed to facilitate career guidance
8. Coordinate the evaluation of student learning experiences and use the resulting data in counseling students, in consulting with the instructional staff and parents, and in modifying the curriculum
9. Coordinate a job placement program for the school and provide for job adjustment counseling
10. Provide individual and group counseling and guidance so that students will be stimulated to continually and systematically interrelate and expand their experiences, knowledge, understanding, skills, and appreciations as they grow and develop throughout life (pp. 13–14)

In December 1974, the Board of Directors of the American Personnel and Guidance Association adopted a statement describing the role and functions of counseling and personnel practitioners in career education. This statement recommended that counselors provide leadership in the following areas:

1. Identifying individual career development tasks and implementing programs to accomplish them
2. Identifying and classifying educational and occupational information
3. Assimilating and applying career decision-making methods and materials
4. Eliminating the restrictions that racism and sexism place on opportunity
5. Expanding the variety and appropriateness of assessment devices and procedures necessary for sound personal, educational, and occupational decision making
6. Emphasizing the importance of career counseling and of achieving its goals (pp. 3–4)

These six functions are considered to be inseparable leadership duties for counselors in career education. The APGA statement also considers it essential for counselors to participate actively in the career education process in seven additional ways:

1. By serving as liaison between educational and community resource groups
2. By conducting assessment surveys of career education needs among students
3. By organizing and operating part-time and full-time educational, occupational, and placement programs
4. By conducting job adjustment activities
5. By contributing to revisions of the curriculum
6. By helping involve the family in career education
7. By participating in efforts to monitor and assess activities and communicating the results of those activities to other practitioners and clientele (p. 5)

In 1976, the Association for Counselor Education and Supervision adopted a position paper on counselor preparation for career development and career education (Association for Counselor Education and Supervision, 1976). This position paper contends that counselors engaged in career guidance, regardless of their employment setting, should be knowledgeable of and competent in the following fifteen areas:

1. Career and human development theory and research: the skills necessary to translate this knowledge into developmental career guidance and career education programs
2. Career information resources: to assist teachers, administrators, community agency personnel, paraprofessionals, and peers in integrating this type of information into the teaching-counseling process
3. Career assessment strategies: to assist individual using these data in the decision-making process
4. Individual and group counseling practices: the skills necessary to assist individuals in career planning using both approaches
5. Career decision-making processes, and implement programs designed to facilitate career decision-making for clientele in educational and community agency settings
6. Job placement services: to assist their clientele to seek, acquire, and maintain employment
7. The unique career development needs of special clientele groups (women, minorities, the handicapped, disadvantaged, adults), and assist them in their development
8. Sexism and racism: the necessary skills to reduce institutional discrimination in order to broaden the career opportunities available for all persons

9. The roles that life style and leisure play in career development, and in assisting clientele to select and prepare for occupations that coincide with various preferences
10. Consultation strategies and the skills necessary to assists others (teachers, parents, peers) to deliver indirect career guidance services
11. Synthesizing strategies: the skills necessary to assist individuals understand of their career decisions and life roles
12. Program development and curricular infusion strategies: design and implement career awareness, self-development, career exploration, and job placement programs within educational and community agency settings
13. Organizational development and change processes, and in facilitating change in educators' attitudes toward career education
14. Program evaluation techniques: to acquire evidence of the effectiveness of career guidance and career education programming
15. Educational trends and state and federal legislation may influence the development and implementation of career guidance programs (pp. 10–11)*

The position paper on the counselor's role in career education, promulgated in 1974, was subsequently revised after additional experience. In 1980, as a result of a national study of the role of the school counselor in career education, a matrix of career guidance competency requirements emerged that was related to different functions and purposes in which the counselor might be expected to engage. Figure 1.1 presents this matrix. Although it is not directly linked to an implementation of the matrix, the reader might find it useful to review the position paper entitled "The Role of the School Counselor in Career Guidance: Expectations and Responsibilities," published by the American School Counselors Association (1985). This paper provides a useful philosophical background for career guidance as a school counselor function.

The various position papers previously cited are relatively comprehensive with regard to the counselor's role in career guidance or in career education, but few have addressed in a specific manner the counselor's role in career counseling. That condition was rectified in 1981, when the Board of Directors of the NVGA approved a comprehensive set of counselor competencies essential to the practice of vocational/career counseling. They defined minimum competencies in six areas, including the following selected examples:

General Counseling–Knowledge of general counseling theories and techniques; ability to use counseling techniques in effectively assisting individuals with career choice and life/career development concerns; skills in building a productive relationship with the client; ability to assist the client identify internal factors as well as contextual factors related to life/career decision making.

Information–Knowledge of education, training, employment trends, labor market, and career resources; basic concepts related to vocational/career counseling including career development, career pathing, and career patterns; career development and decision-making theories; resources and techniques designed for use

* Reprinted from pp. 10 and 11 of Association for Counselor Education and Supervision. Position paper on counselor preparation for career development/career education, April 1976. © AACD. Reprinted with permission. No further reproduction authorized without written permission of American Association for Counseling and Development.

Figure 1.1

Competency (Role) Areas and Statements (APGA Study of School Counselor in Career Education) (Reprinted from *The School Counselor's Involvement in Career Education,* edited by Frank E. Burtnett. APGA Press, 1980. © AACD. Reprinted with permission. No further reproduction authorized without written permission of American Association for Counseling and Development.)

Career Guidance Program Components

	Counselor Knowledge/ Expertise Component	Leadership Component	Management Component	Direct Services Component	Indirect Services Component
PLANNING/ DESIGN	Understand program management concepts Understand concepts of career education, guidance, and career development Understand staff development and in-service education techniques and procedures Understand community and labor market composition and trends Understand concepts of collaboration in the delivery of educational programs	Involve educational staff and community resource persons in planning and designing activities Institute communication networks among appropriate populations	Assess student career development needs Apply program management concepts Assess the effectiveness of the existing career guidance program Establish program goals and objectives Design specific career guidance services and activities Coordinate career guidance program with career education and total educational thrust at the institution Prepare budgets Develop calendars and time lines depicting sequence of program activities	Plan and design activities and services to facilitate career development needs of students	Participate in the design of school and non-school activities which extend the goals and objectives of the career guidance program
IMPLEMENTATION	Understand career development theories Understand counseling theory and techniques Understand decision-making theory Understand group dynamics Understand needs of specific groups within institutions and the community (women, handicapped, ethnic minorities, etc.) Understand the role and function of information in education and counseling Understand curriculum design and content Understand measurement and appraisal techniques	Coordinate school and community resources Develop program support from administration, board of education, instructional staff, community and students Develop and implement a public relations system Provide input to curriculum revision	Manage the career guidance program Conduct staff development sessions	Counsel individuals and small groups Conduct student assessment (ability achievement, interest, personality, etc.) Disseminate occupational and educational information Conduct career awareness, explorations and experience programs Operate student service activities (e.g., career center, job placement program, etc.)	Consult with teachers, parents, and administrators regarding students Conduct information programs for parents and community representatives Provide direct input and technical assistance to persons implementing career education activities Conduct staff development training
EVALUATION	Understand essential, integral, and continuous nature of evaluation Understand range and variety of data collection and assessment methodologies Understand program standards and guidelines from government agencies and accrediting and professional associations Recognize exemplary career guidance practices, methods, and techniques	Demonstrate exemplary career guidance program aspects	Conduct comprehensive evaluation of the career guidance program Monitor activities conducted by self and others Utilize broad-based input to the evaluation system (students, teachers, parents, etc.) Prepare and disseminate interpretive communication evaluation results Communicate findings to career guidance program decision-makers Improve and modify the career guidance program decision-makers Improve and modify the career guidance program process Identify exemplary practices, methods, and techniques Conduct evaluation of the effectiveness of staff development training	Evaluate the effectiveness and value of specific career guidance activities and services	Disseminate findings from career guidance and career education programs to appropriate populations

with special groups; strategies to store, retrieve, and disseminate vocational/career information

Individual/Group Assessment–Knowledge of appraisal techniques and measures of aptitude, achievement, interest, values, and personality; strategies used in evaluating performance, individual effectiveness, and program effectiveness; ability to interpret appraisal data to clients and other appropriate individuals or groups of people

Management/Administration–Knowledge of program designs, needs assessment techniques and practices and performance objectives used in organizing and setting goals for career development programs; knowledge of management concepts and leadership styles used in career development programs; ability to prepare budgets and time lines and to design, compile, and report on evaluation of career development activities and programs

Implementation– Knowledge of program adoption and planned change strategies and of personal and environmental barriers affecting the implementation of career development programs; ability to implement individual and group programs in career development for specified populations; ability to implement a public relations effort on behalf of career development activities and services; ability to devise and implement a comprehensive career resource center and to implement pilot programs in a variety of career development areas

Consultation–Knowledge of consultation strategies and models; ability to provide effective career consultation to influential individuals, the general public, and business and professional groups; ability to convey program goals and achievements to personnel in positions of authority; ability to provide data on the cost effectiveness of career counseling and career development activities

As discussed earlier in this chapter, in January 1991 the Board of Directors of the National Career Development Association revised the minimum career counseling competencies adopted by the board of directors of the National Vocational Guidance Association in 1981. Several new categories were added to the original six categories, and additional skills and knowledge emphases were included in some of the original categories. In addition to combining some of the original categories, new categories of minimum skills added in 1991 included those in career development theory, special populations, supervision, ethical/legal issues, and research/evaluation. These additional categories emphasized the following skills:

- Ability to support clients and challenge them to examine the balance of work, leisure, family, and community roles in their careers
- Knowledge about variables such as ethnicity, gender, culture, learning style, personal development, and physical/mental ability, all of which affect the assessment process
- Knowledge of information, techniques, and models related to computer-assisted career information delivery systems and career counseling
- Sensitivity toward the developmental issues and needs unique to minority populations
- Ability to provide effective supervision to career counselors at different levels of experience
- Ability to apply ethical standards to career counseling and consulting situations, issues, and practices
- Ability to design evaluation programs that take into account the needs of special populations, minorities, the elderly, persons with the AIDS virus, and women

Although the list is not exhaustive of all recommended additions, those cited reflect the changing demands upon career counselors and the skills needed to maintain one's currency and competence to deal with emerging issues for clients or students.

The 1981 competency statements of the NVGA were placed into a new and popularized form in the 1985 *Consumer Guidelines for Selecting a Career Counselor,* set forth by the National Career Development Association (the newer name of the NVGA). Under the heading "What do Career Counselors do?" the following is stated:

> The services of career counselors differ, depending on competence. A professional or Nationally Certified Career Counselor helps people make decisions and plans related to life/career directions. The strategies and techniques are tailored to the specific needs of the person seeking help. It is likely that the career counselor will do one or more of the following:
>
> - Conduct individual and group personal counseling sessions to help clarify life/career goals
> - Administer and interpret tests and inventories to assess abilities, interests, etc., and to identify career options
> - Encourage exploratory activities through assignments and planning experiences
> - Utilize career planning systems and occupational information systems to help individuals better understand the world of work
> - Provide opportunities for improving decision-making skills
> - Assist in developing individualized career plans
> - Teach job-hunting strategies and skills and assist in the development of resumes
> - Help resolve potential personal conflicts on the job through practice in human relations skills
> - Assist in understanding the integration of work and other life roles
> - Provide support for persons experiencing job stress, job loss, career transition (pp. 1–2)*

*Reprinted from "What Do Career Counselors Do?", 1985 *Consumer Guidelines for Selecting a Career Counselor.*

Although there are other excellent analyses of necessary skills for career guidance person nel, the statements examined here generally represent the perspectives of professional associations and are therefore both representative of thinking among practitioners and influential in shaping such thinking.

The position papers cited here, although written for somewhat different purposes, share a generally common view about the roles for which the counselor or career guidance practitioner should be responsible. They each view the counselor as an activist involved in both group and individual activities designed to promote knowledge, attitudes, and skills that individuals need for self-definition and career planning. Rather than being confined to a one-to-one model of interaction in an office situations, the counselor is seen as a collaborator, a resource person, and a consultant. In general, each paper advocates that the counselor play a developmental role, providing experiences by which persons can acquire mastery behaviors appropriate to effective career development, rather than only a treatment or remedial role for youth or adults who have had difficulty making choices and found their job skills wanting.

In each of these position papers, counselors are expected to understand career development, to be able to help educators or employers to realize career development implications for curriculum or training modifications, and to create learning opportunities relevant to the broad range of human talent. It is also expected that counselors will work with others in effecting placement of students and adults in educational and occupational opportunities in the community through which their career development can be enhanced.

A developmental approach to career guidance is not likely to mean that counselors will have no further responsibility for crisis counseling, for remediation in the traditional sense, or for assisting students or adults at particular decision points. In all likelihood, such needs will always be present, although it is assumed that the incidence of crises can be reduced if counselors use developmental techniques to equip individuals with self-understanding, career awareness, and decision-making skills. It is also assumed that emphasizing developmental approaches to career guidance allows the counselor to have a positive effect on the lives of more persons than can a counselor who relies exclusively on one-to-one, crisis-oriented approaches. It is not assumed that counselors' eclectic use of developmental career guidance approaches will eliminate the need for individual counseling. Rather, it is expected that such processes will continue to help students and adults personalize and test the insights they obtain from career guidance emphases in curriculum, work experience, simulations, and other approaches. A major assumption is that the counselor functions related to career guidance can be viewed in terms of the skills taught and brought together into a program, and that they can ultimately be related to the outcomes sought by students or adults.

Trends in Counselor Role in Career Guidance

Professional association position papers, proposed or actual legislation, articles on counseling literature, and the mapping of broad trends in student or client needs for career guidance and counseling provide the conceptual fuel that triggers trends in counselor roles. Some of these trends are explicit; they typically extend processes that have been in evolution for a decade or more. Other trends are more vague and ill-defined.

Examples of trends in counselor roles in career guidance that are yet to be discussed in position papers, legislation, or professional literature take many forms. Given the fact that career counseling and career guidance operate at the intersection between individuals and their environments, they represent switching mechanisms, guides, and therapeutic agents in such contexts. As such, counselors or other specialists implementing career services are, in the future, likely to serve as brokers or maximizers of opportunities; as interpreters of the relationships between training or retraining and new career paths; as classifiers and providers of information and collaborators in its use; as support systems by which persons can acquire insight into their own stereotypes and irrational beliefs that have hindered their risk-taking and mobility; as stimuli through which individuals can increase their feelings of self-worth, power, and self-efficacy; as providers of psychoeducational mechanisms by which persons can learn certain skills—for example, assertiveness, anger management, decision making, conflict resolution, stress reduction, and job searching—necessary to exploring and mastering a successful and meaningful work life; as mentors offering feedback, coaching, and advice about career related tasks; and as therapeutic agents who signify hope and possibility in a confused and seemingly unsupportive work world.

Application of Systematic Approaches to Career Guidance. In the first version of this book (Herr & Cramer, 1972), we advocated that vocational guidance be seen as a total system of interacting techniques and personnel that could facilitate the individual acquisition of knowledge, attitudes, and skills leading to effective career behavior. Much of that has been incorporated into current models of career education and guidance. Although we continue to believe that counselors must apply systems thinking to the programming of career guidance, the term *systems* connotes to some a task so formidable that they reject it as a real solution to advancing the effectiveness of career guidance.

As a compromise, then, in the second and third editions and now in this one, we have proposed that, if speaking of a systems approach to career guidance suggests too threatening or too overwhelming a task to be realistic, the term *systematic approach* might be better. Regardless of which term one uses, however, the trend for the counselor seems apparent. In the future, the goals of career guidance and the methods by which these goals will be met must be identified in each setting—educational institution, agency, or workplace—for both accountability and programming effectiveness.

If any criticism of guidance and counseling is enduring, it is that it is difficult to assess its outcomes or to know in any specific sense what it contributes to broad social or educational goals. Shaw (1968) was among the first to note that most descriptions of guidance services have been confined to what is done (such as individual counseling, testing, maintenance of records, and information giving), rather than to why these things are done. Such questions as "How will students or adults be different as a function of career guidance?" or "What specific client outcomes are sought from different guidance and counseling processes?" have not typically been addressed. In short, descriptions of career guidance programs have largely dealt with the processes to be expected rather than the products. However, in an era of accountability, legislators, administrators, and consumers are frequently heard to say, "We want to know what you intend. What are your goals? How do you distinguish your contributions from those of other educational or social processes?"

Systems thinking or a systematic approach endeavors to specify clearly the results sought and the specific methods by which such results will be obtained. In the process, a systematic approach to career guidance would recognize that objectives must be stated explicitly, that the relationship of the counselor's contributions to these objectives must be stated clearly in relation to the contributions of other persons, and that ways of assessing whether or not career guidance objectives are being met must be identified and carried through. The basic question for career guidance programming is "Which resources or combination of resources (people, places, media) are appropriate for fostering what type of development in what type of client under what conditions (time, place, size of group, and so on) to achieve what purposes?" (Phillips, 1966) This requires a statement of program goals, behavioral objectives for students or clients, linkage of career guidance processes and resources to behavioral objectives, and an evaluative procedure.

Such planned approaches to career guidance are outcome-based (Johnson & Johnson, 1982) rather than function-based. Planned programs are assumed to clarify what counselors can contribute to the school, college, or workplace in which they are employed, the differences they can make in the lives of students or adult workers, and the degree to which they can be held accountable for selected outcomes or domains.

Walz and Benjamin (1984) have summarized the advantages of systematic career guidance delivery in the following paraphrased form:

1. A developmental emphasis—the systematic approach gives program planners the opportunity to design a proactive delivery system that anticipates needs and problems and develops appropriate strategies for dealing with them.
2. Effective use of available resources—program designers can tailor components of the delivery system (for example, counseling, media, information resources, computer-based guidance) to desired outcomes. This customizing avoids the shortcoming in traditional methods of overusing a particular guidance resource such as counseling.
3. Amenability to change and innovation—with clearly stated goals and objectives and

specified modes of delivery, it becomes easier to locate difficulties and target areas needing change or improvement and then to provide the training and resources needed by the staff to accomplish the new or revised goals and objectives.

4. Relative ease of evaluation—evaluation is an integral and necessary component of the systematic approach. Specific standards for judging behavioral change allow for more objective evaluation, and where there is a discrepancy between proposed and actual outcomes, new methods can be developed and implemented.
5. Avoidance of faddism—clarity in objectives and in modes of delivery provides a source of insulation against faddism or opportunistic responses to "catchy" ideas that have not been tested systematically.
6. Promotion of community effort—knowledge of what the program is about fosters a higher degree of articulation by community members and stimulates them to find ways that they can be involved. (pp. 28–29)

Chapter 6 will deal with planning for programs of career guidance or career education in considerable detail.

The Counselor as Applied Behavioral Scientist. In order to plan systematically for career guidance and to respond to individual differences, the counselor will likely become more eclectic in the future. Rather than being theory-bound or a practitioner of a single process (such as individual counseling), the counselor will need to use a range of techniques and processes both with groups and with individuals. The application of these techniques will need to be tailored to specific problems presented by individuals or to developmental purposes. In general, the application of these techniques will cause the counselor to have a broad acquaintance with a range of theories, concepts, and ideas bearing on career development and the empirical evidence of the effectiveness of these ideas. There seems to be no question that among the techniques to be employed by future career guidance practitioners, there will be heavy reliance on psychoeducation techniques and structured group experiences to build skills required by particular clients.

As the career counselor increasingly becomes an applied behavioral scientist, the model of systematic eclecticism wedded to an ongoing concern for evaluation and research will incrementally expand the science and knowledge base on which career counseling and guidance rest. Fundamentally, such a model assumes that specific approaches to career guidance or counseling are effective for some purposes and not for others, and that students or adult clients come to counselors for a variety of reasons. In response, the career counselor practicing systematic eclecticism collaborates with the client to select those approaches that are most relevant to the problem presented or to other unique needs of the client. A further assumption is that the career counselor should be trained in a repertoire of approaches—individual, group, assessment, psychoeducation, self-monitored, and so forth—that would be based on scientific analysis of their effectiveness under certain conditions and for specific purposes.

The trend for the career counselor to be an applied behavioral scientist who practices systematic eclecticism suggests levels of analysis, goal setting with counselees, and perspectives that go beyond those historically emphasized in career guidance and counseling. For example, systematic eclecticism suggests that it is not now possible to view any single theory as having sufficient explanatory power to cover all of the needs for career services brought to counselors. Rather, it suggests that the future will require an increase in the conception of career guidance and counseling approaches and counselee outcomes as a matrix of possible interactions; that most counselees will have more than one problem that needs to be addressed; and that the counselor's role will be to help the counselee experience a combination of approaches, treatments, and experiences effectively matched to his or her needs.

Implicit, if not explicit, in the paradigm of the counselor as an applied behavioral scientist is the parallel concept of a scientist-practitioner, as advanced by the American Psychological Association's view of the Counseling Psychologist. Inherent in such notions is a respect for and a professional commitment to engaging in research and evaluation of career counseling and career guidance processes used with different populations and for different reasons. Of relevance to the systematic planning for and the effective execution of career guidance and career counseling are familiarity with and contribution to the research findings of relevance to one's professional domain. Although this book contains many such findings, it is also useful to be knowledgeable about summaries thereof; one such summary is that of Campbell et al. (1983). These researchers classified empirical studies of positive effects of career guidance into five broad categories:

1. *Improved school involvement and performance* (41 studies). These researchers conclude that the majority of the studies reported gains in student career development outcome that they attribute primarily to interventions involving individualized career development learning experience (for example, experience-based career education, special guidance classroom activities, career exploration, and counseling).
2. *Personal and interpersonal work skills* (31 studies). Nineteen studies used as a dependent variable self-awareness; five, interpersonal and life skills; and six, work values. The majority of the studies that examined the effect of career interventions on these outcomes reported positive effects (26 of the 31).
3. *Preparation for careers* (14 studies). Twelve of the 14 studies examined showed positive gains in career preparation among people exposed to each of four types of intervention: counseling, classroom career guidance instruction, employer-based career education, and hands-on career exploration activities.
4. *Career planning skills (34 studies).* Twenty-seven of these studies demonstrated positive outcomes. Although the researchers who performed these studies tended to employ a variety of types of intervention to increase career planning skills in students and adults, they identified career or vocational counseling as the major process in over half the studies.
5. *Career awareness and exploration* (44 studies). Thirty-one of these studies showed positive results. Career and vocational exploration, experience-based career education, counseling, and career education classroom activities gave the best results.

Based on their review of empirical studies, Campbell et al (1983) came to the following conclusions:

- Vocational guidance interventions achieve their intended outcomes primarily if guidance personnel provide structured interventions in a systematic developmental sequence.
- Vocational guidance has demonstrated its effectiveness in influencing career development and adjustment of individuals in the five broad outcome areas.
- Vocational guidance has been successful in assisting individuals representing a wide range of subpopulations and settings, including those in correctional institutions, vocational training centers, community colleges, and those susceptible to academic, economic, and psychological problems.

The Counselor as Change Agent. In providing a comprehensive program of career guidance, the counselor will probably depart from the one-to-one mode of interaction with clients as principal strategy. Counselors will be increasingly involved in collaborative efforts with teachers, parents, administrators, community agency personnel, and employers to modify the environments that shape their clients' lives. Examples of the activities in which counselors are likely to become engaged include creating positive climates for learning; modifying curriculum content; working with employers to provide work-study experiences, exploratory opportunities, realistic employment requirements, and more mentally healthful work environments; and actively seeking job placement for clients. There seems to be little question that counselors will need to persist in giving their skills to educators, parents, and management or supervisory personnel in industry to sensitize these individuals to the needs of all persons for self-esteem, achievement, and opportunities to share in decision making and governance. In such circumstances, the counselor will likely serve as a consultant or a resource person to these "significant others" who influence the lives of various groups in different educational settings or in workplaces.

Career Guidance and Leisure. Comprehensive career guidance programs of the future will need to concern themselves with the range of roles affected by whether work is seen as a central commitment of individuals. As suggested at several places in this book, one of those roles is leisure (Super, 1981). In some types of work, it may not be possible to find personal fulfillment, satisfying human relationships, or a sense of achievement. In such instances, persons need to look elsewhere for outlets for such needs. The leisure world of volunteer activity, hobbies, and nontechnical learning may serve such needs for self-fulfillment. Some people may be forced into extended periods of leisure because of work dislocation, reduced work time, or early retirement. Some may seek leisure opportunities because they are not committed to work as a central concept in their lives. Regardless of what reason motivates persons to engage in leisure activity, how they choose and conceptualize the use of leisure in their lives will be a legitimate and growing emphasis in career guidance. As McDaniels (1982) has advocated, leisure will need to be integrated as an idea important to other concepts of career development.

McDaniels (1989) has persuasively argued that career counseling must embody both leisure counseling and work counseling. He suggests that counselees may increasingly seek help in leisure or work or both. In his view, "A skilled career counselor of the future should be able to provide assistance in both areas separately or in a combined holistic approach. . . . Individuals need a holistic, not a compartmentalized approach in order to find satisfaction in the changing world of work and leisure in the 1990s and beyond." (p. 182) McDaniels is not alone in his advocacy of more attention to leisure within the concept of career counseling; Bloland and Edwards (1981) have argued for a career counseling conceptualization that blends work and leisure. They recognize work and leisure as playing complementary roles in the lives of people but also hold that leisure can play two roles when it seeks to make up for dissatisfaction felt in work. They build their theoretical structure on the work of Kando and Summers (1971), who suggest that leisure can respond in two ways to dissatisfaction at work: (1) supplemental compensation (positive feelings through leisure are also adequately experienced through work); (2) reactive compensation (avocational activities are used to recover from unpleasant work experiences).

Rimmer and Kahnweiler (1981) have studied the potency, evaluation, and activity associated with the terms work, leisure, education, the future, and self among college students and found them to be perceived as interrelated components of their lives. Whether such relationships would also be true for other subpopulations is not known, but some evidence suggests that leisure time is a mixed blessing for many people (Herr & Watts, 1981). Obviously, the availability of leisure time varies among people, and their ability to use it without additional stress or conflict also varies widely. Clearly such ambivalence and ambiguity about how leisure fits into life priorities, how decisions about effective uses of leisure can be made, and how leisure can fulfill needs unmet by work are important elements of future models of career education and career guidance.

Career Guidance as Content or Curriculum. One of the major outcomes of developmental career guidance during the past 20 years has been the rise of career guidance workshops, group approaches, self-directed modules, and other programs. Some of these are designed to facilitate individual decision making by "educating persons to choose." Others are built around specific clusters of career development tasks found to be most significant at different chronological life periods or at particular transition points. They may include attempts to influence the development or acquisition of a positive self-concept, interpersonal skills, control over one's life, the discipline of work, presenting oneself objectively, knowledge of resources, preferred life styles, and other career management tasks (Tennyson, Hansen, Klaurens, & Antholz, 1980). Some researchers advocate training youth and adults in affective work competencies (Kazanas, 1978). Nelson (1979) has described the methods and materials for teaching occupational survival skills. Hopson and Scully (1981) have presented a British version of life skills teaching that includes much career-related content.

There are many examples of career guidance content available. Many state departments of education have created career development plans for use by counselors and others to implement systematic career guidance programs at each educational level. In 1988, the National Occupational Information Coordinating Committee published *The National Career Counseling and Development Guidelines,* which give examples of how to plan career guidance programs for adults in human service agencies, for students in post-secondary institutions, and for students in elementary, middle/junior, and high schools. The guidelines suggest relevant content at each of these levels. Whatever the source of content, it must be tailored to the special needs of different youth or adult subpopulations. As integral parts of comprehensive career guidance programs, content can be expanded to focus on whatever type of self-development, skill acquisition, or exploratory behavior is necessary in different work environments or educational settings.

Herr (1982a) and Herr and Johnson (1989) have suggested that, depending on the population and the purpose to be served, career guidance content in group programs tends to deal with three categories of skills: work context skills, career management (including career planning and job search and access skills), and decision-making skills.

Work context skills are related to the psychological aspects of the situation in which work activity is carried on but can be viewed separately from the technical skills of work performance.

In some nations observers would suggest that these are the elements of industrial discipline; in others they would be called affective work competencies. In any case, they include knowledge and skills associated with employer-employee relations and supervisor-worker relations, interpersonal skills with co-workers, willingness to follow rules, adaptability, punctuality and regularity in attendance, pride in work, self-discipline, and efficiency. Such work context skills tend to be those that research studies and surveys of employer preference have shown repeatedly to be at the heart of work adjustment, job satisfaction, and work satisfactoriness. Their lack is at the core of reasons for workers being discharged; with some modification in language, the lack of these skills probably also contributes to school vandalism, mediocre achievement, tardiness, and other behavioral problems. Although more subtle and psychological than work performance skills or numeracy and literacy, they can nevertheless be analyzed and taught.

In many ways, however, the teaching of work context skills is incomplete without attention to a second category of individual learning described as *career management*. Indeed, it is conceivable that many of the problems now associated with work context (such as worker alienation and mid-career crisis) are really problems of self-learning or deficits in career planning or job search and access skills. These skills, like work context skills, are more psychological than technical, and they can be taught. They are typically now described under the rubric of career development, concentrating on helping people to become aware of their self-characteristics (such as aptitude, values, and interests), their career opportunities (such as occupational alternatives, educational options, and the relationship between subject matter and jobs), and the bringing together of self- and career opportunities into a plan for action. In essence, guidance learning is designed to help individuals become more purposeful, goal directed, and capable of self-management. It includes attention to decision-making skills, job search and interview strategies, and general planfulness. They also include concern for such emphases as the ability to use exploratory resources to reality-test choices, constructive use of leisure, personal economics skills, and other pertinent areas of behavior by which one is helped to get and keep a job. In general, they argue that forging a career requires two types of knowledge: self-knowledge and job knowledge.

With respect to self-knowledge, individuals need to come to terms with who they are; what kinds of commitments they are willing to make; what their aptitudes, interests, values, and goals are; and how competent or confident they feel. In essence, self-information is a base for anything else; that is, knowing one's strengths and weaknesses, preferences, and goals defines an evaluative foundation to which any option or action can be referred to determine its relevance. This base of information also helps one determine what information one has, what one needs, and what should be secured.

Job knowledge includes the range of work options available and the ways in which these might be accessed. This requires having knowledge about and considering the personal relevance of such matters as the characteristics of curricular majors available, their prerequites and content; the relationship between subject matter and occupations in which that subject matter is required; the outcomes of pursuing various curricula (What is the placement record? Into what kinds of jobs are people placed?); the matching of personal characteristics with those required in preferred curricula or occupations; and so forth.

In addition, considerations of occupational and other opportunities will probably require information about methods of access. Are the preferred occupations available locally? If not, where are they available? How are potential employers identified? What is the best procedure for contacting an employer? What information or procedures are pertinent to the completion of letters of inquiry, resumes, applications? What types of questions or other conditions are likely to prevail in an interview situation? How does one follow up a contact with an employer?

A third area of emphasis beyond that of work context or career management skills is that dealing with the *decision-making* process itself. One could argue that such a distinction is overly pedantic, and that this learning is typically incorporated into the knowledge previously described. That may be true, but decision-making skills are, nevertheless, a type of content that has integrity in its own right as a systematic method that can be applied repeatedly to process information, weigh alternatives and project consequences of actions. Perhaps most important, decision making is the way people can establish relations between actions in the present and the future expectations about the consequences of those decisions. Thus, decision making becomes an important way of establishing an internal locus of control.

Career Counseling and Mental and Behavioral Health

Although career counseling has been historically portrayed as primarily oriented to economic health, choice of an occupation, the development of pre-vocational skills, and the preparation for work, that perspective will probably be viewed in the future as too restrictive. As suggested by the expanding definitions of career counseling proposed by such theorists as Crites (1981), Brown (1985), and Rounds and Tinsley (1984), career counseling is being increasingly seen as a therapeutic modality, a specific application of personal adjustment counseling, or even psychotherapy when it is applied to specific problems related to work. In this context, Herr (1989a) has addressed the growing research base that links career development, work, and behavioral and mental health. This research, which will be more fully explored in Chapter 2, suggests that among other roles career counseling is critical to giving unemployed and underemployed youths and adults a sense of purposefulness and positive self-efficacy, thus to reducing the stress-related side effects of hopelessness and despair. Such outcomes are not benign. The past decade has seen a growing number of research findings that demonstrate the variety of life difficulties and physical and mental health problems that ensue when work life is unsatisfactory or when job dislocation or unemployment occurs. Distress about work and particularly about unemployment is associated with a range of personal and social problems—for example, depression, anxiety, physiological effects (cardiovascular disease, early death), suicide, spousal or child abuse, abuse of alcohol and other drugs, anger, violence, impaired interpersonal relationships, grief and mourning, and feelings of victimization. As Spokane (1989) has observed, "it is reasonable to assume that there is more to career development than has met the eye for the past 75 years, and that it is no longer possible to avoid the overlap between career development and psychopathology." (p. 23)

The stress reactions and stress-related physical and psychological diseases that accompany problems of work adjustment, work choice, and the exit from work bring career counseling directly into the realm of the emerging movement in behavioral health and, more broadly into the realm of behavioral medicine and mental health. Such career counseling approaches in business and industry can provide dislocated workers, unhappy workers, maladjusted workers, and unemployed or underemployed workers information, support, encouragement, skill building, or some combination of these to facilitate hope and reduce feelings of being an unworthy social isolate. Skill building approaches can deal directly with such matters as anger management, assertiveness, planning, interpersonal competencies, and openness to constructive supervision. Such approaches are not just matters of occupational choice and adjustment; they also help people create reality and meaning for themselves within the context of work and career. The latter is directly related to behavioral and mental health.

Basic Academic Skills and Career Development

Just as there are rapidly emerging relationships between career development and mental health, there are also relationships between basic academic skills and career development that will significantly affect what career counselors will do and how they will do it. Given the changes in the global economy and the fact that workforces who are literate, flexible, and teachable are necessary to successful engagement in international competition, the possession or lack of basic academic skills will, perhaps for the first time, become major elements of individual career development. The assessment and analysis of the status of individuals' basic academic skills will become prime ingredients in what occupations they are likely to be able to consider, for what training they are likely to be eligible, and whether they can find employment in technological occupations or are relegated to occupations in which the career ladders are much shorter. In a society in which knowledge has replaced experience as the primary requisite for employment in an occupational structure in which more than half of the workers are now engaged in "knowledge work" (Drucker, 1989), basic academic skills—computation skills, literacy, communication skills—become primary employability skills. As projected in many reports, given the ability of this nation to automate many of its unskilled and semiskilled jobs and to export other low-skill jobs to other nations where wage rates are low and desire for such jobs is high, very few new jobs will be created in the future for persons who cannot read, take and act on instructions, do basic mathematics, and communicate effectively. Such requisites will be seen as fundamental employability skills in order to avoid reductions in economic development of individual firms and other enterprises caused by employees who are unable or unwilling to learn new production systems or new management strategies. Such basic academic skill development will also need to include the development of the other general employability skills discussed at length elsewhere in this book. As a reflection of the need to combine both types of skills, one national study has recently suggested that "today's new mathematically-based technologies require better computational and literacy skills, and the structures require employed with more interpersonal and organizational skills. The increased importance of the working team suggests the need for better communications and teamwork skills" (Carnevale & Gainer, 1989). These combinations of basic academic skills, general employability skills, and technical skills will maximize the personal flexibility and the life options of the workers entering the labor market and those retraining to remain within it. Thus, career counselors will increasingly need to attend to each of these three skill sets as interdependent elements of individual career development.

The Counselor as Technologist. Many counselors have been trained to believe that the primary, if not total, explanation for behavioral change in their clients is counselor personality (for example, the provision of empathy, unconditional positive regard, and so on). Assuming that such a premise is too limited a concept of the counselor's role with diverse client needs, career guidance has incorporated into the counselor's professional repertoire several forms of technology that extend the counselor's potential to effect behavioral change. Games, work samples, films, problem-solving kits, self-assessments, and computer interactive systems are but a few of the means developed recently to provide learning and simulated experience designed to increase client exploration and planning.

As Sampson and Reardon (in press) have effectively described, computer-assisted career guidance (CACG) systems are rapidly becoming a core element in the delivery of career and educational guidance services in the United States. Trends in computer-assisted career guidance system development include increased diversity of systems, increased availability of information within the systems, greater potential for integrating CACG systems with existing career guidance services and programs in different types of organizational settings, closer collaboration among system developers, and interest in international and non-English-language versions of CACG systems. Technology applied to career guidance is likely to expand rather than recede, and thus the career guidance person of the future will need, in addition to expertise already cited, to have a conceptual framework and personal competencies by which to effectively use such resources. To these ends, Peterson, Sampson, and Reardon (1991) have placed the counselors' role in using various forms of technology within a cognitive information processing paradigm. Their approach provides a theoretical approach to how students or clients process information about themselves and career options and become effective decision makers. Such views clearly accord with the need for counselors as technologists to also be applied behavioral scientists and planners as they select career interventions, design a career service center, or use career information and media.

With particular attention to the use of computers in career guidance, it is possible to conceptualize the competencies required and the broader contextual understanding in three ways: (1) computer as method, (2) computer as process, and (3) computer as subject matter of content. Each of these emphases becomes critical to the counselor's role as technologist and to knowledge not only of *what* one does with technology, in this case the computer, but *why*. (Herr & Best, 1984)

Although computers and other technologies have redefined the repertoire of skills and resources counselors can bring to bear on career related concerns, computers and technology are valuable only to the degree that the outcomes they facilitate are appropriate to the program planning or counseling outcomes to be achieved. Such a reality affirms again that counselors as applied behavioral scientists and planners must be proficient in the selection and implementation of multiple interventions. Career counselors must learn to view the use of computer-assisted approaches to individual career development as part of a plan—as one of the treatment options—not the only, or even the preferred, approach for all counseling problems. Thus, counselors must see technology of any kind as a tool by which to extend their skills and to potentially meet certain counselee needs, not as a separate and autonomous system.

Special Needs Populations. The United States is a nation of immigrants who have carried with them from Europe, Africa, Asia, and South America the traditional values with which they were imbued in their land of origin. Nations do differ in the psychological character they embrace (Peabody, 1985), and such models are perpetuated in the lives of persons across generations through family traditions, ethnic churches, community groupings, and other media. An emerging challenge to career guidance is how to attend to the cultural diversity inherent in the widening portions of the population to be served. What does this diversity mean for programs of career guidance, the counselor as technologist, the content and curriculum of career guidance, or other topical categories?

But suggesting that all persons have special needs derived from their cultural history does not suggest that such a condition eliminates the need to attend to more restricted and focused definitions of special needs populations. Although the specific group characteristics may change, there will continue to be groups of persons who have special needs for career guidance. Ordinarily, these are groups who have been denied equity in their access to educational and occupational opportunities because of racial and sexual bias or discrimination because of age or disability. Bias or discrimination of any kind is a waste of human resources, and it is a matter that career guidance counselors and specialists can help reduce or eliminate.

As the pressures and demands upon citizens intensify and additional at-risk groups come into public visibility, the constituent groups who have experienced bias and discrimination and need career guidance and counseling become more comprehensive. For example, one such group for whom discrimination has been the rule is the mentally ill. Although many people assume that mentally ill individuals neither want to nor can make a contribution to society, Loughead (1989) has disputed this point, arguing that research suggests that work is therapeutic and leads to independent living for the mentally ill, reduces taxpayer expense, and has other benefits to the person and to society. To this end Loughead has developed a career development curriculum for mentally ill clients that is appropriately integrated with career counseling for this population. The point here is that there are many different types of populations having special needs for career guidance and counseling that are not now being met.

Counselors have many possibilities for action both at the client level and at the institutional level. In the first place, it is a matter of helping youths and adults free themselves of the psychological limits on choice that they experience because they have incorporated other people's beliefs that females (or males, for that matter) or persons of particular racial, age, or physical disability characteristics should not consider certain educational or job options. Frequently they have also internalized the implied reasons for restricting such choices; for example, they may believe that if one has some set of group characteristics (such as race or sex), one is ipso facto inferior or less able than others. In the second place, it is a matter of trying to keep employers, parents, teachers and other gatekeepers of opportunity from restricting free access to jobs and education on the basis of such stereotypes. The reduction of bias will include the whole repertoire of counselor and career guidance strategies, including those of cognitive restructuring and support groups as well as resource, collaborative, and consultative roles. The requirements for such emphases are basic to any rationale for a planning model for career guidance.

Techniques useful in dealing with other types of special career problems experienced by different special needs populations are discussed elsewhere in this book. Of particular note is the growing recognition in the literature and in legislation that special needs populations comprise not only persons denied equality because of historical social discrimination based on race, gender, or age. In addition, research and theory of the last decade have also demonstrated that persons at significant points of transition in their lives (for example, divorce, loss of a loved one, sudden unemployment) become vulnerable, and thus, at least temporarily, people with special needs. Although such a condition may be dynamic, not fixed as are race and gender, it can nevertheless cause problems for the person at work and in other parts of life; career guidance and counseling can be helpful in such situations.

INTERNATIONAL APPROACHES TO CAREER GUIDANCE

As suggested at the beginning of this chapter, career guidance, career education, and more traditional forms of vocational guidance have become international phenomena. They are not exclusive inventions or provisions of the United States. Many nations have implemented or refined mechanisms designed to facilitate individual decision making, reduce underemployment, and aid job adjustment. Different nations arrange their counseling or career guidance systems in ways reflective of the placement of their career specialists in ministries of labor, ministries of education, in school districts, regional catchment areas, or in local job service bureaus. Reflective of both the programs and practitioners, there are now annual or biennial conferences of such specialists under the auspices of such associations as the International Association for Educational and Vocational Guidance, the International Association of Applied Psychology, the International Round Table for the Advancement of Counseling, and even the American Association for Counseling and Development, which has a large international membership.

Obviously, the approaches taken to career guidance, career education, or career counseling by other nations are colored by their own political belief systems, economic conditions, cultural traditions, and conceptions of free and informed choice of educational and occupational opportunity. As a result, such approaches are not necessarily interchangeable across national boundaries. This is not the point. The point is that as nations experience particular levels of industrialization, occupational specialization and diversity, and as available information about the possibility structure existing in that nation expands, needs for career guidance grow and change.

In a study of educational and vocational guidance services for the 14 to 25 age group in the European community, Watts et al. (1988a) have contended that there are three key strands in guidance in schools that can be identified. These trends are similar to those in North America or, more specifically, in the United States as reported elsewhere in this book. They suggest some convergence in how career guidance is viewed among industrialized nations and, in particular, how Europe is viewing career guidance in schools.

According to Watts et al. (1988),

> The first [trend] is that educational and vocational guidance is increasingly being seen as a *continuous process,* which:
>
> — Should start early in schools.
> — Should continue through the now often extended period of transition to adult and working life.
> — Should then be accessible throughout adult and working life.
>
> So far as schools are concerned:
>
> — Guidance is more and more being seen not as an adjunct to schools but as an integral part of the educational process.
> — This is resulting in the growth of specialist guidance roles within the schools.
> — It is also producing a recognition of the need to involve *all* teachers in guidance to some extent, and to develop ways of supporting them in their guidance roles.
> — Guidance elements are increasingly being built into the curriculum, in the form of careers education programmes, work-experience programmes, etc.
> — Where external agencies work into schools, their role is now more and more viewed as that of a partner or consultant to the guidance services within the school itself.
>
> The second key trend is the move towards what we have termed a *more open professional model,* in which the concept of an expert guidance specialist working with individual clients in what sometimes appears to be a psychological vacuum is replaced, or at least supplemented, by a more diffuse approach in which:
>
> — A more varied range of interventions is used. These may include:
>   • Guidance elements within the curriculum of education and training programmes.
>   • Group-work alongside one-to-one work.
>   • Use of computers and other media.
> — More attention is given to working with and through networks of other individuals and agencies. This may involve:

- Supporting 'first-in-line' teachers, supervisors, etc. in their guidance roles.
- Involving parents and other members of the community as resources in the guidance process.
- Working with 'opportunity providers' to improve the opportunities available to young people.

Such a model offers the prospect of being a more cost-effective approach to guidance, as well as being based more closely on the ways in which choices actually tend to be made in practice.

The third and final trend, closely linked to the other two, is towards a greater emphasis on the *individual as an active agent,* rather than as a passive recipient, within the guidance process. This can be seen in, for example:

— The growth of programmes of careers education, work experience, etc. designed to provide young people with a range of skills, attitudes, knowledge and experiences which will help them in making their own career decisions.
— The growth of interest in counselling as opposed to advice-giving.
— The reduced emphasis on psychometric testing, and the increased interest in encouraging self-assessment rather than 'expert' assessment.
— The development of self-help approaches in occupational information centres and in computer-aided guidance systems.
— The interest in 'education for enterprise' as a way of developing young people's self-reliance and initiative.
— The participation of young people in the preparation of information booklets and in running youth information centres.

The individual young person is thus now increasingly seen as the active centre of the guidance process, with the guidance specialist being available partly as a specialist referral point and partly as a means of activating other resources for young people to draw upon. (pp. 93–95)*

*From *Educational and Vocational Guidance Services for the 14–25 Age Group in the European Community* by A. G. Watts, in association with Colette Dartois and Peter Plant. © copyright Commission of the European Communities, 1988. Reprinted with permission.

Societies throughout the world are in transition. In some, the changes are revolutionary; in others, evolutionary. It is a rare nation, if it exists, that is not influenced by turmoil surrounding its economic climate, achievement images, value structure, employment or unemployment rates, educational structure, male/female relationships, quality of life, and other matters that bear on the kind of work available, who does it, and how people get access to it and advance within it. Obviously, career development in each nation is a function of the prevailing political, economic, educational, and industrial systems of that nation and of the resources devoted to career guidance or career education and the forms they take.

Societies vary on at least two dimensions in their approaches to helping youth and adults with career development (Watts & Herr, 1976). The two dimensions can be distinguished by (1) whether the primary locus is the needs of society or on the needs of the individual and (2) whether the approach basically accepts the status quo or is concerned with changing it in prescribed directions. Figure 1.2 graphically illustrates this point. Each of the four cells in the figure carry different implications for the nature and content of career guidance. Basically each asks whether the purpose of career guidance is human development, facilitating individual free choice and purposeful action, or developing human capital and deciding how it will be used for the good of the state. Career guidance can be and is developed in various nations from each of the answers possible.

In an important sense, career guidance and career counseling do not occur independently of the political, economic, and social structure of the nation in which they are implemented. They must be understood and appreciated as sociopolitical processes shaped by the legislation and policies of a specific country and by the prevailing aspects of culture. Of particular importance in the latter regard are such elements of culture as "the nature and rigid-

Figure 1.2

International Approaches to Helping Youth and Adults with Career Development (Reprinted from 1981 comprehensive set of counselor competencies of National Vocational Guidance Association. © AACD. Reprinted with permission. No further reproduction authorized without written permission of American Association for Counseling and Development.)

	Needs of Society	Needs of the Individual
Change	Social Change Approach	Individual Change Approach
Status Quo	Social Control Approach	Non-Directive Approach

ity of the class and caste structure, the value system, the relationship of the individual to the group, and the nature of the enterprise system" (Super, 1985a, pp. 12–13). These elements vary in their interaction from nation to nation. Whatever the combination, they are the mediators of the opportunity structure; of which career paths and mobility factors are available; of the social metaphors that translate into sanctioned or supported behavioral models; of contingencies or reinforcements that result in cognitive structures, habits, and information processing; of the in-groups and the out-groups of the society; of the images of individual achievement possible; and of expectations for person-institutional loyalties or identification. They dictate whether the state's goals or those of the individual will be preeminent. These elements define which groups are at risk (or vulnerable) or problems. They create the context within which career guidance and counseling inadvertently or systematically respond to the ethnocentrisms that differentiate societies, political belief systems, and individual choice.

Such cultural artifacts differentiate how people will conceive and play out the self-concept: as a bundle of roles subjugated to the family or other group, as a collectivist society, or as a system of self-pictures available to discriminate behavior in ways unique to the individual (Triandis, 1985). Cultural diversity also is manifested in the type of career counseling problems experienced by persons in different nations and in the varieties of psychopathology that are apparent, how they are understood and interpreted by persons experiencing them and the broader society, and the course from onset to cure they are likely to describe (Draguns, 1985).

Within this broad context of national differences, Super (1974) has suggested that in examining career guidance practices among the developed nations, four conflicting trends are apparent. The current authors have provided commentary about each to accent their viability in contemporary terms.

1. *Manpower utilization versus human development.* In the first situation, career guidance can be viewed as an instrument of national policy by which persons can be directed and trained in educational and occupational areas reflecting economic and social needs. Or, in the latter instance, career guidance can be seen as reflecting a national policy that emphasizes self-fulfillment, social welfare, and personal

happiness. These are not necessarily mutually exclusive views, but it is likely that in most nations one of the two possibilities predominates as the basis for career guidance.

2. *Occupational choice versus vocational development.* The basic conflict here has to do with whether one views career guidance as leading to an immediate occupational choice or as a process of helping individuals clarify and act on intermediate and future goals. In the second perspective, even when immediate choice is under consideration, is it considered in relation to such matters as the place of work in the preferred life style, preferences for leisure, life goals broadly conceived, or the relationship of this job or position to those one hopes to achieve in the future.
3. *Information dissemination versus counseling.* The fundamental issue in this conflict is whether the provision of accurate information about educational and occupational information is adequate in itself or whether people need the assistance of specially trained individuals to sort out the implications of such information in relation to personal interests, values, needs, and abilities.
4. *Professional guidance versus lay guidance.* This conflict has to do primarily with the form and intensity of the training people need in order to do effective "career guidance" and whether a nation can afford to commit the resources and the training necessary to professionalize its career guidance practitioners.

Although each of these four conflicts is couched in international terms, it is possible to argue that there are advocates for each of the positions reflected in different sectors of this nation. Nevertheless, the prevailing professional rhetoric, if not always the practice, of career guidance favors those elements of the four conflicts that emphasize human development, vocational (career) development, counseling, and professional guidance. Saying this, however, does not preclude the fact that in the United States, as in other nations, career guidance is a sociopolitical process significantly affected by the characteristics of the society in which it is found. Theories, techniques, and programs of career guidance are never value free.

Under any model of implementation, career guidance represents some form of environmental modification that in turn carries a set of assumptions with political overtones. In any transactional view of individual-environmental interaction, it is societal factors—political, religious, economic, historical—that largely determine the types of problems that are appropriate for counselors or career guidance practitioners to deal with. This perspective is played out in the legislative entitlements or definitions of service that can be provided, in the policy focus, and in the resources committed to career guidance as counseling.

To pursue further the notion of societal effects on career guidance, it is possible to argue that the types of questions that youths and adults bring to career guidance specialists or counselors are related to how they view the current societal belief systems about such matters as personal choice, achievement, social interaction, self-initiative, marriage, prestige, occupational or educational status, and many other aspects of life. The resulting anxieties, deficits, or indecisiveness that these people experience as they compare themselves with what society in the form of parents, teachers, peers, spouses, employers, self-improvement books, or the mass media say they should believe or do represent a large part of the content with which career guidance specialists or counselors deal (Herr, 1982b).

Flowing from such a point of view is the notion that the questions different societies "permit" or encourage their citizens to ask about themselves and their future and the resources placed at the disposal of the individual to sort out answers to these questions vary cross-culturally in fairly dramatic ways. Herr (1974, 1978a) has attempted to analyze the types of work-related questions populations are likely to ask whose nations differ on an industrial development continuum. In particular he distinguishes among the types of work, information systems, work-related questions, and guidance processes likely to exist in the least developed societies, developing nations, and developed or postindustrial nations.

As one moves across these three categories of industrial development, the roles of families change as information disseminators and reinforcers of certain socially stratified occupational or educational choices; "have nots" change from a majority to a minority position in the society; occupational diversity and service roles increase; work becomes less visible and increasingly "walled off" from those who must choose it; information about opportunities becomes more sophisticated and more abundant; personal questions shift from those primarily addressed to physical survival and increasingly become more existential ("Who am I"? "What do I want to be?"); and career guidance and counseling tend to become more conceptually based and seen as specialized occupations (professions) in their own right. Although such perspectives are overly simplified, and, indeed, caricatures of reality, they do cast into bold relief the fact that career guidance mechanisms do not exist in a political, social, or economic vacuum. They are interactive, if not symbiotic, with the characteristics of the societies in which they exist.

The speed and the comprehensiveness with which career guidance will expand across the nations of the world is difficult to predict. If, however, the relationships previously suggested between industrialism and the diversity of roles available, education and work, the need to provide information about work, and encouragement of achievement in systematic rather than random ways are valid, then career guidance in some form seems inevitable in virtually every nation. Perhaps the more salient point is that in an increasingly technological world, both international organizations and governments have become more aware that the major questions regarding technology are not technical, but human questions (Drucker, 1970). Among these questions are not only those of how to develop workers able to discharge the occupational task-specific skills required to design, operate, and maintain the various forms of technology, but, more importantly, how to help people come to terms with such matters as their work values, work commitments, work productivity, and the personal discipline associated with these matters; in short, their general employability skills.

Acknowledgment of the effects of cultural diversity upon such outcomes should continue to stimulate a search for those elements that are common and effective across national models of career guidance and counseling and those elements that must be considered indigenous to a particular nation or culture (Herr, 1985a).

Summary

In this chapter we have examined briefly the international and historical evolution of the concepts and content of what is now being called career guidance. We have introduced the notion of *comprehensive* career guidance to reflect its importance to all segments of the population—children, youths, and adults—as well as its growing availability in community agencies, business and industry, and educational settings. We have distinguished career counseling and identified the roots of counseling psychology in vocational guidance. In addition, we have discussed the past, present, and future of career education. Although it does represent continuity from the past, career education is more than vocational education. Its roots and its substance speak to ideas deeply embedded in the American society as they reflect education for choice and the development of purposefulness in work. Crucial to the implementation of career education is effective career guidance. We have suggested that it is necessary to think in terms of a career guidance program that is systematically planned, has clear statements of counselor competencies, and reflects a series of national trends that show its future directions. We have also identified a partial vocabulary of terms pertinent to career guidance, as well as some issues that are yet to be resolved. Finally, we have considered some perspectives of the shape and substance of career guidance and career counseling as international phenomena.

In Chapter 2 we will examine contemporary meanings of work and ways to view the characteristics of the workplace and work competencies. In Chapter 3 we will discuss the occupational structure, its changing nature, and its classification. In Chapter 4 we will consider the variety of current theoretical and research models essential to understanding career behavior in both macro and micro terms. In this case macro views attempt to explain the unfolding of career identity, choice, and adjustment across the life span; micro views attempt to explain specific processes of career development—for example, decision making. In Chapter 5 we will explore the career problems of specific population groups (women, handicapped, minorities, and so forth).

Chapters 2, 3, 4, and 5 describe much of the *content* of career guidance and career counseling differences in occupational and life alternatives; influences on work values, career identity choice-making strategies; and the special circumstances relating to access and adjustment to work associated with gender, social circumstances, disability, and other factors. The remaining chapters of the book tend to describe the multiple *interventions* subsumed by the term *career guidance*. Thus, the descriptions of how work behavior is formed, the influences on it, and how it is individually manifested tend to be the objects of career interventions as well as the content with which such interventions are concerned.

CHAPTER 2

WORK: SOME CONTEMPORARY AND EMERGING PERSPECTIVES

Key Concepts

- The term *work* has multiple definitions, its own vocabulary, and different meanings across groups and time.
- When one chooses a job, an occupation, or a career, one also makes decisions, purposefully or inadvertently, about leisure, continuing needs for education, status, prescriptive or discretionary use of time, and the work culture in which job tasks will be performed.
- Job satisfaction is a complex term incorporating matters of job context and job content, overall satisfaction, and facet satisfaction.
- Many research studies link work and mental health, unemployment, stress-related physical problems, work pathology, family disorder, substance abuse, and other forms of interaction.
- The transition to work is comprised of stages and barriers that young workers and adults must negotiate and master if such transitions are to be successful.
- A central organizing goal of career guidance and of career counseling is the choice of and effective implementation of work in one's life.
- The global economy will likely require new forms of personal competence and flexibility. Such behaviors will serve as stimuli to more comprehensive models of career counseling and career guidance.

Work is the term of central concern in this chapter. A central organizing goal of career guidance and of career counseling is the facilitation of the choice and implementation of work in one's life. When one chooses a job, one chooses a whole series of things in addition to the work content or tasks to be performed. One also chooses the persons with whom one will work, the role expectations of others, the social status ascribed to the job, the likely types of leisure in which one will engage and with whom one will likely experience leisure, how much vacation time will be taken and when vacations will occur, the types of continuing education or training required, the style of supervision, whether one's use of time is rigidly prescribed or discretionary, and the "work culture" in which the job tasks will be performed. Put somewhat differently, Landy (1989) has suggested that "Work is something that happens to an individual. It is a treatment of sorts. People go to a work setting and are exposed to various elements. These elements include things such as heat and light and noise. In addition, there are such elements as pay and supervisory style and coworkers. Even the duties and responsibilities that make up the "job" are treatments. Workers are exposed to a work pace, a certain demand for productivity, and accountability" (p. 600).

Given such diverse and interactive outcomes from a choice of work, it is paradoxical that the multiple meanings of work are rarely discussed in the career guidance literature. Indeed, work is frequently treated as a monolithic abstraction, almost as though all work is the same or as if the word *work* has a single meaning.

To treat work as though it has the same meaning for all people is to restrict the vision of how career guidance or career counseling should be tailored to the needs of people who experience work differently. Counseling is a verbal profession. It has, as a major part of its content, words and other symbols by which people communicate their perceptions of themselves and the work world. How a counselor responds to clients' problems and concerns depends on the labels and the definitions by which these questions, problems, or concerns are classified.

Chapter 1 identified some of the terms of major significance to the understanding and practice of career guidance and career counseling. It was suggested there that the career guidance practitioner will function differently if the client's immediate concern is choosing a specific job, considering a choice of occupation and the training required, or deliberating about how such matters might fit with life style, family roles, availability and use of leisure, or personal aspirations as these combine to shape a career. Terms such as *job*, *occupation*, and *career* are not interchangeable. They represent different choices for the client and for the career guidance practitioner. They also embody different meanings, levels of abstraction, time frames, and complexities that need to be reflected in counselor behavior.

DEFINITIONS OF WORK

Although work can be defined in a variety of ways, some definitions summarize several major concepts. For example Super (1976) defines work as

> The systematic pursuit of an objective valued by oneself (even if only for survival) and desired by others; directed and consecutive, it requires the expenditure of effort. It may be compensated (paid work) or uncompensated (volunteer work or an avocation). The objective may be intrinsic enjoyment of the work itself, the structure given to life by the work role, the economic support which work makes possible, or the type of leisure which it facilitates. (p. 20)

This definition does not equate work and occupation, as is often the case. Rather, it allows for work to be nonpaid, to be outside the formal job structure identified as occupation, to include homemakers, members of alternative communities, and those self-employed in the invisible and illegal economy as workers (G. Miller, 1980).

The National Vocational Guidance Association (NVGA) in its glossary of terms defines work as a conscious effort, other than having as its primary purposes either coping or relaxation, aimed at producing benefits for oneself and/or others (Sears, 1982).

Super also proposes definitions for other words appropriate to a language of work. They include the following:

Labor–Productive work for survival or support, requiring physical or mental effort.
Employment–Time spent in paid work or in indirectly paid work such as homemaking.
Leisure–Time free of required paid or unpaid work, in rest, play or avocations.

The NVGA glossary defines leisure as relatively self-determined activities and experiences that are available due to having discretionary income, time, and social behavior; the activities may be physical, intellectual, volunteer, creative, or some combination of all four (Sears, 1982).

Play–Activity that is primarily recreational and relaxing; engaged in for its own sake; it may be systematic or unsystematic, without objective or with a temporary and personal objective; it may involve the expenditure of effort, but that effort is voluntary and easily avoided by the player (p. 22).

Super's definitions of work and related terms are basically psychological; they tend to place the perceptions, definitions, and motivations relative to work within the individual's actions. Another way to define work is from a sociological perspective. In this connection, Braude (1975) contends that

> The sociologist argues that the human being is not an economic animal and that only, nor is he a psychological mechanism and that only, nor is he wholly political or exclusively cultural. If man is human at all, the sociologist says, this humanity stems from the necessary inclusion in groups and in the web of groups that make up society. (p. 4)

Flowing from this perspective, Braude goes on to argue that

> Narrowly conceived, work is simply the way in which a person earns a living. From a broad perspective, a person works in order to maintain or enhance any of the statuses that are his by virtue of his membership in a multiplicity of groups. . . . As long as the person defines, or has defined for him, the activities in which he is engaged as in some manner related to his survival, either physical or social, then we can say that person is working. . . . The work that any individual performs is articulated with that of others who work and with the containing social structure by its location within the division of labor. (pp. 12–13)

These definitions of work and related terms suggest that such concepts are complex. They deal with both individual perceptions and actions as well as the social interactions and roles through which individual behavior is played out. Indeed, Braude (1975) maintains that work needs to be understood within a context of people, position, and purpose.

Definitions of work change across time and across societies. Super (1984b), with respect to recent changed perspectives on work, contends that

> The approach of recent years has shifted from a focus on work alone as *the* central life concern to an interest in the quality of life, life in which work is *one* central concern in a constellation of roles such as homemaking, citizenship, and leisure that interact to make for life satisfaction. The terms *work motivation* and *job satisfaction* are now perhaps not displaced by, certainly incorporated into, the terms *quality of life* and *life satisfactions*. (p. 29)

Even where definitions of work or the structure of values implicit in such definitions are similar from country to country, the hierarchical order or relative importance of work differs within and across societies. Super's multinational Work Importance Study (Super, 1984b, p. 36) has found, for example, that risk taking as a work value is more highly valued in the United States than in Yugoslavia and more by English-speaking Canadians than by French-speaking Canadians. Ronen's research in Japan (1979) has indicated that unlike most Western countries, where economic rewards are a material value, in Japan they are a prestige value, signifying the esteem in which the worker is held by the employer. In a study of 540 employees of a large industrial corporation in Hungary, Elizur and Shye (1990) found that the quality of work life (QWL) was strongly related to the employees' perceptions of their quality of life (QOL) in more general terms; that employees' quality of work performance is affected by both their quality of life and their quality of work life. England (1990) has also demonstrated that patterns of work meanings and related work outcomes are differently distributed among the work forces of Japan, Germany, and the United States.

In sum, work is a term having multiple definitions, meanings that shift across time, and hierarchical elements that differ within and between societies. As such, it needs to be a central concept in the counselor's interpretation of the importance and the practice of career guidance and counseling.

In spite of the conceptual complexity associated with work, frequently in career guidance we talk of choices, options, and decisions without using the word *work*. We act as though everyone understood that work is implied and as though the meaning of work were similarly understood by everyone using it. We also act as though the place of work in the lives of men and women is static, unchanging with age. In doing so, however, we corrupt the richness, diversity, and dynamism that the word work stands for. For example, if we confine our use of work only to task performance or work content, we are likely to emphasize a counselee's aptitudes, achievement, and work performance potential. In doing so, we may overlook the fact that, in either choice of or adjustment to work, the issue for a particular client may not be task performance but rather how one understands the workplace and its expectations, one's ability to get along with co-workers or to share values and interests with them, or one's preferences for the intensity and style of supervision, or one's ambivalence about shifting attachments to work as one ages. As one focuses on each of these emphases, possible assessments, questions, and reality-testing experiences emerge that are different from those appropriate to thinking only about whether one can learn or do work tasks per se.

In the remaining sections of this chapter, we will consider several emphases that derive from work and that are of particular importance in career guidance and career counseling. They include the following: work values and the meaning of work to different groups of people; job satisfaction; work and mental health; employment and unemployment; the transition to work; work and leisure; affective work components; occupational survival skills; and an emerging concern for personal flexibility in a global economy. We will briefly deal with such notions as the division of labor, specialization, work tasks, work roles, and good and bad work. In short, in this chapter we hope to increase the reader's sensitivity to the language of work and its meaning for the practice of career guidance. Because other chapters speak directly to dealing with specific career problems, we will concentrate here on linking various categories and concepts of career guidance to differences in the meanings and concepts of work.

The Concept of Work

From the earliest days of recorded history, work has been the subject of controversy. It has been seen as punishment or as the way to eternal salvation. It has been viewed as fit only for slaves to do so that their masters would have unfettered leisure or as the context in which humankind can achieve its most creative and influential purposes. Anthropologists and historians have argued that work has been instrumental in creating civilizations by causing people to engage in mutual effort to survive and to advance their quality of life. The division of labor that differentiates people into classes of functional activity has been seen by some sociologists as the basis for social stratification, classes, castes, and other types of social systems.

The current issues surrounding work are so pervasive and so central to human existence that Pope John Paul II devoted a papal encyclical on the subject in 1981: "Laborem Exercens" (On Human Work). This was the first such statement the Roman Catholic Church had delivered on work in nearly ninety years. Selected statements from the encyclical strike directly at the meaning of work and its dynamics:

> Because fresh questions and problems are always arising, there are always fresh hopes, but also fresh fears and threats connected with the basic dimension of human existence: man's life is built up every day from work, from work it derives its specific dignity, but at the same time work contains the unceasing measure of human toil and suffering and also of the harm and injustice which penetrate deeply into social life within individual nations and on the international level.

Former U.S. Secretary of Education Bell (Riegle, 1982) has conveyed a sense of the meaning of work somewhat differently from Pope John Paul II, but no less dramatically:

> Work in America is the means whereby a person is tested as well as identified. It is the way a youngster becomes an adult. Work shapes the thoughts and life of the worker. A change in atmosphere and life-style can be effected by an individual by simply changing the way he or she makes a living. For most of us in adult life, being without work is not living. (p. 1114)

Whether viewed through a secular or spiritual lens, such a powerful medium obviously carries diverse meanings for individuals choosing or engaging in work. Although virtually all paid work has the potential to meet the economic needs of human beings, all work, paid and nonpaid, has the additional potential to meet broad social and psychological needs: effective interaction with others, personal dignity, a sense of competency or mastery, identification with some purpose or mission larger than oneself, and human relationships.

Table 2.1 suggests the range of needs or purposes that work can provide. Such purposes or needs are not necessarily mutually exclusive. The same person may attempt to achieve several different types of economic, social, and psychological purposes from work simultaneously, even though one category may be emphasized in shaping work motivation.

The different purposes that work can serve are related to how central work is—to the degree of general importance that working has in the life of an individual—at any given time. Such purposes are also related to the work outcomes sought or the levels of such values as family, leisure, duty, obligation, and so on.

England's (1990) research in the meaning of work across advanced industrialized and technological nations has indicated that eight patterns of the meanings of work could be identified in which work was more or less central to the pattern but in which different perceptions of the meaning of work were expressed. In adapted form, the eight patterns are identified as follows:

> *Pattern A—non-work centered, non-duty-oriented workers.* Lowest work centrality of the eight groups. These persons do not value working very highly nor do they have an orientation toward duty to employers and society through working. Highly leisure- and comfort-oriented in work goals. Value interpersonal relations highly. Characterize working by saying it is work "if you must do it." (p. 36)

Table 2.1

Different Purposes Work Can Serve

Economic	Social	Psychological
Gratification of wants or needs	A place to meet people	Self-esteem
Acquisition of physical assets	Potential friendships	Identity
Security against future contingencies	Human relationships	A sense of order
Liquid assets to be used for investment or deferred gratifications	Social status for the worker and his/her family	Dependability, Reliability
Purchase of goods and services	A feeling of being valued by others for what one can produce	A feeling of mastery or competence
Evidence of success	A sense of being needed by others to get the job done or to achieve mutual goals	Self-efficacy
Assets to purchase leisure or free time	Responsibility	Commitment Personal evaluation

Pattern B—non-work-centered, high duty-oriented workers. Very low work centrality score. Relatively high family, religious, and leisure orientations and comprise the highest number of workers in the eight patterns who defined working as an activity that "is not pleasant." (p. 36)

Pattern C—economic worker pattern. Average work centrality scores. Very high economic values and very low expressive values. Contained highest number of all eight groups who defined workers in terms of "being told what to do" and as "being physically strenuous." (p. 37) Very strong economic orientation to work.

Pattern D—high rights and duties economic workers. Average work centrality, high economic work values, and very high levels of obligation and entitlement. Contained highest number of all eight groups who defined working in terms of "obtaining a feeling of belonging." (p. 37)

Pattern E—low rights and duties non-economic workers. Average work centrality scores, low economic values, low obligation norms, and low entitlement norms. Most status and prestige-oriented of all eight groups. Contained lowest number of all eight groups who defined working in terms of "if it contributes to society." (p. 37) High number who described working as "mentally strenuous" and "not pleasant." (p. 37)

Pattern F—moderately work-centered, non-economic, duty-oriented workers. Moderately high work centrality, low level of economic values. They show a strong company orientation and are highly concerned with the products and services they produce or provide. Of all the groups, they most strongly define working in terms of "contributing to society." (p. 38)

Pattern G—work-centered and balanced work values workers. High work centrality, relatively high economic and expressive values. Second highest group to define working in terms of "something which adds value" and "being accountable for their work." (p. 38)

Pattern H—work-centered expressive workers. High work centrality scores, very low economic values, and very high expressive work values. Highly concerned about the types of tasks they do, the type of occupation in which they work, and the types of products or services they produce or provide. "They give the highest endorsement of all eight groups to the statement, 'Working itself is basically interesting and satisfying.' They are highly concerned with 'contributing to society' through their work and contain the highest number of all groups who defined working "as something which adds value and in terms of 'being accountable.'" (p. 38)*

England's research showed that the labor forces of the United States, Japan, and Germany were represented differently by the proportions of workers who could be described by each of these eight patterns. From his data base England estimated that in these countries, the percentage of workers in each pattern was as follows:

Pattern	United States	Germany	Japan
A	7.0	13.8	8.8
B	2.33	19.7	12.0
C	14.50	20.6	10.4
D	5.4	15.3	4.9
E	12.8	4.0	4.6
F	14.0	6.3	11.1
G	16.8	14.7	32.4
H	6.2	5.6	15.8

*Adaptation from "The Patterning of Work Meanings which are Coterminous with Work Outcome Levels for Individuals in Japan, Germany, and the USA" by George W. England, *Applied Psychology: An International Review*, Vol. 39, No. 1, January 1990, pp. 36–39. © 1990 International Association of Applied Psychology. Reprinted by permission.

Notice the contrast between the labor forces of Germany and Japan and the labor forces of the United States.

In addition to suggesting how work meaning or the centrality of work and related values vary in the labor force of each of these countries, England's research also describes relationships between each of the patterns of work meanings and values for work outcomes: (1) income; (2) quality of work; (3) occupational satisfaction; and (4) job satisfaction. In general, the values of the last relationship increase across patterns A to H, with the outcome values for each occupation for patterns E, F, G, and H generally higher than the outcome value patterns for groups A, B, C, and D.

Although the meaning of work is individually defined and a major mediator of work adjustment, not only are individual purposes for working important, but also what organizations require of workers. Perspectives on what individuals expect to gain from work and what organizations expect to receive from individuals function in complex ways. Morgan (1980, p. 65) has identified these two sets of dimensions:

- Dimensions that individuals have expectations of receiving and organizations have expectations of giving
    - 1. A sense of meaning or purpose in the job
    - 2. Personal development opportunities
    - 3. The amount of interesting work that stimulates curiosity and induces excitement
    - 4. The challenge in the work
    - 5. The power and responsibility in the job
    - 6. Recognition and approval for good work
    - 7. The status and prestige in the job
    - 8. The friendliness of the people, the congeniality of the work group
    - 9. Salary
    - 10. The amount of structure in the environment (general practices, disciplines, regimentation)
    - 11. The amount of security in the job
    - 12. Advancement opportunities
    - 13. The amount and frequency of feedback and evaluation
- Dimensions which organizations have expectations of receiving and individuals of giving
    - 1. Performing nonsocial job-related tasks requiring some degree of technical knowledge and skill
    - 2. Learning the various aspects of a position while on the job
    - 3. Discovering new methods of performing tasks; solving novel problems
    - 4. Presenting a point of view effectively and convincingly
    - 5. Working productively with groups of people
    - 6. Making well-organized, clear presentations both orally and in writing
    - 7. Supervising and directing the work of others
    - 8. Making responsible decisions well and without assistance from others
    - 9. Planning and organizing work efforts for oneself or others.
    - 10. Utilizing time and energy for the benefit of the company
    - 11. Accepting company demands that conflict with personal prerogatives
    - 12. Maintaining social relationships with other members of the company outside of work
    - 13. Conforming to the pathways of the organization or work group on the job in areas not directly related to job performance
    - 14. Pursuing further education on personal time
    - 15. Maintaining a good public image of the company

- 16. Taking on company values and goals as one's own
- 17. Seeing what should or must be done and initiating appropriate activity*

The last combination of expectations of work organization for worker behaviors will be elaborated upon later in this chapter as the transition to work is discussed. It suffices to say here that such individual/organizational purposes may be congruent or in opposition. As such, they may define good work—bad work or job satisfaction–dissatisfaction for any given individual.

The perspectives of England and Morgan are affirmations that cultural traditions and histories give their members particular "world views" or perceptual windows" on events, including acceptable behavior at work, the meaning of work, and interactions with work organizations. Cultural constructions of achievement images and belief systems are likely to be incorporated into the individual citizen's psyche and information-processing mechanisms as well as into the economic organizational systems that prevail in a given nation (Herr, 1990). At least two points can be made in such a context. One is that people moving from one nation to another are likely to bring the perceptions of work and their role in it that predominate in their nation of origin. Thus, in a pluralistic society such as the United States, there will be a profusion of culturally defined meanings of work and work behavior that must be accommodated in the work places of the society. The second point is that institutions, policies, and social technologies in a given nation are likely to be organized and applied in ways that reflect the values and perspectives about human resources or individual behavior that predominate in that society.

To carry the analogy of work meaning, performance, and organizational interaction further, it is useful to contrast the United States and Japan on some of these dimensions. In the United States, unfettered individual achievement, freedom, justice, and liberty are dominant social values, and the burden of achievement in the work place rests with individual action. Given such a set of assumptions, work and other organizations can be and are structured to reflect expectations for individual behavior and responsibility. Japan views such social values differently; dominant social values include loyalty, conformity, hierarchy, duty, and obedience. As a result, organizational forms are created that are different from those created in the United States. For example, Japan's economic and political system is increasingly being called a "developmental model" rather than a "regulatory model"—a term used to describe the United States and the United Kingdom (Dore, 1987). Developmental models set clearly defined strategic economic goals, attempt to ensure that workers are constantly prepared to manage and implement the processes required to meet such goals, and to identify with the economic targets as well as to identify their personal contributions necessary to achieve such outcomes.

The Japanese notion of a "developmentally" oriented work organization includes a major emphasis on harnessing the tacit skills and latent talents of workers from the factory floor to the management office. At each of these levels, workers are put to the task of diagnosing problems and organizing information that will improve productivity and corporate knowledge. In this model, the management objective is to "figuratively" make every worker an industrial engineer designed to help the organization collectively seek continuous improvement and to look beyond a narrowly focused view of immediate job completion. Within such a concept, training of workers is concerned with

*Reprinted from pp. 34–35 in "Career Development: Theories and Issues" by Carole W. Minor in *Adult Career Development: Concepts, Issues and Practices*, edited by Zandy B. Leibowitz and H. Daniel Lea. © AACD. Reprinted with permission. No further reproduction authorized without written permission of American Association for Counseling and Development.

teamwork, multifunctional approaches, interpersonal skills, and problem-solving capabilities. Thus, the intent of the Japanese system of labor management is to create conditions under which workers will be encouraged to cooperate and develop collective awareness and diagnostic skills (Wood, 1990).

A developmental model contrasts with that of a regulatory model, which is more concerned with the processes and rules of competition, not the substance. In the view of some observers, the regulatory model assumes that individuals or organizations will constantly try to "beat the system," that they have a natural tendency to slack off or to abuse power, and that they must be regulated in order to promote equity, access, and fairness in competition (Fallows, 1989). The main point is that the meaning of work and the shape of work organizations will be differently defined in political, cultural, or organizational terms, depending upon whether one's model is regulatory or developmental. In the former view, each person in the corporation or work place is expected to maximize his or her short-term gains and to be autonomous and unconstrained by anything but one's personal ability to cope with market forces and competition. In such a perspective, both success and failure are individual matters. On the other hand, in a developmental view, each person is believed to be part of the whole, to deserve fair treatment and the support necessary to do his or her job, to be respected and consulted, and to be assured of an adequate income and security. The latter view is much more likely to promote personnel development within work organizations than personnel management. It is also more likely to promote cooperation, compromise, identity, and loyalty to the organization rather than aggressiveness, entrepreneurship, risk taking, and individual achievement.

The intent here is not to set up a dichotomy of economic organizations or cultures; clearly, these emphases on regulation or development are on a continuum or spectrum, not simply one or the other. The important point is that individual perspectives on the meaning of work, or on what work values and behaviors should be manifested, do not occur in a vacuum. They are shaped by and reinforced within cultures and in the work organizations and policies that reflect such cultural differences.

Meanings of Work Vary Across Time

The meanings attached to work differ not only across groups and cultures, but also across time. As suggested previously, work has been seen differently through history. Toffler (1980) has described such shifts in terms of three waves of change across the world: agricultural, industrial, and advanced technological. Each of these brings with it different forms of work and meaning. Maccoby and Terzi (1981) suggest that there have been four major work ethics throughout American history and that elements or residuals of each of these coexist today: the Protestant ethic, the craft ethic, the entrepreneurial ethic, and the career ethic. In addition, they contend that a fifth ethic, that of self-fulfillment, is rapidly emerging as a major motivation to work. The point of such observations is that "each work ethic implies a different social character, different satisfaction and dissatisfaction at work, and a different critique of society" (p. 165).

According to Maccoby and Terzi, the Protestant ethic stimulated a character driven to work for the glory of God and for personal salvation and one that could not tolerate unethical and undisciplined behavior. The craft ethic is represented by people oriented toward "savings and self-sufficiency, to independence and self-control, and to rewards on earth. The craftsman is most satisfied by work which he controls, with standards he sets" (p. 165). The entrepreneurial character suggests risk taking, boldness, the exploitation of opportunities and people, and a dislike of the bureaucracy, red tape, and regulation that stifle free enterprise and personal initiative. The career ethic represents other-directedness, a striving to get ahead, to become more attractive and valuable in the marketplace—survival of the fittest rather than seniority and loyalty as the prime requisite of promotion and reward. The emerging ethic of self-fulfillment represents those who seek challenge, growth, and work that is not so consuming that it denies a place for family, community, leisure, and other aspects of life. The presence of such a profusion of work ethics affirms that both those who are in the process of work choice and those who are engaged in work represent a pluralism of purpose and motivation.

Such multiplicity of work values or meanings complicates the task of career guidance significantly. Similarly, it complicates the seeking of answers to such questions as, "Has the motivation to work declined?" The probable answer to such a question is more questions: "What kind of work are you talking about? Which group of workers holding what type of work ethic are you considering?" Beyond such questions, however, it appears that despite certain popular rhetoric to the contrary, Americans' motivation to work is still quite high, although certain jobs and styles of supervision are not looked upon with much favor.

As various observers have reported (Maccoby & Terzi, 1981; Vecchio, 1980a), when they asked people if they would continue to work even if they could live comfortably for the rest of their lives without working, most people choose to work. Indeed, as the rise in the proportion of women and minorities in the labor force indicates, more and more people are trying to gain access to work, and the demand for paid employment of all types continues to grow. Chelte, Wright, and Taosky (1982), in a review of all major studies of work dissatisfaction conducted in the preceding 20 years, concluded that there has been no significant decline in overall worker job satisfaction during the period from 1959 through 1979. Other studies continue to suggest that most workers like and value their work (Rabinowitz, Falkenbach, Travers, Valentine, & Weener, 1983). As we will discuss in the following section, reporting that most people want to work or are seeking work is not the same as saying that people are satisfied with the work available to them or with their personal fit to the job they have.

In a study by the Bureau of Labor Statistics, cited by the Joint Economic Committee of the Congress (1980), it was noted that the commitment to the work force by young adults (ages 20–24) is far stronger than in the past. Indeed, it is now equal to that of the 25–44 age group, where labor force participation is highest. In addition, evidence points to the fact that these workers are eager to make a contribution to the world. Nevertheless, existing literature seems to suggest that subgroups within the youth culture reject the traditional work ethic, materialism, and conventional social norms as they understand them.

JOB SATISFACTION

From the meanings of work just discussed, it is obvious that in most of the work in which people engage we find a confrontation of the individual with the organization. The ingredients of this confrontation yield satisfaction or dissatisfaction, feelings of competence or inferiority, and motivation to be productive or work alienation.

Among the more controversial issues facing the American business/industrial labor complex and, indeed, government policy is that of job satisfaction or job alienation. Sometimes the professional literature, the popular press, and certain research findings leave one with the impression that processes of self-understanding, finding meaning in achievement, or choice are important only during the exploration or anticipation phases of youth. Therefore, efforts to help people deal successfully with such needs are most frequently available in schools and colleges, places primarily occupied by youths, rather than in settings primarily occupied by adults.

Such a perspective belies the reality that adults must continue to cope with trying to implement a self-concept in their life-styles, in their work, in their choices, and in their planning. Efforts to grapple with skills in interpersonal relationships and in learning or relearning continue, for most people, as long as they live. As E. Gross (1975) has observed, "Socialization is far from complete in childhood; it goes on throughout persons' lives, involving adjustment to and becoming members of schools, universities, occupations and becoming socialized to appropriate roles in old age." Caplow (1954) has suggested that organization socialization involves individual accommodations in terms of "skills, self-image, involvements, and values."

Perspectives on Job Satisfaction

Job satisfaction is a complex term as well as a significant one for career guidance and counseling. The importance of the concept is evident in Palmore's (1969) often-quoted fifteen-year follow-up study that indicated that job satisfaction is the best predictor of longevity, better than physicians' ratings of physical functioning, use of tobacco, or even genetic inheritance.

But job satisfaction is not a singular term. As efforts to measure it have shown, at issue is both overall satisfaction and "facet" satisfaction. The latter assesses satisfaction with particular facets or elements of work—for example, pay, co-workers, supervision, working conditions, and types of work. It is possible for a worker to be dissatisfied with specific facets of his or her work but still report an overall sense of job satisfaction (Dawis, 1984).

Inherent in the notions of overall satisfaction and facet satisfaction are the distinctions of job content and job context. Research approaches to job satisfaction have typically treated these as separable and having different implications for job satisfaction. For example, Herzberg, Mausner, and Snyderman (1959) proposed a classic two-factor theory of job satisfaction (also sometimes called dual-factor or motivation hygiene theory), which suggested that satisfaction and dissatisfaction are really two distinct sets of processes. The factors associated with *job content*—achievement, recognition, advancement, responsibility, the work tasks—are the "satisfiers" or "motivators" that lead to job satisfaction. The factors associated with the *job context*—compensation, supervision, co-workers, working conditions, company policies and practices–are the "dissatisfiers" or "hygiene" factors that cause dissatisfaction, but they cannot cause satisfaction. Only the factors associated with job content, the satisfiers or motivators, can lead to satisfaction. Although controversial, the Herzberg et al. theory did lead to a large amount of research on job satisfaction that, while mixed in result, has helped to clarify the importance of facet satisfaction and, particularly, the separateness of external variables into the categories of satisfiers and dissatisfiers.

Another theoretical approach to job satisfaction, equity theory (Pritchard, 1969), added other factors to those of Herzberg's that were also considered relevant to job satisfaction. Of principal interest is the notion that satisfaction depends upon personal feelings of fairness, justice, or equity when what is obtained is compared to what is desired and how this ratio compares to that obtained by other reference persons. Thus, equity theory not only adds to the conception of factors affecting job satisfaction those related to reference outcomes, but it also shifts the focus of attention from a major or exclusive emphasis on what the environment provides or does to the individual to the individual's cognitions about such events.

Many of the theories central to the discussion of career development in Chapter 4 and in later chapters deal directly with job satisfaction and how it is psychologically motivated. In particular, the reader is encouraged to read the work of Vroom (1964), Lawler (1973), and Raynor and Entin (1982), on expectancy theory; Bandura (1977) on self-efficacy theory; Tiedeman and O'Hara (1963) on anticipation and implementation; Holland (1966) on person-situation congruency; Roe's (1956) use of Maslow's prepotent needs theory; and Super's (1980) perspectives on self-concept and career maturity, as each of these relates in some way to job satisfaction or dissatisfaction. Indeed, virtually all of the work in Chapter 4 that deals with either the choice of or the adjustment to work has implications for the understanding of job satisfaction.

In addition to the perspectives considered in Chapter 4, several not discussed there are useful to consider in this section. For example, the task force that considered the status of work in America (O'Toole, 1973, pp. 36–96) attempted to summarize what was then known about worker satisfaction. They noted that the level of satisfaction with one's work is directly related to the levels of the following items:

1. Prestige of the job
2. Autonomy—control over the conditions of work
3. Cohesiveness of the work group, which facilitates interaction
4. Challenge and variety of the task
5. Employer concern and involvement of employees in decision making
6. Wages with respect to both amount and "relative deprivation" felt by the worker; his or her perception of adequacy of wages when compared with those of others performing similar tasks
7. Mobility potential of the job: workers want to feel that there exists in a job a potential for movement upward through the skill hierarchy, the occupational hierarchy, the organizational structure in which the work is performed, or any combination of the three
8. Satisfactory working conditions
9. Job security

These nine perspectives describe the areas in which career guidance programs in business and industry can provide information, support, encouragement, or skill-building approaches that can facilitate job satisfaction. In an elaboration of some of these elements. Hall and Schneider (1973) have proposed a model of organizational career development based on psychological success and failure. In it they suggest that the need for competence leads the individual to seek situations where self-esteem will be enhanced and avoid situations where self-esteem is likely to be reduced. They base their model on three propositions:

1. Increases in career self-image, career commitment, and self-esteem will result from success in attaining a career-relevant goal that satisfies the following criteria:
   - The goal was set by the person.
   - The path to the goal was defined by the person.
   - The goal was perceived as challenging or difficult but attainable.
   - The goal was central to the person's self-image.
   - The goal was attained.
2. The extent to which a person's initial job assignment provides the conditions for psychological success (challenge and autonomy) will continue to be positively related to career commitment, performance, and success in subsequent years. An initial job experience of psychological failure may conversely be related to decreased commitment, performance, and success in later years.
3. The transition from one organizational status to another is often accomplished by significant changes in the person's self-image, satisfaction, and attitudes toward work (pp. 3–8).

In the model proposed by Hall and Schneider, good performance leads to satisfaction. In this respect it is congruent with the various interpretations of expectancy theory cited in Chapter 4. The opposite way to view the relations among motivation, performance, and satisfaction (Steers & Porter, 1975) is that performance follows from satisfaction rather than leads to it. In this regard, another classic approach to job satisfaction will be cited: the theory of work adjustment by Lofquist and Dawis (1969). Basically, in this model the fit among individual needs, skills and abilities, and technical organizational requirements is the seedbed for satisfaction, and if such satisfaction is attained, high performance will ensue.

The Lofquist and Dawis model emphasizes that work is more than the accomplishment of some set of tasks. It is also a place of human interaction and psychological reinforcement, which may be far more significant in creating job satisfaction than merely performing tasks.

Lofquist and Dawis (1969) contend that job satisfaction and work adjustment result from correspondence between individual and environment. The major assumptions that underlie this theory include the following:

- Each individual seeks to achieve and maintain correspondence with his or her environment.
- Work represents a major environment to which most individuals must relate.
- In the case of work, then, correspondence can be described in terms of the individual fulfilling the requirements of the work environment, and the work environment fulfilling the requirements of the individual.
- The continuous and dynamic process by which one seeks to achieve and maintain correspondence with one's work environment is called *work adjustment*.
- This stability of the correspondence between the individual and the work environment is manifested as tenure in the job.
- *Satisfactoriness* and *satisfaction* indicate the correspondence between the individual and the work environment. Satisfactoriness is an external indicator of correspondence derived from sources other than the worker's own self-appraisal. Satisfaction is an internal indicator of correspondence; it represents the individual worker's appraisal of the extent to which the work environment fulfills his or her requirements.
- The levels of satisfactoriness and satisfaction observed for a group of individuals with substantial tenure in a specific work environment establish the limits of satisfactoriness and satisfaction from which tenure can be predicted for other individuals.
- The work personalities of individuals who fall within the limits of satisfactoriness and satisfaction for which substantial tenure can be predicted may be inferred to be correspondent with the specific work environment.

An important aspect of this theory and the program of related research is the correspondence between the individual's needs and the reinforcer system that characterizes the work setting. Such a view is similar to the early work of Henry A. Murray (1938) and the work of Holland (1973a) in assessing the importance and the degrees of tolerance associated with person-situation congruence. Lofquist, Dawis, and their various colleagues have distinguished work settings and occupations on the basis of their profile of reinforcers of individual behavior: 20 different reinforcers are seen as potentially comprising a work setting (see Table 2.2); these are distributed in six categories—safety, comfort, status, altruism, achievement, and autonomy (Rounds, et al. 1981); different persons will have needs profiles that accord with or are incompatible with the reinforcer profile of any given occupation or setting. Their job *satisfaction* and tenure in that setting will vary accordingly.

Table 2.2

Occupational Reinforcers

Ability utilization	Recognition
Achievement	Responsibility
Activity	Security
Advancement	Social service
Authority	Social status
Company policies & practices	Supervision-human relations
Compensation	Supervision-technical
Co-workers	Variety
Creativity	Work conditions
Independence	Autonomy
Moral values	

To assess an individual's job *satisfactoriness* one can compare the individual's scores on ability tests, such as the General Aptitude Test Battery, with Occupational Aptitude Patterns, published by the U.S. Department of Labor for different occupations. Together these two assessments—of individual satisfaction (correspondence of needs and occupational reinforcers) and satisfactoriness (correspondence of individual abilities with occupational requirements)—were integrated into the Minnesota Occupational Classification System in 1975 and coordinated with the *Dictionary of Occupational Titles* and the Holland Codes cited elsewhere in this book.

Findings About Job Satisfaction

In a major review of the job satisfaction literature, Dawis (1984) has suggested that "from a cognitive standpoint, job satisfaction is a cognition, with affective components, that results from certain perceptions and results in certain future behaviors. As a cognition, it is linked to other cognitions, or cognitive constructs, such as self-esteem, job involvement, work alienation, organizational commitment, morale, and life satisfaction. To understand job satisfaction, we must examine its relationship to these other constructs" (p. 286).

In considering the consequences of job satisfaction, Dawis goes on to contend that "from a behavioral standpoint, job satisfaction is a response (a verbal operant) that has behavioral consequences. On the positive side are tenure, longevity, physical health, mental health, and productivity; on the negative side, turnover, absenteeism, accidents, and mental health problems" (p. 289). "The turnover literature documents a negative relationship between job satisfaction and turnover. . . . Quitting the job is the means by which the individual avoids the aversive condition that is job dissatisfaction . . . .The absenteeism literature has likewise documented a negative relationship between job satisfaction and absenteeism; like turnover, absenteeism is a form of avoidance adjustment" (p. 289). "Negative but low correlations have been reported between job satisfaction and accidents" (p. 289). Dawis also reports that job dissatisfaction is related to mental and physical health problems including psychosomatic illnesses, depression, anxiety, worry, tension, impaired interpersonal relationships, coronary heart disease, alcoholism, drug abuse, and suicide.

Dawis concludes his analysis by contending that "it would seem best to think of job satisfaction as an outcome of job behavior. As an outcome, or consequence of job behavior, job satisfaction can be seen as a *reinforcer* that has consequences for future job performance and other work behavior (absences, turnover). Future satisfactory job performance can be maintained by present job satisfaction. Future absence or turnover behavior can be made more likely by present job dissatisfaction, acting as a negative reinforcer" (p. 291).

Person-Job Fit

Fundamental to the issues inherent in the job satisfaction literature is the matter of person-job fit and who has commitment to work.

Many national reports made during the 1970s and 1980s generated public debate about the quality of work life. Embedded in such debate are experimentation with new approaches to designing work organizations, employee health and well-being, workplace participation and democratic management, productivity and the quality of work life, the relationship of satisfaction to performance, and work-related stress and dissatisfaction (Lawler, 1982). The core of such concerns is the *fit* between person and job.

Hackman and Oldham (1981) have picked up this theme in their research. Unlike many other theorists about job satisfaction and productivity, they link these directly to the fit of person to job. They state that

> One of the major influences on organizational productivity is the quality of the relationship between people who do the work and the jobs they perform. If there is a good "fit" between people and their jobs, such that productive work is a personally satisfying experience, then there may be little for management to do to foster high motivation and satisfaction—other than support the healthy person-job relationship that exists. But if that fit is faulty, such that hard and productive work leads mainly to personal discomfort and distress, then there may be little that management can do to engender high productivity and satisfying work experience. (p. 173)

They further maintain that

> Even as work organizations have continued to get bigger, more mechanical, more controlling of individual behavior, and more task specialized, the people who work in these organizations have become more highly educated, more desirous of "intrinsic" work satisfaction, and perhaps less willing to accept routine and monotonous work as their legitimate lot in life. . . . Ways of structuring jobs and managing organizations that worked in this century, it is argued, cannot work now because the people who populate contemporary organizations simply will not put up with them. (p. 175)

Another way of saying this is that the descriptions of workers as passive, confused, irrational, and nonresistant to manipulation by management, which were promulgated by the Hawthorne studies, are now being viewed as more mythology than fact (Bramel & Friend, 1981).

Various social psychological and sociological studies of work have documented the importance of numerous aspects of work experience for adult self-esteem. Schwalbe's (1988) research, for example, has suggested that self-perceived competence in the workplace is the most important source of self-esteem, with reflected appraisal (for example, having co-workers think of you as a good person) next, and their social comparisons with the skills and abilities of other persons as third most important. Schwalbe has suggested that one can think of person-environment fit as self-esteem centered. If persons attach various degrees of importance to different sources of self-esteem, the issue of fit in the workplace becomes a complex one for a career counselor or an employer. Apparently, trying to maximize the fit between an individual and a work environment is not only related to sources of self-esteem that people seek but also how these differ by age, For example, Mortimer and Finch (1986) found that the experience of autonomy at work and related conditions of work are consequential for the self-image at different age periods.

Such perspectives argue that an extremely important role for career guidance in business and industry is that of worker classification and assessment, as well as job redesign, based on models of management that allow for greater worker participation in decisions about work processes, flex-time, quality circles, worker ownership of product quality, worker autonomy, perceived self-competence, and so forth. The current infatuation of American management with Japanese management styles relates directly to such issues.

Against this background of person-job fit, there continues to be a concern about the effects of underemployment or overeducation of many Americans. O'Toole (1975) has, for example, written about the "Reserve Army of the Underemployed." He means that there are far fewer challenging jobs than there are persons with educational credentials that qualify them for such jobs. Although the educational level of the population has continued to go up, and in particular the number of college-educated persons has risen significantly as a proportion of the total labor force since World War II, the economic system has not kept up with the "job content inflation" associated with the rise in educational credentials or with the employment expectations of younger workers.

In the past decade, the perspectives of O'Toole on the relationships between education and work have been modified. As the global economy increases, so do the levels of international competition experienced by nations; it has become clear that the fundamental resource that will give nations a competitive edge is a work force that is literate, flexible, teachable, and therefore able to adapt quickly to new production methods and management styles. More jobs in the economy are requiring workers to be able to engage in lifelong learning in order to remain current with the information processing and methodological requirements of high-technology occupations and technology-intensive occupations. The availability of work forces with sufficient training and competence to meet the demands of the new economic alliances, the global economy, and the tidal wave of new technologies being integrated into the production and service sectors of nations across the world is one of the growing international issues of the 1990s. A major trend in the evolving job configurations of world economies is the likelihood that machine systems and robots are likely to replace many of the low-skilled and semi-skilled production jobs now occupied by poorly educated or untrained workers.

In effect, the application of advanced technology in the workplace is a central factor in the redistribution of learning requirements in the society. For example, as forecast in the United States, "very few new jobs will be created for those who cannot read, follow directions, and use mathematics" (Hudson Institute, 1987, p. 1). In one study that ranked new or emerging jobs according to the skills required rather than by education, the rising educational requirements can be seen in fairly dramatic terms. When compared across six skill categories according to the math, language, and reasoning skills they require, only 27 percent of all new jobs fall into the lowest two skill categories, compared to 40 percent of current jobs that can be performed with these limited skills. By contrast, 41 percent of new jobs are in the three highest skill groups, compared to only 24 percent of current jobs (Hudson Institute, 1987, p. 1).

In a very real sense, basic academic skills are becoming the ultimate employability skills. Drucker (1989) has argued that the biggest shift—bigger by far than the changes in politics, government, or economics—is the shift to the knowledge society in all developed non-Communist countries. Until quite recently, there were few jobs requiring knowledge. But, in the twentieth century, knowledge has rapidly become the economy's foundation and its true capital: knowledge has replaced experience as the primary requisite for employability. Thus, it is not difficult to predict that undereducation will intensify as a major problem for many segments of the population into the twenty-first century. Problems of educational deficits will be major issues in person-job fit; these will need to be considered as major concerns for the career guidance practitioner of the 1990s and beyond.

Although unemployment and undereducation are dramatic concerns in person-job fit, the concern expressed by O'Toole about underemployment in the 1970s will likely intensify as a major issue in the 1990s. Highly qualified workers often "bump" slightly less qualified workers from their jobs and push them further down the status hierarchy as advanced technology replaces middle management, clerical, semi-skilled, and unskilled labor. As higher levels of skills and capabilities are unused and highly qualified people are underemployed, they are likely to be dissatisfied with their jobs. In such instances, they have great potential for occupational and social pathology and for problems with person-job fit.

The implementation of advanced technology in the economic structure has created a new form of underemployment that is only now becoming visible. As the available mix of occupations changes from manufacturing to service industries, and as changes in the organization of work require the displacement of middle managers and others, the quality of life and the earning power of those affected change. For example, the service industries tend to pay roughly two-thirds of the annual salary paid in manufacturing industries. Therefore, if a steelworker suffers displacement and finds a job in a service industry (such as electronics repair), the former steelworker, although still employed, is likely to experience a significantly lower wage and quality of life. Coupled with the loss of seniority rights and the probability of reduced benefits packages, the result is a substantial drop in the standard of living for workers in many durable goods industries (for example, automotive and mining workers) as the economy and occupational structure is being transformed into situations predominated by information-based and service industries.

Rochelle and Spellman (1987) contend that as advanced technology pervades the workplaces of the nation, "for those who want to work and have the skills, technological displacement is not likely to mean unemployment so much as lesser employment—a shift to what work is available—generally at lower pay" (p. 82). They go on: "the American working population faces a difficult and contradictory situation. Work will be available, but not necessarily the work people are prepared for and, it appears, not at the wages they are conditioned to expect" (p. 90).

Counselors involved in the delivery of career services in businesses and industries as well as government agencies or private practice will have major roles in working with the unemployed and the underemployed. While the specifics of these roles will be discussed at greater length in other chapters, counselors will need to provide support and psychological assistance, as well as assistance to people in reevaluating their self-concepts and needs. Counselors will also be increasingly involved in learning systems for youth and adults as brokers of training and retraining opportunities that increase the possibilities of person-job fit; formal educational qualifications will become more important mediators of such fit.

Career Guidance and Job Satisfaction

The models of job satisfaction, motivation, and work performance discussed here and in Chapter 4 provide both conceptual stimuli and a potential blueprint for the variety of activities in which counselors and career guidance persons can engage effectively in business and industry. These will be detailed more fully in Chapters 11 and 13. What is known about job satisfaction supports such counselor activity as the following:

- Educating first-line supervisors and managers about current perspectives on job satisfaction, work motivation, and work performance
- Providing information to workers about career paths, career ladders, and the avenues

and requirements for mobility within the organization

- Classifying workers by technical skills and psychological needs to maximize person-job fit with regard to content, supervisory style, and related factors
- Conducting workshops and seminars to increase workers' understanding of their educational opportunities, their employability skills, and their understanding of the organizational characteristics with which they interact
- Consulting with managers about job redesign and work enrichment schemes
- Providing support groups for workers in various types of transitions (such as new jobs, geographical relocations, overseas transfers, shifting family structures)
- Providing individual counseling about work behavior and career development
- Conducting assessments of facet satisfactions and worker aspirations
- Intervening in the workplace environment to help shape policies that improve quality of work life or that modify jobs to allow workers with particular handicaps to perform effectively
- Identifying effective reinforcers in the work setting and translating them into person-job fit
- Brokering in-plant and formal training and retraining opportunities to increase worker competencies

WORK AND MENTAL HEALTH

One of the major themes that both emphasizes the important meaning work has for many and the difficulties that ensue when one's work life is unsatisfactory is that of work and mental health. In the previous section we discussed the mental and physical problems that are corollaries of job dissatisfaction. Such corollaries have also been found in an historical line of data that has become increasingly visible, particularly in the psychological literature of the past two decades.

In 1985 McLean traced the previous 100 years of occupational mental health efforts. In the United States, such emphases took root in the second decade of this century as industrial psychiatry, and questions about the mental hygiene of industry and about unemployment and personality began to emerge. In the 1920s, behavioral scientists from a broad range of disciplines began to address studies of worker turnover, employee morale, working conditions, work productivity, and individual worker needs and characteristics. In 1924, Mayo conducted the classic, but flawed, studies of the working conditions at the Hawthorne plant of the Western Electric Company near Chicago. More than 20,000 employees were interviewed, and several small experimental groups were intensively observed as changes were made in their work situation. As McLean observed,

> The Hawthorne studies concluded that a work organization has both economic and social functions. The output of a product may be considered a form of social behavior and all the activity of a plant may be viewed as an interaction of structure, personality, and culture. If any of these variables is altered, Mayo noted, change must occur in each of the other two variables. Further, reactions to stress on the part of the individual employees arise when there is resistance to change, when there are faulty control and communication systems, and when the individual worker must make adjustments to his structure at work. (pp. 33–34)

As the decades since the 1920s have intensified the interest of mental health professionals in occupational mental health, it has become an accepted axiom that business and industry, the workplaces of the nation, turn out two main commodities: material goods and human satisfactions. Analyses of the implications of such an axiom as it is mediated by organizational characteristics, the presence of satisfiers and dissatisfiers, the application of psychiatric insights to attempts to understand the outcomes of persons under the stress of war, in or out of combat, the problems of defense workers under intense production pressure, and workers performing in less-than-optimal working conditions has laid the base for the current understandings of the work-stress connection identified in Chapter 11 and the diverse workplace responses known as human resource development (HRD), employee assistance programs (EAPs), and related programs. As discussed in Chapter 11, these programs deal with a broad range of issues from alcoholism to family mediation to educational counseling to financial planning, outplacement, or preretirement planning. Major conferences and the professional literature deal increasingly with issues of worker absenteeism, stress management, drug abuse in industry, the changing meaning of work, the emotionally troubled employee, or mental health and work organizations. Specific attention seems to ebb and flow between focusing on the mentally ill worker and the prevention of work stress, and the creation of an occupational setting that is mentally healthy, between delivering mental health services directly to workers and considering the work organization to be the patient. However the issue is conceived, it accents the relationships that exist between work and mental health.

Many existing research studies link work and mental health. In a major study of mental health in America and the contrasts in patterns of helpseeking from 1957 to 1976, Veroff, Kulka, and Douvan (1981) report that about 10 percent of their respondents in 1957 and in 1976 either used help or could have used help with job problems or vocational choice (p. 190). Undoubtedly, this number is understated, since several other problem areas reported probably also included job-related problems (such as situational problems involving other people, nonpsychological situational problems, "nothing specific—a lot of little things," and marriage). The researchers also found that younger workers are more distressed in their work, more aware of their own shortcomings, and more sensitive to difficulties, and that they seek greater gratification from their work life. Older people are more often locked into a job to which they have already adapted and hence tend to make the best of the situation. Such findings indicate that some groups are more likely to risk psychological distress associated with work than others. However, the findings of Veroff, Kulka, and Douvan suggest that distress about work is only minimally related to readiness for self-referral.

> Evidently adaptation to work is a psychological process which if unsuccessful is as likely to stimulate thoughts of self-help as of seeking help from professionals. Indeed one might surmise that people often diagnose their own psychological problems at work as being ones which require that they "get themselves together" or find other work or another job. This option of leaving a job as a solution to a work problem may possibly reduce the association between work distress and readiness for self-referral (p. 89).

Career Development and Mental Health

Whether it leads to readiness for self-referral or not, distress about work is associated with a range of social and personal problems. Counseling psychology, and counseling theory in general, is just beginning to make the link between career development and mental health (Herr, 1989). Until now, for the most part, the focus of attention has been on the structure of career development and its changes over time (Chapter 4 focuses on such content), not on the relationships between career patterns and mental health. But there is a growing and compelling body of evidence suggesting that such relationships do exist; that the characteristics of work (for example, Lewin-Epstein, 1989), absence of work, or underemployment are reflected in behaviors that suggest various problems in living or, indeed, mental illness; and that there may, in fact, be psychological and mental health consequences of difficult career decisions (Spokane, 1989).

Until the past decade, with few exceptions, career counseling and career guidance have been historically portrayed as significantly more oriented to economic health, to choice of an occupation, and to the development of pre-vocational skills and the preparation for work than to the reduction of stress and other factors that put people at risk of experiencing physical and mental disorders. However, as suggested in Chapter 1, traditional and restrictive views of the purpose and potential of career counseling are slowly changing in the face of growing evidence that career development and human development are connected; satisfaction or dissatisfaction in one of these affects the other. Thus, in national policies, commission reports, and a growing segment of professional literature, career counseling and guidance are being seen as critical ingredients in giving underemployed, unemployed, vocationally dissatisfied, or indecisive youth and adults a sense of purpose and self-efficacy; in so doing, career guidance or counseling is expected to be helpful in diminishing the stress-related side effects of hopelessness and despair associated with a work life that is seen as unsatisfying or mismatched to the individual's aspirations and abilities.

Implicit in such perspectives is the reality that problems with work may be intrapsychic, environmental, or interactive. Work problems that are intrapsychic may involve individual preoccupations with self-esteem, deficits in interpersonal skills, inability to appropriately tolerate constructive supervisory relationships, or involvement in additive processes or substances. Work problems that are environmental in etiology (causative factors) include exposure to a management or supervisory style that is negative for that person and creates a pathological work situation, a work setting that provides no opportunity for advancement or for the levels or kinds of rewards to which a person aspires, or a work context that is racially or sexually biased and stifles individual mobility or security. An interactive work environment is one in which there is a mismatch between the individual's skills and environmental expectations—a lack of person-job fit. In each of these situations, the workplace becomes an environment in which both positive and negative, healthy and unhealthy, good and bad outcomes are stimulated; a context in which conflicts, thwarted ambitions, and emotional distress from one's life outside that workplace can be brought into the workplace to shape one's life as a worker. As such, the workplace becomes a crucible for mental health issues that revolve around work and become the content of career counseling and career guidance.

Good Work—Bad Work

Some types of work do not gratify many of the needs in Table 2.1, whereas other types potentially gratify all. In part, this distinction occurs when work tasks are routine and repetitive, seen only partially by their participants as contributing to a final product, when the individual is made servant to the machine and deskilled in the process, or when only limited possibilities for personal achievement are offered. Such notions raise in the minds of observers a dichotomy of "good work versus bad work" (Schumacher, 1981). Bad work is an unpleasant necessity; good work is a process that ennobles the product as it ennobles the producer. Meaningless work is seen as an abomination, as bad; good work is seen as giving purpose to life, speaking not just to one's physical engagement but to how the work engages the soul and the spirit.

However metaphysically uplifting such thoughts are, they tend to cast the organization and content of work into a simple dichotomy that, for the most part, does not exist in absolute terms. Rather, individuals tend to define work as good or bad depending on how it meets their particular needs.

As O'Toole (1981) has argued, "When it is said that work should be 'meaningful' what is meant is that it should contribute to self-esteem, to the sense of fulfillment through the mastering of one's self and one's environment, and to the sense that one is valued by society" (p. 15). These are psychological processes that individuals perceive and attribute to work differently. Indeed, as O'Toole has suggested in another context, what almost all authors find when studying workers in different types of "bad" work—work that could be better done by machines or animals—is that such people attempt to interject some meaning into the hours in which they labor; they cope with unrewarding work by creating a sense of community. "If the task itself is meaningless, meaning can at least be attached to the social interaction with fellow workers" (p. 8).

In this connection, Fretz and Leong (1982), after a comprehensive review of pertinent research studies, concluded the following:

> One finding that occurred with striking frequency in studies in the life span and worker adjustment sections was the moderating impact of the interpersonal context. When workers desire and have satisfying affiliative relationships on the job, the descriptive effects of limited job scope, job dissatisfaction, person-environment misfit, and the like were often minimized. If more direct investigation of affiliative context support these scattered findings, there are obvious intervention implications—facilitating more satisfactory affiliative conditions may often be easier and less expensive than employee relocation, job enrichment, and the like. Some jobs are simply not pleasant; maximizing the value of the interpersonal context may be the most direct route to maximizing employee stability and performance. (p. 152)

Given the propensity for workers to master, cope, or interject meaning into work that by some external criterion would be seen as bad or repetitive, it is not difficult to understand that even when workers report boredom and monotony they also report that work is a prime source of personal definition or identity, and they would continue to do it even if they became wealthy enough to stop working (Vecchio, 1980). Although that attitude may be true in general, as noted above, England (1990) and Super (1982, 1984b) have noted differences in the salience of work to people in different nations and regions of nations. Yankelovich (Calhoun, 1980; Yankelovich, 1981; Yankelovich & Lefkowitz, 1982), among other observers, reports that in the United States work values are changing. His surveys suggest that

> Under the impact of [women's liberation] the rigid division of labor in the family is beginning to break down. People are growing balky on the job; they seem less willing than in the past to endure hardships for the sake of making a living. Some unions are now stressing non-economic issues at the bargaining table. Many people are seeking jobs that may pay less well but offer a more agreeable life style. And even the high value we place on economic growth as the main goal of our society is cast in doubt. (p. 33)

Changes in the Meaning of Work

Yankelovich contends that we are now in the throes of a transformation of work values and the work ethic. In this view, the work ethic is so central to American culture that if its meaning shifts, the character of our society will shift along with it. In the next chapter we will exam-

Table 2.3

Trends in the Work Ethic in the 1960s and the 1980s

1960s	1980s
The Good Provider Theme The breadwinner—the man who provides for his family—is the real man *The Independence Theme* To make a living by working is to "stand on one's own two feet and avoid dependence on others." *The Success Theme* Hard work always pays off *The Self-Respect Theme* Hard work of any type has dignity whether it be menial or exalted. A man's inherent worth is reflected in the act of working.	*Reduced Fear of Economic Insecurity* For most people economic security continues to dominate their lives. But today people take some economic security for granted. A substantial minority say that they are now prepared to take certain risks with their own economic security for the sake of enhancing the quality of life. *Economic Division of Labor Between the Sexes* The economic discipline that maintained the rigidity of sex roles in the past has weakened. The idea of women working for purposes of self-fulfillment rather than economic motives gains wider acceptance all the time. *The Psychology of Entitlement* A broad new agenda of social rights is growing and a psychological process is developing whereby a person's wants and desires become converted into a set of presumed rights. *The Adversary Culture Challenges the Cult of Efficiency* The average American has begun to wonder whether too great a concern with efficiency and rationalization is not robbing life of the excitement and pleasure desired. *The Changing Meaning of Success* An increasing number of people are coming to feel that there is such a thing as enough money. A "big earner" who has settled for an unpleasant life style is no longer considered more successful than someone with less money who has created an agreeable life style. People are no longer as ready to make sacrifices for economic success as they were in the past.

Source: Adapted table from "The Meaning of Work" by Daniel Yankelovich in *Working: Changes and Choices*, edited by James O'Toole, Jane L. Schneider and Linda C. Work. Copyright © 1981 by Human Sciences Press.

ine the shifts from goods-producing to service- and knowledge-producing as the major outcomes of work. We will talk about the nature of the knowledge explosion and the effects on work of such technological advances as silicon chips and microprocessors. But it is important to realize that those changes have to do with content of work. What Yankelovich and others in this chapter are concerned about is how people view the "meaning" of work in relation to themselves, how central it is to their self-definitions. In Yankelovich's view, such meanings are changing. He has compared his studies of American life themes in the 1960s with those of the 1980s. Such themes link work with people's life values and are the ingredients of the term *work ethic*. Table 2.3 compares the themes identified by Yankelovich in the mid-1960s with those from his research reports in 1981.

Ginzberg and his associates in the Conservation of Human Resources Project and several earlier projects at Columbia University have been studying work in America since 1939. They avoided proposing a general theory of work throughout the years because of the complexity of the forces affecting work shifts in America and throughout the world. Ginzberg, however, reported a series of propositions in 1975 that describe the views he and his colleagues hold about the fundamental shifts occurring in the role of work in the lives of individuals in contemporary America. Many of them complement the findings of Yankelovich or are precursors of them. Among the major observations are the following (Ginzberg, 1975):

- It is erroneous to postulate a marked decline in the work ethic in America and especially to attribute it to youth alone. We believe that changes have been underway for some time in the ways in which large numbers of Americans of all ages relate to work.
- Similarly, we believe it is an error to single out any particular occupational group, such as blue-collar or service workers, and argue that they have lost pride in workmanship and are no longer willing to give a day's work for a day's pay. Our counterpoint is that if such trends can be validated, they can be found in all occupational groups, although not necessarily to the same degree . . . .
- Today, more and more young people do not get regular jobs until they are in their early or mid-twenties. There is little doubt that this markedly elongated preparatory process affects their expectations and responses as members of the labor force.
- An interesting clue to what may well be a deep malaise is seen in the small but growing number of people who have had successful careers but who decide in midstream to make a break and seek a new occupation. Although the reasons for these attempts at breakaway are many and diverse, they seem to be rooted in varying degrees of dissatisfaction with the work these individuals have been doing.
- It is often difficult to assess the specific contribution of the individual in our society, because work is increasingly performed in groups and because the key to group cohesion and performance lies in "political arrangements" among the members and the leadership. Thus, personal acceptability is often confused with technical competence. . . .
- Another important concomitant of how large organizations operate and one that has an impact on how people work is the restricted room at the top—a limitation that quickly becomes clear to most employees. Once they recognize it, many recalculate the probabilities of attaining one of the key prizes and the costs that attach to the effort . . . .
- About 40 percent [in 1990, about 50 percent] of all working persons are women; we know little about what different groups of women want from work, except that many of them have begun to fight against the discrimination to which they have been subjected. Moreover, most working women are married, and changes in their career aspirations will inevitably lead to changes in the lives of their husbands and children.
- Finally, we must recognize that the close links that formerly existed between work and income have been loosened with consequences that are just beginning to surface. (pp. 63–65)*

To argue that the meaning of work is changing is not to say that all persons in the work force accept such changes or act in accordance

*Reprinted with permission of the publishers from Eli Ginzberg, *The Manpower Connection* (Cambridge, MA: Harvard University Press). Copyright © 1975 by the President and Fellows of Harvard College.

with them. Yankelovich attributes what he calls the nontraditional values, those now emerging, primarily to persons under thirty-five and particularly to the college-educated. In his view, although the percentage is shrinking, the majority of workers still hold traditional values in which work motivation derives from money, status, and security.

But there are other ways to suggest the meaning of work to people and its relationship to how they live. For example, Mitchell (1984) has described the work of SRI International (formerly the Stanford Research Institute) in its Values and Lifestyles (VALS) Program. The resulting typology was derived from national sampling in this country and has been applied to the population of a number of other nations to examine the differences in the proportions of persons in the life-style emphasis of each nation and the variance such differences create in elements of national character. The VALS typology comprises four comprehensive groups that can be divided into nine life-styles, each defined by its distinctive array of values, drives, beliefs, needs, dreams, and special points of view. The four groups and nine life-styles are described as need-driven groups—survivor life-style, sustainer life-style; outer-directed groups—belonger life-style, emulator life-style, achiever life-style; inner-directed groups—I-am-me life-style, experimental life-style, societally conscious life-style; and a combined outer- and inner-directed group—integrated life style.

In succinct terms, the need-drive groups are struggling to meet their basic needs. The survivor subgroup constitutes about 4 percent of the United States population, is very poor, typically elderly, poorly educated, lacking in self-confidence, depressed, and essentially unable to take advantage of the work opportunities that might help them improve their position. The other need-driven group, the sustainers, are likely to be somewhat better off financially but still living on the edge of poverty, frequently engaged with the underground economy rather than the secondary or primary labor markets, angry, resentful, and rebellious. About one-fourth of this group is looking for work or works only part-time. Few of these people get much satisfaction from their work, which primarily occurs in machine, manual, and service occupations. Persons in this life-style category make up about 7 percent of the United States population. While these persons have not given up hope and seek financial security and economic improvement (many are hard-working and ambitious), they frequently have a difficult time finding opportunities because they are often immigrants without good English skills, minorities with poor educational backgrounds, or single parents on welfare or with marginal incomes.

The outer-directed group includes about two-thirds of the American adult population. Belongers are the biggest group in this typology, about 35 percent; emulators make up about 9 percent; and achievers, 22 percent of the population. In a collective sense, these are the people who dream the American dream, and many within their typology also live it. As the name of the typology implies, outer-directed people pay considerable attention to what others think, to what the media says is important, to the visible, tangible, and materialistic aspects of life. The research of Mitchell and his colleagues suggests that the belongers are likely to be highly patriotic, conventional, happy, aging, and quite traditional members of the middle class. They want to fit in, not stand out. They follow the rules. They cherish their family, church, and job. They need acceptance and are dependent and conformist to get it. They tend to live in small towns and rural areas, not large cities. The second life-style group in this typology, the emulators, tend to be younger than the belongers and much more intense in their striving to be like those who are richer and more successful than they are. They are hard-working, ambitious, and competitive. They are not likely to have completed college, although they may have one or two years of college or graduated from technical school. Thus, they are not likely to achieve the highest levels of professional, technical, or administrative occupations for which they strive, although, of course, some do. However, many experience rejection and feel that the system has been unfair and their primary ambitions have been frustrated, frequently because there is a mismatch between their goals and their abilities or preparation. They nevertheless ask much of themselves and of the system, and they often take great responsibility to achieve success. The achievers, on the other hand, are the members of the outer-directed group who have made it. They are the people the emulators hope to be. They are typically gifted, hardworking, self-reliant, successful, and happy. They typically live a comfortable and affluent outer-directed life. They are generally middle-aged, self-assured, and prosperous leaders and builders of what is considered to be the American dream. Very few of these people are minority: for example, approximately 2 percent are black. They tend to include many members who have attended college and graduate school. They are often self-made successes, politically and socially conservative.

The inner-directed typology includes the I-am-me life-style possessed by about 5 percent of the adult population, and the experiential group, about 7 percent of the population. As contrasted with the outer-directed group, the inner-directed are oriented to how they feel internally about different aspects of their lives as compared to what other people or external systems suggest that they should feel. Thus, their attitudes toward their jobs, personal relationships, spiritual matters, and other daily satisfactions become preeminent to them. Many of these people are active in social movements. They are less driven by money and social status than other groups. They tend to have excellent educations and frequently hold good jobs of a professional or technical nature. These people are likely to have been raised in relatively prosperous, outer-directed families where they were relatively satisfied with material comforts and are no longer driven to acquire them as a sole raison d'être. Within the inner-directed typology, the I-am-me and the experiential life-style groups tend to differ in some ways. Although both are likely to be younger than the outer-directed group, the I-am-me group tends to be in a turbulent stage of transition from outer-directed values and characteristics to those that dominate in the inner-directed classification; there is considerable anxiety as they give up what have been secure and comfortable lives for more uncertain, contradictory situations. These are people in the throes of seeking out new life-styles, new ways of life, new personal identities. They are, on balance, energetic and active participants in whatever they engage. In some contrast to the I-am-me are the slightly older inner-directed group of experientials. For this latter group, action and interaction and direct, vivid experience with people, ideas, and events are their driving force. These people tend to be independent, self-reliant, and excellently educated, with high-level technical and professional positions. They are concerned with quality-of-life issues, natural rather than artificial products, spirituality, and skepticism. They are participative, self-assured, interested in personal growth and learning, and socially sensitive.

The final life-style typology is the combined outer- and inner-directed group, those who Mitchell's research suggests are the integrated types. Such people, estimated to make up 2 percent of the population, combine outer-directed and inner-directed styles into an integrated outlook on life. They tend to adapt easily to existing norms and mores and have a fully developed sense of what is fitting and appropriate. They find ways to balance work and play and to combine close relationships with people with the motivation to accomplish. These are people likely to be middle-aged and above and very well-educated, working in very well-paid occupations in which they can either lead or follow when action is required.

What the research of Mitchell and his colleagues indicates is that groups with different life-styles or values view work through lenses that vary in their focus on the utility of work, the meaning of work, and the centrality or fragmentation of work. These windows on work are associated with different behaviors in the workplace and in one's life beyond the job.

Changes in the Meanings of Work Across Political and Economic Systems

In a pluralistic society like the United States, groups that differ by gender, ethnicity, education, and socioeconomic structure are likely to differ in the meanings they attribute to work. An extension of that point can be made about differences in the meaning of work and how work is organized in different political and economic systems. Work is interpreted differently by different cultures, and the skills and values considered important from one nation to another reinforce some work values and behaviors and not others. As Fallows (1989) has suggested, different societies find different ways to make individual behavior serve the collective good.

Put somewhat differently, Segall et al. (1990) contend that "more sophisticated cross-cultural research underscores the plausibility of expecting that people in different cultural settings would vary in the way they learn to solve problems and in the patterns of skills they acquire. . . . Cultures vary in the salience attached to certain skills, in the combination of basic cognitive processes that are called upon in any given context, or in the order in which specific skills are acquired" (p. 94). As Segall, Dasen, Berry, and Poortinga further note, "in any society, there is likely to be a meaningful relationship between child training emphases and adult behavior. . . . Children are likely to be induced to behave in ways compatible with adult roles that they will have to assume, with these roles in turn reflective of socioeconomic complexity and social organization" (p. 236). Thus, "all human beings are capable of a far greater repertory of behaviors than any single person ever exhibits. Each of us, because of the accident of birth, begins life in a particular social context, within which we learn to make some responses and not others" (p. 237).

Unemployment and Mental and Emotional Distress

Probably the most dramatic example of the connection between mental and emotional distress and work is that of unemployment. For example, Levine (1979) has reported on both the reactions to unemployment and the emotional consequences of unemployment. He reports that reactions to unemployment tend to unfold in three stages: (1) optimism, (2) ambiguity, and (3) despair. Although there are individual differences in coping with these stages, the virtually predictable emotional and cognitive consequences, according to Levine, include the following: boredom, identity diffusion, lower self-esteem, guilt and shame, anxiety and fear, anger, and depression. These are not benign emotional reactions.

Borgen and Amundson (1984), in a major study of the experiences of unemployed persons from a variety of educational, cultural, and work backgrounds in Canada, extend the findings of Levine. They contend that the experience of unemployment depicts an emotional roller coaster that is comparable in its impact and stages to those found by Kubler-Ross (1969) when she described the grief process associated with loss of a loved one: denial, anger, bargaining, depression, and acceptance. In regard to Maslow's model of prepotent needs, which suggests that as needs at the bottom of a hierarchy are satisfied, other needs emerge, Borgen and Amundson suggest that unemployment brings with it a needs shift that involves tumbling down the hierarchy from need levels attained under previous employment to more primitive need levels that are dominant under unemployment. According to Maslow, the categories of needs that emerge as lower levels of needs are routinely met or taken for granted begin with the most basic, the physiological needs, and proceed next to the safety needs (security, stability), to the love and belonging needs (relatedness), to the esteem needs (prestige, self-worth, recognition), and, finally, to the self-actualization needs (creative self-expression). Although it is rare that people actually attain the highest level of self-actualization in their work, it can be assumed that most persons successfully employed will be able to attain needs beyond the most primitive physiological necessities and to meet needs for safety, love, belonging, and esteem. The 1989 research of Borgen and Amundson suggests that whatever needs are attained in employment shift downward significantly under unemployment. The psychological reactions under such circumstances are not only those of loss as defined by the Kubler-Ross paradigm, but also feelings of victimization similar to those experienced by persons who find themselves in the role of victim as a result of rape, incest, disease, and crime. Such feelings include shock, confusion, helplessness, anxiety, fear, and depression (Janoff-Bulman & Frieze, 1983).

Borgen and Amundson's (1984) research is important for at least two other reasons. One is that unemployment is experienced differently by different groups of males and females who did or did not anticipate job loss and by immigrant populations. The second is that the factors that vary among these groups and mediate the emotional reactions to unemployment include the following: attachment to the job, social status, individual personality variables, financial situation, social support system, and future expectations.

In applying Borgen and Amundson's model to the situation that occurs when a long-established plant closes, Hurst and Shepherd (1986) found similar emotional stages to occur among workers anticipating job loss. In such instances, the emotional roller coaster is likely to be prolonged as older workers remain while younger workers are laid off to pare down the work force of the plant to be closed. In this research, that of Lopez (1983), and in that of Amundson and Borgen, groups varied in their reactions to job loss. Hurst and Shepherd found in their sample that employees most likely to experience prolonged depression are the few who are handicapped by physical, skill, and age barriers, and those with very low self-esteem. But even for those workers who do not experience clinical depression, as reported in other research as well (Lopez, 1983), there tend to be "feelings of loss, sadness, resentment, and anger because of the end of the company, close collegial relationships and way of life for most employees" (Hurst & Shepherd 1986, p. 404).

Lopez's research (1983) has suggested that counseling approaches to working with employees dislocated because of business failures could include such paraphrased possibilities as the following:

1. Clarifying with workers their marketable, transferable, and work skills and helping them to develop short-term plans by which such skills might be realistically applied in other situations
2. Creating opportunities for displaced workers to vent their feelings about vocational and personal concerns
3. Helping workers to identify and assess their sources of financial, familial, marital, and other types of personal support
4. Helping clients to obtain and use timely information on referral services, employment outlook, and available placement services
5. Reinforcing with workers the ideas that they are skilled and mature and that the job losses they experience are not because of

their personal incompetence or negligence, but rather that this experience is not something that they caused

Borgen and Amundson's research highlights what other theorists and researchers have also observed in relation to the interaction of mental health with state of the economy or unemployment or related phenomena. One is that such relations are likely to include multiple variables, not simply unidimensional relationships. Different people experience economic downturns and unemployment differently, and mental health outcomes can be precipitated by factors in the environment (sociogenic), as well as factors within individuals (eugenic) (Berg & Hughes, 1979). Thus, there are questions of social causation, social selection, precipitating factors, and individual predispositions that relate to how work and mental health are related. Brenner (1979) has attempted to clarify the differences among some of these concepts. For example, physical and mental health are not unitary concepts. Some people react to stress in physical terms (for example, cardiovascular disease, cirrhosis, hypertension, chemical dependency, early death); others in behavioral terms (for example, aggressiveness, violence, spouse abuse, child abuse); others in psychological terms (for example, depression, anxiety). Thus, precipitating factors in the environment (for example, a plant closing, losing a job) can cause different reactions among people (physical, behavioral, psychological) depending upon individual predisposing factors to stress. In reference to making the connection between precipitating factors and predisposing factors, Brenner suggests three important questions: "(1) Will any member of the population react? (2) Who will react? (3) What will be the reaction?" (p. 71).

As we alluded to briefly in Chapter 1, the social context or social ecology of a situation in which precipitating and predisposing factors operate is linked to both. In other words, the social context specifies whether or not precipitating factors are really meaningful problems. Similarly, the previous or current social ecology that the individual occupies mediates how precipitating factors are interpreted and how predispositional factors are likely to be played out. For example, the regularly observed inverse relationship between socioeconomic status and mental health problems may be caused by class differences in access to quality medical care, including prenatal care, or to social selection factors—poor people living in the midst of a deteriorating inner city in which employment opportunities of high quality are few in number—rather than to any actual class differences in reaction to stress. The question, then, pertains to whether or not the different resources of individuals and the different access to the resources on which the social status of individuals is based lead to different social sanctions, different vulnerability and reactions to stress, and more severe social reactions to economic and employment problems (Dohrenwend, 1975).

The links between unemployment and other individual or social costs are complex. Liem and Rayman (1982), among others, have reviewed studies of the social and private costs of unemployment. They indicate that "prolonged unemployment is commonly a serious threat to health and the broad quality of life. These costs, furthermore, are borne not only by individual workers, but also by their families and communities" (p. 1116). They go on to say that "there is good evidence that losing one's job can increase health risks, exacerbate chronic and latent disorders, alter usual patterns of health-seeking behavior, and exact numerous other social and interpersonal costs" (p. 1116).

Economists have shown that the state of the North American economy over the past 100 years or so is a useful predictor of rates of hospital admissions for mental illness and of suicides (Brenner, 1981). In these studies, job loss or underemployment is frequently a proxy measure for the state of the economic climate. Warner (1985), a psychiatrist, has studied the prevalence and outcome of schizophrenia in relation to the political economy and he has found a close relationship between illness onset, treatment outcome, changes in employment, and the economic situation. Warner's evidence is that first-time admissions to the hospital increase in times of high unemployment and that those socioeconomic classes, specifically the poorest or lowest socioeconomic classes, that are most negatively affected by labor conditions and unemployment happen to be at a greater risk for schizophrenia. He also finds that the incidence of schizophrenia among immigrants is higher than in their country of origin if they encounter harsher labor conditions in their new country. Examining historical data, Warner found that during the Great Depression of the 1930s there was a decreased rate of recovery from schizophrenia, apparently because of the joint effects of economic stress and unemployment on patients in the community. On the positive side of this equation, however, some studies suggest that when schizophrenic patients receive adequate social resources, including jobs, counseling, rehabilitation training, and income, rehospitalization and disability can be significantly reduced (Estroff, 1981).

Other research supports the findings that unemployment, problematic work relationships, and stressful work conditions play significant roles in the development of physical and mental health problems (for example, Brenner, 1987, Frese & Mohr, 1987; Joelson & Wahlquist, 1987; Levi, 1984; Rose, Hurst, & Herd, 1979). Life event changes perceived as stressful—job loss or major career changes are typically so identified—have been repeatedly shown to precede the onset of mental illness. Thus, demoralization and despair associated with severe work or economic or family problems trigger distress that has biological and physiological, as well as psychological, correlates (Kleinman, 1988). In the language of stress, difficulties at work are not only stressful life events, they are stressors that may cause the individual to attempt to cope with or adapt to the resulting stress and strain until he or she runs out of physical and mental resources or gets beyond the capability of existing support systems to buffer him or her from feelings of uncontrollable threat. Depending upon the cultural or social meanings attributed to work conflict or unemployment by the person, his or her family, or the community, he or she may consciously or unconsciously seek ways to express the problem. Sometimes the expression is a physical one (for instance, backache); sometimes it is mental (for example, depression, anxiety, or other symptoms). Which of these "symptoms" of work problems is likely to occur is probably a function of the particular cultural symbols of such distress that the individual has been conditioned to believe are appropriate (Helman, 1985). This does not mean that all cases of backache are somatic expressions of mental distress, but rather that in some cultures or social groups, work conflicts or other aspects of career distress may be "somaticized," symbolized by backache, chronic pain, or other physical symptoms rather than depression or anxiety or other more clearly psychological disorders. One has to be careful not to blame the victim or to overgeneralize the translation of distress into physical or psychological terms, but such transformation of stressors and symptoms does occur in relation to distress at work.

Among the other specific problems in the research literature found to be associated with unemployment and economic decline are first admissions to psychiatric hospitals, rises in rates of infant mortality, increased deaths from cardiovascular and alcohol-related diseases, sharp increases in suicide rates, greater demand for mental health services due to increased psychological impairment of the population (Brenner, 1973, 1979), the probability of suffering a disability (Leigh, 1987), problems with a person's routine use of time and the creation of changes in the life-style and in perspectives of the world (Peregoy & Schliebner, 1990), threats to the structural interdependence between the family and the workplace (Kantor, 1977), stress in the children of unemployed parents—such as moodiness at home, new problems in school, strained relationship with peers (Liem & Rayman, 1982), digestive problems, irritability, and retarded physical and mental development (Riegle, 1982), child and spouse abuse, and juvenile delinquency (Riegle, 1982). The "ripple effect" of unemployment touches not only the individual who is unemployed but all parts of the system of which he or she is a part. For each of the persons involved it is common to manifest a wide range of physical, emotional, and social stresses and strains. In Chapter 13 further discussion of unemployment and its effects is presented.

Work Pathology

Beyond the general relationships between work and mental health just cited, there are also more serious matters. For example, there are problem employees whose work pathology and psychopathology often merge. These are persons for whom corporations have long provided units dedicated to occupational mental health (McLean, 1973). Staffed by psychiatrists or clinical psychologists, such units are frequently augmented by the referral of problem employees to outside consultants through employee assistance plans or through various health care or insurance plans. As counseling psychologists and other career guidance specialists are increasingly employed by corporations and government agencies, treatment of such problems in the workplace may become more common.

In considering serious problems of mental illness in the workplace, it is sometimes difficult to know whether work induces mental illness or people bring mental illness to work. Huffine and Clausen (1979) have engaged in one of the few long-term studies of the effects of mental illness on careers. They intensively studied 36 married white men after they had entered a Washington, D.C., area mental hospital between 1952 and 1958 as first-admission patients with diagnoses of functional psychosis, affective disorder, severe psychoneurosis, or character disorder. Their data revealed that, in itself, being labeled mentally ill does not determine the course of a man's career even though he may be confined for months in a public mental hospital. They found that men whose symptoms subsided—either at the end of the initial episode or within a few years thereafter—did not suffer gross occupational setbacks. Indeed, it was found that the career of a man who was able to establish his competence before the initial onset of mental illness stands a good chance of surviving prolonged, even severe, symptoms.

However, about one-third experienced lower occupational status and more repeated failure than before admission. Success in spite of mental illness tends to depend on success of previous socialization into a work role and competence developed before becoming mentally ill. In situations where these two conditions exist, the result seems to be a resilient work role, making it unnecessary to sacrifice a career to mental illness. Although this study did not pursue them, factors in the character and structure of the workplace may also facilitate or impede reestablishment of a career after an episode of mental illness.

The interaction of the dynamics of the workplace with the individual's needs and characteristics is not confined to how such environments respond to or support people who are recovering from mental illness. Earlier in this chapter, we also spoke about how organizational forms were reflections of cultural images about expected work behavior in terms of individual achievement or collective identity and teamwork, and in organizational terms such as regulatory or developmental models. In the last decade, there have been many books addressed to how organizations stimulate excellence in worker performance, and how some leading corporations organize their environments to enhance worker productivity, innovation, and personal growth.

But there are also books and articles that attempt to describe and explain how some work organizations reinforce or create conditions of worker pathology. For example, Schaef and Fassel (1988) have addressed what they have described as "addictive organizations," organizations that reflect the characteristics of individual addicts: denial, distrust, anger, manipulation, and coercion. At one level, they suggest, given the large number of employees who are addicts to processes or substances, that

> scores of nonrecovering addictive and co-dependent employees are inevitably replicating their dysfunctional family in the workplace. Family systems theory has long recognized that problems not solved at one level always occur elsewhere; this is also true of addicts and co-dependents in corporations. They do what they know best, and that is to operate addictively wherever they are. (p. 7)

At a second level, they address the effect on organizational pathology that occurs when dysfunctional managers, active addicts themselves, negatively affect the climate of the system they are administering and the employees with whom they relate. A third level of perspective is how organizations can and do function as the addictive substance in its mission, its products, its centrality as an organization in employees lives, and in the loyalty it expects. Depending upon how those characteristics are arranged, organizations can both stimulate and reward workaholism while denying its negative meaning to the person's family life and mental health. They further argue that addictive organizations tend to perpetuate and patch up problems instead of facing and solving them.

According to such perspectives, addictive organizations are likely to be characterized by problems of communication, gossip, fear, isolation, dishonesty, suppressed feelings, sabotage, projection, disrespect, confusion, control, denial, forgetfulness, self-centeredness, grandiosity, and planning as a form of control. These negative organizational dynamics and their support or stimulation of worker pathology are seen as in contrast to those organizations that are moving out of or avoiding an addictive system. The latter manifests such positive organizational dynamics as the following: supporting the mission of the organization by a structure that is congruent with the mission; promoting self-responsibility in employees; providing permeable rather than rigid boundaries between levels and elements of the organization; multivaried-multidirectional communication throughout the organization; integrated work teams and situational leadership; a sense of morality in the way of working and in product development; congruence in formal and informal goals; and a commitment to a process model of change (Schaef & Fassel, 1988, p. 9).

Although they do not define the issue in terms of an addictive model of organizations, London and More (1987), specialists in employee development and organization effectiveness at AT&T, also contend that

> individual, environmental, and organizational factors interact to affect how people make career decisions and transitions. The environment, in the form of the company, boss, job, and larger socioeconomic conditions, affects the decisions and transitions people are likely to face, as well as strengthens or weakens their career motivation. (p. xvi)

> . . . Organizations have considerable influence over how their employees feel. Organizations can create stress, but they also have the potential for reducing and preventing it. (p. 195)

The sources of career stress in organizations take many forms. They include role conflict, role or task overload or underload, role ambiguity, discrimination and stereotyping, marriage/work conflicts, interpersonal stress, feelings of inadequacy, discordant values, and progress toward career goals.

Depending upon the structure of organizations and how closed or open they may be, threats and psychological injuries to workers are a part of work life (Hirschhorn, 1988). How stressful or problematic they become is dependent on personality characteristics of the workers, previous experience, the nature of the psychological boundaries that exist in a work setting, and other factors. But frequently, workers perceive that work entails risk, and "risks are experienced psychologically as threats that must be aggressively met, contained, and ultimately transformed into challenges and opportunities" (p. 33). However, many people who experience role conflict, role overload, or lack of confidence, or whose understanding of the work organization's expectations or dynamics is inadequate, experience anxiety that, in turn, can become a precursor of a more serious problem as it progresses or persists. Hirschhorn has suggested that

> "feelings of anxiety are the fundamental roots of distorted or alienated relationships at work. . . . A work group manages its anxiety by developing and deploying a set of social defenses. By using these social defenses, people retreat from role, task, and organizational boundaries. They may try to manage their anxiety by projection of blame or scapegoating others, by bureaucratizing their work, resorting to excessive paperwork to reduce face-to-face communications, or engaging in excessive checking and monitoring of their work to reduce the anxiety of making difficult decisions. Such social defenses may depersonalize relationships at work and distort the worker's capacities to accomplish his or her primary work task. As a result potential individual-organizational pathologies can arise and spiral in complexity toward more difficult physical and mental reactions to distortions with the meaning of work or, indeed, to various forms of mental distress or illness.

The factors associated with work pathology and worker-organizational structure are only now being more fully probed, but insights arising from research in such areas are likely to have important implications for the supportive role that can be played by the career guidance specialist or counseling psychologist in industry. It is likely that such professionals will at least need to assist managerial and supervisory personnel as well as the afflicted person's co-workers in understanding what behaviors might be expected in different forms of mental distress or illness and, indeed, that it is likely that no symptoms will be observable at all because of the control exerted by medication or other treatment, or a combination thereof. They will also probably actively attempt to improve person-job fit or, indeed, efforts to make organizations more developmental, supportive, and reparative environments in which workers can grow and be productive.

Work pathology per se is not one of the 18 classes or groups of conditions described by the American Psychiatric Association (1981) in the third edition of its *Diagnostic and Statistical Manual of Mental Disorders* (DSM-III) or in the 1987 revision, the DSM-III-R. Rather, any of the 18 categories of mental, social, and behavioral disorders included in this manual can appear in the workplace as a function of workers' distress or upset. Beyond that, however, the DSM-III-R does identify occupations, job changes, and related work processes as psychosocial stressors that can produce aberrant behavior as one copes with or adapts to the stress related to such processes. Occupational functioning is also one of three areas of adaptive functioning by which mental illness can be diagnosed; the other two are social relations and leisure time. Furthermore, occupational and social impairment comprises one of the 15 symptom groups included in the DSM-III-R. Within such a context, then, work is both a condition of mental health and a condition of mental disorder (W. S. Neff, 1985, p. 7).

W. S. Neff (1985), in an insightful and useful perspective, indicates that it is important to distinguish between the necessary and the sufficient conditions of work:

> By the former set of conditions, we are referring to the fact that most work situations present us with an irreducible aggregate of requirements, which we must meet in order to be able to work at all. Some degree of moticity, a measure of manual dexterity, the ability to comprehend and follow instructions, the ability to perform a task—all of these can be described as the necessary requirements of work. On the other hand, the ability to meet these requirements may not be *sufficient* to make us workers. We cannot be so fearful of authority, for example, that the mere presence of a supervisor reduces us to a state of apparent paralysis. We cannot (usually) decide for ourselves how long we shall work, when we shall begin, or at what pace we shall proceed. Work situations are *social* situations, characterized by very complex sets of norms, rituals, customs, and social demands. It is thus possible for an individual to be able to meet the necessary conditions of work without being able to meet the sufficient conditions. (p. 13)

As a function of etiology, of content, and of manifestation, some norms of mental or social pathology may require specific types of differential treatment in the workplace. W. S. Neff (1977, 1985) has suggested several broad patterns of what might be considered work psychopathology. The underlying theme of such problems may be difficulty with authority figures, with interpersonal relations, with the meanings of work, or related conflicts. In particular, he reports five patterns of behavior that lead to failure at work. The patterns, in paraphrased form, include the following:

Type 1. These are people who appear to have major deficiencies in work motivation and a negative conception of the role of worker. Such people have not been socialized to value work for themselves or they attribute negative stereotypes to the work role (such as "work is for squares"). They may view work as societal pressure for them to conform to a regimentation they prefer to avoid or resist. They pursue impulse gratification now, rather than deferred gratification and planning for the future. Persons so characterized, particularly in the extreme cases, may be made to work under powerful social coercion but will likely meet only minimum standards of productivity and will require continuous, close supervision. From a counseling view such people need to be assisted in developing an internal locus of control and to be placed in work settings that provide graduated incentives for productivity.

Type 2. These are individuals who experience fear and anxiety as the predominant responses to demands to be productive. A fairly common type, such persons may be fearful of inability to perform effectively or have little positive self-regard. Their previous life is likely to have been a series of failures. They may interpret constructive criticism as personal threat; be acutely uncomfortable, perhaps immobilized by anxiety, in a competitive situation; treat opportunities for cooperative work with others as situations likely to expose personal vulnerability. Such people are likely to respond favorably to conditions arranged to offer them success experiences. These individuals probably require supervisory support and encouragement while discovering that there are work roles that can be performed without constant personal deprecation. They may sometimes require a constantly sheltered work role that does not demand new and rapid challenges or expectations. Therapeutically, such persons could likely profit from cognitive restructuring or rational-emotive approaches that focus on their self-labeling and its behavioral consequences (Ellis, 1962; Meichenbaum, 1977).

Type 3. This type includes people whose basic behavioral style is open hostility and aggression. They perceive supervision and criticism as attacks to which to respond with anger or violence. In such people the work expectations of society are internalized as restrictive and hostile demands on them. Such people are frequently energetic and able if placed in work they can do independently of others. They frequently do not have difficulty in finding employment, but rather in maintaining it. The typical reason for dismissal or quitting is inability to get along with others because of, in the extreme circumstances, manifestations of paranoid psychosis or in other situations, intense irritability, physical aggression to others, or constant anger. This type of behavioral problem is very difficult to deal with in a work setting, although it may respond to long-term therapy or newer approaches to anger management and reduction (Novaco, 1976; Schlichter & Horan, 1981).

Type 4. Included here are people whose behavior is characterized by marked dependency. Because of socialization problems in early childhood, the individual internalizes precepts that personal welfare depends on pleasing authority figures; that independent behavior by the worker can threaten such a relationship; and that childlike compliance is the chief defensive strategy to be used in any circumstance (home, school, work) where others are perceived as all-powerful authority figures. Such people may work effectively to please a supervisor as long as close and continuous management is present. They typically require constant emotional support from the supervisor, whose patience is likely to be sorely tried in attempting to respond to the constant personal irresponsibility and emotional immaturity displayed by the worker.

These people are likely to require selective placement in situations where they receive considerable personal approval and support. Therapeutically, they need assistance in examining their view of authority relationships and the types of trade-offs they are consciously or unconsciously engaging in through their dependency behaviors.

Type 5. These people display a marked degree of social naivete. They simply lack knowledge about themselves as workers, about work content, and about the realities and demands of the work environment. In such cases, the focus of the counselor is not on the individual's rejection of work or resistance to components of the workplace but on ignorance. The procedure is to provide the worker with social learning or a specific educational experience in which information about the organization and expectations of work is primary.

The five types of inadequate work patterns suggested by Neff are hypothetical but represent some of the potential interactions between work and the mental health of some workers. Without some type of intervention, people characterized by such work behaviors will likely fail, quit, or be dismissed. Career guidance practitioners, counseling psychologists, or other human resource development specialists will need to provide differential treatment to cope with the variety of problems.

Persons who are having mental health problems in their workplace may not display psychiatric symptoms—paranoia, character disorders, severe psychoneurosis—although they may be depressed, preoccupied with family problems, abusing alcohol, or otherwise behaving ineffectively. In short, they may have become problem employees.

Peace (1973) suggests that problem employees can be seen first as simply employees with problems. If sufficient help is not received, they may become problems to themselves. If self-understanding and other forms of assistance do not occur at this point, the employee may then become a problem for management. In this view, employees never become a problem for management until they have first become problems to themselves. The problem employee is a person who has an emotional problem that he or she has neither solved nor escaped. Becoming a problem employee is not a voluntary process but one that evolves as the worker acts in ways that make sense in the tangled emotions being experienced but that alienate or anger co-workers, supervisors, and others.

From a somewhat different perspective, Nolan (1973) defines a problem employee as "one who does not conform to the social vocational role expected of him at his place of employment" (p. xi). From this standpoint, physical disability, psychological maladjustment, neurosis, and so forth are not in themselves characteristics of problem employees. Nor is a person in good physical and psychological health necessarily a nonproblem employee. The actual definition of a problem employee depends on the standards set by the work organization. Many factors affect such definitions and thus preclude a simple listing of personality traits or deficits as problematic in themselves. The possibilities across a spectrum of worker types have been identified by Nolan (1973) as follows:

1. Some job applicants have psychological problems at the time of hiring; they may get worse, improve, or stay the same upon employment.
2. Some employees who may or may not have been maladjusted at the time of employment develop problems at a later date. These problems may or may not be influenced by the job setting.
3. Some employees show average or superior job performance in spite of—or because of—their problem.
4. Some employees who are not technically regarded as psychologically handicapped still cannot function effectively under certain work conditions or leadership types (p. xiii).

Obviously, counseling psychologists, career counselors, and other career guidance practitioners involved with industry will have many opportunities to engage in counseling, skill-building, classification, consultation, education, and referral as the relationships between work and mental health attract more attention in the future.

WORK AND LEISURE

The values ascribed to work and leisure and the interaction between the two have been matters of significant discussion for many centuries. The debate has escalated in the past two decades as the onset of automation, robotics, and other machine-machine systems have altered the character of many forms of work. Supposedly, technological advances have freed people to engage in more leisure activities. For some, leisure seems synonymous with idleness or fewer hours of work. To other observers, the effective use of leisure is in itself a serious matter since idleness and the inadequate use of leisure can bring with them anxiety, frustration, crime, and other social problems.

In the most obvious counterpoint, the type of work one engages in affects how much time one has for leisure pursuits, what these pursuits are likely to be, and with whom and when they will occur. But leisure and how it is used also have to do with quality of life. For example, some observers describe retirement and aging as representing for many a transition from a work role to leisure role. Others suggest that persons must balance work and leisure as sources of need satisfaction (Leclair, 1982). The questions in such cases are, "Can leisure also provide the self-esteem potentially available from work? Can leisure be growth-producing just as work can be? Does leisure deserve the same sort of attention and resources as does planning for work or other aspects of career?"

The answers to such questions are debatable. In recent decades, leisure has rarely been seen as having merit in itself either as a lifestyle or in excessive portions as a complement to work. As the meanings of work and work ethics in this society change toward greater emphasis on holistic approaches to well-being and self-actualization, the part that leisure plays in such circumstances is being reexamined by many observers. Some of these implications directly related to career counseling were discussed in Chapter 1. There are some additional conceptual insights relevant here.

Concepts of Leisure

One of the concepts useful in thinking about leisure is that time is a commodity to be rationally used (Wilson, 1981). Therefore, the planning of a career involves considering how one will use the time available. It has been suggested that the only thing all humankind shares is 24 hours a day. The way we use these hours differentiates us. Obviously, the partitioning of time available into work, leisure, family and community roles, idleness, and learning is a matter of values as well as of resources and information.

The use of time interacts with the use of language. As has been said both here and in the first chapter, language shapes how we view people and problems and what we do about them. Language sets limits on perception; we can see only that which we have been linguistically trained to see. As Wilson (1981) has so effectively articulated,

> our language is beautifully adapted to the world of organized work, but ill-adapted to the world of unorganized leisure. We have many words and many perceptual frames to describe the product of goods or the rules of bureaucratic behavior. But one's tongue twists or falls silent when we try to tell of contemplation or love, of writing a poem, or pondering a philosophy. (p. 283)

Wilson reminds us, "One of our great hazards in considering leisure is that it is so commonly thought of as a residue, an empty category of experience that is 'left over' when other life sustaining activities have been accomplished" (p. 284). Instead, in his view, leisure requires alertness, involvement, and immersion. It is an active rather than passive process, in which one is not compelled to engage but is frequently the condition to which "peak experience," growth, and self-actualization can occur. Kelly (1981) goes beyond this position in his wedding of leisure sociology and existential theory to contend that the essential variety of leisure offers "an especially apt environment for trying out identities not fully established and the nonserious consequences of play affording opportunity for risk in self-presentation" (p. 312).

Leisure has other positive attributes as well. For example, various studies (such as Ragheb & Griffith, 1982) have found that higher frequency of participation in leisure activities provides higher life satisfaction, and the same holds true for leisure satisfaction; in addition, the greater the leisure satisfaction, the greater the life satisfaction. Thus, effective participation in leisure is likely to be therapeutic and to yield more life satisfaction. However, such outcomes are apparently not simple matters of engaging in leisure and getting greater life satisfaction. The research of Sneegas (1986), for example, has shown that there is a complex relationship between perceived social competence and types of leisure activities. Thus, many persons choose interpersonal leisure activities based upon their sense of self-efficacy in social situations or their social skills. By extrapolation it can be argued that "the quality of life of adults is influenced by the effect of perceived social competence on leisure participation and leisure satisfaction" (p. 257). Such observations suggest the importance that counseling holds for persons grappling with issues related to leisure.

E. L. Jackson (1988) acknowledges that leisure provides psychological as well as practical benefits for persons of all ages but indicates that such benefits can only be realized if one is aware of the role of leisure and how to utilize it in order to receive these benefits. In particular, Jackson suggests that individuals experience many constraints or obstacles that prevent them from obtaining the potential benefits of leisure. Included as constraints are work commitments, family commitments, lack of awareness of opportunities, shyness, and low motivation. Pertinent to such obstacles to the life satisfactions afforded by leisure are counseling models intended to be useful for different populations and purposes.

Tinsley and Tinsley (1982), for example, have suggested four categories of leisure counseling or guidance: *leisure guidance* dealing with such foci as values clarification and self-knowledge related to leisure issues; *leisure decision making* focusing on affective and cognitive dimensions, self-awareness, and self-exploration of potential leisure impediments; *leisure education* dealing with didactic instruction about types of leisure, potential benefits, and assessment of potential difficulties in leisure and how these might be overcome; *leisure counseling* in which leisure is seen as a state of being and counseling is viewed as a process by which people are helped to attain a "state of leisure." Such an approach is a holistic model, which focuses on how the individual may make leisure a meaningful component in personal development. Burlew (1989) has reported on the use of the Life-Long Leisure Graph, a tool to help counselors investigate client leisure needs, as a method of helping clients implement the concept that psychological needs are satisfied through both work and leisure activities. His research with graduate students using the Graph suggests that it can be helpful in identifying patterns of needs and values, defining how needs and values are being met, planning to meet needs and values, and examining developmental patterns, as these provide a visual framework for a comprehensive career guidance or counseling approach to individual clients that includes leisure as a major component.

McDaniels (1984), one of the few counseling leaders to write prolifically about the work/leisure connection, contends that an adequate conceptualization of career must include both work and leisure in a holistic framework. He uses the formula $C = W + L$ to advance the notion that career equals work plus leisure. He also proposes the formula $CC = LC + WC$ (p. 574) to reinforce the point that career counseling should include both leisure counseling and work counseling. He strongly asserts that "a skilled career counselor of the future should be able to provide assistance in both areas separately or in a combined holistic approach" (pp. 574–575). He advocates a life-span approach to work and leisure that clearly articulates the role of leisure in career development. In doing so, he describes six stages in which to conceive developmental tasks related to leisure development throughout life. These stages provide a framework for systematic responses by parents and the home, schools and youth groups, workplaces, and community agencies assisting adults.

McDaniels identifies unresolved issues in dealing with work and leisure in career development and career counseling as well as changes in work and workers that make imperative more serious attention to the work/leisure connection. In his view, unresolved issues include, Do we live in a work or a leisure society? Is *leisure* a dirty word? Do schools prepare students for leisure? Can leisure satisfaction replace job satisfaction? How should leisure counseling be done? For each of these questions, McDaniels effectively examines the issues and their meaning for more systematic attention to leisure as a way of responding to the changes in the Western industrial nations that give the topic increasing importance:

- shorter work days and work weeks
- longer and more frequent vacations
- earlier and financially better retirement
- greater availability and acceptability of leisure options
- higher levels of interest in leisure by many
- more unemployment and underemployment (p. 558)

In 1989, McDaniels elaborated the concepts he articulated in 1984. He emphasized that work and leisure counseling should be incorporated into a life-span approach. Within such a context, he argued that counselors should engage in a variety of actions that enhance institutional and individual responses to the changing role of leisure and work in America. Among the examples of such action he supports are the following:

- Encourage parents to promote leisure in the home
- Help schools and youth groups become involved in leisure activities
- Emphasize leisure in the workplace
- Encourage community agencies to assist in leisure development (pp. 188–191)

McDaniel has also given examples of how counselors can help people discover what they are good at. One of these examples is to help people see leisure in the broadest possible way by examining specific possibilities within such dimensions as the following: creative, physical, intellectual, social, volunteer, and combined dimensions. Beyond such analyses, he advocated the use of courses, clubs, inventories, leisure-work models, and community resources by which persons can be encouraged to explore, participate in, or put their leisure to work.

A Leisure Typology

Gunter and Gunter (1980), using concepts of freedom of choice, time, and involvement, have identified several modes or styles of leisure that can be useful as reference points for career counselors.

Pure Leisure. Pure leisure represents an ideal state in the blending of individual choice and involvement. In reality, it is a type of sporadic experience rather than an ongoing lifestyle: the fantasy of child's play, the separation and timelessness that often accompanies the reading of a good book or the hearing of a beautiful symphony, the spontaneity of a comfortable evening with friends, the simple escape from work and other distractions that sometimes occurs in travel or games. Usually experiences of pure leisure are temporary rather than continuous leisure-styles. In fact, there is increasing evidence that much leisure of great importance for maintaining psychological equilibrium may be "interstitial" and found in minutes and moments interspersed through any day (Csikszentmihalyi, 1975).

Anomic Leisure. How to use the increased leisure options society bestows on us, particularly in the absence of institutional roles and involvements, is a problem. Although some persons would consider such a situation the essential element of the good life, the lack of structural constraints and obligations may cause leisure to be viewed with dislike, antipathy, confusion, and a sense of powerlessness. At various points in life (unemployment, retirement, shortened work weeks, enforced vacations or holidays), individuals may have an abundance of free time and for a variety of reasons be unable to cope with it. A variation on this classification has been described as a polarity, compensation, or oppositional view of leisure in which the distinctions between work and leisure are sharply defined. Leisure is seen as filling the void left by work.

Institutional Leisure. One's work involvement or involvement with other institutions, such as family, community, politics, or religions, may be so intense as to minimize one's freedom of choice outside of the penetration of these institutions throughout our life style. The most negative form of institutional leisure occurs for the workaholic. A more positive form occurs for the individual who is so wrapped up in the work role being played that the choice of leisure tends to blend institutional involvements with free time. This may happen through continuing education, travel, conducting business on the golf course, reading, or meetings that are work related but seen by the individual as interesting, rewarding, growth producing. It is the quality rather than the form of the activity that makes it leisure. Allen (1980) has described this type of leisure as a fusion, spillover, or extension model in which no clear distinction exists between what is one's leisure and what is one's work.

Alienated Leisure. Although the institutional pervasiveness of leisure may be similar to that in the previous category, in this form of leisure there is little personal satisfaction or positive psychological identification with it. Here the institutional structure may consume the person's leisure time out of necessity, not choice. Family responsibilities—such as many children or aged parents—may require constant attention and time; work roles may require constant community involvement in meetings, dinners, and other tasks to preserve image and public relations. Persons in this category pursue leisure activities from duty or habit but really do not derive satisfaction or choice from them.

Leisure Counseling

Although such a typology does not exhaust personal approaches to leisure, it nevertheless draws a crude map of the different roles counselors might play in helping clients come to grips with leisure issues. In some cases, the question is one of identifying the leisure opportunities that exist. In others, the question is one of values clarification toward work and leisure. In still other cases, the individual needs to be helped to consider in depth the lack of leisure they are experiencing and their unhappiness about such a situation. Counselors need to help some persons find leisure "moments" during their daily activity or consider leisure to try on personal roles that may not yet be fully formed. It seems obvious that the constructive choice and control of leisure in one's life are extremely important to self-esteem, holistic health, and other positive characteristics. A lack of such conditions is conducive to stress "burnout," possible antisocial acts of vandalism, crime, and so on.

McDowell (1976) has defined leisure counseling as "a helping process which facilitates interpretive, affective, and/or behavioral changes in others toward the attainment of their leisure well-being" (p. 9). Edwards (1980) maintains, "Leisure counseling is a process that occurs when a trained leisure counselor helps one person or a group of persons, of any age, to determine their present leisure interests, attitudes, and needs—then assists them in choosing and following leisure pursuits that are practical, satisfying, available, and unharmful" (p. 1). Leclair (1982) suggests that leisure counseling is "a process using contemporary counseling techniques to facilitate the awareness of client's thoughts, feelings, and values toward leisure as well as to develop the client's decision-making skills involved in leisure participation" (p. 294). Just as in other areas of controversy and possible stereotyping, counselors must consider their own values about leisure and the different models of leisure in which clients might engage so that they can provide resources and effective planning assistance.

THE TRANSITION TO WORK

The transition to work brings the individual's employability into conjunction with opportunities for employment. Employability and employment are not synonymous terms. *Employability* refers to one's potential for gaining access to, adjusting to, and being productive in the workplace. Therefore, employability refers to a composite set of traits and skills which permit the individual to meet the demands of the workplace (Herr, 1984). Employability relates to the ability to hold a job even if no jobs exist. Most observers now believe that employability can be broken into subsets of skills. Usually these are divided into such emphases as general employability skills, occupational-specific skills, and firm-specific skills. The latter two sets of skills usually refer to those that are technical and refer to the content of work. General employability skills usually refer to the emotional, affective self-management, and decision-making or planning aspects of choosing, preparing for, and adjusting to the demands of the workplace. In a society where teamwork, occupational diversity, and adjusting to different management styles and organizational entities become major issues in both choosing and adjusting to work, the quality and scope of an individual's general employability skills become extremely important aspects of career development.

The term *employment*—in contrast to the term *employability*—refers to holding a job. One can have highly developed employability skills but be unemployed. *Employment* means that the occupational structure has opportunities in which one's employability potential can be realized. Obviously, the smaller the gap between one's employability skills and the requirements of available jobs, the more likely it is that an individual will be employed. But these relationships are complex. At different stages of the transition to work, mobility through work structures, or changes in one's career paths, different types or combinations of general employability skills are required. Similarly, as the job market, the occupational structure, or the organization of work moves through various transformations, the general employability skills they require are likely to change as well. Later in this chapter, the changing demands on workers' "personal flexibility" as a function of the emerging global economy will illustrate the reality, discussed earlier in the chapter, that employability skills are not absolute but are likely to change across time, cultures, political systems, and nations.

Counselors need a thorough understanding of the skills and perspectives embodied in the term *general employability*. They also need to understand challenges and employability skills for workers at the beginning of their work life and at various points along a continuum of consolidation and advancement at work.

The Initial Transition to Work

Research shows that, as a group, young workers in the United States enter the labor force gradually rather than abruptly on the completion of school (Stevenson, 1978) and that their career attitudes are substantially formed prior to the first job itself (Raelin, 1980). Then a trial-and-error period typically precedes complete assimilation into the labor force. Large numbers of teenagers and young adults combine school and work before completing the transition. This process is made possible largely through opportunities for part-time employment in the secondary labor market (including fast-food restaurants, service stations, agriculture, odd jobs, and retail stores). However, a growing body of research indicates that beyond a predictable period of experimentation, joblessness among out-of-school teenage youth carries with it a "hangover effect." Adams and Mangum (1978) show,

> those who have unfavorable early labor market experiences are less likely than others to have favorable experiences later, education and other background characteristics held constant. Thus, early labor market experiences are related to subsequent measures of labor market success. They cannot be treated as benign phenomena which "age out" nor as simple individual problems which have no implications for social policy or governmental intervention. (Garraty, 1978)

Frequent unemployment and other poor labor market experiences during the early years have a deleterious effect later, in part because periods of unemployment represent loss of work experience, information, and skills that may put the person at a competitive disadvantage in the eyes of an employer and may also have an injurious effect on attitudes toward work.

The demoralizing effects of prolonged unemployment have been documented in many reports in the United States and elsewhere (for example, Peregoy & Schliebner, 1990). Unemployment has been characterized as a global phenomenon and one which is unequally distributed among the nations of the Third World and the industrialized societies. Such studies have shown that unemployment is destructive enough for adults, who have already achieved a work identity, and who because of their life experience and knowledge may find it possible to see unemployment as a social rather than a personal problem. Young persons or women entering the labor force for the first time have no such identity or experience to sustain them, and their resulting sense of rejection and worthlessness may well reinforce negative self-images that have already been established at school or in the family. Borow (1989) has indicated that

> the net effect of youth's limited contact with and uncertainty about the working world has not been so much to engender anti-work attitudes, as is often claimed, as to create persistent anxieties about the nebulous vocational future. Attending these anxieties, in any case, is an insidious form of avoidance behavior, a reluctance to plan and to explore, and a resultant slowing of the process of career development. (p. 9)

The most serious problem in this regard is found among those youths who are both out of school prematurely and out of work. In addition, major transition problems are frequently experienced by certain groups of disadvantaged youth, particularly but not exclusively black males and females, Hispanic youth, Native Americans, and inner-city and rural poor. According to Borow (1989),

> a disproportionate number of youths among socio-economically disadvantaged populations appear to exhibit depressed levels of achievement motivation, self-efficacy expectations, and other important indicators of competitive coping behaviors. (p. 9)

Many disadvantaged youth are likely to experience disordered career patterns and be characterized by the following:

- negative self-image and feelings of inadequacy as workers-to-be;
- fatalistic attitude and distrust in the efficacy of rational planning;
- unrealistic picture of the world of work;
- poor understanding of the sequence of preparatory steps leading to a stated vocational goal (Borow, 1989, p. 10).

Employment Transition Problems

Persons entering the labor force without a substantial base of experience are likely to experience a variety of transition problems to which career guidance programs and career counselors must be prepared to respond. The sophistication and the organization of contemporary work frequently walls off young people from what jobs they might choose and how information about available work might be obtained. Many counselors and teachers suffer from the same lack of knowledge. In some cases, students find that what they studied in school is unrelated to available jobs or to new processes, materials, or technological developments. Furthermore, as a nation, energy crises and international complications have directly affected the content and organization of work. Our nation has come to realize the incredible complexity and intense interaction of the technological and human problems facing us in the foreseeable future. It has become evident that many of the problems experienced by our work force are not simply technical, but psychological and sociological.

As much as many persons need to acquire occupational task skills, they also need assistance to clarify or strengthen their self-attitudes and to change their personal habits, emotional responses to life situations, attitudes toward work, planning skills, and methods of adjusting to new jobs.

Haccoun and Campbell (1972) conducted an extensive study of the work entry problems of youth. The results of their survey were used by Crites (1976) in his discussion of "thwarting conditions" that new workers may experience as they attempt to become established in a job. According to Haccoun and Campbell and to Crites, there are two classes of thwarting conditions: (1) those dealing with job performance problems and (2) those dealing with job entry, career planning, and management problems. Each of these classes of "thwarting conditions" contains a number of pertinent problems, as shown in Table 2.4.

Table 2.4

Work Entry Problems of Youth

I. On the job performance problems	II. Job entry, career planning, and management problems
Responsibility, maturity, attitudes and values	Job-seeking
Work habits	Interview and test-taking
Peer and supervisory adjustment	Geographic mobility
Communication	Family and personal situational adjustment
New roles	Job layoffs and rejections
Automation and changing technology	Educational preparation and job placement
Self-image	Career planning and management
Alienation	Occupational aspirations and job expectations
	Youth Image
	Military
	Prejudice and discrimination
	Prior work experiences
	Trade Unions

Source: Based on research of Haccoun and Campbell (1972), "A Comprehensive Model of Career Development in Early Adulthood" by J. O. Crites, *Journal of Vocational Behavior,* 1976, Vol. 9, pp. 105–118. Orlando, FL: Academic Press, 1976. Reprinted by permission.

Research adds increasing insight into the "thwarting conditions" related to the transition to work and work adjustment. Ashley et al. (1980) studied in depth the adaptation to work of 38 males and 30 females, from 17 to 30 years of age. The results of the study indicate that for those who adapt to work successfully, a sequence of adjustments in five areas may be involved.

Performance Aspects. In the initial phase of adjustment, upon job entry, the performance aspects of adaptation occupied the center of employees' concern. Some of the performance-related adjustment problems they encountered included learning what was expected and how to do the new job tasks, doing unusual job tasks (often not in the job description) or learning new ways to do old ones, coping with idle time or sporadic work schedules on the job, and dealing with a great volume or variety of work tasks or unexpectedly complex job tasks, physical or mental fatigue or inefficiency, and production quotas and standards.

Organizational Aspects. Informal (unofficial) rules, procedures, and hierarchies presented a major challenge to most workers coming into a new job. They frequently found a distinct difference between the official and the unofficial rules of the job. Workers seemed to feel that satisfactory adjustment had a lot to do with a good initial orientation. Most workers recognized a need to know about the company, its functions and activities, and how workers fit into the total organization of the company.

Interpersonal Aspects. Overlapping in time with performance aspects was the need to begin to adapt to co-workers because their assistance was needed in order to achieve adequate adaptation in performance. Subjects who could not relate to co-workers were unhappy in the work situation. Many of the subjects reported feeling that they had adjusted to the new job when they "felt accepted" by their co-workers. Several workers reported difficulties in adjusting to supervisory styles that conflicted with their own attitudes, values, or work styles. For some of the young workers, especially those in a full-time work environment for the first time, interpersonal aspects of the jobs (such as teamwork, dealing with disagreeable co-workers, adjusting to supervisors, getting assistance from others) represented the most difficult part of adjusting in the work environment.

Responsibility Aspects. As adaptation proceeds and performance and interpersonal aspects of the job come under control, adjustment problems related to responsibility tend to emerge. These include proving oneself, making use of training opportunities, getting ahead, getting raises, and related tasks.

Affective Aspects. Throughout the adaptation process, adjustment to work is affected by the worker's attitudes and feelings. Subjects indicated the importance of maintaining a good work attitude and a willingness to work hard, regardless of how good or bad the particular job was seen to be. They also reported that self-awareness and good feelings about oneself and one's job performance were important aspects of adaptation to the job.

In another study of functional competencies for adapting to the world of work. Selz, Jones, and Ashley (1980) asked four national respondent groups (general adult population, high school seniors, public school teachers, and employers) to establish the priority of competencies important to occupational adaptability. Fifty percent or more of all samples thought one would have a great deal of difficulty at work if one did not have the following abilities:

- use reading, writing, and math skills the job calls for

- use tools and equipment the job calls for
- get along with others
- deal with pressures to get the job done
- follow rules and policies
- have a good work attitude

As a function of in-depth interviews with some 135 owners, managers, and supervisors and 130 entry-level employees, Hulsart (1983) identified skills needed by entry-level workers. The 121 employability skills defined were able to be classified within 12 skill groups as follows:

1. Job Seeking/Career Development
2. Mathematics
3. Computer
4. Reading
5. Writing
6. Communications
7. Interpersonal
8. Business Economics
9. Personal Economics
10. Manual Perceptive
11. Work Activity
12. Problem Solving/Reasoning

Hazler and Latto (1987) asked some 91 employees in Western Kentucky to identify the usefulness of skills and attitudes on the job using a 7 point Likert scale, with 7 indicating "greatly needed" and 1, little or not at all. Forty-six of the employees responded to the surveys. Their perceptions suggested that attitudes generally received higher ratings than did skills. The four skills with a combined average of 6.68 on a 7 point scale were being dependable, getting along with other people, staying with a task until it is finished, and recognizing the importance of good health. The skills that were identified with a 6.16 and 6.65 average respectively were following spoken instructions and reading and understanding what has been read. Those with a 5.84 to a 5.46 average included following written instructions, speaking and listening, thinking and solving problems, using shop tools, writing skills, and using basic arithmetic.

A final example of employee perceptions of skills and attitudes needed by students in the transition to work is available from a project funded by the Parker Pen Company in cooperation with the Wisconsin Department of Public Instruction (Oinonen, 1984). This study was concerned with both the skills that students need for job entry and the degree to which schools are preparing students for the transition. In the project, some 7,400 surveys were sent to some 2,500 businesses employing 50 or more workers. As in similar studies, high schools are seen as preparing students for the world of work only adequately and only in some areas. For example, in the Wisconsin study, 34 percent to 42 percent of the employers reported that high schools were preparing students at a good to excellent level in these competencies:

- works with others, improves job skills
- accepts advice and supervision
- speaks well enough to be understood
- maintains personal health
- follows through on assignments

At the other end of the spectrum, only 3 percent to 10 percent of the employers thought that high schools were preparing students at a "good" or "excellent" level in the following:

- understands U.S. economic system
- has general knowledge of business operations
- recognizes, solves problems by self
- understands career ladders, advancement
- writes well
- demonstrates spelling and grammar skills
- applying and interviewing for a job

Put in a somewhat different way, employers in this survey felt that it will be increasingly necessary to emphasize the following skills for high school students engaging in the transition to work:

- writing, spelling, grammar
- arithmetic
- flexibility, learning new skills
- oral communication, speech
- applied computer literacy
- reading/interpretation of blueprints and instructions
- business economics
- technology (applied science)
- human relations
- decision making

The types of transitional or entry-level skills reported here permit counselors to alert students and new workers to the types of preparations, skills, and attitudes they will encounter as they enter the workplace. For some persons, these competency sets will serve as diagnostic tools to help identify why some persons are having difficulty in these transitions. Finally, much of what career counselors will be concerned about is helping students and others develop the attitudes and general employability skills that are of primary significance in choosing, implementing, and adjusting to work.

Affective Work Competencies

In the studies reported here of either transition to work or work adjustment, what seems to be repeated is that, although job skills and "task teachability" are important, so, too, is what some nations call "industrial discipline," and what Kazanas (1978) has described as "affective work competencies." Many of us have long contended that people typically do not lose their jobs because they cannot perform them but rather because of "personality." We have used that term in a vague, almost glib, way to represent some complex of behaviors that do not fit the expectations of the work setting, and so we have dismissed the person. Kazanas' research confirms that what has so often been characterized as personality factors in unemployment can really be defined in terms of the characteristics, habits, values, or attitudes comprising affective work competencies. He contends that within management theory and behavioral research in industry, there has been a shift in emphasis from cognitive and psychomotor behavior to the social and psychological components of affective behavior.

A review of the research on why employers discharge or fail to promote employees identified fifteen behaviors, the first seven of which were common across studies (Kazanas, 1978, p. 32):

1. carelessness
2. laziness
3. absence/tardiness
4. disloyalty
5. distraction
6. too little or too much ambition
7. lack of initiative
8. dishonesty
9. noncooperativeness
10. lack of courtesy
11. unwillingness to follow rules
12. troublemaking
13. irresponsibility
14. lack of adaptability
15. misrepresentation

The opposite of the reasons for being dismissed are the affective work competencies identified by employers as important to work adjustment (Kazanas, 1978, p. 34):

1. punctuality
2. honesty
3. reliability
4. dependability
5. initiative
6. helpfulness
7. cooperation
   a. willingness to cooperate
   b. ability to get along with others
   c. character skills—performance as a co-worker
8. willingness to learn
9. sense of humor

Affective work competencies, like other work context skills, can be taught and must be seen as part of the content of career guidance programs. Such skills reflect a worker's understanding of the sociology and psychology of the "work culture." With such an understanding of the organizational structure and expectations that mediate the performance of work, career guidance personnel can encourage the development of affective work competencies not simply as arbitrary or capricious value sets but as "occupational survival skills" (R. E. Nelson, 1979).

Indeed, these emotional dimensions of work have been found to be mediators of a variety of career-related tasks. For example, Kivlighan, Johnsen, and Fretz (1987), in a study of the role of emotional components in career problem solving, suggested that if career interventions are to be effective, clients need to have an opportunity to express their feelings, to confront issues related to personal responsibility, and to develop a sense of universality and acceptance in the individual or group counseling process. Other studies of career interventions have similarly indicated the importance of dealing with affective or emotional problems or deficits if the issues involved in career indecision or problem solving are to be resolved (Clarke & Greenberg, 1986; Sepich, 1987). The role of the emotional or affective interactions of workers within the workplace is seen in other surveys of employees, which validate the research. The major reasons high school graduates or dropouts lose their jobs include the following:

- Poor work habits (tardy, undependable)
- Poor work attitude
- Work lacks quality (inaccuracies, wasteful)
- Work lacks quantity (low output)
- Inability to accept advice and supervision (Oinonen, 1984)

Although worker deficits in employability skills reported here have been studied primarily in young workers as they enter the labor force, a growing research base has shown similar deficits in information, planning, and job-seeking skills among older workers experiencing occupational dislocation. The studies of Northcutt (Knowles, 1977), for example, suggest that only 40 percent of the American adult population is coping adequately with typical life problems (such as getting work and holding a job, buying things, managing one's economic life, and parenting). Evidence suggests that such persons need to experience skill-building approaches that are organized around the type of life crises they are facing. These observations are supported by findings from the National Assessment of Educational Progress (Westbrook, 1978), which indicate that a large percentage of adults are weak in basic skills and in occupational information; they have had little opportunity, tested or otherwise, to examine their personal characteristics with a counselor; and they are unclear about their educational or career needs.

As the occupational structure changes, the inadequacies in skills of the adult population as identified above are exacerbated. For example, according to a joint publication of the U.S. Department of Education and the U.S. Department of Labor (1988), "New technology has changed the nature of work—created new jobs and altered others—and, in many cases, has revealed basic skills problems where none were known to exist" (p. 3). Such findings have stimulated the need for "literacy audits" among workers and the necessity of introducing basic skills training directly into the work place where such audits show that it is needed. In such processes, it has become clear that many workers requiring retraining do not have the basic academic skills which permit them to learn new tasks and procedures. Such persons are, in fact, often functionally illiterate.

Other studies also speak to such problems. One national study of employers found that 30 percent of those surveyed reported that secretaries have difficulty reading at the level required by the job; 50 percent reported managers and supervisors unable to write a paragraph free of grammatical error; 50 percent reported skilled and unskilled employees, including bookkeepers, unable to use decimals and fractions in math problems; 65 percent reported that basic skills deficiencies limit the job advancement of their high school graduates (Berlin & Sum, 1988). In another example, the New York Telephone Company, in a major recruitment effort, found that from January to July 1987, only 3,619 of 22,888 applicants passed the examination intended to test vocabulary, number relationships, and problem-solving skills for jobs ranging from telephone operator to service representative (U.S. Department of Education & U.S. Department of Labor, 1988). Such issues affect the economic security of the United States in a global economy and, indeed, the job access and mobility of many adults. They will increasingly become formidable concerns in career counseling and career guidance.

Multidimensional Barriers to Work

For disadvantaged adults particularly, but not exclusively, transition to work and work adjustment are multidimensional problems. Often when people are provided job training or occupational information or encouragement or career counseling and they still do not get work and adjust to it, we assume that they do not really want to work, they prefer welfare, or they are lazy. It is more likely that we have provided help in only one of the dimensions of life that is affecting their transition to and effective induction into work. C. D. Miller and Oetting (1977) identified some 37 specific barriers to work in 11 categories, which were reported by 409 economically and vocationally disadvantaged persons in the Denver area. These barriers included child care, health, transportation, social and interpersonal conflicts, financial problems, legal problems, emotional-personal problems, drug and alcohol abuse problems, job qualifications, discrimination, and language and communication problems. In such perspectives we again see the need for career guidance approaches to take a multidimensional view of individual problems with work and a differential treatment approach to the resolution of the various problems experienced by any given individual.

It is useful to reaffirm that the transition to work and the adjustment to work are not single events but dynamic ones likely to recur throughout the life of adults. In 1978, the College Entrance Examination Board conducted a major study probing career changes for adults (Arbeiter, Aslanian, Schmerbeck, & Brickell, 1978). They concluded that some 40 million adults in the United States anticipated making a career change and were engaged in various life transitions—entering, progressing in, and exiting not only specific jobs, but also career fields. As part of this study, it was found that the spur to much career change lies in requirements for learning or, on the other side of that issue, life transitions tend to trigger learning, either voluntary or mandatory. These findings have been further explored in another national study that has examined life changes as reasons for adult learning (Aslanian & Brickell, 1980). Clearly, the nature of work in America is interwoven with the need to learn as one moves into a new job, adapts to a changing job, and advances in a career. Therefore, as work in the American society increasingly replaces experience with knowledge as a major criterion of admission and success, career guidance programs and practitioners must also respond to such conditions. We will need to provide clients with assistance in sorting out alternative and often nontraditional forms of learning and their implications for personal time commitments, travel, residency, and occupational preparation. Such assistance must be provided with an awareness of the fact that adults deciding to return to school also have many personal responsibilities and emotional demands on their time and energy. Also at issue may be adult problems with learning, such as lack of self-confidence in one's ability to learn, unrealistic expectations of progress, theoretical or irrelevant learning tasks, seeking help too late or from the wrong sources, lack of efficient reading and study habits, press of time, and related matters (Porter, 1970).

Papalia and Kaminski (1981) have discussed various counseling skills required in an industrial environment. They indicate that career counselors should advise and counsel on programs offered by local and regional institutions of higher education. They should help employees prepare and process material related to tuition reimbursement, matriculation, admission, or assessment of prior learning. Of particular importance is the career counselor's role in negotiating for an industry the offering of special credit and noncredit courses, either in-house or at a campus location, locating special resource personnel needed to offer special programs and renting space and equipment from area educational facilities so that industry can conduct its own programs in these locations.

Adult Career Problems

As discussed in Chapter 1, Campbell and Cellini (1981) have developed a diagnostic taxonomy of adult career problems. In doing so, they have indicated that across the stages of adult career behavior, four common tasks tend to recur: (1) decision-making; (2) implementing plans; (3) achieving organizational/institutional performance at an acceptable level; and (4) accomplishing organizational/institutional adaptation so that the individual can effectively take part in the work environment. They then develop a diagnostic taxonomy of problems in each of these areas that can be used to classify client problems (see Table 2.5).

In broad terms, this taxonomy represents an array of adult career problems to which differential treatments can be related. It also provides a structure from which groups of persons needing similar assistance could be inferred and relevant skill-building efforts constructed.

In using such a classification scheme, other research reminds us that it is a mistake to lump together all midlife or, indeed, other career changes that occur throughout adulthood. L. E. Thomas (1980), for example, found four distinct groups of changes among seventy-three men who had left professional and managerial careers between the ages of 34 and 54. The four groups—labeled the drift-outs, opt-outs, force-outs, and bow-outs—differed on several variables including amount of education completed, additional education undertaken to change careers, time taken to make the change, radicalness of change, and the importance of personal values in deciding to leave their former careers. Undoubtedly, other differentiations could be made among blue-collar changers and other subpopulations. However, the needs for content and process in career guidance will likely differ from group to group. Subsequent chapters address many of these issues in depth.

COUNSELING FOR PERSONAL FLEXIBILITY

As discussed in chapter 1 and briefly noted in this chapter, the structure of the world's economy is changing rapidly. National economies are eroding and being integrated into an interdependent global economy. This process is setting new standards for the quality of a nation's work force and for the creation of educational and counseling processes that will imbue students, citizens, and workers with the knowledge, attitudes, habits, and skills that are necessary in the societies they hope to create for the twenty-first century. As the occu-

Table 2.5

Diagnostic Taxonomy Outline: Problem Categories and Subcategories

1.0 Problems in career decision-making
- 1.1 Getting started
  - A. Lack of awareness of the need for a decision
  - B. Lack of knowledge of the decision-making process
  - C. Awareness of the need to make a decision, but avoidance of assuming personal responsibility for decision-making
- 1.2 Information gathering
  - A. Inadequate, contradictory, and/or insufficient information
  - B. Information overload, i.e., excessive information which confuses the decision maker
  - C. Lack of knowledge as to how to gather information, i.e., where to obtain information, how to organize, and to evaluate it
  - D. Unwillingness to accept the validity of the information because it does not agree with the person's self-concept
- 1.3 Generating, evaluating, and selecting alternatives
  - A. Difficulty deciding due to multiple career options, i.e., too many equally attractive career choices
  - B. Failure to generate sufficient career options due to personal limitations such as health, resources, ability, and education
  - C. The inability to decide due to the thwarting effects of anxiety such as fear of failure in attempting to fulfill the choice, fear of social disapproval, and/or fear of commitment to a course of action
  - D. Unrealistic choice, i.e., aspiring either too low or too high, based upon criteria such as aptitudes, interests, values, resources, and personal circumstances
  - E. Interfering personal constraints which impede a choice such as interpersonal influences and conflicts, situational circumstances, resources, and health
  - F. The inability to evaluate alternatives due to lack of knowledge of the evaluation criteria—the criteria could include values, interests, aptitudes, skills, resources, health, age, and personal circumstances
- 1.4 Formulating plans to implement decisions
  - A. Lack of knowledge of the necessary steps to formulate a plan
  - B. Inability to utilize a future time perspective in planning
  - C. Unwillingness and/or inability to acquire the necessary information to formulate a plan

2.0 Problems in implementing career plans
- 2.1 Characteristics of the individual
  - A. Failure of the individual to undertake the steps necessary to implement his/her plan
  - B. Failure or inability to successfully complete the steps necessary for goal attainment
  - C. Adverse changes in the individual's physical or emotional condition
- 2.2 Characteristics external to the individual
  - A. Unfavorable economic, social, and cultural conditions
  - B. Unfavorable conditions in the organization or institution central to the implementation of one's plans
  - C. Adverse conditions of or changes in the individual's family situation

pational structure of a nation changes due to the pervasive influence of advanced technology, transnational commercial interaction, or a pool of jobs to choose from that are more international in scope, it is likely that the meaning of work, as well as the skills necessary to work, also change. The behaviors, skills, and attitudes the industrialized societies are seek-

Table 2.5 (Continued)

3.0 Problems in organization/institutional performance
- 3.1 Deficiencies in skills, abilities, and knowledge
  - A. Insufficient skills, abilities, and/or knowledge upon position entry, i.e., underqualified to perform satisfactorily
  - B. The deterioration of skills, abilities, and/or knowledge over time in the position due to temporary assignment to another position, leave, and/or lack of continual practice of the skill
  - C. The failure to modify or update skills, abilities, and/or knowledge to stay abreast of job changes, i.e., job obsolescences due to new technology, tools, and knowledge
- 3.2 Personal factors
  - A. Personality characteristics discrepant with the job, e.g., values, interests, and work habits
  - B. Debilitating physical and/or emotional disorders
  - C. Adverse off-the-job personal circumstances and/or stressors, e.g., family pressures, financial problems, and personal conflicts
  - D. The occurrence of interpersonal conflicts on the job which are specific to performance requirements, e.g., getting along with the boss, co-workers, customers, and clients
- 3.3 Conditions of the organization/institutional environment
  - A. Ambiguous or inappropriate job requirements, e.g., lack of clarity of assignments, work overload, and conflicting assignments
  - B. Deficiencies in the operational structure of the organization/institution
  - C. Inadequate support facilities, supplies, and resources, e.g., insufficient lighting, ventilation, tools, support personnel, and materials
  - D. Insufficient reward system, e.g., compensation, fringe benefits, status, recognition, and opportunities for advancement

4.0 Problems in organizational/institutional adaptation
- 4.1 Initial entry
  - A. Lack of knowledge of organizational rules and procedures
  - B. Failure to accept or adhere to organizational rules and procedures
  - C. Inability to assimilate large quantities of new information, i.e., information overload
  - D. Discomfort in a new geographic location
  - E. Discrepancies between the individual's expectations and the realities of the institutional/organizational environment
- 4.2 Changes over time
  - A. Changes over the life span in one's attitudes, values, life style, career plans, or commitment to the organization which lead to incongruence between the individual and the environment
  - B. Changes in the organizational/institutional environment which lead to incongruence between the individual and the environment, e.g., physical and administrative structure, policies, and procedures
- 4.3 Interpersonal relationships
  - A. Interpersonal conflicts arising from differences of opinion, style, values, mannerisms, etc.
  - B. The occurrence of verbal or physical abuse or sexual harrassment

Source: From "A Diagnostic Category of Adult Career Problems" by R. E. Campbell and J. V. Cellini, *Journal of Vocational Behavior,* Vol. 19, pp. 175–190. Orlando, FL: Academic Press, 1981. Reprinted by permission.

ing for their work force can be summarized under the term *personal flexibility* (Herr, 1990).

Personal flexibility as the target of career guidance and counseling in a global economy is not likely to have an absolute meaning across the world. Nevertheless, there tend to be clusters of knowledge and skills that will be important for those workers in the industrialized societies who will be either directly or indirectly affected by the changes in the meaning or content of work or the shifts in work organizations necessitated by the global economy. Since the concept of a global economy is just emerging without the previous terminology of East versus West, non-Communist versus Communist, or other geopolitical barriers with which to contend, the notion of "personal flexibility" is itself a term in the very early stages of development. What is described here is undoubtedly a primitive treatment of how models of personal flexibility are likely to be mediated by political, cultural, and organizational structures across the world and what the behavioral elements of such models are. Nevertheless, there are categories of skills subsumed under the broad rubric of personal flexibility that, at this early stage of conceptualization, seem relevant to working within the context of global economic transformations, intense psychological change, shifts in the organization of work, and career opportunities that are not confined to one community, culture, or nation, but may be chosen from a larger pool or globally defined career possibilities. Such emerging concepts will inexorably broaden the role of career counselors in the future. In the next section, some of the ingredients of personal flexibility for workers in a global economy will be described.

The Elements of Personal Flexibility in a Global Economy

Basic Academic Skills. Given the characteristics of the emerging technologies that are increasingly critical to international competition, basic academic skills—literacy, numeracy, communications—are perhaps the ultimate employability skills. Within the industrialized nations, very few new jobs will be created for those who cannot read, follow directions, and use mathematics. In an information era, knowledge has replaced experience as the requisite for a growing proportion of the jobs being relocated or created around the world. Without basic academic skills, it is difficult to comprehend how individuals can possess personal flexibility, teachability, or be capable of engaging in life-long learning, a condition that increasingly will be required to maintain personal flexibility. Personal possession of these skills will certainly depend upon the quality and nature of schooling and training one receives in one's life and in the personal understanding that, in many of the emerging jobs across the world, working and learning have become blurred and essentially interchangeable concepts.

Although it is not accurate to argue that the only skills of value in the future will be high level intellectual skills, it is certainly accurate to suggest that basic academic skills and the ability to acquire the knowledge bases necessary in the occupational structure as it is emerging will be minimal requirements for many workers in the global economy. Not every worker is or will be directly involved in a high technology occupation or one that is technology intensive, but the pervasive application of advanced technology throughout the occupational structure is causing the educational skills required in the workplaces of the world to rise. This phenomenon is related to the fact that the automation of work is easiest in the lower-skilled jobs; by eliminating many unskilled and semi-skilled jobs through technology, the average education or training required in the remaining jobs or in the emerging occupations is increased. Undoubtedly, there will continue to be a large number of jobs with medium to low-skilled requirements, but jobs that are currently in the middle of the skill distribution will be the least skilled occupations of the future, and there will be very few *net* new jobs created for the unskilled workers (Hudson Institute, 1987). The future of the occupational structures in the industrialized world is to eliminate more and more such unskilled jobs and to put an increasing premium on higher levels of reading, computation, communication, and problem-solving or reasoning skills. In essence, the skills learned in school and the skills learned on the jobs will be increasingly seen as complementary and interactive.

Given such realities, career counseling for personal flexibility will need to acknowledge, perhaps for the first time in history, that educational skills and choices must be clearly seen as major components of career development and, therefore, that career counselors must be seen as integral to learning systems for youth and for adults, cognizant of the likely outcomes of different education and training options, and brokers of such opportunities tailored to the needs of different individuals.

Adaptive Skills. But personal flexibility will not be confined to intellectual skills. As technological adaptation of a variety of forms continues to be implemented in the occupational structures and work places of the world, the economic development of individual firms and other enterprises will suffer if its employees are not able or willing to learn new production systems or new management strategies. While academic skills in reading, mathematics, and science are important to such processes, there are other qualitative skills likely to be critical in such employment environments as well. One set of such overarching skills has been defined by the U.S. Congress's Office of Technology Assessment as including the following:

- skills of problem recognition and definition
  - recognizing a problem that is not clearly presented
  - defining the problem in a way that permits clear analysis and action
  - tolerating ambiguity
- handling evidence
  - collecting and evaluating evidence
  - working with insufficient information
  - working with excessive information
- analytical skills
  - brainstorming
  - hypothesizing counter arguments
  - using analogies
- skills of implementation
  - recognizing the limitation of available resources
  - recognizing the feedback of a proposed solution to the system
  - the ability to recover from mistakes
- human relations
  - negotiation and conflict resolution
  - collaboration in problem solving
- learning skills
  - the ability to identify the limits of your own knowledge
  - the ability to ask pertinent questions
  - the ability to penetrate poor documentation
  - the ability to identify sources of information (documents and people)

These skills are important not only to manufacturing but to service industries. They represent the survival skills necessary in an environment of rapid change and one which is information-rich.

In addition to the skills cited above, an increasing number of employers are extending their conception of basic skills to include self-discipline, reliability, perseverance, accepting responsibility, and respect for the rights of others (U.S. Department of Education & U.S. Department of Labor, 1988). Other observers are discussing the needs for adaptive skills and for transferable skills. Adaptive skills are also referred to as coping skills, occupational employability skills, work survival skills, or, sometimes, career employment skills. They frequently involve skills necessary in positive worker-to-worker interaction or worker-work organization interaction. Thus, they frequently include work context skills, self and career management skills, and decision-making skills (Herr, 1982a). Transfer skills "enable a person to draw upon prior learning and previous experience for application to new and different situations" (Pratzner & Ashley, 1985, p. 19). Such skills include those involving learning to learn, dealing with change, being a self-initiator, coping, and self-assessment skills. Mobility skills are those related to making a career or job change and include job-seeking and job getting, interviewing skills, resume preparation, and carrying out alternative job search strategies. Each of these skill sets are increasingly subsumed under the notion of general employability skills discussed earlier in the chapter. Such general employability skills are important across the spectrum of work and are, in that sense, very elastic in their application and less likely to become quickly obsolescent than are technical or work performance skills. Like technical skills, general employability skills must be learned through some complex of modeling, reinforcement, and incentives. The elementary and secondary schools have major contributions to make to such learning if they see such skills as important to their broader educational mission. Certainly, vocational education needs to include the teaching of such skills in concert with other entry-level occupational skills (The National Commission on Secondary Vocational Education, 1985). These general employability skills do not substitute for the basic academic skills or job performance skills but they are clearly mediators of how such academic or job performance skills will be practiced, and they are important dimensions of personal flexibility.

There is another set of skills, only dimly perceived, in a societal trend that is only vaguely understood. In addition to the shift from manufacturing to service in the United States, there has also been a shift from Fortune 500 companies, large multinational organizations, to companies which employ less than 100 workers as the sources of new jobs in this economy. In part because of the adaptation of advanced technologies to their work processes and in part because of the effects of international competition, the Fortune 500 companies in this nation have essentially created no new jobs since 1978. They have rearranged jobs and career ladders, but they have not added significant numbers of new jobs for a decade. Thus, the United States is experiencing a major rise in self-employment and in small businesses, which require sets of skills embodied in such terms as *entrepreneurial behavior* and *innovation*. It has also been contended that, as the larger corporations require down-scaling in size and "deinstitutionalizing," there are needs for entrepreneurs within such organizations. As the workplace, the organization of work, or the content of work undergoes transformation, there are needs for persons who have the skills and desires to manage innovation and change.

Some of the skills associated with entrepreneurial behavior are taught in courses which stress the pragmatics of owning and running a business: accounting, marketing, deploying resources, sources of risk capital, and time and resource management for example. But, in a large sense, the skills associated with entrepreneurial behavior involve acquiring understanding of systems, risks, and change. These are combined behaviors, strategies, and traits. They are essential to systematic innovation, whether in creating a new, small business or modifying an existing one to take advantage of new market forces and potentiality. By definition, "systematic innovation therefore consists of the purposeful and organized search for changes, and in the systematic analysis of the opportunities such changes might offer for economic or social innovation" (Drucker, 1986, p. 35). Systematic innovation requires the entrepreneur to be able to monitor the unexpected, the incongruities between reality as it actually is and as it could be or ought to be; innovation based on process needs, filling missing links, redesign of old processes around new knowledge; changes in industry structure or market structure that catches everyone unaware. Systematic innovation also requires the entrepreneur to monitor demographic changes; changes in perception, mood, and meaning; and new knowledge, both scientific and nonscientific.

One might argue that being an entrepreneur is to be a manager of information and, in turn, of innovation. It is to be a futurist. It is to be one who views needs in systems terms. It is to be cross-disciplinary in one's reading and analysis. It is to be a professional learner, if you will, frequently a generalist, not a specialist in a restricted sense.

Entrepreneurial behavior will be an important ingredient in the future in many aspects of the global economy, in government, in service industries, in manufacturing, and in education. The skills needed are directly related to working and learning, although our perceptions of these skills are yet to be fully understood and addressed in most of our learning environments. It is likely that, whether such behaviors are manifested in self-employment, in small venture industries, or in transforming older industries into new economic structures, entrepreneurial behavior will be critical to many nations in both domestic and international economic development.

Career Motivation

Given the world of uncertainty and complexity that characterizes the global economy, there are other competencies that need to be embodied in personal flexibility. One such model is that of London and Stumpf (1986) that is directed to the ingredients of career motivation. There are three parts of career motivation that fit well within a concept of personal flexibility, as we have been shaping it. These include "being resilient in the face of change, having insight into one's self and the environment, and identifying with one's job, organization, and/or profession as career goals" (p. 25). Each of these dimensions includes sub-elements. For example, career resilience is comprised of belief in oneself, need for achievement, and willingness to take risks; career insight means having clear career goals and knowing one's strengths and weaknesses; and career identity is comprised of job, organization, and professional involvement, need for advancement and recognition, and wanting to lead. By definition, *career resilience* has to do with "the extent to which we keep our spirits up when things do not work out as we would have liked. This includes how resistant we are to career barriers or disruptions affecting our work" (p. 26). Such a perspective suggests that individuals need to feel that they are competent to control their responses to what happens to them, that one can effectively discriminate how to act in cooperation with others or independently. In some sense, this interpretation of career resilience is not unlike concepts such as an internal versus an external locus of control. *Career insight* refers to the extent to which people are realistic about themselves and their careers and how accurately they relate these perceptions to their career goals, set specific career goals, and formulate how they can achieve these goals. *Career identity* is the extent to which they are involved in their jobs, careers, and professions.

The concept of "personal flexibility" is not unlike that of "personal competence" or "life development skills." In each of these perspectives, personal flexibility or competence can be defined as a series of skills or forms of knowledge that an individual acquires either through processes of socialization or training (Danish, Galambos, & Laquatra, 1983). More subtle, perhaps, is an assumption that

> all human beings are capable of a far greater repertoire of behaviors than any single person ever exhibits. Each of us, because of the acci-

> dent of birth, begins life in a particular social context, within which we learn to make certain responses and not others. (Segall, Dasen, Berry, & Poortinga, 1990, p. 23)

Thus, it is possible to suggest that personal flexibility represents not a substitute for culturally defined perceptions of necessary life development skills, but another repertoire of skills, an alternative set of cultural competencies, that people need to learn about and possess as these relate to their ability to master change, cross-cultural migration, and other career dimensions influenced by the global economy. Indeed, in a related view, Gladwin (1967) suggests that competence includes an ability to utilize various alternatives in reaching a goal; an understanding of social systems of which one is a member and ability to use their resources; and testing.

In such a view, the targets of intervention for counseling for personal flexibility may be one or more of the following skill sets for particular individuals: *cognitive or physical skills,* that is, alternative models of conceiving problems, problem solving, or reasoning about self or others or ways of performing or doing certain tasks; *interpersonal skills* such as initiating, developing, and maintaining relationships (for instance, self disclosing, communicating feelings accurately and unambiguously, being supportive, and being able to resolve conflicts and relationship problems constructively); and *intrapersonal skills* such as developing self control, tension management and relaxation, setting goals, taking risks, and so on (Danish, Galambos, & Laquatra, 1983).

Amundson, a Canadian counseling psychologist (1989), has approached the concept of personal flexibility as we are describing it from the perspective of competence. In his perspective, "competence refers to a state of being as well as to a state of doing. A competent person is one who has the capacity (or power) to adequately deal with emerging situations." (p. 1) Amundson suggests that there are eight components required to define his model of competence and that to be competent in almost any job demands some capability in each of these eight areas. They include: A sense of purpose, self/other/and organizational understanding, communication and problem-solving skills, theoretical knowledge and understanding of facts and procedures, practical experience, a supportive organizational context, which, at minimum, has elements that allow people to achieve without wasting time and resources, a support network that allows competent people to give and to receive help as part of maintaining their competency, and self confidence, including acceptance of oneself, the strength to learn from mistakes, and perseverance.

It is likely that, as research into the requirements for human behavior within global economies evolve, conceptions of the elements of life coping skills, of competence, or of personal flexibility will gain credibility as organizing themes for career guidance and career counseling in many settings. Such research will serve to demystify the problems of living, which require different combinations of the skills integral to personal flexibility in interpersonal relations: coping with cultural identity confusion; work adjustment in a culturally different environment; geographic rootlessness, uprooting and reestablishing family and other social support systems; anticipating and handling change; managing anxiety and stress more consciously and with more control; assuming personal responsibility for one's life; gaining an internal locus of control; and increasing feelings of power or reducing feelings of powerlessness. Among others, these involve developing skills of interpersonal communications, anger management, assertiveness training, decision-making values clarification, intercultural sensitivity, and stress reduction as major foci for career counselors' work with clients. Such emphases are consistent with the perspectives of Krumboltz and Menetee (1980), who suggested that the future will require counselors to concentrate on prevention rather than only on remediation, to give increased attention to helping people develop self-control and the skills they need to regulate their behavior, and to adopt a more integrated approach to the interactive effects of how people think, feel, and act. The promotion of personal flexibility in workers of the future will necessitate at least these emphases.

CONCLUSIONS

The rationale for career guidance and for continuing research into career development implies that work is fundamental to how one feels about oneself. In addition, virtually any analysis of human development indicates that access to work is crucial to the ability to move effectively from adolescence to adulthood. Such a concern has particular vitality in those nations with highly developed technology and great affluence, such as the United States and other industrialized nations.

Tyler, Sundberg, Rohila, and Greene (1968) found in an extensive cross-cultural study of vocational choice patterns of adolescents that the more complex and affluent a society becomes, the freer one is from choice constraints, and thus the more the choice process becomes internalized. At the current level of American societal development, it's likely that the direction of one's life is determined more by one's own choices than by external social conditions. Finally, the premise on which this book rests is that career behavior and development, as well as access to work, are based on knowledge, skills, and attitudes that can be fostered rather than left to chance.

This chapter has emphasized that the knowledge, skills, and attitudes important to the transitions to work and to work adjustment are dynamic. As the national and, indeed, global economies are transformed and create new possibilities for choice, new forms of knowledge and new skill patterns emerge. A contemporary metaphor for the new combinations of information and skill that an increasing number of workers across the world will need to possess is *personal flexibility*. This term represents a summary of the perspectives held in parallel with such terms as *personal competence* and *life development skills*. As such, the term *personal flexibility* creates a focus toward the likely interaction of person, occupational opportunities, and the dynamics of the work places in the twenty-first century.

Since 1945 our society has largely replaced the words "stability" and "scarcity" as characteristics of our economy with the words "change" and "abundance" even though all groups in the population do not share such conditions equally. This reversal has occurred largely because of science and technology's fantastic abilities to harness energy and to translate this energy into person-machine systems. No occupational group is unaffected by the explosion of knowledge, changing social values, movement to corporate hierarchies, occupational and geographic mobility, new housing patterns, and similar phenomena that attend the fundamental realignment of our occupational structure and our economic base. These processes are now escalating under the influence of international competition and the economic interdependence of nations.

To assume, however, that work is disappearing, or that a society with leisure as its principal characteristic has emerged, is still premature. It appears more accurate to suggest that many new types of work are appearing and that much of the work to be done requires new levels of personal commitment and capability. To emphasize this latter point, one can compare the help-wanted ads of any metropolitan newspaper with similar ads of twenty or twenty-five years ago. The job titles alone reflect significant changes in the type of work being done now and the number of job choices possible.

In the future, work may become less attractive as an economic necessity because of growing welfare benefits or the possibilities of guaranteed income; it may occupy fewer hours each week, even though it is more central in one's life due to the continuing education necessary to perform it; or it may occupy a longer period in one's total life because of longer life expectancy. But there is no evidence that work will cease to be a central force in defining individual life styles in the foreseeable future. Therefore, a broad understanding of work and its potential meaning to different clients is crucial to the effective practice of career guidance, career counseling, and counseling psychology.

Summary

We have talked in this chapter about the terms that are associated with work and its differences in meaning across groups and across time. We have examined current perspectives on job satisfaction and the relationships between work and mental health. Finally, we have considered the transition to work including multidimensional barriers to work, adult career problems, and the affective work competencies important to work. We have introduced the term "personal flexibility" as an emerging target of career counseling and guidance for persons involved in the global economy of the 1990s and beyond. These topics have been discussed in terms of their implications for the practice of career guidance and counseling, their critical importance in the industrialized nations, and their significance for new paradigms of purpose and function.

CHAPTER 3

THE AMERICAN OCCUPATIONAL STRUCTURE

Key Concepts

- Career counseling is future-oriented and requires some reasonably accurate ideas about the occupational contours that are likely to exist when an individual is ready to enter the labor market. Although current forecasting methods are relatively crude and imprecise, they are broadly useful in career counseling.
- The information society requires that those who have the best jobs have the most education, but education will not guarantee the best jobs.
- By whatever system jobs and occupations are classified, the aim is to achieve order and to reduce the potential chaos of information overload. Getting the occupational structure reduced to manageable proportions facilitates decision making.
- The occupational structure is the centerpiece of a matrix of work options, educational avenues, tasks and contexts, personal investments and outcomes that combine to comprise the American "possibility structure" that counselees must conceptualize, explore, anticipate, and choose from, and to which they must gain access.
- The occupational structure can be conceived of in terms of subsystems of requirements and rewards that when classified reflect such factors as interests, aptitudes, competencies, educational requirements, points of entry, tasks, settings, supervisory structures, enterprises, income, and prestige. These factors provide ways to tailor exploration and analysis of the occupational structure to individual needs.
- The occupational structure is in constant flux, as are the characteristics of those in the labor force.

It is important for counselors to understand the characteristics of the occupational structure because individuals must know what is possible—what opportunities exist now and will exist in the future—if they are to make effective decisions. In one sense, career decision making is the process of relating relevant characteristics of self to appropriate aspects of the worlds of work, education, and training. Intimate knowledge of that external world is necessary if counselors are to help counselees reduce that huge universe to manageable proportions. When career counseling is directed toward immediate placement, only an understanding of the current occupational structure is required. However, when career counseling has its more common emphasis—on some future point of choice and entry—counselors and counselees must operate on the basis of informed speculations about the changing occupational structure.

THE CHANGING SCENE

Futurism is popular today, and a great many futurists are attempting to predict what the United States will be like ten, twenty, fifty, or a hundred years from now (McDaniels, 1989; Naisbitt, 1982; Theobald, 1987; Toffler, 1980; Wegmann, Chapman, & Johnson, 1989). All agree on only one point: the future will bring change. Beyond this simplistic conclusion, however, futurists agree on very little. Whether predictions emanate from historical and qualitative analyses or from more empirical and quantitative bases, conclusions suggest that the occupational structure of the United States is one of those societal elements that will undergo the greatest upheaval. What precise form this flux will take, however, is arguable. We may view this problem in terms of the difficulty of making occupational projections and in terms of scenarios for the future.

Occupational Projections

The relative accuracy of occupational forecasts is moot. Virtually everyone, including labor forecasters and their critics, agrees that forecasts are not completely accurate, nor can they ever be. Consequently, the Bureau of Labor Statistics generates numbers that such publications as the *Occupational Outlook Handbook* translate into broader employment growth phrases such as "much faster than the average for all occupations" and "more slowly than the average for all occupations." Errors in prediction are caused by a number of factors, including recession or boom periods, inaccurate estimates of the rate and type of technological change, devastating diseases of unprecedented impact such as AIDS, obsolescent data on projections of employment by industry, changes in the demand for products or services, the composition of the population, work attitudes in flux, changes in training opportunities, and alterations in retirement patterns. The clear message is that caution must be applied in utilizing occupational projection data in career counseling.

To improve occupational projections, the Bureau of Labor Statistics provides forecasts based on alternative assumptions about the future in terms of economic growth (Carey, 1981b). In addition, it has created an industry-occupation matrix that describes industry employment by occupation. These changes in forecasting help to gainsay the arguments of critics such as O'Toole (1982) who maintain that the two major errors of past prognosticators have been in assuming that the future is a simple extrapolation of the present and in basing forecasts on a singular view of coming events rather than on the interactive effects of several simultaneous forces.

Although propensity for error will persist, and although our forecasts are likely never to be very elegant, the data on labor forecasting are accurate enough to be useful to counselors and to individuals in career planning. Indeed, we have no choice; we *must* use future-oriented data. The lag between preparation for an occupation and entry into that occupation is frequently protracted over years. One needs some idea, however imperfect, of what the occupational demand is likely to be at the time of entry as well as at the time of choice.

Future Scenarios

Futurists present their visions as *scenarios*, potential slices of future history. As we read the work of various futurists, we are struck with the great number who are akin to the biblical Jeremiah. The future, they maintain, will be terrible unless we repent our ways. Unfortunately, even downside futurists do not seem to agree on what it is that we have to repent. Contrasted to this outlook are the Pollyanna futurists. Everything will be all right, they claim, smiling brightly. "We have survived and flourished until now; we shall prevail in the future." Sandwiched between the doom-and-gloom crowd and the head-in-the-sand bunch are the realists, many of whom offer fascinating predictions that have implications for career guidance and counseling.

The American labor force is now largely occupied with information handling. In fact, more people are engaged in manipulating information than in mining, agriculture, manufacturing, and personal services combined. This change is largely the result of advances in microelectronic technology, wherein data can be handled in a few picoseconds (one second contains as many picoseconds as there are seconds in 31,700 years). The shift has moved America from an agricultural society to an industrial society, and now to a service-based, information-oriented society. The term "compunications" is sometimes given to this phenomenon of the marriage of microelectronics and information processing. In this age of high technology, we are talking about a society that is service- rather than goods-oriented and that is dominated by a professional-technical class (rather than the business people who dominated the industrial society).

The increase in technology brings new occupations and different work modes. The incipient field of robotics is one consequence. Robotics takes us one step further along the automation-cybernetics continuum. We are witnessing ever more complex machines under the control of people. This, is turn, will lead to greater needs for training as individuals do more intellectual, higher-level work. We are also witnessing machine-machine systems that monitor, control, initiate, and terminate work with only a little supervision, done by a few skilled technicians. Eli Ginzberg (1982) points out the profound influences of our mechanized society and the increasing effects of mechanization in the future—mechanization of agriculture, mining, design and manufacturing, commerce, and office work. He observes that in 1820, approximately 70 percent of the American population was engaged in agriculture; now about 3 percent are in agriculture and approximately 70 percent are in service. Goods are produced with fewer operatives as our machines get bigger and better. Even in a very large goods-producing company such as General Electric, only 40 percent of employees are directly involved in production. The obvious consequence of the new technologies and machines is job displacement.

On the other hand, care should be taken not to overemphasize the types of employment created by the technological revolution. Levitan (1987) points out that in the next decade, "for every computer specialist, operator, or technician added to the workplace, there will be three additional unskilled laborers, three salesworkers, and seven clerical workers." (p. 31)

It is clear that the advance of our scientific technology has not been accompanied by similar progress in our social technology. Gordon (1979), for example, sees little progress in the development of social policies to encourage the career development of women while protecting the welfare of the family. Issues such as maternity benefits, child care, and part-time or flex-time work are still not resolved. Currently, child care is available to only a small percentage of working mothers. Occupational stress and the quality of work life also await the development of effective social technologies. Many, for example, are predicting a more participatory work force. Raskin (1980) predicts, "Autonomous work teams, the opportunities of rotated leadership, two-way communication on everything important to the worker in his job, plus a widening list of joint policy decisions at the shop level are inevitable." (p. 97) Although this view may be overly optimistic, it is clear that we shall have to spend more energy in improving the quality of work.

Some are predicting that family-supportive company policies will increase because the baby-boomers are reaching upper-management levels and are more sympathetic to family concerns than were their predecessors. Hence, for example, they foresee an increase in on-site child care opportunities, flexible working hours, and sick leave for children's illnesses. Others envision a time when employees will select their own supervisors, leading to increased morale and productivity. All of these social changes are predicated on the assumption that job satisfaction is at least as important to American workers as are traditional incentives such as job security and wages. Thus, employers must offer more quality-of-worklife benefits to attract the best workers.

Current occupations will, of course, serve as the foundation for new occupations in the future. Whether they stem from technological progress or from social concerns, new occupations are invariably related to old. A gene splicer is still likely to be a biologist. A fiber-optics technician probably will be a physicist. Environmental engineers can be air pollution control engineers, radiological health engineers, solid-waste engineers, industrial hygiene engineers, sanitary engineers, water pollution control engineers, and environmental compliance engineers, but they are still engineers. New occupations tend to spring from existing ones. They do, however, tend to merge disciplines (biochemists, geophysicists, bionicists).

One of the major problems generated by a movement toward a knowledge society is overeducation. Several commentators have indicated an oversupply of college graduates. The U.S. Department of Labor suggests that only approximately one-quarter of all job openings will require four or more years of college. Given current rates of college attendance and economic growth, that figure translates into an annual surplus of approximately 140,000 graduates. This situation is seen as one of inflated credentialism and has led some observers to maintain that problems of job satisfaction, underemployment, and unfulfilled ambitions will be exacerbated (Berg, 1975; Harrison, 1973; O'Toole, 1975). In fact, in the very near future, there will be no profession for which supply does not exceed demand (unless, of course, *demand* is redefined). Various solutions to this potentially dangerous situation have been proffered: educational upgrading; equalizing access to higher education; ending credentialism; equalizing income distribution; job redesign or profit sharing; total employment; reducing college enrollments; upgrading job requirements; a national person-power policy; and career education, among others. There is obviously no easy solution. For years we have known that too little education is a career handicap; now we must cope with what was once unthinkable—that too much education may be equally constricting.

Despite the fact that college graduates now account for one-fourth of all adult workers, there are some surprising findings that the effects of overeducation are not nearly so dire as they were predicted to be. (Rumberger, 1980) An occupational mismatch in terms of overeducation apparently does not cause graduates to suffer any loss of relative income. There is also no evidence that overeducation produces nonmonetary effects in terms of alienation, disaffection, or other harmful psychological states, with the exception of reduced job satisfaction. (Burris, 1983) Smith (1986) neatly summarizes the situation by stating, "A college education was once sufficient for the attainment of a good job. It is clearly no longer suffcient, but, at the same time, it is all the more necessary" (p. 95).

This relatively new development should in no way obscure the fact that undereducated and unskilled workers are still the major problem in the labor force. The less people are educated, the more likely it is that they will be unemployed. Labor force entrants—particularly those entering the labor force for the first time—account for the majority of unemployed teenagers. At the other end of the spectrum, men aged 55 to 64 without a high school diploma leave the labor force in significantly greater proportion than high school and college graduates of comparable ages. The undereducated are also the unskilled and the poor. Of this group, many have latent ability, and, if motivated and trained, could contribute meaningfully to the labor force. Unemployment is typically low in the professional and skilled occupations and is generally high for the less skilled segments of the labor force.

Although the general educational attainment of the American worker is rising, a substantial proportion of the population remains undertrained for specific skilled jobs and undereducated for general adult competency. As we have observed, people do not need just more education. There is ample evidence to suggest that individuals can be retrained and gain entrance to an occupational level previously unavailable to them. Hence *undereduction* may not be as much of a problem as is *inappropriate* education.

Kutscher (1989), in reviewing the projections for the occupational outlook in the year 2000, concludes, "The projections indicate that the managerial, professional, and technical occupations, which require the most education, will have faster rates of growth than occupations with the lowest educational requirements, some of which are even projected to decline." (p. 39) This finding has implications especially for minorities, since African-Americans and Hispanics are currently overrepresented in occupations with the projected slowest rates of growth and underrepresented in the occupations projected to have the higher growth rates. One should keep in mind, however, that occupations with the fastest growth do not necessarily provide the most *new* jobs—just the *better* ones.

Later in this chapter, we shall investigate further some likely changes in the American occupational structure. For now, it is sufficient to remind ourselves that a few decades ago there was no aerospace industry, no computer industry, no airport security guards, and no television industry.

THE PAST, PRESENT, AND FUTURE OF THE LABOR FORCE

The Past

Several striking changes have occurred in the American occupational structure during the last forty years.

- The number of employees in goods-producing industries has remained relatively constant, while the number of employees in industries providing services has increased dramatically. Consequently, more than twice the number of workers are now involved in the provision of services as are employed in the production of goods.
- The number of employees in blue-collar occupations have increased relatively little, while the number of employees in the white-collar occupations have increased markedly. Currently, approximately 60 percent of workers are classified as white collar.
- The average educational attainment of the labor force has risen appreciably. More than 87 percent of workers now have at least a high school education.

About 36 percent of all workers age 18 and over have completed at least one year of college (Young, 1980). Currently, three out of four jobs require some education or technical training beyond high school. At the same time, one of every four ninth-grade students will not graduate high school (and a higher percentage of minority and poor students will dropout (National Alliance of Business, 1986). In some states the drop out rate is mind-boggling (for example, 42 percent in Florida, 39 percent in Georgia, Arizona, and Louisiana, 38 percent in New York, 35 percent in Texas and South Carolina, and 34 percent in California).

In an insightful analysis of data in occupational projections, Hoyt (1988) argued that the large number of college graduates offers a challenge to career development professionals to assist those who will *not* graduate from college. Citing the huge projected increase in the number of salespersons, secretaries, and nurses aides, for example, and arguing that about one-third of the jobs in the year 2000 will require less than a high school education, he states, "Career guidance professionals have clear responsibility for heeding such figures. We cannot, in effect, afford to continue concentrating our career guidance efforts on those who least need help (the bright college-bound students) while essentially ignoring those whose career development needs are greatest." (p. 34) Although this does not imply that the college-bound have less need for career guidance, it is certainly accurate to assert that both groups have career needs that must be met and that neither can be ignored.

- The proportion of women in the labor force has increased significantly. About one-quarter of all managers are now women, and over 50 percent of American women now work outside the home. The pollster, Louis Harris (1989), suggests that marriages are increasing, divorces are leveling off, and families are remaining together more. Less than 10 percent of mothers will stay home and raise their children. Consequently, he predicts that by 2001, 8 of 10 women will be working.
- The number of minorities in the professions has increased. About 12 percent of blacks are now in professions (Erickson, 1980). Occupational mobility for minorities is not now nearly so formidable a barrier to be overcome as it once was. By the start of the next century, over one-third of the American population will be nonwhite, with perhaps the majority of children being nonwhite.
- Part-time work has increased considerably. Over one in every five workers is a part-time employee.
- Job turnover has increased; that is, the average number of jobs held over a work lifetime has gone up (for males).
- The number of self-employed workers decreased strongly until the 1970s. It has, however, increased steadily since 1972. (Fain, 1980)
- The elderly who dropped out of the labor force to retire are predicted to reenter; some nearing the age of retirement may decide not to retire because of labor shortages in some areas. (Harris, 1989)

The Present

The current labor force (all persons working and looking for work) in America is probably most accurately portrayed in Table 3.1. This table was chosen for presentation because it displays the labor force not only in terms of its occupational structure but also in terms of the educational attainment and earnings of the workers who constitute the various occupational groups. The accuracy of these data in describing the current labor force will vary; the national unemployment rate changes, and consequently, this affects the proportion of workers in various categories.

The Future. Now let us look at the more difficult task. Given the flaws in forecasting discussed earlier in this chapter, what will the occupational structure be in ten or fifteen years?

Because of the pig-in-the-python phenomenon of the baby-boom generation aging, the age distribution of the labor force has changed, reflecting a smaller proportion of young workers and an increasing proportion of middle-aged workers. By the year 2000, 16- to 24-year-olds will constitute 16 percent of the labor force, 25- to 34-year-olds 22 percent, 35- to 54-year-olds 49 percent, and 55-year-olds and older 12 percent. (Bureau of Labor Statistics, 1990, p. 9)

The median age in America rose from 28.1 in 1965 to about 33 in 1990. Geographically, the Northeast and north central states continue to lose population, while the South gains and the West gains somewhat less.

The changing age of the labor force has a potentially deep effect. Jackson et al. (1981) suggest that

> As the baby-boom cohorts entered the labor market, there were large numbers of applicants for most jobs, and as a result, companies could afford to ignore human-resource development. As

Table 3.1
Occupation of employed persons 16 years old and over, by years of school completed and sex (March 1988)

Sex and occupation	Total employed, in thousands	Percentage distribution, by years of school completed								Median school years completed
		Total	Elementary school		High school		College			
			Less than 8 years[1]	8 years	1 to 3 years	4 years	1 to 3 years	4 years	5 years or more	
1	2	3	4	5	6	7	8	9	10	11
All persons										
All occupational groups	112,585	100.0	2.9	2.3	11.2	39.7	20.5	13.8	9.6	12.8
Managerial and professional specialty	29,007	100.0	0.5	0.4	2.5	17.7	19.3	29.4	30.3	16.3
Executive, administrative, and managerial	13,928	100.0	0.7	0.7	3.7	27.1	23.6	27.5	16.7	14.9
Professional specialty occupations	15,079	100.0	0.2	0.1	1.4	9.0	15.4	31.2	42.7	16.8
Teachers, except college and university	3,981	100.0	0.1	(*)	1.2	6.8	7.8	38.5	45.6	16.9
Teachers, college and university	772	100.0	0.4	(*)	(*)	3.6	9.6	14.0	72.4	18+
Technical, sales, and administrative support	35,267	100.0	0.7	0.7	7.4	44.6	26.2	14.2	4.3	12.9
Technical and related support	3,506	100.0	0.3	0.1	2.3	29.5	35.6	22.5	9.7	14.4
Sales occupations	13,509	100.0	1.0	1.1	11.1	39.4	24.4	17.8	5.2	12.9
Administrative support, including clerical	18,252	100.0	0.5	0.5	5.7	51.3	29.7	9.9	2.5	12.8
Service occupations	14,809	100.0	5.4	4.4	21.0	45.2	18.0	4.7	1.2	12.4
Precision production, craft, and repair	13,178	100.0	4.4	3.6	14.8	53.4	18.3	4.3	1.2	12.5
Operators, fabricators, and laborers	17,338	100.0	6.7	5.0	21.5	50.9	12.1	3.1	0.7	12.3
Farming, forestry, and fishing	2,966	100.0	13.6	6.6	16.1	43.7	12.4	5.6	1.9	12.3

Men										
All occupational groups	61,538	100.0	3.7	2.7	11.8	37.4	19.1	14.2	11.1	12.9
Managerial and professional specialty	16,120	100.0	0.6	0.5	2.6	15.6	17.2	29.1	34.3	16.5
Technical, sales, and administrative support	12,273	100.0	1.0	0.8	6.9	33.7	28.7	21.4	7.4	13.8
Service occupations	5,800	100.0	6.2	4.1	19.2	41.6	20.6	6.3	2.0	12.5
Precision production, craft, and repair	12,012	100.0	4.3	3.6	14.9	53.6	18.4	4.2	1.1	12.5
Operators, fabricators, and laborers	12,840	100.0	6.2	4.7	21.1	50.2	13.5	3.5	0.7	12.4
Farming, forestry, and fishing	2,493	100.0	14.5	7.1	16.0	43.3	12.0	5.1	1.9	12.3
Women										
All occupational groups	51,027	100.0	2.1	1.8	10.5	42.5	22.3	13.2	7.8	12.8
Managerial and professional specialty	12,887	100.0	0.3	0.2	2.3	20.2	21.9	29.8	25.2	16.2
Technical, sales, and administrative support	22,994	100.0	0.4	0.6	7.7	50.4	28.0	10.3	2.6	12.8
Service occupations	9,009	100.0	4.9	4.6	22.2	47.6	16.4	3.6	0.8	12.4
Precision production, craft, and repair	1,166	100.0	5.3	4.5	14.4	51.2	17.3	5.3	2.0	12.5
Operators, fabricators, and laborers	4,499	100.0	8.1	5.8	22.5	52.8	8.1	2.1	0.5	12.3
Farming, forestry, and fishing	473	100.0	8.9	3.8	16.7	46.1	14.6	8.5	1.5	12.4

NOTE—Because of rounding, details may not add to totals.

[1] Includes persons reporting no school years completed.

[2] less than .05 percent

SOURCE: U.S. Department of Labor, Bureau of Labor Statistics, Office of Employment and Unemployments Statistics, "Education Attainment of Workers, March 1988," (This table was prepared December 1988.)

> the smaller cohorts born in the late 1960s replace the baby-boom cohorts . . . this will change. Companies will have to compete for entry-level workers, and the resources they devote to this competition will increasingly reduce those available to reward continuing employees. But continuing employees will demand rewards. Their numbers will make the typical nonpecuniary reward, promotion, possible for a decreasing percentage of cohorts, and with neither money nor promotion, employees' dissatisfaction will increase. (p. 130)

It is apparent that in the 1990s, the extraordinarily large proportion of so-called "prime age" workers (75 percent) will lead to greatly increased competition for higher level jobs and will necessitate more lateral job moves to increase job satisfaction.

Drucker (1982) addresses this situation, indicating that, in fact, jobs for the young will have to be restructured. No longer will fast promotions prevail, for even capable individuals will have to spend many years not far removed from the entrance level. Consequently, he makes an eloquent plea for career assistance in the workplace:

> But, above all, there is need to counsel the young. There is need to make sure they have someone to whom they can talk in the organization, if only to unburden themselves. There is need of someone who is concerned with the problem of the young getting to the place in the organization—or outside the organization, for that matter—where their strengths are most likely to be productive and recognized. (pp. 170–171)

In Chapter 11, we will detail some of the possibilities for this type of career counseling within organizations.

This relative shortage of youth and the great increase in prime-age workers—those with expectations of promotions—will inevitably lead to increased competition for desirable jobs. Therefore, the labor force will probably have to be more mobile in seeking employment and advancement. From the late 1960s through the 1970s, the labor force increased by over 2 percent annually. Beyond 1985 it is expected to increase less than 1 percent per year—barring a new baby "boomlet" or female participation increasing at a greater rate than predicted (Fullerton, 1980). Even though the growth rate of the work force will decrease, minorities will be represented at a higher rate: 25 percent of new entrants. Such increase will be attributable to higher immigration rates, the increasing number of illegal aliens entering the labor force, and the generally higher birthrate of minorities.

Hence, although there will be fewer youth entering the labor force, there will be a greater percentage of minorities. In fact, well into the twenty-first century, there are predicted to be relatively fewer children and youth and a growing proportion of middle-aged and older individuals.

Occupations expected to provide the best opportunities for employment to the year 2000 (in the sense that they are growing much faster than average) include paralegals, medical assistants, home health aides, radiologic technologists and technicians, data processing equipment repairers, medical record technicians, medical secretaries, physical therapists, surgical technologists, operations research analysts, securities and financial services sales representatives, travel agents, computer systems analysts, physical and corrective therapy assistants, social welfare service workers, respiratory therapists, and correction officers and jailers.

Because of the larger number of people that they employ, 20 occupations will account for approximately 40 percent of all the new jobs in this decade. They are retail salespersons, registered nurses, janitors and cleaners, waiters and waitresses, general managers and top executives, general office clerks, secretaries (except legal and medical), nursing aides and orderlies, truck drivers, receptionists and information clerks, cashiers, guards, computer programmers, food counter and related workers, licensed practical nurses, secondary school teachers, computer systems analysts, accountants and auditors, and kindergarten and elementary school teachers.

According to U.S. Department of Labor projections, the three fastest-growing occupational groups will be technicians, professionals, and executives, administrators, and managers. These groups have the highest proportion of workers with college degrees and earn the highest wages. Figure 3.1 also displays the fact that the slowest-growing occupational groups (operators, fabricators, laborers, and agricultural forestry and fishing workers) have the highest proportion of workers with less than a high school education and the lowest earnings.

There are only a few occupational groups that are expected to actually decline in number over the next decade. These include order clerks; stenographers; typists, processors, and data entry keyers; private household workers; farm operators and managers; timber cutting and logging workers; communications equipment mechanics; line installers and cable splicers; telephone installers and repairers; precision assemblers; inspectors, testers, and graders; metal-inking and plastic-inking machine operators; steel workers; welders, cutters, and welding machine operators; stationary engineers; apparel workers; textile machinery operators; and railroad and water transportation workers. (Brand, 1990, Davis, 1990)

The point that all these changes emphasize is that trends in occupational and industrial growth necessitate continual adjustments in career decisions. Using the best information now available, counselors and counselees can plan for the future insofar as supply and demand factors affect career decisions. For example, we have already witnessed the fact that reduced openings for teachers caused many college students to major in other fields and caused those who majored in education to enter other occupations. In the past, two out of every three women college graduates entered teaching. Obviously, even with upturns in the employment of teachers at the elementary school level, in certain speciality areas, and with existing shortages in several secondary school subject areas, women who chose to major in education have been forced to broaden their outlook on career opportunities.

One ominous demographic factor is the fact that the less educated proportion of the population is growing faster than any other segment. It is estimated that 23 million adults are functionally illiterate. (National Alliance of Business, 1986) Typically, they are the least prepared for work; their dropout rates are high and will continue to grow as will the incidence of teenage pregnancies. Simultaneously, entry-level jobs are requiring more and more basic skills, analytical skills and interpersonal skills. In addition, millions of manufacturing jobs will be restructured and millions of service jobs will become obsolete. Therefore, continuing and increased dislocation and disruption in people's career patterns are likely. Current efforts at improving education and training to respond to these needs (such as requiring competency tests, more schooling, specifically mandated subjects, restructuring the schools, and so forth) may or may not be successful. Lifelong education will obviously need to be expanded. In the information age, those with education are the rulers, those without education, both preparatory and continuing, are the peasants.

Feingold and Miller (1983) present a comprehensive listing and discussion of almost 200 occupations that they classify as "emerging careers." They also identify another 350 emerging occupations that they do not discuss; These occupations include such exotic work as behavioral pharmacologist, cable TV auditor, tectonic statistician, selenologist, limnologist, cognitive neurophysiologist, genetic counselor, insect toxicologist, nursing home

Figure 3.1

Growth of Occupational Groups, Educational Attainment of Workers, and Earnings

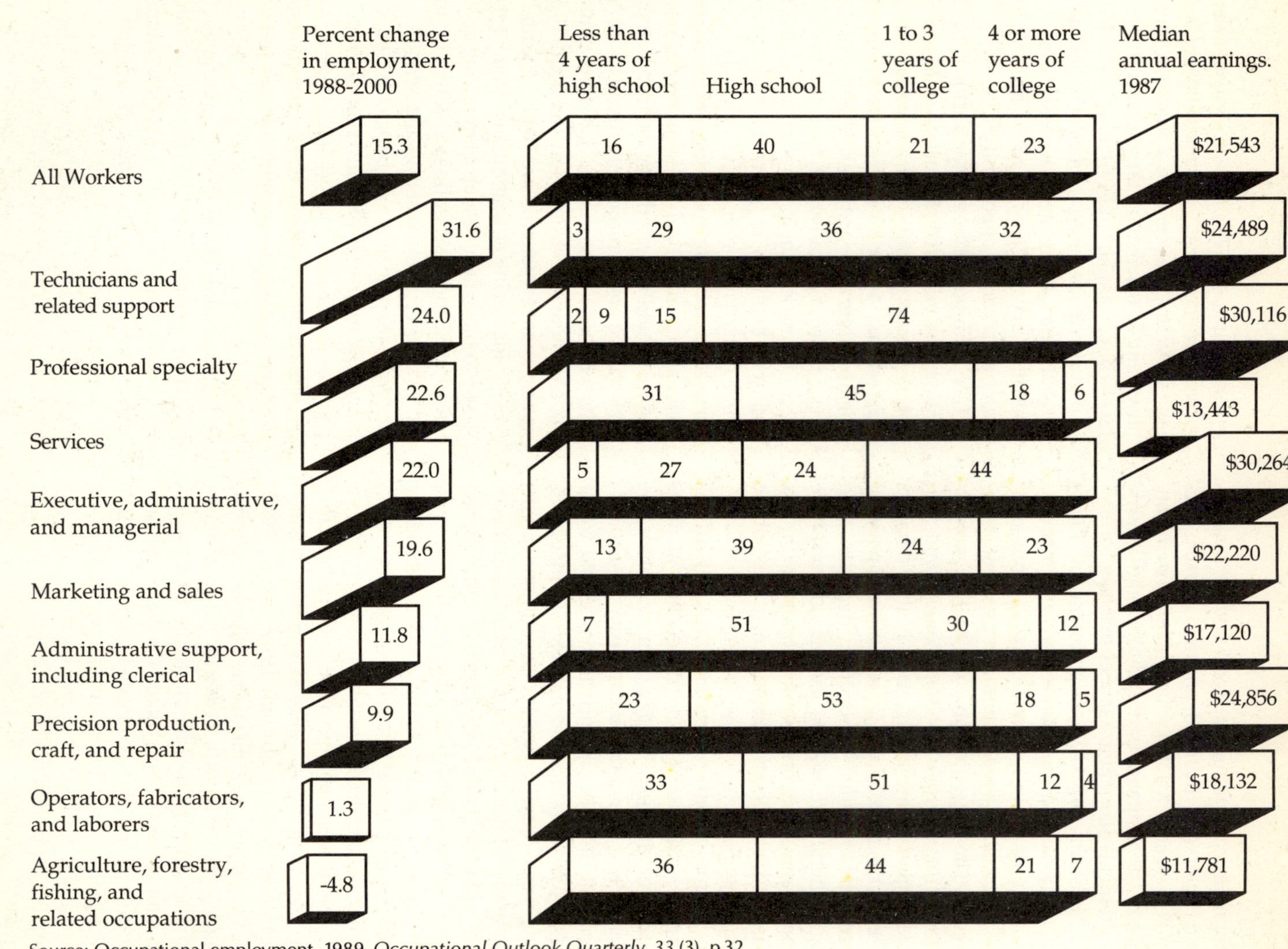

Source: Occupational employment, 1989. *Occupational Outlook Quarterly, 33* (3), p.32.

counselor, thanatologist, population ecologist, neutrino astronomist, and paleomagnetician. Not all of these occupations involve traditional high technology—technical or scientific skills in fields where advances are taking place with incredible rapidity. Many involve social technologies but nonetheless require high and continuing levels of education and training.

As technology creates new hardware and techniques, new jobs are created. Consider the case, for example, of some relatively recent inventions in the medical field. Computerized axial tomography (CAT) scanners, ultrasound, nuclear scans, gene splicing, and fiber-optic instruments all require technical and support personnel. The microcomputer explosion has obviously led to the creation of a great number of jobs, ranging from software and hardware design to entrepreneurial ventures to retailing. The majority of jobs will soon require computer skills. Relatively recent developments, such as superconductors and ceramic engines, will likely have equally stunning impact on the configuration of and the skills required in the world of work. Some countries are more geared than others to respond to the challenge of technology. In the United States, less than 10 percent of the baccalaureate degrees are awarded in engineering; but in Japan, engineering degrees account for 21 percent; in the USSR, 35 percent.

There are many predictions about changes in the *nature* of work as well as in the *type* of work. It is difficult to know which, if any, of the incipient efforts to change the nature of work are likely to become popular. A simple cataloging of some of these predictions should illustrate the potential effect on career counseling:

- *Job redesign* to utilize the particular talents of individual workers and accommodate higher levels of education
- *Job sharing* in which two or more individuals share a full-time position on a less than full-time, full-pay basis
- *Flexible scheduling*, or flex-time, whereby individuals put in an eight-hour day but are able to choose (within prescribed parameters) when these daily eight hours are worked
- *Quality control circles* whereby workers negotiate and are responsible for quality standards of both work and materials
- *More part-time jobs* and temporary workers to allow homemakers and retirees to earn supplementary income
- *Sabbaticals*, much as in academia, for personal and organizational development
- *Job rotation* to relieve monotony and to increase breadth of worker understanding
- *Flexibility of rewards* wherein workers may choose the combination of pay and benefits that best fits their needs
- *Power sharing*, or democratization, leading to greater cooperative group governance
- *Flexible retirement*, including time of retirement (earlier or later than usual) and type of retirement (phase out, as in a four-, three-, or two-day week, or all at once)
- *Nontraditional rewards*, such as time off for high-quality work, bonuses for safe work
- *Improved career ladders* so that individuals may perceive an escape from plateauing at a terminal level
- *Home-based work* whereby individuals produce goods or perform services in their own homes
- *Educational benefits*, both through the formal educational system and at the work site, paid for by the organization (including opportunities for retraining and retooling)
- *Copreneurs*, married entrepeneurial couples who give new meaning to the "mom and pop" business (Barnett & Barnett, 1988)

The shape of the future with regard to the quantity and quality of work in America is not sharply focused. However, counselors and counselees who are willing to try to form some sense of what those contours will be are likely to be rewarded.

RELATION OF THE OCCUPATIONAL STRUCTURE TO CAREER GUIDANCE AND COUNSELING

Several parts of this text have and will identify the antecedents and the processes of career decision-making. Weaving throughout this discussion are the factors that produce individual differences shaping personal styles of approach to choice and implementation of choice. In this chapter, perhaps the important point to be made is that such considerations are valid only if many choices exist, and if any given individual has the political and social freedom to choose among opportunities. The fact that these two conditions do exist in the United States has historically impelled the provision of career guidance to foster not only freedom of choice but informed choice as well.

Individuals must choose something; in terms of this book, they must choose an occupation and, indeed, a career pattern from among the thousands of existing possibilities. For example, the *Dictionary of Occupational Titles* (DOT) lists over 20,000 jobs. New jobs are created each day, and obsolescent jobs are phased out of existence.

If, however, as we have contended several times, personal identity is acquired through such characteristics as commitment, planning, and seeing oneself and what one does in the present as affecting the future, then career guidance should aid the choice of an occupation within the broad context of "career." This context connotes not simply a choice at a point in time, but also a series of immediate and intermediate choices made to achieve one's goals at a future time.

In order for individuals to relate themselves to the educational and occupational alternatives available to them, they need some "handles" to help them see how these alternatives differ. Later in this text (Chapter 15) we will detail many types of occupational information, both regionally and nationally based and directed toward current vacancies and likely future developments.

To bring some order into what can well be a chaotic situation, various schemes have been devised to classify, in logical ways, the thousands of individual jobs and the variety of educational and training programs. Each scheme emphasizes at least one characteristic for differentiating occupations. As will be indicated in Chapter 6 (career guidance objectives), in Chapters 7 through 12 (the application of career guidance practices at different developmental levels), and in Chapter 15 (information systems), these occupational differences can be used to give substance to efforts at assisting career development and choice; to reality-test one's characteristics against job requirements; and to create filing systems or person-machine interaction systems to provide better access to information.

One of the prime differences between occupational alternatives relates to levels and kinds of education or training. A system of classifying differences in educational and training opportunities by overt and covert criteria will not be elaborated on here—except as it is included in the variables for classifying occupational characteristics in the DOT. However, it is important, when considering the range of opportunities in the American occupational structure, to recognize the relationship between level and kind of education or training and level and kind of work.

Occupational Classification Systems

People have made attempts to classify occupations from ancient times. Hopke (1979) points out that primitive societies classified workers into two categories: physical laborers and nonlaborers (such as priests, chiefs, and medicine men). Others talked of the three-class system: peasants, nomads, and the priestly or educated classes. As society became more complex, so did work and its classifications. Some of the classifications were indeed fanciful and curious. For example, there have been classifications by physical characteristics, such as brain weight and head size. (Sorokin, 1927) The brains of physicians and university teachers average 1500 grams; the brain weight of unskilled laborers averaged only 1410 grams. The head size of full professors was 35.79 centimeters; of associate and assistant professors, 35.72; of instructors, 35.64; and of students, 34.58.

As we have become more sophisticated, classifications of occupations have been formulated for various purposes on both a priori and post hoc bases and with their roots in economics, psychology, and sociology. Some are careful attempts at empirical derivation; others are slightly better than incense burning. Among the major classification systems are the following:

- By *industry* as in the Census classification below
- By *socioeconomic group*, for example, bourgeoisie, proletariat; blue collar, white collar; lower, middle, upper
- By *ability and/or aptitudes*. Ghiselli (1966) has demonstrated, as indicated in Chapter 4, that "in terms of their requirements, jobs are not organized into clear cut and separate groups. Rather there is a continuous variation among jobs, and they form clusters which do not have distinct boundaries. Second, jobs which superficially appear to be similar in terms of nature of work may have quite different ability requirements, and jobs which appear to be quite different may have very similar requirements." (p. 111) This finding that, despite mean occupational differences on ability dimensions, the heterogeneity of ability within occupational groups is substantial has been verified over the decades. (Fryer, 1922; Stewart, 1947; Thorndike & Hagen, 1959)
- By *occupation*—an obviously cumbersome method if one uses single occupations, since there are over 20,000 titles listed in the *Dictionary of Occupational Titles*; by groupings of occupations according to the Census Classification or the DOT, the system is sensible.
- By *interests*. Most interest inventories classify occupations by interest patterns of those in the occupations. Jackson and Williams (1975) contend that they have isolated 23 distinct occupational clusters on the basis of interest. The U.S. Employment Service (USES) operationalizes the worker trait by occupational group concept in terms of 11 basic occupational interest factors (Droege & Padgett, 1979), which are now used in the U.S. Department of Labor's *Guide to Occupational Exploration* and for which an interest inventory is available. Thus, one can combine the General Aptitude Test Battery (GATB) and the Interest Inventory for a broader assessment than was previously possible with USES materials. The USES Occupational Interest areas are artistic, scientific, plants and animals, protective, mechanical, industrial, business detail, selling, accommodating, humanitarian, leading-influencing, and physical performing. Holland's classification, although based on personality types, may also be considered an attempt at classification by interests. Holland himself, however, has indicated that different occupations include a variety of types and subtypes (Holland & Holland, 1977).
- By *field and level*. Anne Roe's two-dimensional classification by eight fields of interest and six levels of occupations, described in detail later in this chapter, has proven to be a useful taxonomy. Meir (1978) has demonstrated that the field-level matrix is indeed orthogonal; that is, fields and levels are mutually independent.
- By *field, level and enterprise*. Super (1957) suggested adding a third dimension to Roe's scheme to indicate the enterprise or the general setting where work is performed.
- By *income*. The range of income within occupational groups is so wide as to make

classification on this basis almost meaningless. As with ability classification, there are mean differences among occupations, but the within-occupation variability is substantial.

- By *type of work.* This type of classification can take many forms, ranging from dichotomies such as physical-nonphysical to the more sophisticated descriptions of people-data-things activities outlined later in this chapter and contained in the discussion of the DOT. The Minnesota Occupational Classification System attempts to classify occupations by a combination of ability requirements, work reinforcers (need satisfiers), and environmental style dimensions (Dawis, Lofquist, Henly, & Rounds, 1979). The ACT World-of-Work Map is also a extension of the DOT.
- By *educational or occupational prerequisites.* Again, the DOT system of classifying occupations according to educational level is a good example of this type of taxonomy. Classifications such as these are easily implemented in practice by means of occupational materials such as the Bureau of Labor Statistics' "Jobs for Which You Can Qualify If You're a High School Graduate," "Jobs for Which You Can Train through Apprenticeship," or "Jobs for Which You Will Probably Need a College Education."
- By *occupational duties performed.* Part of the DOT presents occupational descriptors—the tasks performed by people in the occupation. Although such information is basic to anyone considering an occupation, it is so narrow that classification solely on this basis is rather unwieldly.
- By *life span.* It is possible to classify occupations according to such dimensions as early entry–early leaving, early entry–late leaving, or late entry–late leaving. A professional athlete, for example, would have an early entry–early leaving occupation, whereas a physician would have a late entry–late leaving occupation.
- By *rewards.* Rewards can comprise financial or honorific benefits or improvement in working conditions, or a combination of these factors. In one sense, the status classifications of occupations described later are examples of this type of taxonomy.
- By *age.* Kaufman and Spilerman (1982) have demonstrated that the majority of detailed census occupations conform to one of five basic age profiles: (1) occupations in which young workers are overrepresented (such as entry-level occupations); (2) occupations in which middle-aged workers are concentrated (such as supervisors, foremen, managers); (3) occupations in which the elderly are overrepresented (such as contracting occupations); (4) occupations with a uniform age distribution (such as crafts); and (5) occupations with a U-shaped age distribution (such as undesirable jobs).

The USOE Clusters

The career education movement stimulated the development of a new occupational cluster system by the USOE. Because of the prestige of that office and because of the funds for career education that emanated from that source, the fifteen-cluster taxonomy quickly became a highly utilized classification system. Commercial materials, especially, were rushed to market, packaged within the USOE cluster framework. Similar to many other clustering models, the USOE clusters begin with the assumption that all work can be classified, involving either the production of goods or the provision of services. These two activities are then organized into 15 occupational clusters. Within each cluster there is a hierarchy of occupations ranging from professional to unskilled.

1. *Business and office* (for example, data processor, bookkeeper, accountant, file clerk)
2. *Marketing and distribution* (for example, salesperson, marketing researcher, economist, systems analyst)

3. *Communications and media* (for example, reporter, photoengraver, script writer, electronic technician)
4. *Construction* (for example, architect, paperhanger, bricklayer, roofer, plasterer)
5. *Manufacturing* (for example, machine operator, chemist, welder, tool and die maker)
6. *Transportation* (for example, pilot, truck driver, auto mechanic, aerospace engineer)
7. *Agri-business and natural resources* (for example, farmer, miner, farm agent, wildlife manager)
8. *Marine science* (for example, sailor, diver, fisher, marine biologist)
9. *Environment* (for example, forest ranger, meteorologist, geologist, tree surgeon)
10. *Public services* (for example, counselor, fire fighter, police officer, probation officer)
11. *Health* (for example, psychologist, veterinarian, dentist, speech pathologist, chiropractor)
12. *Recreation and hospitality* (for example, waitperson, chef, golf pro, cashier)
13. *Personal services* (for example, beautician, priest, mortician, TV repairperson)
14. *Fine arts and humanities* (for example, dancer, author, jeweler, piano tuner)
15. *Consumer and homemaking education* (for example, interior decorator, seamstress or tailor, home economist, model)

The USOE cluster classification system is not without its critics. Some of the criticisms revolve around issues of cost and other practical considerations of implementation. Some center on challenging the theoretical assumptions underlying the categories. The most obvious perceived disadvantage of the USOE clusters, however, is the problem of overlap. A number of occupations can be located in more than one cluster; the categories are thus not mutually exclusive. Although this criticism is not unique to the USOE clusters (it applies equally to several other category systems), it does point out potential weaknesses in the system that must be overcome if it is to be more effective than other systems. There are several attempts currently underway to construct an empirically based cluster taxonomy of occupations (Perlman, 1980). In general, the USOE clusters have been utilized less as the career education movement has lost its momentum.

Census Classifications

Since 1970 the U.S. Bureau of the Census has conducted a decennial accounting of the demographics of this country. Recent legislation increases the frequency of that nationwide census of population. In order to provide a framework within which to classify the work world, the Bureau of the Census has devised two distinct classification systems: one that is descriptive of the industries in which people work, and another that is related to occupational categories. Each of these is briefly discussed below.

Industrial Classification. A commonly employed classification model is the federal government's Standard Industrial Classification System (SICS). It offers a comprehensive listing of types of industry within eleven major categories (note similarities to USOE clusters):

1. Agriculture, forestry, and fishing and mining
2. Construction
3. Manufacturing
4. Transportation
5. Communications and other public utilities
6. Wholesale trade
7. Retail trade
8. Finance, insurance, and real estate
9. Business and repair services

10. Personal, entertainment, and recreation services
11. Public administration

These categories, in turn, are divided into 84 less broad industrial classifications. For example, retail trade is composed of eight subcategories:

1. Building materials, hardware, garden supply, and mobile home dealers
2. General merchandise stores
3. Food stores
4. Automotive dealers and gasoline service stations
5. Apparel and accessory stores
6. Furniture, home furnishings, and equipment stores
7. Eating and drinking places
8. Miscellaneous retail

Finally, these 84 categories are further delineated by specific industries within them. Basically, the SICS describes *where* people work; it gives little or no indication of what people do. It is a classification system that is useful in gathering statistics and sometimes in filing occupational information. Otherwise, it has little utility for direct career guidance and counseling.

Occupational Group Classification. The 1980 Census of Population Occupational Classification is as follows:

- *Managerial and professional specialty occupations*
  - Executive, administrative, and managerial occupations
  - Professional specialty occupations
- *Technical sales, and administrative support occupations*
  - Technicians and related support occupations
  - Sales occupations
  - Administrative support occupations, including clerical
- *Service occupations*
  - Private household occupations
  - Protective service occupations
  - Service occupations, except protective and household
- *Farming, forestry, and fishing occupations*
- *Precision production, craft, and repair occupations*
- *Operators, fabricators, and laborers*
  - Machine operators, assemblers, and inspectors
  - Transportation and material moving occupations
  - Handlers, equipment cleaners, helpers, and laborers

These census classifications are valuable, because the U.S. Bureau of the Census periodically updates the distribution of workers into occupational categories and by industry. Thus, they provide data to a variety of consumers in terms of an accepted classification system.

Status Classifications

Another classification system is based on the status of occupations. Status level is usually determined by the perceived prestige of an occupation, which, in turn, is based on such factors as the amount of money earned, power, the type of work involved, the degree of responsibility for social welfare, the amount of education necessary, and other prerequisites. Some people mistakenly believe that earning power is the primary criterion of status. That this is not so is evident by examining the various prestige scales. For example, one scale ranked 100 occupations according to prestige (Smith, 1943); ranked highest was U.S. Supreme Court Justice (Smith 1943); ranked lowest was the occupation of professional prostitute. Available data suggest that a "successful" prostitute makes considerably more money annually than does a jurist sitting on the highest court.

The classic prestige scale is the one established by the National Opinion Research Center of the University of Chicago. It is generally referred to as the NORC Scale of Occupational Prestige and presents the following prestige hierarchy of occupations (National Opinion Research Center, 1947):

- Government officials
- Professional and semiprofessional workers
- Proprietors, managers, and officials (except farm)
- Clerical, sales, and kindred workers
- Crafts and kindred workers
- Farmers and farm managers
- Protective service workers
- Operatives and kindred workers
- Farm laborers
- Service workers (except domestic and protective)
- Laborers (except farm)

The NORC Scale closely parallels another prestige ranking system, Duncan's Sociometric Status Index of 1950. The average status score for all occupations is 30. In relation to that average, the following occupational group scores prevail:

- Professional, technical, and kindred workers 75
- Managers, officials, and proprietors (except farm) 57
- Sales workers 49
- Clerical and kindred workers 45
- Craftsmen, foremen, and kindred workers 31
- Operatives and kindred workers 18
- Service workers (except private household) 17
- Farmers and farm managers 14
- Farm laborers and foremen 9
- Private household workers 8
- Laborers (except farm and mine) 7

These occupational status rankings as well as others have remained relatively stable for the past half-century (Hodge, Siegel, & Rossi, 1964; Counts, 1925; Deeg & Paterson, 1947; Hakel, Hollman, & Dunette, 1968; Braun & Bayer, 1973; Medvene & Collins, 1974; Kanzaki, 1976). The results may be somewhat suspect, because perceptions of the status of newer occupations cannot be compared with earlier perceptions since the occupations did not exist. Also, most respondents utilized to establish prestige hierarchies are college students. This fact could prejudice the results. Hence, it may be dangerous to generalize the results of occupational status studies.

Usually, only a relatively few occupations are included in these types of ranking hierarchies. More recently, however, researchers (Chartrand, Dohm, Denis, & Lofquist, 1987) drawing on data from the Minnesota Occupational Classification System have developed a regression equation that allowed them to assign prestige rating estimates to about 2000 occupations.

The relative constancy of occupational prestige over time is not to say that the occupational structure is unresponsive to generational changes. A classic example was the great upsurge of scientific and engineering careers stimulated by Sputnik and the resulting reactions all the way through the space program. Then, because of federal deemphasis of the space program and subsequent massive technical and scientific unemployment, the United States found itself with a surplus of scientists and engineers. Thus, fewer students opted for training in these areas. Now, however, scientists and engineers are again in demand. Also in the late 1960s and early 1970s, we witnessed a reluctance of college graduates to enter large corporate business and industrial structures because of the perceived depersonalization of such organizations, because of a movement away from material goals on the part of many students of that generation, or because of some other factor. Now, one of the "hot tickets" in colleges and universities is the business major, and corporate recruiters on campus are inundated with interviewees.

The point is that, to some extent, the way in which occupations are perceived and consequent interest in entering them are contingent on supply and demand. Supply and demand, in turn, are shaped by priorities in the society and by the prevailing work ethic of each generation. To an equal extent, some occupational areas seem to endure, as is the case with the health sciences.

In any case, occupational status classification systems are useful in that they permit individuals in the process of career development and choice to project into the future in order to discern probable changes in occupational status levels. If young people are to appreciate the dignity that they can bring to all work, they must understand the bases on which some occupations are perceived as prestigious and on which others are not. If occupational prestige is a consideration in career decision making, it is important that individuals understand the factors that determine prestige.

Holland's Classification System

Many classification schemes are based on the psychological characteristics of workers. One example is the system developed by John Holland and his associates at the Johns Hopkins University (Holland, 1973b, 1985). In Chapter 4, Holland's theory of career development is described; one should note that it is based on a theory of personality types. Evolving out of this theory are six classes of occupations: realistic, investigative, artistic, social, enterprising, and conventional. Each of these has five to sixteen subclasses; within each subclass, occupations are arranged by the years of general education required. In all, 1156 common occupations are included. All occupations are arranged in a system that uses the six Holland code letters:

- Realistic occupations (R) include skilled trades and many technical and some service occupations.
- Investigative occupations (1) include scientific and some technical occupations.
- Artistic occupations (A) include artistic, musical, and literary occupations.
- Social occupations (S) include educational and social welfare occupations.
- Enterprising occupations (E) include managerial and sales occupations.
- Conventional occupations (C) include office and clerical occupations.

The two or three classes that people in a specific occupation most resemble are designated in order by the code letter for those classes. Thus counselors, for example, are designated SEA, meaning that they most of all resemble people in social occupations, that they next most resemble people in enterprising occupations, and that they still less resemble people in artistic occupations. If one takes the six categories and looks for possible combinations, over 100 emerge. One of the difficulties with the Holland system is that for some combinations, few occupations have as yet been identified. One form of the Holland system, therefore, uses only a two-letter designation, thus, counselors are SE.

To relate his classification scheme to a more familiar system and one that provides occupational information, Holland further identifies occupations by their fourth edition DOT code numbers. These numbers provide a description of the occupation and estimates of interests and aptitudes associated with it. Thus, the occupation of counselor is described by in DOT designation, 045.107–010, and by the three occupational classes or types that counselors must resemble, SEA.

Finally, a 1 through 6 designation describes the level of educational development demanded by an occupation. Levels 5 and 6 refer to college training; levels 3 and 4 mean high school and some college, technical, or business training; and levels 1 and 2 mean only elementary school or no special training. We now have the complete Holland classification for the occupation of counselor.

DOT	Ed	Code
045.107–010	5	SEA

The Holland classification system has been applied to interest measurement and to a variety of other aids in career planning. Many of these will be described in later chapters. There has been a great deal of research that attempts to validate Holland's occupational groupings and to establish their effectiveness in career research, career guidance, vocational education, and social science. Thus far, the Holland taxonomy has generally withstood the rigors of close empirical scrutiny and stands as an excellent example of an attempt to classify occupations psychologically. As shall be seen in Chapter 16, the Holland system has been converted into a career guidance delivery system, through the *Self-Directed Search*, and it provides one of the reporting frameworks for the Strong Interest Inventory. Moreover, the SDS has lately been utilized by the Department of Defense as a career guidance aid to be used with the results of the Armed Services Vocational Aptitude Battery (ASVAB), an instrument administered over a million times a year. There remain some very real questions regarding aspects of the translation of Holland's theoretical model to an operational model (such as the validity of self-estimates of aptitudes and the relationships of the six categories to each other in terms of their hexagonal arrangement), but the system has value in that it does what any good occupational classification scheme should do—it leaks down the complex and confusing occupational world into manageable categories to which individuals can then relate important self-characteristics.

Field and Level

Most occupational classification systems are unidimensional—that is, they classify occupations on the basis of a single factor or variable. As previously noted, it is possible (and desirable) to classify occupations by combining two or more variables into a multidimensional scheme. One of the first attempts of this sort was made by Roe (1954) and later modified by Moser, Dubin, and Shelsky (1956) (see Table 3.2). Her classification system combines eight fields and six levels. The eight fields, which are based on the work of interest measurement researchers, are outdoor-physical, social-personal, business contact, administration-control, math-physical sciences, biological sciences, humanistic, and arts. Her levels are based on the responsibility, education, and prestige involved in an occupation. These levels are professional and managerial (higher), professional and managerial (regular), semiprofessional and low managerial, skilled support and maintenance, semiskilled support and maintenance, and unskilled support and maintenance.

The field-level classification system is another attempt to bring order into the potential chaos of our awareness of the thousands of existing jobs. The assumption is that no single dimension is adequate to do this job; therefore, dimensions must be combined. If counselors understand such a multidimensional structure and also understand their counselees, then they can help individuals relate their self-characteristics to the occupational structure.

Standard Occupational Classification Manual

Development of a Standard Occupational Classification (SOC) Manual started in 1966; it is basically an attempt to bridge the Census Classification and the DOT. It includes the best features of the International Standard Classification of Occupations (ISCO), the Canadian Classification and Dictionary of Occupations, and the British Classifications of Occupations and Directory of Occupational Titles. The

Table 3.2

A Classification of Occupations (Revised from Roe)

Level	I Service	II Business Contact	III Business Organization	IV Technology
1. Professional and managerial$_1$ (higher)	Research scientist (social)	Sales manager (large corporation)	Cabinet member President (large corporation)	Inventor (industrial research) Research scientist (engineering)
2. Professional and managerial$_2$ (regular)	Administrator (social welfare) Manager (penal institution) Probation officer Social worker	Personnel manager Sales engineer	Banker Broker CPA Hotel manager	Air Force (pilot) Engineer Flight analyst Superintendent (factory)
3. Semi-professional and managerial	Employment interviewer Nurse (registered) Physical director (YMCA) Recreation therapist	Confidenceman Freight traffic agent Salesman, auto, insurance bond, real estate Wholesaler	Accountant Owner (small grocery) Postmaster Private secretary	Aviator Brine foreman (DOT Foreman II) Contractor (general, carpentry, etc.) Engineer (locomotive)
4. Skilled	Army Sergeant Barber Chef Headwaiter Policeman Practical nurse	Auctioneer Canvasser Survey worker Salesman (house to house)	Compiler Morse operator Statistical clerk Stenographer	Blacksmith Carpenter Dressmaker Paperhanger Plasterer foreman (DOT Foremen I) Shiprigger
5. Semiskilled	Chauffeur Cook Elevator operator Firemen (city) Fortuneteller Navy, Seaman	Peddler Salesclerk Ticket agent	Cashier Clerk (file) Mail carrier Telephone operator Typist	Carpenter (apprentice) Crane operator (portable) Meat curer Railroad switchman Truck driver
6. Unskilled	Bellhop Janitor Streetsweeper Watchman	Newspaper Boy	Messenger	Carpenter's helper Deckhand Laborer foundry

Table 3.2 (Continued)

V Outdoor	VI Science	VII General Cultural	VIII Arts and Entertainment
Research engineer, mining	Dentist Doctor Research Scientist (Physics, Chemistry)	Judge Professor (History, Math, etc.)	Orchestra conductor TV Director
Conservation officer Fish and wildlife specialist Geologist Petroleum engineer	Chemist Geneticist Pharmacist Veterinarian Physicist	Clergyman Editor News commentator Teacher (high school, primary)	Architect Baseball player (major league) Critic Sculptor
Apiarist County agent Farmer (small independent owner) Forest ranger	Chiropodist Embalmer Physical therapist	Justice of the Peace Law clerk Librarian Reporter	Ad artist Athletic coach Interior decorator Photographer
Landscape gardener Miner Rotary driller oil well)	Medical technician		Chorine Illustrator (greeting cards) Window decorator
Farm tenant Fisherman Gardener Hostler Nursery worker Trapper		Library attendant	Clothes model Lead pony boy
Animal tender Ditcher Farm laborer Nursery laborer		Copy boy	Stagehand

Source: From *Journal of Counseling Psychology,* Vol. 3, pp. 27–31. Published by the American Psychological Association.

classification covers all occupations in which work is performed for pay or profit but does not include volunteer work. The SOC tries to reflect the current United States occupational structure on the basis of work performed and place of work. It is structured on a four-level system: division, major group, minor group, and unit group. It runs from gross description to finer detail as one goes from division to unit; and it includes DOT numbers and census occupation codes.

There are 21 divisions. Each division has major groups (designated by a two-digit number) minor groups (designated by a three-digit number), and unit groups (designated by a four-digit number). The divisions are as follows.

1. Executive, administrative, and managerial groups
2. Engineers and architects
3. Natural scientists and mathematicians
4. Social scientists, social workers, religious workers, and lawyers
5. Teachers, librarians, and counselors
6. Health diagnosing and testing practitioners
7. Nurses, pharmacists, dieticians, therapists, and physicians' assistants
8. Writers, artists, entertainers, and athletes
9. Health technologists and technicians
10. Technologists and technicians, except health
11. Marketing and sales occupations
12. Clerical occupations
13. Service occupations
14. Agriculture and forestry occupations, fishers, and hunters
15. Construction and extractive occupations
16. Transportation and material-moving occupations
17. Mechanics and repairers
18. Production-working occupations
19. Material handlers, equipment cleaners, and laborers
20. Military occupations
21. Miscellaneous occupations

To illustrate the progressively finer distinction, let us consider the division of natural scientists and mathematicians:

- 17 Computer, mathematical, and operations research occupations (major)
  - 171 Computer scientists (minor)
    - 1712 Computer systems analysts (unit)
    - 1719 Computer scientists, not elsewhere classified
  - 172 Operations and systems researchers and analysts
    - 1721 Operations researchers and analysts
    - 1722 Systems researchers and analysts, except computer
  - 173 Mathematical scientists
    - 1732 Actuaries
    - 1733 Statisticians
    - 1739 Mathematical scientists, not elsewhere classified
- 18 Natural scientists
  - 184 Physical scientists
    - 1842 Astronomers
    - 1843 Physicists
    - 1845 Chemists, except biochemists
    - 1846 Atmospheric and space scientists
    - 1847 Geologists
    - 1849 Physical scientists, not elsewhere classified
  - 185 Life scientists
    - 1852 Forestry and conservation scientists
    - 1853 Agricultural and food scientists
    - 1854 Biological scientists
    - 1855 Medical scientists

This system is obviously useful for research and classification purposes. It remains to be seen how utilitarian it will be for the development of career-related materials and for other practical applications.

The *Dictionary of Occupational Titles* (DOT)

Perhaps the most widely used occupational classification system is that employed in the *Dictionary of Occupational Titles*. The DOT was first issued in 1939 to meet the needs of the public employment service system to standardize occupational information in order to facilitate job placement, employment counseling, career guidance, labor market projections, and person-power accounting. Subsequent editions of the DOT appeared in 1949 and 1965. The fourth edition was published in 1978, and a brief supplement appeared in 1982. The fourth edition was somewhat revised and updated in 1991.

The fourth edition of the DOT contains information relating to approximately twenty thousand jobs. This figure represents about fourteen hundred fewer jobs than in the third edition and is a consequence of the deletion of some thirty-five hundred jobs and the addition of approximately twenty-one hundred new occupational definitions.

All jobs in the fourth edition of the DOT are designated by a nine-digit number. Previously, a six-digit number had been used; however, three additional digits have been added to provide each occupation with its own code in order to expedite computerized analyses. The first of the nine digits refers to an occupational category, of which there are nine:

0/1. Professional, technical, and managerial occupations
2. Clerical and sales occupations
3. Service occupations
4. Agricultural, fishery, forestry, and related occupations
5. Processing occupations
6. Machine trades occupations
7. Benchwork occupations
8. Structural work occupations
9. Miscellaneous occupations

These nine occupational categories are divided into 82 two-digit occupational divisions, which are then subdivided into 549 three-digit occupational groups. For purposes of illustration, the two-digit occupational divisions and the three-digit occupation groups relating to the 0/1 occupational category and the 00/01 division are presented below.

Example of two-digit division
0/1 professional, technical,
and managerial occupations

- 00/01 Occupations in architecture, engineering, and surveying
- 02 Occupations in mathematics and physical sciences
- 04 Occupations in life sciences
- 05 Occupations in social sciences
- 07 Occupations in medicine and health
- 09 Occupations in education
- 10 Occupations in museum, library, and archival sciences
- 11 Occupations in law and jurisprudence
- 12 Occupations in religion and theology
- 13 Occupations in writing
- 14 Occupations in art
- 15 Occupations in entertainment and recreation
- 16 Occupations in administrative specializations
- 18 Managers and officials, n.e.c. [not elsewhere classified]
- 19 Miscellaneous professional, technical, and managerial occupations

Example of three-digit group
00/01 occupations in architecture,
engineering, and surveying

- 001 Architectural occupations
- 002 Aeronautical engineering occupations
- 003 Electrical/electronics engineering occupations
- 005 Civil engineering occupations
- 006 Ceramic engineering occupations
- 007 Mechanical engineering occupations
- 008 Chemical engineering occupations
- 010 Mining and petroleum engineering occupations

011 Metallurgy and metallurgical engineering occupations
012 Industrial engineering occupations
013 Agricultural engineering occupations
014 Marine engineering occupations
015 Nuclear engineering occupations
017 Drafters, n.e.c.
018 Surveying/cartographic occupations
019 Occupations in architecture, engineering, and surveying, n.e.c.

The middle three digits of the nine-digit code number refer to worker traits. Jobs require that people function in relation to data, people, and things. Each of these three items has a hierarchy of relationship levels, and the code digit refers to the highest level within the hierarchy at which a worker is required to function. Following are the hierarchies for each digit.

Data (fourth digit)

0 Synthesizing
1 Coordinating
2 Analyzing
3 Compiling
4 Computing
5 Copying
6 Comparing

People (fifth digit)

0 Mentoring
1 Negotiating
2 Instructing
3 Supervising
4 Diverting
5 Persuading
6 Speaking-signaling
7 Serving
8 Taking instructions—helping

Things (sixth digit)

0 Setting up
1 Precision working
2 Operating—controlling
3 Driving—operating
4 Manipulating
5 Tending
6 Feeding—offbearing
7 Handling

Hence, the more a worker functions with complex responsibility and judgement, the lower the number on each list; the less complicated the function in relation to data, people, and things, the higher the number. Compiling data is a more complex task than copying data; instructing people is more complicated than serving them; and precision work with things is more intricate than manipulating them.

The final three digits of the nine-digit code indicate the alphabetical order of titles within the six-digit code groups. Many occupations may have the same first six digits. Therefore, the last three digits serve to differentiate a particular occupation from all others. If a six-digit code is applicable to only one occupational title, the last three digits will be 010.

To illustrate, let us "read" the nine-digit codes for a sample occupation: marine architect.

Marine Architect (001.061–014)

0 = A professional, technical, and managerial occupation
0 = An occupation in architecture, engineering and surveying
1 = An architectural occupation
0 = Synthesizes data
6 = Speaks to people
1 = Precision work with things
014 = Alphabetically distinguishes from other 001.061 occupations (for example, landscape architect)

Each entry in the DOT contains the following information: (1) the occupational code number; (2) the occupatoinal title; (3) the industry designation; (4) alternate titles (if any); (5) the head statement (summary of occupation); (6) task element statements (specific tasks worker performs); (7) "may" items (duties performed by worker in some establishments but not in others); (8) undefined related titles (if applicable). To illustrate, the entry for marine architect follows:

001.061–014 ARCHITECT, MARINE (profess. & kin.) architect, naval; naval designer.

> Designs and oversees construction and repair of marine and craft and floating structures, such as ships, barges, tugs, dredges, submarines, torpedoes, floats, and buoys; Studies design proposals and specifications to establish basic characteristics of craft, such as size, weight, speed, propulsion, armament, cargo, displacement, draft, crew and passenger complements, and fresh or salt water service. Overseas construction and testing of prototype in model basin and develops sectional and waterline curves of hull to establish center of gravity, ideal hull form, and buoyancy and stability data. Designs complete hull and superstructure according to specifications and test data. In conformity with standards of safety, efficiency, and economy. Designs layout of craft interior including cargo space, passenger compartments, ladder wells, and elevators. Confers with MARINE ENGINEERS (profess. & kin.) to establish arrangement of boiler room equipment and propulsion machinery, heating and ventilating systems, refrigeration equipment, piping, and other functional equipment. Evaluates performance of craft during dock and sea trials to determine design changes and conformance with national and international standards.

The fourth edition of the DOT is a single volume of 1371 pages and provides essentially the same data that were packaged in the two volumes of the third edition. The DOT user will find it separated into nine sections: an introduction and summary listings, master titles and definitions, term titles and definitions, occupational group arrangement, glossary, alphabetical index of titles, occupational titles arranged by industry designation, an industry index, and an appendix that explains the data, people, and things system.

There are three basic arrangement of occupational titles. The *occupational group arrangement* is appropriate if the user has sufficient information about the job tasks, wants to know about other closely related occupations, and/or wants to be sure he or she has chosen the most appropriate classification using the other arrangements. *Occupational titles arranged by industry designation* is appropriate if the user knows only the industry in which the job is located, wants to know about other jobs in an industry, and/or wants to know about work in a specific industry. The *alphabetical index of occupational titles* is appropriate if the user knows only the occupational title and cannot obtain better information.

In summary, the fourth edition of the DOT presents few problems of usage for the counselor. Besides its direct value as a comprehensive reservoir of information on approximately twenty thousand separate jobs, the DOT provides a framework for use in a variety of other career-related resources) such as Holland's SDS, CIS, and so on).

Maps

A number of classification schemes designate themselves as "maps"—representations of the world of work based on various criteria. Two examples of such maps are the ACT World-of-Work Map (ACT, 1985) and the Occupational Aptitude Patterns (OAP) Map (Gottfredson, 1986).

World-of-Work Map. The World-of-Work Map was devised by the American College Testing Program (ACT) and is used as an aid in their Career Planning Program (CPP). The World-of-Work Map begins with an addition to the DOT people-data-things dimensions: ideas. According to ACT, data/ideas form one similar set of work task dimensions, while people/things constitute another. In a circular arrangement (see Figure 3.2), things lead into data and things on one side and ideas and things on the other; similarly, the remaining three dimensions flow into neighboring realms. Six job clusters can be located within the eight work task combinations: business contact, business operations, technical, science, arts, and social service. Each of these, in turn, can be further refined. The social service job cluster, for example, consists of general health care, education and related

Figure 3.2

World-of-Work Map (2nd Edition). (From *ACT (1985) Interim Psychometric Handbook for the Third Edition ACT Career Planning Program (Levels 1 and 2)*. Copyright © 1985 by The American College Testing Program. Reprinted with permission.)

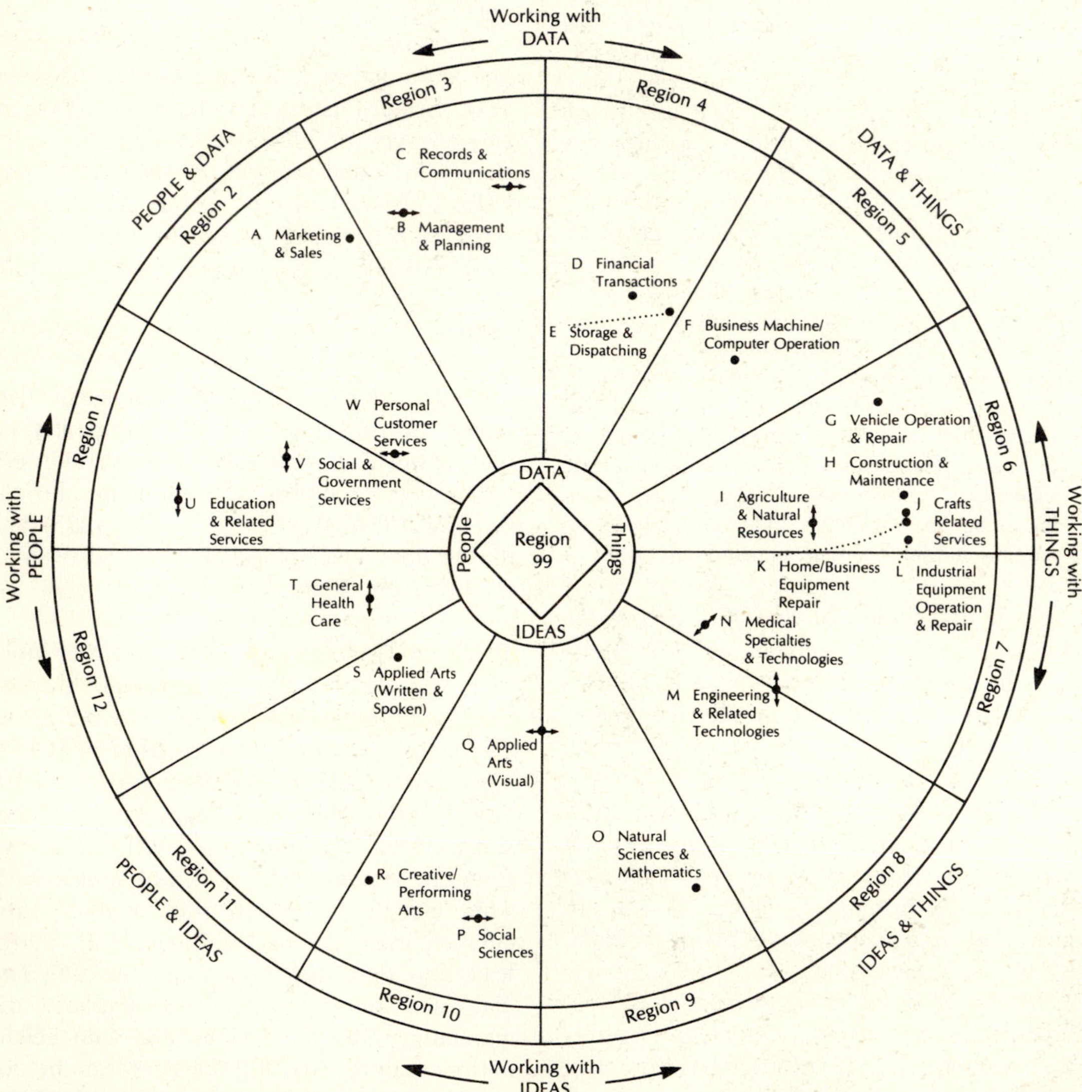

The location of a Job Family on the map shows how much it involves working with DATA, IDEAS, PEOPLE, and THINGS. Arrows by a Job Family show that work tasks often heavily involve both PEOPLE and THINGS (↔) or DATA and IDEAS (↕). Although each Job Family is shown as a single point, the jobs in a family vary in their locations. Most jobs, however, are located near the point shown for the Job Family.

Figure 3.3

Occupational Aptitudes Pattern (OAP) Map (From "Occupational Aptitude Pattern (OAP) Map: Development and Implications for a Theory of Job Aptitude Requirements" by L.S. Gottfredson, *Journal of Vocational Behavior*, Vol. 29, pp. 254–291. Orlando, FL: Academic Press, 1986. Reprinted by permission.)

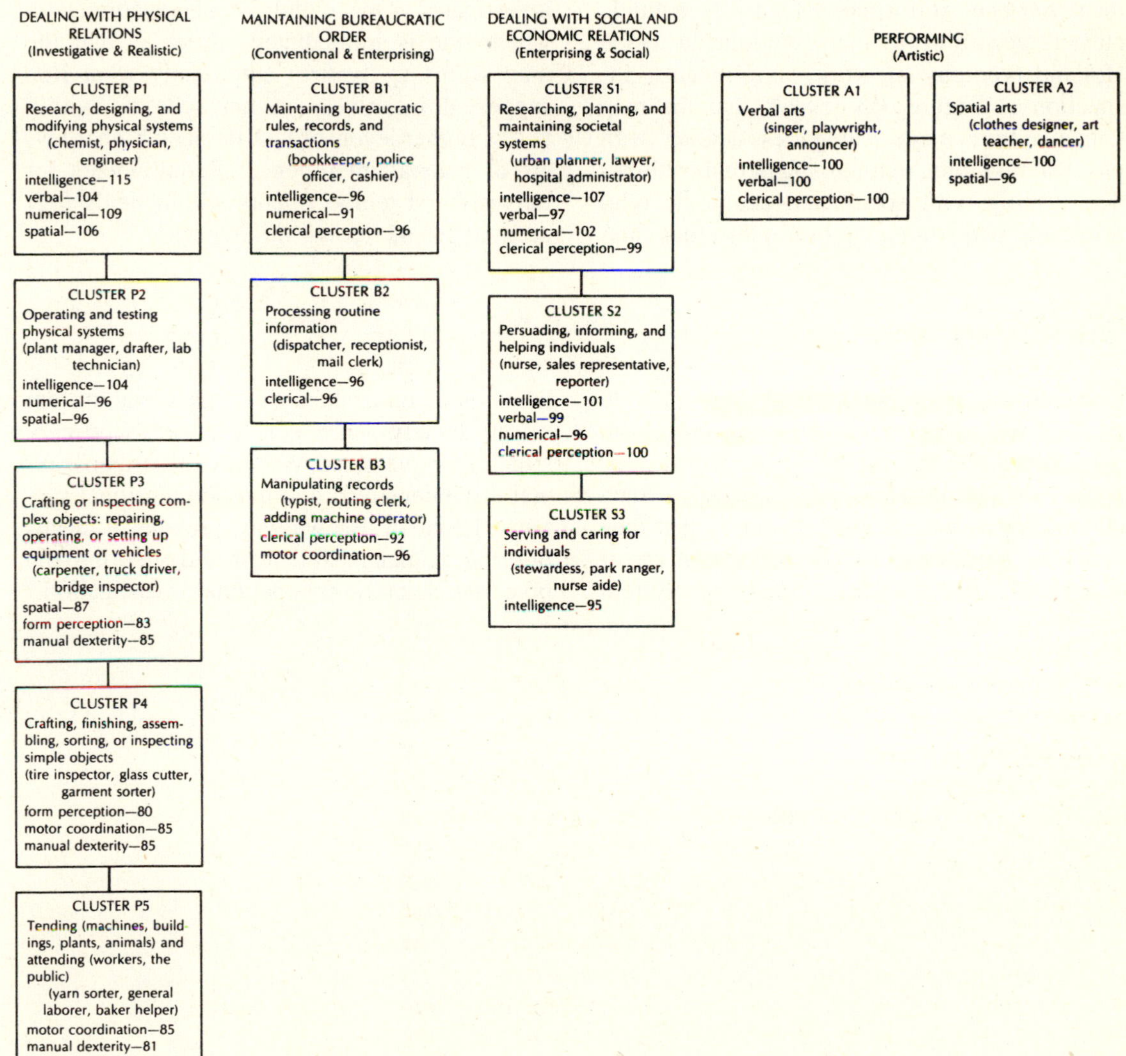

services, social and government services, and personal/customer services. All of these are located in Regions 1, 2, and 12 of the World-of-Work Map.

It is arguable whether such a system is an improvement over other systems. Initially, the World-of-Work Map presents the information seeker with a seemingly complex task that may discourage its use. On the other hand, it does offer some refinement of the accepted and respected *Dictionary of Occupational Titles*.

Occupational Aptitude Patterns Map. The Occupational Aptitude Patterns (OAP) Map is based on an analysis of Occupational Aptitude Pattern scores derived from the General Aptitude Test Battery of the United States Employment Service. It further categorizes aptitude clusters according to their relationship to the Holland typology of work environments. Inspection of Figure 3.3 reveals that the map contains four major categories dealing with physical relations, maintaining bureaucratic order, dealing with social and economic relations, and performing. In turn, these four categories are comprised of thirteen clusters, each of which displays a general intellective or psychomotor aptitude characteristic.

This map is relatively new, and the practical applications have yet to be thoroughly investigated. One interested observation with which one is immediately struck is that the map seems to confirm empirically what Roe suggested intuitively in her scheme: within fields, higher levels of task demand higher levels of general intelligence. Requirements for interests and temperaments within fields may account for additional differences.

Summary

Occupational classification schemes provide ways of examining the American occupational structure, an understanding of which is essential to career guidance and counseling. Such classification systems are valuable in that they provide a framework for the delivery of career guidance services. The occupational system helps us to understand the total social system of our society, since it is a society's primary structuring element. We have described several unidimensional and multidimensional systems. Each, in its own way, provides a means of bringing manageable form and order into the potential chaos of occupational investigation.

CHAPTER 4

THE DEVELOPMENT OF CAREER BEHAVIOR AND CHOICE

Key Concepts

- Career development approaches encompass perspectives from multiple disciplines that provide windows into both the structure of and the longitudinal changes in career behavior.
- The influences upon and outcomes of career development are one aspect of socialization as part of a broader process of human development.
- For purposes of classification, theoretical and research approaches to career development can be divided in many ways. In this chapter, five major emphases will be described: trait-and-factor, actuarial, or matching approaches; decision theory; situational, sociological, or contextual approaches; psychological approaches; and developmental approaches.
- A major emphasis within most career development theories is the creation of choice-making paradigms; ways to understand the interdependence of decisions, risk-taking behavior, time perspectives, and the interaction of personal self-referents and choice strategies.
- Theories and research describing career behavior provide the conceptual glue for as well as describe where, when, and for what purpose career counseling, career education, and career guidance should be implemented.

The conceptual perspectives reviewed in this chapter deal with several interacting emphases: (1) the flow of understandings, experiences, commitments, values, and skills by which one forges the many facets of personal identity—self, educational, occupational, and career; (2) the process of decision making as the way one expresses personal identity in a choice; and (3) the functional relationships between time, social structures, and personal attributes. This does not imply that we will review all possible conceptual perspectives here. That is not possible within the limited space available in this chapter. Rather the intent here is to highlight major conceptual approaches or families of approaches that attempt to explain the acquisition of work-related behavior, the anticipation of career options, and adjustments to the settings in which that behavior will be implemented.

As studies pertinent to career development have ensued, the concepts involved have tended to broaden and become more interdisciplinary.

Super (1990) has contended that

> The pioneers of career development are people from four disciplines. They are differential psychologists interested in work and occupations, developmental psychologists concerned with "the life course," sociologists focusing on occupational mobility as a function of social class, and personality theorists who view individuals as organizers of experience. (p. 197)

To these representatives of core disciplines in career development, one can also add the growing perspectives of political scientists, economists, and organizational development theorists as people concerned about the development and allocation of human resources in national and global economies and the interactive effects of persons and environments as new forms of work organizations emerge in service- and information-based economies.

As a function of the diversity of disciplinary lenses applied to career behavior, some research is more pertinent to occupational choice at a specific point in time or to adjustment within a work setting than to career development across time. Some research is concerned with the structure of choice, work behavior, or "career maturity" within a particular life stage, whereas other research is concerned with how such structures change over time, the role of chance in career choice, and the continuities and discontinuities in career patterns throughout life. Increasingly, research and speculation in career development have shifted from almost a total concentration on adolescence and young adulthood to greater attention to career behavior in middle and late adulthood. As a result, it can be argued that career development theory and life-span developmental psychology are growing more congruent in their perspectives and methodology, if not deliberately, then certainly inadvertently.

Life-span developmental psychology is an empirical, multidisciplinary science that is concerned with the description and explication of ontogenetic (age-related) influences, normative history-graded (evolutional) influences, and nonnormative life events as they influence behavioral change from birth to death (Goulet & Baltes, 1970), as well as with the relationship between intervention and life-span development (Danish, 1981; Fuchs, 1978; Vondracek, Lerner, & Schulenberg, 1986). In their idealized sense, both life-span psychology and career development, as a special instance of life-span psychology, are more than the additive result of different age-related studies with different groups of subjects in different educational or work settings. The intent in both cases is more holistic and longitudinal in understanding the influences on and the life histories of persons as they engage in the various roles available to them across time. In fact, the available career development theory and research do not meet the idealized criteria just suggested but derive, for the most part, from less systematic, segmental theories and more disparate sources.

Career development theory is, as yet, relatively fragmented and incomplete, particularly when addressing women and the socially and economically disadvantaged members of society. Osipow (1983), for example, has observed that

> few special explanations or concepts have been devised to deal with the special problems of the career development of women . . . most of the masculine-based tests and theories fail to really provide a useful vehicle for the understanding of the career development of women. (p. 187)

While true, it is also useful to observe, as does Fitzgerald and Crites (1980), that

> existing theories of career choice, although developed on men, have much to offer . . . unless [one] assumes that males and females are somehow fundamentally different in their needs and aspirations. It seems reasonable to assume that all individuals, regardless of sex, share the basic human need for self-fulfillment through meaningful work. (p. 46)

Despite the large amount of research now attempting to identify factors related to how male and female career behaviors differ, the unique influences on each, and, particularly the effects of stereotyping, organizational discrimination, and socialization on gender differences in psychological development (Gilligan, 1982), it is fair to contend that what is known about women's career development has not resulted in a "relevant theoretical conceptualization . . . which is capable of integrating existing knowledge and guiding future research and intervention" (Hackett, 1985, p. 48).

The perspective of this book, however, is that, with due respect for the voids in necessary knowledge about women, minorities, and other groups in the society whose career behavior has been particularly affected by the magnitude of social change in the last quarter century, what is currently known provides a basis for programmatic efforts to spur the development of effective career behavior. If one views the confluence of approaches, theory, and research with objectivity and boldness, one finds tentative sets of constructs and propositions to explain differential career behavior and decision making, as well as to provide guidelines for aiding such processes.

Speaking to several of the theories discussed in this chapter, Bell, Super, and Dunn (1988) suggest that when taken together they can form "a composite picture for career and personality theory and practice, yielding a dynamic and diagnostic anagram to both widen and deepen our understanding of personal adjustment and career development. When these perspectives are integrated, they embrace both personal and career counseling" (p. 3). These observers further suggest how these theories contribute to the career counselor's pool of diagnostic and conceptual insights. For example,

> the psychodynamic approaches of Bordin and Roe focus on *why* clients behave as they do, Roe going beyond Bordin in dealing with later interpersonal as well as intrapsychic forces. . . . Both Super and Ginzberg supply a time perspective, looking ahead and asking *when* important decision points are likely to occur. . . . Occupational information gathered according to Holland's hexagon or Roe's occupational descriptions can be used to acquaint clients with occupational options that fit their career goals and show them *how* to discover more satisfying work environments. (pp. 3–4)

Although this is not the whole of the chapter's content, the observations of Bell, Super, and Dunn indicate both the rationale for and the integrative nature of the theoretical perspectives about career behavior explored in this chapter as the conceptual frame of reference to which interventions can be addressed.

CAREER DEVELOPMENT AND VOCATIONALIZATION

M. Katz (1973, p. 89) has stated that "the content of vocational guidance is defined as the opportunities for choice that society permits among educational and occupational options." Placing that idea in a broader view suggests that the content of career guidance includes not only choices among educational and occupational options but also those of life style—the degree to which work will be a central way of fulfillment for a particular individual and the ways the person will cope with the possibility of free and informed choice in pursuing personal direction and planning.

An overriding goal in career guidance is the facilitation of free and informed choice in the individual. The assumption is that choice cannot be free unless it is informed. A further assumption is that the types of information available to an individual depend on how free the person is to consider different options or life styles. The latter, of course, can be diminished or strengthened by political conditions, historical events, family circumstances, the rigidity of social class constraints on mobility, and many other phenomena. Given that reality, however, in order for one to choose freely, one needs knowledge, not only about what is available from which to choose but also about the personal characteristics that might be emphasized in evaluating and acting on available choices. This latter goal requires, in addition to knowledge, clarification of personal values, interests, and attitudes as these relate to self-characteristics; environmental alternatives (occupational, educational, personal, and social options); and the decision-making process itself.

Career development, as the term will be used in this chapter, refers to the body of speculation and research that focuses on understanding the factors underlying free and informed choice, the evolution of personal identity in regard to work, and the transition, induction, and adjustment to work. Borow (1961) has summarized the matter well in his statement that theories and research that examine career development are in reality "a search for the psychological meaning of vocationally relevant acts (including the exploratory vocational behavior of youth) and of work itself in the human experience." More recently, Super (1980, p. 283) has stated that "careers have been viewed variously as a sequence of positions occupied by a person during the course of a lifetime" (Super, 1957), as a decision tree portraying the decision points encountered by a person going through school and into the world of work (Flanagan & Cooley, 1966), and as a series of life stages in which differing constellations of developmental tasks are encountered and dealt with (Buehler, 1933; Super, 1957).

The latter view has been significantly advanced by Vondracek, et al. (1986), who contend that vocational and career development is a life-span phenomenon, properly studied from a multidisciplinary viewpoint in which a contextual perspective to understanding career behavior is essential as is a *dynamic interactional* view that emphasizes that the individual and the context change interdependently over time. Osipow (1983) has summarized many of the emerging attempts to integrate a wide range of perspectives in his discussion of a "systems view of career behavior." He states that such a view

> explicitly recognizes that various situational and individual factors operate to influence career behavior in a broad way. With a highly sophisticated systems approach to career development questions about the role of the biological, social, and situational factors in occupational behavior would become more explicit and . . . understandings of the interactions between these views would be more likely to emerge. (p. 314)

Osipow's notion of a systems view of career behavior is important not only because it acknowledges that such behavior is interactive and complex but also because it is congruent with a systems view of career guidance and counseling that is responsible to the complexities found in career behavior. Thus, the position taken by Osipow and the position of this book and its previous editions is that a systems approach that recognizes the multidimensional influences on and character of career behavior needs to be responded to by an intervention system that reflects the multidimensional ways that can alter such behavior. The intent of such analyses are to help counselors both with problem identification and with intervention design (Jepsen, 1984b, p. 136).

While career development is a part of and interactive with the broader range of human development, it also emphasizes one aspect of socialization, what Crites has called "vocationalization" (1969, p. 88) and Borow has called "occupational socialization" (1984, p. 161).

In Borow's terms, "Socialization then, is the intricate birth-to-death process by which one acquires one's view of the human world and its institutions, one's beliefs, loyalties, convictions of right and wrong, and habitual response modes. The learning is both formal and informal, deliberate and incidental, conscious and unconscious" (p. 161). "The socialization process, then, speaks to the articulation of the motivational system of the personality with the structure of the social system" (T. Parsons, 1951, p. 32). As E. Gross has observed (1975), "although traditional studies of socialization have focused on infancy and childhood, recent research has turned to adult socialization. Such research suggests that socialization is far from complete in childhood; it goes on throughout persons' lives" (p. 141). The importance of Gross' observations has been amplified in the virtual explosion of perspectives on adult career development that have become available in the recent past.

The processes of vocationalization or occupational socialization, as a part of career development, as it is described throughout this book, speaks to the various factors—psychological, sociological, cultural, economic—which, across time, result in self-career identity, decision-making ability, and career maturity. Such socialization processes, as we see it, have to do with those processes and factors that aid or impede one's acquisition of the values, knowledge, and skills leading to effective career behavior.

Most importantly, however, our contention is that the individual processes of occupational socialization or vocationalization, as described by career development concepts, can be understood, anticipated, and influenced by systematic programs of career counseling, career guidance, or career education. Career development concepts, then, are not descriptions of the inevitable; rather, they describe the possible and sometimes the probable behavioral results, if no intervention occurs to help the individual cope consciously with such possible or probable outcomes as they relate to his or her goals.

APPROACHES TO CAREER DEVELOPMENT AND CHOICE

Career development is concerned with broader phenomena than those represented by the term *occupations*; it is synonymous with the earlier term *vocational development*. The emphasis in the psychological or sociological study of careers (career development in this context) is on the continuities and discontinuities in the lives of groups (Super, 1954). The psychology and sociology of occupations, on the other hand, stress characteristics of single or categorized occupations (Super, 1969b).

The occupational model is primarily concerned with prediction from one point in time to another. "It takes prediction data at an early stage of the career and uses regression methods to predict success to one occupation, or uses discriminant analyses as a means of assessing the likelihood of being found, later, in each of several possible occupations." On the other hand, the career model "is one in which the individual is conceived of moving along one of a number of possible pathways through the educational system and on into and through the work system" (Super, 1969a, p. 3). Both of these models are important for different reasons. To make an arbitrary distinction, the occupational model, which stresses matching or actuarial relationships of person and job, is central in career counseling applied to an immediate job or occupational choice; the career model undergirds career guidance or counseling as a stimulus to intermediate and long-range career planning. Put another way, the major unit of concern in an occupational model is the differences in work content across occupations and their relationship to individual aptitudes and interests. The major unit of concern in a career model is the clarity and accuracy of the self-concept as the evaluative base by which to judge available options.

The approaches describing career development or some aspect of it have been classified in several ways. Hilton (1962) originally labeled them as models of attribute matching, need reduction, economic man, social man, and complex information processing. Osipow (1968, pp. 10–11) classified such approaches as trait-factor approaches, sociology and career choice, self-concept theory, and vocational choice and personality theories. Crites (1969) discusses them as nonpsychological theories (such as accident, economic, cultural, and sociological) and the psychological theories (such as trait-and-factor, psychodynamic, developmental and decision). Pitz and Harren (1980) have described those theories dealing specifically with career decision-making as normative (or prescriptive) and behavioral (or descriptive). In the former case, the theorist focuses on procedures for making optimal decisions, decisions that best meet some criterion. In the latter, the theorist is concerned with describing the decision-making process itself. Holland and Gottfredson (1976) have described the two main traditions for understanding careers as the developmental view and the differential view. Jepsen (1984a) has divided career theories into those that are structural or developmental.

Young (1988) has attempted to divide career theories into those that describe behavior as either empowering or enabling. Empowering behavior is seen in this perspective as deterministic and predictable. Enabling behavior is seen as more flexible; it is that which takes advantage of contextual events, such as those due to happenstance or chance, and uses them for purposes of self-development. Holland's theory (1985) of personality typologies and personality-environment matching is an example of an empowering theory. Krumboltz, Mitchell, and Jones (1976), whose research emphasizes influences on change and development, is an example of enabling theory.

Other observers classify career development perspectives with somewhat different systems. Super (1981) has contended, "The approaches and theories of the past 75 years fall into three main categories: those that match people and occupations, those that describe development leading to matching, and those that focus on decision making" (p. 8). As shown in Table 4.1, several types of approaches are included under each of the three main categories.

These attempts at classification highlight the factors, emphases, or disciplinary bases that distinguish one theory or research effort from another. In general, the categories depicted are not mutually exclusive or independent, but they attempt to explain differential career behavior and choice from somewhat varied vantage points.

Indeed, Osipow (1990) has suggested that the major theories of career development are converging as data about career behavior accumulates and the theories are continuously revised. He indicates that his analysis of the four major theories suggests that each includes common themes: biological factors, parental influences, outcomes, personality, methods,

Table 4.1

Types of Approaches to Occupational Choice and Career Development

Matching	Developmental	Decision-Making
Differential Aptitudes Personality	Life-stage and identification	Process
Situational Structure Context Socialization	Life-span, life-space and personal constructs	Style
Phenomenological Self-concept Congruence	Stage and determinants Path models Regression models	Process-style-situation

(From *Career Development in Britain,* edited by A.G. Watts, Donald E. Super, and Jennifer M. Kidd. Copyright ©1981 by A.G. Watts, D.E. Super, J.M. Kidd. Reprinted by permission of Hobsons Publishing plc.)

and life-stage influences. Although such common themes do exist, it is also true that different theoretical approaches address these themes with different emphases and make each of them more or less central to a particular theory's perspective. Osipow's analysis of major theories include those of Holland, Super, Mitchell and Krumboltz, and Lofquist and Dawis. Although each of these theoretical approaches is treated in this chapter and in other places in the book, we believe that there is a broader array of concepts in the literature of career development, choice, and adjustment than is captured by these four emphases. Nevertheless, Osipow's fundamental premise seems correct that some convergence in theoretical perspectives is evident and that, "should we find that sufficient similarity exists, we may discover that we are further along toward the creation of a unified theory of career development than we have thought. If so, we might profitably devote our efforts toward the identification of each theory's special utility and the population its concepts best describe and serve" (p. 123). We think that such observations are valid and predict increasing future emphases in research and conceptualization. However, for the early professional in the field of career development, we believe that it is still useful to look separately at theoretical efforts to understand their basic and unique premises.

For our purposes in this chapter, career development approaches and their proponents will be considered in the following sequence: trait and factor, actuarial, or matching; decision; situational or sociological; psychological; and developmental. Where possible, the disciplinary antecedents or roots of each approach will be identified.

TRAIT-AND-FACTOR, ACTUARIAL, OR MATCHING APPROACHES

Trait-and-factor or matching approaches, coupled with actuarial methods, constitute a venerable theme in career guidance. Rooted in the psychology of individual differences, applied psychology, and differential psychology, these approaches conceive of the person as an organization of capacities and other properties that can be measured and related to the requirements of training programs or occupations. Based on empirically derived information on differences among people occupying various occupations or correlates of choice or satisfaction, trait-and-factor approaches are more descriptive of influences on choice than they are explanatory of career development.

In the trait-and-factor approach, the individual is conceived as possessing a pattern of traits—such as interests, aptitudes, achievements, personality characteristics—that can be identified through objective means, usually psychological tests or inventories, and then profiled to represent the individual's potential. Trait-and-factor approaches consider occupations similarly, that is, as susceptible for profile according to the "amounts" of individual traits they require. When one profile is overlaid on the other, the probable degree of fit between person and job can be identified.

Such an approach represents the essence of the *occupational model* previously identified in this chapter and in Chapter 1. As Super (1969b) has noted, vocational psychology, from its beginnings until shortly after 1950, was essentially a psychology of occupations. The occupation was the subject, and the persons in it were the sources of data on the occupation. Thus, from an actuarial standpoint, predictions can be made using individual traits as predictors and the degree to which these traits are possessed by successful persons in different occupations as the criteria. Further, the techniques and results of the numerous studies combining different traits and different occupational requirements also provide a means of appraising an individual's possibilities.

C. H. Miller (1974) has suggested that the assumptions underlying the trait-and-factor approach include:

1. Vocational development is largely a cognitive process; decisions are to be reached by reasoning.
2. Occupational choice is a single event. In the spirit of Parsons, choice is stressed greatly and development very little.
3. There is a single "right" goal for everyone in the choice of vocation. There is little or no recognition that a worker might fit well into a number of occupations.
4. A single type of person works in each job. This is the other side of the coin of the third assumption. Taken together, these two notions amount to a one-person, one-job relationship—a concept congenial to the trait-factor approach.
5. There is an occupational choice available to each individual. (p. 238)

D. Brown (1984), paraphrasing a review of trait and factor theory by Klein and Wiener (1977), suggested that current thinking includes these premises:

1. Each individual has a unique set of traits that can be measured reliably and validly.
2. Occupations require that workers possess certain traits for success, although a worker with a rather wide range of characteristics can be successful in a given job.
3. The choice of an occupation is a rather straightforward process, and matching is possible.
4. The closer the match between personal characteristics and job requirements, the greater the likelihood for success (productivity and satisfaction). (Brown, 1984, p. 12)

Historically, trait-and-factor studies have provided the technical foundation for elaborating the three-step process of vocational guidance as laid down by F. Parsons (1909) and described in Chapter 1. As psychological instruments have been developed to assess individual traits, and as knowledge has been accumulated about differences in occupational and educational requirements including aptitudes, interests, and personality factors, career guidance processes, under the influence of trait-and-factor approaches, have become an increasingly scientific aid to choice. This approach stands in contrast to pre-Parsonian assumptions that subjective descriptions of occupational or training requirements are a sufficient basis for choice.

The assumptions on which trait-and-factor approaches rest, while contributing historically to the current practice of career guidance, can lead to a narrow perspective on career development. Trait-and-factor approaches have been primarily oriented to specific occupations or tasks as the criteria toward which predictor variables such as aptitudes, mental ability, socioeconomic characteristics, interests, values, personality manifestations, and other variables are directed. However, career development is not concerned solely with the choice of an occupation; it is also concerned with the process by which such choices can be purposefully integrated within a patterning of decisions, thereby maximizing freedom of choice and implementing the personal meaning of the way one conceives his or her traits.

The trait-and-factor problem today is not simply the task of relating a predictor, such as a test score, to some final occupation, but the consideration of patterns of attributes and their relationship to the sequence of decisions young persons must make in establishing themselves in the world of work. As these procedures are used, they diminish a major weakness of trait-and-factor approaches—the view of individual traits and environmental requirements as relatively static rather than dynamic.

Clearly, if used with insight into the predictive limitations of trait-and-factor procedures, such information can be valuable in providing a person with a sense of the "odds" one faces in pursuing specific choices or the incremental differences that exist between where one is now and where one hopes to be in terms of various educational or occupational options.

A persistent finding limiting the overall usefulness of trait-and-factor, or actuarial, approaches has been that the typical measures used predict training success more effectively than job success. For example, on the basis of various traits, one can reasonably predict with accuracy whether an individual will successfully complete a carpenter's apprenticeship or some type of formal education (such as medical school). Those trait patterns are less likely to predict whether the person will be a successful carpenter or physician after completion of training.

Even though there are limitations on predictions from traits, D. Brown (1984) has asserted that "Generally, trait measures have been positively related to job success and job satisfaction. When our best available (not our average) validity coefficients are considered, these measures have not only been positive but relatively strong" (p. 14).

Brown's enthusiasm for trait-oriented thinking and results is not shared by all observers. Some observers believe that trait and factor ideas have been absorbed into other theoretical approaches (Osipow, 1983), that the rigidity of trait-oriented notions of matching individuals and occupations has led to a decline in the adherents of trait-oriented thinking (Weinrach, 1979), or that practitioners are not current with trait techniques and the procedure is in incipient decline (Crites, 1981).

Regardless of which of these positions one takes, the fact remains that even though the trait-and-factor approach has much to commend it—statistical sophistication, testing refinement, and technological application—the resulting predictions of individuals' success in specific occupations have been less precise than one would like. D. Brown (1984) has acknowledged this situation when he states, "As the situation stands, trait measures do not account for any more than 36 percent of the variance associated with various criteria and usually the portion is less" (p. 14).

The point is that aptitudes and other predictors of occupational success are important, but so are other manifestations of personality, such as values, energy levels, perseverance, person-situation fit, and so on. The latter are likely to explain the variance not predicted by trait measures.

If one were to subscribe to the trait-and-factor approach as the sole description of career development and decision making, one would have to assume that people have a much greater degree of self-insight than most seem to have—self-insight not simply of the measurable aspects of the self but of the self as a wholly functioning organism, and the relationships between self and the personally important components of the options among which one can choose. In addition, if one considers the counselor as the major source of information about self-characteristics and occupational factors, one must face the possibility that the counselee is accepting such information on the basis of faith in an authority figure. Consequently, choices made are not affirmations of identity developed from insights into self-characteristics and a personal view of the world. Rather, they are made because it is expedient to assume that the person will find success in an occupation on the basis of statistical findings indicating that he or she fits into certain occupational populations.

As indicated previously, trait-and-factor approaches maintain that choice is primarily conscious and cognitive. Such a premise seems more hopeful than valid as succeeding approaches to career development in this chapter will demonstrate. Choice occurs not only as a function of relating an individual's traits to the characteristics of alternatives, but also as a function of complex interaction between the person's developmental history and environment. In fact, the richness or impoverishment of the reservoir of experience, the accuracy and relevance of the information possessed, the distortion in appraisal of self-characteristics or possibilities of reaching aspirations, the scope and nature of the self-concept system, as well as many other combinations of factors, also enter into choice, frequently making it more psychological than logical.

With due respect to the important research that has given substance to trait-and-factor approaches, it is useful to highlight some of the major predictor variables of importance to this approach. Because of space limitations, no attempt will be made here to discuss the voluminous literature pertaining to each of the prediction-criterion interactions that a full treatment of this topic deserves.

The Primary Predictors Used in Trait-and-Factor Approaches

The decades of research studies exploring individual traits and their significance in different settings and in various forms of career-related behavior has yielded a large number of significant variables. Each of the following has shown a significant relationship either to educational achievement, to success in particular types of training, to choice of particular occupations or curricula, to realistic decision making, or to job satisfaction: abilities (scholastic achievement, spatial relations, abstract reasoning, clerical speed and accuracy, eye-hand coordination, fine or gross manual dexterity); needs and interests; stereotypes and expectations; work values; influences of significant others; size of community in which one is reared; childrearing patterns; socioeconomic background; general psychological adjustment; risk-taking; levels of aspirations; level and type of occupational information possessed; career maturity (vocational choice attitudes and competencies); sex differences; racial differences; personality characteristics (acceptance of responsibility, honesty, and so forth); curriculum pursued in school.

The large number of these variables suggests the validity of a rather simple point: given sufficient ability to perform a particular work activity, the choice of, satisfaction with, or advancement in that work activity is dependent upon a complex range of psychological, personality, and possibility factors. Within such perspectives there are variables or combinations of variables that set ceilings on likely choices or performances and other variables that mediate the satisfactoriness of possible choices or whether specific options are acceptable or desirable. Among the most important of these are aptitudes and abilities, needs and interests, values, stereotypes and expectations, adjustment, risk-taking, and aspirations.

Aptitudes. A person's intelligence and other aptitudes play a significant part in the occupational level he or she is likely to attain, the training the person is likely to be admitted to or succeed in, and the work he or she is able to perform. Intelligence and aptitudes do not relate in the same fashion to each of these possibilities. Intelligence and/or specific aptitudes typically correlate more highly with success in training than with success in work performance—principally because the latter is based on a wider range of expectations and criteria than the former. There are differences between learning to do something and applying one's knowledge in a work setting in which one's work skills must be integrated with those of others, performed under rigid deadlines, or conditioned by other dimensions eliciting personality traits.

Research studies also tend to support the relationship between ability and the levels attained within career fields. Thus, while personality, values, or interests may lead to the selection of a particular job family or occupation, ability influences the particular career role attained within that field.

In one of the most comprehensive of recent studies on aptitudes and jobs, Gottfredson (1986) has studied the occupational aptitude patterns used by the U.S. Department of Labor and their implications for a theory of job aptitude requirements. In constructing an Occupational Aptitude Profile (OAP) Map, comparing it to other skill-based and aptitude-based classifications as well as to the Holland (1985) typology of work environments, and with ratings for complexity of involvement with data, people, and things, Gottfredson concluded the following: (1) general intelligence is the major gradient by which aptitude demands have become organized across jobs in the United States economy; (2) within broad levels of work, the aptitude demands of different fields of work differ primarily in the shape of their cognitive profiles; and (3) different aptitude demand patterns arise in large part from broad differences in the tasks workers actually perform on the job. Gottfredson elaborated her first conclusion by further stating that "differences in the general intelligence demands among jobs not only constitute the single most important aptitude distinction among jobs, but also influence or constrain all other aptitude demands in some way. . . . Intelligence is more useful than any other aptitude factor, whether group or general, for predicting job performance across the full spectrum of jobs and job families." She also goes on to conclude that the higher the job level, the more important intelligence is; the lower the job level, the more useful motor aptitudes are, relative to cognitive ones, in predicting job performance.

Gottfredson's (1986) research conclusions are essentially validated in other research. For example, Baeher and Orban (1989) have indicated that research demonstrates that general cognitive ability is important at all levels of the occupational structure. In addition, higher-level positions require higher levels of general cognitive ability. However, this research also suggests that, although cognitive ability is of importance in all the higher level occupations, predictive validity in these occupations would be increased by adding a personality measure. The best prediction is increased by a combination of these measures. In addition, both sets of predictors are differentially important for different occupational specialties and levels of organizational functioning. At the lower level of occupational complexity, although general cognitive ability continues to be important, general psychomotor ability becomes important, and such measures add substantially to the prediction of performance in less complex jobs. Thus, regardless of which general cognitive ability is the most significant single predictor of job training success or job performance, the point is that in less complex jobs, cognitive ability has an important analog in psychomotor ability, and in highly complex jobs, general cognitive ability has an analog in personality measures such as drive, self-reliance, and potential for creative and innovative behavior. In stressful jobs such as police work, the additional predictor of major consequence beyond general cognitive ability is likely to be measures of emotional health, and in some technical jobs, measures of spatial relations ability.

Needs and Interests. Needs and interests typically have been found to be closely related. The relationship between needs, occupational interests, and personality identifications has been demonstrated in the extensive research related to Holland's theory, described later. It also has been found that inner-directed and other-directed personalities differ in their occupational interests, as do persons who are decided and undecided.

The relative importance of interests to vocational decisions has been studied by Bordin, Nachmann, and Segal (1963). Certain occupations evidently satisfy specific needs, and these needs are related to interests (Kohlan, 1968). In response to these relationships, there has been a significant merger between the work of Strong and that of Holland, perhaps most clearly seen in the format and scoring of the Strong Interest Inventory. Although the rationale and empirical base of each differs, they do identify differences in occupations similarly in regard to the interests held by people who occupy them (Campbell & Holland, 1972). With respect to career maturity, Wigington (1982) has demonstrated that high scores on the Kuder Occupational Interest Scales are significantly correlated with scores on the Career Maturity Inventory.

Melamed and Meir (1981) have also demonstrated relationships between interests, job congruity, and selection of avocational activity. Using employed persons from 21 to 65 years of age in Australia and in Israel they found (1) people tend to select leisure activities congruent with their personality patterns; (2) people in congruent occupations (as measured by personality pattern and occupational code) were vocationally satisfied and conceived their preferred activities as an extension of the type of activities they do at work; and (3) people in incongruent occupations are vocationally dissatisfied and compensate for this by selecting compensatory leisure activities, and they tend to show higher salience (importance) for their avocational activities than for their work activities.

Values. There is considerable evidence that what an individual values both in work itself and in the rewards that work is perceived as offering affects vocational decisions and is internalized fairly early in development. Values, however, cannot be viewed in isolation. The values a person holds are the products of upbringing, environment, cultural tradition, education, and a host of other variables.

Available data are clear that occupational groups can be differentiated by discriminant analysis in terms of the values and personalities of their membership. Some research also suggests that the patterning of work values is positively related to the vocational maturity of persons and to academic success (Knapp & Michael, 1980). Thus, vocational maturation for both males and females involves the development of differentiated work values (C. H. Miller, 1974). Jurgensen (1978), over a 30-year period, ranked the importance of 10 factors that make a job good or bad as perceived by some 57,000 applicants for jobs in a public utility. He found the order for men to be security, advancement, type of work, company, pay, co-workers, supervisors, benefits, hours, and working conditions. Women considered type of work more important than any other factor, followed by company, security, co-workers, advancement, supervisor, pay, working conditions, hours, and benefits. The interesting finding was that changes in these rankings over thirty years were almost inconsequential. Other research suggests that work values are independent of job knowledge. Therefore, it cannot be assumed that being clear about one's work values also means having enough job knowledge to make realistic choices. It would seem then that work values and job knowledge need to be addressed separately in the career counseling process (Sampson & Loesch, 1981).

Stereotypes and Expectations. Expectations and stereotypes also appear to influence vocational decision making. Information that people have regarding occupations is often indirect and stereotypic. Such stereotypes have been found to develop by the beginning of elementary school or earlier (Rosenthal & Chapman, 1980; White & Brinkerhoff, 1981) and are frequently sex-linked (Garland & Smith, 1981). As they go about making a vocational choice, persons may search for environments that they perceive will meet their needs and expectations (Holland, 1963), and it seems likely that stereotypes of occupations are held by such searchers and that these are part of a foundation for vocational choice (Hollander & Parker, 1969, 1972). Research shows that persons have well-developed stereotypes about the personalities and persons in different occupations particularly as these relate to achievement orientation vs. helping orientation (Levy, Kaler, & Schall, 1988).

It is also likely that vocational decisions are affected by the prestige or status people assign to various occupations. Typically, high school students express preference for high-status or prestige occupations, even though they cannot realistically expect to enter these occupations (Clack, 1968). Students eventually realize that abilities, interest, and skills directly affect access to and success in occupational and educational options and must be considered in choice-making.

Adjustment. General psychological adjustment also affects vocational choice. The career development pattern of emotionally disturbed students is not so smooth as that of well-adjusted students (Osipow & Gold, 1967). For example, Schaffer (1976) studied the work histories of male psychiatric patients. The results indicate that the more severe the maladjustment, the less likely the men were to have been employed above the semiskilled level, and that there was a direct relationship between severity of disorder and unemployment time. In addition, job satisfaction and success were found to vary as a function of the personality characteristics of the different diagnostic groups. Heath's research (1976) has shown that psychological maturity, whether measured in adolescence or adulthood, consistently predicts vocational adaptation.

Risk-Taking. Another personality variable that seems to be related to vocational choice is risk-taking. Early work by Ziller (1957) found that there was a significant relationship between vocational choice and a propensity for risk-taking. Subsequent studies (Burnstein, 1963; Mahone, 1960; and Morris, 1966) also found evidence that risk-taking plays a part in vocational decision making. However, a large-scale study by Slakter and Cramer (1969) has demonstrated that although there is some evidence that risk-taking is related to vocational choice, the current measures of risk-taking are too crude to capitalize on this relationship. Witmer and Stewart (1972) have reported findings showing that a preference for taking risks reflects a general life-style. Thus, the high-risk person's openness to new experiences and that person's rejection of tradition may indicate self-confidence in dealing adequately with life contingencies.

Aspirations. Level of aspiration appears to contribute to vocational choice. At least in males, level of aspiration seems relatively constant during secondary schooling (Flores & Olsen, 1967). Level of aspiration is also frequently related to level of self-esteem, with persons of higher aspiration also persons of higher self-esteem (Prager & Freeman, 1979). Level of aspiration usually affects curriculum choice and hence vocational choice. These findings about aspiration have been extended in a national sample of young men and women between the ages of 14 and 24, showing that the category of a person's earlier job (using Holland's classification) forecasts the category of later jobs, and that there is significant agreement between a person's current occupation and vocational aspiration (Nafziger, Holland, Helms, & McPartland, 1974). It also has been found that aspirations, expectations, and vocational maturity are related in graduate students and rehabilitation clients. Thus, whether one's expectations are similar to one's aspirations appears to depend on past success-failure experiences, education, and consequent vocational maturity (Walls & Gulkus, 1974). When vocational aspirations and job opportunities as determinants of later jobs held are studied, it is found that men more often achieve congruence between their aspirations and their field of employment by changing aspirations to match the job field rather than the other way around, and that early jobs are more predictive of later field of work than are early aspirations (Gottfredson & Becker, 1981).

Summary of Traits and Factors. Although the above analysis is not exhaustive, it is clear that a great many variables enter into career decision making: abilities, work values, occupational stereotypes and expectations, residence, family socioeconomic status and child-rearing practices, general adjustment, personality factors including needs and propensity for risk-taking, educational achievement, level of aspiration, and gender. Each of these is influenced by and overlaps with the others. They are in dynamic interrelationship. The preponderance of one or more variables in vocational decision making depends heavily on the individual making the choice. Some individuals are more influenced by certain factors than others. A major characteristic of trait-and-factor approaches is that they describe relationships between variables and choices, but they do not explain how such variables develop. We must turn elsewhere for such insights.

DECISION THEORY

Decisions are not simply benign, independent behaviors that persons emit impulsively. Rather, decisions are the conjunctions between self and environment. Decisions are the public testimonies people make about how they view themselves, how they view their opportunities and the relationships between them. Decisions are like tips of icebergs; they symbolize but do not describe all of the hidden meanings of a choice, the factors that shape it, or the hope or despair that attended the particular decision taken. As Alfred North Whitehead has reminded us, "People create their realities by the decisions they make." Until the act of choice occurs, possible choices remain potentialities. Once the choice is made, what was a possibility now becomes a reality, an entity that forever remains a part of one's life as a chemical trace or in some other form.

The importance of the decision process has made it a central construct in career guidance and career counseling as well as a major focus of inquiry in theory and research. Increasingly apparent in the professional literature are attempts to theorize about educational and occupational choice through the use of decision models. The major factor that differentiates these models from others reviewed in this chapter is their primary emphasis on the *process of decision making*. For purposes of this section, a variety of approaches with diverse conceptual roots are reviewed, such as cognitive, economic, mathematical, and social learning.

In historical terms, decision-making models are economic in origin. A fundamental assumption in many of these approaches, based on Keynesian economic theory, is that one chooses a career goal or an occupation that will maximize gain and minimize loss. The gain or loss is not necessarily money but can be anything of value to the individual. A given occupation or career pathway might be considered as a means of achieving certain possibilities—for example, greater prestige, security, social mobility, or a spouse—when compared to another course of action. Implicit in such an approach is the expectation that the individual can be assisted to predict the outcomes of each alternative and the probability of such outcomes. The assumption is that the person will then choose the one that promises the most reward for his or her investment (such as time, tuition, union dues, delayed gratification) with the least probability of failure.

A major notion in decision theory is that an individual has several alternatives or courses of action. In each of them, certain events can occur. Each event has a value for the individual, a value that can be estimated through some method of psychological scaling. Also, for each event a probability of its occurrence can be estimated through actuarial prediction. If, for each course of action, the value of each event is multiplied by its probability and these products are summed, the sound choice from this point of view would be the alternative in which the sum of the expected "values" is the greatest. Such a perspective has led to the use of decision trees, flow charts, and game trees to describe the decision-making process. The different paradigms explaining decision theory provide counselors with models, graphs, and concepts that help them to discuss the process of decision making directly with their clients. As such, the paradigms provide cognitive maps of the decision-making process itself as well as how different variables or behaviors affect the process.

Expectancy Theory

Decision theory is frequently expressed in mathematical terms as an expectancy × value theory of motivation (Raynor & Entin, 1982) or as expectancy/valence theory (Vroom, 1964; Lawler, 1973). For more than fifty years, many investigators have used the concepts embedded in these approaches to understand relationships among variables in a dynamic state as they affect individual behavior or as they have attempted to understand the relationship among inputs to choice or work motivation more generally. In a cognitive theory of motivation, individuals are viewed as rational persons who have beliefs and anticipations about future events in their lives. Steers and Porter (1975) summarize the theory in the following way: "It argues that motivational force to perform—or effort—is a multiplicative function of the expectancies, or beliefs, that individuals have concerning future outcomes times the value they place on those outcomes." Vroom (1964) uses the term valence to refer to affective orientations, positive or negative, toward outcomes, but distinguishes these preferences (valences) from the actual satisfaction they offer (their value). In general, it is assumed that means acquire valence as a consequence of their expected relationship to ends. But, in this view, positive valence, particularly in the face of uncertain outcomes, is not sufficient to motivate choice or action. It must be combined with expectancy, the degree to which the individual believes that preferred outcomes can be attained (are probable). Finally, it is assumed that people choose from among alternative acts the one that has the strongest positive or weakest negative force (value) and the most likelihood of occurring.

Lawler (1973), in a similar approach to that of Vroom, also uses the terms *valence* and *expectancy* to explain individual action. He suggests that all of the theorists using such a framework maintain that the tendency to act in a certain way depends on the expectancy that the act will be followed by a given consequence (or outcome) and on the value or attractiveness of that consequence (or outcome) to the actor. Lawler (1973) continues this line of thinking by distinguishing two types of expectancies about which people are concerned; ($E \rightarrow P$) and ($P \rightarrow O$). The first, effort → performance, has to do with the person's estimate of the probability that he or she can accomplish the intended performance (such as perform the tasks required, meet a deadline) in the particular situation. The second, performance → outcomes, has to do with subjective probability estimates that if a particular performance is achieved it will lead to certain outcomes (a pay raise, promotion, or some other reward). In extending Vroom's position, Lawler argues that motivation or choice is a function of both the attractiveness of outcomes, the valence, and the two expectancies cited: that one can do what needs to be done and if one is able to do so, the probability that a desired outcome will result. An additionally useful characteristic of Lawler's view is his analysis of how people achieve perceptions of $E \rightarrow P$, their ability to perform. Among others, he cites communications from other people, learning, personality factors, self-esteem, and past experiences in similar situations as influencing one's perceptions about the ability to perform as required in a particular situation.

A recent extension of expectancy × valence notions has been used by Raynor and Entin (1982) as the basis for a general theory of personality, motivation, and action. The basic hypothesis of the theory is as follows:

> When doing well *now* is seen by the person as a necessary prerequisite for earning the opportunity to try for later success (termed a contingent path), individual differences in achievement-related motives (the motives to achieve success and to avoid failure, M_S and M_{AF}, respectively) are accentuated and become apparent in action, so that success-oriented individuals ($M_S > M_{AF}$) are more motivated to do well but failure-threatened individuals ($M_{AF} > M_S$) are more inhibited by the prospect of failure, as compared to when immediate activity has no such future implications (termed a noncontingent path). (p. 3)

Raynor and Entin integrate these concepts and others with theory concerning self-identity, self-image, self-evaluation, and self-esteem. In oversimplified form, they found that earning the opportunity to continue along a contingent path was important for self-evaluation because attainment of the future goal that was contingent on immediate success is anticipated to provide feelings of self-worth.

Wheeler and Mahoney (1981), in applying an expectancy model to occupational preference and occupational choice, reinforce the fact that economic and psychological models have not tended to distinguish between occupational preference (occupations to which people are attracted), and occupational choice (the occupations persons actually choose to enter). The former is a function of valence as it was discussed in the previous section; the latter is a function of the attraction to an occupation, the expectancy of entering an occupation, and the costs of preparing for an occupation. Applying such a model to the preferences and choices of 98 business and 30 psychology students, they found strong support for the distinction between the two concepts. Occupational preference was a function of pure attraction. Choice involved a compromise among attraction, expectancy of attaining an occupation, and expected costs. They also found that this process is likely to differ for various groups since different groups are more strongly influenced by economic cost-benefit analysis and other groups are primarily influenced by the attractiveness of the occupation regardless of how much it costs to attain that occupation.

Brooks and Betz (1990) applied Vroom's model of expectancy and valence to predicting occupational choices in college students. Their results, as a sophisticated test of Vroom's concepts, were important. For example, they found that the expectancy × valence interaction for an occupation accounted for from 12 percent to 41 percent of the variance in tendency to choose that occupation, and that expectancy alone was essentially as good a predictor as was the product of expectancy × valence. Gender differences in occupations chosen were marked and consistent with the traditionality or dominations of occupations by gender. These gender differences were reflected in and consistent across expectancy, valence, and likelihood of choosing an occupation. Finally, it was found that the concept and measurement of expectancy is very similar to that of career related self-efficacy expectations as earlier reported by Betz and Hackett (1981) in their adaptation of Bandura's model.

Self-Efficacy Theory

Bandura (1977) has proposed a view of behavior change that he has called self-efficacy. Bandura contends that behavior change and therefore decisions made are mediated by expectations of self-efficacy: expectations of beliefs that one can perform a given behavior. The theory states that the level and strength of self-efficacy will determine (1) whether or not a coping behavior will be initiated, (2) how much effort will result, and (3) how long the effort will be sustained in the face of obstacles. This model proposes four principal sources from which expectations of self-efficacy are derived: performance accomplishments, vicarious experience, verbal persuasion, and emotional arousal. As does Lawler, previously cited in expectancy theory, Bandura also distinguishes between an outcome expectancy and an efficacy expectancy. An outcome expectancy refers to the person's estimate that a given behavior will lead to particular outcomes. An efficacy expectation is an estimate that one can successfully execute the behavior required to produce the outcomes sought. Efficacy expectations vary on such dimensions as magnitude, generality, and strength.

According to Bandura (1977) self-efficacy appears to be able to be increased and strengthened as a result of various types of treatments, but several general concepts are important to the understanding of the theory. First, people cognitively process information differently. Depending on how they judge the many factors bearing on their performance, they will vary in their perceptions of self-efficacy. Second, people have many different types and amounts of efficacy-relevant experiences. Providing one new source of efficacy information will not necessarily affect the overall level of self-efficacy. However, research data (Bandura, 1977; Bandura, Adams, & Meyer, 1977) suggest that with understanding of the concept of self-efficacy, the sources from which it is derived, and its potential effect on vocational behavior, intervention procedures can be devised to increase individual levels of self-efficacy.

Self-efficacy theory has become an important explanatory system relative to many different forms of behavior: social skills, stress reactions, phobias, coping behaviors, achievement, sports performance, and so on (Bandura, 1982). In several important studies, self-efficacy has been found to relate to mathematics performance, to career entry behaviors such as choice of college major and academic performance, and to gender differences pertinent to a variety of career behaviors (Betz & Hackett, 1981; Betz & Hackett, 1983; Betz & Hackett, 1986; Campbell & Hackett, 1986; Hackett, 1985; Hackett & Betz, 1981; Lent & Hackett, 1987). In general, these studies have found significant gender differences in self-efficacy relevant to perceived career options and in male and female mathematics performance. Because mathematics is so critical as a foundational skill or knowledge set for scientific and technical occupations, avoidance of such skills also likely eliminates women or men who have low self-efficacy in mathematics from such occupations. While these studies of self-efficacy suggest that such behavior is complex and that tests of the concept do not always yield the expected results, in general it is found that success experiences produce increases in self-efficacy, in task interest, and in ability ratings, but failure depresses these ratings. Although not all studies have shown gender differences in self-efficacy vis-á-vis career options or mathematics performance, where such is not observed there do tend to be differences in the strength and direction of self-efficacy for men and women in either failure or success groups, with women in failure groups typically rating themselves lower on evaluation of performance and on potential ability than men. On the other hand, women in success conditions are more likely to rate luck as a significant influence on their performance than men.

In direct and indirect ways, the concepts and the language of both expectancy theory and self-efficacy theory permeate many of the career guidance interventions designed to facilitate the decision-making process. The observant reader will note such relationships in many of the approaches that follow.

Decision-Making Paradigms

Many paradigms describing the decision-making process have evolved from earlier conceptions of problem solving or scientific analysis. Pitz and Harren (1980), for example, have indicated that any decision problem can be described in terms of four elements:

1. the set of *objectives* that the decision-maker seeks to achieve
2. the set of *choices*, or alternative courses of action, among which the decision-maker must choose
3. a set of possible *outcomes* that is associated with each choice
4. the ways each outcome might be assessed with respect to how well it meets the decision-maker's objectives, the *attributes* of each outcome (pp. 321–322)

In turn, a typical view of the sequence of events in decision making might include the following steps:

- defining the problem
- generating alternatives
- gathering information
- processing information
- making plans and selecting goals
- implementing and evaluating plans (Bergland, 1974)

Or, instead, as Krumboltz and Baker (1973) identified as Task Approach Skills important in career decision making, the following steps:

1. recognizing an important decision situation
2. defining the decision or task manageably and realistically
3. examining and accurately assessing self-observations and world-view generalizations
4. generalizing a wide variety of alternatives
5. gathering needed information about the alternatives
6. determining which information sources are most reliable, accurate, and relevant
7. planning and carrying out the above sequence of decision-making behaviors

Clarke, Gelatt, and Levine (1965) would suggest a somewhat different labeling of the decision-making paradigm that has implications for the information required by the person doing the choosing. In paraphrased form, the stages are as follows:

Information about Alternative Actions–Before deciding what to do, a person needs to know what alternative courses of action are possible.

Information about Possible Outcomes–The person needs to know to what results the alternative actions available are likely to lead.

Information about Probabilities Linking Actions to Outcomes–How likely are alternative actions to lead to different outcomes? What are the probabilities—high, medium, low—of certain results occurring from different actions?

Information about Preferences for the Various Outcomes–The person needs to consider the values he or she wishes to apply to different outcomes.

Together these emphases in decision making suggest that the individual needs both a prediction system and a value system to make decisions among preferences and expectancies for action within a climate of uncertainty. Gelatt (1962) proposed a decision-making framework in which information is the "fuel" of the decision-maker and actions taken may be terminal (final) or investigatory (that is, instrumental in both acquiring and requiring more information). Within this framework, Gelatt contended that there are essentially three elements of the decision-making process, each of which requires different information. Figure 4.1 summarizes this point.

In 1989, Gelatt amended his 1962 model to respond to new knowledge about the conditions under which decision making occurs. Gelatt has argued for Positive Uncertainty as the new decision-making framework for counseling. He suggests that, "the new view of the decision-making world does not mean destroying the old approach and erecting a new one. It means discovering new connections between the old view and new insight. . . . What is appropriate now is a decision and counseling framework that helps clients deal with change and ambiguity, accept uncertainty and inconsistency, and utilize the nonrational and intuitive side of thinking and choosing" (p. 252). In this view, Gelatt is not proposing a new decision strategy as much as he is accenting the decision-maker's legitimate use of nonobjectivity or subjectivity in the choices they make in the constant presence of uncertainty. Thus, in the information society with its ambiguity and paradoxes, Gelatt has suggested a new definition of decision making as "the process of arranging and rearranging information into a choice or actions" (p. 253).

Gelatt specifically contends that in his amended model, reflections, flexibility, and both rational and intuitive thinking must occur in a holistic way. "In his current view, the future does not exist and cannot be predicted. It must be imagined and invented. . . . Rational strategy is not obsolete, it is just no longer sufficient" (p. 255). Therefore, "helping someone decide how to decide must move from promoting only rational, linear, systematic strategies to recommending, even teaching, intuitive situations and sometimes inconsistent methods for solving personal problems or making decisions" (p. 253).

While Gelatt's new insights into "positive uncertainty" are useful in a world of increasing decision ambiguity and unpredictability, it is useful to return to his original concepts of risks in decision making. This perspective remains a useful one to the career counselor.

The Gelatt perspective emphasizes the need for accurate and complete information in each of the systems necessary to a choice of and values about a particular situation, and it implies that risks vary among outcomes of possi-

Figure 4.1

A Graphic Conception of the Gelatt Model

	Information Necessary
Predictive System	Alternative actions
	Possible outcomes of actions
	Probabilities of outcomes of actions
Value System	Relative preferences among probable outcomes
Decision System	Evaluation of priorities or rules

ble actions. In one sense, the better the information a decision-maker has, the clearer are the risks that the person takes in implementing different actions. The risks are not necessarily reduced, but it is assumed that knowing them provides the chooser a more rational basis for deciding what magnitude of risk is worth taking or whether the probabilities of a pay-off occurring for the risk involved are too low. Obviously, the degree of risk one is willing to take varies among persons and leads to different choice-making styles—some people are highly aggressive, others quite cautious, still others are in between these bipolar reference points. Jepsen (1974) has reported research showing that individual differences in decision making can be classified in terms of strategy types in adolescents. He clustered groups of adolescent decision-makers into twelve types based on how they organized data about themselves and career options. These clusters reflect differences in planning activity. Examples of three of the twelve types will illustrate Jepsen's view of individual differences in this area:

Strategy-type 3–Sought little career information and viewed current actions as relevant to planning. Considered only a few occupational alternatives and few reasons for considering either occupations or post-high school actions. Few outcomes were anticipated for preferred post-high school activity.

Strategy-type 6–Named many alternative occupations and post-high school activities and reasons for each. Many possible outcomes were anticipated, many intrinsic and self-appraised reasons were given. Planning activity was very high.

Strategy-type 9–Very few actions were taken on plans and little information was sought. Vaguely stated and low-level occupational alternatives were reported, and a single class of reasons was given for considering them.

Subsequent research by Jepsen and Prediger (1981) demonstrates that career decision styles are unique components of vocational behavior and development. Factor analytic studies by Phillips, Friedlander, Pazienza, and Kost (1985) lend support to that view.

Arroba (1977) has also studied styles of decision making and suggested several categories: for example, the compliant, no-thought, emotional, intuitive, logical, and hesitant. Arroba contends that any one individual may use a number of styles at different times and in different situations. Thus, a person may be logical in important new situations, compliant in unimportant familiar situations, and hesitant in important situations that contain unfamiliar elements and for which relevant data are lacking.

Other investigators have followed from Jepsen's research to seek additional insight into decision styles and the mechanisms that differentiate them. For example, Nevill, Neimeyer, Probert, and Fukuyama (1986) have examined aspects of cognitive structure in relation to vocational information processing and decision making. In particular, they have focused on individual differentiation—the number of different dimensions of judgment contained in a vocational schema—and integration—the level of organization or interrelationship among these dimensions. They did find differences among persons who were high and low on these variables. One finding was, for example, that under conditions of high differentiation, greater self-confidence was associated with high levels of integration.

In an elaboration of his earlier work on decision-styles, Jepsen (1989) has more recently combined several concepts related to the process of adolescent decision making with the antecedent conditions that prompt decisions and to which they are responses. He discusses the developing ability to cope successfully during important career decision points. He suggests that adolescent career development includes mastering decision-making *processes* as well as finding satisfying *content*:

> it involves learning effective ways to decide in addition to finding actions that lead to pleasing outcomes. . . . successful decision making provides the maturing person with a heightened sense of potency, competency, and identity that form the basis for continued growth in the adult years. Failure to master the challenges of career decision points during this age may leave the person with dampened hopes, self-doubts, regrets, and confusion about his/her identity. (p. 78)

Jepsen (1989), in this model, identifies the factors in the social context that prompt the adolescent to deal with a career decision point and the internal mechanisms by which such messages are received and processed. He suggests that the adolescent's social environment is composed of several primary reference groups which are principal agents of socialization as well as the purveyors of messages about expectations for action by the adolescent. These social groups may include the family of origin, classes and activities in school, peer friend groups, the extended family, the coworker group on a job, a religious group, or the group of families constituting a neighborhood. In turn, these groups send intermittent powerful messages, not delivered to all adolescents in the same way or with the same power, but nevertheless with content conveying aspects of a general expectation for the adolescent to take actions necessary to enter productive work roles. Adolescents, then, respond overtly and covertly to these messages. Overt responses typically include statements or actions and covert responses involve private thoughts and feelings. The two forms of response may not be consistent with each other. As Jepsen indicates, "adolescents may say things publicly that are not consistent with what they are thinking privately" (p. 85). The expectations for such inconsistency may lie elsewhere in this chapter as described by expectancy-valence or self-efficacy conflicts or the presence of vocational beliefs concerning oneself or other processes of doubt, lack of confidence, defensiveness, or feelings of vulnerability shaping their internal or covert self-talk.

Depending upon how the messages are appraised by the adolescent, overtly or covertly, the adolescent's emerging goals and anticipated means (a plan) for reaching such goals will likely be revised or strengthened within the limits of his or her available strategies, rules or criteria, risk-taking style, cognitive resources, and emotional states.

While this brief summary does not fully describe all of the elements and dynamics of Jepsen's model, it does connect adolescent decision making to the social context that stimulates and shapes the content and strategies likely to be employed. It also suggests counselor actions of relevance. They include the following:

> First, counselors can help adolescents to distinguish and clarify the powerful messages communicated by the particular groups in their social environment. . . .
>
> Second, counselors can help adolescents to focus on their covert responses and thus reveal what they are telling themselves. . . .
>
> Third, counselors help adolescents to appraise the content of powerful messages. . . .
>
> Fourth, counselors help adolescents to inventory their resources for meeting the demands of the decision. . . .
>
> Fifth, counselors help to orchestrate the delivery of powerful messages through organizing and facilitating discussions between adolescents and representatives of the reference groups identified earlier. (pp. 88–89)

In Jepsen's analysis of possible counselor roles in relation to a linking of several psychological and sociological explanations of the social context and the processes of adolescent decision making, he also distinguishes two general categories of theory and practice in the decision-making literature. One line of research and inquiry has dealt with *prescriptions* about the elements and the processes that comprise rational behavior. The thrust of such approaches is the assumed need to derive a set of recommended steps for reducing errors in decision making. The second approach is to develop *descriptions* of behavioral patterns. According to Jepsen,

> The prescription of external, rational principles, while important, is secondary to the identification of internal perceptions and conceptions about past and anticipated future experiences. The decision-making model provides a conceptual framework for organizing and assessing the adolescent's critical experiences. Rather than using the framework as a more-or-less fixed ideal from which to prescribe next steps, counselors use the framework to organize inductively the decision-maker's thought and feelings into a general strategy and, then, to assess the strategy for desirable attributes of the decision-making process such as thoroughness, detail, consistency, and continuity. The decision-making concepts serve as categories into which the decision-maker's reflections or experiences—past, present, and future—are sorted. (p. 82)

Another important line of inquiry relative to decision-making style has to do with career indecision. Researchers (for example, Osipow, Carney, Winer, Yanico, & Koschier, 1976) have focused on developing measures of indecision and taxonomy systems in the elements of indecision.

One important outcome of this line of research has been the construction of the Career Decision Scale (Osipow, 1980), described more fully elsewhere in the book. Basically, the 19 items of the CDS were designed to examine different dimensions of career indecision. Slaney (1988), in a review of the literature of career decision making, suggested that career indecision research has shown inconsistent or contradictory findings because researchers have been unable to differentiate between persons who are undecided about their career and those who are generally indecisive. He proposed that the former may be a normal developmental state, which career information or career interventions can modify. In contrast, indecisiveness may be more a characteristic trait of the individual and require more intensive and lengthy treatment. Other researchers have arrived at similar distinctions between problems of indecision and indecisiveness (for instance, Tyler 1961; Salomone, 1982). In response to Slaney's perspective, Vondracek et al. (1990) used four factor-based CDS scales to describe career decision behavior among 266 junior high and 199 senior high school students, consisting of 222 boys and 243 girls. Among these students, the researchers were able to differentiate between different types of undecided clients as well as between undecided and decided clients. Using CDS factor scales described as Diffusion, Support, Approach-Approach, and External Barriers, they were able to identify students who were undecided because they are confused and lack information about occupations (high score on Diffusion); those who are undecided because several occupations have great appeal for them (high score on Approach-Approach); students who need support and reassurance for a tentative decision (high score on Support); and those who cannot reach a decision because they perceive either internal or external barriers to decision making (high score on External Barriers). Obviously, each of these types of indecision suggests interventions that differ by type.

Undecidedness has also been studied among university students. Lucas and Epperson (1988; 1990) conceive such a phenomenon as involving multiple variables. In their 1990 study, 196 students undecided on career options completed a battery of personality questionnaires that included emphases on State and Trait Anxiety, Self-esteem, Work Salience, Relationship or Leisure Orientation, Locus of Control, Vocational Identity, Perception of Barriers, Need for Information, and Planful, Intuitive, or Dependent Decision-Making Style. The results from these variables were submitted to cluster analyses to determine subtypes. The results confirmed the view that different forms of career indecision exist and that in this study five clusters or types of such undecidedness could be identified. The types identified varied, for example, from high anxiety to little or no anxiety; from low self-esteem to high self-esteem; from external to internal locus of control; from dependent to nondependent decision styles and across the other variables examined. While such variables may not be inclusive of all relevant variables, they do support the differences in factors producing career undecidedness in clients and in the need for different forms of career guidance intervention to be considered by type.

Phillips, Pazienza, and Walsh (1984) studied the effectiveness of different decision-making styles on career decision making and found that although the evidence did not show that a rational style was the most effective, a style that included dependence on others could be damaging early in the decision process. Osipow and Reed (1985) applied the Johnson (1978) model of decision-making styles to a measure of decision/indecision among college students. The Johnson model includes four characteristics on two bipolar scales of decision making: spontaneous-systematic and internal-external. Spontaneous decision-makers make decisions holistically and quickly; systematic decision-makers collect information carefully and proceed logically in making a decision. Internal individuals process information privately and quietly; external deciders think out loud and talk to others about decisions. Osipow and Reed's research suggested a continuum of most to least undecided among these types including the most undecided (spontaneous-external) followed by spontaneous-internal, systematic-external, and systematic-internal, who are the least undecided. Graef, Wells, Hyland, and Machinsky (1985) constructed measures of vocational indecision from a variety of biographical indicators used with college students. They were able to predict typologies of student characteristics that did or did not relate to vocational decidedness, vocational identity, and vocational maturity. Their results indicated that the overall construct of vocational decidedness differs for males and females, both with regard to the specific parts of the construct and the life history factors that are antecedents to each criterion element of the decidedness construct.

Building from the research described above and other work that has focused largely on variations in career decidedness, Blustein, Ellis, and DeVennis (1989) are among researchers dealing with the steps that take place beyond making a choice. These researchers are concerned about commitment to an occupational choice; the sense of attachment to a choice mode. In their preliminary findings, they have demonstrated that commitment is a developmental process that begins with an uncommitted, exploratory phase and progresses to a highly committed phase. And, in addition, that persons can be described in terms of their openness or closedness to the exploratory and developmental experiences of the commitment process.

Some researchers have begun to link problem-solving self-appraisal to career decision and indecision. Holland and Holland (1977) suggested that career decision making could be viewed as a specific instance of problem solving with the latter defined as the complex chain of goal-directed events, including both cognitive and overt responses, that are intended to reduce some unsatisfying element of a problematic situation (for example, marital conflict, indecision about educational or occupational choices, or depression). Larsen and Heppner (1985) studied differences between those who appraised their problem-solving skills as positive or negative in relation to their scores on two measures of career decision/indecision. They found that persons who perceived themselves as positive problem-solvers were more confident about their decision-making ability and occupational potential, less likely to view the source of indecision outside themselves, more likely to have related their abilities to an occupational field, and they endorsed fewer antecedents of career indecision than did the self-perceived negative problem-solvers.

Zakay and Barak (1984) have proposed a model of decision making that accents the meaning of the values involved in the decision. More specifically, the investigators suggest that in such a meaning model, an "ideal alternative" (IA) is formed in a decision situation. Such an ideal alternative has meaning values and importance weights assigned by the chooser to each meaning dimension. The psychological distances between the meaning vectors of IA and each alternative are calculated by the chooser, and the alternative that offers the smallest difference or distance between its dimensions and those of the IA is chosen. Such a view suggests further that the greater the distance between the closest alternative to the ideal alternative and the ideal alternative itself, the higher the level of the individual's indecisiveness; the smaller the distance, the higher the chooser's choice confidence. The meaning viewpoint of the model proposes that any variable is possible and important. They also emphasize the attention that personal preferences, beliefs, perceptions, interests, habits, and needs should receive in such a model, as these represent elements of the individual's personal "decision-space." In two tests of the model, the investigators demonstrated that their data supported the validity of the model, its utility in understanding cognitive and behavioral indecisiveness, and its potential use in modifying the decision-making process.

A similar point can be made relative to the valuing of outcomes likely from different actions. Each person clearly or vaguely applies a scale of values important to him or her to each available alternative in a decision. The strength of the values in relation to the probability of the outcome actually occurring is seen by some observers as the crux of the decision process (Katz, 1963, 1966, 1969). Katz (1966) has suggested, in a model of guidance for career decision making, that an index of "investment" be developed to represent the substance of what an individual risks or loses in preparing for or electing any career option. This assumes that the person can be helped to determine the "odds," the chances of success in entering or attaining some alternative. More importantly, however, it means that knowing the odds is insufficient for decision making. As Katz has indicated, persons must also assess the importance of success to themselves in each option or the seriousness of failure. To make such assessments immediately places one's decisions in a value domain. Thus, decision-making includes the identifying and the defining of one's values: what they are and what they are not, where they appear and where they do not appear.

Another way of conceiving the application of decision theory to choice is seen in the approach of Kalder and Zytowski (1969). In this model, the elements consist of inputs (such as personal resources, intellectual and physical characteristics, time, capital), alternatives (possible actions at a choice point), and outputs (the probable consequences of various actions). Again one undergoes a process of scaling what one has to give up to get various outcomes and how probable such occurrences are. The chosen alternative is assumed to be the one that offers the highest net value—the best value available when input costs and output costs are balanced. Implicit in such a model is the assumption that the decision-maker has sufficient information about personal characteristics and the alternatives available to rank the values, utilities, and sacrifices associated with each possible action.

Brayfield (Brayfield & Crites, 1964) has stressed the importance of considering choice as occurring under conditions of uncertainty or risk. According to him, the individual assigns a reward value (utility) to alternative choices and appraises the chances of being able to realize each of them (subjective probability). As a result, the person will attempt to maximize the expected value in making a decision. Thoreson and Mehrens (1967) have also addressed this point. They state, "Objective probabilities are not directly involved in the decision-making process, but are only involved insofar as they are related to subjective probabilities, The question that arises is the extent to which certain information (objective probability data) actually influences what the person thinks are his chances (subjective probability) of an outcome occurring" (p. 167).

Although formal decision theory conceives of decision making as (1) a process, (2) having an essentially rational base, and (3) involving the selection of a single alternative at a particular point in time (Costello & Zalkind, 1963), the influence of individual subjectivity in interpreting information about oneself and about various options gives substantial credence to Hansen's (1964–1965) position that decisions are frequently more psychological than logical. Every counselor must keep the possibility of personally introduced bias in information constantly in mind, as clients are assisted to determine what sorts of information they need and what the acquired information means. Rather than assuming that the client will process information rationally and comprehend its full implications instead of filtering it through a personal set of incomplete or stereotyped images, the counselor must be directly involved in ensuring that the client considers pertinent information with as much objectivity as is possible.

A Social Learning Approach to Decision Making

Krumboltz, Mitchell, and Gelatt (1975), Krumboltz, Mitchell, and Jones (1979), and Mitchell and Krumboltz (1984; 1990) proposed and subsequently refined a social learning theory of career selection. In their view, the social learning theory of career decision making is an outgrowth of the general social learning of behavior, proposed and essentially by Albert Bandura, with its roots in reinforcement theory and classical behaviorism. "It assumes that the individual personalities and behavioral repertoires that persons possess arise primarily from their unique learning experiences rather than from innate developmental or psychic processes. These learning experiences consist of contact with and cognitive analysis of positively and negatively reinforcing events" (Mitchell & Krumboltz, 1984, p. 235). Such an approach does not imply that humans are "passive organisms that are controlled by environmental conditioning events. Social learning theory recognizes that humans are intelligent, problem-solving individuals who strive at all times to understand the reinforcement that surrounds them and who in turn control their environments to suit their own purposes and needs" (p. 236).

Krumboltz and his associates have indicated that "real life is always more complicated than our theories" but that it is possible to call attention to the events most influential in determining career selections. In particular, they point to the following four categories of influencers:

1. Genetic endowment and special abilities (such as race, sex, physical appearance and characteristics, intelligence, musical ability, artistic ability, muscular coordination)
2. Environmental conditions and events (such as number and nature of job and training opportunities, social policies and procedures for selecting trainees and workers, neighborhood and community influences, rate of return for various occupations, technological developments, labor laws and union rules, changes in social organizations, physical events (earthquakes, floods), family characteristics, community and neighborhood emphases)
3. Learning experiences such as *Instrumental Learning Experiences* (ILEs), in which antecedents, covert and overt behavioral

responses and consequences are present. (Skills necessary for career planning and other occupational and educational performances are learned through successive instrumental learning experiences. *Associative Learning Experiences* (ALEs) in which the learner pairs a previously neutral situation with some emotionally positive or negative reaction, observational learning, and classical conditioning are examples.)

4. Task approach skills (such as problem-solving skills, work habits, mental set, emotional responses, cognitive processes that both influence outcomes and are outcomes themselves)

These four types of influences and their interactions lead to several types of outcomes:

1. Self-observation generalizations (SOGs)—overt or covert statements evaluating one's own actual or vicarious performance in relation to learned standards
2. Task approach skills (TASs)—cognitive and performance abilities and emotional predispositions for coping with the environment, interpreting it in relation to self-observation generalizations, and making covert or overt predictions about future events. With relation to career decision making specifically, might include such skills as value-clarifying, goal-setting, alternative-generating, information-seeking, estimating, planning
3. Actions—entry behaviors that indicate overt steps in career progression (such as applying for a specific job or training opportunity, changing a college major)

The Krumboltz and associates model accents the instrumentality of learning experiences in producing preferences for activities as well as task approach skills. Krumboltz, Mitchell, and Gelatt (1976) state, "It is the sequential cumulative effects of numerous learning experiences affected by various environmental circumstances and the individual's cognitive and emotional reactions to these learning experiences and circumstances that cause a person to make decisions to enroll in a certain educational program or become employed in a particular occupation" (p. 75). Within a decision theory frame of reference, then, this model suggests that becoming a particular kind of worker or student is not a simple function of preference or choice but "is influenced by complex environmental (e.g., economic) factors, many of which are beyond the control of any single individual." These factors can be learned by the individual, and career decision-making skills can be systematically acquired.

Mitchell and Krumboltz (1984; 1990) have discussed a comprehensive inventory of empirical studies over the past two decades that provide considerable evidence to support the processes of the social learning theory of career decision making. It is apparent that the systematic research work of Krumboltz and his colleagues has provided significant evidence to support many of the hypotheses that can be generated by the theory and has also provided insight into possible career counseling interventions.

Among the many practical applications of Krumboltz's recent work is that which deals with the private rules of decision making and how these can be influenced by irrational beliefs (1983). For example, Krumboltz has identified several types of problems that can arise from faulty self-observation, generalizations, or inaccurate interpretation of environmental conditions. The problems he identifies include the following:

1. Persons may fail to recognize that a remediable problem exists
2. Persons may fail to exert the effort needed to make a decision or solve a problem
3. Persons may eliminate a potentially satisfying alternative for inappropriate reasons
4. Persons may choose poor alternatives for inappropriate reasons
5. Persons may suffer anguish and anxiety over perceived inability to achieve goals

Accordingly, Krumboltz suggests that beliefs that can potentially cause distress in career decision making are based on faulty generalizations, self-comparison with a single standard, exaggerated estimates of the emotional impact of an outcome, drawing false causal relationships, ignorance of relevant facts, and giving undue weight to low-probability events. Krumboltz contends that some of these beliefs and private rules in career decision making are related to the fact that making decisions is a painful process that involves at least four causes of stress: threat to self-esteem, surprise, deadlines, and absence of allocated time for decision making. These stresses, in turn, lead to such reactions as impaired attention, increased cognitive rigidity, narrowed perspectives, and displaced blame. Finally, Krumboltz contends that there are methods for identifying and acting on the private beliefs and stresses identified above. They include assessment of the content of the client's self-observation and world-view generalizations and the processes by which they arose; structured interviews; thought listing; *in vivo* self-monitoring; imagery; career decision-making simulations; reconstruction of prior events; behavioral inferences and feedback; use of psychometric instruments; use of cognitive restructuring techniques to help alter dysfunctional or inaccurate beliefs and generalizations; use of simple positive reinforcement; providing appropriate role models; use of films including problem-solving tasks for viewers; use of computerized guidance systems to provide and reinforce problem-solving tasks; teaching belief-testing processes; analyzing task-approach skills and teaching those in deficit (Krumboltz, 1983; Mitchell & Krumboltz, 1984); the use of the Career Beliefs Inventory (Krumboltz, 1988) to identify presuppositions that may block people from achieving their career goals.

The comprehensive conceptualization by Krumboltz and his colleagues about decision making and interventions in it has made extensive contributions to the professional literature in terms that have been summarized above but for, perhaps, a more important reason. Unlike many other theories, which tend to emphasize either environmental factors, particularly social and economic influences on decision making, or intrapsychic individual processing of psychological events, the social learning approach as articulated by Krumboltz has attempted to provide insight into each of these sets of factors and their interactions.

Cognitive Dissonance

A final approach still within the general domain of decision theory—with particular relevance to the outcomes of premature choosing and the resulting restrictions on full career development—is what has been called complex information processing (Hilton, 1962). The advocates of this approach contend, "the reduction of dissonance among a person's beliefs about himself and his environments is the major motivation of career decision-making." Although James (1963) has recommended that Hilton substitute "conflict" for "dissonance," the roots of this approach are Festinger's (1957) early theory of cognitive dissonance. That theory, here grossly oversimplified for purposes of space, indicates that the magnitude of information and the number of factors to be considered in decision making are so great that the individual chooses prematurely, without fully considering the implications of the choice, in order to reduce the besieging pressures as the torrents of information relevant to the choice are sorted out. The person then reinforces the choice by rationalization: selective attention to those data making the choice appear satisfying to self and to external observers. Although the chooser "knows" there are other options and better ones, particularly over the longer range, it is comforting to make a selection and suppress the costs of its unrealism by a variety of self-deceptive devices. Such a process is not unlike what happens when one is "bitten by the new car bug." Suddenly, the tires on the old car seem balder, there exist previously unheard noises in the engine, the newspaper seems to be full of warnings that in another year new car prices will escalate dramatically, and so on. Such selective perceptions help to reduce the dissonance in the choice. Career choices are rationalized through a similar process.

Hershenson and Roth (1966) have suggested in their four-phase portrayal of the vocational decision process that cognitive dissonance reduction operates to reinforce a course of action to which a person has committed him or herself. Harren (1979), too, has included cognitive dissonance in his model of vocational decision making among college students. His perception is that cognitive dissonance operates in such a way as to permit the individual to exaggerate both the positive characteristics of an alternative that has been chosen and the negative aspects of rejected alternatives. Thomas and Bruning (1984) have recently reported support for the work of Hershenson and Roth and that of Harren in their study of changes in cognitive-dissonance-related variables among 224 undergraduate students engaged in a program of professional training.

Many of these decision theory models, as well as others, are discussed in Chapter 14. Together with the preceding section, these treatments of the decision-making paradigms suggest their extreme importance to career development and choice and to counselor functions in support of such development.

SITUATIONAL, SOCIOLOGICAL, CONTEXTUAL APPROACHES

The social structure, as it is organized in a particular nation, is entwined with the characteristics of the majority and minority cultures that comprise it. But regardless of whether a particular society is culturally pluralistic or homogeneous it will create roles and achievement images for individuals to follow that serve as mechanisms to match individual self-interest to the collective good, whether such "good" be economic development, political stability, or some other goal. Such societal definitions of roles, who occupies them, how they are played out, and to what ends are reflected in the information people receive and the behaviors or skills that are rewarded. Segall et al. (1990) suggests that

> more sophisticated cross-cultural research underscores the plausibility of expecting that people in different cultural settings would vary in the way they learn to solve problems and in the patterns of skills they acquire. Now it is understood that cultures vary in the salience attached to certain skills, in the combination of basic cognitive processes that are called upon in any given context, or in the order in which specific skills are acquired. (p. 94)
>
> . . . in any society, there is likely to be a meaningful relationship between child training emphases and adult behavior. . . . Children are likely to be induced to behave in ways compatible with adult roles that they will have to assume, with these roles in turn reflective of socioeconomic complexity and social organization. (p. 236)

Such cultural constructions of achievement images, appropriate behavior, and belief systems are likely to be incorporated into the individual citizen's psyche through family, school, and religious institutions as well as embodied into the economic and organizational systems that prevail in a given nation. Thus, cultures represent templates or guides that encourage children, youth, and adults to embrace some values, information, behaviors, personal goals, and not others. For reasons of history, tradition, religious influence, and other factors, the occupations, knowledge, and skills valued are likely to differ from those of other societies or cultures.

In pluralistic societies, such as the United States, environments that people occupy are not unidimensional. They are physical, social, and cultural. The interactions among these aspects of one's "life space" exert influences or limits on how gender and family roles are conceived, the achievement images likely to be nurtured, the resources available, and the accuracy and form of knowledge provided about opportunities.

In some contrast to more psychologically-oriented theories of career development, which accent the effects of individual action in creating one's own reality and in forging careers through choices made, sociological perspectives tend to accent the environmental factors that facilitate or constrain individual action. As Hotchkiss and Borow suggest (1990),

> Psychologists are interested in how constellations of personal attributes, including aspirations, aptitudes, interests, and personality traits, shape subsequent job performance and satisfaction. Sociologists, by contrast, generally are more interested than psychologists are in how such institutional factors as formal rules, informal norms, and supply-and-demand forces shape the settings in which individuals work. . . . Sociologists have generally viewed paid employment and occupational choice as embedded in a broad system of social stratification. (p. 263)

Thus, sociologists are primarily concerned about the structural factors that condition individual choices and their consequences.

Sociological or situational emphases portray change from place to place and from time to time. In other words, the context in which career behavior unfolds is different across nations, communities, and families. It is different from one socioeconomic group to another. The career context is also different across time. As social, economic, and technological conditions change at a national or global level, they reflect the decrease of some types of work opportunities and life-styles and the emergence of others. Similarly, one's place in a birth order of siblings in a family modifies the career context available. Thus, the course of one's development is dependent on when one is born, how many others are growing up at the same time and competing for opportunities available, how sex roles are defined in one's historical time, and other phenomena. Whether one is born in a "baby boom" or at a time of relatively few births; at a time of "women's liberation" and enlightened attitudes toward racial minorities; in a time of economic depression or abundance are each elements of both the psychological and the literal "opportunity structure" with which persons interact as they form their personal values, interests, and plans of action. People, then, are in dynamic interaction with their environment. Vondracek, Lerner, and Schulenberg (1986) portray such interaction as follows: "Dynamic interaction means that the context and organism are inextricably embedded in each other, that the context consists of multiple levels changing interdependently across time, and that because organisms influence the contexts that influence them, they are able to play an active role in their own developments" (p. 37).

There are several notions in the professional literature about the multidimensionality of environments as they effect career development. Gibson (1979), for example, has discussed the idea that environments offer "affordances"—objects, events, people—that can provide information, stimulation, and possibilities to people who can perceive such "affordances." Indeed, it is possible to think of formulating taxonomies of the affordances provided by different environments and their possible responses to different individual needs or perceptual systems.

In another view, Bronfenbrenner (1979) has also emphasized the importance of the interaction between the developing person, the environment, and the interaction between the two. His concern is that while the behavioral sciences tend to acknowledge such interaction between the person and the environment, the major theoretical and research attention has been focused on the properties of the person rather than on the characterization of environments and their implications for the person. Bronfenbrenner introduces a number of concepts that are of importance within the present section, but that are also important to the last part of this chapter, when we discuss developmental approaches more directly and, in particular, perspectives on adult transitions. For example, Bronfenbrenner describes such events as finding a job, losing a job, and retiring as *ecological transitions* that occur throughout the life span when "a person's position in the ecological environment is altered as the result of a change in role, setting, or both" (p. 26). These transitions reflect the consequences of both changes in the person and in the environment across time.

Another concept important to a sociological, situational, or contextual view of career development is Bronfenbrenner's *principle of interconnectedness*. This principle envisions the environment as being comprised of several interrelated systems that affect each other and individual psychological development. He offers four ecological structures to define the environment. These include the *microsystem*, in which occurs the more intimate aspects of the individual's development in the family, in the school, or in the workplace; it is comprised of the interpersonal relationships, goal-directed molar activities, and system-defined roles and expectations a person experiences in a given setting such as a family or school; the *mesosystem* links together the major microsystems, the child's family and school, the family and workplace expectations at a particular point in the parent's life; the *exosystem*, which includes indirect effects upon a person from a spouse's or parent's microsystems, for example, the workplace; the *macrosystems*, which include the major cultural-, national-, societal-level belief systems, ideologies, and morés about sex-roles, personality models to be emulated and similar social metaphors (Vaizey & Clark, 1976) that organize majority or dominant visions of appropriate behavior and sanctions on it. Each of these systems has its own impact as a career context, as a generator of environmental circumstances and situations, that both affects and is affected by individual psychological development.

One's social class membership is, for example, a function of family heritage, resources, and status. This is a microsystem issue. How the family or child interacts with the school is a mesosystem issue but obviously is affected by the social class membership of the child and how that is interpreted in intellectual, power, or behavioral terms by the school. The child's social class membership is also an exosystem issue in the sense that a child, or a spouse in many instances, inherits from the parent (or spouse) a level of financial or social status that derives from the occupation of that parent or spouse. The child does not generate the social class membership but is characterized by such status as an indirect effect of the parent's role in a particular exosystem. Finally, at the most generalizable level, the macrosystem may be the generator of images that suggest that certain family structures (microsystems) or social classes are better than others or are problematic. In turn, such reinforcement and interaction ripple through the four ecological systems defined by Bronfenbrenner and affect the child's or the family's conceptions of self, opportunities, values, or other cognitive structures.

The above description grossly oversimplifies the interaction of person and context. It does not begin to address the many intricacies and subtleties that comprise the psychological processes by which individuals accommodate the physical, social, and cultural aspects of their environment, or, indeed, how the four ecological systems defined by Bronfenbrenner vary for individuals or for nations. Nevertheless, such differences do prevail.

Without using the term macrosystem, Watts, Super, and Kidd (1981) have illustrated the variance of that structure in a comparison of the evolution of career development theory in Britain with that of the United States.

> It is intriguing that theories of career development in the USA have been so heavily dominated by psychologists whereas in Britain the contributions of sociologists have been much more prominent. The dominant focus in the USA has been on the actions of individuals, while in Britain indigenous theoretical work has been more preoccupied with the constraints of social structures. . . . The failure of the American social-structural evidence to have much influence on career development theory seems to be due basically to cultural and historical factors. From the beginning of its independent existence, the USA has been formally committed to the proposition that all men are created equal. . . . As a result, there is belief that the individual controls his own destiny; that if he has appropriate abilities, and if these can be appropriately developed, his fate lies in his own hands. (p. 3)

The observations of Watts are very helpful in capturing the essence of situational or sociological perspectives on career development. Such approaches remind us that decision making, the development of self-identity, and life changes do not occur in a vacuum. They occur within political, economic, and social conditions that influence the achievement images and belief systems on which individuals base their actions. They occur as person-environment interactions (Super, 1957).

Person-Environment Interactions: The Family

During most of the twentieth century, observers from many disciplines have reported on the effects of social or socioeconomic class on occupations chosen, educational goals, and on other aspects of work identity and career (Borow, 1989; Hotchkiss & Borow, 1990). Underlying those observations are the attainments of parents and the effects of different family constellations of values and information as important predictors of occupational choice and of work adjustment. Although not the only important mediator of social class or social status in children, family characteristics are conduits for their particular culture, history, and meaning systems and, as such, they represent the seedbed for differences across classes in the socialization, or vocationalization, of the young (Steward & Healy, 1989). The research of Chusid and Cochran (1989) found that work is pervaded by the reenactment of family themes, and that the meaning of a career change can be understood as a significant development of dramas from the family of origin that were restaged in work.

Hotchkiss and Borow (1984), speaking to the major sociological work on family effects on status attainment, contend that the basic premise in such a model is that

> career statuses, such as education, occupation, and income are passed from generation to generation by a sequence of interpersonal processes. Parental status in particular influences the status achieved by their children indirectly through a chain of effects. Attitudes characteristic of different status levels are passed from parent to child, both immediately by parent contact with the child and less directly through the youth's contact with adults other than parents and with peers who come from similar backgrounds. This process is termed *significant-other* influence. Interpersonal relations with significant others help to shape the career plans of youth, and those plans affect career attainments. (p. 139)

Family influences, including childrearing patterns and socioeconomic level, also appear to have an effect on occupational choice and on career maturity. Indeed, Levine (1976) has suggested that the influence of social and economic origins on later life is so well documented that it could almost be considered axiomatic. Some representative studies of such phenomena follow. Basow and Howe (1979) examined the influences of various models on the careers of 300 randomly chosen college seniors. They found that parents were the most influential models, and nonparent, nonteacher adults were the least influential. They also found that females were significantly more affected by female models than were males.

Hollander's (1972) studies of male high school and college students found that maternal influences on vocational interests are stronger in high school and paternal influences stronger in college years. Oliver's research (1975) indicated that a girl's father is more important than her mother in determining the degree of her career commitment as a collegiate undergraduate. Oliver concluded that antecedent family variables influence the development of motivational patterns that are associated with career and homemaking orientation in college women. Smith's findings (1980) showed that whether the mother worked was a major influence on high school girls' orientation toward the role of housewife versus paid employee. Anderson (1980) found that high school seniors used the educational achievement of their same-sexed parent as a primary factor in setting their educational goals. In general, such a process served to lower the educational goals of the females in the sample.

Roe's theory of vocational choice, described later in this chapter, rests on the hypothesis that childrearing processes partly determine subsequent vocational choices. Medvene (1973) found that the long-term developmental effects of parental avoidance, concentration, and acceptance of their children are important to both emotional-social and educational-vocational clients who come to college counseling centers.

Available evidence suggests that family socioeconomic status is comprehensively related to career choice. Socioeconomic differences are associated with differences in information about work, work experience, and occupational stereotypes, which, in turn, affect vocational interests. Dillard's study (1976) of black youth concludes that socialization or vocationalization processes, significantly influenced by the family, rather than ability differences in reading achievement, account for career maturity differences in this sample. MacKay and Miller (1982) found that elementary school children from middle and upper socioeconomic backgrounds choose white-collar and professional occupations as goals more often than children from lower socioeconomic backgrounds; that these attitudes are firmly established by the time a child is in grade three; and that there is a positive relationship between socioeconomic level and complexity of data manipulation in occupational choices.

Friesen (1986) has contended that in trying to understand the positive effects between socioeconomic status in families and the vocational attainment of children, it is necessary to comprehend both opportunity and process. In the first instance, the higher the socioeconomic status (SES) of the family, the more likely parents are to have the resources to finance educational opportunities that lead to higher-status occupations. With regard to process, there are other matters involved. For example, different socialization patterns exist among SES groups. As illustrative, the research of Kohn (1977) has shown that middle-class parents tend to value self-direction in their children, and lower SES parents tend to value conformity. These findings also suggest that the values at the job may be transmitted to the home, which, in turn, are translated into childrearing practices. Schulenberg, Vondracek, and Crouter (1984) contend that the childrearing practices employed by parents with their sons as compared to their daughters lead to differences in their vocational development. Weitz (1977), Block (1983), and Hoffman (1977) have also reported studies that indicate that parents tend to reinforce certain behaviors in males that they do not reinforce in females. In such research, it tends to be found that parents expect their sons, more frequently than their daughters, to be independent, self-reliant, highly educated, hard-working, ambitious, career-oriented, intelligent, and strong-willed. In contrast, the daughters are expected to be kind, unselfish, attractive, loving, well-mannered, have a good marriage, and be a good parent.

In applying family systems theory to the effects of families in the decision-making process, research by Kinnier, Brigman, and Noble (1990) indicates that familial dynamics and the process of career decision making are intertwined. Indeed, family enmeshment, where families are undifferentiated from or overly dependent on each other, was found to be related to difficulty in making decisions about their careers, and to career indecision. In a somewhat different approach using sophisticated sociometric processes, Rockwell's (1987) research has demonstrated that occupational preference is socially constructed and is highly influenced by the career decision maker's expectations of approval from significant others for making certain occupational choices.

Given the rapid growth of the application of systems theory to the understanding of and therapy with families in psychology, several perspectives seem to be related to this context. As is reflected in the situational and sociological views reported in this section, psychology in general has become aware that understanding of the individual requires an understanding of his or her social setting, a primary aspect of which is the family. But, in addition, it has become clear that to understand the family, a counselor needs to understand its position in the larger social setting and in relation to other social institutions. As reported elsewhere in this book, work choice and adjustment are not simply individual matters. They are also affected by and affect family harmony, resources, emotional conditions, and other matters. Hoffman (1986) has identified some of the processes by which research shows that work affects families:

1. Work provides material resources that affect the families' economic well-being.
2. Being employed or not employed and the particular occupation confer status that affects the family's status in the community, the worker's status in the family, and the worker's self-concept.
3. Behaviors at work are repeated in the home.
4. Work experiences affect ideas about what qualities are important in adulthood and thus influence child-rearing patterns.
5. Work affects the worker's personality and intellectual functioning and thus influences his or her behavior in the family. The child is affected through parental child-rearing practices and identification with the parent.
6. Authority structures at work are repeated in the family and are reflected in child-rearing patterns.
7. Moods generated at work are carried over to the family.
8. The family may be used as a complementary source of need satisfaction: the worker may seek to satisfy in the family needs unsatisfied or engendered at work.
9. Work takes time, energy, and involvement from the family. In addition to the loss itself, this can lead to stress from overload or guilt.
10. Work can be a source of stress either because of the above processes or because it is intrinsically dangerous or insecure. (pp. 179–188)

While each of these processes deserves to be discussed at length, the simple statement of them suggests the types of situational effects on families and on children that different combinations of these processes might produce. As the reader examines other theoretical approaches in this chapter, certain of these processes will be reflected in many of them. In a collective sense, the processes identified here show both the power and the complexity of the family in inducting children into work roles and providing a source of security and satisfaction for the working parent whose needs at work may not be fully satisfied.

In sum, whether from a contextual, sociological, or a situational perspective, the family is a facilitator of experiences that expand or limit family members' knowledge of occupations, a reinforcement system of contingencies and expectations that subtly or directly shape work behavior, and a purveyor of socioeconomic status. The home is itself a workplace and a center in which social and occupational roles are modeled either by the members of the nuclear family or the network of friends and acquaintances with which this unit interacts (Herr & Best, 1984).

Accident Theories

In addition to the family as a major instrument of contextual, sociological or situational effects upon career development, some authors have advanced an accident theory of occupational choice or career development. Some observers suggest that the term accident theory refers to the "accident of birth" (Shafer, 1987). But in broader terms the perspectives usually encompassed by accident theory gives primary visibility to the role of chance or unforeseen events as major determinants of personal opportunities for choice. Such perspectives recognize that most of the major career theories attempt to describe normative and, in that sense, predictable patterns of behavior that are typical and frequent in different populations. But accident or chance theories are also acknowledgements that career development occurs in social and economic contexts in which unforeseen events may deflect or disrupt patterns of choice and development that were rationally planned. These views suggest that chance encounters, influential people, fortuitous or other events are likely to occur and shape or change individual career behavior.

Chance Encounters. In one exposition of such a view, Bandura's (1982), the central thesis is that chance encounters play a prominent role in shaping the course of human lives. For his purposes, "A chance encounter is defined as an unintended meeting of persons unfamiliar to each other. . . . Human encounters involve degrees of fortuitiveness. People often intentionally seek certain types of experiences, but the persons who thereby enter their lives are determined by a large element of chance" (1982, p. 748). Bandura also describes how fortuitous symbolic encounters mediated through another's actions profoundly affect life paths. Symbolic encounters might include hearing a particular lecture, reading a particular book, unexpectedly witnessing a particular event on television or in reality, which has such an effect on an individual that it stimulates the pursuit of a new life path. According to Bandura, some chance encounters "touch people only lightly, others leave more lasting effects, and still others branch people into new trajectories of life" (1982, p. 749). He suggests that psychology is not able to predict fortuitous occurrences, nor does it have much to say about their occurrence except that personal bents and social structures and affiliations make some types of encounters more probable than others. Here we find the particular importance of social class, family background, geographic residence, and similar contexts increasing the likelihood of some encounters and decreasing the likelihood of others.

Bandura further suggests that if psychology cannot predict the likelihood of chance encounters, it can provide the basis for predicting the nature, scope, and strength of the effect they are likely to have on human lives. He suggests that "neither personal proclivities nor situational imperatives" operate as independent shapers of the course of lives. Chance encounters affect life paths through the reciprocal influence of personal and social factors. He then outlines the personal and social factors that are likely to determine the effect of chance encounters. Table 4.2 shows these factors in paraphrased chart form from his narrative of the process.

Table 4.2

A Synthesis of Bandura's Perspectives on Factors Influencing Chance Encounters

Personal Determinants of the Effect of Chance Encounters	Social Determinants of the Effect of Chance Encounters
Entry Skills Interest, skills, personal knowledge likely to gain acceptance or sustain contact with another	*Milieu Rewards* The types of rewards and sanctions an individual or group provides if a chance encounter alters a life path
Emotional Ties Interpersonal attractiveness tending to sustain chance encounters so that certain social determinants might operate	*Symbolic Environment and Information* Images of reality provided by other than direct experience; different individuals or groups furnish different symbolic environments
Values and Personal Standards Unintended influences more likely to be important if persons involved share similar standards and value systems	*Milieu Reach and Closedness* Chance encounters with a relatively closed milieu — e.g., cults, communal groups — have the greatest potential for abruptly reordering life paths
	Psychological Closedness Belief systems provide structure, directions, and purpose in life. Once persons, through chance encounter, get caught up in the belief system of a particular group, it can exert selective influence on the course of development and erect a psychological closedness to outside influence. Beliefs channel social interactions in ways that create their own validating realities.

Bandura's work to date rests primarily on observation and biographical data. It is an attempt to develop into an effective conceptual framework the psychological processes that are subsumed or activated by what is more popularly called chance or accident. In this sense, he makes the following point: "Fortuitous influences may be unforeseen, but having occurred, they enter as evident factors in causal chains in the same way as prearranged ones do" (p. 749). Bandura has not attempted to speculate about the number of people whose career development is a function of chance encounters or how such a view applies across occupational groups. There are other findings, however, that bear on such matters.

Preparation and Planning. Hart, Rayner, and Christensen (1971) studied the degree of preparation, planning, and chance in occupational entry among sixty men representing professional, skilled, and semiskilled occupational levels. They found that most men at the professional level entered their occupation primarily through planning and preparation. At the skilled level, some men entered their occupations through planning, whereas many others were primarily influenced by chance events. Those who entered occupations at the semiskilled level were primarily influenced by chance events. Partially based on the earlier work of Hart et al., Salomone and Slaney (1981) studied the perceived influence of chance and contingency factors on the career choices of 447 female and 470 male nonprofessional workers. In some contrast to the findings of Hart et al., Salomone and Slaney found that chance factors were much less important than were personal qualities in influencing vocational decisions. The authors conclude as follows:

> Perhaps the "chance theory" was seen as a reasonable alternative by sociologists writing in the 1940s and 1950s but clearly, the workers of the 1970s—including nonprofessional skilled and unskilled workers—appear to assess their personal inclinations (interests and needs), their skills and abilities, and their personal and family responsibilities before making vocational choices. . . . In large measure, they perceive themselves as using rational processes to arrive at their occupational decisions. (p. 34)

Not agreeing fully with the findings of either Hart or Salomone and Slaney, Scott and Hatalla (1990) examined the perceptions of women college graduates regarding the influence of selected change and contingency factors upon their career patterns 25 years after graduation. Their findings indicated that a significant proportion of the sample perceived eight contingency factors as influential in their career pattern and that the chance factor "Unexpected Personal Events" was also perceived as influential by a significant proportion of the women in the sample. Although contingency factors were more likely to be perceived as having influence on career patterns than chance factors, "Unexpected Personal Events" was a consistent and influential factor across the various career patterns of women observed in the study. Consistent with other studies, the contingency factors perceived as most influential by the highest percentage of respondents were awareness of skills and abilities, perception of interests, educational level, and awareness of intelligence. These were primarily internal determinants of identity and in comparison with chance factors are predictable and available to the person's awareness as they engage in career planning and choice.

Cabral and Salomone (1990) have synthesized the literature on choice factors, particularly as they relate to adult career development. They offer a number of concepts that extend the role of chance in career behavior, individual ability to control or cope with chance, and the relationship between chance and personality. With regard to the control of chance, they contend that there are two conclusions to be drawn. One is that "chance operates on a continuum from events or encounters that are totally unforeseen (a natural disaster, the sudden death of a spouse, or a conversation on an airplane, for instance), to those that are at least in part under the control of the individual (overhearing information concerning a job opportunity during a meeting of a professional organization, or deciding to enter graduate school in a newly-emerging field after learning of that field through one's mentor)" (p. 10). A second conclusion is that persons respond differently to unforeseen encounters or events.

Cabral and Salomone explain the latter in terms of two possible personality dimensions: *locus of control* and *self-concept*. They argue that persons "with external locuses of control, as well as those who offer empowering-deterministic explanations for their behavior, will be more susceptible to the influence of chance events or encounters. More importantly, these individuals will be less likely to be proactive when chance events or encounters do occur" (p. 11). In contrast, it would be assumed that persons with an internal locus of control would be somewhat less affected by unforeseen events and encounters, would attempt to control or diminish the uncertainty they represent, or would instead embrace these encounters and events as opportunities to seize and act on. How individuals function in terms of chance, according to Cabral and Salomone, is also a function of the individual's self-concept or self-conceptions, which act as filters through which the individual perceives events and people in his or her contexts, guides and edits information received in memory, serves as cognitive schemata that aid in the definition of people and events, and provides a basis for choice and evaluation. Individuals are likely to behave in ways that reinforce and implement their self-concept.

Cabral and Salomone conclude their discussion of chance and its effects on career decisions with the following key points:

- Chance, defined as foreseen and uncontrollable events and encounters, is inevitable and plays an important role in shaping career decisions.
- Career decisions in the lives of individuals are rarely purely rational, nor are they in most instances based purely on chance. Some combination of planfulness and happenstance seems to drive the decisions and development of an individual's career.
- The critical dimensions of chance encounters or events are their timing in relation to the individual's development and the contexts within which they occur.
- "Chance" actually encompasses a range of events or encounters that vary greatly in the degree of control that the individual has over them. It is possible to affect the potential for certain types of chance events or encounters by entering or avoiding different contexts.
- Individuals are most vulnerable to the effects of chance during life transitions, particularly those that occur early in the career and those that have not been anticipated. (p. 14)

Culture and Social Class Boundaries. But the factors bearing on choice or development are not restricted to chance or intervening variables. The breadth of the individual's culture or social class boundaries has much to do with the choices that can be considered, made, and implemented. No more vivid an example exists than that of people raised in poverty. Poor people are not just rich people without money. Their life space, possibility structures, level and types of reinforcement, models, and social resources all differ as a function of their social status. Therefore, an important factor in the career development of an individual is the effect of the culture and society on the goals one is conditioned to value. Within this context are found such elements as family income levels, social expectations, levels of social mobility, and psychological support for patterns of educational and occupational motivation.

Lipsett (1962) argued almost three decades ago that counselors must understand the implications of the following social factors for a particular individual as they interact with career development:

1. Social class membership—for example, occupation and income of parents, education of parents, place and type of residence, ethnic background
2. Home influences—for example, parental goals for the individual, influence of siblings, family values and counselee's acceptance of them
3. School—for example, scholastic achievement, relationships with peers and faculty, values of the school
4. Community—the "thing to do in the community," group goals and values, special opportunities or influences
5. Pressure groups—the degree to which an individual or his or her parents have come under any particular influence that leads him or her to value one occupation over another
6. Role perception—the individual's perception of self as a leader, follower, isolate, and so forth; the degree to which one's perception of self is in accord with the way others perceive one

The important concern here is that the factors identified by Lipsett operate directly or indirectly in every individual's life. The degree to which they operate as determinants or constraints in development and choice, however, can be assessed only in the individual case. Counselors must be alert to how much clients have accepted the attitudes and values held by the various aspects of their environments, have personally tested such perspectives, and whether those perspectives facilitate or restrain choice-making.

Feck (1971), in a major study of urban disadvantaged youth, identified fifteen basic needs, including those that are career-related. These needs included

(1) security and stability in one's environment
(2) successful education experience
(3) recognition for achievement
(4) love and respect
(5) legal sources of finance
(6) financial management
(7) proper housing
(8) good health
(9) development of basic communication skills
(10) salable work skills
(11) an appreciation of the meaning and importance of work
(12) successfully employed or adult peer-group models
(13) positive self-concept
(14) job opportunities and qualifications
(15) socially acceptable attitudes and behaviors

In a land that prides itself on its freedom and opportunity, such needs should be comprehensively met for all citizens. But, again, when context, situational, and sociological perspectives are invoked, it becomes evident that social class factors create barriers or complications that thwart such need fulfillment. For example, Kessler and Cleary (1980), in their research on social class, found that lower social classes experienced more undesirable life events that require extensive readjustment than did middle or upper classes. Thoits (1982) also found that disadvantaged persons are more vulnerable and reactive than their more advantaged contemporaries to life stressors, particularly to the impacts of health-related events. In order to meet the needs specified by Feck, the disadvantaged need an open system of opportunity (Griffiths, 1980), information on world of work and available resources (Williams & Whitney, 1978), relevant and appropriate education, training, and counseling, (Smith, 1980) and, perhaps, as much as anything else, a strong sense of control. Without a strong sense of personal control, a feeling that one's personal action makes a difference, life comes to be viewed as a big crap game in which the individual simply does not count.

A major study of youth unemployment has clearly shown that social class and racial differences exist in the amount of unemployment experienced by various subpopulations of youth (Adams & Mangum, 1978). Indeed, such social class differences are also apparent in the use of resources and other types of mechanisms to aid in the transition from school to work. Similar findings have been reported in another major work on the youth labor market (Osterman, 1980).

Perhaps the most important point gleaned from sociological studies of career development and choice is that although the preferences of individuals across various social or economic classes are essentially the same, lower-class expectancies of being able to achieve their preferences are less. In other words, what they would prefer to do is not what they expect to be able to do. Such inconsistency may stem from a recognition of their inability to do what they prefer because of lack of intellect or aptitude (Osipow & Gold, 1967; Clack, 1968). But the more pertinent reason seems to be their perception of cultural constraints that will prohibit them from access to their preferred choices. Thus, it is likely that occupational preferences will reflect the family's occupational level and, therefore, the child's socioeconomic milieu.

Although the personal aspirations of an individual raised in an environment unsupportive of planfulness or commitments to long-range goals may be the same as for those reared in more favored circumstances, if the person does not have the knowledge or the techniques to cope with the environment, that individual is at a considerable disadvantage in achieving the prerequisites for reaching personal goals.

Some sociologists even argue that developmental notions of career guidance based on individual choice are unrealistic. Roberts (1977), a British sociologist, is one of the foremost proponents of such a view. In essence he does not believe that most people choose, in any precise sense of that term. Instead, they are chosen or act as opportunities arise rather than in some longitudinal preplanned way. He summarizes the point as follows: "The notion that young people possess freedom of choice and that they can select careers for themselves upon the basis of their own preferences is pure myth. It is not choice but opportunity that governs the manner in which many young people make their entry into employment" (p. 145). As factors affecting such a circumstance, he identifies the mechanisms of educational selection, the patterns of recruitment into different types of employment, home background, and other social structure factors.

Whether or not one is as adamant about social structure factors in career development as is Roberts, situational approaches to career development suggest that the socioeconomic structure of a society operates as a percolator and a filter of information. In essence, one's position among the social strata making up a nation has much to do with the kind of information one gets, the alternative actions one can take, and the kind of encouragement one receives. Persons are often selectively rewarded or reinforced in certain kinds of behavior depending on the group to which they belong. Women's Liberation, Black and Brown Pride Movements, Gay Liberation, and the Grey Panthers are examples of reactions against the constraints in opportunity imposed because of stereotyped images held by various segments of our society.

In a pluralistic culture such as America today, persons of different ethnic or racial backgrounds are likely to differ in the types of role models available to them. Perhaps more important, different cultures allocate values differently and these values have consequences for behavior. Unfortunately, these value differences are rarely responded to by school or by helping professionals (Harrington, 1975).

Although the mass media, and television in particular, may convey general achievement images that all of us are encouraged to emulate, information about how such images are accomplished or planned and prepared for is not as accessible. Thus, career guidance has a major responsibility to reduce the correlations between membership in certain groups and success. Individual competence and desire, not group membership, must become the criterion by which relevant information and encouragement are provided to people regardless of their sex, race, or other situational determinants. Having a pluralistic population does not mean having a caste system in which some persons remain at low status levels, because they are denied information or opportunity to seek other levels in the society.

Finally, in considering many of the situational effects on the choice in graphic form, it is useful to consider the Blau, Gustad, Jessor, Parnes, and Wilcock paradigm (1956). Although more than three decades old, their schematic of the choice process is a classic synthesis of the factors occurring together within the individual and the environment as the person moves toward occupational entry. Essentially, this paradigm accents the effects of the social structure on choice.

> The social structure—the more or less institutionalized patterns of activities, interactions, and ideas among various groups—has a dual significance for occupational choice. On the other hand, it influences the personality development of the choosers; on the other, it defines the socioeconomic conditions in which selection takes place.

> These two efforts, however, do not occur simultaneously. At any choice point in their careers, the interests and skills in terms of which individuals make their decisions have been affected by the past social structure, whereas occupational opportunities and requirements for entry are determined by the present structure. (p. 539)

This twofold effect of the social structure is schematically presented in Figure 4.2. The left side of the figure suggests that the molding of biological potentialities by the differentiated social structure (Box 3) results in diverse characteristics and individuals (Box 2), some of which directly determine occupational choice (Box 1). At the same time, as indicated on the right side, the social structure changes (Box III), resulting in a socioeconomic organization at any point in time (Box II), some aspects of which directly determine occupational selection (Box I). These two developments, separated only for analytical purposes, must be joined to explain entry into occupations.

The Blau et al. paradigm suggests that geography, the historical moment in time, occupational characteristics, political factors, and the occupational possibility structure and its requirement affect anyone's career development. Stopping there, however, understates situational effects on choice, because while interacting with such external circumstances, the individual has also incorporated and will act on the belief systems held by family, peers, neighborhood, ethnic, and religious groups that also define his or her "situation."

PSYCHOLOGICAL APPROACHES

Psychological approaches to career development stress intrinsic individual motivation more than the other approaches discussed thus far do. Tying the psychoanalytic, need, and self-emphases into a single body of psychological approaches, Crites (1969, p. 91) observes, "each of them proposes that the most significant factor in the making of a vocational choice is a motivational or process variable. For this reason, they contrast sharply with the trait-and-factor theories, which emphasize the observable characteristics of the individual and not the inferred states or conditions which prompt him to behave as he does."

The major assumption of the psychological approaches is that because of differences in personality structure, individuals develop certain needs or drives and seek satisfaction of these needs or drives through occupational choices. Thus, it is contended that different occupational or, indeed, curricular areas are populated by persons of different need types or personality types. These approaches rather consistently develop a classification of personality or need, and then relate it to gratifications available in different environments—occupational or educational. In one sense, the distinguishing characteristics of these approaches are the disciplinary lenses through which career-related phenomena are viewed and the emphasis on the antecedents of vocational behavior as a function of some form of self-classification, conscious or unconscious.

Freud's Psychodynamic View. At the core of any psychodynamic view of work or other aspects of life is the "depth psychology" of Sigmund Freud. As is well known, Freud devoted much of his life to creating a theory of personality encompassing both its conscious and unconscious aspects and the notions of how childhood personality development profoundly influences adult life, including one's work life. However, the most comprehensive application of classic psychoanalytic concepts to occupational choice or career development has been made by Bordin, Nachmann, and Segal (1963), called the Michigan Group. Although preceded by Brill's (1948) psychoanalytic concepts of guilt and exhibitionism and of the pleasure and reality principles to explain the choice attraction of various vocations, Bordin, Nachmann, and Segal have extended the

Figure 4.2

The Blau, Gustad, Jessor, Parnes, and Wilcock Paradigm. (Reprinted with permission from Peter M. Blau et al., "Occupational Choice: A Conceptual Framework," *Industrial and Labor Relations Review,* July 1956, 9(4), p. 534. Copyright © 1956 by Cornell University. All rights reserved.)

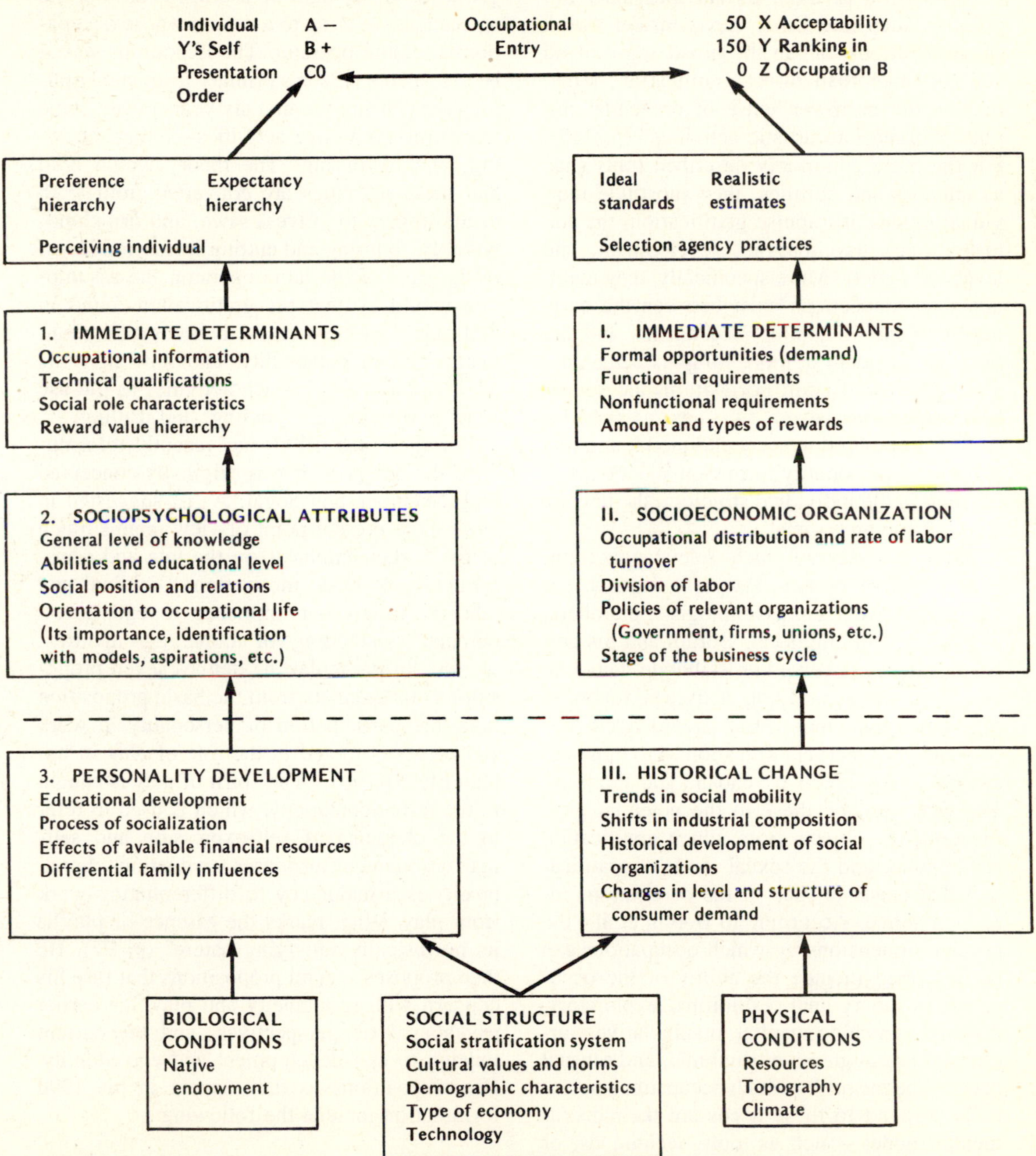

emphasis on the gratification that various types of work offer to meet certain individual impulses. Much like Brill, they consider "work as sublimation—but in the broad sense of all activity other than direct gratification, rather than in the narrower sense of pregenital impulses turned into artistic activities" (p. 110). For the more commonly described traits such as interests and abilities, they substitute individual modes of impulse gratification, the status of one's psychosexual development, and levels of anxiety. More specifically, they maintain that connections exist between the early development of coping mechanisms and the later development of more complex behaviors. They assert that adult occupations are sought for their instinctual gratifications, as need for these is developed in early childhood, and that in terms of personality formation and the needs inherent in the individual structure, the first six years of life are crucial.

From analyses of such roles as accountants, creative writers, lawyers, dentists, social workers, clinical psychologists, plumbers, physicists, and engineers, Bordin and his colleagues have conceived an elaborate matrix of the basic need-gratifying activities found in different occupations. They have divided psychic and body-part classifications into those activities important to psychoanalytic thinking. They then related these to the potential gratification, the objects from which gratification is available, and the sexual mode of gratification that exists in each of the occupations indicated above. According to Bordin et al., the psychic dimensions by which occupations can be described include the ability of the occupation to satisfy anal, exhibiting, exploratory, flowing-quenching, genital, manipulative, nurturing, oral, aggressive, rhythmic, and sensual needs. The means by which occupations potentially respond to these needs are their instrumental modes—such as tools, techniques, or behaviors used—and the objects dealt with—such as needs of clients, pipes and plumbing fixtures, and money.

To illustrate the Bordin, Nachmann, and Segal position, it might be useful to consider the antecedents relating to a person whose occupation is a lathe operator. The hypothesis would be that such a person's primary instinctual gratifications during the first six years of life came from oral aggressive activities—biting, chewing, and devouring. The theory would hold that these activities are converted from teeth to the fingers to knives, saws, and drills and, possibly, to biting and cutting words and ideas. In the case of the lathe operator, the assumption would be that the gratification found in oral aggressiveness tends to become fixation, manifested in personality, and now finds its adult counterparts in such activities as the use of tools for cutting, grinding, and drilling.

Bordin (1984; 1990) has recently reformulated the theory as it was originally conceived with Nachman and Segal. As he suggested in 1989, "the present point of view retains much of the earlier emphasis on the fate and transformation of basic motivations (libidinal and others) but gives prominence to ego development . . . including, of course, ego identity" (p. 96). In particular, he defines seven propositions that emanate from the basic proposition that "the participation of personality in work and career is rooted in the role of play in human life" (p. 96). "The spirit of play is caught in the term spontaneity, which is used to refer to the elements of self-expression and self-realization in our responses to situations. Spontaneity is a major key to differentiating work from play. What marks the essence of play is its intrinsically satisfying nature" (p. 97). He then proposes several propositions that fuse his concern with spontaneity and play, his earlier psychoanalytic perspectives, and his current linkage to ego development and ego identity. His propositions as they appear in his 1990 formulation include the following:

1. This sense of wholeness, this experience of job, is sought by all persons, preferably in all aspects of life, including work (p. 105).

2. The degree of fusion of work and play is a function of an individual's developmental history regarding compulsion and effort (p. 108).
3. A person's life can be seen as a string of career decisions reflecting the individual's groping for an ideal fit between self and work (p. 109).
4. The most useful system of mapping occupations for intrinsic motives will be one that captures life-styles or character styles and stimulates or is receptive to developmental conceptions (p. 115).
5. The roots of the personal aspects of career development are to be found throughout the early development of the individual, sometimes in the earliest years (p. 116).
6. Each individual seeks to build a personal identity that incorporates aspects of father and mother, yet retains elements unique to oneself (p. 116).
7. One source of perplexity and paralysis at career decision points will be found in doubts and dissatisfactions with current resolutions of self (p. 117).

Adler's View. Although Freud's work has been acknowledged repeatedly as the dominant conception of psychology, namely personality theory, future historical writings may give a larger share of that prominence to Alfred Adler. Many current emphases in holistic psychology, the importance of the self-concept as a stimulus to behavior, the individual's ability to hold goals consciously and to plan in accordance with them, the transactional nature of individual personality as a product of social forces, and many concepts of normality have their roots in Adlerian perspectives.

In strong opposition to Freud's major premise that human behavior is essentially determined by inborn instincts, Adler believed that such behavior was motivated by social urges. He fashioned a humanistic theory of personality that was the antithesis of Freud's view (Hall & Lindzey, 1957).

Adler stressed a subjective, creative system of behavior through which persons search for experiences that aid in fulfilling their unique style of life. The self, then, is an important cause of behavior and, indeed, the focus of individual uniqueness. The individual is conscious of inferiorities and of goals held. According to Adler (1927), the major goal of individuals is to overcome inferiority and to obtain superiority within some notions of social interest. There are innumerable ways to strive for superiority, and how this is accomplished fits into a unique style of life. In a sense, persons perceive, learn, and retain what fits the style of life and ignore everything else. In doing so, however, Adler believes that humankind possesses a creative self by which personality is built out of the combined material of heredity and experience. The creative self gives meaning to life and formulates both goals and the means to goals (Adler, 1935).

Although Adler did not make work a central concern of his theory, there is no question that his concepts of personality describe work motivation and the work setting as a place to implement social interest, unique life styles, and superiority. Many of Adler's concepts will appear in different guises in more recent theories described in this chapter.

Jung's View. A contemporary of Adler and Freud, and a competitor to Adler for being considered one of the world's great thinkers in psychology overshadowed only by Freud's impact on psychology's view of human behavior, Carl Gustav Jung developed what came to be termed Analytical Psychology (Jung, 1916). Both his theory of psychoanalysis and his method of psychotherapy, Analytical Psychology, rejected Freud's emphases on sexual gratification, the repetition of instinctual themes, and the influences on a form of childhood personality development as predictive of adult life. Jung wedded "causality" (the conditioning of one's individual and racial history) with teleology (one's aims and aspirations) to explain behavior. Thus, Jung argued that both "the past as actuality and the future as potentiality guide one's present behavior. . . . For Jung, there is constant and often creative development, the search for wholeness and completion, and the yearning for rebirth" (Hall & Lindzey, 1957, p. 78). Jung viewed personality as a complex of interacting systems, and he introduced a rich vocabulary of terms and ideas to the psychological literature to provide explanations for the concepts he advanced. Many of the notions now prominent in present-day psychology and in theories of career development originated with Jung's voluminous writings. In some cases he borrowed terms from other psychologists; in other cases he borrowed terms and concepts from mythology, religion, archeology, and other disciplines; in other instances, he created his own terms. Among the systems about which he was concerned were the ego, the personal unconscious and its complexes, the collective unconscious and its archetypes, the persona, the anima and animus, and the shadow. He talked of psychic energy and psychic values. Although few contemporary writers acknowledge it, Jung introduced the term self-actualization as the goal of individual development, the ultimate end to which humankind strives, the progression of development from a global to a differentiated to an integrated state.

With respect to the principal connection of Jung's theory to contemporary manifestations in career counseling and career assessment, the conceptual origins upon which the Myers-Briggs Type Indicator rests would probably be the most recognizable to readers. Jung distinguished two major attitudes or orientations of personality, the attitude of extraversion and the attitude of introversion. An extraverted attitude orients the person toward the external, objective world; an introverted attitude orients the person toward the inner, subjective world (Jung, 1933). In addition, Jung described four fundamental psychological functions: thinking, feeling, sensing, and intuiting. It is these functions in combination with extraverted-introverted orientations that create the base for the Myers-Briggs assessment of types and its attempt to measure the basic differences in the way individuals prefer to use their perception and judgment. The Myers-Briggs Type Indicator measures 16 MBTI types which are reflected in different combinations of the four separate indices that emanate from Jung's work: attitudes related to Extraversion (E) or Introversion (I); processes of perception assessed by Sensing (S) or Intuition (N); processes of judgment as reflected in Thinking (T) and Feeling (F); and the style of dealing with the outside world as shown by Judgment (J) or Perception (P) (Myers & McCaulley, 1985, p. 3). Thus, the type that is identified from the four basic preferences reflects the dominant process by which people are likely to habitually direct their transactions with their environment, education, work, and social interactions.

Maccoby's Research. Maccoby (1980) examined Fromm's extension of Freud's concepts as related to how work influences the potential for pathological versus healthy development. Fromm contended that individual development occurs through stages, from helplessness and dependency to the increasing capacity for independence, reason, mutuality, and creative expression. This process depends on biological maturation and social training, which derives from family influences and those of other agents of society, including work. Maccoby points out that within Fromm's model, psychopathology can be understood as a person's regressive attempt to recreate an infant's sense of total protectiveness, by controlling the world and by seeking a feeling of omnipotence. The result is to become more unconsciously driven, more helpless, and ultimately more despairing. Within this context, work can be viewed as playing a major role in determining an individual's developmental level. Work can stimulate life-affirming attitudes and growth and development, or through frustration and oppression stimulate regressive attitudes. As Maccoby points out, for those on the borderline between normalcy and psychopathology, stressful work or an unhealthy work environment can trigger regressive solutions and behaviors, unproductive attitudes, and similar negative behavior. Presumably decisions made in such a psychic frame of reference would reflect the individual's view of work as repressive or as challenging and growth producing.

Maccoby (1976) has also applied psychoanalytic and socioeconomic concepts to the understanding of upward mobility in high-technology corporations. He described this process of social selection as a function of the corporate "psychostructure" that selects and molds certain kinds of behavior in order to achieve congruence between the work requirements and the character of those who do the work. Maccoby found that in these corporations, individuals who move upward on the career path must be highly motivated to do what the organization requires them to do and to restrain personal traits that do not fit the requirements of the workplace and the images afforded by the psychostructure. Again, on the negative side, depending on the psychostructure operating, such requirements can attract certain types of emotional disturbance, or stimulate dependency, compliance, and other regressive behavior leading in turn to substance abuse, underdeveloped feelings of compassion and affection, and other related phenomena.

The psychoanalytic view of occupational choice or career development has less research to validate its assumptions than most of the other emphases discussed in this chapter. In addition, criticisms have been leveled at the theory's inadequacy to consider the effects of external forces on choice such as economic, cultural, or geographic limitations, although such criticisms are not often focused on such persons as Adler, Jung, or Fromm. Finally, the psychoanalytic position of Freud, in particular, suggests that career guidance or career education could do very little after early childhood to alter individual career development. The role of the counselor would be limited to helping persons identify the pertinent mode of gratification they seek and the occupations that might satisfy those needs.

Roe's Approach. The theoretical and research efforts of Roe (1956) also apply personality theory to career development. Roe marries two major personality theories to vocational behavior: (1) the earlier work of Gardner Murphy (1947)—in particular, Murphy's canalization of psychic energy and emphasis on the relationship between early childhood experiences and later vocational choices; and (2) Maslow's (1954) theory of prepotent needs. Roe also accents genetic factors as these interact with need hierarchies to determine vocational behavior and choice. "In other words, given 'equal' endowments genetically, differences in occupational achievement between two individuals may be inferred to be the result of motivational differences which theoretically are likely to be the outcomes of different childhood experiences" (Osipow, 1968, p. 18).

In a retrospective view of her work (Roe & Lunneborg, 1984), Roe has stated, "My theoretical concerns have focused on two apparently disparate areas and their subsequent integration—personality theory and occupational classification. My purpose has been to view the whole range of occupations in terms of their relationship to individual differences in backgrounds, physical and psychological variables, and experiences" (p. 31).

Roe's early conceptualizations derived from her studies of different types of scientists (1953). From such research she concluded that some personality differences evolve from childrearing practices (such as rejecting, overprotecting, democratic) and that these differences are related to the kinds of interaction that such persons ultimately establish with other people—toward them or not toward them—and with things. Affected strongly by the psychoanalytic notion that the first few years of life encompass the primary experiences shaping adult behavior, she identified the substance of three primary childrearing practices.

She describes the first as *emotional concentration on the child*, which includes the opposite extremes of overprotective and overdemanding behavior. Children who have been intensely conditioned to receive need gratification from their parents if certain contingencies were met might choose occupations that would give them a high level of feedback and reward—such as the performing arts. The second childrearing pattern is that of *advoidance of the child*. The continuum of parental responses in this pattern might include emotional rejection of the child as well as physical neglect. The hypothesis here would be that the child would look to nonpersons and things, and would have limited contacts with others as bases for gratification. In such instances, scientific and mechanical interests are likely to develop as ways of finding gratification without reliance on others. The third childrearing practice is *acceptance of the child*, which might involve either casual acceptance or loving acceptance, incorporating the child into the family unit as one among equals in a democratic process. In this third childrearing practice, it is assumed that a child's independence is encouraged, and that he or she may seek occupations that balance personal and nonpersonal interests without the need for isolation from others or intense approval from them.

Roe suggests then that there are relationships between the psychic energy, genetic propensities, and childhood experiences that shape individual styles of behavior, and that the impulse to acquire opportunities to express these individual styles is inherent in the choices made and the ensuing career behavior. Thus, the strength of a particular need, the delay between the arousal of the need and its satisfaction, and the value that the satisfaction has in the individual's environment are the conditions—shaped by early childhood experiences—that influence career development. These inputs to Roe's thinking can be summarized into two perspectives on the origin of vocational interests, that (1) career directions are first determined by "the patterning of early satisfactions and frustrations," and that (2) "the modes and degrees of need satisfaction will determine which needs will become the strongest motivations" (Roe & Siegelman, 1964, p. 5). Roe's 1984 summary of her research findings shows that there is no direct link between parent-child relations and occupational choice. But, she concludes that this finding does not invalidate her propositions concerning needs and interests as determinants of motivation and accomplishment (Roe & Lunneborg, 1984).

As Roe's work was taking shape after World War II, so was that of Maslow, whose theory has probably been the most influential yet developed in shaping the concepts of needs. To elaborate her need constructs, Roe applied Maslow's theory of prepotent needs to career behavior. Maslow (1954) arranged human needs in a hierarchy in which he conceived the emergence of higher-order needs as contingent on the relative satisfaction of lower-order, more primitive needs. The needs in ascending order are as follows:

1. physiological needs
2. safety needs
3. needs for belongingness and love
4. needs for importance, self-esteem, respect, independence
5. need for information
6. need for understanding
7. need for beauty
8. need for self-actualization

Perhaps one or two simple illustrations of the meaning of Maslow's hierarchy will be useful here. For example, one might cite the instance of a child doing poorly in school who comes from a home where food is scarce and the parents are considering divorce. A teacher might chastise the child for not doing his or her homework and not caring about school. The more accurate view is that the child is preoccupied with satisfying physiological and safety needs. Until these can be relatively taken for granted, the child is unlikely to be motivated by needs for information or understanding. A similar translation can be made in seeking certain kinds of work. The person who has lived through a depression where work is limited and large numbers of people have no money or little food is likely to view the security aspects of work more positively than the person who has not been exposed to such poverty and is freer to seek high-order needs in work.

Roe's concerns with specific childrearing practices, the manner in which the parents interact with the child, the resulting need structure, and the ensuing orientation toward or away from persons were measured by the Parent-Child Relations Questionnaire, constructed by Roe and Seigleman in 1963 (Roe & Lunneborg, 1990). The results were translated into a useful field and level classification of occupations, including the following (Roe, 1956, pp. 143–152; Roe & Lunneborg, 1984; 1990):

Fields	*Levels*
I. Service	1. Professional and Managerial (1)
II. Business Contact	2. Professional and Managerial (2)
III. Organizations	3. Semiprofessional, Small Business
IV. Technology	4. Skilled
V. Outdoor	5. Semiskilled
VI. Science	6. Unskilled
VII. General Culture	
VIII. Arts and Entertainment	

This conceptualization of the occupational structure has been variously represented as a two-dimensional matrix, a circular array, and as a cone. The original notion was that this was a two-dimensional classification of fields or job families that were primarily defined by their content expressed by a things-versus-person orientation. The second dimension, levels, deals with the work complexity or responsibility involved in a particular job. The choice of fields is considered to be a function of interests; the level attained is dependent on genetic factors manifested in intelligence as well as the style of environmental manipulation.

This field and level classification, which also has been described as a circular array (Roe, 1956) of occupational groups contiguous in their emphasis on people (Groups I, II, III, VII, VIII) or on things (Groups IV, V, VI), has been supported by Perrone (1964). He found that high school boys with similar scores on cognitive measures tend to prefer similar occupational groups as defined by Roe's eight groups. Indeed, when job changes are examined they are found to be nonrandom. That is, people typically move from one job in one group to another in the same group as defined by Roe's classification scheme. They do not typically move to a group in which the orientation or activity is in direct opposition to the initial group (Hutchinson & Roe, 1968). The research of Knapp and Knapp (1977), among others, has also supported such findings.

While studies of Roe's model of the occupational classification structure have been supportive, although less so for women than for men, as Roe has suggested herself, the research on the effects of parent-child relations and occupational choice has not shown direct links or have yielded negative results, even though there exists some evidence that adult attitudes toward or not toward persons are affected by early childhood experiences (Roe & Lunneborg, 1984; 1990; Green & Parker, 1965).

The personality approach of Bordin, Nachmann, and Segal earlier discussed (and that of Roe) imply that occupational choices are made as aspects of self-classification, whether the central focus is impulse gratification or need satisfaction. Thus, occupational choices and career patterns are affirmations of personal behavioral styles.

In sum, Roe's pioneering work in career development has had an important impact on interest assessment and on career development research. Although more difficult to trace, it is also likely that her work on early family determinants of vocational choice and needs satisfaction have been incorporated into the practice of career counseling as a stimulus to hypotheses that might be tested with individual clients and that might be related to analyses of occupational classifications that could be personally relevant (Roe & Lunneborg, 1990).

Holland's Theory. Holland's (1966, 1973, 1985) approach gives explicit attention to behavioral style or personality type as the major influence in career choice and development. In this sense, Holland's work is part of a long tradition of conceptualizations of individual differences in personality type encompassing the work of such persons as Spranger (1928) and Murray (1938). Spranger described six basic types of individuality: theoretic, economic, aesthetic, social, political, and religious. Murray proposed a series of needs and press (environmental characteristics, reinforcers, rewards) that he combined into a need-press paradigm designed to explain differential behavior in organizations.

Holland's theory has been described as structural-interactive "because it provides an explicit link between various personality characteristics and corresponding job titles and because it organizes the massive data about people and jobs" (Weinrach, 1984, p. 63).

Holland has suggested that structural-interactive approaches share several common themes. They include the following:

(1) The choice of an occupation is an expression of personality and not a random event, although chance plays a role.
(2) The members of an occupational group have similar personalities and similar histories of personal development.
(3) Because people in an occupational group have similar personalities, they will respond to many situations and problems in similar ways.
(4) Occupational achievement, stability, and satisfaction depend on congruence between one's personality and the job environment. (Holland, 1982, p. 2)

As might be expected from the content of such propositions, Holland (1985) has indicated that the intellectual roots for his theory are in differential psychology—primarily interest measurement—and in typologies of personality (p. x).

Indeed, Holland's contributions are equally prominent in the area of environmental assessment and in understanding person-situation interactions as they are in understanding individual behavior. Much of his effort has been devoted to developing structures for understanding and predicting the behavior of persons in different types of environments. Holland and his associates have also made extremely important contributions to the understanding of vocational interests in relation to personality characteristics; to the importance of both academic and nonacademic accomplishments to life; and to the development of instruments useful both in testing his theoretical propositions and in translating his theory into career guidance tools. The most notable of the latter are the Vocational Preference Inventory, My Vocational Situation, the Self-Directed-Search and the Holland themes used in the Strong-Campbell Interest Inventory. Finally, Holland's theory has generated hundreds of studies in the past two decades that have tested, refined, and extended his propositions with diverse populations, in different settings, and in many nations of the world (Holland & Gottfredson, 1990). We will identify a few studies to suggest some of the lines of ongoing inquiry after we identify the primary assumptions of the theory.

Holland assumes that the individual is a product of heredity and environment. As a result of early and continuing influences of genetic potentialities and the interaction of the individual with his or her environment, there develops a hierarchy of habitual or preferred methods for dealing with social and environmental tasks. The most typical way in which an individual responds to the environment is described as *modal personal orientation*.

Four assumptions constitute the heart of Holland's theory:

> 1. In our culture, most persons can be categorized as one of six types; realistic, investigative, artistic, social, enterprising, or conventional.
> 2. There are six kinds of environments: realistic, investigative, artistic, social enterprising, and conventional.
> 3. People search for environments that will let them exercise their skills and abilities, express their attitudes and values, and take on agreeable problems and roles.
> 4. A person's behavior is determined by an interaction between his personality and the characteristics of his environment. (Holland, 1973, pp. 2–4; 1985)

To emphasize the interactive character of his theory, found in person-situation correspondence, Holland has classified work environments into six categories analogous to the six personal orientations. In other words, he describes the person and the working environment in the same terms. Accordingly, Holland makes explicit, more than do most of his contemporaries, that occupations are ways of life, environments that manifest the characteristics of those inhabiting them as opposed to being simply sets of isolated work functions or skills. In addition, Holland has extended his examination of types of occupational environments to educational environments, particularly collegiate.

In condensed and paraphrased form, the major emphases of the six personality types and their relationships to pertinent occupations are as follows:

1. The *Realistic (R)* type has a preference for activities that require the explicit, ordered, or systematic manipulation of objects, tools, machines, animals; this type has an aversion to educational or therapeutic activities. Examples of occupations that meet the needs of Realistic types are surveyor and mechanic.
2. The *Investigative (I)* type has a preference for activities that entail the observational, symbolic, systematic, and creative investigation of physical, biological, and cultural phenomena in order to understand and control such phenomena; this type has aversion to persuasive, social, and repetitive activities. Examples of occupations that meet the needs of Investigative types are chemist and physicist.
3. The *Artistic (A)* type prefers ambiguous, free, unsystematized activities that entail the manipulation of physical, verbal, or human materials to create art forms or products; this type has an aversion to explicit, systematic, and ordered activities. Examples of occupations that meet the needs of Artistic types are artist and writer.
4. The *Social (S)* type prefers activities that entail the manipulation of others to inform, train, develop, cure, or enlighten; this type has an aversion to explicit, ordered, systematic activities involving materials, tools, or machines. Examples of occupations that meet the needs of Social types are social science teacher and vocational counselor.
5. The *Enterprising (E)* type prefers activities that require the manipulation of others to attain organizational goals or economic gain; this type has an aversion to observational, symbolic, and systematic activities. Examples of occupations that meet the needs of Enterprising types are political scientist, salesman, and executive.
6. The *Conventional (C)* type prefers activities that entail the explicit, ordered, systematic manipulation of data, such as keeping records, filing materials, reproducing materials, organizing written and numerical data ac-

cording to a prescribed plan, operating business machines and data processing machines to attain organizational or economic goals; this type has an aversion to ambiguous, free, exploratory, or unsystematized activities. Examples of occupations that meet the needs of Conventional types are accountant and clerk. (Holland, 1973, pp. 14–18)

Obviously, it is unlikely that persons fall solely into one of the major personality types described. Therefore a coding system has been devised to indicate the person's primary and secondary types (Holland, Vierstein, Kuo, Karweit, & Blum, 1970). These codes are reflected in three-letter combinations—each letter corresponding to the first letter of one of the six types. For instance, a code of RIA would indicate that the person is most like the Realistic type, next most like Investigative, and third most like Artistic. Holland and his colleagues have also classified hundreds of occupations according to the same three-letter code system. For example, for the code RIA, two occupations are listed—architectural draftsman and dental technician. It is assumed that a person obtaining the code RIA should begin to explore these two occupations and then break into related areas through the use of the *Dictionary of Occupational Titles* and other pertinent references. Holland and his colleagues have also devised a *Dictionary of Holland Codes* which list occupations alphabetically that are related to the various, major permutations of Holland codes (Gottfredson, Holland, & Ogawa, 1982).

Holland, like Roe, addresses himself to level hierarchies within occupational environments. The level hierarchy, or the particular responsibility or skill level within an occupational field that one gravitates to, is dependent on the person's intelligence and self-knowledge. Self-knowledge refers to the amount of accuracy of self-information as contrasted with self-evaluation, which refers to the worth the person attributes to him or herself. A complementary description of Holland's scheme was offered in the previous chapter.

In summary, Holland's theory (1973, 1985) contends that individual behavior is a function of the interaction between one's personality and environment, and that choice behavior is an expression of personality. Thus, people seek those educational and occupational settings that permit expression of their personality styles. Since persons inhabiting particular environments, occupational or educational, have similar personality characteristics, their responses to problems and interpersonal situations are likely to be similar. For these reasons, interest inventories are personality inventories, and vocational stereotypes held by individuals have important psychological and sociological implications. Put another way, it is possible to suggest that, as persons explore occupational possibilities, they use stereotypes of themselves and stereotypes of occupations to guide their search. If their preferences are clear and their information about self or occupations accurate, they will likely make effective choices. If their understanding of their personality type or appropriate occupations is unclear, they are likely to be indecisive and vacillate among possible choices. In Holland's view, the adequacy of information about the self and various occupational possibilities is crucial.

Finally, Holland hypothesizes that congruent interactions of people and environments belonging to the same type or model, in contrast to incongruent interactions, are conducive to more stable vocational choice, higher vocational achievement, higher academic achievement, better maintenance of personal stability, and greater satisfaction.

In 1976, Holland and Gottfredson extended and clarified some of the earlier theoretical propositions. They did so by exploring four major questions:

1. How do personal development, initial vocational choice, work involvement, and satisfaction come about?

> People grow up to resemble one type or another because parents, schools, and neighborhoods serve as environments which reinforce some behaviors more than others and provide different models of suitable behavior. The reinforcement consists of the encouragement of selected activities, interests, self-estimates, and competencies. . . . Different cultural influences as well as other aspects of the interpersonal milieu, such as sex-role socialization, race, religion, and class promote the development of some types more than others by differential encouragement of the experiences (activities, interests, competencies, etc.) that lead to different types. (p. 21)

2. Why do most people have orderly careers when the individual jobs in their work histories are categorized using an occupational classification scheme?

> The majority of people manage to find work that is congruent with their type. More explicitly, the average person searches for or gravitates toward work environments in which his/her typological predilections and talents (activities, competencies, perceptions of self and world, values, traits) are allowed expression and rewarded. . . . By definition, well-defined types know what activities and competencies bring them satisfaction and congruency. . . . Orderly careers are also encouraged by the stereotyped ways in which employers perceive a person's credentials. (p. 21)

3. Why do people change jobs? What influences their search for new jobs?

> People change jobs because they are dissatisfied, because they are incompetent, because other workers wish them to leave, and for other personal and environmental reasons: better climate, physical disability, dissatisfied relatives, more money, and other influences. In theoretical terms, people leave because of excessive person-environment incongruency, or because of an opportunity to increase their congruency. (p. 21)

4. Why do some people make vocational choices that are congruent with assessment data, others do not, and still others are undecided?

> People with consistent and well-defined personality patterns are expected to be "good" decision-makers because of the implications of differentiation and consistency; integration of preferred activities, competencies, occupational preferences and self-estimates; and compatibility of primary dispositions. . . . [Some personality] types may be better decision-makers than others. . . . The making of decisions at appropriate times (end of high school, end of sophomore year, when to change jobs, when to marry, etc.) may reflect only different rates of development and different environmental contingencies. (p. 22)

In the 1985 refinement of his theory, Holland discussed the secondary assumptions that augment the four key assumptions addressed previously. These secondary assumptions—which can be applied to both persons and environments—include the following:

Consistency–Some types of persons or environments have more relationship to each other than do others. Thus, "degrees of consistency or relatedness are assumed to affect vocational preference" (p. 4).

Differentiation–"The degree to which a person or an environment is well-defined is its degree of differentiation. . . . Personal identity is defined as the possession of a clear and stable picture of one's goals, interests, and talents. Environmental identity is preset when an environment or organization has clear, integrated goals, tasks, and rewards that are stable over long time intervals" (p.5).

Congruence–Different personality types require different environments. "Incongruence occurs when a type lives in an environment that provides opportunities and rewards foreign to the person's preferences and abilities—for instance, a realistic type in a social environment" (p. 5).

Calculus–"The relationships within and between types or environments can be ordered according to a hexagonal model in which the distances between the types or environments are inversely proportional to the theoretical relationships between them" (p. 5).

Following the earlier emphases on the four key assumptions identified earlier, Holland added a fifth assumption (Holland, 1984), that of identity. In essence, identity has to do with the possession of a clear and stable picture of one's goals, interests, and talents. With regard to identity in organization, the focus is on the organization's clarity, stability, and integration of goals, tasks, and rewards.

As indicated at the beginning of this section, Holland himself and his associates have been extremely productive in both generating and testing his theoretical propositions. As one might expect with a theory that is both comprehensive in the questions it stimulates and dynamic, the findings reported are somewhat mixed, although they typically support the theoretical propositions. To illustrate the range of research engendered by Holland's theory, a few selected studies will be described.

1. Personality type and values—Laudeman and Griffith (1978) studied the relationship among personality typology, environmental orientation, and values of six different groups of male seniors at a midwestern university. Each group represented one of Holland's primary personality types through the following majors: mechanical engineering, electrical engineering, elementary education, accounting, marketing, and art or music education. Holland's Vocational Preference Inventory (VPI) was used to assess personality types and the Allport-Vernon-Lindsey Study of Values was used to measure six basic values or motives in personality. Although there were some inconsistencies among engineering and education majors with regard to their highest mean scores on the VPI personality scales, the researchers concluded that male college seniors in this sample did generally reflect personality types and value dimensions that correspond with their major field of study in accordance with what would be predicted by Holland's theory.

2. Consistency—Holland's notion of consistency has also been tested in different ways. This concept, advanced in 1973, is related to his six major personality types, which are arranged in a model that corresponds to their intercorrelations (see Figure 4.3).

In looking at the hexagons for men and women, one can see that those personality types with the highest positive correlations are arranged together on the outside of the hexagon, whereas those types with the smallest correlation are the farthest apart on the diagram. The intermediate distances have correlations of intermediate size.

Consistency, according to Holland, is the degree to which the dominant and subdominant interest types (the first two expressed vocational choices) of a person or an environment are similar to each other as demonstrated by their adjacent position or closeness on the hexagonal model. The assumption is that persons whose dominant personality (interest) types are essentially consistent would be more integrated in their characteristics (traits, values, perceptions) than persons whose interest types are much more disparate. Such consistent persons would be more vocationally mature. Further, consistent persons would likely be more predictable and higher achievers than inconsistent persons. Erwin (1982) examined changes in college majors, course withdrawals, and other indices of academic performance in relation to Holland's construct of consistency but found only weak support for the construct as it was measured in this study. However, Wiley and Magoon (1982) studied the construct of consistency in social person-

Figure 4.3

Holland's Hexagon for Men and Women. (Reprinted from *Perspectives On Vocational Development,* edited by John M. Whitely and Arthur Resnikoff. APGA Press, 1972. © AACD. Reprinted with permission. No further reproduction authorized without written permission of American Association for Counseling and Development.)

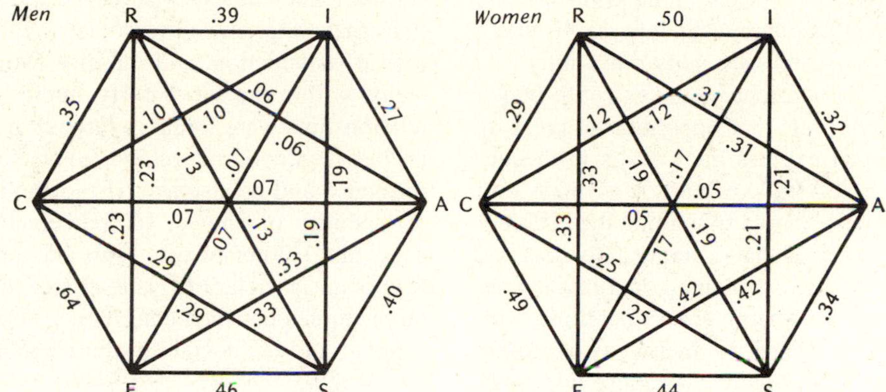

ality types (211 college freshmen) in relation to persistence in college and academic achievement. They found significant results in favor of the construct. For example, high- and medium-consistency subjects persisted in college at a higher rate than low-consistency subjects and the relationship between consistency and college grade point averages was also significant.

3. Congruency—Related to the studies of Erwin and Wiley and Magoon of the usefulness of Holland's typology for predicting persistence and performance in college, Bruch and Krieshok (1981) studied Holland's notion of congruence and person-situation compatibility among theoretically-oriented engineering majors. The researchers hypothesized that high congruence (an investigative student in an investigative major) compared to moderately high congruence (a realistic student in an investigative major) would result in greater persistence and better academic performance. The hypotheses were confirmed in that high student-curriculum congruence (I-type student in I-type major) demonstrated greater academic achievement and persistence in the initial engineering major over a two-year period than did student-curriculum congruence, which was moderate. Spokane (1979) followed up 232 women and 386 men in their senior year who had taken the Strong-Campbell Interest Inventory in their freshman year. He found that congruent students were more satisfied and differentiated than incongruent students and that they perceived themselves to be more congruent. Barak and Rabbi (1982), in a study of 293 undergraduate students randomly stratified across majors representing different Holland categories, found that consistent students tend to persist in college, do not change majors, and achieve more than inconsistent students. Consistency in this study related to people who possess a consistent personality pattern and an integration of similar interests, competencies, values, traits, and perceptions, and was reflected here in the degree to which students at registration made the first two choices of major in the same or adjacent Holland category (investigative-investigative, investigative-realistic, and so on).

Meir (1989) and other researchers have expanded the concept of congruence and its demonstrated relationship to satisfaction and well-being in several ways. In particular, they have tested the cumulative effect of three kinds of congruence: (1) occupational congruence as originally proposed in the Holland theory; (2) avocational competence—the degree to which one's avocational choice suits one's interests; and, (3) skill congruence—the extent to which the individual feels that opportunities exist by which one can express one's skills in the occupational role. In two studies of male and female teachers, it was found that the different types of congruence had a cumulative effect on well-being. Those with one congruence were higher on the well-being scale than those with no congruences. Those with either two or three congruences were higher than those with only one.

Gottfredson and Holland (1990), in a longitudinal and statistically complex study of 345 newly hired bank tellers (75 percent female, 74 percent between 18 and 26 years of age) over a four-month interval, found that person-job congruence did have substantial correlations with job satisfaction in a well-defined, homogeneous sample. Such results support the hypothesis that congruent work environments allow the expression of a person's interests and competencies. However, in some contrast to expectations from other research, the study did *not* find that person-job incongruence resulted in counterproductive work behavior, role ambiguity, or role conflict.

Spokane (1985) conducted a comprehensive and insightful review of the major studies of person-environment congruence in Holland's theory of careers. He divided the studies into two basic categories of research design. The first category incorporated those studies that typically take place at one point in time, employ correlational techniques, and compare subjects classified as congruent or incongruent on some set of criterion variables. The second design category contains time series or experimental designs that study change in congruence over time. Spokane included in his analysis forty correlational and twenty-three change studies.

His summary of the conclusions from the correlational studies supports Holland's predictions that congruence is associated with performance, satisfaction, and stability. More specifically, within the set of forty studies, positive relationships were found in three or more studies between congruence and (a) academic performance and persistence, (b) job satisfaction, (c) stability of choice, (d) perceived congruency, and (e) personality (ego strength). Nonsignificant correlations were found in three or more studies between congruence and (a) self-concept and (b) sociability-based measures of personality.

The conclusions from the change studies suggest that adjustments or shifts from science to nonscience occupations are largely complete by age 30 and that personality modifications accompany such changes and are geared in the direction of the shifts. People who remain in an environment become and perceive themselves to be more similar to the modal personality type found in that setting. When placed in a congruent environment, individuals feel a better fit.

In summarizing his review of congruence research, Spokane indicates that such research "reveals a consistent relationship between congruence and a number of measures of vocational satisfaction and adjustment. We also conclude that incongruence can be resolved by a change in the person, a change in job, or both" (p. 336). He also cites some important implications of congruence for counseling; for example, the concept of congruence is a useful organizer for a client as long as it is not used to suggest that the client is likely to find a perfect job. Citing the perspectives of Gottfredson (Gottfredson, 1981), his review suggests that counselors should help clients "to outline ranges or zones of congruent occupations that are delimited by (a) field, (b) level, (c) sex type, and (d) amount of effort and education required" (p. 336). Two other important counseling implications that flow from this review are that (1) frequently, incongruence may more likely be resolved by a change within the client or a change in personal aspiration than by a change in job, and (2) individuals whose measured interests are incongruent with the job or college major they have chosen can be identified early in their careers and helped to examine their situation through counseling or other means.

4. Occupational classification—In 1973, Helms suggested that the Holland Occupational Classification system could be used to organize occupational information, analyze work histories, and develop occupational exploration plans for clients. These possible uses exist at least partially because Holland's system organizes occupations "into homogeneous groups based on their psychological similarities" (Helms, 1973, p. 69).

Scanlan (1980) has applied Holland's occupational classification system to self-employed men and found it useful in differentiating what he described as craft entrepreneurs and opportunistic entrepreneurs. He also found that, in accordance with the theory, the educational interests of the respondents, the types of occupations they held before self-employment, and the types of work on which craft and opportunistic entrepreneurs spend their time in the course of operating their businesses all reflect the three-letter Holland codes by which they were differentiated. Jones (1980), for example, has shown how the Holland typology can be useful with the *Guide for Occupational Exploration* published by the U.S. Department of Labor in 1979. Rounds, Davison, and Dawis (1979) used a multidimensional scaling procedure to examine the fit of Holland's hexagonal model to the General Occupational Theme scales of the Strong-Campbell Interest Inventory, which are based on the Holland model. The fit for males was good. For females, the relationship was less good, suggesting caution in the use and interpretation of the SCII occupational themes for females.

Holland, Gottfredson, and Baker (1990) have extended earlier research in the predictive validity of vocational aspirations—categorized according to an occupational classification system based on the Holland theory—which suggests the efficiency of such an approach as compared to the use of an interest inventory. This study of Navy recruits (467 men and 250 women) was designed to examine the coherence and validity of vocational aspirations (concurrent, retrospective, and predictive), and to provide a more explicit psychological interpretation of such phenomena. The main findings were that expressed vocational preferences—singly or in combination—were superior to the interest inventory (in this case, the Vocational Preference Inventory) in tests of predictive, concurrent, or retrospective validity. The conclusions of the authors were that these results, as tests of relationships to their retrospective preferences about civilian occupations and preferences for Naval occupations early and late in base training, were "consistent with the literature showing the substantial predictive validity of categorized self-expressed aspirations or preferences" (p. 340).

5. Gottfredson (1980) compared six schemes for describing occupations in order to examine the construct validity of Holland's typology of work environments and to estimate the amount of information shared by these commonly used classification systems. The five occupational classification systems studied, in addition to the Holland system, included occupational prestige, activities and requirements presented in the DOT, self-direction, the twelve major census categories, and the occupational reinforcer patterns formulated in the Minnesota Theory of Work Adjustment (Lofquist

& Dawis, 1969). Acknowledging limitations in both the data available for the occupations examined and the differing or uncertain validity of the classification schemes used, Gottfredson's evidence does support the construct validity of Holland's occupational scheme. She finds that it is superior to the census classification scheme in its potential flexibility and interpretation. She does recommend, however, that the Holland work typology be supplemented by a measure of occupational prestige so that the resulting information would include a paradigm of work type by level. Gottfredson also contends that a greater specificity is needed in the domains of job characteristics to which Holland's constructs apply than has been true in the past. For example, Holland's characterizations are more applicable to some types of occupational differences (for example, worker traits required and job activities performed) than to others (for example, work products or job context).

6. Rounds, Shubsachs, Dawis, and Lofquist (1978) classified 181 occupations, for which reinforcer rating data were available, into the six Holland environmental models. The Minnesota Job Description Questionnaire provides ratings of twenty-one reinforcers (such as ability utilization, achievement, activity, advancement, and authority) in different occupations (see Chapter 16). The authors concluded that the results provided only modest support for Holland's environmental formulations, particularly that of consistency. They also reported finding a different order of intercorrelations among the Holland Scale that has been used to construct the hexagon (RCSIAE or REAISC rather than RIASEC as proposed by Holland). Finally, they suggested that descriptions of occupational environments based on vocational interests and vocational preferences, as is Holland's, differ from those based on environmental characteristics (occupational reinforcers and behavioral requirements) such as the Minnesota Theory of Work Adjustment. Gottfredson (1980) has suggested that the data of Rounds et al. be reevaluated to account for the effects of prestige level. Super (1981), however, would likely be somewhat more supportive of the findings of Rounds et al. since he contends that the one fundamental methodological flaw in most of Holland's work "is the fact that both Holland's predictors and his criteria have been preferences. . . . The predictor has usually been either the score on an interest inventory consisting of occupational titles or expressed vocational preferences classified according to Holland's hexagon. The criterion has been the vocational preference (another occupational title) expressed at some later date" (p. 20).

7. Validity by sex and by minority group—Another line of research dealing with Holland's theory has to do with its validity for men and women and across racial groups. Doty and Betz (1979) studied the concurrent validity of Holland's theory for men and women employed in an enterprising occupation. In general, the findings suggested that, at least within an employed sample, Holland's theory is valid for both men and women as defined by equally high scores on the E-theme in the Strong-Campbell Interest Inventory and the Self-Directed Search and by relationships between enterprising scale scores and job satisfaction. Walsh, Bingham, Horton, and Spokane (1979) studied the differences between 155 college-degreed black and white women employed in three traditional male occupations (engineering, medicine, and law). They found that white and black women in the same occupation tended to obtain similar mean scores on the VPI and the SDS. Ward and Walsh (1981) also studied the concurrent validity of Holland's theory for employed noncollege-degreed black women. The subjects were 102 black women working in occupations representing each of the six vocational environments described by Holland. Four scales of the VPI and four scales of the

SDS successfully differentiated the work environments of the women consistently with Holland's theoretical propositions.

8. How people acquire their characteristics—One line of research inquiry that has not been fully explored deals with how people become various types. Perhaps the central assumptions about the matter lie in Holland's perception that "a person becomes oriented toward some occupations as opposed to others because of a special life history of activities, competencies, self-perceptions, values, and so forth. Consequently, if we desire to change the vocational aspirations of a person or a special group, we must change the experience of people before they arrive at the age when they must go to work" (Holland, 1973b, pp. 5–6).

Holland's theory has been characterized by its comprehensive attention to the structure of career behavior and the determinants of career choice; it has not professed to be a process or developmentally oriented approach to change in such factors over time. Such emphases lie more nearly in the section that follows.

In sum, then, Holland's theory continues to stimulate other lines of inquiry, raise new questions, and find new applications. Although much research remains to be done on the hypotheses generated by the theory, it continues to be a major conceptual structure for considering choice, persistence, and performance in educational and occupational settings.

Weinrach and Srebalus (1990) have summarized the most important changes in Holland's theory over the course of its history presented here in abridged form:

> (1) The theory has expanded its constructs, becoming more comprehensive and explicit.
> (2) Throughout its evolution, new concepts (for example, identity) have been added to prop up others. The theory's limitations are more explicit.
> (3) The theory remains in the tradition of differential psychology. . . .
> (4) It has moved away from all-or-none distinctions among environmental and personality types and toward statements of degree and patterning.
> (5) All major constructs have operational definitions, and these enable careful empirical verification of the theory.
> (6) A two-dimensional scientific model (the hexagon) has been added.
> (7) Empirical evidence, pro and con, has been generated in more than 450 studies across populations of diverse characteristics.
> (8) Application of the theory to career planning and counseling has been encouraged through the development and refinement of practitioner and self-help tools.
> (9) Procedures have been developed to teach the theory and evaluate mastery of it.
> (10) While continually open to revision based on empirical evidence, Holland's theory has successfully resisted modifications intended to satisfy prescriptive cultural and political pressures. (Weinrach & Srebalus, 1990, pp. 47–48)

DEVELOPMENTAL APPROACHES

Developmental emphases on career behavior and decision making differ from the approaches previously discussed, not because they reject the latter but rather because they are typically more inclusive, more concerned with longitudinal expressions of career behavior, and more inclined to highlight the importance of the self-concept. They tend to be process-oriented in their conceptions of how career behavior develops and changes over time.

Ginzberg, Ginsburg, Axelrad, and Herma. Ginzberg, Ginsburg, Axelrad, and Herma (1951)—a team composed of an economist, a psychiatrist, a sociologist, and a psychologist respectively—were early leaders in speculating about career development as a process that culminates in an occupational choice in one's early twenties. In particular, they asserted that "occupational choice is a developmental process: it is not a single decision, but a series of decisions made over a period of years. Each step in the process has a meaningful relation to those which precede and follow it" (p. 185). Ginzberg and his colleagues identified four sets of factors, the interplay of which influences the ultimate vocational choice: individual values, emotional factors, the amount and kind of education, and the effect of reality through environmental pressures. These factors undergird the formation of attitudes, which converge to shape occupational choice. More particularly, Ginzberg et al. saw choice as a process delimited by life stages, in which certain tasks are faced by preadolescents and adolescents. Within the interaction that occurs as these tasks are confronted, compromises between wishes and possibilities contribute to an irreversibility as the process unfolds.

Ginzberg and his associates have labeled the gross phases of the vocational choice process—the period of development—as fantasy (from birth to age 11), tentative (11 to 17), and realistic age (age 17 to early twenties). Except for fantasy, each of these periods has subaspects. Thus, the tentative period is divided into stages of interest, capacity, value, and transition. Following this period, there emerges the realistic period, which is broken into exploration, crystallization, and specification.

Ginzberg et al. have given credence to the notion that vocational behavior finds its roots in the early life of the child and develops over time. They have indicated that vocational behavior and career choice become increasingly reality-oriented and specific as one moves toward the choice itself.

In the reformulation of his theory 20 years after the first statement, Ginzberg (1972) suggested some modifications. First, he contended that the process of occupational choice-making does not end at young adulthood. Rather, it is likely to occur throughout the individual's working life with changes in goals or work situations requiring decision making and remaking. Second, Ginzberg has dampened his emphasis on the irreversibility of occupational choice. Finally, he has substituted the term *optimization* for the earlier term *compromise*. The point here is that individuals constantly try to improve the occupational fit between their changing selves and circumstances. As shifts continue to occur in work and other aspects of life, the person must deal with new decisions designed to balance possible gains against economic and psychological costs. Ginzberg's reformulated theory now includes the following elements (paraphrased):

1. Occupational choice is a process that remains open as long as one makes and expects to make decisions about work and career. Often occupational choice and working life are coterminous.
2. The decisions made during the preparatory period (principally schooling through adolescence) will help shape later career, but changes occurring in work and life will also influence career.
3. Decisions about jobs and careers are individual attempts to optimize the fit between personal priority needs and desires and the work opportunities and constraints that occur.

In 1984, Ginzberg again reviewed his 1951 and 1972 theoretical constructs and suggested their modification. By the time of his most recent reformulation, Ginzberg's three original colleagues had died, and, therefore, the 1984 formulation was his own summary of the research he had engaged in for three-and-a-half decades in the Institute for the Conservation of Human Resources, which he headed at Columbia University.

In the 1951 formulation of their theory, Ginzberg et al. had focused on three concepts; process, irreversibility, and compromise. Originally, they gave little attention to the possibility of reopening decisions and their effects upon career development after the age of 20 or so. By 1984, however, Ginzberg had modified the early perspectives to suggest that "what happens to a person before he reaches twenty will affect his career, but he retains considerable scope for later decision-making" (1984, p. 179).

In 1972, and again in 1984, Ginzberg suggested a reformulation of the factors involved in a lifelong choice process, including the original choice (essentially what the 1951 formulation addressed), the feedback between the original choice and later work experience, and economic and family circumstances. Ginzberg contends, then, that "if the original choice did not lead to the anticipated satisfactions, the individual was likely to reopen the choice process, which in turn would be conditioned and influenced by the degrees of freedom permitted by his family circumstances and the economy" (1984, p. 179). Such a perspective led to a third and current restatement of the core concepts of his theory: "Occupational choice is a lifelong process of decision making for those who seek major satisfactions from their work. This leads them to reassess repeatedly how they can improve the fit between their changing career goals and the realities of the world of work" (1984, p. 180). Ginzberg goes on to say that "these emendations, improvements, and corrections of our original theory, first developed in 1951, still conceive of occupational choice as a process in which the early decisions an individual makes will restrict his or her later scope of action. Our theory predicts that the individual will make a career choice that will balance competing interests and values and take into account the opportunities available and the costs of pursuing them" (1984, p. 180).

Super's Developmental Approach. Probably the developmental approach that has received the most continuous attention, stimulated the most research, influenced the field of vocational psychology most pervasively, and is the most comprehensive is that promulgated by Super and his many colleagues in the longitudinal Career Pattern Study, which provided much of the data to test his theoretical perspectives (Super et al., 1957; Super et al., 1963; Super, 1969a, 1969b; Jordaan & Heyde, 1979). This approach is an integrative one, stressing the interaction of personal and environmental variables in career development.

Super had provided early input into the Ginzberg statement but believed that it was deficient in several respects (Super, 1953). According to his view, the Ginzberg position did not take into account previous pertinent research (such as the nature of interests in vocational choice); it failed to describe "choice" in an operationally acceptable way; it made a sharp distinction between choice and "adjustment" when, in fact, the two were blended in adolescence and virtually indistinguishable in adulthood; and it failed to delineate the process of compromise.

In response to these conditions, Super formulated his own theory consisting of 10 major propositions, each of which was testable and, indeed, could provide the framework for a longitudinal research study. The original 10 propositions were put forward in 1953, expanded to 12 in 1957 (Super & Bachrach, 1957) and expanded again in the 1970s and 80s. In 1990, they include the 14 that follow:

1. People differ in their abilities and personalities, needs, values, interests, traits, and self-concepts.
2. People are qualified, by virtue of these characteristics, each for a number of occupations.
3. Each occupation requires a characteristic pattern of abilities and personality traits, with tolerances wide enough to allow both some variety of occupations for each individual and some variety of individuals in each occupation.
4. Vocational preferences and competencies, the situations in which people live

and work, and, hence, their self-concepts change with time and experience, although self-concepts, as products of social learning, are increasingly stable from late adolescence until late maturity, providing some continuity in choice and adjustment.

5. This process of change may be summed up in a series of life stages (a "maxicycle") characterized as a sequence of growth, exploration, establishment, maintenance, and decline, and these stages may in turn be subdivided into (a) the fantasy, tentative, and realistic phase of the exploratory stage and (b) the trial and stable phases of the establishment stage. A small (mini) cycle takes place in transitions from one stage to the next or each time an individual is destabilized by a reduction in force, changes in type of manpower needs, illness or injury, or other socioeconomic or personal events. Such unstable or multiple-trial careers involve new growth, reexploration, and reestablishment (recycling).
6. The nature of the career pattern—that is, the occupational level attained and the sequence, frequency, and duration of trial and stable jobs—is determined by the individual's parental socioeconomic level, mental ability, education, skills, personality characteristics (needs, values, interests traits, and self-concepts), and career maturity and by the opportunities to which he or she is exposed.
7. Success in coping with the demands of the environment and of the organism in that context at any given life-career stage depends on the readiness of the individual to cope with these demands (that is, on his or her career maturity). *Career maturity* is a constellation of physical, psychological, and social characteristics; psychologically, it is both cognitive and affective. It includes the degree of success in coping with the demands of earlier stages and substages of career development, and especially with the most recent.
8. Career maturity is a hypothetical construct. Its operational definition is perhaps as difficult to formulate as is that of intelligence, but its history is much briefer and its achievements even less definitive. Contrary to the impressions created by some writers, it does not increase monotonically, and it is not a unitary trait.
9. Development through the life stages can be guided, partly by facilitating the maturing of abilities and interests and partly by aiding in reality testing and in the development of self-concepts.
10. The process of career development is essentially that of developing and implementing occupational self-concepts. It is a synthesizing and compromising process in which the self-concept is a product of the interaction of inherited aptitudes, physical makeup, opportunity to observe and play various roles, and evaluations of the extent to which the results of role playing meet with the approval of superiors and fellows (interactive learning).
11. The process of synthesis of or compromise between individual and social factors, between self-concepts and reality, is one of role playing and of learning from feedback, whether the role is played in fantasy, in the counseling interview, or in such real-life activities as classes, clubs, part-time work, and entry jobs.
12. Work satisfactions and life satisfactions depend on the extent to which the individual finds adequate outlets for abilities, needs, values, interests, personality traits, and self-concepts. They depend on establishment in a type of work, a work situation, and a way of life in which one can play the kind of role that growth and exploratory experiences have led one to consider congenial and appropriate.

13. The degree of satisfaction people attain from work is proportional to the degree to which they have been able to implement self-concepts.
14. Work and occupation provide a focus for personality organization for most men and women, although for some persons this focus is peripheral, incidental, or even nonexistent. Then other foci, such as leisure activities and homemaking, may be central. (Social traditions, such as sex-role stereotyping and modeling, racial and ethnic biases, and the opportunity structure, as well as individual differences, are important determinants of preferences for such roles as worker, student, leisurite, homemaker, and citizen.) (Super, 1990, pp. 206–208)*

In a major sense, Super has made explicit the intimacy of career development and personal development. He has synthesized much of the early work of Buehler (1933), Hoppick (1935), and of Ginzberg, Ginsburg, Axelrad, and Herma (1951) in his longitudinal attempt to focus developmental principles on the staging and the determination of career patterns. He has characterized the career development process as ongoing, continuous, and generally irreversible; as a process of compromise and synthesis within which his primary construct—the development and implementation of the self-concept—operates. The basic theme is that the individual as a socialized organizer of his or her experience chooses occupations that will allow him to function in a role consistent with his self-concept and that the latter conception is a function of his developmental history. (The male pronoun is used precisely here, because Super's research and theory have primarily dealt with men not women, although others have extended his work to women. And, in his later theoretical work and empirical studies, he has addressed the applicability of his theory to both genders (Super, 1990).) Further, because of the range of individual capabilities and the latitude within occupations for different combinations of traits, he has indicated that most people have multipotentiality.

Although Super's approach has been labeled typically as a developmental self-concept theory (Osipow, 1968, p. 117), Super himself has labeled it differential-developmental-social-phenomenological psychology (Super, 1969b). Such a label indicates the confluence of knowledge bases to explain career development that this approach has attempted to synthesize and order. Super (1984; 1990) has suggested that what he has contributed is not an integrative, comprehensive, and testable theory but rather a "segmental theory, a loosely unified set of theories dealing with specific aspects of career development taken from developmental, differential, social, and phenomenological psychology and held together by self-concept or personal-construct theory" (p. 194) and by learning theory (1990, p. 199).

Super's conception of a career model, as contrasted with an occupational model, is intended "to denote a longitudinal, developmental approach rather than a single-choice, matching approach such as that of differential psychology and of congruence theory as used by Holland" (Super, 1984, p. 198). Super has suggested,

> that self-concept theory, as I have used it, is both very similar to and very different from congruence theory as Holland has used it. It is similar, in that occupational choice is viewed as the choice by the individual of a role and a setting in which the person will fit comfortably and find satisfaction, as the implementation of a self-concept. It is different in that Holland's interest has been

*From "A Life-Span, Life-Space Approach to Career Development" by D.E. Super in *Career Choice and Development: Applying Contemporary Theories to Practice*, Second Edition by Duane Brown, Linda Brooks, and Associates, p. 200, figure 7.1. © 1990 by Jossey-Bass, Inc., Publishers. Reprinted by permission.

> primarily in the single choice and in the assessment of people and occupations for more effective matching, whereas mine has been in the nature, sequence, and determinants of the choices that constitute a career over the life span. (1984, p. 205)

In 1990, Super suggested that self-concept theory and the term *self-concept*, as he has used these terms during the course of his research, might have been better called *personal construct theory* and *personal constructs* (Kelly, 1955) to show the individual's dual focus on self and on situation. In addition, the use of personal constructs by Super may have, in his view, given greater emphasis to individuals' perceptions of and construction of their environment within the social, economic, and political determinants of careers, as well as the psychological and sociological perspectives in the family context. Such notions of the individual's dynamic organization of and action about conceptions of self and society is implicit through many of the central elements of the theory. For example, Super depicts "a career as the life course of a person encountering a series of developmental tasks and attempting to handle them in such a way as to become the kind of person he or she wants to become. With a changing self and changing situations, the matching process is never really completed" (Super, 1990, pp. 225–226). Similarly, "career maturity is defined as the individual's readiness to cope with developmental tasks with which he or she is confronted because of his or her biological and social development and because of society's expectations of people who have reached that stage of development. This readiness is both affective and cognitive" (Super, 1990, p. 213). It involves affective variables such as career planning, or planfulness, and career explorations, or curiosity. It also involves, among others, such cognitive characteristics as knowledge of the principles of career decision making and ability to apply them to actual choices; knowledge of the nature of careers, occupations, and the world of work; and knowledge of the field of work in which one's occupational preference falls.

Super gives prominence to individuals' mastery of increasingly complex tasks at different stages of career development. Here he has attempted to synthesize the work of Miller and Form (1951) and of Havighurst (1953) by integrating these two perceptions of life-stage phenomena into a more elaborate set of constructs. Miller and Form, after extensive analysis of the work histories of a sample of men, conceived the following work periods as descriptive of a total life perspective: initial (while in school), trial (early, short-lived, full-time work), stable (normally mature adult), and retirement (after giving up employment). These work periods, in concert with those of Buehler (1933)—growth (childhood), exploration (adolescence), establishment (young adulthood), maintenance (maturity), and decline (old age)—provided the outline of Super's thesis, although he originally focused on the exploratory and establishment stages.

These two stages are divided into substages. The exploratory stage breaks down into the tentative, transition, and trial (with little commitment) substages; the establishment stage, into the trial (with more commitment), stabilization, and advancement substages (Super, 1969b). He has further formulated gross developmental tasks—crystallization, specification, implementation, stabilization, and consolidation—which rest on substages and metadimensions contributing to increasing vocational maturity (Super et al., 1963). Within these stages are factors, internal as well as external to the individual, that influence the choices made. These factors continue to narrow the array of options the individual considers. There is an emphasis, then, on vocational convergence and greater specificity in behavior.

For more than a quarter of a century, Super, his colleagues, and a great number of doctoral students have carried on the Career Pattern Study to attempt to validate and refine this theory. This longitudinal effort has studied the lives of more than 100 men from the time they were in ninth grade until they were well into adulthood, 35 years of age and beyond, as they have gone about occupational choice, preparation, and participation in work.

In the course of the Career Pattern Study, insights into life stages and the developmental tasks that comprise them have become refined. These are portrayed graphically in Figure 4.4. (Also see Table 6.3 in Chapter 6, which synthesizes from writings by Super and Jordaan a broad view of Super's perspectives on the life stages and their composition.)

Each of the career development tasks identified in Figure 4.4 can be further subdivided into the specific behavior required to complete the task. For example, Table 4.3 reports a factor analytic model of vocational maturity in ninth grade that provides an outline of elements to which either instruction or guidance processes might be related. This level of speci-

Figure 4.4

Life stages and substages: Super's 1957, 1963, 1981 formulation. (From Donald E. Super, *New Dimensions in Adult Vocational and Career Counseling,* (Columbus, Ohio: Center on Education and Training for Employment (formerly NCRVE, Ohio State University). Copyright 1985. Used with permission.)

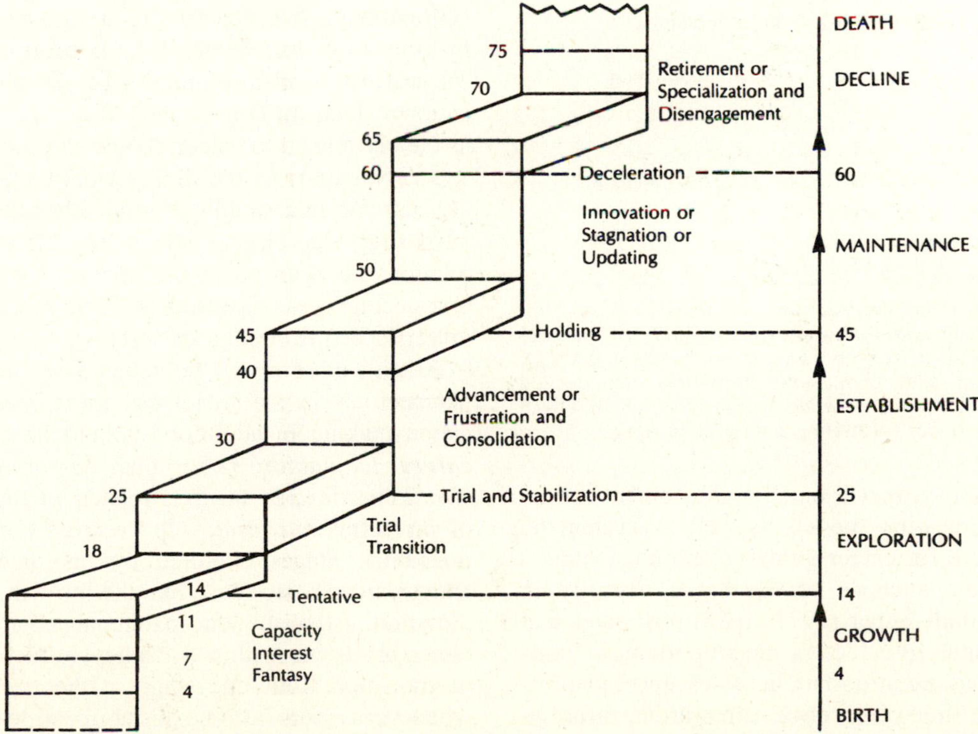

Table 4.3

A Factor Analytic Model of Vocational Maturity in Ninth Grade

Factor I	Planning Orientation
	A. Acceptance of Responsibility
	B. Specificity of Information (more immediate types)
	C. Specificity of Planning
	D. Steps Taken to Obtain Information
	E. Awareness of the Need for Choices
Factor II	The Long View Ahead
	A. Awareness of the Need for Ultimate Choices
	B. Specificity of Information (remoter types)
	C. Entry Planning
	D. Awareness of Factors in Choice
	E. Awareness of Contingency Factors
	F. Acceptance of Responsibility
Factor III	The Short View Ahead
	A. Specificity of Planning
	B. Awareness of the Need for Immediate Choices
	C. Acceptance of Responsibility for Choice
	D. Steps Taken to Obtain Information for High School
Factor IV	The Intermediate View
	A. Awareness of Factors in Choice
	B. Awareness of Need for Intermediate Choices
	C. Specificity of Post-High School Plans
	D. Awareness of Contingency Factors

(Reprinted from *Measuring Vocational Maturity for Counseling and Evaluation,* pp. 13 and 14. National Vocational Guidance Association, 1974. ©AACD. Reprinted with permission. No further reproduction authorized without written permission of American Association for Counseling and Development.)

ficity has provided much of the content for career education models as well as systematic planning for career guidance and counseling.

In his analysis of vocational maturity in adulthood, Super (1977, 1985) postulates that the same five factors are important in midcareer as are important in adolescence; planfulness or time perspective, exploration, information, decision making, and reality orientation. However, he contends that the tasks, the topics to be explored, and the kinds of information needed by 40-year-old adults are different from those important to adolescents. He further contends, "Although the content of decisions differs, decision-making principles are the same at any age and in dealing with any life stage" (p. 9).

To date, empirical evidence supporting some of these propositions has been mixed. For example, Blustein (1988) studied the relationship between Career Choice Crystallization (CCC) and the behaviors considered to be part of Vocational Maturity (VM): career planning, career exploration, decision-making skills, world of work information. In a study of 158 community college male and female students, Blustein found that the career planning component of the Career Development Inventory, the scales used to measure vocational maturity, was related to career decidedness as career commitment but not to the other components of vocational maturity, career exploration, decision-making skills, and world of work information. These clusters of developmental tasks and vocational maturity components seem not to be as clearly related to career choice commitment and decidedness as the theory would support, at least for this sample. Some other studies have suggested similar low to moderate correlations between vocational maturity and career decidedness (for instance, Fretz & Leong, 1982; Jepsen & Prediger, 1981).

Among more recent refinements in Super's perspectives is that readiness for career decision making in adulthood should be called *career adaptability* rather than *career maturity.* This view, in turn, is related to his use of the terms *maxicycle*—to describe the five major life stages explored by his theory—and *minicycle*—to describe the growth, exploration, establishment, maintenance, and decline that occur within a maxicycle at points of transition from one stage to the next (or whenever careers become unstabilized, leading to new growth, reexploration, and reestablishment). Within such contexts, he has reaffirmed

(1984, 1990) that in his life-stage model, the terms *trial* and *transition* have been intended to denote recycling of tasks through minicycles. These continuing processes of reexploration and reestablishment are analogous to what other theorists describe as transitions.

From 1976 to 1979, Super lived and worked in England and began to test his theoretical propositions in that nation. While doing so, he also elaborated aspects of his conceptual models.

One aspect of his more recent formulations is a Life-Career Rainbow (1980, 1981, 1984) to depict how various roles emerge and interact across the life span. He suggests that most people play nine major roles in their life, which emerge in approximate chronological order as follows: (1) child (including son or daughter), (2) student, (3) leisurite, (4) citizen, (5) worker (including unemployed worker and nonworker as ways of playing the role), (6) spouse, (7) homemaker, (8) parent, and (9) pensioner. The constellation of interacting, varying roles constitutes the career (1980, p. 284). The principal theaters in which these roles are played include (1) the home, (2) the community, (3) the school (including college and university), and (4) the workplace. Although there are other roles and other theaters, the ones identified tend to be the most common.

Each role tends to be played primarily in one theater, although some roles, such as worker, may spill over, for example, from the workplace to the home, and cause conflict and confusion. It is in role shaping, redefining the expectations of others and of the role itself with one's conception of it, as well as in the choice of positions and roles, that the individual synthesizes personal and situational role determinants.

With respect to the relationship between earlier performance and later positions and roles, Super maintains, "The nonoccupational positions occupied before the adult career begins influence both the adult positions which may be occupied and the way in which their role expectations are met. Thus the amount and type of schooling is one determinant of occupation entered, and the first occupational position, both its type and job performance, is one determinant of later occupational positions open to the individual" (1980, p. 286). Similarly, relationships occur between earlier and later performance throughout life and, indeed, between preretirement and satisfaction with one's life in retirement.

Super goes on to suggest that the fact that people play several roles simultaneously in several theaters means that occupation, family, community, and leisure roles affect each other. "Success in one facilitates success in others, and difficulties in one role are likely to lead to difficulties in another" (1980, p. 287).

Super indicates, "The simultaneous combination of life roles constitutes the *life style*; their sequential combination structures the *life space* and constitutes the *life cycle*. The total structure is the *career pattern*" (1980, p. 288). Accordingly, roles increase and decrease in importance with the life stage and according to the developmental tasks that are encountered with advancing age.

Decision points occur before and at the time of taking on a new role, of giving up an old role, and of making significant changes in the nature of an existing role (1980, p. 291). Super has identified a graphic model of career decision making that involves cycling and recycling and is rational, prescriptive, developmental, and emergent. It is shown in Figure 4.5. What this model does not portray is that the time intervals at any one step may vary greatly. Depending on the circumstances that surround the career decision point, the total model may emerge over years, days, or weeks.

Super (1980) contends:

> The decision points of a life career reflect encounters with a variety of personal and situational determinants. The former consist of the genetic constitution of the individual modified by his or her experiences (the environment and its situational determinants) in the womb, the home, and the community. The latter are the geographic, his-

Figure 4.5

A Developmental Model of Emergent Career Decision Making. (From "Life-Span, Life-Space Approach to Career Development" by Donald E. Super, *Journal of Vocational Behavior,* pp. 282–298, figure 4, p. 295. Orlando, FL: Academic Press, 1980. Reprinted by permission.)

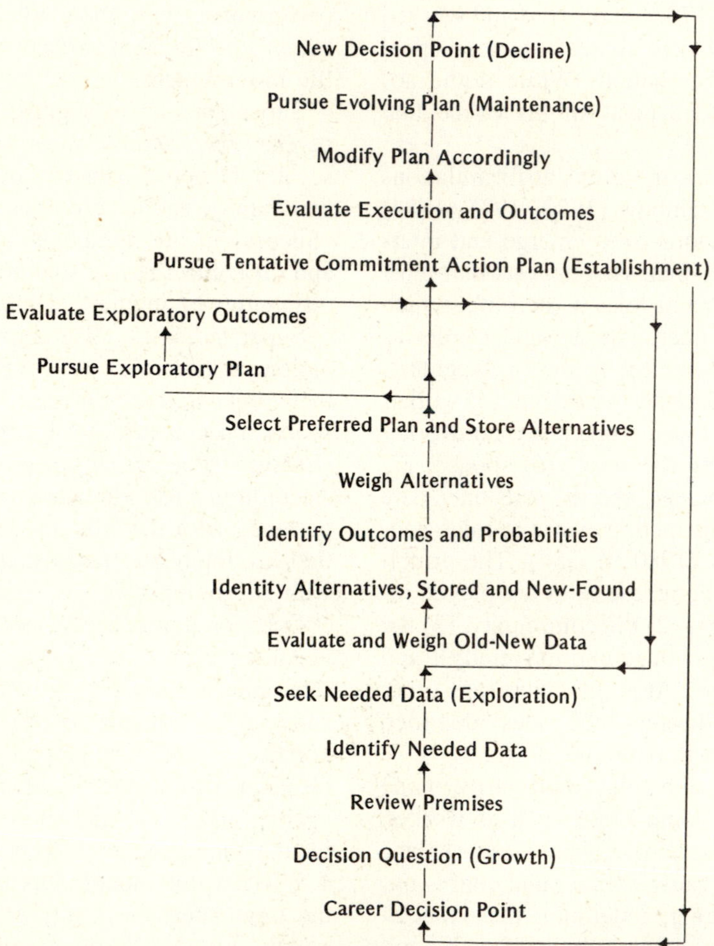

toric, social, and economic conditions in which the individual functions from infancy through adulthood and old age. (p. 294)

These determinants affect *preferences, choices, entry* into the labor force and assumption of the worker role, and role *changes*. Figure 4.6 portrays these two categories of determinants lifting up or pressing down on the individual.

Throughout the 1980s and the early 1990s, Super has redefined and clarified the intention of the Life-Career Rainbow: to bring into one model the maturing and playing of a changing diversity of roles by individuals as these occur

Figure 4.6

Personal and Situational Determinants of the Worker Role

SITUATIONAL DETERMINANTS

	Social Structure and Economic Conditions						
Remote Deter-minants	↓ Historical Change ↓						
	Socioeconomic Organizations						
	↓ ↓ ↓						
Immediate Deter-minants	Employment						
	School						
	Community						
	Family						
	↓ ↓ ↓						
Life Stages	Growth	Exploration		Establishment		Maintenance	Decline
Worker Role	⊕ ⊕			⊕			
Age	10	20	30	40	50	60	70
	↑ ↑ ↑						
Immediate Deter-minants	Situational Awareness						
	Self-Awareness						
	Attitudes						
	Interests						
	Values						
	Needs						
	Academic Achievement						
	Specific Aptitudes						
	Intelligence						
Remote Deter-minants	↕ [Situational ↕ Determinants] ↕						
	Biological Heritage						

PERSONAL DETERMINANTS

across the life span and as they structure the life space, as continuously influenced by biological, psychological, and socioeconomic determinants. The result has been a new model, called the Archway Model, "designed to bring out the segmental but unified and developmental nature of career development, to highlight the segments, and to make their origin clear. . . . It tells the same story as the Rainbow but tells it in a different way" (Super,

1990, p. 199, 201). It also incorporates the determinants included in Figure 4.6. Figure 4.7 depicts the Archway Model.

Using a Normal Arch as the graphic representation of the Archway Model, the doorstep portrays the biographical-geographical foundations of human development. The large stone on the left supports the person (psychological characteristics) and the large stone on the right supports the society (economic resources, economic structure, social institutions, and so on). These societal factors act upon the person, and the person acts upon them as he or she grows and functions as a unit in society—the context in which the individual pursues his or her educational, familial, occupational, civic, and leisure careers.

The left-hand column of the Archway depicts the qualities of personality that constitute a person: the *biological base*, the *needs* and *intelligence* that develop from it in interaction with the environment, and the *values* that derive from needs as objectives that are sought in activities thought likely to lead to the attainment of those values; activities are synthesized as *interests*. Also parallel to these personality traits on the left-hand column are aptitudes as derivatives of general intelligence and special aptitudes. The top of the left-hand column is denoted as *achievements* that result from "the use, misuse, or disuse of personal resources."

Although the vectors and arrows reflecting the reciprocity of influences between the left-hand column, personality, and the right-hand column, society, are not shown in the model, Super clearly intends to stress the interaction between the factors depicted in these two columns. He states, "natural resources, the economy, and the family influence the development of aptitude, values, and interest, as does their use in school and at work. The individual, using his or her abilities and seeking outlets for interests, acts on society in visible ways (for example, as a leader, as a protagonist in enacting equal rights legislation) and in ways that escape notice (for example, by quietly fitting into and helping a new and innovative organization to function)" Super, 1990, p. 203). The right-hand column culminates in societal factors producing such outcomes as social policy and employment practices, whereas the left-hand column's emphasis on personality factors is manifested in achievements.

Joining the columns is the Arch, which depicts the career. It, too, is comprised of stones, representing conceptual components or segments. These components include the developmental stages of childhood and adolescence, young adulthood, and maturity, as well as the positions (child, worker, spouse, and so on) that one plays in moving through these developmental stages. The *keystone* of the Archway is the person who, through decision making, reflects the bringing together of personal and social forces as these are organized into self-concepts and roles in society. According to Super, the cement that holds all of these stones or segmented theories about the person and society together is learning theory. "Today we would say that interactive learning is the theory that explains the relationships of the segments of the Career Archway; social learning . . . but also learning in encounters with objects, facts, and ideas. . . . Interactive experiential learning, self-concept, and occupations-concept formation takes place through the interaction of the individual and the environment. This is what the Career Archway is designed to bring out" (Super, 1990, p. 204).

Tiedeman's Paradigms. The work of Tiedeman and his associates, particularly O'Hara, added perspective to some elements of Super's original propositions. In regard to Tiedeman particularly, Super (1969a) has stated;

> Some men continue to change occupations throughout life, while others have stable periods followed by new periods of trial, which in turn lead to stabilization for a second or third time. Thus, there are stable (direct en-

Figure 4.7

A Segmental Model of Career Development. (From "A Life-Span, Life-Space Approach to Career Development" by D.E. Super in *Career Choice and Development: Applying Contemporary Theories to Practice,* Second Edition by Duane Brown, Linda Brooks, and Associates, pp. 206–208. © 1990 by Jossey-Bass, Inc., Publishers. Reprinted by permission.)

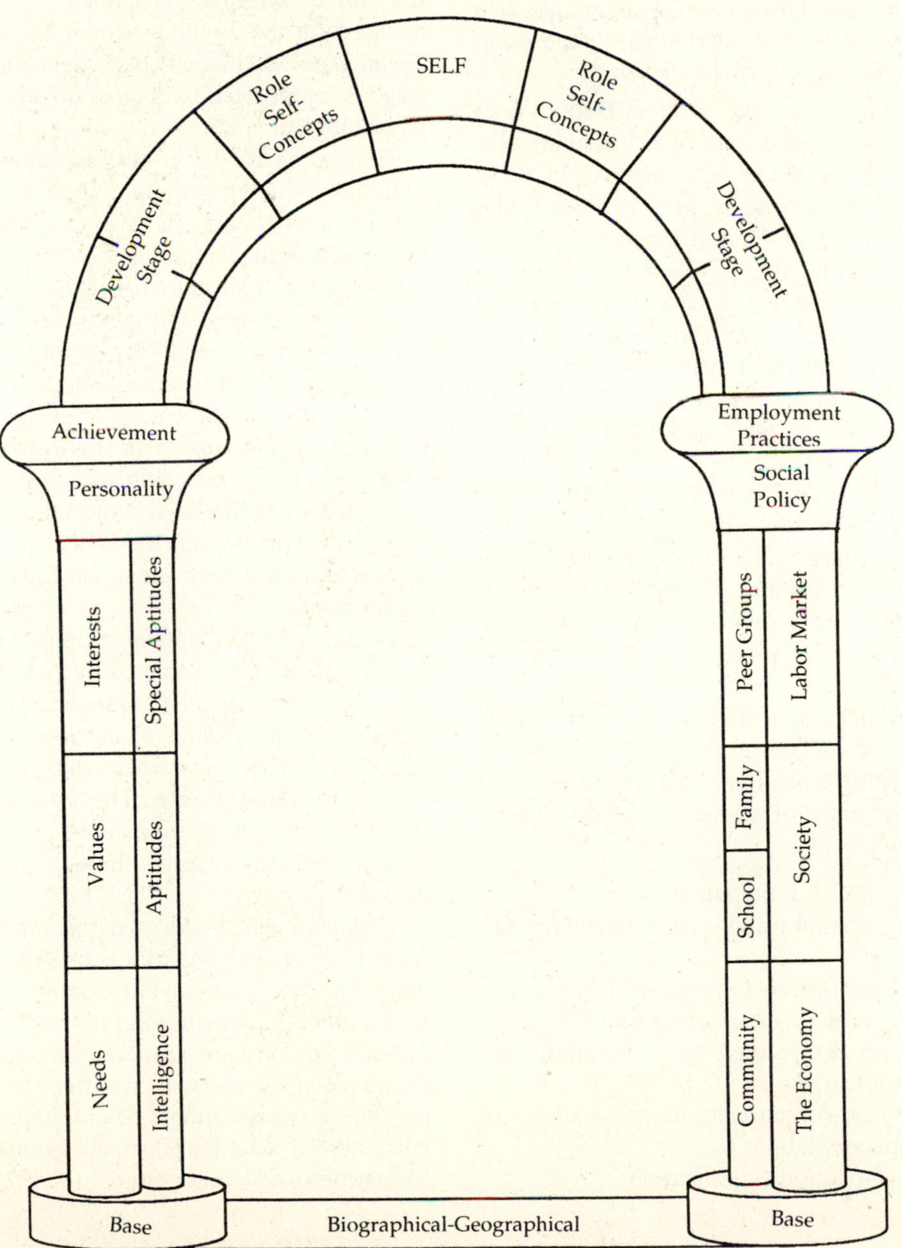

> try into the lifework), conventional (trial leading to stability), unstable, and multiple-trial careers. The life stage processes continue more or less throughout life, repeating themselves in the sequence: INITIAL—TRIAL—STABLE—DECLINE. Tiedeman's (1958) use of this concept in theorizing about position choice, each decision concerning the occupancy of a position involving exploration, establishment, and maintenance, is a useful refinement. (p. 4)

Tiedeman, alone and with O'Hara, views career development as part of a continuing process of differentiating ego identity. In these terms, how a person's identity evolves is dependent on early childhood experiences within the family unit, the psychological crises—as defined in terms of Erikson's constructs (1963)—encountered at various developmental stages, and the agreement between society's meaning system and the individual's meaning system, as well as the emotional constants of each.

In essence, Tiedeman has emphasized an occupational decision-making paradigm within the staging phenomena (á la Erikson) making up career development. Tiedeman has maintained that Super's developmental perspective is probably an accurate way of viewing the process of career choice, but he further believes that an explicit statement about the characteristics of individual decisions needs to be made. To this end, Tiedeman has offered the following model of decision making (Tiedeman, 1961):

I. The period of anticipation
   A. Exploration (random and acquisitive activity)
   B. Crystallization (emerging of patterns in the form of alternatives and their consequences leading to clarification and comment)
   C. Choice (organizing in preparation for implementations)
   D. Specification (clarification)

II. The period of implementation and adjustment
   A. Induction (person largely responsive)
   B. Reformation (person largely assertive)
   C. Integration (satisfaction)

Each of these stages is intended to represent a change in the dominant condition of the decision process. Indeed, each decision-making stage is represented by a qualitatively different psychological state.

Tiedeman's model is not limited to the formulation of a choice (anticipation) but also considers what happens when one attempts to implement that choice (induction). Basically, this process indicates that there is constant reciprocity between the person's self-concept and the environmental expectations as decisions are made and implemented. If the individual's ability to take on role expectations as defined by the environment is not stretched beyond tolerance, the person will stay in the position and integrate these expectations into the ego concept. However, if this does not happen, the person will likely reinstitute the process of anticipation.

Tiedeman and O'Hara also suggest that individual personality is shaped by perceptions of career choices and also somewhat by the individual's conformance to the norms and values of those persons already established within the occupational setting. They stress the intimacy of self-concept and career concept as a person gradually matures through many small decisions.

Tiedeman's later work has become increasingly independent and critical of Super's developmental perspectives. For example, in 1977, Dudley and Tiedeman observed, "In brief, Super did not provide any conceptualization of the personality as an active force with complex inner organizations; he did not provide an adequate notion of the person as an agent in formation of a career pattern" (p. 6).

In his evolving collaboration with others (Dudley & Tiedeman, 1977; Peatling & Tiedeman, 1977; Tiedeman & Miller-Tiedeman, 1977), Tiedeman has been increasingly instrumental in emphasizing the power of the individual to create a career and in advancing notions of autonomy, competence, and agency as major ingredients of such processes. He and his colleagues are pursuing ways to facilitate conceptions of the human career as a holistic concept, in which career and the process of career development are one. In so doing, Tiedeman is continuing to add substance to his self-constructionist concept of the ability of individuals to exercise control over the development of their own career and over the career decision-making process.

Tiedeman and his colleagues have viewed career development as a "within to without" phenomenon rather than the reverse, which is more typical in conceptions of career development. In this view, anticipation of choice, the first major category of behavior in the original Tiedeman paradigm (1961) is seen as a creative process of hierarchical restructuring in which the individual continues to transform self and environmental subsystems as movement toward accommodation or implementation occur. The conceptualizations have been aided by the evolution from a cubistic model to a pyramidal one. The cubistic model (Miller & Tiedeman, 1972) suggests that three dimensions are involved in leading a decision-guided life that is proactive (from within to without) rather than reactive (from without to within). Each of the basic conditions is comprised of three steps along the way to greater maturity, sophistication, or consciousness in action: (1) *problem condition*—steps: problem forming (vicarious), problem solving (acting out), solution using (autonomous use); (2) *psychological states*—steps: exploration, clarification, accommodation; (3) *self-comprehension*—steps; learning about, doing, doing with awareness (Miller & Tiedeman, 1972). This schematic provides a language system by which one can help the individual with self-comprehension and movement toward greater control of personal decision making and the recycling of it. Miller-Tiedeman (1977) subsequently simplified the cubistic model into a pyramid containing many of the same concepts and others particularly important to her efforts to facilitate decision making with adolescents. The pyramidal model of decision-making comprehension includes four levels—learning about, problem solving, solution-using, solution-reviewing—which are each elaborated and coupled with a hierarchy of decision strategies.

As Tiedeman and Miller-Tiedeman's work unfolds (1984), it continues to build on the early work of Tiedeman and O'Hara, to which has been added more recent conceptions of ego development, decision-making strategies, and values. The latter are incorporated into the counseling and education processes designed to help persons become more consciously and proactively engaged in career decision making.

In summarizing their perspectives, Tiedeman and Miller-Tiedeman characterize them as follows:

> Ours is not a theory that allows another to predict the behavior of a subject (common reality). Rather, ours is a value-laden model that allows a person to put his or her own decision-making activity into perspective for him- or herself (personal reality). The model is therefore merely a description of what may be internally experienced during decision-making. However, as the individual comes to understand what occurs as he or she thinks, while acting on information from the common reality, she or he will have the capacity to be proactive. With this kind of awareness and confidence, the personal reality will then reign over the common reality. (Tiedeman & Miller-Tiedeman, 1984)

In sum, Tiedeman and, in particular, Miller-Tiedeman are evolving a conceptual, linguistic, and process structure designed to accept the power of the person to create and to be in a human career. Although other approaches to career development do not oppose such notions of individual power to create a career, Tiedeman and Miller-Tiedeman seem dedicated to self-empowerment as the central proposition in such a process.

Gribbons and Lohnes' Career Development Study. Gribbons and Lohnes (1968, 1982) engaged in a longitudinal study of career development, entitled the Career Development Study (CDS), for more than twenty years. The 111 subjects of the study (57 boys and 54 girls) began to be studied when they were eighth graders in 1958 in five eastern Massachusetts communities. These families were scattered in socioeconomic status and fathers' occupations. The students had a common exposure to an eighth-grade group guidance treatment based on *You: Today and Tomorrow* (Katz, 1958). Throughout the years of the study, the subjects were interviewed intensively and were contacted by questionnaire, correspondence, and by telephone. Early in 1980 a final data collection was completed when the subjects were 34 and 35 years old. Contact was made with 91 of the 108 living subjects.

Much of the data were collected by first using the Readiness for Vocational Planning Scale, which was subsequently abbreviated and retitled the Readiness for Career Planning Scale. To a large extent the CDS has attempted to validate many of the concepts first proposed in the research framework for Super's Career Pattern Study.

In their first major report in 1968, Gribbons and Lohnes examined the concept of Readiness for Vocational Planning as a measure of vocational maturity during adolescence. Their research identified eight variables, which in combination correlate highly with readiness for vocational planning at the eighth-grade and postsecondary school levels. They are as follows:

Variable I. Factors in Curriculum Choice–Awareness of relevant factors, including one's abilities, interests, and values and their relation to curriculum choice; curricula choice to occupational choice

Variable II. Factors in Occupational Choice–Awareness of relevant factors, including abilities, interests, values; educational requirements for choice; accuracy of description of occupation

Variable III. Verbalized Strengths and Weaknesses–Ability to verbalize appropriately the relation of personal strengths and weaknesses to educational and vocational choices

Variable IV. Accuracy of Self-appraisal–Comparison of subject's estimates of his general scholastic ability, verbal ability, and quantitative ability with his actual attainments on scholastic aptitude tests, English grades, and mathematics grades

Variable V. Evidence of Self-rating–Quality of evidence cited by subject in defense of his appraisal of his own abilities

Variable VI. Interests–Awareness of interests and their relation to occupational choices

Variable VII. Values–Awareness of values and their relation to occupational choices

Variable VIII. Independence of Choice–Extent of subject's willingness to take personal responsibility for his choices (pp. 15–16)

Gribbons and Lohnes found that vocational maturity—as measured by the eight Readiness for Vocational Planning scales cited—increased from grades 8 to 10. They also indicated that an overlapping of scores in these two grades showed that some eighth graders had already achieved considerable vocational maturity while some tenth graders evidenced a considerable lack of it. More important as a rationale for vocational development is their findings that levels of eighth-grade vocational maturity are predictive of educational and occupational planning, educational aspirations, and level of occupational aspirations in the twelfth grade; of field and level of actual occupation two years after high school; and of two-year, post-high school career adjustment. The RVP scales failed to discriminate among those students manifesting Differential Career Processes—constant maturity, emerging maturity, degeneration, and constant immaturity—but they did demonstrate a trend from idealism in the eighth grade to realism in the twelfth grade, with brighter students (above IQ 105) appearing to choose more consistently with their measured intelligence than less bright students.

Following the portion of their study reported in 1968, Gribbons and Lohnes revised the Readiness for Vocational Planning because it had proven to be too time-consuming and cumbersome. Its place was taken by the Readiness for Career Planning, a shorter scale, 22 items rather than 45, that was simpler to score.

When the authors compared their 1980 data with the variety of data they had examined at different decision points throughout the preceding 22 years, they made a number of conclusions. These are selectively summarized and paraphrased as follows:

1. By 1980, very few of the subjects were in the occupations to which they had aspired as eighth graders in 1958. Only six men and six women were in the same or closely related occupations. As a result, Gribbons and Lohnes contend that career guidance in secondary education should not focus on counseling about specific occupational titles, but only as these illuminate principles that apply to discriminations among broad career fields and levels (p. 115).

2. By 1980, eight women and six men remained in the same socioeconomic class that their families had occupied in 1958, whereas 24 women and 23 men moved one or more levels higher and 15 men and 15 women moved lower in socioeconomic level from that occupied by their families in 1958.

3. By 1980, only 20 of the 52 persons who aspired to college as eighth graders had actually achieved the goal (54 percent males, 15 percent females).

4. A general result of the longitudinal study is that career patterns can be conceptualized, operationally defined, measured, and predicted. Career transitions are in part predictable from probability laws fitted to career process variables and in part predictable from antecedent trait profiles of subjects (p. 126).

5. The Career Development Tree from Project TALENT research appears to be the most useful mapping of career patterns over adolescence and into young adulthood. A curriculum that would produce understanding of this mapping would produce a considerable sophistication in world-view and a frame of reference for exploring personal multipotentiality (p. 126).

6. Inputs to the computation of career predictions need to include:

- Current career plans
- Sex
- Socioeconomic
- Ability factors (verbal knowledge, mathematics, English, visual reasoning)
- Vocational maturity factors
- Scholasticism
- Interest factors (science, cultural, business, outdoors, and shop) (pp. 126–127)

7. The majority of adolescents are poorly oriented with respect to career development tasks and fully one-third to one-half of young adults at age 25 appear to be in career development troubles (p. 127).

8. Educational variables prefigure career variables. "We think it is in their failure to sponsor understanding of the career values of

education that educators miss their main opportunity to promote best career development possible in students" (p. 128).

9. "Career guidance in our schools should begin in the elementary years with curriculum units designed to teach understanding and the value of careers and education as they intertwine in our civilization. In the junior high years, students should begin to interact with a computer measurement system that will help them to assess their personality and project their multipotentiality. . . . Ways must be found to communicate the scientific knowledge we now have about career development to young people in our schools, in modes that encourage better relations of self to society, better self direction and greater acceptance of responsibility for personal history. The knowledge is technical, involving probability laws and trait-statistical maps. It requires computer communications. We must have a computerized career information system as an integral part of a career guidance curriculum in our schools" (p. 128–129).

10. Finally, in comparing the men and women subjects over the 25 years of the study, women, as a group, were able to aspire to less and to achieve less than men. Sex-role stereotypes appear to have been the primary source of the special difficulties for women.

The most mature stage of career development in this process model suggests that career maturity can also be conceived in terms of self-actualization as used in other places in this book.

Savickas's Model of Time in Career Development. Savickas's conceptualization and research has linked how people experience and structure time to their conceptualization of their career and to how they enact vocational behavior. He contends that optimal career success and satisfaction follow from an experience of time that is characterized by an orientation to a future that is densely populated with events clearly connected to present behavior.

Savickas contends that persons require a sense of subjective career that allows them to experience self-conscious thoughts about the vocational past, present, and future. In essence, a subjective career emerges from beliefs about and attitudes toward time. In his view, unless individuals envision a subjective career that extends into the future, they rarely seek career counseling. In contrast, he views the model career counseling client as one who seeks to reduce anxiety about the future; who wants the counselor to help them take responsibility for their lives and to design their occupational futures.

In Savickas' view, some persons have not learned how the culture, particularly the middle-class culture, in the United States conceptualizes and uses time to structure life roles. Thus, they may orient themselves to the past or present, not the future, and lack a sense of the future as the major emphasis of subjective career, or they may view time so differently from the dominant occupational culture that they experience vocational failure and dissatisfaction.

Although, as described in the previous section of this chapter and in Chapter 6, Super's theoretical perspectives on career development have emphasized time perspective as one of the five major factors in career maturity in adolescence and in career adaptability in adulthood, few career interventions have been designed to incorporate this concept. In contrast, Savickas has built his concept of career interventions on three organizing constructs as they relate to time. They are (1) time perspective; (2) time differentiation; and (3) time integration.

According to Savickas, (1990), *time perspective* refers to how individuals view and orient themselves to time. . . . Time imagery related to achievement motivation" (p. 5). An individual's time perspective also includes an orientation to time zones: past, present, and future. "The career culture considers future orientation as the prime precursor of mental health and career achievement. A future orientation enables one to deal with gratification and work for tomorrow. A future orientation increases anxiety and, in turn, occupational commitment because work is outgrowth of anxiety about survival in the future. . . . Career interventions typically work to create or reinforce a future orientation by making the future seem important and by creating anxiety about what one will do in the future" (p. 7).

In this view, *time differentiation* is seen as making the future real. The density and extension of events within time zones tends to define which time zone is the more real for the client. "An individual who densely populates the future with anticipated events which extend far into the horizon has a schema ready for career planning. A differentiated future provides a meaningful context for setting personal goals . . . . While a future orientation may create anxiety, future differentiation alleviates anxiety by envisioning the future and one's place in it" (Savickas, 1990, p. 8). Teaching persons about anticipated events, how to think about and label them may be important interventions. In this context, career counseling involves "helping people create, articulate, and enact their dreams." (p. 10).

In the third dimension of this approach, *time integration* enables planning. "Temporal integration refers to the sense of connectedness among events across time zones. . . . Continuity among them, how, and when provides the cognitive schema for realistic planning. . . . Discontinuity reduces predictability and makes planning illusive. When life is viewed as an unbroken thread, individuals can become aware of enduring themes and patterns in life, strengthen their sense of identity, and choose activities that require a perseverance. . . . Optimism that present behavior can be organized to achieve future goals moves enactment of plans" (Savickas, 1990, p. 11). Career interventions used to deal with time integration combine attention to planning attitudes, competencies, contingent planning, and purposeful action.

Much more deserves to be said about Savickas' model of career interventions appropriate to dealing with each of the three time constructs—perspective, differentiation, integration—as fundamental to a conception of a personal subjective career. These constructs and interventions are fundamental to a conception of career development as movement across life stages and time. Research directed to such views can be found in the following references: Savickas, Silling, & Schwartz, 1984; Wolf & Savickas, 1985; Ringle & Savickas, 1983.

The Gottfredson Model of Occupational Aspirations. Among her other research and theoretical writings, Gottfredson has proposed a developmental theory of occupational aspirations in which she has sought to integrate, in a broader approach, a variety of principles from psychological theories as well as type theories of vocational choice. According to Gottfredson, her theory "accepts the fundamental importance of self-concept in vocational development, that people seek jobs compatible with their images of themselves. Social class, intelligence, and sex are seen as important determinants of both self-concept and the types of compromises people must make, thus the theory integrates a social systems perspective with the more psychological approaches" (1981, p. 546).

Gottfredson's theory is a stage theory that, like Ginzberg et al. and Super, conceives of the self-concept becoming increasingly differentiated and complex as a child grows. Thus, as the child and adolescent ages, refining occupational aspirations, one of the major processes involved is the continuous adding of self-concept characteristics. Like self-concepts, occupational images held by people can be characterized by their complexity and differentiation and their comprehensiveness and specificity. Gottfredson suggests that persons construct cognitive maps of occupations in which the similarities and differences among such occupations tend to include only a few major dimensions: sex-type (masculinity/femininity), level of work (prestige), and field of work. While persons across gender and socioeconomic classes tend to agree on how occupations can be placed in hierarchies within these categories, Gottfredson also suggests that persons create their own cognitive maps of acceptable alternatives based upon one's conception of one's social space—the person's view of where he or she fits into society. Within the construction of such individualized cognitive maps of job-self compatibility, children and adolescents create boundaries of acceptable jobs based on tolerable sex-type images, tolerable levels of prestige, and tolerable levels of effort to attain them.

Gottfredson (1981) portrays the developmental stages and their effects on occupational aspirations by describing four major stages with assorted substages or elements. In paraphrased outline form, they appear as follows:

Stage 1. Orientation to size and power (ages 3–5 years)
Stage 2. Orientation to sex roles (ages 6–8)
Stage 3. Orientation to social valuation (ages 9–13 years)
- Awareness of social class
- The development of preferences for level of work
- Differences in preferences by social class and ability level
- Circumscription of range of preferences

Stage 4. Orientation to the internal, unique self (ages 14+)
- Perception of self and others
- Specification of vocational aspirations (p. 555)

Gottfredson provides many interesting concepts to describe boundaries and motivational dimensions related to the development of occupational aspirations. For example, she states that

> Some aspects of self-concept are more central than others and will take priority when compromising occupational goals. One's occupation constitutes a very public and continuing presentation of self, and some people have priorities for what aspects of self they want to emphasize or present unambiguously. . . . Gender self-concept will be the most strongly protected aspect of self, followed by the maintenance of one's social standing or worth, that is one's social class and ability self-concepts. . . . Thus, people will tend to sacrifice interest in field of work to maintain sextype and prestige, and to some extent will sacrifice prestige level for sextype if that is also necessary. (p. 572)

Within this context, she also suggests two other manifestations of compromise: "Exploration of job options ends with the implementation of a satisfactory choice, not necessarily the optimal potential choice" and "People accommodate psychologically to the compromises they make."

Gottfredson's concepts have begun to initiate research by others to test her perspectives. In particular, Gottfredson's theory suggests that elements internalized at an earlier age (for instance, sex type) will be more resistant to change then elements internalized later in development. Thus, "vocational interests are sacrificed first, job level second, and sex type last" (1981, p. 549). The findings of Hesketh, Elmslie, and Kaldor (1990), who studied the Gottfredson theory of compromise with 73 career-dissatisfied adults and 90 high school students, suggested an alternative model of compromise that indicated that interests were more important in career choices then either sex type or prestige, because interests are of a compound nature, incorporating the latter. Such a view also suggests that counselors may be able to help clients who have rejected occupations on the basis of one attribute (for example, sex type or prestige) to understand the basis of their rejection and to reconsider such choices on the bases of such more complex attributions (for example, interests).

ADULT DEVELOPMENT

Although adult career development is a major focus of the work of Super, Tiedeman, Ginzberg, and, certainly, Holland's work on the structural aspects of career behavior, there is also a group of persons who have targeted their theorizing and research on adult development exclusive of concerns about the total life span or about the early stages, childhood or adolescent, of career development. As suggested elsewhere in this chapter, much of the early work in career development theory and research was focused on adolescent exploration, anticipation, and the formulation of preferences, although major theorists have speculated about adult development as well as adolescent development. Research of the last two decades or so has made clear that exploration and change do not end with adolescence but continue throughout life. Adulthood is also dynamic; it is a time of changes of self-concept and aspirations, a time of transitions, crises and reformulations, a time of minicycles and personal redefinitions.

Just as is true in the range of theories described in the earlier segments of this chapter, adult development theorists view adult career behavior and the adult experience from different perspectives. Schlossberg (1986) has suggested that there are four such perspectives: one which explains adult behavior within the cultural context, a second which focuses on the psychological developmental stages of the individual, a third view that discusses the adult experience in terms of transitions, and a fourth perspective that examines continuity and change over the life span.

Schlossberg has classified the major theorists in each of these four categories by the major concepts they espouse and by the counseling or institutional practices that such concepts support. Table 4.4 represents her analysis of such perspectives, concepts, and practices.

Schlossberg's Work. As suggested in the above analysis, Nancy Schlossberg is among the major theorists of adult development and adult career development. In addition to her own important concepts, Schlossberg has synthesized the work of other adult theorists into perspectives that are pertinent to career guidance and counseling. Summarizing the work of major theorists in adult development, Schlossberg (1978) has advanced five propositions about adult development that reflect some of the change that occurs. These propositions follow in paraphrased form:

1. *Behavior in adulthood is determined by social rather than by biological clocks*. In childhood and adolescence, biological development or deterioration is a greater factor than in adulthood. Beyond the changes occasioned by menopause or the possible rapid physical change of late, late adulthood, most of the effects on behavior in adulthood are social, not biological. Social norms about when and how certain behavior should occur—when one should marry, settle down in a job, or retire—tend to affect perceptions of and stimulate action regarding major life events. To be out of synchronization with such events may cause feelings of uncertainty, anxiety, or inadequacy. Although these age-related norms may be changing under the influence of the increasing numbers of adults returning to school, changing careers in midlife, entering new careers after retirement, and trying out new marital and life styles, socially defined age-appropriate behavior remains a very powerful influence on life-career behavior.

2. *Behavior is at times a function of life stage, at others of age*. Many theorists have

Table 4.4

The Adult Experience: Perspectives, Concepts, and Practices

Perspectives	Concepts	Practices
Cultural:	*Bertaux* • Life Stories depend on work structure *Rosenbaum* • Career mobility results from organizational structure *Kanter* • Individual progress is determined by opportunity structure	Change or modify system Examples: • Hire and promote older individuals • Gear admissions and financial aid to older part-time individuals
Developmental: Age/Stage	*Levinson et al.* • Invariant sequence of developmental methods • Life structure • Dream, mentor • Polarities *Erikson* • Unfolding of life and restoring of inner issues • Hierarchical stages *Gould* • Release from childhood assumptions • Tinkering with inadequacies *Perry, Loevinger, Kohlberg* • Hierarchical sequence • Sequence in ego development and moral development *Fiske, Gutman* • Men and women express the dormant part of themselves at midlife *Gilligan* • Critique of models based on men and applied to women • Hierarchical models obscure other voices • Widening cries of attachment • Renegotiation of interdependence over time	Design programs for people at different stages Examples: • Programs for returning students, preretirees Design programs for people who process work differently Examples: • Differential teaching, advising, and counseling Assess congruence of supervisor, supervisee along dimensions of personality, learning style, achievement Sensitize faculty, counselors, and others to age, social class bias

Transitions: Life Course/ Life Span/ Life Events	*Neugarten, Moore, & Lowe* • Socially created rather than biologically determined transitions *Lowenthal (Fiske), Chiriboga, Thurnher* • Life span • Stage not age • Coping with transitions; balance of resources to deficits • Sex differences *Schlossberg* • Types of transitions: anticipated, unanticipated, nonevents • Coping moderators: transition, environment, self • Transition process: over time, for better or worse *Pearlin* • Coping, not life events, is central issue • Classification of life strains and coping responses	Design programs for people in similar transitions • Support from others who have successfully negotiated the same transition • Provide cognitive map • Offer programs at several times: before, during, after transition Teach individual coping skills • To change situation • To modify meaning of situation • To relax
Life Span: Continuity and Change	*Neugarten* • Capacity of individual to select, ignore, or modify socializing influence • Fanning out and variations • Fluid life span *Vaillant* • Early trauma not predictive of later behavior *Pearlin* • Variability • Differential distribution of strains by sex, age, different patterns of coping *Brim, Kagan* • Orientation (not yet theory) toward constancy and change • Discontinuities rather than sequencing are studied • Importance of variability based on cohort, sex, age, social class	Multiple programs for larger population • Individual and group programs • Media • Other

Source: Table 1, pages 9–11. Schlossberg, N.K. Adult Development Theories: Ways to Illuminate the Adult Experience. Chapter 1 in *Adult Career Development: Concepts, Issues, and Practices.* Edited by Zandy B. Leibowitz and H. Daniel Lea. Alexandria, VA: National Career Development Association, 1986. (©AACD. Reprinted with permission. No further reproduction authorized without permission of American Association for Counseling and Development.)

identified distinct chronological periods in which specific tasks, problems, structures, and states of mind are likely to occur. Levinson et al. (1978), to be discussed in the next section, advocates such a view. Other theorists (such as Lowenthal, Thurnher, & Chiriboga, 1976) attribute less importance to age per se and much more importance to what types of events or the tasks the person is actually dealing with. This is a "stage approach."

3. *Sex differences are greater than either age or stage differences*. In the various adult life stages, men and women differ dramatically, partly because of early socialization and partly because their identities tend to be defined differently. The identities of men tend to be defined primarily in terms of direct achievement. Women, on the other hand, define their identities more in terms of vicarious achievement, not through their own activities and accomplishments but through those of the dominant people in their lives (usually men) (Lipman-Bulman & Leavitt, 1977).

4. *Adults continually experience transitions requiring adaptations and reassessment of the self*. In opposition to notions that adulthood is one of stability and certainty, the concept of transitions suggests that adults are constantly experiencing change either deliberately, because it is chosen, or inadvertently, because of forces external to the self. Such changes can engender growth, new concepts of self, or crisis and deterioration. In either case, stress frequently accompanies the transition and requires adaptation.

5. *The recurrent themes of adulthood are identity, intimacy, and generativity*. Identity, intimacy, and generativity, as defined by Erickson (1950), recur throughout the individual's life. Identity may become an issue whenever the individual faces a transition. This in turn raises questions of generativity: What meaning does my life have? What have I contributed to the world? What have I created? Intimacy refers to free, open, spontaneous, affectionate, trusting responses with all of those with whom we have close human ties. These relationships tend to sustain energy and motivation to develop identity and to cope with matters of generativity. They are apparently crucial to successful adaptation to transitions.

In a 1984 book, Schlossberg (1984) has explored many of the perspectives that underlie a framework for helping adults in transition. In particular, she suggests that adults must be looked at as individuals who relate differently to transitions. The transition itself must be examined in terms of its type, context, and impact, with the transition process considered in relation to how the person reacts to it over time. In addition, the individual's coping resources need to be examined to determine if they are assets or liabilities, resources or deficits, either intrapsychically or environmentally. Certainly, a major ingredient of understanding adult variability in transitions is an understanding of some of the major views of adult development.

The Importance of Adult Transitions. As the propositions of adult development provided by Schlossberg suggest, transitions are the central focus of much current theoretical attention. Indeed, Perry (1982) has contended that "special needs populations" can be conceived of in two ways: (1) as those who are experiencing equity difficulty in gaining access to education and work because of bias, discrimination, quotas, prejudice, and other forms of social gate-keeping; and (2) those who are at risk because of transitions—changing families, midcareer job dislocation, retirement. In much of the literature, transitions are portrayed as frightening or traumatic. Indeed, as Schlossberg (1981) has asserted, the current definitions of transition have actually grown out of crisis theory. However, some theorists (such as Parkes, 1971) prefer the term *psychosocial transition* to play down the notion of crisis.

It is in this perspective that Levinson et al. (1978) talk of *developmental transition* to represent "a turning point or boundary between two periods of greater stability" (p. 57).

Levinson, Darrow, Klein, Levinson, and McKee (1978) have extended the models of Havighurst, Ginzberg et al., and Super et al. by adding the notion of transition to each of the life stages portrayed in those models. In other words, one does not abruptly change life stages (exploration to establishment, establishment to maintenance), but instead engages in a period of activity over time that represents a transition to the next life stage. Levinson et al. use the term *era*, much as other theorists use the term *stage* or *phase* (p. 18). According to Levinson et al., there are four such eras in life: childhood and adolescence, ages 0–22; early adulthood, 17–45; middle adulthood, 40–65; and late adulthood, 60 on. The transition between eras consistently take four or five years—not less than three and rarely more than six. Transitions are developmental periods that link the eras and provide some continuity between them, a boundary zone. "The nature of each era is reflected in the evolution of a man's careers in work, family, and other settings, his involvement in solitary and social enterprises, and his broader life plans and goals" (p. 30). The pronoun "his" is used precisely here because Levinson's work, like that of Super, was based on research with men. He and his colleagues studied 40 men in considerable depth over several years as the empirical base for his theoretical perspective. They split the subjects into four groups of 10 men each from one of four occupational subgroups: hourly workers in industry, business executives, university biologists, and novelists.

In addition to eras and transitions, Levinson et al. use several other terms to describe career development as they see it. Primary among these is *individual life structure*. The life structure refers to the patterning of one's life at a given time and to the engagement of the individual in society. Levinson (1977) contends that a life structure has three aspects:

1. The nature of the man's *sociocultural world*, including class, religion, ethnicity, race, family, political systems, occupational structure, and particular conditions and events, such as economic depression or prosperity, war, and liberation movements of all kinds.

2. His *participation in his world*—his evolving relationships and roles as citizen, worker, boss, lover, friend, husband, father, member of diverse groups and organizations.

3. The *aspects of his self* that are expressed and lived out in the various components of his life; and the aspect of the self that must be inhibited or neglected within the life structure (1977, p. 100). In Levinson et al. (1978), this aspect is expanded to reflect the idea that a man selectively uses and is used by his world, through his evolving relationships and roles as citizen, lover, worker, boss, friend, husband, father, and member of diverse groups and enterprises. Participation involves transactions between self and world. (p. 42)

In this view (Levinson, 1977; Levinson et al., 1978), adult development is the evolution of a life structure through alternating stable periods and transitional periods. The primary developmental task of a stable period "is to make certain crucial choices; build a life structure around them and seek to attain particular goals and values within this structure" (p. 100). Each stable period has its distinctive tasks that reflect the requirements of that time in the life cycle. The primary developmental task of a *transitional period* is "to terminate the existing structure and to work toward the initiation of a new structure" (1977, p. 100). In this process, a man reappraises the existing life structure, explores possibilities for change in the world and in the self, and moves toward the crucial choices that will form the basis for a new life structure in the next stable period. Each transitional period also has its own distinctive tasks reflecting its place in the life cycle.

Levinson et al. (1978) describe choices as the primary components of the life structure. To describe and analyze the life structure is to consider the choices a person makes and how he deals with the consequences. "Every choice is saturated by both self and world. To choose something means to have a relationship with it. The relationship become a vehicle for living out certain aspects of the self and for engaging in certain modes of participation in the world" (p. 44). (See Chapter 6 for specific development tasks in adulthood according to Levinson et al. [1978].)

Kanchier and Unruh (1988) conducted a study of 464 managers and former managers (298 non-changers, 166 changers) who were employed in middle and senior executive positions by one large Canadian organization. The purpose of the study was to attempt to clarify the process of occupational change by identifying, exploring, and describing the transition periods of the life cycle and the disengagement stages of the occupational cycle to determine if they are interrelated, and to ascertain if changers and non-changers differ on the variable used to assess these transitions.

Using the Job Descriptive Index and the Self and Work Perception Questionnaire, as well as two-hour semi-structured interviews, they found that changers were significantly more dissatisfied than non-changers with their corporate positions. A significantly larger percentage of changers than non-changers (in the Age-30 and Mid-Life Transition categories) underwent critical self-evaluation with respect to personality traits and career values and goals. Significantly more changers than non-changers experienced traumatic events other than job dissatisfaction, such as marital break-up, death of a parent, illness, extensive travel, or birth of a child. Many changers said that these experiences precipitated and encouraged self-appraisal and were related to the changes they noted in personality traits and career values and goals. The researchers suggested, as would be described by Levinson and colleagues (1978) and by such other transition theorists as Graham (1969), that career life cycles seemed to be interrelated; that the transition periods of changers' life cycles seemed to be integrated with the disengagement stages of their occupational cycles. During the disengagement stages of their occupational cycles, changers were also questioning their career and life goals. These self-appraisals were often intensified by traumatic events and associated with shifts in values. Changers felt they were growing and developing in their careers and indicated that they would probably enter, master, and disengage themselves from several occupations or job tasks throughout their lives to enhance their career and personal growth. For changers, career development seemed to be a continuing search for a better fit between their occupations and their developing personalities.

The researchers, in addition to linking career change to transitions at different age periods and with regard to different events, suggested that counselors should give positive recognition to job changes as real opportunities for personal and professional growth and enhanced career marketability. Thus, "Adults, including those in their 50's or older, should be encouraged to view transitions as suitable times to (a) describe, explore, and evaluate the nature of the conflicts they are experiencing; (b) challenge, revise, or modify their career and life goals; and thereby (c) acquire a sense of mastery over their lives" (p. 136).

The importance of adult transitions as the focus of counselor behavior has also been addressed by Watts (1980), who has suggested three roles which derive from theory about adult career development. One addresses *developmental stages* in the life cycle, as these are related to various periods of chronological age. In such a perspective, the role of the career counselor with adults would be to help persons understand, adapt to, and master the requirements of the developmental tasks characteristic of each stage. A second model focuses upon *roles*. This model views aging as a process of learning new roles and relinquishing old ones. The career counseling response here would involve periodic stock taking about roles and about the interactions and transitions between them, learning to let some roles go and developing the skills and insights to take on new roles. The third model focuses on *life events* which involve significant transitions. Here the career counseling role is one concerned with coping with crises and realizing the growth potential that may be innate with such crises. Each of these approaches has relevance to where particular adults are in their career development and in their transitions.

Other Major Approaches to Adult Development. Several other approaches to adult development are useful in extending our views of career development. Unfortunately, space here does not permit a fair treatment of them although several of them have been summarized in Table 4.4. Suffice it to say they can be divided into those that emphasize "phasic" or "stage" approaches (Lasker, Moore, & Simpson, 1980). Phasic approaches are those in which certain types of development are seen to occur during relatively fixed periods of life: they are age-related. Levinson et al. (1978), Super (1957), Ginzberg et al. (1951), Erikson (1950), and Gould (1978) would be examples. The stage approach involves identification of levels of maturity that are essentially independent of age but vary with the psychological capabilities and development of different individuals. Loevinger (1976), Perry (1968), and Knefelkamp and Slepitza (1976) are representative of such approaches. Together, these theoretical approaches reinforce the importance of change for notions of career development, of differences in individual interpretations of events and in their capabilities to act on them, and of the interactive nature of self and society.

Just as Levinson et al. have proposed major transitional tasks that adults must deal with, several other theorists have also proposed such tasks. Gould (1978), for example, has suggested that major themes in adult development that begin in late adolescence/young adulthood and continue throughout the life span include the following:

1. Leaving our parents' world.
2. I'm nobody's baby now.
3. Opening up to what's inside.
4. The life of inner-directedness finally prevails; I own myself.

In his classic work, Havighurst (1964, p. 216, 1972) has also portrayed major tasks that correspond to the evolving requirements of adult development. (See Chapter 6 for selected perspectives.)

Career Stages in Organizations. Although there are many other adult developmental theories that might be cited, it will suffice here to report only one other perspective, that is, that different settings are comprised of or trigger different types of career transitions or organizational career stages. For example, Dalton, Thompson, and Price (1977) have suggested four progressive career stages in organizations: apprentice, colleague, mentor, and sponsor. Schein (1978) divides the career life cycle into four stages: entry, socialization, mid career, and later career. Hall (1976, 1978, pp. 81–81) discusses early career, middle career, and later career stages. As examples of his later career stages, spanning ages 45 to 60, he identifies the following tasks and levels:

- awareness of advancing age
- awareness of body changes related to aging
- knowing how many career goals have been or will be attained
- search for new life goals

- marked change in family relationships
- change in work relationships
- sense of work obsolescence
- feeling of decreased job mobility and increased concerns for job security

Regardless of which model is used to explain career transitions within organizations or the more global models of adult career development, each stage portrayed involves different activities, relationships, and developmental tasks. They, in turn, require different emphases in the delivery of career guidance and counseling.

Although many of the adult development models described in this section—and earlier theoretical perspectives described in other sections of this chapter—have validity for or have been related to women, such is not always true. The next chapter will portray some of the theoretical dimensions unique to women and minority groups; however, it is useful here to cite Gilligan's perspectives about women's career development: (1) there are qualitative differences in how men and women process and interpret the world, and (2) there are sex differences in adult development not reflected in many of the current models. Gilligan (1982d) asserts that "women define themselves in a context of human relationships" while men tend to devalue such relationships. She further contends that "attachment and separation anchor the cycle of human life . . . the concepts of attachment and separation that depict the nature and sequence of infant development appear in adolescence as identity and intimacy and then in adulthood as love and work" (p. 151). "This reiterative counterpoint . . . tends to disappear" in many developmental models. Gilligan's view of Levinson's concept of the dream is tied to achievement. Gilligan contends, "In all these accounts the women are silent . . . thus there seems to be a line of development missing from current depictions of adult development, a failure to describe the progression of relationships toward a maturity of interdependence"(p. 155). Gilligan (1928b) rightly contends that even where sex differences are identified and examined, they are not effectively incorporated in most adult development models.

> Male and female voices typically speak of the importance of different truths, the former of the role of separation as it defines and empowers the self, the latter of the ongoing process of attachment that creates and sustains the human community. . . . Since this dialogue contains the dialogue that creates the tension of human development, the silence of women in the narrative of adult development distorts the conception of its stages and sequences. (Gilligan, 1982a, p. 155)

IMPLICATIONS FOR CAREER GUIDANCE AND COUNSELING AND CAREER EDUCATION

In the several approaches covered in this chapter, career development is described as a process shaped by an interplay of self-references, self-knowledge, knowledge about training, educational and occupational opportunities, genetic and early childhood influences, evolving personality styles, and patterns of traits that individual express cognitively and psychologically in their choice behavior and career identity. The collective finding of these descriptions of career development is that like all human behavior, it is complex and is part of the total fabric of personality development.

Osipow (1986) has captured much of the complexity of career development as it has been explored in this chapter when he compares his views of 1969 and 1986 on how careers unfold by stating that

> There is nothing that I said in 1969 that I would not say now. Career development still seems essentially socially bound. Careers are still subject to considerable change over the life span. Career choice and implementation, as well as adjustment, expose individuals to a great many

> stresses. Abilities still significantly affect how people's careers unfold and their levels of attainment, and the environment appears to provide an important context in which career development takes place. (p. 161)

The development of career-related behavior is characterized by progressive growth and learning operating from infancy through adulthood within a network of impinging forces internal and external to the individual. Within this context, choice behavior involves a series of interdependent decisions that are to some extent irreversible but are efforts to optimize the individual's situation and are intimately tied to the individual's personal history, to personal perceptions of the future, and to both antecedent experiences and future alternatives.

Many of the existing approaches to career development are based on limited samples of rather privileged persons; most often these samples are of men rather than women. They are, in general, addressed to those in the middle range of socioeconomic characteristics rather than to those who veer from this classification in either direction. Consequently, these approaches tend to emphasize the continuous, uninterrupted, and progressive aspects of career development that seem possible primarily in those whose choice barriers are minimal, for whom both psychological and economic resources are available to aid purposeful development, and in whom a high correspondence between self-concept and vocational concept is most probable. Such criteria do not fit all the persons about whom career guidance practitioners or educators must be concerned.

Another characteristic of these current approaches to career development is that al though they predict that individuals with particular need hierarchies or self-concepts will reject occupations and career patterns that do not seem compatible with their personal characteristics, little attention is given to the possibility that work itself is not central to the life-styles or aspirations of some persons, or that it has connotations that repel rather than attract. For many persons, choices are based not on what they want to do but on what they do not want to do. For these people, choice seems to be more nearly a matter of moving away from the undesirable rather than moving toward an ideal. For other persons, work is not the central commitment for investment of identification or energy that many theories assume. The multinational studies of work salience by Super and his colleagues are clarifying the importance of work salience as a central concept in how people approach career development.

Another point of concern in present descriptions of career development is the age or level of maturity required to make choices. "Most would feel that a certain maturing process must take place before youth (ages 14 to 18) can sensibly make choices—especially vocational ones" (McDaniels, 1968). McDaniels rebuts this assumption by stating that youth "are not too young to choose, only too poorly prepared to make choices." Thus, in much of the thinking about career development, there is insufficient attention to the heterogeneity in every group within the population whether classified by age, sex, race, social class, or any other basis.

Perhaps the most important point of all in analyzing current approaches to career development is that the theories of career behavior largely describe what happens if nothing is done to influence the process. Other chapters in this book discuss theories of intervention in such behavior. Thus, theories of career development describe the targets of intervention: which behaviors should be developed; what influences should be diminished in effect; what cognitive or psychological structures should be strengthened. Although several longitudinal approaches have emerged—for example, Super's Career Pattern Study (1957), Crites' Vocational Development Project (1969), Gribbons and Lohnes' Readiness for Vocational Development (1968)—their purpose has not been to systematically influence career development, but only to describe it at different stages of life.

Other theories have been focused on the structural properties of career behavior (Holland, 1967, 1973, 1985; Krumboltz, 1983) or on the specifics of decision making. While each of these has been important to understanding the evolutionary complexities of career identity and choice, they have focused only on selected interventions in such processes. Taking due cognizance of the caveats expressed, the following career development implications would seem to provide a conceptual base for planning career guidance or career education activities and for implementing career counseling.

1. The concept that people are only economic animals and that work is chosen only for the livelihood it offers is too simplistic. Work also provides a means for meeting needs of social interaction, dignity, self-esteem, self-identification, and other forms of psychological gratification.

2. Individual differences ultimately characterize the style, preference, and performance of people occupying various occupational and educational roles.

3. Personal, educational, occupational, or career maturation is comprised of complex learning processes that begin in early childhood and continue throughout life.

4. Choice occurs not as a single point in time but in relation to antecedent experiences and future alternatives. Decisions interact and are interdependent as they shape choices.

5. Decision making is continuous, tentative, and often more psychological than logical. Specific choices are triggered by messages, directly or subtly expressing expectations for action from reference groups, the mass media, or institutions that comprise the social context in which decisions are made.

6. Because of the importance to adult behavior of early childhood experiences in the family, the school, and the community, intervention to facilitate positive career development needs to begin during the first decade of life. This is the nursery of human nature, when attitudes are formed that are ultimately reflected in career commitment or rejection.

7. Career development is comprised of tasks with which persons must cope in each life stage. Many of these tasks are culturally defined; some are age related; some are stimulated by transitions.

8. Value systems, both individual and cultural, are important in shaping career development.

9. Career information must include not only objective factors such as earning possibilities, training requirements, and numbers of positions available, but also the social and psychological aspects of careers as well.

10. To be effective, career information should be provided in contexts, actual or simulated—for example, gaming, field trips, career-sensitive curricula, work study, role playing, computer-mediated information retrieval—by which individuals can project themselves into possible career roles, act them out, and test their meaning.

11. Since occupational and career choices are methods of implementing an individual's self-concept or expressing their personality style or type, information about self-characteristics—attitudes, aptitudes, values—is as necessary as career or occupational information. Unless the person knows what personal resources he or she has to commit to choice and the outcomes sought, the person has no guidelines by which to evaluate whether anything is of value to him or her.

12. Career development concepts provide the substance for program goals for career guidance and career education that can be translated into behavioral expectations for students or adults and pertinent experiences created to facilitate such behaviors for persons in different life stages. Such concepts represent hypotheses to be tested with individuals in career counseling.

13. Career development theory indicates that decision making involves action. There-

fore, ways need to be found to help persons take responsibility for their own learning and for their own direction. Persons need to be helped to develop planning skills and the courage to execute their plans.

14. Persons need to be helped to develop an awareness that they do have choices, to determine at any given time what kind of decision is involved and the factors inherent in the decision that make a personal difference.

15. An individual's career development is not isolated from development in physical, emotional, and mental areas.

16. Choice opportunities for most persons are so complex that career guidance provided solely in the family or neighborhood is likely to be inadequate for today's realities.

17. Occupational choices and career patterns are basic to one's life-style and reflect developmental experiences, personality, goals, and so forth.

18. Career choice can be an essentially rational process if the person knows how to select and obtain appropriate information and then is able to apply the decision-making process to it. However, all choices have elements of uncertainty about them.

19. Career choice is frequently a compromise between the attractiveness of an alternative, the likelihood of attaining it, and the costs of attaining it. Major elements of choice-making are one's feelings of self-efficacy about performing the tasks required in a choice alternative and the likelihood that it will lead to the outcomes sought.

Summary

In this chapter, the concept of career development has been defined and applied to such terms as vocationalization and occupational socialization, and the possibility of influencing such development rather that leaving it to random events has been discussed. Five major approaches to describing career development—trait-and-factor, decision, situational, psychological, and developmental emphases—have been discussed and some of their implications identified.

Whatever the process of occupational or career decision making, it is clear that choice involves a series of minidecisions made over a relatively long period of time. If systematic assistance in making these decisions can be provided, there is an increasing likelihood that the decisions will be "good"—appropriate for the chooser. The factors that enter into a job, occupation, or career decision and the process by which that decision is made are highly complex. Content and process are intricately related. What a systematic approach to career guidance accomplishes is to bring some order into what is typically a chaotic, haphazard choice.

Finally, it is important to reassert that the present perspectives of career development are incomplete in describing the behavioral development at issue. They have not been formulated as a result of or in conjunction with repeated or longitudinal studies as much as one would hope. Neither do they use enough samples from female, disadvantaged, or culturally different populations so that one can feel confident of the similarities or dissimilarities across subcultures that are implied in some of the theoretical speculation. The particular career problems and the ways theoretical approaches fit various special populations will be discussed in Chapter 5.

CHAPTER 5

CAREER DEVELOPMENT AND COUNSELING OF SPECIAL POPULATIONS

Key Concepts

- Although career development theory and research, as described in Chapter 4, applies in general to special populations, these populations also have unique concerns or problems that need specific attention.
- Career interventions with special populations emphasize techniques somewhat different from those used with the general population or call for different emphases in the use of common techniques.
- Of particular importance to the provision of career services to special populations is the reduction of stereotypes, discrimination, environmental barriers, and other forms of bias that typically impede the career development of such groups.
- No special group is homogenous in its characteristics, problems, or treatment by the larger society. There is as much variability within such groups as there is between special populations and majority groups. Therefore, counselors must guard against unconscious stereotyping, leading to bias, in their personal interactions with members of special populations—whether women, the culturally different, immigrants, homosexuals, or persons with disabilities.

Chapter 4 presented a summary of what we know about so-called majority groups. Several other populations are thought to be sufficiently distinct from these groups on whom career development normative data have been gathered that they should be treated differently. We agree that these other populations have some unique concerns; we also believe that much of what we have learned about career development can, in fact, be applied to them. Differences between their career development and that of the "norm" may, in fact, be more a matter of degree than of kind.

There are a great many possible special populations. For example, workers on late shifts represent one of every six full-time employees. It is assumed that these workers have unique problems that cause them to suffer from sleep disturbances, digestive and nervous disorders, and disruptions of family life, all of which negatively affect marriages. Hence, we might well treat this population separately. Because of space limitations, however, we must limit the populations we will discuss. The populations we have chosen are women, the culturally different, immigrants, homosexuals, and persons with disabilities.

In each case, we will present an overview of research relating to the population and offer suggestions for counseling. In some of these areas, the research findings conflict. We have tried to make as much sense as possible out of these inconsistencies and to be temperate in our conclusions. With each group, we would suggest, the counselor can draw on a great deal of conventional career development theory. This chapter should provide information to supplement that knowledge.

WOMEN

Throughout this volume, we will look specifically at the unique career development needs of females. We emphasize women because of their recent large-scale entry into the labor market and because we are learning more about their career development each day. That knowledge guides practice and instructs us how to apply differential interventions to enhance female career development.

During the 1970s and 1980s, the number and percentage of women in the labor force rose continually. Although the curve of female participation in the labor force has begun to flatten, the proportion of women in the American work force is expected to continue to increase modestly. Most women work because of economic necessity, whether they are single, divorced, separated, widowed, or part of a dual-worker household in which the husband's wages are less than is necessary to exist beyond the poverty level. Women account for a bit less than half of all workers, although a relatively large proportion of females (about one-quarter) hold part-time jobs. The average woman can expect to spend about three decades of her adult life in the labor force; and the more she is educated, the greater the probability that she will be employed. Females are still heavily employed in low-paying, dead-end jobs and in the so-called traditional occupations (e.g., clerical workers, service workers, retail sales workers, and so on). More than half of all children under 18 have working mothers. All these data reflect a relatively recent phenomenon. The number of working mothers has increased tenfold since the period immediately preceding World War II, and the number of women workers has more than tripled (Women's Bureau, 1982).

These data clearly indicate the effect of women in the work force. However, they do not emphasize the increased female participation in many professional and managerial occupations.

Apparently, *tokenism,* or the low proportion of one sex in a workplace dominated by the opposite sex, has different consequences for men and women (Zimmer, 1988). For instance, studying policewomen and male nurses, Ott (1989) concluded that being a minority had opposite effects on men and women. (Male-majority police teams resist women when they have large enough numbers to constitute a "critical mass," but female nurses exhibit no similar resistance to males when their numbers increase.) Jolly, Grimm, and Wozniak (1990) probed sex desegregation patterns in professional and managerial occupations and determined that desegregation is very much present and increasing in these higher-status fields. The desegregation rates are highest, however, in occupations in which men are paid less and the number of workers is declining. Fields that pay the most to their professional and managerial workers are the most resistant to sex desegregation. All in all, then, the great strides made by women in the recent past may still leave them short of occupational equity.

Two factors have combined to cause the significant change in the gender composition of the work force. Antidiscrimination laws and executive orders have been enacted or enforced more rigorously. Simultaneously, the consciousness-raising of women, in regard to careers, has been a target of women's rights groups and professional helpers (counselors and other human relations workers). Both of these endeavors have attempted to alter the composition of the labor force. In large measure they have succeeded. The still obvious imbalance in the labor force has resulted from discriminatory practices in employment and in entry to advanced training for certain occupations and from a low level of aspiration among women. The career "undershooting" of women, in turn, has been ascribed to occupational stereotyping, early childhood conditioning, fear of failure, fear of success, problems of self-efficacy, and a variety of other child-rearing and socialization practices. Hence, attempts at changing the sexual composition of the labor force have centered on legally removing discrimination barriers on the one hand, and on changing the career aspirations of women on the other. It is clear from the preceding data that the strategy has been successful (although still too slow in the opinions of many).

In addition to legislative and aspiration-raising efforts, another factor is causing changes in the work force. Traditional women's occupations are now precisely those that are most in oversupply—teacher, librarian, social worker, and so on. Women in higher education are forced by the labor market to select non-traditional careers or to be unemployed. Research on the career development and behavior of women is one of the most popular areas of investigation in vocational psychology. Reviewing the literature for 1984, Borgen and colleagues (1985) determined that it was *the* most popular topic, with 66 articles addressing women's careers and gender roles.

In the following sections, we will summarize the research on various aspects of the career development of women. Specifically, we will investigate stereotypes, time parameters, traditional versus pioneer versus homemaker career studies, role models, male-female differences, and discontinuities in female career development. We will then present implications for the counseling of women.

Stereotypes

As we shall see in Chapter 7, the sexual stereotyping of occupations begins at a very young age. For many individuals, this stereotyping remains endemic to careers throughout life. For example, using a sample of third- and fifth-grade students, MacKay and Miller (1982) discovered that boys had more complex interaction with things in their occupational choices (environments) than did girls. Interacting with things is perceived as masculine, interacting with people is perceived as feminine, and interacting with data is seen as both masculine and feminine. That young boys' perceptions are even more stereotyped than those of girls is given support in the work of Teglasi (1981), who found that boys' selections of both toys and occupations in grades 1–6 were more sex-typed than were the selections of girls. Hence, the need for early elimination of sexual stereotyping in careers is as important for males as it is for females.

By high school, the sexual stereotyping of interests and mathematical ability has become well ingrained (C. E. Lunneborg, 1982a) and may be fostered even further by brief self-assessment instruments (they make males appear less interested in service and females appear less interested in technical jobs than do more standard measures of these characteristics). One study (Robinson-Awana, Kehle, & Jenson, 1986) asked seventh-grade boys and girls to respond to a self-esteem inventory as themselves and again as they thought a person of the opposite sex would respond. Results showed that both boys and girls believed girls had lower self-esteem, thus concurring with a stereotypical belief (an exception was that the more academically talented females rated boys significantly below themselves). This study serves as yet another example of the negative consequences of stereotyping.

Women in adolescence and young adulthood also demonstrate that they select from only a few occupational possibilities and too often on a sex-typed basis. Results of research with adolescents consistently show that females have lower occupational expectations than males, largely as a consequence of traditional sex-role socialization. For adolescent females, there is reason to believe that domestic and work-role expectations are related to both generalized sex-role attitudes and specific plans for adult domestic roles (Aneshensel & Rosen, 1980). In short, too many females see the sexes in stereotypical ways and feel that women and men should enact different domestic and occupational roles. Even at the college level, students' interest in an occupation may be altered by suggestions of male or female domination in the occupation. When, for instance, male college students are told that in 10 to 15 years, women will constitute 50 to 60 percent of all attorneys, their interest in law as an occupation is significantly less (Collins, Reardon, & Waters, 1980). This finding, however, has not been replicated in studies utilizing more sophisticated research designs (Kluth & Muchinsky, 1984). Nevertheless, the fact that many occupations are sex-traditional simply perpetuates sex-role stereotpyes, sustaining the division of labor as a self-fulfilling prophecy (Yount, 1986).

One promising approach to the dynamics of sex-role stereotyping in careers is suggested by Hackett and Betz (1981), who explain it in terms of self-efficacy theory. This theory suggests that because of differential socialization, women lack strong expectations of personal efficacy for a variety of career-related behaviors. Hence, they fail to realize their capabilities and talents in work. Self-efficacy expectations, it is assumed, are lower among women than men. If one performs a task successfully, expectations of efficacy for the task are increased. It is hypothesized that women have fewer opportunities to demonstrate successful task accomplishments. They may also have fewer chances to watch other people succeed, to experience success vicariously. It is thus thought that they may lack same-sex models. Anxiety frequently prevents the development of facilitative efficacy expectations, and females are considered more likely to have anxiety responses. Finally, information about personal efficacy comes from the verbal encouragement and persuasion of others. It is thought that females receive less encouragement from counselors and others. So expectations of personal efficacy tend to be weakened for women.

In support of Hackett and Betz, Nevill and Schlecker (1988) conducted a study that demonstrated a relationship between perceived career options and self-efficacy expectations and consequently suggested that counselors should reinforce the behaviors of their female counselees that lead to enhanced exposure to and experience of nontraditional occupations (e.g., modifying females' mathematics self-efficacy beliefs).

Stereotypes insinuate themselves into career decision making in various insidious ways, most of which are inimical to both males and females. For example, Yanico (1986) reports a study designed to determine college students' self-estimated and actual knowledge of gender-traditional and nontraditional occupations. She determined that

> college women view themselves as less informed about non-traditional occupations than about traditional, female-dominated occupations, they also report knowing less about male-dominated occupations than college men report. . . . Women significantly underestimated their degree of information about non-traditional fields. . . . The women also significantly overestimated their knowledge of gender traditional fields, and compared to the men in the study, saw themselves as more informed about female-dominated occupations. Generally, college males view themselves as equally knowledgable about fields that are traditional and non-traditional for men. (p. 237)

Thus, women erroneously think that they know more about traditional fields and less about nontraditional ones, reflecting the way they may think about themselves and impinging upon self-efficacy expectations. Further, some decision-making penalty is apparently associated with being nonstereotypical. Those who are nontraditionally sex-typed seem to be more vocationally undecided than males or females who are traditionally sex-typed (Gianakos & Subich, 1986).

Related to the concept of stereotypes is the idea of expectations. Do the work expectations of males and females differ in terms of a variety of parameters, such as income, performance, and so on? The research data available to us suggest that there are indeed significant differences in gender expectations. Hartman and colleagues (1988) and Bridges (1988) both conducted studies that demonstrate these differences in perception. In the former study, both male and female part-time college students viewed high job performance as more masculine and poor performance as more feminine. In the latter study, women proved much more likely than men to base their career choices on stereotypical considerations. Bridges states, "Thus women may tend to select their careers on the basis of either the perceived sex-related skills or the sex-appropriateness associated with the occupation, whereas males may be more likely to consider less stereotypical characteristics, such as salary, personal interest, and value on achievement in the field" (p. 88). In terms of differences in income expectations, H. L. Smith and Powell (1990) asked male and female college seniors to reveal their expectations for income after graduation. While both male and female respondents were equally informed and relatively accurate about the earnings of other college graduates, they differed in the estimates of their own incomes. Men were more likely than women to "self-enhance"—that is, to see themselves competent enough to earn "top dollar."

Stereotypes, of course, also apply to men entering female-dominated occupations. We are just now beginning to see some work on the psychology of men in terms of gender differences in career development. Research such as that of Lemkau (1984) indicates that the same stereotyping factors that operate for women also work for men in nontraditional occupations: lower adherence to traditional sex roles, behavior less sex-stereotyped, and more tendermindedness (as measured by the Cattell 16 PF). Nozik (1986) supported these results and also found that men who enter nontraditional occupations (both professional and skilled) generally came from families in lower socioeconomic strata. Fitzgerald and Cherpas (1985) conducted a study that determined male and female counselors could be equally guilty of sexism.

An instructive study of female marines and male nurses (Williams, 1989) suggests that whereas women marines are segregated and harassed, male nurses are welcomed and encouraged, receiving far less overt stereotypical treatment. The psychoanalytic interpretation that the investigator provides for the results may or may not be accurate; but if it is accurate, it suggests deeply ingrained, not necessarily conscious reactions that will not be changed in the short run. In addition, some recent work argues that not only are men and women treated differently at work because of stereotypes, but they actually work differently; that is, in male-dominated work women tend to be more service-oriented to clients, have a more nurturant attitude toward colleagues, and use power differently from men (Lunneborg, 1990). This focus of inquiry may help to establish whether males and females in comparable positions indeed have different work styles or work personalities attributable to gender.

Chusmir's (1990) review of the relatively scant research on men who make nontraditional career choices (i.e., occupations that have less than 30 percent of same-sex workers) revealed that these men can be described modally as follows:

> They likely possess many of the same traits and characteristics often attributed to women. Contrary to stereotypes, nontraditional men generally

> are comfortable with themselves and their masculine sexuality. They have a well-balanced gender role identity. . . . Their background as well as their personality is nontraditional. Nontraditional women tend to come from a background of family stability and close contact with both a supportive father and mother, whereas nontraditional men likely grow up in a family environment of instability—children whose parents were divorced or in which one of the parents was deceased. Their greatest influence came from women (mothers and important other females), and they often had a distant relationship with their father. (p. 14)

In a later chapter, we shall discuss the effects of stereotyping and the psychology of attractiveness on decisions relating to job-seeking behaviors, such as interviewing for employment. Clearly, in some cases, gender stereotyping has an effect when applicants are assertively feminine (for example, too much makeup, too strong a perfume scent) or excessively masculine (for example, unshaven, slovenly, overly aggressive). There is some encouraging research, however, suggesting that sex effects, in general, are minimal or absent in performance appraisals by supervisors (Kinicki & Griffeth, 1985; Morrow & McElroy, 1984; Thompson & Thompson, 1985), and that sex stereotypes are decreasing among college students (Beutell & Brenner, 1986). If such is indeed the case, the outlook is improving. Unfortunately, most such studies are analogue in nature (that is, simulated rather than real-life), and there may be differences between laboratory-type results and those found in the actual workplace.

The sad fact is that American youth still cling to traditional stereotypes regarding division of labor in the home and occupational attainment of men and women. Male perceptions of life roles, on average, are far from egalitarian, and while there certainly is movement toward more equity, it is not likely to come in the majority of relationships for some time. It is more likely to come occupationally than domestically, in our judgment. The more females can be encouraged by teachers and counselors to expand their career aspirations and view of life roles and the more both males and females can be helped to examine their own restrictive and restricting attitudes, the more likely it is that a genderless egalitarianism will exist in the future. The primary point of attack is, logically, at the earliest age possible; intervention becomes increasingly difficult as stereotypes become more ingrained.

Time Parameters

The career needs, aspirations, and life plans of women need to be continually evaluated and upgraded. Research quickly becomes obsolete, and the findings of the very recent past do not necessarily apply to the present or the future.

Two studies, conducted independently and using different instrumentation, compared female college students' attitudes toward education, family, and work in 1969 and 1973 (Parelius, 1975; Voss & Skinner, 1975). Both reported differences in female sex-role perceptions between the 1969 and 1973 groups (for example, an increase in the percentage planning a "double-track" career-homemaking pattern, a reduction in the percentage planning to interrupt their careers for childrearing, stronger commitment to sexual equality, and, in general, a greater extrafamilial orientation). Voss (1980) later compared groups from 1966, 1973, and 1976 on their perceptions of the female sex-role. She discovered that men are indeed expressing a more liberal female stereotype, but that they may not behave as they talk. She also discovered subgroup differences in male perceptions of female sex-roles (such as college major differences).

Spitze and Huker (1980) looked at data on sex-role status from 1938 and 1978 and concluded that there were strong historical effects; that is, trends in attitudes over time may be explained more by the general climate during a given period than by changes in specific individual experiences and attributes.

In addition, Harmon (1989) has examined the extent to which changes over time in women's career aspirations can be attributed to developmental causes, historical influences, or both. She studied college female cohorts from 1968 and 1983 and determined that both developmental and historical influences were operative. Among her conclusions: "Overall, there are several differences which suggest that historical effects have produced a group of young women who are more aware of the need for women to be employed and are considering less traditional careers for women than their older counterparts at the same age" (p. 60).

In another longitudinal study of women's career development, S. R. Jenkins (1989) studied a group of 111 college women as seniors in 1967 and followed them up in 1981. Among other findings, she discovered little sex difference in factors that predict occupational attainment in teaching and entrepreneurial business; what was predictive for men was also predictive for women. The other remarkable finding, among many, was the migration of these women out of planned teaching careers and into other fields, probably because these other opportunities opened to them at this period in history.

Of course, sometimes the more things change, the more they remain the same. At the college level, Frank (1988) researched male and female students' acceptance of women managers. Demonstrating that perceptual stereotypes have not radically changed from those reported in the 1970s, she determined that men "perceived women managers as being less knowledgeable and possessing poorer managerial skills than male managers. . . . Female students showed a greater preference for a male boss" (p. 107).

Fiorentine (1988), in a time series analysis of college freshman from 1969 to 1984, determined that the value women placed on status-attainment goals increased substantially. Simultaneously, however, the value they placed on domestic-nurturant goals did not greatly decrease. Thus, while the sexes are apparently becoming more alike in career values and goals, women are experiencing more conflict regarding homemaking versus career values.

In 1983, Pirnot and Dustin (1986) administered the Study of Values to 93 women categorized as career-oriented or homemakers. The results were compared to those of a group of women who responded to the instrument in 1966. The researchers discovered substantial differences in both groups from 1966 to 1983: religious values decreased and economic and aesthetic values increased. Other intergenerational differences gleaned from cross-sectional research have been observed by Faver (1984), who found the relationship between career orientation and achievement orientation is stronger in younger women (22–44) than in older women (45–64). The inference is clear: counselors must remain in touch with the literature and developments of the times. We are all aware of counselors who appear to be caught in a time warp, assuming that everything is as it was. When dealing with the changing status and needs of women, especially, such ingenuousness can be harmful.

Traditional Versus Pioneer Versus Homemaker

Studies of the factors that distinguish career-oriented women from non-career-oriented women or women in traditional occupations from women in "pioneer" occupations offer few guidelines for practice. Their results are frequently conflicting, and their conclusions simplistic. Among the more instructive studies, however, are those that hint at factors distinguishing one group of women from another in terms of career orientation. These studies make the following suggestions:

- A female exposed to a maternal model of work competence tends to be more career-oriented.
- Those who are career-oriented or who are planning nontraditional careers achieve higher grades, make a career choice later, come from more advantaged homes, and experience more personal identity and acceptance conflicts.
- They have fathers with higher educational levels and are more likely themselves to be childless (Greenfeld, Greiner, & Wood, 1980).
- They tend to receive more encouragement from teachers, counselors, friends, and significant others.
- They exhibit higher esteem needs (Betz, 1982).
- They may have a greater propensity for risk taking in the sense that women who score higher on the Strong Interest Inventory Adventure scale tend to enter more nontraditional occupations than do lower-scoring women (Douce & Hansen, 1990).
- They manifest stronger career-centeredness and career salience (Illfelder, 1980; Marshall & Wijting, 1980; Yanico, 1981).

An exception to the finding of stronger commitment to work in nontraditional women is demonstrated in a study by Ellermann and Johnston (1988), who found that college women in both traditional and nontraditional majors were highly committed to their future careers (although women in nontraditional majors were significantly less committed to a home and family). None of these studies, however, provides truly definitive answers.

We have not progressed a great deal in our knowledge of these differences (traditional versus pioneer versus homemaker). For example, Lemkau's (1979) review of studies from 1932 through 1976 turned up no characteristic constellation of personality and background factors for the woman who pursues a male-dominated occupation. Lemkau does, however, conclude with a description of what might be a typical or model woman in a male-dominated occupation (at least in 1976).

> She is the oldest child of a stable marriage. Her mother is probably as well-educated as her father and was employed during her childhood. Her father is better educated than most and employed in a professional or managerial position. In keeping with the educational and employment status of her parents, her family tended to be upwardly mobile. If her atypical role is one requiring high education, the probability that she, or one, or both parents was foreign born is higher than expected in the general population.
>
> This prototypic woman reports having been close to both parents. She recalls that her parents emphasized achievement, hard work, and education, conveying by work and example that competence was as appropriate for girls as for boys. She reports that they were supportive of each other in diverse endeavors, and that they encouraged her to experiment with "masculine" as well as "feminine" activities and behaviors.
>
> As an adult, she shares with her male counterpart those characteristics related to competence on the job, having even more than he of such "right" traits as assertiveness, intelligence, and imagination. Except for a tendency to be more oriented toward ideas and things and less to the social environment, she does not differ from the more typical woman on positive aspects of the feminine stereotype. She does not fit the stereotype of the "castrating" career woman whose competence is developed at the expense of sensitivity or expressiveness. While she is experiencing some stress in her role, she is generally emotionally healthy with unusual resources for coping with difficulties she encounters. (pp. 236–237)

Holms and Esses (1988) reached much the same conclusion in their 1988 study of the motivation of Canadian high school girls for a traditional or nontraditional type of career. They state:

> Girls who obtained higher marks in school, identified with either masculine or androgynous trait dispositions, had more liberal attitudes toward

> women, and were from higher socioeconomic backgrounds aspired to higher levels of education, were more highly committed to a career, and aspired to more highly prestigious occupations. (p. 313)

In terms of career-oriented women versus homemakers, Betz (1982) has demonstrated that they have at least one characteristic in common: their highest need appears to be self-actualization, simply pursued in different ways. There are also obvious differences. For instance, as one might suspect, employed women are more feminist (liberal in sex-role attitudes) than are full-time homemakers (Feree, 1980). Ultimately, whether a woman works outside the home or not seems to depend on the interaction between career and family task demands and her own values (Faver, 1982). Mazen and Lemkau (1990) compared women in traditional and nontraditional occupations in terms of their scores on the California Psychological Inventory (CPI). Their analysis revealed a high number of similarities, but five of the CPI scales did differentiate (in rational directions) traditional and nontraditional women: Femininity, Communality, Self-Control, Capacity for Status, and Dominance.

Comparing women in traditional occupations to pioneers to homemakers is, in the final analysis, highly complex. It has been repeatedly demonstrated that female career patterns are much more complex than those of males (Stockton et al., 1980). Add this finding to the fact that there is extreme overlap among these three groups of women on almost all variables—within-group variation is almost as large as between-group variation—and it is easy to understand why no clear and consistent findings have emerged.

A few studies have sought to link Holland's theory of careers and female occupational choice differences. One study (Wolfe & Betz, 1981) substantiated a strong association between congruence and traditionality of choice; that is, women who choose nontraditional career fields are significantly more likely to make choices congruent with their personality type than are women who choose traditional career fields. Another study (Swatko, 1981) showed that women in nontraditional occupations score higher than those in traditional occupations on Holland's investigative and enterprising scales, both of which represent predominately masculine environments.

One fascinating study followed up 352 of Terman's gifted women who were part of his original sample (Holahan, 1981). The mean age of these women was 66 at the time of follow-up. This population of very bright individuals was categorized into three groups: homemaker (N = 139), job (N = 57), or career work history (N = 136). In general, the homemakers were not dissatisfied with their lives (although they said that they would have chosen careers had they to do it all again). Career women were generally satisfied; job holders were not (a job holder is one who has done work for income but who would not call it a career). The group with lowest life satisfaction was composed of those who worked for income alone and who had lost a spouse through death or divorce. However, in a backward look from the vantage of young old age, the majority of Terman's women, careerists and homemakers, expressed high life satisfaction.

Finally, sex-role self-concept (masculine, feminine, androgynous) does not appear to be related to curriculum choice in college (Lyson & Brown, 1982) or to persistence in either traditional or nontraditional majors (Yanico & Hardin, 1981). It does, however, seem related to career ambitions in both traditional and nontraditional occupations.

One of the difficulties in research relating to differences among so-called traditional and nontraditional occupations is that of definition: What constitutes an atypical or nontraditional occupation? Hayes (1986) catalogued 10 different terms in studies used to describe the sexual segregation of labor, including asextypical, gender-concentrated, gender-dominant, gender traditional and gender nontraditional, sex-congruent and sex-incongruent, sex labeling, sex-linked, sex-segregated, sex-typed, and sexual separation of labor. Depending on definition and source, percentages of males and females in an occupation can vary considerably.

All in all, then, we can say little with certainty about differences among women who choose pioneer careers compared to those who select traditional careers and compared to those who elect to be full-time homemakers. Although we can speak of some modal characteristics, there is great variance in each of these three groups.

Role Models

Earlier literature suggested that career models, especially female models, appeared to exert a strong influence on the career aspirations of women (Almquist, 1974; Angrist, 1972; E. D. Elliott, 1973). Whether the model is a working mother, an occupational model—who is also enacting simultaneous roles of wife, mother, and worker—or a professor, career-oriented women have reported that she has been influential in the formulation of their career goals. Although it is clear that role model influences are predictive of women's career-related aspirations and choices, G. Hackett, Esposito, and O'Halloran (1989) confirmed that these models are not necessarily female.

The popular media have played up the idea of "mentor" in the work progress of successful career women. The notion here is that of an established powerful figure in an occupational field (usually male) who takes a female under his aegis and guides and, in a sense, manipulates her rise in that field. Subsequently, the idea of mentor (also termed, occasionally, "patron" or "rabbi") in the career development of women has proven useful. We know that mentors beget mentors in that those who had a mentor become mentors for others; we know that mentor relationships are most often established in the first five years of one's career; we know that more women are becoming mentors as their numbers increase in top management positions; we know that women experience a mentor relationship much less seldom than males; we know that as workers, in general, get older, they generally get more interested in mentoring; and we know that most women are now advised that the route to upper-level jobs is through a mentor (Baruch, Barnett, & Rivers, 1983; Clauson, 1980). Cesari (1985) advocates intrapersonal mentoring, that is, teaching women to take control of their own job socialization. Ryan (1985) would see this teaching role as appropriate for counselors. F. A. Kaufman and colleagues (1986) maintain that counselors are in a good position to help in the development of mentor relationships:

> First, they can provide information to potential mentors and proteges about the advantages of mentorships. Second, they can assist in identifying and matching individuals on the basis of teaching and learning styles, values, and interests. Third, they can establish and monitor mentorship programs in schools and professional organizations. Fourth, they can provide ongoing training in the mentorship process. (p. 577)

Several studies have confirmed the importance of role models in the career development of women. Lunneborg and Lunneborg's (1985) research has demonstrated that both male and female role models influence the careers of women who hold a nontraditional work orientation. These models (in high school, college, and graduate school) were positive influences and included parents, siblings, teachers, friends, and other adults. In terms of parents, the encouragement and support of *both* a mother and a father is most important in fostering nontraditional careers (Auster & Auster, 1981). In a somewhat more detailed study, Weishaar, Green, and Craighead (1981) attempted to determine how college major choice is influenced by role models who serve as reinforcers, for males as well as for females. Their major finding was that *no one* was reported most frequently as an influencer of college major. When an adult was mentioned, it was most often a same-sex parent, although clearly fathers and other adult males gave their daughters reinforcement, especially those selecting nontraditional careers. On the basis of their findings, the authors recommend the use of vocational role models to influence women to pursue nontraditional careers. The suggestion is very strong, then, that for both males and females the developmental support and encouragement of important adult figures is an essential variable in career development.

Aspects of Sex Differences

There is presently no clear theory relating to the career development and choice of women. H. A. Rose and Elton (1973) and Zytowski (1969), among others, have argued for a separate theory of career choice for males and females. Barnett (1971) has offered some interesting thoughts that might lead to such a theory, but her effort illustrates the confounding of sex with other personal variables in decision making. For example, she states:

> For a college woman, her decision to pursue a career is intimately related to her femininity, her need for independence, her self-concept, and her plans for marriage. It is influenced also by the expectations of her social group, family, and college peers and her responses to these groups. For each woman, the planning process and the feelings accompanying it reflect her position with respect to these four factors. (p. 31)

That statement seems sensible. But it would appear equally sensible if one substituted male adjectives and pronouns. Perhaps male-female distinctions in career development and career choice are not so much a matter of kind as a matter of degree. Notions of masculinity and femininity are certainly important in career choice. Are they more important for women? Probably. Plans for marriage are important in the general life planning of both men and women. Are they more important for women? Probably. Perhaps what is needed is a theory of career development and career choice that applies to both sexes, but that might weight various factors according to gender and weight other factors according to such variables as age, race, socioeconomic class, and so on.

Astin (1984) provides one of the most thoughtful attempts in recent years to move toward a theory of career development that more adequately encompasses the possibility of differences in degree—rather than kind—by gender. This model (alluded to in Chapter 4) attempts to describe the career-related behavior of both men and women, albeit in a first-step, rudimentary form that requires testing. Astin proposes four constructs in her need-based sociopsychological model of career choice and work behavior:

1. *Motivation* in the form of three primary needs (for survival, pleasure, and contribution), which are the same for both sexes. Work—defined as activity intended to produce or accomplish something, and which can take the form of paid employment, volunteer work, or family work—has the capacity to satisfy these needs.
2. *Sex-role socialization,* whereby social norms and values are inculcated, through play, family, school, and early work experiences. In the process of satisfying the three needs through these childhood activities, the individual develops certain experiences that directly influence career choice and work behavior.
3. *The structure of opportunity,* which includes economic conditions, the family structure, the job market, the occupational structure, and other environmental factors that are

influenced by scientific discoveries, technological advances, historical events, and social/intellectual movements.

4. *Work expectations,* including perceptions of one's capabilities and strengths, the options available, and the kinds of work that can best satisfy one's needs. The individual's expectations are initially set by the socialization process and by early perceptions of the structure of opportunity. They can be modified, however, as the structure of opportunity changes (pp. 124–25).

Astin's ideas certainly merit research to determine their usefulness in explaining and predicting career choice and behavior. Although there has been initial enthusiasm for her constructs, she is not without her critics who, perhaps unfairly, harshly attack her work not as an early piece designed to elicit research but as though it were a fully developed theory. Fitzgerald and Betz (1984), for instance, take issue with Astin's work for not being integrated with extant knowledge of career choice and behavior, for offering poorly defined constructs, for failing to give suggestions for measurement, for not generating predictions, and for not giving credit to the women's movement, among other perceived shortcomings.

Farmer (1985) also attempts to provide a theoretical perspective that applies to both males and females. She investigated possible differential effects of background, personal, and environmental influences on aspiration, mastery, and career commitment. Her multidimensional model warrants continued research and development. So too does a model developed by Fassinger (1990).

King (1989) offers an additional causal model for career maturity as a result of her investigation of sex differences among high school students. She found a basically similar causal pattern for these male and female adolescents, but also found sex differences, with a higher level of career maturity in girls largely related to their sense of control over events in their lives and a cohesive family that provided cultural opportunities.

Gilligan (1982a) is another theorist whose work is exciting a number of researchers. Hotelling and Forrest (1985) have considered the implications of Gilligan's theory of sex-role development for counseling in general, but it remains for someone to test her constructs specifically in terms of career development. Gilligan argues that dependence-independence and relationships are experienced differently by the sexes, leading to differences in intimacy and empathy. She challenges Erickson's classic ordering of identity and intimacy, suggesting that while it may hold true for men, it is insufficiently descriptive of women. The result is extreme responses by women. As Hotelling and Forrest described the condition,

> From Gilligan's perspective, a woman's development is restricted because she fails to realize that she must incorporate both self-care and care for others into her identity. Many women may view this as an overwhelming task. Two responses, both of which can be maladaptive, are the "superwoman" phenomenon (an attempt to uphold extremely high standards both at work and home) and the "male" model (which requires one to excel at work only). The consequences of the first model are emotional and physical strain and overload; often the woman feels not only exhausted and confused but guilty if she does not perform all tasks perfectly. The second model, which defines self through separation, may result in a woman progressing in her career but ignoring her need for connection with others. The expectation to maintain autonomy and independence in a vacuum of human intimacy at work can be painful, confusing, and lonely to a woman who has learned that connection with others is essential. (p. 184)

The dichotomous thinking expressed by Gilligan and her supporters has been criticized by those who deny that males have any less need for intimacy than females and who see Gilligan's different voices as a dangerous perpetuation of stereotypes. However, critics should take note that much here is potentially useful to explore.

There are studies on a variety of sex differences in career development, career choice, and career behaviors. Siegfried and colleagues (1981) found support for the idea of sex differences in job preference, that is, preference for various job characteristics classified as either motivators (such as challenging work, voice in decision, contribution to society) or hygienes (such as salary, fringe benefits, job security). They concluded that both males and females in college ranked the motivators high in importance, but females also gave nearly the same importance to hygiene factors. Sex differences were so real that, using multivariate analysis, the investigators were able to predict a subject's sex simply by looking at the rank of motivators and hygiene factors. On the other hand, investigating reactions to work of over 3500 men and women factory workers, Loscocco (1990) found that male and female workers were very similarly influenced by specific personal and job characteristics and that both were most affected by the intrinsic and financial rewards of their jobs.

Studying 204 female managers, Ornstein and Isabella (1990) questioned whether Levinson's age stages or Super's psychological stages (see Chapter 4) were descriptive of changes in career attitudes. Their conclusion was that Super's career development model was *not* supported and that Levinson's stages were closer, but offered far from robust support. These results are interpreted to mean that there are major differences between men and women in terms of career development, largely because women's careers are less continuous, their career development is less heterogeneous than men's, and/or employing organizations may exert more influence on their career development than do career stages. In any case, a woman's age was more predictive of her career experiences than was her career stage.

Another study of sex differences, using Project Talent data (Card, Steel, & Abeles, 1980), determined that although women had higher grades and higher test scores than men in high school, 11 years after high school the men had acquired more education and were earning more money. The authors attributed these sex differences primarily to greater conflict for women between the roles of spouse/parent and the roles of student/worker. Variables that measured the onset, duration, and extent of family-related commitments were more strongly related to female than to male realization of potential.

These types of very real male-female aggregate differences in earnings are much-discussed issues in the popular media. Several refinements in the way these data are examined help to explain the differences somewhat. Rytina (1981) has demonstrated that when women constitute only a small proportion of the workers in an occupation, their earnings are much lower than those of their male counterparts. In the female-dominated and low-paying occupations, the earnings of women are closer to those of men. Hence, occupational sex segregation negatively affects female earnings and perpetuates male-female earnings differences, although these differences are not translated into lesser job satisfaction for females (R. Lee, Mueller, & Miller, 1981). Further refinement comes in a study by McLaughlin (1978), who studied occupations of equal prestige for which male-female earnings were decidedly unequal. He discovered that

> the earning potential of prestige-equivalent occupations differs such that males tend to be clustered in occupations with greater income potential even within categories of prestige. This is consistent with the notion that many men and women who attain equally prestigious occupations do not attain equal occupational earning potential. (p. 920)

Karpicke (1980) provides another example of sex differences that substantiates the degree-versus-kind argument made earlier in this chapter. She studied college students to determine sex differences in success avoidance, home-career conflict, and attitudes of significant members of the opposite sex as influences on career planning. She was also interested in determining the sex differences in and the accuracy of counselors' perceptions regarding these variables. Her results suggest that undergraduate females have significantly more success avoidance and home-career conflict than male students, but that this fact may not be so important in career planning as originally thought. She concludes,

> The results of this study suggest that the theoretical career development literature for women is not accurate in its emphasis on the integration of the female sex role into a woman's career plans. Although two of the variables measured (success avoidance and home-career conflict) were more important to women than to men, they do not appear to be focal concerns for the career planning process of either sex. Continuing efforts need to be made to determine factors that influence the career planning processes of both sexes and to provide counselors with empirical data on which to base career counseling intervention strategies. (p. 245)

Occasionally, the mass media promulgate the findings of writing that appears in the professional literature and tag it with a "cute" descriptor. Such was the case in 1989 when F. N. Schwartz published her notions about a dual-track managerial career for women and promptly found it labeled the "mommy track." Briefly, this argument states that women managers cost companies more than men managers because of career interruptions, greater turnover and plateauing, and so on. Schwartz suggests that there are two types of women managers: one type resembles men (career-primary women) and are career-first people; the majority of women, however, are what she terms career-and-family women, those who want to pursue serious careers while also rearing children. Schwartz maintains that corporate America can bring the costs of women managers in line with those of men by allowing women certain accommodations, among which are family supports (e.g., maternity leave, flexibility of work hours, child care, etc.). This would, in effect, create two tracks—a fast track for men and a slower track for women—but both would eventually end up in the same place: at the very top rungs of the corporate management ladder.

There are those who maintain that women face a "glass ceiling" that limits their advancement in top management (a phenomenon also allegedly present in minority career development). This "glass ceiling" implies an invisible barrier put up by white males to deter the upward mobility of women beyond middle management. Whatever the reason—conscious or unconscious discrimination, systemic barriers, or the like—it is clear that substantial gender and racial differences exist within corporate management (A. M. Morrison & Von Glinow, 1990) and that equity is not a realistic short-term prospect.

The meaning of leisure is apparently different for women than for men. Although relatively little research has emerged regarding women and leisure, Henderson (1990) did review the sparse collection of extant scholarship and determined that women experience leisure in a different context from men and give it less time and a lower priority. Further, women tend to perceive their leisure as a family activity, in that they use the home as a "container" for leisure. Strikingly, many women apparently feel that they are not entitled to leisure; they feel that they are undeserving because of the way they perceive their role obligations in life.

Men and women also evidently experience divorce differently with respect to work. R. R. Peterson (1989), for example, investigated the issue using a cohort of almost 4000 women, aged 30–44, about whom data were available from 1967 to 1977. In general, these women responded to divorce and consequent economic hardship by work adjustment, achieving at least partial economic recovery, but their predivorce work history determined the degree of economic resiliency.

With television situation comedies and standup comedians focusing on premenstrual syndrome (PMS) and with all the other media attention given to the topic, it is not surprising that PMS has been addressed with regard to work. It is certainly a topic that lends itself to distinctions between men and women. Although no specific research exists in relation to work, A. S. Phillips and Bedeian (1989) have reviewed the general PMS literature and concluded that there is currently no scientific proof that PMS affects behavior (including work behavior). However, both men and women believe that it does. Therefore, they view wellness programs within employee assistance programs as appropriate sites in which to address attitudes toward PMS. They cite corporations that hold PMS awareness days to inform women about the etiology of PMS and about palliative measures. Employer education is also necessary, they feel, so that PMS will not be used as an artificial barrier to higher-paying, more responsible jobs for women.

Discontinuities in Female Career Development

Although more and more women are displaying uninterrupted career patterns, discontinuities obviously abound. The major source of male discontinuity was formerly the military draft. This discontinuity has not been a problem for several years. For women, the primary source of discontinuity is children.

J. E. Walker, Tansky, and Oliver (1982) examined 1973 interview data gleaned from the Quality of Employment Survey conducted by the University of Michigan Survey Research Center. The 1455 workers surveyed included 470 regularly employed women, 179 of whom were sole wage earners. The researchers analyzed the data in terms of male-female differences in work values. They concluded that only one value—convenience—was consistently different for men and women. Women assigned it a higher priority. The presence of children in the home (preschool or school age) was negatively related to most work values for women. In other words, working mothers experience reduced work involvement, perhaps because the presence of children causes working women to reassess the importance they give to work. Although the data on which these conclusions are based are almost two decades old, there is little reason to doubt their current applicability.

Another study investigating women's careers (Rosenfeld, 1979) used data on 5083 women surveyed from 1967 to 1977. The conclusion was that men are likely to remain continuously employed whereas women tend to have intermittent employment. Once again, the discontinuities were generally related to changes in the extent of home responsibilities. The discontinuity of career development in women is seen as a paramount barrier to occupational upward mobility.

Lassalle and Spokane (1987) identified 17 women's career patterns, based on degree of participation (full time, part time, or out) and occupational level, at four different age points (18, 22, 25–26, and 29–30). They found evidence to suggest that "the more consistent and extensive the labor force participation, the greater the respondent's occupational advancement. The data also indicated that a woman's attachment to the labor force tends to be bimodal: either strong or almost nonexistent. Very few women were in patterns in which labor force participation was primarily part-time or sporadic" (pp. 63–64).

Some see a chicken-egg argument in relation to women's fertility and employment.

Which causes which? Does childbearing constrain labor force participation, or can we use labor force activity to predict a woman's expected fertility? Cramer's (1980) research suggests that the dominant effects are from fertility to employment in the short run and from employment to fertility in the long run. Some argue that race and sex-role attitudes are among variables that may affect this conclusion, but this has not been demonstrated. In fact, the research of Spitze and Waite (1980) failed to predict a fertility-employment link on the basis of sex-role attitudes.

One study of about 500 midwestern female college students (K. L. Peterson, 1985) suggests that discontinuity is not foreign to women in higher education. While anticipated levels of work involvement were important, women in the study experienced considerable doubt and confusion about working throughout their lifetime; that is, they anticipated that they would not be continuously employed. Such an attitude would obviously affect career choice. On the other hand, lifelong career commitment may be related to the particular major a woman chooses; for example, Katz (1986) found no differences in the relative career commitment of males and females in baccalaureate-level management majors and MBAs. Hock, Morgan, and Hock (1985) report that women generally adhere to these earlier-determined plans to work continuously or not. Using a longitudinal approach, they found that of 172 new mothers, 75 percent of those planning to stay home did so, and only 25 percent of the mothers who planned to stay home worked instead. They concluded that "married women of low career orientation appear to meet their needs through home, family, and non-work roles" (p. 399).

In any case, career interventions with women should include assurance that females understand the nature of continuous and discontinuous career patterns and the effect of fertility on those phenomena. In Chapter 12, we will further discuss these consequences for women who seek to return to the labor force or who seek to enter it for the first time after a protracted period of childbearing and childrearing. Such women have rarely considered the consequences of discontinuity before the fact and frequently, therefore, experience trauma after the fact.

The Career Counseling of Women

Given differences in the career development of women, what are the implications for the career counseling of females in contemporary society? One must assume that at all levels, but especially at the higher occupational levels or in nontraditional careers, women will exhibit more conflict than men, will experience differences in job-seeking patterns, and will have to overcome more obstacles to career advancement (Leviton & Whitely, 1981). The techniques applicable to the career counseling of women are the same as those used for men, but they differ in the intensity with which they must be pursued.

Such techniques as networking, peer counseling, and professional support are especially useful with women clients. Networking is "a process of identifying existing social networks, enhancing connecting networks along new lines, and channeling information through these created guidance networks" (Voight, Lawler, & Falkerson, 1980, p. 106). These networks are made up of contact persons for educational and employment advice and placement. It is ironic, in contemporary society, that while old-boy networks are being vilified and legislated against as a job-finding technique, networking can be valuable for women in job-finding and promotion. Not the least important network is that of the family, which, in addition to providing social support, also helps members get jobs, especially blue-collar jobs (Grieco, 1987). Employees serve as sources of information and sponsors for family members in the job market.

Peer counseling can range from simple support groups to more action-oriented endeavors. Professional support and counseling can assume a variety of forms.

The counseling of adult women college students is another professional intervention to aid women. Smallwood (1980) surveyed a sample of this population and concluded that their four major needs are (1) adequate child care facilities, (2) accommodating job schedule realities (help with securing off-campus employment coordinated with class schedules, flexibility of class scheduling, and so on), (3) academic reentry (such as special academic counseling and encouragement), and (4) financial and personal counseling needs (such as divorce or major life change). Again, while these needs are applicable to males, they are no doubt more pressing for females.

Early counseling interventions with females are thought to be important influencers of career decision making. One study (Sauter, Seidl, & Karbon, 1980) demonstrated that women who elected traditional or nontraditional career paths experienced different high school counseling and held different attitudes toward women's roles. Women who chose traditional career paths were more conservative and sex-dichotomized in their attitudes. Further, high school counseling was reported as an influence only by women who selected traditional female careers, suggesting that counselors encourage sex stereotyping. Thus, early counseling interventions in themselves are apparently not so important as the type of intervention. What is called for, according to the authors, is nonstereotyped counseling that addresses career opportunities for women and helps them appraise their abilities and ambitions.

A number of techniques are appropriate in counseling women. Various stress-reduction programs have proven successful in decreasing emotional exhaustion and personal strain. Higgins (1986), for example, reports that both a progressive relaxation and systematic desensitization program and one emphasizing instruction in time management, rational-emotive therapy, and assertiveness training were equally effective in reducing stress among working women. In fact, the reduction of stress for women who are experiencing conflict because of multiple role demands is the focus of much writing and research (e.g., Ashurst & Hale, 1989; Mowbray, Lanir, & Hulce, 1984; G. Nelson, 1990; Swanson-Kauffman, 1987). Specific techniques, ranging from mutual-support self-help groups to professional interventions, are discussed in Chapter 11 in the section dealing with occupational stress.

Foss and Slaney (1986) conducted a videotaped career intervention with 80 college women to determine its effect on the woman's traditionality of choice and that of a hypothetical daughter. Results indicated that while the use of the videotape was effective, subjects were generally "aware of the advantages of less traditional careers but were not reflecting this awareness in their own career choices as clearly as in the choices for their daughters" (p. 199).

The idea of counselor stereotyping and sex bias is, of course, not new. Male counselors seem to ascribe different motivations (such as success avoidance) to male and female undergraduates, and even female counselors do not accurately perceive sex differences in motivating factors (Karpicke, 1980). Mercado and Atkinson (1982) offer evidence that male counselors encourage male and female high school students to explore occupations along sex-stereotypic lines. Further, a physical-attractiveness bias may enter vocational counseling. Indeed, given what we know about the psychology of attractiveness—that attractive individuals are ascribed all sorts of positive characteristics and nonattractive people are not—it would be surprising to discover that it did not. Such biases are difficult to counteract. One attempt to do so is reported by Rudnick and Wallach (1980). They organized a conference for counselors and math and science teachers to explore nontraditional female choices. This type of preservice and inservice education is apparently necessary on an ongoing basis. Another successful workshop for women, entitled "Choices and Changes," is reported by Sandmeyer (1980). She organized groups to explore four themes: Expanding Horizons, Narrowing the Focus, Translating Self to the Employment Context, and Looking Ahead. Initial evaluations were positive.

Gaming and simulation are other techniques that have been applied to the career counseling of women. For example, Hammer-Higgens and Atwood (1989) describe *The Management Game,* a psycho-educational intervention for both counselors and clients that gives them some forewarning and enables them to experience vicariously some of the hostile elements that women will face within the corporate structure. It also suggests ways of overcoming these barriers.

Finally, Sundal-Hansen (1984) suggests a career futures scenario in which sex equity produces a future society with 10 characteristics. The first three of these ideal characteristics provide a resounding finis for this section of Chapter 5.

1. Women and men will be able to make choices and decisions more according to their authentic interests, talents, values, and preferences and to explore a wide variety of fields, subjects, and activities not labeled by sex. These changes will allow for the development of the multipotentialities of both women and men. Children will be exposed to and will be free to explore a wider variety and range of options in activities, hobbies, interests, roles, and behaviors. They will experience sex-fair childrearing at home and sex-fair education, counseling, and curriculum at school.

2. There will be more equitable distribution of men and women in education and work. Movement will be away from occupational and educational segregation toward more equal distribution of the sexes in all kinds and levels of education and occupation. Business and industry will pay more attention to human needs in the workplace, with flextime and flexplace, parental leave, childcare services available to employees, multiple benefit options, and other kinds of employee assistance programs reflecting a new corporate perspective on, responsibility for, and commitment to the personal and family needs of workers.

3. Women and men will have more solid relationships because they will be able to relate to each other as equals, instead of women being "less than" men and men "more than." They will learn to respect each other at home and in the workplace, to resolve conflicts constructively, to negotiate roles and share tasks. They will find creative new patterns for working out work/family relationships in dual careers, in blended families, and in single-parent and other family types (pp. 240–41).

THE CULTURALLY DIFFERENT

There are many minorities on which we might possibly focus. We will limit our attention to only four: African-Americans, Hispanics, Asian-Americans, and Native Americans. The amount of space devoted to each is probably representative of the amount of research that appears in the professional literature.

Miles (1984) suggests that the overall term *economically disadvantaged* should be applied to a large group that cuts across racial and ethnic boundaries, for while each minority group certainly has unique concerns, the core problem is poverty. Poverty tends to characterize minority groups in greater proportion than the majority. Thus, the key element is not race or ethnicity so much as poverty. This is not to say that discrimination is not real; it obviously exists. Only after poverty is dealt with, however, can we turn to concerns unique to each culturally different segment of society.

African-Americans

In support of Miles's observation, the data indicate that the plight of African-Americans, especially inner-city males, is horrific. According to one study (Glaberson, 1990), nearly one of every four young black men (20–29 years of age) in New York State is in a state prison or local jail, on probation, or on parole. The number of young black men in custody on any given day (45,000 out of 193,000 in New York State) is double the number of black men enrolled in all the colleges in the state. This pattern is mirrored across the country. Over 50 percent of young urban black men were unemployed in the 1980s, worked part-time jobs involuntarily, or earned poverty-level wages (Lichter, 1988). Forty-eight percent of African-American families are headed by women, and more than half of all black children are born out of wedlock (Staples, 1986).

In the past two decades, the situation has worsened. Taylor (1990) argues that "industrial decentralization, combined with structural shifts in city economies from centers of goods-producing or manufacturing activities to higher order service-providing industries, has severely affected the employment opportunities of inner-city Blacks, especially the job prospects of poorly educated Black youths. . . . Such structural changes have substantially reduced the number of unskilled and semiskilled jobs in those industries that have traditionally attracted and economically upgraded previous generations of Blacks." (p. 7) The consequences for African-American families are obvious, as are the effects on crime rates.

Lest one automatically blame the African-American family structure for so many ills, it is instructive to read the work of Lewis and Looney (1988). Their research looked into 18 inner-city, poor black families and compared them with middle- or upper-middle class white families that they had previously studied. They concluded that the white and black families were much more alike than different and what appeared to "work best" in fact worked best for both black and white families. L. E. Jenkins (1989) reminds us that the family is embedded within a larger-scale social system that sometimes does not act in a manner designed to enhance the psychological health of that family. The inner-city black family is thus frequently regarded in terms of its negative aspects rather than its strengths. If black parents (including female heads of households) have good parenting skills, achievement in children emerges much as it does with whites. Obviously, the more compatible the cultures of the home and the school, the greater the probability of successful academic achievement.

Simultaneously, however, middle-class minorities are growing. It is true that about 30 percent of African-Americans (who constitute about 13 percent of the population) live in poverty, but about one-third can be considered middle class. Nearly half of all blacks own their own homes, and about 1.5 million work as managers, business executives, and professionals.

An examination of some of the research related to the career development of African-Americans reveals that although there has been a recent increase in research on career development and behavior of precollege blacks, there has been relatively little on higher education and adulthood. Most research on post-secondary subjects has concentrated on access: Do black students in compensatory programs achieve as well as regularly admitted students? Are admissions tests as predictive for blacks as for whites? Much less research has been devoted to process and exit-related concerns: What effect does the collegiate experience have on the values and attitudes of blacks? Why do blacks tend to gravitate toward certain occupations? What are unique black career-related problems?

Nevertheless, there are some useful findings. First, one should not assume that black students come to higher education with anything but ambition, an appreciation for work, and high career expectations. At the same time, however, the career development of African-Americans is more likely than advantaged populations to be delayed or impaired. This lag can manifest itself at the college level in such problems as a discrepancy between a desire for a college education and a career choice that does not require that level of education, a general lack of knowledge of alternatives, possible skills deficits, and an unclear picture of self in relation to the world of work. These problems are hardly unique to blacks, but they may be more characteristic of black students as a group than of whites.

The school obviously has a role to play in the development of African-American youth, and according to many observers, it has failed to exercise that role with vigor and skill. Grant and Sleeter (1988) longitudinally (over a 7-year period) studied 24 lower-middle-class junior high school students who were of different racial backgrounds. They found a gradual narrowing of dreams as the students went through secondary school. In junior high, these youngsters projected themselves into a wide band of future career roles, with no anticipation of racial, social, class, or gender barriers. The concept of institutional racism was alien to them; they valued education, visualizing it as a way to achieve their dreams. Because of the school's low demands on them, however, they put forth minimal effort. Their dreams were largely abandoned as the students progressed through school, and the school itself assumed an important role in that abandonment. "In spite of students' interest in further education, in spite of their good behavior in school, and in spite of the fact that the majority had normal learning ability, both the junior and senior high school faculty (with the exception of a very few individuals) accepted students' failure to empower themselves through education, and in doing so, ensured that they would fail" (p. 38). It is moot whether the increased number of black children in private schools (Slaughter & Johnson, 1988) will change this conclusion.

One researcher who has produced a body of solid information on the career development of blacks is Dillard (1980). He cites several factors that impede the career development of blacks, ranging from restricted opportunities to background factors. These impediments, according to Dillard, make theories based on white, middle-class vocational development inappropriate for blacks. He argues, for example, that lower-class blacks have few positive work-related experiences, limited educational experiences, poor environmental resources, negative orientations to work, and restricted access to career and employment information. Further, he observes that few opportunities are available for young blacks at lower socioeconomic levels to view and accept work habits from a role model, especially a paternal model. He maintains that black women are forced to give greater consideration to family and racial and sexual discrimination in work decisions than white women. Dillard also suggests that because of situational factors, the primary work values of lower-class blacks are likely to be extrinsic rather than intrinsic: self-expression is less a concern than is bread on the table. Finally, in terms of aspirations, Dillard proposes that rather than studying black-white differences, we ought to be investigating within-group black differences: male versus female, urban versus rural versus suburban, lower-class versus middle-class, and so on. Dillard's ideas are sensible and worthy of implementation. He recognizes the ever-present confounding variable of socioeconomic class. Until we can control clearly for socioeconomic class in racial comparisons, research on between-group and within-group differences in career development will be less helpful than it might otherwise be. For example, Dillard and Campbell's (1981) study of parental influences on the aspirations of Puerto Rican, black, and Anglo children demonstrated no clearly direct linear influence. The aspirations that some parents hold for their children are influences in adolescent vocational development. For others, however, there seems to be no influence, regardless of ethnicity of race. Why, we do not know.

There is no doubt that in the aggregate blacks are disadvantaged, not only compared to the white majority but also compared to other minorities. To be sure, strides have been made. Since World War II, the earnings of black men have increased faster than those of white men. Since 1975, however, these gains have stabilized. Up to 1975, the gains were usually attributed to the declining proportion of blacks in the South, increased education, and a period of relatively full employment. In general, additional education translates into additional earnings for blacks at about the same rate as for whites. On-the-job training, however, seems to pay off more for whites (D. E. Taylor, 1981).

At one time in America there were considerable differences among blacks in the North and in the South in terms of occupational earnings and status. In some respects these differences persist (Hogan & Pazul, 1982). For example, northern-born black men pursue different career patterns from blacks who migrate from the South. Blacks who are native to Milwaukee, Wisconsin, emphasize the intrinsic rewards associated with jobs, whereas southern-born migrants to Milwaukee emphasize the extrinsic rewards. "As a result, the northern natives tend to value a high status job, even if it is low-paying, while the migrants prefer a job with higher pay even if it is relatively low status" (Hogan & Pazul, 1981, p. 127). This situation is changing, however. Regional differences in black occupational attainment and status are declining as a result of decreased emigration from the South and some selective return of migrants to the South (LaGory & Magnani, 1979).

With so many blacks unemployed, it is natural that many would see discrimination as a major cause (along with skills deficits and lack of work readiness). Indeed, how a worker perceives the possibility of employment discrimination affects several attitudes, including locus of control. Becker and Krzystojiak (1982) studied labor market discrimination and concluded that beyond racial identity, blacks' perceptions of employment discrimination influenced their tendency to blame external forces for their plight (blacks who feel they are discriminated against experience twice as much externality as blacks who report no awareness of discrimination). Clearly, those blacks who perceive discrimination in employment are affected in terms of their subsequent work attitudes, values, and behaviors.

Interestingly, however, one study (G. J. Johnson, 1990) has reported that being underemployed and/or underpaid did *not* seem to lower the self-esteem of African-American men. The explanation given was that "perhaps Black men compensate for underemployment and underpayment by developing coping strategies whereby they assess their self-worth by personal and familial achievements which actually enhance their self-esteem" (p. 37).

What is bias and what is not bias in employment? Research has not yet provided definitive answers. Several studies have investigated aptitude measurement, for example, as a source of bias. Work sample examinations, especially, have been carefully examined for ethnic differences that might lead to a conclusion of bias. Backman, Lynch, and Loeding (1979) concluded that the TOWER System of Vocational Evaluation produced higher mean scores for whites than for blacks in all aptitude areas except motor skills. These differences were not attributable to amount of education. Further, the work samples were designed to represent job tasks rather than academic achievement. These findings suggest that the use of a separate set of norms, for ethnic, sex, and disability groups may be appropriate. These norms are provided. Although the differences are apparently real, for whatever reason, it is also possible to exaggerate black-white differences. Brugnoli, Campion, and Basen (1979), for instance, used work sample ratings for mechanics to show that when observers are asked to make global evaluations after viewing an applicant's performance on a task representing an irrelevant job behavior, race-linked bias tended to be present. When observations were of relevant behaviors and were required to be specific rather than global, however, the work bias was not present. This finding suggests that careful training of evaluators can make reported differences in aptitudes less vulnerable to distortion through racial bias.

Other studies have investigated the validity of interest inventories with African-Americans. Carter and Swanson (1990) reviewed eight studies of the Strong and concluded that there was "little evidence of the Strong's psychometric validity with Black samples" (p. 195). The instrument under examination was the old SVIB, not its later refinements; further, there was also no evidence that it is *not* valid. On the other hand, Hansen's (1987) research suggests that at least some Westernized interest inventories can be successfully used in other cultures. If African-Americans can indeed be said to represent a different culture, cross-ethnic use is appropriate. The bulk of evidence, though scanty, points toward the judicious use of inventories with blacks.

The occupations that African-Americans choose (or that are available to them) are relatively constricted. It is well known that in terms of the Holland classification, blacks are underrepresented in the Enterprising and Investigative categories and overrepresented in the Realistic and Social categories. Enterprising occupations (such as sales and management) usually provide high income with less education than do other job families. Black youth, it is thought, should be exposed to more information about and experience in enterprising occupations. Why blacks are not more highly represented in enterprising occupations is difficult to know. Past discrimination may have been directed more to managers, administrators, and salespersons than to educators, health personnel, ministers, and other social service workers. Whatever the reason, blacks should become more involved in types of work that offer higher income differentials. Entrepreneurial business activities represent one such occupational category.

Similarly restrictive choices are made by blacks in their tendency not to opt for science and engineering curricula in higher education. In 1988 African-Americans constituted 1.3 percent of the total graduate enrollment in the physical sciences at doctorate-granting institutions, 1.4 percent in the mathematical sciences, and 1.7 percent in both computer science and life sciences (National Science Foundation, 1989). From 1975 to 1989 the number of doctoral degrees awarded to blacks in the physical sciences, life sciences, and engineering remained stable, fluctuating narrowly between a low of 101 in 1980 and a high of 133 in 1978 (Vetter, 1989). Blacks tend to choose majors predominately in the fields of social science, education, and health. Clearly African-

Americans need to be encouraged to explore careers that have been nontraditional for them. Malcolm (1990) suggests one way of getting blacks attracted to such occupations:

> Only by increasing the amount of time Black children are engaged in meaningful educational activity in mathematics and science; by reaffirming the historical, contemporary and future role of Blacks in science and engineering; and by valuing and recognizing participation in these fields within our communities and families can we ever expect to change the trickle of talent which currently flows from the pipeline into a flood. (p. 257)

The restricted choices of minority students are also noted by Turner, Johnson, and Patterson (1981) who view the problem as basically one of an expectation-readiness gap. Hence, they advocate training in career decision making as an appropriate focus for minorities in higher education. They describe a program for minority undergraduates at Western Michigan University that begins with summer orientation. The goals of the program are

- To promote and facilitate students' involvement to continuous evaluation
- To provide the resource materials and guidance necessary to enhance effective career exploration
- To assist students in reality testing of their tentative career choices
- To facilitate reality-based career decisions
- To encourage and assist in the development of a life plan to support and strengthen career decisions
- To encourage minority students' use of counseling, testing, and placement services

It is hoped that this emphasis on self-assessment and initial career exploration, reality testing, and implementation will lead to a more comprehensive distribution of career choices among blacks and other minorities.

There has been relatively little research to determine the difference between the expressed needs of blacks for career planning and those of the majority population. One may hypothesize that African-Americans express the same basic needs as their white counterparts in college: résumé-writing skills, job-interviewing skills, career-planning workshops, and so forth.

Among the solutions proposed is that of Cheatham (1990), who in a thoughtful article proposes that the emphasis of interventions be *Africentric* for African-American students. He argues that counselors must pay heed to a group's cultural uniqueness; specifically, the African-American's values, truths, and meanings. Cheatham alleges that the dominant U.S. culture is Eurocentric and therefore clashes with values, attitudes, and beliefs that are strongly influenced by African origins. Consequently, Cheatham suggests different career interventions with blacks. He proposes "the use of culture-specific information that enables the helper to distinguish between an African-American client's psychosocial dynamics and behaviors, and those behaviors that are products of obligatory, grudging accommodation to normative majority culture (i.e., Eurocentric) structures" (p. 336). Included in such interventions would be a recognition of structural or racial discrimination, culturally influenced perceptions of the meaning of work, differential availability of career information and guidance, and economics and labor market forces that affect African-Americans differentially. It remains for someone to operationalize this idea. One must resist a temptation, however, to throw out the more universal, Eurocentric aspects of career interventions, for they indeed work with African-Americans as well as the majority culture. Once again, we are talking of differences in degree rather than kind and the necessity to combine what is catholic to every person's career development with what is parochial to a unique subgroup's needs. The lack of either focus in an intervention diminishes the treatment.

Hispanics

Hispanics or Latinos are a heterogeneous minority constituting approximately 8 percent of the population of the United States (U.S. Bureau of the Census, 1989). Their heritage may be from Mexico, Cuba, Puerto Rico, Central America, South America, or Spain itself. The largest Hispanic ethnic group is the Mexicans, followed, in order, by Puerto Ricans and Cubans.

Each of these major Hispanic groups has different unemployment rates and sex differences in workforce participation, although all groups are basically less well off than the general population. Among the Puerto Ricans, there is a great deal of movement between the mainland and America.

Cubans, on the other hand, have little or no movement back to Cuba. Cubans and Mexicans tend to be unemployed for shorter durations than do Puerto Ricans. These figures emphasize the heterogeneous character of Hispanics.

Hispanic workers are concentrated more in the lower-paid, lesser-skilled occupations than the total work force. More than half of the employed Hispanic women are either clerical workers or nontransport operatives (dressmakers, assemblers, machine operators, and so on), both low-paid occupations. Hispanic men are disproportionately employed as operatives, service workers, and craft workers. Although a great percentage of Hispanics are *not* employed in agriculture, contrary to popular stereotype, about 7 percent work in that area compared to 1 percent of the white population. Although these data present a picture of Hispanic ethnic groups as generally underrepresented in the more remunerative occupations of society, some progress is being made. The children of first- and second-generation immigrants expect higher-status and better-paying jobs in the economy. The major task facing these groups is to acquire the education and occupational skills necessary to realize these aspirations.

As with any socioeconomically disadvantaged minority, young Hispanics generally have a constricted knowledge of and exposure to occupations. Consequently, they choose from a relatively limited array of alternatives. They may not have basic job-seeking skills (such as filling out applications), and they may need encouragement, motivation, and reinforcement to pursue occupations and opportunities not traditionally considered reachable by Hispanics.

Of course, the major difference between Hispanics and some other major American minorities is language. The United States is the fifth largest Spanish-speaking country in the Western Hemisphere (after Mexico, Argentina, Columbia, and Peru). Those whose native language is not English tend to complete fewer years of schooling. Since over half of the American Hispanic population are children or adolescents, this lack of language facility translates into very high dropout rates. From this dilemma springs the controversy of bilingual education. Some want Spanish to be the first language of instruction and bilingualism the goal. Add to this strong family ties and cultural traditions (for example, Hispanics tend to have a deeply engrained sense of fatalism and destiny), and the career counselor has more than the "normal" problems with which to contend. There is not only heterogeneity among ethnic groups of Hispanics; there are also clear individual differences. Treating people as individuals while recognizing the cultural context from which they come is a fine-line activity.

Several organizations are dedicated to providing services especially for Hispanics. These organizations provide college financial assistance (for example, National Hispanic Scholarship Fund), special career and academic counseling (Aspira), and vocational training and job placement (the Puerto Rican Forum). In addition, Hispanics are a targeted and preferred group for various federal programs because of their lower levels of educational attainment, occupational and employment status, and income compared to the general population.

As with blacks, Hispanics have been the focus of a number of studies that seek to determine occupationally relevant differences between them and the white majority. These studies have not always provided useful data. It may be that, as Dillard advocates for blacks, we are better off studying within-group differences for Hispanics. One study (Gould, 1982) investigated the career progress of 111 Mexican-American college graduates and concluded that differences in their career progress were largely attributable to individual differences rather than ethnicity. Further, he found that

> in spite of the number of cultural differences enumerated for Mexican-Americans, the personal factors related to career progression were not unlike those which one would expect as being salient for a group of Anglo Americans. Hence, based on the results of this study, there is no reason to believe that the correlates of upward progression which have been identified in the literature are inappropriate for identifying Mexican-American candidates who have the greatest potential for career progression. (pp. 107–108)

These correlates include such factors as grades, tolerance for ambiguity, work ethic, psychological success, and need for achievement. Regarding the last variable, Gould (1982) had previously determined that those Mexican-Americans with a moderate need for achievement have higher upward mobility than those with high or low need achievement, suggesting that employing organizations resent either too high or too low a level.

In a similar vein, T. B. Scott and Anadon (1980) investigated the ACT Interest Inventory profiles of Native Americans and Caucasian college-bound students and found the profiles of both groups to be very similar. In general, whenever the responses of white and nonwhite racial groups to interest inventories are compared, they are found to be basically alike.

The attribution research with Chicana women produces similar results to that reported for blacks in the previous section. Romero and Garza (1986) had a group of Anglo, black, and Chicana women make causal attributions and rate occupational outcomes for females of all three ethnic groups in terms of task difficulty, competence, effort, luck, personal connections, gender, and ethnicity. The attributions for occupational outcome differed not only with the ethnicity of the rater but also with that of the person being rated. Anglo women are relatively color-blind in that ethnicity does not seem to affect attributions of occupational success or failure. Chicana women, on the other hand, attributed the occupational success of Anglo women and the occupational failure of minority women to ethnic origin. Thus, ethnic factors do appear to affect attributions made for occupational success or failure.

Hispanic students are as open to career interventions as any other subpopulation. Rodriguez and Blocher (1988) demonstrated that diverse career interventions with academically and economically disadvantaged Puerto Rican college women in a special admissions program in a large urban college were effective in raising their career maturity and in changing their locus of control (moving them farther toward a belief that they can control their environments and their futures).

Reviewing the relatively sparse literature on career counseling with Hispanics, Arbona (1990) reached several conclusions:

> Occupational aspirations and interest measurement among Hispanics are the two areas that have been examined most extensively by research. From the findings, it may be concluded that, in general, Hispanics want to educate themselves and enter demanding occupations. However, very little is known regarding their career decision-

making process or the difficulties they face in pursuing their aspirations. The research reviewed also supports the notion that the Holland model may be used to assess the career interests of Hispanics and to help them explore the world of work. Research related to career progression behaviors, job satisfaction, and work values among Hispanics is very limited and does not allow for any firm conclusions.

In terms of content, the career counseling research related to Hispanics is very limited and, for the most part, lacks a theoretical base. This research has not yet addressed the application of career development theories to Hispanics, nor has it examined the nature of career-related problems confronted by this group. With the notable exception of the research on vocational interests, we know very little about the applicability of career counseling instruments and the effectiveness of career interventions in working with this ethnic group.

This review of the literature, however, underscores important issues. The findings of this body of research contradict traditional views that assume that Hispanics lack high educational and occupational aspirations. Instead, it suggests that the lack of occupational mobility among Hispanics is related to structural factors, such as socioeconomic status and lack of opportunities, and not to cultural traits. The literature reviewed also shows that Hispanics are not a homogeneous group and suggests that there are important differences between the various Hispanic sub-groups as well as between Hispanics from different socioeconomic backgrounds. Also, it is important to be sensitive to regional differences among Hispanics of the same ethnic group. (pp. 313–14)

Asian-Americans

The Asian-American student has received a great deal of press in the last few decades. Much of this publicity has promulgated the notion of a sort of "superstudent" who is able to leap curricula in a single bound and, faster than a speeding bullet, master all sorts of difficult tasks. The attractiveness of this image is further enhanced by the fact that the student is likely to be the son or daughter of first-generation immigrants.

In fact, Asian-Americans (who number about 4 million) do seem as an ethnic minority to have, on average, achieved educationally at a high level, especially when compared to African-Americans, Hispanics, and Native Americans. This ethnic group—like any other—is diverse; it has members of such origins as Japanese, Chinese, Cambodian, Vietnamese, Indian, Pakistani, Filipino, and Thai, among others, and they tend to achieve differentially (Sue & Abe, 1988). There is, of course, the unpublicized aspect of Asian-Americans; that is, a very large percentage of them have little or no education (Sue & Padilla, 1986), they have sociopathic groups within their communities, and they tend to be underemployed. Hurh and Kim (1989) have traced the image of Asian-Americans over a century in which they moved from being regarded as "unassimilable immoral heathens" to a successful model minority. They determined, however, that if success is equated with the principle of earnings equity, the image is primarily a myth, for underemployment is prevalent among Asian-Americans. The fact remains, however, that over 8 in 10 Asian-American high school graduates are in college two years after high school graduation. The search for the cause of this phenomenal achievement has not produced definitive answers.

Sue and Okazaki (1990), for example, systematically reviewed the research relating to Asian-American achievement, including the evidence for both hereditary differences in intelligence and family cultural values that foster educational achievement. They found no compelling evidence to support either hypothesis. Rather, they propose that these results were produced by Asian-American culture interacting with the larger society. Specifically, they argue that Asian-Americans perceive education as a vehicle for mobility, without which, because of discrimination and other restrictions to occupational mobility, their vertical movement is severely limited. This argument does not, of course, explain why Asian Americans would be thus motivated and other ethnic minorities, which experience similar barriers to occupational attainment, would not. On the other hand, there are those who make a persuasive case for the influence of the family on the achievement of Asian American students. Caplan, Whitmore, and Choy (1989) studied "boat people," Indochinese refugees who came to the United States, and concluded that "it is the family's ability to translate cultural values into a life style . . . that helps its members to confront adversity and prepares them for future success" (p. 148). Education begins in the home and is always tied to the values of the home. One could speculate from this conclusion that if assimilation leads to denial of cultural values in subsequent generations, achievement will be adversely affected.

As with other ethnic groups, the career counseling of Asian-Americans requires the application of some specific knowledge and skills, sometimes in addition to traditional approaches and sometimes in place of more generic interventions. Much of what we assume about counseling Asian-Americans is based on cross-cultural research that emanates from studies of samples in foreign countries rather than Asian-Americans themselves. For example, Khan, Alvi, Shaukat, Hussain, and Baig (1990) demonstrated the utility of Holland's Self Directed Search with college and university students in Pakistan. Should we assume that the findings pertain to Pakistani-Americans? Exum and Lau (1988) researched 50 students from Hong Kong who were studying at a midwestern American university regarding their preferences for directive versus nondirective counseling. They concluded that a directive counseling approach was preferable, since these students require a counselor who is authoritative without being authoritarian. What these students apparently wanted was a counselor who projects self-confidence and provides structure, interpretation, and a solution to a problem. Again, can we transfer these findings to the counseling of Chinese-American students? Fernandez (1988) also addresses the counseling of Southeast Asian students, who compose over 40 percent of the total foreign enrollment in U.S. colleges and universities. Considering the problem of culture shock, she argues that it is inappropriate to counsel these students in modes that require introspection, reflection, and extreme client verbalization. Behavioral approaches seem more appropriate. Also, individuals are not likely to make decisions without the advice and consent of their families, so working toward family cooperation would be useful. Can we hypothesize the same for Asian-Americans? For all generations?

Applying this family emphasis with an American sample of Chinese- and Korean-American parents, Evanoski and Tse (1989) provided culture-specific, bilingual career awareness workshops. Using bilingual role models and bilingual materials, these workshops were held in community settings and enhanced the career awareness of thousands of Chinese- and Korean-American parents who—presumably—have enormous influence on the career choices of their children. These workshops were three hours long and emphasized exposure to various occupations and the role of the community college in facilitating access to those occupations.

Kitano and Matsushima (1981) list the cultural styles preferred by Asian-Americans; these include "indirect communication, deference to authority, emphasis on confidentiality, the importance of family and community, and group orientation" (p. 178). For first generation? Second? Much more research on the career counseling of Asian-American students is required, just as it is on career interventions with all minority groups.

Native Americans

No other minority group in America has experienced deeper prejudice or is in a less-advantaged posture than Native Americans. There are approximately 1.6 million American Indians in the United States, many of whom are concentrated on reservations. They are composed of many nations and numerous tribes, each with a rich heritage and unique character. The latest census data indicate a marked increase in the number of people declaring themselves to be Native Americans, perhaps signalling a heightened pride.

Despite the poverty that they have experienced and continue to experience, Native Americans have both reasonable career aspirations and formidable barriers to overcome in achieving these career goals. Herring (1990) believes that certain "career myths" exacerbate the already imposing roadblocks to the career development of Native American youth and lead to irrational beliefs. These are in fact, the same myths that affect every minority; they include limited research findings about their career development and behavior, stereotypes, and lack of awareness and opportunities. As a result, Native Americans have extremely high unemployment rates and tend to enter a restricted number of occupations (one-third of Native Americans, of the relatively few who attend college, earned their degrees in education or social sciences). Herring suggests that utilization of Native American occupational role models from nontraditional occupations would be beneficial in expanding their career horizons.

The most common traditional occupational stereotype of the American Indian is that of the skilled structural steel worker, daringly risking his life as he adroitly maneuvers thousands of feet above the ground. While Native Americans do account for a disproportionately large percentage of structural steel workers, the total number so employed is a very small percentage of the Native American work force. In one study, nontraditional, gender-based occupations were clearly considered by Navajo students on reservations, but the researchers attributed the findings of acceptance of nontraditional occupations to "limited contacts with the institutions and materials that transmit the biases of the majority culture" (p. 270). Thus, the students were less aware of the sex types associated with particular jobs (Beyard-Tyler & Haring, 1984). It would be interesting to replicate this study with American Indians living off-reservation.

Thus far, the career needs of American Indian students do not seem a great deal different from those of any other minority. To investigate the possibility of differential career attitudes of black, white, and American Indian high school students, C. C. Lee (1984) surveyed over 500 tenth-grade rural students in the Southeast. Included in the sample were 70 Native American males and 75 Native American females, 92 black males and 114 black females, and 87 white males and 82 white females. Participants took both the Career Maturity Inventory and the Tennessee Self Concept Scale and also responded to questions designed to elicit demographic and other data. Multiple regression analysis demonstrated that "different equations would be required to predict career choice attitudes, one each for Blacks, Whites, and Native Americans" (p. 181). Further, it was discovered that minority parents apparently had a greater impact on the career choices of their children than did white parents. Replication of this study with a nonrural sample would be useful. This study is cited because it demonstrates that there do indeed appear to be differences between the career development needs of Native Americans and the majority culture, and, in fact, there may be differences between American Indian career needs and those of other minorities. Currently, however, we are unable to delineate those needs without further research.

As is the case with every minority group, the use of standard assessment instrumentation with Native Americans has received some research attention. Results have been mixed. Some studies have reported that differences in the results of interest measurement are so slight between American Indian and white populations that routine use of existing instrumentation would be appropriate (Scott & Anandon, 1980); other studies have found differences of sufficient magnitude to call for separate tribal norms (Epperson & Hammond, 1981; Gade, Fuqua, & Hurlburt, 1984). A more recent study of the Strong (Haviland & Hansen, 1987) found no differences between female white and Native American college students but substantial differences between male white and American Indian students. Clearly, a great deal more research is necessary before any definitive conclusions can be reached. At this time, the best guidelines for a counselor to use in interpreting tests and inventories with any minority would apparently be to exercise caution and always interpret in light of a counselee's sociocultural history.

We do not have the space to detail the aspects involved in the career counseling of Native Americans. In the absence of more extended instruction, Trimble's (1981) observations offer a suitable *caveat* for counselors:

> Conventional counseling techniques are often inappropriate for use with certain American Indians, especially ones from more traditionally oriented communities. Some Indians, like many first-time clients, simply don't know what to expect, and their subsequent silence and apparent nonattentiveness are construed by the counselor as hostility. Other Indians, more familiar with counseling, conform their behaviors to the counselor's ethnocentric expectations of "good client behaviors." In the latter instance, little if any conflict-reduction or problem solving occurs as the client is merely role playing and not being helped by the relationship. In either instance, an internalization of appropriate client-like behavior fails to occur, presumably resulting from the incompatibility between the counselor's technique and the client's cultural orientation. (p. 220)

Counseling Minorities

Several books are available that are useful to the counselor who is assisting minorities with career development and choice issues (Vacc, Wittmer, & DeVaney, 1988; Pedersen, 1988; Axelson, 1985; Dillard, 1983). In fact, however, guidelines are little different from those used in counseling people in general. Perhaps, as we maintain is the case with women, differences are more in degree than in kind. The counselor should know the cultural milieu of culturally different clientele, just as he or she should understand the cultural context of any client. Professional helpers should possess certain characteristics for performing culturally skilled work with various ethnic groups (or a representative of any cultural context, for that matter). These characteristics include beliefs/attitudes, knowledge, and skills (Division 17 Education and Training Committee, 1982).

Beliefs/Attitudes

1. The culturally skilled counseling psychologist has moved from being culturally unaware to being aware and sensitive to his or her own cultural heritage and to valuing and respecting differences.

2. A culturally skilled counseling psychologist is aware of her or her own values and biases and knows how they may affect minority clients.

3. A culturally skilled counseling psychologist is comfortable with differences between himself or herself and the client in terms of race and beliefs.

4. The culturally skilled counseling psychologist is sensitive to circumstances (personal biases, stage of ethnic identity, sociopolitical influences, etc.) that may dictate referral

of the minority client to a member of his or her own race or culture.

Knowledge

1. The culturally skilled counseling psychologist has a good understanding of the U.S. sociopolitical system's treatment of minorities.

2. The culturally skilled counseling psychologist possesses specific knowledge and information about the particular group he or she is working with.

3. The culturally skilled counseling psychologist has clear and explicit knowledge and understanding of the generic characteristics of counseling and therapy.

4. The culturally skilled counseling psychologist is aware of institutional barriers that prevent minorities from using mental health services.

Skills

1. At the skills level, the culturally skilled counseling psychologist is able to generate a wide variety of verbal and nonverbal responses.

2. The culturally skilled counseling psychologist is able to send and receive both verbal and nonverbal messages accurately and "appropriately."

3. The culturally skilled counseling psychologist is able to exercise institutional intervention skills on behalf of his or her client when appropriate.

These suggestions for desirable characteristics are certainly beyond contention, but they also apply to *any* clientele, not simply the culturally different. There is surely no doubt about the counselor's need to understand the characteristics of the counselee's ethnic or racial group and to have all the attending and responding skills characteristic of a good counseling relationship.

These guidelines are interesting, however, because they suggest that culturally different counselors may sometimes need to refer clients to others who may be more skilled with problems that center on membership in that group. This strategy is quite different from that recommended by some who would have only members of a given ethnic, racial, or sexual group counsel individuals in that group.

We reject the implication that in the long run only like-ethnics should counsel ethnics; by extension, only substance abusers should counsel substance abusers, only gays counsel gays, only divorced counsel divorced, only unemployed counsel unemployed, only schizophrenics counsel schizophrenics, and so on, *ad absurdum*.

A thoughtful model of Minority Identity Development (MID) has been offered by Atkinson, Morten, and Sue (1983). Although this model has not been tested to any appreciable extent, it does offer a framework for intervention with minorities at various developmental stages. In summary form, the model appears in Table 5.1.

This model suggests that in stage 1, minority individuals prefer the cultural values of the majority culture over their own. In stage 2, dissonance sets in and results in confusion and conflict. The dominant culture no longer seems clearly superior to the minority member's own culture. In stage 3, the minority individual rejects the dominant culture in a sort of reaction formation and totally endorses the minority views. In stage 4, the person begins to think less in terms of minority group dogma and more in terms of forming individual reactions. Finally, in stage 5, conflicts are resolved and individuals become comfortable with themselves and with their heritage. The recurrent theme throughout each of these stages is oppression, first as an individual experiences it and later as he or she strives to eliminate it both in his or her own life and in society. We have previously referred to the great heterogeneity on all variables that exists within any minority group. The MID model is another example. Within any given cultur-

Table 5.1

Summary of Minority Identity Development Model

Stages of Minority Development Model	Attitude Toward Self	Attitude Toward Others of the Same Minority	Attitude Toward Others of Different Minority	Attitude Toward Dominant Group
Stage 1 — Conformity	self-deprecation	Group depreciation	Discrimination	Group appreciation
Stage 2 — Dissonance	Conflict between self-deprecation and appreciation	Conflict between group depreciation and group appreciation	Conflict between dominant views of minority hierarchy and feelings of shared experience	Conflict between group appreciation and group depreciation
Stage 3 — Resistance and Immersion	Self-appreciation	Group appreciation	Conflict between feelings of empathy for other minority experiences and feelings of culturo-centrism	Group depreciation
Stage 4 — Introspection	Concern with basis of self-appreciation	Concern with nature of unequivocal appreciation	Concern with ethnocentric basis for judging others	Concern with the basis of group depreciation
Stage 5 — Synergetic Articulation and Awareness	Self-appreciation	Group appreciation	Group appreciation	Selective appreciation

(From D. R. Atkinson, et al., *Counseling American Minorities.*

ally different ethnic or racial group, identity issues may be resolved to a greater or less degree by individual members. The task of counselors is to determine at which stage an individual is functioning and how facilitating or self-defeating that stage might be in terms of career development.

Pederson (1990) argues that multicultural counseling should be organized around the construct of *balance*, by which he means "the identification of different or even conflicting culturally learned perspectives without necessarily resolving that difference or dissonance in favor of either viewpoint" (p. 552). In other words, what is advocated is a "walk-in-his-moccasins," nonjudgmental, sensitive approach to multicultural counseling in which there are no assumptions of "better" in terms of conflicting cultures. Similarly, writing from a framework of *nigrescence* (the process of becoming black), Parham (1989) also urges that counselors help African-Americans (and, by extension, any minority) to confront the question of how much to compromise their ethnicity or race in order to assimilate into the larger culture. Specifically, he identifies three issues: (1) self-differentiation versus preoccupation with assimilation (a feeling of being personally worthwhile without needing the validation of the majority culture); (2) body transcedence versus preoccupation with body image (coming to grips with self-image in relation to the "European" majority look); and (3) ego transcendence versus self-absorption (the development of ego strength by contributing to one's people as well as to oneself alone). All these compromises entail feelings of worth. The attitudes addressed by both Pederson and Parham would be especially important in career counseling.

All these research findings and suggestions for practice distill to the following guidelines for career counseling of the culturally different:

1. Counselors should, above all, possess all the generic counseling knowledge, skill, understanding, ability, and behavior thought to be appropriate in any helping relationship.
2. Counselors should recognize their own attitudes and values as these impinge on counseling specific ethnic and racial groups; they must work to ensure that these internal frames of reference do not form road blocks to successful counseling. Obviously, white, majority counselors should uncover any possible biases toward blacks, Hispanics, or other groups; but professionals who are themselves culturally different should undergo similar self-scrutiny regarding the majority.
3. Counselors should be aware of the cultural context from which individuals come, but they should not assume that individuals are bounded by that culture. They are first and foremost *individuals* and only secondarily representatives of a specific racial or ethnic group.
4. Counselors should understand what aspects of career helping may need special attention with specific culturally different groups. All groups, minority or majority, will need the same career skills, attitudes, knowledge, and so forth; some groups may need emphasis on a particular aspect of career development.
5. Counselors must help minorities to understand and internalize the fact that they *do* have a choice in career development, that given certain decisions and behaviors, certain consequences are likely to occur.
6. Counselors should help culturally different individuals understand that although they may encounter discrimination, they cannot be discouraged by it or consider themselves perpetual victims of it. They can be taught to deal with it and to use the vehicles available to surmount it.
7. Counselors must be sure that they understand which deficits and discontinuities in the career development of the culturally different are consequences of socioeconomic class and which are the result of membership in some specific racial or ethnic group.

IMMIGRANTS

America, of course, is a land of immigrants as are, most notably, Canada and Australia. Massive occupational assimilation has challenged American social service agencies for over a century. There are both legal and illegal immigrants to America, and recent immigration laws have confounded the two.

Legal and Illegal Immigrants

The legal immigrants in recent years have emigrated primarily from Southeast Asia (most notably the Indochinese, Laotians, Cambodians, Taiwanese, and Filipinos); Cuba, Haiti, and other West Indian islands; Colombia, Honduras, and other Central American countries; and Russia (specifically, Russian Jews). In addition, immigration quotas have been maintained for other countries that have traditionally supplied the United States with new citizens.

In general, the last few decades have witnessed decreased immigration from northeastern and southeastern Europe, while evidencing dramatic increases from the Western Hemisphere and Asia. Huge influxes of refugees are both a threat and a promise to America. The promise is one of enhanced human resources and the richness of cultural pluralism. The perceived threat is to indigenous minorities. For instance, putting together data supplied by Bach and Bach (1980) with U.S. Census data, we conclude that there are as many Southeast Asian refugees in America who have come since 1975 as there are Native Americans.

Some say that the large number of immigrants (a little fewer than 800,000 per year, accounting for the greatest proportion of population growth) creates jobs and stimulates demand; others argue that immigrants take jobs away from natives—an assertion for which little evidence has been found. Some view immigrants as a drain on welfare and a peril to unilingualism; others perceive them as adding a richness that moves us closer to the reality of a truly multiracial society. While a fairly large number of natives may hold attitudes of resentment and hostility toward immigrants, there is relatively little overt antagonism, with the exception of a few pockets of protest.

The basic challenge for these refugees is to find adequate employment to ensure economic self-sufficiency. This task is not so easy, considering that refugees, especially those whose emigration was largely unanticipated, frequently are not fluent in English. Others who are admitted for humanitarian reasons come with severe health problems. They have adjustment difficulties, but after a while the labor force participation of most immigrant groups tends to match that of the general population. Those who leave a country under considerable stress, however, tend to work a longer work week, to represent a smaller proportion of white-collar workers, and to have a greater proportion of service workers.

Refugees are likely to settle in geographical enclaves, probably since the majority are prone to have friends or relatives already there. It is well known that Southeast Asians have gravitated to California and Texas in large numbers, both initially and through secondary migration (movement from one state to another, once in America). Louisiana and Virginia are also states with large Southeast Asian populations. Cubans and West Indians have settled heavily in Florida; Russian Jews and Colombians in New York City.

Some come to this country in hard economic times, and the assistance available to them is, therefore, minimal. Add that fact to the language problem, exploitation by employers, union barriers, nonrecognition of skills, licensing restrictions, lack of information about the job market, and the normal anxiety of being a stranger in a strange land, and it is easy to comprehend some of the difficulties faced by immigrants.

The experience of the Cuban refugees is instructive (Bach, 1980). They came in two waves: early, beginning in 1959, and late, in 1980, when Castro loosened restrictions on emigration. In some respects, these immigrants were more fortunate than most Third World immigrants who settle in American cities, for most had some urban industrial work experience. Most Cuban immigrants, like most immigrants of whatever country of origin, soon became members of an ethnic working class—in this case, the Cuban-American working class. The jobs they got were likely to be as craftsworkers, machine operatives, or unskilled laborers. Few (especially in the latest wave) were professionals or managers. Many earlier immigrants had to take positions at a lower status than they had held in Cuba. All in all, occupational adjustment, especially in hard times, is not easy for immigrants, but they eventually assimilate. Obviously, the more help they get, the easier the task.

The Cuban experience is less painful than that undergone by some other immigrant groups. Disparate vocational experiences of Cuban and Haitian refugees in South Florida show that Cubans have access to an enclave employment option providing the same financial (and other) returns for work that are provided by employment in the primary labor market. Haitians, on the other hand, lack an employment enclave; consequently, they tend to cluster into secondary and informal employment—if they work at all (Portes & Stepick, 1985). Thus, enclaves provide a buffer between the immigrants and the new country (Cobas, 1986).

A disproportionately large number of immigrants in certain groups (for example, Koreans, Greeks) seem to gravitate toward self-employment, which may be necessitated by disadvantages in the job market, possession of a business background in the country of origin, participation in the ethnic subeconomy, or some other reason (Cobas, 1986). In some immigrant groups, self-sacrifice and almost around-the-clock labor are prices willingly paid for self-employment in order that ensuing generations can lead the proverbial better life.

Illegal immigrants, on the other hand, have an even more difficult task, since they are in constant danger of deportation and thus subject to exploitation. Sehgal and Vialet (1980) point out that over 1 million illegal aliens are apprehended in America each year (mostly Mexican because of concentration on the border—more than double the total, on average, admitted legally each year. These are only the ones who get caught. Estimates of total numbers of illegal immigrants range from 2.9 to 5.7 million. Some slip illegally into the country; others enter legally and later violate the terms of their visas. The illegals and visiting labor force participants, it is assumed, are a source of cheap labor to exploiters who do not have to pay much attention to working conditions. It is argued that illegals thus displace native workers. It is more likely, however, that they replace legal immigrants. Unfortunately, the problem is such that counselors are not typically involved.

Once immigrant groups are in the country for a time, both generational changes and occupational advancement tend to lead to greater exogamy (marrying outside the immigrant group) and thus greater assimilation into American culture (Schoen & Cohen, 1980). Assimilation usually takes place as people start at the bottom occupationally and gradually move up. Some people, however, remain in an all-enclave economy, working within immigrant-owned firms.

Legal immigrants, especially those whose emigration has been sudden, unanticipated, externally induced, and stressful, face many adjustments. Occupational adjustment may be the greatest of these.

There is a difference also in the adjustment of white as opposed to black immigrants. DeFreitas (1981), for example, discovered through his research that black immigrants in New York City experience significant occupational mobility during their first few years after arrival. Downward mobility is especially severe among those with high level occupational backgrounds in the country of origin. These results are consistent with hypotheses derived from previous research on the adjustment difficulties experienced by white immigrants. However, unlike most white immigrants who are able to subsequently recover much of their lost occupational status through upward mobility, foreign-born black professionals, managers, and craftsmen appear less likely to regain their former occupational levels. Despite certain employment advantages when compared with indigenous blacks, foreign-born blacks are subsequently underrepresented in high-pay, high-status occupations relative to white males.

Counseling Immigrants

How can immigrants best be counseled about career concerns? To answer this question intelligently, we really need to know more about the vocational development of immigrants than we do now. In most cases, immigration represents a discontinuity in career development for an individual. The nature and effect of that discontinuity has not been studied in very much depth.

One exception is the excellent work under way in Israel by Krau (1981, 1982). Although the findings from the Israeli experience are not completely applicable to the American scene, they have enough face validity to be worth further exploration and testing here. For example, Krau investigated how individuals cope with basically unanticipated emigration and whether cognitive dissonance might be a motivator explaining immigrants' behavioral strategy. Using 89 new, educated immigrants to Israel (mainly from Russia and Romania), who were provided an accountancy training program by the Ministry of Absorption, Krau discovered that any preparation for a career change took place basically *after* arrival in the new country. To cope successfully after the fact of immigration, some people reduce their self-image to become congruent with the lower status of their new career. For example, they tend to become less self-assertive. Some people, however, deny that their status has been lowered. Such denial results in less expressed satisfaction. In short, one can accept a lowered status and adopt a self-image that is congruent with that lowered status and, eventually, over time, work back to a higher level. Or one can deny the reality of lowered status and risk a poorer adjustment. Counseling such individuals thus involves helping them to minimize denial efforts.

Krau (1984) found that immigrants, when compared with indigenous white-collar workers and executives, scored higher on measures of work centrality and job involvement and held more positive attitudes toward authority figures. Apparently, one method of coping for immigrants is to focus on work. The workplace may be regarded as a smaller societal unit, an environment that is a more hospitable surrounding with which to identify than is the larger society.

Krau has built a model of the career development of immigrants. The stages of the model include crystallization, vocational retraining, job entry and trial, establishment, and maintenance. Although immigrants experience discontinuity because of emigration, Krau's model suggests that once they reach a new country, the process of career reconstruction is one of continuity. In his model, he matches coping behaviors with specific career development tasks of immigrants. His paradigm is partially presented in Table 5.2.

Preliminary research on the validity of the model is encouraging. From these early findings, it appears that the model of career stages accurately represents what most immigrants go through as they become integrated into the work world and culture of their new nation. Further, "skills critically defining the adjustment to one career stage are success predictors for the acquisition of behaviors of greater complexity needed to adjust to the requirements of the following period" (Krau, 1982, p. 328). Some highly educated, skilled immigrants who are fluent in the language of their new country may pass directly from the crystallization stage to job entry and trial, skipping the retraining stage. If the model holds, the counselor must determine where the individual is likely to experience the greatest difficulty in coping behavior and work preventively to ensure a smoother transition.

Most refugees, with time, appear to adapt to a changed occupational structure and their place in it. Anh and Healy (1985) studied 210 Vietnamese refugees in Los Angeles and Orange counties and determined that "refugees in the United States 3 or more years were more satisfied than were those present 1 or 2 years, and those in the United States 2 years were more satisfied than were those 1 year or less" (p. 81). Hence, those in the country the longest

Table 5.2

A Career Development Model of Immigrants

Career Stage	Problem-creating Condition	Coping Behavior
Crystallization	Language difficulties	Learning
	Lack of information on labor market and job requirements	Help-seeking behavior
	Cognitive dissonance over status incongruence	Reduction of cognitive dissonance
Vocational Retraining	Cognitive dissonance over status incongruence	Reduction of cognitive dissonance
	Need to accept unfamiliar occupation	Emotional acceptance of new occupation
	Lack of skill in new occupation	Acquisition of occupational knowledge and skills
Job Entry and Trial	Competition on the labor market	Competitive behavior
	Short employment interviews and tests	Efficiency in test situations and display of vocational knowledge and skills
Establishment	Job requirements	Conformity to requirements
	New work community	Openness to social contacts and new values
	Need for enculturation	
	Need for economic security	Effort to achieve a permanent income
Maintenance	Job requirements	Conformity to job requirements
	Need to heighten living standard and position in community	Effort to catch up economic community standards
		Effort to assert oneself in the community

Source: "The Tested Career Development Model of Immigrants," in "The Vocational Side of A New Start in Life: A Career Model of Immigrants" by Edgar Krau, *Journal of Vocational Behavior, 20,* 1982, pp. 313–330. Reprinted by permission of Academic Press, Inc.

were more fully employed and more satisfied with their jobs.

Finally, a caveat: simply because immigrants are grouped for census purposes does not mean that they are alike. Southeast Asians are a good example. Not only are the cultures different among the countries, but within nations immigrants represent divergent cultures. Longstanding regional and national antipathies may make emigrants from one country loathe to be in a group with others from another nation or even their own. Great care should be exercised in setting up any career intervention to be certain that the group is not so heterogeneous that is is unworkable.

Most attempts to intervene in the career development of immigrants have focused on language training and vocational skills training. Lobadzinska (1986) urges that acculturation—formal learning about the American way of life—also be a focus of effort. One vocational training program for Indochinese adolescents has typical objectives (Vertiz & Fortune, 1984):

1. Identification of personal values, interests, aptitudes, and abilities
2. Communication of personal qualities to others
3. Identification of at least two types of preentry-level jobs that would provide vi-

able experience toward tentative career options

4. Location of possible employment sites
5. Establishment of personal contact with potential employers to inquire about part-time jobs
6. Completion of job application
7. Interviews in small groups with personnel specialists from business and industry, and a one-to-one situation with videotape (p. 231)

There is a tremendous need for research in this country on the vocational development and behavior of immigrants. No comprehensive study exists, and the few small studies that we have are inadequate to provide a truly sound foundation upon which to construct either a theory or a repertoire of interventions. The work of W. Borgen and Amundsen (1985) in Canada offers a good example of the type of attention to immigrant career development that is needed in the United States.

In general, immigrants will have strong needs for information (job market, skills required, and so on) and will want a structured counseling procedure. Language deficits must be addressed, and there must be a systematic effort to translate their skills to the American culture. Career counselors must also confront issues of alienation and disorientation in immigrants. Refugees pose additional problems that require attention. Gold (1988), for example, points out that compared to immigrants, refugees would most likely not leave their homes voluntarily, would not typically have as strong a support network, would not have planned their new life as thoroughly, would have brought fewer resources, and would probably have greater mental health problems.

GAY MEN AND WOMEN

That sexual preference should have an impact on career development and choice is, in many ways, repugnant. Nevertheless, homosexuals are, in fact, barred from certain occupations (e.g., the armed services) and find vertical mobility blocked in other occupations simply because of their sexual orientation. This result of homophobia is one of the major reasons that homosexuals often hide their sexual preference, living in fear of being "discovered," since their livelihoods are sometimes tied in with appearing "normal."

The negative bias against homosexuals is often more intense than that directed at any other minority group (Goleman, 1990). Whether homophobics doubt their own sexuality and seek reassurance in "gay bashing," whether some combination of fear and self-righteousness impels them to save the morals of the world, whether they follow religious dicta (e.g., homosexuality is equated with evil), or whether some other reason prevails, homosexuals are indeed targets of institutional and individual bias. There are those, for example, who feel that homosexuals should not be teachers because of the alleged temptation to molest children, despite the fact that child molesters are overwhelmingly heterosexual.

Given the deliberate, systematic exclusion of gays from many occupations and the de facto segregation of gays in many others, it is surprising that very little scholarly attention has been paid to their career development issues. Two enlightening articles in this regard have relatively recently appeared in the professional literature typically read by counselors.

Hetherington, Hillerbrand, and Etringer (1989) addressed the career issues of gay men, who are reputed to have more uncertainty about their career choices and less job satisfaction than either heterosexual men and women or lesbians. Knowledgable and sensitive career counselors should be aware of several of the issues they identify. One issue is *negative stereotyping*, for example, equating homosexuality with mental disturbance or assuming that certain occupations are dominated by gay men (e.g., photographer, interior decorator, nurse, and so on). A second issue is *employment discrimination,* since the legal status of those who have a different affectional preference from the majority appears to be moot and still evolving. Employment ads that include a declaration of no prejudice on the basis of sexual orientation are a good start. A third issue is that of *limited role models,* since gay men in the work force are more or less an invisible minority. Limited role models may be presumed to have the same effect on gay men as the absence of competent occupational role models has on any minority.

In terms of implications for career counseling, it is advocated that specialized programming be provided to address the needs of gay men. In addition to the traditional career interventions, gay men may need counseling to help them negotiate life-style and relationship issues, interviews, and the choice of whether to divulge sexual orientation. For instance, should activities in gay organizations be listed on the résumé? Help in planning the transition from school to work is another focus area, since, in general, academic institutions provide a less hostile environment for gays than does the world of work. Other career areas to confront are geographical concerns (e.g., whether to look for work where there is a substantial population of gays) and concerns of dual-career couples (much as with heterosexual couples—see Chapter 13). Utilizing gay occupational role models would appear to be an effective strategy.

Females who prefer a lesbian life-style also have special needs, some of which overlap with those of gay men and some of which are unique (Hetherington & Orzek, 1989). Lesbian women are apparently relatively certain about and satisfied with their career choices when compared with gay men and heterosexual men and women. Which aspects of lesbian career development can be ascribed to gender and which to sexual orientation is arguable (e.g., the influence of sex-role attitudes). Standard career development issues such as self-concept formation and exposure to role models may be more complex phenomena for lesbian women than for heterosexuals. Occupational harassment and negative stereotypes are as real for lesbians as they are for homosexual men. Finally, lesbians grapple with unique dual-career and life-style issues. In addition to the usual career needs complicated by gender, lesbians must also determine what occupations are accessible and offer advancement and how to negotiate the job search.

Clearly, a great deal of research needs to be conducted to determine how best to meet the identified career needs of gays and to discover what other needs exist. Do gay men and women, for example, experience more stress at work than do "straights"? What career development decisions are influenced by gender, by affectional preference, and by sex-role attitudes? What are the effects of the interaction of these dimensions? How can gays best negotiate work systems? How can they best change restrictive systems? Do gay men and women fall into different configurations from the general population in terms of Holland categories? All these questions and many more await the results of research.

PERSONS WITH DISABILITIES

This section is intended to consider career-relevant aspects of a final special population, persons with disabilities.

Career Development of Persons with Disabilities

A person with disabilities is one who is usually considered to be different from a normal person—physically, physiologically, neurologically, or psychologically—because of accident, disease, birth, or developmental problems. Persons with disabilities, including the physically or mentally challenged, typically feel less adequate than others, either situationally or generally. A disability, then, need not be a handicap. Physicians try to cure or palliate a disability; counselors try to remove or reduce a handicap, whether or not the disability can be helped, including looking at handicapping conditions within the individual's environment. Some, in fact, believe that persons with disabilities should be viewed as a minority group; as such, their problems are considered not so much physical as social and psychological (Fine & Asch, 1988), and problems are caused not so much by the disability itself as by the environment.

Hence, by *the disabled,* we mean a population that has a disability or several disabilities that may or may not be a vocational handicap. The disability may be *physical* (such as amputations, birth defects, cancer, heart problems, burns, deafness, blindness, multiple sclerosis, muscular dystrophy, orthopedic involvement, spinal injury), *intellectual* (mental retardation, learning disability, brain damage, speech and language disorders), *emotional* (mental illness, substance abuse, alcoholism, obesity and other eating disorders), or *sociocultural* (as discussed earlier in this chapter). In any case, best estimates are that in the United States over 10 percent of the population have chronic physical, mental, or emotional conditions that limit their activity sufficiently to make a substantial career difference.

It may be reasonably expected that severe disability, either congenital or adventitious, will have a profound influence on an individual's career development. To a great extent this is true, but the effect is largely unpredictable by type of disability. Classic studies by B. A. Wright (1960) and Shontz (1975) have demonstrated that for persons with disabilities, the within-group variability in terms of personality patterns and general adjustment is as great as the variability between them and the rest of the population. To be sure, those with disabilities may have certain functional limitations that restrict their freedom in choosing from among the vast array of occupations, and if the disability is not congenital, there is bound to be some discontinuity in career development.

These exceptional individuals are presumed also to be the victims of considerable prejudice by potential employers and possible bias by counselors (Ioracchini & Aboud, 1981). It is no doubt true that attitudes rooted in the concept of stigma affect behavior toward the disabled, just as sexism, ageism, and racism exist; but some research suggests that attitudes toward the disabled vary by type of disability. In the past, for example, employers appeared to be more willing to hire the physically disabled than to hire the functionally disabled (such as the psychiatrically disabled).

These attitudes may be softening (C. I. Stone & Sawatzki, 1980). As is the case with many stereotyped attitudes, they can frequently be altered by providing experiences permitting the development of greater emphathy with the subject of the stereotype. With the disabled, for instance, Ibrahim and Herr (1982) used a role-playing situation in which individuals assumed a disability, and the experience had a significant effect in building positive attitudes toward those who actually had that disability.

Curnow (1989) contends that certain misconceptions of disability have limited the application of vocational development theory to persons with disability. The umbrella rationale for these misconceptions is the idea that compared to the nondisabled population, persons with disabilities have special needs that preclude the use of extant theories. In actuality, current vocational development theory may indeed be appropriate for the disabled population if, in addition, counselors consider the parochial or unique needs that the disabled bring to rehabilitation. The reader will recognize that this argument has been advanced earlier in this chapter in relation to several of the special populations discussed (e.g., women, minorities). In the case of the disabled, these considerations would include (1) limitations in early experiences (e.g., less opportunity for exploration, restrictive view of vocational options, etc.), (2) decision-making ability (e.g., persons with disabilities have fewer opportunities to rehearse decision making), and (3) self-concept and disability (e.g., negative social attitudes and stereotypes contributing to less than positive self-image).

It is obviously impossible to deal with every disability within the confines of this volume. Each disability is, in fact, the focus of a large body of literature related specifically to career development within that disability. Further, the reason rehabilitation counselors are available is to assist in the vocational rehabilitation of those with disabilities. In fact, a current emphasis in vocational rehabilitation is *transitioning,* a term used to indicate the importance of helping the disabled to function vocationally and educationally within the larger society. All we are attempting to do in this chapter is to make the "generalist" career counselor aware of the possible functional limitations and the possible delayed, discontinuous, or impaired career development of those with disabilities.

Career Counseling of Persons with Disabilities

In a classic 1963 article, McDaniels argued that in cases of traumatic disability, the individual was required to regress to the tentative and realistic phases of the exploratory stage. In these substages, the task of the disabled is to define and accept a modified self-concept with certain new limitations, to test these formulations in reality, and to find new ways to satisfy aspirations. Ultimately, according to McDaniels, the process of vocational redevelopment will be affected by pretrauma experiences in career, personal, and social circumstances; the types of concepts and decisions requiring modification; the specific type of disabling factors; and the availability of assistance and information. In the three decades since McDaniels's original theoretical conceptualization of vocational redevelopment for persons with disabilities, little has changed. We have more sophisticated tools, but the basic idea of career redevelopment and what it entails has not appreciably changed, even though different theoreticians may offer different contexts for redevelopment. Two examples are presented here, both of which deal with needs: one is based on Maslow's need hierarchy, and a second is based on a trait-and-factor orientation applied to the theory of work adjustment.

Maslow's need theory has been operationalized by Lassiter (1981) to apply to persons with disabilities and their vocational redevelopment. Within this context, he describes needs and their applications to work and work adjustment in competitive work settings:

1. Physiological needs
   a. Need to learn to work in a wheelchair (for example, using the bathroom, traveling from home to job, taking a coffee break, meeting with fellow workers, dealing with different job performance tasks)
   b. Need to learn new ways of being productive (for example, coping with a work schedule different from others; using specially structured pieces, instruments, or machines to meet job demands; receiving an individualized instructional program in mobility)
   c. Need to accept responsibility for personal hygiene (for example, attend to toilet and other personal needs, learn to care well for his or her body and avoid

medical complications and illnesses in order to avoid absenteeism, loss of productive activity, and more severe disablement)

2. Safety needs
   a. Strong desire to remain in work similar to previous job and a preference for association with familiar people on the job
   b. Need for a job that appears to offer tenure and stability with decent health and retirement plans, and so on
   c. Need for a smoothly functioning, orderly position
3. Belongingness and love needs
   a. Need to find new ways of developing feelings of belongingness
   b. Need to analyze the potential for caring and being cared for that might be provided in the job setting if certain job modifications or support groups were developed
4. Esteem needs
   a. Need to experience new feelings of competence and self-confidence that come from a person's exposure to new interpersonal skills and new tasks
5. Self-actualization needs
   a. Need for self-awareness and self-actualization
   b. Need to develop one's inner space (thoughts and feelings)
   c. Acceptance and optimization of a life of severe disability

A different needs perspective is provided by those who advocate the use of the theory of work adjustment with the disabled (Dawis & Lofquist, 1978; Lynch & Maki, 1981). The theory of work adjustment is discussed at several points throughout this volume, and many are enthusiastic about its application to the disabled. The theory suggests, in part, that individuals have work needs; occupations provide work reinforcers; if reinforcers equal or exceed needs, people will be satisfied at work. In other words, individuals adjust to work through the interaction between work personality and work environment. Melding this theory with a trait-and-factor approach, Lynch and Maki suggest that the counselor working with a disabled client use the traditional trait-and-factor steps: (1) *analysis*—getting information about the client; (2) *synthesis*—interpreting information about the client; (3) *diagnosis*—using interpretation of the data, combined with consideration of the functional limitations of the client, to identify assets of the individual; (4) *prognosis*—determining future options and developing a plan of action; (5) *counseling*—helping clients to know themselves and to use available resources to achieve their potential; and (6) *follow-up*—monitoring adjustment in the placement situation.

Various other curricula for individuals at a given developmental stage, such as school age (Brolin & Gysbers, 1989); for the hearing impaired (Happ & Altmaier, 1982); or for the mentally ill (Loughead, 1989) have also been developed. There are many examples of such curricula, and they are easily found in journals with a focus on one or another disabled population.

In vocational rehabilitation, counselors will engage in some or all of the following activities: vocational testing, vocational assessment (work sampling, vocational evaluation), counseling, work adjustment training, prevocational activities, skills training, employment preparation, job development, job referral and placement, and postplacement counseling. Skills training is especially important with certain disabled populations, such as substance abusers (Deren & Randell, 1990), because "therapeutic counseling, psychotherapy, and/or chemotherapy intervention alone are not likely to ameliorate many of these clients' social, educational, and vocational deficits, and when clients complete treatment, many of the pressures that initially contributed to anti-social and substance abuse behavior may again become prominent" (p. 4).

In the vocational counseling of persons with disabilities, assessment is problematic. The Education of All Handicapped Children Act (PL 94-142), together with the Carl D. Perkins Vocational Education Act (PL 98-524), requires that school districts conduct vocational assessments for students with handicapping conditions in occupational education programs. These assessments must include the identification of vocational interests, abilities, and special needs in relation to each student's specific handicapping condition. No later than ninth grade, schools must provide students and their parents with information about occupational education opportunities for students with handicapping conditions. To effect a vocational assessment, counselors may simply have to conduct an interview with the student, parents, and teachers; use specialized vocational evaluation instruments (e.g., APTICOM, McCarron-Dial, MICRO-TOWER, MESA, TAP, etc.); or in some relatively few cases, engage in a comprehensive vocational evaluation that employs work itself (real, simulated, or situational) as an assessment tool. A comprehensive assessment usually results in a report that includes an evaluation of occupational interests, vocational strengths and weaknesses, learning style, language proficiency, recommendations for occupational program placement and/or exploration, modification or support services required (e.g., adaptive equipment), and some prognosis regarding rehabilitation success. Caston and Watson (1990) studied 185 cases in a state Bureau of Vocational Rehabilitation (BVR) office and discovered that only about one-quarter were provided a vocational evaluation. Although relatively few of these reports made specific job recommendations, about two-thirds of the clients ignored specific job recommendations and chose to work at different jobs. In other words, based on this sample at least, vocational evaluations were sparsely used and of modest impact. Other rehabilitation specialists believe that vocational evaluations have enormous importance for counseling persons with disabilities.

In any case, we must exercise caution in the use of tests with the disabled. Willingham and colleagues (1988) investigated the use of tests to predict academic performance with hearing-impaired, learning-disabled, physically handicapped, and visually impaired examinees to determine the appropriateness of "flagging," (i.e., identifying scores that may not be comparable to those in standard tests because they were earned under nonstandard conditions). They determined that academic performance is somewhat less predictive from the test scores of students with disabilities than from those without, but if time limits could be established for both those with disabling conditions and those without, admissions tests would be technically comparable.

Another area of importance in counseling persons with disabilities is job readiness. To help disabled clients become job ready, the counselor provides training in such job-relevant aspects as increasing their motivation and willingness to work, getting them medically stabilized and ensuring their ability to function well interpersonally and emotionally, to follow orders. to have specific work skills, and to demonstrate good work habits. These attempts to mold the work personalities of the disabled extend to all disabled populations—the physically impaired, the sensorily impaired, alcoholics, and so on.

Another major consideration in the career counseling of the disabled is placement, which receives much more emphasis in the rehabilitation literature than in the more general career literature. Studies of the effectiveness of placement in vocational rehabilitation have consistently demonstrated that the time spent in this activity has a high "payoff," in the sense that total rehabilitation increases and the number of cases regarded as failures decreases.

Career education and similar experiences also are frequently used in the vocational development or redevelopment of persons with disabilities. Marinoble (1980), for instance, advocates the use of community jobs, just as with nondisabled students, to provide a direct, independent career education experience for disabled students. In such a situation, students can reinforce social skills and put to use work behaviors learned in the classroom. In colleges PL 93-112 requires career offices to provide services to persons with disabilities without discrimination. Many career centers have adapted their services to assist persons with disabilities. The visually impaired, for example, are provided specially designed materials in braille and specific programs directed toward meeting their unique needs.

Herr (1982a) has collated a list of the knowledge and skills necessary for counselors who work frequently with persons with disabilities (pp. 21–22).

Knowledge

1. Federal and state legislation, guidelines and policies dealing with exceptional persons
2. Rigors of exceptional persons
3. Types of classification, diagnostic tools or processes and their limitations vis-á-vis work potential or skill
4. Informal assessment procedures for assessing interests, values, goals
5. Characteristics of different types of exceptionality, their etiology, and their likely effects upon work behavior
6. Opportunities available in the local labor market for persons with different types of skills and different types of difficulties
7. The meaning of functional limitation and its use in counseling
8. Models of career development applicable to the congenitally or adventitiously disabled
9. The effects of social stigma, labeling, and stereotyping on the self-concept of exceptional persons
10. Characteristics of the handicapped related to employment skills, training programs, and potential occupational and educational opportunities
11. Ways of working with other specialists to facilitate a comprehensive approach to career exploration, career preparation, and career placement of exceptional persons
12. Examples of job redesign by which employers can accommodate the capabilities and/or functional limitations of various types of exceptionality
13. Methods of developing individual educational programs (IEPs) or individual employment plans
14. Fears, concerns, and needs of parents or spouses of exceptional persons and ways to work with total family unit
15. Models of developing daily living, mobility, job search, and work skills
16. Reference materials and directories pertinent to different categories of exceptionality

Skills

1. Ability to interpret and advise about legislation, policy, guidelines, and rights that affect exceptional persons and their family members
2. Ability to use diagnostic and informal assessment procedures with exceptional persons
3. Ability to assess functional limitations and use them in helping clients engage in occupational exploration and career planning
4. Ability to apply knowledge of career development theory to assist in the analysis

of self-concept portrayal or developmental task deficits of individual clients
5. Ability to provide effective individual and group counseling of persons of different types of exceptionality and their families
6. Ability to work with other specialists in team approaches to clients for educational or employment planning and placement
7. Ability to work with employers in developing job restructuring for different types of exceptional persons
8. Ability to plan and implement different types of skill-building workshops or experiences necessary for employability and work adjustment*

For those people who have some type of disability, various rehabilitation agencies in the community can provide invaluable career help. To qualify for the career services of an agency of this type, an individual must be handicapped in seeking or keeping employment because of some mental or physical disability. Further, there must be some reasonable probability that the services will indeed bring employment benefit to the individual.

The generally accepted goal of vocational rehabilitation is to assist the individual with a disability to gain the ability to work and thus be self-sufficient. The major community agencies for helping to achieve this goal are the local offices of the Division of Vocational Rehabilitation (DVR). Specialty agencies (for the blind, cerebral palsied, and so on) also provide career services to the disabled. Besides providing guidance and counseling, such agencies help clients by providing physical and mental restoration services, training, maintenance and transportation, family services, interpreters for the deaf, readers for the blind, and placement, to cite just a few types of assistance.

We have observed that there is employer discrimination and prejudice toward persons with disabilities. These employer attitudes largely reflect those of the public in general. Hence, vocational rehabilitation counselors must not only work with clients to get them ready for employment, but also educate employers to get them to hire the disabled. Work readiness for clients may entail providing work at a rehabilitation center or in a sheltered workshop—"a work-oriented rehabilitation facility with a controlled working environment and individual vocational goals, which utilizes work experience and related services for assisting the handicapped person to progress toward normal living and a productive vocational status" (Association of Rehabilitation Facilities). Such a workshop may be transitional or long-term. About one-half million individuals per year are in such workshops. It may further involve providing clients with job-seeking skills or using vocational exploration groups to offer information and feedback. In general, vocational rehabilitation consists of intake, work tryout, work conditioning and training, job placement, and follow-up. Evaluation is usually by means of traditional psychometric instruments as well as by work samples.

There is ample documentation that for mental patients work is a needed form of activity (MacKota, 1980); community-based settings lead to more successful vocational rehabilitation than hospital-based settings (Stein & Test, 1980); and employer-hiring bias toward the psychiatrically disabled continues to exist. Ciardello and Bingham (1982) have demonstrated that even the most chronically disturbed individuals are capable of work.

The process of career helping for such individuals is really no different from that for other populations (although some of the sub-

*From "Counselor Education Programs: Training for Career Development with Exceptional People" by E. L. Herr in *Careers, Computers and the Handicapped*, edited by Michael Bender, Lee J. Richmond, and Nancy Pinson-Milburn. Austin, Texas: PRO-ED, Inc., 1985. Reprinted by permission.

stance obviously changes). As Anthony (1980) describes the process, it involves (1) determining client needs, (2) developing a rehabilitation plan, (3) providing work adjustment training, and (4) engaging in placement.

Several guidelines pertain not only to the psychiatrically disabled but also to other populations with disabilities:

1. Past general history and prior work history are good predictors of future work adjustment.
2. Continual support, at least for the short term, is necessary.
3. A step-by-step, systematic career-helping program is best (see, for example, Beley & Felker, 1981).
4. Vocational skill building (rather than a concern with diagnosis or symptomatology) is extremely important.
5. Tests of self-concept or ego strength are probably more useful predictors of work adjustment than are more traditional psychological tests.

Whether the service is provided in a rehabilitation center, a rehabilitation workshop, or a rehabilitation residence, the goal is still to remove both internal and external barriers to a client's working. These barriers, as defined by G. N. Wright (1980), consist of an *occupational handicap* (the inability to perform at a satisfactory level all the essential requirements of an occupation), an *employment handicap* (difficulty in getting a suitable job because of discrimination), a *placement handicap* (difficulty in job place because of an occupation or employment handicap (or both), or a *vocational handicap* (difficulty in adjusting or readjusting to the world of work). The rehabilitation literature is replete with references to the concept of *vocational adjustment* or *work adjustment*. This concept is actually nothing more than the confluence of the worker's job satisfaction with the employer's idea of job satisfactoriness.

Since the 1973 Rehabilitation Act, counselors are responsible for providing each client with an Individualized Written Rehabilitation Program (IWRP). This movement toward systematic delivery and accountability requires a written statement of counselor and client responsibilities in the rehabilitation process, services to be provided, intermediate and long-range vocational goals, criteria for evaluation, review process, and postemployment services.

Toward the end of the phase in which barriers to seeking and keeping employment are removed, the rehabilitation career helper assesses, counsels, or engages in job development and placement. Job development usually involves securing job opportunities for those disabled clients who are not easily placed. As counselors actually place the clients, they must attend to such considerations as work tolerance (capacity for protracted effort), work readiness, job-seeking skills (including employment interviewing, job orientation, and possible job modification to accommodate a disability).

Roessler (1987) has provided an agenda for vocational rehabilitation intervention. He suggests 10 needed initiatives in the provision of services and in public policy:

1. On a national level, vocational training policies should stress development of two tracks: (a) basic literacy and employability preparation for general service jobs and (b) training in computer programming and information processing for high-technology positions.
2. Employers must have significant involvement in the development of curricula and employment transition mechanisms in vocational preparation programs.
3. The Social Security program needs to decrease disincentives to employment such as loss of medical coverage for persons with disabilities earning above a certain wage level.

4. Tax incentives to employers to hire "targeted groups" and to make necessary job accommodations must continue.
5. Deregulation efforts that affect worker safety and affirmative action should be resisted.
6. Vocational rehabilitation counselors must be informed about national economic projections, shifts in their local economies, vocational preparation opportunities, and entry requirements of new employment areas.
7. Evaluation of rehabilitation outcomes should expand to include both quantity and quality (Primary market placement of case closures).
8. Rehabilitation services for many clients must include employability preparation (i.e., teaching clients how to complete job applications, respond in the job interview, and meet the interpersonal and task performance demands of work).
9. Counselors need to promote the supported employment movement and to clarify the ways in which they can contribute to its success.
10. Employers should expand employee assistance benefit programs to realize the cost savings possible through attracting and retaining a qualified work force (p. 19).

In total, rehabilitation agencies provide excellent career services for persons with physical, emotional, intellectual, or sensory disabilities. Although they are relatively new organizations (in existence largely since 1920), they have established a fine record of helping individuals with disabilities become useful workers.

Summary

In this chapter we have considered five populations, which are not necessarily mutually exclusive: women, the culturally different, immigrants, gay men and women, and persons with disabilities. For each, we have pointed out unique aspects of career development or redevelopment that require counselor interventions. These interventions emphasize techniques somewhat different from those used with the general population or call for different emphases in the use of common techniques. Also, we suggested that unconscious stereotyping, leading to bias, may be present in counselors and employers; and we offered information to gainsay such stereotyping. Finally, we are persuaded that when we learn more about the career development of these special populations, we shall ultimately conclude that the career differences between each of these groups and the majority are differences more of degree than of kind.

CHAPTER 6

SYSTEMATIC PLANNING FOR CAREER GUIDANCE AND COUNSELING

Key Concepts

- Systematic planning for career guidance and counseling can be defined in terms of five stages.
- Different purposes for career guidance and counseling require different types of content.
- Theory and research findings represent the conceptual bases on which program planning rests.
- Selection of career guidance program goals and objectives should precede the selection of the activities or content of the program.
- There are multiple methods of evaluating career guidance and counseling programs.

According to Katz (1974), managers at all levels need three distinct types of skills: (1) the ability to produce the organization's goals or services, *technical* skill; (2) the ability to work in groups as a leader or member, *human* skill; (3) the ability to see how organizational units and functions are integrated, *conceptual* skill.

Fitz-enz (1990) would extend these points in this way:

> To be good managers, we must use both strategy and tactics. We use tactics for short-term problem solving and day-to-day administration. Strategy provides us with a frame of reference for operating and administrative systems, as well as for employee behavior. Strategic thinking requires a vision of what might be, creativity, risk taking, flexibility, and ambition. Effective strategists work with their staffs to set objectives and define priorities. They approach their function from a systems perspective. They acknowledge the inevitability of change as an antecedent of growth. Finally, they track progress and feed the data back into the system to optimize both efficiency and effectiveness. (p. 99)

The views of Katz and Fitz-enz apply to the role of the career guidance professional as a planner and manager of career development programs regardless of setting: business and industry, education, community agency. The language of these authors may depart somewhat from that often used by career counselors, but the perspectives provided are in concert with the intent and content of this chapter. The primary purposes here are to consider the conceptual skills of counselors and career guidance specialists as they apply to systematic planning for career guidance and career counseling, to acknowledge that different settings and populations require modifications in the application of such systematic planning processes to accommodate their unique characteristics and needs, and to be conscious that change of any kind must proceed within the "institutional culture," the interactive pattern of norms, values, and behavior present in any level of organizational setting.

If career guidance is to be more than a series of random events or activities and limited encounters between counselors and counselees, it must be built on systematic planning, or a systems approach. Such planning requires the completion, in a logical order, of a set of steps that seek to answer several general questions: (1) Why have a career guidance program? (2) What will be the goals of the career guidance program? (3) How will the goals of the career guidance program be achieved? and (4) How will the achievement of career guidance goals be determined?

Systematic planning for career guidance is consistent with a national climate of support for program accountability and for efforts to implement results-based or outcomes-based human services, guidance, or counseling programs rather than rely on traditional models of process- or services-based programs (Gysbers, 1990). Implicit in results-based approaches to program planning and implementation is the assumption that planned programs can clarify what counselors could or, indeed, should contribute to the mission of the corporation, school, university, or other facility in which they are located; what differences counselors can make in the lives of children, youth, or adults in such settings; and the degree to which they can be held accountable for selected outcomes, knowledge bases, or behavioral domains.

In some contrast to outcomes-based approaches, process- or services-based programs tend to advocate making specific functions or roles to be performed by each counselor available in each setting. The assumption is that if the designated functions or processes are in place, the outcomes of the service or program will be positive. One criticism of process- or services-based approaches is that because counselors are invariably busy people, if they do not have clearly specified outcomes and plans to achieve them, it is not clear what results may accrue from their efforts. A further criticism is that simply having traditional processes of guidance and counseling in place does not ensure the flexibility or creativity in a program to cope with the changing needs of client populations in the United States today.

Johnson and Johnson (1982), leading advocates and practitioners of results-based approaches to guidance and counseling, suggest that when a program has a clear set of outcomes to be achieved, there are likely to be many processes that can be implemented to achieve individual outcomes. Focusing on the content of a specific program outcome and then determining what process or processes are likely to be effective in achieving it are different from focusing on putting in place a traditional process that may not be relevant to the needs to be served or the outcomes sought. In addition, outcome-based programs typically assume that clients in a setting—whether children, youth, or adults—learn differently and deserve to have access to more than one process or activity to help them achieve the desired results. Further, unless outcomes for a guidance or counseling program are specified and defined, it is virtually impossible to hold such programs to accountability criteria or determine their effectiveness.

It is important to acknowledge that results- or outcomes-based programs and process- or services-based programs are not mutually exclusive. Aspects of both can and do exist within a programmatic framework. The overriding issue is the systematic and planned effort to put into place those activities or services that are relevant to the needs of the client populations and the mission of the setting within which they are implemented.

Given the context just described, the planning for career guidance, carer counseling, or employee counseling programs does not occur in a vacuum. Such programs must be designed to achieve the purposes of the organization within which they are located as well as to facilitate the career development of those who are directly served. For example, "Employee counseling programs are meant to provide effective means of dealing with problems in the workplace" (Lewis & Lewis, 1986, p. 209). Career development programs in corporate organizations "are comprised of two separate but interrelated functions: career planning, which is an individual process, and career management, which is an institutional process" (Gutteridge, 1986, p. 55). As business and industry place increased attention on workers as assets to be nurtured and developed—not just hired and fired—one focus has been on forecasting and establishing plans for fulfilling the firm's overall employment needs. As schools are increasingly the target of national concern about the quality of the future work force, career education and counseling programs have come to be seen as important to student needs for career exploration and planning as well as to the school's responsibilities to provide graduating students with the personal habits, knowledge, and skills to make an effective transition into the workplace. As suggested in subsequent chapters, career guidance and counseling in schools are concerned with facilitating students' exploration of the educational and career alternatives available to them; sharpening their understanding of their own abilities, interests, and values as bases for career choice; teaching them how to implement career planning; and helping them acquire the skills necessary for the transition to work or to postsecondary education.

Each of the institutional goals identified above is interactive with the provision of direct services to students or to employees. Therefore, they represent the administrative and mission-oriented context against which programatic planning must proceed.

Gutteridge speaks to such a point, using the language of industry, when he states that "human resource management is comprised of four distinct yet interrelated job systems: organizational design, human resource (manpower) planning, career development, and control and evaluation. . . . All of these subprocesses are influenced by a variety of internal and external environmental pressures" (1986, p. 53). Together, regardless of setting, such approaches are designed to create value through and for people (Fitz-Enz, 1990). Such value is reflected in the knowledge, attitudes, skills, and behaviors for which career guidance or career counseling becomes responsible in a specific setting.

THE PROCESS OF SYSTEMATIC OR STRATEGIC PLANNING

A systematic approach to program planning rests on the concept of systems analysis, which in turn is concerned with the examination of the interrelationships among the parts of a system in order to formulate goals and objectives. Science, the defense establishment, and industry have used systems analysis and related methodology for several decades to make complex, interactive units manageable and more amenable to monitoring and evaluation. Depending on its relationship to other components within an institution, career guidance may be seen as a system in its own right or as a subsystem of a larger whole (see, for example, Byham, 1982).

Program planning, whether for career guidance or other purposes, is required to ensure that the goals are clearly understood, that the techniques or processes constituting the program are related to the goals, and that the criteria on which the program will be judged are explicit. These elements underlie the program's accountability and are the steps leading to its evaluation.

Systematic planning, as we use the term, is not inconsistent with what others describe as strategic planning or strategic management. Although strategic planning can be done in various ways, it is fundamentally a process of answering such basic questions of organizational management as the following:

1. Who are we?
2. What is our purpose?
3. On what will we focus?
4. What are we able to do?
5. What is absolutely necessary?

6. How will we operate?
7. What have we achieved? (Fitz-Enz, 1990, p. 81)

Or, said another way,

- What are our most important organizational issues?
- How are things different today from what they were three or five years ago?
- How are things likely to be different three to five years from now?
- What types of external changes can we expect in the near future?
- What types of internal changes can we expect in the near future?
- How do we compare to our competition in critical areas?
- Is our technology state-of-the-art?
- What can we do to close the gap between what we are and what we must become? (Fitz-Enz, 1990, p. 84)

Kurpius, Burrello, and Rozecki (1990) have proposed a strategic planning model for practitioners in human service organizations that summarizes many elements common to comprehensive planning models. The steps in their plan are

1. Articulating the foundation
   a. Beliefs
   b. Creating a vision
   c. Defining a mission
2. Assessing the forces
   a. Analyzing external and internal factors
   b. Generating and assessing essential policies
3. Formulating the plan
   a. Specifying objectives
   b. Generating strategies
   c. Implementing action plans
   d. Recycling (p. 5)

In essence, whether you follow the steps of a strategic planning model or a systematic approach to career guidance, the intent is the same: If you wish to end with a particular type of employee, student, or client behavior (for example, career maturity, self-understanding, decision-making skills), you build toward that goal by comprehensively taking into consideration the functional relations between the elements and people who affect such a goal. In conceiving such a system, the counselor or career administrator needs to take into account the interdependent effects of such variables as

1. Learner, worker, or client characteristics
2. Resource characteristics available in a school, employment, or community setting (such as budget, materials available, referral sources, exploratory sites, personnel who can be involved)
3. Counselor characteristics
4. Effectiveness of counselor techniques
5. Administrative characteristics or management requirements
6. Community or institutional expectations

In systematic planning, then, one must begin with a statement of what is to be achieved in career guidance and counseling: what goals are to be accomplished; and what student, employee, or client development is to be facilitated. A basic premise of this book is that an understanding of the various approaches to career development provides the *content* for these considerations. (Chapter 4 identified the major emphases in career development theory and research, and much of this chapter extends the analysis of career development approaches more specifically. These aspects of career development should be reviewed as appropriate here.) This emphasis on beginning with goals for the program is in contrast to beginning with counselor techniques that can be performed. In too many instances, counselors do what they know how to do without questioning what they are attempting to achieve. In the process, they lose sight of answers to such questions as, Why career guidance? or How will students, employees, or clients be different as a result of exposure to career counseling? Without answers to such questions, however, career guidance programs lack direction and are likely to be pressured into areas for which counselors are not prepared or in which their skills are ineffective.

A Systems Approach to Career Education

Ryan (1974) has identified six functions necessary to a systems approach to career education. In modified form, they include

Establishing a conceptual framework–Determine the rationale, define the basic concepts, specify the basic assumptions on which the program will be based.

Possessing information–Gather, evaluate, and store data about the community, available resources, facilities, the population to be served. Determine what other information is necessary.

Assessing needs–Compare the ideal program as built from the rationale, assumptions, and concepts of step 1 with the existing situation in the setting where this program is to be installed. Determine the discrepancies between what the program should be and what it now is. Assess the perceptions of parents, employers, managers, employees, teachers, students, or other consumers, administrators, and community representatives about what priorities the program should meet; these could be described as the assessed needs to which the program will be directed. Which of these groups you query depends on whether you are implementing a career guidance program in business and industry, a community agency, or an educational setting.

Formulating the management plan–Specify program goals and performance objectives for students, employees, or clients. Identify the processes that will be related to the program goals. Specify the resources and constraints that need to be considered in putting the plan together.

Implementing the program–Put the program plan into action. Provide in-service training to staff involved, order materials or resources necessary, offer the experience or processes related to program goals.

Evaluating the system–Monitor ongoing operations as well as the changes in knowledge, skills, and attitudes of the participants. Determine whether the program is meeting its goals and whether individual elements are effective.

These steps are equally valid for career guidance programs across settings.

A Career Development and Assessment Process Model

In a graphic effort to illustrate the flow of activities or subsystems that underlie systematic planning, Scott, Davis, and Dieffenderfer (1984) have proposed a Career Development and Assessment Process Model designed to coordinate vocational or career guidance services that would allow social service agencies to link their services "in common goals to help targeted individuals lead productive lives" (p. 18). The model is designed to have a variety of benefits: to eliminate duplication of services, use available funds most efficiently, establish credibility with employers, develop standards for vocational services delivered to clients, be the focus of training for employers who are going to deliver services, and establish linkages with training, educational sources, the business community, and job bank sources.

Figure 6.1 portrays the schematic characteristics of this model. Although space does not permit a complete rendering of the narrative for each activity, it would be necessary to establish detailed procedures and define levels of responsibility for carrying out the activities.

Figure 6.1

Service Components Career Development and Assessment Process Model (From "Career Development and Assessment Process Model for Coordinated Vocational Services" by M. L. Scott, G. N. Davis and R. Diefenderfer, *Vocational Evaluation and Work Adjustment* Bulletin, 1984, Spring issue, pp. 18–21, figure 1. Reprinted by permission.)

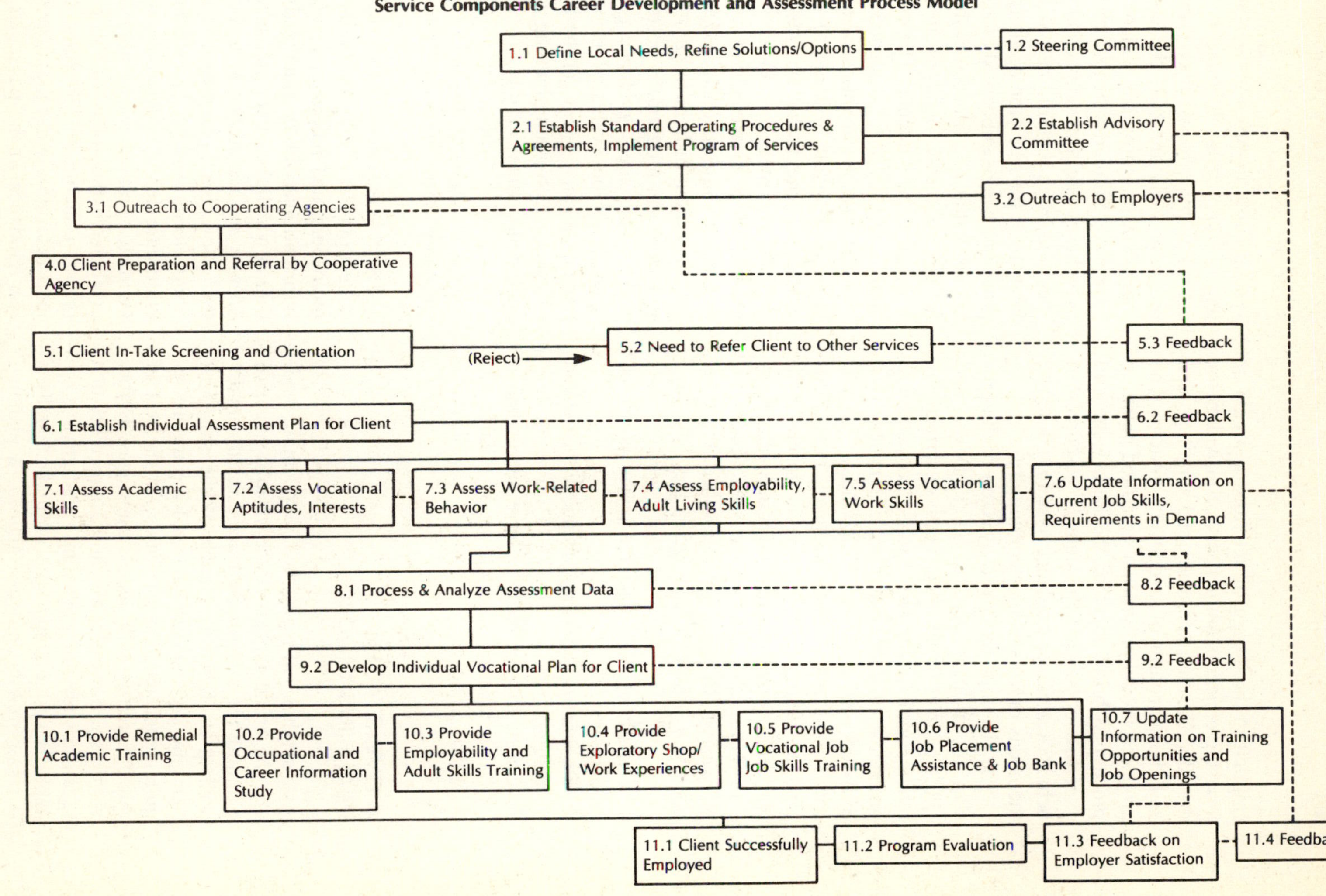

Implicit in the design of activities is a goal of arousing concerns among service providers for the identification of needs and target groups and the selection of a delivery system. The proposed model provides a structured planning process to bring together the knowledge and expertise of several community resources in behalf of a career guidance system tailored to the needs of a particular community.

The six steps described by Ryan or the process model portrayed by Scott, Davis, and Dieffenderfer have also been described by others, with variations applied to particular problems or emphases (see Mannebach & Stillwell, 1974; AIR, 1975; Chiko, Tolsma, Kahn, & Marks, 1980; Rimmer, 1981; Gutteridge, 1986). In fact, there is no one right way to accomplish such planning, but, however it proceeds, it should be logical and comprehensive. Reduced to its essence, the three phases of designing a program are

1. Determine and describe what is to be achieved.
2. Do what is necessary to achieve the desired result.
3. Check to see that you have succeeded in doing what you set out to do (Gammuto, 1980, p. 84).

A FIVE-STAGE PLANNING MODEL

As a synthesis of many possible planning models, the broad aspects of the various stages of planning for a career guidance program are described in Table 6.1. Each of the stages of planning portrayed in Table 6.1 has unique requirements and characteristics. In the rest of this chapter we will discuss the stages. Before we do so, however, we should remember that regardless of which planning paradigm one accepts, a systems approach is fundamentally a decision-making process. Indeed, a planning system really involves the generation of a system of hypotheses. In stage 1, program goals are really hypotheses; they imply that if such program goals are met, the conditions existing before the program will be eliminated or improved. Similarly, behavioral objectives are hypotheses that if persons obtain the behaviors specified, the program goals will be achieved. In stage 3, the selection of alternative program processes can be conceived of as a series of hypotheses that one process is more likely than another to result in the desired behavior for which it is accountable. The evaluation, summative or formative, designed to monitor the program is really a series of tests of the hypotheses implicit in stages 1–3. Indeed, the evaluation scheme that evolves can be conceptualized almost as a pre/posttest with the program elements considered to be treatments; the original conditions considered as baseline data; and the output or behavioral outcomes that result from the program as posttest data. Obviously, most career guidance programs cannot or will not be evaluated using pure experimental designs, but it can be helpful to think of much of program planning as analogous to such conceptualizations.

Stage 1—Developing a Program Rationale and Philosophy

Stage 1 includes all the thinking and data collection that relates to developing a program philosophy and rationale. It includes securing information about the characteristics of the setting in which the career guidance program is to operate and the resources to be committed to that effort. Such planning also includes developing needs surveys (questionnaires or structured interviews) to determine what consumers (students, employees, or other adults) and others believe the focus of the career guidance program should be. Together, these data will help determine what the current status of career guidance in the particular setting is and

Table 6.1

Stages in Planning for and Implementing a Career Guidance Program

Stage 1	Stage 2	Stage 3	Stage 4	Stage 5
1. Develop a program philosophy. 1.1 Review research and theory pertinent to career guidance and career development. 1.2 Specify program rational. 1.3 Describe theoretical and philosophical basis for program. 1.4 State assumptions. 1.5 Define concepts. 2. Collect comprehensive data on what consumers (students, employees, adults) and others (parents, employers, teachers, administrators, community representatives) believe should be program priorities. 3. Collect data on the current program—goals, resources, etc. 4. Identify where the target population—students, workers, other adults—currently stand on their career development. 5. Determine discrepancies between what current program is and what it should be.	1. Specify program goals. 2. Specify individual behavioral objectives to be achieved.	1. Select alternative program processes. 2. Relate program processes to problem goals or specific behavioral objectives. 3. Identify resources necessary to implement various program processes. 4. Identify personnel (teachers, counselors, human resource specialists, administrators, community representatives, first-line supervisors, parents) who have contributions to make to various program processes.	1. Describe evaluation procedures. 1.1 Summative evaluation to assess whether total program goals are being met. 1.2 Perform formative evaluation to assess whether program elements are contributing effectively to program goals. 1.3 Identify evaluative data to be secured, from whom, and by whom. 1.4 Build or secure data collection instruments. 1.5 Decide on the form of data analysis and who will be responsible. 1.6 Identify persons or groups to whom evaluative data will be provided and in what form.	1. Identify milestones (crucial events) that must occur for program implementation. 1.1 When staff in-service will occur. 1.2 When information about the program must be prepared and sent to consumers. 1.3 When materials and resources for the program must be ordered. 1.4 When base-line data on participants will be collected. 1.5 When program will be introduced.

what different groups believe it should be. At the conclusion of stage 1, counselors should have formulated a statement that clearly answers such questions as, Why career guidance? Why career counseling? Why a career development system?

Needs Assessment. As a device by which to clarify the difference between the current status and the desired state of career guidance, the process of needs assessment has become frequently used. As Cook (1989) contends,

> All human service programs are developed based on the . . . implicit assumption of need in the population at risk. Programs will eventually fail or succeed depending on how well they address those needs. Consequently, need assessment is the first step in the program planning cycle and is essential for the effective delivery of services and the efficient allocation of resources. . . . Need is a relative concept that can be viewed as a discrepancy from some recognized standard or as the gap between an individual's desired and actual situation. . . . Need assessment usually seeks to define and prioritize an individual's expressed needs and then link these needs to service provision such as providing vocational counseling to a person who is disabled. (p. 462)

Needs assessments can be used for many planning purposes; for example, demands for accountability, ways to clarify evidence of widespread criticism for unsolved problems in a program, and methods to respond to the increasing competition for scarce resources. Needs assessments go beyond such reasons to allow significant others of relevance in particular settings—consumers, employers, administrators, parents, the public at large—to participate in identifying appropriate program rationales, goals, directions, or even interventions.

Needs assessments are basically processes to document the difference between a current state of affairs and some target or desired state of affairs. As such, a needs assessment is a technique by which to identify the discrepancies between what is and what ought to be and determine how these discrepancies might be reduced. Like most other planning processes,needs assessments are exercises in logic and include a process of implementation that involves appropriate persons, minimizes time and personnel costs, and yields the documented needs and the planning priorities that are of concern to stage 1 expectations as they are described here.

While there are many models of needs assessment, the Counseling and Personnel Services Clearinghouse at the University of Michigan has suggested the following four-phased structure (ERIC/CAPS, 1982):

Phase I. Planning and Designing the Needs Assessment

Step 1. Carry out preliminary activities.

- Set up needs assessment committee.
- Identify external priorities or limiting factors.
- Determine scope of assessment.
- Establish needs assessment schedule.
- Review committee resources and obtain commitment.

Step 2. Make specific plans and design needs assessment.

- Specify process and product goals (e.g., process goals refer to the intervention process itself, and product goals refer to student or employee outcomes as a result of the intervention process).
- Develop statements of program objectives with clarity, precision, measurability, feasibility, appropriateness, relevance, and logic.
- Set standards for all objectives.
- Discuss and agree on kinds of data to be gathered (performance, description, opinion, attitude, perception).
- Determine sources of data.

- Determine sample for data gathering (groups, sizes, strategies/methods).
- Select/modify/develop data collection methods and instruments (quantitative and qualitative).
- Design analysis of existing variables.

Phase II. Conducting the Needs Assessment

Step 3. Obtain, organize, and summarize NA data

- Categorize all data to be collected (program, clients, resources, stakeholding groups).
- Collect and summarize data (existing and new) in each category.

Step 4. Analyze and interpret data to derive meanings

- Employ arithmetic/statistical analysis.
- Identify specific qualitative elements.

Step 5. Conduct analysis of apparent relationships

- Determine factors for each documented need according to standards and to category.
- Designate needs related to factors that can be addressed immediately, later or over extended periods of time, and not at all.

Phase III. Using the Needs Assessment Results (A prior review of the anticipated utilization of results and an evaluation of the appropriateness of such utilization may be advisable. The early identification of possible barriers to the consecutive use of results prevents inefficient use of resources.)

Step 6. Select priorities

- Assign priorities to each need(s) set.
- Assign priorities on basis on criticality over time (in consideration of currently available resources, limits of action authority, and so on).

Step 7. Plan program

- Identify new program elements and/or modifications.
- Establish performance objectives.
- Allocate resources by priority and relative cost.
- Provide for coordination of resources.
- Assign tasks to individuals, teams, and groups, with timeless and milestones for accomplishment.

Step 8. Implement program

- Provide resources for program change according to documented needs and priority assignments.
- Identify measures and means of data collection for each objective.

Phase IV. Review of Meta-Assessment

Step 9. Determine impact of change process

- Decide on indicators to be accepted as evidence of improvement.
- Gather data to determine actual occurrence of improvement.
- Identify relationships between observed improvements and program changes.
- Relate observed improvements to originally documented needs (pp. 1–2).*

The purpose of Phase IV is to look back at the process as a whole, relate the results to the objectives, determine the extent to which the process has succeeded, and modify the process for greater or further success during the next needs assessment cycle. Although such a process appears to encompass the whole of planning for career guidance, it does not. Needs assessments are only stage 1 techniques and must be coupled with other considerations as the development of a program rationale and philosophy is undertaken.

*From The Counseling and Personnel Services Clearinghouse, University of Michigan: ERIC/CAPS, 1982.

Another aspect of stage 1 is to review current research and theory on what the program's directions might be, what knowledge or behaviors might be affected by the program, and what basic concepts and assumptions should be considered. In Chapters 1 through 5, possible contributions have been made to such an analysis and should be reviewed. Chapter 4, in particular, speaks to the conceptual elements that give career guidance or career counseling its general rationale. Many of these insights could be translated into program philosophy for a particular setting.

Basically, programs in career guidance will have one of three emphases or a combination of these three. (1) In a *stimulus approach*, consumers are assisted in anticipating and exploring opportunities and how these relate to their personal abilities, preferences, and circumstances. In essence, the intent is to facilitate career development. (2) In *induction and adjustment* to a setting, the intent of the career guidance program is to assist persons in translating their preferences or choices into action, consolidating these choices, and advancing within the settings in which they are implemented. (3) In a *treatment approach* individuals may anticipate and explore but also must undergo remediation or reconstruction of their attitudes, knowledge, and skills often to facilitate their work adjustment.

However a program emphasis is conceived, planning for it needs to include insights into the behaviors that the program intends to affect. These insights need to be translated into a program philosophy and rationale. For example, if the career guidance program is to emphasize a stimulus approach, then career maturity and the elements comprising it may be helpful input to conceptualizing a program philosophy and rationale. Although the usefulness of insights into the behavioral structure of career maturity is not confined to the stimulus approach to career guidance, the other two career guidance program emphases are likely to require other bodies of theory and research that are useful in conceptualizing and planning their particular intent.

Concepts of Career Maturity as Input for a Stimulus Approach. Before one can properly specify program goals or performance objectives for the career development, vocationalization, or stimulus of students or adults, one must identify the overall goal. Goals that appear most frequently in the literature and that seem to have the most face validity are career maturity and career adaptability. In Chapter 2, the emerging goal of personal flexibility was also introduced. Although useful as ultimate goals, however, terms such as career maturity, career adaptability, and personal flexibility are too global to be useful for intermediate purposes unless they can be dissected into specific elements. Thus, for example, it is necessary to convert the elements of career maturity into unifying themes and behavioral descriptions and place these along a developmental line leading to career maturity at some point in life, such as high school graduation, tenth grade, sophomore year in college, release from a rehabilitation facility, or at specific career transition points, such as when an employee is ready to be promoted to a new role.

When attempting such a task, however, one must realize that, just as in other developmental processes, individuals will differ in their readiness for various elements or aspects of career development and in the ways they develop this readiness. Not everyone will reach the same point at the same time, nor will all proceed through the elements of career development at the same pace. As previously indicated, the speed of such movement and the readiness for it will depend on the individual's personal history and many extrinsic and intrinsic factors.

The objectives of career development, then, rest on statements of expectations for specific target groups, which necessitate judgments of what individuals ought to be able to achieve and behavioral descriptions of these activities. But one must also realize that for optimum effect, career development should be personalized. Although the literal realization of such a goal may be too much to expect, any systematic attempt to aid career development requires an emphasis both on diagnosis and on the provision of diverse learning experiences. It is simply not enough to say to a person, "Be career mature." One needs to understand what being career mature means, what the consequences of career maturity are, how one acquires career maturity, and what opportunities are available to aid such an effort.

In essence, a systems approach to career maturity at its best would represent a planned continuum of experiences for individual students, employees, or clients. The individual should be exposed to the program on the basis of assessed readiness and move progressively toward the goal of career maturity or career adaptability.

Fostering career maturity seems to require both individualizing and personalizing (Shane, 1970). As will be shown later in this chapter, there are certain elements of effective behavior that all persons need to acquire individually. But there are also times when, as individual goals become clearer, the person needs the opportunity and the assistance to "create him or herself"; that is, to develop ways of creating goals and a life-style independent of others.

Before directing further attention to goal setting, it is important to consider career maturity itself more specifically. For example, Ginzberg, Ginsburg, Axelrad, and Herma (1951) reported, "To some degree, the way in which a young person deals with his occupational choice is indicative of his general maturity and, conversely, in assessing the latter, consideration must be given to the way in which he is handing his occupational choice problem" (p. 60). Extending this definition, Super (1957, p. 186) indicated that in a gross sense career maturity can be described as "the place reached on the continuum of vocational development from exploration to decline." Later still, Crites (1961, p. 259) described it as "the maturity of an individual's vocational behavior as indicated by the similarity between his behavior and that of the oldest individuals in his vocational life stage."

A clarification of these definitions of career maturity is provided by Super (1957), who differentiated Vocational Maturity I (VMI) from Vocational Maturity II (VMII). He defines VMI as "the life stage in which the individual actually is, as evidenced by the developmental tasks with which he is dealing in relation to the life stage in which he is expected to be, in terms of his age" (p. 132). VMII is defined as "maturity of behavior in the actual life stage (regardless of whether it is the expected life stage) as evidenced by the behavior shown in dealing with developmental tasks of the actual life stage compared with the behavior of other individuals who are dealing with the same developmental tasks" (pp. 57, 132).

These definitions of Vocational Maturity I and II raise several other points. One is that career maturity differs when defined as the vocational behavior expected of persons at different points in life. What is career maturity at age 10 will not be at age 16 or 25 or 35. Second, although in VMI there is an expectation that gross characteristics of career development describe broad chronological periods in life, VMII attends to how a particular individual is coping with career development in a personal sense. In other words, it asks, Where is this person now, and what knowledge, attitudes, or skills does he or she need to progress to higher levels of career development? Similarly, it would be possible for corporations and other settings to define the types of career maturity necessary at different transition points within the career paths available. Third, VMI and VMII introduce the concept of developmental tasks as means by which career development progresses.

Most of the examples of ingredients important to career maturity, reported on later in this chapter, have evolved from the work of Super and his colleagues in the Career Pattern Study. Some readers may consider this an imbalance. However, as Norton (1970) has noted, whether one examines the concurrent, related work of Vriend (1968), Crites, (1965), Gribbons and Lohnes (1968), Nelson (1956), or Westbrook (Westbrook & Cunningham, 1970), the essential criteria of career maturity remain fairly constant. What does change, however, across these approaches to career maturity are the methods of measuring the presence of specific elements of career maturity. In Chapter 16 we will discuss these measurement strategies and their availability for counselor use.

It is important to realize that if career maturity or career adaptability or personal flexibility or another goal is to be used as the goal of career development, and if a systems approach to achieving it is to be mounted, relevant measures are needed (1) to assess personal readiness to make educational-vocational decisions or to participate in particular types of career development experiences; (2) to serve as diagnostic instruments for determining treatment; and (3) to evaluate the effectiveness of strategies for aiding vocationalization (Westbrook & Cunningham, 1970). Many such assessment devices are described in Chapter 16.

The Mastery of Development Tasks as a Function of Career Guidance. Several theorists have either directly or indirectly wedded particular developmental tasks with stages of increasingly mature vocational behavior. Thus, we can assume that the developmental task concept is useful, both as a description of the changing demands on individuals as they move through life and as a means of organizing those demands—whether knowledge, attitudes, or skills—into a systems approach to career development.

In terms of the first use of developmental tasks just cited, Havighurst (1953, p. 2) has provided the following definition: "A task which arises at or about a certain period in the life of the individual, successful achievement of which leads to happiness and success with later tasks, while failure leads to unhappiness in the individual, disapproval by society, and difficulty with later tasks." This definition has come to be accepted almost universally.

The developmental task concept can be used to describe an average set of demands with which the individual must cope, as well as a way of looking at how a given individual is attaining such an expectation, at what points he or she is having difficulty, what specific experiences or competencies the person needs to acquire, and what resources might aid his or her development. Such a concept makes it possible to provide sequential developmental experiences that will prepare the individual to meet emerging developmental tasks and to prescribe (on an individual basis) alternative methods of coping with developmental task difficulties. In short, facilitation of developmental tasks offers a rationale for career guidance as well as a potential organizing theme for program planning.

Further, individual variation in accomplishing developmental tasks can be considered in the following ways: "A given task has a unique meaning to each individual. . . . Secondly, individuals vary with respect to their general approach to developmental tasks. . . . The third idiographic dimension of developmental tasks is the patterning of developmental tasks" (Zaccaria, 1965, p. 374). Lo Cascio (1967) has identified three basic patterns for mastering developmental tasks: continuous developmental pattern, delayed developmental pattern, and impaired developmental pattern. The individual differences that produce such differential patterns are values, attitudes, need systems, age, sex, and temperament, as well as cultural factors, such as socioeconomic status.

If one accepts developmental tasks as an organizing structure for conceptualizing career development or facilitating career adaptability or maturity, one must then determine what the developmental tasks are that move one along a continuum to such goals. Chapter 4 presents many conceptualizations from which to draw. Table 6.2 presents major emphases in selected approaches that illustrate the point. Table 6.3 summarizes such developmental tasks from Super's perspectives. The two tables are not parallel in the sense that each discusses developmental tasks as Havighurst defined them. Nor do they agree on the exact time span in which particular development ensues. They do, however, agree that career development occurs in crucial steps with each systematically related to those preceding and succeeding it. These steps also relate to turning points in each developmental stage, where individuals either progress or fall back as a function of their success in grappling with the central issues of the stage. As such, they become useful in diagnostic terms and as planning content for career guidance programs or for career counseling protocols.

Although the illustrations in Tables 6.2 and 6.3 are too gross to be directly translated into goals for career guidance, other pertinent points are discernible. For example, what does Havighurst's first stage (identification with a worker) suggest for a student who comes from a home and a culture in which there are no productive workers? If the achievement of later tasks depends on such identification, then education or some other intervention (such as career guidance) must respond to that lack. In accordance with the general rationale of developmental tasks that missed stages leave a deficit in dealing with later tasks, the question becomes, What resources, what role models, what experiences can the school, the corporation, or agency provide to help this particular person acquire a concept of work as a part of his or her orientation for the future? Or, suppose we are talking about a male who has, in Super's terms, never been able to advance in an occupation. Do we simply consider this person a "loser" and try to dismiss him from the workplace or instead allow him to drift along at a mediocre level of productivity, assuming he can do no better? Or, do we attempt to determine what prevents him from advancing? Is it his fear of responsibility? His preoccupation with family problems? His lack of clarity about the requirements of particular career paths in the work setting? Each of these and other hypotheses is reasonable and can be pursued in a career conference with the worker. Once the problem is defined, a career guidance or career counseling approach can be instituted to help the person become more purposeful and productive.

Table 6.2 provides a frame of reference for formulating specific program goals and individual objectives. The themes presented are more global than objectives should be. It does not provide behavioral descriptions that permit evaluation of an individual's accomplishment of the goals set for him or her. Before turning to the development of program goals or the matter of behavioral descriptions, let us consider some current research findings on career maturity as an example of how theory and research pertinent to a particular goal might be used.

Current Research Pertinent to Career Development and Career Maturity. Research of particular relevance to career maturity has been accomplished in the Career Pattern Study (Crites, 1974a, 1985; Jordaan & Heyde, 1979; Super, 1969a, b; Super, Starishevsky, Matlin & Jordaan, 1963); and in the Career Development Study (Gribbons & Lohnes, 1968, 1982). Each of these research studies has identified the el-

Table 6.2

Selected Examples of Theoretical Conceptions of the Developmental Tasks Related to Career Behaviors

Havighurst (1964, p. 216)

Age 5 – 10

I. Identification with a worker — father, mother , other significant persons. The concept of working becomes an essential part of the ego-ideal. Principal developmental tasks of middle childhood

1. Developing fundamental skills in reading, writing, and calculating
2. Learning physical skills necessary for ordinary games
3. Learning to get along with age mates
4. Learning an appropriate masculine or feminine social role
5. Developing concepts for everyday life
6. Development conscience, morality, and a scale of values
7. Achieving personal identity

Age 10 – 15

II. Acquiring the basic habits of industry: Learning to organize time and energy to get a piece of work done (school, work, chores). Learning to put work ahead of play in appropriate situations

Age 15 – 25

III. Acquiring identity as a worker in the occupational structure; choosing and preparing for an occupation. Getting work experience as a basis for occupational choice and for assurance of economic independence. Principal developmental tasks of adolescence.

1. Achieving new and more mature relations with agemates of both sexes
2. Achieving masculine or feminine social role
3. Achieving emotional independence of parents and other adults
4. Achieving assurance of economic independence
5. Selecting and preparing for an occupation
6. Acquiring a set of values and an ethical system as a guide to behavior
7. Preparing for marraige and selecting a mate
8. Starting a family
9. Getting started in an occupation

Age 25 – 45

IV. Becoming a productive person; mastering the skills of an occupation; moving up the ladder within the occupation

V. Maintaining a productive society.

— Achieving adult civic and social responsibility
— Assisting teenage children to become responsible and happy adults
— Developing adult leisure-time activities
— Relating oneself to one's spouse as a person
— Adjusting to aging parents
— Accepting and adjusting to the physiological changes of middle age
— Reaching and maintaining a satisfactory performance in one's occupational career

Age 45 – 65

VI. Contemplating a productive life

— Adjusting to decreasing strength and health
— Adjusting to retirement and reduced income
— Adjusting to the death of a spouse
— Establishing an explicit affiliation with members of one's age group
— Establishing satisfactory physical living arrangements
— Adapting to social roles in a flexible way

Erikson (1963, 2nd Ed.)

Birth to approximately age 25

Basic trust (basic mistrust)

Autonomy (shame and doubt)

Initiative (guilt)

Industry (inferiority)

Fundamentals of technology

First sense of division of labor and of differential opportunity

Outer and inner hindrance

Identity (role confusion):

Ego identity and the tangible promise of career

Occupational identity

Sexual identity

Intimacy (isolation):

The capacity to commit oneself to concrete affiliations and partnerships and to develop the ethical strength to abide by such commitments

Ethical sense

True genitality

Table 6.2 (Continued)

Age 45 – 60

Generativity (stagnation) productivity creativity

Ego integrity (despair)

After Age 60

Integrity vs. Despair (disgust)

Levinson (1978)

Early Adult Transition (17 – 22)

1. Terminate pre-adulthood
   — start moving out of the pre-adult world
   — question the nature of the world and one's place in it
   — modify or terminate existing relationships with important persons, groups, and institutions
   — Reappraise and modify the self that formed it
2. Begin early adulthood
   — Explore its possibilities
   — Imagine oneself a participant in it
   — Consolidate an initial adult identity
   — Make and test some preliminary choices for adult living

Four major tasks from 17 to approximately 30

1. Forming a dream and giving it a place in the life structure
2. Forming mentor relationships
3. Forming an occupation
4. Forming love relationships and family

Entering the Adult World (22 – 28)

Fashion a provisional structure that provides a workable link between the valued self and the adult society

1. Explore possibilities for adult living; keep options open; avoid strong commitments; maximize the alternatives
2. Create a stable life structure
   — Become more responsible and make something of my life

Age 30

Transition (23 – 33)

— Make important new choices or reaffirm old ones

Settling Down (33 – 40)

1. Tries to establish a niche in society
   — anchor life more firmly
   — develop competence in a chosen craft
   — become a valued member of a valued world

Age 25 – 45

— define a personal enterprise, a direction in which to strive

2. Work at advancement
   — strive to advance, to progress on a timetable
3. Becoming one's own person
   — accomplish the goals of the settling down enterprise
   — become a senior member in one's world
   — speak more strongly with one's voice
   — have a greater measure of authority

The Mid-Life Transition (40 – 45)

1. A period of questioning of the life structure

Hall (1978, pp. 81 – 84)

Start at 45 – 60

— awareness of advancing age
— awareness of body changes relating to aging
— knowing how many career goals have been or will be attained
— search for new life goals
— marked change in family relationships
— change in work relationships
— sense of work obsolescence
— feeling of decreased job mobility and increased concerns for job security

Table 6.3

A Synthesis of Super's Conception of Life Stages and Developmental Tasks

Growth	Exploration	Establishment	Maintenance
Birth Self-concept develops through identification with key figures in family and school needs and fantasy are dominant early in this stage; interest and capacity become more important with increasing social participation and reality testing; learn behaviors associated with self-help, social interaction, self-direction, industrialness, goal setting, persistence. Substages: *Fantasy* (4 – 10 years) Needs are dominant; role-playing in fantasy is important. *Interest* (11 – 12 years) Likes are the major determinant of aspirations and activities. *Capacity* (13 – 14 years) Abilities are given more weight and job requirements (including training) are considered.	*14 years* Self-examination, role try-outs and occupational exploration take place in school, leisure activities, and part-time work. Substages: *Tentative* (15 – 17) Needs, interests, capacities, values, and opportunities are all considered, tentative choices are made and tried out in fantasy, discussion, courses, work, etc. Possible appropriate fields and levels of work are identified. Task — Crystallizing a Vocational Preference *Transition* (18 – 21) Reality considerations are given more weight as the person enters the labor market or professional training and attempts to implement a self-concept. Generalized choice is converted to specific choice. Task — Specifying a Vocational Preference *Trial-Little Commitment* (22 – 24) A seemingly appropriate occupation having been found, a first job is located and is tried out as a potential life work. Commitment is still provisional and if the job is not appropriate, the person may reinstitute the process of crystallizing, specifying, and implementing a preference.	*24 years* Having found an appropriate field, an effort is made to establish a permanent place in it. Thereafter changes which occur are changes of position, job, or employer, not of occupation. Substages: *Trial-Commitment and Stabilization* (25 – 30) Settling down. Securing a permanent place in the chosen occupation. May prove unsatisfactory resulting in one or two changes before the life work is found or before it becomes clear that the life work will be a succession of unrelated jobs. *Advancement* (31 – 44) Effort is put forth to stabilize, to make a secure place in the world of work. For most persons these are the creative years. Seniority is acquired; clientele are developed; superior performance is demonstrated; qualifications are improved.	*44 years* Having made a place in the world of work, the concern is how to hold on to it. Little new ground is broken, continuation of established pattern. Concerned about maintaining present status while being forced by competition from younger workers in the advancement stage. Tasks: Accepting one's limitations. Identifying new problems to work on. Developing new skills. Focusing on essential activities. Preservation of achieved status and gains. **Decline** *64 years* As physical and mental powers decline, work activity changes and in due course ceases. New roles must be developed: first, selective participant and then observer.

Tasks: Developing a picture of the kind of person one is. Developing an orientation to the world of work and an understanding of the meaning of work.	Tasks: Implementing a Vocational Preference. Developing a realistic self-concept. Learning more about more opportunities.	Tasks: Finding opportunity to do desired work. Learning to relate to others. Consolidation and advancement. Making occupational position secure. Settling down in a permanent position.	Individual must find other sources of satisfaction to replace those lost through retirement. Substages: *Deceleration* (65 – 70) The pace of work slackens, duties are shifted, or the nature of the work is changed to suit declining capacities. Many men find part-time jobs to replace their full-time occupations. *Retirement* (71 on) Variation on complete cessation of work or shift to part-time, volunteer, or leisure activities. Tasks: Developing non-occupational roles. Finding a good retirement spot. Doing things one has always wanted to do. Reducing working hours.

ements of career maturity, particularly as they have implications for preadolescents and adolescents, and more recently, for adults.

The Career Pattern Study has focused principally on the exploratory and establishment steps of career development. It has been assumed that these are the stages crucial to education and, in particular, to curriculum development and guidance. As Table 6.3 illustrates, the developmental tasks that span these two life stages (from approximately age 14 to 25 plus) are as follows (you might wish to review the appropriate sections discussed in Chapter 4):

- Crystallizing a vocational preference
- Specifying it
- Implementing it
- Stabilizing in the chosen vocation
- Consolidating one's status
- Advancing in the occupation

Crystallizing a vocational preference has to do with the individual's "formulating ideas as to fields, and levels of work which are appropriate for him, self and occupational concepts which will enable him, if necessary, to make tentative choices, that is, to commit himself to a type of education or training which will lead him toward some partially specified occupation" (Super, Starishevsky, Matlin, & Jordaan, 1963, p. 82). Specifying a vocational preference is the "singling out of a specific occupation and the attitude (not the act) of commitment to it" (p. 82). Implementing the preference is converting it into a reality. Thus, these separate stages are divided between all the factors in formulating a preference, on the one hand, and those in formulating an actual choice on the other. In this context, choice can be represented by entering a postsecondary educational program designed to prepare one for a preferred goal or in entering employment and receiving on-the-job training in a particular area of work performance.

The implication of this line of reasoning is that the major emphasis in career development to the twelfth-grade level is on enabling the individual to crystallize and specify preferences or to anticipate the act of choice. However, it is also obvious that many adolescents or high school graduates have not attained such maturity. Thus, college student personnel programs, industrial relations efforts, and rehabilitation programs or other community-based programs will need to provide opportunities for clients and workers to develop these same insights and skills in an abbreviated, accelerated time frame. Indeed, as other parts of this book indicate, many adults served by community agencies or by career services in business and industry are as ignorant about themselves and their opportunities as are children and youth. Therefore, the same type of planning content will be useful in developing programs focused on a stimulus approach.

What, then, are the behaviors or attitudes that foster the crystallization or specification of a vocational preference? What subelements could be set forth in a chart similar to Table 6.3? One such list is as follows, paraphrased from the work of Super, Starishevsky, Matlin, and Jordaan (1963):

1. *Awareness of the need to crystallize*—Fundamentally, this attitude acts as a precursor of those which follow. It has to do with developing an attitude of readiness to involve oneself in the succeeding elements. This is perhaps more adequately described by Jordaan (1963) as becoming oriented to the need to explore.

2. *Use of resources*—This element is principally a set of instrumental behaviors by which one copes with exploration, whether it is focused on self-understanding or occupational description; it is present in relation to many persons or objects: parents, counselors, teachers, materials, part-time jobs, employers.

3. *Awareness of factors to consider in formulating a vocational preference*—This involves knowledge of the possible bases for preferences—whether intellectual requirements, relationship between interests and appropriate outlets, need for alternatives, or availability of outlets for different self-characteristics, that is, security, prestige.

4. *Awareness of contingencies that may affect vocational goals*—The existing evidence suggests that this element and items 2 and 3 collectively contribute to narrowing preferences and adding stability to those preferences which remain. Fundamentally, this element concerns the factors that may impede implementation of a particular preference, and the alternatives that can be actualized if necessary.

5. *Differentiation of interests and values*—This element refers to the ability of the individual to differentiate the personally important from the unimportant and to concentrate attention on certain objectives and activities rather than others as a basis for decision making and for action.

6. *Awareness of present-future relationships*—This factor is concerned with coming to terms with the interrelationship between present activities and intermediate or ultimate vocational activities: for example, understanding educational avenues and their requirements as these provide access to different fields or levels of occupational activity.

7. *Formulation of a generalized preference*—All the factors described to this point should culminate in the formulation of a generalized preference, or crystallization. This level of preference is less a specific occupation than a general one out of which further specification will ensue. In such cases, the preference represented by a particular occupational title is likely to symbolize related activities that are liked rather than a specific occupation.

8. *Consistency of preference*—Consistency may be primarily verbal, or it may be manifested instrumentally in course selection and in such areas as extracurricular or part-time occupational activities.

9. *Possession of information on the preferred occupation*—This element represents possession of more specific information about the generalized preference. It is characterized by greater variety and accuracy of information and by better understanding than is represented by the formulation of a generalized preference.

10. *Planning for the preferred occupation*—The focus here is on deciding what to do and when and how to do it. As Super and Overstreet demonstrated in their work in 1960, specificity both of planning and of information are measurable characteristics of vocational maturity in early adolescence.

11. *Wisdom of the vocational preference*—This is in large measure a criterion of the previous elements. Although certain external criteria can be applied, it is generally assumed that wisdom is really more a function of the process by which a preference is developed than the preference itself.

12. *Specification*—This level of vocationalization represents elaboration of the preference, that is, more specific information and planning, a greater commitment to the preference, and a refinement of the steps already described, with a sharper focus on the particular preference and the steps preceding implementation (pp. 84–87).

Analyses (Jordaan & Heyde, 1979, Super, 1974,1969a) of the studies within the Career Pattern Study concerned with the elements just identified affirmed the importance of planfulness and time perspective at the ninth grade. Also, although ninth-grade boys did not understand themselves or the world of work enough to make sound vocational or prevocational decisions, these manifestations of career maturity were related to ability, to opportunity for the arousal of interest and the use of abilities, and to taking advantage of such opportunities.

Further, these studies found that career maturity factors common at both the ninth and twelfth grades included occupational information (educational, psychological, and economic) as well as planning, independence, crystallization of interests, and specification and implementation of preferences (Super, 1969a). Super further reported that the available data suggest that the "realism of the late teens is more the reality of the self, of its abilities and interests, than that of opportunities beyond the realm of personal experience." More important, however, is this finding:

> Vocational maturity in the ninth grade, judged by occupational information, planning and interest maturity, was significantly related to vocational success in young adulthood. . . . In the twelfth grade vocational maturity, judged by the same measures as in grade nine, proved even more valid. Information about training and education required for the preferred occupation yielded a significant number of anticipated relationships. Those with educational and occupational level attained by age 25 were moderately high, and those with career development and stabilizing-floundering were fair . . . measures of awareness of choices to be made and of information and planning bearing on the choices, which seemed to have some construct validity in ninth grade and twelfth grade have predictive validity for vocational development in young adulthood. (pp. 5–6)

These studies have somewhat tempered earlier findings (Super & Overstreet, 1960) that ninth-grade boys cannot yet make sound decisions about fields or even levels of work. In other words, these later studies show that aspects of career maturity at the ninth grade more accurately predict career maturity at the twelfth grade and at age 25 than had been found earlier. Further, since these studies demonstrate that some students reach a level of career maturity at ninth grade that predicts career maturity at age 25, they support the theory that career guidance or education can stimulate career development for a great many other students and that career behavior can be modified.

Additional support for direct attention to career development as a dimension of general education is implicit in findings reported by Super (1969b, p. 18), in which he states, "Boys who are given opportunities in school and out-of-school and who use these opportunities during their school years tend also to make good use of their later career opportunities." Thus, it has been found that measures of career maturity in high school predict career success better than do the conventional predictions based on test scores or grades, and better than occupational success; in other words, how boys deal with developmental tasks at one stage tells something about their maturity later in life. It further stresses that in the early growth years, the foundations of later careers are laid.

In comparing career maturity in adolescence and in middle adulthood, Super (1977, p. 296) contends that although the decision-making principles remain the same, the content differs, particularly in the "universality of awarenesses and information needed in adolescence, compared to the particularity required in adulthood." These aspects of particularity can be seen in the dimensions of the Adult Center Adaptability model he has recently identified and presented here as Table 6.4 (Super, 1985, p. 12). Thus, while the same behavioral factors—planfulness, exploration information, decision-making and reality orientation—are important in adolescence and in adulthood, the content in adulthood becomes more specific in its focus.

As indicated in Chapter 4, throughout the history of the Career Pattern Study, the self-

Table 6.4

A Model of Adult Career Adaptability

I. Planfulness
  A. Autonomy-Responsibility
    1. Educational Planning
    2. Occupational Planning
  B. Time Perspective
    1 Past: Reflection
      a. Crystallizing
      b. Specifying
      c. Implementing
    2. Present-Immediate Future
      a. Stabilizing
      b. Consolidating
      c. Advancing
    3. Intermediate Future-Present
      a. Holding
      b. Keeping up
      c. Innovating
    4. Distant Future
      a. Tapering off
      b. Preparing to retire
      c. Retiring
II. Exploration
  A. Querying
    1. Self
      a. In time-life stage
      b. In space-roles
    2. Situation
      a. In time-organization
      b. In space-life style
  B. Resources (Attitudes toward)
    1. Awareness
    2. Valuation
    3. Willing to Use
  C. Participation-Use
    1. In-House
    2. Community
III. Information
  A. Life Stages
    1. Time Spans
    2. Characteristics
    3. Developmental Tasks
  B. Coping Behaviors
    1. Coping Options
    2. Appropriateness
  C. Available Outlets
    1. Organizational
    2. Job
    3. Occupational
  D. Implementation-Access
    3. Probable Outcomes
IV. Decision-Making
  A. Principles
    1. Knowledge
    2. Valuation
  B. Applications
    1. Use in Past: Styles
    2. Use at Present
V. Reality Orientation
  A. Self-Knowledge
    1. Traits
    2. Performance
  B. Realism
    1. Resources-Access
    2. Prospects
  C. Consistency of Preferences
    1. Current
    2. Over Time
  D. Crystallization
    1. Self-concept Clarity
    2. Goal Certainty
  E. Work Experience
    1. Floundering vs. Stabilizing
    2. Stabilizing or Maintaining vs. Declining in Midcareer

Source: From Donald E. Super, *New Dimensions in Adult Vocational and Career Counseling*. (Columbus, Ohio: Center on Education and Training for Employment (formerly NCRVE), Ohio State University. Copyright 1985.) Used with permission.

concept in career development has been the synthesizing agent. Super (1951, 1953) has proposed that

> In expressing a vocational preference, a person puts into occupational terminology his ideas of the kind of person he is, in entering an occupation, he seeks to implement his self-concept, and in stabilizing in an occupation he attempts to achieve self-actualization. In a chronological sense, three phases of self-concept evolution occur: formation, translation and implementation. Through growth and learning as well as the constant interaction of the individual with external influences the self-concept system is modified and adjusted until a synthesis is finally evolved. (p. 185)

Each of the crucial phases of the evolving self-concept has certain emphases and processes integral to it (Super, 1969b):

> 1. The formation process includes exploration of the self and of the environment, the differentiation of the self from others, identification with others who can serve as models, and the playing of these selected roles with more or less conscious evaluation of the result (reality testing).
>
> 2. The translation of self-concepts into occupational terms may take place through identification with an adult role model ("I am like him" or "I want to be like him"), experience in a role in which one has been cast, or learning that some of one's attributes should make one fit well into a certain occupation.
>
> 3. The implementation process involves action as in obtaining the specialized education or training needed for the preferred occupation or finding employment in it (p. 19).

In sum, theory and research support the self-concept as a dynamic factor in shaping individual behavior. As Herr has noted (1970),

> Motivation, perseverance, choice, and generalized behavior each relate to the labels persons apply to the different aspects of the self and to the elements which comprise the contexts or situations with which they do or expect to interact. Self-labels, or self-concepts, represent the pieces making up the composite self-picture, the self-concept system, one uses to trigger or restrain particular modes of behavior under specific contingencies. One's self-concept may be an accurate representation of the self, it may be distorted, or it may be obscure either in general or under specific conditions (p. 67).

Suggested Input to Program Goals of Stimulus or Exploration. The theory and research emanating from Super's Career Pattern Study, the related work of Gribbons and Lohnes, and the perspectives of Havighurst, Erikson, Levenson, and Hall have been treated as examples of appropriate input in formulating career guidance program rationale, program goals, and indeed, performance objectives that are concerned with facilitating exploration, choice, anticipation, and adaptability. However, before turning to the specific matter of formulating program goals and objectives per se, some synthesis of the aforementioned data is necessary.

In order to attain different aspects of career maturity, students, employees, or other adult clients need a comprehensive body of information that links what they are doing educationally at particular times to future options in both education and work. They need to know what curricula or training opportunities will be available to them, what factors distinguish one curriculum or training opportunity from another, what components make up separate curricular pathways, what personal factors are relevant to success in different curricula, and how the various curricula are linked to different field and level responsibilities in the occupational world.

Students and adult clients also need self-knowledge. They need to be able to differentiate personal values and personal interests as these relate to personal strengths and weaknesses in abilities—verbal, quantitative, and scholastic. They need to be able to assess these elements of the self, to incorporate their meaning into the self-concept, and to relate this self-information to the choices with which they will be confronted.

Students and adults also need to understand the characteristics of the organizations in which they work or are likely to work as these determine role relationships, social relations, flexibility of coping behavior, level and kind of consumption, and changes probable throughout their occupational history.

Transcending this necessary base of knowledge is the motivation to use it in purposeful ways, or, as Clarke, Gelatt, and Levine (1965, p. 41) observe, to develop "an effective strategy for analyzing, organizing, and synthesizing information in order to make a choice." In the making of decisions, there are skills that can be learned. Once a person has made a plan for some segment of life with which he or she is content to live, that person can make the next plan more intelligently and with less hesitation or conflict. But it must be remembered that one cannot make occupational or career decisions without educational implications and vice versa. Nor can effective planning and choice making occur without one's recognizing and assessing the psychological and emotional implications of various decisions.

The studies of Super and his colleagues emphasize attitudes of planfulness, recognition of possible alternative actions, and ways to assess the desirability of outcomes on the basis of personal preferences and values. Students and adults can be helped to evaluate the sequence of outcomes of immediate choice—proximate, intermediate, ultimate—as well as the factors that are personally relevant at experiential branch points, the probabilities associated with these factors, and the personal desirability of the three outcomes in the sequence. The fostering of planfulness and of career development involves providing the person not only with knowledge, but also with opportunities to apply the knowledge to his or her personal characteristics. Vocationalization efforts must, among other things, help individuals bring to work a sense of value, ego-involvement, personal endeavor, and achievement motivation.

Table 6.5 synthesizes, in gross terms, some of the emphases within the time spans most appropriate to vocationalization, through young adulthood, thus providing an organizing framework for developing goals and objectives for career guidance programs emphasizing exploration and choice. Although these tasks normally occur in adolescence and young adulthood, career guidance programs for older adults that focus on exploration and choice will probably need to include such content as the recurring minicycles of choice and career redirection described in Chapters 12 and 13.

Input for Programs of Induction or Orientation. Before leaving stage 1, it is important to note that conceptualizations of input to the ingredients of career maturity are basic to planning for career guidance programs that have stimulus, career exploration, or the facilitation of anticipation or choice as their major goals. To date, most planning concepts have been devoted to such purposes rather than to induction or orientation. The lack of conceptualization appropriate to these areas is fertile soil for both the application of theory and research. Nevertheless, there are career guidance programs in which the major goals are induction or orientation. Such programs have various settings. They are particularly prevalent in colleges and universities and in business and industry. They are concerned with the behaviors of persons as they attempt to implement their preferences in the realities of a curriculum or a work setting and as they advance beyond exploration and anticipation to actual implementation of their preferences, induction into the realities of the work environment, and advancement in the occupation or the corporation they have chosen for themselves.

Table 6.5

Synthesis of Inputs to Vocationalization and Career Maturity Through Young Adulthood

Approximate Ages ⟶

Pre-school	5-9	10-14	15	18	19-25

Formation of self-concept ⟶ Translation of self-concept into vocational terms ⟶ Implementation of self-concept

Developing preference or anticipation ⟶ choice ⟶ induction ⟶ reformation ⟶ integration

Fantasy ⟶ Tentative ⟶ Realistic

Trial (with little commitment) Trial (more commitment) ⟶ stabilization ⟶ advancement

Awareness of the need to crystallize (orienting) ⟶ Use of resources (exploring) ⟶

⟶ Formulating interests ⟶ Relating interests and capabilities Relating interests and capacities to values
⟶ Developing a vocabulary of self ⟶
⟶ Developing a vocabulary of work ⟶
⟶ Rudiments of basic trust in self and others ⟶
⟶ Rudiments of initiative ⟶
⟶ Rudiments of industry ⟶
⟶ Knowledge of fundamentals of technology ⟶
⟶ Differentiating self from environment ⟶
⟶ Identification with a worker ⟶
⟶ Developing sex social role ⟶
⟶ Learning rudiments of social rules ⟶
⟶ Learning fundamental intellectual, physical and motor skills

Awareness of factors to consider in formulating a vocational preference
Awareness of contingencies which affect vocational goals
Differentiation of interests and values
Awareness of present-future relationships
Accepting oneself as in process
Relating changes in the self to changes in the world
Acquiring basic habits of industry
Learning to organize one's time and energy to get work done
Learning to defer gratification, to set priorities
Achieving personal identity

Acquiring knowledge of life in organizations
Preparation for role relationships
Preparation for level and kind of consumption
Preparation for an occupational career
Formulation of generalized preference
Possession of information concerning the preferred occupation
Planning for the preferred occupation

Choosing and preparing for occupation
Achieving more mature relations with peers of both sexes
Achieving emotional independence of parents and other adults

Preparing for marriage selecting a mate
Developing capability for intimacy
Starting a family
Becoming a productive person
Mastering the skills of an occupation
Moving up the ladder within the occupation
Acquiring career resilience, career insight, career identifications

Developing planfulness
Developing decision-making strategies
Independence of choice

Role-playing, Identification ⟶ Role-playing, curricula exposure ⟶ reality testing ⟶ work study
attitudes of others ⟶ identification ⟶ self-appraisal

If Super's work in specifying the ingredients of career maturity is the major input to planning career guidance programs concerned with exploration and anticipation, Tiedeman's (1961) concepts are helpful in considering induction or orientation. As discussed in Chapter 4, Tiedeman has described the period of implementation and adjustment, which follows the period of anticipation, as consisting of three emphases: induction, reformation, and integration. This process suggests that in the early stages of *implementation*, the individual is largely responsive to environmental expectations, work norms, role definitions, personal possibilities available in the setting, and so on. If the individual's ability to take on these role expectations is not stretched beyond limits of tolerance and can be accommodated in the self-concept system, the individual is likely to remain in the position and move to the second stage, *reformation*. In that stage, the individual is likely to become more assertive, take more control of the setting or job, begin to impose certain personal demands on it, and begin to shape it to fit personal preferences and characteristics. In the third stage, *integration*, both the individual and the work setting are likely to have undergone some reciprocal shaping and change. Many of the role expectations of the setting have become part of the individual's work identity and self-concept, resulting in the individual's job satisfaction, and the environment has been rearranged to accommodate the personal idiosyncrasies of the worker as he or she plays out the role expectations. As the environment reinforces the individual worker's satisfactoriness and the worker gains satisfaction, integration leads to consolidation and advancement.

Schein (1971) has described induction into an organizational career in a conception of stages and transitions that also provides input to the planning of a career guidance or career development program. This is portrayed in Table 6.6.

Schein's work connects the stages of one's career in an organization with the processes that might be put in place in a career guidance program to facilitate that stage. The latter reflects what will be discussed in stage 3 of this chapter. Additional input to induction or orientation goals is also found in the research of Haccoun and Campbell (1972) and Campbell and Cellini (1981), discussed in the latter parts of Chapter 2, as well as in the models of Adult Career Adaptability recently proposed by Super (see Table 6.4).

What Schein's concepts and those of Campbell and Cellini, among others, illustrate is that it is not only the maxi- and minicycles of individual career development that are important in career guidance programs, but that such career development is also affected by organizational structures and expectations. Thus, different settings consist of or trigger different types of career transitions or organizational career stages. As reported elsewhere in the book, Dalton, Thompson, and Price (1977) have identified four progressive professional career stages in organizations: apprentice, colleague, mentor, and sponsor. Hall (1976) speaks of early career, middle career, and later career stages within organizations. Schein (1978) divides the career life cycle for organizations into four stages: entry, socialization, midcareer and later career. London and Stumpf (1986) speak of career motivation in the workplace as consisting of career resilience, career insight, and career identity. Regardless of which model one uses to explain career transition within organizations, each stage involves different activities, relationships, and psychologically related developmental tasks for different types of workers. As such, these stage requirements must lead to career guidance/career counseling programs that are tailored to the characteristics of the different industrial and corporate settings in which they are to be implemented.

Super's model of Adult Career Adaptability is less concerned with the organizational

Table 6.6

Interaction of Worker and Organization in Career

Basic Stages and Transitions	Statuses or Positions	Psychological and Organizational Processes; Transactions between Individual and Organization
1. Preentry	Aspirant, applicant, rushee	Preparation, education, anticipatory socialization.
Entry (trans.)	Entrant, postulant recruit	Recruitment, rushing, testing, screening, selection acceptance ("hiding"); passage through external inclusion boundary; rites of entry; induction and orientation
2. Basic training novitiate	Trainee, novice, pledge	Training, indoctrination, socialization, testing of the man by the organization, tentative acceptance into group.
Initiation, first vows (trans.)	Initiate, graduate	Passage through first inner inclusion boundary, acceptance as member and conferring of organizational status, rite of passage and acceptance.
3. First regular assignment	New member	First testing by the person of his own capacity to function; granting of real responsibility (playing for keeps); passage through functional boundary with assignment to specific job or department
Substages 3a. Learning the job 3b. Maximum performance 3c. Becoming obsolete 3d. Learning new skills, etc.		Indoctrination and testing of person by immediate work group leading to acceptance or rejection; if accepted further education and socialization (learning the ropes); preparation for higher status through coaching, seeking visibility, finding sponsors, etc.
Promotions or leveling off (trans.)		Preparations, testing, passage through hierarchical boundary, rite of passage; may involve passage through functional boundary as well (rotation).
4. Second assignment Substages	Legitimate member (fully accepted)	Process under No. 3 repeat.
5. Granting of tenure	Permanent member	Passage through another inclusion boundary.
Termination and exit (trans.)	Old-timer, senior citizen	Preparation for exit, cooling the mark out, rites of exit (testimonial dinners, etc.).
6. Post-exit	Alumnus emeritus retired	Granting of peripheral status

context in which such adaptability unfolds and much more with the behavioral elements that need to be addressed in facilitating such adaptability. In this model, planfulness, exploration, information, decision making, and reality orientation represent the major factors or themes to which either individual career counseling or career guidance programs might be addressed as essential elements of orientation or induction or, possibly, treatment.

Input to Treatment Program Goals. In the third emphasis in planning a career guidance program, one must often anticipate the need for treatment for some group of counselees. These are persons whose career development has been arrested or impaired or who have undergone trauma or disease sufficient to make their ability to choose or to experience work adjustment problematic. Many paradigms exist to explain such phenomena. A classic one is that of Leona Tyler (1969), who has differentiated counseling into choice and change. The assumption is that persons who need to accomplish personality change, independence from others, and similar psychological maturity cannot deal with choice dilemmas until they resolve the more fundamental personality issues with which they are currently preoccupied. Another useful paradigm is that of Goodstein (1972) who portrays indecision and indecisive behavior in relation to anxiety as an antecedent or a consequent of behavior. D'Alonzo and Fleming (1973) have suggested that the main psychiatric factors among employees and therefore the problems encountered in mental health programs in industry (as well as career guidance programs in business and industry) are as follows:

1. Improper discipline during childhood and youth ("Momism" at home or on the job)
2. Job adjustment and responsibility; the need of all people to face reality with its attendant successes and failures; learning to accept criticism and to compensate for defects
3. Family problems
4. Health worries
5. Miscellaneous fears, phobias, anxieties, and so on. (p. 164)

Together these types of behavior are manifested in absenteeism, excessive turnover, alcoholism, industrial accidents, lowered productivity, and labor strikes (Dawis, 1984).

As discussed in Chapter 2, Neff (1977, 1985) has identified several types of problem employees and the characteristics of their work psychopathology.

> Type I includes people who appear to have major lacks in work motivation; they have a negative conception of the role.
> Type II includes individuals whose predominating response to the demand to be productive is manifest fear and anxiety.
> Type III includes people who are predominantly characterized by open hostility and aggression.
> Type IV includes people who are characterized by marked dependency.
> Type V includes people who display a marked degree of social naivete (pp. 238–243).

Each of these types of persons requires differential treatment typically of significant intensity as well as differences in level of supervision, information, and personality change.

Within the growing trend to connect career counseling to mental or behavioral health as it relates to problems of unemployment and underemployment (Herr, 1989), as discussed in Chapter 1 and elsewhere in the book, there are also major implications for treatment of persons so affected as a major career guidance problem.

On balance, neither career guidance programs nor career counseling emphasizes treatment of severe psychological problems, however they are defined. But persons with severe problems of motivation or adjustment do come to career guidance programs and to career counselors for many reasons, including denial of the severity of their problems, because the career guidance program or counselor is the only mental health provision available, or because these persons believe philosophies and activities of career counseling will be helpful to them. Therefore, the career guidance and counseling practitioner must be prepared to deal with such treatment issues or to include, in program planning, procedures by which such persons will be referred or therapists will be placed on a consultative retainer to deal with such cases as they arise.

A Program Rationale for Planning. In summarizing stage 1 (developing a program rationale and philosophy), a particular school or college, corporation, or agency may synthesize from the foregoing steps a program rationale that includes the following assumptions:

1. Individuals can be equipped with accurate and relevant information translated into terms of personal development level and state of readiness.
2. Individuals can be assisted to formulate hypotheses about themselves, the choice points that will be in their future, and the options available to them.
3. Individuals can be helped to develop appropriate ways of testing these hypotheses against old and new experiences.
4. Individuals can be helped to come to terms with the educational and occupational relevance of what they already know or will learn about themselves and their futures.
5. Individuals can be helped to see themselves in process and to acquire the knowledge and skills that will allow them to exploit this process in positive, constructive ways.
6. Individuals acquire feelings of personal competence or power from self-understanding and the ability to choose effectively.

In addition, analysis of community, administrative, and consumer groups will have offered support or rejection of these assumptions and their priority in a career guidance program. Information will be acquired about whether or not the students or adults to be served by the program already possess such knowledge, skills, and behaviors or whether such outcomes need to be facilitated. As these judgments are made, they need to be translated into actual program goals and behavioral specifications for the students or adults who will be involved with the program.

Preceding the statement of program goals and behavioral objectives, most programs would typically have an introductory statement dealing in broad terms with several topics explaining, "Why career guidance?" These topics might include the following:

- Current social and occupational conditions faced by youth and adults
- Needs for career planning and other career guidance elements as perceived by students (adults) and community groups
- The present career guidance program
- Assumptions that guide new program thrusts
- Basic concepts of program directions

The particular content of such preliminary statements will vary from one setting to another. What is important in one setting with one type of population may not be important in another. The resources available (personnel, materials, money) to support the program as well as the amount of time the program will be in contact with the student or adult population to be served (12 years, 3 years, 4 years, 6 months, 3 sessions) will need to be considered as the actual program goals to be adopted are decided upon.

Stage 2—Stating Program Goals and Behavioral Objectives

Following the formulation of a rationale and philosophy for the career guidance program that answers, Why career guidance? it is necessary to decide on what will actually comprise the program. A review of career development theory will suggest many behaviors, types of knowledge, or skills that a career guidance program might facilitate. Conducting needs assessments, analyzing resources available, and deliberating on the characteristics of the target groups to be served in a particular setting will likely reduce the many possibilities to those that constitute the most important goals for a particular program.

In stage 2 of systematic planning, the primary purpose is to translate the needs for career guidance in a particular setting, as identified in stage 1, into program goals and behavioral expectations that are actually hypotheses saying that, if these goals are accomplished, the needs to which career guidance responds in this setting will be met or reduced, consistent with individual differences manifested by persons served by the program.

Program Goals. Program goals and behavioral expectations for students or clients differ in their specificity and in their purpose. Program goals are general statements of program purposes or outcomes. Program goals should not deal with the processes by which they will be accomplished but concentrate instead on the outcomes to be achieved. Program goals should reflect the philosophy, theory, and assumptions underlying a program as defined in stage 1 of systematic planning.

Examples of program goals in a particular setting might be as follows. As a result of the career guidance program all clients will do the following:

1. Develop vocabulary for distinguishing self-characteristics such as interests, aptitudes, values, roles, and self-concept
2. Understand their unique pattern of personal characteristics (such as abilities, interests, values, attitudes, and so on)
3. Attain a positive self-concept (that is, a sense of self-respect, personal worth, and respect for one's own uniqueness)
4. Understand the variety and complexity of occupations and career opportunities available locally and within the state
5. Understand the relationships between educational opportunities and occupational or career requirements
6. Determine the basic characteristics and qualifications related to preparation for and performance of various occupational roles
7. Understand the concept "life-style" and its relationship to career development
8. Learn how to effectively use a range of exploratory resources
9. Develop effective decision-making strategies and the skills necessary in carrying them out

These goals are client- or student-centered. In general terms, they make explicit the career guidance program's purposes, and they imply criteria by which their accomplishment might be judged. These are the global statements of outcomes around which the program will be structured. Decisions about behavioral expectations, processes, resource needs, and evaluative strategies will each flow from the statement of program goals.

Again, depending upon the particular setting, there are many such outcome statements or goals. For example, LaVan, Mathys, and Drehmer (1983) have identified some of the outcomes expected from counseling practices provided by major American corporations. They include the following:

Career Counseling

- The retention of middle and upper levels of managers compared to some base year
- Preparation of candidates for various positions selected from within versus hired externally
- Attitude survey results indicating such dimensions as the degree of satisfaction with promotional opportunities, or the degree to which personal interest and/or preferences are used in selection
- The degree to which the organization's counseling activity compares to known successful systems

While LaVan, Mathys, and Drehmer also talk about outcome indicators for out-placement counseling, personal problem counseling, retirement counseling, and alcoholism and drug counseling, those cited for career counseling within the corporate environment accent the importance of program goals being seen in terms of the expectations and outcome indicators indigenous to particular settings.

Another way to consider the development of program goals and their associated competencies and indicators is through use of the resources provided by the National Occupational Information Coordinating Committee (1988). In particular, the multi-volume work *National Career Counseling and Development Guidelines* provides recommended competencies and indicators for each competency for elementary schools, middle/junior high schools, high schools, postsecondary institutions, and human service agencies. The competencies represent general goals and the indicators represent specific knowledge, skills, and attitudes that individuals should master in order to deal effectively with lifelong career development tasks. The competencies at each level are consistent with the general developmental capabilities of individuals at that level.

Program goals, as we describe them, could be extrapolated from competencies as described by the National Occupational Information Coordinating Committee (NOICC). To illustrate how such goals might appear for young adults across the three areas of emphasis included in the Guidelines referenced above, the following goals could be cited:

- Career planning and exploration
  - Skills in making decisions about educational and career goals
  - Understanding of the impact of careers on individual and family life
  - Skills in developing career plans
- Self-knowledge
  - Maintenance of a positive view of self in terms of potential and preferences and assessment of their transferability to the world of work
  - Ability to assess self-defeating behaviors and reduce their impact on career decision
- Educational/vocational development
  - Ability to relate educational and occupational preparation to career opportunities
  - Skills for locating, evaluating and interpreting information about career opportunities
  - Skills for seeking, obtaining, keeping, and advancing on a job

Behavioral Objectives. Behavioral objectives, as compared to program goals, are more specific expressions of behavior. The specifying of statements of behavioral expectations for students or clients that underlie program goals is one of the most difficult aspects of systematic planning. It necessitates making value judgments of what people ought to be able to achieve, and it requires describing these in behavioral terms. Further, it frequently requires a range of behavioral expectations underlying each program goal so that individual differences in readiness or experience can be recognized.

As compared with program goals, behavioral statements for clients or students should describe observable performance or behaviors—outcomes that describe what individuals will be able to do, not what will be done to them. Program goals are usually stated so broadly that it is difficult to know when an employee or student has reached them, but behavioral objectives are measurable. Writing objectives require you to think of the performances that indicate that the program goal has been reached. In addition to writing objectives that are likely to be important to all consumers of the career guidance program, it is always important to remain flexible enough to accommodate individual objectives of a crisis nature or those that do not fit directly within the planned program emphases.

Approaches to Writing Objectives. The current emphases in objective development stress the importance of defining the outcomes of career guidance in terms of observable human peformance, citing the conditions under which they should be demonstrated, and determining the standard or criterion of success. Within this context, however, there are several ways of stating objectives based on different purposes.

The frame of reference used by the National Occupational Information Coordinating Committee's *National Career Counseling and Development Guidelines*, cited under the section on program goals, proceeds from competencies (Program Goals) to indicators (behavioral objectives). For example, one might use as an illustration the second competency under the area of self-knowledge, "Ability to assess self-defeating behaviors and reduce their impact on career decisions." According to the NOICC Guidelines, the indicators (behavioral objectives) important for a young adult to reach such a competency are as follows:

1. Identify symptoms of stress, fear, anxiety, avoidance, and ambivalence and apply coping strategies to deal with these.
2. Identify strategies for reducing discriminating attitudes and behaviors.
3. Recognize the symptoms of depression in self and others and identify sources of assistance.
4. Identify disadvantages of sex-role stereotyping and assess his/her behavior in relation to both women and men.
5. Develop behaviors, attitudes, and skills that contribute to the elimination of stereotyping and bias in education, family, and work environment.
6. Develop skills to manage resources.

The reader will note that the indicators (or behavioral objectives) used as examples do not describe broad, general career development goals as do program goals. Rather, these indicators describe specific attitudes, knowledge, and skills that students or adults need in order to develop the competencies or program goals to which the indicators are related. As such, they describe the outcomes sought and can be wedded to standards that identify the conditions under which they will take place. For example, when merged with a standard, the first indicator cited above might be rewritten in this way:

1. Identify 10 symptoms of stress, fear, anxiety avoidance, and ambivalence and present a 15-minute lecturette on coping strategies to deal with these symptoms.

This form of writing behavioral objectives is consistent with the history of writing behavioral objectives in its emphasis on the skill or behavior involved, the domain of concern, and some standard by which to judge whether the intended behavior has been achieved. Probably the best-known approach to writing objectives using such a model is that advanced by Mager (1962).

According to the Mager approach, a statement of objectives is a collection of words or symbols that describe an educational intent. Such a statement should include (1) what the individual will be doing (terminal behavior) when demonstrating his or her achievement, (2) the important conditions under which the terminal behavior is to occur, and (3) a criterion of acceptable performance or standard that indicates when the learner has successfully demonstrated his or her achievement. An objective relevant to career guidance developed in line with these criteria is as follows: Given ten occupations, the student must be able to correctly identify, by labeling, the minimum educational requirements of at least nine of them.

The latter format for writing objectives provides, to a greater degree than others, behavioral descriptions that, when analyzed with other data, permit evaluation of whether an individual has accomplished the established goals. However, such a format represents the potential dangers of becoming too restrictive either in criterion of success used, the evaluation activities, or the requirement that all persons accomplish goals in the same way.

Obviously, each career guidance program will need to develop independently a set of operationally stated objectives to guide its program's effort in fostering career development in the students or clients for whom it is responsible. The particular objectives developed will reflect the clients' characteristics as well as the available resources. Measures of individual performance of these objects will also be necessary. In schools, agencies, business or industrial settings, or other career guidance settings, where there is great variability in the personal histories of the students or the clients, it will also be necessary to assess the degree to which individuals or groups can already perform the behavior. Finally, as such a system is implemented, it will be necessary to continuously evaluate whether the career guidance activities designed to accomplish the objectives are actually bringing about changes in the behavior of the persons exposed to them.

Table 6.7 presents some sample objectives that might be used at different educational levels to facilitate particular emphases on career development. They are not exhaustive, nor are they necessarily the right objectives for a given situation. Indeed, they make sense only as they relate to different program goals, and as they describe behaviors that seem to relate to such goals. They do blend, however, some of the research inputs contributing to career maturity, previously discussed in this chapter, with strategies for developing objectives. As the key illustrates, separate objectives roughly approximate different levels of the cognitive and affective domains. For example, an objective followed by a (C,K) indicates that the objective is from the *cognitive domain* and assesses *knowledge*; an (A,Re) means that the objective is the *affective domain* and assesses *receiving*. The reader is also encouraged to study the work of Simpson (1972), if the development of psychomotor objectives is called for.

Table 6.7 indicates that the development of behavioral objectives, using a Mager approach, should include either quantitative or qualitative criteria for assessing the behavior. If used for a career guidance program that will extend over a long period of time, these behavioral objectives should be consistent with student or client capability at different developmental levels. This same format can be used in developing career guidance objectives for college student personnel programs, or for adults in business and industry, although the time available for such programs will probably be less than in the public schools and the clientele more diverse.

Gronlund (1970), in reviewing the format proposed by Mager for developing objectives, suggests that such an approach is most useful when the desired outcome is to have all students or clients perform alike at a specified minimum level. Gronlund maintains that in addition to stating objectives in terms of minimum essentials, it is necessary to state more complex objectives in such form that they encourage each person to progress as far as possible toward predetermined goals. Thus, the objective to be attained is stated in a general form and is followed by specific samples of representative behaviors at different levels of complexity. Being able to accomplish any one of the behaviors is sufficient to satisfy the goal. However, not every person must accomplish the same behavioral objective and, therefore, individualization is possible. An example of this kind of objective appropriate to career guidance is as follows:

Objective: Understands the interdependence of the occupational structure

1. States the principle of interdependence in his or her own words
2. Gives an example of the principle
3. Identifies work orientations—such as data, people, things—which contribute to interdependence
4. Distinguishes between field and level lattices in job families as representative of interdependence

None of the methods of writing objectives is more correct or desirable than any other. The format to use depends on the purposes to be served, the general style of the planning system being developed, or the previous format for goal and behavior being used in the particular setting. Indeed, many exiting models of systematic planning blend the NOICC, Mager, or Gronlund models of writing objectives into a system that is locally relevant.

With the rise of career education since 1971, many efforts have been undertaken to formulate models of tasks that persons need to perform in order to master the many elements comprising career maturity. One such model is the specification of career management tasks by Tennyson, Hansen, Klaurens, and Antholz (1975). Their paradigm reflects a developmental view of career development, including the specification of tasks appropriate to different life stages. These career management tasks and the stages associated with them are shown in Table 6.8.

Each of these tasks could be considered a program goal around which career guidance efforts would be implemented. This model also identifies career management tasks appropriate to persons beyond high-school, or, indeed, into adulthood. These tasks include the following:

I. Developing interpersonal skills essential to work
II. Developing information processing skills about self and the world of work
III. Reintegration of the self
IV. Acquiring a sense of community
V. Commitment to a concept of career
VI. Acquiring the determination to participate in change
VII. Creative application of management skills to life roles

In relation to each of these tasks are behavioral indicators that research suggests underlie the task identified. Each of the career management tasks is broken down into performance objectives and enabling objectives. For example, at the senior high school level, the first management task is "reality testing of a self-concept." The performance objective and enabling objectives associated with this task are as follows:

PO #1 Describes his own abilities, aptitudes, and other personal resources in relation to the requirements for preferred occupations

EO #1 Identifies both actual and potential personal objectives

EO #2 Describes the physical, mental, social, economic, and educational requirements of his preferred occupation

The Minnesota model (Table 6.8) just described is illustrative of a number of models that have evolved from a comprehensive theoretical base and systematic planning. Another is the National School-Based Comprehensive Career Education Model I developed in 1971. The planning in this model included the identification of elements, themes, goal statements, and performance objectives. Each element is composed of several themes and these, in turn, are further reduced to more explicit statements

Table 6.7

Sample Objectives to Facilitate Career Development at Different Educational Levels

Elementary School	Junior High School	Senior High School
In an oral exercise, the student can identify at least six types of workers who contributed to building his school (C,K)	The student verbally differentiates self-characteristics (e.g., interests, values, abilities, personality traits) and expresses tentative occupational choices that might provide outlets for each (C,C)	The student reality-tests broad occupational preferences systematically relating them to personal achievement in different courses, part-time work, extracurricular activities (A,O)
In a flannel-board presentation, the student can label, according to their tools or clothing, ten different types of workers found in the community (C,K)	The student can accurately appraise on a written profile his or her measured ability, achievement level, and current interests (C,An)	The student analyzes his or her present competency in skills necessary to broad occupational preference and develops a plan by which these can be enhanced where necessary (C,An)
The student can check vocabulary items correctly as being names of interests, aptitudes, or abilities (C,K)	The student can place on a skilled/unskilled continuum twenty occupations about which he or she has read (C,K)	Given a part-time job in school or out of school, the student is able to list the advantages and disadvantages it might offer in terms of personal interests of values (C,C)
The student can select from a list of ten alternatives the five best reasons for planning his or her time (A, Re)	From a dramatization portraying five different ways of valuing different methods of handling daily events, the student can consistently identify and describe the value set with which he or she feels most comfortable (A,V)	From a series of case studies about working conditions as they affect individuals with different characterstics, the student can identify patterns of coping behavior and discuss their personal implications under similar circumstances (C,E)
The student can correctly list major breakdowns of the occupational structure: e.g., communications, manufacturing, distribution, transportation, or professional/skilled/semiskilled/unskilled (C,C)	The student can weigh alternative outcomes from different kinds of work in relation to the public welfare and rank order these outcomes in terms of personal preference (A,O)	The student executes plans to qualify for an entry-level position by choosing appropriate courses at the high school level (A,V)
The student can prepare a graph showing the different educational alternatives available: junior high school, high school, community college, area vocational technical school, college, apprenticeships, armed forces (C,Ap)	The student observes the five films and then lists the major differences in the technological processes observed (A,Re)	The student produces a plan of alternative ways of accomplishing educational (occupational) goals if the first choice is not successfully implemented (C,Sy)
The student can arrange in appropriate rank order the number of years of schooling associated with different educational alternatives in (C,C)	Using the *Dictionary of Occupational Titles,* the student can identify ten occupations that are ranked highest in dealing with people, things, or data (C,Ap)	The student can differentiate between the major occupations that make up a broad occupational area or a job cluster in terms of (1) the amount and type of education needed for entrance, (2) the content, tools, setting, products, or services of these occupations, (3) their values to society, (4) their probability of providing the type of life style desired, and (5) their relationship to personal interests and values (C,E)
The student can classify the titles of courses available in the junior high school and senior high school and the types of content with which they are concerned (C,C)	After a field trip to a factory, the student can tell in his or her own words the differences in work conditions or procedures observed in different parts of the plant (C,An)	
The student voluntarily discusses the importance of work and how education helps one to work effectively (A,Rs)	The student is able to assess in rank order the personal value of each of ten occupational clusters (C,An)	

The student can select from a table models of tools or instruments used in ten different occupations (C,An)

The student can role play three occupations which are of most personal interest (C,Sy)

The student can demonstrate how certain knowledge and skills acquired in different school subjects are applied in different work roles (C,Ap)

The student can identify the skills in which he or she feels most confident and role plays workers who might need these skills (C,E)

The student can role play interpretations of the values workers might hold in four different occupations (C,E)

The student is willing to share with others the planning and presenting of a play about work and being a worker (A,V)

The student discusses the importance of teamwork in different work settings, cooperates with others in order to reach a common goal, and can express the importance of his or her contributions and that of others in reaching a common goal (A,O)

During school activities, the student expesses or demonstrates a positive attitude toward self, others, edutation, and different types or work roles (A,CCV)

The student can describe in essay form how knowledge and skills acquired in different subject matter areas relate to performing different work roles (C,Ap)

The student can identify and define ten forms of continuing education following high school including apprenticeships, on-the-job training, correspondence courses, armed forces service schools, evening schools, reading (C,C)

The student completes an assigned job analysis according to instructions and on time (A,Rs)

The student can compare correctly the social roles which describe a supervisor and a follower (C,Sy)

The student can identify, locate, and describe the use of five directories listing post-secondary educational opportunities at college, junior college, and technical levels (C,Ap)

The student can identify in a gaming situation future decisions to be made in order to reach different goals (C,Sy)

The student can identify, assess, and defend an anaylsis of possible steps that might be taken to minimize personal limitations and maximize assets (C,E)

The student continuously explores and synthesizes the relationships between tentative choices and demonstrated abilities (A,V)

The student can describe personal and environmental contingencies that could impinge on future decisions (C,E)

The student can differentiate occupational areas in terms of (1) a potential satisfaction each might offer, (2) the work tasks performed, (3) the future impact technology could have on occupational areas, (4) the future demand for workers in those areas (C,E)

The student considers five different categories of post-secondary education, chooses one, and defines the reason for choosing it (C,C)

The student develops a plan of access to the next step after high school, either educational or occupational, listing possible alternatives, whom to contact, application dates, capital investment necessary, the self-characteristics to be included on a resumé (C,Ap)

Given an identified social problem — e.g., air pollution, rehabilitation of drug users, the development of new uses for materials, creating by-products of fishery harvesting — the student can create a lattice of occupations at different levels which might contribute to resolving the problem. (The student may use as a reference the *Dictionary of Occupational Titles* or the *Occupational Outlook Handbook*) (C,E)

The student makes adjustments in planning, use of resources, and exploratory experiences necessary to maintain progress toward achievement of goals (A,O)

The student verbalizes feelings of competence and adequacy in those tasks which have relationships to personal vocational preference (A,CCV)

The student takes specific steps to implement a post-secondary educational plan (A,CCV)

The student takes specific steps to implement a post-secondary vocational preference (A,CCV)

The student demonstrates ability to judge personal choices in terms of situations, issues, purposes, and consequences rather than in terms of rigidity or wishful thinking (A,CCV)

KEY: (C,K) = Cognitive-Knowledge; (C,C) = Cognitive-Comprehension; (C,Ap) = Cognitive-Application; (C,An) = Cognitive Analysis; (C,Sy) = Cognitive-Synthesis; (C,E) = Cognitive-Evaluation; (A,Re) = Affective-Receiving; (A,Rs) = Affective-Responding; (A,V) = Affective-Valuing; (A,O) = Affective-Organization; (A,CC) = Affective-Characterization by a value or value complex.

Table 6.8

The CDC Career Management Tasks

Attending Stages — Grades K–3
1. Awareness of self
2. Acquiring a sense of control over one's life
3. Identification with workers
4. Acquiring knowledge about workers
5. Acquiring interpersonal skills
6. Ability to present oneself objectively
7. Acquiring respect for other people and the work they do

Responding Stage — Grades 4–6
1. Developing a positive self-concept
2. Acquiring the discipline of work
3. Identification with the concept of work as a valued institution
4. Increasing knowledge about workers
5. Increasing interpersonal skills
6. Increasing ability to present oneself objectively
7. Valuing human dignity

Asserting Stage — Grades 7–9
1. Clarification of a self-concept
2. Assumption of responsibility for career planning
3. Forumulation of tentative career goals
4. Acquiring knowledge of occupations, work settings, and life styles
5. Acquiring knowledge of educational and vocational resources
6. Awareness of the decision-making process
7. Acquiring a sense of independence

Organizing Stage — Grades 10–12
1. Reality testing of a self-concept
2. Awareness of preferred life style
3. Reformulation of tentative career goals
4. Increasing knowledge of and experience in occupations and work settings
5. Acquiring knowledge of educational and vocational paths
6. Clarification of the decision-making process as related to self
7. Commitment with tentativeness within a changing world

Source: Tennyson, Hansen, Klaurens, & Antholz, 1975.

of expected behaviors. An example might be the element "self-awareness," as it applies to grade nine. The appropriate theme under that element would be, "The student will come to recognize the relationship of his interests, aptitudes, and achievements to realization of his career aspirations." This element and theme are in turn translated into goal statements and performance objectives as shown in Table 6.9.

Another approach that graphically identifies the various levels of planning is the one formulated in the Career Guidance, Counseling and Placement Project at the University of Missouri—Columbia (1973). In this project,

Table 6.9

Goal Statements and Performance Objectives for one Aspect of Self-Awareness at Grade 9

Goal Statement	Performance Objective
A1.0 Students will utilize their aptitudes as measured by The General Aptitude Test Battery to access and explore related occupational information (WTG's).	A1.1 Students will be able to identify occupations (WTG's) which are related to their aptitudes.
B1.0 Students will develop a definitive notion (in their own words) of their aptitude strengths and weaknesses.	B1.1 Students will be able to rank their aptitudes (9 aptitudes of the GATB) according to their strengths.
	B1.2 Students will be able to list aptitude clusters representing their overall strengths and weaknesses (e.g., strengths in perceptual areas, strengths in performance areas, strengths in intellectual and academic areas.
C1.0 Students will utilize their aptitude strengths and weaknesses, likes and dislikes, personal achievements, etc. to project themselves into possible satisfying occupational situations (WTG).	C1.1 Students will be able to name and describe in essay form at least three occupations which they feel would be satisfying to them and explain why they feel the occupation would be satisfying.
D1.0 The student will apply or utilized understanding about his interests, personal achievements, aptitudes to develop educational and career goals.	D1.1 The student will compile a list of occupational and educational goals and explain his reasons for formulating his goals and objectives.
	D1.2 Given all the curriculum alternatives for the local school district, the student will be able to plan a course of studies consistent with his educational and occupational goals.

four domains facilitating a "career conscious individual" have been identified as pertinent to career guidance. They include self-knowledge and interpersonal skills, knowledge of work and leisure worlds, life-career planning knowledge and skills, and basic-studies and occupational preparation. Within each of these domains there are several steps: the identification of concepts pertinent to the domain, the specification of goals related to the concepts identified, the identification of developmental goals tied directly to an educational level, the translation of developmental goals into performance objectives indicating specific behavior an individual will be able to demonstrate as a result of a particular learning experience, and the identification of activities that will facilitate such learning. Table 6.10 portrays the presentation of only one such concept within the domain of life-career planning knowledge and skills.

Various state models also use variations on goals, objectives, competencies, and activities formats for planning career programs. For example, in 1990 the Florida Department of Education's *Blueprint for Career Preparation* described a six-year action plan that began in 1988. That "blueprint" included the following six steps:

1. Begin in kindergarten through fifth grade by developing in students an awareness of self, the value of work an exposure to careers and technology.

Table 6.10

Approach to Planning for Career Guidance, Counselor Placement for State Departments of Education Developed by University of Missouri—Columbia (1973)

Domain: Career Planning Concept: One's future is influenced by present planning. Goal 3.2: For the individual to understand the relationship between present planning and future outcomes.			
Dev. Goal 3.2: K–3 For the individual to understand the consequences of his decision-making.	Dev. Goal 3.2: 4–6 For the individual to understand that previous decisions will affect present and future decisions.	Dev. Goal 3.2: 7–9 For the individual to understand the need to re-examine decisions regarding future long-range career responsibilities.	Dev. Goal 3.2: 10–12 For the individual to understand the need to reconsider goals and formulate new plans when necessary.
Objective 3.22: The individual will describe situations in which his decisions affect others.	Objective 3.21: The individual will identify situations in which one decision has led to a series of other decisions.	Objective 3.21: The individual will identify skills or knowledge utilized in a preferred occupation which may transfer to another.	Objective 3.23: The individual will describe situations in which new information might cause him to reconsider his goals and formulate new ones.
Activity: Glasser Classroom Meetings	Activity: Decision Logs	Activity: Interviewing	Activity: Career Exploration Groups

2. By grade six, students—with the help of their teachers and parents—should assess personal aptitudes, abilities and interests, and relate them to careers. They should also learn the role of technology in the world of work.

3. In grades seven and eight, students should set career-oriented goals and develop four-year career plans for grades nine through 12. These plans may change as they are reviewed annually, but it sets students on a course and provides a basis for curriculum selection. It also gets parents involved.

4. During high school, a new "applied curriculum" will make academic concepts relevant to the workplace, especially in communications, math and science. Vocational courses are coordinated with academic instruction.

5. Students choosing postsecondary education programs should be able to successfully gain employment, advance within their fields or change occupations. These programs include vocational technical centers, community colleges and universities.

6. Educators should intensify efforts to share information and to involve parents, business and the entire community in this process. Partnerships and the involvement of people beyond educators are critically important. (p. 4)

In order to monitor the progress of the state and the schools involved toward such goals, these six steps or program goals have sample competencies associated with them. For example, under Step 2, self and career awareness for grades kindergarten through five, the sample competencies include the following:

- Acquiring knowledge of the importance of a positive self-concept to career development.
- Developing skills for interacting with others.
- Becoming aware of the importance of emotional and physical development in career decision making.
- Acquiring an awareness of the interrelationship of lifestyles and careers.
- Becoming aware of changing occupational roles for males and females. (p. 9)

Given the goals of personal assessment and technological literacy in grade six, the sample competencies encompass the following:

- Developing and utilizing a positive self concept for career development.
- Understanding the emotional and physical development required for proactive career decision making.
- Understanding the value of personal responsibility, good work habits and planning for career opportunities.
- Comprehending the significance of technology in the world of work.
- Identifying career opportunities in the field of technology.
- Demonstrating technological literacy. (p. 10)

Similar sample competencies are identified for each of the other steps in the career preparation blueprint. These in turn are wedded to activities and processes that meet the overarching or ultimate goal for the plan, that "students graduating from Florida's public schools shall be prepared to begin a career and continue their education at a postsecondary technical school, community college or university" (p. 9).

Business and industry, as well as various government agencies, have begun to introduce career development systems that use the types of program goal statements and behavioral objectives cited in the previous examples. Specificity of the goals and behavioral statements is frequently less elaborate but the general models are similar. For example, Leibowitz and Schlossberg (1981) have identified a framework from which career planning skills can be identified, defined, and operationalized. These skills are arranged in stages of importance to both employees and managers. As such, they can serve as the planning framework for training workshops or for the development of career guidance programs in which managers have a major role. For each of the cells of this model, specific behavioral objectives can be defined and specific strategies identified to accomplish such goals. Table 6.11 presents the planning model proposed by Leibowitz and Schlossberg for industry.

Many other models of systematic planning could be identified here. Virtually all states and many industries and government agencies have now developed such approaches to career education and career guidance. These many examples offer a pool of goals and objectives from which one might select those appropriate to a given setting and, most importantly, to the conceptual framework for career guidance that one develops in stage 1 of one's planning.

In summary of stage 2 in systematic planning, a few points need reinforcement.

1. The specification of program goals and behavioral objectives for students or clients should not occur in a vacuum. These program directions should flow from a conceptual framework and a needs assessment pertinent to the local agency setting.

Table 6.11

Career Planning Process Model

	Stage 1	**Stage 2**	**Stage 3**
Employee Responsibility	Explore	Understand	Take Action
Manager Responsibility	Listen and Support	Identify Clarify	Select Strategy
Manager Roles Required	Communicator Counselor	Communicator Appraiser	Communicator Counselor Appraiser Coach Mentor Advisor Referral Agent Advocate

2. Behavioral objectives provide an inventory of possible emphases that can help a counselor and counselee define what problems or skill deficits should be worked on.
3. Depending on the form in which behavioral objectives are written, both the career guidance activities to facilitate them and the criteria on which they might be evaluated can be specified.

Stage 3—Selecting Alternative Program Processes

The major problems in systematic planning for career guidance occur in stages 1 and 2—deciding what needs exist, developing a conceptual framework for the program, and translating such insights into program and performance goals. Once the directions for the program are specified, it is then necessary to identify those processes that can facilitate the identified goals.

A major question in selecting program processes in relation to either program goals or performance objectives is what behavior is intended. The second question is, What processes might facilitate these behaviors: individual counseling? group career development? work-study? behavior modification? values clarification? role-playing? It is conceivable that any one of these processes or many other acceptable techniques might be useful. However, it is necessary to decide which available technique or process is likely to be the best. Viewed in this context, any career guidance technique or process must be considered a means to an end. It must also be evaluated in terms of the time available, resources required, competencies of personnel available, costs involved, and other such criteria as are appropriate in a particular setting. Table 6.12 suggests examples of the broad range of techniques or processes that could be used to facilitate career development and from which decisions can be

Table 6.12

Examples of Techniques to Facilitate Career Development

- films
- discussions
- developing bulletin boards
- making occupational role books
- creating listings of characteristics of self in relation to educational and occupational alternatives
- analyzing expectations of work
- collecting newspaper articles or magazine stories
- writing short themes
- developing games about interests
- self-ratings
- field trips
- resource people
- examination of want ads
- work samples
- work study
- part-time work
- panels of recent graduates in different work or educational settings
- profile census data
- individual counseling
- testing
- group career counseling
- social modeling
- desensitization
- seminars on career paths/career ladders
- peer discussion groups for women and minorities
- career path publications
- in-house career counselors
- reading biographies
- formulating a written career development plan
- completing genograms of occupations held by extended family members or ancestors
- defining terms
- committees
- role play
- job analyses
- debate
- interview: workers, employers, employment service counselors, college admissions people, post-secondary AVTS personnel
- gaming
- test interpretations
- making posters
- contrast or compare characteristics of work or education
- library research
- keep personal records for purposes of analysis
- publishing newspaper about career development concerns
- doing follow-up study
- shadowing workers
- apprenticeships
- internships
- computer-assisted programs
- career guidance curriculum
- work simulations
- relaxation tapes
- behavioral rehearsal
- career resource center
- individual counseling
- skills inventory — job matching system
- on-the-job training
- job rotation

made in relation to different program goals or behavioral objectives.

Figure 6.2 indicates how many such techniques are combined in one corporation's career development system. A leader in this kind of programming, Connecticut General Insurance Company, the employer of over 14,000 people, has had a continuing commitment to employee career mobility. A brief portrayal of the techniques used in this process includes

Figure 6.2

Connecticut General's Overall Career Development System

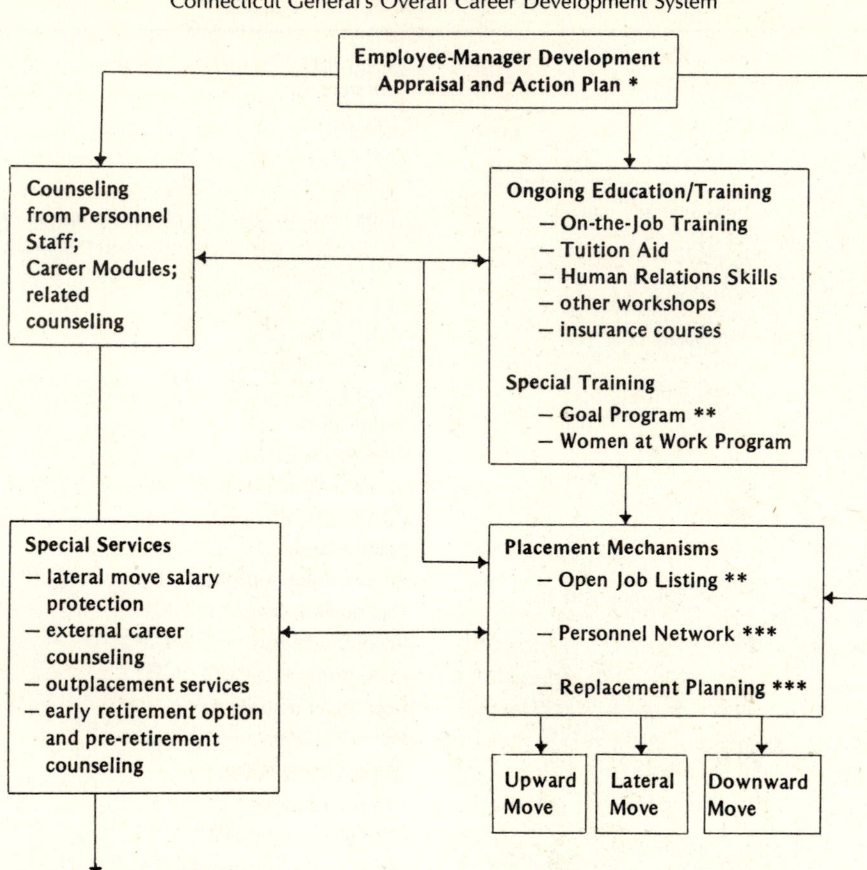

various combinations of counseling, special services, education/training, and referral and placement activities.

Extending such points further, Table 6.13 indicates how input from a needs assessment conducted on a particular target population, in this case female undergraduate students living in a dormitory of apartment suites, can be related to processes (programs) tailored to meet such needs. This depiction also includes in the right column examples of criterion variables by which to evaluate the effectiveness of the various processes of concern.

Hypothetical examples of how program goals, performance objectives, and activities/techniques can be presented for planning

Table 6.13

Counseling Service Planning Chart

Sample Population Sub-group Description	Goal Area of Strongest Need and Goal Statements Within That Area	Examples of Programs to Serve Needs	Examples of Criteria for Goal Achievement
Female undergraduate students living in dormitory of apartment suites	Work-Study Skill Development:		
	Know how to manage finances	Discussion seminar; Speakers	Answer correctly 90% of items on written test
	Outline and take notes effectively	Study skills group	Take notes during classroom lecture that cover 90% of main points
	Write in manner that is coherent and interesting	Writing improvement lab	Write paper that includes all basic elements of good writing
	Speak so easily understood	Speech course: group counseling	Satisfactory rating by all members of the group
	Increase reading rate and comprehension	Speed reading course	Rate increase of 25% and comprehension increase 20%
	Concentrate for longer time on studies	Individual counseling; group counseling; peer support network	25% increase in time spent reading textbooks
	Complete assignments on time	Group counseling; peer support network	Meet all assignment deadlines
	Prepare effectively for tests and exams	Study skills group	Receive satisfactory score on at least two tests
	Know how to use a library	Study skills group; library workshop	Can describe to satisfaction of group how to find library resources

Source: Reprinted from "Needs Assessment and The Design of Service Delivery Systems" by James A. Fruehling, *Journal of College Student Personnel,* 1979, Vol. 20, No. 4, pp. 322–328; Fig. 2, p. 327. © AACD. Reprinted with permission. No further reproduction authorized without written permission of American Association for Counseling and Development.

purposes follow. (See Table 6.14.) A longitudinal program would include goals, behavioral objectives, activities, and evaluation methods arranged at different educational levels or within sequences appropriate to a particular agency or corporate constituency. Obviously, a total program would include more goals than are identified here, but the essence of their formulation is reflected in the examples given. Again, it should be noted that any format may be used in a systematic approach to programming, as long as it is structurally

Table 6.14

Examples of Presenting Program Goals, Performance Objectives, and Activities/Techniques

Ninth-Grade Program in Self- and Career Awareness

Program Goal	Subgoal	Performance Objectives	Career Guidance Techniques
1. To increase individual self-awareness.	1.A. Reinforce awarenss of one's strengths.	1.A.1. The student will be able to show, in front of the group, a 5–10 minute oral description of him or herself as if his or her best friend were describing him or her for membership in a club.	1.A.1. The counselor will introduce a group discussion on the various components of a person (e.g., physical, emotional) and how these form a self-concept.
		1.A.2. The student is able to write a two-page report for the counselor describing how his or her three greatest strengths have helped in situations with people within the previous two weeks.	1.A.2. The counselor will explain the concept of a personal journal and its place during the entire course. The students will begin theirs with a one-page feeling reaction write-up of their responses.

Vocational Rehabilitation in a Regional Correctional Facility

Program Goal	Behavioral Objectives	Career Guidance Techniques
1. To help the client use available educational and occupational information for formulation of tentative vocational goals.	1.A.1. The client can verbalize a basic understanding of the personal and situational factors and decisions which shaped his work history.	1.A.1.1. Group sessions with a counselor.
	1.A.2. From the "help wanted" columns in regional newspapers the client can identify jobs which (1) he is prepared for now, (2) he could probably do with some remedial education and/or vocational training, and (3) are probably out of his reach.	1.A.2.1. Test and interest inventory results interpreted and discussed in individual counseling sessions. 1.A.2.2. Use of career information kits and occupational briefs adopted to client's reading level. 1.A.2.3. Use of tape recording of job descriptions, films, and displays to reach those clients with low reading levels.
	1.A.3. In a gaming situation, the client can identify future decisions which must be made to reach the tentative goal he has set.	1.A.3. Department-made adult game adapted from the life-career game.

Table 6.14 (Continued)

A College Program for Returning Women Students		
Program Goal	**Behavioral Objectives**	**Career Guidance Techniques**
1. To help students develop decision-making skills.	1.A.1. The student will identify and assess specific reasons for selecting a particular course of study or career choice.	1.A.1.1. Role play the decision-making and assess paradigm in regard to an interview with a department head about reasons for choosing a course of study.
		1.A.1.2. Discussion groups to provide support for decisions being made and carried out. Groups will challenge, suggest, foster, and support decisions.
		1.A.1.3. Taped interviews with representatives of various curricula will be considered in terms of placement record, role expectations, content in various courses of study.

Business and Industry		
Program Goal	**Behavioral Objectives**	**Career Guidance Techniques**
1. To help employees achieve desired job or career change.	1.A. The employee will be able to identify the career change resources available in the Counseling/Career Planning, Education/Training and Job Opportunities units of the corporation.	1.A.1. Provide the employee with a copy of organizational chart of major career change mechanisms available in the company. Discuss the functions of each component and what services are available in each unit.
		1.A.2. Have the employee identify intermediate career goals and identify the company provisions for job information and job transfer, programs of education and training provided, and career planning workshops available on topics of personal interest.
2. To increase employee's awareness of career paths and placement of information.	2.A. The employee will understand the use of career paths for personnel classification steps, placement, and mobility within the company.	2.A.1. Lunchtime discussions will be held with all employees to acquaint them with the use of career paths charts in their department as well as open job listings, personnel networks, and replacement planning.
		Representatives of the training section will identify the various training opportunities available to support different career path moves.

sound and contains objectives consistent with the experiences required by those serviced by the program.

Stage 4—Developing an Evaluation Design

Although stages 1 and 2 of systematic planning require the most deliberation and compromise among the different directions a career guidance program might take, stage 4, the evaluation stage, seems to be the most threatening to many counselors. Apparently, some counselors equate evaluation with some highly sophisticated and esoteric skills beyond their ability to comprehend. Such a perspective is incorrect but widely held.

Evaluation has been defined by Trantow (1970) as "essentially an effort to determine what changes occur as the result of a planning program by comparing actual changes (results) with desired changes (stated goals) and by identifying the degree to which the activity (planned program) is responsible for the changes" (p. 3). The key word here is "planned." Evaluation cannot occur unless it is effectively planned. Nor can it occur if we are not clear about the goals we wish to accomplish or the ways these will be measured. If we have completed the stages of the systematic planning process outlined earlier in this chapter, the goals and the behavioral objectives the program seeks to accomplish should be clear. The question we need to raise now is, "What evidence will we accept that the goals or objectives have been met?" Some possibilities might include the following:

- Ratings of student, employee, or client performance by teachers, parents, counselors, or employers
- Judgments by experts of whether program goals have been met
- Follow-up studies of how students, employees, or clients plan, apply decision-making skills, make accurate self-estimates after exposure to career guidance
- Scales of student or client attitude about themselves or career exploration or work
- Staff reaction sheets about changes in student or client behavior during a career guidance program
- Student or client opinion of how their behavior has been changed or improved as a result of career guidance
- Observations of student or client understandings and skills in role playing or actual situations
- Changes in school attendance, work punctuality, or other quantitative indices related to career guidance goals
- Scores on published standardized instruments:

  Assessment of Career Development
  Career Maturity Inventory
  Career Decision Scale
  Career Development Inventory
  Readiness for Vocational Planning
  Adult Career Concerns Survey
  My Vocational Situation

These instruments measure different aspects of personal knowledge about career development behaviors with regard to (1) what the person *knows about* personal attributes, occupational information, job selection, course and curriculum selection, school and career problem solving; (2) what the person *has done* in regard to involvement in career planning activities, involvement in a wide range of worker activities, involvement in activities related to preferred occupation(s); and (3) one's attitudes, preferences, and perceptions with regard to self, work, and information resources. For a comprehensive analysis of the specific content of each of these instruments, with regard to the emphases cited above, see Kapes and Mastie (1988, Cook, Hepworth, Wall, and Warr (1981), or the most recent *Mental Mea-*

surements Yearbook. There are also other published instruments dealing with work values, interests, and planning that are pertinent to evaluation and that will be discussed in Chapter 16.

The basic point to be made here is that the type of evaluation and the resulting data will differ in accordance with the setting and the type of behavior being assessed. It depends on what the program goals are, what types of energy and personnel time can be committed to evaluation, what fiscal support is available for evaluation, and what evaluative competencies exist in the career guidance staff or can be obtained from outside experts.

A system of evaluation is concerned with whether the total program is meeting its goals, typically referred to as summative or product evaluation; and whether the individual processes or activities designed to accomplish particular goals or behavioral objectives are doing so effectively, or more effectively than other possible processes or activities, typically referred to as formative or process evaluation.

Put in a very simplistic way, summative or product evaluation requires that you have data about student or client performances in areas related to program goals before the career guidance program or procedure was implemented and similar data about the students or clients after the career guidance effort. This is necessary so that you can judge what changes took place, whether they were sufficient to justify the program, and what they mean for future program efforts. Summative or product evaluation is essentially concerned with the aggregate effects of the program in terms of its goals, rather than how well specific techniques or activities contributed to such outcomes.

Process evaluation is usually concerned with more experimentally oriented questions than is product evaluation. It seeks answers to whether individual behavioral objectives are met effectively by the techniques related to them, whether particular activities are more effective with some subgroups rather than others, and which program techniques or activities are most effective for what purposes with what groups.

The National Occupational Information Coordinating committee (1988) depicts the evaluation process and its inclusion of process or product evaluation, as well as the uses of evaluation results, as shown in Figure 6.3.

Lombana (1985) has extended the viewpoint expressed above by discussing empirical and perceptual evaluation procedures. In doing so, she has created a two-by-two figure that has four quadrants contrasting client objectives with program objectives and empirical evaluation with perceptual evaluation. In her perspective, empirical measures assess whether or not a given objective was accomplished, whereas perceptual measures allow one to determine how the counselors' efforts were viewed by others. Program or client objectives can be measured through either empirical or perceptual evaluation, depending upon what information is being sought for whom and for what purpose. Such a conceptual model is very useful in sharpening the questions that need to be addressed in stage 4, Developing an Evaluation Design, in the systematic planning model. Figure 6.3 portrays the quadrants and questions included in each as proposed by Lombana.

Regardless of whether the intent is to evaluate the products or the processes of career guidance, there is a logical sequence of steps that should be undertaken (Herr, 1976a).

1. *Identifying goals and stating objectives*. This step has been covered sufficiently in this chapter so it will not be discussed further here.

2. *Choosing criterion measurements*. This is a crucial step. After evaluation criteria have been identified—goals for the program and objectives for the processes—ways of measuring them must be identified or devised. Cri-

Figure 6.3

Evaluation Process

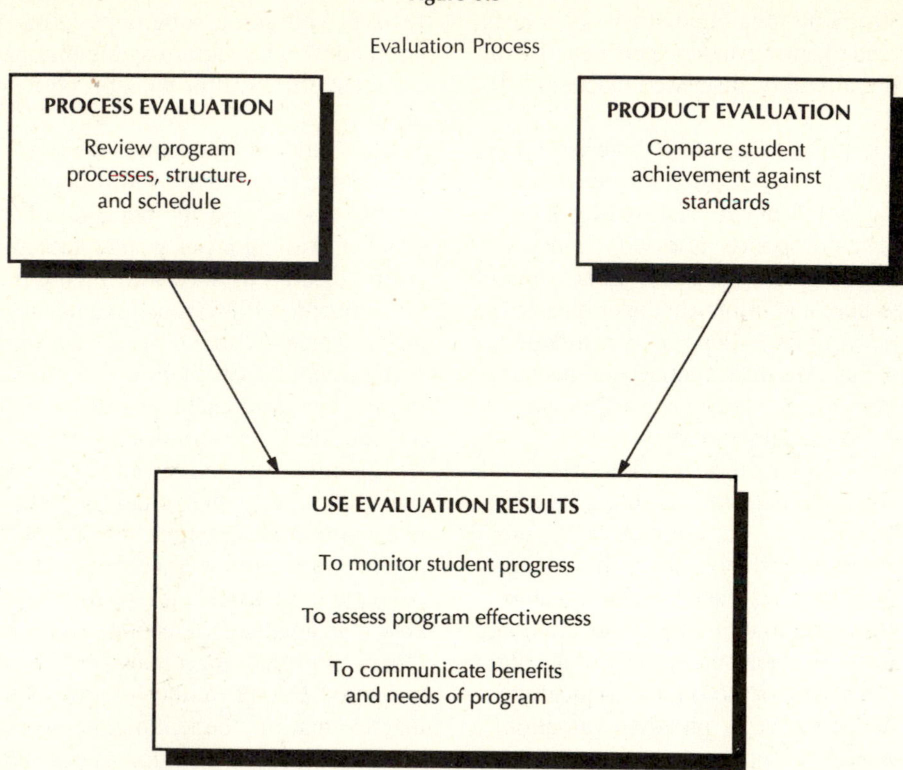

teria differ in the precision with which they can be measured. Commercially published instruments are available which can be used to evaluate some career guidance goals; for other goals, locally devised rating scales, self reports, observations, and questionnaires will have to suffice. The point of overriding importance is ensuring that whatever information is gathered is clearly relevant to what the program goals and objectives are, not something else.

3. *Establishing levels of performance or standards*. It is necessary to decide at an individual or a group level what is acceptable. From an individual standpoint, this may mean deciding, for each program goal, how many behaviors (1, 3, 5) must be successfully demonstrated or how many examples (1, 5, 10) must be listed, labeled, or otherwise shown within a particular behavior. From a group standpoint, it may be necessary to decide that some percentage of persons meet some portions of objectives (at least 70 percent of the group will complete 75 percent of the required objectives) for the project to be considered successful. There is no magical formula here. The judgment will likely be a judgment of what might be a reasonable improvement over baseline data.

4. *Specifying program elements*. In summative evaluation, the boundaries of the career guidance program need to be identified. The question is what specific elements in an agency, a school, a corporation, or a college are considered to compromise the career guidance effort. By considering this question care-

Figure 6.4

Four Types of Accountability Procedures. (Reprinted from "Guidance Accountability: A New Look at An Old Problem" by Judy H. Lombana, *The School Counselor*, 1980, Vol. 82, No. 5, pp. 340–346; Fig. 3, p. 345. ©AACD. Reprinted with permission. No further reproduction authorized without written permission of American Association for Counseling and Development.)

Four Types of Accountability Procedures

EMPIRICAL EVALUATION

PROGRAM OBJECTIVES	I Primary Question: Did the counselor accomplish the task identified in the objective?	III Primary Question: Did the students (or other clients) change their behavior as a result of the counselor's efforts?	CLIENT OBJECTIVES
	II Primary Question: How effective was the counselor's accomplishment, as perceived by others?	IV Primary Question: How effective were student (or other client) behavior changes as perceived by others?	

fully, we can reassess the validity of the career guidance program goals and reinforce their distinctiveness from those being carried on by other parts of the agency or institution in which the career guidance program is located.

In process evaluation, the critical issue is identifying the behavioral objectives or goals for which a particular activity or technique is being done. How do these differ for different program processes? Do all the techniques or activities implemented have clear purposes in client or student behavior or are they being done for their own sake?

5. *Designing the evaluation*. This step is analogous to planning the preparations for a trip. It involves laying out the data collection format and identifying the persons who will participate. The specific questions to be considered include the following:

a. Who will be involved?—Will the career guidance staff conduct the evaluation alone? Will outside experts, state agency personnel, or some other group be involved in collecting or analyzing information? What amount of staff time is available for evaluative efforts and how will other responsibilities be covered?
b. Sampling—From whom and about whom should information be obtained? What size groups will be involved? How can we ensure that the data we collect are representative of the persons about whose behavior we are most concerned?
c. Timing—When will information about the products or processes of career guidance be collected? Continuously? Immediately when a student or client completes an encounter with a career guidance activity? Six months after a person finishes his career guidance experience? At random times? Such decisions obviously affect the amount of effort which the evaluation process will require, what kinds of questions can be raised, how comprehensive the design will be.

6. *Collecting data*. How will the desired information be obtained? Questionnaires? Interviews? Observations? Commercial Instruments? Are you going to purchase them or develop them locally? How much lead-time will

be required to get these things accomplished before evaluation can begin? Can the information be machine scored and/or coded to protect confidentiality? Does the content of the data collection instruments clearly relate to the goals and objectives (criteria) to be evaluated?

7. *Analyzing data*. How you analyze the information you collect depends upon the kind of information you collect. Are the data ranked or on an interval scale? Do you have baseline data about students or clients for comparison purposes with post-career guidance information about these persons? Do you need between-group or within-group comparisons? The form of the information collected, the purpose of the evaluation, the research skill of the evaluator, and the time and money devoted to the evaluation will each affect the kind of information analysis that needs to be undertaken. Some people equate evaluation with statistics. Different statistical methods do help you summarize numerical information and, to be used appropriately, these methods each require particular types of information. For many purposes, simple comparisons by frequency count, percentages, or graphic representation (pie chart, bar graph) will be adequate to answer the evaluation questions. In other situations, correlation, analysis of variance or covariance, or path analysis may be more appropriate.

8. *Interpreting data*. While statistical treatment of data can provide answers to many kinds of questions, the meaning of these answers becomes a matter of value judgment by someone or some group. The findings may be that 70 percent of the program goals were met for 60 percent of the persons involved. That's a statistical fact, but is it an acceptable indicator of program quality? Does it point to areas of needed program improvement? How does it compare with the characteristics of persons before the program began? The meanings of these questions are not matters of statistics but matters of counselor or administrative judgment—the ultimate substance of evaluation. As a part of systematic planning, it is important to know who will make such judgments and for what purposes.

9. *Reporting and using data*. Evaluating a career guidance program or procedure always implies that the results may signal the need for change or a clearer indication of the status of the counselor's or the program's accountability. In either case, it is likely that administrators, boards of education, corporate boards of directors, trustees, and legislators will need to be apprised of the outcomes of the evaluation process. Although these persons may be influential in deciding on personnel, facilities, resources, or program directions, they may have little understanding of either career guidance or research. Therefore, the information collected and its analyses, no matter how complex, must be put into terms that these decision-makers can understand. Pictures, graphs, slides, and a clearly presented verbal report are typically preferred over statistics to convey essential information about career guidance to those who need to know. If handled effectively, such approaches represent major methods of communication, public relations, as well as accountability, to the counselor's various publics. The major focus of evaluation here is on assessing a program's impact in such a way that decision-makers can consider the support to provide it in the future and what changes need to be. Nevertheless, it is important to note that the basic data on which evaluative judgments are based are also important as feedback to the individual, so that insights pertinent to career maturation can be gained (p. 2).

The evaluation stage constitutes a feedback loop in systematic planning of career guidance programs. It both provides insight into whether the program is meeting its goals and also provides the base for action to improve the program.

Stage 5—Milestones

The last stage of systematic planning is really an adjunct to the other four stages. It is the specifying of critical times when major events must take place if the career guidance program is to become functional, or different, or evaluated a some specified time. In simple terms, milestones can be considered the time frame for the implementation of the planned program.

Let us assume that a school district, college, or corporation has totally reconstructed its career guidance priorities and developed a planned program that is due to begin in September. It is now the previous December and the four stages of systematic planning have been accomplished. We are now beginning stage 5, the specification of the things that must happen if the career guidance program is going to become operational in September. What schedule of events should we consider? Some examples might include the following:

Milestones

February 15—Develop an inventory of all equipment and resources that need to be ordered for the career guidance program.

March 1—Complete all purchase orders for resource and equipment needs. Begin assembling an in-service package to be presented to all staff involved in the career guidance program.

March 15—Schedule presentations on program progress for administrative group and board of directors in May.

March 20—Identify evaluation instruments that need to be purchased and order them.

April 15—Complete in-service package. Schedule in-service presentations in early June.

May 15—Present orientation to program progress for administrators and directors.

June 15—Complete in-service of career guidance staff, community representatives, and instructional staff or first-line managers to goals, objectives processes, and evaluative design for the career guidance program.

July 1—Check on the status of resources and equipment purchases. Follow-up on missing items.

July 15—Check on the availability of evaluative instruments. Meet with consultant personnel to finalize rating scale satisfaction inventory, or other such services.

August 1—Assemble a public information package for news media and institutional publication. Describe the needs for the program, its goals and objectives, and when it will be implemented.

September 1–10—Collect baseline data on how students, clients, employees currently stand on behavioral expectations (knowledge, attitudes, skills) underlying program goals.

September 15—Implement program.

These are possible milestones that need to be met before a program is implemented. In many instances, these milestones would be more detailed or there would be more milestones to accomplish. Upon implementation, another set of milestones pertaining to data collection, analysis, and interpretation would need to be followed for the first year of operation. Both the milestones and the events described are changeable. Nevertheless, systematic planning is aided by utilizing milestones. In the last analysis, that is the central point of this chapter—to demonstrate the need for systematic planning and the incorporation of the techniques that will facilitate it.

Summary

In this chapter, we have proposed that the systematic or strategic planning of a career guidance program occurs in five stages. These include developing a program philosophy, specifying program goals and behavioral objectives, selecting alternative program processes, describing evaluation procedures, and identifying milestones. In each of these stages, a number of questions and decisions must be dealt with. We have discussed examples of each of these stages and the types of content appropriate to them.

CHAPTER 7

CAREER GUIDANCE IN THE ELEMENTARY SCHOOL

Key Concepts

- Career guidance in the elementary school involves systematic provision of knowledge and skills throughout the curriculum and extensive cooperation of teachers and counselors.
- Career guidance in the elementary school is not intended to force children to make premature choices but to avoid premature closure of future options.
- Major emphases of career guidance in the elementary school are on positive attitudes toward self and opportunities, feelings of competence, and ways in which school experiences can be used to explore and prepare for the future.
- There are relationships between work habits and attitudes developed in the elementary school and work habits in adulthood.
- Parental influence on children's career development is a major variable in the provision of career guidance in the elementary school.
- Career guidance programs in the elementary school can be planned and sequenced to respond to the changing developmental characteristics of elementary school children.

The provision of career guidance in the elementary school is not a new add-on to or a dramatic reversal of typical elementary school emphases. Self-knowledge, knowledge of future educational and occupational alternatives, and development of the rudiments of decision making by students generally have been considered important in both elementary school philosophy and practice. Current models of career guidance reinforce the need for systematic activities and information to occur throughout the elementary school curricula and to involve parents, teachers, and counselors in many forms of cooperative effort.

As Staley and Mangiesi (1984) have observed, it is widely acknowledged that children begin to formulate career decisions at a relatively young age. They acquire impressions of the work people do, the kinds of people employed, the compensations offered, and the abilities required for acceptable performance. On the basis of these impressions, they enthusiastically embrace some occupations as possible careers for themselves and absolutely remove others from either present or future consideration. Career guidance in the elementary school is not intended to force children to make premature choices but instead to avoid premature foreclosure of choices. Career guidance focuses on awareness of choices that will be available, ways to anticipate and plan for them, and their relation to personal characteristics. Many students need to know that they will have opportunities to choose and the competence to do so. These students also need to become aware of themselves, how they are changing, and how they can use school experiences to explore and prepare for the future.

Miller (1989), among other authors, has stated emphatically that in the elementary school the initial stage of career development is self-awareness. Without self-awareness other stages of career development such as career awareness or decision making become meaningless. Thus, central to career guidance activities in the elementary school are those that address a child's awareness of self, feelings of autonomy and control, need for planful behavior, and desire for explanation.

But it is not simply the formulation of career decisions and a sense of opportunity that is at issue in the elementary school; some researchers suggest that early classroom learning strategies may help predict the individual's tendencies to engage, dissemble, or evade in difficult workplace situations, particularly in early employment (Hansen & Johnson, 1989). Using an expectancy-valence model similar to that described in Chapter 4, Hansen and Johnson have described how learning strategies observed in the classroom as early as in the elementary school and reinforced in the junior and senior high schools can lead to productive or nonproductive work strategies in early adulthood. To simplify the matter, a taxonomy of four classroom learning strategies is used by these researchers to describe the interaction of learning related to high or low task confidence or task value. These, in turn, lead to engaging, dissembling, evading, or rejecting tasks in the classroom or in the workplace.

To be more specific, *task engaging* means that the individual sees relative value in the required performance and is relatively confident of his or her ability to meet its demands. In a state of situational challenge, "the individual strives for an accurate understanding of the task and of the means to accomplish it, and enters into the required effort with intentionality. Ambiguity of assignment is met with efforts to clarify, interpret, and resolve" (p. 82). In *task dissembling*, "the individual sees a relative value in the required performance, but lacks confidence in his or her ability to meet its demands. In a situational quandry, the individual wants to perform, but is uncertain of what to do or how to do it, or whether it can be done. In the desire to succeed, to appear successful, not to fail, or at least not to appear to fail, the individual dissembles, pretending to understand, making excuses, denying, distorting, or engaging in undifferentiated thinking that includes elements that may not appear to be part of the situation. New situations and unfamiliar assignments are seen as threatening, rather than challenging, and are met with further dissembling" (p. 83). In a third learning (workplace) strategy, *task evading*, the individual feels relatively confident of his or her ability to meet the demands of the assignment, but sees relatively little value in it. He or she is in a situational dilemma, feeling ready and able to take on a challenge, but being unable in this particular situation to identify a task of sufficient value. . . . The individual may go through the motions of task performance in an automatic fashion, usually accomplishing at least an acceptable minimum of output. But the task is neither actively engaged nor rejected: it is simply evaded. The individual is removed from the task, his or her attention is scattered, given only partially to the performance and perhaps in more important part to other competing interests such as daydreaming, distracting a neighbor, worrying about lacking money, planning a party, recalling a television drama or even mentally rehearsing another more compelling performance in an area that is found challenging (p. 83). The final learning/work strategy is *task rejecting*. In this situation, "the individual lacks confidence in his or her ability and sees little value in the assigned task. . . . In a situational state of psychological withdrawal, the individual neither actively engages assignments nor defends against them. He or she is in situational malaise, neither having a clear goal or valued task, nor feeling able to secure one in this situation. He or she may appear passive, working within a system of understandings that are unresponsive to the present demands and restrictions of the situation" (p. 84).*

This taxonomy of learning or work strategies is not only present in the elementary schools but can be found in junior high or senior high schools as well. Its use makes several points. One, the roots of work strategies that lead to productive or nonproductive results take hold in the early years of schooling, as do the sense of self-confidence and valuing of different tasks that underlie the different forms of individual behavior reflected. Two, everyone uses the dissembling, evading, or rejecting of tasks in some situations. The problem is that for some people they can become habitual strategies that may be employed with increasing frequency in response to decreasing levels of situational distress or discomfort. Third, preliminary research suggests that, whatever their genesis, nonproductive learning strategies can be reversed by situational and interactional interventions. With particular application to career guidance and career counseling, efforts to help individuals learn to recognize and control their tendencies to evade, dissemble, or reject tasks may be accomplished through individual and group work. Certainly, efforts to increase student self-efficacy and self-confidence to take on a wider range of tasks, with less feeling of threat, and efforts to help students gain assertive skills by which to clarify assignments or to indicate their lack of understanding when faced with ambiguity represent the types of behaviors that can be identified and reinforced in career counseling strategies in the elementary school and at other educational levels. In doing so, such interventions acknowledge that the effectiveness with which students can deal with challenge and threat within the learning environment is likely to be related to personal experiences of self-efficacy with particular situations or tasks, and that these experiences in turn are likely to be reflected in career decisions made.

The importance of the behaviors and attitudes that students incorporate in the elementary school can be seen from another perspective. Analyses of research addressing school dropouts suggest that the antecedents to the withdrawal from school at age 16 or so likely occur over a long period of time, probably beginning in the elementary school. As Finn (1989) has suggested, there are currently two major models that attempt to explain the underlying variables that lead to early school leaving. One of these is a *frustration-self-esteem model* that contends that poor school performance is hypothesized to lead to an impaired self-view (low self-esteem) and, in turn, to the child's opposing the context (the school) that is seen as responsible. This oppositional behavior may take different forms: disrupting the instructional process, skipping class, or even committing delinquent acts. There are many reasons for a child to evidence frustration at the instructional process—for example, poor psychological support from the home, a lack of continual evidence of adequacy through school-related success experiences, poor interaction with teachers, or a growth of acute distress and alienation from the world of school and adults in general.

These observations are not intended to suggest that oppositional behavior is entirely or even primarily the student's fault. Such behaviors can arise because schools have not provided programs or created environments that challenge students to feel competent and valued by teachers or peers. Indeed, alienation of students from the expectations of the school is often a self-protecting way of responding when one has been hurt, bored, or made to feel inferior by the climate or the activities of the school. The fundamental point is that what happens in the life of the child in the elemen-

*From *Adolescence and Work: Influences of Social Structure, Labor Markets, and Culture*, edited by David Stern and Dorothy Eichorn. Copyright ©1989 by Lawrence Erlbaum Associates, Inc. Reprinted by permission.

tary school does create patterns of behavior, positive or negative, that are likely to persist into the secondary school and adulthood. Thus, they need to be the focus of the counselor's sensitivity and intervention, either to assist children in developing positive attitudes of self-esteem and ability, or to help teachers and administrators create climates and classrooms that motivate such characteristics.

The second model is described as a *participation-identification model*. This model manifests two major variables; one behavioral, *participation*, and the other psychological, *identification*. Participation requires that the student have curricular experiences available that both retain his or her interest and engagement and result in learning and development. The second variable, identification, connotes a form of bonding, a sense of belonging, shared value, a feeling of being able to deal with and be congruent with the social group (other students, teachers, institutional norms). Identification and self-esteem have been found to be correlated—not independent.

The fundamental point to be made here is that the research reported by Hansen and Johnson and by Finn is illustrative of the power of the early developmental experiences of children in the elementary school to be precursors of persistence at later educational levels and in acquiring behaviors that are antecedents of work performance in adulthood. Thus, they are both challenges to and opportunities for career guidance and counseling in the elementary school.

Against such contexts, the assumptions that give career guidance credibility in the elementary school are as follows:

1. Awareness that styles of choice behavior in adolescence and adulthood are affected by the types of developmental experiences that occur in childhood
2. Evidence that many of the materials and texts used in elementary schools portray the world of work or of future education inaccurately and foster unnecessary sex-typing of occupations or restricted views of available educational or occupational possibilities
3. Acknowledgment that feelings of personal competence to cope with the future grow with knowledge of one's strengths, ways to modify weaknesses, skills in planning and using available exploratory resources, and understanding of relationships between schooling and its application in work and other community roles

A consideration of the characteristics of elementary school children will help to place some of these assumptions into perspective.

THE ELEMENTARY SCHOOL CHILD

Children of elementary school age are fundamentally generalists, in the sense that they are typically open to and they interact with, a broad range of stimuli and modes or behavior. In their unbridled enthusiasm and curiosity, they have not yet been constrained by many of the social realities and stereotypes that plague and distort the perceptions of their older brothers and sisters and many adults with whom they identify. Yet they are vulnerable in the sense that attitudes and perceptions about life and their place in it are formative and are readily influenced by the environmental circumstances surrounding them, including accurate or inaccurate information and sex stereotyping.

Environmental Influences

Environmental circumstances take many forms and have varied relationships to the growth and development of elementary school children. For example, Rich (1979) has demonstrated that children are most knowledgeable about occupations located in their own community. Therefore, if they come from a predominantly rural community, for example, with few occupations and these mostly of low status, it is these to which they will likely aspire. She argues that such circumstances put rural students at a comparative disadvantage to their urban counterparts. She further contends that acquiring knowledge "about nonlocal occupations or more specifically about middle- and high-status occupations, could provide rural students with an equal opportunity to make more varied and more optimal occupational choices" (p. 325).

Environmental circumstances go beyond geography. A particularly powerful one is socioeconomic status. Holland (1981) found, in a study of 300 randomly selected sixth-grade students enrolled in twenty-two public schools in Georgia, that socioeconomic status was more useful in predicting the maturity of career attitudes than self-concept, race, sex, place of residence, or age. The data indicated that the higher the student's socioeconomic status, the higher the score obtained on the Attitude Scale of the Career Maturity Inventory (CMI).

Gender and socioeconomic characteristics can be either separate or interactive influences on career exploration. Hageman and Gladding (1983) studied children's willingness to accept men and women in various occupations and their own willingness to aspire to nontraditional occupation. The participants were 90 sixth graders (47 females and 43 males) and 84 third graders (39 females and 45 males) in two elementary schools that differed in the socioeconomic composition of their students. Although both schools were in suburban areas, a majority of the children in one school came from upper-middle and lower-upper-class families, while the other school's children were from upper-lower- and lower-middle-class backgrounds.

The results of the Hageman and Gladding study indicated that a number of differences in perceptions of occupations prevailed among the groups. Sixth-grade girls were very willing to accept both men and women in sixteen traditionally male occupations; sixth-grade boys differed significantly from girls in this regard. The boys thought that only males should be employed as auto mechanics, architects, electricians, carpenters, doctors, school principals, astronauts, pilots, pharmacists, professional athletes, lawyers, dentists, truck drivers, police officers, radio announcers, and reporters. These sixth-grade boys also differed from girls in their belief that dental assistants and cleaner/servants should be women only.

When the perceptions of third-grade girls were compared to sixth-grade girls, they differed in their view of only one occupation, that of lawyer. The older girls were more willing to accept both men and women as lawyers. The study also found that sixth-grade girls chose nontraditional jobs as occupations they would like to have considerably more often than did third-grade girls (that is, 40 percent versus 25 percent). While the research suggested that a large number of the girls were considering nontraditional occupations, it was also evident that, in line with other research on sex-stereotyping, most of the girls did not feel free to pursue a nontraditional career. A final finding of the study was that children from lower socioeconomic backgrounds were more conservative in their perceptions of appropriate occupations for males or females or for themselves than were children of higher socioeconomic background. Part of the explanation for such differences undoubtedly relates to role models available as well as to the children's perception of their own freedom of action in exploring or participating in career options.

Research findings also suggest that there is a connection between childhood play activities and later career choices. For example, the research of Cooper and Robinson (1989) of retrospective descriptions of childhood games, activities, preferences, and aspirations by 214 males and 51 females enrolled in a variety of science, mathematics, and engineering courses at a Midwestern technical university corroborate earlier studies that masculine and androgynous childhood activities may play a role in the development of skills necessary for later achievement in math and physical sciences. Implications of these findings by the researchers suggest that elementary school counselors who are concerned about eliminating or reducing gender limitations should promote a greater level of masculine and androgynous experiences for female children. In addition, counselors could work with students individually and in groups to modify attitudes that negatively influence girls' participation in these activities. Greater exposure to childhood activities found to be related to females' subsequent participation in nontraditional curricula or occupations could be coupled with the use of selected female role models to strengthen self-efficacy and interest in previously male-dominated roles in the technical and scientific fields.

In a different but related line of inquiry, Hughes, Martinek, and Fitzgerald (1985) have examined the role of self-esteem among boys and girls in relation to nontraditional career choices. The sample studied consisted of 66 students (35 girls and 31 boys) in a private laboratory school. The result of the study strongly supports the notion that for girls the relationship between self-esteem and nontraditional attitudes is reliably established as early as the primary years in school. In addition, the study showed that boys with high self-esteem persisted in maintaining stereotyped attitudes toward sex roles while girls with high self-esteem made less traditional career choices. This study is not able to project how such sex-role stereotypes or, in contrast, freedom to consider nontraditional sex roles will translate into actual work choices in the future. It does, however, affirm that attitudes likely to undergird adult role behavior have antecedents in the early life of children.

A further major environmental circumstance affecting the career attitudes of children is their relationships with their parents and the attitudes of the latter toward work. Miller (1978) has examined the childhood antecedents to career maturity attitudes in young adulthood and found some support for the hypothesis that parental attitudes and behavior reported as having occurred during childhood are positively associated with career maturity attitudes among community college students. Parental attitudes and behavior that impede general development and well-being were found to be associated with attitudes indicative of career immaturity. As discussed in Chapter 13, prolonged unemployment also tends to be associated with increases in child abuse, substance abuse, marital discord, intense anxiety, and insecurity. Such circumstances are likely to influence the views of work held by children in families significantly affected by unemployment.

Berry (1979) has reported that research indicates that many problems of older children, youth, and adults are a result of unresolved communication problems stemming from childhood (p. 515). She argues the importance of this matter for communication theory, which she contends "explains human growth and development itself because it is the social matrix from which the self-concept emerges and takes shape and it is the self-concept that gives direction to human life. . . . It is communication that (1) puts the individuals in touch with their own thoughts and feelings and (2) ties person to person and every person to a group" (p. 516). In this view, social interference with communication development takes place when the pattern of communication between the parent and child is unsatisfactory, at least from the child's point of view. Obviously, such disturbed communication patterns will affect not only the child's view of self but interactions with others in the school and, subsequently, in the workplace.

Seligman, Weinstock, and Owings (1988) studied the role of family dynamics in the career development of five-year-olds. They found that children with a positive family orientation are likely to obtain information about their parents' activities and to receive more encouragement. These factors contribute to the child's career development. The researchers also found that the children's perceptions of their fathers as powerful, important, attractive, approachable, and warm were related to the development of articulated future goals in the children. Part of the explanation for this finding may be the fact that children at this age are attracted to power and mastery. Thus, the father, by his size and his accomplishment of having both a career and a family, can serve as a role model for the integration and the value of both endeavors. Such circumstances probably permit these children to identify with both aspects of their father's life and imagine themselves in similar roles.

These findings do not denigrate the role of the mother in determining the general climate of the family. Rather, they suggest that career guidance practitioners need to pay considerable attention to the role of the father and to the father-child relationship in shaping and promoting the career development of the young child.

As a function of such environmental circumstances and others, levels of aspiration, achievement motivation, and self-perceptions have their genesis in the early years of the family and of schooling. Here are the roots of the behavior that will manifest itself many years later under the labels of career identity and commitment, or conversely, juvenile delinquency, early school leaving, and underemployability. If Luchins's primacy effect (1960) is a valid premise—that the information obtained first carries the most weight in ultimate decisions—then in the case of elementary school age children, education and career guidance must focus considerable attention on attitude development, decision processing, and self-awareness, as well as on knowledge of the broad characteristics and expectations of work. These are the ingredients of career development that underlie growing career maturity.

Children's Values Toward Work

Many people believe that the elementary years are too early for career guidance goals. They believe that concerns about self-understanding and planning for the future are better saved for the junior high school and beyond. Although adults might feel more comfortable if they did not need to plan career guidance responses to children's developmental needs in the elementary school, children do have such needs.

As elementary school children move through the elements of fantasy so characteristic of growth and learning at that life period, work is an important concern to them. By the time they have completed the first six grades of school, many of them have made tentative commitments to fields of work and to self-perceptions. The point here is not that the choices are irreversible or that this phenomenon is good or bad, but, rather, that it occurs. Parker (1970), for example, found that fewer than 10 percent of 29,000 students in the seventh grade in Oklahoma described themselves as not having vocational goals. Simmons (1962) discovered that the elementary school children in his study were very much aware of occupational prestige. Creason and Schilson (1970) found that of a sample of 121 sixth graders who were asked about their vocational plans, none indicated that they had no vocational plans, none indicated that they had no vocational preferences, and only eight indicated that they did not know why they chose their particular preference. In a related study, Davis, Hagan, and Strouf (1962) found that out of a sample of 116 twelve-year-olds, 60 percent had already made tentative choices. Nelson (1963) has demonstrated that as early as the third grade, children have well-developed attitudes regarding occupations and levels of education and that as early as ages 8 and 9, children tend to reject some occupations as holding no interest for them.

Rosenthal and Chapman (1982) have shown that children are aware of the sex stereotypes of certain occupations, and that, from an early age, children employ "linguistic markers" (for example, "lady doctor" or "male nurse") to denote those in nontraditional occupations. Using Krefting and Berger's (1979) findings that indicated that interacting with things is perceived as masculine, interacting with people is perceived as feminine, and interacting with data is perceived as both masculine and feminine, McKay and Miller (1982) studied third- and fifth-grade students. They found that boys had more complex interactions with things in their choices of occupational environments than did girls.

In studying subjects of several different ages, Shepelak, Ogden, and Robin-Bennett (1984) asked college, high school, and students in third and fifth grades to evaluate whether fictitious occupations arbitrarily assigned a gender label were positions appropriate for women, men, or both sexes. The use of imaginary occupations allowed the authors to circumvent the students' prior knowledge of the normative work world. There were very few differences in the way students from the four age groups responded. Third and fifth grade students were likely to initially classify more occupations as open only to males. In general, however, all students were more likely to perceive those occupations with masculine labels as appropriate for men and not for both men and women.

Fitzgerald and Betz (1983) found in a review of the literature that female self-esteem correlates highly with nontraditional career choices. In their own study with boys and girls in grades three through six, they found for girls that the relationship between self-esteem and nontraditional attitudes is established as early as the primary school year. In addition, they found that girls but not boys with high self-esteem made less traditional choices concerning their future occupations than did girls with low self-esteem.

Gottfredson's (1981) research in occupational circumscription, reported in some depth in Chapter 4, suggests that as children grow older, the occupations acceptable to them are progressively reduced in number. This process of circumscription or reduction begins as early as age 6. According to Gottfredson's perspective, the occupations children first eliminate from consideration are those they perceive to be inappropriate for their sex. Between ages 9 and 13, children enter into a second phase of circumscription in which they begin to rule out occupations of insufficient prestige for their social class self-concept as well as occupations requiring effort beyond their view of their general ability level. Such research has indicated that by the time children are in the fourth grade, they have constructed a job-prestige hierarchy similar to that constructed by adults (Gottfredson, 1981). Miller (1986) has suggested that career education in the upper elementary grades should focus on counteracting the effects of occupational elimination based on social class inappropriateness or sex stereotyping. Thus, career education or career guidance in the elementary grades should include nontraditional role models, guest speakers, photographs and films, presentations, discussions, books, and field trips that focus on offsetting the premature foreclosure of options that tend to operate on sex and social class criteria unless interventions are planned and comprehensively provided.

Hales and Fenner (1972, 1973) have reported research findings indicating that values related to work begin to form in childhood and that these values enter into preadolescent vocational behavior. In particular, their research has shown that "although sixth-grade pupils differ in the work values which they hold, the work values of different groups (male-female, social classes) are more alike than they are dissimilar" (1973, p. 31). They further contend that an exploration of work values by elementary pupils may be useful in initiating analysis of the world of work from a perspective that is less dominated by sex and social class roles than is true of interests and aspirations. Borow (1970), too, has proposed that career development in the elementary school can be better understood if it is presented within the context of values and the valuing process. Cooker's research findings (1973) are similar to those of Hales and Fenner (1973), although he suggests somewhat sharper sex differences in values, with boys who value such things as money and control more than girls, and girls who place more importance on altruism and helping others than boys; this finding suggests that the valuing process does begin in the preschool period. In other words, whether or not education and career guidance respond to this fact, the evidence shows that elementary school students have already begun to assimilate perceptions and preferences that may be wholesome and meaningful or distorted and ultimately harmful to aspirations and achievement.

Additional Perspectives

Some additional perspectives on the ability of elementary school children to conceive of themselves in occupational terms, the sex differences in such behavior, and the knowledge of elementary children about occupations and related phenomena can be obtained from the findings of the National Assessment of Educational Progress's Career and Occupational Development Project. The national study included some 28,000 nine-year-olds, (Miller, 1977). Selected findings from this assessment include the following:

1. Nine-year-olds can describe things they do well and things they cannot do well, although for the most part they are too young to relate these directly to occupational activities. It is harder for them to state their limitations than their strengths. More whites and children from homes where parents possess education beyond high school than blacks or children whose parents have not completed high school are able to list both strengths and weaknesses.
2. Nine-year-olds have limited methods of evaluating their own abilities or are unable to do this. Females more often judge by what others say or by tests and grades, whereas males more often judge by personal comparison or comparison with a piece of data.
3. Most nine-year-olds are able to state strong and weak interest activities but fewer are able to state weak interests than are able to state strong interests.
4. Nine-year-olds generally have much knowledge of the duties and requirements of visible occupations, although there is evidence of sex differences in the knowledge of specific occupations.
5. When given a list of 26 household skills and maintenance-building skills that are work-related and done without assistance, most nine-year-olds indicated that they had done many of the activities (for example, babysat, repaired a toy, shopped at the store, planted vegetables or flowers, painted an object).
6. About 60 percent of nine-year-olds have participated in out-of-school learning experiences such as special training and lessons. Males, blacks, and children whose parents have less than a high school education have had fewer such experiences than other groups.
7. Most nine-year-olds can give acceptable responses to exercises that measure their skills in working effectively with peers, co-workers, and others.
8. Most nine-year-olds do not perceive themselves as being responsible for their own behavior.
9. Most nine-year-olds show resourcefulness in completing a task assigned to them when the instructions are clear. However, fewer nine-year-olds are able or willing

to take the initiative to seek assistance in completing a task that is unclear to them.

10. About 60 percent of nine-year-olds see the responsibility for selecting what work they will do for a living as belonging to someone other than themselves. Blacks and those whose parents do not have high school diplomas are less apt to see their future work as their own decision than are whites or those whose parents have more than a high school education.

National findings such as these provide information relevant to career guidance program planning and also to the variability of children's development.

Importance of the School Years

The first ten years of life have been called, correctly, the "nursery of human nature." This is the period of life when a child's goals, achievement motivation, and perceptions of self as worthy or inferior begin to be formulated. The concepts children acquire during this life stage directly influence later school success, career identity, adult interests, and general perspectives on life.

Elementary school children, in their play and school groups, are concerned with individual differences, work, adult life patterns, and personal feelings of competence, which they translate into self-perspectives and preferences for some work or educational activities to the exclusion of others. Whether based on accurate information or not, such perspectives direct the child's behavior unless subsequent experiences change such directions.

One can speculate that not all the information and influences from which these preferences and perceptions are derived are appropriate or accurate. Frequently, unrealistic career plans are made at this level because of the emphasis in parent and community attitudes, as well as in textbooks, on prestige fields, frequently defined as those requiring college preparation. Such an emphasis obscures consideration of other occupations that employ large proportions of workers, offer equally potent gratifications, and are growing in demand. During the past twenty years, various studies have shown that only a small fraction of the many existing types of work are presented to children in elementary school texts and in basal readers. Frequently, the occupations presented reinforce sex-typing (male chef, female waitress; male physician, female nurse) or other unfortunate distortions (Herr, 1977b).

This phenomenon is but one evidence of the increasingly rigid walls between the preadolescent (and the adolescent) and the occupational niches and educational options to which they must relate. Far too often, large segments of the student population—those from the culture of poverty and those from homes in which the children are economically favored but psychologically disadvantaged—have no systematic models of effective behavior or of enthusiasm to which to relate and no environmental support for developing personally and socially fulfilling behavior. Although all children have some adult models, they probably do not all have models who display a range of adequate behavior and also a consistent vocational identity that provides a stable base for the child's self and occupational explorations.

The effects of a stagnated or unresponsive home or school life can be inferred from Hunt (1961). He points out that, according to Piaget,

> The rate of development is in substantial part, but certainly not wholly, a function of environmental circumstances. . . . The greater the variety of situations to which the child must accommodate his behavioral structures, the more differentiated and mobile they become. Thus, the more new things a child has seen and the more he has heard, the more things he is interested in seeing and hearing. Moreover, the more variation in reality with which he has coped, the greater is his capacity for coping. (pp. 258–259)

There is, then, the danger that when the educational process does not create flexibility of behavior and awareness of ways to obtain goals, the seeds of an anomic situation are inadvertently planted. If we hold a carrot up to children, a culturally valued goal, whether a prestige occupation or a certain level of educational attainment, without expending equal energy in developing command of the means whereby children can obtain these goals, we have negated our concepts of individual differences and education as a process of development. Further, we are operating from a narrow view of ability and reinforcing a restrictive definition of individual talent.

Research indicates that many youngsters who drop out of school physically at age 16 have already dropped out of school psychologically as early as grade three. Frequently, this occurs because they fail to sense relationships between what they study in school and life as they experience it outside of school. Some generalize school failures or feelings of incompetence to all academic experiences. They acquire a psychological set that generates resistance to schooling and to the possibility of working toward a self-fulfilling future. Such children probably do not comprise the majority of elementary school children. Many children do develop awareness of their personal uniqueness, possible life options, methods of planning, and ways of becoming responsible for their futures. Unless opportunities for the last behavior to occur are systematically planned and the elementary school curriculum is augmented with career guidance activities, many other children may learn inadequate behaviors or incorrect information about themselves or their opportunities.

Many of the career guidance goals and career education emphases identified in this chapter or earlier ones have long been a part of the elementary school's philosophy. Dewey (1931), for example, believed that the child's knowledge began by doing and that industrially oriented themes, problems, and activities provided the potential to satisfy native tendencies to explore, to manipulate tools and materials, and to construct and create. Indeed, Dewey saw that industrial themes or problems could serve as a correlating medium for other subjects (1931), and as opportunities to acquire knowledge of the industrial world, the fundamental processes of economic life (1931), and the sociocultural backgrounds of vocations (1931). Unfortunately, restricted or incomplete information and a lack of systematic planning have reduced the power of many schools to achieve these goals. By implementing the stages of planning identified in Chapter 6 and incorporating many of the activities identified later in this chapter into a school's offerings, however, one should be able to make such goals accessible to more students.

COUNSELORS AND CAREER GUIDANCE

The elementary school counselor has many responsibilities and techniques for discharging this professional role. Historically, the processes used by elementary school counselors have been defined as the three C's: counseling, coordinating, and consulting. How much each of these is used depends on the needs and resources that characterize a local setting. The American School Counselors Association (1977) has stated, "Consistent with the philosophy of education, elementary school counseling concerns itself with children in the developmental process of maximizing their potential. The elementary counselor works within the educational framework and the child's total environment to enable each child to arrive at an identity and learn to make choices and decisions that lead to effective functioning as a worthwhile being" (p. 1).

It is within such a context that planning for career guidance becomes important for an elementary school counselor. There are many ways to conceive the planning process; several examples follow. Halverson (1970) has proposed several principles of career development that are useful to planning, based on characteristics of elementary school children.

1. [One principle is] the need for goals and objectives that are defined in terms of educational needs and interests of students at this stage of development.
2. The consideration of career development within the larger concept of all the goals of the elementary school [is also a factor]. It should not be a new, fragmented, or separate piece of the curriculum, but an integral part of goals already validated for elementary education.
3. Curriculum planning as it is influenced by career development should not be dominated by college-preparatory emphases.
4. Readiness for learning in terms of career development must take into account what has already been learned or experienced by the student, the projected goals that relate to the student's expressed or identified needs, and the level of his or her intellectual, social, and emotional maturity.
5. Concrete experiences and learning must precede learning of the abstract. Younger children function more successfully in the concrete realm than in the abstract, with the readiness for abstractions increasing with age.
6. If goals for career development are adopted, experiences and activities must be sequenced in such a way as to maximize the likelihood that students will achieve these goals.
7. There are many subject areas and activities in the elementary school which can be vocationalized. Thus, career development can be integrated with other instructional goals.

As the elementary school child moves through increasingly complex phases of awareness about self-characteristics and the local world, he or she also moves from being a nonspecialized consumer of input to a more action-oriented investigator of selective types of input, and finally in the junior and senior high school years becomes a candidate for future educational experiences or for a particular work role. This general overview of career development roughly parallels the paradigms of Ginzberg, Super, Tiedeman, and O'Hara, as discussed in Chapter 4. It also reflects the notions of Piaget (1929) about the stages of cognitive development, of Kohlberg (1968) about moral reasoning, or of Dewey (1931) about behavior-appropriate learning. Collectively these views suggest that the content of guidance or education—in this case career development concepts—will be most effective when they are atuned to the patterns of thought that are natural to a child of the age concerned. For elementary school children such content is learned better when approached at a concrete rather than an abstract level.

GOALS FOR CAREER GUIDANCE IN THE ELEMENTARY SCHOOL

There are several perspectives on appropriate goals of career guidance in the elementary school. One such view is that career guidance in elementary schools should provide experiences by which students can do the following (Herr, 1976b):

1. Realize that understanding one's strengths, values, and preferences is the foundation for education and occupational choices
2. Understand that it is possible to achieve future goals by planning and preparation in the present
3. Achieve a sense of personal competence to choose and to meet the requirements of educational and occupational alternatives
4. Consider the implications of change in one's self, in one's options, and in relation to the need for continuing education throughout life
5. Understand the similarities between problem-solving and personal decision-making skills

6. Develop an unbiased, nonstereotyped base of information from which to plan later educational and occupational decisions
7. Understand that schooling is made up of many opportunities to explore and to prepare for life
8. Recognize the relationships between academic skills—reading, writing, computation—and other subject matter and how these are used in future educational and work options
9. Identify occupations in which people work with others, with ideas, or with things
10. Consider the relationships between occupation, career, and life style
11. Describe the purposes that work serves for different people
12. Consider the importance of effective use of leisure time (pp. 1–2)

The National Occupational Information Coordinating Committee (1988) has identified 11 competencies, as well as the behavioral indicators for each, that the committee views as representative of "the basic skills and attitudes that children should acquire to deal effectively with daily life, to make the transition into the middle/junior high school and to start developing an educational plan to insure their academic growth and continuing career development" (p. 12). As such, they also provide the bases for developing goals for career guidance in the elementary schools. The NOICC competencies (goals) for the elementary school are listed here not in order of priority but include the following:

1. Knowledge of the importance of a positive self-concept to career development
2. Skills for interacting with others
3. Awareness of the importance of emotional and physical development on career decision making
4. Awareness of the importance of educational achievement to career opportunities
5. Awareness of the interrelationship of work and learning
6. Skills for understanding and using career information
7. Awareness of the interrelationship of personal responsibility, good work habits, and career opportunities
8. Awareness of how careers relate to needs and functions of society
9. Understanding of how to make decisions and choose alternatives related to tentative educational and career goals
10. Awareness of the interrelationship of life roles and careers
11. Awareness of different occupations and changing male/female roles

Depending on the setting and the characteristics of the children being served, many other goals might be developed for a local program of career guidance. Others have been suggested in Chapter 6, and a careful reading of this text will suggest still others. Indeed, it may be more important for "significant others" to understand the developmental needs of children than for the children to understand their own needs. Such goals for career guidance in the elementary school can be useful in parenting classes or in efforts to stimulate community volunteers of PTAs to help give children work-relevant exploratory experience. Regardless of which goals are finally chosen, however, several thoughts need to be kept in mind.

The goals and the characteristics of elementary school children discussion earlier in this chapter should make one point very clear: if career guidance in the elementary schools is to make a difference, simply providing periodic occupational units in which students are told about work is not sufficient. As a result of a study of the types of occupational information used in vocational decision making by 294 boys in grades four, six, eight, ten, and twelve, Biggers (1971) concluded, "Less effort might be devoted to novel ways of disseminating information and more effort given to helping students learn to use the information." He further maintains, "Guidance programs beginning in the elementary grades must recognize the need and plan appropriate experiences to increase the student's ability to use information in vocational decision-making, which is the reason for disseminating vocational information in the first place" (p. 175).

Biggers's observations are well worth noting. To be useful in the elementary school, information must be available in a wide range of reading levels and other sensory modes. In addition, activities will have to meet the diverse needs of students in their initial forays into career development. Parents need to be involved, and when this is not possible, some children need to be provided with adult occupational models. Counselors will have to be activists, initiating and coordinating experiences for different children both within and outside of the educational process. Educational materials and the attitudes of teachers need to be influenced to contribute to vocationalization. Speaking specifically about the role of elementary school counselors in facilitating such processes, the American School Counselors Association (ASCA) states, "As children reach the upper elementary grades, effort is directed through the curriculum toward increasing student awareness of the relationship between school and work, especially the impact of educational choices on one's life style and career development" (ASCA, 1981, p. 9).

Parental Influences

The involvement of parents in this process is not limited to their role as the prime source of influence on their child's occupational perceptions at the time he or she begins school. Rather, at the elementary school level in particular, counselors should develop strategies to help parents answer these questions: "Why career guidance? When does career development begin? Is home environment related to career development? When should my child begin to explore occupations? What are schools and employment agencies doing in this field? How much education will my child need to succeed in different careers? Should a parent ever choose an occupation for his or her child? Should a parent encourage a child to work part-time while in high school? Do young people give sufficient thought to the choice of an occupation?" (Knapp & Bedford, 1967). By using such a strategy, counselors are making parents collaborators rather than isolates in the guidance process and in the education of their children.

As suggested in Chapter 4, because parents have direct control over the environment in which their children are raised, they have the unique opportunity to expose them to experiences designed to enhance their self-fulfillment. As their children enter education, parents share but do not give up the responsibility for their development. Unfortunately, the complexity and dynamic quality of the current occupational structure make it very difficult for most parents to serve as the chief career guidance agents for their children. Indeed, parents are frequently worried about their own occupational future, unsure of how their work contributes to a final product or fits into a total institutional pattern, or confused about the multitude of jobs they see around them.

Such circumstances are exacerbated when economic turmoil and major occupational restructuring are occurring, as in the present American environment. However, for many elementary school children, the problem of stable and informed parental support has been made more difficult because of the changing family structures within which so many children live. Owing partially to economic circumstances and partially to shifting social values, the single-parent household is becoming the new norm for childhood experience. Fifty-nine percent of the children born in 1983 will live with only one parent before reaching age 18. More infants are beginning life with one parent, a mother who herself may still be a child. Many of the children who live in households headed by females also grow up in or near poverty. One child in five under age 19 and one child in four under age 6 is now classified as poor by national standards. Black and Hispanic children living in households headed by females are at the greatest risk of growing up in poverty (The College Board Commission on Precollege Guidance and Counseling, 1986, p. 6; Herr, 1989b)

In such situations, many parents feel incapable of providing career guidance or other support to their children—some, because of economic and personal stresses, do not have the psychic energy to do so. Other parents are simply unclear about how they can be an effective part of their children's development. Often they need reassurance from counselors that they can make such a contribution, as well as an understanding of what form it might take. Although not confined to the elementary school, specific ways that parents can contribute to the career guidance program include these:

1. Parents can encourage and help their children to analyze their interests, capabilities, and limitations.
2. In the work areas with which they are most familiar, they can help their children relate worker traits, conditions of work, lifestyles of workers, and potential opportunities for work.
3. They can discuss work values that they have experienced in themselves and others and relate some of the consequences.
4. Parents can discuss the economic condition of the family and help the youth to plan what education and training will help him or her break out of the constraints of these conditions.
5. Parents can provide encouragement and information as to how their child can use the knowledge, experience, and services of relatives, friends, fellow workers, and community or state agencies in exploring, planning, and preparing for their work role.
6. Parents should provide the necessary example and counsel to their children during crucial developmental periods to help them establish and maintain a positive self-concept.
7. They should display the attitude that *all* persons have dignity and worth no matter what occupational position they hold.
8. They can provide situations in which their children can experience decision making and carry responsibility for the consequences of their decisions.
9. They should provide open communication between home and school so that the experiences and the consultation possibilities in both environments can be used to meet the children's needs.
10. Parents should encourage their children to explore a wide spectrum of alternatives, both educational and occupational, without stereotyping or labeling any alternatives to discourage the child's consideration of them.
11. They should be sensitive to and acceptant of the ambivalence or tentativeness that children frequently exhibit about self-images or images of future career alternatives.
12. Without defensiveness about their lack of specific information, parents can help their children contact specialists or find information relevant to their concerns.
13. They can learn about the relationships between specific educational patterns and occupations in order to help their children to plan their educational experiences effectively.
14. Parents can provide opportunities for work within the home and the community with the opportunity to accept responsibility.

In a study of 382 parents of children in kindergarten, third, and fifth grade in five Maryland public schools, Birk and Blimline (1984) focused on both the importance of parental influence on elementary school children and parental perspectives of their role in their children's career development. They found that, although parents are for the majority of children the most influential agents of occupational exploration, many parents also convey biases and stereotypes about occupational goals and, particularly, sex-appropriate goals. Thus, these researchers recommend that school counselors help parents develop attitudes to do the following:

1. Accept the challenge to actively collaborate with counselors and teachers in the career development process
2. Acknowledge and accept the importance of the parental role in career development
3. Maintain a belief in the importance of a child's self-concept in career decision making
4. Acknowledge the presence and value of work within the home family structure
5. Advocate increased career opportunities for all without regard to social or sexual stereotypes (p. 316)

In addition, Birk and Blimline suggest that counselors need to help parents to acquire accurate information about "(a) the role of parents in children's career decisions, (b) changing career choices and broadened options for males and females, (c) educational opportunities, (d) wage and salary statistics, (e) the importance and stages of career planning, (f) barriers to the career development process, (g) career resources in the school and community, (h) myths involved in sex-role stereotyping, (i) sex equity laws, and (j) ways to improve communication skills between the parent and the child" (p. 316).

THE RELATIONSHIP OF GOALS TO PROGRAM FUNCTIONS

As indicated in Chapter 6, program goals and behavioral statements of career guidance objectives should precede functions. Program goals should be cast as behavioral descriptions so that the counselor or teacher can evaluate whether the student has met the objectives specified for a grade or other educational level. Assuming for the moment that one has selected from Chapter 6 or has developed locally objectives pertinent to one's school setting and students, one must determine which functional options are available to accomplish the objectives. Several suggestions have already been offered in this chapter. The strategies should be concrete rather than abstract, at least in grades one though three; they should involve action rather than simply verbalization; and they should use multimedia approaches as much as possible. As stated previously, children are doers. They need to explore and try on different work roles.

Concrete Strategies for Implementing Goals. O'Hara (1968) adds several other observations that can be used to guide the selection and use of functions for fostering vocationalization or career development. First, the characteristics of career development discussed in this book are largely acquired needs pertinent to students in the United States and other developed nations of the world but are not necessarily part of the developmental needs of children in other cultures. Therefore, one must prepare children for career guidance or career education. One way to do this is to positively reinforce, through social approval from teachers, counselors, and parents, behaviors of children that are oriented to consideration of choices, information seeking, and participation in exploratory activities. If some teachers provide these experiences and encourage children to participate in or exhibit career development, but other teachers convey by attitude or behavior that these things are unimportant, many students are not likely to persist in the behavior. For example, if an elementary school child is trying to raise questions about work or choice making but is constantly patted on the head and told not to worry about those things now, the child is not likely to continue to consider them important. If they were, this teacher, who is a significant influence in the child's life, would deal with them.

Second, because many of the problems to which early efforts at career development are directed are remote, real or simulated experiences must be provided in which children can make decisions and experience the consequences of those decisions. This may be done by permitting children to plan a particular project and then analyzing the results, or by working through illustrative case materials or games, identifying decision factors and alternative outcomes. From such immediate experiences, bridges are built from the academic world to the world of work. Furthermore, ways must be found to convert daily intellectual problems into occupational problems, thus allowing children to learn a variety of responses to problem-solving circumstances.

The child must also be helped to develop cues by which personally important concepts and ideas can be distinguished from unimportant ones. The child needs to have translated into his or her terms such concepts as relative importance, compromise, irreversibility, synthesis, and developmental process.

In order to differentiate or integrate self-characteristics and characteristics of the occupational world, the child must be assisted in developing a broad repertoire of pertinent words—the language of occupations. Without them, students lack the tools for manipulating and symbolizing the world as it pertains to them.

Hunt (1970) has stressed the importance of symbolization to the student's ability to deal with the physical, social, and the inner worlds as they relate to career development. She sees each of these three abilities as competencies that children must acquire as foundations for career development. In extending this line of reasoning, she recommends that children study workers primarily as problem solvers. Regardless of whether the medium used to help students develop an understanding of different occupations is a field trip, demonstration, film, or reading, students should be encouraged to ask these questions:

1. What is the nature of the problem of living that this person routinely solves?
2. What is the nature of this person's competencies?
3. What special tools does this person use for solving problems?
4. What special facilities does this person need?
5. Could I do what this person is doing?

In addition, Hunt has argued that from kindergarten through the third grade, the emphasis should be more on manipulative direct experience than on vicarious experience. The emphasis at these grade levels is on "Who am I?" rather than "What do others do for me or tell me about?" This also means that the tools or the media that are made available in these experiences must be physically manageable. Besides gaining an understanding about work, children must gain perceptions of themselves as successful with these tools or media. At the fourth- to sixth-grade levels, Hunt suggests that although concrete direct experiences are still vital, the array of tools and media needs to be expanded to provide more and more problem-solving challenges requiring exploration of information and acquisition of basic skills.

What is implicit in the positions of O'Hara and Hunt is that people and work are irrevocably related. Thus, occupational information is valuable to the degree that it can diminish an outside-the-person focus and stimulate the child's earning and exploration as a part of seeing himself or herself in process as having and exhibiting freedom of choice. This emphasis on people as workers and as problem solvers also reinforces for the elementary school child the importance of "me" and "my characteristics" as primary influences on "my future."

Sequencing Career Guidance Experiences. The previous observations about how elementary school children learn and grow reinforce the importance of sequencing career development experiences from concrete to abstract. First-grade activities should differ from sixth-grade ones, even though the themes or the attitudes to be developed remain constant. In considering sequencing, one must also consider gender differences, as these affect knowledge about or realistic attitudes toward career development.

Norris (1963) has suggested a career guidance sequence in the elementary schools, particularly in terms of occupational information:

Kindergarten.The child learns about the work activities of his mother, his father, and other members of his household.

Grade 1.The child learns about work in his immediate environment—his home, school, and neighborhood.

Grade 2.The child learns about community helpers who serve him as well as about familiar stores and businesses in the neighborhood.

Grade 3.The child studies the expanding community. Emphasis is placed upon transportation, communication, and other major industries.

Grade 4.The child learns about the world of work at the state level including main industries of the state.

Grade 5.The child's studies broaden to cover the industrial life of the nation. Major industries of the various sections of the United States are selected.

Grade 6.The child's program is expanded to include the entire western hemisphere. Life in Canada and in South and Central America is contrasted with life in the United States (p. 56).

Bank (1969, p. 285) has provided a derivation of Norris' grade-level theme by focusing on occupational role models exemplifying particular emphases:

Kindergarten	School role — models	Principal Teacher School secretary University professor
First grade	Community role — models who help feed us	Grocer Milkman Waitress
Second grade	Community role — models who protect our health	Dentist Nurse's aide Doctor
Third grade	Models who protect our health — personal hygiene	Barber Beauty operator
	Models who provide shelter	Plumber Building cleaner
	Models who protect us	Lawyer Fireman Policeman
Fourth grade	Models who provide transportation	Gas station manager Bus driver Airline stewardess
Fifth grade	Models who provide communication	Postman Printer Photo-journalist
Sixth grade	Models who provide for business	Banker Office secretary Salesclerk

Beyond the examples of using occupational role models to sequence career guidance experiences for elementary school children, many career education projects have identified specific concepts appropriate to each grade or educational level by which to organize activities or experiences for children. These approaches are very much like those suggested in Chapter 6. Although there are many examples available, two will illustrate the point here.

The Concepts of Awareness and Accommodation. Bailey and Stadt (1973, pp. 351–359) have suggested that kindergarten through sixth grade can be divided into two stages: awareness (kindergarten through grade three) and accommodation (grades four through six). These in turn can be broken into subgoals as follows:

Awareness (K–3)

1. Awareness of self
2. Awareness of different types of occupational roles
3. Awareness of individual responsibility for own actions
4. Development of the rudiments of classification and decision-making skills
5. Learning cooperative social behavior
6. Development of respect for others and the work that they do

Accommodation (4–6)

1. Development of concepts related to self
2. Development of concepts related to the world of work
3. Assuming increased responsibility for planning one's time
4. Application of decision-making and classification skills
5. Development of desirable social relationships
6. Development of work attitudes and values

Each of these concepts stimulates the development of career guidance experiences that will facilitate the behaviors, attitudes, or knowledge involved. Somewhat similar is the sequence of concepts that guides the career development exemplary project in the District of Columbia Schools (1976). There are many subconcepts distributed across kindergarten through grade six, but the subconcepts and career development activities at each grade level are derived from five:

1. There is dignity in all work.
2. The life of a culture depends on its workers who produce goods and services.
3. There are many different kinds of work.
4. Mankind uses tools for work.
5. Work has rewards.

In addition to such concepts, children would likely benefit from the realization that school is a child's work and that its rules, expectations, and content are organized in many ways parallel to the adult world of work.

EXAMPLES OF PROGRAM CONTENT

These approaches to sequencing show awareness of the developing radius of the interests of elementary school students and their increasing capacity for abstractions. They do not, however, directly suggest what content to include or what emphases would lead to the outcomes suggested. There are many possibilities.

In Chapter 6, the Florida Blueprint for Career Preparation was cited as an example of the development of programs of career guidance at various state levels. As part of the follow-up to the Blueprint, the Florida State Department has identified what it describes as "best practices." Some of these follow for the elementary school (Florida Department of Education, 1990, p. 4).

GRADES K–5

At the elementary school level, the *Blueprint* calls for a career development program that infuses self-, career-, and technology-awareness activities into the curriculum.

Schoolwide. Dream Lake Elementary, in Apopka, offers an annual event called "Careers on the Move." On this day, community members bring the vehicles they use in their work to school and give brief presentations about their careers and how the vehicles are used in them. These presentations also include information about how math, reading, computer, or other skills are used; what specialized education the careers require; and the importance of timeliness and dependability. Students who view the vehicles also get to talk with the drivers and learn about such wide-ranging occupations as furniture deliver, tire service, telephone installation and repair, vehicle towing, cement mixing, carpentry, garbage collection, street sweeping, insurance investigation, and undertaking.

Grade K–1. Some methods are developing career resource centers—collections of puzzles, games, toys, tools, and other information that can be used for activities to help students understand what goes on in various careers. To increase parental involvement and interest, instruct students to ask their parents to donate something representative of their careers to the resource center. For instance, a carpenter might donate a measuring tape; a practice session on using the measuring tape would teach both a valuable skill and awareness of what a carpenter does.

Grades 1–2. A simply drawn map of the local neighborhood can be used to teach students at this level about their local streets as well as various careers. By following an imaginary bus driver or mail deliverer through these streets, children get practice in reading maps, counting turns, reading street signs, and experiencing what these people do when they work.

Grade 3. In a dark room, pour hot water into a wide-mouthed jar, then place ice cubes on top of the jar. Shining a flashlight through the middle of the jar will reveal the formation of a cloud. A discussion of how weather affects our lives can lead to lists of careers directly influenced by or dependent on weather—meterologist, air-conditioning and heating mechanics, clothing manufacturers, builders, and health care workers.

Grade 4. After a class discussion of career clusters and the life-styles associated with various careers, students can complete a brief written self-appraisal which determines some of their likes and dislikes. When they share the results of this interest inventory with others in the class, other students can suggest careers that might satisfy their preferences.

Grade 5. By videotaping interviews with workers at various job sites around town about their jobs, students can develop map-reading skills, interviewing techniques, technological (VCR) expertise, and awareness of the careers they observe. While on the job sites, they can collect information about the location, type of environment, tools used, noise and/or comfort level, risks involved, attitudes of the people they observe, and a multitude of other factors.

Another way of sequencing content has been advocated by Ridener (1973). Based on 23 concepts that are to provide the kindergarten through sixth-grade curricula, this approach emphasizes careers of the month, in which instructional guides tie occupations and careers to specific subject matter at each grade level. Thus, each month careers associated with different subjects are highlighted, but no one curriculum reinforces the career concepts throughout the year. The suggested sequence is used to introduce career concepts in a variety of ways throughout the school in September; in October, language arts careers are highlighted; November, math careers; December, science careers; January, social science careers; February, fine arts careers; March, vocational educational careers; and April, health and physical education careers. Finally, in May, activities occur by which the concepts focused on throughout the year can be reviewed and reinforced.

Schmidt (1976), working with a team of elementary school teachers and counselors in the Colorado Springs School District, designed a career guidance program built around two components. The first was concerned with increasing self-concepts of elementary children, and the second built on the first to help students explore careers. The self-concept component was divided into four basic areas: strength-building, in which students were taught how to identify strength in others; values identification, by which students could be helped to clarify their own value systems; goal-setting, in which students established minigoals important to larger aspirations and monitored their progress in achieving these; and life management, in which they discussed obstacles to their self-made goals and developed strategies for overcoming them. The second component, career awareness, involved the use of several types of commercial resources. One, *Career Kits for Kids*, was used at the kindergarten through second grade level and allowed students to role-play different types of workers and wear hats and uniforms that fit each particular role. Real workers in the selected areas were invited in to provide actual work process examples for the children and show them the tools used in the occupations. In addition, puppet shows and songs were made up by the children about different forms of work. The second commercial resource used in this component was a series of six filmstrip units (*Career Discoveries*—Guidance Associates) that dealt with broad career areas such as "people who influence others" and "people who make things." The emphases here were on the types of persons in different jobs, their lifestyles, and the strengths, values, and goals they brought to their job. Again, guest speakers were brought in and students compared their personal profiles developed in the self-concept component to those appropriate to different work options.

Related to the content and method suggested by Schmidt, it was implied by Sander, Westerberg, and Hedstrom (1978) that the world of children's literature offers a wide variety of ways to explore decision making or other career guidance objectives. They summarize ten stories from children's literature that could be useful. Included are stories dealing with decision making and the consequences of making unwise choices, self-awareness and economic awareness, and other topics.

Somewhat similarly, Nelson (1979) has described the CREST program, which through three storybooks for children and related materials and activities translates the concepts of choice awareness in a way that is intended to be understandable and engrossing for children. It helps them see the many ways in which they are in charge of themselves and the many alternatives they have as they choose their ways. Research on the project indicated that children in the experimental condition were able to produce more choices, and those choices were judged to be more positive, than were those of children in the control condition. Teacher responses were also found to be quite positive about the value of the CREST program.

The T4C program operates from kindergarten through grade six in many New Jersey schools (New Jersey State Department of Education, 1973). This approach integrates world-of-work concepts within traditional subject areas and emphasizes hands-on experiences by which students can become acquainted with various technological processes. Each T4C classroom has a complete set of hand (and sometimes power) tools and teachers have guides for 47 learning episodes that can be tied into various subjects at different grade levels. Episodes include "Discovering Machines" and "Merchandising" in kindergarten, "Writing Poems for Silk Screen Cards" in first-grade language arts classes, "Exploring Electricity," in third-grade natural sciences, and "Weather Station" in sixth-grade science. In each episode, simple problems using appropriate technologies are completed by the children, written about, and demonstrated in other ways.

Wircenski, Fales, and Wircenski (1978) reported on a project for a combined second- and third-grade class in the Lafayette, Indiana, schools. The specific objectives were to help the children learn the following concepts:

1. That the world of work is composed of many interrelated jobs in order to plan, design, advertise, manufacture, distribute, and service goods
2. That all jobs are important
3. That cooperation among all workers is very important

These objectives were met by engaging the class in constructing a small wooden wagon and by carrying out activities related to the manufacture of the wagon in various subject areas. Students were assigned to various manufacturing tasks after job specialization required to assemble the wagon was studied. Examples of the uses of related subject areas included the following: music—a promotional song was written and sung by the students; art—a company logo was designed and advertising materials produced; English—various writing assignments dealing with the history of work, the importance of manufacturing, and career opportunities available were produced; math—material and supply needs were calculated and related production times and likely salaries were computed; social studies and science—the principles of manufacturing were studied. As part of the project each student was interviewed, hired, and trained for his or her job. In engaging in the project, students were also exposed to the importance of work ethics, leadership, cooperation, and respect for others.

Fifield and Peterson (1978) have described the use of job simulation to enhance vocational exploration in the elementary schools. At the time of the report, more than thirty units based on the fifteen USOE career clusters, discussed in Chapter 3 and in other places in this book, were being rotated through classrooms in Logan, Utah. The units were either located in classrooms or in mobile units moved among elementary schools. According to the authors, the following steps were taken to develop each simulation unit:

1. A mock-up site was prepared (for example, for the auto brake repair unit, a car fender appropriately mounted with backing plate and brake parts was provided; for the plumbing unit, the section of a wall in which a wash basin and pipe fixtures were installed was provided). In most cases, the mock-up used a workbench or work area where materials and tools were organized. . . .
2. Appropriate materials and tools were assembled and made available for each unit. . . . The student was required to perform only the essential tasks in completing each simulated unit. Real tools associated with the respective jobs were used and the mock-up for the job was designed as realistically as possible.
3. Instructions and directions were narrated on a cassette tape that was accompanied by a set of written directions and appropriate pictures. . . .
4. Supportive career materials, such as videotapes, catalogues, career brochure, and other literature pertaining to the occupations were used as the principal source of illustrative materials. (p. 329)

Each unit was designed to be completely self-contained so that the teacher could serve strictly as a monitor.

In addition to using the USOE clusters as organizing themes and content for career development in the elementary schools, McGee and Silliman (1982) use interest measurement as a basis for career awareness activities. In particular, they describe the five sections of *What I Like To Do* (Meyers, Drinkard, & Zinner, 1975)—play, academics, the arts, occupations, and reading—as the basis for developing small-group guidance activities. They then suggest sample activities that can be used in working through the individual sections of the inventory. Included would be use of slides and newspaper or magazine picture showing different people working, student journals in which written assignments related to "what I want to be" are maintained, interest trading corners, library research, writing brief job descriptions, bulletin board projects, and interviews with workers.

Handel (1973) has suggested three techniques found to be useful as career guidance activities: career corner, seminar special, and brainstorming. Found to be useful with fifth and sixth graders, career corner comprises a large pegboard with manila packets containing information about various careers placed in an activity area. Pertinent film loops, filmstrips, and tapes can also be placed in the activity area and keyed to the information on the pegboard. Students can develop their own synopses of information in which they are interested and place them into a personal job bank folder for future use. The seminar special consists of devoting periodic morning meetings to visits from people in the community who bring objects they use in their work for the children to handle. These objects provide a focal point to discuss the career area each adult visitor represents. With some cross-class scheduling, several adults can be involved in adjacent rooms each morning, and students can move between them. Brainstorming in this situation was confined primarily to counselor-teacher discussions of the range of possibilities by which teachers could reinforce career development concepts in their subject matter. Although ultimately providing career guidance input to classrooms, this technique was found to increase rapport between the counselor and teachers and promote a team effort in career guidance.

Enhancing career awareness in the elementary school does not necessarily require expensive and sophisticated devices or processes. In line with the intent of the career education movement discussed in Chapter 1, it is important to meld diverse instructional materials and teaching strategies into a sequential program of career awareness, exploration, and preparation from kindergarten through grade twelve and beyond. Within that context, Staley and Mangiesi (1984) have described the use of books to enhance career awareness and to help elementary school students learn about career options.

Use of a wide assortment of informational, fictional, and biographical material provides children with vicarious experiences and the necessary background for dreaming and fantasizing about career options. In some instances, different types of books can be used as a supplement to discussions, field trips, and specific units about work. In other situations, books will form the nucleus for achieving particular career objectives such as providing positive role models, illustrating men and women in nontraditional occupations or with equal opportunities and commitments to work, and reinforcing opportunities for sexual and racial balance in the workplace.

Staley and Mangiesi have suggested four strategies for using books in career development: (1) choosing books that appeal to both younger and older children with diverse interests; (2) reading aloud to the class those books likely to appeal to most students, providing them vicarious career experiences to talk about, write about, and think about; (3) allowing students blocks of time for sustained silent reading of books of their choice; and (4) using trade books as background material for teachers and counselors to work together to prepare career awareness units on preplanned themes appropriate to different grades.

In Detroit, Michigan, an elementary school employment service has been developed to give children the opportunity to learn about the rules of work and to have work experiences in and after school (Leonard, 1972). Additional goals are for children to learn how to fill out job applications, develop positive attitudes toward work and a sense of responsibility toward a job, and understand the relationship between their school life and the world of work. Procedures are developed by which students can apply for, consider the requirements of, interview for, and be hired for such jobs as safety patrol member, service squad member, future teacher, lunchroom helper, room helper, audio-visual aide, office helper, custodian's helper, and library staff member. Hedstrom (1978) has described a similar project in the Kentwood, Michigan, schools.

All the projects reviewed here, although derived from somewhat different sets of objectives, give evidence of being responsive to the guidelines in this chapter. Their activities are also congruent with Kaback's (1966) observation, "The younger the child the greater the interest in the actual job performance itself. Most children are natural born actors; they want to act out in order to understand what it feels like to be a carpenter or a ballplayer" (p. 167).

There are several important implications in Kaback's statement. First, in terms of the media of career development, dramatizations, role-playing, and simulation have potential for children to figuratively project themselves into the characteristics of roles important to differences in occupations. Second, it is possible to help students identify with attainable occupations represented in their immediate neighborhoods or community. Finally, if children base their occupational preferences on job performance itself, this is a prime time to introduce them to the relationships between interests and occupational areas.

Laramore and Thompson (1970) have suggested encouraging students to fantasize about what they would like to do as adults and then pantomime those jobs, letting other students guess who they are and what they are doing. Other suggestions they provide include the following:

1. Have students discuss their hobbies and attempt to relate them to occupations.
2. Have upper-grade, elementary school children discuss any part-time jobs which they hold around the home or in the community with regard to what they like, the satisfactions they get, or how they spend the money obtained.
3. Have students write a résumé of their own skills (weeding, cutting grass, baby-sitting, ironing) and have them discuss how they might sell these skills to prospective employers in their neighborhood. (pp. 263–264)

Some elementary schools actually provide employment opportunities and personnel offices to serve different career guidance expectations. For example, the Schulte School in Sturtevant, Wisconsin, takes the position that children should assume responsibilities and make a meaningful contribution to the operation of the school. They also believe that students should understand the relationship between their activities in school and the real world outside the classroom (Elleson & Onnink, 1976). To these ends, they have created an employment office, Jobs, Inc., operated by the school counselor, which helps school staff members find needed workers and to help elementary school students find school jobs that they prefer.

Other interesting examples of providing students with hands-on experiences to take responsibility and to learn work procedures in the elementary schools are available. For example, Leonard (1972) has described an effective way to build career guidance experiences into a self-contained classroom situation and curriculum. He advocated the creation of a Popcorn Factory in which students play the roles of various workers in the factory and the teacher can use such content to make spelling, reading, writing, and arithmetic more meaningful while expanding each student's perspective on work and on himself or herself.

Johnson (1980) has described an elementary school career education program for kindergarten through sixth grades that was designed to help students learn about the free enterprise system and to develop an awareness of various jobs and job responsibilities within such a system. All students participated in a six-week course that highlighted job information through team teaching, lectures, group discussions, filmstrips, field trips, and guest speakers. After the six-week overview of the free enterprise economy, students moved into the specific teams dealing with one of four areas: banking, farming, manufacturing, or retailing. After learning about jobs in these specific categories, the children selected the jobs they could best perform and, in doing so, actually made managerial decisions. For example, the bankers set up the Loaning Ranger's Bank, which provided procedures whereby students could deposit from one to five dollars per week or borrow from established funds. In the process of this activity, the children served in such positions as tellers, posters, filers, bookkeepers, and couriers. Similar environments for hands-on experiences were created by the farmers who developed a cultivatable plot of land into the Green Acres Farm and participated in the decisions and actual tasks involved with land preparation, seed planting, fertilizing and watering plants, harvesting, and selling crops to local retailers. The retailing group organized an emporium in which students served as managers, supply clerks, bookkeeping staff, and salespeople. They took a loan with interest from the Loaning Ranger's Bank to purchase stocks of school supplies, paper, pencils, and so on, sold vegetables on consignment from the Green Acres Farm, and brokered craft items produced by the last group, the manufacturers, in their factory. Students in the Purple Polka-Dot Factory sold stock certificates for 25 cents each to obtain initial operating capital, elected a board of directors to supervise factory operations, and manufactured such products as purple polka-dot necklaces, fuzzy wuzzy pencils, big-nose bookmarkers, and faculty favorite cookbooks.

Activities for the four teams were integrated with school curricula—math, science, spelling, social studies, and language arts—necessary to perform the various functions in the clusters. Pre- and post-test data indicated that student participants gained knowledge about the vocabulary and processes of the free enterprise system. Informal reactions solicited from students, teachers, parents, and the community were overwhelmingly positive.

Obviously, either of the projects reported by Leonard or Johnson, or those previously described, represent major career guidance thrusts of importance to counselors. They constitute both the substance and the planned sequence of activity that can yield important insights and skills to empower elementary school children to grow in career consciousness, self-awareness, and optimism about future opportunities.

CAREER GUIDANCE TECHNIQUES IN THE ELEMENTARY SCHOOL

Throughout this chapter we have suggested many career guidance techniques appropriately used in the elementary school. However, many others can be used to achieve particular program goals and behavioral objectives. Even the extensive list of techniques that follows is not exhaustive, since creative elementary school counselors and teachers will find additional ways to achieve selected career guidance goals. These may be used with individual students or groups of students, by the counselor or by a teacher. Many can also be used by the counselor in serving as a resource to teachers.

As suggested by the National Occupational Information Coordinating Committee (1988) career guidance and counseling programs in schools are based on seven processes: classroom instruction, counseling, assessment, career information, placement, consultation, and referral. The issue is what kind of content will they include. The following techniques represent examples that might be integrated with one of these seven processes.

Curriculum Infusion—Career Units

Provide reference books or biographies that portray personal decision making.

Show guidance films on selected topics.

Read poems such as Robert Frost's "The Road Not Taken" and have students compare them to decision making in their own lives.

Have students create and then discuss "I wish" poems.

Analyze short stories based on characters portraying different interests or values.

Select a career cluster requiring competence in particular subject matter (such as math, science, language) and identify occupations related to it.

Have students research some aspect of change—such as a means of transportation—compile pictures depicting changes and occupations affected, and arrange a bulletin board display related to the project.

Do oral reports on different occupations with the student pretending to be the worker in the report.

Have students write a paper on "The kind of person I am," "The kind of person I want to be," or "How I have changed in the past year."

Make a movie with students serving as plot writers, camerapersons, and graphic artists to illustrate communication careers.

Have students prepare an autobiography and address at least three ways in which their life is influenced by family, school, and peers.

Display words in a prominent place that refer to leisure-time occupations such as lapidary, numismatist, spelunker, philatelist, bibliophile. Have students look up the meaning of these words and consider how they relate to the use of leisure time.

Build interest centers around different career clusters or ways to assess self-characteristics.

Provide listening centers that include individual earphones, recording devices, record players, tapes and cassettes dealing with worker interviews, study skills, and topics related to self-understanding.

Group Activities

Play "Let's Pretend" or "What's My Line" using occupations or careers as the content.

Role play photo problems for children in grades 1 through 3. Mount photographs depicting various problems or situations pertinent to self-understanding or occupational differences on display board, and have children role-play their interpretation of the photos.

Have students discuss unfinished stories available in the *NEA Journal* and in other sources that cause them to consider alternative solutions to various problems.

Have students design posters depicting the steps or conditions important to responsible decision making.

Have students probe a problem-solving situation by making up the behavior of puppets.

Have students design table games in order to play different approaches to decision making, career options, or other life situations.

Divide class into "green" and "purple" groups, for example. Have students simulate discrimination of one color, analyze the behaviors involved, and relate to interpersonal skills or work adjustment.

Write a skit using terms from the world of work.

Develop crossword puzzles using terms from the world of work.

Use the help-wanted section of a newspaper to identify words from the world of work.

Have students compose questions and take part in a class "quiz show" based on occupations and educational alternatives.

Have students compose a help-wanted advertisement for a particular job.

Bring in a tool or material, or a uniform or a picture of one, and use these as the basis for a creative writing lesson about the objects or workers who use them.

Have students write about a fantasy or daydream about doing a certain job, draw pictures of themselves doing it, and identify the tools necessary. Discuss in class.

Using local job-related events, have students develop career pyramids to illustrate the interdependence of jobs required to accomplish the goal (such as build a new apartment house, airport, supermarket).

Have students produce a short cartoon strip about some aspect of the world of work that went wrong.

Have students collect pictures of workers whose occupations are clearly a means of self-expression, such as writer, musician, artist, and generate class discussion on the way in which other occupations are a means of self-expression; pictures may be used for bulletin board.

Have students participate in everyday decisions such as what to do in free time, which homework assignment to do first, where to eat lunch.

Have students plan a class party or field trip, identify the compromises that must be made, and list the risks or consequences.

Have students design creative drama skits that deal with self-concept, values, making choices, and other pertinent topics.

Have students compare lists of interests, abilities, and achievements with occupations in which these are important.

Have students identify feelings from pictures (sad, happy, and so on) and relate them to past situations in which they experienced these feelings.

Have students identify different roles they play, list them on the board, and have discussions on how these roles are learned or why they are important.

Have students maintain a diary in which they note things that make them feel unique, worthwhile, and deserving of respect.

Have students construct a career pyramid that illustrates the different types of jobs in a career area at different levels of education and responsibility. For example, in health careers, discuss the range of opportunities from the ambulance driver or sanitary inspector to the most sophisticated specialist.

Have students compose a brief job profile for a worker in each of the career clusters.

Given a series of pictures illustrating various community workers (police officer, truck driver, salesperson, teacher, construction worker), have the students give a job title for each, discuss the work activities involved and the problems they solve.

Have students describe ten different workers who built, maintain, or operate the school.

Have students list major problems facing society and then identify an occupation or career cluster that they think will have greatest effect on solving the problems.

Using a list of twenty to fifty occupations, have students give an example of a need or function of the community that is met by each occupation.

Using a list of ten to fifteen common occupations, have students describe those that are (1) mostly outside work, (2) mostly inside work, (3) both inside and outside work.

Using pictures of people at work, have students distinguish between those involving the production of goods or services.

Have students match pictures of tools and what they are used for (for example, rake-leaves, hammer-nails, saw-boards, screwdriver-screws). Discuss the use of tools for different purposes in school and in work.

Have students identify two commonly used tools in each career cluster.

Have dress-up clothes available for children to try on and pretend to be the workers. Discuss how they feel when they act out a particular worker's role and what would they like to know about such a worker.

Students will select an occupation of their choice and through a variety of media (resource books, filmstrips, interviews), develop an accurate description of a typical life-style for the worker in a chosen occupation.

Using a supply of magazines, have students locate one picture that breaks down the traditional male-female occupational role-typing (male nurse, female physician, male secretary, female truck driver). Discuss.

Students may keep a log of all the examples of occupational stereotyping that they discovered while watching TV.

Using a list of leisure-time activities (baseball, art, photography, rock collecting) have each student identify at least one occupation that could result from an interest in each activity.

Have students pantomime a leisure activity in which they engage. Other students try and guess the activity. Play "Twenty Questions" based on leisure-time activities of the students.

Have students plan and carry out a Hobby Fair in which each student is invited to bring an example of his or her hobby, and demonstrate or describe the hobby to the class.

Have students make a class display of various famous people engaging in their leisure field career.

In a role-playing situation, have students break into pairs and role-play an employer who is interviewing an applicant for a job. The interviewer wants to know why the person wants the job—besides the money.

Have children engage in comparison shopping while visiting a shopping center. Have children compare the costs of a box of eight crayons. Discuss.

Community Involvement—Career Surveys

Take field trips to sites that allow students to see how subject matter is applied to solve work problems or is necessary to facilitating work activity.

Invite resource persons to discuss how personal characteristics contribute to daily functioning or ask them to discuss their vocational history in relation to what they now do.

Have students "shadow" selected workers on the job to view the work activity in which they engage and the other types of workers with whom they interact.

Invite the director of the local adult education class to visit the school, discuss the program with students, and explain why adults take courses.

Develop and organize lists of resource speakers and field trips to observe the workers' roles in various occupations.

Visit a local factory and observe the entire production process. Assign small groups to study one aspect of the process thoroughly, make a display of it, and present it to the total class.

After an opportunity to interview a worker, have the student orally describe the career exploration of the worker, and the way in which the worker applied career exploration to the process of deciding to enter the career in which he or she is presently employed.

After talking with two adults in very different occupational roles, have students list four ways in which their occupation influences the life-style of each (amount of spare time available, money to buy various items, travel versus staying in one location, hobbies, friends).

Interview a parent or relative to discover the personal satisfactions obtained from working and leisure activities.

Have students visit a local sports equipment store and discuss with the manager the growing demand for sporting equipment for leisure time.

Have the class visit a local craftsperson or invite the person to visit the class. Have that person discuss his or her work in terms of speed, efficiency, economy, and quality. If possible, have the students compare the handcrafted product with its mass-produced counterpart. Stress that society needs both type of products.

The career guidance techniques identified here are of little use unless they are planned for and integrated into a systematic effort. For example, a field trip is often merely a reward for students or teachers and has little intrinsic value. Its value can be significantly enhanced if students are prepared to look for certain things while at the field site, and if they have an opportunity to discuss their observations on return from the site. The same is true of most of the other items mentioned in the foregoing list. In isolation, these techniques are of very little value. When tied to specific program goals and behavioral expectations for children, introduced in a planned and meaningful way, and opportunities made available to reinforce the learning they represent, such techniques have a powerful cumulative effect in moving elementary students toward progressive career maturity.

To achieve such goals in career guidance, the elementary school counselor, in cooperation with teachers, needs to consider the following:

1. How to individualize those career guidance techniques that will be used
2. How to increase teacher, parent, and student knowledge of career development and the ways career guidance techniques facilitate it
3. How to coordinate career guidance activities
4. How to develop or acquire special materials
5. How to implement cooperation, planning, and evaluation, as suggested in Chapter 6

Obviously, some students will not achieve the behaviors identified throughout this chapter as necessary to career development by means of curricular or other group modes. Problems involving personal relationships, decision making and problem solving, adjustment to one's failures and successes, and meeting the demands of everyday living (Gibson, 1972) are best handled in an individually tailored counseling mode. The stimulus modes identified in most of the chapter examples lay an information base from which self-understanding, career awareness, and related coping or mastery tasks can arise. Individual and group tasks supplement each other depending on individual readiness and the tasks to be achieved.

Summary

In this chapter, we have described an array of themes and practices that can be used in elementary school career guidance efforts to stimulate career development in children. Attention has been given to the characteristics of development manifested by elementary age children, and these characteristics have been set forth as the criteria to which career guidance efforts must be attuned. The major themes discussed were the importance of the elementary school as a shaper of attitudes toward the self and toward different aspects of the environment, the relationships between work habits developed in the elementary school and work behavior in adulthood, and the need of individual students to develop a vocabulary for distinguishing environmental characteristics and important aspects of their evolving selves. Relationship of goals to program function and the sequencing of career guidance program content and techniques have also been discussed.

CHAPTER 8

CAREER GUIDANCE IN THE JUNIOR HIGH/MIDDLE SCHOOL

Key Concepts

- Planning for career guidance and counseling in the junior high school/middle school must acknowledge the transitional character of this period and the importance of student exploration and planning.
- An important emphasis in career guidance and counseling in the junior high school is to help students understand the consequences of curricular and course choices made now—and planned for the senior high school—so that later options will not be prematurely closed.
- Students cannot explore or choose educational or occupational goals if they do not know about them. Timely, relevant, and accurate information is important to quality career guidance programs.
- Sex differences in information, models available, self-efficacy, and bias toward or away from particular choices become major factors in planning and delivering career guidance and counseling in the junior high school.

When examining the guidance needs and characteristics of students at separate educational levels—elementary school, junior high school/middle school, and senior high school—it is tempting to declare that one of these is more important than another. Yet the essence of career development is that each of these life stages demands mastery of different emphases within an evolving consciousness of self-characteristics and of the life options to which these characteristics relate. In other words, career development, as mediated through the educational process, must be responsive to the developmental tasks that surface as children grow, as well as to the characteristics of the institutions that influence their mastery of these developmental tasks. If either career guidance or career education is going to be a developmental process, the program must be continuous and cumulative. The outcomes obtained by students at one educational level must serve as the foundation for the next educational level. Developmental tasks appropriate to each level were discussed in Chapters 4 and 6; you may wish to review them here.

In most career education models, programs for grades seven through nine emphasize exploration and planning. This does not imply that the elementary school emphases of self- and career awareness have been completed, but rather that as children grow, they face new demands. Thus, they must develop increasingly complex behaviors. Indeed, it is likely that, for most students, self- and career awareness will continue to be refined as self- and career exploration and planning proceed in the junior high or middle school and beyond.

The need for pre- and early adolescents to acquire knowledge and skills important to exploration and planning comes from their opportunities to engage in activities farther from home and independent from the family, as well as from the nature of the school itself. The eighth and ninth grades are the first instances in the typical student's life of formal choice-points; times when the individual is faced with external pressures to make a public decision and a potentially long-range commitment among competing alternatives. Such decisions are reflected in expectations of choice among specific courses, high school curricula, a particular high school or area vocational technical school to attend, or, in some instances, whether to remain in school at all.

The junior high/middle school is a transition period between childhood and adolescence as well as between general and specialized education. As such, its processes and goals reflect either solutions or further exacerbations of what Coleman (1974) perceives as the gap between "youth and adulthood" or what Marland (1974) sees as the gap between "education and work."

It is a period that observers are increasingly citing as a time of particular vulnerability, a time when young adolescents may adopt self-damaging behavior patterns that can sometimes shorten their lives or diminish their prospects for the future. "Young adolescents experience biological, cognitive, and psychological changes that lead them to reappraise themselves and their relationships to their families and communities. These changes are often accompanied by disengagement from school, the onset of experimentation with alcohol and other drugs, and sexual activity. Research shows that problem behaviors manifested early tend to persist into later life" (Hamburg & Takaniski, 1989, p. 826). Many of the potential behavioral problems that begin to be visible among this age group are interrelated and are accompanied by poor school achievement. "Thus, early adolescence is a period when young people are choosing life-styles rather than among specific behaviors, life-styles that become progressively integrated and consolidated as the adolescent grows older" (Jackson & Hornbeck, 1989, p. 834).

Factors such as present-future relationships, values, delayed gratification, personal responsibility, and choice consequences have real implications for individual students. How and to what degree the attitudes, knowledge, and skills making up these factors are acquired has implications beyond immediate adjustment at the junior high or middle school level. Such development is also predictive of success and satisfaction in the senior high school years and beyond.

Before turning to specific aspects of career guidance in the junior high school/middle school, it is useful to think about the developmental characteristics of students at this age. Unless these matters are taken into consideration, much career guidance activity is likely to be irrelevant. For ease of writing, "junior high school" will be used in this chapter to include both middle school and junior high school students.

CHARACTERISTICS OF JUNIOR HIGH SCHOOL YOUTH

Junior high school students are not the same creatures who inhabited the elementary schools a year or two earlier. As a result of experience and growth, their horizons have widened. With pubertal changes near, either in themselves or their peers, their perceptions of life have changed. Junior high students are more able than elementary age children to comprehend relationships and to use abstract terms and symbols. They are preoccupied with belonging and conformity, being highly influenced by their like-sexed peers and less so by their opposites; they are also taking tentative steps toward independence from their families. They are making more definitive strides in sorting themselves from the mass of students with whom they interact as they try on the multiple social roles that accompany school and community experience.

Kimmel and Weiner (1985) suggest that the primary developmental tasks of these early adolescent years is adapting to mental and biological changes, accepting how one looks, and learning to use one's mind and body effectively. Lefstein and Lipsitz (1986) have summarized the needs of this age group as follows:

- Diversity
- Self-exploration
- Meaningful participation
- Positive interaction with peers and adults
- Physical activity
- Competence and achievement

This list of needs reflects both the characteristics of the young adolescent and a template of emphases to which career guidance programs must be structured if they are to effectively meet the developmental needs of this age group. The needs of the typical junior high school child suggest that career guidance programs must offer them a wide variety of experiences and opportunities so that children at various rates of development can find something that fits their present stage of development and the issues with which they are preoccupied. Such programs must provide opportunities for these children to receive feedback about who they are becoming, the opportunities opening to them, and their relationships with others. They need time and space to gain new experiences and to contemplate the meaning of these experiences for their lives. Young adolescents want to be active and to demonstrate their ability to be responsible for themselves and others. They seek opportunities to use their skills and to participate meaningfully. Within such contexts, young adolescents want positive experiences with adults and peers as they seek affection, support, information, and criticism.

Junior high school students are immersed in the continued development, refinement, and strengthening of "basic skills begun in the elementary school, and they are beginning to converge on the more specialized experience of the senior high school. Their time focus is shifting, however subtly, from the immediate present to the future. Because choices of curricula and of the specific high school or vocational school they will attend a year or two hence are rapidly approaching, their sensitivity to work and its relevance to them as persons in the process of becoming is accentuated.

These problems of selecting a high school to attend and choosing courses in high school are matters of significance in the junior high school. Frequently, this is true because junior high school students or their parents are unaware that when one chooses an educational course of action, he or she reduces, or at best alters, the alternatives available in the future.

Educational decisions made in the junior high school are obviously not benign, although they may be reversible. The fundamental point is that the problem of committing oneself to an educational plan, advertently or inadvertently, in the junior high school as one prepares for the transition to high school is one with ramifications that ripple throughout one's life. One can keep open or foreclose future opportunities by the course content and the course patterns that one chooses in the junior high school and in the transition to the intermediate or senior high school. When one makes such choices, one essentially limits or establishes an interactive network of future alternatives. For example, if one chooses to avoid courses in advanced mathematics, the likelihood of entering scientific, technological, or engineering curricula or occupations beyond high school is minimal to nonexistent.

Jordaan and Heyde (1979) observe,

> Although they may not realize it, these curricular choices are also for many students prevo-

> cational choices. The commercial curriculum is in effect prebusiness; the industrial arts curriculum, preparation for a skilled trade; the college curriculum, preprofessional; and the general curriculum, a sort of no man's land with no clear-cut prevocational implications. . . . In pursuing a given curriculum they are, whether they know it or not, increasing the probability of being admitted to or excluded from certain fields of work and training programs. (p. 2)

As suggested previously, these perspectives are particularly true in the election of those courses that permit the student maximum freedom to qualify for educational opportunities beyond the secondary school while the student is reality-testing whether or not such further education is necessary for goal achievement. Because at the junior high school level in particular, school *is* work, the opportunity to use personal encounters with the different content and context of courses in order to explore present and future alternatives is important; it is also manageable.

Although the alternatives from which a junior high school student can choose are limited, they nevertheless represent the opportunity to practice collecting and analyzing information about alternatives, to anticipate outcomes, and to develop decision plans. Because such dimensions are crucial to successful career development, curricular decisions made in the junior high school provide the opportunity to help students consider how to maximize freedom of choice and assume responsibility for choices made while there is still time for reversing a choice and charting new educational routes if necessary.

Evidence from the national data base *High School and Beyond* reported in a 1986 publication of The College Board, *Keeping the Options Open: An Overview* (The College Board Commission on Pre-college Guidance and Counseling, 1986) indicates that junior high school students frequently do not understand and act on the consequences of their early academic choices. For example, data revealed that only 46 percent of students who expected in grade 9 that they would enter college reported being enrolled in the academic (as opposed to the general or vocational) curriculum in grade 10. By their senior year, only about half the students reported being on a path that was congruent with their college expectations. Part of this phenomenon can be explained by the lack of assurance many students feel about being able to actually achieve the goals they set for themselves. Thus, if one uses the decision to go to or prepare for college as an example, when crucial choices about courses are made, it is important for students to believe that college is a real possibility for them, financially as well as academically. If younger adolescents and their families do not get timely and effective financial aid information, they are likely to make educational choices that limit rather than advance their academic aspirations (National Student Aid Coalition, 1985).

A similar situation arises when junior high school students and their families are at a crucial point of decision about choosing a vocational educational curriculum. Unless they have timely and accurate information about access, work opportunities, and future post-secondary educational possibilities associated with attending a vocational education curriculum, they are likely to exclude such choice options from their deliberations (National Commission on Secondary Vocational Education, 1985).

The years of junior high school are, by design, transition years. Intensive, almost frenzied, exploration can be expected whether the school aids it or simply allows it to proceed (Stamm & Nissman, 1973). It is a period when such career development concepts as compromise and the congruence or incongruence between aspirations and expectations become operational as realities, and when idealistic fervor or naivete get their initial temperings in the reality-testing of curricular, athletic, and part-time work experiences. It is also a time when values emerge with enough continuity to be measureable (Perrone, 1973). Indeed, research shows that the development of work values is well underway by the fifth grade and that eighth graders display value profiles like those of fifth graders (Hales & Fenner, 1972). Unless the educational experiences provided students at this level are timely and appropriate to the questions that students are asking themselves, it is unlikely that they will have a significant influence on student behavior or choice making. This is a time, then, when change in the self and the world can be used as a focal point for planning, and when student responsibilities through participation in planning can be related to the consequences of decisions. The research of Campbell and Parsons (1972) has shown that the majority of junior high students exhibit a readiness for vocational planning. The question is, Are schools and counselors prepared to help in this process?

Sex Differences

The junior high school years are also a time when sex differences exert important influences in curriculum choice, and when choice considerations become different in kind for males and females.

In the previous chapter, little emphasis was placed on differences in career development strategies based on sex. The intent was not to gainsay the influence of sex-typing on occupational stereotypes or on appropriate choices to be considered. Rather, the assumption was that boys and girls both need a language of vocations, an orientation to preference, and the rudiments of how to differentiate interests and aptitudes and relate them to future educational options and the occupational clusters available. These experiences should be gained within a context that is not sex-biased. In the junior high school, sex effects become far more pronounced and perhaps make different guidance emphases necessary. As indicated in the conclusions of Chapter 4, career development theories give only cursory attention to differences between males and females, but it is obvious—if for no other reason than the advanced biological maturity of girls—that differences will occur in the ways young men and young women approach occupational and career choices.

Kammer's (1985) study of rural, eighth-grade boys and girls indicated that many girls do not expect to attain their career goals and that boys and girls differ in their occupational choices according to traditional sex-role expectations as early as eighth grade. Haring and Beyard-Tyler (1984) suggest that such differences occur and are likely to keep women from pursuing nontraditional occupations because of three, if not four, factors: (1) sex-role socialization, (2) poor self-efficacy, (3) negative attitudes held by women and their peers, and possibly (4) counselor bias. Zytowski (1969), Fitzgerald and Crites (1980), Gottfredson (1981), and Betz and Hackett (1981), among others, are adding to our preliminary theories of career development for women. The reader might wish to review Chapters 4 and 5 to reconsider these perspectives.

Fortner (1970) reported that in one sample of 400 junior and senior high school girls, when compared with a similar sample of 170 boys, the girls tended to show preference for professional, managerial, and skilled positions more than did the boys and tended to show preference for semi-professional, small business, semiskilled, and unskilled less than did the boys. Measured intelligence or scholastic aptitude was significantly correlated with these levels of preference.

Entwisle and Greenberger (1972) explored the effects of sex, race, IQ, social class, and residential locus on adolescent attitudes toward women's work roles. The sample consisted of 270 male and 305 female ninth graders attending six Maryland schools described as black inner-city, white inner-city, black blue-collar, white blue-collar, white rural, and white middle-class. The findings showed a marked difference between boys and girls concerning the women's role, with boys consistently holding more conservative opinions. Both sexes disapproved of women holding "men's" jobs. Black students were less opposed to women working than were white students, but they were just as negative toward their doing the same work as men. Both black and white inner-city students were generally willing for women to work. Blue-collar girls were more conservative than inner-city girls on women's roles. The greatest differences between girls' and boys' views were found among the middle-class white sample. High IQ girls were generally found to hold more liberal views than average and low IQ girls, and high IQ girls from blue-collar homes were found to be the most liberal about women's roles.

Although it might be readily assumed that findings about gender differences in self-concept or in choice of work would be significantly different today as compared to findings of 20 or so years ago, that is not necessarily true. As research by the Search Institute (1988) reports, "some things remain puzzlingly the same" (p. 1). Some excerpts from these findings follow:

> Test scores continue to reveal persistent differences between boys and girls on crucial matters of self concept and self esteem. There are also differences between boys' and girls' self-descriptions. In many instances, the girls' self-descriptions are unflattering even when the objective data contradict them. Young adolescent boys, for example, are more likely to rate themselves as "smart" than are girls, even though in the aggregate girls school grades at that age are higher than boys'. Boys also tend more readily to attribute mistakes and failures to bad luck while girls tend to attribute them to their own inadequacies. . . . As compared with boys their own age, young adolescent girls give overall evidence of a lower self-image. . . . As compared with boys, girls are more afraid of success. And they are less pleased about being female than boys are about being males. (p. 1)
>
> . . . One of the questions young adolescents consciously put to themselves is, What am I good at? What can I do? Boys tend to answer with a list of their skills and abilities. Girls to answer with a self-deprecating, "Not much!"

However,

> girls like school better than boys do throughout the middle school or junior high years. They also have higher educational aspirations. In our study, 81 percent of girls said they intended to go on to college or to graduate school, as compared with 68 percent of boys with plans for higher education. . . . In general, girls are more socially competent in early adolescence, finding it easier to make friends and share their feelings than boys do. Yet those abilities don't appear to change their suspicion that they are basically losers. (p. 1)
>
> We find that some young adolescent girls develop fear of success. . . . It is likely that a number of the differences between boys and girls discussed here contribute to this fear of success. . . . One of them is the need to have friends. . . . Another of the causes may be an increasing desire to be attractive to boys. . . . She is probably convinced . . . that you can't get a guy interested in you if you're smarter than he is. (p. 2)
>
> It is natural for both boys and girls, at about sixth or seventh grade, to begin to feel an increased compulsion to conform to traditional gender-role images. Boys want to conform to whatever they believe to be the masculine role and girls want to conform to the feminine. . . . Girls are also aware of what the traditional occupations are for women. Even though there are more women in traditionally male occupations, girls know which are expected and which are exceptions. They know that there is, for many of the traditional roles for women, no history of vocational training—for being a housewife, for instance, or being a waitress. They know that the pay in virtually all of the traditionally female occupations is low.
>
> In spite of some positive social changes, girls are still bombarded with messages that being fe-

> male is not as good as being male. . . . Look at the premium our country still puts on competition and achievement—qualities more frequently displayed by males—versus the value accorded to the more frequently female qualities of comparison and human connection. . . . Growing up female in the U.S. is still a hazardous business. (p. 3)*

The findings of the Search Institute's research in junior high school students is echoed in other research. As suggested, but not pursued, in the elementary school chapter, ideas and beliefs that reinforce the notion that most occupations are more appropriate for one sex than the other develop early in children's lives and persist throughout the process of schooling. Post-Kammer and Smith (1985) replicated Betz and Hackett's (1981) study of college women using a self-efficacy model of women's career development that suggests that many career-related problems faced by women may be due to low or weak self-efficacy expectations. Because efficacy expectations result from experience, traditional sex-role socialization of females, which includes occupation sex-role stereotypes, works against women developing high efficacy expectations in terms of specific career-related behaviors and skills. Self-efficacy expectations, when low or weak, constitute an internal barrier to women's career behavior and choices. In addition, external barriers to women such as discrimination or lack of support systems require strong self-efficacy expectations if they are to be overcome.

Post-Kammer and Smith (1985) used a population of eighth and ninth grade college-bound students to determine whether or not self-efficacy differences were present in this population. They were. Each sex had greater self-efficacy expectations about occupations traditional for their sex than for nontraditional ones.

A related issue for sex differences is that of work values in the junior high school. Post-Kammer (1987) examined the relationships between work values and career maturity among both sexes in the ninth and eleventh grades. Sex differences were reported for half of the work values, as measured by Super's Work Values Inventory, and 3 out of 5 for Crites Career Maturity Inventory subscales. There were no significant differences in the career maturity scores of the ninth and eleventh graders. However, different work values predicted the career maturity of boys and girls. It was found that "fewer values emerged as a result of the regression analysis for boys than for girls indicating that understanding the career maturity of girls may be more complex than understanding that of boys" (p. 65).

Wijting, Arnold, and Conrad (1977) studied the variance in work values of 1402 boys and girls in grades 6, 9, 10, and 12. They reported that the most salient pattern of work values in this sample was an intrinsic work orientation, with high values being placed on activity, involvement, and pride in one's work, and a devaluing of extrinsic rewards (such as money and social status). With minor variations, they found this pattern to be true of girls, not boys. They found that boys generally devalued the intrinsic rewards of work and positively valued money and social status. These researchers also found that these work values tend to increase in their crystallization from grade 9 to grade 12. With respect to vocational maturity attitude, Herr and Enderlein (1976) found, in a study of 1553 students from ninth to twelfth grades in three school systems and across sex and curricular classifications, that females displayed a higher mean Vocational Development Inventory—Attitude Scale score at all grade levels than did males. Crites (1978) reports,

> Recent longitudinal research . . . indicates . . . that sex differences do emerge during the high school

*From "The Risky Business of Growing Up Female" by the Search Institute, *Source,* 1988, Vol. 4, No. 1, pp. 1–4. Reprinted by permission.

> years. . . . At each succeeding grade level (above the seventh grade) females had statistically reliable higher mean scores on the attitude scale than males. In other words, their attitudes toward the process of career choice matured at a faster rate than that of males. (p. 5)

Pedro, Wolleat, and Fennema (1980) indicate that, for whatever reason, there is growing evidence that women's educational and occupational options are limited by the preparation in mathematics they receive while in high school. In this study they compared plans to study mathematics in high school among 400 female and 322 male ninth- and tenth-grade students from nine high schools in midwestern communities. Even though this sample was skewed toward higher-than-average enrollment in mathematics, they found the female students planned to study less mathematics than their male classmates, both during and after high school, even though they were achieving as well as their male counterparts. In addition, when career plans were studied, they found that the ninth- and tenth-grade females in this sample tended to select the stereotypical female career areas that generally require little mathematics. As the authors note, with only the minimal preparation in mathematics, the female students will not be able to choose from the full range of options should they change their occupational plans later. This is particularly true in a society where the emerging occupations are those of high technology. As discussed in Chapter 5, Hackett and her various co-researchers have been targeting mathematics self-efficacy as a crucial variable—one they are testing interventions by which to strengthen. To this end, Hackett (1985) has indicated that counselors must work not only with the interests, values, and abilities of each client but also with their perceptions of the gender appropriateness of the options available. Specifically, counselors must actively bolster women's career and math-related self-efficacy expectations if more informed and nonstereotyped career choices are to occur.

In related research, Neely (1980) has reported the results of a comparison of the scores on the Career Maturity Inventory of 72 male and 52 female ninth-grade students in a midwestern town of 25,000 residents. The girls' mean scores on the Attitude Scale fall significantly higher than the boys' mean scores. The girls' scores on the competency subtests were also found to be significantly higher than the boys' on self-appraisal, goal selection, and problem solving.

Research by Westbrook, Sanford, and Donnelly (1990) in which 112 rural ninth-grade public school pupils were administered the goal selection scale of the CMI Competence Test and the ACT Career Planning Program found no significant ethnic or gender differences in career maturity of ninth-grade students. This study, and earlier studies by Westbrook et al. (1988), found that goal selection and appropriateness of career choices have more in common with scholastic aptitude than they have with each other. Viewed from this perspective, the career choice process, at least at this developmental level, is, to a great extent, a cognitive process. High-ability students in grade nine are likely to make more appropriate career choices than low-ability students. According to Westbrook et al. (1990), such a finding is understandable, "because high-ability students qualify for more jobs and are not as likely to choose a job that is incongruent with their attributes" (p. 30).

The work patterns and the proportions of women in the labor force have changed significantly during the past several decades. It is expected that for the foreseeable future, women will enter the labor force in greater percentages than will men. Thus, as cultural constraints about what is acceptable work or schooling for women continue to fall away, it is expected that women will continue to seek more schooling and more employment than ever before.

Attitudes toward women working—and toward the job of homemaking—have undergone profound changes. The proportion of women in the work force, particularly wives and mothers, has increased dramatically. Now approximately one-half of all married women work outside the home and most have children under 18. Only 3 out of 10 women are full-time homemakers (Herr, 1989b). By 1990, 30 percent of all children will have been in single-parent families and half of all children will have spent some time in a single-parent family before reaching age 18. Most single parents are women. At present, almost half of all black children and a fifth of Hispanic children are being raised in single-parent families (Family Service America, 1984).

In particular, young women's relationship to the world of work is dramatically different from that of their mothers. Many more enter the labor force now, doing so at an earlier age; and most intend to work indefinitely. The primary activity of nonstudent young women in the late 1950s was more likely to be keeping house and caring for a family. Today's youth enter the labor market earlier and most combine school with work. Many more are from single-parent families and a significant minority are single parents themselves (Wetzel, 1989).

Government projections (Bureau of Labor Statistics, 1986) indicate that increasing participation of young women and stable or declining participation for teenage males will continue for the rest of this century and into the next. By the year 2000 the labor force will have a larger share of young women and a smaller share of young men.

Although such processes of women's involvement in work are accelerating, the pathways and the continuity with which these pathways can be pursued are still different for boys and girls. Homemaking is still a major role for women even though it may be as a part of a two-earner family or as a single parent. In either case, homemaking and work outside the home are likely to be combined for many women. Bearing at least one child continues to be pervasive among married women. These factors of home-making and child-bearing cause either temporary or long-term discontinuities in the career development of women, even though they often negate the important presence of women in the labor force for much of their lives. As day-care centers, financial subsidies for home care of children, and other supports to working mothers are expanded, women will become more significant in their leadership and in their distribution throughout the occupational structure. These possibilities need to be considered in multiple role planning.

The other reality factor remains. Even though social reinforcement for working women is increasing and legislation bars overt obstacles, psychological barriers still tend to cause girls to have fewer job choices than do boys. Reasons for this phenomenon can be found in curriculum content selected by girls as well as in factors in the larger society.

Nieva and Gutek (1981) suggest that the continuing tendencies to consider jobs as male or female encourages the development of two labor markets—a male labor market and a female labor market (p. 5). As Hawley (1980) has indicated, although occupational segregation is slowly diminishing as women in greater numbers begin to enter male-dominated fields, "over one-half of the female workers in the United States are now concentrated into clerical, operative, or service positions while professional women are concentrated in the areas of teaching and nursing" (p. 1).

Similar to the discrimination that prohibits access to some occupations because of racial criteria, sex-typing can be expected to restrict women's access to some occupations in the foreseeable future even though women jockeys, coal miners, baseball umpires, commercial airline pilots, and long-haul truckers are no longer without precedent. Counselors continue to have a major job in helping to reduce high correlations between sex and occupation.

Girls tend to be "set" in a career earlier than boys (by about age 15), even though they may enter a career pattern with less thought than boys because of the residual effects of stereotyping of choices they are encouraged to pursue. According to Hollender's research (1974), significantly more females than males report a definite vocational choice during this period. For these reasons, some observers advocate that counseling for girls should be different from that for boys. Whether counseling should be different in fact or should emphasize different things earlier is debatable, but it is not debatable that since the male's identity has been more historically cloaked in a career fabric than has the female's, girls have a different problem of identity achievement from that of boys. Cultural influences have historically assigned to boys in this country a primary role as the breadwinner and, thus, have reinforced in many ways that career development of males is more important—not necessarily because of the benefits to the male himself but because of the importance of the choices he makes to the well-being of his future family. Although this notion is changing, many of the historical effects remain in the attitudes of various persons.

Research also indicates that the occupational preferences of males and females at the junior high level and beyond are not the same, and this is true for both whites and blacks (Nafziger, Holland, Helms, & McPartland, 1974; Powell & Bloom, 1963; Woal, 1974). Although it is not clear why these differences occur—perhaps the incorporation of early sex stereotyping, maybe a lack of information across occupations—counselors need to help the student be clear that such differences are consciously held and are not simply a result of information or experiential deficits. Thus, if career guidance strategies are to respond to the needs of females and to help them come to terms with career development—career maturity and identity—these strategies must be mounted no later than the junior high school period. To wait diminishes the likelihood that career development can be influenced for females in optimum ways.

Approaches to Gender Differences in the Junior High School

A very basic strategy by which counselors can attempt to facilitate realistic exploration of career motivations in junior high school girls is by exposing them to nontraditional role models. Cramer, Wise, and Colburn (1977) examined the use of "stereotype debunking" as a method of combating sex stereotyping. It was found by Piost (1974) that showing a female computer programmer in a career film significantly increased the career motivation of eighth-grade girls for that career compared to their considerably lessened preference for the career when a male model was used in the same film.

Wilson and Daniel (1981) used a role clarification and decision-making workshop to help seventh- and eighth-grade students overcome sex-role stereotypes. Using a variety of activities—such as considering the lives of famous women, songs illustrating social norms and social change in men's and women's roles, discussion of characteristics required for different occupations, interest inventories, analysis of nontraditional jobs—they found in comparing an experimental with a control group that a relatively brief workshop (five sessions) is effective in influencing traditional sex-role attitudes.

Vincenzi (1977) has examined a related approach to minimizing occupational stereotypes that, although it used sixth graders as subjects, could be adapted to the junior high school. In this instance, 80 girls and 97 boys from nine sixth-grade classes were chosen randomly and assigned to experimental and control groups. The experimental group students were exposed to two 30-minute sessions a week for 10 weeks. During these sessions, the experimental group did the following:

1. Reviewed and discussed magazine articles concerning women working at jobs traditionally sex-typed as masculine and men at jobs traditionally sex-typed as feminine
2. Examined and discussed the definitions of a stereotype and identified stereotypes other than occupations
3. Met seven women who work in traditionally masculine occupations. Each woman spoke for thirty minutes, gave a short demonstration, and explained her job and why she chose it. Occupations discussed were doctor, lawyer, chemist, television reporter, architect, telephone linesperson, and auto mechanic

The research findings of this approach indicated that the number of occupations viewed as sex-typed by the experimental group was significantly reduced and that the experimental group improved significantly over the control group in the incidence of occupational stereotyping.

Another method of dealing with such concerns is to use women in nontraditional careers as guest speakers or as persons for students to shadow on the job. Such persons can also demonstrate the efficacy of multiple role planning. Beyond these types of recognition of sex differences at the junior high school level, counselors also need to help teachers and parents recognize sex stereotyped activities and reinforcement in teaching materials, in educational policies about course options segregated by sex (such as home economics and shop), and in reading materials of various kinds. Title IX of the Education Amendments of 1972, as amended in 1974, 1976, and 1980, has made quite clear that segregation of the sexes in courses, athletics, or other school-related activities can be inappropriate at best and illegal at worst. Counselors obviously have responsibilities to advance the gender-fair notions implicit in this legislation. Put more positively, counselors can help teachers and parents to enthusiastically support career exploration that is unfettered by traditional sex biases. Such efforts, once begun, must continue in the senior high school, in higher education, and among adult populations.

Differences in Maturity

Of the entire educational span, the junior high school years have the widest range of maturity levels in the student population. The effects of pubertal changes, differences in the rates of male and female growth, and the general unevenness of physical, emotional, and intellectual development within and between the population of girls and boys contribute to this spectrum of maturational differences. Differences in readiness, questions of general academic progress, preoccupations with bodily change, peer conflicts, boy-girl relationships, and rebellion against family restrictions—each coexists with and often confounds the continuing process of career development.

Differences in maturity among junior high school students, particularly with regard to career development, is apparent in data provided by the National Assessment of Educational Progress's Project on Career and Occupational Development (Aubrey, 1977). Selective findings about a national sample of some 38,000 thirteen-year-olds follow:

1. Most thirteen-year-olds can state things they can do well and things they cannot do well. Females are slightly better able to do both than males and whites are some-

what better than blacks at these types of self-appraisal.

2. While almost all thirteen-year-olds can identify something they would like to do better, only about three-fourths have actually tried to find out how to do it better. Blacks and students whose parents have not completed high school are somewhat less able to state how to find out how to improve their abilities and limitations, although both of these groups indicate an extremely strong interest in school and academic areas and a desire to improve in these areas.
3. Males more often judge how well they do a preferred activity by a personal comparison while doing an activity, whereas females tend to more often judge by what others say.
4. Overall, males and females are equally knowledgeable about highly visible occupations. However, there is some evidence that there are sex differences in the understanding of specific occupations.
5. Approximately 70 percent of thirteen-year-olds are interested in a current hobby, sport, game, or activity that they feel would be of use for obtaining a job. Group and individual sports are the major categories selected as most useful in obtaining a job. School and academics rank near the bottom.
6. The vast majority of thirteen-year-olds state that at least one school subject has taught them something of use in a job. Of 11 academic areas, mathematics receives a larger percentage of responses linking this discipline to work and jobs than the combined total of the remaining 10.
7. When asked to list 10 things to be considered in choosing a job or career, most thirteen-year-olds can list two things and less than half of them can list more than five. While they have difficulty in stating specific factors to consider in choosing a job or career, most do think about a future job.
8. The first choices of thirteen-year-olds for future jobs tend to be occupations generally requiring college degrees or lengthy training periods beyond high school rather than jobs now held by the majority of the work force.
9. Practically all are able to state types of work they do at home. The work done by thirteen-year-olds at home could provide career development programs with a starting point for an exploration of future careers and occupations.
10. There is a difference among subgroups of thirteen-year-olds with regard to how many have visited places of interest in the community and acquired related learning experience.
11. Nearly 80 percent of thirteen-year-olds have participated in out-of-school learning experiences such as special training and lessons. Blacks and children whose parents have not graduated from high school have had fewer such experiences.
12. In general, thirteen-year-olds have been exposed to a host of out-of-school experiences without assistance. By connecting their present skills and interests with future career choices, they could begin the process of initial planning on a positive note with individual student direct involvement.
13. Over half (59 percent) have attempted to find a part-time or summer job.
14. A high percentage of thirteen-year-olds are able to list three or more ways people their age could earn money, but minority group students and those whose parents have not completed high school have less information in this regard.
15. Thirteen-year-olds seem to have sensitive and aware attitudes toward work.
16. Three-fourths of thirteen-year-olds feel they ultimately should make the decision

as to what job they would take to make a living.

A Time for Early School-Leaving

The junior high school years are a period when many students will permanently absent themselves from formal education. Some of these students will have begun to drop out of school psychologically in the elementary grades. Others will do so in grades seven, eight, or nine. Still others who have found no meaning in school will not only terminate their psychological interaction with the education process, but they will also remove themselves physically. In several other places in this book, what the future holds for those without a high-school diploma or marketable skills is discussed. Career guidance and the broader educational process, then, must respond to potential dropouts not merely by encouraging these students to remain in school or by lecturing them about the monetary value of a high school diploma, but by altering the educational structure to make it more meaningful.

The reality is that many students who drop out are not getting anything in school that helps them get a better job, and they know it! In many instances, ways have not been found to move concrete, task-oriented instruction into the junior high school, where these students can get hands-on experiences that relate to real work as they see it. Nor is there opportunity to combine general education and work-study opportunities at the junior high school level.

The point is that for some youngsters at this level, purely academic content holds no appeal at all unless it has immediate relevance to salable skills and this relevance is made obvious. These students in the junior high school need access to a skill-centered curriculum like that contained in vocational education at the comparable level. If they do not receive this opportunity, the chances are that they will leave the school as unemployable. Some of these young people do not have the tolerance or the ego-strength to wade through a morass of personally meaningless experiences until the ninth, tenth, or eleventh grades, when they can get more meaningful educational experiences. However, these students should still be provided with experiences other than occupational task-specific skills to foster career development. Indeed, within the context of skill development, not only can they be helped to see where they might go, but prescriptions of the specific ways of implementing their goals can be developed. For those for whom skill-centered training is most relevant and is the prime source of success experiences, training in decision making and planning that transcends job layouts can facilitate self-understanding and recognition of alternative ways of using evolving skills. Within this context, the concept of continuing education as a way of refining one's skills and becoming a more effective problem-solver at work can be wedded to a knowledge of available apprenticeships, on-the-job training, postsecondary vocational technical schools, military service schools, and other pertinent experiences. It is clear that such task-centered, skill-oriented, and concrete experiences would be helpful to all students if used to relate self-characteristics to the alternatives available, but it is even clearer that such experiences are critical to preventing dropouts.

In a national report, the Hispanic Policy Development Project singles out the junior high school years as a crucial time to work on student motivation and aspiration. Research reported in this document revealed that 43 percent of Hispanic students who drop out leave school before grade 10, and 25 percent of all Hispanic students enter high school overage. The study ties Hispanic students' lack of motivation to continue their education to the anonymity many of them feel in the junior high schools and the lack of recognition of or respect for their cultural values (National

Commission on Secondary Education for Hispanics, 1985).

PLANNING CONSIDERATIONS

Although there are commonalities between the role of the middle/junior high school counselor and the roles of elementary and senior high school counselors, there are also differences. For example, the American School Counselors Association (1977b) contends that "orientation to junior and senior high schools, educational placement, career development, and group activities to promote greater self-direction, particularly in value formulation and decision-making, are all areas with special implications for the middle/junior high school counselor" (p. 3). Obviously, such experiences must be planned and coordinated.

In addition to the general planning considerations for career guidance discussed in Chapter 6, the introductory sections of this chapter suggest several specific characteristics of junior high school students that must be considered.

1. Since the junior high school is a transitional experience from the structured and general education of the elementary school to the less structured but more specialized education of the secondary school, students must be provided broad opportunity to explore their personal characteristics as well as those of the educational options from which they must choose. Opportunities to relate curricular options to the possible and subsequent educational and occupational outcomes seem highly desirable.

2. Since wide ranges in career maturity, interests, values, and abilities characterize junior high school students, a wide variety of methods is needed to accommodate the range of individual differences. Minority students and students whose parents have not completed high school frequently have not had the developmental experience or occupational knowledge enjoyed by whites or students from homes in which parents are well educated. These students may need special programs to facilitate their understanding of opportunities available to them, their requirements, and how to access them.

3. Since females are more likely than males to have made definitive vocational choices, career guidance programs must ensure that such choices were made deliberately and on the basis of accurate, pertinent information.

4. Although students in the junior high school are capable of verbal and abstract behavior, exploration will be enhanced if they are given concrete, hands-on, direct experiences as well.

5. Fundamental to the rapid changes that students experience in the junior high school is a search for personal identity. Therefore, career guidance programs must encourage students to explore their feelings, needs, and uncertainties as a base for evaluating educational and occupational options. Values clarification and other similar processes are helpful in this regard.

Goals for Career Guidance in the Junior High School

There are many statements of career guidance goals for junior high school youth. One example is that developed by the Wisconsin Department of Public Instruction (Wilson, 1986), which has recommended the following objectives:

- Understand decision-making skills
- Learn to cope with transition in school, home, and community lives
- Become informed about alternative educational and vocational choices and preparation for them
- Relate personal interests to broad occupational areas
- Understand and use communication skills

- Learn human conflict management with adults and peers
- Learn that sex-role stereotyping, bias, and discrimination limit choices, opportunity, and achievement (p. 7)

Another example of career guidance objectives in the junior high school (Herr, 1976) suggests that students should learn to do the following:

1. Attain realistic understanding of themselves
2. Develop skill in using various sources of self, educational, and occupational information
3. Understand different educational options available in high school and beyond, the nature and purpose of these, and the types of postsecondary education or career options to which they lead
4. Distinguish between career clusters in terms of the major occupations which make them up and in terms of such matters as (1) the amount and type of education needed for entrance, (2) the content, tools, settings, products, or services with which these occupations are associated, (3) the potential of such occupations to satisfy personal interests of such occupations to satisfy personal interests and values, (4) the potential of such occupations to provide the type of life style desired
5. Consider life in an organization and the various roles played
6. Identify ways of effectively managing work and leisure time
7. Consider the behavioral implications of taking personal responsibility for what one wants to become
8. Identify broad career areas and levels of educational aspiration which are personally appropriate
9. Plan their high school program based on accurate information, tentative career goals, and accurate self-appraisal
10. Formulate plans for implementing the decisions made (pp. 1–2)

Another excellent statement of objectives relevant to the junior high school is found in the CDC management tasks (see Table 6.8) and the references to that plan (Tennyson, Hansen, Klaurens, & Antholz, 1975).

EXAMPLES OF PROGRAM CONTENT

Career guidance programs or activities designed to incorporate many of the goals we have cited are now available in many middle and junior high schools. Both the substance and the format of these career guidance approaches vary widely. Some examples follow.

The concept of change—change in characteristics of the self and in environmental options—has been mentioned elsewhere in this book as a possible unifying thread in career development and decision making. At the junior high school, such a theme can be related to the accelerating application of new technological discoveries to the occupational structure; it can reinforce the validity of preparing oneself to be versatile and yet firmly grounded in the fundamental processes that undergird all occupations. The concept can be related to work habits, mechanical principles, electrical principles, structural design and architectural evolution, chemical and biological principles, numerical operations and measurements, or verbal communication as this relates to different role relationships. Therefore, students can be increasingly encouraged to ask of occupational and educational areas, Do I like it? What does it take? Do I have what it takes? Such questions can be tested in various courses, as well as in the simulated or work experiences that will be discussed later in this chapter. Students can be encouraged to ask, Why am I taking chemistry or algebra or English? and How can I use it? Teachers must be encouraged to respond to these questions as meaningful, with fairly specific answers. This is the sort of climate that supports career development and connects what students are being exposed to educationally with the occupational world. It can expand students' awareness of possibilities.

When teachers are asked to consider how the subject they teach is related to occupations or careers at different levels of education or in different interest categories, a basic difficulty often is that their formal backgrounds have not prepared them to respond to such questions. One important resource to offset this condition has been prepared by the Minnesota Department of Education. The Bureau of Pupil Personnel Services of this agency has developed a series of charts describing the relationship between subject-matter courses and selected careers. An example of these is available in Table 8.1, presenting information on careers related to social studies.

Obviously, this table does not exhaust all the possibilities, but it does represent a method of connecting what one studies with how it might be used. At any point in the educational process, discussions, role-playing, field trips, or other activities could be conducted to point up how social studies might be used in that particular occupation. One could relate social studies to a people-data-things conception of the occupational structure or to other emphases, always trying to extend student perceptions or possibilities and the ways of access to them.

In order to offset the limited experience of some teachers in involvement with work-related material on their subject matter, various school districts have taken different approaches to this circumstance. Some districts pay groups of teachers to work during the summer, developing short units in the major subject areas on specific career topics. In this fashion, the regular curriculum can continue but with a change in emphasis that accommodates more career-oriented content. For example, in a Utah school district, as a result of such a summer workshop, sample units were developed by teacher teams and then distributed to all teachers in that subject area within the school district for testing and refining in the school curriculum. One such unit was newspaper reporting as a career in ninth-grade English classes. Many other school districts have developed learning activity packages that can be integrated into various educational levels and subject matter. Coordinators of Career Education in State Departments of Education are prime resources to identify examples of these in each state.

Career Clusters. One method of helping students relate their characteristics to occupational alternatives through exploration as well as develop increasingly sophisticated skills important to a family of occupations is career clustering. Career clustering has been integrated into many school-based career education models or projects.

In junior high school, the objective of career clustering has been to expose students to the full range of occupational choices that will be available later and to the notion of the relationships among occupations comprising a particular career family, to knowledge of the relative advantages and the requirements of each, as well as to provision of entry skills appropriate to a broad family of related occupations (such as construction or health care).

Career education has strongly emphasized career awareness and career exploration prior to career preparation. It has further advocated that career preparation makes the student occupationally flexible. In this context, then, occupational or career clusters can be used to organize curriculum directed toward the preparation of students with skills, knowledge, and attitudes required for job entry into a family or cluster of occupations. This means that instructional teams can be developed to integrate mathematics, science, communications, and social studies around typical problems found in career clusters. Techniques such as flexible or

Table 8.1

Selected Careers Related to Social Studies

Level	Service	Business, Clerical, and Sales	Science and Technology	General Cultural	Arts and Entertainment
B.A. or above	Social worker Psychologist FBI agent Counselor YMCA Secretary Clergy	Government official Industrial executive Market analyst Economist Buyer Arbitrator	Archaeologist Paleontologist Anthropologist	Judge Lawyer Philologist Editor News commentator Reporter Librarian	Museum curator Historian (Dramatic arts)
High School plus technical	Police sergeant Detective Sheriff Employment interviewer	Union official Bank teller Salesperson Wholesaler Retailer		Justice of the peace Radio announcer Law clerk	Tour conductor Travel bureau director Cartoonist
High School graduate	Police officer Religious worker Bus driver	Floor walker Interview (poll) House canvassers and agents		Library assistant	Museum guide
Less than High School graduate	Train porter Taxi driver Bellhop Elevator operator Usher	Peddler Newspaper carrier		Library page Copy person	

modular scheduling, team teaching, independent study, and individualized instruction can be used to address differences in content or learning styles. Career clusters are also career guidance devices in that they provide students with awareness and exploratory opportunities across several clusters of occupations. As indicated in Chapter 3, there are 15 career clusters developed by the USOE and used in most national career educational models.

Each of the clusters has been divided into sub-clusters, which are further divided into discrete occupational functions at increasing levels of specificity requiring various types of education, from unskilled levels to graduate or professional education. Some states have developed modifications on these 15 clusters. Some cities have developed curriculum guides that can be used in exploratory or group guidance programs at grades seven and eight. Many commercial materials and audiovisual products have also been developed to deal with one or more of the 15 clusters to stimulate student exploration and career awareness.

Winter and Schmidt (1974) reported on how they used a cluster approach to integrate career education into the eighth-grade language arts curriculum at Scott Carpenter Junior High School in Westminster, Colorado. In particular, they developed seven modules including an introduction to careers, self-awareness, decision making, occupational clusters, economic awareness, investigating an occupational cluster, and planning for the future.

The first module caused students to define the word *career*, to identify typical career patterns for men and women, and to identify reasons for working. The filmstrip, "Why Work at All?" was shown to stimulate student discussion on reasons for working.

In the self-awareness module, students were expected to identify their strengths and weaknesses as related to their abilities and interests and to match these with at least two potential careers. The relationships between school subjects and possible jobs were also examined. Workbooks, personal checklists, interpretations of results of the Ohio Vocational Interest Survey, and the writing of personal character sketches were activities used to support this module.

The major content of the decision making module was the curriculum on decision making, entitled *Deciding*, developed by the College Entrance Examination Board in 1972.

The occupational clusters module was presented through the "Popeye" comic books published by King Features Syndicate, which use cartoon characters to present information about jobs in each cluster. Students also constructed people pyramids showing how people from different clusters work together to produce different products.

The economic awareness module focused on how economics affects each student's life. Such concepts as economic systems, supply and demand, inflation, depression, and elements of production were discussed.

A variety of approaches was used in the module on investigating an occupational cluster. The Widening Occupational Roles Kit (WORK), *Job Family* booklets, and *Job Experience* Kits (all from Science Research Associates) were used as major resources for students in identifying a specific preferred cluster or area within a cluster to study. In addition, students wrote to at least one firm that offered jobs in the preferred cluster asking for information about the job and the firm. Students also took field trips to pertinent sites and had resource speakers from different occupations come to class to discuss their jobs.

In the planning module, students compiled lists of skills they would need to meet the requirements of jobs in the occupational cluster most related to their interests and aptitudes. Students also planned a tentative high school program of studies that would provide the necessary skills. During this module, the relevance of flexibility and tentativeness in planning as well as employment trends and the rapidity of change were considered.

The model reported by Winter and Schmidt is an excellent application of clustering and related concerns now developed in the junior high school. The possibilities for expanding or modifying such modular approaches to serve career guidance objectives in a local school are restricted only by the initiative and ingenuity of the local staff.

Other Sequential or Comprehensive Approaches

There are many other forms of comprehensive or sequential approaches to career guidance in the junior high school. One such program, entitled Project Career Reach, was developed at West High School, District 129, Aurora, Illinois (Bollendorf, Howrey, & Stephenson, 1990). Combining a career development model of junior high school career needs, a model of guidance objectives for program planning, a generic individualized career plan, and a marketing scheme to stimulate students to make use of the program offered by the guidance department, the six high school counselors designed Project Career Reach. They used five steps to develop the program: mission analysis, market analysis, resource analysis, strategic planning, and measures of program outcomes. The result was a multifaceted program intended to be systematically delivered. Included in Project Career Reach were the following:

- College Night
- Achievement Testing
- Peer Counseling
- Registration
- School-Business Partnership
- Mini-Workshops (such as Financial Aid Seminars)
- Career Speaker Service
- Grade Boosters
- College Representatives
- Career Center
- Practical Composition (Career English)
- GIS searches of career-related information

After putting such program components in place, the counselors used all forms of media to reach students with different learning modalities and to encourage them to use the career programs. The school newspaper interviewed staff members and publicized activities for student readers. Signs were used as visual stimuli to publicize the career speaker series, the School-Work-Connection, the regional Career Fest, and other program emphases. Community newspapers and local radio and television announcements were also used to create visibility for the career guidance program.

As a result of the program, career information searches increased by 149 percent in the year following implementation of Project Career Reach. Nearly half of the students surveyed at the end of the program indicated their intent to be involved in other career development activities during the next school year. Students surveyed who were involved in the program indicated that they better understood careers and career information resources.

Another type of comprehensive career guidance program for junior high school students is likely to be found in many state manuals on career education or career guidance. For example, the State Education Department of New York State has created a Home and Career Skills curriculum for implementation in grades seven and eight. This program is intended to develop skills that lead to effective decision making, problem solving, and management in the home, school/community, and workplace; develop concepts and skills basic to home and family responsibilities; and develop personal skills which will enhance employment potential. These objectives are intended to be met by applying the principles and process skills of decision making, problem solving, and management to all areas of daily living. The program or curriculum is comprised of a series of interrelated modules that can be combined in one unit or taught in sequence within other relevant courses.

Without dealing with the content, specific objectives, or activities in each module, the topical outline of the three modules directly related to career content includes the following:

- Process skills
  - How do I decide? (Decision making)
  - How do I solve problems? (Problem solving)
  - How do I manage? (Management)
- Personal development
  - What makes me, me? (Self)
  - How do I relate to other? (Others)
- Career planning
  - What does working mean to me? (Introduction to work)
  - What kind of work can I do? (Tentative plans)
  - Can I make working work for me? (Entrepreneurship)

Using Community Resources in Career Guidance. One approach to facilitating career development among junior high school students is to systematically involve the use of community resources. Pinson (1980) has made the helpful observation, "Community in the abstract can be simplified if one views it through a student's eyes as three sets of establishment adults: school staffs, parents, and employers (less clear to the students is a fourth set of adults . . . : organized labor)." Throughout Chapters 6, 7, 8, and 9 a variety of suggestions have been made about how school staff can facilitate the career development of students within subject matter areas. In Chapter 4, the role of parents in facilitating the career development of their children was discussed. Those observations about parents, like those about the characteristics of school staff, are relevant here as well.

As suggested in Chapter 1, during the 1970s some school districts began to deal with the lack of career awareness among elementary, junior high, and senior high school students by developing community-based career education programs. While the organization of such programs can become quite complex, they do permit the community to be used as a classroom. Links between the school and the business community frequently result in multiple outcomes. For example, students learn more about occupations and about themselves—their skills, interests, personality characteristics, and values. In addition, the school system gains cost-free expertise from community resources and, frequently, schools receive for instructional purposes equipment and materials that businesses are replacing.

In any community-based career education effort, there are major needs to locate resources, find community sites, recruit and schedule students for programs, orient students to expected behaviors at sites and to the information potential that should be sought, provide information about the program to school officials, parents, and community members, and carry out follow-up procedures. Milburn (1983) has identified the dimensions of such program development and the role of the career counselor as a community liaison.

Pinson (1980) has extrapolated from various documents and statements recommendations from business and industry about how they can be useful in career guidance. Selected recommendations and priorities include the following:

1. Using the business and industry community to validate civic and social outcome measures as well as the work competency indices developed by schools as exit requirements

2. Utilizing community work stations as frequently for observation and exploration by elementary and middle-school youth as for actual work experience at the secondary school level
3. Involving business and industry in ways that further curriculum objectives in all subject areas: i.e., assisting students to conduct a job search in the yellow pages could indirectly increase their reading achievement levels (p. 138)

With respect to the contributions of organized labor to career guidance, Pinson recommends such ideas as the following:

1. Ongoing career development programs should more closely reflect the interests and needs of today's adult workers, as opposed to "the child as an adult."
2. Reconsider and revise the framework of work experience to take into account labor's views of economic realities; for example, more nonpaid work experience during school tenure.
3. Encourage the infusion of labor studies as part of a comprehensive thrust at all school levels. Involve union representation at the curriculum design level.

Although many of these perspectives are equally valid for the senior high school, there are some specific programs oriented to the use of community resources in junior high school career guidance programs that are worthy of note.

In Concord, Massachusetts, students work with a team of teachers and counselors in a community program (Ryan, 1972). The first part of the program is designed to alert students to the world of work. As part of that phase, students are asked to choose one of four concurrent courses that have been jointly developed by Rotary Club members from the community and the counselor/teacher team. Each course is given on a Friday morning for five weeks at an appropriate community site. Supervision at the site is provided by a teacher, a Rotary Club community course reader, and parent volunteers. The four courses offered are Health/Medicine, Manufacturing, Food and Its Processing, and Community Retailing. Throughout these courses, students maintain journals describing perceptions of adults observed in the occupation studied. In the sixth week of the program, students in the separate courses are brought together for the sharing of impressions, knowledge, and recommendations. During the next five weeks, students may choose from four additional courses: Knowing Your Town, Construction and Home Building, Food and Its Retailing, and Service Industries. Finally, for several Friday mornings, students are placed with adult workers who are in occupations preferred by individual students.

This approach has many virtues. One of them is its systematic integration of learning and observation. Another is its purposeful use of the community as a learning laboratory. Third, such a program brings adults into contact with the concerns and interests of young persons and provides a natural method for the two groups to interact. Fourth, perhaps less directly, the program helps students develop reasons for a sense of pride and accomplishment in their schoolwork, beyond that of academic achievement.

The St. Louis Public Schools have extensive collaboration between the schools and resource persons from business and the community (Katzman, 1989). These include the following:

- *Traveling career panels* in which seventh graders learn the importance of basic skills within the world of work and how these skills are applied by individuals on the job. A panel of two persons from business or industry visits a seventh grade classroom, bringing tools and a classroom activity that typifies their job. A math panel, for example, might include a chef who brings a chili recipe for 20 people that needs to be converted to serve 100 and a corporate budget director who brings ledger sheets and teaches the students to form a personal budget. The class follows up with career-related field experiences to view the panelists in their work environment.

- *College planning conferences* in which eighth graders spend the day on a college campus as a way of helping students who never felt that they could have opportunities to envision such directions and to reinforce an incentive to enter high school, graduate, and plan for the future.
- *Career awareness fair* in which eighth graders have an opportunity to watch career role models demonstrating their jobs. The fair is a way for over 780 (in 1989) business persons and community members to reinforce how important it is to master the basic school subjects, remain motivated about learning, stay in school, and explore the diversified world of work. The 1989 fair had some 7,000 eighth graders in attendance. Activities included building inspectors demonstrating blueprint reading: flight attendants showing students how to prepare for a flight; chefs demonstrating the use of their utensils and the preparation of recipes. Students complete a number of pre- and post-fair activities and conduct career interviews while at the fair.
- *Business/school mentoring* in which a business or community agency pairs with a middle or an elementary school to communicate with, provide career and motivational information for and guide students over an extended period of time.*

*Abridged from "A Response to the Challenges of the Year 2000" by Susan Katzman in *Career Development: Preparing for the 21st Century* by the Comprehensive Career Development Project for Secondary Schools in Tennessee. Copyright © 1989 by The University of Tennessee, Knoxville, Department of Techological & Adult Education. Reprinted by permission.

When considering community involvement in career guidance at the junior high school level, parents are frequently a neglected resource. Fletcher (1976) has suggested several possible ways parents can become integral parts of the career guidance program. They can volunteer to take students to work with them, and they can have students work with them as interns if they own a business. They can drive students to field trips, serve as career center aides, or serve as resource speakers in classes on career guidance seminars. Retired grandparents can come into career guidance classes and show students how hobbies can be related to careers. Fletcher suggests further that it is useful to develop a resource file of parents' careers for various uses in career guidance. Such a file could classify these occupations by the U.S. Office of Education career clusters described in Chapter 3 and earlier in this chapter. Finally, Fletcher indicates that parents often feel left out of career planning, because they do not understand the relationship of classwork to future careers. Helping them through PTAs or other methods to understand these relationships is likely to stimulate their positive involvement in the career development of their own children and to provide a powerful resource bank to supplement the career guidance efforts of the counselor or teacher.

A school/community-based project that combines many of the previously described examples in behalf of a comprehensive approach to career exploration for middle school youth has been reported by Rubinton (1985). A joint effort of the schools, a community college, the community, and the family, this federally funded project, Career Exploration for Youth (CEY), served children in public and parochial middle and junior high schools and their teachers, counselors, administrators, and parents in Brooklyn, New York.

The program contained four components emphasizing experiential learning. The first component was comprised of hands-on career courses presented to students. These courses were activities-oriented and emphasized exploration in four career clusters: business and office, marketing and distribution, communications and media, and public service. The intent of the activities in each cluster included, examination of myths about careers; examination of biases against and for careers familiar to children; motivation to explore unfamiliar and nontraditional careers; generation of career-related options in cluster areas of interest to children; provision of direct participation in career experiences; introduction of role models; and relating of careers to values of children.

The second component of the program was comprised of a career decision-making course for parents. The course, which was designed to help parents facilitate the career development process among their children, allowed parents to explore careers in relation to their interests, aptitudes, abilities, values, and life experiences. Instruction included discussion, lectures, guest speakers, self-exploration exercises, administration of an interest inventory, a research project, and visits to a work site.

The third component was a course for teachers, counselors, paraprofessionals, teacher aides, school secretaries, and administrators that was designed to prepare school personnel to infuse curriculum with career development concepts. The activities contained in this course involved the provision of basic knowledge, understanding, and methods of teaching career education, assistance with the integration of career education into the existing school curriculum, and implementation of ideas, goals, and methods of career education in teachers' classrooms or school settings.

The final component of the program consisted of offering children who participated in the project a recreation component to complement the activities in the career clusters in which they engaged. To the degree possible, recreation activities were used to complement that which was occurring in the career clusters.

An extensive evaluation system found that children significantly increased their career awareness and knowledge. School personnel reported increased confidence in their ability to incorporate career education into their curricula, and community response was found to be overwhelmingly enthusiastic.

Career Guidance Strategies for Decision Making and Problem Solving

The examples just cited respond to elements of career development at a rather gross level and are basically similar to those activities recommended for the elementary school. To meet more specific goals, some differences in strategy or context are useful. Paolitto (1977) has maintained that the junior high school is a natural setting for group counseling as a major vehicle of personal learning for early adolescents. More specifically, Kinnick (1968) has connected the use of group discussions and group counseling to increased student ability in problem solving and decision making.

Kinnick has described group discussion as "the cooperative and constructive deliberation on a common problem by a group attempting to reach agreement on a solution to that problem" (p. 350). Typically, group discussion involves a group of 8 to 15 members engaged in exchanging information, knowledge, and ideas for the following purposes; (1) to provide a means of helping students learn problem-solving skills, (2) to help particular students improve their ability to solve their particular problems, and (3) to help students learn to work with others toward a common goal. Group discussion could be stimulated by the use of case materials presenting different types of problems with which junior high school students can identify (such as choosing curricula, decision making, choosing a college, how to study, job analyses); or by the use of film strips or films dealing with similar content, field trips, or resource persons. Variations on the discussion method could be initiated through the use of role-playing, sociodrama, or plays focusing on particular content or problem areas.

Group counseling that focuses on problem solving, according to Kinnick, does not depart markedly from group discussion. The emphasis of the latter is on problems, whereas the stress in group counseling is on the person's approach to problems, and thus involves more personal references, identity issues, and emotionality. One may assume, then, that more personal problems would be examined in group counseling than in most group discussions. In either of these groups, however, problem solving as a creative process of evaluation, information collection and analysis, synthesis and planning can be aided by means of (1) lifelike, group settings for making decisions and choices, (2) the influence of peers through group interaction and group norms, (3) the opportunity for free expression of opinions and emotions with less personal reference, and (4) the opportunity to give and receive support as a group member.

Wood (1990) has advocated the use of "group career counseling" to aid ninth graders in making career plans. In her view, it is useful to seek permission from teachers of classes in which all students are enrolled (such as English) to actually work with such classroom-sized groups for four days in sequence. She developed a unit that can be done in four sequential class periods. The content includes getting acquainted, learning about the services of the counseling office, discussion of career plans, completion of a career interest survey and feedback about the meaning of the results, researching at least one career using available materials in the counseling office and the media center, and planning a tentative high school schedule for the next three years. These activities are conducted within a group counseling context that allows students to raise personal issues about career-related concerns and experience how other ninth-graders are processing such concerns in their own lives. In follow-up to the four-day sequence, these activities provide the stimulus to arrange individual counseling sessions, interviews with parents, and further uses by students of the resources available. In order to implement such an approach, Wood addressed the essential importance of collaborating with teachers to inform them about the career group objectives, to arrange times convenient to them, and to provide some evaluative feedback about student participation and initiative using a point system that teachers can incorporate in their grading system to cover the students' involvement for four days of the particular marking period.

Regehr and Herman (1981) undertook to teach the skills of career decision making and self-assessment to ninth-grade students. Two of four classes were selected from 10 ninth-grade classes in a large junior high school in Calgary, Canada, to serve as experimental and control groups for the study. The experimental program was conducted over three months in eleven 50-minute periods. Sessions 1 through 7 were directed at teaching self-assessment skills to the students. These skills were continually viewed in a work or career context. Sessions 8 through 11 dealt with teaching the skills of decision making and examining them within a career framework. Following each session, students were instructed to keep a log of their reactions, thinking, and feeling about each of the sessions. Prepost testing was done exclusive of the sessions and included the Attitude and Competence Scales of the Career Maturity Inventory (CMI), the Internal-External Locus of Control Scale (I-E), and a questionnaire specifically designed for this program.

Surprisingly, a multivariate analysis found no significant difference in overall career maturity between the experimental and control groups. It appeared that since the control group was in a group guidance class that included a career unit, they may have been taught essentially the same skills as those taught more directly in the experimental program. Beyond this possibility, the researchers indicated that other explanations were differences in student readiness to explore career related information and the lack of familiarity they had with discussing personal values and beliefs about themselves, and that isolated programs intended to foster career development may not be able to compensate for what Wise, Charner, and Randour (1976) have described as the influences of career development. These influences include family, school, mass media, and community groups, which represent interactive components of comprehensive and systematic approaches as described elsewhere in this book.

Motsch (1980) studied the efficacy of peer social modeling in assisting girls with career exploration. She assigned 180 ninth-grade girls to one of four treatment conditions or to a control group. She assigned an additional 36 girls randomly selected from another high school to a second control group. A videotape of a female counselor and a female high school student discussing different career information-seeking behaviors presented the modeled behaviors. The four treatment conditions and controls include (1) videotape only, (2) videotape plus reinforcement, (3) videotape plus reinforcement plus stimulus materials, (4) stimulus materials plus reinforcement, (5) Control Group I, and (6) Control Group II. The findings were,

> Peer social modeling is related to increasing both the variety and frequency of information-seeking behaviors; more specifically, that a counseling group using modeling, positive reinforcement, and overt practice of the modeled behaviors with stimulus materials is more likely than the other treatment conditions investigated to provide an increase in the variety and frequency of information seeking behaviors among ninth grade girls. (pp. 238–239)

Even more directly focused on the fostering of decision-making skills is the work of Krumboltz and his students. Ryan and Krumboltz (1964) found that systematically reinforcing decision and deliberation statements of students in counseling did increase the rate of deliberation and decision statements significantly and that this reinforced behavior generalized to noncounseling settings.

Yabroff (1969) has demonstrated the importance of specific information if the counselor wishes to increase the realism of choices of ninth-grade students. He used experience tables (probability tables based on what has happened to students having different levels of achievement, and so on, when such students entered colleges, employment, or high school courses) to reinforce the importance of obtaining (1) specific facts about the choice, (2) a knowledge of alternatives, and (3) some estimate of the possible consequences. Yabroff found that his sample of ninth-grade students selected high school courses and made post-high school plans more commensurate with their abilities than did students who did not receive such information.

Much of the work in social modeling and imitative learning as stimuli to information seeking or decision making has been designed for use with senior high school students. Many of these techniques will be described in Chapter 9. Chapter 14 will contain a more complete analysis of decision making and the career guidance intervention strategies designed to influence it.

Simulation as a Career Guidance Strategy. In discussing simulation, This (1970) has stated the following:

> Desirable as it may be, it is not always possible to bring reality into the classroom or into the training situation. When this is not possible, we try to replicate in the learning experience the nearest thing we can to the phenomenon of the real world. It does not matter whether we are talking about a piece of equipment or an emotional experience. We call this simulation. (p. 20)

The following elements are generally considered to be necessary for an effective simulation program:

1. A supportive climate
2. Exposure of the individual's normal behavior
3. Feedback
4. Experimentation
5. A cognitive map
6. Practice
7. Planning application

In a sense, most of the work reported in the previous section has used some form of reality simulation to stimulate exploratory behavior in students. In each instance, some form of technology, such as films, modeling, or audiotapes, has been used. Until recently, educational technology has been more concerned with how to communicate than what to communicate. It has, however, clear and powerful potential for simulating real-life experiences as an aid to career development, decision-making processes, contingencies, and outcomes. It can also serve as a medium for information retrieval accessed on the basis of student characteristics.

Johnson and Myrick (1971) have described the use of a simulation technique for middle school students called MOLD (Making Of Life Decisions). In this simulation each student follows six basic steps:

1. He completes a personal profile sheet describing abilities and interests.
2. She becomes involved with small group procedures that assist him or her in self-appraisal.
3. He explores career fields and makes a tentative career choice based on his or her abilities and interests.
4. She plans on paper the next year of his or he life, making decisions about his or her education, job, home life, and leisure activities. The student chooses from alternatives actually available in the community, not fictional or hypothetical possibilities.
5. He receives feedback on his or her decisions, such as grades earned in each course and whether or not he or she got a job applied for. This feedback is derived from probability tables which take into account such variables as ability, study time, and chance.
6. She uses the results and plans the following year. In this way, contingency plans and consequences of immediate decisions can be accounted for.

This simulation was used with a filmstrip on career and educational planning, a review of materials in the guidance center, and small-group discussion of reasons for personal choices, where personal strengths were identified and reinforced.

Information Retrieval

In recent years, several projects have attempted to tie together exploration, simulation, and information retrieval with computer technology. Such computer-based systems will be discussed in Chapter 15. Here we will look at approaches to the use of information in the middle/junior high school. In a larger sense, the examples cited throughout the chapters on the elementary school, the junior high school, and the senior high school are ways of delivering information, of responding to the characteristics of the consumers, and of giving students a context in which they can project themselves into the information and reality-test its personal meaning.

Harris and Wallin (1978) studied whether occupational information does influence the career choices of seventh-grade students. The sample for the study included 133 (63 girls, 70 boys), seventh-grade students who were randomly assigned to three groups varying in the amount of information about occupations provided to the students. The results of the study supported the "idea that the career horizons of [seventh grade] boys and girls can be expanded by helping them to become more aware of occupational requirements, duties, conditions of work, and opportunities" (p. 53). Group C, the group that received the most comprehensive information about job descriptions, training needed, and potential earnings, was found to consider a wider range of career alternatives than did the other two groups.

A growing method of providing self- and career information to junior high school students is through the use of self-directed career planning instruments. These devices are particularly useful in schools where resources are limited and needs exist to provide career guidance at a low counselor time investment. Jones (1983) evaluated the use of two frequently used self-directed career planning tools—a self-guided occupational card sort known as the Occu-Sort (O-S) (Jones, 1977, 1981) and the Self-Directed Search (SDS) (Holland, 1970).

Jones studied the outcomes obtained by 578 eighth- and tenth-grade students from a school system in North Carolina who were randomly assigned to the use of the Occu-Sort, the Self-Directed Search, or neither. The evaluation focused on six types of outcomes important to career guidance: (1) proportion of nontraditional occupations (for the person's sex) suggested to the person by the instrument and subsequently being considered; (2) number of occupations suggested and later being considered; (3) understanding and recall of the three-letter occupational code found in the Holland approach; (4) stimulation toward seeking occupational and educational information; (5) student satisfaction with this vocational counseling experience; and (6) the reliability of the self-scored occupational code for the O-S. The findings were that students considered both instruments to be helpful. The Occu-Sort in contrast to the Self-Directed Search was found to be more effective in (1) encouraging students to consider nontraditional occupations, (2) suggesting potential occupations to students, and (3) communicating the meaning of the occupational code and its relation to Holland's theory (1973a). No differences were found between the Occu-Sort, Self-Directed Search, and the no-treatment groups with respect to the number of occupations the students were considering after the experience or in other information-seeking behavior.

Barker and Patten (1989) studied the effectiveness of the Career Area Interest Checklist as compared to students' expressed interests after participating in a career guidance module. On the basis of a sample of 19 eighth grade boys and 22 girls, statistically significant agreement was found between the order of career preference measured by CAIC work tasks and expressed student preference. They also found that junior high school students understand 144 work tasks used in the CAIC and that this tool can be useful in facilitating student awareness of career options that may make high school subject planning more focused and meaningful. Finally, the preliminary evidence about the CAIC tends to validate student preferences about work tasks for which they express preferences or certain dislike and helps with clarification of work tasks about which they should engage in more exploration.

These findings and others (Otte & Sharpe, 1979) affirm that the ingredients of career development discussed throughout this book are important to all students, not just a certain stratum. They also reemphasize that although information availability and help with sorting out one's self-implications are not the whole of vocationalization or career development, they are an important component of it. Finally, by implication, it is clear that the provision of information cannot be delayed until students are at the point of leaving school. Useful, meaningful data must be continuously accessible throughout the course of education.

Career Guidance Strategies and Work

For many students, work is the best try-out experience. For some, organized work-study programs are ways of shortening the period of economic and psychological dependence under which so many youth chafe. If such work experience is also to facilitate career development, it should be more than casual, unsystematic ventures into whatever chance opportunity presents itself. The behavioral goals cited in Chapter 6 are pertinent here also. They represent motivational as well as diagnostic possibilities to which work can be related. However, if such goals are to be realized, education and the business-industry complex must come together in mutually creative exchanges in order to provide such opportunities systematically. One requirement would be that schools accept responsibility for helping youngsters find part-time or summer jobs in which they can use what they have learned. Equally important, guidance and counseling activities must be directed to helping students examine the work they are doing as they are doing it, if it is to help the vocationalization of these students.

One attempt in the junior high school to use work as a way of accomplishing some of the goals cited here is the Forsyth Program conducted in Forsyth County, Georgia. This is an effort to reconstruct, at grades seven through nine, the total educational environment so as to make it meaningful to socioeconomically disadvantaged students who are indifferent to existing curricula or to work. The concrete elements of a particular vocational program such as industrial arts, home economics, or agriculture are used as the core of the basic academic curriculum (math, science, and communication skills). Students are placed in work stations within the school or outside the school, and their experiences are used as the basis for group counseling sessions. The group counseling sessions are conducted by an educational and work-experience coordinator (a person with both counseling and vocational education background). This person also places and supervises students in their work stations and coordinates the activities of those teachers assigned to work with students in the project (Bottoms & Matheny, 1969; Royston, 1970).

It is obvious that paid work has limited possibilities for fostering behavioral modification or career development in the junior high school in many parts of the nation because of federal, state, or local restrictions on age, the amount of time a student can commit to work, and the type of work he or she can do. There are, however, junior high school students to whom none of these restrictions apply. There are others for whom opportunities could be made available if job needs were communicated to educators or counselors by such community agents as the Chamber of Commerce, industrial personnel people, representatives of the National Alliance of Business, or the United States Employment Service. As discussed at some length in Chapter 9, it is also possible to use combinations of work shadowing, work visits, and work experience with junior high school students to introduce them to selected career development concepts (Herr & Watts, 1989).

Other Career Guidance Activities and Techniques in the Junior High School

As is obvious, career guidance in the junior high school can be accomplished in many ways and related to many objectives. Teachers can achieve some career guidance objectives by making their subject matter more career oriented. Teachers and counselors can collaborate in some program efforts. Counselors can achieve many career guidance objectives alone. Activities that take students into the community for exploratory purposes can be helpful. In addition to the approaches to career guidance that have already been described here, the following list of other possible activities or techniques that have been tried in career education or career guidance settings across the nation might suggest ways to meet needs:

Curriculum Infusion

- Using census data, have students compare and contrast the composition of the United States labor market in 1940 and currently. Have them consider the percentages of workers employed in such areas as blue-collar versus white-collar families, or goods-producing versus service-producing industries. Discuss why shifts have occurred in these percentages.
- Divide class into small groups and have them compete in naming the most occupations in goods- or service-producing occupations.
- Given a unit in consumer economics or similar topic, have students define in a two-page paper what job rewards mean to them. Consider such areas as fringe benefits, salary, vacations, shift work, life-style, supervision, independent action.
- Given a list of activities (hobbies, sports, pets, clubs, and so on), have the student differentiate between those that require interpersonal skills and those that do not.
- After reading a biography of a famous person, have students identify risks the person took in implementing a career goal. Discuss.
- Have students write a theme describing a decision they made in the past that involved compromise.
- Teach students good study habits and relate these to good work habits.
- Develop "student days" in which students follow school and community officials in their daily job tasks. Have students report back to the class on what they learned about the various occupations and their responsibilities.
- Present students with a description of a hypothetical individual whose job was done away with through technological change. Have students work in groups to decide what that person might do to capitalize on existing skills and knowledge.
- Following group discussion on the effects of technology on the world of work, have students identify at least six occupations that existed twenty years ago and have now been combined with other occupations or have ceased to exist.
- Develop a bulletin board display illustrating the variety of tools and materials used by various occupations relating to subject areas taught in school.
- Given a situation of poor interpersonal relations between a subordinate and a supervisor, have the students role-play three ways to improve those relations.
- Following a class discussion on the effects of technology on our society, have students name two areas (such as marine science, space exploration, ecology) that are most likely to create new occupations within the next 10 years.
- Display posters in each subject matter area illustrating the contributions of workers in related occupations.
- Have students prepare bulletin board displays depicting marketable skills relating to subject area.
- Have students look through job ads in local newspapers to identify as many marketable skills as possible. Have them relate identified skills to specific subject areas taught in school.
- Given a preferred occupation, have the student demonstrate in a role-playing situation examples of communication skills necessary for successful performance of the occupation.

- Examine current events in the news media with regard to present career, economic, social, political climate and changes that will confront students when they plan for and enter the work world.
- Set up career cluster explorations in industrial arts classes that give pertinent hands-on experience in each cluster.
- Organize extracurricular career interest groups.
- Develop bulletin board displays illustrating the educational pathways to various careers (that is, four-year college, graduate, and professional schools, two-year college, trade school, on-the-job training, apprenticeship programs, and so on).
- Select a consumer product and trace it back to its original raw material, showing the interdependency of various occupations necessary to produce the product.

Decision Making and Acquisition of Career Information

- Tape record a simulated interview between a counselor and a student engaged in the decision-making process or some aspect of it. Have students listen to the tape and discuss their view of what went on.
- Use a variety of simulated decision-making games and compare the steps they portray (such as Life Career Game, Consumer, Economic System).
- Given a curriculum decision that students will confront in the future, have them list the alternatives, advantages, and disadvantages of each, and make a tentative decision. Consider the consequences likely to occur in terms of future educational and occupational possibilities.
- Have students list major decisions regarding their future which they must make:

  1. Within two years (such as high school course selection)
  2. Within five years (such as trade school, college, occupation)
  3. Within ten years (such as where to live, work, marriage)

Have them consider at least three alternatives in each decision that will be available and discuss the implications of each.

- For a hypothetical situation in which an individual clearly made an inappropriate occupational selection, have students identify reasons why the occupation was inappropriate for the person in question.
- Using a tentative identification of a preferred occupation, have the student list chronologically the steps that need to be taken to prepare to enter the occupation.
- For the 15 USOE career clusters, have students give at least two reasons why they would or would not consider occupations within each cluster.
- For a preferred career cluster, have students select four occupations within that cluster and gather information about them. Have them state the criteria by which they chose the four and on which they might rank them.
- Provide role models who not only have nontraditional careers but are also raising children to help both female and male students understand ways in which career and lifestyle decisions can be integrated.
- Use any or all of the following systematically to reinforce the need and the way for females to do career planning: role-plays, creative problem solving, values clarification, goal-setting activities, conflict resolution, assertiveness training, guided fantasy, and work exploration.
- Provide group sessions for parents to increase awareness of their attitudes about the career development of girls, the changing role of women, the issues their daughters face, and ways to help their daughters keep their options open.
- Through individual or group counseling, have students develop a set of personal criteria for use in exploring occupations.

- Using a list of ten qualities desired by individuals in fellow workers, have the students discuss at least one way in which each quality could improve individual chances for advancement in a selected career.
- Using a list of twenty common occupations, have students classify each in terms of its relationship to data, people, and things using the categories "highly related, related, not related."
- Have the students list examples of talents or other contributions they might make to a hypothetical talent show.
- Create a series of posters or displays illustrating women doing a variety of occupations previously thought of as masculine roles and men in such occupations as nursing, secretarial work, and so on.
- Use a "Problem Bucket" to which students anonymously contribute problems facing them. Discuss problems in small groups and explore possible solutions.
- Conduct job clinics relating to those jobs open to junior high school students, such as babysitting, lawn work, newspaper delivery, and so on.
- Play match-up games in which students are expected to choose the correct types of educational requirement for various occupations.
- Have the student develop a tentative outline of the course of study he or she plans to pursue in high school including program choice, required courses, and electives.
- Have students list ten occupations in which socialization skills and interpersonal relationships are crucial (such as salesperson, teacher) and ten occupations in which these skills are less important (such as research scientist, chemist, veterinarian).
- Invite business personnel into the school to conduct mock job interviews with students and discuss the results with them.
- Using a list of six occupations commonly stereotyped as to sex roles, have the student look up each occupation in available resource materials and be able to give specific reasons why such stereotyping is wrong.
- Have students role-play a decision situation involving the need for compromise.
- Make posters illustrating various phases of the decision-making process.
- Have students solve a scrambled letters puzzle based on decision-making terminology.
- Have students identify the entry-level skills for five occupations within an occupational cluster of their choice. (Make use of career information, field trips, talks with workers in the field, and so on.) Have the student identify those skills he or she feels could now be performed and those in which additional training needs to be acquired.

Community Involvement

- After listening to a resource speaker on a career of his or her choice, have students list at least four new ideas concerning that career area that each had not previously considered.
- Have students tape record an interview with a worker whose job has come into existence in the past ten years as a result of scientific technology. Discuss the implications for planning that the interviews suggest.
- After a field trip to a setting representative of a particular occupational cluster, have the student list tools or materials he or she observed workers using.
- After having interviewed a person who works in the student's general field of interest (career or group discussion how this person's occupation is an integral part of his or her total life-style).
- Develop a directory of entry-level jobs in the community including job descriptions, requirements, contact persons, and procedure for applying.
- Have students engage in volunteer community service work in hospitals, nursing homes, orphanages, and so on. Discuss their experiences in helping others in class and

explore the potential occupations related to them.

- Invite local employment service counselors to talk with students about jobs available in the community.
- Develop a Youth Employment Service to bring students seeking part-time work together with employers having short-term or odd jobs.
- Develop performance contacts with students relative to community projects that would help them acquire career awareness.
- Given an opportunity to observe an experienced individual and a trainee in a specific career cluster, have the student compare at least five different levels of capability between the two individuals as they perform their work roles.
- Design a Human Resource Book that lists members of the community who are willing to share their knowledge and expertise with students. Identify these persons by address, phone number, occupational title, and area of expertise.

Summary

In this chapter we have examined the implications for career guidance of youth occupied primarily by exploration, planning, and identity formation. We have noted the effects on the development of career guidance programs that are associated with gender, differences in maturity, and early school leaving. Themes and practices recommended in Chapter 7 for use at the elementary school level have been longitudinally extended and reshaped to make them appropriate for the middle/junior high school. Examples of program content, activities, and techniques appropriate to youth are described and, where possible, relevant research findings are presented.

CHAPTER 9

CAREER GUIDANCE IN THE SENIOR HIGH SCHOOL

Key Concepts

- Students in the senior high school vary in their career development and in their needs for career guidance and counseling.
- Career guidance in the senior high school can be conceived of in terms of three emphases: stimulating career development, providing treatment, and aiding placement.
- Major goals of career guidance for senior high school students are specific planning of next steps in education and work; values clarification of life roles as a worker, a consumer, a leisurite, and a family member; and assuming responsibility for decision making and its consequences.
- Career guidance techniques in the senior high school include structured classes, group and individual counseling, topical workshops, computer-assisted programs, self-directed activities, use of information systems, assessment, mentoring, the integration of work and education for reality-testing, exploration and behavioral modification, and job placement.
- Consistent with the setting, resources, and program design, the facilitation of some career guidance goals is best achieved by teachers, others by counselors, and still others through cooperative activity between school personnel and specialists in the community.

The major factor that senior high school students must deal with is the imminence of reality as defined by the rapidly approaching separation from senior high school and passage into the independence of young adulthood. Like other factors in decision making and intermediate choices, reality—defined as how the alternatives of postsecondary school life are considered by the individual—will have different implications for each individual.

Postsecondary school reality might be cast in any one of the following forms:

1. Choosing a postsecondary vocational or technical school to pursue some skilled specialty
2. Gaining access to a college and selecting a major field of study with its myriad implications for later vocational endeavors
3. Converting part-time work experience while in school into a full-time position in the labor market
4. Entering the labor market for the first time
5. Deliberating about military service, marriage, combining work and continuing education
6. Acquiring an apprenticeship opportunity

However, there will also be many students for whom none of these possibilities seems viable or appealing; for them, the future represents threat or trauma. Some of these students see the future beyond high school as a confrontation with their indecisiveness about life and their place in it. Others will find the burden of decision making untenable and will try to escape or postpone facing such an awareness directly (Hayes, 1982). Still others will experience a generalized anxiety about the decisions they face.

In both sociological and psychological terms, many teenagers are apparently worried that for them the American dream is being jeopardized and their visions of the future are restricted by the problems of money, future, the complexity of choices, and health. The Survey of American Teens, undertaken by the American Home Economics association (1988), reported that when some 32 topics were presented to 510 junior and senior high school students, 3 in 10 said they were "extremely concerned" or "very concerned" about the following:

- Being able to pay for college (39 percent)
- Making the wrong decisions about their future and not being able to change them (34 percent)
- The United States is headed for a big depression (30 percent)
- Not earning enough money to enjoy the better things in life (29 percent)
- Learning in the future that some of the things they eat will cause cancer or a heart attack (28 percent)

Although 8 in 10 teens say that they are basically happy with their lives, nearly 6 in 10 say they have a friend who has considered suicide, and 5 in 10 indicate that some of their friends are flirting with disaster by taking drugs. Although some 55 percent of the teens turned to friends for advice and help in overcoming problems and 47 percent of teens do seek parental guidance, one in six teens report that they have no one to turn to for advice in making important decisions. Over half of these teens report feeling that they do not have a handle on life.

Hamburg and Takaniski (1989) have indicated that recent historical events have drastically changed the experience of adolescence, in some ways making it more difficult than ever before. Among these events are the lengthening period of adolescence; the disjunction between biological and social development; confusion about adult roles and difficulty in foreseeing the future; the erosion of family and social support networks; and greater access to potentially life-threatening activities (p. 825). These events have introduced a high degree of uncertainty into the lives of many adolescents and have potentially, or actually, affected their decision-making styles and career maturity.

As Mangum (1988) has observed, "the transition from adolescence into the adult world of work is inherently difficult in a society which persistently separates home and workplace and extends adolescence. There is a substantial minority, primarily from culturally and economically deprived backgrounds, who are permanently scarred by their unsuccessful experiences" (p. 1). Many youth have been cast into a marginal role in adolescence—one that is likely to be reflected in economic marginality in adulthood—because they have grown up in families with lower economic resources, they have experienced parental divorce, a lack of significant adult role models, poor educational outcomes or the noncompletion of high school, or, possibly, involvement in alcohol and drug abuse, teenage pregnancy, or crime. A sizable proportion of these youth are from minority groups who have faced discrimination in education and the workplace, and as a result have become alienated from the larger society or lack aspirations to have a meaningful job that will provide sufficient income to permit them to support a family. Indeed, among Hispanic and black adolescent populations, the unemployment rates have continued to be two to three times that of the white adolescent population, especially in inner cities.

CAREER DEVELOPMENT AMONG SENIOR HIGH SCHOOL STUDENTS

Although little is known specifically about when adolescents state their occupational choices or the numbers of them who are essentially decided about such commitments, some rough estimates are available. Crites (1969) reviewed several pertinent studies and concluded that about 30 percent of students are undecided during the high school and college years. This is somewhat more than Fottler and Bain's finding (1980a) of 18 percent undecided among a sample of high school seniors in Alabama and less than Marr's longitudinal study (1956), which reported that 50 percent of the subjects did not make a choice until about age 21. Hollender's research (1974) has shown that decisiveness among senior high school students varies with their intellectual characteristics. Among male students, decidedness increases significantly from the lowest intellectual quartile to the highest. Females showed a similar trend, although the percentage decided dropped in the top intellectual quartile, perhaps because of the conflicts bright girls continue to experience between nurturant roles and further educational achievement.

The research of Super and Nevill (1984) has demonstrated that career maturity among high school students is not simply a function of sex or socioeconomic status. They have shown instead that work salience, the relative importance of work to the individual, is directly related to career maturity. Thus, if work and career have not yet become important to some high school students, it is not likely that much career development has taken place for them. Similarly, if career development is minimal, expressed preferences and scores on vocational interest inventories are not likely to have much permanent meaning. Without studies of large numbers of high school students across the nation, it is difficult to know the proportions of such students as stratified by their attributions of work salience or their career maturity, but it is clear that the population is quite diverse in these dimensions. To the degree that the facilitation of career planning, participation in work, and commitment to work are goals integral to the educational mission of the school, findings such as those of Super and Nevill affirm that "career education and counseling must in such cases aim first at arousal, at creating awareness of the place of work in life, its possible meanings, and how to make it real and meaningful" (p. 42).

Whichever of the numbers or trends regarding decisiveness in the senior high school population one accepts, it is clear that career development needs among senior high school students are wide-ranging.

One window into both the career needs of high school students and the status of responses to those needs is found in a 10-year nationwide follow-up study of career development among high school students. Prediger, Roth, and Noeth conducted a study in 1973 of students in grades 8 and 11 in 133 schools across the United States. In 1983, Prediger and Sawyer conducted a 10-year follow-up of students in grades 8, 10, and 12 in 115 schools across the nation and developed estimates from these data about eleventh graders so that comparisons could be made with the 1973 data. Selective comparisons of student views of their needs for help with career planning and the status of their career-related behavior is abstracted from Prediger and Sawyer (1985) as follows:

1. In 1973, 78 percent of the eleventh-grade students in the nationwide survey indicated their desire for help with career planning; in 1983, this figure for eleventh-grade students had decreased to 71 percent. Thus, although it can be argued that more students are receiving help with career planning now than ten years ago, clearly most high school students still desire help with their career planning.

2. In 1973, 50 percent of eleventh graders reported receiving "some" or "a lot" of help with career planning from their schools. In 1983, that figure had risen to 66 percent. Apparently, high schools nationwide are offering more assistance with career planning than was true a decade ago, but at least 33 percent of eleventh graders are receiving very little such help and whether or not it is available, 71 percent of eleventh graders would like more.

3. When asked how certain students were about their occupational preferences in 1973, 22 percent of the eleventh graders answered, "I am not sure at all," and in 1983, 27 percent answered in that fashion.

The survey asked many other questions concerning student beliefs about career development and the types of occupational preferences in which they were interested. The answers to many of these questions suggested the impact of social events, various consciousness-raising activities (such as efforts to reduce sex-stereotyping), and increased efforts by schools to provide courses dealing with career planning. In the final analysis, however, it continues to be evident that high school students vary in the status of their career development and that most of them profess major needs for help with their career planning. In the final analysis, such data indicate that high schools vary widely in the status of their career planning services including planning for postsecondary and collegiate education.

Need for Increased Availability of Career Guidance Services

The evidence cited about the unevenness of career guidance services in high schools has been echoed in a range of national reports arguing for more such services for youth in schools, for more school-community cooperation on behalf of such needs, and for the necessity of parental involvement in more systematic and comprehensive ways if the career guidance needs of diverse populations of students are to be met. Some examples follow.

The Business Advisory Committee of the Education Commission of the States (1985), in a national report dealing with the growing problem of alienated, disadvantaged, disconnected, and other at-risk youth recommends "new structures and procedures for effecting the transition from school to work or other productive pursuits. . . . Young people today need more and better guidance than ever before" (p. 26). The report discusses the need for coordinated programs including career counseling, financial assistance, summer jobs, cooperative education options, and role models if such at-risk youth are to be reconnected to schooling and to work. Such perspectives imply the need for community involvement in the career guidance of youth and in the provision of opportunities by which they can be supported and encouraged to move forward with purpose and productivity.

The Research Policy Committee of the Committee for Economic Development (1985), in a major report dealing with business and the public schools, strongly recommended that schools provide employability counseling and exploratory programs to assist in career choice, job search, and general employability. This report specifies the legitimate role for the business community in interacting with and supporting quality education in schools and in the community. The report talks about the range of the business community's involvement in schooling: for example, serving of business representatives on school boards, providing vocational education and, particularly, cooperative education, sponsoring of athletic and extracurricular activities, adopting schools, providing resource personnel for instructional or guidance purposes in schools, serving on guidance advisory groups, offering student internships in business and industry, providing mentoring of disadvantaged and minority students, providing project funding for educational purposes, and offering school-to-work programs, donations of equipment, and teacher or student awards and recognitions. (Research and Policy Committee, Committee for Economic Development, 1985).

The National Alliance of Business and the National Advisory Council on Vocational Education (1984), in a major analysis of the nation at work and particularly of relationships between education and the private sector, has argued for more school-to-work transition programs including job placement assistance, career counseling, cooperative career education activities with business, and counseling about vocational-technical program alternatives to college degree programs. Many of the recommendations about the business community's interaction with the schools are essentially the same as those proposed in the report previously cited.

Also concerned with children at risk and counseling for employment, the 1988 report of the William T. Grant Foundation Commission on Work, Family, and Citizenship goes further than the others cited to describe needed community involvement with the guidance needs of children. The following excerpt is an example:

> In the United States, the almost exclusive responsibility for youth's transition to work is lodged with parents and the schools. Many parents have networks and associations that allow them to give their teenagers a hand in finding jobs. But particularly in poverty families, these informal but important connections are too often absent, leaving teenagers dependent on their own initiatives or on the schools. Yet our schools are largely isolated from the community and from the workplace. A host of blue ribbon panel recommendations calling for an end to the school's isolation from the larger community have been largely ignored. (p. 39)
>
> Obviously, this is not a problem that can be solved by the schools alone. The Commission urges school authorities, business leaders, and community officials to join together in greatly expanded efforts to aid youth. The image of these foundering young people should not be seen as evidence that young people have failed, but rather that adults of the community have failed to give them a fair chance to get started. (p. 40)
>
> The Commission urges new consideration by state policymakers, school and community leaders of a variety of out-of-school learning possibilities which use the schools as the nexus of community-based programs and resources. (p. 41)

The Commission report then goes on to identify examples of programs in which the community and parents can play major roles. The listing of these is as follows:

- Monitored work experience
  - Cooperative education
  - Internships
  - Apprenticeship
  - Pre-employment training
  - Youth-operated enterprises
- Community neighborhood services
  - Individual voluntary service
  - Youth-guided services
- Redirected vocational education incentives
  - Guaranteed postsecondary and continuing education
  - Guaranteed jobs
- Career information and counseling
  - Career information centers
  - Parents as career educators
  - Improved counseling and career orientation
  - Community mentors and community-based organizations
- School volunteers

Although these suggested possibilities do not exhaust the potential of either communities or parents to become more intimately involved with schools, they do illustrate ways to augment the schools' programs and processes, on the one hand, and, on the other, to create a sense of community responsibility for socializing youth to the behaviors, skills, and opportunities important to their future mobility, as well as to create a sense of the community as a large learning laboratory in which resources, persons, and programs exist to provide diversity in where and by whom children and adolescents are taught.

These national perspectives reinforce the need for expanded conceptions and availability of career guidance services in the United States and, at least implicitly, contend that differences in career aspirations and developmental experiences require comprehensive approaches to career guidance and counseling.

Differences in Career Aspirations

Available data tend to confirm that within the subpopulations comprising senior high school students there are substantial differences in career development and maturity needs for career guidance. Many factors produce these differences: levels of parental support, work salience, gender and racial background, self-concept, and health and physical development.

Racial Background. For example, Jaramillo, Zapata, and McPherson (1982) in a study of 213 Mexican-American college-bound high school students found that there were subgroups within such a population as related to gender and rural or city location. They found, in particular, that females in the sample were more concerned than males about the financial condition of the family and their own personal vocational and educational future. Dillard and Campbell (1981) compared the influence of 304 Puerto Rican (154), black (154), and Anglo (99) parents on the career behavior of their 194 adolescent children in grades 9 to 12. Represented were both intact and non-intact families with middle and lower socioeconomic characteristics. They found that these parents differentially affected their children's career development. For example, it was found that parental career *values* did not have much influence on their children's career aspirations in any of the three groups. However, the parental career *aspirations* for their children were significantly related to the child's career aspirations in both black and Puerto Rican families but not in the Anglo families. Mothers in the black group seemed to contribute more strongly to their children's career development than did fathers of the same ethnic membership. In general, Anglo parents' career values or aspirations are much weaker predictors of children's career development than are those of black or Puerto Rican parents.

In related research on the career choice attitudes of rural black, white, and Native American high school students, Lee (1984) found that parental influence has a greater impact upon the career choice attitudes of black and Native American students than on that of white students. Using a sample of 520 tenth-grade students in five public high schools in rural North Carolina, Lee also found that self-concept interacted with ethnicity to produce different groups of predictors of career attitude maturity for black, white, and Native American students. It seemed clear that the cultural and ethnic differences in views about self among these groups had important implications for their career behavior. For example, the research suggested that in the case of Native American students, historic socioeconomic hardships and unique cultural traditions may "affect the development of self-perceptions and their influence on behavior and attitudes in ways that are different from the other two ethnic groups" (p. 192). Thus, this study suggests that more needs to be known about how parenting differs across the rural ethnic groups studied here and about how such effects impact upon their self-concept development and career behaviors.

Parental Effects. Studies of the effects of parents on their children's values, aspirations, and achievement show that such effects can also be indirect. For example, children whose parents do not have much education or financial security are not likely to receive information about postsecondary opportunities or assistance in choosing curricular patterns that will give them the most challenging future options. As suggested in the previous chapter, many of these students take the easiest academic route they can and thereby prematurely foreclose many educational or occupational alternatives or, indeed, drop out of school before graduation. One national report (College Board Commission on Pre-College Guidance and Counseling, 1986) indicates that children of lower-income families turn to the school for information and academic support that their families cannot provide. Unfortunately, in many schools where low-income children predominate there is insufficient counseling or career guidance available to meet their needs. Where it is available, however, the research shows that counselor and teacher influence on students' post-high school plans increases as socioeconomic level and parental educational level decreases (p. 11). Counselors do make a difference to these students.

Other research has examined the relationships among student employment status, family structure, socioeconomic position, and adolescent academic success. In one study of 4587 high school students in Washington State (Schill, McCartin, & Meyer, 1985), it was found that families do pass on employment advantage—or disadvantage— to their children, depending upon the characteristics of the family structure. For example, students who had part-time employment while in high school were likely to be from intact, middle-income families rather than lower-income families, thus deriving more financial advantage and experience from adult contacts than did lower socioeconomic students. The latter were doubly disadvantaged in that they were less able to obtain part-time employment and less able to acquire the information and experience of those who did. Other findings were that employed students were likely to have higher GPAs and have a mother or father employed in a higher-status occupation. While middle-income students are more likely to have a job than the lower socioeconomic status student, they are apt to work fewer hours than the latter. Working mothers seem to have positive effects on their offspring, providing a model (much like the father) for their employment experiences. The research also found a curvilinear relationship between hours worked and GPA, with those students working less than twenty hours a week having higher GPAs than students working more than twenty hours a week. These data suggest an intertwining of family variables and student adolescent employment experiences and, indeed, the effects of such experiences upon subsequent employment.

Another interesting evidence of family effects upon high school student career choice is found in the research of Noeth, Engen, and Noeth (1984). In this research, 1200 juniors in Washington State were randomly sampled from 21,060 who were college-bound and had taken the Washington Pre-College Test. These students completed a survey instrument designed to examine the factors that they felt influenced their educational and occupational plans by helping them make career decisions. Both males and females reported that interesting classes (93 percent) and students' families (91 percent) were most helpful in terms of assistance with career decisions in the expected college major. The next level of helpfulness was ascribed to grades (87 percent), friends (76 percent), WPC test scores (74 percent), and teachers (73 percent). The two factors seen as providing the least help were counselors (59 percent) and out-of-school activities (54 percent). Similar findings were reported for receiving help with the planned occupation.

The role of parents as primary determinants of children's career development has been identified in a number of studies (Birk & Blimline, 1984; Otto & Call, 1985). Parents also have a dominant role in their children's anticipation and preparation for college (College Board Commission on Pre-college Guidance and Counseling, 1986). Parental influence has much to do with children's self-concepts, values, and personality as well as with the focus of their aspirations and achievement. Therefore, parents must be empowered to be positive motivators of children's ambition, work habits, and commitment to study.

One approach to such empowerment comes from the work of Cochran and his colleagues through the use of planning workbooks, activity self-exploration workbooks, and career grids combined into a Partners Program that parents used in helping their children's career planning (Cochran & Amundson, 1986). The research of Palmer and Cochran (1988) found that such approaches were effective in supporting parents as agents of career guidance for their children. Indeed, this research suggests that even though counselors can offer group career programs in interest testing, computer-assisted interactions, and other techniques, parents can be enabled through workshops tailored for parents to help their children sort out ideas, information, values and so on, particularly when provided a structured program they can follow.

Parents must have access to resources and training to play a positive role in meeting the career guidance needs of children. Among the useful possibilities are creating parent resource libraries, distributing to them lists of practical suggestions about ways they can help their children in study habits, exploration, and information seeking, and offering parent group meetings at convenient places and times. School counselors can conduct parent study groups and can help them to serve in liaison roles between the school and the community. Parents can be invited to and supported in roles as mini-course instructors or resource persons in the classrooms, teacher aides on field trips, members of advisory or planning committees, and technical advisors on particular work settings, colleges, or other postsecondary opportunities. Parents can be the major target of information about college or career nights and can provide incentives for their children if they attend together. Student/parent handbooks on educational planning and financial aid can be prepared and reinforcements developed to have parents and children jointly examine such information.

Career Maturity in Special Populations

Plata (1981) compared the occupational aspirations of 40 normal and 40 emotionally disturbed male adolescents randomly selected from a midwestern public school (twenty from a general studies program and twenty from vocational education) and from a special education program administered in a state institution for the mentally ill in which the students were residents (20) or part of an outpatient population (20). He found, using the Occupational Aspiration Scale, that the level of occupational aspiration for regular normals (students in general secondary school studies) was significantly higher than for either of the emotionally disturbed groups. The latter scores reflected that emotionally disabled adolescents do maintain their aspirations "at a low level or that their level of occupational aspiration vacillates" (p. 134). This finding is consistent with a series of earlier research studies. However, in addition, it was found by Plata that the level of occupational aspirations of normal, vocational students did not differ significantly from either of the emotionally disturbed groups but was significantly lower than the scores of normal students enrolled in general academic secondary school studies. Thus, we find again that there are subgroups of secondary school students who differ on their occupational aspirations. Although emotional disturbance apparently depresses such aspiration it does not explain the fact that the normal, vocational students in the sample also had low occupational aspirations.

Pound (1978) studied the self-concept of some 500 male and 500 female students randomly sampled from six high schools in western New York in attempting to predict career maturity for race and sex subgroups. Using the attitude scale of the Vocational Development Inventory (now CMI) and the Tennessee Self-Concept Scale(s) as predictors he found that the self-concept does appear to have a different effect on career maturity depending on the race and sex of the participants. He indicated that

> when male students evaluate self concept, they are heavily influenced by external sources. . . . For white females, the findings suggest that internal resources play a major role in developing an evaluative statement of self-concept. Finally, the results would indicate that for Black females, statements related to positive or negative feelings toward self are developed from multidimensional sources favoring neither internal nor external frames of reference. (p. 67)

He further contends that when predicting career maturity, different predictors are important for different racial and gender groups and, similarly, different influences affect "the frame of references chosen by students in evaluating their self-concept."

In a study somewhat related to that of Pound, Karayanni (1981) compared the career maturity of emotionally maladjusted and emotionally well-adjusted high school students in two medium-sized schools in north central Florida. Eighty-nine students were classified as emotionally maladjusted from their scores on the Minnesota Counseling Inventory (MCI) and 92 were classified as well-adjusted using the same procedure. Using the Attitude Scale of the Career Maturity Inventory as the dependent variable, Karayanni found significant differences in career attitude maturity between well-adjusted and maladjusted students. The well-adjusted students had a significantly higher score on the CMI-Attitude Scale than did the emotionally maladjusted students. He interpreted this to mean that any disturbance in personality will affect an individual's vocational development. Although he did not find sex differences in career attitude maturity scores, when they were pooled without regard to level of adjustment, he did find significantly higher scores for white students than for black students.

Perrone, Male, and Karshner (1979) have studied the career development concerns of talented students. Their findings include the following:

> 1. The talented are often told, "You can be anything you want," which somewhat negates and denies what and who they already are, placing them on a treadmill of continually becoming something beyond their immediate selves. This anything-is-possible attitude often makes it difficult for talented students to acknowledge their weaknesses and any evidence of personal limitation is ignored or rejected.
>
> 2. Talented persons may receive a great deal of reinforcement from others for their endeavors, making it difficult to sort out what they value from what others value for them. In attempting to set priorities they often adopt the value systems of powerful or influential models, which makes it hard to measure up.
>
> 3. Talented persons sometimes have a tendency to commit themselves to career choices prematurely, based on subject-matter fields in which they achieve considerable recognition and success (p. 18).

In a follow-up study of 648 talented high school students in young adulthood, Post-Kammer and Perrone (1983) extended these findings about talented students and their career guidance needs. In particular, they found that approximately 30 percent of the respondents reported that upon high school graduation they felt unprepared to make career decisions; about one-quarter of the sample indicated that in high school they did not know how their interests and abilities related to various career possibilities. By young adulthood, approximately one-quarter of the talented students did not believe they had lived up to their educational and occupational abilities. Although males and females did not differ in their perception of measuring up to educational abilities, females were more self-critical about not living up to their occupational abilities.

As suggested in other studies, these findings indicated that for many gifted individuals, work is a form of self-expression; indeed, careers contribute significantly to their self-concept. Sometimes gifted students experience tension between careerism and intellectualism; between strong professional commitment based on the desire to become affluent and other career interests based more on a search for satisfying work. (Pendaris, Howley, & Howley, 1990)

In addition, while work is equally important to both males and females, talented females value relationships and marriage more highly than do males. Within work itself, relationships were also found to be more important for females than males, suggesting that many talented females continue to have attitudes consistent with sex-role stereotyping. In sum, then, gifted and talented males and females experience needs for career guidance to

1. Help with educational and career decision making
2. Learn how their values can be used in career planning and career decision making
3. Relate choice of college majors to their career implications
4. Differentiate the career expectations they have for themselves as compared with expectations others hold for them
5. Acquire ways to identify careers by which to satisfy their needs for challenge and continual skill development

The research of Dayton and Feldhusen (1989) among secondary schools in Indiana has made clear that it is important to recognize that gifted students are not found only in academic or college-preparatory curricula. There are also vocationally talented high school students. These latter students tend to manifest academic talent or high ability, vocational talent or high ability, high levels of motivation/persistence, study skills, and leadership. Among the difficulties these talented students had as enrollees in vocational education were difficulties in scheduling both academic and vocational classes, boredom and maintaining self-motivation, the lack of articulation between vocational and postsecondary programs, and dealing with parent, teacher, and counselor pressure to stay in the academic track even though as students they wanted to be involved in vocational education. Career guidance services for such students were seen as needing to deal with the unique pressures they face, to assist them in scheduling and clarifying options, and to provide career education in more depth than usual.

Fottler and Bain (1980b) studied the occupational aspirations of 2112 seniors from 14 high schools in Alabama. The sample was described as 54.3 percent females, 26.4 percent nonwhites, 50.8 percent enrolled in a college preparatory program, average age 17.4 years. A comparison of the career aspirations of males and females indicated that approximately twice as many males (5.6 percent) as females (2.8 percent) aspired to a managerial position. Beyond this finding, however, the data do not suggest that females' aspirations are lower than males'. Indeed, females tended to aspire to professional and technical occupations slightly more than the males, while aspiring to managerial occupations less.

At lower levels of occupational aspirations, traditional patterns emerged: females aspire to clerical and service positions, and males aspire to be craftsmen, operatives, or laborers. Professional and sales were the only two occupational groupings for which there were not statistically significant differences in the proportion of male and female aspirations. At least two concepts are evident in these data. First, compared to earlier studies the "motivation to manage" among students of all ages is low and declining. Second, there apparently are deep-rooted attitudes that continue to direct both sexes toward traditional occupational roles.

Gender Differences

Garrison (1979) also studied gender differences in career aspirations of high school seniors. He compared three statewide surveys of twelfth-grade students (1970, 1973, and 1976) in public high schools in Virginia. The number of students in each survey was 57,195, 58,558, and 62,181 in 1970, 1973, and 1976 respectively. He found that the career choices of high school males and females are becoming more similar, particularly in regard to high status professional occupations. His data suggest that male aspirations for these jobs are declining while female aspirations are rising dramatically, lessening gender differences in choice. He also found a declining percentage of females choosing clerical-sales jobs and middle-status professions. In sum, he sees the potential for a reduction in sex segregation growing as men's and women's orientations to the labor force become more similar.

Dunne, Elliott, and Carlsen (1981) found somewhat similar results to those of Fottler and Bain. They studied the occupational aspirations of 1900 tenth, eleventh, and twelfth graders in 26 rural high schools in five regions of the United States. They found that the females had both higher educational and occupational aspirations (when measured by the Duncan SEI Scale) than did males. In addition, they found that although the young rural women tended to aspire to female-stereotyped jobs, they did not restrict themselves to so narrow a range of choice as has been found in many other studies. However, beyond the female-stereotyped occupations, females tended to consider neutrally perceived occupations (such as artist, draftsperson), not jobs stereotyped for the opposite sex (such as logger, plumber, construction worker). Females in this sample did not seem to consider homemaking to be a career to which they aspired.

Aspirations by high school students toward particular types of occupations have been studied by Heilman (1979). She found that projections of more balanced sex ratios (30 to 50 percent) encouraged greater occupational interest among women, but a totally balanced sex ratio (50/50) tended to reduce their occupational interest. Heilman suggests that, for males, changes in sex composition appear to alter the perception of social rewards to be derived from a career, whereas for females they alter the perceived likelihood of success. In addition, the data suggested that gradual increments in the number of women in nontraditional occupations, for example up to 30 percent, did not cause major changes in men's interests or images of the field while increasing women's likelihood of viewing these occupations as realistic possibilities.

Koski and Subich (1985) examined sex differences among high school students concerning prestige and sex stereotypes of their realistic and fantasized occupational choices. These findings suggested less balance in the consideration of traditional and non-traditional occupations among males and females than some of the other studies cited. Specifically, male students' realistic and fantasied occupations had few female workers. Female students chose occupations either with more women than men workers or equivalent numbers of both sexes.

Women's realistic choices were less prestigious and more heavily populated by female workers than were their fantasized choices. Overall, the males' fantasized and realistic choices were primarily in the traditionally male, high prestige occupations. Females aspire to such jobs, but expect to be actually employed in less prestigious occupations traditional for their sex.

Macke and Morgan (1978) studied the work orientation of some 1067 high school senior girls, both black and white, in Louisville, Kentucky. It was found that such work orientations were related to mothers' work *behavior* rather than to work values or proscriptions against maternal employment. It was also found that with equal commitment to families, black girls were 20 percent more likely than white girls to expect to work after having children because of economic circumstances.

In the aggregate, the studies reviewed here show that high school students tend to fall into groups whose career development is different and reflective of family influences, ethnicity, and gender. Thus, the responses of career guidance and counseling need to be tailored to accommodate such differences.

Differences in Career Development

Another view of the differences in career development that can be expected among senior high school students comes from the National Assessment of Educational Progress Project on Career and Occupational Development referred to in the previous two chapters. About 37,500 seventeen-year-old boys and girls from across the nation were included in the sample. Selected findings follow (Mitchell, 1977):

- Most seventeen-year-olds have talked seriously to someone about their future plans. Their plans are discussed with parents twice as often as with counselors, advisors, or peers. Only about two-thirds felt that the person(s) they talked to were aware of their abilities.
- Males tend to have more confidence in their ability to do things well than females.
- When asked to match occupations with required physical characteristics or learned skills, most seventeen-year-olds are able to match at least five of nine correctly but less than 10 percent could match all correctly. Blacks and persons from low socioeconomic backgrounds in cities were significantly lower than other groups in their ability to make such occupational matches.
- Prestige and status are cited more than twice as often as challenge and responsibility, personal satisfaction, or opportunity and advancement as reasons for accepting a promotion to a supervisory job.
- Only 2.2 percent of the respondents saw school or academic areas as activities that might be useful for a job. Students are not able to draw linkages between formal or informal academic learning and performance on a job.
- The principal resource named for finding out the requirements of a job is observation of the job field. Reading about it and contacting a personnel office are also frequent responses. Only about one-quarter of the respondents see the counselor among their top five sources of job requirement information. The responses to the questionnaire item indicate that students are not sufficiently aware of sources of job information or how to access these sources.
- Nearly all seventeen-year-olds have thought about the kind of job they would like to have in the future. More than two-thirds have considered professional jobs, with more males than females aspiring to be professionals.
- Females see themselves as clerical workers in service occupations, and as homemakers and housewives. Males see themselves as craftspersons, farmers and farm managers,

laborers, managers or administrators, proprietors and owners, in the military and in protective services. Thus, the data indicate that seventeen-year-old males and females choose sex-stereotyped jobs.

- Most have worked at a part-time or summer job; economic independence is the main reason for doing so. Females more than males name part-time clerical, sales, and service jobs, whereas more males name craftsperson, farm laborer, laborer, and operative.

Work Values

Of particular importance in understanding senior high school students is the status of their work values. In essence, work values represent one of many decision schemes by which to give coherence and meaning to an occupational choice. As Cochran (1986) has suggested, "In trying to make a vocational decision, a decider is faced with varying possibilities of what values can be realized in work. In response to this situation, people must form some view or theory of what values can be realized together and what cannot" (p. 25). Cochran's research with senior high school students in Vancouver, British Columbia suggests that the most important values for setting occupational preferences need to be harmonious in their relationship to each other. If a person's most important values are disharmonious or conflicting among themselves, the decision scheme is in jeopardy. Thus, for a given individual it makes considerable difference how values are given priority. Such perspectives lead to the validity of considering work values and their clarification as a major function of career guidance for senior high school students.

Perrone's seven-year longitudinal study (1973) of 170 students in a suburban Wisconsin village found that students beginning in the junior high school and continuing into grades 11 and 12 expressed rather constant value levels of three types: security, affiliation, and independence. More specifically, boys valued a good income more than girls did. Girls valued helping others, working with people, and having time for one's family more than did boys. Senior boys valuing independence had higher IQ scores than did those valuing security and affiliation. Senior girls valuing independence and affiliation had higher IQ scores than did those valuing security. Boys and girls valuing security had lower grade point averages than did those valuing independence and affiliation. As seniors, boys had higher occupational aspirations than did girls—the first time this difference occurred in this sample from the junior high school forward.

In a study of work values of 116 fifth-, eighth-, and eleventh-grade students in a small Appalachian school system, Hales and Fenner (1972) found that the development of work values was well underway for most children by grade 5 and continued with remarkable consistency through grade 11. As compared with the fifth and eighth graders in this sample, eleventh graders valued altruistic jobs and work that permits self-realization more highly than did the fifth or eighth graders. This finding did not suggest a value shift as much as an apparent response by eleventh graders to the immediacy of choice and an apparent determination to embark on such choice from a position of one's own strengths. Reflecting the farming, small retail, and semiskilled trades characteristic of their geographic region, students in this sample generally gave priority to work that is steady and dependable, pays well, permits the use of personal skills and interests, and benefits other people. However, the deviation of scores on the scales measuring such values suggests that there were many variations in the student values profiles, even though this group of students was quite homogeneous in socioeconomic and other characteristics.

With respect to the consistency or inconsistency of work values among students from the junior high school through the senior high school, other research indicates that they are affected by several factors that have implications for working with any student. For example, sex differences in work values have been reported in the studies cited here and in others (see Olive, 1973; Wijting, Arnold, & Conrad, 1977). The social positions of parents and racial differences are also related to students' work values (Ermalinski & Ruscelli, 1971; Thomas, 1974).

Post-Kammer (1987) studied the work values and career maturity of some 402 boys and 483 girls in ninth and eleventh grades of a suburban public high school in a large midwestern city. She reported that work values and career maturity were not highly correlated in her analyses, which suggests that they are essentially independent constructs. She also found that boys and girls in her sample differed in their work values and in their career maturity: girls valued achievement and variety to a greater extent and security to a lesser extent than did boys. Boys more highly valued management, economic returns, and independence, whereas girls more highly valued altruism and way of life. On career maturity scales, she found that girls scored higher on involvement and independence that did boys. Given the differences in scale scores between the girls and the boys, this study suggested that understanding the career maturity of girls may be more complex then that of understanding boys' career maturity. Finally, she found that values tend to change from extrinsic to intrinsic between ninth and eleventh grades. For example, eleventh graders score significantly higher than ninth graders on three intrinsic work values (achievement, altruism, and creativity) and one extrinsic work value (variety). The ninth graders scored higher than eleventh graders on the extrinsic value (associates). The remaining three intrinsic values and seven extrinsic values were not significantly different in score between the ninth and eleventh graders.

Relationships Among Curricula, Work Values, Work Salience, and Career Maturity

A longitudinal study by Kapes and Strickler (1975) suggests somewhat less consistency in work values from ninth to twelfth grades than do the other studies reported. Particularly significant is their finding that different high school curricula appear to cause different changes in work values. For example, home economics students tend not to change their work values from ninth to twelfth grade, whereas college preparatory students change their work values much more during the same period. Thus, some curricula tend to reinforce a set of work values whereas others tend to challenge such values. This research further clarifies the status of work values in the senior high school. Rather than having totally different shifts in work values, students are more likely to have work values changing in intensity, with strong values growing stronger and weak values growing weaker.

Herr and Enderlein (1976) found similar relationships between high school curricula and career maturity, as did Kapes and Strickler (1975) with work values. Their research indicated that students in the academic program were more career mature in ninth grade than students in vocational education, general, or business education. Although academic students were still the most career mature at twelfth grade, students in business education had almost equaled them. Students in the other two curricula remained significantly less career mature than either the academic or business education students. Apparently, curricular content interacts with student characteristics differently in stimulating both work values and career maturity.

In a subsequent longitudinal study of 1007 of Herr and Enderlein's students, Herr, Weitz, Good, and McCloskey (1981) examined the relationship of high school curricula and personal characteristics while in high school to postsecondary educational and occupational patterns when these persons were 24 to 27. Young adults from an academic curriculum background were found to be significantly more career mature in their career-related exploratory behavior at ages 24 to 27, using the adult form of the Career Development Inventory as the criterion measure, than persons from vocational curricula. Apparently postsecondary school educational or occupational experiences do not equalize the gap in career maturity observed between academic and vocational students during the secondary school. Indeed, these data suggest that persons who have completed a vocational education curriculum in high school enter the career establishment with significantly fewer and less complete developmental exploratory experiences than do persons from academic curricula. These findings are undoubtedly confounded somewhat by differences in ability and socioeconomic background found among persons who enter the academic or the vocational curriculums in secondary schools. Nevertheless, career development knowledge and experiences for students in the secondary school apparently differ in major ways, and the resulting differences in career maturity persist into young adulthood.

What this longitudinal study did not find, as compared with the earlier study of Herr and Enderlein (1976), were sex differences in career maturity. They earlier found that female students were significantly more career mature than boys regardless of curriculum in high school. However, as measured by their concern about and completion of career development tasks, Herr, Weitz, Good, and McCloskey (1981) found no sex differences in career maturity by ages 24 to 27. Thus, it appears that following high school, women do not capitalize on the advantage they experience in career attitude maturity during high school, either because of homemaking and child-rearing experiences or institutional discrimination. An alternate hypothesis (Pedro, 1982) developed in a study of high school females in a nonurban high school in the Midwest is that one needs to understand whether females plan to achieve directly or vicariously in career and job areas in order to understand the extent of involvement for planning in these areas. Thus, gender-specific and general career maturity variables need to be considered in understanding the career development of female high school students and their subsequent career behavior.

In attempting to identify specific predictors of post-secondary educational and occupational behavior, Herr et al. (1981) found that in addition to sex and curriculum, the best predictors of postsecondary educational level completed were high school GPA and father's occupation. Of present occupational status, in addition to sex and curriculum completed, the top three predictors were satisfaction with current occupational plans and progress toward them, high school GPA, and career maturity in high school as measured by the Attitude Scale of the Vocational Development Inventory (now the CMI). The top three predictors of current salary, in addition to sex and curriculum, were satisfaction with current occupational plans and progress toward them, career maturity in high school as measured by the Attitude Scale score of the Vocational Development Inventory, and certainty of occupation plans.

Koski and Subich (1985) investigated the curriculum background of males and females relative to their homemaking commitment and career commitment as well as the prestige and sex-stereotype ratings for fantasized and realistic career choices. In a sample of 93 (41 male, 52 female) vocational education seniors and 48 (27 female, 21 male) college preparatory seniors, the investigators found differences in the career plans and desires of students from different curriculum tracks. More specifically, they found that vocational education students aspire to less prestigious careers than do college preparatory students and that the gap between their fantasized choices and their realistic choices is less wide than that of college preparatory students. Such findings lead to the intriguing view that while the aspirations of vocational education students are substantially lower than those held by college preparatory students, they also may be considerably more realistic than those of college preparatory students, leading to the view that the latter group would be well-served in career guidance by a major focus on reality-testing while they engage in career exploration.

Jordaan and Heyde (1979) completed a comprehensive longitudinal analysis of the vocational maturity of high school boys. This study traces the vocational development of a group of boys from approximately age 15 to 18, or grades 9 to 12. Some of their findings follow. Few twelfth graders and still fewer ninth graders had decided on an occupation or a specialty within an occupation. Vocational preferences from the ninth to the twelfth grade tended to be "unstable, uncertain and unrealistic," with twelfth-grade preferences having little similarity to those expressed in the ninth grade. Some two-thirds of the twelfth graders and even more ninth graders had no confidence in their goals. In twelfth grade nearly half of the boys were considering goals that were not consistent with their socioeconomic background or their measured interests and abilities. Most boys in the twelfth grade, as in the ninth grade, knew little about the occupation they thought they might enter; their use of appropriate resources of information, their knowledge of the world of work, and their plans for achieving their goals were often seriously deficient. Only about half of the twelfth-grade boys knew what they would or should do to qualify for their prospective occupations, and few had done any contingency planning.

As compared with the ninth grade, even with the deficits in knowledge and planning, twelfth-grade boys are considering fewer occupational possibilities and fields of work. There is, as theory would suggest, a movement toward greater crystallization and specificity in choice from the ninth to the twelfth grade. In speaking of the typical twelfth grader, as compared to the typical ninth grader, Jordaan and Heyde suggest that

> His interests are more adult, and he has somewhat more confidence in them. He is more aware of the significant characteristics of occupations and has more information about occupations that interest him. He has more specific plans for obtaining the required training, education, and on-the-job experience. He shows greater readiness to assume personal responsibility for securing a beginning job or the required education and training. However, his vocational preferences are no more realistic or appropriate, judging by intellectual requirements, interests involved, or socioeconomic accessibility, than they were when he was in the 9th grade. (p. 186)

In theoretical terms, Jordaan and Heyde (1979) contend that the data they examined support the conclusion "that awareness of concern with present and future decisions, awareness of factors to consider in making decisions, occupational information, and planning are important aspects of vocational maturity in adolescence" (p. 195). These findings have also been found to be true of Canadian youth in research reported by Borgen and Young (1982). As suggested elsewhere, particularly in Chapters 4 and 6, such behaviors are also related to career behavior at age 25 in other studies by Super and his colleagues. As such they represent important organizing themes around which program goals and career guidance activities in the senior high school can be planned.

The Transition to Work

There are a variety of perspectives not yet discussed in this chapter that address the place of work while in high school and after. These perspectives are also descriptive of the senior high school student. For example, most youth do not abruptly leave high school and enter into a stable job with a firm that provides security and mobility. Rather, as has been suggested elsewhere in this book, "For many youths, the process of entry and adjustment to the labor market is lengthy and involves distinct periods. The behavior of the youths changes over time, moving from a period of casual attachment to an increasing commitment to work and to stable behavior" (Osterman, 1989, p. 255). Osterman has explained this transitional period in the engagement of work as a moratorium. Specifically, he states,

> in the first several years after leaving school, young people are frequently in what might be termed a moratorium period, a period in which adventure seeking, sex, and peer group activities are all more important than work. Some years later comes a settling down, a stage characterized by a very different set of attitudes about work (p. 244).
>
> This moratorium stage tends to be reflected in the reality that most youth spend their initial years after school in the secondary labor market (e.g. the fast food industry). Firms in such categories do not invest resources in training youth nor are there career ladders available to provide incentives to youth to settle into the firm and identify with it as an occupational commitment for an extended period of time. Such firms, with little investment in training, benefits, or long-term commitments to these workers, can accept the unstable behavior of youths in ways that primary firms cannot or will not. These secondary jobs meet the requirements of young people in the moratorium period because they are typically casual and unskilled, with little responsibility, and few penalties attached to unstable behavior.

As youth complete the moratorium period and begin to "settle down" they gravitate to the primary labor market—the firms that are large, stable, and likely to provide long-term jobs, security, and reasonable opportunities for promotion and advancement through well-defined internal career ladders. Because of the benefits, the expectation that those hired will remain with the firm for a long time, the investments in training, and job security, jobs in the primary labor market are rarely available to students directly out of high school. Employers in the primary labor market are interested in stability, some evidence of positive attitude and employment credibility as reflected in a period of work in the secondary labor market, and to the individual's teachability, flexibility, and dependability (Mainquist & Eichorn, 1989).

Before leaving this topic, it is useful once again to acknowledge that there are connections between a student's part-time employment in high school, the nature of that work, and the student's subsequent experience in the labor market. For example, graduates who had jobs during high school that gave them opportunity to exercise and improve their skills in dealing with people, things, or data were able to earn more pay per hour and spent less of their time looking for work. Thus, there is both a quantitative and a qualitative dimension to the work in which students engage during high school. For example, less unemployment and higher hourly earnings were obtained by new graduates who spent a larger number of hours per week in paid employment during their junior and senior year (for example, 16 compared to 10 hours per week) and in qualitative terms had jobs during high school that gave them more chances to develop and use skills (Stern & Nakata, 1989). Obviously, the transition to work is a complex process that deserves intense and comprehensive attention within career guidance programs.

Vondracek and Schulenberg (1986) have observed that the reality is that youth in the United States, as in other nations, learn about and are trained to carry out work tasks in both formal and informal ways. Informal mechanisms include experiences in the home, where transferable skills sometimes develop from the home chores for which youth are held accountable by parents (such as the care of younger siblings, food preparation, grounds or building maintenance and repair). Children also learn about work tasks vicariously as they hear parental conversations about such matters or observe family members engaged in different types of work. In addition to being a place for specific learning about work tasks, the home is a place in which images of work are portrayed and reinforced, work habits are developed, and networks of job-access opportunities, whether limited or wide-ranging, find their roots (Herr & Best, 1984).

Another informal mechanism through which youth learn about work is part-time employment. At its best, part-time employment has significant potential for providing "bridges" to full-time work by inducting youth into the adult normative culture in which work occurs and by training them in the cognitive and psychomotor tasks that comprise work content. Such part-time employment or other formal work-related learning—career education, career guidance, vocational education—can reinforce the insights inherent in the notion that work adjustment involves more than learning to cope with the technical demands of job-related tasks. Successful adjustment at work requires mastery of a range of social learning tasks such as when to take a work break, how and when to give advice to a co-worker, how to respond to and accommodate authority in the workplace, and perhaps more important, how to understand and manipulate the culture of the workplace to one's personal benefit (Borman, Izzo, Penn, & Reisman, 1984). The problem is that the influences of home, part-time employment, and other informal or formal work-related learning mechanisms are unevenly distributed across student populations and by the time they enter the high school the career development of many students is uneven, if not impaired.

IMPLICATIONS FOR CAREER GUIDANCE IN THE SENIOR HIGH SCHOOL

Students in the senior high school arrive at the differing degrees of career maturity described in the previous sections by differing routes of continuity or discontinuity. Vondracek and Schulenberg (1986) describe the categories of influence on adolescent career development as (1) normative, age-graded influences, either biological or environmental, that might include the development of physical characteristics requisite to certain careers or early socialization to work experiences; (2) normative, history-graded influences that may also be biological or environmental in nature and may include the effects of historical events such as depression, war, or famine; and (3) nonnormative, life-event influences such as the unexpected death of a family breadwinner, illness, or injury that can alter previously made career plans. The combination as well as the single effect of these categories of influence upon individuals shape the differential profiles of career development in adolescence that are described throughout this chapter.

Just as the categories of influence upon career development differ, so must the career guidance activities or interventions provided to adolescents (Niles & Herr, 1989). In our perspective, career guidance activities must have three emphases: stimulating career development, providing treatment, and aiding placement (the latter refers to student movement to the next educational level or to the immediate life of worker, consumer, and citizen). Conceptually, it is important to recognize that in terms of career development, some senior high school students will be no more mature than are elementary school students. Therefore, they will need to acquire, in a shorter time, the vocabulary, self- and career awareness, and exploratory experience that might have been expected to occur earlier. Treatment will need to occur when, even after being provided information and other exploratory experiences, students are still unable to make a choice or a commitment to some plan of action (Crites, 1981).

Which of the three career guidance emphases is implemented must depend on where the individual student is in career development and what he or she needs most at a given time: reassurance, information, reality-testing, emotional release, attitude clarification, or work exposure. Obviously, career guidance activities at the senior high school level, as at other educational levels, must be predicated on individual needs, readiness, and motivations.

The principal emphases in career guidance activities for different individuals must be on the intensity of planning, readiness to participate in life as an independent person, and goal-directedness of the individuals to be served. These objectives must be elaborated and cast in behavioral terms as recommended in the preceding chapters, particularly Chapter 6. But the significant point here is that career guidance activities in the senior high school must take each student from where he or she is in coping with developmental tasks integral to career development and lead that person to the creation and the achievement of a set of specific preferences and plans to implement them. For many students, the senior high school years are the crucible in which they test their vague aspirations by developing specific strategies for converting these aspirations into reality. Career guidance, in its repertoire of emphases, represents the last opportunity for many students to rehearse different coping behaviors and alternative actions and plans in a protected context, and to assess these against a backdrop of self-characteristics and value sets before their induction into the adult society.

Planning Considerations in the Senior High School

Within the systematic stages of planning for career guidance outlined in Chapter 6, there are several concerns of particular importance in relating career guidance to senior high school students.

1. Because many students will complete their formal education with the senior high school and thereby terminate their opportunities for the systematic analysis and facilitation of their career development, efforts need to be undertaken to reach all students with career guidance opportunities.

2. The major career guidance emphasis in the senior high school needs to be on the specific and comprehensive planning of immediate, intermediate, and future educational and occupational choices after high school. However, for many reasons, not all senior high school students will be ready for such planning. Many students will need intensive self- or career awareness and exploration opportunities, either because they did not have such experiences in the junior high school or because they were not ready to profit from them at that time.

3. Due to the nature of senior high school students and the diversity of their goals, career guidance in the senior high school should include counseling and developmental guidance experiences dealing with study habits, human relations at work, career and educational planning, job search techniques, and job interview skills.

4. Decisions must be made about how career guidance and placement will correspond or differ in the senior high school. Will placement be seen as a process spanning the total senior high school period or an event primarily dealt with in the twelfth grade? Will counselors take sole responsibility for educational and occupa-

tional placement or will they share these elements with other persons (such as vocational teachers or employment service counselors) in the school and the community?

5. The senior high school student is confronted with internal and external pressures to make decisions and to pursue specific types of outcomes. Career guidance can help students deal effectively with these pressures.

6. The verbal and conceptual skills of high school students are more developed than those of junior high students, permitting career guidance to proceed along multiple and complex dimensions.

7. Since the major combinations of possibilities following high school are reasonably clear—college, other postsecondary education, work, nonwork, military, or governmental service (such as VISTA, Action)—career guidance should help senior high school students to consider the advantages and disadvantages of each.

Goals for Career Guidance in the Senior High School. Unlike goals for elementary and junior high school populations, those for senior high emphasize specific planning and awareness of life roles as a consumer and as one engaged in leisure time pursuits. Examples of program goals that might be adapted to a particular senior high school (Herr, 1976c) include helping students learn to

1. Show relationships between their achievements, values, preferences, educational aspirations, and career preferences
2. Analyze current personal competency in skills necessary to career preferences and develop plans to strengthen these skills where necessary
3. Assume responsibility for career planning and its consequences
4. Prepare to qualify for entry-level jobs by taking appropriate courses, by cooperative education, or by on-the-job training
5. Prepare to qualify for post-secondary education by taking courses required by the type of program and institution desired (community college, college, trade, or business school)
6. Develop knowledge and skills pertinent to life as a consumer
7. Develop skills pertinent to effective use of leisure time
8. Systematically reality test career preferences by relating them to achievement in courses, part-time work, or extracurricular activities
9. Identify alternative ways of accomplishing desired educational or occupational goals if preferred choices are not available
10. Describe the major forms of continuing education following high school (for example, apprenticeships, on-the-job training, correspondence courses, military service schools, evening schools, reading, college), and list those most related to career preferences
11. Identify the steps required to gain admission after high school including whom to contact, application dates and procedures, and the capital investment necessary
12. Make accurate estimates of personal traits and achievements and present these effectively on a résumé and in an occupational or educational interview
13. Develop specific plans to implement career goals
14. Execute career plans (pp. 1–2)

Consistent with the setting and the program design, the facilitation of some of these goals might be best achieved by teachers, others by the counselor, and still others in cooperative activity among various specialists or community persons.

Sequencing Career Guidance Experiences in the Senior High School. A persistent theme in the chapters on career guidance in the elementary and junior high schools has been the need for many of the objectives of career development to be met within the goals of particular curricula. Implied has been the need for students continuously to connect what they are doing educationally with consequences in terms of occupational and educational alternatives, the life-styles they represent, and their general requirements. Mention has also been made of the importance of teacher attitudes in encouraging planfulness among students, an appreciation of the spectrum of occupational alternatives in which knowledge of various subject matter is useful and in some cases necessary, and other elements of career maturity.

Exploring Educational and Career Opportunities. At the root of these recommendations is the fact that students need to come to terms with a variety of personal questions and with clarifying a self-concept. Hoffman (1973), in discussing self-understanding for productive living, has observed, "The questions teachers should be encouraging students to ask are 'Who am I?' 'What influences me?' and 'How can I control the influences upon me?' Once these answers are found, or at least sought, the most neglected area of education will take its proper place as the most important" (p. 79). Livingston (1970) has viewed the matter in the following perspective:

> One reason university graduates have had so much difficulty making the transition from academic life to the world of work is that they have failed to develop in school the self-identities needed to enable them to make firm career commitments. Their formal education has not nurtured the traits of individuality, self-assurance, and responsibility or developed the attributes that would permit them to become active agents in their own career success. (p. 40)

Bruner (1973) has offered this opinion: "Neuroses of the young are far more likely to revolve around work than around sex. The delay of vocational or job decisions fostered by our school system has provided difficulty for students to identify themselves in adult roles." He suggests that the "first order of business in the transformation of our mode of education is to revolutionize and revivify this idea of vocation or occupation" (p. 22).

The school counselor has a role in directly encouraging the development of such experiences as well as in collaborating with teachers to assist them in the career development of students. The school counselor needs to exert leadership in helping administrative and curriculum groups respond to the architect's dictum that form should follow function as plans are made to incorporate more flexibility, interdisciplinary integration, variable time blocks, individualized programming, multimedia approaches, and self-teaching devices than now exist in many educational systems.

Some Examples of Programs. The examples of comprehensive sequential career guidance or career education activity at the senior high school level differ from those at the elementary or junior high school. Presumably, this is because the organizational structures of these three educational levels vary. In particular, the typical senior high school structure is built around the need for students to acquire the knowledge and skills inherent in a subject rather than adapting subject matter to specific students' needs.

In essence, career education and career guidance both rest on the need to infuse general education subject matter with a greater career orientation. At a fundamental level, this requires incorporating and adopting many of the themes and activities emphasized in Chapter 6 and supplementing them with simulation, group processes, or work-study opportunities. For example, a continuing career development theme in courses designed to prepare students for college will diminish the persistent assumption that college is an end in itself. College, too, is an intermediate occupational choice for the vast majority of students who enter. With such an emphasis, students can be helped to see college less as a way of deferring career thinking and more as one way to achieve particular career goals. As will be indicated later, many of the students for whom college immediately follows high school can also profit from direct work experience or from access to vocational education experiences in the school itself, in order to heighten the purpose with which they approach college.

Not all the students to whom career development strategies have relevance in general education and career guidance will have college as their major intent or work after high school as their immediate goal. Hoyt mounted a major research project some years ago concerned with those whom he has described as "the specialty oriented" (Hoyt, 1965). He contrasted the specialty-oriented with the liberal arts-oriented student. The former also has postsecondary education aspirations but is inclined to trade, technical, or business school training rather than college. He speaks of the specialty-oriented as those whose prime educational motivation is to acquire an occupational skill or set of skills that could be used to enter the labor market.

Hoyt indicates that for the specialty-oriented student, guidance practices should include increased use of information in the counseling process and counseling for specific decision making. He asserts, "I think far too many students leave the secondary school today with, at best, some general notions of what they may do but without the slightest idea of when or how they will be able to convert these general notions into realistic actions" (p. 235).

The reader will note that many of Hoyt's concerns about schooling's lack of commitment to teaching decision-making skills to students are similar to the concerns that initiated the career education movement in the United States in the early 1970s. Those perspectives are discussed in Chapter 1 and the reader might wish to review that material here. These concerns about what experiences and skills students need to make an effective transition from school to work remain a national issue. In addressing this matter, Mangum (1988) has stated, "There are cultural norms, labor market realities and human development processes which compose the transition environment. No program to improve a transition can expect success which does not take into account these constraints. Employers control and dispense jobs and any successful program must ultimately help youth to meet employer expectations" (p. i.). Mangum goes on to state that "irresponsibility is a far more serious barrier to successful youth access to the labor market than inexperience and lack of skill. No more then one-third of U. S. jobs require pre-entry training and most job skills are learned on the job. Thus, job-getting and job-keeping skills are more critical to youth attractiveness as employees then are job-doing skills" (p. 1).

The perspectives of Mangum and Hoyt, as well as the analysis of employment transition problems in Chapter 2 and the examples of career development content recommended as part of the planning process for career guidance in Chapter 6, take different forms in the senior high school programs. For example, Herr (1984) and Herr and Johnson (1989) have suggested that work context skills, career management skills, and decision-making skills comprise the major elements of general employability skills and may be used as the objectives for programs aimed at increasing employability.

Work Context Skills. Work context skills relate to the psychosocial aspects of the situation in which work activity is carried on. They include emphases on employer-employee relations; accepting constructive supervision, interpersonal skills, willingness to follow rules, adaptability, punctuality, pride in work, self-discipline, efficiency, dependability, and understanding of life in an organization.

Career Management Skills. These are skills by which one brings self-information and career information together into a plan of action. They include career planning, job search and access skills, the ability to use exploratory resources and to reality-test alternative choices, engaging in the constructive use of leisure, personal economics skills, self-knowledge, and knowledge of occupational and educational opportunities.

Decision-making Skills. Skills in this category include systematic methods of processing information, predicting and weighing alternatives, clarifying values, examining risk-taking styles, and projecting action consequences.

The categories briefly noted above represent the types of sequential content that can be directed to facilitating the transition to work, that reflect the types of skills employers expect, and that facilitate the acquisition of general employability skills. Such skills have their own substance and integrity as elements of career development; they can be conceived as a specified set of outcomes; and planning is essential to foster them.

Table 9.1 lists some of the major types of interventions that can be used in school or out of school to enhance the acquisition by high school, and often by junior high school, students of general employability skills.

The interventions identified in Table 9.1, although not exhaustive of all such possibilities, are representative of those used as program content in career guidance programs in senior high schools. Some examples follow.

One of the most comprehensive approaches to career development and career guidance in the senior high school is that found in Mesa, Arizona. One of the original six field-test sites for the national school-based career education model, Mesa went through an extensive process of system-wide evaluation and project developments using a variety of consultants from around the nation. Using essentially a systems approach, guidance personnel built into the guidance program an accountability component that could be based on student needs. The steps on which the Mesa guidance personnel designed their efforts included the following:

1. A detailed needs assessment that included assessing the demographic characteristics of the students to be served and the outcomes from guidance which students desired in four areas: intrapersonal, interpersonal, academic learning, educational-vocational

   At the senior high school, the top priority outcomes were as follows:

Academic Learning

- I need to improve my memory.
- I need to improve my understanding of what I need.
- I need to improve my ability to concentrate.
- I need to know how to study better.
- I need to become more comfortable when giving information or speaking in class.

Educational-Vocational

- I need to understand my abilities, interests, and other characteristics.
- I need to consider more than one alternative for what I should do after high school.
- I need to know how and where I can find occupational and educational information and guidance.
- I need actual on-the-job experience to know what it's like to be employed and to learn more about jobs.

Table 9.1

Interventions for developing employability skills

	IN SCHOOL	OUT OF SCHOOL
WORK CONTEXT SKILLS	Role Models	Role Models
	Skill-centered curricula	Interview parents/relatives
	Enhancing slef-concept	Utilize community resources
	Group Counseling	Work visits
	Exploring work values	Work Participation
	Interpersonal Skills Training	Work Shadowing
	Assessing/Modifying Self-Efficacy	Mentoring
CAREER MANAGEMENT SKILLS		
—Career Planning	Infusing Coursework with Career Concepts	Work Visits
	Work Study	Work Study
	Career Counseling	
	Career Libraries	Work Shadowing
	Career Information and Planning Courses	Mentoring
	Countering sex-typing	
	Career Awareness Programs	Utilize family and community role models
	Work Simulation	
—Job Search & Access	Job Search Training	
	Job Finding Clubs	Job Clubs
	Interview Skills Training	
	Stress Management	Stress Management
DECISION MAKING SKILLS	Distinguishing Indecision & Indecisiveness	
	Testing for decision-making	Information gathering
	Group Guidance Programs	Career Decision-Making for Parents
	Decision-Making Programs	
	Group counseling/exercises in problem-solving	Family and Community Role Models
	Values and Needs Clarification	Reality-testing

Source: Herr, E.L. and Johnson, E. (1989). General employability skills for youths and adults: Goals for Guidance and Counseling Programs. *Guidance & Counseling. 4*(4), p. 20. (Reprinted with permission. ©Guidance Centre, The Ontario Institute for Studies in Education.)

- I need to know what jobs are available to me.

Interpersonal

- I need to better solve problems I have with my parents.
- I need to be a better listener and more responsive to the feelings and needs of others.
- I need to accept criticism better.
- I need to have more confidence so I can be at ease with other people.

Intrapersonal

- I need to be more satisfied with my life, my achievements, and myself.
- I need someone to talk to when personal problems arise.
- I need to set goals so I can stop drifting along with no particular purpose in life.
- I need to be more skillful in making decisions and solving problems.

2. An objective status assessment of on-going programs in terms of how counselors were using their time and toward what end
3. A reconciliation of the "What is" with "What ought to be"
4. A guidance model based on the outcomes of steps 1 and 3

Designed a program based essentially on student needs

Programmed an implementation schedule for delivery of the program to the target population

Designed evaluation strategies to determine if, in fact, the program delivered its objectives

Built in a systematic evaluation and feedback system to insure that all parts of the program remained sensitive to changing student needs

Began a task analysis to determine competencies required by practitioners to deliver the program

Did a beginning competency analysis to determine present competency level of practitioners

Began the design of in-service programs to bring practitioners to appropriate competency levels

Began the development of transportable practitioner training packages (Mesa Public Schools, 1974)*

What has emerged from this analytic process are a series of guidance "units" administered in various subjects through a teacher/counselor team relationship and a reconceptualized counselor role in career guidance. A major emphasis of the guidance program is the delivery of various guidance learnings as an integral part of the existing curriculum and classroom activities. The format for the guidance learnings sought in the curriculum were teacher-counselor booklets or resource guides for each unit. In each of these guides the following topics were included:

1. Goal statements and performance objectives of the unit
2. Length of unit and each lesson within it
3. Materials necessary to deliver the unit
4. Enrichment activities
5. New vocabulary
6. Teacher preparation tasks
7. A brief descriptive statement of each lesson
8. Answer keys to end-of-unit tests, where appropriate
9. Points to cover in individual or group discussions with students

In originally implementing these units, the counselors did the teaching. Subsequently, teachers took responsibility for the teaching

*Developed by the Mesa Public Schools, 1974. Reprinted by permission.

but, as necessary, counselors continued to monitor units, lead group discussions, counsel individual students, and assist in other ways. In such circumstances, both the teachers and counselors became resource people. They checked on student progress; led small-group discussions on important points; conferred with individual students when the need dictated; suggested supplementary activities to both fast and slow learners; helped students with end-of-unit evaluation procedures; and facilitated student learning by making certain that appropriate materials, resources, and people were available as the students needed them.

Another comprehensive sequential approach to career guidance is that developed through in-depth planning in the Corning-Painted Post Area Schools (N. Y.). Table 9.2 presents the program outcomes for which the guidance program became accountable. As can be seen, the guidance program is responsible for five goal areas, each with specific themes around which guidance programming takes place in each grade.

Table 9.3 presents the activities of the guidance program in each of the goal areas by grade. Referring back to the planning concepts of Chapter 6 will help reinforce your understanding of these commitments to activities as hypothesis testing. The assumption is that each of the activities cited by grade and by goal will be instrumental in achieving the outcomes in each of these cells. The overall matrix provides administrators and the public with information about what the guidance program includes, how it changes over time, and what broad goals it is accountable for. What is not included here because of space limitations is the specific behavioral outcomes for students that the processes are intended to facilitate as the broad goal areas are translated into student knowledge, attitudes, and skills at each grade level.

In many parts of the nation, states and large cities have created sequential programs of career guidance or programs that blend career guidance and career education. For example, in the St. Louis School District such programs include classroom curriculum modules in self-awareness, career awareness, career orientation, and career preparation. There is also a major emphasis on providing experiential career education learning components that embrace collaboration between education and the business community (Katzman, 1989). At the senior high school, the latter includes such joint activities as the following:

- *Career Prep Club* in which business and community persons team teach with the classroom teacher. This 12-lesson program draws upon businesspersons to present job-seeking and helping skills. Topics include career planning, how to find job openings, applications (college, armed services, and jobs), résumés, interviews, job attitudes, and how to advance on the job. Every student is responsible for completing a personal job/college portfolio.
- *Decision-making seminars* in which ninth graders learn from government and business speakers about individual and group decision making and how knowledge of social studies is used in public and private sector jobs.
- *Shadowing* in which a tenth, eleventh, or twelfth grader investigates his/her interests at a business site. Usually designed as a three-hour experience, shadowing provides students an opportunity to observe in an actual work environment what a job entails. These shadowing sites vary extensively in their focus and provide not only direct experience for the students engaged in shadowing at a particular site but also content for classroom sharing and the vicarious learning about the workplace for other students.
- *Men and Women of Tomorrow Plan Today* in which high school juniors are paired with

Table 9.2

Corning-Painted Post Area Schools Core Guidance Program by Outcomes

Goal	Grade						
	6	7	8	9	10	11	12
Knowledge of self	Values	Interests	Aptitudes	Aptitudes	Work values	Interests	Values Aptitudes Interests Achievements
Knowledge of Work and Education	Sex-role stereotyping		Local opportunity	Occupational and educational resources Occupational structure	Attitudes toward and rewards of work	Job Seeking survival skills Leisure Education work link	Education/ work link
Decision-Making		Decisions and values	Course selection Curriculum selection	Course selection	Course selection Decision-making skills	Course selections Post-high school planning	Post-high school planning
Remedial and Consultation	Behavior change	——▶——	——▶——	——▶——	——▶——	——▶——	——▶——
Placement	Academic adjustment	Academic adjustment	Academic adjustment Course selection Curriculum selection	Academic adjustment Course selection	Academic adjustment Course selection	Academic adjustment Course selection	Academic adjustment Post-high school plans

professional role models in the community for a day in a conference setting outside of school. The adult role models and the students attend sessions together on self-esteem, goal setting, manhood and womanhood, and communication skills. The adult role model and the student spend the day together, developing a contract about goals the student hopes to achieve and designing a follow-up shadowing activity.

- *Pre-employment skills work programs* in which juniors and seniors have an opportunity to work as well as attend school. Designed as an afterschool program, students work two hours a day, five days a week in the private sector and attend a Career Prep Club class every two weeks. Funding is provided by the Job Training Partnership Act.*

In Newburg High School, Oregon, counselors take responsibility for enabling students in each grade from 9 through 12 to attain specified career goals and a set of objectives that support the goal for each grade. (Oregon Occupation Information Committee, 1989) For example, the overarching career development goal for each of the four years include the following:

- *Ninth grade*—The student will make tentative career development plans.
- *Tenth grade*—The student will assess career development plans and develop job search techniques.
- *Eleventh grade*—The student will assess career development plans as they relate to academic and personal choices.
- *Twelfth grade*—The students will assess career development plans and prepare for appropriate post-high school plans.

*Abridged from "A Response to the Challenges of the Year 2000" by Susan Katzman in *Career Development: Preparing for the 21st Century* by the Comprehensive Career Development Project for Secondary Schools in Tennessee. Copyright © 1989 by The University of Tennessee, Knoxville, Department of Technological & Adult Education. Reprinted by permission.

To illustrate how objectives are identified to support the grade-level goals, all students have four objectives that underlie the twelfth grade goal just identified:

1. Review and update the educational plan and develop post-high school direction
2. Update his/her resume to be reflective of current goals and experiences
3. Gain firsthand insight into one of the following post-high school opportunities: entry-level employment, military, college/technical school training
4. Investigate the role of employment and labor market conditions in the economy

To tie the objectives cited for twelfth grade students to the activities designed to facilitate these objectives, seniors are expected to engage in the following activities: counselor conference; personal resume preparation; attendance at a job fair, military interviews, or college fair; and completion of the Employment and Labor unit in economics classes. Other activities are used at other grade levels. For example, at the tenth grade level students will engage in such activities as taking a standardized aptitude test, interest survey, and career profile; completing a job search unit in a personal finance class; obtaining a Social Security Number and work permit; and finding job openings, filling out application forms, writing a resume and cover letter, learning techniques for interviewing, and writing follow-up letters. Other individual and small group activities are used at the ninth and eleventh grade levels.

A specific example of a particular activity that might be included in a state, district, or city plan is what Brown (1980) has described as a Life-Planning Workshop (LPW) for high school students. The LPW is conducted in structured small groups that cover seven components in six to eight one-hour meetings. The components are as follows:

Table 9.3

Corning-Painted Post Area Schools Core Guidance Program by Activities

Goal	Grade						
	6	7	8	9	10	11	12
Knowledge of Self	"Bread and Butterflies" "Deciding" Discussion	SRA, "What I Like to Do" "Picture Inventory Exploration Survey" (P.I.E.S.) Discussion	Differential Aptitude Test (DAT) Discussion	Guidance Information Systems Continued Interpretation of DAT and SAT	"Work Values Inventory" Value Clarification Exercises (e.g., values auction) Guidance Information System "Harrington-O'Shea" System Continued Interpretation of DAT and SAT	"Strong Interest Inventory" or "Career Assessment Inventory" Guidance Information System "Armed Services Vocational Aptitude Battery" Continued Interpretation of DAT and SAT	Senior Interviews "CEEB" and "ACT" "ASVAB"
Knowledge of Work and Education	"Jobs and Gender" "Job Prejudice" Discussion		Speakers Field Trips Career Days Interviews Shadowing Lecture and discussion Want ads	Media Center "Hands-on" Lecture and discussion Career Days Guidance Information Sys tems Audio-visual Presentations Reading Assignments	Media Center "Hands-on" Lecture and discussion Career Days Guidance Information Sys tems Audio-visual Presentations Reading Assignments	Media Center "Hands-on" Lecture and discussion Career Days Guidance Information Sys tems Audio-visual Presentations Reading Assignments	Media Center "Hands-on" Lecture and discussion Career Days Guidance Information Sys tems Audio-visual Presentations Reading Assignments

Decision-Making		"Deciding" Discussion	Course Selection Curriculum Selection	Course Selection	Course Selection "Harrington-O'Shea System" Guidance Information System	Course Selection Post-high School Planning "Career Motivation Process"	Post-high School Planning "Career Motivation Process" "Short Job Search"
Remedial	Identification →	→	→	→	→	→	→
	Counseling →	→	→	→	→	→	→
	Referral →	→	→	→	→	→	→
	Consultation (team conferences, individual conferences, in-service training, departmental meetings, articulation meeetings, curriculum review, special needs, faculty meetings, staff development days, case conferences, parent conferences, perant-counselor advisory groups, parent group meetings, home visits, newsletters, industry visitations, career days, industry internships, periodic meetings with industry, agency consultations, media communications, college days, agency board participation, health and welfare associaton						
Placement	School Visitations Principal-Counselor Presentations Student Handbooks Open Houses Newsletters Team-Parent Conferences Individual Conferences	Student Handbooks Open Houses Newsletters Temp-Parent Conferences Individual Conferences	Student Handbooks Open Houses Newsletters Temp-Parent Conferences Individual Conferences High School Visit	Course Selection Group and Individual Conferences → Individualized Test Interpretation and Achievement Review →	→ → →	→ → → Post-high School Plans	→ → Post-high School Plans

1. Why People Behave as They Do—Emphasizes that behavior is goal-directed and explores the concept of accepting responsibility for one's own behavior
2. Winners and Losers—Emphasizes how losers can become winners by accepting responsibility, making good decisions, and planning ahead
3. Your Fantasy Life—Explores the relationship between fantasy and planning
4. Your Real Life—Outlines what students consider to be a set of realistic life expectations regarding education, career, close relationships, leisure and community involvement. Compares fantasy and realistic expectations and uses a lifeline exercise (Knickerbocker & Chesney, 1975) to help students note where they are now and where key decisions are made throughout life
5. Setting Life Goals—Deals with the decision-making process and planning using a force-field analysis approach that requires students to list forces that contribute to or retard goal attainment
6. Short-Term Life Planning, High School Graduation—Helps students identify all requirements for high school graduates and the positive and negative forces relating to the attainment of that goal
7. Long-Term Life Planning—Takes students through both short-term and long-term planning in education, career, close relationships, leisure, and community development. Shows students that each of these areas is related to all others and is potentially a source of personal fulfillment

Because the field testing of such an approach has shown initially positive results, it could be used within curriculums or as the substance of group counseling or special career guidance units.

A sequential two-week-long unit focused on helping high school students clarify their life-role preferences as part of their career development has been described and evaluated by Amatea, Clark, and Cross (1984) and by Amatea and Cross (1986). This unit is comprised of 10 structured class sessions designed to be introduced by a counselor into a regular class. (The authors have used sociology, psychology, and family life classes in four schools for this purpose.) Each of the 10 sessions has a theme and is devoted to activities intended to achieve specific unit objectives. Activities include didactic presentations on life roles, students planning a day in the future, structured interviews of parents, role-plays, case simulations of decision making, completing a Role Conflict Assessment Scale, discussions of perceived ideal qualities of sex-roles, developing lists of characteristics of ideal mates, checklists depicting simulated work and family commitments, assessments of the life-styles of different family structures with and without children and with both spouses working or not, development of individual time lines related to such roles as marital, occupations, parental, and self-development roles, and methods of managing or reconstructing role commitments to moderate stress.

The objectives of the unit were (1) to increase students' awarenesses of their own values and preferences regarding work, family, and marital life roles; (2) to help students examine the sources of such life-role preferences; (3) to increase students' awareness of the relative benefits and costs of a variety of life-style choices; and (4) to help students examine their own unique styles of choosing a set of life-role priorities and planning for a particular life style. A variety of evaluation strategies were carried out to test the effects of the unit in the four schools and by gender. Results of Analyses of Covariance between treatment and control groups on the Attitude Scale of the Career Maturity Inventory and two of the scales of the Life Role Expectations Inventory—career-role salience and marital-role salience—were somewhat mixed. Although there were posttest differences found on the CMI in favor of the experimental groups, there were no significant effects by treatment or by sex on the scales of the Life Role Expectations Inventory. In qualitative terms, students who participated in the units were quite enthusiastic and recommended that the unit be lengthened. Analyses of their evaluative comments suggested that they had been helped to become aware of long-range time, life-style planning (rather than only discrete decisions), and the affirmation or clarification of existing values.

Another career development class was implemented and evaluated by Mackin and Hansen (1981). The population for the class was eleventh- and twelfth-grade students at an inner-city high school in Minneapolis students were administered the attitude scale and three of the Competency Subscales of the Career Maturity Inventory (CMI) as part of a pre/post design. The Career Development Curriculum designed by the senior author served as the independent or treatment condition provided over 11 weeks. The Career Development program was based on development tasks for high school students drawn from the Career Development Curriculum developed by Tennyson, Hansen, Klaurens, and Antholz (1975) that has been described at several places in this book. The goals of the curriculum are (1) to increase self-awareness; (2) to increase career awareness; and (3) to increase decision-making and planning skills. Self-Awareness consists of four units—self-concept, interests, abilities, and values and needs. Activities include student completion of a self-esteem measure, an adjective list, an occupational family tree, the Strong-Campbell Interest Inventory, Holland's Self-Directed Search, standard achievement and aptitude assessments, selected readings, values auctions, and a paper dealing with self and society.

Career Awareness included two units: Career Development and The Future. Activities included constructing personal lifelines, life-career rainbows, guest speakers, field trips, and occupational fantasy trips. Guest speakers included persons who would provide role models counteracting prevailing stereotypes of sex-typed or racially typed roles.

Decision Making and Planning was devoted primarily to "teaching decision-making skills and helping students identify goals and plans for the attainment of these goals. Emphasis is on learning a process of decision-making. Activities used include selected exercises from *Decisions and Outcomes*" (Gelatt, Varenhorst, Carey, & Miller, 1973), analysis of decision-making styles, a force-field analysis of student plans, and a career plans paper.

Although the sample size was small (N = 15) and there was no control group, the results were quite positive. Students were found to have significantly increased their scores on the attitude scale, self-appraisal scale, and goal-selection of the CMI. On class-evaluation scales, the students indicated that the class was helpful in the eight areas of intended effect: interests, values, skills, needs, occupational and school information, setting goals, making decisions, and making plans.

Variations on this approach that are specifically addressed to the reduction of sex-role stereotyping have been stimulated by Project BORN FREE. Training materials and approaches as well as the conceptual bases for this program are described in several important articles (such as Hansen & Keierleber, 1978).

More recently, Hansen and Minor (1989) have described emphases that need to be included in career development curriculum of students, particularly as it reflects the changing roles of young men and women. Recommended as major topical areas in such curricula are (1) career decision-making skills; (2) work and family issues in the United States and across cultures; (3) changing roles of men and women gender issues; (4) changes in the workplace and the job market; (5) changes in the family; (6) life-role planning; (7) economic independence and survival skills; (8) entrepreneurship and job creation; and (9) managing change, negotiation, and transitions. Hansen and Yost (1989) have also suggested a career planning model that incorporates many of the topics identified above. Entitled *Integrative Life Planning* (ILP), the model is intended to provide knowledge and skills by which students can identify primary needs, roles, and goals and integrate them into one's definition of self, work, and family. Included in the ILP are exploration of "such potential conflict areas in family and work as the power of gender in career; family and work priorities; societal, organizational, family, and individual goals and values; developmental tasks and priorities at different life stages; and how roles, contexts and domains can be integrated in individuals, couples, families and the community" (Hansen & Yost, 1989, p. 142).

An additional example of a sequential approach has been designed to create a team effort to support career planning for academically disadvantaged students in East Lyme High School, Connecticut (Matthay & Linder, 1982). The team included two special educators, two counselors, and two cooperative work experience coordinators. Fifty-one tenth-grade students comprised the population of students who were included because of lack of decision-making skills, lack of motivation toward finishing high school, and low academic test scores (significantly below grade level and below state and local norms in standardized reading and math tests).

Participants in the program's career awareness classes met for 45 minutes every day for one semester, participated in weekly individual counseling with the school counselors, and received tutoring from the special educators as needed. The classes consisted of action activities, individual assessments of interests, aptitudes, and exercises, values clarifications discussions, activities, maintenance of journals, career decision-making exercises, audiovisual presentations, speakers, field trips, interviews with workers, assigned readings, and individual and group counseling. The content of the program included self-awareness, career awareness, and specific career discovery.

Based on pre/post testing, open ended feedback from students, and the observations of students by teachers and counselors, the results of the program were found to be as follows:

1. Students became more familiar with regional career opportunities and trends and increased their job-search and decision-making skills.
2. Thirty-nine of the 51 students were found to have improved academic performance, improved class and school attendance, more positive self-images, more dedication to their school work, greater drive toward choosing career goals, and increased initiative to make meaningful choices about future goals.
3. Thirty-eight of the participating students planned to enter the cooperative work experience program in either their junior or senior year. Eight others felt the program was helpful in assisting them to consider entering vocational education programs.
4. Twenty-four of the students indicated that the program provided them an impetus to complete their high school education.
5. Students reported improved understanding of the relationship of school courses to specific careers and an understanding of the background knowledge and skills essential for successful job performance.

The program reported by Matthay and Linder includes many of the elements suggested by Levinson (1985) as necessary to sequential programs for emotionally disturbed secondary school students. Levinson suggests that programs designed for emotionally disturbed children must be highly structured, and the counselor should be involved with others—special educators and vocational educators—to deliver a series of career-related elements, including the following paraphrased elements:

1. *Behavior management system* of rules and behavioral contracts designed to reduce socially undesirable behavior
2. *Social skills training* comprised of instructional modules formulated to help students develop such skills as those of hygiene, cooperation, self-initiative, sensitivity and concern, responsibility, attentiveness and emotional expression
3. *Employment education,* which includes instructional modules to strengthen basic academic competencies necessary for employment
4. *Work adjustment training* designed to assist students to acquire general employability skills: punctuality, industriousness, thoroughness, acceptance of criticism, pride in workmanship, and knowledge of safety rules
5. *Occupational and career self-awareness activities* including role-playing, field trips, printed materials focused on helping students acquire knowledge of the world of work
6. *Stress identification, management, and reduction* designed to help students identify sources of stress in their lives and acquire relevant coping skills
7. *Decision-making skills* including the elements necessary to process choices and develop a decision-making style
8. *Work experience activities* in which students are placed in actual work settings, the characteristics of which would differ depending upon the students' vocational readiness and emotional control

In a strategy to facilitate the employment of handicapped students, Elksnin and Elksnin (1991) advocate that school counselors use job clubs. Since an important component of career development for handicapped students is counseling them to use effective job strategies, there is empirical evidence, according to Elksnin and Elksnin, that the job club approach results in higher rates of employment than other more traditional job search methods. When implementing a job club approach, for adult or handicapped students, several emphases are essential to the program:

- Defining job search skills in behavioral steps
- Regarding job seeking as a full-time job which requires the job-seeker to plan a structured job-seeking schedule
- Obtaining job leads on a systematic basis from friends, relatives, and acquaintances
- Learning how to use the telephone as the primary contact for job leads after identifying leads from various sources including yellow pages and classified want ads in newspapers
- Participating in a group of other job seekers for support and assistance
- Learning to emphasize personal characteristics in résumés and applications
- Learning to identify and emphasize work skills acquired through work and leisure experiences
- Receiving training and practice in traditional job-seeking skills such as interviewing, resume and letter writing, and completing of applications
- Monitoring job-seeking progress as the basis for adjusting the process if needed

Space does not permit the examination of such other excellent examples of sequential career guidance approaches as Careers in Literature and Life (Bienstock, 1981), the Career Search Program (Castricone, Finan, & Grumble, 1982), or Operation Guidance, which is a comprehensive and systematic approach to career guidance developed by the Center for Vocational Education at The Ohio State University (Campbell, Suzuki, & Gabria, 1972). The last system involves carefully designed modules to assist schools to perform context validation, state behavioral objectives, methods selection, and testing. Although other examples of sequential career guidance activities in senior high schools might be cited, those given suggest examples of the content and organization that are frequently found.

Career Guidance Strategies to Foster Decision Making

In most of the sequential approaches to career development in the senior high school, helping students acquire decision-making skills is a major objective. In some cases, this goal is made explicit and in other cases it is assumed to be a by-product of the other career guidance activities implemented. Regardless of whether these are seen as part of a sequential program, many guidance techniques have been used to promote decision-making behavior among senior high school students.

Many appropriate techniques are discussed in other parts of this text. Those discussed here relate directly to senior high school students. In one study, Jones and Krumboltz (1970) examined the matter of stimulating occupational exploration through film-mediated problems. The experiment was replicated in two high schools; one a predominantly white middle-class school and the other a school in which 46 percent of the students were Mexican-American and Puerto Rican, 7 percent were black, 1 percent were Oriental, and the remainder were white. In both of these high schools, three versions of an experimental film were shown; the film presented five jobs that represented a cross-section of employment opportunities available for men and women in banking. A representative problem situation in each job was enacted on film for five or six minutes to the point where a decision had to be made.

The three versions of the film differed in the type of response each requested from the students in the experimental group: active-overt participation (students recorded their solutions in workbooks), active-covert participation (students were asked to think about their solutions but did not write them down), passive participation (no questions were asked of the students). One control group of students viewed regular banking career films; another read printed banking career information, and questions for them to consider were suggested; a third control group read printed general career information. The conclusions were (1) that the experimental film versions were more effective than were materials selected for comparison, and (2) that the participative versions of the experimental film were more effective than the passive version.

In another study, Krumboltz and Schroeder (1965) randomly assigned 54 eleventh-grade volunteers for educational and vocational counseling to three treatments: (1) reinforcement counseling (information-seeking responses reinforced), (2) model-reinforcement counseling (tape-recording of a male counselee played to each student prior to reinforcement counseling), and (3) a control group. The findings were (1) that the experimental groups engaged in more information seeking outside the interview than did control-group members; (2) that reinforcement counseling produced significantly more information seeking outside the interview (such as reading resources, talking about opportunities) for females but not males as compared to control-group behaviors; (3) that model-reinforcement counseling produced significantly more information seeking outside the interview for males than for females as compared to controls; and (4) that the ratio of information seeking to other responses in the interview was positively correlated with external information seeking.

In a related study, Krumboltz and Thoresen (1964) randomly assigned 192 eleventh-grade pupils to individual and group counseling settings in which the following four procedures were used by counselors: (1) reinforcement of verbal information-seeking behavior, (2) presentations of a tape-recorded model interview followed by reinforcement counseling, (3) presentation of film or filmstrip plus discussion as a control procedure, and (4) inactive control. The findings were (1) the model-reinforcement and reinforcement counseling produced more external information seeking than control procedures; (2) that with a male model, model-reinforcement counseling surpassed reinforcement counseling for males but not females; (3) that group and individual settings were about equally effective on the average, but interactions were found to be affected by counselor variables, schools, set of subjects, and treatments.

Meyer, Strowig, and Hosford (1970), in a similar study, assigned 144 female and male eleventh-grade students in three rural high schools to four behavioral-reinforcement counseling treatments and controls in individual and small-group settings. Baseline data on the information-seeking behaviors of the students were collected before initiating the treatments. Local high school counselors were trained and used as the experimental counselors. The treatments used were (1) reinforcement of verbal information-seeking behavior, (2) tape-recorded model interview plus reinforcement, (3) sound film plus reinforcement, and (4) no-treatment control. The findings were (1) that all behavioral-reinforcement treatments produced significantly more information-seeking behaviors than no-treatment control procedures; (2) that on average, reinforcement counseling was as effective as model reinforcement and film reinforcement for promoting the criterion behaviors; (3) that insignificant differences occurred between small-group and individual counseling settings; and (4) that for most treatments, females showed a greater amount and variety of information-seeking behavior than males.

Young (1979) compared the effectiveness of a value confrontation procedure with a procedure based on verbal operant conditioning in enhancing career development attitudes and increasing the frequency of information seeking in ninety rural adolescent males. The subjects were identified as internally or externally controlled, according to their locus of control scores, and were then randomly assigned to one of the two experimental treatment groups or a control group. The specific purpose of the value confrontation was to create an awareness of dissatisfaction about one's career planning and to relate this to inconsistencies in one's belief system. For these students, the dissatisfaction about their career planning had already been reported on the Career Development Inventory-Secondary School Form. It was brought to their attention by the counselor. The counselor then related how "good" career planners and "poor" career planners ranked the focus values "logical" and "responsible" and the priority of the values "ambitious," "logical," and "responsible" over other values (p. 16). At four times during the procedure students had the opportunity to examine their own hierarchy of values. The reinforcement counseling treatment was to make the subjects aware of the relative strength of their career planning orientation, resources for exploration, and information and decision making. After the interpretation of the CDI, the counselors verbally and nonverbally reinforced those statements of the subject that were evidence of vocationally mature responses. These were expressions of behavior or of intentions. Seven weeks after the treatments it was found that the value confrontation procedure resulted in significantly greater frequency of information seeking for internally controlled subjects when compared to the reinforcement counseling and control procedures. No statistically significant differences on the career planning orientation criterion between the cognitive and behavioral treatment groups were evident.

Collectively, the studies reported here, although not exhaustive, provide insight into the potential of reinforcement-behavioral counseling, modeling, imitative learning, and filmed and audiotaped presentations of specific stimulus materials to influence different components of decision-making and information-seeking behavior among high school students. Perhaps more important, they demonstrate that gender and other individual characteristics are related to the effects of these approaches. In other words, they emphasize the necessity of matching technique with individual characteristics and needs.

Approaches Involving Parents and Group Counseling. Amatea and Cross (1980) described a career guidance program designed for ninth- through twelfth-grade students and their parents, entitled *Going Places*. The program includes six components that are presented through discussion, small-group activities, reading materials, skill rehearsal, and at-home tryout and specialization. The program consists of six two-hour sessions, one per week. Through the use of a behavioral contract, participants commit themselves to homework that applies skills learned in the group sessions. The unique aspect of the program is the combination of parents and their children in the same group systematically learning about personal and occupational data and other specific career-planning skills. The goals of this program are

> (a) to develop a supportive family environment to encourage career planning and decision-making; (b) to provide an overview of the important elements involved in career planning and decision-making; (c) to encourage the development of self-management skills in goal setting and decision-making as useful tools in career planning; (d) to develop self-exploration skills and compile a base of self-information; (e) to encourage the development of organizing principles for viewing the work world as a method for expanding job options and comparing self and occupational data; (f) to develop systematic information-getting skills useful in exploring occupational and training paths; and (g) to provide information on various occupational and training paths. (pp. 277–278)

Evaluated by anecdotal data from 24 students and 24 parents who participated in three different programs, reactions to the content and the format of the program were found to be very favorable. However, the authors did suggest several caveats. For example, because the program is designed primarily for literate, motivated parents and students, its content and format will not suit all types of students, parents, and family groups. In addition, the program is not designed to deal with deep-seated conflicts between parents and children in which career is a central issue; thus, families need to be screened before inclusion in the group. Finally, in order to accommodate the needs of parents, such a program typically needs to be offered in the evening.

Laramore (1979), too, has outlined a process of group career counseling for families that requires eight to ten three-hour sessions, one per week. The first session is devoted to providing an information base for the parents and children, rapport-building activities, and an effort to dispel some common myths about career choices. In sessions 2 through 6 activities that reveal skills, attitudes, interests, and values are introduced and shared. During this time group members maintain a data sheet about each of the other group members and they clip want ads and other information that they think will be useful to each of the other members. These are filed in individual envelopes and given directly to the member in the seventh session. At this "career options" session, members share why they chose which information for each other. Then decision-making steps are discussed and related to the possible career options for each individual. For the eighth session, members must have written a letter of application, a resume, or a qualification brief for one of the jobs. General information on effective job-seeking skills is then given. In sessions 8 through 10, group members role-play job interviews, and these are videotaped when possible and critiqued so that individual performance can be improved. In the last hour group members share their plans of action and discuss implications and possibilities.

Neely and Kosier (1977) report using the 18 sequenced tasks of the Vocational Exploration Group (Daane, 1971) with both handicapped and nonhandicapped high school boys and girls. Using self-ratings and observations about work potential as criteria, the findings tended to support the utility of short-term group approaches in the career development of high school students, including the handicapped. Myers, Lindeman, Thompson, and Patrick (1975) have reported that the Educational and Career Exploration system (ECES), a computer-based system, significantly affected experimental students' planning orientation and uses of resources for occupational exploration but did not significantly increase their possession of occupational information or their decision-making skills as compared with students exposed only to a regular guidance program. Thus, it was suggested that this system might supplement a local guidance program in those areas where the latter was less effective than ECES. At the end of this chapter, other methods of facilitating decision making in senior high school students are listed. General helping strategies are also provided in Chapter 14.

Career Information Systems

Although in Chapter 15 we will discuss in depth the use of career information, it is useful here to consider the findings of a national survey of career information systems in secondary schools conducted by Educational Testing Service and funded by the National Institute of Education (Chapman & Katz, 1981, 1983). This study included stratified samples from the 17,856 secondary schools in the United States that have grades 10 through 12 and are not devoted exclusively to special populations. School questionnaires were sent to 3412 schools, and student questionnaires were sent to 4883 students in 155 schools stratified from the total school sample.

The findings of the questionnaires indicated that a wide variety of offerings is available to students. These include six categories of publications, computer systems, guidance activities, and contact with educational professionals. Obviously, no school has all of the resources identified, and some schools have very little. About a quarter of the schools in the sample have a computer system of some sort; only 18 percent use simulations. The top ten resources and the nationwide percentage of schools that use them are as appears at the top of the next column. (p. 248)

Management of these guidance resources is typically in the hands of professionals—the director of guidance and staff or the coordinator of career education and staff. Over 60 percent of the schools reported that they have a staff member who serves as a director or head of career guidance, and fewer than 6 percent of the schools nationwide said that they did not employ a full-time equivalent guidance counselor. Although counselors report spending less than a quarter of their time with students discussing occupational choice and career planning, roughly two-thirds of the counselors indicate that "a great deal" of this time is spent in directing students to occupational information or in answering students' questions about occupational information. More than half of the counselors said that they spent "a great deal" of this time interpreting occupational information and assisting students with career decisions.

On the negative side, the findings do indicate that although 92 percent of the schools have the *Occupational Outlook Handbook* some 8 percent or 1400 schools do not. Some

Resource	*Percentage of Schools Using*
Occupational Outlook Handbook	92
Conference with counselors	83
Dictionary of Occupational Titles	83
Career days, speakers, etc.	75
Occupational handbooks for the military	75
Vocational school directories	74
Externally produced AV materials	71
College directories arranged by occupation	70
Occupational information units in subject matter course	62
Job site tours	59

6 percent of schools do not have a full-time equivalent guidance counselor. That figure translates into over 1000 schools. Thirty-five percent of schools (6000 or more) have no one serving as director of guidance. In at least 30 percent of the schools it is likely that much of the career resource material is obsolete.

When one turns to the information in the student questionnaires, there is considerable evidence that the resources students use most, although not exclusively, are *not* those provided by the school. Students seem to use informal resources more than formal ones. Parents or relatives, friends, and employed workers ranked 1, 2, and 3 as persons students had talked with about occupations. Counselors and teachers lagged far behind. Parents or relatives and someone in the proposed line of work were named as frequently as formal publications, and considerably more frequently than counselors and teachers, as the source of information about the education and training requirements for entry into an occupation the student was considering, and about its earnings, job security, the opportunity it provided to help others, and the activities the work entailed.

Additional information about the use of reference materials is also reported on the student questionnaire. Although reference books have been used at least once by almost 80 percent of the students, less than 50 percent of the students have used them more than once. Magazines are used a little less frequently than reference books, and pamphlets and briefs less than that. Half of the students who are aware that their school has a computer terminal have ever used it and the same applies to microfiche. Although over 60 percent of the students have been exposed to a film or other audio-visual medium for career information, fewer than 50 percent of them have ever participated in any of the other eight experiential activities about which they were asked: simulation, special course in career planning, career day, work-study, job shadowing, tour of a business, meeting with former students, meeting with employed workers. These student reports exist in the face of the finding that over 75 percent of the schools offer career days and over 40 percent offer special courses in career planning.

The survey found a relationship between the type of student and the resource used. For example, low-ability females in nonacademic programs tended to use teachers as their career resource more than the average of other students; tenth and eleventh graders used counselors more than the average; nonwhite, high-reading-ability females used books, magazines, and pamphlets more than did the average. Similar relations of resource and student type were found for other groups. The researchers were appropriately cautious in interpreting these findings but they do give credence to the importance of offering experiences and resources that differ on the basis of the ability, experience, development, learning style, and interests of the users.

A final point to be made is that this survey suggested that students do not lack career resources but rather a usable context in which to place the information. In essence, as Katz suggested more than two decades ago, students "often don't know what information they need, don't have what information they want, or can't use what information they have" (Katz, 1963, p. 25). The problem, then, for any career guidance system is to help students determine what questions to ask, what information will answer their questions, and where to find the information they need; to help them structure the information and interpret it; and to help them arrive at a strategy for making decisions based on information (Chapman & Katz, 1981, p. 252). However mundane it sounds, students need to be educated to a paradigm of decision making in which information plays a role and is seen as naturally integrated into the awareness, exploration, and action elements of such a paradigm.

Also at issue in such a survey is counselors' intentions and preparations to serve as career resources themselves. Sobol (1978) studied the characteristics and activities of 69 counselors in high schools in the Dallas, Texas, area. It was found that 87 percent of the counselors help students choose college, 75 percent help students choose between college and vocational education, 70 percent help students get jobs, and 51 percent set up job interviews for students. In addition, it was found that most of these counselors try diligently to keep abreast of their field. Seventy-two percent reported that they study job opportunities by various means: for example, 58 percent use labor market forecasts, 43 percent bring in guest speakers, 62 percent talk to business representatives. The other side of the matter is that the school counselors tend to emphasize the current job market rather than the projected job market of five or ten years in the future. About 42 percent of the counselors do not use labor market forecasts at all and about 16 percent are not aware that such forecasts are available to them. Obviously, for those counselors who do not know about or use labor market forecasts their use as a career resource to students is limited, as is the likelihood that students will develop a context for their information-seeking behavior that includes consideration of intermediate and future goals as well as immediate choices.

An interesting technique for disseminating information on the relationship of curricula to specific job titles, to conceptualize jobs held by graduates of different programs, or to help students identify specific career opportunities in local industry has been described by Lipsett (1980b).

Figure 9.1 illustrates how different emphases within a business administration curriculum are related to clusters of jobs. Figure 9.2 illustrates how jobs held by graduates of a particular curriculum could be portrayed. Figure 9.3 depicts career paths in local industry. As Lipsett has suggested, although such career charts are not panaceas, they can be integrated into career counseling, a career information course, or other career exploration activity. Obviously, such visual display of important information can be an important adjunct to any of the career information systems we have identified.

CAREER GUIDANCE AND VOCATIONAL EDUCATION

One of the most fruitful efforts of the school counselor will be direct collaboration with vocational educators to reshape both the image and the substance of their disciplines. From a career guidance standpoint, the important thing to remember about vocational education is that it has been seen for too long as useful to only a highly restricted sample of the total student population rather than to all or most students. Its image has been that of a second-class alter-

Figure 9.1

Business Administration

Typical Job Titles Related to Principal Curricular Areas

Economics	Accounting	Marketing	Personnel	Finance
Economist	Public Accountant	Sales Representative	Employment Interviewer	Bank Loan Officer
Labor Market Analyst	Tax Accountant	Sales Manager	Recruiter	Bank Branch Manager
Long Range Planner	Cost Accountant	Branch Sales Ofc. Mgr.	Employee Benefits Specialist	Bank Operations Manager
Utility Rate Specialist	Auditor	Market Researcher	Job Evaluator	Bank Examiner
Municipal Research Specialist	Bank Examiner	Advertising Copy Writer	Training Specialist	Broker (stocks & bonds)
Business Forecaster	Estimator	Advertising Manager	Job Analyst	Treasurer
	Budget Director	Account Executive	Employee Counselor	Investment Counselor
	Credit Manager	Buyer (store)	Labor Relations Specialist	Controller
	Controller	Merchandise Manager	Personnel Director	
	Office Manager	Store Manager	Industrial Relations Director	
		Publicity Director	Compensation Administrator	
		Market Forecaster		
		Circulation Manager		
		International Trade Specialist		

Typical Job Titles in Functional Subspecialties

Traffic	Purchasing	Banking	Factory Operations	Information Management	Real Estate	Insurance
Traffic Manager	Purchasing Agent	Operations Manager	Production Control Mgr.	Computer Programmer	Appraiser	Underwriter
Shipping Clerk	Buyer (industrial)	Branch Manager	Production Planner	Systems Analyst	Broker	Actuary
Operations Manager	Inventory Control Manager	Loan Officer	Cost Accountant	Manager of Information Systems	Sales Representative	Claims Examiner
	Warehouse Manager	Cashier	Foreman		Property Manager	Sales Representative
		Investment Officer	General Foreman		Mortgage Officer	
		Investment Counselor	Manufacturing Manager			

Source: Reprinted from "Career Path Charts as Counseling Aids" by Laurence Lipsett, *Vocational Guidance Quarterly,* 1980, Vol. 30, No. 4, pp. 360–370, chart, p. 364. ©AACD. Reprinted with permission. No further reproduction authorized without written permission of American Association for Counseling and Development.

Figure 9.2

Jobs Held by Retailing Graduates

Entry Jobs	First Level Management	Second Level Management	Higher Management
Assistant Buyer	Buyer	Division Manager	Store Manager
Salesperson	Department Manager	Merchandise Manager	Area Manager
Assistant Interior Designer			V.P. Merchandising

Specialized Professional Jobs	Related Jobs Outside of Retailing
Sales Forecaster	Account Executive
Manager, Visual Design	Sales Manager
Credit Manager	Sales Representative
Personnel Manager	Manufacturer's Representative
Interior Designer	Advertising Manager
Fashion Coordinator	Chamber of Commerce Executive
Market Researcher	
Training Specialist	
Training Supervisor	

native for those with low verbal skills or for those with interests in working with their hands rather than their minds. In the process, many students in such programs and many vocational educators have become defensive about their alleged inferior status, have moved further into an isolationist stance divorcing themselves from so-called academic education, and have tied themselves to training experiences rigidly defined by time and content. This latter condition has occurred not necessarily because vocational educators want it that way but because factors such as legislative funding and union or apprenticeship regulations have, in some instances, forced such restrictions.

Regardless of the reasons for the situation, many students who desperately need what vocational education can offer have been blocked from this access. Such a condition has added fuel to the arbitrary separation of students into supposedly homogeneous categories of college-bound and non-college-bound, with the educational experiences offered each group seen essentially as mutually exclusive.

The means of releasing more of the potential contribution of vocational education to career development and, indeed, to career guidance lies not in assigning or recruiting more students for a vocational education track but in making vocational education an equal partner with all other aspects of the educational process. All the relationships between "general education" and career development that have been suggested throughout this book apply to vocational education with equal force. They must be incorporated into a reshaping of the many thrusts of vocational education in such a way that the lines, or at least the images, that presently separate vocational education and general education are made to blur or vanish.

Current legislation (such as The Carl D. Perkins Vocational and Applied Technology Education Act, reauthorized in 1990) and reports of relevant national research (such as the National Assessment of Vocational Education, 1990) have contended that a major priority for the 1990s is an integration of academic and

Figure 9.3

Company's Career Opportunities with a Bachelor's Degree in Business or Equivalent

Division	Grade 07	Grade 08	Grade 09	Grade 10	Grade 11
FINANCE DIVISION	Accountant		General Accountant	Supv. Gen. Accounting	
				Supv. Cost Accounting	
	Applications Programmer I		Sr. Applications Programmer	Mgr. Applications Programming	
	Systems Analyst			Senior Systems Analyst	Mgr. Systems Analysis
					Mgr. Credit & Collections
MARKETING DIVISION			Sec. Supv. Administrative Services		
					Advertising Manager
MANUFACTURING DIVISION			Asst. Traffic Manager		
			Production Control Mgr.		Mgr. Order Analysis
					Mrg. Customer Service

vocational skills in the secondary schools of the nation. These trends reflect the changing requirements of the occupational structure and the importance of the direct connections between academic and vocational education.

These comments about vocational education are not intended to preclude the continuation of specific job training for some students, but rather to convey the urgent need to broaden the present interrelationships and pathways within vocational education and between it and other educational experiences. Indeed, it is important that even more specific vocational education programs be developed that truly respond to both the low and the high ends of the intellectual continuum—whether the preparation is for becoming a helper, a waiter, a lawnmower repairperson, an industrial landscape gardener, a heavy construction equipment operator, or a computer programmer. The need is to create more tactics not only for fitting youth to programs but also for fitting programs to youth. The existing lock-step in many states of rigid training durations and specified training experiences as the only route to vocational education must be broken to exploit the enlarging

Figure 9.3 (continued)

Labor Grades				
Grade 12	**Grade 13**	**Grade 14**	**Grade 15**	**Grade 16**
Chief Accountant				Mgr. Accounting Operations
Sec. Mgr. Cost Accounting	Mgr. Cost Accounting		Chief Factory Accountant	
	Mgr. Systems Analysis & Applications Programming			Mgr. Data & Office Services
Asst. Mgr. Purchasing		Manager Purchasing		
		Mgr. Order Processing		
Traffic Manager				
Mgr. of Prodn. Ordering				
				Mgr. of Services

Source: reprinted from "Career Path Charts as Counseling Aids" by Laurence Lipsett, *Vocational Guidance Quarterly,* 1980, Vol. 30 No. 4, pp. 360-370, chart 3, p. 366. ©AACD. Reprinted with permission. No further reproduction authorized without written permission of American Association for Counseling and Development.

opportunities in the occupational structure for individuals with a wide range of capability. If career guidance is to be fully effective, vocational education courses must not only teach skills for specific occupations or skills across families of jobs; they must also develop within students the elements of career development that will free them to discern the alternative ways to use these skills and to attain the personal competence to capitalize on these skills. Further, more avenues must be created for all students to move freely between general and vocational education, with the criteria for such movement being individual need, readiness, interest, motivation, and a blend of academic and vocational experiences to meet these criteria.

For a variety of reasons, including (1) concerns about high youth unemployment among some special needs populations; (2) the need to reduce dropout rates from secondary schools in some parts of the nation, and (3) international economic competition, there is substantial evidence that vocational education is being reconsidered and redefined as a major national educational strategy, and that career guidance is being reaffirmed as a critical element of vocational education. These observations rest on two major resources, although others could be cited. The first is the Carl D. Perkins Vocational Education Act of 1984, which has provided nearly one billion dollars in federal support to states to provide strengthened and improved vocational education to major segments of secondary school populations and to groups with problems of access to the occupational structure. Thus, the Perkins Act is concerned with providing vocational education that manifests its own form of excellence and that is a major instrument to facilitate educational and occupational equity for subpopulations who have been denied equal opportunity for training and jobs. The Perkins Act—in addition to funding new program models and delivery systems and updating the capability of vocational education to deal with advanced technologies in the workplace—has made a major commitment of funds to tailor vocational education to the special needs for sex equity, the handicapped, disadvantaged, single parents and displaced homemakers, the criminal offenders, and adults needing retraining. Throughout the Perkins legislation career guidance is mentioned time and again in addressing both excellence and equity issues.

Reauthorized by the U.S. Congress in 1990 until fiscal year 1995 to become effective on July 1, 1991, the Carl D. Perkins Technology Education Act was revised and renamed the Carl D. Perkins Vocational and Applied Technology Education Act Amendments. Although some aspects of the 1984 version of the law will change, the Perkins Act will continue support for career guidance programs for their major role in meeting the Act's purposes of providing equity in the choice of vocational education for underserved populations and excellence in the programs chosen as reflected in likely placement into emerging and rewarding occupations for those served by these programs.

A second document having major implications for a renewed national emphasis on vocational education is the 1984 Report of the National Commission on Secondary Vocational Education. After a year of deliberation, this fourteen-person Commission comprised of persons representing business and industry, economics, guidance and counseling, and secondary and higher education published its report entitled *The Unfinished Agenda* (National Commission on Secondary Vocational Education, 1984). This report was partially a response to the report of the National Commission on Excellence, *The Nation at Risk* (1983), which advocated significant upgrading of the high school graduation standards in the United States (particularly in science and mathematics) and in so doing, either ignored vocational education or treated it negatively. The *Unfinished Agenda* was an attempt to correct the stereotyped image of vocational education and to propose a series of recommendations that would strengthen vocational education in American schools.

Although the report of the National Commission on Secondary Vocational Education includes too many recommendations to be dealt with effectively here, there are several emphases deserving particular note, for example, the purposes of vocational education. In many stereotypes, vocational education is seen as focusing only on training for entry-level occupations for students who do not have the capability or motivation to go on to college. In contrast, the National Commission contends that vocational education in the secondary school should be and generally is concerned with the development of the individual student in five areas: (1) personal skills and attitudes, (2) communications and computational skills and technological literacy, (3) employability skills, (4) broad and specific occupational skills and knowledge, and (5) foundations for career planning and lifelong learning (p. 3). In stating such purposes, several other perspectives are evident. First, vocational education and academic education are not competitors but complementary; in an occupational climate where advanced technology is pervasive, effective training in vocational education must rest upon a firm foundation in the basic academic skills. Second, vocational education is not a monolith. It is comprised of a diversity of content and curricula ranging from those of less academic rigor to those that are highly technical. Third, vocational education programs differ in specificity from courses designed to train students for entry into a specific occupation (such as auto mechanics) to those designed to prepare people to enter a cluster of occupations that tend to share common entry-level skill requirements (e.g., construction). Fourth, vocational education is not only concerned with teaching the technical aspects of job performance but also with work habits, career planning, and job-access skills.

Of particular interest to the major focus of this book is the National Commission's concern for improved and strengthened career guidance both as integral to vocational education and in broader terms of its availability for all students. As a rationale for its support of career guidance, the Commission contends that

> Inadequate student knowledge subtly but formidably constrains student access to vocational education. Students and parents need to be accurately informed about what vocational education is, how it relates to their personal and career goals, and how it can be used to help them achieve their goals. . . . We need comprehensive career guidance programs that will provide this information and remove some of the subtle status distinctions involving vocational education. Comprehensive guidance means counseling that is available to all students, covering all subjects, leading to all occupations. . . . We cannot achieve this goal of comprehensive guidance when counselors must deal, on the average, with 400 or more students. Nor can this goal be achieved unless counselors and teachers cooperate in new approaches to facilitate the career development of students, and unless counselors expand their use of group techniques, computer-assisted career guidance, comprehensive career information systems, and other methods designed to provide assistance to all students. Counselors must serve as a resource to integrate career guidance concepts and occupational information in the classroom. In addition, the amount of shared information between vocational educators and school counselors should be increased to reinforce the likelihood that counselors will effectively advise students to consider vocational education as an option. (p. 10)

Integrating the Work Experience with Schooling

Obviously, the traditional concepts of vocational education, the newer forms such as the cluster concept, and a greater freedom of movement between or integration of academic and vocational education are not mutually exclusive ways to provide career guidance and career development. At the senior high level, the integration of work experience with schooling can be a reality. The age and sex of the student are no longer the contingencies they were at the junior high school level. Blocks of time can be developed when students will actually report to jobs instead of school for two or three weeks or a term at a time.

Although the economic appeal is obvious, the training and exploratory value of work experience must be fitted to individual needs. Hence, if a particular student is interested in electronics, a program can be made available by which he or she can complete required high school work and simultaneously secure on-the-job training through part-time employment. With creative business-industry-education cooperation, programs can be mounted that provide training at work stations in the community in the late afternoon or morning hours, with the rest of the day devoted to general education in the school. For some students, this can be pretechnical training, for others, a permanent job, and for still others, precollege exploration. The integration of such experiences is inherent in the school-based and experience-based models of career education described in Chapter 1.

Probably the most common name for programs of work-study is *cooperative education*. A specific definition of this term is found in Section 195 of Title II of the Education Amendments of 1976, where the Vocational Education Act of 1963 is amended.

> The term "cooperative education" means a program of vocational education for persons who through written cooperative arrangements between the school and employers, receive instruction, including required academic courses and related vocational instruction by alteration of study in school with a job in any occupational field, but these two experiences must be planned and supervised by the school and employers so that each contributes to the student's education and to his or her employability. Work periods and school attendance may be on alternate half days, full days, weeks or other periods of time in fulfilling the cooperative program.

Cooperative education or work experience programs are essentially a process of behavioral change for students through experience. At one level, experience comes from immediately determining how what one learns in the classroom is applied at work. At another level, it comes from being adult-oriented at the work station rather than adolescent-oriented. In this sense, students have the opportunity to experience work norms as lived by adults rather than speculate about such things with one's adolescent peers. Finally, cooperative education programs assist students to see themselves and the work done as a whole. Frequently, classroom study fragments employability traits, work habits, human relations, and communications into small increments for purposes of learning. But in the real world all of these elements are part of a complete and constantly unfolding fabric that requires individual judgment and discrimination if career maturity is to result.

Work experience programs also allow the student to test which career development tasks have already been incorporated into his or her behavioral repertoire and which still need honing. In this way, work experience programs provide goal direction to learning and to student planning. A work experience in these terms is not just experience for its own sake but is related to employability. It represents a prime medium for career education and for developing effective work behaviors that help students acquire a positive career identity. In sum, cooperative education can be seen as a powerful tool in career guidance on the secondary school level.

It might be noted here that elements of cooperative education are similar to those described in the literature on mentoring. For those school systems unable to develop cooperative education programs, mentoring programs may be a useful alternative. Mentoring has been mentioned elsewhere in this book as a process of providing role models from the community for students who will profit from being able to observe firsthand the work context and activity of a mentor. Mentoring programs are evident in business, in community colleges, and in other educational contexts. Borman and Colson (1984) have described the use of mentoring as a career guidance technique for high school students in the West Nyack, New York, schools. In this program eighth-, eleventh-, and twelfth-grade students were assigned to professionals (mentors) to learn about career fields of interest in the community. Students explore some 25 career fields a year by spending after-school hours with their mentors for one semester: students in twelfth grade spend 3 hours per week or a total of 60 hours with their mentors; eighth-grade students tend to spend 1 to 1 1/2 hours per week. Although the specific process of evaluation is not described, Borman and Colson indicate that most students and mentors judge the program as excellent. Colson, Borman, and Nash (1978) earlier developed such a mentoring program for gifted high school seniors in College Station, Texas. At the beginning of the program an eight-week guidance laboratory in career investigations involved students with selected college professors for two months before they went into the mentorship experience. This program included a three-phase working internship in which the high school participants were placed in the community in career areas of interest to each student.

Work Shadowing. Another formal learning process related to mentoring or work experience is *work shadowing*. Although the term is virtually unmentioned in American career development literature, it has achieved increasing attention in British research. According to Watts (1986), "work shadowing describes schemes in which an observer follows a worker around for a period of time, observing the various tasks in which he or she engages, and doing so within the context of his or her total role" (p. 1). Although observation is critical to British models of work shadowing, this element does not stand alone. Rather, three other elements can be usefully added to observation: "*integration* with the work-guide (the worker being shadowed)—i.e., asking questions about what he or she is doing; *participation* in the work-guide's work—i.e., carrying out tasks for him or her; and *contextualization*—i.e., observing or talking to other workers with whom the work-guide comes into working contact" (p. 40).

When one compares work shadowing to work experience and work visits, clear conceptual distinctions can be drawn among these processes. Herr and Watts (1988) have suggested that "in work shadowing, the *prime* element is observation of work roles. In work experience, the prime element is performance of job tasks. In work visits, the prime element is contextualization and observation of the range of work processes performed within the work-place" (p. 81). In particular, "the student engaged in work shadowing will learn about the *tasks* in which the worker engages, about the *processes* within the workplace in which he or she is involved, and—often particularly striking to the young visitor—about the *environment* of the workplace as a whole" (Watts, 1986, p. 41). Because work shadowing focuses on the work role(s) of a particular individual (work guide), it can provide insight into informal aspects of human relationships at work, including power relationships. Such insights are obviously valuable within the broad context of vocational education; but the potential learning from work shadowing can also make it a powerful career guidance mechanism.

The whole spectrum of work-based learning, including apprenticeships, is likely to see a major resurgence in the United States during the 1990s. In contrast with other nations with whom we will increasingly compete economically, American policies concerning the transition to work of adolescents and young adults has been very limited. As suggested in several places in this book, more systematic approaches to school-business collaboration in support of career guidance and of vocational training and apprenticeship systems will be required.

Although it is thought that we have the finest higher education system in the world, our children are being outdistanced in the acquisition of mathematics and science skills in the precollege grades. In addition

> we have the least well articulated system of school-to-work transition in the industrialized world. Japanese students move directly into extensive company-based training programs, and European students often participate in closely interconnected schooling and apprenticeship training programs. . . . In Austria, Sweden, West Germany, and Switzerland, it is virtually impossible to leave school without moving into some form of apprenticeship or other vocational training. . . . {in the United States} High school and beyond follow-up interviews with a representative sample of high school seniors from the class of 1980 revealed that only 5 percent of graduates were participating in an apprenticeship training program within the first year following graduation from high school, and only 1 percent of graduates reported being enrolled in an apprenticeship program three years after graduation from high school. In sharp contrast, between 33 and 55 percent of all those who left school at ages sixteen to eighteen in such European nations as Austria, Germany, and Switzerland had entered apprenticeships in the late 1970's. (Berlin & Sum, 1988, p. 23)

An informed perspective on the present and future requirements of the American economy must accept the reality that education, training, employability, and employment are tightly linked. However, the linkages are complex in their content and character. Training and employability depend on the availability of an employment environment that provides opportunities for those who are trained in both general and specific employability skills. The employment possibility structure is dynamic as a function of economic policies and events, both domestic and international. Therefore the linkage of training, employability, and employment is influenced by providing information to training settings about areas of emerging demand so that structural mismatches between the employability potential of the labor force and the requirements of the employment structure can be minimized. Such information must also be made available systematically and with sufficient lead time to workers and potential workers so that choice of preparation through training related to occupational availability will be facilitated. Career counseling and career guidance must be seen as integral parts of the learning system.

The Relationship of Career Guidance to Vocational Education[1]

Hohenshil (1980) has aptly reported the prevailing view of vocational education toward guidance and counseling:

> Vocational education has long been a strong supporter as well as critic of guidance and counseling. On the one hand, there is no other area of education that has financially supported guidance as much for so long. . . . On the other hand, [vocational editors] have also believed that many counselors are neither well prepared nor have the interest in making career development a priority in their guidance programs. There is a generalized feeling that school counselors place too much emphasis on "college and therapy" at the expense of the development and implementation of well planned career guidance. (p. 668)

In general, as partial validation of Hohenshil's observations, the literature on career guidance, vocational guidance, or vocational counseling *in* vocational education is not large. Rather, the literature speaks primarily, and more broadly, to vocational guidance or career guidance in secondary schools, sometimes differentiating the needs and treatment of vocational education students and sometimes not. There are, however, studies that suggest that vocational students receive less vocational or

[1]Parts of this section are adapted from Herr, E. L. Career Development and Vocational Guidance. Chapter 6 in *Education and Work*. Edited by Harry F. Silberman. Chicago, Illinois: The University of Chicago Press, 1982.

career guidance than other students. Examples of some of these studies follow.

In 1966 Campbell and his colleagues undertook a national study of the status of guidance and counseling in secondary schools by comparing the viewpoints of school administrators, counselors, teachers, and students on guidance issues. Some 353 high schools and 7000 respondents were included in the study. Among other findings it was reported that in most schools no one assumed the primary responsibility for assisting students to decide on and enter into vocational programs (Campbell, 1968).

Kauffman and his colleagues (1967) in two major studies of vocational education found that over half the vocational students, but less than one-third of those who followed an academic or general program reported that they had never discussed their course choices with a counselor; of those students who reported that they had had some formal guidance, three-quarters had a favorable estimate, but vocational students were less likely than students in other curricula options to report favorably.

Palmo and De Vantier (1976) studied the counseling needs of vocational students over an academic year in one vocational-technical school. A similarity of concerns and problems existed among the students. The majority expressed difficulties with teachers, failure in school, peer relationships, home problems, and vocational/career plans. In particular, although vocational students have tentatively chosen a vocational path by enrolling in a vocational curriculum, approximately 30 percent of the students in this study were dissatisfied or confused by their choices and were not really aware of the alternatives available to them. The vocational students expressed a need "for more vocational counseling and additional materials that might help them with impending decisions" (p. 174).

Stern (1977) has summarized other studies of students or graduates that reflect, however indirectly, their needs for career guidance. Such findings are that vocational students are no more knowledgable about the world of work than nonvocational students, as likely to drop out as other students, no more satisfied with their jobs than graduates of the general track, and somewhat less satisfied than commercial and college preparatory graduates.

Career Guidance in Vocational Education. Career or vocational guidance *in* vocational education is typically seen as a *support* to the latter. Although there is a historical rhetoric as well as more recent legislative support for vocational guidance and vocational education as a partnership, that view does not always predominate in practice.

Support services can be defined in many ways. By tradition aspects of education tend to be included that facilitate the central role of instruction but are not themselves primarily instructional. Guidance and counseling generally meet these criteria and can play important support roles before and after vocational education instruction. For example, career or vocational guidance has a significant role in attracting, recruiting, or selecting students for vocational education options. Because of the many educational choices for youth, attracting appropriately motivated and talented students becomes a major concern to vocational educators in any setting. Vocational guidance can convey the image and possibilities of vocational education to potential enrollees, parents, sending schools, and other sources of input to vocational education programs.

The view of career guidance as a process of support to vocational education seems to be a reality in many instances. For example, Sproles (1988) studied 100 traditional and 100 nontraditional finishers of vocational education in West Virginia and the influences upon their choice of and completion of vocational education. As summarized by Sproles,

> This research suggests that many sources influence students' choices of programs in vocational education. Guidance counselors seem moderately helpful and supportive, but many influential individuals were perceived to be equally or more helpful to most of these vocational educational students. This implies that counselors need to be aware that they may be only one source of information in a network of many sources, and there are times when their roles complement or supplement advice from others. The counselor's main role is likely to be in presenting factual information about vocational programs and careers. Thus, the counselor must be well-informed about vocational education, and objective in presenting the vocational choices. This seems especially true when a nontraditional student is counseled. (p. 21)

The school counselor is a supporter of vocational education and its appropriate choice by students; this should not be confused with being a salesman for vocational education. Counselors must be able to apprise students of the utilitarian value of particular courses of study as these are related to skills and credentials of importance to college or work after high school (DiRusso & Lucarino, 1989). But such roles must be cast with consideration given to the readiness of students to make such choices, levels of work salience, and their levels of psychosocial or career development as antecedents to career decisions, not in terms of meeting enrollment quotas in various vocational education curricula or courses.

A second role for career or vocational guidance in vocational education is that of *assisting* in the selection of students for admission to various vocational education programs. Such a role involves individual assessment of aptitudes and preferences that, in turn, must be considered in relation to probabilities of success and satisfaction as these derive from *research* about differences in vocational education curricula and the characteristics of those who are successful in them. When individual desires and the realities of course availability or probabilities of success come into conflict, school counselors can help potential enrollees consider the alternatives in as nonarbitrary a manner as possible. Whether or not such conflict exists, school counselors have a major role in ensuring that students are properly motivated and equipped to take advantage of the vocational education instruction chosen. Where such a condition does not occur, career guidance personnel need to assist students in choosing a different option in vocational education or to exit from it into another option that promises to meet their current needs.

A third role of career or vocational guidance in vocational education is directly related to instruction itself. As will be discussed in the following section on placement, vocational education students need access to instruction in work-context skills and guidance or career-development skills as well as in specific technical and occupational skills. Since these skills are composed of attitudes, emotions, psychological factors, and cognitive and informational aspects, school counselors often become involved with their provision. Counselors may work with vocational teachers as collaborators or consultants as such learnings are infused into curricula. Or, in some instances, school counselors may take direct responsibility for providing such instruction. Through separate group courses, seminars, interactive computer-assisted instruction, gaming, role-playing, and other techniques students can gain work-context and personal guidance learnings. As this occurs, career guidance as a support service tends to blur into career guidance as subject matter.

A fourth support service contribution to vocational education is the role of career guidance in the placement of students. Conceived in traditional terms, placement of vocational education graduates into suitable employment or postsecondary education has been seen as an event, not a process. The assumption has been that, in the case of work, for instance, when a student is about to complete the vocational education program, he or she would be brought into direct contact with an employer(s) seeking a person with such training. The rationale for such an assumption is that the student is employable—possesses the appropriate attitudes, marketable skills, job search and interview behaviors—and only needs assistance to obtain a suitable employer. The role of career or vocational guidance was conceived as that of matchmaker at the point when the student exited the vocational education system.

Increasingly, placement is being conceived as a process, not an event. As such it is seen as a stream of career development and guidance learnings that are acquired concurrently with occupation-specific task learnings throughout the students' vocational education experience, not just when the student is about to enter work full-time. In this sense, assisting vocational education students to focus on their learning and performance capabilities; gain decision-making capacity; formulate an awareness of their options, how to prepare for them and gain access to them; and acquire job search and job interview behavior are seen as preparing these persons not only for the school-to-work transition but for placement as a natural extension of all vocational education. Career guidance, then, is seen as a central component of this process, not something abrupt and different from it.

Perspectives in Vocational Placement

Historically, career guidance, counseling, and placement have been considered mutually exclusive functions. Our contention is that although they are not synonymous, neither are they mutually exclusive or discrete.

There are obviously many ways to think about the vocational placement of students in the workplace or other educational settings after they finish their secondary schooling. As suggested in the previous section, many people treat placement as an event; an independent activity that can be seen differently from other dimensions of a career guidance program. Such a view can create problems where none need to exist, because it assumes that placement is different or unable to be accommodated within guidance programs or by their personnel.

In some contexts, the term *placement* is used vaguely. As a result, it is hard to determine if placement means locating jobs, or creating awareness of job needs and then matching students with the available jobs, or building capabilities within students to handle job search and job adjustment. It would seem that both aspects of placement—job development and student development—should be combined if the program is to be effective. Such a view would see placement as integral to career or vocational guidance.

If there is a difference between career guidance and placement, it lies largely in the fact that the first concept is heavily involved with facilitating self- and career-awareness, exploration, and formulating and choosing preferences. Placement, though not excluding these concerns, is more oriented to creating processes by which choices can be converted into action through gaining entry into available jobs or educational opportunities consistent with such preferences. Thus, career guidance is concerned with anticipating and sorting among alternatives; placement is concerned with implementing choices and adjusting to them. These differences in emphasis, however, do not preclude both objectives or processes being included in a career/vocational guidance program.

Part of the way to handle such disparities is to think about placement as a process, not an event. In a systems approach, career guidance as a stimulus to career development is a process that leads to placement. In a very real sense, effective placement of students into the labor market is the end result of their readiness for vocational planning, crystallizing a vocational preference, and acquiring job search and employability skills and other attitudes, knowledge, and skills pertinent to the career guidance process.

Viewing placement as a process does not preclude the fact that individuals come to placement in different conditions of readiness for decision making and for assuming the responsibility for implementing a choice. The assumption is that these conditions will depend on the students' exposure to elements of career development, career education, or career guidance in concert with reinforcement, encouragement, and modeling in their family background and general or vocational educational experiences from elementary school through the senior high school. If such development has not occurred in the personal history of the student to be placed, the counselor alone or in cooperation with others needs to assist the student, within an abbreviated time frame, with the placement prerequisites the individual lacks. This obviously may include some type of assessment to find out where the student stands with regard to the *process of choice*—independence, planfulness, possession of occupational information, knowledge of the decision-making process, his or her attitude toward choice—and to help him or her think about the *content of choice*—which includes the placement alternatives available, their characteristics, and their likely consequences.

If placement is viewed as a transition process as well as a point in time, then as part of the career guidance program, the school counselor can, among other things, help the student prepare psychologically for placement. This may require role-playing interview situations, assistance in completing or recognizing the importance of employment applications, or making compromises because of the restricted provision of jobs available in the local setting. It will also involve support and follow-up while the individual is moving through the placement process. In some cases, the counselor must lend strength to individual students who encounter initial rebuffs in the job-seeking process until the student's self-confidence and self-esteem are reinforced.

To be effective in the placement process, it is obvious that the school counselor needs to have the time and the ability to communicate with persons outside the school who are active in placement—personnel or training people in business and industry, employment service counselors, rehabilitation counselors, and others. Such communication requires that the counselor be able to talk knowledgeably about the competence, goals, and characteristics of persons to be placed, as well as to secure information about openings that is relevant, accurate, and localized. In this regard, knowledge of regional labor trends as well as knowledge of available local jobs is important to the counselor, as is knowledge of training opportunities, career paths, and career ladders in local industry.

Placement of handicapped persons poses a particular challenge to the counselor to know the competencies and aspirations of individual disabled persons and the specific competencies required in different occupations. Unless the counselor persists in being as precise as possible in determining what a particular handicapped person is capable of doing and what is actually required in jobs, it is very easy to lapse into generalized stereotypes about what the handicapped person can or cannot do and what jobs require. As an example of the importance (for placement) of going beyond generalities and stereotypes, Gottfredson, Finucci, and Childs (1984) studied the adult careers of persons who had been diagnosed in adolescence as dyslexic. "Dyslexia is a specific type of reading disability, and the term is generally applied to people who fail to learn to read with facility despite normal intelligence, good health, and ample opportunity" (p. 356). The sample of 579 dyslexic men in this study were compared to 612 nondisabled men of the same age, social class, and intellectual levels. In contrast to the nondisabled populations, the dyslexic adults rarely become professionals—physicians, lawyers, or college teachers—probably because of the emphasis put upon academic skills, reading, and higher degrees. Rather, the dyslexic sample tended to have high-level, primarily in management or sales, occupations in which skills other than reading (such as taking initiative, being responsible, being persuasive) are accented and the importance of a higher degree is diminished. These data show that placement activities with special groups, particularly those with conditions that are remediable, require learning about the cognitive, social, and physical skills that are actually critical in different occupations, not simply assumed to be important. Such information provides a better sense of the field of opportunities available to such handicapped individuals and ways to identify those skills that the student might strengthen to become more competitive.

Since not all students to be placed will be high school graduates, school counselors concerned with placement will need to know of jobs available for the school dropout as well. At the point of placing dropouts, the counselor needs to reject the temptation to admonish them about how much monetary difference exists between them and high school graduates or why this choice condemns them to a lifelong position of unskilled or semiskilled work. In some instances such an admonition would be in error. For instance, as Redfering and Cook (1980) have shown in their study of high school dropouts (N = 100) and high school graduates (N = 100) in which half of each group had received vocational training and the other half had not, the existence or absence of vocational training was a more potent influence on income level and job complexity than was completion of high school. Therefore, rather than moralizing about the decision of the student, the appropriate course of action is to provide the dropout with help in obtaining employment, information about ways to continue the student's education, and the reassurance that opportunities exist for resuming a high school program.

A further question that needs attention is, What will we include in the *placement* domain? Do we mean by placement facilitating student entry into jobs or post-secondary educational opportunities? Or do we mean, in addition, student placement into cooperative education, part-time employment, volunteer placement, summer employment, and a range of exploratory opportunities? Crawford (1976) has indicated that at the secondary school level one must consider at least five goals: (1) placing graduates in full-time or part-time jobs, (2) placing dropouts, (3) placing students in part-time jobs, (4) coordinating preplacement training, and (5) advising students of occupational opportunities available through continuing education. Whether or not one accepts Crawford's goals, the answers to the preceding questions will have significant implications for who should be responsible for placement, how much time should be committed to placement, what resources are needed, and what the content of placement should be.

The fact is that placement for students entering the labor market has seldom been seen as a major responsibility of the school. It is true that vocational educators in different curricula, business teachers, and some school counselors have engaged in placing students. But it is less true that these activities have been performed with purpose under the rubric of career guidance or have been seen as a natural extension of this process.

And yet job placement, like other educational outcomes, cannot occur effectively unless it is seen as important and planned effectively. A study conducted at the National Center for Research in Vocational Education (1982) examined the factors relating to the job placement of former secondary vocational education students. They found that a strong commitment to job placement is one of the most important factors affecting job placement. National Center researchers found that higher job placement seems to exist in those schools where administrators, counselors, and teachers possessed both a clear understanding of the importance of job placement and a consistent belief that the major purpose of vocational education is the placement of students in jobs related to their training. They further found that enthusiasm for the goal of job placement is also an important part of this process. McKinney, the project director, stated, "There has to be a philosophical position on the part of the school system that job-related training and effective job placement programs are two very important and two very interrelated processes" (p. 1).

Ways to Facilitate Job Placement

The study suggested that several activities seem to facilitate higher job placement rates in all labor markets. These include the following:

- Maintaining regular contact with employers regarding the job placement of students
- Providing coordination for job placement activities through a centralized job placement service and including teachers in job placement activities
- Helping students acquire the basic education skills needed to obtain a job and to perform on the job
- Orienting the vocational education curriculum to the needs of the employers in the community

We reemphasize that placement is more than an isolated event; it is a process that brings students and employers together. If the school already participates in work-study or cooperative education programs, part of this task has already been accomplished. If it does not, strategies to enlist school-industry-business cooperation must be devised. Cooperative linkage with employment service counselors is one step in this direction; vocational resource conferences, community advisory groups, utilization of chambers of commerce, and the National Alliance of Business are others.

In our experience, developing a part-time job brokering system within a career resource center or trying to set up summer employment for juniors, seniors, or students of legal age has been very helpful to the students and it has raised the consciousness of employers that the school exists, that there are students seeking work, and that the counselors are interested in learning about employer needs and the characteristics of work in their firms. This is particularly helpful in the urban area, where the students of several local high schools are competing for placement. Goeke and Salamone (1979) have described several useful related projects such as developing a rent-a-kid program to foster part-time work, job-finding clubs for seniors, or informal work-study apprenticeship programs in conjunction with employers in the private sector.

Buckingham and Lee (1973) have recommended that placement programs include job clinics. Essentially, job clinics are workshops on broad topical areas that help students acquire job search and acquisition skills related to such areas as

- Effectively completing job applications
- Personal appearance
- Employers tests—civil service testing, scholastic testing
- Job interview behavior

- Telephone tips for talking with potential employers
- Transportation to work
- Job referral cards to employers
- Tips in applying for jobs

Also of concern in placement is the identification of a person or persons responsible for placement and, possibly, the location of a placement center. Although placement is clearly a part of career guidance, a pertinent question is, Should counselors take the total responsibility for placement, or should they serve to coordinate a variety of placement activities? There is no one correct answer to this question. It depends on school resource commitments and structures. Whether or not counselors should assume total responsibility for placement, they must consider it a significant part of their responsibilities. The existence of a placement center is again dependent on school structures and resources. In many instances, placement centers have been included as part of *career resource centers*. In this sense, placement information and procedures can be integrated with computer terminals, manpower information, career guidance references, student follow-up data, group processes, resource persons, and other aspects of the career guidance program.

Regardless of who does the job placement, Brown and Feit (1978) contend that five categories of skill are required:

- Determining students who need placement
- Survey of job opportunities
- Prereferral assessment and training
- Referral
- Placement follow-up

Each of these skills has been part of the repertoire of most counselors, although frequently they have not been brought into the direct service of job placement. That such application needs to become a more integral aspect of career guidance programs seems no longer to be debatable.

CAREER GUIDANCE TECHNIQUES FOR THE SENIOR HIGH SCHOOL

Throughout this chapter, examples of career guidance techniques have been discussed for use with different student populations and for different purposes. The following inventory of career guidance techniques used in various programs throughout the nation may provide additional ideas for adaptation in the local setting. Many of these activities could be directly integrated into various subject matter areas as part of a career education infusion strategy or equally well used as part of group or individual career guidance strategies.

Curriculum Infusion

After reading a vocational biography, have students describe how a career decision made by the subject influenced areas of his or her life such as choice of friends, family life, location of residence, and so on.

Have students complete a sample job and/or college application, write a job résumé, and successfully role-play a job or college interview.

Have students engage in appropriate research and prepare a term paper discussing the concept of supply and demand as it relates to a changing labor market.

Develop a short unit in each subject matter area on how technology has affected the occupations related to that subject area (for example, implications of technology for office clerical workers as part of business education program, and so on).

Have students demonstrate in a written assignment the ways in which technology has multiplied the number of jobs, and have them associate this fact with the necessity for interdependence among workers in a particular industrial setting (that is, steel plants, space industry, and such).

Have students define in writing the specific steps they must go through to obtain some future educational or vocational goal. The steps should be listed in chronological order.

In art class have students design and prepare a brochure describing student skills, desires for part-time work, and related matters to be sent to the community.

Have students prepare a résumé listing the various skills they possess.

After reading a biography in which the "career pattern" of a famous individual is described, have students identify the decision points in that person's life, the occupational roles played, and the stages of preparation leading to each role. Have students use this information to prepare a written assignment describing the "career pattern" of the subject in question.

After studying "industrialism," the student might write a short essay on the factors leading up to and resulting from mass production techniques as they developed in the United States during World War II.

At the beginning of any course, the teacher might help each student write a brief assignment as to the relationship of the course to some educational or occupational goal of the student. Students could also formulate a list of individual goals pertaining to the course, that is, skills, knowledges, or attitudes they hope to develop.

Group Guidance Processes

Have students construct an occupational family tree in which they research the occupations held by each of their grandparents, parents, and siblings. Have them examine gender-specific reasons for choices as appropriate. Apply specific questions to the tree: Which family member am I most like? Why? What do my family members want me to choose? Why?

Develop life planning workshops in which life roles and the coping skills required in them are analyzed and shared.

Given a career-related problem (such as selection of a college, trade or technical school; comparison of two or more occupations; need for financial assistance), have students locate appropriate informational resources.

Given ninth-grade educational plans, have senior high school students modify the plan to correspond with changing concepts of the self.

For a series of case studies illustrating examples of people making career decisions, have the students identify those examples that represent poor planning, and indicate what steps could have been taken that were not.

Have the students write a long-range career plan identifying the specific steps each must take to reach preferred future goals.

Have students develop a tentative long-range occupational plan on entering high school. This should be in writing and kept on file. It should include short-term as well as long-term goals and steps to reach such goals. The plan should be periodically reviewed and evaluated in individual counseling sessions.

Have each student develop in writing a plan of access to his or her next step after high school, either educational or occupational, listing possible alternatives, whom to contact, application dates, capital investment necessary, and self-characteristics to be included on applications or resumes.

Have students differentiate between the major occupations that make up the occupational cluster of their choice in terms of (1) the amount and type of education needed for entrance and advancement; (2) the content, tools, settings, products, or services of these occupations; (3) their value to society; (4) their probability of providing the type of life-style desired; and (5) their relationship to personal interests, abilities, and values. Discuss in group sessions.

Have students list at least six factors they are seeking in a career (such as opportunity to travel, meeting new people, responsibility, opportunity for advancement, and so on). Discuss in group sessions.

Given information concerning labor force trends from 1970 to 1980 or beyond, have the students discuss ways these trends might affect their own career selections.

Use the Decisions and Outcomes curriculum prepared for the College Entrance Examination Board as the basis for a group guidance unit on decision making.

Discuss the kinds of decisions people of varying age groups must make: 5-, 10-, 18-, 21-, 35-, 50-, 65-year-old persons. Relate these to long-term planning concerns.

Present students with a series of hypothetical situations describing an individual with a decision-making dilemma (an individual who wants to be a professional athlete but has not displayed sufficient ability). Have students discuss and consider what compromises exist.

Devote a section of the school newspaper to profiling the skills and abilities of selected graduating seniors, to posting job openings, and to providing various job tips.

Create a job-finding club for seniors to facilitate the learning of job-search and related procedures.

Draw on past experiences in decision making, and have students discuss how a decision that was made was influenced by some external factor (family, friends, geography).

Have students list the relative advantages and disadvantages of each of the career alternatives they are considering in terms of their relationship to expressed life-style goals.

Have students take specific steps to implement a career-based decision before leaving high school (such as apply to a job or post-high school training program, engage in job or college interview).

Using appropriate resources, have each student develop a list of entry-level skills needed for an occupational area of his or her choosing.

Have students engage in mock job interviews.

Have each student list at least six courses or school experiences in which he or she has been successful and relate these successes to the attainment of marketable skills currently possessed.

For an identified social problem, such as air pollution, rehabilitation of drug users, the development of new uses for materials, or creating by-products of fishery harvesting, have students create a lattice of occupations at different levels (professional to unskilled) that might contribute to resolving the problem.

Have students read books that depict work as a means of self-expression and discuss what this means for choice.

Have students identify important skills or competencies related to some educational or occupational goal. Have them compare their progress in attaining these with that of the previous year in terms of (1) little or no progress, (2) fair progress, (3) great progress.

Have students list 10 means of furthering their education beyond high school (such as college, trade school, apprenticeship, on-the-job training, military, peace corps, reading, and so on), and discuss the advantages and disadvantages of each.

Have students differentiate between the major occupations that make up a preferred career cluster in terms of the amount and type of education needed for entrance.

For an occupational area of his or her choice, have the student list in order the educational experiences (courses and training) needed to enter and advance in that occupation.

Have students contrast and compare a recent interest inventory with one taken in junior high school.

Have students do a genogram of the occupations of members in their family of origin as a way of defining parental and family influences across generations and potential role models in the family who were previously unknown.

Community Involvement

Invite outside resource persons to review their own career patterns and emphasize the planning in which they engaged, the information they used, and information they would like to have had but did not.

Establish a placement service to provide (part-time, summer, or simulated) job experiences for students to try out job skills.

Have resource persons from the local Bureau of Employment Security discuss such matters as local employment trends, unemployment rates, and related factors.

Take field trips to local industries followed by a discussion of how new technologies or automation has affected each one.

Cooperate with the local Bureau of Employment Security to establish a program designed to inform students of local job opportunities.

Establish a rent-a-kid activity program to facilitate the development of and information about part-time jobs in the community.

Interview employers regarding personal qualities they look for in employees. After they interview employers in management or supervisory positions regarding qualities necessary for career success, have students write a short paper relating job attitudes to job success.

After an opportunity to observe and interview workers in job settings relating to an occupational cluster of his or her choosing, have the student list the materials, tools, and processes associated with the observed occupations.

Have students do a "job analysis" of an occupation of their choosing.

Have students participate in part-time work experiences in a job related to an occupational cluster of their choosing.

Using a list of community agencies, businesses, and so on and a description of their functions, have students select one and work there for a week, demonstrating punctuality, regular attendance, and the ability to perform tasks under the direction of a supervisor. Success will be judged by the job supervisor.

Send follow-up questionnaires to working graduates, requesting their assistance as contact persons for students wanting occupational information about the kind of work in which they are now employed or as job-lead resources for current students.

Summary

In this chapter we have discussed career development in the senior high school as it is conditioned by the imminence of various forms of reality with which students must cope. Continuing themes regarding a systematic approach to career development which were begun in elementary school finally converge at the senior high school level. Implications for intensity of planning and the fostering of goal-directedness in different individuals are considered as correlates of different forms of behavior following high school. The mutual contributions of vocational education and academic education to career education are examined as recommendations are developed for greater meshing of these two elements of the educational process. In addition, career guidance and placement processes have been discussed. Finally, career guidance techniques appropriate to the senior high school have been identified.

CHAPTER 10

CAREER GUIDANCE AND COUNSELING IN HIGHER EDUCATION

Key Concepts

- Research studies tend to show repeatedly that 50 percent or more of all college students have career-related problems.
- The college-going population in the United States is composed of subgroups who differ in age, reasons for going to college, and motivation for achievement or other goals. Career guidance and counseling must provide differential services to persons in such groups.
- Comprehensive career guidance programs in higher education should provide a complete range of services including career advising, career counseling, and career planning involving cooperative activities between academic departments and career specialists.
- Colleges and universities typically have used four major approaches to deliver career guidance: (1) courses, workshops, and seminars that offer structured group experiences in career planning, job-access skills, decision making, and related topics; (2) group counseling activities; (3) individual counseling; and (4) placement programs.
- College placement activities tend to be seen increasingly as part of a process, not an event. Thus, many career guidance activities throughout the college experience are sequenced to bring the college student to a point of maturity and decision making that can culminate in effective placement.

An extraordinary proportion of Americans are enrolled in either two-year or four-year postsecondary and higher educational institutions. In 1990, approximately 13.2 million students were enrolled in higher education; of these, about 8.3 million were enrolled in four-year institutions, and 4.9 million were in two-year institutions. About 11.4 million were undergraduates; 1.5 million were graduate students; and about 0.3 million were pursuing first professional degrees. In 1990 about one million bachelor's degrees were awarded—a figure that has not changed markedly over the past decade. The United States Department of Education projects that the number of students in higher education is likely to remain relatively constant until 1994, when it is expected to dip for a few years until it returns to its current level by the end of the decade (*Department Chair*, 1990).

The number of high school graduates is expected to decline by 12 percent in 1992 compared to 1988 figures and then to increase beginning in 1995. At the same time, an increasing proportion of high school graduates are enrolling in colleges. In 1990, 58.9 percent of 16 to 34 year olds who said they received a high school diploma in 1988 reported that they enrolled in a two-year or a four-year college. Compare this figure to data 10 years earlier when, in 1978, only 49.6 percent enrolled in colleges. The increase in enrollment percentage is part of a continuing trend in which formerly non-attending segments of the population are returning to school—divorced women, veterans, older people, members of minority groups, and so on. Further, some believe that the continuing school reform movements of the past decade have affected college-going rates.

Although traditional college-age students (18–24) are still a majority in higher education, the increased enrollment of older students is an undeniable trend. Traditional students account for about 56 percent of college enrollments; older students (25 years and older) account for about 42 percent; the remainder are under 18 years of age (U.S. Department of Education, 1988). In every state, the majority of college enrollees are from within-state, although the percentages vary from less than 60 percent in Alaska, New Jersey, and New Hampshire to 95 percent and over in Texas, California, and Arizona.

Although enormous gains have been registered in the past few decades, the proportion of minority students in higher education continues to lag behind that of whites, especially in terms of graduation rates (Carter & Wilson, 1989).

> As of 1987, Hispanics, African Americans, and American Indians continued to be underrepresented among degree recipients compared to their enrollment levels in higher education. Hispanic Americans comprised 5.3 percent of the undergraduate population in 1986 but earned only 2.7 percent of all bachelor's degrees awarded in 1987; correspondingly, African Americans made up 9.2 percent of all undergraduates but received only 5.7 percent of all bachelor's degrees. Similarly, American Indians comprised 0.8 percent of the undergraduate enrollment, yet they received only 0.4 percent of all baccalaureate degrees. (p. iv)

Of course, there is virtually a linear relationship between family income and college attendance. Only 14 percent of families with income under $10,000 have a college-goer, while 56 percent of families with incomes over $50,000 have one or more members in college. The percentage of college students who are minority group members also varies by state with lower representations (less than 8 percent) in states such as Maine, Vermont, New Hampshire, Rhode Island, West Virginia, Kentucky, Minnesota, Wisconsin, Iowa, Nebraska, North and South Dakota, Wyoming, Montana, Utah, Idaho, and Oregon. States with higher proportions (more than 25 percent) of minority college students include Texas, California, New Mexico, Louisiana, Hawaii, and Mississippi.

Another observation regarding the demographics of higher education pertains to foreign students, whose presence continues to grow on American campuses. In the academic year 1988–1989, 366,354 foreign students were enrolled in U.S. colleges and universities. About 47 percent of these students were undergraduates; 45 percent were graduate students; and 7 percent pursued other studies (such as intensive English language courses). The 10 leading sending countries, in order, were China, Taiwan, Japan, India, South Korea, Malaysia, Canada, Hong Kong, Iran, and Indonesia—a decidedly Asian presence (*The New York Times*, November 29, 1989). The 10 leading receiving schools, in order, are Miami-Dade Community College, University of Southern California, University of Texas at Austin, Boston University, University of Wisconsin (Madison), UCLA, Ohio State University, Columbia University, University of Pennsylvania, and the University of Illinois (Urbana). These students tend overwhelmingly to major in the career areas, which might account, at least in part, for the substantial rise in "career" degrees (computer and information sciences, business and management, health sciences, and engineering).

Another study assessed the academic, career, and personal needs of 1625 students at the University of Georgia (Weissberg et al., 1982). Career development needs were expressed by a greater percentage of students than either academic or personal needs. For example, over 80 percent of the students wanted to explore job opportunities related to their majors and to obtain work experience in a career area; 77 percent desired to develop effective job-seeking skills; and 72 percent wanted to learn how to prepare for their careers. Over half said they would very much like to explore their career interests, values, and abilities, to obtain information, to talk to a counselor about career plans, and to learn how occupations can affect their future way of life. In contrast, only four personal needs (time management, relief of speech anxiety, budgeting, and self-confidence) and only five academic needs (study skills, writing skills, test anxiety reduction, ease in class participation, and effective library use) were cited by more than 50 percent of undergraduates, and none of these needs was expressed by more than two-thirds of the students. Clearly, in this study career needs were perceived as paramount when compared to personal and academic needs.

Affirmation of this finding comes in a needs analysis conducted by Walters and Saddlemire (1979). They surveyed freshmen at Bowling Green State University and concluded that 85 percent of students indicated need in six areas of career information:

1. Information on the occupations that my chosen major will prepare me for
2. Knowledge of places and people on campus that can help in my career planning
3. More direct experiences such as part-time work or job visits in occupations that I am considering
4. Better understanding of myself to choose an occupation that closely fits my values, goals, and life-style preferences
5. Knowledge of the job market
6. Help to plan college courses that will give more flexibility in choosing among different occupations (pp. 227–228)

All of these studies taken together and others (for example, Koplik & DeVito, 1986) make clear the need for career guidance and counseling services in our postsecondary institutions—technical, two-year, and four-year. Furthermore, the findings pertain to younger and older students (Warchel & Southern, 1986), to traditional and reentry women (MacKinnon, 1986), to students with disabilities (Schriner & Roessler, 1990), and to virtually every other segment of the postsecondary population.

There is some indication, however, that the career needs of older students are different from those of so-called traditional students. Looking at older community college students, Healy and Reilly (1989) determined that the career needs of this group differed enough from those of their younger counterparts to warrant adult-specific career interventions. For example, vocationally-oriented older students may not be able to engage so readily in occupational exploration by means of extracurricular activities, and they may have more need for assistance in placement in work-related experiences than in learning to make suitable choices. Bauer and Mott (1990), using intensive interviews with a very small sample of older students (ages 28 to 35), concluded—against the usual findings—that while some of their subjects had career needs, these needs were largely overshadowed by personal needs and that there was very little unity of work, love, and play in their life space structures. Nevertheless, the preponderant finding is that the career needs of both younger and older college students figure highly in their expressed needs hierarchy.

The fact that needs are strongly expressed by students, however, does not mean that there will be high demand for interventions designed to meet those expressed needs. Barrow, Cox, Sepich, and Spivak (1989) conducted a study that found only modest relationship between the services students said that they needed and those that they actually used. Of the eleven highest ranked needs, only two—stress management and time management—drew heavy outreach workshop attendance. The other nine highly rated needs—career planning, understanding interests, setting reasonable expectations, communicating more effectively, finding written information regarding career and educational programs, making decisions and solving problems, enriching relationships, improving relationships with others, and getting energized to tackle goals—were not highly requested or attended.

CHARACTERISTICS OF THE POPULATION

Certain selected characteristics of the college-going population have a bearing on the provision of career guidance services. Among these are reasons for choosing higher education, student cultures, age distribution of the clientele, outcomes of advanced schooling, and socioeconomic backgrounds of students.

Reasons for Going to College

Higher education in America is not a part of the compulsory educational system; consequently, going to college involves a deliberate choice. The reasons for that decision are many and varied. There is a large body of research that pertains to student motivations for attending college. Basically, these studies suggest several categories of college-goers:

The Self-Fulfillers—These students are primarily concerned with a search for personal identity and self-fulfillment. They expect the collegiate experience to offer a flexible and supportive environment in which self-expansion can occur. Although vocational ends may be present, they are neither immediate nor primary. For many others, college is seen as a setting in which to pursue assortative mating.

The Careerists—These students view themselves as attending college primarily for vocational reasons; that is, to receive the specific preparation or credentials necessary to enter into a specific profession or occupation or to prepare for advanced training and education. The collegiate experience is seen as a means to an end rather than as an end in itself. Other motivations may be present, but they are peripheral to the major goal of occupational preparation.

The Avoiders—For these students the college decision is more a matter of avoidance than it is of positive, conscious, and deliberate striving for a goal, either career- or self-fulfillment oriented. In the 1950s and 1960s, these were the students who pursued higher education in order to avoid the draft. They are individuals who seek to put off choosing other alternatives, either because of lack of readiness to make these choices, because of a perceived repulsion in the alternatives available, or because of an inability to make a choice. In effect, they are buying time.

These three categories, which, of course, are not mutually exclusive, describe most of the reasons for the college choice, albeit in simplified form. The point is that many students in each category—the self-fulfillers, the careerists, and the avoiders—will ultimately have a need for career guidance. The self-fulfiller, at some point, realizes that although personal development and enhancement of mind and spirit are indeed laudable goals, most people in our society are expected and required to work. The careerist not infrequently discovers that an original career choice is inappropriate and searches for occupational alternatives. The avoider eventually becomes cognizant that one cannot procrastinate career choice forever.

Student Cultures

Related to the notion of student motivations for higher education attendance is the idea of student cultures. There have been many classifications offered to delineate the clientele of higher education according to the diverse systems of values and activities to which they subscribe. Perhaps the most widely cited of these taxonomies is that devised by Clark and Trow (1966). They perceive four dominant student cultures: collegiate, vocational, academic, and nonconformist.

The *collegiate* culture is one with a college orientation, involving "expensive play." Students in this category are engaged primarily in the pursuit of fun. The *vocational* culture is composed of those students who view college as a kind of off-the-job-training, an organization of courses and credits leading to a diploma and a better job than they might otherwise expect. Their pursuit is for skills and a diploma. The *academic* culture is made up of those students who have an identification with the intellectual concerns of the serious faculty members. They are pursuing knowledge. Lastly, the *nonconformist* culture is seeking an identity. They are students who are involved with ideas, and who use off-campus groups as points of reference. They maintain a critical detachment from college and evidence a generalized hostility toward the college administration.

Still another taxonomy is offered by Katchadourian and Boli (1985). They looked at the dimensions of careerism and intellectualism on a college campus and defined students as *careerists* (high careerism, low intellectualism) who were mostly men; *intellectuals* (high intellectualism, low careerism), two-thirds of whom were women; *strivers* (higher careerism, high intellectualism); and *unconnected* (low careerism, low intellectualism). The site of this research, Stanford, might not be called typical. Nevertheless, the findings are that careerists make most academic decisions on the basis of better career preparation; intellectuals assume that academic interests are pursued for their own sake and will somehow eventuate in an occupation; strivers want a liberal education but also want successful careers; and the unconnected are indifferent to both a liberal education and to a career.

In terms of the vocational culture, from the 1973 to 1974 to the 1983–1984 schoolyear, there was a dramatic rise in the number of so-called professional degrees awarded. Bachelor's degrees in career-specific fields increased markedly whereas those in general fields (social sciences, humanities, and so on) declined. These career degrees (such as computer and information sciences, health services, engineering, business, and management) grew tremendously; the only notable exception to this trend was in education degrees. There is some evidence that in the last few years, however, the more traditional arts and sciences majors are making small gains.

As with initial motivations for college attendance, student cultures are not mutually exclusive. Further, students can slide from one to another with relative ease. Changes in student cultural identification usually entail alterations in career thinking to which career specialists must respond.

Sex Composition

A nineteenth-century male bastion, higher education in the twentieth century has experienced a rapid and continued growth of female students. From 1972 to 1978, the number of women 25 years old and older attending college more than doubled (The National Center for Education Statistics, 1981). The latest data show that females are in the majority in higher education. As we have indicated frequently, females at various developmental stages present a different and, in many ways, a more complicated set of career guidance concerns than do males. The clientele of higher education is no exception.

Outcomes of Advanced Schooling

Most people choose higher education because they feel it will lead to worthwhile personal or monetary returns. However, it is very difficult to assess the outcome of advanced schooling. Despite some recent contrary reports in the mass media, it is reasonably clear that as a group, college graduates will earn significantly more than high school graduates. Yet it is not easy to partial out the influence on earnings of a college education considered apart from ability and other personal factors.

Smart (1986) has attempted to research this problem in a longitudinal study involving 4626 students. He was interested in determining what vocational outcomes could be ascribed to the cognitive attributes of the college attended (for example, how selective the college is), to the student's educational performance (academic integration within the institution and overall educational degree attainment), to affective attributes of the collegiate experience (such as social integration and college satisfaction), and to attendance at certain types of institutions (public versus private, large versus small, and so on). He determined that for *professional* career attainment, the major influencers are cognitive attributes of the college and students' educational performance and degree attainment, while for *nonprofessional* careers, affective attributes and attendance at private institutions were paramount as influencers. Thus, "the kind of undergraduate institutions that students attend and their performance and experiences in those institutions do influence the occupational attainment process. At the same time, social origins and precollege characteristics continue to exert a substantial influence on occupational status attainment, although in an indirect manner" (p. 93).

In summary, students in higher education are a heterogeneous group in terms of age and socioeconomic status, motivation for college attendance, and sophistication of career planning. Women and minorities are attending college in increasing numbers and present career concerns that require special attention. Diverse student cultures offer a framework within which to view and to understand the college population. Finally, the outcome of higher education suggests a payoff in terms of careers, although many of the reasons for that advantage may have relatively little to do with the collegiate experience itself.

PLANNING CONSIDERATIONS

Eli Ginzberg (1971) has suggested that higher education has been remiss in carrying out responsibility for career guidance. He states the following:

> We have seen that the college setting is not a sympathetic environment for the provision of educational and career guidance. The presumption is that when students encounter problems in these areas the faculty is available to counsel them. But most faculty members know little about the world beyond academe. They are generally able to assist prospective graduate students, but often cannot help undergraduates who plan to enter the world of work. Colleges still have to recognize and respond to the need of many students for career guidance as a contribution both to increasing the value of the educational experience as well as to facilitating later work adjustment.
>
> We have spoken earlier of the special problems of the community college. Thus it should suffice here to note that they, too, frequently neglect vocational guidance despite the fact that occupational training is probably the most important function they perform. Unfortunately, the prestige associated with an academic rather than a

> technically oriented program of studies has led many administrators and faculty to downgrade students in the latter track and to neglect their guidance needs. (p. 135)

Ginzberg is probably correct even today. As one searches the professional literature, one can discover few statements, until recently, relating to the provision in higher education of a comprehensive career guidance and counseling service. Placement, in the narrow brokerage sense of bringing employers and prospective employees together, has traditionally existed on most campuses. So, too, has the opportunity for contacts, whereby a professionally trained counselor assists a student to consider various career alternatives. These two activities—placement and limited individual career counseling—have historically existed as discrete pursuits on college campuses. Only recently has there been a movement toward combining the career planning and placement functions; only lately has the concept of programmatic, integrated, and systematic delivery of career guidance services in higher education become a visible phenomenon.

Institutional Commitment

The first planning consideration relating to the provision of career guidance and counseling in higher education involves *institutional commitment*. Two- and four-year colleges and universities must recognize the legitimacy of the career helping function as a bona fide part of the total higher educational enterprise. Further, these institutions must provide the trained labor and facilities necessary to effect the career guidance function.

There is evidence that institutions of higher education have made this commitment. Koehn's (1978) survey of the status of career-planning programs in California colleges indicates a great broadening from the simple broker role. Skills identification, values clarification, and speakers on the content of particular fields and job search skills were activities common at every institution. Credit-bearing career planning courses were offered at over 40 percent of the schools. About two-thirds offered sequential experiences at a somewhat less than course level. Still, problems existed including unpredictable attendance, staffing difficulties, space, lack of academic credit for courses, and general faculty ennui or, in some cases, antipathy. Further evidence comes from Reardon, Zunker, and Dyal (1979). Their survey of 302 institutions demonstrated the frequency of career planning programs and services shown in Table 10.1. In general, the larger the institution, the more varied the career services and the higher the career counselors' satisfaction with them.

Some go even further in expanding the old brokerage role beyond career planning and career counseling and advocate a complete amalgamation of counseling and placement on the college campus (Robb, 1979). As phrased by Chervenik, Nord, and Aldridge (1982),

> Career planning and placement are a wedded pair, interlocked and interrelated. The emphasis that may be given to one or the other depends on the operation's constituency, location, and direct assistance from employer representatives. In short, the objective of career services is to help students to understand the career planning and placement process, so that throughout life they will be prepared to cope with the inevitable changing situation: a future with jobs and circumstances unknown at this time. (p. 51)

Commitment of faculty, even with institutional commitment, remains a troublesome problem. There is still a sort of antivocationalism in many faculty who represent arts and sciences disciplines. No cure for this vexing condition has yet been discovered, but there is some evidence to suggest that faculty who are involved in in-service training for career guidance in higher education are more likely to infuse career concepts into their classrooms than are faculty who receive no special training (Ryan & Drummond, 1981).

A second planning consideration in higher education relates to the *immediacy* of students' career guidance needs. Procrastination, dilatory behaviors, and other delaying tactics in decision making become less attractive alternatives as the imminence of the real world intrudes into students' lives. The Scarlett O'Hara syndrome—"I'll think about it tomorrow"—produces an increasing sense of uneasiness; one's tomorrows become fewer as one approaches a choice of major field or a career. As the graduation rite of passage comes closer, most students receive intensified pressure from parents, relatives, friends, and others to specify career goals. A few short years ago, the student was being asked what he or she wanted to be "when you grow up." Now, grown up, the student can no longer have the luxury of responding with some vaguely conceived career goal. The problem is in the here and now, not in the long-range future.

Table 10.1

Frequency of Career Planning Programs and Services and Chi-Square Differences for Institutional Size

Activity	% Yes
1. Occupational Information	88
2. Resume Preparation	81
3. Interview Preparation	81
4. Educational Information	78
5. Individual Assessment Information	76[a]
6. Referral (Campus)	74
7. Referral (Community)	72[b]
8. Self Help Materials	71
9. Group Career Counseling	68
10. Faculty Consultation	61[b]
11. Testing	58
12. Resource Speakers	56
13. Advising Undeclared Majors	52
14. Decision-Making Training	51
15. Multimedia Materials	36[a]
16. Academic Advising	36
17. Orientation	35
18. Mini-Career Courses	33
19. Study Skills	30
20. Special Women's Programs	30[a]
21. Staff In-Service Training	30[b]
22. Assertiveness Training	39
23. Career Planning Course (Credit)	39
24. Career Planning Course (Noncredit)	29[a]
25. Card Catalogue (Cross Referenced)	28
26. Job Simulation	26
27. Employability Skills Training	26
28. Curriculum Infusion of Career Materials	19
29. High School Visitation	17
30. Faculty In-Service Training	16
31. Computer Assisted Guidance	11

[a] $p < .05$.
[b] $p < .01$.

This principle of immediacy affects delivery of services in times of tight budgets. Blocher and Rogers (1977) report that when limited funds caused a shortage of career helping personnel at George Mason University, a decision was made to concentrate priorities on services to seniors rather than on underclass students, since the needs of seniors were more immediate.

This concentration in the later years of college is indeed unfortunate, since Keller, Piotrowski, and Rabold (1990) concluded in their study of student needs that because many undergraduates make career choices early in college, career orientation and planning courses should commence in the first year of study and, prior to senior year, students should be exposed to job-seeking skills.

Third, in planning comprehensive career guidance programs in higher education, institutions should offer a *complete range of services*. Hale (1974) has proposed some useful distinctions among the types of career guidance services that should exist on a campus. *Career advising* is viewed as academic advisement by a faculty member, who translates career choices into educational goals and programs and relates academic curricula to career opportunities. *Career counseling* is perceived as psychological procedures used to assist students with self-evaluation and recognition of capabilities and interests. *Career planning* is seen as a process of relating the outcome of self-evaluation to information currently available about the world of work. These services should lead to an integrated, coordinated system that is composed of five elements: (1) a structured and comprehensive university-wide program of career education; (2) a central agency offering career information, career counseling, and career planning and placement in a one-stop service for students and academic advisors; (3) a cadre of specially qualified and prepared academic advisors selected from among faculty of the many subject disciplines; (4) a central administrator in academic affairs who can devote full-time to the supervision and coordination of the career education, counseling, and academic advisement system; and (5) a Commission on Academic Advisement and Counseling (for advisory and coordinating functions).

In summary, the primary planning considerations relating to the provision of career guidance and counseling in higher education include institutional commitment, responsiveness to immediate needs, and comprehensive, articulated delivery of services.

Another way to view planning is in terms of evaluation standards. In this regard, twenty-one professional associations combined to contribute to the Council for the Advancement of Standards for Student Services/Development Programs. This consortium of professional associations in higher education devised and published *Standards and Guidelines* (1985), a document that recommends criteria for evaluating all aspects of student services. One of the important functional components of the 16 considered is, of course, career planning and placement. In highly abbreviated form, their standards suggest the following:

Mission–Career planning is a developmental process and must be fostered during the entire period of a student's involvement with the institution.
The primary purpose of career planning and placement must be to aid students in developing, evaluating, and effectively initiating and implementing career plans.

Program–Career planning and placement services must offer the following programs:

1. Career counseling, which assists the students at any point in time to do the following:
   - Analyze interests, aptitudes, abilities, previous work experience, personal traits, and desired life-style to promote awareness of the interrelationship between self-knowledge and career choice
   - Obtain occupational information including, where possible, exploratory experiences such as cooperative education, internships, externships, and summer and part-time jobs
   - Make reasoned, well-informed career choices that are not based on race/sex stereotypes
   - Set short-range and long-range goals
2. Placement counseling and referral, which assists the student to do the following:
   - Clarify objectives and establish goals
   - Explore the full range of life and work possibilities including graduate and professional preparation
   - Prepare for the job search or further study
   - Present oneself effectively as a candidate for employment or further study
   - Make the transition from education to the world of work
3. Student employment, including part-time, vacation, and experiential education programs, which assist students in obtaining work experiences, financial resources, and/or the opportunity for academic credit

Organization and Administration–Career planning should be integrated with placement. Career planning and placement may be offered by a separate student services unit and may be offered by other student services or institutional units such as counseling centers, financial aid offices, and academic departments.

Human Resources–Professional staff members must be skilled in career planning, placement, and counseling, and must have the ability to function effectively with students, faculty, administrators, and employers.

Funding–Funds should be provided for adequate career/employment information, and for the preparation and maintenance of student placement credentials.

Facilities–Space for at least the following is recommended: reception area, staff offices, a private office for the unit head, interview and counseling rooms that allow privacy, employer lounge, student registration and sign-up area, career resource center, office equipment, bulletin boards, work areas, storage, filing, and rooms for group meetings and conferences.

Campus and Community Relations–The career planning and placement service must do the following:

Develop job opportunities on a continuing basis from a variety of employers

Provide all employers the opportunity to consider candidates for employment

Maximize students' exposure to employers through a variety of programs

Collect information on occupational trends and employers' needs

Encourage dialogue among employers, faculty, and administration concerning job needs and trends

Encourage employers to recognize career planning and placement services through public acknowledgment and/or other avenues of support

Develop a working relationship that encourages the academic administration and faculty to maximize and give support to an effective program for students and graduates

Promote better understanding between the institution and employers of the relationship of curricula and other activities to the career needs of and opportunities for students

Promote a systematic flow of information to faculty members and students from alumni concerning their academic preparation and employment experiences

Ethics–

Referral of an employed graduate to another employer must be preceded by that person's request for referral.

Career planning and placement office personnel must use their best efforts to ensure that the student's selection of a career or a graduate school is protected from improper influence by faculty, administrators, placement staff, and employers.

Conditions of employment and salary offers made to an individual by an employer must not be divulged in a personally identifiable form by career planning and placement office staff members.

Unless permission is given by the student, information disclosed in individual counseling sessions as well as information contained in records must remain confidential. (pp. 21–31)

These sorts of criteria are deceptively innocent at first glance; in fact, however, each presents a potentially volatile activity. For instance, the seemingly naive statement that career planning and placement should "provide all employers the opportunity to consider candidates for employment" gives no hint of the spirited debates and occasional confrontations that occur on campuses when organizations try to recruit who bar the employment of homosexuals or who represent activities loathsome to some (such as the military, industries that manufacture weaponry, businesses that trade with nations such as South Africa, and so on).

GOALS FOR CAREER GUIDANCE

Goals for career guidance in higher education should be such that all types of career concerns and needs are addressed. It is, therefore, unlikely that many students will require each of the outcomes that follow; however, almost all students in higher educational institutions could probably benefit from one or more. In a truly comprehensive career guidance program, provision will be made to achieve the following goals:

Assistance in the Selection of a Major Field of Study. A majority of freshmen will change their major field at least once during their collegiate experience. Indeed, this phenomenon is to be expected, for the first two years of study at most colleges and universities are so structured as to allow students to explore academic experiences. Each change of academic discipline entails a commensurate alteration in career planning to which career guidance should respond.

At South Dakota State University, for example, undeclared majors take a one-credit course in career planning and development and meet with an advisor at least twice each semester (Menning, 1981). The course allows them to explore various alternatives before declaring a major. For many college students, choice of major is tantamount to choosing a future vocation. Goodson (1978) has conducted research at Brigham Young University that suggests that in the chicken-egg type of relationship between choice of major and choice of occupation, the more career-oriented students choose an occupation first, whereas the less career-oriented students choose a major first. There is some evidence that the faculty adviser system produces few effective results in terms of student career decision making (Moore, 1976; Russel & Sullivan, 1979). Something more substantial is required. Finally, unique subgroups may have special concerns regarding selection of a major. Women are one such example (Gianakos & Subich, 1988).

Assistance in Self-Assessment and Self-Analysis. As we have repeatedly stated in this book, career planning presumes self-knowledge of several types. Reasonable career choices cannot be made by individuals who do not have a fairly clear notion of who they are, their strengths and weaknesses, what they value, their motivations, their psychological characteristics, and their interests. In short, students must be aided to discover both a personal and a vocational identity that can subsequently be related to the world of work.

Assistance in Understanding the World of Work. At the collegiate level, it is likely that most students will have a broad and basic understanding of the occupational structure. However, many students may need help in exploring specific segments of that structure in personally relevant terms (for example, What work is related to a given major? What is the employment outlook in a specific occupational field? What are the diverse opportunities available within a single chosen field?).

Assistance in Decision Making. Information, whether pertaining to the self or to some area external to the self (that is, career options), is of little use if it is not effectively processed. Such information must be translated into short-range and long-range career goals and then reality-tested. A personal plan must be developed that, ideally, is consistent with the information that one has gathered.

Assistance with Access to the World of Work. Placement, in a broad sense, is more than an attempt to dovetail students seeking employment with available jobs. It consists of an array of services designed to help students with access to the world of work. It ranges from the scheduling of students for on-campus recruitment interviews to the dissemination of placement folders to prospective employers; but it also entails assistance in developing student skills in selling oneself: resume preparation, interviewing behaviors, job-searching procedures, and so forth. In fact, in one survey of the needs of graduating students, four of the top five expressed needs related to these types of activities. They were writing a resume, finding graduate school and scholarship information, getting to graduate school, and conducting a job search (Gallagher & Scheuring, 1979).

Assistance in Meeting the Unique Needs of Various Subpopulations. Some identifiable segments of the college population present special concerns for the career counselor. Among these subpopulations are visible minorities (such as African-Americans, the disabled, Hispanics, Native Americans, certain Asians, older men and women, and so on) and less visible minorities (such as gay students). Campuses with relatively large proportions of distinct minorities may well wish to mount programs directed toward meeting the career guidance needs of such groups, insofar as these needs extend beyond "normal" boundaries (that is, coping personally and legally with discriminatory practices, locating specialized sources of assistance, and such). Another group that may require additional career aid is women. Chapter 5 in this volume deals with the unique career concerns of various minorities and women. Here we point out some examples of other types of collegiate groups that may need special attention.

As indicated earlier in this chapter, foreigners constitute a substantial number of students in American colleges and universities. Several observers (Walter-Samli & Samli, 1979; MacArthur, 1980) have pointed out that these students present specific career concerns. For instance, they study in America for so many years that they frequently are not aware of current career opportunities in their own home countries. Counselors need to be sensitized to their culturally engendered modes of coping with complex decision making. They need periodic reviews of progress and evaluations of the training to be sure that there are links to opportunities in their home countries. Preparation for reverse culture shock is another problem. Life-style, equipment, and role expectations will all be different from what they experienced in America. Some will expect the college or university to offer assistance in job placement at home. Foreign graduate students seem to have realistic career plans, but foreign undergraduate students frequently do not (Salimi & Hsi, 1977). These undergraduate students, therefore, present an even more intense need for career assistance. Finally, international students are more likely than American students to prefer help from faculty and counselors rather than from friends for various problems (Leong & Sedlacek, 1986), thus making them receptive to professional interventions.

Another college subpopulation with some unique career concerns is the adult student. Returning or first-time entrants to the college classroom are increasing, and there are those who argue that new and different career services are necessary for adults (Hitchcock, 1980). Others, however, maintain that modification of existing services is sufficient (Heppner & Olson, 1982). For example, the University of Missouri at Columbia responded by hiring older peer counselors, offering expanded hours for counseling, and providing in-service training in 13 areas, including such topics as the process a person goes through in returning to school, the process a person goes through in changing jobs or whole career fields, time and money management, issues faced by special groups, and the appropriateness or inappropriateness of various assessment tools for adults. College students over 28 years of age are more likely than younger students to be high achievers. Married women are more likely to achieve than unmarried women (Von der Embse & Childs, 1979). It is argued that adults' problem-solving orientation to learning and a desire to apply new knowledge immediately contribute to this higher academic achievement. Life experience and motivational factors seem to make adults more ready for learning and more open to career counseling. Some colleges offer a separate reentry course for these adults, especially women (Lance, Lourie, & Mayo, 1979; Levin, 1986; Flynn, Vanderpool, & Brown, 1989) and provide them with a designated counselor and other specific resources to meet their common needs.

A third subpopulation requiring a special type of career attention is the liberal arts student. Especially in an age of vocationalism, liberal arts majors may require different services from their more career-oriented counterparts. Several of the specific techniques for career interventions with these students are described later in this chapter. Because their needs are unique, specific sources of jobs for liberal arts students have been compiled (Zehring, 1979), and studies have concluded that liberal arts graduates do not face so terrible an employment prospect as many fear. Cappeto (1977), for example, traced the immediate and long-term employment prospects of undergraduate business majors versus liberal arts majors. He discovered that business graduates had a large advantage in terms of initial employment (for example, on graduation day, 75 percent of the business graduates had job offers as compared with 44 percent of social science graduates, 41 percent of humanities graduates, and 26 percent of science graduates). Within five months after graduation, however, employment differences were much less sharp: 2.17 percent of business graduates were unemployed compared with 4.19 percent of science graduates, 4.9 percent of social science graduates, and 9.52 percent of humanities graduates. Still, the problem of helping students to translate liberal arts education into employable skills is formidable and requires special effort. Some studies (Buescher, Johnston, Lucas, & Hughey, 1989) suggest that early intervention with liberal arts students is the key to helping them vocationally.

Yet another group that some believe should receive special attention in terms of career and personal counseling is the gifted college student. By definition, any student in college could be considered gifted, but Schroer and Dorn (1986) describe an intervention for 71 academically talented college students at Texas A&M University. Their program was a six-hour group effort in career counseling, utilizing the Career Motivation Program (CMP), a series of 10 structured activities exploring interests, values, strengths, and personality in a group-interactive context. "At the conclusion of the group experience, gifted men and women demonstrated significant positive change on Certainty of Career and Major, significantly less indecision, significantly less anxiety about choice, and significantly less difficulty in deciding about several attractive options" (p. 570). A similar program has been reported for gifted students at the Ohio State University (Gordon, 1983).

These are but four examples of specific collegiate subgroups that may require intensive effort by career counselors. The list of such groups could be expanded. Some colleges, for instance, pay special attention to the career needs of student athletes (Wittmer, Bostic, Phillips, & Waters, 1981). Others provide special career services for veterans, especially Viet Nam veterans.

SEQUENCING CAREER GUIDANCE EXPERIENCES

The primary thrust of this book is that career guidance experiences at every life stage should proceed in an orderly, systematic, sequenced, integrated, and articulated fashion in accordance with the common and unique needs of the particular clientele. Career guidance in higher education is no exception.

The first requisite in sequencing career guidance experiences in higher education is that activities either logically emanate from or fit into a theory of student development. For example, a systems approach, TRIPOD, has been instituted at Moravian College, Bethlehem, Pennsylvania, and is based on Holland's theory of career development (Kirts & Fischer, 1973). This approach provides sequenced phases of career assistance, beginning with self-assessment, progressing through an educational and occupational exposure phase, and culminating in training for job hunting techniques, evaluation of job opportunities, and interview-taking. The advantages of TRIPOD are precisely those to be gained from any systematic, developmental program:

1. It provides a sequential developmental process which facilitates the natural occurrence of vocational maturing.
2. It promotes increased self-awareness on the part of the student and helps him relate that awareness to the world of work.
3. It is designed to be operated in a way that produces minimal conflict with academic philosophies and functions, yet seeks to use the academic community as a vital and integral resource to aid the program.
4. It promotes a team approach involving both counseling and placement personnel, each with its own thrust and emphasis, yet bound together by common overall objectives.
5. It provides maximum flexibility in that students may take advantage of as many or as few activities as they deem necessary and as their time allows. Entering freshmen have the opportunity to fully utilize the entire program, but even seniors may participate to the extent that they can make an intelligent search into the job market.
6. It allows for academic planning on the part of students in a way that assists them in selecting courses of study that will better prepare them to meet their objectives. (p. 49)

A variation of the comprehensive program model may be found in the notion of modular service delivery. Abbott, McLean, and Davidshofer (1978) and Hageseth (1982) describe a two-session workshop format (50 minutes or less per session) in which activities are carefully structured and the subject matter is restricted to a single theme. At Virginia Commonwealth University, these modules are conducted by graduate students. Modules include workshops on life planning, vocational exploration, decision making, and choice implementation.

The point with all systematic programs is that each stage builds on a previous stage to ensure comprehensive interventions. Simultaneously, a student may enter at any stage of self-perceived or counselor-perceived need. Finally, all segments of the career-helping community have clearly delineated responsibilities in order to minimize the possibility of fragmented services.

EXAMPLES OF PROGRAM CONTENT

Basically, colleges and universities have used four major approaches to deliver career guidance: (1) courses, workshops, and seminars that offer structured group experiences in career planning; (2) group counseling activities that are generally less structured and emphasize broader, more affective aspects of human and career development; (3) individual counseling opportunities that accentuate diverse theoretical orientations to career concerns; and (4) placement programs that culminate the career planning and decision-making process.

Courses, Workshops, and Seminars

An increasingly popular career guidance delivery mode is the structured group experience in the form of a course, workshop, or seminar. At Dickinson College, Carlisle, Pennsylvania, the PATH Program was devised to assist liberal arts students to relate their studies to career alternatives, to recognize the marketable skills they possess, and to provide a framework for future job-hunting (Figler, 1973). Presumably, liberal arts students have developed communication skills and a breadth of viewpoint in problem solving; but these skills must be related to the job market. The PATH Program attempts to help liberal arts students to dovetail their skills and the world of work by exposing them to four group sessions of approximately 90 minutes each. These sessions are conducted with certain ground rules;

1. Imagine that your vocational future is completely open. Make no prior assumptions about your vocational goals or inclinations.
2. Try not to censor your responses to the exercises. You will not be forced to disclose anything that you would prefer to keep to yourself.
3. Job labels are to be treated as just symbols, within which you can move around and create your own type of work experience.
4. The objective is to create your own vocation, weaving it together like a patchwork quilt, from the many different things you like to do.
5. The expectation of this program is *not* that you will have a clear, final idea of what you want to do when the program is completed.
6. This program can be used and reused at any of several times in your life. (p. 48)

In Session I, students are exposed to structured exercises that focus on the Present Self. These include a discussion of childhood fantasies, a listing of things one likes to do, and a description of both achievements and failures with emphasis on the personal qualities or traits that contributed to each successful or unsuccessful outcome. Session II emphasizes the Future Self. Students respond to the question, Who will you be? in as many as 10 different ways, both vocational and nonvocational. They discuss an ideal vocation and summarize antivocations; in other words, they consider both points of personal attraction and repulsion in future work. Session III is devoted to Self-Assessment. The stress is on the relationship of major field of study to career possibilities, along with a self-inventory of abilities, personal traits, and satisfactions. Finally, participants are asked to review occupational literature and to tentatively choose four occupational titles that seem most attractive. Session IV emphasizes an Evaluation of Occupations. Occupations are considered one at a time in relation to abilities, personal traits, and satisfactions rated on a 10 point scale. Each student compares his or her ideal occupation developed in Session II with the occupations evolved in the later sessions.

At Cornell University, female students took a course entitled Career Environment and Individual Development (Babcock & Kaufman, 1976). This credit-bearing course met seven weeks, once a week, for two hours. The primary focus was the relationship between careers and individual behavior. To accomplish this end, value clarification exercises were employed, and students were taught decision-making methods, theories of occupational choice, job satisfaction factors, sources of occupational information, workpower projections, and techniques of career planning. Large- and small-group discussions were frequent, and videotapes were used. Assignments included reading an interview with a worker in a chosen occupation, "shadowing" a person at work, keeping a decision-making diary, and writing a final paper on personal career plans. Students who took the course were matched with comparable samples who had received individual counseling and with a no-counseling control group. The course was more effective than individual counseling and no-counseling in facilitating the career development of women as measured by Super's Career Development Inventory and by Graff and MacLean's Counseling Assessment Form.

1. Students in the class showed a significantly greater gain on self-knowledge and the relation of that knowledge to occupations than did students in the other groups.
2. Students in the class reported having engaged in a greater number of planning activities to become informed about careers than did the students in the other groups.
3. Students in both the class and the walk-in (counseling) groups reported greater gains in changes in expressed occupational choice than did the students in the control group.
4. Students in the walk-in group reported much assistance in interviewing techniques and writing resumes and cover letters; students in the class reported no assistance in these areas.
5. Students in class reported much assistance in making a comprehensive self-appraisal but the walk-in group reported little or no assistance in that area. (p. 265)

The authors concluded that "a systematic learning experience structured around values clarification strategies, decision-making exercises, and readings and discussions on job satisfaction and workpower projections can be employed effectively in a college setting as a model for facilitating students' vocational development" (p. 265).

In another study comparing the effectiveness of various career guidance delivery modes, Smith and Evans (1973) confirmed the superiority of a structured career guidance program over individual counseling and no-counseling in increasing the career development of students. Meeting once a week for five consecutive weeks, students convened in large and small groups to focus on decision making, values, interests, behavioral traits, and social influences. The individual counseling consisted of two to four sessions and included test interpretations and discussions of values and decision making. A control group received no treatment. The authors concluded that a systematic learning experience structured around a strategy for decision making can be effectively employed in a college setting to facilitate career development.

These courses, seminars, and workshops are illustrative of those prolific in higher education. Each, in its own way, seeks to bring a systematic order to the often chaotic process of career planning. For further information on such structured group experiences see Cochran, Hetherington, and Strand (1980); Crouse and Weiss (1984); Garis & Hess (1989); Garis & Niles (1990); Gordon and Grites (1984); Henley (1986); Jones, Gorman, & Schroeder (1989); Quinn & Lewis (1989); Schrank (1982); and Sherry and Staley (1984).

Group Counseling

The distinction between group counseling and more structured group guidance activities is frequently subtle, and the boundaries between the two are often obfuscated. Traditionally, group counseling has involved less formal structure, more affect, and greater utilization of the resources of group members. However, attempts at group counseling with a career focus in higher education often combine both structure and relative nonstructure, as the following examples of group counseling efforts illustrate.

Pickering and Vacc (1984) reviewed 47 research articles in refereed journals between 1975 and 1981 that addressed the effectiveness of career development interventions for college students and reached several conclusions. Although their method of analysis is relatively crude when compared with more sophisticated metanalytic procedures, there is little reason to believe that other statistical techniques or approaches would produce contrary results. Among their findings were the following:

- More than half of the studies were reports of short-term interventions, 79 percent of which reported positive gains.
- About one-quarter of the reported programs were self-help interventions, with 67 percent of these demonstrating improvement.
- About another one-quarter were long-term (such as career courses) and 93 percent reported success.
- A few studies compared methods; in all, 79 percent of the studies reported positive gains or differences between treatments.
- The most frequently utilized outcome variables were career maturity and decision-making skills.
- The most common personality variables investigated were anxiety, locus of control, and self-concept.
- A majority of the interventions used behavioral interview techniques; trait and factor was the next most popular orientation.

The general conclusion was that "short-term interventions, designed to facilitate career maturity and the development of decision-making skills through a behavioral orientation, have been most widely used, and their effectiveness has been supported. Ideally, a comprehensive program consisting of self-help, short-term, and long-term (course) interventions should be available to students for their career development needs" (p. 156).

Davis and Horne (1986) compared the effectiveness of small-group counseling and a career course on the career decidedness and maturity of students at a mid-western university. The course met three times per week (50 minutes) for a 16-week semester and contained 16 to 19 students per section. It combined lectures on educational and career topics, a text, testing, guest speakers, homework, and discussion. The small-group treatment met for 12 sessions of one hour each and consisted of 12 members per group. Each session was loosely structured and emphasized group interaction, discussion, feedback, and sharing. There was no reading, tests, or homework. Using the Career Decision Scale (CDS) and the Career Maturity Inventory (CMI) as outcome measures, Davis and Horne found that both types of groups were effective in decreasing undecidedness and increasing maturity and that there were no significant differences between the two treatments.

Other group counseling of a career nature has emphasized one theoretical orientation or another. For example, Kurtz (1974) describes the use of a Transactional Analysis format in vocational group counseling.

There have been many comparisons regarding the relative career helping effectiveness of structured group experiences versus more counseling-oriented groups. A study by Perovich and Mierzwa (1980) is typical of the design and results of this type of research. They compared Vocational Information Groups (VIG) to Self-Growth Groups (SGG) to Control Groups (CG). VIGs in eight work sessions considered eight specific content areas for which vocational information was provided in a group context that allowed group member interaction (such as career development, strategies for employment, decision-making skills, sex-role stereotypes). The SGGs were aimed at self-growth through greater self-understanding by means of encounter with other group members; FIRO-B techniques were used as a starting point; T group techniques were employed for the remainder of the eight work sessions. The control group received no treatment. With the VIG, college students achieved desirable gains in vocational maturity, planning awareness, and self-esteem, and there were no sex differences. With the SGG, vocational maturity increased but not self-esteem or planning awareness. Both types of groups achieved results significantly better than the control group. The conclusion is that a structured group experience is preferable in meeting the vocational needs of college students.

Robbins and Tucker (1986) provide an example of a more sophisticated investigation of the effects of workshops in that they attempt to account for differences in client attributes in relation to outcomes. In this case, they studied the relation of goal instability (a general instability or absence of orienting goals) to self-directed and interactional career counseling workshops at the University of Maryland. Outcome measures were career information-seeking, career maturity, and satisfaction with the workshop. The self-directed intervention consisted of three two-hour sessions and emphasized self-directed and individualized problem solving (for example, information gathering and self-reflection, various exercises, Holland's Self-Directed Search). The interactional intervention also was comprised of three two-hour sessions, but the leaders emphasized group interaction and self-disclosure (which they, themselves, modeled). The results indicated that individuals with high goal instability did better on the criteria when they were in interactional rather than in self-directed workshop formats. Further, participants seemed to consistently prefer the interactional workshop. The researchers conclude that an "emphasis on leader modeling and participant self-disclosure can boost the effects of information-oriented interventions for high and low goal instability people alike" and ". . . that matching personality types with treatment strategy increases the outcomes of career intervention workshops" (p. 422).

Individual Counseling

It is probably fair to say that most individual counseling of a career nature in higher education (at least in the past) has been of the "test 'em and tell 'em" variety. Although continuing to recognize the importance of human assessment as a requisite to career planning and decision making, most modern counselors are placing increased emphasis on the importance of value clarification and the recognition of total life patterns in the counseling process. The trait-and-factor orientation that so long has dominated individual career counseling is still prevalent, but it has been supplemented by a consideration of the total life goals, commitments, and values of the individual.

The number of individual career counseling sessions and the sophistication of the counselor appear to have little effect on a student's gaining an increased certainty of career choice. Ullrich (1973) has demonstrated that students report an increased certainty of career choice whether seen for only two interviews or more frequently and whether the counselor is experienced or inexperienced. Satisfaction with that career choice, however, was not increased as a result of counseling. It appears that most students who seek individual career counseling are experiencing some discomfort with their situation.

Allied to the counseling strategy for the delivery of career guidance in higher education is consultation. Conyne and Cochran (1973) have noted the influence of faculty members on the career development of students and have suggested an outreach consultation strategy for influencing the academic press of an institution in the service of career development. To accomplish this goal, the career development specialist both acquires information from faculty and disseminates information to them.

Cooper (1986) compared the effects of group and individual vocational counseling on career indecision and personal indecisiveness. Both group and individual counseling were judged to be successful in reducing career indecision and personal indecisiveness.

The foci for career counseling at the collegiate level are indeed broad. One example is that of early dual-career couples. Almost one in five college students is married. On the assumption that many of these couples may be experiencing marital difficulty as a result of enacting dual roles of student and spouse (for instance, diversity of goals, strong achievement needs of both individuals, demanding schedules, and multiple-role responsibilities), Houser, Konstam, and Ham (1990) investigated coping strategies that are related to marital adjustment. They found that unsuccessful techniques for couples were confrontive coping (aggressive efforts to alter the situation) and escape-avoidance (wishful thinking and trying to avoid situations that are stressful). For men, distancing also was not a very useful coping strategy. The authors suggest that "counselors in college counseling centers can potentially increase their effectiveness by identifying the coping strategies used by married couples who seek counseling and facilitate the acquisition of knowledge of alternative coping patterns that lead to greater marital adjustment. Furthermore, counselors can use coping skills training to increase adaptive mutual coping strategies for couples" (p. 329).

Rotberg, Brown, and Ware (1987) studied community college students and tentatively concluded that career choice is "influenced by both career interest and career self-efficacy expectations, which are themselves modified by gender and sex role orientations" (p. 166). The question for counselors thus becomes not only what *are* a person's aptitudes and interests, but also how do people themselves *view* their ability to perform the tasks of various occupations. Thus, their self-efficacy may require change to become more consonant with reality, and this focus would represent a further reason for counseling.

Peer Counseling

One development that is apparently gaining in popularity on the college campus is the use of peer counselors. Ash and Mandelbaum (1982), Knierian and Stiffler (1979), and Zehring (1976) have advocated the effective use of peers in career counseling to supplement understaffed programs. Such paraprofessionals, it is argued, have a natural rapport with their peers and can be trained to perform the more rudimentary tasks attendant to counseling. One interesting side effect is that professional staff evidently are stimulated by the enthusiasm of the peer counselors.

Kenzler (1983) has pointed out that peer counselors, with training, can handle initial assessment interviews and provide general job-search assistance. In such matters, they can be very effective. For example, Pickering (1986) compared three methods of career planning for liberal arts majors: career counselors, peer tutors, and self-study. All treatments were accomplished by means of groups, and sessions met six times for 60 to 90 minutes, focusing on Figler's PATH, which contains 18 individual exercises. Criterion measures were Crites' Career Maturity Inventory and an examination on PATH. No significant differences in treatment were discerned, and all groups gained. The investigator concluded that structured career planning using tutors was effective. It should be recalled, however, that no deeper counseling was considered.

These brief examples have been presented to illustrate that individual career counseling should take into account the whole person and an individual's given need at a specified developmental time. There is little evidence that any theoretical counseling orientation is superior to any other in the totality of career counseling. Techniques from a given school of counseling may be appropriate for certain types of career counseling (such as behavioral for increasing information-seeking behaviors) and techniques from another orientation for other types of career counseling (such as "insight" counseling for self-awareness and understanding). Individual career counseling appears to be effective in achieving a variety of desirable outcomes (for example, anxiety reduction, increasing certainty of career choice, decision making, and so on); however, as noted previously in this chapter, group methods have been demonstrated to be at least as effective in achieving certain types of career-related outcomes.

Although over two decades old, the types of career counseling described by Morrill and Forrest (1970) still represent an appropriate descriptive continuum.

Type 1.–Counseling that aids the client with a specific decision by providing information and clarification of issues

Type 2.–Counseling that aids the client with a specific decision by focusing on decision-making skills rather than only on the decision at hand. This has application for the specific situation as well as later choice points

Type 3.–Counseling that views career as a process rather than an end-point toward which all decisions lead. Thus, the focus changes from the objective of making the correct ultimate choice and once-and-for-all pronouncement of identity to the process of making a continual series of choices

Type 4.–Career process counseling that focuses on creating in the individual the ability to utilize his personal attributes to achieve self-determined objectives and to *influence* the nature of future choices rather than merely adapt to external pressures. (p. 301)

They propose that career counseling should be consonant with the developmental process. The focus should be narrow when only a specific decision in the developmental process is being considered and broad when the concern is the individual in relation to his or her career process.

Placement

In the early days of higher education in America, the placement function was largely carried out through the old-boy network. Mentors helped their students to get jobs. Over the years, a formal placement structure evolved. Over two decades ago, Thomas (1966) surveyed 82 placement offices at colleges and universities throughout the country in order to determine the purposes to which these offices directed themselves. On the average, the following seven goals emerged in rank order:

1. To assist students in the investigation of career opportunities
2. To assist in the fulfillment of the purposes of the university
3. To maintain liaison between the university and employers of its products
4. To assist alumni in matters pertaining to employment opportunities
5. To provide part-time, temporary, and/or summer student placement services
6. To act in a public relations capacity
7. To perform research in areas related to placement activity (p. 87)

These purposes still exist; however, increased attention is being afforded the career planning function. What used to be almost purely employment counseling is now expanded to career counseling in most college and university placement settings. To be sure, placement offices are still repositories of both occupational information and employer information, are a vehicle for bringing together industrial, business, and educational recruiters with student and alumni job-seekers, and are dispensers of student and alumni career dossiers to potential employers. But many placement offices are offering a broader array of career guidance and counseling services. In addition to increased career planning with individual students, placement offices are keeping academic departments aware of changes in particular labor markets, offering orientation to the world of work programs, and enacting other structured group experiences to produce better work-world citizens. In short, the days are gone on most campuses of simply posting job openings and scheduling recruiters.

A survey of the effectiveness of placement offices at 50 business schools presents a good-news/bad-news finding regarding how effective they were in meeting student needs (Landau, Somers, & Amoss, 1984). Landau et al. found that these centers were perceived by students as effective in supplying information about career alternatives and assisting them in finding their first job. They got high ratings for providing career counseling, job-search advice, campus recruiting programs, and preparation for job interviews. On the other hand, these career centers were perceived as lacking in a number of areas. One was their apparent failure to provide students with a realistic picture of the world of work. Another was their lack of success in helping graduates cope beyond the first job. They also were taken to task for not helping graduates deal with personal and professional conflicts, especially those of dual-career couples. Finally, they were not regarded as effective in preparing graduates for job and career changes. In one sense, what they were doing well was the old, narrow notion of placement; what they were not doing well is the newer, life-style idea of career helping.

Placement-type activities in colleges include the preparation of manuals to help students in the job-search process (O'Neil & Heck, 1980), alumni panels (Cherichello & Gillian, 1980; Sampson, 1980), assisting with the graduate school application process (Marshall, 1979), public relations activities (Dwight, 1979), informational interviewing of employers (Boll & Briggs, 1979), and interchanges with business and industry (Lamb, 1980; Ottke & Brogden, 1990). One interesting study in this latter realm was conducted by Ducat (1980) who investigated the effects of cooperative education placements on the career exploration and occupational self-concepts of community college students. She discovered that the internship experience seems to activate uncertainty that stimulates vocational exploratory behavior and ultimately leads to a more favorable view of self. In short, cooperative internships may be better laboratories than the classroom for enhancing vocational exploratory behavior and self-perceptions.

Arp, Holmberg, and Littrell (1986) describe a six-session structured job-search support group for adult students at Iowa State University. In the first session, emphasis was placed on participants' developing an awareness of internal barriers to their job search and setting short-term goals to remove barriers. Session two was devoted to skill assessment. During session three, the focus was on conducting informational interviews, establishing networks, and using library resources on employment to encourage awareness of job opportunities. Session four emphasized successful ways of finding employment. The penultimate session concentrated on résumé writing. The final session dealt with employment interviews.

Related to the placement function, Figler (1978) has delineated 20 generic life skills in five categories that individuals should use when they conduct a career search. Counselors can also use this skills inventory to diagnose client deficiencies. Thus, the skills inventory can serve as a needs assessment.

Self-Assessment Skills

1. identifying and clarifying one's *values*
2. sensitivity to one's *feelings*
3. indentifying one's *skills*
4. *creativity* in imagining new career possibilities
5. recognizing extent of one's *risk-taking* proclivities
6. translating self-assessment into action by *goal-setting*

Detective Skills

7. building a *prospect list* of people, organizations, and so on
8. learning how to create contacts through a *personal referral network*
9. taking initiatives in the search process through *assertiveness*

Research Skills

10. using available *printed materials*
11. obtaining information from people in careers as an *inquiring reporter*
12. gathering data about a field or employer through *participant observation*

Communication Skills

13. gathering information by effective *listening*
14. encouraging people to talk by *questioning*
15. expressing oneself with *self-disclosure*
16. communicating through *writing*

Transition Skills

17. involving others as a *support group*
18. selling oneself through *self-marketing*
19. preparing to move to a target area through *long distance*
20. surviving financially through an *interim job*

This is a typical array of job-seeking skills, job survival skills, job-advancement skills, and the like. Aspects of these important skill areas are addressed throughout this book. At this juncture, however, we would note that how-to books on these skills represent an obvious growth industry and that writing them provides employment for many people.

These books have certain common elements. The writing is typically of the "selling" genre and leans heavily on metaphor and alliteration. The message is intended to be inspirational and uplifting, almost a homily on the need for faith and endurance in the process. The advice is slanted toward assertive, aggressive selling of a product—oneself. Not infrequently, the book is addressed to some specific segment of the population (women, business types, redundant workers, and so forth).

At the present time, the best that can be said about these books is that they do not seem to do any harm. As far as we know, there has not been a published study that demonstrates the superiority of any of these methods over hit-and-miss efforts or over any other of these methods. We recommend none of them; we recommend all of them.

One of the problems to be overcome in the provision of career guidance and counseling in higher education is the potential destructiveness of "territorial imperative" thinking. As higher education has increasingly accepted its role in enhancing the career development of students, various campus bailiwicks of helpers have staked claim to the career assistance function—placement, counseling, and advisement offices; academic departments; and units directed at specific subpopulations in academe (such as minority programs). This compartmentalization has the potential of producing a fragmented, piecemeal, hit-or-miss, redundant provision of services or of resulting in a coordinated, comprehensive, integrated program. Care should clearly be taken to ensure the latter outcome.

CAREER GUIDANCE TECHNIQUES

In addition to the techniques previously described in this chapter, the following procedures and ideas illustrate the types of activities that can be used in the career guidance and counseling of college students.

- Arrange seminars involving recruiters and faculty in various allied fields.
- Set up internship programs to provide field experiences in subject matter disciplines.
- Role-play job interviews and videotape them for student feedback.
- Have students interview individuals currently working in their field of interest.
- Videotape recruiters and amass a library of such tapes for student viewing on demand.
- Administer personality assessment instruments and provide group and/or individual interpretation (such as Eysenck Personality Inventory, Edwards Personal Preference Schedule, Omnibus Personality Inventory, and so on).
- Conduct a credit-bearing or credit-free course or seminar on general or specific aspects of career planning.
- Administer various interest inventories and provide group or individual interpretation (such as Strong Vocational Interest Inventory, Kuder Form DD, and so on).
- Develop shadowing programs to enable students to experience real day-to-day work situations.
- Have students study Roe's field and level occupational classification system.
- Administer various career planning forms and discuss the results (such as Self-Directed Search, Career Key, Career Navigator, and Programmed Guide to Career Decision-Making).
- Teach the use of the *Dictionary of Occupational Titles* and the *Occupational Outlook Handbook*.
- Administer and interpret various career development or career maturity inventories (such as Super's Career Development Inventory, Crites Career Maturity Inventory, and so on).
- Arrange faculty-staff panels to talk about curriculum and careers in their fields.
- Conduct values clarification exercises as they relate to career planning and decision making.
- Arrange student panels composed of various majors to talk about their studies and aspects of making a decision about a major.
- Devise illustrative case study materials for use as a stimulus in career group guidance.
- Have individuals in a group present themselves as "cases" to the other group members.
- Use status rankings of occupations as a discussion vehicle.
- Use the residence halls, the student union, and other areas as outreach career guidance possibilities.
- Set up mobile career information units (such as vans) and circulate around the campus.
- Locate jukeboxes, tape machines, VCR's, computers, or other media in high traffic locations around the campus to disseminate curricular and career information.
- Establish career information libraries or resource centers in libraries, unions, residence halls, and so on.
- Utilize electronic bulletin boards to disseminate career information
- Utilize the campus radio or TV stations for a regularly scheduled career program.
- Have a regularly appearing career planning column in the student newspaper.
- Organize cooperative work programs for students in various courses.
- Integrate a career planning unit within an existing academic course (such as Speech, any introductory course).
- Establish a computer-based academic advisement or career guidance system.

- Engage in in-service, updating workshops with faculty advisors.
- Have students write vocationally relevant autobiographies.
- Use films and filmstrips to stimulate discussions.
- Teach students to write a résumé and have them write their own résumé.
- Engage in decision-making simulation and gaming activities (such as those in *Women and Deciding*).
- Have students engage in individual study of an occupation or an occupational field.
- Have students take a job satisfaction inventory and discuss the results.
- Directly teach theories of career development or theories of career decision making.
- Show the film *Future Shock* and discuss the implications for career planning.
- Study the occupational structure according to one or more classifications (such as industrial, census, Holland, cluster).
- Use the "Looking Ahead to a Career" slides to acquaint students with current and future labor power needs (available from the National Audiovisual Center, Washington, D.C., 20409).
- Have students conduct a career-related project as part of an academic course requirement.

Summary

In this chapter, we have considered characteristics of students in higher education as they relate to career planning and decision making. Interventions designed to assist students with career concerns have been discussed. Guidelines were offered relating to the effective and efficient delivery of career guidance services. If students were exposed to the type of career-related interventions described in earlier chapters of this volume, the need for such intensive career assistance at the collegiate level would probably be lessened. Currently, however, the higher educational setting is replete with students who have career problems to which career helpers must respond.

CHAPTER 11

CAREER COUNSELING IN THE WORKPLACE

Key Concepts

- Both remedial and developmental functions of career counseling are important in the workplace.
- Adjustment in the workplace affects life adjustments.
- Human resources management, employee assistance programs, and career development in organizations are descriptions of major activities that include career counseling in the workplace.
- Work organizations create career patterns for their employees that may differ in timing and in substance from setting to setting.
- Career counselors working in business and industry engage in some functions that are different from those of career counselors employed in schools or colleges and universities, requiring them to understand both individual career development and organizational development.
- An important component of career development in the workplace is the recognition and management of occupational stress.

This chapter concentrates on the types of career counseling activities taking place in the diverse organizational structures that constitute the workplace—stores, factories, laboratories, offices, agencies, and other institutions—in which people vocationally function. The principles pertaining to both remedial and developmental functions described in earlier chapters can be put to use in the workplace. The career function is broadened somewhat to include a wider array of functions, such as those typically found in employee assistance programs. In addition, we offer a discussion of one of the most endemic problems of modern times—work stress.

WORK ADJUSTMENT AND PERSONAL ADJUSTMENT

Throughout this volume, we have emphasized the central place of work in life. Personal adjustmemt and work adjustment appear to exist in a symbiotic relationship. Underwood and Hardy (1985), for example, studied 923 nonprofessional, nonmanagerial workers to determine the relationship between personal and vocational adjustment. The relationship was significant, with poorly-adjusted individuals being poorly-adjusted workers and well-adjusted individuals being well-adjusted workers. They concluded that vocational adjustment appears to be a specific aspect of personal adjustment, although it would be possible to conclude that work adjustment affects life adjustment. We are all familiar with the worker who has a bad day on the job and comes home to exhibit the kick-the-dog syndrome—transferring to those in the immediate home environment the anger and the frustration of unhappiness at work.

When we are at work, it becomes a center of intense feelings and beliefs. We are just now beginning to study the interrelationships between work and leisure that increase or decrease career salience and other values. Lounsbury and Hoopes (1986), for instance, investigated the effects of vacations on such variables as job involvement, life satisfaction, and turnover intention in a group of 128 employees in technical, administrative, clerical, and service jobs. They did so by taking measures one week prior to a vacation and one week following a vacation. Their primary finding was that the relative salience of nonwork domains increased and work domains decreased after the vacation.

Walter Neff (1985) states that there are three primary life domains—work, love, and play. In Chapter 2, we presented Neff's speculations regarding five types of inadequate or maladjusted work personalities. To these we might add several others. For example, it might be argued that the so-called *workaholic* has concentrated on work to the exclusion of love and play in his or her life. The compulsivity of work consumes this person's life; work is taken home (such as it is) constantly, the person feels guilty if not working, works very long hours, is uneasy with leisure, cannot relax, and is unable to engage happily in any activity except work (Spruell, 1987). It has yet to be determined when work ceases to be merely high career salience and becomes pathological. When does career commitment become an obsession and a compulsion? Naughton (1987) suggests that the true workaholic is a person who is high in both job involvement *and* compulsive behavior. Thus, workaholism as a characteristic of committed persons would be viewed as nonpathological while workaholism as a compulsion would be viewed as maladaptive behavior.

This discussion emphasizes a recurrent theme in this book—the central place of work in the lives of most adults. Consequently, the workplace becomes an environment in which both positive and negative, healthy and unhealthy, good and bad outcomes are stimulated. There are those who believe that the workplace is the proper setting for facilitating positive outcomes and preventing negative outcomes. Based on a variety of motivations, career interventions in the workplace are becoming more observable.

The Rise in Interest

One of the fastest growing opportunities for career assisting is that pertaining to business and industry in its broadest sense. Fast growing, however, does not mean common. Two surveys of the extent of career development activities in corporations, for example, demonstrate that the movement is, at best, incipient. A. R. Griffith (1980) received responses from 118 of the Fortune 500 companies from which he solicited information. He concluded that less than 25 percent of workers in the 118 responding corporations were being reached by career development services. These services included the ones shown as Table 11.1.

In a more comprehensive study, Walker and Gutteridge (1979) report on career planning practices in 225 of the 1117 firms they surveyed. Their results (Table 11.2) indicate that career planning practices in industry are more informal than systematic.

Other surveys (Abdelnour & Hall, 1980; Cairo, 1983; Griffith, 1981; Portwood & Granrose, 1986; Levine 1985; Gutteridge & Otte, 1983) report similar stirrings within organizations, both private and public. Many of these surveys are unsophisticated in construction and analysis, are based on inadequate samples, and are atheoretical. Nevertheless, they do demonstrate that career development in the workplace is receiving increased attention and thought. In some ways the current state of the literature pertaining to career planning in organizations is reminiscent of the writing and research related to the condition of school counseling in the late 1950s and early 1960s—role studies, suggestions, reports of tentative programs, recommendations for practice, rudimentary attempts to link theory with

Table 11.1

Rank of Career Development Services Offered by 118 Corporations to All Employees by Frequency

Rank	Service	Frequency n (%)	Median Years Offered
1	Support for external training	98 (83.1)	8
2	Alcohol/drug counseling	67 (56.8)	6
3	Retirement planning	66 (55.9)	5
4	Support groups for minorities/women	56 (47.5)	4
5	Job separation counseling	51 (43.2)	6
6	Career exploration	35 (29.7)	3
7	Career ladders	25 (21.2)	3.5
8	Teaching of advancement strategies	17 (14.4)	2
9.5	Personal financial planning	12 (10.2)	3
9.5	Family/marital counseling	12 (10.2)	2

Source: Reprinted from "A Survey of Career Development in Corporations" by A. R. Griffith, *Personnel and Guidance Journal,* April 1980, pp. 537–543, table, p. 540. ©AACD. Reprinted with permission. No further reproduction authorized without written permission of American Association for Counseling and Development.

practice, and very little empirical or evaluative research.

Why the increased attention? It would be pleasant to report that corporate America is motivated by humanistic concerns to let employees become all they are capable of being. Alas, that is probably not the case, although certainly every company gives the idea lip service. In fact, a variety of pressures external to the workplace and a growing recognition that good career management is also "good business" have led to the enhanced emphasis on career planning and development. Equal employment opportunity enforcement, union bargaining for career ladders, shortages of certain specialized personnel, and other pressures on organizations have combined to cause extant, narrowly defined programs to expand or to goad companies into establishing initial programs. Employee health care costs and increasing litigation by employees against their companies also are factors. Of course, the serendipitous byproduct of inaugurating a program to foster organizational development is that the individual, too, benefits. Hill (1985) reports that over the past decade, attitude surveys of employees at a major oil company state that a lack of career counseling is their predominant concern at all levels of the organization.

Work life is basically an arena in which various types of conflict are likely to occur at all occupational levels. The solution to many conflicts in the workplace is probably best applied in the setting in which they occur. Safety and health hazards, and hazards stemming from threatening interactions on the job (such as police work) can be addressed in the setting from which they arise. Factors such as work overload, work underload, working conditions, changing causes of stress throughout an individual's work life (Cooper & Marshall, 1980), supervision problems, role ambiguity and conflict, and other problems of work are addressed throughout this volume. In the most pessimistic manner possible, Williams (1980) points out the stressors pre-

Table 11.2

Career Planning Practices[a]

Practice	Doing	Planning	Discontinued	Never Done
Informal counseling by personnel staff (n = 222)	197 (88.7%)	11 (5.0%)	1 (0.5%)	13 (5.9%)
Career counseling by supervisors (n = 217)	121 (55.8%)	38 (17.5%)	0	58 (26.7%)
Workshops on interpersonal relationships (n = 213)	104 (48.8%)	26 (12.2%)	5 (2.3%)	78 (36.6%)
Job performance and development planning workshops (n = 210)	89 (42.4%)	46 (21.9%)	0	75 (35.7%)
Outplacement counseling/ related services (n = 212)	79 (37.3%)	4 (1.9%)	4 (1.9%)	125 (59.0%)
Psychological testing and assessment (n = 211)	74 (35.1%)	17 (8.0%)	40 (19.0%)	80 (37.9%)
Workshops and communications on retirement preparation (n = 212)	71 (33.5%)	51 (24.1%)	0	90 (42.5%)
Testing and feedback regarding aptitudes, interests, etc. (n = 208)	68 (32.7%)	20 (9.6%)	28 (13.5%)	92 (44.2%)
Referrals to external counselors and resources (n = 209)	61 (29.2%)	8 (3.8%)	8 (3.8%)	132 (63.2%)
Training of supervisors in career counseling (n = 212)	53 (25.0%)	67 (31.6%)	2 (0.9%)	90 (42.5%)
Career counseling by specialized staff counselors (n = 210)	43 (20.5%)	16 (7.6%)	2 (1.0%)	149 (71.%)
Individual self-analysis and planning (n = 211)	33 (15.6%)	39 (18.5%)	2 (0.9%)	137 (64.9%)
Assessment centers for career development purposes (n = 213)	31 (14.6%)	37 (17.4%)	8 (3.8%)	137 (64.3%)
Life and career planning workshops (n = 210)	24 (11.4%)	36 (17.1%)	2 (1.0%)	148 (70.5%)

[a] Bases of percentages vary with responses. Nonresponses are excluded from percentage calculations.

Reprinted by permission of the publisher from "Career Planning, an AMA Survey Report" by J. K. Walker, et al., *AMA Management Briefing,* 1979.

sumably caused by the work environment, and suggests that the organizations in which people work have a responsibility to eliminate or assuage the stressors.

> The work environment in twentieth century society is also one of stress. People congest in large cities working for impersonal companies or governments. They hurry to and from work engaging in work that is often personally unsatisfying and under conditions that could be labeled inhumane. Natural bodily rhythms are subjected to clock time, and the noise of the factory often impedes communications. White collar co-workers are frequently competitors, while labor and management engage in posturing and confrontation. (p. 23)

We may conclude that there is increasing excitement about the prospects of career development programs within organizations. At the same time, such programs are typically neither comprehensive nor common, and several issues and problems require resolution.

A Lexicon of Workplace Terminology

Within large organizations, there are a number of terms that require definition, either because they are used differently from standard usage within the counseling profession or because they are unfamiliar to counselors.

Human resources management is an organizational aspect of institutions that includes such activities as training, education, appraisal, recruitment, selection, career development, succession planning, workforce planning, employee assistance programs, job enrichment, and organizational staffing (Vetter, 1985). Bowen and Greiner (1986) suggest that the human resources function is viewed, at least in theory, as essential to successful management in a high-tech, services-based, global economy. On the other hand, in practice, managers often complain that the human resources function does not provide needed assistance, uses esoteric techniques, is out-of-touch and paper-ridden and too costly. This description does not sound too different from the way administrators frequently describe school guidance or college student personnel functions. Human resources management is an umbrella term and usually consists of organizational development, training, personnel, and career development.

Employee assistance programs (EAPs), according to Lewis and Lewis (1986), are concerned with the potential and real productivity losses involved with the mental and physical health of workers (for example, stress, alcoholism, chemical dependency, family conflicts, interpersonal difficulties, financial pressures, and so on). Presumably, these programs reduce absenteeism and the incidence of accidents, and increase productivity. There are now over 5000 EAPs in the United States, and the number continues to grow (Land, 1981).

Most studies of the effectiveness of EAPs originate with management and are conducted by those who provide the services. Few are effected by third-party, independent evaluators. Most of these studies, not surprisingly, demonstrate that an EAP has value to the organization (few concentrate on value to the employee). Kurtz, Googins, and Howard (1984) argue that if adequate research and evaluations are to be accomplished, evaluators will need to concentrate on single concerns (such as alcoholism, wellness, counseling, and such) rather than all concerns at once, since so many independent variables attenuate results. Furthermore, the criterion measure of success is nebulous. Does it mean percentage of employees using the service? Does it mean productivity increase? Does it mean service provided? In addition, it is difficult to know what part of changes to attribute to EAP interventions and what part to associate with other aspects in an individual's life. Thus, lack of sophisticated design in evaluations and nebulous outcome measures make most evaluations of EAPs suspect.

All of these weaknesses in demonstrating the effectiveness of EAPs notwithstanding, we regard the activities of EAPs as important and as appropriate for career counselors in the workplace—providing they have the necessary preparation to confront the wide range of presenting problems. In all, they address the symbiotic nature of work, family, and self roles and can be approached from both a preventive and remedial orientation. The object of EAPs, then, is to provide people who are having problems on and off the job with a place to go when they are having difficulties in order that their work will be more effective.

Career development within organizations is a recent concept in terms of popularity, although it has existed to some degree for a long time. Knowdell (1984) defines the role of the career counselor in industry by noting that relatively recently we have witnessed

> . . . the emergence of a new occupation, that of the human resource development (HRD) specialist. Often these practitioners are industrial trainers or personnel specialists going under a new name. Some are recent graduates with human

> resource development specializations in graduate schools of business and organizational behavior. A few are professional counselors who have made successful transitions from the public sector. Whatever their origin, these new professionals must assume a major role for ensuring the success of the organization's career development program. In many cases, they act as career counselors, conducting assessments and providing occupational information. Many conduct training classes to equip supervisors with career coaching skills. Others consult with top management to ensure organizational support for career development. Some have taken on the unfamiliar tasks of marketing and promoting career development within the organization. Others are conducting outplacement and preretirement counseling for obsolete employees. (p. 490)

A career development system is best defined as "an organized, formalized, planned effort to achieve a balance between the individual's career needs and the organization's work-force requirements. . . . It is an ongoing program linked with the organization's human resource structures rather than a one-time event" (Leibowitz, Farren, & Kaye, 1986, p. 4). Lewis and Lewis (1986) view career development programs as focused within the organization's human resource management and development area to help workers make and implement career decisions. Derr (1986) views career development as a set of activities and resources that a company provides to help its employees to achieve their career objectives (career enhancement), coupled with the organization's own attempts to recruit, develop, and move its employees according to its own short-term and long-term human resource needs (career management).

Just as with EAPs, career development programs allegedly bring about better retention and communication and lead to workers who are more motivated, loyal, and productive, whose lives are enriched, and who achieve a host of other positive outcomes. Unfortunately, there are not yet any definitive studies to support these contentions.

AN OVERVIEW OF CAREER DEVELOPMENT FUNCTIONS

Career-related functions performed within organizations vary from setting to setting. They also change according to who is performing the role of career helper—career development specialist, supervisor, consultant. One of the most comprehensive listings of career functions in industry is provided by Leibowitz and Schlossberg (1981) and is reproduced in Table 11.3. Their perspective is that of how a manager or supervisor can perform a career-helping role. There is a potential problem, of course, when the person who evaluates work performance is also the person who serves as the counselor. Although some people maintain that the task is not only possible but also desirable (Meckel, 1981), there is clear potential for role conflict and employee suspicion in these dual relationships.

The difficulty in reconciling the apparently incongruous tasks of assessment of individuals by the organization and of career counseling by those who perform that function is made explicit by Burack and Mathys (1980) who list the essential differences between these two modes of operation (Table 11.4). In any case, Table 11.4 hints at the broad array of possible *supervisor* activities. On the level of the functions of a *career counselor* in industry (or the career development specialist as opposed to a supervisor or manager) the literature is less instructive. One article (Merman & McLaughlin, 1982) suggests 11 counselor activities to achieve a like number of desired outcomes. The work is presented here in adapted form:

	Role	Employee or Organization Outcome
1.	Advisor or Information-giver	Acquiring needed information to make informed choices.
2.	Teacher/ Facilitator	Developing of skills needed for present and/or future positions.

Role	Employee or Organization Outcome
3. Process consultant	Improving of self-concept through awareness of goals, values, strengths, and weaknesses.
4. Strategic planner	Taking personal responsibility to manage one's own career and market self for internal or external career opportunities (for example, motivation, assertiveness, marketing, career management, and job search).
5. Consultant to organization	Making organization responsive to employee needs for career development.
6. Creator and Enabler	Taking responsibility for complete control of own career (for example, providing situations for employees to learn in a nonthreatening atmosphere).

Role	Employee or Organization Outcome
7. Facilitator/ Teacher (see #2)	Becoming an active problem-solver and understanding and developing process skills.
8. Integrator	Developing trust that the organization understands his or her needs including the effect of career changes on personal life styles.
9. Consultant/ Mediator	Coordinating personal needs and organizational mission.
10. Facilitator/ Philosopher/ Futurist	Participating in helping the organization identify the effect of current issues, trends, and social values.
11. Manager of a system/Conceptualizer	Organization develops an appropriate and evolving career management system using emerging technologies.

Table 11.3

Roles and Associated Questionnaire Items

Communicator

- Holds formal and informal discussions with employees
- Listens to and understands an employee's real concern
- Clearly and effectively interacts with an employee
- Establishess environment for open interaction
- Structures uninterrupted time to meet with employees

Counselor

- Helps employees identify career-related skills, interests, values
- Helps an employee identify a variety of career options
- Helps employee evaluate appropriateness of various options
- Helps employee design/plan strategy to achieve an agreed-upon career goal

Appraiser

- Identifies critical job elements
- Negotiates with employee a set of goals and objectives to evaluate performance
- Assesses employee performance related to goals and objectives
- Communicates performance evaluation and assessment to employee
- Designs a development plan around future job goals and objectives
- Reinforces effective job performance
- Reviews an established development plan on an ongoing basis

Coach

- Teaches specific job-related or technical skills (OJT)
- Reinforces effective performance
- Suggests specific behaviors for improvement
- Clarifies and communicates goals and objectives of work group and organization

Mentor

- Arranges for an employee to participate in a high-visibility activity either inside or outside the organization

Table 11.3 (Continued)

- Serves as a role model in an employee's career development by demonstrating successful career behaviors
- Supports employee by communicating to others in and out of organization employee's effectiveness

Advisor

- Communicates the informal and formal realities of progression in the organization
- Suggests appropriate training activities which could benefit employee
- Suggests appropriate strategies for career advancement

Broker

- Assists in bringing employees together who might mutually help each other in their careers
- Assists in linking employees with appropriate educational or employment opportunities
- Helps employee identify obstacles to changing present situation
- Helps employee identify resources enabling a career development change

Referral agent

- Indentifies employees with problems (e.g., career, personal, health)
- Identifies resources appropriate to an employee experiencing a problem
- Bridges and supports employee with referral agents
- Follows up on effectiveness of suggested referral agents

Advocate

- Works with employee in designing a plan for redress of a specific issue for higher levels of management
- Works with employee in planning alternative strategies if a redress to management is not successful
- Represents employee's concert to higher-level management for redress on specific issues

Table 11.4

Career Counseling Versus Appraisal Interviewing: Similarities and Differences

Element	Career Counseling	Appraisal Interviewing
Focus	• helps individual take charge of own career	• determines potential value of employee to organization
Time frame	• short-run to long-term	• immediate
Information	• individual gets more information than organization	• organization gets more information than individual
Direction	Individual ⇄ Organization	Individual ⇄ Organization
Type	• career paths, ladders • job requirements • organization politics	• judge past performance • assess potential • establish promotability • compare against performance standards
Climate	• supportive, nonthreatening	• neutral, threatening, and/or at times helpful (developmental)
Result	• helps person to establish goals, means, completeness, logic, and next step in own career • where specific targeted jobs are involved, will involve needs analysis to establish individual developmental requirements along his or her career path	Traditional approach: • hire or reject • recommendation to promote or transfer Developmental approach: • supply useful career-related information • work out means to achieve job objectives

There is the recurring theme pervading the literature of a tension between individual needs, goals, and aspirations on the one hand and the organization's needs and requirements on the other (Lee & Rosen, 1984). Usually, career helping is effected either by a disinterested third party or by a third party who is passionately committed to the individual as opposed to any institution. It is not surprising, then, that human resource management specialists are gingerly entering the career development field *in situ*. Organizations have some fears about possible negative consequences of increased career development activities in the workplace. These roadblocks to progress include the raising of false expectations in the minds of employees regarding promotional possibilities (Zenger, 1981); overplanning that tends to provide more regulation than is necessary; management ignorance about the advantages of career counseling; lack of organizational self-insight; servicing large demand once programs are established; difficulty in evaluating the results of career development programs; and perceptions of getting help as an indication of weakness (Knowdell, 1982). Although none of these concerns has been documented as occurring, they are significant possibilities that must be fully addressed if career planning in organizations is to be effective.

Organizational Career Patterns

Some preliminary work offers tentative paradigms of "normal" developmental career patterns in organizations. The types of career patterns that are possible for individuals in organizations seem to depend very much on the type of management espoused by the organizations. For example, Ouchi (1981) has distinguished three types of management styles in organizations. Type A, American in orientation, is characterized by short-term tenure in employment, quick promotions, and specialized career paths. Type J, Japanese in origin, is marked by more long-range, secure employment, slow promotion, and nonspecialized career paths. It is argued that a third style, Type Z, would be appropriate for American organizations. Type Z would be distinguished by long-term, although not guaranteed employment, slow promotion, and moderately specialized career paths. All three management styles hold implications for individual career development patterns within organizations.

A specific model of career stages is provided by London and Stumpf (1982). Using Buehler's original categories as adapted by Super (described earlier in this volume), they offer developmental requirements associated with mastery of each adult career stage.

Stage I: *Exploration and Trial* (for example, taking a job offer, experiencing training and job challenges, setting goals, getting feedback)

Stage II: *Establishment and Advancement* (for example, developing expertise, experiencing success or failure, reinforcing self-image, forming a career strategy, finding a mentor)

Stage III: *Mid Career*

(a) *Growth* (for example, evaluating goals, fearing stagnation, adjusting career direction, needing change, working through midlife crises)

(b) *Maintenance* (for example, realizing the value of job security, fearing the risk of change, expressing loyalty to the organization, having a feeling of pride in professional accomplishments, becoming a mentor)

(c) *Decline* (for example, sensing failure, insecurity, and crisis, anticipating early retirement with few plans, disengaging from work and nonwork prematurely, developing physical and/or mental illness)

Stage IV: *Disengagement* (for example, psychologically preparing for retirement, finding new interests and sources of self-improvement, learning to accept a reduced role)

Most of the descriptive material relating to career stages in organizations is based on very small samples or on observations of individuals within selective industries or occupational groups. For example, one classification evolved from a study of approximately 200 scientists and engineers who may or may not be representative of other types of personnel in organizations. From the experience of these subjects, the investigators (Graves, Dalton, & Thompson, 1980) postulate four stages of careers that occur within organizations.

Stage 1 is characterized by work in collaboration with and under the guidance of a senior researcher or formal supervisor. Work is never completely one's own, for assignments are part of a larger project or activity. The scientist or engineer tends to do routine, detailed work. A task at this career stage is to balance the need to be dependent and the need to show initiative if one is to advance to a higher stage. Stage 1 is basically an apprenticeship.

Stage 2 finds the engineer or scientist having his own project or area of responsibility. The worker assumes responsibility for a specific portion of a project or for a process. He works with relative independence and is judged by the results that are produced. It is in this stage that the worker acquires a reputation for competent work and establishes his credibility. It is a stage characterized by independence and specialization.

In Stage 3, the worker assumes responsibility for the guidance of others. He applies a greater breadth of technical skills and works for the benefit of others in the organization. His task is to develop and stimulate others through ideas and information. He becomes a mentor as he develops from a perspective of self to a perspective of others.

Finally, in Stage 4 the worker becomes a significant influence over the future direction of a major part of the organization. More than a mentor now, the scientist or engineer sponsors and develops many promising people. He has wide interactions both inside and outside of the organization. He becomes either an upper-level manager, an idea innovator, or an internal entrepreneur.

A still more specific delineation of the normal course of careers in organizations is provided by Schein (1978). He divides the career life cycle into four stages: entry, socialization, midcareer, and late career.

Entry Stage Tasks

1. Making a preliminary occupational choice that will determine the kind of education and training to pursue
2. Developing a viable "dream"—an image of the occupation or organization that can serve as the outlet for one's talents, values, and ambitions
3. Preparing oneself for the early career through "anticipatory socialization," in order to develop what one considers to be the attitudes and values necessary for succeeding in one's chosen occupation
4. Facing the realities of finding a first job

Socialization Stage Tasks

1. Accepting the reality of human organization (for example, dealing with people, communicating)
2. Dealing with resistance to change
3. Learning how to work; coping with too much or too little organization and too much or too little job definition
4. Dealing with the boss and deciphering the reward system—learning how to get ahead
5. Locating one's place in the organization and developing an identity

Mid-Career Stage Tasks

1. Finding career anchors (a "career anchor" is an occupational self-concept resulting from self-perceived talents and abilities, self-perceived motives and needs, and self-perceived attitudes and values—in short, the pattern of self-perceived talents, motives, and values to guide, constrain, stabilize, and integrate the person's career).

Five career anchors have been identified; four others are hypothesized. (A tenth career anchor, *warrior*, has been identified among army personnel (Derr, 1980). Warriors have a basic psychological need for high adventure and action).

a. Technical/functional competence
b. Managerial competence
c. Security and stability
d. Autonomy
e. Creativity
f. Basic identity
g. Service to others
h. Power, influence, and control
i. Variety

2. Specializing versus generalizing

Late-Career Stage Tasks

1. Becoming a mentor
2. Achieving a proper balance of involvement in work, family, and self-development
3. Letting go and retiring

Another attempt at defining career stages within organizations is that of Thompson, Baker, and Smallwood (1986). They see four stages occurring, as outlined in Table 11.5.

Each of these attempts at defining the course of careers within organizations, as well as other attempts to describe the work life cycle (see, for example, Miller & Form, 1951), potentially provide a theoretical base for in-house career development programs.

SELECTED FUNCTIONS OF CAREER DEVELOPMENT SPECIALISTS

Although there is all this interest in career development in the workplace, one would do well to heed Dorn's (1986) cautions that industry may not be ready to employ traditionally trained counselors and that the nature of the work may be different from classic notions of career counseling. Up to this point, the reader must surely have picked up on the fact that career development as used in the workplace is a substantially different term from the more historical usage employed in other parts of this book. Nevertheless, some possible functions are identifiable. A discussion of a number of functions selected from a larger possible universe follows.

Working with Plateaued Workers

A number of organizations have attempted to intervene in the career development of so-called plateaued workers—those who have little or no prospect of continued vertical growth in an organization. These are usually competent individuals who, largely because of the pyramidal structure of most organizations, will simply not be promoted. This situation can lead to productive plateaued workers or to unproductive plateaued workers. Hall (1985) has suggested a number of possibilities to counter and assuage what could be a dysfunctional way of coping by the plateaued worker; for example, moving the mature professional to a different kind of work that places a premium on experience and is more generalized than the specialized work currently performed. To achieve this end, organizations could create more project-type jobs, periodically rotate technical specialists, allow temporary moves as well as downward moves, provide internal consulting projects, facilitate job switches, lend employees to other departments within the organization, utilize job redesign and training, and allow for second career chances.

Dual paths have been created by many companies (Raelin, 1987) to try to address the issue of plateauing. For example, technical employees are provided with compensation and advancement opportunities comparable to those of management, thus creating alternatives to plateauing. In one study (Corzine, Buntzman, & Busch, 1988) plateaued man-

Table 11.5

Characteristics of Career Stages

Stage I	*Stage II*
Works under the supervision and direction of a more senior professional in the field. Work is never entirely his or her own, but assignments are given that are a portion of a larger project or activity being overseen by a senior professional. Lacks experience and status in organization. Is expected to willingly accept supervision and direction. Is expected to do most of the detailed and routing work on a project. Is expected to exercise "directed" creativity and intiative. Learns to perform well under pressure and accomplish a task within the time budgeted.	Goes into depth in one problem or technical area. Assumes responsibility for a definable portion of the project, process, or clients. Works independently and produces significant results. Develops credibility and a reputation. Relies less on supervisor or mentor for answers, develops more of his or her own resources to solve problems. Increases in confidence and ability.
Stage III	*Stage IV*
Is involved enough in his or her own work to make significant technical contributions but begins working in more than one area. Greater breadth of technical skills and application of those skills. Stimulates others through ideas and information. Involved in developing people in one or more of the following ways: Acts as an idea leader for a small group. Serves as a mentor to younger professionals. Assumes a formal supervisory position. Deals with the outside to benefit others in organizations—i.e., works out of relationships with client organizations, develops new business. etc.	Provides direction for the organization by: "Mapping" the organization's environment to highlight opportunities and dangers Focusing activities in areas of "distinctive competence." Managing the process by which decisions are made. Exercises formal and informal power to: Initiate action and influence decisions. Obtain resources and approvals. Represents the organization: To individuals and groups at different levels inside the organization. To individuals and institutions outside the organization. Sponsors promising individuals to test and prepare them for key roles in the organization.

Source: Reprinted by permission of the publisher from "Improving Professional Development by Applying Four-Stage Career Model" by Paul H. Thompson, et al., *Organizational Dynamics,* Autumn 1986.

agers (those who were in their current position for at least five years and who indicated that they did not expect to be promoted in the next five years) were studied regarding their Machiavellian tendencies (strategy in interpersonal relationships; for instance, high "Machs" tend to win more, to be persuaded less, to persuade others more, and to behave as predicted). Machiavellian tendencies were found *not* to be related to career plateauing. Stout, Slocum, and Cron's longitudinal three-year study (1988) of 122 plateaued and non-plateaued salespeople indicated that, as one might expect, plateaued workers developed less commitment to the organization, a greater inclination to leave the organization, and a lesser concern with specific career issues. Some workers, however, were self-plateaued for reasons of self-satisfaction with current status and a sense of security. Other observers have suggested downward movement options as an alternative to plateauing or advancement (Mainiero & Upham, 1987).

The problem of midcareer boredom and dead-end prospects is not new, of course. The maintenance stage of careers, as lengthy as it is, offers a petri dish in which can grow all sorts of inimical as well as beneficial organisms that affect the health of a worker's career development. At some point in their careers, a large number of workers become emotionally desensitized to their work. Morgan, Patton, and Baker (1985) offer a number of suggestions to assist the midlife employee. The first step in combating the midcareer blues and blahs is creating an awareness program to sensitize individuals to the possibility of the problem and to provide information and professional counseling to prevent the occurrence. In terms of remedial activity, an organization can provide continuing education and opportunities for retraining to change jobs or careers, allow voluntary reductions of pay and responsibilities, develop a mentoring program, offer more autonomy and independence, provide support groups, and give sabbaticals for selected employees.

Clearly, plateauing, lateral moves, and downward moves are becoming much more common in today's work world as slower corporate growth and population demographics combine to have their effects. The task for career helpers in the workplace is to provide the necessary assistance to assure that plateaued and/or demoted workers remain both productive employees and mentally healthy individuals.

Training and Education Programs

Another aspect of the role of the career development specialist in the workplace is that of providing education and training programs. These programs can range from training in supervisory and management skills, to technical and communication skills, to new employee orientation programs, to training in performance appraisal, leadership training, word processing, interpersonal skills and time management, hiring and selection, and stress management, among others. Training may be conducted both on-site and off-site, and it typically includes all of the standard pedagogical techniques (for example, lecture, discussion, demonstration, role-playing, simulation and gaming, and so on). According to LoBosco (1985), the purposes of training include helping workers to perform better on their current jobs, to achieve self-improvement that is not necessarily job-related, to prepare for a higher-level position, and to make lateral moves (retraining).

A large part of the training performed by a career development specialist will be working with managers to improve their coaching and counseling skills in the career intervention process. Managers are encouraged to guide and develop their employees and are provided with the necessary information and attending/responding skills to do so.

Another part of the training and education function is providing workers with information of various sorts. Most large organizations have some systematic way of informing employees about career-related matters, whether done through a career information center or by some other method. Included here are such dissemination techniques as brochures, computer-accessed data, workshops, videotape presentations, general reference libraries, and other methods that diffuse information about career opportunities within a company. This function might include gathering, storing, retrieving, and disseminating information about such career-relevant aspects as career paths, career-related benefits, on-site and off-site courses and programs, company philosophy about career development, job postings, family-related benefits, and job matching.

Mentoring

In Chapter 5, we briefly alluded to the concept of mentoring as a means by which women could enhance their career development. Mentoring for both men and women within the workplace has received a good deal of attention. Bowen (1985) defines the mentoring function as follows:

> Mentoring occurs when a senior person (the mentor) in terms of age and experience undertakes to provide information, advice and emotional support for a junior person (the protege) in a relationship lasting over an extended period of time and marked by substantial emotional commitment by both parties. If opportunity presents itself, the mentor also uses both formal and informal forms of influence to further the career of the protege. (p. 31)

Mentors engage in a range of activities to assist their proteges. By means of in-depth interviews, Kram (1984) studied managers in a northeast public utilities firm (N = 18 mentoring relationships) and a Fortune 500 manufacturing company (N = 15 peer relationships). She discovered that mentors appear to serve both a *career* function (aspects of the relationship that enhance career advancement) and a *psychosocial* function (aspects of the relationship that enhance one's sense of competence, identity, and effectiveness). Career functions included sponsorship, coaching, challenging assignments, exposure (visibility), and protection. Psychosocial functions included acceptance, confirmation, role-modeling, friendship, and counseling. According to Kram, the mentor relationship is characterized by phases: initiation, cultivation, separation, and redefinition; and these phases are tied to one's career stage (early, middle, and late career). Cross-gender issues tend to heighten within the mentor relationship. Kram argues that mentorship can be of as much benefit to the mentor as to the protege, that all mentor relationships are not positive, that mentor stages and functions may vary according to the setting, and that all people do not have mentor relationships open to them. Finally, in another work, Kram (1985) points out barriers to constructive mentoring, including opposition of potential mentors because they never received mentoring, potential mentors who experience career blocks that impede their desire to help junior colleagues, potential proteges who distrust the motives of senior managers, a lack of respect for the capabilities of senior colleagues, and lack of interpersonal skills to engage in mentoring.

Of course, mentoring is not necessary for all individuals, but it is certainly a help whether it is of a formal or informal nature. Roche's study (1979) indicated that almost two-thirds of 1250 executives said they had at least one mentor. Clauson (1985) surveyed 76 managers and asked them to rate the degree of influence the three most influential people in their lives had in 14 different aspects of life. In general, managers tended to emulate their mentors in intellectual sharpness, job skills (managing, doing), managing a career (organizational life), social skills, and emotional characteristics. He found that although mentorship was not essential to success in the sense of being a necessary and sufficient condition, it was surely helpful. In yet another study, Reich (1985) determined that mentors were perceived as most valuable for offering concrete help: early transfer to more challenging jobs, opening up new positions, assignment to special projects, and providing autonomy in difficult projects. Less concrete was the function of offering political assistance (for example, pressure applied to key people to obtain promotions, advisement on good positions and company politics, and so on). Seventy-two percent of Reich's respondents indicated that mentors contributed substantially to their career development.

In terms of cross-gender mentoring, Bowen (1985) compared same-sex mentoring (MM, FF) with cross-sex mentoring (MF, FM). Although there is clearly a potential for mischief and misperception in cross-gender mentoring, Bowen found that it was not the sex of the mentor as such that accounted for self-perceptions of career enhancement due to the relationship but rather the functions provided by the mentor. Envy, jealousy by significant others in one's life, snide remarks, and so on are all possible evocations as a result of cross-gender mentoring, but sex-related problems appear to be minimal.

In their interview study of male and female faculty members, Stonewater, Eveslage, and Dingerson (1990) investigated perceptions of past career helping relationships. Two major themes emerged. In terms of mentor influences, men and women on the faculty expressed differences. The men more often reported a sense of direction and professionalism; women generally seemed less confident about themselves and indicated less planning in their careers. In terms of mentoring, almost all who indicated that they could not have accomplished what they did without the assistance of a helper were women. Secondly, the type of support reported by women was either emotional caring or a combination of personal and work-related support. Conversely, men were likely to report support in terms of work-related assistance. These results suggest that men and women need different types of mentoring.

Carden, on the basis of her review of the mentoring literature, suggests the following research needs in terms of mentor-protege relationships (MPRs) (1990):

> Future research on mentoring and adult career development must begin with clearer definitions, better control of extraneous variables, and inclusion of subjects from populations that have been largely ignored thus far (e.g., racial and ethnic minority group members, male tokens in traditionally female occupations or professions, blue-collar workers, physically handicapped individuals, and mid-life career changers). In addition, studies aimed at identifying the cognitive and affective processes underlying the influence of "isms" (racism, sexism, ageism, etc.) on the formation, development, and effectiveness of MPR's are needed. (p. 293)

The message of all of these studies is clear—whether mentoring is a formal, organization-sponsored and -encouraged activity or the more prevalent informal activity, having a powerful mentor greatly facilitated upward career mobility. For the career counselor within an organization, tasks built around the mentoring function might include setting up and monitoring mentorship programs and working with mentors to assist them in helping their proteges.

Career Ladders

Career ladders or career path charts are detailed descriptions employed to demonstrate possible job movements, laterally and vertically, that are available within an organization. They depict graphically a sort of road map for negotiating an organizational hierarchy and they present information useful primarily for professional, technical, and managerial staff.

According to McRae (1985), there are three kinds of career paths:

1. *Historical* paths are the informal paths easily analyzed by examining biographical histories of those who currently hold the job

in question. Historical paths tend to perpetuate past practice.

2. *Organizational* paths are those defined by management; such paths are reflected in business plans, needs, and organizational structures. Representing relationships outlined in job descriptions, they are usually consistent with the salary progressions followed in practice.
3. *Behavioral* paths represent the logical and possible sequences of positions that people could follow in light of an analysis of what they actually do. Behavioral paths are rational definitions of what is possible rather than what has been done in the past or what is desired by management. (p. 58)

Within organizations, the career development specialist's role is to define and promulgate these career ladders or career path charts, trying to ensure that equal opportunity is available to all segments of the organization.

Wellness Programs

One of the growing aspects of EAPs is represented by wellness programs. As we indicated earlier in this chapter, there is no reason why career counselors in the workplace should not get involved with typical EAP activities, providing they have the training and skills to do so. Wellness programs are a case in point. Solomon (1985) indicates that wellness programs typically have several components: distribution of health information (ranging from chemical abuse to nutrition), workshops and seminars, fitness programs, and health screenings.

The most common foci of these efforts have been stress, weight control, nutrition, fitness, first-aid, preventive health care, safety, and smoking. Obviously, the underlying motion is that a sound mind in a sound body will lead to enhanced productivity.

Outplacement Counseling

A major stress inducer among workers is both the prospect and the actual act of an organization or a component of it ceasing to function. We have all witnessed the dread and anxiety caused by a plant closing, as longtime workers, many of whom have limited skills, are put out of work. Sometimes, companies provide outplacement counseling for such dislocated workers, although the extent of services and the target populations vary considerably.

Levine's (1985) survey of outplacement and severance pay practices in organizations indicates that although many companies appear concerned about employees who are terminated through no fault of their own, relatively few help in anything but a monetary way. These relatively few programs, designed to assuage the personal and organizational trauma of involuntary job loss, are growing, but are still far from common. They are also sometimes provided by a source other than the company—unions.

Most companies who do support outplacement counseling use outside consultants exclusively. Fewer use both outside consultants and in-house staff; fewer still use exclusively in-house staff. Usually a high-level personnel or human resources manager effects whatever program is determined to be appropriate. Most programs concentrate on helping displaced workers to find new employment and on helping them to cope psychologically. Severance pay is almost always a part of the package. The primary technique utilized seems to be training in job-search skills (such as location of opportunites, résumé writing, interviewing, training opportunities, and so on). Eves (1986), for example, describes a program implemented during and after the process of a plant shutdown in which small-group sessions were held over a three-day period.

These sessions focused on getting organized for the search, determining interests, analyzing experience/life history, preparing résumés and cover letters, targeting companies, interviewing, negotiating, and accepting an offer. Some organizations provide office space, telephone usage, secretarial assistance, and so on, but usually limit such aid to executives. Less common is counseling assistance for families and referrals to community agencies. Lewis and Lewis (1986) see the basic activities involved in outplacement counseling as (1) dealing with affect, (2) self-assessment, (3) goal setting, (4) strategy formulation, and (5) action or implementation.

Healy (1982) succinctly defines the purpose of outplacement counseling as an effort "to reduce anxiety and tension produced by career disruption; to increase attractive job leads; to assure systematic, constructive job searching; to decrease unemployment time; and to effect a career change which improves or at least does not reduce the worker's return from working" (p. 566). A number of consulting firms are making substantial amounts of money from outplacement contracting in attempting to achieve these objectives. There is a wide variation in fees, and the amount charged does not necessarily appear to be related to the success rates in placing and adjusting clients.

Retirement Planning

In Chapter 12, we describe the career counselor's role in preretirement and retirement counseling, as this stage of life is the last in the work cycle. Some of this type of counseling is taking place within the workplace, although it can be more accurately termed planning than counseling. Federal legislation prohibits forced retirement in most types of work prior to age 70 (if at all), yet people seem to be retiring prior to that age, especially in industry. A minority of organizations has some form of organized assistance for employees in the retirement process, and most of these provide for an early retirement option. Information is provided to employees on such aspects of retirement as financial planning, tax information, company- provided postretirement benefits, group insurance conversion, company pension options, medicare, estate planning, health care, legal considerations, housing, and the availability of volunteer work and occupational opportunities.

Often this information is imparted by outside experts who come into the workplace: Social Security staff, financial and legal experts, health care specialists, accountants, and so on. The major vehicles for information dissemination are lectures and seminars, written materials, group discussions, and referrals. Many organizations attempt to provide a mechanism so that retirees can continue some form of contact with the former employer (for example, through communications, benefits, part- time employment, and so on). There is evidence (Kamouri & Cavanaugh, 1986) that preretirement planning programs can be effective in sensitizing participants to the issues of planning for retirement, acquiring information about aspects of retirement, and participating in retirement roles. Therefore, it is a useful activity for career development specialists.

Employee Assistance Programs

Whether staffed in-house or simply a referral service (the latter is more prevalent), EAPs—usually located within personnel, human resource, or medical departments—attempt to prevent and remediate personal problems of workers in order to increase productivity, reduce absenteeism, enhance retention, and improve morale. Those organizations that do provide in-house services typically employ trained staffs, consisting of such personnel as counselors, nurses, doctors, psychologists, and/or social workers.

Even with in-house staffs, referrals to outside agencies is a major function of EAPs. These referral sources include alcohol and drug rehabilitation facilities, mental health and social agencies, psychiatrists and psychologists, and self-help groups (such as Alcoholics Anonymous). In addition to referrals, EAPs provide an educative function in that they work with supervisors and managers to teach them how to recognize the need for assistance in those they supervise, and they work with employees to help them gauge whether they need help. The most common problems brought to EAPs are chemical dependency, marital difficulties, financial problems, on-the-job interpersonal difficulties, sexual harassment and discrimination (often handled by other than EAP), disruptive family relationships, and stress. For a complete discussion of EAPs, the reader is referred to Lewis and Lewis (1986) and Pickman, Challenger, Emener, and Hutchison (1988).

Some see the efforts of EAPs and career planning and development programs industry as simply attempts by organizations to enhance the self-esteem of their employees in order to bring about greater productivity. Brockner (1988), for example, argues that everything from layoffs to negotiation behavior can be assuaged or enhanced by attention to employees' self-esteem. In a broad sense, he is probably correct, although our current understanding of the construct of self-esteem and the sophistication of its measurement are less than adequate. In general, supervisors seem to require employees to evidence some blatant and overt maladaptive behaviors before they will refer them to EAPs. These behaviors typically include high absenteeism, irritability, decreased productivity, and apathy (Bayer & Gerstein, 1990).

Analyzing 91 employee assistance programs in Ontario, Canada, Macdonald and Dooley (1990) concluded that current programs contain improved procedures to enhance the protection of confidentiality and to emphasize the voluntary aspects of referrals. Unions are becoming increasingly involved in EAPs. Nevertheless, issues persist. Although confidentiality protection has increased, for example, confidentiality typically does not guarantee anonymity. Also, awareness and education programs are less fully developed than is desirable; after-the-fact responses are much more prevalent.

THE CAREER COUNSELOR IN THE ORGANIZATION

Several people have urged career counselors to intensify their role in organizations, especially in industry. Indeed, such a concept is not new; one can point to isolated instances of counseling by psychologists within industry as far back as the 1920s (Baker, 1944). Several contemporary writings about psychologists functioning as counselors within industry described in a sort of "how I spent my summer vacation" way the activities of academics on sabbatical leave who tried to link "town and gown" more closely by working within industry in their geographical area. One such endeavor was undertaken by Lipsett (1980a). During his sabbatical, he set up an office within a 1700-person plant and counseled employees. These employees had four basic categories of problems. The first group wanted help in changing from perceived routine occupations (such as secretary) to those perceived as less routinized and more satisfying (such as sales). The second group desired educational counseling, mainly in order to qualify for job advancement. The third group wanted to explore qualifying for management. The fourth group brought to the counselor problems of work adjustment (such as relations with supervisors). Lipsett concluded that disseminating information played an important part in his functioning and that test results, career path charts, and educational and occupational information resources were necessary in the industrial setting.

A college counselor used another leave to set up services at a 200-person Smith-Corona laboratory (Papalia & Kaminski, 1981). These services then continued on a part-time basis after the leave. The counselor typically spent his time focusing on personal adjustment, academic counseling, and career decision making. In addition, the counselor helped to develop training programs that carried academic credit at his institution. He further acted as a group facilitator for human relations, problem solving, decision making, organizational development, leadership training, and communication skills. Part of his role also included referrals to local agencies (for example, Catholic Charities) and outplacement counseling. Finally, he arranged for the offering of flex-time courses dealing with such topics as "Transactional Analysis for Managers" and "The Psychology of Personal Adjustment."

A somewhat less provincial approach is taken by Leonards (1981) who speaks more universally about the possibilities of corporate psychology. He believes that counseling psychologists are most appropriate for corporate clientele because of their emphasis on working with healthy personalities. Foci would include counseling resolution of midcareer issues, preretirement planning, and specific career development concerns. Further contributions to the corporate body would come from the counselor's assisting in organizational development, program evaluation, and general psychological consultation.

Continuing with speculation regarding the role of a counseling psychologist in industry, both Toomer (1982) and Osipow (1982a) offer ideas about how psychologists can transcend a career role in organizations and can contribute to many areas. Toomer's ideas of the roles and relationships of counseling psycholgists in business and industry appear to speak to almost everything *but* career counseling. Figure 11.1 indicates a broad range of roles and functions he would propose.

Osipow's ideas about applications in organizations for counseling psychologists are more specific in their career-relatedness. He suggests, for example, 16 possibilities for useful contributions:

1. Helping employees and managers identify hazards in work
2. Training people to identify their work styles (especially those that might be deleterious to them) and teaching them to change them
3. The effects of repetitive work on people
4. The effects of transfers to new locations, especially if forced
5. Special stresses and strains in the two-career couple family
6. Special stresses experienced by people employed in boundary spanning roles (for example, jobs which require employees to "split" allegiances)
7. The special stresses in people with high interpersonal demands in their jobs
8. Preparation for retirement
9. Dealing effectively with the process of job evaluation
10. Dealing with the special problems of entrepreneurs
11. Dealing with the problems of job loss
12. Dealing with the special problems of small-business people
13. Dealing with the special problems of professionals
14. Health care issues
15. Self-help and self-care
16. Family counseling

Gutteridge and Otte (1983) surveyed forty major corporations in order to estimate the scope of career development practices within organizations. Their results caused them to offer a number of recommendations directed to ward enhancing the establishment and imple-

Figure 11.1

Counseling Psychologist in Business and Industry: Roles and Relationships From "Counseling Psychologist in Business and Industry" by J.E. Toomer, *The Counseling Psychologist, 10*(3), 9–18. Reprinted by permsission of Sage Publications, Inc.

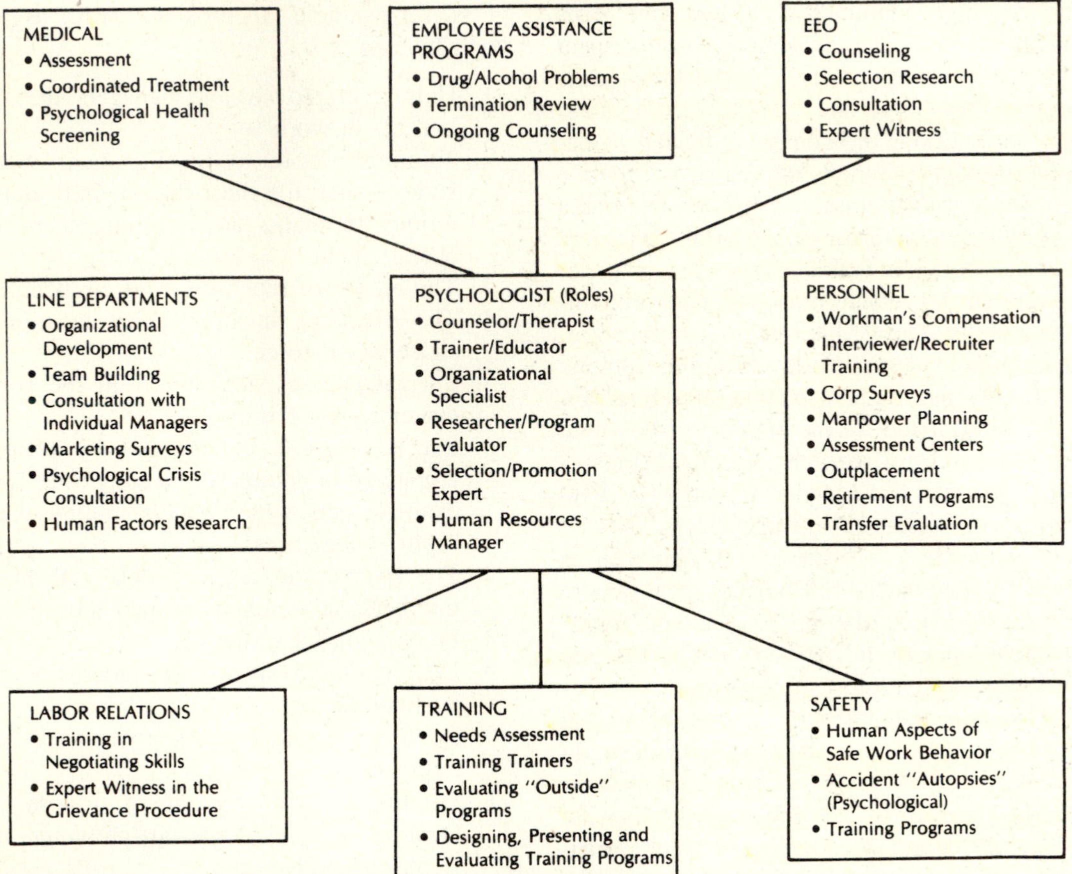

mentation of career programs in the workplace. Among these are that practitioners should do the following:

- Be trained in both organizational development and career development processes
- Be assured of support by both top management and operating-level personnel
- Explicitly state objectives and evaluation methods
- Integrate career development activities with other components of the personnel/human resource system
- Communicate roles clearly to employees, managers, and counselors
- Provide a training program for supervisors

Further, they recommend a ratio of one professional counselor to each 2000 employees (or less) in order that the counselors can engage workers and management in individual counseling, teach career planning seminars, and instruct supervisors how to conduct career discussions.

Verlander (1985) argues that the effectiveness of a career management system (CMS) depends on how well it is integrated with all of the other human resource functions within an organization. Typical programs include management and supervisory training, career planning, career counseling, equal employment efforts, and career information systems. Almost all systems provide for performance appraisal and feedback. Lewis and Lewis (1986) advocate that counselors in the workplace develop a broad set of competencies to address these concerns, including skills in program development and management, counseling and assessment, resource utilization/networking, organizational consultation, education and training, and marketing and public relations. These competencies represent a formidable repertoire for any single discipline to master, and few, if any, formal preservice preparation programs address them in any complete sense.

Hall (1986), after reviewing the current state of career development in organizations, arrived at seven conclusions:

1. No organization has the ability (in terms of either resources or information about the future) to manage an employee's career or to plan well-ordered career paths.
2. Therefore, the employee must assume responsibility for his or her own career development (or at least 80 percent of it).
3. To be responsible for one's own career in today's turbulent organizational environments, the employee needs new *career competencies*, not just job skills. These career competencies might be called "metaskills," because they are skills in acquiring new skills. The most important metaskills are adaptability (routine busting), tolerance of ambiguity and uncertainty, and identity change.
4. It is in the best interests of the organization to help both the employee and his or her spouse assume the career responsibility and to develop their own career direction. (This makes it easier for the organization to pursue its own future directions.)
5. The organization should provide information and support to facilitate the person's assumption of career responsibility.
6. The organization should make possible wide degrees of freedom of movement for the individual. All directions of movement should be possible and valued by the culture: down, across, up, and out.
7. To provide an environment that is supportive of good career planning and career management, the organization needs a good strategic human resource management process. Career development activities are performed most effectively when they are one part of an integrated strategic human resource management system. This means that the organization must have clear business objectives and a clear set of human resource objectives and priorities growing out of those business objectives. (pp. 348–349)

Each of these articles is representative of the current state of the career counselor in industry. They offer tentative, exploratory proposals of how specialists can function to enhance career development in the organization. There are not, as yet, definitive answers to a number of questions. These questions are addressed later in this chapter.

Cairo (1985), acknowledging the absence of data, presents some tentative conclusions related to the design and implementation of career programs in organizations.

1. Program development should be preceded by a systematic and thorough assess-

ment of the career development needs of the target population. This should include some effort to distinguish between employees who require help in obtaining the standard career development competencies and those with different, but equally important, career development needs.

2. To avoid the problems associated with employees' unrealistic expectations of career planning and development programs, information about career opportunities should be honest, accurate, and up-to-date. Whenever possible this element of a program should include information about job requirements, career paths, training and development resources, and promotional possibilities.

3. Efforts to facilitate employees' appraisal of work-related skills must include the recognition that some important skills might be extremely difficult, perhaps even impossible, to acquire regardless of subsequent developmental activities. In such cases, employees might be encouraged to focus on finding positions that maximize strengths and minimize weaknesses rather than searching for suitable developmental activities.

4. Organizations that expect supervisors to take a central role in the career development of their subordinates should provide incentives and rewards for these efforts and ensure that supervisors possess, or acquire, the knowledge, skills, and attitudes required to be effective helpers.

5. Methods for helping employees monitor their career plans should be part of every program. This will require coordination among other career-related activities to provide employees with ongoing opportunities to review earlier goals and plans and modify them in light of any new information or circumstances.

6. Finally, there is a clear need for more and better program evaluations. Given the large number of existing career planning and development programs and the likelihood of continued growth in this area, it is important that we begin to examine carefully the effects of our efforts. (pp. 245–246)

Examples of Career Programs

As indicated by survey results, many organizations have formal, functioning career development programs. General Electric, AT&T, AirCal, Aetna, and Xerox, for example, all have formal materials and procedures to assist their employees with career development concerns. We here offer a brief description of several illustrative programs in order to give a flavor of the activity that is taking place.

Since 1975 a program at Livermore Laboratory in California has served the 7000-plus person workforce by means of three major components: a career assessment center, individual career counseling, and several career assessment workshops. The workshops are conducted during working hours for about seven weeks. They are limited to 18 participants per session, and require approximately 40 hours of participant time. Workshops progress from overviews of career planning to assessment of values and interests, to decision-making concerns, to an achievement motivation program. Evaluations based on participant self-reports have been generally positive (Knowdell, 1982).

Related to this program is the establishment of a Career Resource Center at Livermore (Moir, 1981). This is a typical example of such centers that are, of course, common outside of business and industry but are rarer within the workplace. The center is run by a full-time office assistant who is supervised by a professional career resource specialist. It contains educational information, career planning information and resources, data on the world of work, books and cassettes related to the personal growth, supervisory/management training materials, computerized career information, professional periodicals, self-study courses, and announcements of off-site training.

One common strategy related to career development in organizations is the assessment center. There is little doubt that the assessment center is used more for personnel selection than for individual development, more for identifying potential managers than for diagnosing employee strengths and weaknesses. The concept began in World War II with selection of spies for the OSS and now concerns itself largely with selection for higher management and for management trainees. In a few situations, the assessment center is also used to select sales and technical personnel and other nonmanagement workers. Techniques used in assessment centers include in-basket exercises (an individual is provided with data relating to problems and must, within a specified time period, demonstrate effective decision making); related management games and simulations; leaderless group discussions; analysis and presentation of complex situations; role-playing exercises; essay writing; psychological aptitude and personality tests; and others. These techniques are designed to assess oral and written communication skills; leadership; ability to organize and plan; decision-making ability; tolerance for stress and behavioral flexibility; and energy, forcefulness, creativity, and risk taking among other traits. There is obvious potential for byzantine behaviors by assessors; consequently, those involved in assessment center activity have produced a guiding document, *Standards for Ethical Consideration for Assessment Center Operators*. Noe and Steffy (1987) studied those who had undergone an assessment center intervention to predict their potential for advancement. The results indicated that participants increased their information-acquisition behaviors regarding future career paths.

It should be no surprise that computerized career interventions have been injected into the organizational career planning and development process. These range from simply computerizing an assessment device to more comprehensive systems. For example, Vale (1990) describes the use of the Minnesota Clerical Assessment Battery (MCAB) as an aid in personnel selection, while Forrer, Leibowitz, and Dickelman (1989) offer Career Point: A Computer-Based Career Development System for Organizations. Since this latter approach is likely to proliferate, we offer a description of its components. This system consists of 12 computer modules for use with an IBM PC (and compatibles). These modules include an introduction to the system, knowledge of the organization (made specific to the particular employer), several assessment modules (values, interests, and preferences; skills; goals), identifying job opportunities, planning for reaching goals, job search skills, and résumé writing. Incorporated in the system are such well-known career planning aids as The Work Environment Scales, the Meyers-Briggs Type Indicator, the Career Leverage Scale, and the Self-Directed Search. We anticipate that similar systems that combine extant instrumentation with the opportunity to customize the intervention to the particular organization will become very common in the future.

The Gulf Oil Corporation in Pittsburgh and Chatham College have combined resources to offer a program to help women assume an active personal role in future planning and to use information effectively in implementing plans (Fort & Cordisco, 1981). These ends are addressed by means of assessment activities (values, interests, temperament, and selected aptitudes), individual advising (by one person from Gulf and one from Chatham and directed at educational information and career goals), and workshops (lectures, discussions, homework, and so on). Evaluations are loose but suggest positive growth on the part of participants.

Many organizations have excellent in-house educational and occupational information materials. One is the Aetna Life and Casualty

Company. They publish several volumes for their employees in a *Develop Yourself* series. For example, *Develop Yourself: A Guide to Education and Training* is an almost 250-page catalog of all the education and training offered at Aetna. Each course is listed in terms of the purpose of the course, for whom it is designed, what its content is, how long it lasts, what the prerequisites are, how to get registered, and how much, if anything, the course will cost. This document puts to shame many college catalogs. A companion volume. *Develop Yourself: A Career Path Handbook*, is intended to provide Aetna's 36,000 employees with information about job possibilities within the company in 14 job clusters and the career progression usually followed.

At Coco-Cola USA (Slavenski, 1987), the career development system has at its heart performance planning and review. These are followed by individual career development discussions in which employees can communicate career interests to their managers. Information from both the performance review and career discussion then is utilized in department career development and succession planning reviews called People Days. The next step is finding a fit between available positions and people. This is done through a number of publications and job postings and through a two-day Career Strategies Workshop. Coca-Cola USA also offers an extensive in-house training program as well as 100 percent tuition reimbursement aid for outside courses.

These examples of program content indicate that many of the techniques developed outside of organizations are being put to use within the workplace. Also, however, specific techniques and materials are being developed to meet the unique needs of particular organizations.

There certainly are no extant rules for providing career assistance in the workplace. Developers are relatively unfettered in their attempts to implement a concept. That same freedom, however, leads to several questions.

Issues and Needed Research

Throughout our discussion in this chapter we have pointed to several unresolved issues and questions that lend themselves to researchable answers. To conclude our exploration of career counseling in the workplace, we summarize these concerns.

1. Can career counseling effectively occur within the workplace when there appears to be a basic conflict between the necessity for performance evaluation and the desirability of threat-free career development activity? Can both organizational and individual needs be met within the corporate body?
2. Who should provide career development services within industry? Supervisors? Career counseling specialists? Generic training and development personnel? Some new hybrid of human resource development specialist and career counselor?
3. What are the appropriate functions necessary to achieve which career development outcomes in organizations?
4. What methods and materials are best for what types of adult clients and/or concerns?
5. What evidence can be gathered to prove, disprove, or alter current theoretical notions about adult career development?
6. How do career identities develop? How are they shaped by work experiences?
7. How can we define success in career development? What criteria are appropriate? Are money earned, satisfaction, career maturity, and other outcome measures appropriate?
8. How can we best evaluate to demonstrate the effectiveness of career development programs in organizations? Can we suc-

cessfully reconcile equal employment concerns and organizational needs?

9. What can be done to secure pervasive organizational support for career development program?
10. Is there a "critical mass" of personnel and materials necessary in order to provide minimally acceptable career development services? Is there a minimum number of employees required before a program should be established?
11. Is it possible to use generic career development systems to apply in various organizations, or must systems be tailored to the unique needs and populations of each institution in the workplace?
12. What types of research are required to produce improved performance appraisal, a greater understanding of superviser/supervisee relations, and so on?
13. What are the differential career development needs of diverse subpopulations within the organization (such as clerical, supervisory, managers, production, sales)?
14. How can many of the adult career concerns and special populations described in Chapters 5, 12, and 13 best be addressed within the structure of workplace organizations?
15. Are career development concerns best handled at several locations or at a "home" office?

OCCUPATIONAL STRESS

Although unemployment or the lack of work creates stress, as we shall see in Chapter 13, actual employment can also cause problems in terms of the stress provided within the work environment. The Occupational Safety and Health Administration (OSHA) was created by the United States government to deal with unhealthy conditions in the workplace. For years, this governmental agency concerned itself primarily with hazardous conditions and substances (for example, excess noise, dangerous chemicals and gases, and so on). Now, many believe that the major responsibility of this agency is to address the problem of occupational stress as well as other problems unique to work in the information age (such as the possible effects of CRT screens on secretaries).

Stress is endemic in contemporary society. It is seemingly a common phenomenon, even among children (Humphrey, 1988). Occupational stress has been postulated to be a contributor to the increase in morbidity in industrialized nations. However, there have been few empirical studies to verify this hypothesis (Cooper & Baglioni, 1988).

In this section we offer a relatively brief discussion of the stress of work and the work of stress. Stress, in general, is one of the most investigated aspects of psychology; and occupational or organizational stress, in particular, is one of the most heavily researched topics in all of vocational psychology. Therefore, because of space considerations we shall simply present an overview of the area. The reader should recognize, however, that the amount of space devoted is not in direct proportion to the topic's importance.

Definition of Stress

The human stress response system is now fairly well known. Usually, conditions are presented to individuals, either within work or outside of work, that cause them to call upon their resources to adapt to the conditions. When these conditions (stressors) are greater than a person's abilities to cope or when they cause individuals to utilize their coping resources to the maximum degree possible, stress may be induced. People may see possible harm, threat, or challenge in the environment, and this perception starts a potential stress-strain chain. Strain does not result, however, unless the stressors are first filtered through people's psychological systems (Lazarus & Folkman, 1984); and once strain occurs, it may be more or less debilitating depending upon individuals' differing capacities to cope. The sequence, then is as follows:

1. There is a perceived work stressor in the environment.
2. People make cognitive appraisals of the stressors and view them in a way that makes people unclear about how to respond because the effects of response are important.
3. People experience the level of stress differentially, both physiologically and behaviorally.
4. People bring into play coping behaviors or strategies.

When the situation is both uncertain and important, the stress chain is evoked. In other words, when the environment imposes demands that are out of balance with the person's capacities to respond, strain may result. It should be noted that stress may originate within the individual as well as the environment as we impose demands on ourselves.

The father of stress research, Hans Selye (1976) pointed out that there can be too much stress or too little stress, good stress and bad stress within environments. *Overstress* (hyperstress) is obviously a condition wherein presenting stressors exceed or overtax one's abilities to deal with them; *understress* (hypostress) is the obverse condition wherein the environment presents no stressors and therefore does not challenge. Therefore, one's capabilities may grossly exceed demands, or demands may greatly exceed capabilities, In either case, stress may result. *Good stress* (eustress) is stress that provides an acceptable degree of challenge, a facilitating sort of anxiety. *Bad stress* (distress) produces reactions inimical to the physical and mental health of the individual.

Osipow and Spokane (1984) summarize the situation in this manner: "It now seems clear that social stress occurs in the workplace with effects similar to those of stress outside the workplace. Work and nonwork (e.g., family) stress probably interact to a large extent" (p. 68).

Stressors at Work

Certain aspects of the work environment and the demands of work are thought to have the potential to be stressors. These include lack of control over the pace, output, and methods of work (Tetrick & LaRocco, 1987); repetitive work that requires no great skill; work with highly limited movement and/or social interaction; work with a very fast pace; work involving quick decisions and major responsibility; work with high levels of physical discomfort (such as noise, heat or cold, light, pollution); perilous work; work in which there is a lack of role clarity or conflict between or within roles; and work in which the expectations are greatly incompatible with the realities.

Among the stressors frequently cited in the literature are poor physical working conditions, shift work, work overload or underload, physical danger, person-environment fit (P-E), job satisfaction, home-work pressures, and dual career stress (Cooper & Marshall, 1980). Firth (1985), utilizing cases of managerial/professional clients referred to a psychology clinic for assistance in coping with high stress, identified four types of presenting problems: (1) high investment in work alone (such as overwork, worry, uncertainty); (2) poor relationship with colleagues (for example, cannot work in group, poor relationship with subordinates); (3) promotion problems (too much responsibility, avoidance of promotion, and so on); and (4) role conflicts (for example, conflicts about success, career).

In addition, Schwartz (1980) reports that stress can be generated by such factors as too little or too much competition and ongoing contact with stress carriers (such as demanding workaholics, highly anxious people, indecisive individuals). Shostack (1985) adds another potential stressor—de-skillinization, a phenomenon whereby one's talents are not put to use because of technology or for some other reason. A number of "lacks" have been reported by Crabbs, Black, and Morton (1986) to be major stressors: lack of support from boss, lack of expected promotions, lack of job security, and lack of participation in decision making. Holt (1982) conducted a comprehensive review of the literature on occupational stress and categorized stressors as *objectively* defined (such as physical properties of the work environment, time variables, social and organizational properties of the work setting, and changes in jobs) and *subjectively* defined (for example, role-related, person-environmental fit, off-job stress, and miscellaneous).

More general descriptions of work stressors can be gained from examining the categories found on major instruments that measure work stress, whether these categories have been rationally derived or are a result of factor-analytic techniques. Some are intended for specific occupations; others are generic and meant to be used with all occupations. The Job Stress Questionnaire (JSQ) was factor-analyzed by Hamel and Bracken (1986) who examined the rational categories given by the instrument constructors: work load, role conflict, role ambiguity, and underutilization of skills. They found that factor analysis did *not* support the four factors for diverse occupational levels (blue-collar, white-collar, and professional). Jenner's (1986) Stress at Work Scale was factor-analyzed and yielded four factors: human relationship issues, demand issues, role issues, and leadership issues. In the specific case of university professors, Gmelch, Wilke, and Lovrich (1986), using the Faculty Stress Index (FSI), identified five stressor factors: faculty reward and recognition, time constraints, department influence, professional identity, and student interaction. Rizzo, House, and Lirtzman (1970) developed a Role Questionnaire that measures the major factors of role conflict and role ambiguity. Osipow and Spokane (1984) devised a measure of primarily social role stressors, the Occupational Environmental Scales (OES), that has six subscales (role overload, role insufficiency, role ambiguity, role boundary, responsibility, and physical environment), and the rationally derived scales have been generally confirmed through factor analysis.

We have been discussing stressors that primarily emanate from the work environment. But they also may stem from the person. For instance, the concept of Type A behavior is very well known from the attention devoted to it in the popular press. Type A people are characterized by ambition, competitiveness, personal striving upward, and achievement orientation. Type A personalities are presumed to experience greater occupational stress. In fact, however, the relationship is unclear (O'Rourke, Houston, Harris, & Snyder, 1988; Benight & Kinicki, 1988; Byrne & Reinhart, 1989).

The upshot of all of these studies and many others is that anything in the workplace is a potential stressor for given individuals, whether it be the extremes of any continuum of demand (for example, too much or too little of any aspects of work), role-related issues, or the physical environment. What causes some individuals to perceive a potential stressor as negative and fail to cope and other people to view it as positive and cope easily will be addressed later in this chapter. First, we need to know the effects of occupational stress.

The Consequences of Occupational Stress

The results of occupational stress are described very much in terms used to delineate the effects of burnout as described in Chapter 13. The consequence of stress is usually described in broad strokes as *strain*. A variety of symptoms are believed to be overt manifestations of that strain; for example, fatigue, anxiety, fear, inability to relax, tension, sleep and digestive disturbances, self-esteem effects, headaches, chemical and person abuse, depression and other psychiatric disorders, and a number of physiological responses, ranging from hormonal symptoms to cardiovascular strain, among others. Thus, consequences can be both mental and physical, although it is thought that the mental effects are greater for younger workers and the physical effects are greater for older workers. Specific to work, stress consequences can include job dissatisfaction, boredom, work alienation, strikes, early retirement, employee stealing and other counterproductive behaviors, absenteeism, accidents, and interpersonal conflicts. In short, stress responses can be physiological, affective, and behavioral, and some effects of stress can also be causes of stress.

In terms of physiological consequences. Fried, Rowland, and Ferris (1984) conducted a review of the physiological measurement of work stress, including cardiovascular irregularities (for example, increased heart rate, blood pressure), biochemicals in the blood and urine (abnormal levels of uric acid, blood sugar, cholesterol, catecholamines, and so on), and gastrointestinal disorders (such as peptic ulcer). They concluded that because of deficiencies in the procedures used to measure physiological systems, the failure to differentiate between acute and chronic work stressor effects, and the inability to control confounding factors, there was no strong evidence of a valid link between physiological symptoms and stress at work (except possibly for cardiovascular symptoms). This finding does not mean that such a link does not exist; it means simply that the research has so many methodological flaws that no clear conclusions are possible.

It is rare that occupational stress causes a major psychiatric disorder of the magnitude of a stress-inducing traumatic event such as war, natural disaster, terrorism, and such. The DSM-III recognizes two syndromes as the result of the recognizable stressor that would be expected to evoke stress in most people. These are stressors that are outside the range of usual human experience and thus not typical stressors: one is termed brief reactive psychosis; the other is called posttraumatic stress disorder. The former has a sudden onset immediately after a stressful event, lasts anywhere from a few hours to a week or two, and clinically is characterized by emotional turmoil and at least one psychotic symptom. The latter syndrome is an anxiety disorder that may recur long after the precipitating event and last indefinitely. Clinically, it is characterized by recurrent dreams or flashbacks related to the trauma, emotional numbing, and possibly several other symptoms such as insomnia and impaired concentration. It is obviously rare for work stress to cause these types of psychiatric disorder.

Work stress has been indicted, however, as the cause of a variety of abuse, once again illustrating the symbiotic relationship of work, family, and self roles in people's lives. For example, Barling and Rosenbaum (1986) conducted a study of abusive husbands and determined that overall work experiences are associated significantly with wife abuse. In general, abusive husbands experience more stressful work events and perceive them more negatively. Work stress can also cause self-abuse in the form of chemical abuse such as smoking, caffeine, drugs and alcohol. Gupta and Jenkins (1984) suggest that the reasons for this apparent association may be because certain forces in the organization push the individual away from the organization in the direction of substance use whereas other forces draw the individual and the organization closer together and lessen the probability of abuse. Thus, they believe that employees are likely to use substances only when pushing forces (distancing forces and constraints) are stronger than pulling forces (attractions).

Moderators in Coping with Stress

We believe that the stress-strain sequence is cognitively mediated; otherwise, all individuals would perceive stressors in the same way and react similarly. People obviously differ in their reactions to a possible stressor and to levels of work stress. One person is overwhelmed by demands; another thrives on the same demands. Certain variables are thought to be buffers of stress, moderators that affect individual reactions to stressful events and thus permit either poor or effective coping.

One way to summarize coping behaviors is to look to what is measured by common instruments designed to assess aspects of coping. Coping, in general, refers to efforts to master conditions that tax or exceed adaptive resources. Latack (1986) identified three broad coping strategies related to job stress: *control* (for example, "Get together with my supervisor and discuss this"), *escape* (for example, "Avoid being in this situation if I can"), and *symptom management* (for example, "Get extra sleep or nap"). Osipow and Spokane (1984) developed a coping measure, the Personal Resources Questionnaire (PRQ), that contains four subscales (Recreation, Self-Care, Social Support, and Rational/Cognitive Coping).

Social support in the form of family, friends, professional assistance, and so on has long been thought to be a significant mediator of the impact of stress on the individual. The theory goes that social support modifies the effect of stress in the sense that those with adequate sources of social support more effectively cope with stress. Although there are a number of studies to support this hypothesis, at least one study (Aneshensel & Stone, 1982) suggests that social support goes beyond simply moderating and actively plays a role in support; that is, the presence of support is beneficial in and of itself and its absence is itself a source of stress. Another study (Kaufman & Beehr, 1986), however, found that contrary to all expectations, social support actually strengthened the positive relationship between stressors and strains, thus contradicting most theories and models of job stress and social support. The type of social support given may account for this difference.

For example, supervisors at work also provide social support. In Beehr, King, and King's 1990 study of nurses, the social support of supervisors was found to act as a buffer and to moderate the stressor-strain relationship. They categorized three types of social support: positive job-related communications, negative job-related communications, and non-job-related communications. In general, supervisors' positive job-related communications and non-job-related communications were found to buffer the stress-strain effect. A similar finding is reported by Cummins (1989) who concluded that social support as a buffer is effective only when the support relates to issues at work and when people feel that they have control over their situation (internal locus of control).

Milsum (1985) suggests that stressors are factors that may result in increased stress in the individual, and de-stressors are factors reversing such effects. Stressors tend to stimulate a fight-or-flight response and de-stressors stimulate a relaxation response. Some specific coping de-stressors or moderators or buffers might be financial resources, sick and health care, exercise, stress management, knowledge, problem-solving skills, morale, beliefs, culture and religion, and wellness orientation. Also, moderators might include certain situational variables in the work setting: size and cohesion of work group, autonomy, support from supervisors and co-workers, organizational climate, and so on.

Coping strategies and their effectiveness differ. In a study of New York City teachers (Schonfeld, 1990), advice seeking and direct action were judged to be the most effective strategies; selectively ignoring stressors also appeared to buffer strain symptoms. These results are different from those involving other occupational groups, suggesting that the effectiveness of stress-coping strategies may vary by type of occupation. One classification often investigated in the literature is the dichotomy between emotion-focused coping and problem-focused coping. In this study, problem-focused coping seemed to be more useful in more situations. These results also appear to hold for most studies (Kuhlmann, 1990).

Cox (1987) has delineated the steps necessary in the use of rational problem solving as a coping mechanism to moderate the stress-strain chain. He outlines a six-step process (not too different from the decision-making steps limned in Chapter 14). These are as follows:

1. *recognition* that a problem exists,
2. *diagnosis*: analysis of the situation, involving information acquisition, negotiation of an appropriate language for problem definition, and negotiation of problem description,
3. *design 1*: statement of implied solutions and creative generation of a range of other possible solutions,
4. *design 2*: identification and agreement on criteria of success and immediate evaluation of different possible solutions, and integration of most acceptable into feasible strategy,
5. *development/implementation 1*: implementation, and support for implementation, and
6. *development/implementation 2*: monitoring, feedback and learning. (p. 12)

Finally, coping responses may well be moderated by resources within the individual. Such personal characteristics as age and stage of career development, sex (Haw, 1982; D'Arcy, Syrotuik, & Siddique, 1984; Martocchio & O'Leary, 1989), Type A or B behavior (Heilbrun & Renert, 1986), locus of control (Marino & White, 1985), approach-avoidance proclivities (Roth & Cohen, 1986), race (Neff, 1985), and work values, among many other personal variables, may mediate the stress response. The literature in this regard is substantial, although it yields no clear and unequivocal results.

Moos and Billings (1982) classify appraisal and coping responses into three domains:

> *Appraisal-focused coping* involves attempts to define the meaning of a situation and includes such strategies as logical analysis and cognitive redefinition. *Problem-focused coping* seeks to modify or eliminate the source of stress, . . . to deal with the tangible consequences of a problem, . . . or actively to change the self and develop a more satisfying situation. *Emotion-focused coping* includes responses whose primary function is to manage the emotions aroused by stressors and thereby maintain affective equilibrium. (p. 218)

Clearly, there is not a direct relationship between occupational stress and negative outcomes. Rather, the relationship is complex, intricate, and moderated by a number of processes and variables. We require better research to get at these processes and variables.

Many suggestions have been offered to improve the research on characteristics of stress, its moderation, and its consequences. Newton (1989) asserts that researchers need to concentrate on a person's cognitive "sense-making" of stresses (how and why stress occurs and how people cope); to determine the relationship between occupational coping behavior and longer-term coping style; to utilize a broader conceptualization of strain (beyond anxiety/satisfaction/depression); and to employ a more qualitative methodology rather than depending on existing quantitative measures. Eulberg, Weekley, and Bhagat (1988) point out that we need more research on factors that influence a person's unique perceptions of stressful events. What are the nature of cognitive appraisals that serve as moderators and how do these perceptions affect the experience of stress? Ganster and Victor (1988) call for more "experimental studies that carefully examine the behavioral, psychological, and physiological mediators of social support. Such investigations will most likely involve testing of complex models of social support interacting with individual differences, stress levels, and delivery timing" (p. 33).

Intervening and Managing Stress

The literature is replete with studies that demonstrate the effectiveness of stress management interventions, both for the short-term and for the long-term (Rose & Veiga, 1984). Both Fielding (1982) and Murphy (1984) report the success of intervention programs.

Fielding reviewed studies on the effectiveness of health improvement programs in the workplace, including efforts directed at hypertension, smoking, weight reduction, and physical fitness. Both hypertension and smoking programs were determined to be cost-effective in their reduction of excess morbidity or mortality. No definite conclusions were possible regarding physical fitness and weight reduction programs.

Murphy reported 13 published and unpublished studies that evaluated the effectiveness of stress management techniques applied at the workplace, He found that interventions varied from one session to fifteen treatment sessions, each session ranging in time from 40 minutes to two hours. In general, studies that used more contact hours reported larger reductions in physiological measures and greater reductions in self-reported symptoms of stress. Studies that allowed more time for practicing desired behaviors also appeared to be more successful. Stress management methods utilized in these studies included muscle relaxation, biofeedback, meditation, cognitive restructuring/behavioral skills training, and combinations of these methods. The provision of stress education information was also a major component of most programs. Virtually all of these techniques proved effective when compared with control groups, although relatively few studies have compared methods, and those that have compared methods typically find no clear differences. Few studies reported on how durable or lasting the changes were.

Stoyva and Anderson (1982) propose that a person's reaction to stress is a two-phase process. There is an active coping phase and a rest phase, and our daily existence sees constant shifts from one mode to the other. Individuals who are highly vulnerable to stress, they believe, are likely to exhibit signs of high physiological arousal and, under stress, have difficulty shifting from a coping to a rest mode (that is, they are slow to get accustomed to and recover from the stressful situation). Stoyva and Anderson see this as a defect in the person's capacity to shift to a rest condition. Relaxation techniques help a person to achieve this state and thus alleviate stress. Using this model, they propose that certain interventions are most appropriate for the active coping phase (for example, assertiveness training; social skills and motor skills retraining; self-statements; and imagery, such as guided waking imagery and behavioral rehearsal). Other management procedures are more appropriate to the rest phase (such as relaxation retraining, including progressive relaxation, autogenic training, EMG feedback, and meditation; specific biofeedback, such as hand temperature, electrodermal response, and EMG from particular muscle groups; and systematic desensitization).

Garfield (1986), on the basis of a large number of interviews with "successful" individuals, summarized the characteristics that seemed common to these "peak performers." These included having a purpose in life, formulating plans to accomplish goals, not getting trapped in a comfortable stage of life or plateau for very long, taking risks after determining the consequences, basing their self-confidence on past successes, solving problems rather than placing blame, rehearsing future events with positive mental imagery, taking control, being concerned with quality, and training and utilizing those around them. Bruhn (1989) advocates that counselors assist clients to understand how they experience stress, which of their needs are threatened by diverse types of stresses, and the options available to assuage the stress, as well as to generate new alternatives to meet their needs.

Matheny, Aycock, Pugh, Curlette, & Cannella (1986) conducted a metanalysis of coping studies (*coping* defined as "any effort, healthy or unhealthy, conscious or unconscious, to prevent, eliminate, or weaken stressors, or to tolerate their effects in the least hurtful manner." (p. 509) They determined that of all possible coping treatments (for example, cognitive restructuring, relaxation, stress monitoring, problem solving, social skills, self-reference, wellness, social support, positive diversion, and negative diversion), cognitive restructuring and relaxation seemed to be the most widely used and effective. Used alone, wellness and stress monitoring were relatively ineffective, but when they were combined with other treatment domains, they produced a larger effect size. Problem solving was also effective when combined with other treatments. Finally, individual interventions were judged to be more effective than instructional groups. As a result, the investigators offer a coping model that is organized around four classes of preventive strategies: "(1) avoiding stressors through life adjustments, (2) adjusting demand levels, (3) altering stress-inducing behavior, and (4) developing coping resources" (p. 531). They offer a taxonomy of strategies that are either primarily preventive or primarily combative (Table 11.6).

All of these interventions for stress management are, we believe, appropriate, for application in the workplace in both remedial and preventive modes (stress inoculation).

Table 11.6

Model of Coping

Primarily Preventive Strategies	Primarily Combative Strategies
Avoiding stressors through life adjustments	Monitoring stressors and symptoms
Adjusting demand levels	Marshaling one's resources
Altering stress-inducing behavior patterns	Attacking stressors
Developing coping resources	problem solving
physiological assets (wellness factors)	assertiveness
psychological assets	desensitization
confidence and sense of control	Tolerating stressors
self-esteem	cognitive restructuring
cognitive assets	denial
functional beliefs	sensation focusing
time management skills	Lowering arousal
academic competence	relaxation
social assets	disclosure and catharsis
social support	self-medication
friendship skills	
financial assets	

Source: "Stress Coping: A Qualitative and Quantitative Synthesis with Implications for Treatment" by K. B. Matheny, D. W. Aycock, J. L. Pugh, W. L. Curlette, and K. Cannella, *The Counseling Psychologist, 14,* pp. 499–549. Reprinted by permission.

Summary

In this chapter, we have presented a discussion of a variety of topics related to career counseling (broadly conceived) in the workplace. This area of the career helping domain is relatively uncharted territory, and attempts at intervention are, therefore, tentative and little informed by research and evaluation. An important component of career development in the workplace is the recognition and management of occupational stress. A discussion of this area of inquiry—necessarily brief because of space limitations—served to highlight to central place that attention to work stress should have in career development systems in the workplace.

CHAPTER 12

SPECIAL ADULT CAREER CONCERNS I

Key Concepts

- Attention to the development of career theory focused upon adults is recent in origin; until the past decade, most career theory was concerned primarily with the first two decades of life, not the last five.
- The adult population is heterogenous and comprised of several different subpopulations for whom the career problems and career interventions differ. Groups of particular interest in this chapter are (1) midcareer changers, (2) women entering or reentering the labor force after a period of child rearing, (3) the older worker, and (4) preretirees and retirees.
- Planning models of career guidance or career counseling for adult populations are more recent than those developed for younger persons. Major principles underlying such program planning, however, should include specificity of planning as well as awareness that most adults have family obligations that will affect their planning and that adults typically have immediacy, urgency, and concreteness to their concerns.
- Career counseling techniques useful with younger people are likely to be useful with adults. The career counselor of adults needs to understand principles of adult development and decision-making models, as well as whether a particular person is primarily concerned with anticipation of or implementation of career issues.

Until fairly recently, anyone interested in career counseling might well have wondered if there is a career life after adolescence. Early work in career development and behavior focused on factors and processes leading to the initial choice of an occupation and rarely addressed adult career development. Furthermore, researchers and theorists generally were grounded in the specialties of child and adolescent psychology and ignored the portion of the career life span subsequent to exploration and initial choice.

Awakening to adult career behavior began with an interest in gerontology—the branch of knowledge dealing with aging and the aged. Thus, the last of the career life cycles was probably the first to be studied intensively with adults. Concerns about preretirement and retirement spawned a good deal of research. In fact, most postadolescent research since World War II has been related to old age, and the development of the middle-aged and older worker was still given little attention.

Developmental psychology, which is concerned with changes in behavior over periods of weeks, months, or years, has begun to investigate whether career changes with age extend beyond young adulthood. Specifically, developmental and vocational psychologists have been taking initial steps to determine whether career behaviors and other psychological characteristics are ontogenetic (age-related). Increasing attention, both in the popular press and in professional journals, has been given to the notion of adult life stages. Scholars such as Farrell and Rosenberg (1981), R. Gould (1972), D. J. Levinson (1986), D. J. Levinson, Darrow, Klein, M. H. Levinson, and McKee (1978), Raynor and Entin (1982), Vaillant (1977), and Wortley and Amatea (1982), and lay writers such as Gail Sheehy (1976, 1981) have turned the search for an explanation of the adult life cycle into a chic pursuit. This early research is tentative and is based on population samples that are both small and narrowly delimited. Yet it is a beginning. In relation to career behavior, this new and enthusiastic interest in adults is evidenced by the creation of various committees, commissions, and special interest groups within professional organizations, by a rapidly increasing number of articles relating to adult career behavior, and by new legislation.

Indeed, the language applied to the career development and behavior of adults reflects these popular concerns. Terms like *career menopause* or *career climacteric* are used with an assurance that is in direct contrast to what is actually known about the important changes that may occur in adult career behavior. In fact, we are only beginning to collect systematic data on adults, and there is some question about whether we possess any useful theory of general development in which to use these data. Of the human being's three score and ten years, relatively little attention has been focused on the last five decades of life. Using the work of Piaget and Erickson (or other behavioral scientists), we can build a reasonable model of development from infancy through adolescence; however, beginning with the young adult and through senescence, we are merely in the earlier stages of acquiring knowledge.

Certainly, as discussed in some depth in Chapter 4, there are those who, in the past, have addressed themselves to adult behavior in general and adult career behavior in particular. Not the least of these has been Charlotte Buehler (1933), to whom Donald Super and others have acknowledged a great debt in the development of their own work. Her attempts to evolve a comprehensive psychology of the entire course of life have provided a stimulus and a framework for many subsequent researchers. Among others, Tiedeman and O'Hara (1963) have also provided some valuable thoughts and data on adult career stages. And we are beginning to receive the benefit of data from longitudinal studies such as the Career Pattern Study (Super, 1977, 1980; Super & Kidd, 1979) and Project Talent (Abeles, Steel, & Wise, 1980; Flanagan, 1978), whose initial early adolescent subjects have now reached early adulthood or incipient middle age. One example will suffice to point out the kinds of data that are emerging from longitudinal studies. The 21 year follow-up of the original 111-person sample in Gribbons and Lohnes's (1982) Career Development Study (CDS) compared the original stated 1958 career aspirations of the then eighth graders with the actual occupations for the 91 remaining subjects in 1980. Results reveal the substantial changes that occur between early adolescence and adulthood; few were in their original choice occupation. Since much previous career development research has been accomplished using expressed vocational choice of students rather than actual entry into an occupation, these differences represent significant implications for theory building. In general, the CDS sample showed major shifts for males to business from the sciences and for females to homemaking from education, the humanities,and the arts.

Savickas, Passen, and Jarjoura (1988) compared two of an increasing number of adult career-related inventories: Super's Adult Career Concerns Inventory (ACCI) and Crites's Career Adjustment and Development Inventory (CADI). They determined that—for a group of salespeople at least—the two instruments actually measure different constructs.

The CADI, in their judgment, measures vocational development, while the ACCI does not; instead it assesses concern with how requirements or opportunities for development, adaptation, or change in a career are being met. They consequently recommend that the instruments be used in tandem. On the other hand, Whiston (1990) urges caution in the use of the ACCI because of few validation studies, inadequate normative data, and lack of support for distinct stages.

There is increasing support for a *renewal* stage in the career development of adults. C. P. Williams and Savickas (1990) examined workers in the maintenance stage of their careers to test Super's notions about the developmental tasks necessary at this point in one's career development. They found that, in general, the tasks that these workers identified as important did correspond to Super's hypotheses, although some were suggested to occur sooner or later than Super surmised. These tasks included keeping up with new developments, struggling to hold on, shifting focus (developing new competencies, expanding, and so on), and preparing for retirement (decelerating). A fifth component—continuing education—was a task that was identified but that was not in Super's schema. Similarily, a sixth task—questioning future directions and goals—did not match Super's speculations. It is this last task that suggests a renewal component in the maintenance stage of career development.

Thus, we do know something about adult behaviors and needs—at least enough to make an informed start at comprehensive delivery of career facilitating services; but there is much more to learn before the "science" of career facilitation with adults replaces the current "art." This chapter summarizes some of the existing knowledge, describes some of the delivery systems in use, and generally provides an introduction to the career counseling of adults. Osipow (1983) has summarized our current condition:

> Clearly, attention to mid-career transitions is burgeoning. Many interventions have been devised to try to help people deal with the associated stresses and strains. These interventions remain to be proven with respect to their effectiveness. What does appear to be clear is that the cultural determinants that have indicated career stages and development in younger people seem as they get older to operate to produce predictable stages in many people, at least in professional and managerial levels and very likely in other levels as well. Probably these events are subject to continual revision as a function of changes in society and the continuing reorganization of its work structure, as well as demands for different kinds of human resources. (p. 223)

FACTORS UNDERLYING COUNSELING ADULTS

Obviously, the adult population is completely heterogeneous. It is not a population contained within a single institution, such as the school. The targets of career counseling, therefore, potentially include each person in the labor force and each adult seeking to enter the labor force. However, for our purposes here, some delineation is necessary. In Chapter 13, we will discuss several adult subpopulations: (1) unemployed, dislocated, and discouraged workers; (2) "burned-out" workers; (3) working mothers; (4) dual-career couples; (5) job seekers; and (6) dissatisfied workers. In this chapter, however, we will concentrate on the four adult subpopulations mentioned at the beginning of the chapter.

Characteristics of the Population

Career counseling of adults should be viewed within the context of changes in society, many of which have been discussed in Chapter 3. In general we may point to the following characteristics that significantly affect the career counseling of adults:

1. *Changing marital patterns.*The marriage rate remains lower than in times past, women are getting married later in life, and the divorce rate is substantial (for example, one out of every three married women 30 years old has been or will be divorced).
2. *Changing child-bearing and child-rearing patterns.*The birth rate has declined significantly from the past. Changes in the birth rate have caused increases and decreases in the number of workers in various age groups of the population, affecting both the opportunities open for workers and the types of goods and services in demand by society. Because of divorce, less than 70 percent of all children under 18 live with both of their natural parents.
3. *Changing occupational patterns.*The alteration of the occupational structure causes unemployment, underemployment, and frustration as well as opportunities. The information economy and the service economy require different workers from those needed in a goods-producing, industrial economy. The nature of work itself is in flux.

All of these factors can have a profound effect on the kind and frequency of career counseling services required by the adult population.

Within this context of external changes, adults are also experiencing internal changes—mental, physical, and emotional—that are in symbiotic relationship with their work. The process of aging is indeed complex, stemming from endocrine changes; aspiration-achievement discrepancies; stagnation-versus-growth Ericksonian issues; the more apparent reality of death and dying; changes in relationships with spouse, children, and parents; role changes; and other factors. Each of these changes in life may affect attitudes toward and performance at work, just as the experience of work can affect attitudes toward and general behavior in one's nonwork life. By far the most common psychological difficulty of aging workers is depression (Yolles, Krinsky, Kieffer, & Carone, 1984).

The types of career problems with which adults may need to cope are numerous. One attempt at a taxonomy of these problems is that devised by R. E. Campbell and Cellini (1981). They categorize adult problems into four groups: (1) problems in career decision making; (2) problems in implementing career plans; (3) problems in organizational/institutional performance; and (4) problems in organizational/institutional adaptation. The full taxonomy is presented in Chapter 2.

Work by S. D. Phillips (1982a, 1982b) offers some further instructive data about adult career development and behavior. She investigated career decision making behavior over time in 95 males who participated in the Career Pattern Study and discovered that exploratory behavior tends to decrease and that decisions are less exploratory and more terminal from age 21 to age 36. Career decisions, then, are made differently at different stages of development. Phillips also discovered that, strangely, increasing commitment with age (a condition thought to be highly desirable) did not necessarily lead to higher levels of career outcomes (such as career success, job satisfaction, or systematic career progression). Whether this finding was an artifact of her sample or whether this result is indeed the case is important, since current career development theory is postulated on the desirability of increasing career commitment.

There are those who urge that as much attention must be given to educational opportunities across the lifespan as are now devoted to approximately the first quarter of one's lifetime. Harootyan and Feldman (1990), for example, note that by the year 2000, about two-thirds of all persons 65 and older will be high school graduates (compared to just over one-half currently) and that they will be a much more diverse population than they are presently. These better educated, more diverse people will be using lifelong education in a wide variety of ways, ranging from survival skills (for example, basic literacy and work-related learning) to exploring new roles (for instance, leisure, career shifts, and so forth). Some of this learning will be self-directed; some will involve technical support. Learning will occur in diverse locations, from shopping malls to community centers. In short, lifelong learning is an activity expected to increase substantially from what exists now, and what is extant in stores, factories, laboratories, the military, and so on is already a huge enterprise.

Studies that investigate the counseling needs of adult students offer additional data to guide career interventions. H. H. Goodman (1981, p. 468) lists 19 appropriate potential adult client groups:

1. Adults seeking general personal counseling in the areas of self, family, work, and social interaction
2. Personal and family resources planning and management seekers
3. Life planning, career planning, and career management clients
4. Persons seeking job search, job campaign, and placement coaching
5. Unemployed and underemployed college graduates (men and women) exploring career alternatives
6. Middle-aged men and women (mostly empty-nest housewives) seeking to enter or reenter gainful employment
7. Middle-aged men and women seeking to make a change in employment or career
8. The laid-off or fired middle-aged, middle-class, educated male
9. The female executive or professional under career or job stress
10. The black professional or executive dealing with career problems and stress that accompany transfer or promotion
11. People moving into and out of government and academic employment
12. The certified school teacher seeking career alternatives
13. The fledgling entrepreneur attempting to become self-employed by starting a small business
14. The second-, third-, and fourth-career planner
15. Adults in alternative work patterns such as share-a-job situations where two or more workers share one position and income
16. New careers for older workers: part-time and volunteer work
17. Counseling in employee assistance programs: both public and private sector employer-provided employee assistance programs
18. Counseling for avocational and leisure time activities
19. Counseling institutionalized populations in prisons, rest homes, nursing homes, hospitals, and so on

Given all of this documentation of the career needs of adults, we turn now to discussions of planning considerations with adults and of career counseling techniques with adults.

Planning Considerations

The framework for service delivery with adults is more problematic than it is with younger clients. Compared to programs and theory effected in educational institutions and with younger counselees, the field lacks historical perspective, empirically verified techniques, validated materials, and pertinent theory. Nevertheless, the career counseling of adults will probably be made more efficient and effective if attention is given to the following suggestions regarding planning.

1. Goals and objectives should be based on some model of the needs of adults at various stages of adult life and with diverse presenting problems. Although the body of knowl-

edge pertaining to the needs of subpopulations of adults (as described in this volume) is currently rather small, it is growing daily; there is enough useful material to begin. Particularly helpful to the counselor will be journals about which many counselors new to counseling adults may not be aware: *Industrial Gerontology, Journal of Gerontology, Monthly Labor Review, Industrial Sociology, Journal of Employment Counseling, Personnel Administration, The Gerontologist*, and *The Family Coordinator*.

2. The physical centrality of adult career counseling services, the hours of operation, and the publicizing of such services should be such that the populations to be served readily know what career counseling opportunities exist and that the facilities can be reached with minimum discomfort and maximum ease. Preretirement counseling located in places of employment; women's programs attached to continuing education programs of high schools, colleges, and universities; improved dissemination efforts by the U.S. Employment Service branches; and counseling with senior citizens in centers for the aged are all examples of attempts to expedite service delivery.

3. Middle-class adults who seek career counseling are typically highly motivated. People in earlier stages of career development frequently must establish readiness; the challenge for the counselor of adults is to capitalize on the readiness and motivation that the adult brings to career counseling.

4. Adults generally will have little tolerance for the abstract in career counseling. There is an immediacy, an urgency, and a concreteness to their concerns. They are, on the average, able to phrase their questions in self-referent terms that are concise and meaningful.

5. The bases on which adults ought to make decisions are probably little different from those required by decision makers at an earlier stage of development. They should have a knowledge of self, a knowledge of the world of work, and decision-making skills. In some subpopulations of adults (such as mid-career shifters), these characteristics may be relatively well developed; in others (such as women seeking to enter the nonhousehold labor force for the first time at a relatively advanced age), these requirements may be as undeveloped as in the average adolescent.

6. The delivery of services should be systematic, although the progression may be accelerated because of the accrued experience of the clientele. In short, goals must be translated into activities, suitable materials for the conduct of these activities must be discovered or invented, and evaluation should occur to determine the extent to which goals have been achieved as a result of the activities provided.

7. Specificity is a key in planning. Throughout most of the school years, relatively broad and broadening goals such as career awareness, exploration, conceptualization, perceptualization, and generalization are laudable ends in themselves. With some adults, it may be necessary to achieve these goals, but the counselor must go on from that point to help adults to narrow generated alternatives, to negotiate systems, to focus interests, to secure employment, or otherwise to deal in self-relevant specifics. Expansion is a primary goal for the young; specificity is an aim with the adult.

8. For many adults, career counseling will have to occur within the context of a strong awareness of family implications. Adults' decisions affect more people than simply themselves unlike most earlier decision-making. Often, career decisions of adults will involve simultaneous demands on spouses, children, and the extended family. The obverse may also pertain; that is, marital crises seem increasingly to stimulate a career change.

9. A great many adults will simply want information. Others may want counseling in addition to information. Thus, information dissemination becomes a highly important service for adults.

S. S. Moore (1985) suggests six beliefs that might undergird the practice of counseling adults, no matter what specific theory of adult development a counselor espouses:

1. Adulthood is full of conflict and choice. Adults can expect to encounter change in their lives.
2. The work of psychological development does not end with the onset of maturity—personality development, character formation, adaptation to and interaction with the external environment and the internal self all continue well beyond the age of 21.
3. As people grow older, they grow more and more different from one another—diversity increases with age.
4. Career development cannot be separated from the individual's physical, emotional, and cognitive development. It is connected to all aspects of one's life—leisure, education, values, motivation, lifestyle, and self-concept.
5. Counselors can help adults negotiate change by helping them to identify and build on their natural strengths.
6. Counselors are caregivers, not caretakers. We are there to support, teach, and help individuals reach their own potential. We are not there to direct them into what we think is right for them or what we want for them. We believe that they are the architects of their own lives. (p. ix)

Career Counseling Techniques

Almost any career counseling technique used with younger populations can, of course, be used with adults. Basically, the goals are the same: self-knowledge of various types, its relationship to the worlds of work and education or training, and effective decision-making skills, among others. Many of the techniques that the counselor will use in working with adults are implicit in the goal statements for each adult subpopulation and in the planning considerations just presented. Specifically, as counselors work with adults, they should remember the following unique considerations that should be added to their repertoire of career helping strategies and behaviors.

1. Especially with unskilled adults from lower occupational levels, *motivation* is a primary focus of career assistance. Readiness and motivation for work are frequently lacking in some adults, despite the axiom that people want to work. Counselors must, then, seek to establish within some adults the desire to work.

2. Although much career counseling with adults can be developmental (in the sense of commonalities at given stages of life), a good deal of the focus of adult career counseling will be crisis-generated and crises-centered. Frequently, therefore, what have come to be termed *crisis intervention* techniques will be utilized. Crisis intervention provides quick, short-term relief in an emergency situation. The counselor deals with the immediate problem rather than with the underlying causes of the problem in providing the temporary relief.

3. Many adults will be searching for what has loosely been defined as *self-actualization*. However, their expectations and perceptions that some future work will enable them to achieve self-actualization often prove to be unrealistic. Counselors should work with adults within a framework of *reality*. This is not to say that adults ought to be discouraged from having their heads in the clouds; rather, they should be simultaneously aided to keep their feet on the ground.

4. The *dissemination of information*, a cognitive activity anathema to some counselors, is an important strategy in the career counseling of adults. Adults want answers to specific questions; counselors should provide those answers, or they should assist clients in finding answers for themselves.

5. *Testing* and the use of test results with certain adult subpopulations should be approached, tentatively. Several researchers have pointed out that norms for adult populations are frequently nonexistent, and that there is often not a demonstrated relationship between test score and job performance for a specified adult clientele. On the other hand, certain types of test data, especially discriminant data that tell people how much they resemble certain groups, are very useful. Rounds (1990), for example, has concluded on the basis of his research with adults that they require both values and interest data in career counseling. Hence, he recommends the administration and interpretation (in no particular order) of both types of inventories.

6. *Counseling techniques* that have evolved from work with younger adults (such as reflection of feelings) may not be appropriate for older adults even though they have been successful with younger clients and, in fact, may ignore the developmental needs of this chronologically advanced population (such as historical perspective). They should test their current repertoires of counseling techniques in terms of their salience for adults. Furthermore, counselors should engage in self-examination to be sure that they are not consciously or unconsciously guilty of ageism (negative attitudes toward any age group).

MIDCAREER CHANGERS

It is difficult to discover exactly how many Americans change careers each year, partly because of differing definitions of exactly what constitutes a career change (a shift from one Holland or Roe category to another, from one occupational title to another, or from one job to another). We estimate that approximately 5 percent to 10 percent of Americans change occupations each year and that about one-half of these changers are over 30 years of age. It is safe to say that millions of other workers would like to change but do not or cannot.

Reasons for Change

The reasons that people voluntarily change jobs are many and varied. Sometimes interests, capacities, and values do not fit with the demands of an initial occupational choice. Expectation-reality gaps quickly become apparent upon one's entry into an occupation. Perhaps original occupational choice was determined more by the demands of a significant other (for example, a parent) than by the chooser's own expression of free will. Material needs or wants may have increased to the point where a current occupation fails to meet these enhanced living standards. Employer practices, work environments, the lack of variety in some occupations, too much or too little pressure, too many physical demands, no time for leisure activities, plateauing, boredom—all of these factors and many others may impel individuals to leave an originally chosen occupation, to *push* them out. Other factors may *pull* someone into a new occupation because the change seems attractive. Some changes are anticipated, while others are unforeseen. For example, unanticipated events such as illness, divorce, death of a spouse, and job dislocation cause individuals to change occupations.

H. Thomas (1980) identified career changers who experienced high or low pressure from the environment to change and those who evidenced high or low pressure from themselves to change. Thus, those who had high self-pressure but low environmental pressure would be self-determined "opt-outs" from an occupation, while those who showed high environmental pressure but low self-pressure would be situationally determined "force-outs." To summarize, some major event may cause a career shift, some people may be pushed out because of internal or external circumstances, and, though reasonably satisfied in a current occupation, others may be pulled by the prospects of even more satisfaction in a new occupation.

Not too long ago there was a prevalent notion that voluntary career shifters were "oddballs," individuals who because of some personality flaw or character disorder were deficient in adaptive skills, were professional malcontents, or were otherwise lacking in some way. In fact, most studies of career shifters versus career persisters indicate no differences in emotional adjustment; midcareer change does not necessarily constitute floundering or pathological behavior (Neopolitan, 1980). We believe that voluntary midcareer shifts are generally acts of a mentally healthy personality.

Developmentalists see midcareer changes as simply an alternative available in a predictable stage of adult life. D. T. Levinson et al. (1978), in their taxonomy of adult male development, suggest that midcareer shifts are most likely to occur during what they have termed the Becoming One's Own Man (BOOM) stage (about age 35 to 39). It is during this stage that men are evidently most prone to experience constraint and oppression in work and to seek resolution of these feelings. This study receives support in the research of R. E. Hill and Miller (1981). In their study of academics, Entrekin and Everett (1981) identified a similar stage that comes a bit later in life. The ages from 30 to 44 are described as a "settling in" period; 45 to 49 are seen as a span of years in which the individual reaches out and becomes restless, exhibiting more change needs; 50 to 54 are viewed as a settling down time; and after 55, the individual academic is thought to be finishing his career. Others have described a similar phenomenon that can occur anywhere from the late thirties to the early fifties as "midolescence" (Sagal & DeBlassie, 1981).

Others see midcareer change as a case of incongruity based on Holland's categories. Congruency in terms of Holland's theory has been found to be related to more stable careers in women and men (H. A. Rose & Elton, 1982), and to more career-mature individuals (Guthrie & Herman, 1982). Isaacson (1981) believes that changing worker needs and interests are major reasons for career change. This thesis is supported in a study by Meir (1988) that suggests that the lack of congruence between within-occupation interests and specialty in midcareer may be an impetus to career change. He contends that occupational choice satisfaction is more than a function of choice of correct occupational field in young adulthood; in the career maintenance stage, it is more a function of appropriate occupational specialty. Thus, it may be that original choice of occupation was reasonable, but later choice of specialty was inappropriate and could lead to career change.

Perosa and Perosa (1983) compared people who had changed careers with those in the process of career change (for example, those who had returned to school to prepare for new occupations), and with those who wanted to change careers but nevertheless persisted in their current situation. A career shift in this case was judged to occur when the move was to a different Holland code. They found that the changers engaged in a period of intense self-examination as a result of feeling frustration, stagnation, self-doubt, and depression in their work. In fact, about one-third reported a sense of meaninglessness in their lives and a desire to gain self-respect. This perceived threat to self led to action in the form of decision making. The major variable that separated the changers from nonchangers was apparently the willingness and capacity of the changers to deal with serious risk.

Although most midcareer shifts occur in populations that are at the upper levels of the occupational hierarchy, in some cases, midcareer shifts take place among lower-level occupations. Such is the case, for example, with individuals who are disadvantaged and suffer from delayed or impaired career development. Manuele (1984) worked with a group of 20 such adults who had a mean age of 40.8 and exposed them to the Adkins Life Skills Program: Employability Skills Series. After this intervention, there was a significant increase in the participants' career maturity scores.

Henton, Russell, and Koval (1983) studied 20 wives of career shifters to determine what effect a husband's career change had on his spouse (in her 30s and 40s) and family. By means of an interview technique, the wives indicated that their husbands were looking for increased challenge in their work lives and expressed discontent with their present jobs. About 40 percent reported a drop in financial status because of the change. Approximately two-thirds of the wives perceived themselves as encouraging. The results of the study reinforced the idea that a change in any life role (for example, husband, worker, father, and so on) can profoundly affect other life roles. More generally, any alteration in the space, time, and energy dimensions resulting from the career change will affect the distribution of rewards to all members of the family.

Doering and Rhodes (1989) studied career change among teachers (defined as movement to an occupation that is not part of a teacher's traditional career progression). Using a semistructured, in-depth interview technique with 20 participants, they determined that the top five reasons that were cited for career change were push-out types of considerations: inadequate pay, lack of challenge, stimulation, or opportunity to grow, lack of advancement opportunities, dissatisfaction with classroom, and too demanding a workload. They also determined that the time between thinking about a change and deciding to change ranged from one month to 6 years, with a median of 2 years. Apparently, the gestation period is usually quite long. The three major factors that facilitated a change were support of family, friends, and spouse, financial aid, and self-confidence. Interestingly, very few of these career shifters availed themselves of career counseling opportunities.

In any case, whether midcareer changes are caused by frustration and anxiety, by growth, achievement, and expansion motives, by a recognition of one's individual differences, or by some other factor or a combination of factors, the midcareer shifter should be viewed, in general and barring evidence to the contrary, as a mentally healthy individual. Those in the process of midcareer change are usually at least in their late twenties and beyond. In a chronological sense, they are middle-aged, and with middle age come many changes.

Those Who Change

Who goes through midlife career change? Every occupation is represented, but some are more visible than others. Classic cases of midlife career change can be found in the ranks of those who put in 20 years or so in the military or in municipal activities, such as fire and police protection, and then retire at a relatively young age, free to pursue a second career. In the 1970s, thousands of engineers and scientists became unemployed because of substantial cuts in space and defense spending; these workers in declining industries were often forced to seek unrelated types of employment, or to take lower-paying jobs in the same occupation. More recently, the field of education experienced cutbacks, causing teachers and other educational personnel to switch career paths. In the late 1980s, thousands of workers in the financial community lost their jobs. Whether voluntary or involuntary, it is clear that midlife career change is a visible phenomenon and that a significant proportion of workers will not fit the one life–one occupation mode.

There are various ways of describing career changers. Lieberman and Lieberman (1983) investigated a group of second-careerists who were working in Florida at an arts fair. As a result, they described seven patterns of second careers:

- Mid-life career changers
- Early retirement—force out
- Early retirement–by choice
- Normal retirement—second career
- Post–Child rearing
- On-going career but new work setting
- Combine first and second career

Early research in career patterns gave little attention to the idea of *voluntary* career changes. Drawing on D. C. Miller and Form (1951), Super (1957) described four types of career patterns for men.

> 1. *The stable career pattern.*In this category are found most professional careers, many managers, some skilled workers and to a lesser extent semi-skilled and clerical workers. They are persons who have gone directly from school or college into a type of work which they have consistently followed: in other words, they have essentially skipped the trial work period.
> 2. *The conventional career pattern.*In this pattern the sequence of jobs follows the typical progression from initial to trial to stable employment. This pattern is most typical of managerial, skilled, and clerical workers, but characterizes some professionals and domestic workers.
> 3. *The unstable career pattern.*Here the sequence is trial-stable-trial: the worker does not succeed in establishing himself permanently in what might have been a lifetime job or occupation, but instead gives up his potential career in one field and goes off in a different direction in which he may or may not establish himself. This sequence is seen most often in semi-skilled, clerical, and domestic workers.
> 4. *The multiple-trial career pattern.*This is the pattern of frequent change of employment, with no one type sufficiently prolonged or dominant to justify calling the person established in a career. This type of sequence is observed most often in domestic, clerical, semi-skilled workers, who not infrequently shift from one type of work to another and accumulate the most disconnected of work histories. (pp. 73–74)

Categories 3 and 4 pertain to midlife career shifters, but there is little cognizance of the voluntary or involuntary shifts of well-established workers within an occupation. As we have seen, such shifts by those who have indeed established themselves in an occupation are not at all rare.

In summary, midlife career changes—second careers—are becoming increasingly common. Those in the midst of such voluntary or involuntary shifts require assistance in career planning. There is currently no pervasive delivery system for providing this aid, although isolated programs directed toward this end do exist.

Counseling Midcareer Shifters

Unlike younger decision makers, midlife career shifters typically have accrued experience and developed judgment which enables them to approach the career decision-making process with maturity and knowledge. Even so, the career counselor working with this population should uncover certain common factors even within this group. Some of these factors are addressed in the following goals.

1. Help the individual to explore, specify, and evaluate the clarity of the reasons for a career shift. Is the individual confused and anxious as a result of an involuntary career shift, secure and optimistic because of the prospects of a voluntary career shift, or some combination of both? Are stress factors with which an individual has diffi-

culty coping in a current job likely to be present in an intended job? Does the individual appear distressed, depressed, or dysfunctional? How carefully has the individual planned? These and other questions relate to the goal of shift clarification.
2. Assist the individual in acquiring all necessary information relevant to a career shift. Does the individual recognize the relationship between education or training and the proposed work shift? What steps are necessary to effect the change? Where and how does one get the necessary information?
3. Help the individual to envision the possible effects of a career shift. Will there be financial ramifications? Will family life be affected? Will life-style change appreciably? Will geographical relocation be required? What will be the immediate, intermediate, and long-range consequences?
4. Help the individual develop appropriate job-seeking or education-seeking behaviors. Can the person write an effective résumé? Does the individual have good skills as an interviewee? Has he or she narrowed down to manageable proportions the education or training universe? Does the person have adequate information? These concerns will be treated in detail in the next chapter.
5. Assist the individual in clarifying abilities, interests, and personal characteristics. Will the attributes of the person facilitate or impede the transition to a different career, occupation, or job? Does the person possess characteristics that would make his or her functioning unsatisfying in a particular job? Are there any physical, mental, or emotional problems to be considered?
6. Assist, if appropriate, in placing the individual in a job. Certain settings wherein counselors work with midcareer shifters will have placement as a goal (such as the Employment Service or outplacement counseling). Other agencies that do not perform a brokerage role may well consider performing this function if no alternative is readily available.
7. Gauge the extent of the individual's support network. Are social support and financial support adequate to meet the demands of the career change? What buffers exist to assuage the sometimes painful effects of a significant life change? (Entine, 1984)

One model for assisting midcareer counselees is offered by Finnegan, Westefeld, and Elmore (1981). Their model is not too different from one designed to work with any population. They present four goals: (1) for people to gain information about themselves in order to make constructive choices; (2) for the participants to gain information about their environment that might influence work choices; (3) for the participants to realize that midlife reassessment is not unusual, that others are faced with it, and that there are ways of coping with it; and (4) for members of the workshop to gain skills in decision making for occupational midlife reassessment and change (p. 70). To accomplish these goals, they concentrate on five major themes: abilities, interests, values, confinements (barriers to moving to a new job), and environment (speculation about an ideal work setting).

It is important that changers utilize the services of counselors. Armstrong's (1981) study of middle-aged returnees to higher education sought to determine how they arrived at their decisions. Few of the sample used counseling services; rather, they relied on habitual decision response patterns that were based largely on choosing from among limited alternatives on the basis of little information. D. Brown (1981) discusses several models for assisting adults at midlife: self-help groups; informational models (career information hotlines, job information seminars, occupational libraries, and so on); developmental models (concern with total life/career development); and structured group models (carefully structured activities based on a systematic model). These are not necessarily mutually exclusive models for assisting midlife clients. Examples of these types of programs can be found in the work of Marlowe (1981) and Gerstein (1982).

Because organizational responses are generally slow (see Chapter 11), it is likely that in the foreseeable future, midcareer shifters will be helped to rearrange their internal structures rather than the organizations within society acting to facilitate changes. In any case, we are now only beginning to understand the dynamics of midcareer shifts and to devise helpful interventions.

Although we have some rudimentary knowledge about midcareer shifters, the research in this area has been relatively sparse and has suffered from a number of methodological deficiencies. First, samples studied have been small and nonrepresentative. Subjects have typically been well-educated, white males with an overrepresentation of academics, both former and current. Second, subjects are often in school or in training for an occupation and have not actually effected a career change. Third, subjects vary considerably in terms of such variables as age and length of time in the first occupation. Fourth, definitions of *voluntary* and *career change* also vary. Fifth, relatively few comparison studies of changers versus nonchangers have been accomplished. Sixth, research designs are usually cross-sectional or retrospective; longitudinal studies would be less limiting. Finally, no standardized instruments of proven validity and reliability and with adequate normative data exist that are designed to operationalize the process of midcareer change. There is also no single overall theory of adult development in which to imbed midcareer research. It is little wonder, then, that research in this area is still in the exploratory stage, and that researchers are trying simply to generate hypotheses rather than to test them.

WOMEN ENTERING OR REENTERING THE LABOR FORCE

In Chapter 5 we discussed some career considerations unique to females. A specific aspect of careers relating to adults is the case of women who enter or reenter the labor force after a period of childbearing and child-rearing.

Career Patterns

Super (1957) has classified the career patterns of women as follows:

1. *The stable homemaking career pattern.* This category includes all women who marry while in or very shortly after leaving school or college, having expected to do so and having no significant work experience.

2. *The conventional career pattern.* In this pattern of working, followed by homemaking, the young woman leaving school or college goes to work for a period of several months or several years, in an occupation which is open to her without training beyond that which she obtained in her general education, in brief professional education substituted for general education, or in some relatively brief post–high school or post-collegiate education. Clerical work, teaching, nursing, occupational therapy, or secretarial work illustrate these types of occupations. They are generally viewed as stop gaps, but may be thought of as life careers, with subsequent changes of aspirations. They are often valuable as an opportunity for developing independence and a sense of being a person in one's own right. Marrying after this relatively brief work experience, the young woman becomes a full-time homemaker.

3. *The stable working career pattern.* The sequence in this type of career pattern is one of entering the work force on leaving school, college, or professional school and embarking on a career which becomes the woman's

life's work. She may perceive it as a life career from the start: a small percentage of young women do have strong career (as contrasted with homemaking) motivation and interest [*note:* this was in 1957]. Or she may at first view her working career as a preliminary to marriage, on a working career to resume after a period of full-time homemaking.

4. *The double-track career pattern.* This is a pattern of the woman who goes to work after completing her education, marries, and continues with a double career of working and homemaking. She may take occasional time out for childbearing. The pattern is most common near the upper and lower ends of the occupational scale, among women physicians and scientists, and among women domestics, presumably because the challenge of the work, or the income it produces, is important to the woman in question. The double role is in neither case easy, for the married working woman usually has two jobs, one with and one without pay.

5. *The interrupted career pattern.* Here the sequence is one of working, homemaking, and working while or instead of homemaking. The young woman works for some time, then marries, and then, when her children are old enough for her to leave them, when financial needs—including those from being widowed or divorced—or interest in working become dominant, she returns to work. . . .

6. *The unstable career pattern.* In women, this type of career pattern consists of working, homemaking, working again, returning to full-time homemaking, etc. It results most often from irregular economic pressures which make extra earnings necessary despite homemaking preferences or needs, or from poor health necessitating giving up employment, or from a combination of these. This pattern is observed most often at the lower socioeconomic levels.

7. *The multiple-trial career pattern.* This pattern is the same in women as the similarly named pattern in men; it consists of a succession of unrelated jobs, with stability in none, resulting in the individual having no genuine life work. (pp. 77–78)*

In this chapter, we are concerned with women in patterns 2, 4, 5, and 6. As we saw in Chapter 5, more women have entered and are entering the labor force; a significant proportion of those women are reentering the world of work and education after a substantial hiatus or are older women entering for the first time. These women feel considerable insecurity, stress, and a variety of emotions and uncertainties that call for professional career interventions.

M. W. Riley (1982) envisions more and more reentry or first-time entry women and labels the process "cohort norm formation." Women in their thirties and forties are responding to social changes by moving in new directions: going to school, pursuing careers, or structuring family lives in innovative ways. When they do, however, as Slaney, Stafford, and Russell (1981) have demonstrated, they experience considerably more career indecision than do high school or college women. This finding adds further evidence to support the need for career interventions for reentry women. In addition, there are social and psychological barriers facing reentry women: job discrimination, lack of marketable skills, guilt feelings, and a low opinion of their own abilities. Coupled with all of these factors is the problem of what Berman (1980) describes simply as being a woman in an era of changing values.

Reasons for Returning to a Career

Women return to careers for many reasons. The most obvious cause is financial. In an age

* From *The Psychology of Careers* by Donald Super. New York: Harper Collins Publishers, Inc., 1957. Reprinted by permission.

of inflation, it is frequently necessary for both husband and wife to work in order to maintain a standard of living gained when only the husband worked, let alone to increase a standard of living. In times of high unemployment, a wife may be the only marriage partner able to find work. Divorce and widowhood also may cause financial strain that necessitates reentry. In any case, financial necessity, however idiosyncratically defined, is a major work motivator for reentry women. A second reason for work outside the home is fulfillment. Declining birth rates mean fewer years of childbearing and childrearing, and housekeeping duties are much easier, thus leaving women technologically unemployed in the sense of traditional motherhood. In many cases, such a condition leads to ennui, frustration, a deficient sense of personal worth and identity, and so on. There is some early research to suggest that for many women the empty-nest period is an acute crisis stage. With the termination of the family life cycle, when children have left the home and nurturant demands are no longer present, many women review their lives, find themselves fighting feelings of impotence, helplessness, and despair, and search for outlets to fill the void resulting from the empty nest. (At least that is the theory.)

On the other hand, Black and Hill (1984) discovered in their sample of 232 educated, married women in their 50s that these individuals appeared to be happy regardless of their employment status, age, socioeconomic status, educational level, husband's attitude toward his spouse, working life stressors, and menopausal symptoms. They conclude that for well-educated, middle-aged women, the empty nest is not an apparent problem. For women with other problems, however, the empty nest may touch off distress with which they have difficulty coping.

Confirming this reassessment of the presumed effects of the empty nest, Raup and Myers (1989) concluded that the period indeed represents a major life change or transition, but that relatively few women experience negative effects because of the loss of an active parenting role. These are women who fail to invest in new life roles. What we do not know currently is how to identify at an earlier stage those who are potentially at risk in this normal phase of family development.

The historical period in which a woman lives is as important in determining her reentry into the labor force as are her personal circumstances. Moen, Downey, and Bolger (1990) looked at the decade of the 1970s and determined that better educated homemakers were more likely and older homemakers less likely to reenter the labor force. Marital dissolution also obviously affected a woman's decision to reenter. For each of these three variables, however, there were differences throughout the decade. In line with previously discussed research findings in this chapter, they discovered that the so-called empty-nest phase was not so strong a predictor of reentry as was the entry of the youngest child into a given phase of schooling (for example, elementary, middle, or high school). The differences in reentry rates throughout the decade were ascribed primarily to social changes during that time—changes in public perceptions of women's roles, the continued growth of the traditional female service sector, and new occupational opportunities for young adult as well as midlife women. Women with more education and those whose marriages had dissolved were most likely to take advantage of these opportunities.

Studying the influences that affect adult women's decisions to enroll in college, Mohney and Anderson (1988) concluded that for many such women, the decision was made in the context of what they perceived as other people's needs—children, spouses, and so on. Barriers to earlier enrollment included such variables as parenting demands, multiple roles (for instance, worker, mother, spouse), lack of spousal support, poor self-image (for example, not bright enough, shy), early marriage and pregnancy, lack of financial resources, and so on. Facilitating factors that enabled them later to enroll in college included their perceptions that their children were "old enough," adequate child care, discretionary time, social supports from friends and spouses, and adequate finances, among other influences. Spanard (1990) confirms the results of this study and identifies institutional, situational, and psychosocial barriers specifically related to adults' returning to higher education:

Institutional barriers

1. Location (place)
2. Schedules (time)
3. Fee structures (cost)
4. Campus friendliness

Situational barriers

1. Job commitments
2. Home responsibility
3. Lack of money
4. Lack of child care
5. Transportation problems

Psychosocial barriers

1. Attitudes, beliefs, and values
2. Self-esteem
3. Opinions of others
4. Past experiences as a student (pp. 340–341)

We are now in an era when home-based work (especially white-collar work) is increasing because of technological advances in information processing (K. E. Christensen, 1988). This type of work may provide a bridge that permits many women to transition from no work to complete labor force participation.

The typical woman in America enters the labor force immediately after schooling and works for a few years before marriage and having a child. Few women permanently leave the labor force. Most return or never leave at all. Shortages of skilled workers in many professional, managerial, clerical, skilled craft, and service occupations offer women an excellent employment prospect. Nondiscrimination legislation helps to break down barriers to higher-level occupations and to traditionally male-dominated fields. New opportunities in expanding occupations are available. When these opportunities are combined with the trend toward more education for women and toward smaller families (thus muting the effects of fertility on work), the likely result is a modest increase in the labor force participation of women.

Counseling Reentry Women

Much of the counseling for reentry women depends on how long the women have been absent from paid employment and how large a hiatus exists between termination of formal education or training and entry into the labor force. For most women in late entry or in reentry situations, the following goals would seem to be appropriate.

1. Reinforce positive feelings about self-worth and ability to make a contribution in the work force outside the home. Many women lack specific saleable skills or possess obsolescent training; they irrationally translate these deficiencies into feelings of little personal worth. They should be aided to separate employability skills deficits from personal worth estimates. Many married women may have difficulty realizing an identity separate from their husbands after years of making their self-development subservient to family needs. They must be encouraged to assume a multiroled existence after a period of essentially restricted roles.

2. Provide any information that may be lacking about basic career decision making: personal assets and limitations, values and attitudes, the world of work, resources, and so on. Despite social sophistication and a gener-

ally mature life orientation, women in this category may be vocationally illiterate and may require the most rudimentary types of career information.

3. Assist in exploring changes in life style that may be occasioned by first-time entry or reentry into the labor force. What are the possible consequences of paid employment on marital relationships, continued child rearing, division of labor in the home, leisure activities, and so forth? Will paid labor result in actual economic benefit? In some cases, it will not.

4. Help clients to understand the implications of full-time versus part-time work. Not all women work full-time the year round.

5. Prepare women to deal with possible discrimination, both overt and covert. What possible discriminatory attitudes may be encountered among management? What possibilities exist for subtle or blatant sexual harassment by employers or by fellow workers? Do hiring, promotion, and retention practices present barriers because of sex or age? Do compensation differences exist that cannot otherwise be explained? What are intentional and unintentional sexist questions posed in an interview? How does one combat discrimination on a personal level?

6. Provide specialized experiences, if necessary, in such areas as consciousness raising and assertiveness training.

7. Explore entry-level jobs with extant education versus jobs attainable with additional education or training. Will any job do because of immediate economic necessity, or does she really want a vocation for the rest of her life, or is it some combination of both? Where and how does she obtain the additional education or training?

8. Provide a referral system for placement assistance; provide placement services if no alternative is available; and provide job-seeking and job-hunting skills

9. Provide follow-up and continuing support. Once the individual has begun to work, there may be needs for assurance, enhancement of coping skills, and general support. Furthermore, the counselor may be able to secure feedback about the types of assistance that might have been provided in the prework situation but were overlooked or not given sufficient attention.

In the best of all possible worlds, reentry women would be provided with mentors to help them negotiate both educational and work transitions (Bauer & Mott, 1990).

Many excellent programs have been devised to deal with issues of gender in the career development of women, and reentry women in particular. These programs have produced some fine materials for use with this subpopulation (for example, EDC/WEEA Publishing Center, 55 Chapel Street, Newton, Massachusetts, 02160).

As for most other special populations, there is a separate statement of principles for counseling and therapy of women (American Psychological Association, 1979). These principles begin where generic counseling competencies leave off and are largely directed toward eliminating sexism in counseling by urging the end of sexist language, banishing of preconceived notions about goals for women, forbidding sexual relationships between counselor and client, recognizing unique women's issues and concerns, and remaining professionally alert to the burgeoning literature on women. Worrell (1980) expands on the theme by defining many populations of adult women, one of which is reentry and adult women. Here she includes women "returning to work or school, displaced homemakers, or empty nest women, and aging and retiring women" (p. 479). She sees reentry counseling as generic counseling with special perspectives on sexual issues, identity crisis management, and aging.

The so-called displaced homemaker is a special case of late entry or reentry. Displaced homemakers are usually women who have no income (because of death or a spouse, divorce, and so on), who usually have grown children, and who want to become employed and thus achieve economic independence. Unfortunately, they typically lack job skills or work experience and thus have difficulty entering the labor market. Welborn and Moore (1985) aptly describe the condition of the displaced homemaker:

> Often the displaced homemaker is in the position of not only actively needing and seeking employment, but also of being required to cope with a number of other issues, such as feeling out of control, feeling isolated from those segments of society in which she must now operate, feeling little sense of personal power, feeling a void where once she felt intimacy, and feeling a keen sense of disorientation as the emphasis on family is necessarily reduced as she prepares to go to work. (p. 104)

On the premise that reentry women require a different type of career assistance than do traditional students in higher education, Arp et al. (1986) have devised a support group approach for adult students. Over a six-week period, 90-minute sessions were used each week to help nine women and one man (ages 25 to 55) to set individual goals within a context of themes for each weekly session. The sessions addressed the following concerns: What is holding you back? What skills do you possess? Where do you fit in the job market? How do you uncover job openings? Does a résumé make a difference? What can you expect in an interview? Initial evaluations were generally positive.

There are many reports of successful programs designed for reentry women. Sandmeyer (1980) offered a three-day workshop called "Choices and Changes," which was intended to aid women aged 26 to 35 in decision making for either late entry into the occupational world or career change. A second example concerns career/life planning aspects of counseling with divorced women. Kitabachi, Murrell, and Crawford (1979) offer suggestions for such counseling, and include the additional variable of *loss* (as in the death of a relationship). They advocate a three-stage group process, progressing from self-awareness through self-appraisal to taking action.

In another study, (Slaney & Lewis, 1986) 34 undergraduate women, ages 25 to 56, who were attending a large midwestern university and were undecided about a career choice, were divided into two groups. One group was given the Vocational Card Sort (VCS), an instrument that simply requires them to rank order and place in piles the six Holland categories and the SCII basic interest titles in terms of their preferences. They were also to read explanatory material. The second group took the SCII and were provided with an interpretive report. Both groups were more decided as a result of these simple interventions, and both were satisfied with the treatments received. There were no significant differences between groups, suggesting that employing either the VCS or the SCII is useful in working with reentry women.

McGraw (1982) has summarized a number of other programs and counseling interventions for the reentry woman. As she points out, however, and as we have repeatedly stressed is the case with other defined adult career groups, our knowledge of reentry women is in a relatively primitive state and very much in need of additional and better research.

THE OLDER WORKER

Generally speaking, the older worker is considered to be over 45 (Some prefer the term "more mature worker"). Currently, one in five Americans is over 55; by 2010, one in every four will be (M. H. Morrison, 1984). Although age discrimination in employment hiring practices has been theoretically reduced by federal employment acts, there is little doubt that this category of worker faces considerable prejudice in terms of hiring or retention policies and that career problems are heightened for this age group. The Work in America Institute (1980) has pointed out this problem and has recommended actions for employers to make policies age-neutral and responsive to our aging work force. These include the following:

- Review of nondiscriminatory hiring and separation practices to be certain that de facto systems are not operating despite apparent compliance with Equal Employment Opportunity
- Review of age distribution of employees within an organization to be sure that older workers are not over- or underrepresented in any area
- Examination of alternatives for older workers, such as part-time work, job sharing, work schedule variations, and flex time

Roscow (1983) echoes some of these suggestions and places the issue of older workers in perspective. He states

> In fact, the raising of the mandatory retirement age to 70 is producing shifts in the labor force trends. By the end of the next decade, employers will be more motivated to attract older workers than ever before. This will necessitate a loosening of social security regulations, more flexible working arrangements for older people (hours, weeks, and months), phased/gradual or tapered retirements, job redesign to accommodate physical and psychological abilities and needs, and a general set of personnel policies that are more responsive to the older character of the work force. This also represents a great area for personnel management experiments and change, in anticipation of the coming age shift. (pp. 16–17)

Discrimination against older workers is both morally reprehensible and economically counterproductive. M. L. Levine (1988) argues that age is a general characteristic, just as race or sex is, and is only peripherally related to productivity. Therefore, ageism has no reason for being. Active hostility to older workers in companies appears to be a relatively rare occurrence, but passive-aggressive policies and acts are somewhat more prevalent (for example, limited opportunities for promotion or lateral moves, early retirement incentives, and so on).

On the other hand, an increasing number of postretirement people are returning to the work force, thus swelling the ranks of older workers. In a study by Fontana and Frey (1990), most returnees chose to go back to work to have more contact with people, to earn money, or simply because they would rather work than stay at home. These workers felt that management held few negatively stereotypical views regarding older workers; in fact, they perceived managers as believing that older workers were more productive than younger workers. The 180 postretirement, over 55-years-of-age workers who returned expressed high job satisfaction. These results are consistent with recommendations of Cahill and Salomone (1987) that counseling should be provided for older workers for work life extension, whether individuals continue in a present career, change careers, or work part-time.

Attitudinal and Developmental Factors

Although unemployment among older workers is generally low, when it does strike, it is likely to be for longer periods of time—the median duration is of eighteen weeks (Morrison, 1984)—and fraught with barriers that produce debasement, humiliation, and frustration. As age increases, occupational mobility decreases, thus cutting down the alternatives for the older worker. These workers experience considerable difficulty getting placed in a job, U.S. Employment Service data have consistently demonstrated over the years that older workers are a substantial proportion of their clientele (more than 30 percent) but that these workers are placed on a less than proportional basis (usually less than 20 percent). Because of their unique problems, the discipline of industrial gerontology has come into being to study the employment and retirement problems of middle-aged and older workers.

The labor force participation of workers over the age of 65 in America has actualy declined in linear fashion since just before the turn of the century. In 1890 about 68 percent of all men over 65 were in the labor force; by 1930 that figure had dropped to 54 percent; and by 1970 only 25 percent of all men over 65 were still in the labor force (Graney & Cottam, 1981). In fact, the industries that employ the most people in America have provided few opportunities for older people's participation. It will be interesting to see how much the raised mandatory retirement age will affect these data and how much the data will be influenced by the declining youth population and the subsequent "graying" of traditional entry-level jobs (such as fast foods, retail sales, and so on).

Many of the problems of older workers are caused by the natural consequences of aging. Some jobs are difficult for those workers who are required to expend considerable physical energy or sustained exertion, to endure highly stressful work environments, or to work very rapidly for prolonged time periods. The fact is that, in general, for most older workers, intellectual functioning is not impaired. Whenever health has been preserved, verbal scores have remained relatively stable. There is, however, a persistent and progressive decline in performance on most speeded tasks. Hence, older workers are likely to remain stable in their cognitive abilities and to deteriorate in their psychomotor performance. Of course, when extreme old age is considered, the general trend in cognitive functioning is downhill. These conditions are perhaps responsible for the fact that the lowest retirement rates are found in white-collar and service occupations, and the highest rates exist in blue-collar and agricultural occupations.

In a comprehensive review of age-related differences in work attitudes and behavior, Rhodes (1983) reached some general conclusions with which we agree. She found that age is related to overall job satisfaction, satisfaction with work itself, job involvement, internal work motivation, and organizational commitment. Age appears to be negatively related to turnover intention. There also seems to be an increase with age in needs for security and affiliation and preferences for extrinsic job characteristics and having friendly co-workers and supervisors. In terms of career development, she states,

> Recent studies based on life cycle and career stage models suggest that determinants of job satisfaction and job involvement change depending on one's career stage. Preliminary evidence suggests that task characteristics are more strongly related to job satisfaction and involvement in the trial or early career stage (after a learning period), personal characteristics achieve salience in the midcareer stage, and reward variables, although important throughout, become particularly important in the late career stage. (p. 356)

The four out of ten American workers who are older face some formidable factors that work against their quickly finding new employment when they are displaced from jobs. Among these factors are (1) many employers' unfavorable attitudes toward older workers; (2) substitution of cheaper labor (such as illegal aliens or women) for older workers; and (3) changes in occupations, industry, and the geographical distribution of jobs that favor the hiring of younger workers who are more flexible and mobile.

This lack of flexibility of older workers is often referred to as the problem of obsolescence. Obsolescence is workers' lack of up-to-date knowledge and skills needed to perform effectively. In terms of employer bias, age does not seem to be a primary determiner of an employer's perception of personal work-related traits, but it does affect the hiring decision because of the potentially shortened work life. The same holds true for older women, who face greater unemployment difficulties than their younger counterparts (Pursell & Torrence, 1980). Employer attitudes are also affected by fears that older workers have more accidents. Root's (1981) data indicate that this is not so; older workers are hurt less often than younger workers, but they are hurt more seriously when they do have an accident. Rhodes (1983) corroborates this finding, explaining that perhaps the negative association between age and accidents is caused by the fact that older workers who are less capable of meeting the physical aspects of jobs leave the more physically demanding and hazardous jobs.

Reducing the Negative Effect of Ageism

Several approaches have been advocated to reduce the negative effect of ageism in hiring, promotion, and retention. One suggestion has involved job redesign. Such a technique is frequently applied on an informal, personal basis in small enterprises, but it is now being advocated on a massive scale. Essentially, job redesign involves a determination of a job's physical demands and the minimum physical capacities necessary for its performance. Particularly noted are points of strain that might suggest job modification or reallocation to the benefit of the older worker. The attempt is to dovetail worker abilities and job requirements, taking into account both worker needs and production demands. Thus, employment opportunities for older workers can be extended by removing pressures in the work environment. Job reorganization might also entail allowing workers of greater experience to handle more complex tasks, while inexperienced workers tend to the simpler, more physical aspects of a job. One must be careful here, for there is some evidence that job enrichment may actually decrease job satisfaction among older workers (Phillips, Barrett, & Rush, 1978).

A related technique has involved the concept of functional age. The theory is that it is unfair and wasteful to judge workers on the basis of chronological age; therefore, the idea is to rate a worker's functional ability on the job—to determine what the worker can do operationally. Two examples of the use of the functional age concept follow.

R. A. Snyder, Williams, and Cashman (1984) advocate the use of functional age rather than chronological age as a predictor of reactions to performance feedback. An analog study by J. A. Lee and Clemons (1985) offers some interesting findings related to the kinds of decision-making input data that may be considered when an employer hires an older worker. According to the investigators, the chances of an older worker getting hired increase if the older worker does not have to compete with a younger worker and if the older worker is able to define performance functionally (that is, a behaviorally stated performance report), thus minimizing age stereotypes.

A third approach to accommodating older workers is retraining them in order to establish eligibility for jobs with specific training requirements. Getting older workers to be motivated for and to engage in retraining is, however, frequently difficult to accomplish. Perhaps some distinctions should be made between the younger older workers (45 to 54) and the older older workers (55 to 70).

Kieffer (1980) summarizes some of the suggestions made to assist older workers now on the job. He advocates the following:

- More effective performance evaluation programs
- Identification of alternative jobs or work arrangements in the same or related organizations
- Alternative job placements
- Development and improvement of counseling services relative to further careers or retirement
- Improvement or adaptation of selection systems for training, development, and promotion

- Updating of advisory services on pensions and fringe benefits
- Review of terminating procedures
- Mental health counseling (p. 11)

Counseling the Older Worker

As we have indicated previously, older workers are likely to experience employment difficulties that make them particularly vulnerable to trauma in the career domain. Therefore, many of the goals of career counseling with these clients involve reassurance and immediate assistance.

1. Provide support in building and maintaining positive attitudes toward one's worth and dignity. Is the individual confusing temporary rejection as a worker with rejection as a human being? Does the individual have a work history of rejection? Does the person express feelings of hopelessness, worthlessness, obsolescence, despair? Is confidence shattered?
2. Explore possible retraining and other avenues for improving employment opportunities.
3. Provide any and all geographic information. Does the individual know where the best markets for employment are? Is mobility a problem?
4. Assess the actual reasons for employment difficulties. For example, is the person coming for assistance because of layoff, resignation, sickness, retirement, or firing?
5. Assist individuals in accurately gauging their present state of motivation, the expectations they hold for future employment, and their perceptions of themselves as workers.
6. Especially with managerial, professional, and technical occupations, help the individual to consider the relative importance of such factors as salary, use of abilities, status, amount of responsibility, security, opportunities for advancement, chance to make a contribution, and so on. Also important is the need to explore the possibilities and consequences of occupational downgrading and salary decrease.
7. Assist in developing job-seeking behaviors, if necessary.
8. Provide placement and follow-up services if no other opportunities exist in the area served; refer to appropriate agencies and institutions if placement services are available.

One example of a program for older workers should provide a flavor of the types of activities in use. S. M. Smith and Golden (1982) report on six-meeting, twelve-hour job readiness workshops, mini-workshops, and an employment information showcase. Fifteen to twenty-eight participants were placed in each of 12 groups. Designed for workers 55 and older, the program had three major goals:

1. To develop a mechanism to disseminate vocational guidance information materials, and training to unemployed or underemployed adults . . . to assist in finding gainful employment or volunteer work to supplement retirement incomes or to enhance life styles
2. To develop and compile vocational guidance materials related to the concerns of older job seekers and those who work with this audience in finding gainful employment or meaningful volunteer work
3. To alert potential employers of the skills and abilities of older individuals as a means of both reversing age discrimination and informing older adults that they possess characteristics desired by employers (p. 30)

One of the difficulties in building a research base to contribute to our knowledge of older workers is that so many of the studies that have been accomplished are analog in nature and not drawn from actual work settings. Asking college students to engage in "as if" behaviors is a questionable practice in any analog research and may be especially problematic when the focus is the older workers. In addition, testing the physical characteristics, reaction times, and other physiological and psychological processes of older workers independent of the work they are performing is less helpful than assessing their function on the job.

PRERETIREMENT AND RETIREMENT

We sometimes forget that retirement and the time immediately preceding it are a part of one's career life; these times are as fraught with potentially anxiety-producing events as are any others. Most of that anxiety for those who have had a work life revolves around the possibility that the loss of work will cause serious problems of adjustment. In Chapter 2 we devoted attention to the purposes that work serves in maintaining an individual's psychological and social well-being.

If employment structures one's time, provides contacts outside the family, contributes to personal identity, enables one to remain active, and satisfies a variety of higher-order needs, the absence of work could have a deleterious effect on some individuals. If nothing is substituted in retirement to contribute to individual well-being, it is logical to assume that loss of work has the potential for inducing psychological malaise. For that reason, some people try to retire partially and ease into the stage, but this partial retirement is prevalent mainly among the self-employed (J. F. Quinn, 1981). Many would like to stay in the job market, but discrimination, a lack of job opportunities, and other factors combine to force them to retire completely (S. Gray & Morse, 1980). Hence, despite the raising of the retirement age, early retirement among men has actually increased. Men, in general, plan to retire earlier than they actually do, however (Ekerdt, Bosse, & Mogery, 1980).

On the other hand, some see loss of work as merely an informal nonceremonious rite of passage (Kaiser, Peters, & Babchuk, 1982), a transition between the world of work and retirement. Even so, retirement for some comes as a great surprise. Several national surveys have indicated that over 40 percent of individuals who state that they never expected to stop working are retired four years later (Goudy, 1981). Many people do not plan for retirement at all (Kragie, Gerstein, & Lichtman, 1989). Some studies describe a "retirement syndrome," characterized by anxiety and depression; other studies find that even people who were strongly committed to work do not demonstrate negative changes in retirement either immediately after the fact or eighteen months later.

Much excellent retirement research emanates from a team of researchers at Duke University. In a relatively recent work (Palamore, Burchett, Fillenbaum, George, & Wallman, 1985), they summarize the findings of seven significant longitudinal studies of retirement. Their analyses take into account the major ways in which retirement may be defined: a subjective assessment by the person; an objective retirement (that is, working less than full time and receiving a pension); or a significant reduction in the number of hours worked. Perhaps the major conclusion is that predictors of actual retirement and of successful retirement very much depend on the definition of retirement that is utilized. Predictors such as demographic variables, attitudes toward work and retirement, health, type of work, and so on seem to be differentially predictive, depending on which of the three definitions of retirement is adopted. In a sense, this finding is corroborated by a study effected by Dobson and Morrow (1984) that determined career orientation variables (for example, job satisfaction, attitudes toward work, work commitment, and so on) to be stronger predictors than demographic factors of retirement attitudes, while demographic factors were found to be more efficient in predicting retirement age and level of preparation for retirement. A second enormously important finding of the Palamore et al. study is that contrary to popular folklore, the average retiree does not experience harmful effects on health. Of course, this may not be so in individual cases, but in terms of normative data, the conclusion of no decline in health as a result of retirement gainsays the conventional belief.

Another example of the potential healthful effects of retirement comes from a study by Howard, Rechnitzer, Cunningham, & Donner (1986). They found that people who were Type A (vigorous verbal and psychomotor mannerisms, sense of time urgency, easily aroused anger and hostility, and extremes of competitiveness, impatience, and achievement striving) decreased toward the more placid Type B behavior one year after retirement. Thus, the mental health of Type A people appears to improve with retirement.

Much of the conflict among findings may be an artifact of the samples used in the studies. We know that several individual differences seem related to successful retirement, and these dimensions may be more or less present in different samples. Among the dimensions that appear to be involved in a positive retirement transition are adequate income (Schmitt & McCune, 1981), voluntary rather than involuntary retirement, health (Spreitzer, Synder, & Larson, 1980), specificity of plans and staying active (L. K. Rockwell, Hood, & Lee, 1980), Graney & Zimmerman, 1981; and history of an orderly rather than a discontinuous career (Glamser, 1981). To extend Super's career maturity idea, some people appear to be retirement-mature whereas others seem to be retirement-immature (R. P. Johnson & Riker, 1981; Kingson, 1981). The notion that stress occurs when individuals are forced into a life stage before they are ready seems reasonable (J. W. Walker, Kimmel, & Price, 1981). Because of these individual differences in adjustment to retirement, studies that seek to place retirement among the hierarchy of stressful life events usually show it to be in the middle range (T. H. Holmes & Rahe, 1967).

Attitudes Toward the Aged

Our society's attitudes toward the aged have been less than benevolent (Offerman & Gowing, 1990). In many ways we have rejected the older population. Some people apparently view age itself as an anathema and shun those who are old. About one-fifth of our current aged population is foreign born, and xenophobia (fear of foreigners) may well cause negative attitudes. Our old tend to have much less formal education than does the general population, and in a society that values educational attainments, the old are likely to experience prejudice because of this. Finally, as is well known, the old are usually poor; a great many who do not work are living on an annual income below that established by the U.S. Department of Labor as representing poverty level. Thus, age itself, discrimination toward the foreign born, lack of education, and poverty combine to evoke negative attitudes toward the aged in America. In a few years, as the aged population becomes more indigenous and their level of education (as well as their numbers) increases, these attitudes may soften. At the present time, however, they are real and destructive and give credence to Jonathan Swift's assertion: "Every man desires to live long, but no man would be old."

Adjustment to Retirement

Ultimately, adjustment to retirement is very much an individual matter. Some will welcome retirement and will embrace leisure and the relative lack of structure with guiltlessness and joy. Others will fret and stew, experience trauma, and never adjust. It has been argued, for example, that "leisure is not quite leisure when you do not have to work." In other words, free time becomes a constant excess with which one must cope rather than a welcome temporary release from a bascially time-structured life. Generally, retirement causes people to think about leisure more in terms of *pleasure* than in terms of *freedom*. Hence, retirement can be either a period of enrichment and opportunity to pursue avocational and leisure interests or a source of depression connected with the loss of a culturally dominant social role.

Much of the literature on retirement conceives that stage as a period of disengagement, a reversal of expansion, a period characterized by less involvement in social participation. Disengagement, however, is perhaps an erroneous concept. Those who adjust well to retirement are more likely to reengage society in a different way than they are to disengage society. To be sure, some retirees disengage, but others simply reorient the direction and intensity of their engagement.

Several studies attempt to categorize retirees according to adjustment in retirement or by activity level. The Americana Health Care Corporation's study, *Aging in America: Trials and Triumphs* (1980), divided its sample of 514 randomly selected older persons into three groups:

- *Enjoyers* (27 percent of the sample) successfully cope with aging. Usually they are healthy, well-educated males who are financially secure.
- *Survivors* (53 percent) are reasonably successful copers with age. They are largely men and women of average health, less than a high school education, and basically adequate financial resources.
- *Casualties* (20 percent) are not very successful in coping. Usually they are female, without much education, in relatively poor health, and of low income.

J. W. Walker et al., (1981) divide their sample of 1511 recent retirees from major corporations into four groups:

- *The Rocking Chair Group* (44 percent of the sample) voluntarily retired at about 62–65, are generally healthy, and are reasonably content with their retirement associates, finances, and activities.
- *The Reorganizer Group* (24 percent) retired voluntarily at 62–65, were generally better educated, more financially secure, and healthier. They looked forward to beginning a new pattern of activities and usually worked as volunteers.
- *The Holding On Group* (about 19 percent) continued to work for pay. Some involuntarily retired and needed the income. Most had not thought about retiring or made plans for retirement. Availability of jobs for this group is absolutely necessary.
- *The Dissatisfied Group* (13 percent) were working neither voluntarily nor for pay and had a hard time keeping busy. Income and health were relatively poor. They had little retirement satisfaction.

In short, these two surveys indicate that people of various educational levels, incomes, and activity focus can retire successfully by adopting different styles. They also suggest that, as Dillard (1982) advocates, teaching specific retirement life-styles may be a useful preretirement counseling activity.

Despite folklore, studies have demonstrated repeatedly that retirement has little effect on physical health (Crowley, 1985). One large-scale study, however, has concluded that retirees report more psychological symptoms than workers, even when physical health factors are taken into account (Bosse, Aldwin, Levenson, & Ekerdt, 1987). This finding seems to hold for both early and late retirees. Of course, we are left with the question of whether retirement affects mental health or whether one's mental health affects the decision to retire. All we can say presently is that there appears to be a reciprocal effect between mental health and retirement.

Most people begin retirement with a higher level of enthusiasm and more satisfaction than they experience a year later (Ekerdt, Bosse, & Levkoff, 1985). Identifying those who are likely to experience trauma because of the loss of work in retirement is not an easy task. One study (Fretz et al., 1989) suggests that the best predictors of preretirement anxiety and depression are low self-efficacy, feelings about being able to cope with retirement, and a low degree of planfulness, in addition to the usual health and financial concerns. This type of research is in its incipient stages, and much more needs to be accomplished before predictive psychological variables are forthcoming.

Counseling for Preretirement and Retirement

Retirement is indeed a time of appraisal and reappraisal. It is simultaneously a look backward and a look ahead. The goals that appear appropriate in working with this group are as follows:

1. Assist in planning. Provide information relating to health, finances, housing, appropriate agencies for the elderly, and a variety of concerns relating to daily living.
2. Clarify affective reactions to retirement. Individuals vary in their reactions to retirement. The counselor should not assume any universal reaction: trauma, joy, anticipation, disengagement, and reengagement, are equally likely responses. Forced versus voluntary retirement will probably evoke within the counselee two appreciably different sets of concern.
3. Make appropriate referrals to community agencies designed to deal with particular aspects of the aged.

In terms of suggestion 1, Blai (1982) has put together a compendium of resources for older people who desire to work. State employment service offices, agencies on aging, YWCAs and YMCAs, and Forty-Plus Clubs are all possibilities. In addition, various volunteer agency programs exist; Foster Grandparents Program (FGP), Retired Senior Volunteer Program (RSVP), Volunteers in Service to America (VISTA), Peace Corps, Senior Companion Program, Service Corps of Retired Executives (SCORE). Also, the U.S. Department of Labor sponsors the Senior Community Service Employment Program (SCSEP), which employs economically disadvantaged older persons in part-time community service jobs.

Corporations have taken increasing action to provide their employees with preretirement programs, although the effect of these programs has not been carefully evaluated (S. K. Olson, 1981). Unfortunately, some of the careful evaluations we do have show few, if any, significant longitudinal differences between groups that have had a preretirement program and those that have not (Glasmer, 1981), although in the short run, there may be significant differences in favor of treatment groups (Morrow, 1981). Nevertheless, their number is growing. A survey of chief executive officers and personnel directors of the Fortune 1000 companies (Research and Forecasts, Inc., 1980) confirms progress.

It is now estimated that about half of all large corporations offer preretirement programs (Feuer, 1985), although these programs obviously vary in terms of scope and depth. Of those that do have a program, Table 12.1 presents a breakdown of the topics covered in terms of three categories: *narrow* programs that concentrate on financial questions; *intermediate* programs that cover finances plus health, leisure, and legal ques-

Table 12.1

Topics Covered by Retirement Preparation Program as Reported by Personnel Directors

□ = reported by more than 50%

	Narrow	Intermediate	Broad
Social Security and Medicare	77%	87%	98%
Financial benefits and options	73	85	97
Physical and mental health	14	81	100
Leisure	9	76	100
Legal aspects	23	68	98
Employment	0	28	92
Housing	0	40	90
Community resources	5	49	88
Options for employment after retirement	18	19	83
Interpersonal relations	9	25	68
Life planning	14	21	61
	*	*	*
	(22)	(53)	(59)

*Adds up to more than 100 percent because individuals give more than one answer.

tions; and *broad* programs that cover virtually everything. Hence, most programs are focusing on both higher-order and lower-order human needs.

Loesch (1980) suggests "life-flow leisure counseling" as an antidote to possible diminution of self-satisfaction and self-definition caused by loss of work in retirement. This system involves exploration of interests, values, satisfactions, and personal characteristics and subsequently integrating and synthesizing this information into leisure pursuits. Leisure counseling, in fact, is a part of virtually every prepackaged retirement planning program. For example, the National Council of Older Americans' eight-module program contains one on leisure and another on life-style (E. W. Fitzpatrick, 1980).

Westcott (1983) has suggested a structured life-review technique in counseling elders who see no meaning in life or who have poor social relationships or who are having difficulty mentally recovering from an illness. The technique is advocated to encourage the elderly to reminisce and engage in a life review of specific events that may affect current adjustment, self-esteem, or intergenerational conflicts. There is no reason why the structured life-review technique could not be applied to retirees who are experiencing adjustment difficulties.

Although we pointed out in the previous section of this chapter that the work force participation of workers over age 65 has declined in almost linear fashion throughout this century, there are those who persuasively argue that participation will increase in the future (Hitchcock, 1984). Part-time reentry into the work force after individuals have completed a career may require that they receive counseling. For example, retirees can be helped to understand their strengths, realize new conditions in the job market, and overcome potential discrimination in hiring.

Liptak (1990) offers a program for integrating leisure planning into preretirement programs. He presents a system of translating desires into specific goal statements for individuals—for example, "I want to utilize my leisure time better" is translated into "I will learn to manage my leisure time and structure my leisure activities more effectively," and "I want to attend more social functions" becomes "I will join groups and clubs associated with my leisure interests." Long-, medium-, and short-range goals are thus effected. Several other examples of preretirement programs may be found in R. Morris and Bass (1988).

Although the research accomplished in the area of preretirement and retirement is much more advanced and sophisticated than that pertaining to most other types of adult career behavior, some unanswered questions persist. Atchley (1979) reports on a conference designed to assess research needs. Among the more interesting research questions are the following:

Physical and Mental Ability for Employment

1. How does functional capacity interact with occupation to influence the decision to retire or the timing of retirement? How do subjective and objective health factors compare as predictors of functional capacity for employment?
2. To what extent do various diseases such as heart disease, diabetes, or arthritis influence functional capacity for employment? Do these factors influence the decision to retire or the timing of retirement directly or do they operate through their effects on functional capacity for employment?
3. How do mental health factors such as anxiety or depression influence the decision to retire or the timing of retirement?
4. How does physical aging compare with health factors in predicting functional capacity for employment?
5. How do the following compare as factors influencing functional capacity for employment?
   a. Physical and mental aging
   b. Disability due to disease or accident
   c. Obsolete psychomotor skills
   d. Obsolete knowledge

   Does the relative importance of these various factors differ by occupation and how?

Economic and Noneconomic Rewards of Employment

1. To what extent does the fulfillment of individual occupational goals influence the decision to retire or the timing of retirement?
2. How are the meanings attached to the job related to the type of retirement, the decision to retire, or the timing of retirement?
3. Do people feel a need to replace job rewards (both economic and noneconomic) in retirement? If so, does this influence the decision to retire or the timing of the retirement?

Social-Psychological Characteristics

1. What are the determinants of attitude toward retirement?
2. What are the determinants of attitude toward the job?
3. How do attitudes toward the job influence attitudes toward retirement?
4. How do significant others influence attitude toward retirement?
5. How do attitudes toward retirement influence the decision to retire or the timing of retirement?
6. How does the perceived effect of retirement on prestige affect the decision to retire or the timing of retirement?

Personality Factors

1. How does a positive orientation toward planning (active manipulation of environment) influence the decision to retire or the timing of retirement?
2. All other things being equal, is the Type A person (i.e., hard-driving, competitive, pressed for time) more or less likely to re-

tire or retire early compared to the Type B person?
3. Do inner-directed people retire more frequently or retire sooner compared to other-directed people?

Information

1. What effects do retirement planning programs have on the decision to retire or the timing of retirement?
2. To what extent is the decision to retire the result of a "rational" process?

System Pressures to Retire

1. What effects do varying employer retirement policies, employer pressures toward retirement, and organizational characteristics have on the decision to retire and the timing of retirement?
2. How do employer policies, unemployment, job retrogression, peer pressures, employer pressure, and family pressures compare as influences on the decision to retire and on the timing of retirement? (pp. 47–48)*

Over a decade after Atchley offered these research foci, definitive answers are yet to emerge. Yet, retirement research is a lively center of attention for many scholars, and we are beginning to determine the factors that influence successful and unsuccessful retirement. Unfortunately, most retirement research has been conducted with men. Some studies strongly suggest that women retirees require separate examination (Dorfman & Moffett, 1987; Erdner & Guy, 1990; Riddick, 1985; Seccombe & Lee, 1986; Szinovacz, 1987). The great bulk of retirement research has also focused on whites. Cultural differences have been found that urge distinct research with people of color (R. C. Gibson, 1987; V. Richardson & Kilty, 1989).

Summary

In this chapter we have outlined factors that contribute to an increasing need for adult career counseling. We have presented characteristics of four adult subpopulations: midcareer shifters, women entering or reentering the labor force after child rearing, older workers, and preretirees and retirees. We have suggested specific foci for the career counseling of these groups. We have further presented general guidelines for the career counseling of adults. In the following chapter we will discuss several additional adult subpopulations for which the counselor requires specialized career knowledge and skills.

* From "Issues In Retirement Research" by R. C. Atchley, *The Gerontoligist*, Vol. 19, No. 1, pp. 47–48. Reprinted by permission.

CHAPTER 13

SPECIAL ADULT CAREER CONCERNS II

Key Concepts

- Most people will need to make career adjustments as they negotiate the various career development stages.
- Involuntary job loss or prolonged unemployment are among life's most stressful occurrences.
- Burnout is basically an emphasis within a job satisfaction–job dissatisfaction continuum.
- Work and family affect each other interactively.
- *Dual-worker* and *dual-career* (families) are not interchangeable terms.
- Job satisfaction is a complex phenomenon, the causes of which vary in different stages of individual career development and in terms of moderator variables.
- Job-seeking skills can be acquired.

As we saw in Chapter 2, even with the most advantageous career development, a person may experience problems related to work. These difficulties, in turn, can frequently affect nonwork behaviors. Most people need to make career adjustments as they negotiate the various career development stages. Some will need only minor fine-tuning; other will be forced to make profoundly troubling changes. Even after adjustments, problems will continue to arise from within the individual (for example, expectancy-reality discrepancies) or from outside the individual (for instance, economic downturns causing unemployment). The potential frustrations in the labor force are many, and counselors can work in both a developmental mode and a remedial mode to help people to address these areas of concern.

In this chapter, we will discuss six more adult career concerns. For each we will present an overview of the particular problem; we will review representative research on the problem; and we will offer implications for counseling those who are experiencing it. We begin with a look at the unemployed, dislocated, and discouraged worker. A discussion of so-called burnout will follow. Attention will then be directed to family effects of working mothers. The family theme will be continued with a consideration of dual-career couples. We will explicate three aspects of job-seeking behaviors—locating job sources, writing application letters and résumés, and interviewing. We will conclude with a reflection on aspects of job dissatisfaction. Much of the literature in these areas is contradictory; consequently, this chapter represents what might best be considered a state-of-the-art report.

UNEMPLOYED, DISLOCATED, AND DISCOURAGED WORKERS

Virtually every stress assessment instrument includes the category of recent job loss. It is generally acknowledged that such an event is traumatic and produces considerable anxiety, stress, and disequilibrium. Indeed, the involuntary loss of a job or prolonged unemployment can be among life's more upsetting occurrences. For career counselors, dealing with those who have experienced involuntary job loss (whatever the reason) is especially challenging.

The Nature of Involuntary Job Loss

The number of people who are involuntarily unemployed will vary, of course, depending on economic conditions and other factors. Obviously, the worse the economic conditions, the greater the unemployment; the greater the unemployment, the larger the number of discouraged workers. Discouraged workers are people who desire jobs but who do not look for them because they believe a search will be fruitless. There are approximately one million such workers (more or less depending on conditions) in America. They want to work and, if jobs were more plentiful, they would be working. Discouraged workers, however, are *not* figured into unemployment statistics, since only those people who are looking for work are included in determining the unemployment rate.

Unemployment can take several forms. *Frictional unemployment* is a term used by economists to designate a temporary problem faced by individuals between jobs, those who have quit their jobs to search for better ones, and those who are looking for their first job. About one-half to two-thirds of the unemployed typically fall into this category. *Cyclical unemployment* refers to job losses caused by level of economic activity (such as recessions) and, unlike frictional unemployment, may see workers out of work for months or longer. This type of unemployment is most deeply felt in the manufacturing and construction industries, but clearly no industry is immune. Finally, *structural unemployment* is long-term joblessness that results from changes in the kinds of workers needed by the economy. These are people replaced by new technology, by import competition, or by changes in the geographical location of industry, for example. Generally, such workers have to be retrained or relocated before they can find employment. In addition, enterprises that are near closing or are in general difficulty or that have poor labor-management relations frequently produce a condition in workers alliteratively described as the job jitters. This state is one characterized by uncertainty regarding the permanence of one's job and can often produce anxiety as powerful as that stimulated by the actual job loss.

There do not appear to be significant racial differences among displaced workers, seniority held constant (DiPrete, 1981). There do, however, appear to be age, race, sex, and education differences in the willingness of the unemployed to relocate in search of work (C.F. Mueller, 1981). In general, the young, blacks, men, and persons with lower educational levels are more willing than others to relocate. Such people frequently rely on the support of friends or relatives in the new setting. All of this is not to say that the young, women, and minorities are not more susceptible to layoffs than other cohorts. They are, simply because of "last in, first out" retrenchment practices.

A congressional study determined that 11.5 million workers lost jobs because of plant shutdowns or relocations from 1979 to 1984 and that only 60 percent of them got new jobs during that period ("Study Finds," 1986). A large proportion of these workers were the older workers described in Chapter 12—people with long and stable job histories. The study further indicated that perhaps only 5 percent of these workers were being assisted by extant programs. Of those who did get new jobs, 45 percent were earning lower pay. These data are amplified by Burke (1986), who reported that employees working in poorer jobs in Canada after a plant closing reported less life satisfaction, more psychosomatic symptoms, and greater alcohol consumption. Objective differences in hourly wages produced stronger negative effects than did differences in job characteristics. In general, goods-producing jobs pay higher than service jobs, in which most displaced workers find new employment. This fact, coupled with the disappearance of longevity-influenced rewards, accounts for the lower pay.

Several social and legislative buffers help to assuage the shock of involuntary job loss. The best known program is *unemployment insurance,* the amount of which varies from state to state. In addition, some workers, through their unions, can qualify for *supplemental unemployment benefits* (SUBs) or some variation of SUB pay (such as layoff benefit security or savings programs). Another program is *worker adjustment assistance,* available to those who have lost their work because of import policies. *Public service employment* is also usually helpful in times of high unemployment, especially for the disadvantaged. We are all familiar with programs like the Job Corps and summer youth programs. Other legislation affects special groups of workers only, such as the railroad industry and the transit and airline industries. These programs vary in number and intensity, depending upon the administration in power in Washington.

In addition to this legislated assistance, other programs are designed to aid displaced workers. Many of these palliative measures are the result of collective bargaining agreements. Work rules that specify standard crew sizes, for example, shelter some jobs—and at the same time, may be responsible for layoffs. Slack work provisions enable work sharing or put restrictions on overtime to protect workers. Employee transfer among company facilities is another negotiated protection. So, too, are plans to absorb cutbacks by normal attrition, seniority provisions that give greatest job security to those with longest service, early retirement opportunities, and advanced notice of layoff (unfortunately, usually only a week or less). It is not easy to design a responsive system that will support involuntary job losers and, simultaneously, encourage them to seek new jobs. Dealing with the material needs of the dislocated, discouraged, and unemployed, however, is easier than dealing with the psychological effects of job loss.

The Psychological Effects of Job Loss

In Chapter 2 we discussed the relationship between work and mental health. Here we will provide more detail on that relationship.

The more an individual is motivated to work, the more likely he or she will be to experience depressive affect as a result of unemployment (Feather & Davenport, 1981). Such individuals are more likely to blame external economic conditions for their unemployment than they are to blame themselves. It is not surprising that depressive affect is a concomitant of the unemployed, motivated worker. There have been some attempts to link reaction to job loss with reactions to more permanent loss (such as death and dying stages or grief stages). Both imminent and actual loss, it is hypothesized, produce predictable stages of reaction.

Schlossberg and Leibowitz (1980) describe five stages progressing from job loss to adaptation: disbelief, sense of betrayal, confusion, anger, and resolution. In general, those who suffer traumatic job loss tend to become immobilized and depressed, ultimately accept reality and test themselves and the job market, and usually reacquire some self-esteem (although they tend to have less than the employed). Of course, some never recover and remain in a depressed state, blaming themselves and falling into a state of inertia. For a few, the experience of downward mobility associated with unemployment can be so intensely traumatic that it may increase the likelihood of suicide. J. Hayes and Nutman (1981) have summarized the relationship between unemployment and mental health by pointing out the financial, social, and human costs of high levels of unemployment.

> In financial and social terms it means that more hospital places are required. In human terms it means that the chances of resettlement, an essential element in the treatment of many disorders, is greatly reduced. Finally, if unemployment is a factor which increases the possibility of mental disorders, then in times of high unemployment not only is there a probability of an increase in the number of people suffering from some sort of mental illness, but the means by which these people may be treated are decreased. (pp. 80–81)

Brenner (1973) and Brenner and Swank (1986) have conducted a series of metanalyses over a period of 30 years that point to the fact that high unemployment periods tend to correlate with an increase in admissions to mental health facilities and in suicides, homicides, imprisonment, and death rates. Disillusionment, disaffection, and boredom because of inactivity are frequent complaints. The unemployed may also report feelings of failure and uselessness; they may express feelings of isolation and rejection that they attribute to their unemployment. Although they do not clinically indicate any specific mental disorder or group pathology, such feelings clearly represent stress reactions that impede optimal functioning.

Others report that although the initial shock of job loss is indeed traumatic, the long-term effects may be less devastating than is typically thought.

What is usually described here is a situation akin to a phoenix rising from the ashes, a rebuilding of a war-torn city, or a successful artificial hip implant. It is clear that it would be much better not to have a condition to which the individual must muster resources and react; however, since the situation exists, those who attack it and gain employment are thought to be the better for it. In short, one must stretch to find the brighter side of dislocation and unemployment.

In a comprehensive review of studies relating to the effects of job loss on the psychological well-being of workers, DeFrank and Ivancevich (1986) concluded that the consequences of job loss were very difficult to isolate, although the general effect indeed seemed to be harmful in terms of both mental and physical health. It was also clear, however, that moderator effects operate to buffer or to exacerbate the job loss. Further, the literature is characterized by conflicting results. DeFrank and Ivancevich suggest that "this lack of agreement among studies may be the result of flaws in the available research, including little use of longitudinal designs, exclusion of groups hit hard by job loss (e.g., women, minorities), focus on small sample sizes, and inconsistency in the type and quality of measurement tolls and procedures" (p. 9). In response, they offer a model of the effects of job loss that takes into account moderating variables such as age, sex, personality, behavior patterns, flexibility, concurrent life stress, social support, family impact, job satisfaction, and so on. Also factored into the model are such variables as the workers' perceptions of the job loss and their coping attempts. This model appears worthy of research to test its validity. One Australian study (Feather & O'Brien, 1986), for example, followed a relatively large sample of school-leaving students from high school to employment or unemployment over a period of time. Thus, the study addressed two of the criticisms of DeFrank and Ivancevich: it used a sample of significant size, and it was longitudinal. The investigators found, not surprisingly, that unemployment led to decreases in perceived competence, activity, and life satisfaction, and an increase in depressive affect.

In a confirming study, Winefield and Tiggemann (1989) studied employed and unemployed school-leavers in Australia and discovered, not surprisingly, that the employed group evidenced significantly higher psychological well-being compared to the unemployed group; but among the long-term unemployed, the longer the unemployment duration, the more improved the well-being. This finding has also emerged in studies of older involuntarily unemployed workers.

Shamir (1986a) discovered that in Israel, among highly educated male and female job-losers, self-esteem was not related to employment status. His sample did experience depressive affect, lower morale, and anxiety, but thought none the less of themselves because of unemployment. Self-esteem may be one of those personality variables that is stable enough to mediate stimulus-response contingencies. Shamir (1986b) also determined that individuals with high work involvement were likely to suffer more from unemployment and to gain more from finding employment than low-involved individuals. On the other hand, the so-called Protestant work ethic did not moderate the relationship between employment status and its psychological consequences (depression, anxiety, general morale).

Kinicki and Latack (1990), in validating a new measure to assess coping with involuntary job loss, determined that the coping process changes over time; thus, different coping strategies are likely utilized at various stages of the dislocation, since stress and coping are dynamic processes. Their instrument measures three control coping strategy factors (positive self-assessment, proactive search, and nonwork organization) and two escape coping strategies (distancing from job loss and job devaluation). Apparently, the higher one's self-esteem, the more likely one is to employ proactive search and positive self-assessment coping strategies. In addition, this study upheld the usual finding of the importance of social support and the need for both instrumental (for example, job search) and emotional (for instance, social support) components in any interventions. Social support is also a crucial buffer in the research of Mallinckrodt and Fretz (1988).

It is clear that the unemployment of a primary wage earner will affect other members of a family (S. H. Cramer & Keitel, 1984). In general, however, a family that functioned appropriately prior to the dislocation will succeed in working through the current crisis.

Counseling Involuntary Job Losers

Needs analyses of unemployed persons, especially minority individuals, have demonstrated that they want career planning help, especially in career assessment and placement. The specific form of such assistance has not, as yet, been determined with certainty. Schlossberg and Leibowitz (1980) have proposed a conceptual model based on experiences with "riffed" (reduction in force) workers at NASA's Goddard Space Flight Center. They base their model on job loss as a transition, a "life change or turning point requiring an alteration in everyday patterns of behavior and thinking and necessitating new coping strategies" (p. 205). Their model consists of three components: (1) the characteristics of the particular transition, (2) the characteristics of support systems, and (3) the characteristics of the individual, particularly the resources brought to the transition.

As a result of applying their model to the Goddard situation, Schlossberg and Leibowitz describe ways in which the trauma and pain of job loss can be mitigated by institutional efforts. They recommend a program that includes job-finding training and job-lead identification. Hiring a consultant firm of outplacement specialists is one response; using internal personnel officers is another. In either case, the atmosphere ought to allow participants to experience and express their feelings. The organization can time the staging of terminating events so that employees are gradually allowed to rehearse new roles. It can further have available information-related events. It can provide support, also, for those who must do the actual firing.

Similar recommendations are made by J. Hayes and Nutman (1981), who suggest five ways in which the unemployed can be helped:

1. Enhancing or maintaining the individual's self-esteem by helping him or her manage anxiety and develop more effective problem-solving skills
2. Improving the fit between the individual and his or her life space
3. Promoting job-seeking skills
4. Developing new work-related skills
5. Developing positive attitudes toward work and acceptable work habits (p. 112)

They suggest that effective work-orientation programs for the unemployed have certain common characteristics:

Job orientation. Preparation for a specific job appears to yield more successful results than preparation for work in general.

Training methods. Role playing and self-directed discussion groups do not appear to be so successful as those methods which involve work experience, feedback on progress toward work related goals and immediate positive reinforcement.

Liaison and support. Counseling and liaison between the training and the work setting are frequently associated with success.

Identity and experience of training staff. Professional educators (especially those based in colleges and universities) appear to be less effective than resource persons who seem to have a more intimate knowledge and understanding of the immediate work environment.

Course content. More successful courses focus on work attitudes and work behavior rather than on the more general issues such as those associated with being disadvantaged and unemployed.

Some programs are directed toward specific occupational groups. For example, it has been estimated that each year a large number of farmers in the United States leave the field of agriculture. Heimlich and Van Tilburg (1988) have devised the Rural Economics: Farmers in Transition (RE:FIT) Program to meet the needs of this particular group of displaced workers by means of counseling, career planning, self-assessment, and referral. Materials are specially designed to utilize the terminology and situations of farmers, and the focus is on buttressing the self-image of these dislocated workers.

One of the more intensive counseling-oriented programs occurred in Fremont, California, with the closing of a General Motors plant that had employed about six thousand workers. Counseling was incorporated into a retraining program—not a unique response. What was different was that counseling took place in the setting of a union hall and was effected by peer counselors. Unlike most counseling, the approach at Fremont was to allow expressions of anger and hostility rather than helping people adjust to their anger, since the causes of their plight lay not within themselves but were reflections of social problems beyond their control. Schore (1984) concludes that this program was highly successful.

Attempts were made to fortify the social support of these workers, and spouses were also provided with counseling. In fact, spousal counseling in the outplacement process is now becoming much more common (Fowler, 1990).

The importance of considering both spouses in outplacement counseling is underscored by Aubry, Tefft, and Kingsbury (1990), who studied involuntary unemployment in blue-collar couples. In addition to the typical effects of reduced psychological well-being, they discovered lower marital satisfaction. Their most remarkable finding, however, was that there was no change in marital behavior (for example, household management chores, interactions, and so on), suggesting that the negative effects of job displacement in blue-collar couples are more psychological than behavioral.

In a series of Canadian studies reported by King (1989a, 1989b), the primary problem reported by dislocated workers was the search for new employment, followed by the displaced worker's loss of social status, material and financial concerns, and health, in that order. To combat these difficulties, the author recommends stress reduction activities as well as self-actualization activities, along with professional consultation. Steinweg (1990) has offered six strategies for working with displaced employees: helping clients develop a broad sense of self-esteem; aiding clients to maintain a sense of structure in their lives and to keep their activity levels high; assisting clients in developing and utilizing a systems of social support; encouraging clients to accept external causal attributions for their unemployment; referring clients to community agencies as necessary; and referring to vocational rehabilitation agencies as appropriate.

An example of the cooperation possible between employers shutting down a plant and the community in which the plant is located is provided by Taber, Cooke, and Walsh (1990). Community agencies were mobilized to aid displaced workers to help themselves to solve problems attendant to job loss. A community service council coordinated the application of resources, and a counseling staff of nonprofessionals helped dislocated employees to define their problems, identify appropriate helping agencies, and take remedial actions.

When dealing with the long-term unemployed, successful programs tend to focus on the participant's work attitudes as well as developing job skills. Programs that deal with the development of job skills in isolation are less successful. Most studies seem to agree that skilled counseling, when combined with specific job training, can contribute to successful programs when dealing with the hard-core unemployed. Counseling is clearly a valuable component in programs directed toward assisting the dislocated, most especially those who have been dislocated from managerial or professional positions. The dislocation from work is, at worst, cataclysmic and, at best, upsetting. The ensuing unemployment causes problems of lack of stimulation (even rats and monkeys are disturbed by lack of activity) and feelings of depression and reduced self-esteem. Long-term and chronically unemployed individuals frequently need to change work attitudes as well as to acquire specific job skills. Other people may require an assessment of work assets and training in job-seeking skills. Underemployment is a frequent result of white-collar dislocation. In all cases, career counseling that is tailored to the unique needs of dislocated, unemployed, or discouraged workers can be a useful part of a total support system.

BURNOUT

Beginning in the early 1970s, a time of disillusionment, Herbert Freudenberger and his colleagues, who were working in free clinics in New York City, first applied the term *burnout* to career behavior (Freudenberger, 1974). Since then, the term has come into common usage both in career literature and in the popular media. It has been variously defined as a phenomenon, a syndrome, and a set of symptoms. Most writing on the issue is anecdotal, informally observational, and confined to consideration of only a few occupational groups (for example, mainly business, child care, mental health, education, health care, law enforcement, and social service).

Webster's Third New International Dictionary defines burnout partially as follows: "to cause to fail, wear out, or become exhausted by making excessive demands on energy, strength, or resources, . . . to cease to be in a condition to perform a normal function by reason of unusually prolonged exposure to fire or heat, . . . to fail, wear out, or become exhausted by reason of excessive demands on energy, strength, or resources." The difficulty in applying a commonly used term in a new way is that it can lose its meaning through careless use. The term burnout is metaphorical and lends itself to facile and loose use of language.

One regrets that the term burnout was ever applied to describe a presumed psychological construct and that professionals have attempted to research the alleged phenomenon as a global concept. When some people speak of burnout, it is clear that they are really referring to the job satisfaction–job dissatisfaction continuum about which there is a vast amount of past and ongoing research. The literature in this area is selectively reviewed later in this chapter. When others refer to burnout, they are apparently alluding to a frequent consequence of the maintenance stage of career development—boredom, ennui, tedium, plateauing, the career blahs, and so on. It is a condition that asks the question, "Is that all there is?" Aspects of this concept are addressed in Chapter 11 in reference to career helping in the workplace. Finally, when some individuals speak of burnout, they are describing an individual's reaction to occupational stressors. The concept of occupational stress is dealt with in Chapter 11 as well. In this chapter, we present a brief summary of the extant research relating to burnout—however ill-defined and ill-measured the concept—simply because the term continues to appear in the literature. Readers are cautioned, however, not to use the term loosely and to define carefully which aspect (of what is being called burnout) a client or a researcher is utilizing. One heartening development is that the number of articles purporting to research the construct of burnout has declined markedly in the last few years, perhaps indicating a more sophisticated approach to isolating variables and measuring them.

What is Burnout?

Freudenberger and Richelson (1980) define burnout symptomatically as a depletion of an individual's physical and mental resources, and they attribute the etiology of burnout to excessive strivings to attain some unrealistic goal imposed by oneself or by the values of society. Symptoms include just about everything: loss of "charisma," fatigue, headaches, sleeplessness, quickness to anger, suspicion, paranoia, and depression, among many others. Such symptoms, of course, can be symptoms of something other than burnout, so it is indeed difficult to isolate their cause. Freudenberger views the work situation as the precipitating factor of burnout, especially in the helping professions, in that devotion to helping and unrealistic expectations combine to lead to burnout.

Cherniss (1980a) is another who has considered burnout in the helping professions. He defines burnout as a "process in which a previously committed professional disengages from his/her work in response to stress and strain experienced on the job" (p. 18). In his conception, burnout is a three-stage process. In stage one, the worker feels *stress* because of an imbalance between resources and demands. In the second stage, the worker experiences *strain,* an immediate, short-term emotional response to anxiety, tension, and fatigue. In the third stage, the worker tries to *cope defensively* by altering attitudes and behavior (for example, treating clients mechanically). It is this third stage that is thought to be "true" burnout. Cherniss's stress-related conception has received some preliminary, rudimentary, and small-scale research validation (1980b).

A third major writer in the field of burnout is Maslach, who, with various associates, especially Pines, has described a variety of behaviors related to burnout (Maslach & Jackson, 1981; Pines & Maslach, 1979). Most of her thoughts pertain to mental health workers. In that context, she views burnout as a loss of concern for the people with whom one is working characterized by an emotional exhaustion in which the staff person no longer has positive feelings, respect, or empathy for clients.

The job induces stress; the worker cannot cope; burnout results and manifests itself in such observable behaviors as low morale, excessive absenteeism, psychosomatic symptoms, and an increase in family and marital conflict, to cite just a few presumed personal consequences. Maslach also contends that dealing with certain *types* of clients and *numbers* of clients make a worker especially vulnerable to burnout. For example, it is alleged that those who work with higher populations of schizophrenics are more likely to burn out and that those who work with too many clients are similarly more susceptible.

Several work-related stages have been described that might be confused with what is thought to be burnout. For instance, *rust-out* is a term applied to individuals who are underemployed, who are in occupations that do not make full use of their education and training, or who do not have enough pressure and challenge on the job. Their skills atrophy and, it is consequently argued, they may develop symptoms akin to those ascribed to burnout. Similarly, some writers attempt to distinguish between *tedium* and burnout (Pines & Maslach, 1980); the former is used to refer to a condition arising from "constant or repeated emotional pressure associated with an intense involvement with people" (p. 15), whereas the latter results from "any prolonged, chronic pressures" (p. 15). It is difficult to comprehend this type of mutual exclusivity. Some speak of *stagnation* in the context of burnout but mean something different (Edelwich & Brodsky, 1980). Stagnation refers to becoming stalled after an initial burst of enthusiasm. One final illustration is that of *plateauing*. Plateauing refers to reaching a vertical position in an organization beyond which one will never progress. The thought of no further vertical (or even horizontal) movement could cause symptomatic reactions similar to those of burnout.

Hence, the term *burnout* is not at all clear in meaning. Just as intelligence is sometimes cynically defined as that which intelligence tests measure, burnout may soon come to be regarded as that which burnout instruments assess. Unfortunately, we do not now have a burnout assessment instrument that has been sufficiently tested, although at least one looks promising. Instruments by Helliwell (1981), Freudenberger and Richelson (1980), and Justice, Gold, and Klein (1981) are in the developmental stages. The most advanced instrument is the Maslach Burnout Inventory (Maslach & Jackson, 1981), which consists of four subscales: Emotional Exhaustion ("I feel used up at the end of the workday"); Depersonalization ("I've become more callous toward people since I took this job"); Personal Accomplishment ("I feel I'm positively influencing other people's lives through my work"); and Personal Involvement ("I feel personally involved with my [students', clients'] problems").

The source of stress or burnout is thought by most observers to be the interaction between personal factors (such as personality) and the situational stress variables of the occupation (supervision, job tasks) as both of these variables are embedded in the culture (attitudes toward work).

The correlates of burnout are just beginning to be recognized (assuming that one accepts the definition of burnout used by various investigators). Forney, Wallace-Schutzman, and Wiggens (1982) surveyed 24 career development professionals who reported that burnout seemed to be associated with such environmental correlates as repetitious work tasks, lack of advancement opportunities, work overload, feedback and supervision issues, organizational policies, boredom, and time pressures. In another study, which utilized a larger sample than is usually found in burnout studies, Schwab (1981) studied 461 teachers and concluded that role conflict and ambiguity were significantly related to burnout. If one regards stress and burnout as tantamount (a la Maslach), then another study of Farber and

Heifetz (1981) indicates that burnout may be correlated with excessive workload and working with very disturbed people. This latter finding has been repeated by Emener and Rubin (1980). All of these reported studies deal with aspects of job involvement and supervision that have traditionally been associated with job satisfaction research.

Another group of studies has looked at the relationship between burnout and life events. Pines, Aronson, and Kafry (1981) report a significant negative correlation between tedium (as defined earlier) and positive life events (conversely, the more negative life events there are in a person's life, the higher the tedium scores). Sarason and Johnson (1979), again using a job satisfaction measure equated with burnout, found that negative life changes are associated with lower levels of job satisfaction. Several researchers have preliminarily determined that males and females tend sometimes to react differently to the same occupational stressors (J. W. Thompson, 1980; Tung, 1980). Other researchers suggest that reactions to occupational stress will differ by *level* of employment (Axelrod & Gavin, 1980; Parasuraman & Alutto, 1981). Some research also points to the relationship of on-the-job and off-the-job stress, including that severe reactions come about only when *both* types of stress are present (Pardine et al., 1981). P. R. Wise (1985) studied the events that school psychologists thought were most stressful and isolated nine factors: interpersonal conflict, high risk to self and others, obstacles to efficient job performance, public speaking, time management, keeping district legal, hassles, professional enrichment, and insufficient recognition of work.

Matthews (1990), using the Maslach Burnout Inventory, Spielberger's State-Trait Anxiety Inventory, and her own instrument, compared burnout responses of workers in the health sciences, banking, social welfare, industry, education, and postal service. The occupational groups arrayed themselves in a hierarchy of burnout, trait anxiety, and emotional exhaustion. In general, social service workers displayed the highest burnout symptoms, trait anxiety, and emotional exhaustion, and education was next for each of these parameters. Other occupational groups, however, varied in terms of the severity of each of these three dimensions (e.g., banking was lowest in terms of burnout, but not so in terms of trait anxiety and emotional exhaustion). Although it was not the purpose of this study to do so, it probably illustrates the nebulous nature of the postulated construct of burnout.

Burnout is usually thought to develop in progressive phases rather than suddenly springing to existence. Burke (1989) has attempted to explicate the nature of these phases. Individuals at a more advanced phase will report more negative work experiences and more negative outcomes (for instance, job dissatisfaction) than individuals in an earlier phase. Some researchers posit three or four phases; others suggest as many as eight phases (Golembiewski & Munzenrider, 1988). The advantage of a phase theory is that it provides a framework for research. However, if the construct is not valid to begin with, there is little to be gained from a structure in which to research it.

To summarize thus far: most investigators of burnout regard it as a reaction to occupational stress (in addition to research previously cited, see, for instance, Cedoline, 1982; Gardner & Hall, 1981; Golembiewski, 1988; Leiter, 1988; Savicki & Cooley, 1982; Savicki & Cooley, 1987; Seidman & Zager, 1987; Veninga & Spradley, 1987). Consonant with the stress literature, these reactions may be physical, mental, emotional, or any combination of these. Most authors agree that burnout is not the result of a single event; rather, it is a cumulative phenomenon, beginning with barely noticeable changes and proceeding through increasingly intense reactions until it becomes a crisis that, if left unresolved, can cause chronic depression, abuse of alcohol and other drugs, and even suicide. All of this does not explain why and how an individual's internal resources and social support moderate external stressors. Why, for some individuals, is the same stressor likely to result, in Selye's (1975) terms, in *eustress* (positive), whereas for other individuals it results in *distress* (negative)? The literature on occupational stress is reviewed in Chapter 11.

There is much, however, that is still unexplained by viewing burnout in terms of stress theory, as a stage phenomenon, or in terms of general job satisfaction. One possible route to filling in missing knowledge may be to view burnout as basically the result of an expectation-reality gap. One comes to a career with high hopes and great expectations, an exuberance of spirit, and overriding ambitions. The realities of the daily work world may intrude to deaden, destroy, or at least soften the sharpness of these aspirations. Garden (1989) offers the intriguing possibility that different psychological types represented heavily in various occupations (for example, human services versus business) may react quite differently in terms of burnout. In all speculations, what remains constant is a situation-person effect. What differs is the extent to which situation or person produces the effect. We do not now have any clear notion of the relationships among stress, coping styles, worker characteristics, career development, job satisfaction, and burnout (however it is defined). Until we do, counselors should be a bit more tentative as they discuss burnout.

The Prevention and Treatment of Burnout

There are two ways in which a worker can cope with burnout (especially if one considers burnout to be a form of stress). The first method is a sort of do-it-yourself response. There are a number of books that offer one system or another for coping with stress (Freudenberger & Richelson, 1980; Potter, 1980; Veninga & Spradley, 1981). At a professional level, somewhere in the literature of most fields there are articles on coping with burnout.

A second way of coping with burnout or preventing it is for professional counselors to address the question. They can do so in two ways: alter the work environment or change the individual. We present several suggestions for effecting each of these approaches. Keep in mind, however, that many of these suggestions are made based on one idiosyncratic definition of burnout or another.

The Environment. Various organizational strategies have been proposed to deal with the problem of burnout:

1. Allowing "time-outs" in which workers are allowed time off from the job to recuperate psychologically and to recharge themselves
2. Training supervisors to recognize and to deal with potential burnout-inducing situations and actual burnout
3. Providing enhanced opportunities for vertical career development (such as career ladders, in-service training, or conference attendance)
4. Allowing worker participation in policy-making
5. Allowing more worker autonomy in decision making
6. Providing more explicit organizational recognition of achievement
7. Permitting reduction of workload and variety in type of client served
8. Experimenting with such variables as flex-time, job rotation, job enrichment, and job sharing
9. Providing for employee counseling within the organization
10. Offering comprehensive employee orientation programs

11. Sponsoring organizational workshops on stress management and support groups
12. Clarifying organizational goals and policies
13. Identifying chronic sources of stress and frustration
14. Providing career planning assistance
15. Reducing the intensity involved in a job
16. Identifying and addressing sources of role ambiguity and role conflict
17. Trying to use more employee abilities and skills
18. Providing workers with adequate resources to perform the required work
19. Reducing busywork (such as too many meetings)
20. Using epidemiological techniques to try to reduce the contagion effect of burnout
21. Reducing isolation of workers
22. Allowing enough lead time for work
23. Providing employees with as much security as possible

The Individual. Individual approaches to the amelioration or prevention of burnout will vary according to what theoretical concept is seen as the cause. If stress is seen as the precipitating factor, for example, then it is viewed differently by theorists of the psychoanalytic, learning and behavioral, developmental, sociological, physiological, neurobiological, or environmental schools. Most of the suggestions to help individuals cope with or prevent burnout are really atheoretical or spring from a preliminary set of frequently random postulates about the nature and etiology of burnout. With this caveat in mind, we present several of these suggestions in order to give a sense of the current activity.

Several suggestions involve preservice preparation for helping workers to cope with the possibility of burnout (Lattanzi, 1981; Partin & Gargiulo, 1980; Savicki & Cooley, 1982). Although there is some danger of a self-fulfilling prophecy here, preservice attention is sensible. It is assumed that such preparation will present a realistic picture of what a particular type of work will be and will thus reduce the potential expectation-reality gap. If the expectations of a new occupation are more in line with the actualities of the work setting, it is thought, stress will be less. If workers are not disillusioned by false ideals in their preparation, it is argued, they cannot be disappointed when they face reality.

In both preservice and in-service programs, the basic concerns are the same. These include training in the recognition of sources of work stress, techniques of dealing with the stress, and evaluation of that application. Writers vary in suggesting how one should specifically cope.

Leiter and Meechan (1986) investigated burnout (as defined by the Maslach Burnout Inventory) in the staff of a residential rehabilitation and mental health center. Perhaps the most instructive aspect of their findings was that both the emotional exhaustion and personalization segments of Maslach's conception of burnout increased when staff concentrated their social contacts within the formally defined work areas. Apparently, it is best to get away from one's job in the sense of separating work and social lives.

If people subscribe to the career plateauing notion of burnout, then there is reason to believe that with more qualified people competing for fewer jobs, lack of promotion will lead to more workers who feel stymied or bored or career-trapped. Rantze and Feller (1985) describe four options that such individuals usually pursue.

1. *Placid Approach*—Accept the situation and "adjust" by hiding frustration and discontent. Continue to do the job and look for satisfaction elsewhere.
2. *Hopscotch Approach*—Stay in the same company but try to move laterally by getting a job in another department or office.

3. *Change of Uniform Approach*—Leave the company and get a job in another company, hoping that the situation will be more favorable.
4. *Entrepreneurial Approach*—Identify what goods and services are needed and start a business or consulting firm outside of the corporate or government job dependent world. (p. 25)

Rantze and Feller suggest a fifth approach—*intrapreneurial,* which basically involves strategies to bring about change within the organization by means of standard organizational development techniques.

Others who advocate holistic health education offer different suggestions (Argeropoulos, 1981). They prescribe vigorous exercise, nutrition, relaxation techniques (such as meditation, self-hypnosis, deep breathing, progressive relaxation, yoga, or autogenic training such as biofeedback), use of support groups to foster self-awareness and self-acceptance, organizational skills, specific coping skills training, and alteration of self-defeating belief systems.

Helliwell (1981) presents a long list of suggestions for helping individuals to deal effectively with burnout. These include encouraging introspection, eliminating negative messages, reducing care and concern (psychological withdrawal), and increasing alternative activities to work (such as family and outside interests). Other ideas are of the "straighten up and fly right" variety: stop feeling sorry for yourself, simplify your life, and don't spend time with pessimistic people, to cite just a few. In a slightly different vein, Freudenberger and Richelson (1980) recommend an Alcoholics Anonymous approach: learning to accept things that cannot be changed, and focusing on things that can be.

Forney et al. (1982) suggest the use of Rational Emotive Therapy (RET) techniques in order to discover various "myths" that foster self-defeating attitudes. These myths include such statements as "my job is my life" and "I must always perform at a peak level and with a lot of energy and enthusiasm" (p. 437). The idea is to challenge such myths with rational thinking.

Cedoline (1982) encourages a balanced life between work/play, challenge/leisure, stress/relaxation, companionship/solitude, and discipline/self-indulgence. This balance would be brought about by a stress management program. In this program, the first step is to identify what kinds of stress one is experiencing, what job conditions are most stressful, and what one does or says to oneself under pressure. The second step is designed to help people read their own stress symptoms. For six weeks they keep a daily log of stressful events. Individuals are told to record what events preceded the feeling of stress, when in the day the stress occurred, what the feelings were like, and what response resulted. Each day is rated on a ten-point scale (1 = disaster; 10 = a cinch). The next step is to selectively apply coping techniques, depending on whether the stress is caused by external locus of control problems, occupational feedback or communication deficits, work overload, role conflict or ambiguity, or training deficits. If specific behavioral objectives are devised for this program, it could hold much promise.

Support groups are frequently advocated as a response to or a prevention of burnout (Gardner & Hall, 1981; Spicuzza & De Voe, 1982). Spicuzza and De Voe have developed a Mutual Aid (MA) group system for burned-out individuals. They see these groups as places where people "can discover or reassess their sense of self, search for their own personal meaning in society, diminish their feelings of solitude within a group structure, and perhaps promote social change" (p. 96). These are lofty goals indeed. They see MA groups as consisting of eight to twelve members and as being either homogeneous or heterogeneous. The groups are directed at a combination of socialization, instruction, discussion of business, and evaluation (of previous meetings). Emphasized are the needs for participants to take risks and to practice and experiment with new behaviors.

Few studies have examined the relative effectiveness of preventive versus remedial interventions in the area of burnout. One study (Firth & Shapiro, 1986) investigated the effects of psychotherapy for job-related distress. They worked with 40 self-referred managerial and professional workers who were seeking help with severe (that is, out of the normal range) job-related distress. Some of these individuals received eight sessions of cognitive/behavioral-oriented therapy; others experienced eight sessions of relationship-oriented therapy. Three months after treatment, a follow-up disclosed that three-quarters showed a reduction in stress to a normal range. Cognitive/behavioral therapy appeared to be more effective in the reduction of overall symptoms, but there were no differences between the therapies for relief of job-related problems. On the basis of this post hoc success, the authors suggest treatment after the fact rather than preventive group work in stress management.

WORKING MOTHERS

The many roles we play in life are obviously interrelated. A worker may also be a daughter, a wife, and a mother, for example. The symbiotic effect of different roles is considerable. In our example, work can affect family; family can affect work behaviors. A mythology has arisen over the years, however, regarding precisely what the effects are. In this section we will consider some of the family factors related to work and attempt to draw some conclusions on the basis of available research.

Effects on Children

According to a *New York Times* poll of women in 1989, the most important problems facing women today are, in order, equality on the job, balancing work and family, child care, abortion, and equal rights. That such a large proportion of these perceived problems should relate to work is not surprising. Currently, over half of all children under 18 have working mothers, and projections indicate that almost seven of every ten mothers with infants and young children will be employed by 1995 (Hoffreth & Phillips, 1987). The traditional pattern has been for women to enter post-school work, to take a hiatus from work for an extended period of childbearing and child rearing, and often to return to work when the last child has reached school age. This traditional pattern is eroding in favor of more continuous work careers.

Although a great many studies address the effects of maternal employment on children, many suffer from methodological shortcomings. For example, some studies try to take into consideration substitute care for children while the mother is at work, but often the quality of that care is not assessed. Also, these studies frequently do not account for the mother's occupational and educational status, the age of the child when the mother started working, maternal job satisfaction, attitudes of other family members toward maternal work, the husband's sharing of the management of the home, parental personality characteristics and sex-role beliefs, the size of the family, and the career pattern of the mother. Add to these complications the facts that sample sizes are often small, that definitions of key terms frequently differ from study to study, that most data are gathered from self-reports, and that there is rarely a theoretical anchor for such studies. Although it would be easy to dismiss the findings of this body of research as unacceptably derived, such an indictment would be too harsh. There is much that is instructive.

Several reviews of the literature (Etaugh, 1974, 1980, 1984; Heyns & Catsambis, 1986; L. W. Hoffman, 1979, 1989; Milne, Myers, Rosenthal, & Ginsburg, 1986; E. J. Smith, 1981) provide us with some summary conclusions. Etaugh concludes, "Available data indicate that high-quality nonmaternal care does not appear to have adverse effects on the young child's maternal attachment, intellectual development, or social-emotional behavior" (1980, p. 309). Etaugh (1974) further emphasizes that strength of attachment between mother and child is related more to the quality and intensity of their interactions than to the frequency. Stable and stimulating caretaking appears to be related to the personal and cognitive development of the child, however that caretaking is defined. Furthermore, adjusted mothers (whatever their role) tend to have adjusted children through adolescence (with the possible exception of lower-class boys and girls whose mothers work full-time). Maternal employment does not appear to affect children's school achievement, but it does seem positively to affect educational and occupational aspirations (especially in terms of daughters choosing less traditional careers).

Very few studies have found a consistent negative effect on the educational achievement of the children of working mothers. One study that did find negative effects was accomplished by Milne et al. Using data from two separate data sets on approximately 15,000 elementary and adolescent students in two time frames about five years apart, they concluded that mother's employment and living in a one-parent family can have negative effects on school achievement but that these effects differ by age, race, and family structure. They also found that income and time allocation mediated the effects of work. Heyns and Catsambis analyzed the same data and respecified the model to include measures of the structural, attitudinal, and socioeconomic determinants of a mother's employment. The result was substantially diminished effects. In their analysis, significant negative effects existed only for women in the labor force for the shortest period of time or for women who decreased their labor force participation as their child got older.

The two major variables affecting a woman's decision to work are the presence or absence of children and the family's financial condition. Childbearing, in general, used to have a strong negative effect on outside employment. Now, both economic exigency and personal satisfaction appear to combine to make working mothers of even small children common. This situation is presumed by many to lead to interrole conflict between the roles of mother and employed worker that, in turn, is thought to lead to stress (Beutell & Greenhaus, 1982; Dunlop, 1981). Not the least source of stress is supposed to be the guilt engendered by a mother's working rather than tending primarily to child care. Ever since Bowlby (1958) introduced the notion of maternal deprivation to explain the cognitive, affective, and social deficits of children in institutions (based on research having severe methodological flaws), and ever since Harlow (1953) did his work with monkeys and maternal behavior, generalizations have been made to the maternal work situation. The leaps made have been huge and inappropriate.

As evidenced in the popular literature of our time, beginning with Philip Wylie and his idea of "momism" and extending into the present, it is fashionable to blame mothers for a variety of society's ills. The fact that professional journals have echoed this popular notion and have apparently scapegoated mothers is perhaps more remarkable. P. J. Caplan and Hall-McCorquodale (1985a, 1985b) have investigated the incidence of mother-blaming in major clinical journals from 1970 to 1982 and concluded that the raised consciousness level of the women's movement did not seem to affect the common practice of mother-blaming. For example, mothers' activity is likely to be blamed for children's problems, but fathers' activity or inactivity and lack of involvement is much less likely to be seen as a causative factor. Caplan and Hall-McCorquodale suggest that simple solutions are available; for instance, whenever possible, emphasis on mother-infant or mother-child interaction should be changed to interaction between *parent* and child. There is, of course, a fine line between denial and reality and the desire for equitable attribution, but the point is well-taken: we ought to be very careful about unsubstantiated cause-effect conclusions regarding maternal behavior and subsequent child behaviors.

Research on the effects of maternal employment on infants and preschoolers and adolescents offer several conclusions about which we can be reasonably certain:

1. When the child is enrolled in high-quality, center-based care, the intellectual effects are neither harmful nor helpful, except for children who grow up in high-risk environments. For these children, quality day care seems actually to help to maintain or to raise IQ scores.
2. Maternal employment does not seem to alter the emotional bond between mother and child.
3. Maternal job satisfaction appears to be positively related to development in preschoolers.
4. There is absolutely no convincing proof of the deleterious effects of maternal employment on preschoolers. At the very least, maternal employment seems to do no harm.
5. Maternal employment likely has a positive effect on a daughter's career involvement and commitment. When combined with factors such as the educational and occupational status of the mother, sex-role ideology, and encouragement of both parents, maternal work has an interaction effect that leads to a decrease in a daughter's sex-typing and to more assertive career planning (Haber, 1980; L. M. Jones & McBride, 1980; E. R. Smith, 1980).
6. Adolescent children of working mothers do not appear to experience any proven, consistently harmful effects (Hannson, O'Connor, Jones, & Blocker, 1981).
7. Female adolescents may react somewhat differently to maternal employment than do male adolescents.

It is frequently argued that greater participation of fathers in actual child rearing and other household management tasks will affect the sex-role attitudes of their children in positive (that is, more androgynous) directions. A study by Baruch and Barnett (1986), however, found the direct effects of paternal participation on children's attitudes to be generally weak. Their findings imply that the mother's attitude toward the father's role is a stronger influence than his actual behavior. For example, if a mother holds traditional values regarding the male role, even if her husband is highly participant, the child may receive a message that weakens the effect of the father's behavior.

One attempt at carefully delineating the type of child care as a variable was that of Benn (1986), who found no relationship between child care (or socioeconomic status) and attachment relationships between employed mothers and their 18-month-old firstborn sons. Rather, she found that the effects of maternal employment on mother-son attachment was mediated by the mother's affective state as indicated by her attitudes toward mothering, sensitivity, satisfaction with child care, attitudes toward husband's participation, and so on. In general, the more integrated the mother was in this regard, the more healthy the style of caregiving and child-care decisions.

Logically, it would seem that high-quality day care is a better alternative than a fatigued, preoccupied, bored mother at home. In fact, studies indicate generally that employed mothers spend almost as much daily time interacting actively with their children as do mothers who are home all day. In some studies, children of working mothers gain some benefits and lose others (for example, school achievement, personality development, recreational activities, absenteeism, and so on), so the net effect across groups is no significant difference (S. H. Cramer, Keitel, & Rossberg, 1986).

In summary, there is, thus far, no clear evidence that maternal employment victimizes children. There are data to suggest, at least in some areas that have been researched, that maternal employment reduces children's sex-role stereotyping and has a positive influence on a daughter's career development. It is important to emphasize that while the literature does not demonstrate any other great gains for children that can be attributed to maternal employment, it also shows, for the most part, that maternal employment, in general, does no harm to children.

Effects on Mothers

In the previous section we alluded to the possibility of interrole conflict and stress as a result of maternal employment. The general conclusion reached in most of the research studies is that there is basically no difference in adjustment and satisfaction between working and nonworking mothers (Keith & Schafer, 1980; D. A. Parker, E. S. Parker, Wolz, & Harford, 1980; Townshend & Gurin, 1981). A few studies have actually indicated measurably positive results as a consequence of maternal employment (Kessler & McRae, 1982; L. S. Walker & J. I. Walker, 1980).

There is no doubt that working mothers experience more stress than do unemployed mothers; however, rewards appear to counterbalance the stress, and, for most maternal workers, the stress stemming from interrole conflict does not become debilitating.

Ferree (1984) reviewed studies that assessed the life satisfaction of working women and those who remained in the home. Her conclusion was that in large-scale national surveys, there were no self-reported differences in satisfaction between the two groups. On the other hand, in small sample studies, satisfaction and mental health indices seemed to slightly favor housewives. Ferree suggests that a social desirability factor may be operating in the smaller studies; thus, social expectations regarding the traditional female role may affect response. As the working mother becomes the norm, these findings may change.

Maternal work does not appear to affect a mother's well-being in any substantially negative manner. A number of studies have underlined the importance of social support as a moderator of stress for working mothers. Suchet and Barling (1985) have demonstrated in a South African study that the husband, especially, can enhance the marital satisfaction and reduce the interrole conflict of working mothers. Work is not invariably beneficial for a woman in terms of her well-being. There are many stresses. Scarr, Phillips, and McCartney (1989) concluded that the greatest number of work-family problems revolve around shared family responsibilities, spousal support, and affordable and dependable child care.

Effects on Families

If maternal employment does not seem to affect adversely either child rearing or the mother's well-being, does it have an effect on the marriage or on the family?

Early research reported an inconsistent but generally weak negative relationship between maternal employment and marital satisfaction. Later research, more sophisticated in design and controlling for more variables, suggests that it is not maternal employment per se that determines marital satisfaction; rather, it is the extent to which that employment infringes on fulfillment of role expectations and thus causes conflict (Houseknecht & Macke, 1981). This finding of lack of effects has been more forcefully presented in a study by Locksley (1980), who provides strong evidence against the hypothesis that such negative outcomes in contemporary society as rising divorce rates, juvenile delinquency, and illegitimacy are attributable to a mother's participation in the wage economy. We are beginning to realize that "the nature and quality of a woman's experiences within a role, not merely role occupancy per se, are critical to understanding the processes affecting her well-being" (Baruch, Biener, & Barnett, 1987, p. 133). In general, wife employment status and marital adjustment research produces trivial differences, if any, between dual-worker versus single-worker families. This finding may vary over the life cycle, however (Keith, Goudy, & Powers, 1981).

Further evidence comes from surveys of work and family life conflicts (Pleck, Staines, & Lang, 1980). These surveys indicate that about one-third of all workers (male and female) living in families report either moderate or severe work-family conflicts. This total is relatively small. What is more significant is that working women did not report any greater conflict than did working men.

It is generally accepted that men are more satisfied with marriage than are women. It is also generally accepted that the pressure of young children is likely to be associated with lower life satisfaction and poorer marital adjustment. Maternal employment does not seem to be a factor in these findings. In general, marital adjustment for working wives is greatly enhanced, as might be expected, by a supportive husband (for example, one who approves of his wife's employment, shares in household duties, and advocates a similar belief system). In general, also, higher occupational and educational status is associated with better marital adjustment in dual-worker couples.

Looking at the division of household labor in America, Berk (1985) found that regardless of the employment status of their wives, the number of hours of husbands' household work remained stable. The primarily white, middle-class couples in this study—not surprisingly—perceived inequity differently; only 6 percent of the husbands reported inequality in household arrangements compared to 21 percent of the wives. These findings are somewhat mitigated when one looks at differences by socioeconomic status. L. W. Hoffman (1989) reports that large-scale studies indicate that maternal employment is much more problematic for fathers with traditional sex-role ideology than it is for those with more liberal sex-role views. Since sex-role perceptions are related to social class, researchers tend to find negative correlations between fathers' morale and mothers' employment status in blue-collar families. There also tends to be a strain in blue-collar families in the father-son relationship when the mother is employed, perhaps because the son views the mother's employment as a result somehow of a failing on the father's part. Lest we believe that the grass is greener in other countries in terms of more equal distribution of household management tasks, Moen's (1989) research in Sweden points out that men do not participate equally in parenting (despite the image of the enlightened Swede). Nevertheless, the well-being of Swedish mothers actually has increased in that country despite a great rise in their employment. Sweden does have public policies, however, that are more responsive to maternal employment than those in the United States (for instance, extended, paid leaves of absence for child care, the right of parents of small children to work 6 rather than 8 hours per day, and so on).

Although it is not a principal focus of this section of Chapter 13, McBride (1990) points out that work-family issues not only concern parenting but also frequently deal with being a son or daughter and providing care for elderly parents or in-laws. This caregiver role adds another layer to the potential conflict of multiple roles.

In an effort to more finely delineate the possible types of single-earner and dual-earner couples. Yogev and Brett (1985) described four patterns of couples in a sample of 136 dual-earner and 103 single-earner couples:

Work and Family Symmetry—Couples have similar level of involvement in both work and family.

Symmetric Family–Asymmetric Work—Among dual-earner couples only. Similarly involved in family (either high or low) but degree of work involvement dissimilar.

Symmetric Work–Asymmetric Family—Among dual-earner couples only. Similarly involved with work, but degree of family involvement dissimilar.

Work and Family Asymmetry—Each spouse's involvement in work and family is opposite from the other spouse's involvement.

They discovered that the role-symmetric couples were the most prevalent among both dual- and single-earner couples. The family role behaviors and attitudes of one spouse are related to those of the other spouse. This sort of more detailed definition of types is most useful in research.

Implications for Career Counseling

The great majority of working women will experience some interrole conflict. They must be helped to anticipate it; those who are having difficulty with the experience should be helped to deal with it. Many young women still believe that worker and mother are mutually exclusive roles, and that if mothers work, some horrendous harm will befall their children, their marriage, or themselves. Young women, before the fact, and mothers, after the fact, should be aided to see that these ideas have no basis in reality. The general rule should be that if a woman feels good about herself, if she has a mate who is supportive of her work and who is willing to help with housework and child rearing, maternal employment will not only be unharmful, but it may be beneficial.

One strategy for lessening career-home conflict is for the couple to delay parenthood and to engage in associated behaviors, such as to drop out of the labor force during perceived "critical" periods of child rearing or to remain childless by choice (Wilkie, 1981). At several points in this book we have stressed the necessity for all individuals, but for females especially, to adopt an attitude of planfulness. Choosing between traditional and nontraditional roles is one such decision. Zaslow and Pederson (1981) offer four suggestions, for example, in counseling couples regarding child bearing:

1. Women assuming full-time caregiving roles may be more satisfied with the choice if they have carefully assessed the options for eventual return to employment as well as considered a means to maintain professional competence while unemployed. Women planning to combine career and family roles may need to assess the availability of substitute care and the possibility of flexible work hours, part-time employment, or employment that does not involve separation from the baby. The evaluation requires an examination of needs, feelings, and options.
2. Couples may be encouraged to seek out other parents who have made similar sex-role choices.
3. After the couple chooses how to delegate career-home responsibilities, the counselor must help the couple deal with the pressure inherent in that choice.

4. The support of the spouse is crucial in adjustment to maternal employment, and the counselor may help each spouse to understand the implications of the other's choice for himself or herself.

Beutell and Greenhaus (1982) suggest a similar intervention strategy:

> It may be useful for spouses to discuss the possible effect of similar/dissimilar career orientations on their work and family roles. Spouse workshops or seminars may be appropriate vehicles for initiating and reinforcing such discussions. (p. 108)

Although there is a great deal of talk about the "subtle revolution" in realigning family roles, and although there is a great deal of attention given by academics to the decline of the "good provider" stereotype (Bernard, 1981), women still assume the more sex-traditional share of burdens in household management. When all is said and done, males must be educated to factors of maternal employment as much as women are.

Clearly, work-family issues have become an increasingly prominent focus for social policy. Russo (1990) points out, for instance, that the NIMH women's mental health research agenda emphasizes research on parenting, work-related stress, and the effect on mental health of multiple roles. These foci would be studied within the context of education, economic status, marital status, age, and race/ethnicity. Frone and Rice (1987) suggest that our present research models of examining work-family conflict should be expanded to include other work-nonwork contexts, such as the work-leisure area.

Finally, Etaugh (1984) has suggested a number of guidelines by which counselors can assist families in which the mother is either currently employed or is considering reentry into the labor force. In abbreviated form, she suggests that counselors do the following:

1. Assess their own attitudes toward the traditional female role
2. Be familiar with theory and research related to occupational choices and development, as well as with career opportunities, and the relationship between family and career cycles in order to help women to explore all their options
3. Help working mothers realize that many of the stresses they are experiencing are caused not by their own shortcomings, but by external pressures arising from family and employment systems
4. Make clear that the role conflicts and role overload experienced by working mothers are caused not by their inadequacies, but by the press of more demands than most people can handle effectively
5. Help working mothers clarify their personal values and realize that those regarding career and family may change over time as circumstances change
6. Help working mothers recognize and derive satisfaction from their personal strengths and achievements
7. Help working mothers and their husbands achieve a sense of equity in their relationship through an exploration of issues related to competition and power
8. Help working mothers by developing such external supports as group therapy sessions with other working mothers or working couples in similar situations and/or at different stages in the life cycle
9. Provide working mothers with accurate information concerning the effects of maternal employment on children, since lack of information or misinformation in this area can increase the stress and conflict experienced by working mothers
10. Provide assistance and information pertaining to practical matters, such as availability of child-care services
11. Encourage family discussions that examine the feelings, needs, and attitudes of

the working mother, her spouse, and her children regarding the mother's multiple roles; alternatives to the traditional mother role; and the sharing of home and family responsibilities

12. Encourage parents to establish open and frequent communication with their child's other caregivers
13. Encourage working mothers to talk to their children about their job, take their children to their place of employment, and introduce their children to some of their co-workers
14. Help working parents to develop skills and responses for coping with any negative reactions shown by their children to maternal employment and/or a substitute caregiver
15. Support changes in social policies to enhance the functioning of working mothers and their families, such as reducing occupational barriers and improving the availability of high-quality child care services*

At the very least, the considerable body of literature on maternal employment indicates that such work probably will not harm children, the mother herself, or the marriage. Maternal employment may actually have beneficial effects in each of these areas. Because the prevailing folklore is different from the facts, a massive reeducation of American men and women is necessary. That education has begun.

DUAL-CAREER FAMILIES

We have just addressed the problems of dual-*worker* families or dual-*earner* families. Now we will consider a growing phenomenon in Western cultures, the dual-*career* family. This term is usually reserved for couples in which work represents a high commitment for both parties in which and the wife's work is continuous. If we define dual-career even more specifically—as requiring both spouses to be in professional, technical, or managerial jobs—then approximately 14 percent of the American labor force would fall into this category. This discussion, then, represents another look at family roles within the context of career development.

The Nature of Dual-Career Families

The idea of dual-career families began to be popularized about 1969 and stemmed from a study of graduates of British universities. Rapoport and Rapoport (1971, 1976) are generally given credit for calling attention to the phenomenon. They viewed dual-career couples as a new structural family type, one in which both heads of household pursue careers and simultaneously maintain a family life together, thus emphasizing the importance of work and family for both males and females.

Since the Rapoports' early work, there have been many studies relating to the dual-career family. These studies have suffered from several methodological limitations. Most of the samples have been small and restricted in their representativeness (for example, too many use academics as their sample). Also very few concentrate on or even include the male perspective; they focus on the woman. The perspectives of both partners would seem to be important. And, definitions of what constitutes a dual-career family vary from study to study. There are virtually no studies of unmarried dual career couples. Finally, the data in these studies are most often collected by means of interviews or other forms of self-report. This technique is, of course, common for sociological studies, but it neglects more psychological aspects and other data-gathering possibilities.

*Reprinted from *Perspectives on Work and the Family*, edited by S. H. Cramer, pp. 31-33, with permission of Apen Publishers, Inc., ©1984.

The accumulated research that we do have, however, even with its methodological shortcomings, offers some instructive findings. One apparent conclusion is that dual-career families—which we presume represent one of our most sophisticated and nontraditional structures—are, in fact, usually asymmetrical in terms of domestic responsibilities (Sundby, 1980; Yogev, 1981). Females apparently do considerably more than half of household management chores. This tolerance for domestication is manifested in nonegalitarian family functions. It may be that the wife is unwilling to change or is willing to assume the burden because of a fear of changing the family environment. Another possible explanation has been offered by Rapoport and Rapoport (1971), who describe an *identity tension line,* a point beyond which the violation of sex-role socialization becomes uncomfortable for the individual, either male or female. In any case, the tendency toward a traditional division of labor in performing domestic tasks means that wives retain the major responsibility for child rearing and for household maintenance.

In general, it would appear that the higher the status of the wife's occupation, the more she expects her spouse to assume the shared burden of household management tasks and parenting. Perhaps responding to the amount of money the wife earns and the high status of her occupation, the husband tends to fulfill the wife's expectations (G. W. Bird, G. A. Bird, & Scruggs, 1984). Also, in general, the less the status and monetary reward of the wife's occupation, the more asymmetrical the marriage is likely to be in terms of family roles. Simply because a man is part of a dual-career couple does not mean that he will be any more androgynous in his attitudes and behavior, nor does a woman's career mean that she will possess any more androgynous attitudes or qualities (E. A. House, 1986).

If asymmetry occurs in the majority of dual-career couples, then it is naturally hypothesized that this combination of family and work roles produces overload, identity and self-esteem dilemmas, multiple role cycling, discomfort, role conflict, violation of norms, and decreased leisure—all of which may result in stress. In fact, stress is prevalent in dual-career families (Skinner, 1980), but couples in such a structure generally believe that the stress would be greater if the wife were not pursuing a career. In short, some heightened stress by the woman is perceived as a relatively small cost. One solid indication of the fact that multiple work and family roles cause strain generated by the stressors is that when 200 teachers were examined in Michigan (Cooke & Rousseau, 1984), family and work overload strain was progressively greater for single teachers, those who are married, and those who have children. The incremental strain caused by children has also been well-documented by Chassin, Zeiss, Cooper, & Reaven, 1985).

The nonegalitarian burden for women in the home may be one reason that the wife's career is frequently subordinated to the husband's. In addition to conscious choice, however, discrimination apparently operates to make dual-career wives less successful, in general, than their husbands. This discrimination runs from overt antinepotism regulations to more subtle forms of sexual prejudice. The dual job-hunting constraints generally favor the male's landing a better job. There is a sort of self-fulfilling prophecy operating here in that managerial skepticism about a woman's ability to handle adequately both work and family sets up a barrier to her entry into higher levels within occupations. Sometimes the only solution is the so-called commuting marriage (H. E. Gross, 1980), where husband and wife are geographically separated for extended periods of time.

If there are all of these difficulties in dual-career families, why bother? The answer is that, in general, those involved in dual-career marriages are happy, and the dual career itself is thought to be a primary contributor to that adjustment.

Studies by both Sekaran (1982) and Hardesty and Betz (1980) suggest that if dual-career wives did not pursue their careers, they would be unhappy, for these women are more similar to working males than they are to nonworking females; that is, there is no difference in career salience between husbands and wives in dual-career families. Yogev (1981) indicates that academic wives strongly feel that their careers improve their marriage. Men and women in dual-career marriages tend each to rank family first and career second in priority. So long as the wife's job status does not have to be lowered to accommodate the dual-career couple, marital adjustment appears to be high (Hiller & Philliber, 1982). Men tend to report more spouse fulfillment and contentment, greater intellectual companionship, and increased income as decided advantages in dual-career marriages. Women typically report greater self-expression and realization of their potential and a greater sense of independence and competence for their children as a result of the dual-career nature of the family.

The benefits of a dual-career marriage have been clearly enumerated by Wilcox-Matthew and Minor (1989). These include feelings of self-worth, accomplishment and control from work roles, more roles in which to define success, marital solidarity, higher standard of living, child-care support policies in some employing organizations, and more egalitarian roles, among other positive outcomes. In general, dual-career marriages offer the advantages of enhanced identity of the wife, increased income, greater intellectual development, and higher self-esteem. Men benefit too from less sex-role stereotyping.

Even if a woman in a dual-career marriage opts for a nontraditional career (for example, engineering or veterinary medicine), she is apparently no different in terms of her work plans from her counterpart in a traditional field (such as nursing). O'Connell, Betz, and Kurth (1989) concluded in their study of women in traditional and nontraditional occupations that plans of women to pursue nontraditional professions do not translate into plans for a nontraditional family life. Both groups held similar gender beliefs, plans for marriage and children, and perceptions of the primacy of family or work roles.

Chance or accident factors can play a part in the career development of dual-career women, since these unforeseen events affect everyone's career development. The influence of these uncontrollable factors, however, may not be so strong as frequently imagined. In a retrospective study of college-educated women, Scott and Hatalla (1990) identified nine contingency factors that these women judged to be influential in their career patterns. These were, in order, awareness of skills and abilities; perception of interests; educational level; awareness of intelligence level; family, community, and cultural factors; unexpected personal events; factors specific to a job; enough money for school; and awareness of occupations open. Only one of these nine factors—unexpected personal events—is a chance factor.

Wilk's (1986) intensive study of the psychological characteristics of women in dual-career marriages and the consequent effect on the decision to have children suggests that dual-career childbearing decisions stem from the interaction of intrapsychic elements, marital elements, career elements, and lifestyle elements. The last three influences are well known; the intrapsychic element may be affected by a quasi-narcissistic personality type described as follows:

> I have found that women who have not successfully managed the very earliest developmental tasks related to the establishment of autonomy, the capacity for intimacy, and to the creation of satisfactory relationships with both mother and father, and who have not developed an adult fem-

inine self-concept that is both social and nurturant, find the childbearing decision extremely conflictual. (p. 286)

Wilk also found in her study that two major issues were related to the career dissatisfaction of dual-career women. One was the organizational mixed message that on the one hand professed a pronatalist bias and on the other manifested a career-first set of behaviors. The second was the almost universal absence of female mentors among successful career women. This finding has been replicated repeatedly since it was first expressed by Hennig and Jardin (1977). Why successful females apparently do not choose to mentor other females remains unclear.

One of the relatively rare researchers who has taken a close and careful look (although still incomplete because of the nature of the sample) at men in dual-career couples is L. A. Gilbert (1985). She intensively interviewed 37 men in parent families and 14 men in nonparent families. Most were white men in their 30s and many were in a remarriage; both they and their spouses reported working considerably more than 40 hours per week. Most men viewed their spouses as having positive or neutral effects on their own career goals. In general, however, although the men in these marriages assumed less of the household and parenting burdens than their wives, the greater their involvement and commitment in household tasks and parenting, the greater the perceived career costs. Just as with women in dual-career families, the men needed to feel the support of a spouse and family. They expressed concern about limited job mobility, but they had few fears about the dual-career marriage affecting their career commitment, career goals, or productivity. In terms of marital satisfaction, the crucial variable appears to be that both partners feel a sense of fairness or equity about the balance of family and professional roles. Imbalance tends to erode the mutual spousal support so necessary in successful dual-career marriages. The men felt that communication and compromise were the bywords by which the marriage functioned. Families were classified as traditional, participant, and role-sharing, depending on the man's involvement; as that involvement increased, so did their stress levels. Conversely, as the man's level increased, the spouse's level decreased. The men articulated the typical costs of benefits usually found in dual-career marriages. On the plus side, there was increased income, greater contentment of spouse, independent spousal identity, greater social intercourse for spouse, greater intellectual companionship, less pressure to provide economically, and greater rewards from parenting. On the minus side, the men expressed stress from physical and emotional overload, decreased leisure, increased household tasks, decreased sexual activity owing to exhaustion or lack of time, decreased opportunities for career placement, multiple role demands, and less time for emotional life together. Echoing Gilbert's findings are the results of a study by Barling (1986) in South Africa. This study examined 67 fathers in terms of interrole conflict and marital adjustment, with hardiness (for example, commitment and challenge) as a moderator variable. These men experienced as much interrole conflict as Gilbert's men (worker, parent, spouse, self). Both hardiness and social support were found necessary to cope with the resulting stress. All in all, Gilbert's work is a valuable addition to the dual-career literature and underlines once again a repeated theme in this text: differences in the career development and behavior of males and females are more a matter of degree than of kind.

Counseling for Dual-Career Couples

Any career-family counseling is essentially life-style counseling. The symbiotic relationship between family and career requires both males and females to understand life roles. Most marriages have relationship issues, but these may be intensified in the dual-career family. Addressing changing spouse needs and identity, the shifting balance of power, competition, and continual revision of the initial marital contract are the sine qua non of any successful marriage.

There are some suggestions for employing institutions to effect changes in order to make life easier and fairer for dual-career couples. These include support groups, career management groups, flexible scheduling, nonnepotism policies, child care, and so on. Companies have not yet advanced to the point where such suggestions are widely implemented. Consequently, adjustment in dual-career marriages is usually effected by the individuals themselves working to deal with internal and external constraints.

The two characteristics that appear in almost every successful dual-career marriage are flexibility and the internal security of the individuals (Maples, 1981). Sundby (1980) enumerates eight other factors that seem to be prevalent in successful dual-career families: (1) knowing each other well before marriage; (2) awareness of self and sense of identity; (3) compatibility in decision style; (4) high energy level for the woman; (5) moderate to low social interchange needs; (6) stable help with child care and household management; (7) adequate or better combined financial earnings; and (8) job security or possibilities for career development. These factors might serve as the structure for discussions with dual-career couples both before and during marriage.

Sekaran (1986a) sees five dilemmas facing dual career couples: (1) role overload because of redistributed homemaking responsibilities, (2) identity with traditional gender-based roles, (3) role-cycling problems of timing (such as when to have children), (4) network problems leading to social isolation, and (5) environmental sanctions caused by clashes with traditionally imposed values. To combat these dilemmas, she suggests counseling that emphasizes helping dual-careerists to define self-concept and self-identity, to explore value orientations and develop functional values, to equalize power distribution and role-sharing in the family, to define success, to manage stress, to establish new functional behaviors, and to develop appropriate skills. Sekaran (1986b) also suggests that counseling couples to enhance their feelings about a sense of competence and self-esteem is important, since both are moderators of the work variables (for example, income, job involvement, career salience, and discretionary time) and job satisfaction relationship.

In general, women may use either role definition or role expansion to cope in dual-career marriages (L. A. Gilbert, Holahan, & Manning, 1981). In the first, they alter the demands made on them either internally or in negotiations with others. In the second, much as with the "superwoman" working mother, they try to meet all of the role demands. Role definition obviously produces less stress than role expansion, and wives can be assisted in defining their dual roles more effectively. In terms of enhancing definition, M. Parker, Peltier, and Wolleat (1981) recommended nine adaptation techniques:

1. Asking each other for assistance and support
2. Talking to other couples who share a similar life-style
3. Limiting the number of obligations that are taken on at any one time
4. Discussing expectations, goals, and needs with each other
5. Scheduling time (especially time for being alone singly and together)
6. Looking for help outside the family for domestic, maintenance, and child-care needs
7. Seeking help from an employer or supervisor to make adjustments in the work setting

8. Taking time to get away from the stress and relax
9. Planning for emergencies—having back-up plans for situations that are not a part of the schedule (e.g., sickness, trip out of town) (p. 18)

L. A. Gilbert and Rachlin (1987) suggest several intervention strategies that are appropriate in working with dual-career couples: marital enrichment (enhancing marital interaction as a couple in front of other couples); stress management (identification of sources and development of coping strategies); and value clarification (ferreting out feelings related to problem areas, such as household management issues).

Some of these ideas have been put into effect by Kahnweiler and Kahnweiler (1980) in a workshop aimed at college undergraduates. The object is to raise awareness in college men and women of issues in the dual-career family. This sort of preventive approach may prove useful, but more careful evaluation is necessary. In such a workshop, a list of eleven myths regarding dual-careers generated by Gingrich (1982) might be useful as stimulators of discussion.

1. A dual-career couple has extra money and is usually financially secure.
2. It's better to marry someone who is in your field.
3. After we get married, we'll see who gets a job first, and the other person will look in that area until they get one.
4. In an equal relationship, neither of us will need to compromise our careers.
5. We want children, but it will work out later after we get our careers established.
6. If our careers come in conflict, it will eventually work out because we love each other.
7. Living together before we get married will be better to see if our careers are compatible.
8. If we find a lot of conflict, the only answer is divorce, separation, or a dissolving of the relationship.
9. Business and most other employers are not aware of the career searching situations dual-career couples face.
10. There is never enough time to keep two careers, a home, friendships, individual activities, and a relationship going.
11. It is difficult to get a job and have others understand your unique situation because the traditional housewife and breadwinner standard is still in the majority. (pp. 28–29)

It is, of course, important that counselors understand their own attitudes toward the dual-career family. Both Boswell (1981) and J. D. Gray (1980) suggest that it is mandatory for counselors to explore their own feelings toward sex roles and to overcome any biases that might be present.

Dual-career couples face potentially heightened stresses and strains when compared with those experienced by dual-worker couples. A knowledge of these possibly harmful issues and a sense of how to intervene to prevent or to remedy them are necessary for the counselor.

JOB-SEEKING BEHAVIORS: THREE ASPECTS

This chapter focuses on some potential problem areas related to work. These areas may be the result of dysfunctional behaviors, or they may be the cause of dysfunctional behaviors. For example, getting a job is the most fundamental of work skills. Failure to get a job—repeated rejection—can lead to so-called *rejection shock;* that is, negative emotional and physical symptoms, depression, low self-esteem, alienation, lack of motivation, and so on. Ultimately, the repeatedly rejected applicant becomes a discouraged worker (as defined earlier in this chapter). We assume that if people in the labor force possess job-seeking skills, they will be more likely to become employed. Three of these job-seeking skills have been researched: job sources, application letters and the résumé, and interviews.

Job Sources

The job search is the initial phase of job-seeking behavior. How do people go about locating potential jobs? Which methods of job location appear to be most useful or effective? The answers to these questions are not yet formed with any precision. There are so many conditions in the research that generalizations are few.

One way to address the question is to ask how employers go about filling the jobs that they have available. Angresano's (1980) study of employer hiring practices provides some information. Unfortunately, the focus of interest in this study was only on small and large firms likely to hire graduates of vocational/technical training institutions. Nevertheless, the findings are instructive. The primary methods used by these employers for recruiting workers to fill vacancies were internal promotion, newspaper advertisements, and selection from a pool of walk-in candidates. The principal criteria used for selecting workers were experience with another employer at a similar job, on-the-job training, and a personal interview (as opposed to the completion of a formal training program). The implication is that, at least for voc/tech blue-collar jobs, workers should be advised to seek entry-level jobs and work their way vertically by means of demonstrated performance.

From the job seekers' perspective, Allen and Kearny (1980) studied the relative effectiveness of alternative job sources for two-year college graduates. They categorized job sources as either *formal* (state employment services, private employment agencies, executive search firms, college placement offices, union hiring halls, and advertisements in newspapers and professional journals) or *informal* (personal references from friends, relatives, and faculty members). Their conclusion was that for two-year graduates seeking initial entry into the labor market, formal job sources resulted in more favorable outcomes. For engineering technology majors, however, this advantage lessened over time; for business alumni, formal sources held up. These results are a little different from those of other studies, which seem to show sightly more favorable results for those who use informal sources (Reid, 1972). Factors such as the level of job desired, general economic conditions, and specific formal or informal source used are apparently powerful moderator variables and thus make generalizations difficult.

The research on the relative effectiveness of various job search strategies has been limited (Kjos, 1988). In her study of over 800 successful and unsuccessful job seekers, she found that classified ads were the most frequently reported resource. Successful seekers also networked with friends and family more than did the unsuccessful job seekers.

The general rule would seem to be that job seekers should use all available job sources, formal and informal, in their search. This area appears to be one where, if people have to err, they are better off using too many sources than too few. The common advice of using all available resources in the job search would indeed seem to be appropriate. In addition to establishing this set in counselees, counselors can work to be sure that job seekers understand all the formal and informal sources open to them.

Before proceeding to the next section, we want to make brief mention of the use of biodata in personnel selection. Next to cognitive ability tests, biodata (biographical data) provide the most efficient validities in job selection. For those not familiar with biodata, an illustration may be in order. Biodata instruments ask a series of questions designed to get the applicant to reveal autobiographical information. An example (Richardson, Bellows, Henry & Co., Inc., 1981) follows:

> Of the following statements, the one which describes me best is:
> (a) more of a talker than a listener
> (b) somewhat more talker than listener
> (c) about as much talker as listener
> (d) somewhat more listener than talker
> (e) much more listener than talker

Some instruments are standardized, while others are unique to the organizational setting for whom applicants are screened. Rothstein, Schmidt, Erwin, Owens, and Sparks (1990) suggest that a general measure is applicable to all hiring settings and predicts just as well regardless of age of the applicant, sex, job experience, supervisory experience, or company tenure.

Letters of Application and Résumés

As indicated in a previous chapter, most authorities view the job-seeking process as something akin to a battle campaign. The literature is replete with military terminology, and there is also a great deal of the old-time football coach at halftime exhorting his players to "get out there and fight." Some go so far as to say that the job hunt is no more nor less than selling a product—in this case, oneself. Consequently, general marketing guidelines should be applied to selling oneself (Pelletier, 1981). Some job seekers, of course, react strongly against the notion of marketing oneself like a new cereal or a detergent. Others argue that if the technique is good enough to elect a president of the United States, it is good enough to get a job. All the Madison Avenue hoopla aside, all job seeking involves presenting oneself in the best light possible. With the exception of face-to-face contact with an employer, the most popular method of depicting one's assets is an application letter and a résumé. These offer both opportunities and potential dangers.

In terms of letters of application, Stephens, Watt, and Hobbs (1979) present the results of a survey of employer preferences regarding the form and substance of such communications.

> It appears that the letter most likely to bring forth a positive response would be short, error-free, and grammatically correct. The format of the letter does not make much difference. The style of the letter is probably not as important as previously thought. An emphasis on employer benefit gets varied responses, although the "hard-sell" approach is viewed negatively and should be avoided. The letter should not rehash the résumé, but should merely introduce it. Attempts at sophistication through the use of metaphor, simile, and quotations are not well received by personnel officers. A succinct, straightforward letter to introduce the application or résumé is the safest way to avoid detracting from the profile displayed in those documents. The potential for prejudicing the reader by a poorly constructed introductory letter appears to be a real possibility. (p. 242)

Hence, it does not really matter, it would appear, what form—block or semiblock, for example—the letter takes. What is most important is that the letter project confidence, emphasize accomplishments, be error-free, and be short and direct. With regard to the résumé itself, several guidelines, based on some research, should prove useful.

Ryland and Rosen (1987) effected the same sort of research on résumés as on the previously reported application letters. They viewed preferences for both content and format of the résumé. Their conclusions are similar to the bulk of research in this area. They suggest that both chronological and functional resumes will be well received if error-free, and that when a functional resume is used, the attachment of a brief work history in addition would be useful. Their specific advice is that "a chronological résumé format should be evaluated highly for job applicants with recent, relevant work experience for a particular position. A functional resume format, on the other hand, should be well suited for job applicants who lack extensive experience or career continuity. Similarly, a functional résumé format should be evaluated highly for individuals seeking a career change or reentering the job market after a lengthy absence" (p. 236).

A persistent question directed toward career counselors concerns whether an applicant's failure to answer all questions on an application will result in negative consequences. The motivation for *not* answering a question is typically that the applicant considers the question to be job-irrelevant or an invasion of privacy. Research by D. L. Stone and E. F. Stone (1987) suggests that the "correct" answer depends upon the type of job being sought and perhaps the race of the applicant; some employers are sensitive to the lack of information for some questions on an application blank (for example, a conviction, recovery from substance abuse or a mental illness), while others are not. In short, there are as yet no definitive answers.

Several of the most valuable surveys relating to the variables considered either positive or negative in the job-seeking process are those of Endicott (1965, 1975) at Northwestern University. Citing negative features that personnel officers report as a result of reading résumés and interviewing applicants, Endicott presents the following list of the most common reasons for not offering a job to a graduate (rank-ordered):

1. Poor personal appearance
2. Overbearing know-it-all
3. Inability to express self clearly; poor voice, diction, grammar
4. Lack of planning for career; no purpose or goals
5. Lack of confidence and poise
6. Lack of interest and enthusiasm
7. Failure to participate in activities
8. Overemphasis on money; interest only in best dollar offer
9. Poor scholastic record—just got by
10. Unwilling to start at the bottom—expects too much too soon
11. Makes excuses, evasiveness, hedges on unfavorable factors in records
12. Lack of tact
13. Lack of maturity
14. Lack of courtesy
15. Condemnation of past employers
16. Lack of social understanding
17. Marked dislike for school work
18. Lack of vitality
19. Fails to look interviewer in the eye
20. Limp, fishy handshake
21. Indecision
22. Loafs during vacations preferring lakeside pleasures
23. Unhappy married life
24. Friction with parents
25. Sloppy application blank
26. Merely shopping around
27. Only wants a job for short time
28. Little sense of humor
29. Lack of knowledge of field of specialization
30. Parents make decision for him
31. No interest in company or industry
32. Emphasis on who he knows
33. Unwillingness to go where we send him
34. Cynical
35. Low moral standards
36. Lazy
37. Intolerant with strong prejudices
38. Narrow interests
39. Spends much time in movies
40. Poor handling of personal finances
41. No interest in community activities
42. Inability to take criticism
43. Lack of appreciation of value of experience
44. Radical ideas
45. Late to interview without good reason

46. Never heard of company
47. Failure to express appreciation for interviewer's time
48. Asks no questions about the job
49. High-pressure type
50. Indefinite response to questions*

One might well ask what some of these factors have to do with job performance, and one might well argue the placement of these factors on the hierarchy; nevertheless, what they tell us about business and industrial managers is useful in preparing individuals to write good résumés and give good interviews.

The Job Interview

A third aspect of the job-seeking process is the interview, either with a recruiter who grants interviews to all or with someone who sees the people who pass some initial screening. In either case, job seekers have an opportunity to present themselves in the best possible light. However, their chances for selection may become imperiled for a variety of reasons, many of which, as we have just seen, are unrelated to the requirements of the job.

One area of research has been interview biases and psychological sets. We are reasonably clear that certain personal characteristics establish a negative mindset in the majority of interviewers. Unfortunately, much of this research is analog and employs college student samples rather than actual interviewers. There is an obvious leap in application in such cases. Nevertheless, we may conclude that certain prejudices are more likely than not to be present in employment interviews. One of these interview biases is age. Although interviewers may not be affected in their perceptions of a person's work-related traits on the basis of age, they tend to make more negative decisions in hiring because of the potentially shortened worklife of the older worker. In addition to age, there is evidence that being overweight affects interviewers; fat applicants are viewed as significantly less desirable employees than are average-weight persons despite objectively identical performances (Kaplan, 1984). Nonverbal behaviors (such as eye contact, smiling, head movements, body movements, tone of voice) also appear to affect interviewers.

Interviewers can frequently learn much from the nonverbal behavior of an interviewee. Gifford, Ng, and Wilkinson (1985), using an actual job, actual job applicants, and 18 judges who were interview specialists, determined that such nonverbal behaviors as rate of gesturing, time spent talking, and formality of dress accurately predicted interviewees' social skills. The applicant's motivation, on the other hand, could not be predicted from nonverbal behavior. Although it is clear that résumé credentials have the greatest impact on employment decision making and that verbal interview behaviors are next in importance, appropriate nonverbal behaviors such as eye contact, smiling, and head nodding can provide the extra something that makes a difference in selection (Rasmussen, 1984). Even such a relatively innocuous matter as artificial scents may have an effect on interview decisions. Baron (1983) conducted a study in which he demonstrated that sex of raters and the presence or absence of scent interacted in affecting ratings of job applicants. Males assigned lower ratings to applicants when they wore perfume or cologne than when they did not; females showed the opposite pattern.

Employment interviews may be either structured or unstructured. The latter is typically the case. Unfortunately, the validity of such interviews in selection is considerably less than other selection devices such as ability tests, assessment centers, biodata, and reference checks. Metanalytic study has suggested,

*From *The Northwestern Endiocott-Lindquist Report*. Published by The Placement Center, Northwestern University, Evanston, Illinois. © by Nortwestern University. Reprinted by permission.

however, that rather than utilizing the unstructured interview, the use of a structured, situational interview (a series of job-related questions with keyed responses that are consistently applied) can appreciably raise the validity of the interview as a selection device (P. M. Wright, Lichtenfels, & Pursell, 1989). Nevertheless, until such time as structured interviews become more common, applicants will be prone to some highly subjective interviewer responses. Assessing the nebulous characteristic of "personal chemistry" is not easy. Subjective responses include making snap judgments, failing to concentrate fully, inability to recognize the interviewee's hidden agenda, and so on (Eder & Ferris, 1989; Uris, 1988).

Vecchiotti and Korn (1980) studied the values of college students in the humanities and sciences and those of recruiters and found a number of differences. Recruiters, for example, seem to prefer the masculine Stereotypic Value Profile as measured by the Rokeach, regardless of the sex of the applicant, thus confirming the match between business values and masculine values. Tucker and Rowe (1979) used college students in another study to establish psychological sets on the basis of expectancy theory and to confirm the notion of self-fulfilling prophecy in the employment interview. For some subjects, an interviewer received a favorable letter of reference; for others, an unfavorable letter; and for still others, a neutral letter. Interviewers who got the unfavorable expectancy seemed to give the applicant less credit for past successes and to hold the applicant personally responsible for past failures. The final decision was closely related to these causal interpretations of past outcomes. One possible way to counteract these tendencies is to use several interviewers and a group-consensus approach. This method, however, is obviously not very cost-effective.

In another study of congruence between interviewer and interviewee values, Giles and Feild (1982) demonstrated that college recruiters consistently overemphasized the importance to applicants of intrinsic factors (such as chance to use one's abilities, interesting work, opportunity for recognition in one's profession) and underestimated the importance of extrinsic factors (fair and considerate supervision, good pay, desired geographical location of job). Hence, college recruiters indeed seem to have inaccurate stereotypes of what job factors, intrinsic or extrinsic, were important to applicants.

In one study (Atkins & Kent, 1988) recruiters indicated that applicants' poor grammar, lack of eye contact, dirty hair, face, or hands, and chewing tobacco were communication and appearance variables that most evoked a negative response. In general, they were most impressed by overall oral communication skills, enthusiasm, motivation, credentials, and degree, in that order. They were least impressed with summer and part-time work experience, extracurricular activities, preparation and knowledge of employer, and references, in that order.

Rosen, Cochran, and Musser (1990) investigated three dimensions of the interview process to determine which took precedence in hiring decisions. The dimensions were reputation of applicant (superior or inferior); accuracy (perceived match versus mismatch with the company); and self-presentational style (boastful versus modest).They determined that—given accuracy—the applicant most likely to be hired was a boastful, superior applicant. Evidently, there is no sense in hiding your light under a bushel basket during a job interview. The accuracy dimension (that is, fit) is further explicated by Rynes and Gerhart (1990), whose research suggests that assessments of *general* employability differ from *firm-specific* assessments, and that interviewers utilize firm-specific components in their evaluation of applicants. That firm-specific fit depends upon the assessment of the applicant's interpersonal skills, goal orientation, and physical attractiveness. Variables such as years of experience, grades, and so on do not seem to be given as much weight.

It is important for job seekers to know their legal rights in the hiring process. Knowing what questions are legal to ask in an interview or on an application and which are not is an example. The act of knowing, however, is different from deciding whether or not to challenge illegal questions. Does an applicant run the risk of antagonizing an interviewer by confronting an illegal query? There is no clear answer in the literature. Nevertheless, it is useful for applicants to have a "ball-park" idea about illegal questions. It is unlawful, for example, for potential employers to ask for information concerning the following topics:

- Your original name if it has been changed, or your maiden name
- The names of anyone living with you
- How old you are
- Your religious affiliation
- Race, complexion, skin, or eye color
- Disability or handicap
- Marital status, future plans for childbearing, or number of children (in some situations)
- Height and weight (unless these variables affect job performance demonstrably)
- Ancestry, lineage, national origin, descent, mother tongue
- Photo on application
- Request for name of religious leader as a reference
- List of organizational memberships that would indicate sex, race, religion, and so forth

Some individuals willingly provide such data when asked; others will not respond; still others will assertively challenge the right of the potential employer to request these types of information. Response is very much an individual matter of conviction and/or expediency.

It is clear, then, that psychological sets, stereotypical reactions, and biases affect interviewers' judgments in the interview process. In addition, as we have noted in an earlier chapter, the time of day in which the interview is conducted seems to be a determining factor as well as the quality of the person who preceded one in the interview room and whether or not the recruiter has a quota to meet. On the assumption that counselors cannot do a great deal to change interviewer behavior, they have turned to coaching interviewees on methods to minimize interviewer bias and to maximize their self-presentation.

As we discussed in Chapter 10, there are many structured group experiences designed to help individuals enhance their job-finding skills. One of the major components of these programs is corrective performance feedback. Mathews, Damron, and Yuen (1985), for example, conducted a 16-session seminar with 20 college senior agricultural students, providing them with opportunity to practice job-seeking skills and allowing the students to offer each other feedback. Evaluations indicated that the overall level of performance of job-finding skills increased for every student. There appears to be little doubt that career exploration activities (such as getting a part-time job, reading information, attending career orientation programs) and interview readiness (practice, discussion, feedback, and so on) are critical factors in successful interviews (Stumpf, Austin, & Hartman, 1984).

Galassi and Galassi (1978) synthesized a great deal of the research on interviews and suggested a four-phase intervention in preparing clients for the interview. They label Phase I "Developing Realistic Expectations." In this phase, clients are instructed about the format (structured or unstructured), content (client-centered), and length (short) of interviews, the roles of the interviewer and interviewee, the probabilities of positive decisions, and the way the interview is used in the decision process. In Phase II, "Developing Interviewing Skills," the focus is on effective self-presentation techniques (such as dressing appropriately, using standard speech, developing other communication skills, expressing work attitudes and traits, minimizing subjective impressions, and handling problem questions). Phase III, "Using Effective Training Procedures," refers to counselors selecting the best methods and techniques available to promote achievement of the desired outcomes. In general, the recommendation is for the use of several techniques rather than a single one (such as modeling, role-playing, video feedback, discussion, written materials, relation training, behavioral rehearsal, systematic desensitization, self-instructions, identification and disputation of counterproductive beliefs, and so on). Five or six hours of total instruction is considered minimally adequate. Finally, the fourth phase, "Preparing for Rejection Shock," involves helping clients to deal with some inevitable rejection through reinforcement, support groups, and keeping life changes to a minimum during the job search.

Troutt-Ervin and Isberner (1989) offered a typical job search course to technical students at Southern Illinois University's college of technical careers. The students involved in this professional development course generally thought the course to be important. The course topics were compensation packages, résumés, psychological inventories, cover letters, drug testing, interviewing, job satisfaction, and self-appraisal of abilities. Of these, cover letters, résumés, and interviewing were rated as highly useful; the remaining topics were judged less useful.

There are several compilations of the most frequently asked questions in job interviews (for example, Martin, 1979; Nealer & Papalia, 1982). Combining these into a single list produces the following questions.

1. What are your long-range goals and objectives? When and why did you establish these goals?
2. What specific goals, other than those related to your occupation, have you established for yourself in the next 10 years?
3. What do you see yourself doing five years from now?
4. What do you *really* want to do in life?
5. What are your long-range career objectives?
6. How do you plan to achieve your career goals?
7. What are the most important rewards you expect in your career?
8. What do you expect to be earning in five years?
9. Why did you choose the career for which you are preparing?
10. Which is more important to you, the money or the type of job?
11. What do you consider to be your greatest strengths and weaknesses?
12. How would you describe yourself?
13. How do you think a friend or professor who knows you well would describe you?
14. What motivates you to put forth your greatest effort?
15. How has your educational experience prepared you for a career?
16. Why should I hire you?
17. What qualifications do you have that make you think that you will be successful in a company like ours?
18. How do you determine or evaluate success?
19. What do you think it takes to be successful in a company like ours?
20. In what ways to you think you can make a contribution to our company?
21. What qualities should a successful ______ possess?
22. Describe the relationship that should exist between a supervisor and those reporting to him or her.
23. What two or three accomplishments have given you the most satisfaction? Why?

24. Describe your most rewarding educational experience.
25. If you were hiring someone for this position, what qualities would you look for?
26. Why did you select the school you did?
27. What led you to choose your major field of study?
28. What subjects did you like best? Why? What subjects did you like least? Why?
29. If you could do so, how would you plan your course of study differently? Why?
30. What changes would you make in your school? Why?
31. Do you have plans for continued study? An advanced degree?
32. Do you think that your grades are a good indication of your academic achievement?
33. What have you learned from participation in extracurricular activities?
34. In what kind of a work environment are you most comfortable?
35. How do you work under pressure?
36. In what part-time or summer jobs have you been most interested? Why?
37. How would you describe the ideal job for you?
38. Why did you decide to seek a position with this company?
39. What do you know about our company?
40. What two or three things are most important to you in your job?
41. Are you seeking employment in a company of a certain size? Why?
42. What criteria are you using to evaluate the company for which you hope to work?
43. Do you have a geographical preference? Why? Will you relocate? Does relocation bother you?
44. Are you willing to travel?
45. Are you willing to spend time as a trainee?
46. Why do you think you might like to live in the community in which our company is located?
47. What is a major problem you have encountered? How did you deal with it?
48. What have you learned from your mistakes?
49. Why did your business fail?
50. Why are you leaving your present job?
51. What can you do for us that someone else can't?
52. How good is your health?
53. Do you prefer line or staff work? Why?
54. What kind of salary do you expect?
55. What are your biggest accomplishments in your present or last job?
56. How long would it take you to make a contribution to our firm?
57. What new goals or objectives have you established recently?
58. Why haven't you obtained a job so far?
59. What is your feeling about alcoholism? Divorce? Homosexuality? Women in business? Religion? Abortion? (Such questions are inappropriate but are sometimes asked. Be careful.)
60. Would you describe a few situations in which your work was criticized?
61. What was the last book you read, movie you saw, or sporting event you attended?
62. How would you define success?
63. Are you creative? Give an example. Are you analytic? Give an example.
64. Have you fired or hired people before? What do you look for?
65. Tell us all about yourself.
66. How do you feel about working for a ______?
67. Do you consider yourself a leader? Give an example.
68. Who thinks more of you, your subordinates or your superior?
69. What interests you the most and the least about the position we have?

JOB DISSATISFACTION

In Chapter 2 we presented an overview of job satisfaction in America; in Chapter 16 we will discuss some of the more common measures of job satisfaction. One of the purposes of this chapter is to explore job dissatisfaction and its implications for adults who require career counseling. We conservatively estimate that there are 4000 articles, books, dissertations, and monographs on job satisfaction. It is clearly impossible to address more than a small proportion of these studies.

Summary of Job Satisfaction Studies

To recapitulate what was concluded in Chapter 2 and to expand those findings, we offer the following summary:

1. Most research in job satisfaction is atheoretical and correlational.
2. Results are often contradictory.
3. National surveys indicate that somewhere between eight and nine of every ten American workers report themselves to be basically satisfied with their jobs (Katzell, 1979; Portigal, 1976; Quinn, Staines, & McCullough, 1974; Weaver, 1980).
4. The proportion of satisfied workers in America has not changed greatly over the last quarter-century.
5. Positive relationships have generally been found between job satisfaction and higher occupational levels; higher educational levels (R. P. Quinn & Mandilovitch, 1980); higher pay—or at least a threshold of pay; enriched jobs (Gerhart, 1987); autonomy; considerate and democratic supervision (Gilmore, Beehr, & Richter, 1979; Tziner & Latham, 1989); positive views of top management (Ruch, 1979); participation in decisions affecting one's work and working conditions (Vanderslice, Rice, & Julian, 1987; Wagner & Gooding, 1987); interaction with influential and significant others; geographical location (Oppong, Ironside, & Kennedy, 1988); relatively small organizations and work groups; adequate resources (Katzell, 1979); commitment to the organization (Shore & Martin, 1989); Holland personal codes and occupational environments (M. Maynard, 1979); age, in the sense that satisfaction tends to increase with age in a nonlinear, U-shaped form (Near, Rice, & Hunt, 1980; Pond & Geyer, 1987); and better health.
6. Low job satisfaction seems to be related to certain other characteristics: unpleasant, hazardous work; physical characteristics of the workplace (Oldham & Fried, 1987); role conflict, ambiguity, and overload (Abdel-Halim, 1981; D. Wright & Gutkin, 1981); inability to use skills; repetitive tasks; inability to interact in a work group; pro-union activity (Bigoness, 1978); poor supervision, such as lack of feedback and recognition; discriminatory hiring practices; lack of mobility in the organization; promotional inequity; and low wages.
7. There appear to be no definitive conclusions regarding the relationship between job satisfaction and a variety of other variables. In some cases, there are no measurable differences; in others, the results are equivocal. Among the variables that have been researched are turnover and absentee rates (Carsten & Spector, 1987; Cheloea & Farr, 1980; R. D. Hackett, 1989); sex (R. Lee, 1982; R. Lee et al. 1981; J. Miller, 1980; Voydanoff, 1980; Weaver, 1980); race (Moch, 1980); work performance (Jacobs & Solomon, 1977); and life satisfaction (Bamundo & Kopelman, 1980; Rice, Near, & Hunt, 1980; Schmitt & Mellon, 1980; Wiener, Vardi, & Muczyk, 1981).

It is frequently stunning to people to realize the lack of relationship between job satisfaction and job performance. After all, a priori, happy workers should be productive workers. To test the accuracy of the conclusion based on traditional methods of analysis regarding the general lack of a strong relationship between job satisfaction and job performance, Iaffaldano and Muchinsky (1985) conducted a sophisticated metanalysis of seventy studies. Their conclusions: "The best estimate of the true population correlation between satisfaction and performance is relatively low (.17); much of the variability in results obtained in previous research has been due to the use of small sample sizes, whereas unreliable measurement of the satisfaction and performance constructs has contributed relatively little to this observed variability in correlations" (p. 251).

Some believe that if an individual's personality type is congruent with that of a work environment, the result will be job satisfaction and higher achievement. Although the literature on person-environment congruence and job satisfaction is generally supportive of this idea (Smart, Elton, & McLaughlin, 1986), at least one other study suggests that the general conclusion is not supported by extant studies (Schwartz, Andiappan, & Nelson, 1986). Obviously, further research is required.

Existing methods and instruments for measuring job satisfaction have their critics. Usually, job satisfaction is assessed by measuring a worker's level of satisfaction with various job aspects or facets, such as supervision, pay, or the work itself. Measures of this type do not usually predict job-related behaviors very well, as we have previously observed. The usual reason offered to account for this lack of predictive efficiency is that powerful moderating and intervening variables soften the relationship. In an effort to account for these variables, investigators have produced an "action tendency" measure that asks how the respondent feels like acting in regard to aspects of a job rather than the more common technique of measuring cognitive beliefs or even direct affect (Hartman et al., 1986). This approach looks promising but will require further development. Other researchers (Mottaz & Potts, 1986) have also questioned the usefulness of current work satisfaction indicators that are constructed of separate measures of work rewards and work values, since the two aspects are usually indistinguishable as measured. Some of the moderator variables that have been examined are self-esteem; locus of control (Cummins, 1989); higher-order need strength (Dreher, 1980); interests; ability; job characteristics (Brass, 1981; Helpingstine, Head, & Sorensen, 1981); job involvement (Lefkowitz & Brigando, 1980; Steiner & Truxill, 1989); career stages (Stumpf & Rabinowitz, 1981); worker alienation (Lefkowitz & Brigando, 1980; Vecchio, 1980a); and religious affiliation (Vecchio, 1980b). Each of these moderator variables has been found to affect the relationship between job factors and job satisfaction.

Age is another moderator variable that makes it very difficult to describe a simple relationship between job factors and job satisfaction. A study by Cohn (1979) is a good example of this situation. He investigated the importance of intrinsic (noneconomic) factors in work satisfaction as determinants of an individual's sense of well-being as related to age. He discovered that, as with most such studies, intrinsic factors were lower for men during the later stages of labor-force participation. Why? These declines were not an artifact of lower levels of satisfaction. Rather it appears that older men derive their satisfactions from the *consequences* of work rather than the *experiences* of work. In other words, noneconomic factors of work assume less importance to individuals as they age—the *type* of satisfaction changes while overall satisfaction, as has been indicated earlier, tends to rise with age—complicated relationship, indeed.

This diverse emphasis on intrinsic or extrinsic factors and on methodological problems in the measurement of job satisfaction—for example, single-question versus multifactor measures—further complicates matters. In any case, we know something about job satisfaction and we continue to learn. What we know and learn can be applied to assist the dissatisfied worker.

Counseling the Dissatisfied

If job satisfaction has no consistently proven relationship to either work productivity or absenteeism and turnover rates (if job involvement is controlled for), then one might well ask why employers should be concerned. Basically, other than the human concern that workers are themselves better off happy than unhappy, there is no compelling utilitarian reason why employers should be involved in trying to ensure the satisfaction of their workers. There is considerable reason, however, why counselors should be well-versed in the job satisfaction literature and should be able to apply its findings in helping dissatisfied workers.

It is important for the individual to recognize the centrality of work in his or her life. This knowledge, in turn, can help individuals to understand their workplace and nonworkplace behaviors (Maurer, Vrendenburgh, & Smith, 1981). And when we consider, as House (1974) determined, that measures of work satisfaction are the strongest predictors of longevity (exceeding even general happiness and physical factors), then we realize how important it is to be satisfied at work.

Dissatisfied workers often express a global sort of malaise—the career blahs—and are unable to articulate, without assistance, the specific facets of their job dissatisfaction. It is important that they know the specifics of their discontent, for that knowledge, in large measure, determines what can be done to remedy the situation. For this reason, we recommend either the formal or informal use of one of the better developed instruments designed to measure job satisfaction. For example, in Chapter 2 we discussed job satisfaction in the context of the theory of work adjustment. The reader will recall that this theory suggests that jobs have differing work reinforcers, that individuals have differing vocational needs or preferences for work reinforcers, and that how closely these two elements are related determines an individual's satisfaction. If the theory is accurate, then people should be helped to find their own vocational needs, as well as to discover whether these needs can be reinforced by occupations and jobs. One can do this formally by administering and interpreting to clients the *Minnesota Importance Questionnaire* (Rounds, Henly, Dawis, & Lofquist, 1981) or informally by trying to assess verbally the same dimensions. The 20 relevant need dimensions are (Lofquist & Dawis, 1975) as follows:

Ability utilization—I could do something that makes use of my abilities.

Achievement—The job could give me a feeling of accomplishment.

Activity—I could be busy all the time.

Advancement—The job would provide an opportunity for advancement.

Authority—I could tell people what to do.

Company policies and practices—The company would administer its policies fairly.

Compensation—My pay would compare well with that of other workers.

Co-workers—My co-workers would be easy to make friends with.

Creativity—I could try out some of my own ideas.

Independence—I could work alone on the job.

Moral values—I could do the work without feeling it is morally wrong.

Recognition—I could get recognition for the work I do.

Responsibility—I could make decisions on my own.

Security—The job would provide for steady employment.

Social service—I could do things for other people.

Social status—I could be "somebody" in the community.

Supervision–human relations—My boss would back up the workers (with top management).

Supervision-technical—My boss would train the workers well.

Variety—I could do something different every day.

Working conditions—The job would have good working conditions.

If the instrument is administered, it can be interpreted in terms of the needs that are indicated as important, in terms of a hierarchy of needs, in terms of normative data that are available, in terms of likelihood of satisfaction with a particular occupation or cluster of occupations, and in terms of basic values. In a less formal way, a counselor might simply encourage an individual to talk about the specific characteristics of a job that appear to be producing dissatisfaction, using the categories as a sort of checklist. If the 20 needs seem too unwieldy, the counselor might want to use the six factors into which the 20 needs seem to cast themselves; *safety* (supervision–human relations, supervision-technical, company policies and practices), *autonomy* (responsibility, creativity), *comfort* (activity, independence, variety, security, working conditions, compensation), *altruism* (social service, moral values, co-workers), *achievement* (ability, utilization, achievement), and *aggrandizement* (social status, recognition, authority, advancement).

Once the satisfiers and dissatisfiers are identified, the client can be assisted in changing those things that can be changed, either within the job or by moving to a new type of job or the same type of job in a different setting; and to accept those things that cannot be changed or otherwise to come to grips with elements of self or work.

Similar use can be made of another very popular job satisfaction instrument—the Job Descriptive Index (JDI)—either by actual administration and scoring or by utilizing the taxonomy devised for the instrument. The JDI emphasizes extrinsic rather than intrinsic rewards of work. It asks respondents to describe their work rather than their feelings about that work. There are five subscales and a total score possible. The five subscales are *work on present job* (fascinating, routine, satisfying, boring, an so on), *present pay* (adequate, insecure, underpaid), *opportunities for promotion* (infrequent promotions, fairly good chance for promotion), *supervision on present job* (hard to please, quick-tempered, knows job well), *people on your present job* (ambitious, stupid, no privacy). One can, in fact, use any instrument to devise a structured interview guide of dissatisfaction. The typical areas to be investigated are job involvement, amount of work and the stress and strain of that work, relations with one's co-workers and with one's supervisors, status, finances, opportunities for advancement, security or lack of it, working conditions (physical and nonphysical), opportunities to express a variety of needs, and progress toward career goals. Examining dissatisfactions with work in this sort of context will ultimately lead to a consideration of general life roles and the place of work in the total life context. Eventually, the counselor and client will need to consider the chicken-egg conundrum of the effect of work on life satisfaction and the effect of life satisfaction on work. Although the results of research are equivocal for groups, as we have indicated previously, they are less obfuscated for any given individual. If job dissatisfactions are affecting other aspects of one's life, it is important that this fact be faced squarely and that alternatives be examined. Likewise, if the converse pertains—if life unhappiness is affecting work—that too should be explored. Testing aspects of self and the work environment that are causing dissatisfaction is the first step in attaining job satisfaction.

For some workers, this quest for causes will focus on extrinsic factors of work; for others, the emphasis will be on intrinsic factors. Causes of stress and dissatisfaction will vary over an individual's career. Consequently, an understanding of where the individual is in terms of career stages will be of use to the counselor. In some careers, there will be little or no opportunity for upward mobility, a situation that inherently encourages dissatisfaction. Alternative sources of gratification, such as community work or a hobby, may be effective substitutes. For some individuals, investigating job dissatisfaction from a Marxian perspective might prove useful. Concepts of powerlessness, alienation, meaninglessness, isolation, and self-estrangement are other ways of expressing the type of dissatisfaction that is described more traditionally as lack of autonomy, relations with co-workers, and so on. It is interesting to note the paradox that Marxian ideology is most often prevalent in time of full employment. In hard times, there seems to be much less talk of powerlessness and alienation.

We have concentrated on what the counselor can do to help the individual deal with dissatisfactions of work. We have avoided discussing what can be done by organizations in terms of various types of job enrichment, better supervision, and so on. The motivation for such organizational changes will have to emanate from a belief that job satisfaction for its own sake is an appropriate end.

Job dissatisfaction is a complex phenomenon, the cause of which will vary according to stage of individual career development, and a variety of moderator variables. Counseling the dissatisfied involves determining the specific extrinsic and intrinsic factors giving rise to the dissatisfaction and applying methods of changing or of dealing with the issues.

Summary

In this chapter, we have considered six special adult career concerns. We have tried to indicate that even in the most continuous and mature of career development patterns, such problems may be present. Enough information has been offered about unemployed, dislocated, and/or discouraged workers, burnout, working mothers, dual-career couples, job-seeking behaviors, and job dissatisfaction to give the counselor a basic understanding of each of these areas and an idea of how to intervene either to prevent or to remedy the problem.

CHAPTER 14

HELPING STRATEGIES IN CAREER GUIDANCE AND COUNSELING

Key Concepts

- Since career choice is unique and relatively unrestrained in Western industrialized societies, individual decision making is fateful and deserving of assistance.
- Since so much of career counseling deals with intellectual variables, concepts from the cognitive therapies are particularly useful.
- A fundamental element of career counseling is appraisal of personal attribute data, possible pathways for action, and personal outcomes preferred.
- Group processes have many potential uses in career guidance and career counseling.
- In career counseling, internal personal attributes and values must be balanced with external opportunities and barriers.
- Career indecision and undecidedness are complex multi-dimensional constructs.

Career guidance and counseling exist because of freedom of choice. Theoretically, individuals in our society (as opposed to some other countries) have an almost unlimited number of career and educational options from among which they can choose, free of political constraints. Because career choice is relatively unfettered for individuals, they must be given assistance in decision making. That assistance typically takes the form of helping individuals to discover those personal characteristics that make a career-related difference; aiding them to be aware of the array of educational and occupational alternatives from which they may choose; and assisting them in processing the dimensions of these two worlds on both affective and cognitive levels.

There are several purposes of guidance and counseling, depending on the particular type of problem. Some counseling is directed at eliminating or improving dysfunctional or maladaptive behaviors. Other counseling emphasizes developmental and preventative aspects of helping in order to, in Shakespeare's words, "Meet the first beginnings (and) nip the budding mischief before it has time to ripen to maturity." Still other counseling is aimed at assisting in decision making. These latter two purposes, development and decision making, are the goals of career guidance and counseling.

To accomplish these goals, two strategies are commonly employed: individual counseling and group methods. Each of these helping strategies will be discussed in terms of its relevancy for career development and decision making.

INDIVIDUAL COUNSELING

Definition

There are hundreds of definitions of counseling, focusing on process, relationship variables, content, techniques, outcomes, counselor characteristics, and so on. We regard career counseling as (1) a largely verbal process in which (2) a counselor and counselee(s) are in dynamic interaction and in which (3) the counselor employs a repertoire of diverse behaviors (4) to help bring about self-understanding and action in the form of "good" decision making in the counselee, who has responsibility for his or her own actions.

Counseling requires some as yet undetermined threshold of verbal ability on the part of the counselees. One can help a person who is not yet verbally fluent but not typically through counseling. For example, some stereotypical behaviors of severe retardates (rocking, self-punishment, and such) can be eliminated by behaviorally manipulating the environment. Counseling, however, entails sensible verbalizations.

Being in dynamic interaction refers to the fact that both the counselor and the counselee(s) are constantly changing as individuals and that the relationship between them is in a continual state of flux. There is movement in the successful career counseling experience toward the development or resolution of factors affecting the decision-making process.

There is mutual participation in the counseling relationship. If the counselor assumes all responsibility for participation, then the interview is nothing more than advice-giving. If the counselee is given all responsibility for participation, then the interview becomes a soliloquy. Although some catharsis may result, little else of value emerges. These extreme examples of the structure-nonstructure or the directedness-nondirectedness continuum suggest that the counseling relationship is not a superordinate-subordinate one; the counselor and the counselee are equally responsible for participation. Because of individual differences in personality, types and levels of training, and experience, some counselors will tend to be more active than others. Likewise, some counselees will tend to be more verbally active in the relationship than others. But both counselor and counselee must interact in dynamic fashion if counseling is to affect the counselee's decision making.

In terms of this relationship, some conditions are thought to be facilitative and others are judged to be impeding. Briefly, this notion suggests that a counselor's effectiveness transcends any theory of counseling or the use of specific techniques. The crucial variables in success are assumed to be attitudes and sensitivity that create a "therapeutic" atmosphere. For example, Carkhuff (1983) maintains that the primary dimensions are the counselor's empathic understanding of the counselee, the respect shown for the counselee, the counselor's genuineness within the counseling session, and the concreteness or specificity with which problems are confronted. Other conditions might be equally facilitative: communicated competence, authoritativeness, confidence, self-disclosure, wisdom, noncondemnation of the counselee as a person, objectivity, ability to make accurate predictions, flexibility, high intelligence, absence of serious emotional disturbance, absence of communicated disruptive personal values, personal style, and so on. There is neither space nor intent to review exhaustively the counseling literature. The point is simply that there do seem to exist some conditions that facilitate career counseling. We may assume that their absence retards the progress or, at the very least, does not help the process or assist the counselee toward counseling relationship goals.

The career counselor employs a repertoire of diverse behaviors. Each theory of counseling proposes its unique and sometimes not-so-unique set of procedures and techniques for dealing with the counselee. We are convinced that there are very few "truths" in counseling. Each counseling approach can lay claim to its share of successes—at least insofar as one can gauge successes from reports of clinical activity and can accept varied definitions of the term. Clients, however, vary; each comes with need systems, backgrounds, psychological sets, and states of readiness that militate against undifferentiated treatment. Some counselees want information; some want help in thinking through a problem; some wish assistance in exploring feelings; some desire aid in ridding themselves of unwanted anxieties. And so it goes. Each counselee stimulus presents the counselor with an opportunity to make a differentiated, tailored response. Counselors frequently speak of inappropriate responses made by a counselee; however, the obverse is equally possible. The counselee who seeks information and finds himself or herself confronted by a counselor who clarifies, explores, diagnoses, reinforces, extinguishes, or engages in all sorts of behaviors *except* giving information has reason to wonder about the appropriateness of the counselor's response. All of these behaviors are appropriate as responses to various stimuli; their indiscriminant use, however, is likely to be counterproductive. Counseling procedures or behaviors ought to vary according to the needs of the counselee.

Certain types of counselor behaviors, then, are appropriate in certain situations and are inappropriate in others. For example, if one goal of career counseling is to promote counselee information-seeking behavior, evidence suggests that the behavioral technique of reinforcement is effective. On the other hand, there are specific career counseling concerns (such as valuing) that might be better approached by other procedures or techniques. It may help at specific times to clarify or reflect feelings. It may be useful at other times to summarize, restate, or interpret. There are occasions when a counselee is ready for confrontation, and that technique will be effective. On a more cognitive level, the counselor may want to point out alternatives directly or to provide information. At still other points, in the manner of some behavioral, rational-emotive, or transactional analysis counselors, homework assignments may be given. At times, the counselor might even want to persuade the counselee. These examples of counselor behaviors are by no means exhaustive; however, they do exemplify the diversity of approaches in a career helping individual relationship, and their very diversity argues for their discriminative use.

As an illustration of the diverse repertoire needed by career counselors, Olson, McWhirter, and Horan (1989) offer a paradigm of counseling for career decision making that includes a wide variety of counseling orientations and techniques that are dovetailed with the status of the client. Table 14.1 displays these techniques.

Finally, career counseling should bring about self-understanding and action. Knowledge of self and its subsequent relationship to the worlds of work, education, or training are the aims of career counseling. Action suggests that the clearest criterion of counseling success is outcome, that is, decision-making behavior of an appropriate nature. The individual, not the counselor, selects from informed alternatives and acts on that choice. Career counseling is action-oriented in that it is ultimately concerned with affecting behaviors (decision making). It is helpful, therefore, just as with any other segment of a comprehensive career helping service, to approach individual counseling on a systematic basis: specifying goals in behavioral terms, evolving procedures to accomplish those behaviors, utilizing whatever resources may be required, and evaluating to determine if behaviors have been achieved.

From the general areas of cognitive and behavioral psychology have emerged the so-called cognitive restructuring or reframing therapies, all of which lend themselves particularly well to career counseling. Attribution theory and self-efficacy theory suggest that people engage in perpetual internal monologues in which they make causal attributions about their behavior (and that of other people).

Table 14.1

Assessment Questions and Intervention Strategies in Decision-Making Counseling

Summary Model	Assessment Questions	Intervention Strategies (when the anwer is no)
Conceptualization	(1) Is affective arousal low?	listening (extinction) relaxation training desensitization and variations cognitive restructuring
	(2) Can client correctly define problem as one of choice?	paraphrasing probe (cuing and reinforcing) socratic dialoguing
	(3) Can client explain the decision-making paradigm?	cognitive restructuring emotional role playing cognitive modeling verbal reinforcement
Enlargment of response repertoire	(4) Has client avoided an impulsive response?	thought stopping-substitution covert sensitization outcome psychodrama emotional role playing cognitive restructuring skill-building interventions
	(5) Has client identified all alternatives known to counselor?	creative instructional set originality training brainstorming metaphorical thinking modeling
	(6) Will client search for additional alternatives?	verbal cuing and reinforcement modeling simulation strategies
Identification of discriminative stimuli	(7) Has client identified all discriminative stimuli known to counselor?	outcome psychodrama modeling
	(8) Will client search for additional discriminative stimuli?	verbal cuing and reinforcement modeling simulation strategies
Response selection	(9) Does client support adaptive utilities and probability estimates?	cognitive restructuring emotional role playing outcome psychodrama induced cognitive dissonance awareness of rationalizations peer modeling
	(10) Can client explain a response-selection paradigm?	modeling variations
	(11) Are client's skills sufficient to implement the selected response?	comprehensive behavioral programming stress inoculation emotional inoculation

(From "A Decision-Making Model Applied to Career Counseling" by C. Olson, E. McWhirter, and J.J. Horan, *Journal of Career Development,* 1989, Vol. 16, pp. 107–117. Reprinted by permission.)

Hence, the emphasis is on cognitive processes. Such theorists as Beck (Beck, Rush, Shaw & Emery, 1979), Meichenbaum (Meichenbaum & Jaremko, 1983), Trower, Casey, & Dryden (1988), and Ellis (Ellis & Grieger, 1977) have taken this idea and have developed cognitive therapies whose goal is basically to help people think straight.

This type of counseling is based on three premises: 1) emotions and behavior are determined by the way we think; 2) emotional disorders and dysfunctional behaviors are the consequence of negative and/or unrealistic thinking; and 3) changing this type of thinking will bring about reduction or elimination of emotional disorders and dysfunctional behaviors. Consequently, counselors work to help their clients identify maladaptive thinking. Nevo (1987) indicates 10 such irrational thoughts frequently encountered in career counseling.

1. There is only one vocation in the world that is right for me.
2. Until I find my perfect vocational choice, I will not be satisfied.
3. Someone else can discover the vocation suitable for me.
4. Intelligence tests will tell me how much I am worth.
5. I must be an expert or very successful in the field of my work.
6. I can do anything if I try hard, or, I can't do anything that doesn't fit my talents.
7. My vocation should satisfy the important people in my life.
8. Entering a vocation will solve all my problems.
9. I must sense intuitively that the vocation is right for me.
10. Choosing a vocation is a one-time act.

Mitchell and Krumboltz (1987) studied the comparative effectiveness on enhancing career decision making in college students of a cognitive restructuring intervention versus a decision-making skills intervention and a no-treatment control. They found the cognitive restructuring intervention to be the most effective. This intervention consisted of five elements: "(a) didactic instruction about the role of maladaptive beliefs and generalizations in career indecision, (b) training in the monitoring of personal beliefs and their effect on behavior, (c) modeling by the counselor of the rational evaluation of beliefs and modification based on that evaluation, (d) feedback to the clients on attempted modification of generalizations and beliefs, and (e) performance (homework assignments) designed to test new beliefs for their accuracy and usefulness" (p. 172).

It is obvious that since so much of career counseling rests on a cognitive base, the cognitive therapies are highly usable. What people tell themselves about their abilities, appropriate aspiration levels, and so on are clearly the stuff of career counseling. Techniques such as conditioning, modeling, homework, behavioral rehearsal, and so on that are common in the cognitive therapies lend themselves to application in career counseling.

Krumboltz (1983) has offered an application of the cognitive therapies specifically to career counseling. He argues that certain faulty cognitions cause trouble in career decision making (for example, "If I change, I have failed" or "I can do anything as long as I'm willing to work hard enough"). The result is that people fail to recognize that a remediable problem exists, or they fail to make the effort needed to make a decision or solve a problem, or they eliminate a potentially satisfying alternative for inappropriate reasons, or they choose a poor alternative for inappropriate reasons, or they suffer anguish and anxiety over a perceived inability to achieve goals. Krumboltz suggests a number of ways that individuals can be helped to achieve straight thinking, ranging from structured interviews to client self-monitoring to thinking aloud. Among the repertoire of counselor behaviors are such techniques as examining client assumptions and presuppositions of the expressed belief, looking for inconsistencies between words and behavior, testing simplistic answers for inadequacies, confronting attempts to develop an illogical consistency, identifying barriers to the goal, challenging the validity of key beliefs, and building a feeling of trust and cooperation.

To illustrate the heavy cognitive component of some types of career counseling, we cite a study by Taylor (1985) that investigated what career counselors in Australia actually do in interviews (10 counselors and 81 clients). He discovered that the typical interview was primarily concerned with presenting, reviewing, and classifying information, and then evaluating the information in terms of the client's interests, values, and abilities, and, subsequently, in terms of institutional barriers. Some time was also spent discussing and evaluating the client's vocationally relevant self. In this sample, tests were infrequently used, and there was rarely a concern with the client's general adjustment. The emotional climate of the interviews was basically neutral (that is, neither cold nor warm), and the stress was on the cognitive aspects of making a decision. Overall, it appears that the modal interview focused on specific vocational-educational concerns of the client by means of the counselor's providing information, rationally reviewing it with the client, and encouraging the client to evaluate alternatives. This mode is what has been called the "thinking man's" approach to sorting out alternative courses.

On the other hand, more affective approaches have also been employed successfully. For some clients, under some circumstances, the technique of mental imagery in career counseling has proved effective (Skovholt, Morgan, & Negron-Cunningham, 1989). Encouraging clients to go on guided mental imagery excursions allows them to visualize themselves in some imagined scene in the future. It formalizes what all of us do—daydream. It becomes a way of assessing one's vocational aspirations (for instance, inviting a client to imagine a typical day in the future, from start to finish). Such exercises typically begin with the application of relaxation techniques and then go on to provide the structure that permits the imagination to take hold. Since most career counseling is based on left-brained (logical) involvement, and since the use of mental imagery calls for the application of right-brained (emotional) skills, the altered focus may be effectively utilized with some clients at an appropriate level of readiness.

Some Systematic Individual Counseling Models

Stewart, Winborn, Johnson, Burks, and Engelkes (1978) have devised an approach called "systematic counseling," in which "the various aspects of the counseling process are clearly identified and organized into a sequence designed to resolve the client's concerns efficiently as well as effectively" (p. 2). Their paradigm could easily be used in career counseling. Drawing on learning theory, systems analysis, and educational technology, the model is designed so that an agreed-on objective is stated in behavioral terms, a wide variety of learning experiences is logically structured to achieve the objective, and constant monitoring and feedback occur. The model is described in terms of 13 sequenced functions. Beginning with the fourth function and proceeding through the tenth, the sequence runs as follows:

Function 4.0–During the first interview, the counselor explains the counseling relationship to the client. This involves explaining briefly the purpose of counseling, the respective responsibilities of the counselor and client, the kinds of things focused on in counseling, and the limits under which counseling is conducted.

Function 5.0–The counselor then proceeds to construct a model of the client's concerns, i.e., he engages the client in conversation about the difficulty so as to understand the problem in all relevant aspects. He then verifies or checks his picture of the client's concerns with the client himself.

Function 6.0–Next, counselor and client decide upon a mutually acceptable goal and specific learning objective for counseling.

Function 7.0–The next major phase is to determine and implement a strategy for attaining the client's learning objective. Major strategies include information-seeking, decision-making, and behavior modification. . . . A plan of attack including intermediate objectives and specific steps to be taken by the client and counselor is decided upon, and these steps are then carried out.

Function 8.0–In this phase, client performance is evaluated both in terms of improvement over the initial, presenting level of problem behavior and in terms of whether the learning objective has been attained. If the objective has not been attained, it is then necessary for counselor and client to "recycle" through (repeat) Function 7.0. . . . after which performance is again evaluated.

Function 9.0–After the objective has been attained and there is no apparent need for further counseling, the counselor proceeds to terminate regular contact with the client. He begins by explaining the rationale and procedures for termination and resolves any client or counselor resistance to termination. Next, he conducts transfer of learning, emphasizing how the strategies and skills learned during the counseling process can be applied by the client to future problems. Finally, he establishes a plan for monitoring the client's performance for a reasonable time after the termination of counseling.

Function 10.0–In this phase, the counselor follows up or monitors the client's performance. This procedure usually involves one or more of the following: (a) observing the client's behavior directly; (b) asking the client how he is progressing in brief checkup interviews; (c) requesting information from others in the client's environment who are familiar with his performance; and (d) examining records and other written data concerning the client's behavior. If the client encounters difficulty, provision is made for further counseling.

Another endeavor to bring a logical, sequenced procedure to individual counseling has been described by Gunnings (1976). What is termed a "systemic approach" to counseling (the art of intervening into the lives of individuals through systems understanding and modification) entails seven progressive steps.

1.0 Identification of symptoms
2.0 Exploration of problem causation (self-concept in relation to environmental variables)
3.0 Discussion of problem-solving strategies and techniques (alternatives and consequences)
4.0 Selection of problem-solving strategies and techniques
5.0 Implementation of selected strategies (long- and short-term)
6.0 Evaluation of effectiveness of problem-solving process
7.0 Expansion of client's use of model (transfer to various situations)

There are other systematic individual counseling models in the literature (Brown & Brown, 1977). These systematic models extend from industrial applications (Marlowe, 1981), to "multimodal" career counseling (Smith & Southern, 1980; Gerler, 1980). It is probably fair to state that currently, whatever the theoretical orientation of career counselors, the preferred mode of delivery is systematic, more or less as delineated in this volume. Each systematic approach has in common the notion that the goals of intervention should be specified in terms of the client's behavior; that a logical, differentiated series of techniques and strategies to achieve those goals should be effected; and that monitoring of progress and evaluation of results is important. No doubt the current push for accountability in mental health services will spawn a great many more models of this type.

A Broad View of Career Counseling

Career counseling should not be viewed in a narrowly defined sense. It cannot be separated from various orientations to counseling that, in general, take into account an individual's total personality, culture, and environment. Super (1983) has delineated a developmental model of career counseling that takes a comprehensive view of the process and contrasts markedly with the old matching model.

A broad perspective on career counseling has been recognized by the Association for Counselor Education and Supervision (ACES) of the American Association for Counseling and Development. An ACES position paper (1976) recommends "that all students and adults should be provided with career guidance opportunities to ensure that they"

1. Understand that career development is a life-long process based on an interwoven and sequential series of educational, occupational, leisure, and family choices
2. Examine their own interests, values, aptitudes, and aspirations in an effort to increase self-awareness and self-understanding
3. Develop a personally satisfying set of work values that leads them to believe that work, in some form, can be desirable to them
4. Recognize that the act of paid and unpaid work has dignity
5. Understand the role of leisure in career development
6. Understand the process of reasoned decision-making and the ownership of those decisions in terms of their consequences
7. Recognize that educational and occupational decisions are interrelated with family, work, and leisure
8. Gather the kinds of data necessary to make well-informed career decisions
9. Become aware of and explore a wide variety of occupational alternatives
10. Explore possible rewards, satisfactions, lifestyles, and negative aspects associated with various occupational options
11. Consider the probability of success and failure for various occupations
12. Understand the important role of interpersonal and basic employability skills in occupational success
13. Identify and use a wide variety of resources in the school and community to maximize career development potential
14. Know and understand the entrance, transition, and decision points in education and the problems of adjustment that might occur in relation to these points
15. Obtain chosen vocational skills and use available placement services to gain satisfactory entrance into employment in relation to occupational aspirations and beginning competencies
16. Know and understand the value of continuing education to upgrade or acquire additional occupational skills or leisure pursuits

As indicated earlier in this volume, there are those who consider career counseling "a great swindle," arguing that career choices defy logic and predictable order (Baumgardner, 1977). The great majority of counselors take a more informed and balanced view. They acknowledge that clients have limiting aspects (see Table 14.2), that counselors have their

Table 14.2

Examples of Self and Environmental Factors Influencing Career Choices

Personal Attribute Factors	Value Structure Factors	Opportunity Factors	Cultural Forces Factors
Intellectual ability	General values	Rural-Urban	Social class expectancies
Differential aptitudes	Work values	Accessibility of occupational opportunities	Family aspirations and experiences
Skills	Life goals	Accessibility of educational opportunities	Peer influences
Achievements	Career goals	Scope of occupational opportunities	Community attitudes and orientation toward education or work
Experiential history	Perceived prestige of occupations and curricula	Scope of educational opportunities	Teacher influences
Achievement motivation	Stereotyped attitudes toward occupations and curriculum	Requirements of occupations	Counselor influences
Responsibility	Psychological centrality of occupations or curriculum in values	Requirements of curricula	General role model influences
Perseverance	People-data-things orientation	Availability of compensatory programs	Image of educational or occupational options within a culture
Punctuality	Attitude toward work	Exposure to interventions	High school climate and reward system
Warmth	Work ethic	Status of the economy	College climate and reward system
Risk-taking proclivities	Leisure		Primary referent groups influences
Openness	Change needs		
Rigidity	Order needs		
Ego strength	Nurturance needs		
Self-esteem	Succorance needs		
Decision-making ability	Power needs		
Vocational maturity	Stability		
Sex	Security		
Race	Altruism		
Age			
Physical strength			
Health			

blind spots and limitations, and that the economy is virtually unpredictable; nevertheless, they point out that a broad view of career counseling, applied with skill, can do a great deal to mitigate malevolent and random influences on career development and choice and to help individuals to adapt to and cope with the buffetings of life. Herr (1977c) and Osipow (1977) provide further cogent argument to rebut the fatalistic approach of Baumgardner.

The Counselor and the Counselee's Internal Frame of Reference

If career counseling is regarded in the broad sense of the term and if career development and choice are more than the results of haphazard external events, then much of career counseling will be focused on the counselee's internal frame of reference. At the outset, the objectives of counseling include helping the counselee to cast in bold relief those factors that are an amalgamation of personal attributes, values, opportunities, and cultural factors (see Table 14.2). About four decades ago, Super (1951) proposed a definition of career guidance that emphasized not solely the provision of occupational information at a particular time or a simple matching of person and job, but rather a "process of helping a person to develop and accept an integrated picture of himself and his role in the world of work, to test this concept against reality, and to convert it into a reality, with satisfaction to himself and to society" (p. 89). This definition blends those dimensions of counselees sometimes arbitrarily separated into the personal and the vocational into a totality with interlocking relationships. Further, this process is seen as oriented to the self-concept, primarily focusing on self-understanding and self-acceptance. To these can be related the relevance of external factors that define the environmental options available to the individual.

This approach also stresses the importance of counseling's resting on a base of self-attitudes and value sets that the individual understands and accepts and uses to maximize his or her own freedom to choose the opportunities that seem to meet needs, desires, and inner urgings. In addition, a counseling relationship so defined means that the counselee and the counselor come to understand which personal characteristics are individual and unchangeable and which are modifiable. The counselee can then proceed from self-understanding to the matter of engaging in appropriate career-related behaviors.

Appraisal Information. In order to deal effectively with the latter dimension of the counseling process, the counselor will need to be an appraiser as well as an interpreter of data abut the counselee. Essentially, three broad classes of information are important (Goldman, 1971). The order in which they are dealt with is in large measure a result of the individual counseling orientation.

The first set of appraisal information is concerned with personal attribute data—predictor variables. Given counselors may determine that they should begin counseling a given individual by presenting what they have learned about the counselee through information from tests of aptitude, achievement, interest, and personality; school grades; hobbies; work history; family background; and expressed attitudes. Frequently, counselors who start from this base treat each of these pieces of information as fixed and unmodifiable, as having immutable relationship to certain future outcomes that the individual should consider. Because of the overwhelming amount of information that can be collected about a given individual, much of it may be irrelevant to the counselee's questions. Or, the counselee may accept the interpretation of the predictor variables as having a sophistication or expertness that permits him or her little room in which to maneuver. More important, counselees may play passive and dependent roles, awaiting with little personal investment or acceptance, the expert's judgment about what they can and cannot do or what they should do or should not do. Recall that counseling is an activity of mutual participation. Such a counseling orientation, however, places the counselor in the role of expert and the client in a subordinate, dependent position, thereby making participation less than mutual.

A second set of appraisal data relates to certain pathways that counselees might follow. Should they take vocational education? Should they take a specific educational sequence? Should they attend a post-high school business or trade school? Should they return to school? Should they change jobs? Should they go into the armed forces? Should they enter college? Some counselors may choose immediately to compare the requirements for each of these avenues with the information available about predictor variables that describe the particular counselee. This approach, like starting immediately with predictor variables, is a trait-and-factor approach that, if treated superficially or mechanically, can be irrelevant to the real issues. For example, students who ask where they should go to college may really be asking whether they should go to college at all, or asking, Why are my parents so insistent on my attending college? Are there some other things I might do that can get me where I want to be? A counselor who senses the underlying questions may choose, instead of immediately turning to college catalogues and the predictor variables that describe the student, to help the student sort out what he or she would expect to gain as a result of pursuing one pathway rather than another.

A third piece of appraisal information with which the counselor might begin is the outcomes that are of consequence to the person at his or her present level of development. What kind of person are you? What do you see as your major strengths and limitations? As you think about the future, are you primarily interested in obtaining satisfaction from the work activity in which you are engaged or from the work situation? Do you feel the need for regularity and security, or do you desire variety and change? Do you like to work alone or with others? Are you principally concerned with income levels? Prestige? What possible choices have you already considered and why? What are your values? What influences are most important to you as you have shaped personal answers to these questions—parents, peers, generalized attitudes in the community, and so on?

A Counseling Cycle. From the beginning of the counseling relationship, this approach encourages the counselee to tune in to himself or herself and to organize those parts of self and self-concept that one thinks are of most significance. Super (1957) addresses this point in the following manner:

> Since vocational development consists of implementing a self-concept, and since self-concepts often need modification before they can be implemented, it is important that the student, client, or patient put his self-concept into words early in the counseling process. He needs to do this for himself, to clarify his actual role and his role aspirations; he needs to do it for the counselor, so that the counselor may understand the nature of the vocational problem confronting him.
>
> This calls for the cyclical use of nondirective and directive methods. Schematically, vocational counseling can be described as involving the following cycle:

1. Nondirective problem exploration and self-concept portrayal
2. Directive topic setting, for further exploring
3. Nondirective reflection and clarification of feeling for self-acceptance and insight
4. Directive exploration of factual data from tests, occupational pamphlets, extracurricular experiences, grades, etc., for reality testing

5. Nondirective exploration and working through of attitudes and feelings aroused by reality testing
6. Nondirective consideration of possible actions, for help in decision-making (p. 308)

Such a frame of reference then gives the counselor and the counselee an opportunity to identify those predictor variables and those avenues that appear to be most relevant to the counselee. Further, having such a frame of reference from which to operate allows the counselor to help the counselee identify and clarify possible distortions between his or her self-perception and the behavior that the information suggests.

For example, people who overestimate their mechanical skills may not perform very effectively as machinists. In other words, such individuals ascribe to themselves characteristics they actually do not possess. Following our previous line of thought, these counselees' personal characteristics and values do not seem to be congruent. Such a situation raises several questions for the counselor and the counselee. Is the degree to which one possesses mechanical skills modifiable? Are the elements of mechanical skills perceived by the counselee to be present but actually lacking a matter of spatial visualization, intelligence, manual dexterity, or experience? If the former types of variables are operative, the chances of becoming an effective machinist are minimal. If experience is the deficit, are there pathways in education or the community through which one can heighten skill proficiency? Another question is, of course, What prompts the person to want to be a machinist? Is it the work activity or the work situation? Is it because the person knows people who are machinists and is influenced by them, or is it because the person has been told that machinists are in great demand and thus gain good income and security? Is it because the person wants to remain in the community and the machining industry is a prominent one? If the person is concerned about something besides the work activity as a machinist, are there other skills or strengths on which to capitalize to gain the same outcomes that were perceived to result from becoming a machinist?

The second part of this concern is that choosing an occupation also includes choosing a life-style. In Western culture, one is largely labeled by one's occupational title. It must be realized that this, too, is an important ingredient of choice—deciding how much of self one desires to express in occupational commitment. How ego-involved is the counselee in work, in a choice of education or training, in school, in family? How committed is the individual? How committed can the individual become? A counselor and a counselee need to understand that a measured interest may indicate that one will direct effort to an area but does not say how much effort will be applied to get there. To cite an extreme analogy, a person may have an interest in going to Tahiti, and this interest may remain constant throughout life. But interest alone does not indicate that the individual will take steps or raise the finances to get to Tahiti. So it is with tentative occupational aspirations. Individuals will have to be helped to examine whether they have the dedicated involvement required by specific choice options. This, too, is a matter of values and characteristics of the self that may or may not be present or possible to acquire.

But the capacity for deep involvement relates also to the meaning one attaches to a particular life-style. How important is it to a particular counselee to be tagged a machinist? Is it important enough to delay certain personal gratifications through a lengthy apprenticeship? Is it important enough to labor over applied mathematics or physics? Is it important enough to accept the midnight shift rather than normal work hours? Is it important enough to gamble on attaining seniority as security against layoffs? Is it important enough to practice being punctual, reliable, dependable? Is it important enough to try to be a machinist even if the odds are high against success? These are not necessarily the right questions, but they are all types of questions counselors and counselees must work through as personal attribute and value factors, as the self and the self-concept, are described and clarified. The process of doing so is the process of decision making.

In Israel, Nevo (1990) assessed student reactions to career counseling they had received at the University of Haifa. Perhaps the most astonishing finding was that while clients certainly perceived interest inventories, objective tests, and counseling to have helped them to understand themselves better, this self-understanding did not necessarily translate into making a career decision. They viewed "good" counseling as help in organizing their thinking and identifying their interests and abilities. Some were disappointed at the end either that they could make no career choice or that they had made a choice not entirely satisfactory to them.

This dichotomy between personal versus vocational outcomes in career counseling has been debated for many years. Although there are still those who try to separate the two domains, the fact is that they are symbiotic; in our judgment, no good career counseling can take place without personal investment and self-discovery. This is not to say that career counseling should have a predominately personal focus. Phillips, Friedlander, Kost, Specterman, and Robbins (1988), for example, studied career counseling outcome and determined that from the counselor's point of view the more vocationally focused the sessions (and the greater the number of sessions), the greater the effect. On the other hand, clients' preferences were not so delimited; they seemed satisfied regardless of the personal versus vocational emphasis. It would be difficult, if not impossible, to visualize career counseling without a degree of personal focus. How personal of a focus is the question.

Niles and Pate (1989) argue that all career counselors must have the basic skills of mental health counselors. A synthesis of the skills needed for both foci would require that in addition to the skill areas outlined in this text, career counselors would need to understand mental health areas such as psychopathology and the effects of psychotropic medications in the interaction between emotional disorders and career-related issues. Similarly, Corbishley and Yost (1989) propose that all but the simplest of career counseling mandates a psychological approach, because career-related decisions have an impact on all other dimensions of a person's life, the psychological characteristics of clients largely determine if they will hold reasonable expectations for career counseling, and the type of intervention utilized may well depend on the way that the client engages the world psychologically. Within the context of this type of psychological orientation, Yost and Corbishley (1987) suggest an eight-stage approach to career counseling: initial assessment, self-understanding, making sense of self-understanding data, generating alternatives, obtaining occupational information, making the choice, making plans, and implementing plans. Although these stages do not seem very different from the typical sequence approaches applied to career choice counseling described in this chapter, what sets them apart is the emphasis given to the client's psychological complexity. In any case, we reaffirm that in career choice counseling there is no such thing as a non-psychological approach (however naively it is applied), and certainly in other non-first-choice life-style aspects of career counseling addressed in this book, psychological complexity is a given.

A number of career counseling approaches are constructed around a particular assessment instrument. For example, Hansen (1985) suggests a counseling sequence for use with the SVIB-SII (Strong Interest Inventory). She proposes a 14-step process that is displayed in Figure 14.1. Clearly, such approaches are basically trait-and-factor oriented. Nevill and Super (1986) provide a further example of how

Figure 14.1

Flow chart for a career-counseling sequence. (From *Users Guide for the SVIB-SII* by J.I.C. Hansen. Palo Alto, CA: Consulting Psychologists Press, 1985. Reprinted by permission.)

Step	
Step 1	Develop rapport
	↓
Step 2	Identify the client's concern
	↓
Step 3	Identify counseling goals
	↓
Step 4	Assess the client's knowledge of self and the world of work
	↓
Step 5	Identify additional information needs
	↓
Step 6	Explain methods for obtaining self-information
	↓
Step 7	Discuss the client's feelings about the self-exploration process
	↓
Step 8	Identify inventories and tests that will help the client to gather self-information
	↓
Step 9	Mutually agree on tests and inventories to be taken
	↓
Step 10	Administer the tests and inventories
	↓
Step 11	Preview the test results in preparation for interpretation
	↓
Step 12	Discuss and interpret results; develop hypotheses with client
	↓
Step 13	Evaluate interpretive hypotheses and integrate new information with data previously gathered
	↓
Step 14	Develop strategies for integrating self-knowledge with an examination of the world of work

particular assessment devices can be incorporated into a staged counseling intervention. They term their approach a Developmental Assessment Model for Career Counseling, and it assimilates instruments that they have developed to measure work salience, work values, and career maturity. Nevill and Super's model is presented in Figure 14.2.

Figure 14.2

A Development Assessment Model for career counseling (From *The Values Scale: Theory, Application, and Research Manual,* Research Edition by D. D. Nevill and D. E. Super. Palo Alto, CA: Consulting Psychologist Press, 1986. Reprinted by permission.)

Step I. Preview
- A. Assembly of data
- B. Intake interview
- C. Preliminary assessment

Step II. Depth-view: further testing?
- A. Work salience
  - 1. Relative importance of diverse roles
    - a. Study
    - b. Work and career
    - c. Home and family
    - d. Community service
    - e. Leisure activities
  - 2. Participation in each role
  - 3. Commitment to each role
  - 4. Knowledge of each role
- B. Values sought in each role
- C. Career maturity
  - 1. Planfulness
  - 2. Exploratory attitudes
  - 3. Decision-making skills
  - 4. Information
    - a. World of work
    - b. Preferred occupational group
    - c. Other life-career roles
  - 5. Realism
- D. Level of abilities and potential functioning
- E. Field of interest and probable activity

Step III. Assessment of all data
- A. Review of all data
- B. Work salience
- C. Values
- D. Career maturity
  - 1. Individual and occupations
  - 2. Individual and nonoccupational roles
- E. Planning communication with counselee, family, etc.

Step IV. Counseling
- A. Joint review and discussion
- B. Revision or acceptance of assessment
- C. Assimilation by the counselee
  - 1. Understanding the present
  - 2. Understanding the meaning of work and other life-roles
  - 3. Exploration for maturing?
  - 4. Exploration in breadth for crystallization?
  - 5. Exploration in depth for specification?
  - 6. Choice of preparation, training, or jobs?
  - 7. Searches for jobs and other outlets?
  - 8. Exploring self and situation for self-realization?
- D. Discussion of action implications and planning
  - 1. Planning
  - 2. Monitored execution
  - 3. Follow-up for support and evaluation

Outcomes of Career Counseling

In other chapters of this text, we have reported research comparing the effectiveness of individual counseling with other helping modes in enhancing the career development and behaviors of counselees. Sometimes individual counseling is found to be less effective in achieving desired career-related goals than are structured workshops, seminars, courses, and other intervention methods. Herr (1976a) has implied that such findings may be specious, because the counseling treatments are rarely as carefully and specifically defined as are the comparative intervention methods. In other words, the counseling treatment is frequently generic, broad, and unstructured, whereas the comparative treatment is goal-specific, narrowly delimited, and structured. Four reviews of career counseling outcome would appear to support Herr's speculations. Holland, Magoon, and Spokane (1981) concluded the following:

> The experimental evaluations of counselors, courses, career programs, card sorts, interest inventories, workshops, and related treatments imply that the beneficial effects are due to the common elements in these divergent treatments; (a) exposure to occupational information; (b) cognitive rehearsal of vocational aspirations; (c) acquisition of some cognitive structure for organizing information about self, occupations, and their relations; and (d) social support or reinforcement from counselors or workshop members. In addition, the strong tendency to find some positive effects for both diffuse interventions . . . and specific interventions . . . occurs because the average client knows so little about career decision making and career problems that a small amount of new information and support makes a difference.
>
> At the same time, the general failure to find different effects for different treatments demonstrates a large hole in our understanding of client-treatment interactions and indicates the need for more analytical and less shot-gun evaluation. (pp. 285–286)

Fretz (1981) also concluded that most career interventions (individual counseling, group-oriented, or self-directed) appear to be beneficial and that there is no consistent body of data to suggest that any one mode of intervention is more effective than any other. Fretz attributed the lack of differential outcome to the failure of researchers to explicitly describe treatments, client characteristics, and outcomes; lack of nonrandom assignment of subjects to treatments; attempts to manipulate too many variables; use of a single outcome criterion rather than several; and not reporting intercorrelations among variables. Spokane and Oliver (1983) reviewed career counseling outcome studies by calculating effect sizes (difference between the mean of a treated group and mean of a control group divided by the standard deviation of the control group on a given outcome measure).This procedure yields a finer delineation of differences between groups in a metanalysis. On the basis of this more elegant statistical treatment of the data, the authors reached the following conclusions regarding differential effectiveness:

1. Clients receiving any vocational intervention are better off, on the average, than 81 percent of the untreated controls.
2. Clients receiving individual vocational interventions are better off, on the average, than 79 percent of untreated controls.
3. Clients receiving group/class vocational interventions are better off, on the average, than more than 89 percent of untreated controls.
4. Clients receiving a variety of alternative treatment (for example, computer-assisted, audiotaped, self-directing) are, on the average, better off than 59 percent of untreated controls.

After a more sophisticated analysis utilizing a massive data set, Oliver and Spokane (1988) arrived at a somewhat different conclusion. First, increasing the number of hours or the number of sessions appears to enhance the chances for a favorable outcome. Secondly, individual treatments were judged to be the most effective (but the least cost-effective), whereas workshops and structured groups were somewhat less effective in the aggregate but also less expensive. Still, they were effective. On the basis of their findings, the investigators suggest that particular treatments be dictated by client preferences and that career counselors be wary of premature termination.

A typical study of the types reviewed by Spokane and Oliver is updated by Davis and Horne (1986), who compared the relative effectiveness of a more-or-less standard career course and a more-or-less standard small-group counseling intervention on the career decidedness and career maturity of students in a midwestern university. They found, consonant with the bulk of studies in this area, no significant difference between the two treatments. Both the more structured group course and the traditionally defined counseling group led to change in positive directions in both career decidedness and career maturity.

In one of the most comprehensive and insightful analyses of the diagnosis and treatment of vocational problems, Rounds and Tinsley (1984) argue that more attention must be paid to the behavior change *process* mediating intervention effectiveness. To do so requires the development of reliable vocational-problem diagnostic systems and, within each of these systems, the mechanisms responsible for vocational behavior change must be specified theoretically, and a relationship demonstrated between the change effects and the particular intervention. In short, we need to know what worked for whom and why.

An example of what Rounds and Tinsley advocate may be found in an article by Rosenberg and Smith (1985). Although they do not base their conclusions on research, Rosenberg and Smith do offer some fascinating speculation about the possible relationship between modal personality types and modes of career counseling that might be most effective. What are the career counseling interaction effects between interventions and client attributes? Specifically, do the various Holland types in college benefit from counseling approaches that dovetail with their type's characteristics? As an illustration, let us look to what Rosenberg and Smith say about Social types along several dimensions (most sub–Ph.D.-level counselors are primarily or secondarily Social types).

General approach–Social types obviously need career counseling that is very verbal. They like to talk and prefer an environment that is friendly, open, and supportive. They will participate in group counseling far more than other types will.

Length and number of sessions–Social students prefer counseling to last several sessions, longer than other types prefer. They enjoy the counseling relationship and often may venture into areas of personal concern.

Self-Knowledge–Several strategies are effective in helping social students discover their career-related needs, values, and interests. Counselors can ask them to describe what they like about people they idolize or about significant others. These admired traits can then be compared with the student's self-perceptions. Asking social types about classroom experiences—preferred teachers (or supervisors), classmates (or co-workers), atmosphere, working style, and tasks—frequently yields relevant information about personal needs and values. Good insights can also be gained by verbally investigating other social experiences such as past jobs, volunteer work, and participation in social clubs and other organizations. It is extremely important that social students have an opportunity to talk to counselors and other students before any real and lasting self-knowledge is acquired. Merely writing ideas on paper is not sufficient and will have a limited impact on these students.

Occupational information–Many methods are available to assist social types in gathering occupational information, but these students appear to benefit best from talking to people employed in occupations of interest. In addition to providing relevant career information, professionals in the field serve as a source of needed support. Only these personal visits can help answer questions such as, "What do you really like about this career?" and "What is the personal atmosphere like?" Also, sustained visits of up to two weeks or internships can lead to solid career decisions.

Decision making and planning–Social types need to discuss their experiences and values with others before making an appropriate and enduring career decision. Counselors should provide a lot of support to these students. Social types are not skilled at planning and may need assistance in developing short- and long-range goals. Providing names of other individuals who might help them plan, such as college advisors, is frequently worthwhile.

Follow-up–Social types appreciate periodic reassurance. Knowing that they can talk to a counselor when needed provides excellent support, but follow-up appointments do not need to be rigidly scheduled. A brief note or a phone call can be reassuring. (p. 45)*

For each of the other Holland types—Realistic, Artistic, Enterprising, Conventional, and Investigative—the authors have presented their impressionistic, experience-based prescriptions. What they have produced certainly has a good deal of face validity. The problem, however, is relatively easily researched, and it would seem to be a useful focus for more rigorous inquiry.

Related to this type of speculation about differential counseling strategies based on client characteristics is the work of Kivligham and Shapiro (1987), who sought to determine if Holland types benefitted differentially from a self-help approach. They found that personality type was indeed a predictor of client's benefit from and interest in a self-help treatment program, with those most likely to benefit and be interested being investigative and conventional types (and perhaps realistic, although the sample in this study included too few of this type to offer a conclusion).

In another example that conforms to the requirements of Rounds and Tinsley, Krumboltz, Kinnier, Rude, Scherba, and Hamel (1986) worked with a group of community college students who were classified as rational, intuitive, fatalistic, or dependent decision makers. All were exposed to a rational decision-making training intervention. Those who had been very impulsive, dependent, or fatalistic in former curriculum choices and those who showed dependency in prior job choices seemed to gain most from the rational training curriculum. Obviously, the major implication of this study is that there do indeed appear to be "different strokes for different folks" in terms of teaching a decision-making strategy.

All in all, the research on career counseling outcome is comforting and, taken as a whole, provides powerful documentation for the continued existence of legitimate career helping. It is, whatever the reasons, perhaps more persuasive than outcome research in any other subset of human intervention activity.

Decision Making

In Chapter 4, we presented a review of decision-making theories of career choice. Chapters relating to the provision of career guidance services from elementary school through adulthood each stress, to various degrees, the importance of decision-making skills. Decision making is a learned process crucial to career choice and behavior. There-

*Reprinted from the Spring 1985 *Journal of Career Planning and Employment,* with permission of the College Placement Council, Inc., copyright holder, and the author.

fore, the nature of decision making and its relationship to helping strategies is discussed below.

The topic of decision making is very complex indeed. It is clearly a multidimensional concept (Hartman, Fuqua, & Jenkins, 1986), and it can be no more than touched upon in this volume. Career decision making is a specific application of general theories and principles related to the way people make choices and exercise judgment. Consequently, the broader field is one of the primary foci in all of psychology and has been approached from both cognitive and noncognitive perspectives (see, for example, Rachlin, 1989; Yates, 1990). Although the study of career decision-making processes is really in only a rudimentary state, we can reach some conclusions that inform current, state-of-the-art practice.

Classifications. For purposes of explication, decision making can be classified in several ways. First, we may consider *institutional decisions* versus *individual decisions*. The former relate to judgments that affect organized groups of people; the latter pertain to choices that have largely personal consequences. The literature of management and administration is replete with discussions of institutional decision making, and the findings are summarized herein as they relate to effecting systematic service delivery within such institutions as schools, colleges, agencies, and others. Second, we may regard decision-making methodology in terms of *mathematical model decisions* versus *nonmathematical model decisions*. Mathematical decisions rely mainly on the rigid logic of the calculus of probability, whereas nonmathematical decisions are the result of a less formal symbolic logic. Statisticians tend to be skeptical of any decision theory that cannot be realized mathematically and experimentally; they assume complete information and rationality. Since human beings are sometimes not rational, and since they frequently make choices on the basis of incomplete information, decision making is often more psychological than logical, and less rigorous methods are employed. These nonmathematical models of decision making are usually called *descriptive* models. Third, we may speak of *group decision making* versus *individual decision making*. Here we are concerned with the process of decision making. The literature of social psychology and group dynamics suggests that under certain types of conditions and for specified types of problems, groups consistently outperform individuals in decision making. Unfortunately, career choice is not one of those problems; it tends to be approached individually and, of course, it should be. Finally, we may regard *decisions under certainty* versus *decisions under risk*. In the former, an individual or institution will know with absolute certainty that a decision will be followed by a 100 percent probability of a given consequence. This state is often not so simple as it appears, for there may be many consequences possible, each a virtual certainty, and a choice must still be made. In the latter case the degree of risk may range from a knowledge of different probabilities of occurrence to complete uncertainty.

When we speak of an individual and career-related choices, then, we refer to individual decisions that are basically nonmathematical in a formal sense (although probability data may be available), that are individually effected, and that, typically, are made under conditions of risk.

In terms of conditions of risk, we may think of four possibilities. *Certainty* is that condition described above wherein choice *A* will surely lead to event *B*. *Objective probability* is a condition of risk wherein an individual becomes informed of the odds relating to the consequences emanating from the making of a given decision. Largely by the use of regression equations or less formal expectancy tables, individuals can be compared with others having similar characteristics and can be given relatively objective, actuarial probabilities of sucess or failure in some future event. *Subjective probability* is a risk condition in which individuals translate objective probabilities into personal or psychological terms. They may overestimate low probabilities or underestimate high ones, depending on their propensities for risk-taking and other factors. *Uncertainity* is a risk condition that exists when the consequences of a decision are not completely known or when the probabilities suggest that the outcome desired is not totally certain.

One of the aims of career counselors is to remove as much uncertainty as possible. The counselor accomplishes this condition by assisting the individual in grasping the objective probabilities (aptitudes, interests, work opportunities, education and training opportunities, and such) and in understanding how these objective data may be subjectively or psychologically processed (attitudes, values, aspirations, and so on). To do so requires a strategy for decision making.

In their review of the literature relating to career decision-making models, Jepsen and Dilley (1974, p. 335) concluded that these models

- Are similar in many ways to decision theory and to each other but certainly not to the point where parts of one can be interchanged for parts of another
- Vary substantially on their assumptions about the decision-maker and the conditions under which the decision is made
- Are applicable to different types of decisions
- Are more complementary than competitive

They consider both long-range and short-range changes in the individual and combine this "distance in time" dimension with an "amount of understanding" or informational dimension in the schematic diagram shown in Figure 14.3

Assumptions Underlying Intervention Strategies. Hence, the decision-making model that the counselor chooses to utilize may well depend on the particular stage of career development of the individual in relation to the immediacy of the career-related decision and the amount of information the individual is assumed to possess. Whatever model one chooses, however, there are certain basic assumptions that undergird all intervention strategies in assisting individuals to make decisions.

1. Many factors in decision making will be outside the control of the decider. These factors include such variables as the state of the economy and accessibility of education and training opportunities.

2. Individuals are rarely able to acquire and to process *all* relevant information in making some career-related decisions. They will tend to select out those data that they deem important or readily available, or that someone else thinks are important. Individuals typically realize their inability to acquire the entirety of information and to define the complete range of possible outcomes, and so settle for a strategy of decision making that will lead to "good enough" decisions. Subsequently, that good enough decision may lead to a rationalization process in which decisions made on the basis of bounded rationality are justified as the best decisions possible.

3. Decisions will generally be made ipsatively. That is, people usually have many objectives; to choose one is to lower the probability of attaining others. Choice optimizes the chances of a given outcome occurring and simultaneously suboptimizes the chances of conflicting outcomes. This condition suggests that short-range decisions that may seem good

Figure 14.3

Theoretical Vocational Decision Types

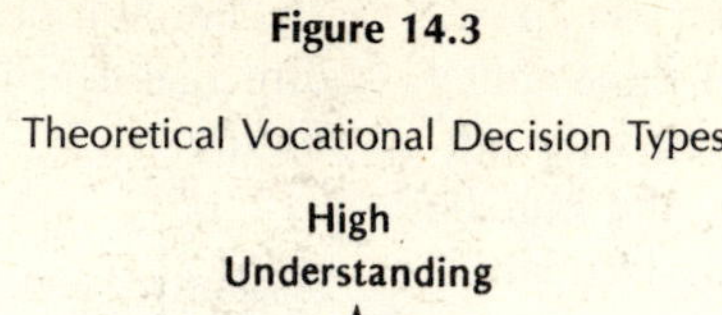

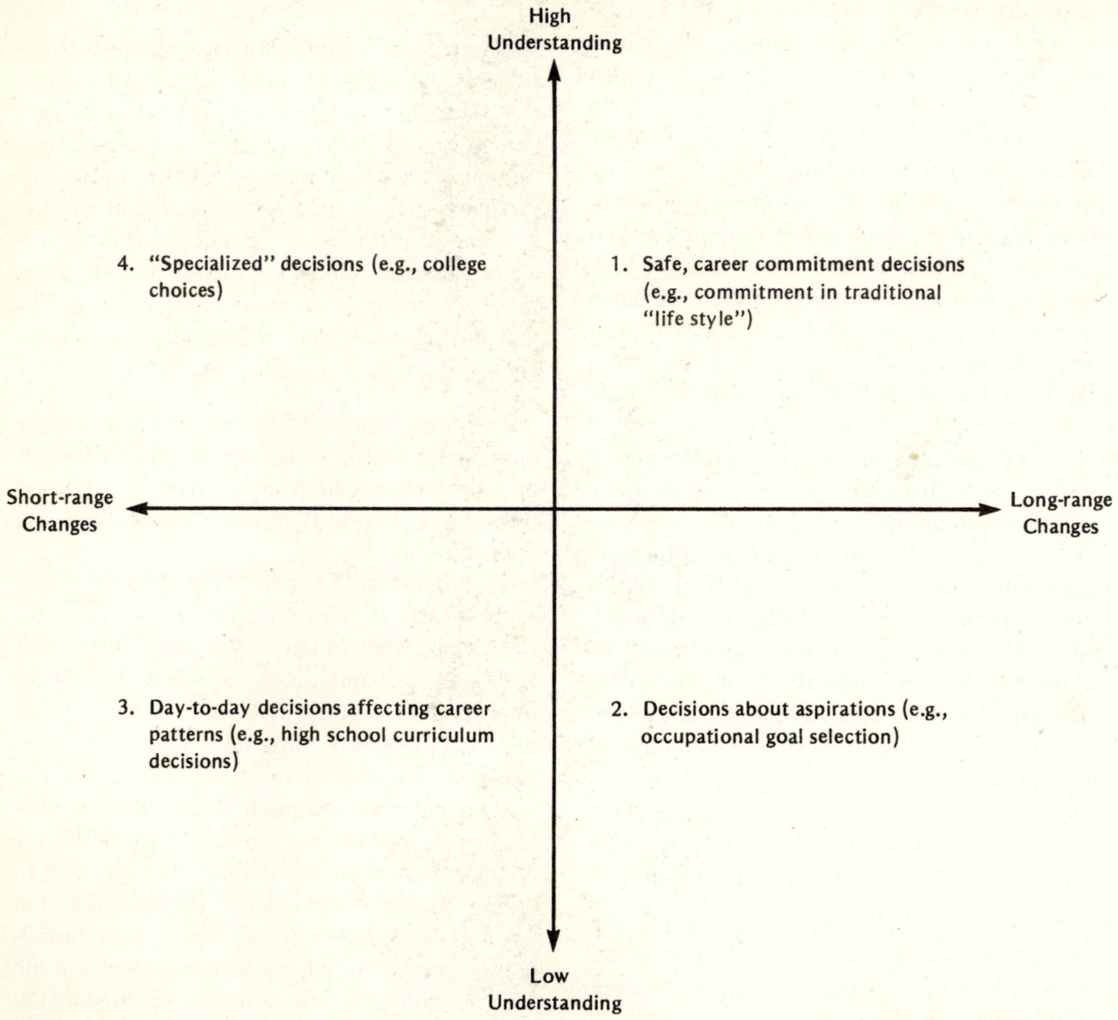

Source: From "Vocational Decision-Making Models: A Review and Comparative Analysis" by D. A. Jepsen and J. A. Dilley, *Review of Education Research,* 1974, Vol. 44, pp. 331-349. Reprinted by permission.

when they are made may be suboptimizing in the sense that they seriously affect the flexibility of a long-range plan.

4. The evaluation of a career-related decision is frequently more a matter of process than of outcome. If outcome is employed as the criterion of a good career decision, then one must look to long-range favorable results. Counselors seldom have that luxury. As a result, process criteria are more frequently used.

We tend to judge a career-related decision as "good" if it is logical and consistent when it is made or if it was the consequence of prescribed procedures and consonant with some specific model of decision making. It is possible, then, for decisions that are judged "good" when they are made in terms of the process to be ultimately "bad" decisions in terms of outcome; conversely, it is possible, though unlikely, that "good" outcomes can result from "bad" process.

5. Individuals can be taught how to make career-related decisions. There are dozens of decision-making programs, each different yet each similar, that have reported at least short-range success. Some of these paradigms will be discussed later in this chapter. Further, it is likely that, once taught, a decision-making strategy and skills in decision making have transfer value.

6. Although we know that a great variety of factors influence individual career decision making, we do not presently have any definitive indication of which factors predominate for which individual under what conditions and of how these differential weightings evolve. We know relatively little about the correlates of decision making (O'Neil et al., 1980). There is some evidence to suggest that the following factors moderate decision-making abilities: values (M. Katz, 1980); propensity for risk (Slakter & Cramer, 1969); achievement motivation (Tseng & Carter, 1970; Wish & Hasazi, 1973); coping style (O'Hare & Tamburi, 1986); prestige (N. B. Taylor & Pryor, 1985); and age (Okun, 1976; Guttmann, 1978). Among the factors that have been investigated and for which the relationship to decision making is conflicting or unclear are: sex (D. J. Milley & Bee, 1982; Slaney, 1980; Foote, 1980); interests (Lowe, 1981); ego identity status (Blustein & Phillips, 1990); vocational maturity (Phillips & Strohmer, 1982; self-efficacy (Taylor & Popma, 1990); anxiety (G. S. Brown & Strange, 1981); and self-esteem (Gordon, 1981). In the final analysis, there may be several correlates (O'Neil et al., 1980).

In terms of the relationship between anxiety and career indecision, Fuqua, Seaworth, and Newman (1987) demonstrated that a substantial, unidimensional relationship exists. Fuqua, Newman, and Seaworth (1988) later determined that although there was indeed a substantial relationship, both state and trait anxiety differentially related to career indecision. They identified four factors in the Career Decision Scale (CDS) and found that measures of anxiety correlated differently with each. One factor (lack of information about self and careers) provided the strongest relationship. A second factor (uncertainty about appropriateness or degree of fit between self and career) and factor four (specific barriers to a previous choice) also correlated substantially with anxiety. The third factor (multiple interests), however, was unrelated to anxiety. Thus, anxiety may relate to certain aspects of indecision, but not to other aspects. In a longitudinal study of college graduates, Arnold (1989) logically concluded that decidedness and well-being were significantly related (especially around graduation). Hence, there can be no doubt that undecided college students are more anxious than their counterparts who have made career decisions with which they are comfortable.

7. We do not have a clear notion of why deciding individuals emphasize one or another of these factors or others and how that situation develops. It is possible to construct a taxonomy that delineates the kinds of influences that impinge on career decision making. The interaction of these internal and external variables is paramount in the decision-making process. Personal attributes and characteristics, value structures, opportunity factors, and cultural forces, separately and in combination, are brought to bear in decisions (see Table 14.2). Their combination, weighting, and content vary from individual to individual.

This fact has led some researchers to propose a taxonomy of decision-making *styles*. Arroba (1977) proposed six styles of decision making:

Logical–situation appraised coldly and objectively, choice made on the basis of what is best
No thought–no objective consideration
Hesitant–postponement of final commitment to an alternative, inability to make a decision
Emotional–decision based on what the person subjectively wants or likes
Compliant–decision made in accordance with the perceived expectations of the situation or of others, passivity
Intuitive–decision based only on a personal feeling of rightness or inevitability (p. 151)

Her proposals were later tested and basically confirmed by Hesketh (1982). Janis and Mann (1977), who have produced some of the most significant work in decision making, have suggested four defective patterns of decision making:

Unconflicted adherence–The individual simply denies any serious risks from current course of action.
Unconflicted change to new course of action–The individual simply denies any serious risks in making a decision or change.
Defense avoidance–The individual avoids anything that might stimulate choice anxiety or painful feelings and gives up looking for a solution.
Hypervigilance–The individual becomes extremely emotionally excited as the time constraints of decision making are made more pressing.

Harren (1979) proposed three vocational decision-making styles in undergraduate students: (1) *rational*, involving objective deliberation and self-appraisal; (2) *intuitive*, involving emotional self-awareness and fantasy; and (3) *dependent*, involving denial of responsibility. This classification system has been the focus of corroborative research by Rubinton (1980) and Daniels (1982), who suggest that rational decision-makers do best with rational interventions whereas intuitive decision-makers do best with intuitive interventions. Harren's decision-making model for college students has also been supported in a study by R. G. Thomas and Bruning (1984) in which the investigators discovered that the effects of nonreduced cognitive dissonance concerning a vocational decision were regression to earlier stages of decision making and revocation of the commitment to the decision.

These attempts at describing decision-making styles differ in terms of the population from which they were derived (secondary school students, college students, adults), the time involved (one point in time or a span of time), and the methodological design. Each,however, offers some potentially fruitful areas for further investigation.

D. J. Walsh (1987) attempted to synthesize the findings regarding individual variations within the vocational decision-making process. She concluded that decision-making approaches appeared to differ along six dimensions:

Internal/external orientation	(self versus others as a resource for the decision task)
Factual/affective focus	(cognition versus emotion in the process)
Systematic/haphazard approach	(within each step of the decision-making process)
Vigilant/inattentive approach	(attention to planning, consequences, and so on)
Amount of time spent	(to complete phases of the process)
Volume of data	(high versus low)

These categories, like most of those in the literature, are descriptive rather than prescriptive.

It is not uncommon that in the behavioral and social sciences certain techniques become popular and their use spurs new research findings or explains more fully some already extant knowledge. Metanalytic techniques and multivariate techniques are two such examples. One of the most recently applied is cluster analysis, a kind of discriminant sorting of data into categories. Using this technique, Lucas and Epperson (1990) sought to determine subtypes of undecided students and to see if previously evolved rational category systems were consonant with those derived through cluster analysis. They confirmed that different forms of career indecision exist, that the cluster-derived categories were consistent with the logically-derived categories previously discovered by the investigators (Lucas & Epperson, 1988), and that each of the five types identified evidenced varying levels of anxiety.

Similarly, Larson, Heppner, Ham, and Dugan (1988) employed the cluster analysis technique to identify four distinct subtypes of undecideds: (1) planless avoiders, (2) informed indecisives (a very small group), (3) confident but uninformed, and (4) uninformed. About 25 percent of the sample in this study of college sophomore students were planless avoiders, individuals who combined a lack of career planning activities with maladaptive coping behaviors and attitudes. These individuals reported poor problem-solving abilities, especially with respect to career-related concerns—a group with no information and no decision-making skills. The confident but uninformed group, also about one-quarter of the sample, evidenced a modest lack of career planning activities, assessed themselves as good problem solvers, but lacked information about the career planning process. The largest cluster (almost one-half of the sample) was the uninformed group. They self-appraised their problem solving as moderate and lacked career information. These were the individuals judged to be most receptive to career interventions.

Further confirmation of the existence of different types of undecided students comes from a study of high school students effected by Fuqua, Blum, and Hartman (1988). Again using the technique of cluster analysis, they identified four groups, generally distinguishable by level of problem and by the characteristic anxiety manifested by each group.

> Group One (42%) seems to represent a career decided group, relatively free of excessive anxiety and relatively effective in terms of attribution and identity formation. Group Two (22%) appears to possess at least moderate career indecision, increased anxiety, less identity formation, and a fairly internalized locus of control. Groups Three (28%) and Four (8%) seem to suffer fairly serious career indecision, are more external in their attribution, and show poorer identity formation. Group Three has moderate levels of anxiety with Group Four alone showing excessive anxiety relative to their peers. (pp. 369–370)

Others have approached the search for subtypes of career indecision by means of the statistical technique of factor analysis, a precursor of cluster analysis that permits a bit more latitude in manipulating data. F. W. Vondracek, Hostetler, Schulenberg, and Shimizu (1990) investigated undecided adolescents and concluded once again that four subtypes existed in their sample, with each group having problems that ranged from minimal to severe.

It seems apparent, then, that there are different subtypes of undecided students that different studies have identified as having more or less the same characteristics, that these differences exist as early as high school and as late as college graduation (with a high probability of the differences extending both upward and downward), and that differential interventions are required based on client characteristics.

8. Each model of career decision making assumes motivation or tries to establish readiness on the part of the chooser to take responsibility for career decisions. Too frequently, career guidance is analogous to the Boy Scout who helped the "little old lady" across the street—when she did not want to go. The intentions are good, but the perceived needs of

the person being assisted are ignored, or the individual is not helped to internalize the importance of the choices that must be made.

9. The effects of information on decision making are highly intricate, as we shall see in Chapter 15. For example, whether a client is decided or undecided, giving positive information appears to enhance simplicity in terms of cognitive differentiation, whereas negative information seems to be associated with greater cognitive complexity (Cesari, Winer, & Piper, 1984).

Some Approaches. These commonalities, then, cut across all programs for teaching decision making. Some of the better known of the decision-making approaches were described in Chapter 4; others will be described below or are treated more fully in order to demonstrate how particular theoretical emphases get translated into practice.

Martin Katz of the Educational Testing Service has spent years developing a system with which to assist two-year college students in the career decision-making process (M. Katz, 1973, 1980). Katz works from the assumption that values are the major synthesizing force in decision making. "The basic choice is essentially a choice between arrays of values, or value systems" (1973, p. 116). Consequently, he has constructed the System of Interactive Guidance and Information (SIGI), a computer-based process designed to help students to examine their values, to explore options, to retrieve information that is related to their values, and to get relevant interpretations of the data. In effect, students are learning a strategy for relating information to values and are thus increasing their competence in decision making. Students may go through the system as often as they like, each time taking an active role in controlling inputs. It is, in fact, a humanistically conceived interactive system that attempts, by means of a detailed exposition of objectives, scope, and sequence, to help individuals to do the following:

- Understand the sequential nature of choices
- Gain a knowledge of options in the domain of human values
- Recognize that value systems can change
- Become aware of the full array of conditions of work and attitudes toward work
- Grasp the rewards and satisfactions characteristic of each specific option at each choice point so the individual can detect the fit of these characteristics to his own values as he perceives them at that time
- Become aware of the cost and consequences of each decision
- Know and understand the probabilities of entry and success in each option considered at any choice point
- Acquire information about ways and means of proceeding (1973, pp. 122–123)

Hence, the content of career decision making might well place a high emphasis on values and valuing. Further, Katz has demonstrated that an interactive, computer-based system can be used an as aid in teaching a decision-making strategy.

Another career-related decision-making process is based on the idea of diverse types of information being equally important as content and on a problem-solving strategy of making choices (J. A. Hamilton & Jones, 1971). This problem-solving model contains six skill areas:

Skill Area #1: *Understanding the Problem*—Being willing to work toward setting and achieving educational and vocational goals

Skill Area #2: *Searching for and Using Information*—(a) Personal information on abilities, interests, preferences, etc., and (b) information about related opportunities in the worlds of education and work

Skill Area #3: *Getting Alternatives*—Thinking of several possible educational and vocational goals

Skill Area #4: *Selecting Goals and Making Plans*—(a) Choosing the goals (first and second choice) that seem like the best bet for the individual, and (b) making plans for reaching them

Skill Area #5: *Carrying Out Plans*—Carrying out plans, switching to a second best goal if necessary

Skill Area #6: *Finding Out If It Works*—(a) Judging whether the first (or the second best) goal has been achieved, and (b) describing what helped and what hindered the individual's efforts along the way

Janis and Mann (1977) propose five distinct stages of decision making: (1) appraising the challenge; (2) surveying alternatives; (3) weighing alternatives; (4) deliberating about commitment; and (5) adhering despite negative feedback. Within this system, a feedback loop permits reversions to earlier stages. The evaluation of a "good" decision is conducted in terms of seven specific criteria:

1. Thoroughly canvasses a wide range of alternative courses of action
2. Surveys the full range of objectives to be fulfilled and the values implicated by choice
3. Carefully weighs whatever he knows about the costs and risks of negative consequences, as well as the positive consequences, that could flow from each alternative
4. Intensively searches for new information relevant to further evaluation of the alternatives
5. Correctly assimilates and takes account of any new information or expert judgment to which he is exposed, even when the information or judgment does not support the course of action he initially prefers
6. Reexamines the positive and negative consequences of all known alternatives, including those originally regarded as unacceptable, before making a final choice
7. Makes detailed provisions for implementing or executing the chosen course of action, with special attention to contingency plans that might be required if various known risks were to materialize (p. 11)

Harren (1979) offers a model of decision making that includes stages of awareness, planning, commitment, and implementation. Within this context, self-esteem and identity are thought to be important. The tasks of decision making are to achieve autonomy, interpersonal maturity, and a sense of purpose. Harren describes the model in terms of four conditions: (1) *interpersonal evaluation* (positive and negative feedback); (2) *psychological states* (level of anxiety); (3) *tasks conditions* (specific career-relevant tasks, defined in terms of imminence, alternatives, and consequences); and (4) *context conditions* (interpersonal relationships defined in terms of mutuality, support, and probability. Pitz and Harren (1980) suggest that a "good" decision under these circumstances should be evaluated in terms of four behavioral criteria:

1. *Information-seeking*. What information has the person sought about alternatives being considered?
2. *Range of alternatives*. How many and what variety of choices has the person identified and considered?
3. *Knowledge of alternatives*. How much knowledge does the person have about the choices and how accurate is it?
4. *Rationality of choice*. How consistent is the person's behavior with the principles of expected utility theory?

Gati (1986, 1990) offers an example of a systematic model for choosing among successive alternatives to bring decisions down to an increasingly specific focus. He calls his model a Sequential Elimination Approach (SEM), and it essentially involves a continual ranking of alternatives, eliminating those that fail to receive higher assessments. Gati believes that it is the responsibility of the counselor to identify the client's type of decision problem (such as lack of occupational information, lack of self-information, inability to deal with uncertainty, and so on) and to determine the client's decision-making style. The SEM is one of several possible intervention modes. Gati suggests that the following sequence of stages might make sense:

1. Identify the counselee's problem
2. Help the counselee define and structure the decision problem (for example, choosing a major)
3. Present the SEM as a framework for career decision making
4. Help the counselee to identify the aspects that are important to him or her and relevant to the elimination process
5. Help the counselee to clarify the relative importance of the aspects enumerated in Stage 4
6. Help the counselee to identify the range of levels considered as acceptable or satisfying with respect to each of the more important aspects
7. Help the counselee to organize the alternatives into meaningful clusters in order to reduce the complexity of the elimination process
8. Provide feedback to the counselee regarding the available alternatives that remain after each additional aspect has been considered
9. Help the counselee to check the relative insensitivity of the results to any particular judgment
10. Help the counselee rank the alternatives that survive the elimination by identifying relations of dominance
11. Help the counselee to outline the steps to be taken to actualize the preferred alternative(s)

Savickas (1990a) offered a career decision-making course to tenth graders, and used didactic instruction based on the content of the Career Maturity Inventory (see Chapter 16) and the Holland typology (see Chapter 4). The course attempted to enhance the students' attitudes toward decision making and concepts about career choice by providing them with cognitive competencies that included self-appraisal skill for evaluating occupational capabilities, knowledge about the world of work, matching personal characteristics with occupational requirements, forming plans to enter an occupation, and developing coping skills to deal with any implementation problems. Designed for adolescents and young adults (grade seven through sophomore in college), the initial course evaluations were positive.

A shotgun approach to enhancing decision making may not be nearly so effective as tailoring interventions to the specific characteristics of clients. For example, Mann, Beswick, Allouache, and Ivey (1989) conducted a decision-making workshop for clients that was based on Janis and Mann's conflict theory and the five types of decision strategies described earlier in this chapter. Their 76 participants consisted of two basic groups: *problem clients* (those who appraised themselves as poor in decision making and with specific problems) and *learners* (those who viewed themselves as competent decision makers but who wanted to improve their ability). These two groups proved to have different reactions to an intervention. The investigators concluded, "We believe that a general 'all-purpose' decision workshop program may succeed when participants are a homogeneous sample but could run into difficulties when participants have quite disparate competencies and reasons for attending" (p. 481).

Each of the preceding programs demands counselee involvement in the choice process. Other programs are more mechanistic, in the sense that the program has inherent in it the capacity to make the actual choice. J. L. Holland's *Self-Directed Search* (1970), for example, processes student input data in such a way that choices on the basis of the data provided by the users are fed back to them for further exploration. In a sense, the system processes the data and makes the choices for the user rather than the user processing the data and making the choice. Even in this type of system, however, the user must subsequently choose from among the alternatives suggested by the mechanical processing.

Common to virtually all of these career decision-making programs and to others not specifically described here are several foci: (1) a knowledge of self, variously defined, but usually including aptitudes, interests, achievements, personality characteristics, attitudes, and values, with different emphases placed on each by different programs; (2) a knowledge of the world of work, variously described, but according to some generally accepted classification system (such as *DOT*, cluster, field and level, and others) and including work-related factors (such as rewards of work, requirements of work, and others); and (3) a decision-making strategy, variously conceived, but usually entailing a step-by-step, rational, logical, by-the-numbers procedure. Currently, no career decision-making system has been proven to be more effective than any other, although each lays claim to success. Comparative studies in this regard would prove interesting and useful.

On the other hand, these models of decision making differ on a variety of parameters. First, they vary in terms of being mathematical or descriptive. Second, they vary in terms of the decision-making variables that are considered most important (values, interests, self-concept, abilities, or motivation). Third, they differ in terms of the emphasis placed on environmental variables (economics, cultural factors, social conditions, and residence). Fourth, they diverge in their assessment of the amount and type of information necessary for good decision making. Fifth, they place differing accents on the probability factor. Sixth, they differ in their perception of the stages that decision-makers experience. Finally, they differ in terms of evaluation (for example, outcome or process).

Bergland (1974), in a thoughtful review and synthesis of the career decision-making literature, has suggested that the basic strategy of decision making is problem solving. Consequently, he offers a series of stages that the decision-maker should be helped to negotiate:

1. Defining the problem
2. Generating alternatives
3. Gathering information
4. Developing information-seeking skills
5. Providing useful sources of information
6. Processing information
7. Making plans and selecting goals
8. Implementing and evaluating plan (p. 352)

Occasionally, someone (O'Hare, 1987) suggests that career decision-making models are simply descriptive and predictive and have not been put into practice in the field because there is a discrepancy between what practitioners say they espouse and what they actually do. Perhaps this type of indictment is too severe, in that the literature clearly demonstrates a theory–intervention link that is constantly growing in sophistication and is producing positive results.

In summary, all of these decision-making models for use in individual counseling are action-oriented. By whatever terminology they are called, they address choice in a staged, systematic manner. They are intended to assist individuals in filtering objective data through subjective systems of risk taking, emotionality, utility determination, and so on. Again, no single model has been determined to be superior to any other; yet each implies its own unique success. They suggest to counselors that virtually any model of assisting an individual in career decision making—extant or yet to be invented—can be successful if based on sound theoretical and research findings, and if operationalized in logical, consistent ways.

Indecision and Indecisiveness. Before leaving the topic of decision making, it is necessary to point out the difference between undecidedness and indecisiveness and to describe several recent decision scales that are largely in the experimental stage. Crites (1969) has defined *indecision* as "the inability of the individual to select, or commit himself to a particular course of action which will eventuate in his preparing for and entering a specific occupation" (p. 305). He specifies three possible cases for indecision: (1) the multipotential individual who is unable to designate one goal from among many choices; (2) the undecided individual who cannot make a choice from among available alternatives; and (3) the uninterested individual who is uncertain about a choice because of lack of an appropriate interest pattern. In contrast, *indecisiveness* emanates from general personal problems rather than from doubts related to a specific career choice, perhaps because of the pain involved in decision making. In indecision there may be lack of information or knowledge of how to sort through alternatives; in indecisiveness a generally dysfunctional personality orientation may cause such choice anxiety that an individual is rendered incapable of making a decision. Seldom are these distinctions made explicit when, for example, counselors speak of decided and undecided students.

Some recent writing (Lopez & Andrews, 1987; Kinnier, Brigman, & Noble, 1990) views indecision as the result of interactional deficits within families. It is argued that a person's indecision might be the outcome of transactional "noise" between the person and the family—a failure in family transformation. Based on clinical intuitions, this idea argues that there is typically an overinvolvement of parents with their indecisive child over career and educational concerns, leading students to achieve inadequate psychological separation from their parents. As Lopez and Andrews suggest, empirical research would be useful to investigate the relationship between indecision or undecidedness and family history, structure, and communication patterns, among other variables. One of these variables might be enmeshment in family of origin.

Several decision scales are now being used, largely for experimental and research purposes. Osipow, Carney, Winer, Yanico, and Koschir (1976) are responsible for the Career Decision Scale (CDS), a 16-item instrument designed originally for college students. It yields scores for four types of indecision: (1) lack of structure (lack of confidence, choice anxiety, potential choice avoidance); (2) perceived external barriers (for example, financial or parental); (3) approach–approach (difficulty in deciding among alternatives); (4) personal conflict (difficulty choosing between occupations that reflect differing personal values) (Osipow, 1980). A study by Barak and Friedkes (1982) found that clients who basically lacked structure received the greatest benefit from counseling; those in the personal conflict and perceived external barrier categories gained the least from counseling. Other studies (B. Hartman & P. Hartman, 1982; B. Hartman, Utz, & Farnum, 1979) apply the scale to both high school students and graduate students.

Another decision scale is the Vocational Decision-Making Difficulty Scale (VDMD) developed by John Holland (J. L. Holland, Gottfredson, & Nafziger, 1975). Slaney, Palko-Nonemaker, and Alexander (1981) identified four factors of indecision measured by this scale: (1) lack of information; (2) lack of clarity of an individual's place in the world of work; (3) choice anxiety; and (4) questions about ability. Slaney (1980) and Slaney, Palko-Nonemaker, and Alexander (1981) discovered significant differences between the VDMD and the CDS. Holland, Gottfredson, and Power (1980) categorized decision-making difficulties as (1) problems of vocational identification, (2) lack of information or training, (3) environmental or personal barriers, and (4) no problems. In an earlier study (J. L Holland & J. E. Holland, 1977) a large majority of an undecided group were identified as simply delaying decisions until reality demanded action. Their indecision was not a matter of lack of information or immaturity. Holland and Holland believe that some students suffer, however, from an "indecisive disposition" resulting from a failure to acquire the necessary cultural participation, self-confidence, tolerance for ambiguity, concept of identity, and environmental and self-knowledge necessary for decision-making. The point that indecision is not necessarily pathological is well taken and should temper the tendency of counselors to feel that decisions need to be made before they are necessary. After all, almost three out of every four college freshmen express some form of indecision, tentativeness, or uncertainty about selecting a major (Grite, 1981; Menning & Whittmayer, 1979; Titley & Titley, 1980).

A third scale, the Vocational Decision Scale (VDS), has been developed by G. Jones and Chenery (1980). Three indecision subtypes were identified: (1) general self-uncertainty (indecisiveness, lack of self-confidence regarding decision-making ability and occupational ability, lack of clarity about oneself); (2) low choice/work salience (lack of relationship between interests or abilities and occupational field, low motivation); and (3) transitional self (scarcity of educational and/or occupational information, conflict with significant others).

Other scales are: Harren's (1979) Assessment of Career Decision Making (ACDM), an instrument based on Tiedeman and O'Hara's stages of exploration, crystallization, choice, and clarification; P. Lunneborg's (1976) Career Decision-Making Questionnaire (CDMQ); and Appel, Haak, and Witzke's (1970) Career Decision Readiness Inventory (CDRI).

L. K. Mitchell and Krumboltz (1984a) point out that the problem with paper-and-pencil measures of career decision making is that they do not test behaviors; they measure only knowledge of decision-making skills. Consequently, experimental instruments focus on behavioral inventories and simulations. Yet, there is currently no persuasive evidence that these newer approaches offer any better data than the paper-and-pencil instruments. Mitchell and Krumboltz also catalog some research needs in the area of career decision making. These include the need for longitudinal as well as short-term outcome measures; the need for teaching clients to recognize situations that require a decision-making strategy; the need for greater research involving varied populations and age groups; the need to investigate more thoroughly the personal cognitions affecting career decision making; and the need for better methodologies, such as causal path analysis (see, for example, B. Hartman, Fuqua, & Blum, 1985), multivariate research designs, and single-subject designs.

Finally, in addition to all those interventions previously mentioned that are designed to enhance career decision making, there is evidence that decision making can be improved through the use of behavioral interventions (Snodgrass & Healy, 1979), group experiences, individual counseling (Kivligham, Hageseth, Tipton, & McGovern,1981), self-administered instruments, simulations (M. Katz, Norris, & Pears, 1978), contract counseling (Brooks & Haigler, 1984), and exploration (Carver & Smart, 1985).

GROUP PROCESSES

The second major strategy for implementing career guidance and counseling programs is the use of groups of one type or another. Many chapters of this text are liberally laced with examples of the use of group processes in such activities as disseminating information, utilizing educational and career information, developing attitudes toward career planning and work, and learning decision making. Therefore, in this section we present only a brief overview of the group strategy in career guidance.

Rationale

It should be evident that in any systematic approach a great many objectives of career guidance and counseling can be achieved through group methods. Traditionally, it has been maintained that group procedures provide *efficiency* and *effectiveness*. If, for example, the dissemination of information is a goal of career guidance at a specific point along the career development continuum, it is clearly more efficient to present the information once to a group than to present it individually to each member of the group. Also, if the goals of career guidance entail problem solving or if the immediate objective of career guidance is to treat dysfunctional behaviors that may be affecting career development, then group methods are appropriate, for groups have been found to perform consistently better in certain types of problem-solving tasks and under certain conditions than do individuals attacking the same problem. In terms of correcting dysfunctional behaviors, it is reasoned that since these behaviors are typically learned in group situations, they are best unlearned or relearned or substitute behaviors learned in the same mileux.

Currently, the majority of all employed persons work within the framework of corporate structures wherein the primary modus operandi is the group as a procedural vehicle. It would seem beneficial for individuals, especially youngsters, to become used to functioning in this manner as a part of their preoccupational experience. Some suggested themes by which such career-related learning might be facilitated in groups are presented in Chapters 7 through 13.

The use of group methods is further justified by the fact that various career guidance curricula and theories of career development suggest universal career needs. These are needs that are presumed to be required or felt by all individuals; therefore, common learnings of this sort may be facilitated in groups. The relevance of these learnings to an individual's unique situation may be recognized through both group and individual methods.

Characteristics of the Group

Counselors may work with collections of individuals or aggregates rather than with true groups. In a social psychology sense, a group is characterized by at least six criteria (J. C. Hansen & Cramer, 1971):

1. Members of the group are in *interaction* with one another; that is, there must be at least two-way communication.
2. Members of the group share a *common goal*. This goal may be set by the group itself, or it may be imposed by external forces.
3. The group members set *norms* that give direction and limits to their activity. Certain behaviors come to be rewarded; others are punished in some way.
4. The members develop a set of *roles*. Certain functions are performed by group members.
5. The group members develop a network of *interpersonal* attraction (likes and dislikes for each other).
6. The group works toward the satisfaction of the *individual needs* of the group members (p. 81).

Clearly, these characteristics will be present in varying degrees, depending on the type of group and the purpose of the group. The more in evidence they are, the more the likelihood that a group exists; the more these characteristics are lacking, the greater the chances that an aggregate or a simple collection of individuals exists. Large assembly programs in a school, for example, typically deal with aggregates. Usually, successful discussions, problem solving, and counseling work through groups. A collection of individuals can still have utility for counselors. The point is simply that a distinction should be made between groups, which offer great potential inner resources for career guidance and counseling, and aggregates, which are a convenience.

If the counselor works with true groups, then there must be some understanding of at least the basic elements of the way in which groups function. As a group interacts, it becomes dynamic; members are constantly adjusting and changing in relation to each other and to themselves. As a group restructures and adjusts, tensions are reduced, conflicts eliminated, and problems solved. The study of the variables underlying group movement is called group dynamics. Understanding group dynamics leads to developing the techniques for effective group actions and decisions by using the forces that facilitate or inhibit group functioning. Such forces include the manner of interaction among the members, the amount of participation, the degree of group cohesiveness, the group values, the kind and quality of group leadership, and the internal structure of the group (degrees of permissiveness, competition, and communication).

The Uses of Groups

The uses to which groups can be put in career guidance and counseling are limited only by the imagination and energy of the counselor. The following section presents some suggestions that provide an idea of the array of possibilities. Purposes for groups in career guidance are offered first; these are followed by a general discussion of the type of focus in career guidance groups.

Purposes.

1. *Information dissemination*. Information about the world of work is required in career decision making. Certain elements of that information are pertinent only for given individuals; others are needed by all people. Information regarding the occupational structure, post-high school or post-college educational and training opportunities, and courses of study at various educational levels, to cite but a few examples, are needed by every counselee and can be transmitted by means of group procedures, which will, of course, require follow-up.

2. *Motivation*. Motivation refers to the concept of convincing individuals of the value of some aspect of career guidance, whether this aspect involves the need for career planning in a broad sense or the need to take aptitude tests, for instance, in a much narrower sense. Readiness, if lacking, and an orientation to planfulness must be established.

3. *Teaching*. The most obvious application of group techniques occurs in the teaching process. In fact, the primary strategy for career education, infusion (that is, teachers highlighting the career relevance of existing subject matter content in the classroom), relies on the teaching strategy. There is certainly a place for teaching in career guidance. Goldman (1962) has argued that group guidance often fails because counselors deal with guidance concerns by means of teacher behaviors. In other words, the *process* of teaching is seen as inappropriate for the *content* of guidance. This charge is certainly true in terms of the more affective elements of guidance content, but, as we have repeatedly stressed throughout this book, much of career guidance begins with a cognitive base. Goals ranging from the development of a vocabulary of work in youngsters to imparting decision-making skills to adults are effectively accomplished by means of a teach-

ing strategy. To deliver a career development curriculum, a counselor simply must use structured groups.

4. *Practice*. Role-playing, dramatization, gaming, and other simulation techniques allow individuals to rehearse or to practice career-related behaviors in groups. Whether the practice is as specific as role-playing a job interview or filling out an employment application, or is as broad as playing the Life Career Game, group situations permit the rehearsal of necessary career behaviors in a protected context.

5. *Attitude Development*. Attitudes are learned predispositions to respond in characteristic ways to certain stimuli. Since they are learned, they can be unlearned. Since they are learned within the family and other groups, they are logically unlearned and relearned within the group structure. Hence, the clarification of career attitudes and values and the crystallization and development of attitudes toward oneself can be fostered within groups.

6. *Exploration*. Since many individuals, whether school-aged or adult, are in the exploratory stage of career development, various group activities designed to enhance that exploration are beneficial. Ranging from field trips to career conferences to less structured activities, groups provide a vehicle for this exploration.

7. *Counseling*. Related somewhat to attitude development but more specific is group counseling. Some view group counseling as simply a remedial activity (for example, dealing with specific fears and anxieties, coping with intrapersonal difficulties, and so on). Others conceive of it as having a developmental focus (such as developing interpersonal and social skills, learning decision-making skills, and so on). In either case, group counseling, as opposed to group guidance, is seen as a means of assisting individuals within a therapeutically created climate of respect and acceptance to recognize and to use their more affective aspects to their benefit.

Type of Focus. Fundamentally, group guidance and counseling should provide an opportunity to test or to discover one's own characteristics as related to particular environmental options. The following questions reflect such an intent: Knowing what I know about myself, how would I probably behave or perform in a situation with identified characteristics? Knowing what I know about a given occupation, what characteristics of mine can I compare and contrast with those required by the occupation? Through role-playing, case studies, selected audio-visual devices, discussion, speakers, structured exercises, and so on, an atmosphere can be created that will encourage individuals to project themselves vicariously into a given choice situation and to analyze how they, personally, would feel in that situation. Of course, it is not possible to create all the situations from which one might be able to choose or to have complete information. Also, it is possible to present irrelevant information to a group or to fail to encourage individuals to consider the characteristics of their behavior and performance that are related to choice making.

Whether one deals with individual counseling or with group processes, the same questions are relevant. Both should support those experiences that reinforce for individuals the validity of the questions: Who am I? Am I able to be what I want to be? What is my life likely to be if I succeed in becoming what I choose to be?

Throughout the career guidance process, individually and in groups, the counselor not only must ensure that counselees have access to accurate, relevant information about their personal characteristics and create conditions that will help them understand the implications of this information, but the counselor also must ensure that counselees have accurate, relevant information about the options open to them. In the final analysis, people's self-perceptions or the self-labels that direct their behavior relate to persons, objects, and possibilities that lie outside the self. In other words, one's self-descriptions, whether they be such adjectives as bright–dull, capable–incapable, or leader–follower, have meaning only in comparing oneself with others and with the requirements of specific situations. Appropriate information, much of which can be gleaned through groups, is vital to making good decisions about oneself as well as about what opportunities exist and what they require as one tests his or her personal fit with these opportunities.

A word of caution: too often a group strategy is employed simply because someone feels that it is time to launch a group guidance venture. Nothing comes before; very little comes after. The group guidance experience becomes a moment in time for its own sake. Group guidance is not "its own excuse for being." In a systematic approach to career guidance, one first determines goals and states them in behavioral terms; one then decides what activities are necessary and appropriate for achieving these goals; finally, one evaluates to discover if these goals have been achieved. One or more of the possible activities might involve the use of groups. This approach is quite a different matter from deciding to use a group strategy and then finding a focus for it. Intent determines strategy, not vice versa.

Much of career guidance and counseling can be accomplished by means of a group-helping strategy of one sort or another. Leading groups requires special skills of counselors, whether the purpose of the group is information dissemination, motivation, teaching, practice, attitude development, exploration, counseling, or some other aim. The use of group techniques is appropriate as a helping strategy in assisting individuals to answer a variety of career-related questions; it is not appropriate as an end in itself.

Summary

We have discussed two primary helping strategies in career guidance: individual and group processes. In one way or another, each of these strategies is designed to facilitate career decision making. The internal personal attributes and values an individual brings to the career decision-making process must be balanced with the external realities of opportunities and cultural factors that constrain one's choices. Each helping strategy can be effected systematically in itself and within a systematic program of career guidance.

CHAPTER 15

INFORMATION IN CAREER GUIDANCE AND COUNSELING

Key Concepts

- Information pertinent to the particular choices to be made—occupational, educational, personal, and social—is the fuel that drives personal decision making.
- Information can be accurate, current, and relevant or not. A major task of career guidance or career counseling is to assist persons in identifying what information they need, determining where such information can be obtained, ensuring that the information acquired is accurate and current, and planning how such information can be used as a basis for action.
- The mere availability of information does not ensure that it will be used or used effectively.
- Information delivery systems have evolved from printed matter to more interactive and personalized approaches such as those found in simulation and computer-aided career guidance systems.
- The fostering of planfulness and effective career behavior involves not only helping counselees to acquire information but assisting them in applying the knowledge gained to personal characteristics—preferences, values, commitments, and capabilities.

Most people are conversant with very few occupations. They are aware, sometimes only vaguely, of the nature of the occupations of their immediate families and perhaps those of a small group of family-connected individuals. Because of the mass media, they may also be acquainted with an additional small number of occupations, frequently stereotyped. During the process of socialization, people have learned that some types of occupations are desirable and that others are taboo, at least within their cultural spheres. In attempting to relate self-characteristics to various occupations, then, they typically have few alternatives through which to sort unless some type of direct intervention occurs. This intervention usually takes the form of exposure to occupational information, mediated by a career guidance practitioner.

In addition to their need for occupational information, individuals require educational and personal information if their career development is to be complete. Since educational decisions are intermediate choices within the total context of career decision making, individuals must possess and be able to use information about various curricular opportunities, post-high school and post-college educational and training possibilities, and the relationship between education and work. If students make decisions to attend college, they need to understand such factors as how collegiate environments differ, how the overt characteristics of institutions of higher education (such as size, selectivity, geographical location, curriculum, and others) affect individuals, how to go about the application process, how to investigate financial aid opportunities, how to determine what national tests are required, and how to cope with many other variables in the process of educational choice. If students or adults are specialty-oriented, they must have similarly important information about opportunities for training. Hence, whether counselees are adolescents in the process of exploration, college students in the process of delimiting choice, or adults involved in midcareer change, preretirement programs, or other career-related decision making, information about educational or occupational opportunities can help individuals accomplish the necessary tasks.

Both educational and occupational information have meaning only insofar as such data are evaluated within the framework of what individuals know about themselves. Self-information is crucial to individuals seeing the relevance of the educational or occupational data that they receive. Counselees need an accurate picture and acceptance of their strengths and weaknesses in both the cognitive and the noncognitive domains in order to realize fully the value of information regarding the worlds of work and education. They must be aware of their diverse aptitudes, interests, values, and attitudes toward learning and work. Only then can they truly evaluate the information they receive. In effect, one asks, "Knowing what I know about myself, how can I use this information?"

Salomone (1989) suggests that *occupational* information is different from *career* information; consequently, counselors should be careful about which term they use. In his judgment, *occupational* and *career* are both adjectives that describe a *type* of information. Since an occupation is different from a career (see Chapter 1), career information is a much broader term than is occupational information (that is, information solely about occupations).

The process of career development requires that information continually reinforce planfulness; the interaction of educational or training alternatives, occupational alternatives, and self-characteristics is mandatory if good career decision making is to occur. Suggestions for enhancing the interaction of these topics have been offered in Chapter 14. People will have different needs for career information depending on their developmental stage in the career life cycle (Bloch, 1989), on their learning styles (McCormac, 1989), and, perhaps, on their sex (Wolleat, 1989).

This chapter suggests processes to achieve the goals for career guidance offered earlier in this book. It offers a range of delivery systems by which the concepts, knowledge, and attitudes integral to career development can be attuned to the needs and characteristics of the various consumer publics. It seeks to identify the range of possibilities available within the many facets of the educational enterprise and within the community for reinforcing vocationalization—for helping the individual develop a vocabulary of work, acquire necessary career knowledge, develop healthy career attitudes, learn adequate decision-making skills, and so forth. Specifically, we will set forth in this chapter some principles for effectively using information and discuss the evaluation of information, types of delivery systems, and illustrations of some of the more promising systems. We include also a discussion of the work of the National Occupational Information Coordinating Committee (NOICC) and its state counterparts (SOICCs). A sampling of some of the specific materials available is also presented. Because of space limitations, we will concentrate primarily on career information and downplay sources of educational and personal information.

The most reliable estimates say that over 7 million people in the process of career decision making each year use computers, manual systems, microfiche, or books to explore the worlds of work, training, and education (Association of Computer-Based Systems for Career Information, 1989).

PRINCIPLES FOR USING INFORMATION EFFECTIVELY

It is obvious that simple exposure to information is insufficient. The mere availability of information about occupations, educational and training opportunities, and the characteristics of an individual does not mean that the information will be used or, if used, that it will be employed effectively. In order to increase the probability that data will be efficiently utilized, one must consider aspects of motivation, the quality of the information, and how information is assimilated.

Motivation

Need is the sine qua non of effective information acquisition and processing. Readiness must be present, since almost all learning is a function of motivation. Motivation, in turn, is based on a person's attempt to satisfy a career-related need. In other words, no need, no action; no action, no career-related learning. Almost all learning theories place a premium on motivation, readiness, and the establishment of a learning set in the learner. Career guidance processes would do well to follow this example. To become motivated, individuals must be assisted to see how their needs are met by whatever information is delivered.

Acquiring information is a mandatory element of occupational exploration. Grotevant and Cooper (1986) conducted a study in which they demonstrated that the wider the career exploratory behaviors in which adolescents engaged, the more congruent their stated occupational choices with dimensions of ability, interests, and personality. M. S. Taylor (1985) has demonstrated some relationship between an individual's occupational knowledge (for example, education-training requirements, job conditions and characteristics, worker relationships, and job knowledge within specific area of study) and job offers for college undergraduates and graduates in management fields. Her study also suggests that occupational knowledge may enhance students' abilities to better present themselves to employers. The major source of students' occupational information seemed to be information provided by others (such as professors, people in a job, outside speakers). Thus, while the possession of good occupational information does not guarantee good decision making, it is unlikely that career decisions will be favorable without the incorporation of occupational information in the decision-making process. Further, having that information seems to have a payoff in terms of enhancing the likelihood of desired outcomes.

Motivation and the establishment of readiness pertain to all scholastic ability levels within an educational setting and to adults. Although there is some evidence that brighter students have more knowledge of high-level than low-level occupations, most research suggests that academic achievers are no more knowledgeable about occupations than are lower achievers, and that the social status of the students is also not a factor in the accuracy of information. The gifted student, for example, has some unique needs in terms of occupational information. Chapman and Katz (1983) have observed that although gifted high school students receive a great deal of educational information, largely related to accessing higher education, they are exposed to very little occupational information. Further, because they are multitalented, as they continue to explore information it constantly opens up new possibilities, often leading to the frustration of choice anxiety (Post-Kammer & Perrone, 1983). All of this has led Fredrickson (1986) to state that

> Gifted persons may be able to acquire and retain more information than most other persons, but

> the use of this information in a career-planning process is still a complex task requiring emotional support and assistance from parents, counselors, and teachers. Gifted students need just as much help as average students, if not more, in career planning. (p. 566)

Accuracy or inaccuracy of information extends to sex-related stereotypes. Yanico (1980) found that college females demonstrated a lack of information about occupations nontraditional for their sex. Males did not. These findings suggest that counselors should not make a priori assumptions regarding who needs occupational information and who does not.

Based on cognitive information processing (CIP) theory, Peterson, Sampson, and Reardon (1991) view the effective use of career information in counseling as a learning event. They maintain that any learning event consists of three components: "(1) an objective; that is, the capability to be acquired; (2) an intervention to bring about the desired capability; and (3) an evaluation to ascertain whether the objective was obtained" (p. 197). Clearly, if the use of career information in counseling is a learning event (and we agree that it is), then career counselors need to be cognizant of the psychology of learning and the learning principles derived from that psychology. This orientation is completely consistent with the cognitive/behavioral counseling approach outlined in Chapter 14.

They urge a CASVE (communication, analysis, synthesis, valuing, and execution) decision making process in which learning is the undergirding structure for decision making and information is required in each phase of the learning process. We have noted at several points in this volume that career decision making is sometimes more psychological than logical, but in those decision-making situations with which the majority of individuals are confronted in career planning and choice, a learning paradigm and the attendant utilization strategies for incorporating self, educational, and occupational information make a great deal of sense. The Peterson, Sampson, and Reardon volume devotes a great deal of space to an excellent discussion of the use of career information in the decision-making process. An example of the use of information in the CASVE cycle may be found in Table 15.1.

These findings point to the necessity of helping individuals learn to use information. This end can be accomplished only after a learning set has been established.

Some people believe that the acquisition of information—not simply occupational, but all types of information—is a fundamental life skill. Hudson and Danish (1980) identify sixteen major categories of life information needs, two of which are related to employment and to education and schooling. These are skills related to defining and locating needed information to cope with a variety of crucial life events.

Readiness and motivation, then, are requisite to the effective use of occupational information at any intervention point in one's life span. Readiness assumes that we can accurately measure the level of an individual's occupational information. There are some instruments available to do so, all of which measure the frequency and variety of vocational information-seeking behavior.

Evaluation of Information

A second factor in the effective use of information is the caliber of the data. Whatever the vehicle through which the information is transmitted—print, film, slide, record, computer, simulation, and such—there is a need to evaluate it in terms of some criteria of "good" information.

One important criterion is the source of the information. Some material is produced for recruitment, and although many such presentations are acceptable, some, because of their overzealousness, are misleading. Other mate-

Table 15.1

Career Information and the CASVE Cycle

Phase of the CASVE Cycle	Example of Career Information and Media
Communication (identifying a need)	A description of the personal and family issues that women typically face in returning to work (information) in a videotaped interview of currently employed women (medium)
Analysis (interrelating problem components)	Explanations of the basic education requirements for degree programs (information) in community college catalogues (medium)
Synthesis (creating likely alternatives)	A presentation of emerging nontraditional career options for women (information) at a seminar on career development for women (medium)
Valuing (prioritizing alternatives)	An exploration of how the roles of parent, spouse, citizen, leisurite, and homemaker would be affected by the assumption of the worker role (information) in an adult version of a computer-assisted career guidance system (medium)
Execution (forming means-ends strategies)	A description of a functional résumé emphasizing transferable skills, followed by the creation of a résumé (information) presented on a computer-assisted employability skills system (medium)

Source: *Career Development and Services: A Cognitive Approach* by G. W. Peterson, J. P. Sampson, and R. C. Reardon. Pacific Grove, CA: Brooks/Cole Publishing Company, 1991. Reprinted with permission.

rials are produced specifically for guidance purposes and thus can frequently be considered more accurate at face value, although there are always decisions made in relation to inclusion and exclusion in preparing information that affect its objectivity to some extent.

Other important considerations are the currency, validity, and applicability of the data. Currency refers to the up-to-date nature of the information. Newness does not guarantee accuracy, but it is likely that information will be more accurate if it is recent. Validity refers to the accuracy of the information, insofar as the data may be affected by such factors as the zealous recruitment motive discussed earlier. Finally, applicability may be considered from two points of view: (1) Are the data presented in such a manner that they can be easily utilized? (2) Is the level at which the data are presented appropriate to the consumer?

Periodically, the National Career Development Association's Career Information Review Service (CIRS) presents reviews of career and occupational information materials in the *Career Development Quarterly* (National Vocational Guidance Association, 1980) based on guidelines determined by the profession.

There are both general guidelines and content guidelines that cover the following areas:

General Guidelines

Accuracy of Information—current and nonbiased

Format—clear, concise, and interesting

Vocabulary—appropriate to target group

Bias and Stereotyping—gender-, race-, and religion-free information

Graphics—current and nonstereotyped

Dating and Revisions—frequent revisions required

Credits—who and where

Content Guidelines

Duties and Nature of the Work—purpose, activities, skills, specializations, and so on
Work Settings and Conditions—physical activities and work environment
Personal Qualifications—specific to a particular occupation
Social and Psychological Factors—satisfiers and limiters associated with an occupation; life-style implications
Preparation Required—length and type, cost, difficulty of entry
Special Requirements—physical, personal, licensing, and so on
Methods of Entering—typical and alternate approaches
Earnings and Other Benefits—current ranges
Usual Advancement Possibilities—typical career ladders
Employment Outlook—short and long range
Opportunities for Experience and Exploration—part-time, summer, volunteer, and so on
Related Occupations—alternate possibilities
Sources of Education and Training—schools, agencies, and so on
Sources of Additional Information—where to go, whom to see

There appears to be considerable agreement among both scholars in the field of occupational information and users of occupational information regarding the criteria of what constitutes "good" information (Bloch & Kinnison, 1989a, 1989b).

Use of Information

How individuals use information in career-related decision making is, in many respects, a highly personalized matter. Usually, information is assimilated, processed, and accepted or rejected in very complex and idiosyncratic ways. Just as the intake of information is individualized, so too is the output of information as it affects career-related decision making.

The field of cognitive science is one of today's "hottest" and most exciting occupational areas. How people process information has captured the attention of computer scientists, cognitive and educational psychologists, and others. Much of this interest is spurred by the desire to create artificial intelligence, but some of the interest is also stimulated simply by the desire to know how more effectively to teach people to engage in a variety of information processing tasks, ranging from learning the three Rs to using career information.

It is clear that people have different learning styles—ways in which they prefer to gather, organize, and process information (Gordon, Coscarelli, & Sears, 1986). This fact obviously affects how they handle occupational and educational information and can indicate how to best present such information to them. Sharf's (1984b) study of occupational information-seeking behavior, for example, indicates that styles of occupational information-seeking vary from client to client; therefore, it is logical to make individual recommendations for occupational information seeking rather than to suggest uniformity to a group of students. He further determined that high school students did not examine all types of occupational information with equal care. He found that descriptions of occupations seem to be read most often, followed by educational information, qualifications, and salary. Students seem to be least interested in working conditions, employment outlook, and more information.

One principle that seems to have been fairly well established through research is that behavioral reinforcement techniques are highly effective in promoting career information-seeking behaviors. Whether used with individuals or with groups, if motivation is present or lacking, verbal reinforcement of information-seeking statements of counselees apparently produces more information-seeking behaviors than not reinforcing. In a sense, counselors are establishing and stimulating a readiness of the type previously discussed.

The role of information in career decision making has not been clearly established. We have some preliminary research from Pitz and Harren (1980) that suggests that a person will seek information only if the perceived payoff is greater than the cost of the information. They cite the example of the impulsive decision maker who wants to terminate the decision process as quickly as possible and who thus makes a decision with minimum information. An agonizing decision maker, on the other hand, "may continually seek information to avoid the act of commitment to a particular choice and its attendant course of action" (p. 325). We do know that occupational information influences occupational perceptions and that the same information can produce varied perceptions on the basis of the perceiver's age and occupational status.

We know also that receiving occupational information tends to increase the simplicity with which one perceives occupations. Learning theorists call this phenomenon *cognitive complexity*.

What is more, the *type* of occupational information also affects cognitive complexity; that is, negative information is likely to produce a less simplified view of an occupation, whereas positive information decreases cognitive complexity (Haase, Reed, Winer, & Bodden, 1979). These studies suggest giving career decision makers both the positive and negative information about an occupation. Since most information now is either neutral or positive, these findings would argue for more description of negative features. Neimeyer (1988, 1989a, 1989b), Neimeyer, Brown, Metzler, Hagans, and Tanguy (1989), Neimeyer, Metzler, and Bowman (1988), Neimeyer, Nevill, Probert, and Fukuyama (1985), and Nevill, Neimeyer, Probert, and Fukuyama (1985) draw upon personal construct theory to explain how people utilize occupational information in the process of career decision making. Whether processing information cognitively or intuitively, people, according to this theory, tend to set up bipolar constructs (for instance, high versus low salary). Individuals will have different sets of bipolar constructs that are important to them; therefore, career information needs to be tailored to the individual. On the other hand, increasing occupational information per se has been found not to lead to an increase in vocational *differentiation* (the number of different judgments and more cognitively complex processes used by the individual). The explanation may lie in the concept of *integration* (how dimensions are organized into an interrelated system of perceptions). In general, the higher the differentiation *and* integration, the more effective the occupational decision making according to a variety of criteria (for instance, self-efficacy, career exploration, recall of information, conflict, and so on).

Finally, it would appear that the level of occupational knowledge can affect even our most basic tools of the trade. There are two ways to assess vocational preferences; by expressing preferences for job titles (such as mechanic) or by expressing preferences for behavioral activities (such as fixing a motor). Loesch and Sampsom (1978) conducted research that suggests strongly that a client's job knowledge is related to the manner of assessing vocational preferences. Those with low-level knowledge should be assessed by behavioral activity preferences; those with high-level knowledge should be assessed on the basis of occupational titles.

Individualizing information appears to be a key requirement for its effective use. This means that there is a variety of approaches for gathering information and the effectiveness of these approaches will vary from individual to individual. As the counselor helps individuals

Table 15.2

Types of Treatment and Interventions Recommended as a Function of Level of Information Processing

Level of information processing	Treatment characteristics	Sample intervention
Very high	*Little needed* Brief, information focused	Assessment (e.g., MIQ, SDS) Occupational information Computer-assisted guidance
High	*Weak supportive* Mentor Short-term information and decision focused	Assessment, brief counseling Occupational information Brief discussion either individual or group based Career workshops
Medium	*Insight* Longer term Broad focus	Analysis of coping/problem solving skills Individual counseling Career course
Low	*Strong supportive* Active guide Longer term Remedial Narrow focus	Teach, instruct, guide Individual counseling

Source: From "Trait-and-Factor to Person-Environment Fit Counseling: Theory and Process" by J. B. Rounds and T. J. Tracey in *Career Counseling: Contemporary Topics in Vocational Psychology,* edited by W. B. Walsh and S. H. Osipow. Copyright © 1990 by Lawrence Erlbaum Associates, Publishers. Reprinted by permission.

to sort through, comprehend, assimilate, and find meaning in information, the effectiveness or lack of effectiveness of such data becomes apparent.

Personalization of career information should indeed be paramount in the counselor's mind. Discussing client information processing in career interventions, Rounds and Tracey (1990, p. 31) propose that the level of the client's information processing should determine the counselor's type of intervention. In general, the higher the level of processing, the more straightforward the intervention. Table 15.2 presents their paradigm.

Drier (1980) has quite rightly indicated that career information is not simply career facts or job data. Career information results, he maintains, when a user attaches personal meaning to information. Borow (1980) also reminds us of two other essentials of occupational information, at least at the secondary school level. He argues that it should be presented to broaden the range of options and stimulate exploration rather than narrow choices and hurry decisions. And he urges that occupational information should evidence greater cognizance of the psychosocial characteristics of work, such as the interpersonal factors and peculiar values identified with various types of work.

Herr (1980) maintains that, again in terms of secondary schools, career information is deficient because (1) it tends to be primarily national rather than state or local and lacks local experience data; (2) it is more useful to adults who are making decisions than to students who are exploring; (3) there is little sharing between the Employment Service and schools; and (4) we have reached few clear conclusions about student uses of information. It is appropriate at this point to survey the types of delivery systems currently available in order to evaluate their potential effectiveness.

TYPES OF DELIVERY SYSTEMS

R. C. Reardon (1984) classifies occupational information into two categories: noninteractive media (such as print, audio, paper-and-pencil inventories, and so on) and interactive (such as computer-assisted career guidance systems, card sorts, structured interviews, and so on).

Until relatively recently, virtually all occupational information was printed and was primarily descriptive (Flanders & Baxter, 1981). Beginning with the *Dictionary of Occupational Titles*, information became more complex and comprehensive and the possibilities for alternate ways of transmitting it became more numerous. The problem before us is a basic and complicated one—the acquisition, storage, retrieval, and dissemination of information. The information or knowledge explosion is a well-known reality. Knowledge in some fields doubles itself every few years. The generation of new knowledge, in fact, as achieved by various research and development programs, is mainly responsible for the changing occupational structure as described in Chapter 3. New jobs and occupations come about because new products, services, and industries evolve from new knowledge; these new jobs, in turn, generate more new jobs and occupations.

Occupational half-lives are continually constricting (Patterson, 1985). The occupational half-life is the amount of time it takes for one-half of the knowledge, training, and skills for an occupation to become obsolete. On average, it is four or five years and decreasing (for example, for technical occupations it is about eighteen months). The assault of information and new knowledge forces us to grope with new methods for storing the information so that it can be retrieved with maximum efficiency and disseminated in the most effective manner. McDaniels (1982) has urged that any future system of comprehensive career information must be built on four foundations:

1. Wide-ranging multimedia approach
2. Wide-ranging location of systems
3. Wide-ranging appeal to users
4. Wide range of sources of career information

The various delivery systems are outlined in the following pages along with representative listings of some of the more common modes.

Printed Matter

The most common and traditional form for career information is published material. These materials range from occupational briefs to the *Dictionary of Occupational Titles* and the *Occupational Outlook Handbook*, from biographies to popular magazines, from booklets, catalogues, and brochures to newspapers. There are diverse prepackaged or home-grown systems available. McDaniels (1980) points out that when counselors adopt a ready-made career information system, they are "buying a theory of career development; a type of access strategy; an evaluation of the appropriateness of the data base; a determination of the counselor component in the system; and a preselected point of counselor intervention" (p. 30). These are decisions that, in effect, are taken away from the counselor, with the quid pro quo being the convenience of the system.

There are all sorts of ways to file printed information. These are described in detail in several excellent texts (see, for example, S. T. Brown & D. Brown, 1990). Also a comprehensive article by C. H. Green (1979) discusses the various accessing systems, ranging from alphabetic to taxonomic.

Unfortunately, experience with occupational and educational literature indicates that all these systems present dissemination problems. The data are easily stored and readily retrieved, but they appear to be insufficiently utilized. Perhaps the motivation of the individual is missing. Perhaps the effort of reading is too much. Perhaps the printed material is dry and uninspiring. Whatever the reason, it is clear that although students are aware of the types of printed information the school has stored and know that it can be retrieved, they do not generally make use of the information. Likewise, adults surely know that they can get information at their public library, but they do not frequently exercise that option. It is apparent that methods other than or in addition to traditional printed materials are necessary or that counselors must deal more effectively with motivational concerns if individuals are to use printed data more extensively.

Acquisition of Information

The acquisition of educational and occupational information is a continual and formidable process. It requires a constant monitoring of commercial catalogues, professional publications, and other sources. Counselors must try to keep current with newer materials. The best way to do so is to consult the *Career Development Quarterly*, which offers periodic reviews of current career literature. There are several bibliographic sources that contain much useful information. Some of the more prominent compendia follow:

- *Career Index*, Moravia, New York: Chronicle Guidance Publications. An annual compilation of an annotated list of occupational and educational guidance materials available from about 700 public and private organizations.
- *A Counselor's Guide to Occupational Information*, Washington, D.C.: U.S. Department of Labor, Bureau of Labor Statistics, July 1980 (Bulletin 2042). An annotated listing of all government publications relating to careers and issued prior to the summer of 1979.
- M. H. Saterstrom (Ed.). *Educators Guide to Free Guidance Materials*, Randolph, Wisc.: Educators Progress Service, Inc., annual. Listing of almost 2500 free films, filmstrips and slides, tapes, scripts, and printed materials that are yours for the asking.
- *Counselor's Information Service*, Washington, D.C.: B'nai B'rith Career and Counseling Services. Published four times per year, this newsletter presents an annotated bibliography of current literature on educational and vocational guidance. Special sections on adult education and the aging and on handicapped and rehabilitation counseling.
- *ACDA Bibliography of Current Career Information* (7th edition). Washington, D.C.: National Career Development Association, 1980. Lists and evaluates, according to ACDA standards, over 2300 books, pamphlets, films, and so on.

Table 15.3 lists several references to occupational filing systems and to printed volumes that are useful for various career guidance purposes. This table is preceded by a listing of magazines and journals devoted to career guidance, as well as a sampling of aids of particular interest to college students and adults.

The following magazines and journals are devoted wholly or in part to career guidance.

Career World–Curriculum Innovations, Highwood, Ill. Published monthly during the school years.

American Education–U.S. Department of Health, Education, and Welfare/Office of Education. Published ten times per year.

Career Education Digest–Education Properties. Published monthly during the school year.

Career Development Quarterly–(formerly *Vocational Guidance Quarterly*). National Career Development Association. Published four times per year.

Table 15.3

A Sampling of Printed Matter

Name	Publisher	Description
Occupational Filing Systems		
Careerdex	Career Associates	1000+ card-file guide to sources of career information
Career Information Kit	Science Research Associates	600 pieces of current literature filed alphabetically by job families. Cross-referenced by Dewey Decimal System
Career Kits and Career Opportunity Boxes	Houghton Mifflin	5 boxes of job information (100–125 cards each) relating to English, social studies, math, foreign languages, and science
Mini-Briefs	Occupational Awareness	Data regarding 1800 occupations related to school subject matter areas
Occupational Library	Chronicle Guidance Publications, Inc.	Over 650 occupations by DOT classification. Supplemented by microfiche and viewdecks. An excellent resource
COPSystem Career Briefs Kit	EdiTS	Over 400 cards describing occupations and organized by cluster sets. Tide to COPSystem interest inventory
Occu-File	Career Aids	346 briefs
Printed Volumes		
Concise Handbook of Occupations	Doubleday & Company	300+ jobs described
Dictionary of Occupational Titles	U.S. Department of Labor	Described in detail elsewhere in this volume. A primary resource

Journal of Career Development–(formerly *Journal of Career Education*).

Monthly Labor Review–U.S. Department of Labor.

Work and Occupations (formerly *Sociology of Occupations*)–Sage Publications. Published four times per year.

Journal of Counseling Psychology–American Psychological Association. Published four times per year.

Journal of Vocational Behavior–Academic Press, Inc. Published four times per year.

Journal of Counseling and Development–AACD. Published 12 times per year.

American Vocational Journal–American Vocational Association. Published ten times per year.

Journal of Employment Counseling–National Employment Counselors Association. Published four time per year.

Journal of College Placement–College Placement Council. Published four times per year.

Measurement and Evaluation in Counseling and Development–Association for Measurement and Evaluation in Counseling and Development. Published four times per year.

Table 15.3 (Continued)

Name	Publisher	Description
Printed Volumes		
Encyclopedia of Careers and Vocational Guidance (Hopke)	J.G. Ferguson Co.	650 occupations and 71 articles
Guide to Careers through College Majors and Guide to Careers through Vocational Training	Educational and Industrial Testing Service	As the titles suggest
Handbook of Job Facts	Science Research Associates	300 major occupations
Occupational Outlook Handbook and Occupational Outlook Quarterly	U.S. Department of Labor	Trends and outlook in over 800 occupations and industries with a quarterly supplement. Another primary resource
Vocational Biographies	Vocational Biographies, Inc.	Almost 400 biographies
The College Handbook and the *College Handbook Index of Majors*	College Entrance Examination Board	Descriptions of over 2000 colleges and universities and indications of what majors are availabe where
Profiles of American Colleges, Vols. I and II	Barron's	Over 1400 colleges and universities described
Guide to Two-Year Colleges, Vols. I and II	Barron's	Information on over 1200 community colleges
College Learning Anytime, Anywhere	Harcourt, Brace, Jovanovich	Alternatives to a traditional college education
Comparative Guide to American Colleges and *Comparative Guide to Two-Year Colleges and Career Programs*	Harper & Row	Descriptions as indicated in titles with special emphasis on admissions criteria
Peterson's Annual Guides to Graduate Study	Peterson's Guides	Graduate and professional programs described in general or by specialty area
Opportunities in *Career Decisions* *Professional Careers* *Looking at Careers*	VGM Career	Work Series

Occupational Outlook Quarterly-U.S. Department of Labor. Published four times per year.

The following is a sampling of aids for college students and adults.[1]

[1]This list is presented solely as a more or less random sampling of the scores of books in this genre. Inclusion is not necessarily an endorsement of any book.

Barkhaus, R. S., Adair, M. K., Hoover, A. B., & Bolyand, C. W. (1985). *Threads: A tapestry of self and career exploration* (3rd ed.). Dubuque, IA: Kendall/Hunt Publishing Company.

Blocher, D. H. (1989). *Career actualization and life planning*. Denver: Love Publishing Company.

Bolles, R. N. (1991). *What color is your parachute?* Berkeley: Ten Speed Press.

Carney, C. G., & Wells, C. F. (1991). *Discover the career within you* (3rd ed.). Pacific Grove, CA: Brooks/Cole Publishing Company.

Cetron, M., & Davies, O. (1988). *The great job shake-out: How to find a new career after the crash*. New York: Simon and Schuster.

Figler, H. (1989). *Liberal education and careers today.* Garrett Park, MD: The Garrett Park Press.

Flores-Esteves, M. (1985) *Life after Shakespeare: Careers for liberal arts majors*. New York: Penguin Books.

Hecklinger, F. J., & Curtin, B. M. (1987). *Training for life: A practical guide to career and life planning*. Dubuque, IA: Kendall/Hunt.

Krannich, C. & Krannich, R. (1990). *Interview for success: A practical guide to increasing job interviews, offers, and salaries*. Woodbridge, VA: Impact Publications.

Leeds, D. (1991). *Marketing yourself: The ultimate job seeker's guide*. New York: Harper Collins Publishers.

Lott, C. S., & Lott, O. C. (1989). *How to land a better job*. Lincolnwood, IL: VGM Career Horizons.

Mitchell, J. S. (1990). *The College Board guide to jobs and career planning*. New York: College Board Publications.

Schwartz, L., & Brechner, I. (1985). *Career tracks*. New York: Ballantine Books.

Strother, J. A., & Marshall, D. R. (1990). *The right fit: An educator's career handbook and employment guide*. Scottsdale, AZ: Gorsuch Scarisbrick, Publishers.

Sukiennik, D., Raufman, L., & Bendat. W. (1986). *The career fitness program: Exercising your options*. Scottsdale, AZ: Gorsuch Scarisbrick, Publishers.

Media Approaches

In addition to printed matter, various audio and visual means of disseminating information are used: bulletin boards and exhibits, commercial, educational, and closed-circuit television, slides, films, records, cassettes, filmstrips, microfilm, and microfiche. At the elementary school level, activities in this category might even include "show and tell" exercises.

The use of an audio aid often encourages students to seek additional career counseling and is an effective way to disseminate occupational information.

A multimedia approach is valuable, especially with low-motivation counselees and with adults.

One of the best known systems is the Vocational Information for Education and Work (VIEW) system that is now over twenty years old and is used in about forty states. It has a microfiche format. Gerstein (1983) sees it as satisfying and effective and superior to other traditional ways of disseminating career information. He does acknowledge, however, that it will one day likely be replaced by a computerized system. The primary advantage of the VIEW system is that it can be tailored to provide information specific to any local labor market.

Colleges and universities now produce their own recruiting videotapes, and students can call 900 numbers to receive, for a fee, a description of many colleges (e.g. 1-900-420-1212–Campus Searchline). Many high schools and colleges also tape the visits of campus and corporate recruiters so that students may view the tapes at their convenience.

Audio and visual approaches provide an interesting and sense-appealing method of transmitting information. The career education movement stimulated a remarkable number of multimedia approaches to occupational information. Table 15.4 represents a sampling of that prodigious output.

Interview Approaches

Educational or occupational information can be gathered by a variety of person-to-person and group interactions with individuals who represent various careers, occupations, jobs, and educational institutions or with individuals also learning about the world of work or educational opportunities. The career confer-

Table 15.4

Examples of Career Guidance Media

Name	Publisher	Description
Films		
Library of Career Counseling Films	Counselor Films, Inc.	Over 30 films and sound filmstrips on the work world
Bread and Butterflies	Agency for Instructional Television	15 TV programs on careers for 9–12 year olds
The Working Worlds	Olympus Publishing	13 films on career clusters
Project WERC Film Series	American Association for Counseling and Development	World of work exploration
Vocational Films	Houghton Mifflin	10 films on general and specific aspects of work
Other Media		
Career Development for Children Project (E)	McKnight	Career awareness, work activities, self awareness
Introduction to Careers Series		Exploration of various careers
DUSO: Developing Understanding of Self and Others (E)	American Guidance Service, Inc.	Understanding social and emotional behavior
TAD: Toward Affective Development (E)		Psychological or affective education
Career Awareness Field Trips (E)	Guidance Associates	7 programs to simulate field trips to various industries
Career Values: What Really Matters to You?		Personal values and career decisions
Changing Work Ethic		Work attitudes and jobs
Jobs and Gender		Sex and career choice
Jobs for High School Students		Entry level jobs
The Paycheck Puzzle		Economic awareness
You and Your Job Interview		How-to-do-it
What You Should Know Before You Go to Work		Employer expectations
Choosing Your Career		Holland's typology and choice
Job Hunting: Where to Begin		Sources of employment information
Career Discoveries Series		6 job groups explored
High School as a Tryout		Career exploration through high school
Focus on Self-Development (E)	Science Research Associates	Self-understanding and understanding of others and the environment

Table 15.4 (Continued)

Name	Publisher	Description
Job Family Series Booklets and Cassettes		Jobs and the clusters
Decision-Making for Career Development		Workbooks and cassettes
WORK: Widening Occupational Roles Kit		Career exploration
KEYS: Career Exploration Program		Career exploration related to interests
KNOW: Knowledge Needed to Obtain Work		64 transparencies related to selecting and applying for a job
Got a Job Interview? Learn the Skills	Pleasantville Media	Videocassette and teacher's guide
Self-Image and Your Career		Videocassette and teacher's guide
Career Awareness Series	Aims Instructional Media Services	Scopes of work in various career areas
Real People at Work (E)	Changing Times	Resource kits K–6
Career Directions: Planning for Career Decisions	Educational Service	4 units for career planning
Career Awareness Laboratory	Singer Career Systems	Electronic media and gaming for career awareness
Careers in Focus	McGraw-Hill	Career exploration and self-discovery
Job Lab 1 and Job Lab 2	Houghton Mifflin	Career exploration via job description cards for elementary and secondary
Vocational Skills for Tomorrow	Coronet	Bilingual career decision-making for non-college bound
Career Training	Westinghouse	6 filmstrips and cassettes and teacher's guide on the how, what, and where of career training
Vocational and Career Planning	Cambridge Career Products	Videotapes
Career Directions	Changing Times Eductional Service	Six units ranging from deciding on a career to work behaviors; filmstrips, cassettes, spirit masters, and teacher's guide
Job Interview Skills	Sunburst	3 filmstrips and cassettes and a teacher's guide
How to Make Good Decisions		Filmstrips on videocassette
COPSystem Occupational Cluster Charts	EdiTS	Visual display of occupations related to COPS clusters
Video Career Library	Chronicle Guidance	20 clusters of occupations
How to Get the Job You Really Want	JIST Works, Inc.	Videotape

(E) = Primarily for elementary school use

ence or career day is one such approach. Here adult individuals represent their vocations, and students are free to talk with or listen to as many as possible within a restricted amount of time. The dangers inherent in this procedure are many: superficial or selective coverage of an occupational area, overemphasis on function to the exclusion of self-factors, proselytizing in the most negative sense, circus atmosphere, and such. Students sometimes go to hear people who represent jobs and occupations in which they are already interested and about which they already know something; thus, no new possibilities are explored. An educational analogue of this activity is the college night. In some cases, a professional organization (such as an AACD branch) organizes and conducts a regional job and educational opportunities fair (Pate, Tulloch, & Dassance, 1981).

This trade fair type of approach can be available to individuals if it is preceded by adequate preparation and followed by ample opportunity for feedback. A remarkably effective program of this type was conducted by Ms. Pam Wise, then a counselor in the Clarence, New York, schools. After determining that the tentative career choices of girls in her high school were typically constricted, she planned and implemented, conjointly with teachers, one-week units in both English and social studies classes. During these sessions, topics ranged from factual material to attitudes relating to women and work. An all-day career conference was held on three successive days; forty carefully briefed women in atypical female careers were brought into the school and interacted with students. Students were excused from class to attend as many sessions as they wished over the three days. All sessions were videotaped to allow students to view any career presentation later that they could not personally attend. Evaluations showed that a large proportion of the girls indicated that they were exploring nontraditional careers as a result of the experience.

In a similar but more in-depth approach, students interview workers in various jobs or personnel directors who are familiar with the requirements of a relatively wide range of jobs. Students are not limited to those occupations represented at a career conference; they can explore any occupation available in the community. Students may be given an interview guide to ensure that important aspects of the occupation are covered in the conference. Again, however, this approach assumes that the student has some prior interest in an occupation and seeks to broaden his or her knowledge of it.

A still more detailed and thorough approach is the job analysis. In this case, students supplement direct-interview data with information gathered from other sources, such as occupational literature. Although this technique offers a comprehensive and intensive view of a single occupation, it can be a tedious exercise that turns off students if their motivation, either intrinsic or extrinsic, is not relatively strong.

A final interview-type approach to occupational information is the job clinic. Whereas the career conference has long-range goals, the emphasis in the job clinic is on immediate goals, usually job placement. The job clinic brings together many individuals who have jobs to offer. Other individuals who need jobs come to the clinic and decide whether their attributes and interests match the available jobs. This type of activity is most common in employment agencies and college placement centers.

Simulation Approaches

There are many simulation or gaming techniques by which counselees can vicariously explore careers as well as educational opportunities. Simulation must be used properly—that is, not in isolation as an end in itself but along with meaningful discussion, follow-up, and explanatory material. Simulation is valuable in that it brings down to manageable proportions a very complicated aspect of life. Although there is some disagreement about the relative merits of simulation, most agree that career exploration through work simulation is effective and that it stimulates students to seek additional information.

The simplest form of simulation is role-playing. For example, individuals may role-play job interviews in order to become more relaxed and prepared when an actual employment interview comes. They may also dramatize potential conflicts in work situations (for example, supervisor-worker tensions) on the premise that such an exercise will serve as a preventive function when a similar situation is encountered in a real work situation.

Taking role-playing a step further, groups of individuals can be exposed to an occupation by means of a role model. Role models may be present in the form of a person, a film, or literature. Role models tell what they do, but, more important, they relate the personal meaning of their work—satisfactions, frustrations, and so on. In short, they give a picture of the kinds of people they are and help the group try for a short time to be a member of the occupation they represent. For example, a psychologist might present the group with a case study on a client and invite the group to attempt a diagnosis and to prescribe treatment. After the role model has been presented, counselees are asked to engage in reflective thinking, to compare and contrast what they know about themselves with what they know about the role model and the role model's work. Thus, individuals vicariously explore the personal relevance of a particular occupation. This type of activity calls for the individual to use educational, occupational, and personal-social information in an integrated manner.

Another potentially valuable simulation technique is gaming. Perhaps the best known occupational game is the Life Career Game, developed by Boocock (1968). The goals are to provide high school and college students with some ideas about the contours of the future, information about occupational and educational alternatives or opportunities, a feeling for the total life cycle of an individual, and practice in decision making. The game is played by teams of from two to fifteen students, who compete against each other in making decisions about a fictitious individual for eight years into the future. Through this simulation, students presumably acquire an understanding of the labor market, educational opportunities, marriage, and leisure patterns.

Career clubs provide still another type of simulation activity. Future Teachers of America and Distributive Education Clubs are examples of this approach. In the former, youngsters with an interest in teaching as a career can hear speakers, go on field trips, and sometimes actually gain some experience in teaching. Prelaw, premedicine, and other professions-related clubs are also in operation. In Distributive Education Clubs, students gain real experience in setting up and running a business enterprise.

Another type of simulation experience—job sampling—is simultaneously an assessment procedure. For example, the Singer Vocational Evaluation System provides actual work sample tasks for a variety of trade and skilled occupations. While the counselee is heuristically exploring some of the occupational functions, the counselor is able to assess aptitudes, attitudes, and interests. This system is but one example of numerous hands-on techniques for exploration. A related technique is that of "shadowing," whereby individuals are permitted to spend time on the job observing a worker who is engaged in an occupation in which they might have an interest.

Field Trips

Field trips (to plants, offices, educational institutions, and so on) are a common method of gaining occupational and educational information. The opportunity to see work performed in an actual job setting and to interview those who perform the jobs, or the opportunity to get the feel of an educational institution can be a valuable experience. Too often, however, field trips are accomplished only en masse with little or no thought given to the interests of students. It is likely that a field trip program, individualized to the extent that arrangements can be made for a single student's visit, will be a better program, at least in relation to the exploratory phase of career development. Group trips can be useful, especially for career awareness and for expanding the educational and career worlds of the culturally different, but they must be preceded by careful planning and followed up with feedback.

Follow-up or debriefing activities include discussions individually and in groups, regarding the values gained from the trip. Such questions as, How does the information that I gained relate to me? and How does what I observed affect my decision making? are appropriate.

Baca (1980) reports on an EXPO Program (Exploring Possible Occupations) for secondary school students. Monthly field trips to occupational sites were combined with speakers who gave presentations at the school. The student evaluations were most positive, although the participants were volunteers, and one might expect a positive evaluation under these circumstances. It is also possible to videotape field trips into local workplaces. Videotaping is a relatively inexpensive technique in institutions that already have the necessary hardware. It may be an acceptable alternative or supplement to actual field trips, which frequently entail insurance, transportation, and supervision problems.

Field trips as exploration can be accomplished on a group or on an individual basis. Given what we have reported earlier in this chapter about the benefits of individualizing exploratory experiences, the individual, tailor-made approach is useful. Satisfactory results, for example, were reported by Heitzmann, Schmidt, and Hurley (1986) at Memphis State University in a Career Encounters Program. In this program,

1. The student works individually with a career counselor and uses career resources, such as books, filmstrips, and computer programs, before arranging a career encounter.
2. The student completes a short application and agrees to spend a day or part of a day with a sponsor.
3. After an interview with the program coordinator, who outlines the kind of experience desired, the student is encouraged to become as familiar as possible with the career through reading and research in the Career Library.
4. A sponsor working in the desired occupation is contacted.
5. The student is provided with the sponsor's name and work telephone number and is then responsible for making the final plans—setting a specific date and time and arranging to meet the sponsor on the selected day.
6. When the visit has been completed, the student reviews the visit with the program coordinator and career counselor to evaluate the visit and consider appropriate follow-up in the form of additional reading, counseling sessions, or other career encounters.

By observing a career *in situ*, the client acquires necessary career information and is an active participant in the process. Another program of on-site visitations to industries to enhance exploration in science and technology careers is reported by Burkhalter, Curtis, Toppins, and Mickler (1983).

Formal Curriculum Approach

Certain aspects of career development are perhaps best effected by means of structured and direct teaching-learning. The question is, which of these experiences can be learned within an existing curriculum structure and which require a career guidance curriculum separate from subject matter classes? The career education strategy of infusion is consistent with developmental theory and, as research has demonstrated, it has proven effective when adequately planned and implemented. The great advantage of infusion is that in addition to career learnings, it seems to be a potent force in increasing student achievement. The state of New York, for example, now requires specified units of career-related instruction for all junior high school students in what used to be required home economics classes. On the other hand, the effectiveness of "acceleration" in career guidance has been repeatedly demonstrated in cited studies. Especially at secondary education, higher education, and adult levels, the use of concentrated intensive workshops, seminars, and courses has been shown to achieve desired goals of career guidance.

We do not want to imply that infusion and separate career guidance courses are an either-or proposition. Both can be useful. Our impressions of the career education infusion methodology is that in the elementary grades through junior high school, teachers have generally embraced the concept. At the senior high school and higher educational levels, teacher resistance has appeared to be more marked; consequently, infusion has been less successful. Infusion may well be the primary method in elementary and middle schools, and discrete, structured career guidance group experiences the primary delivery mode beyond the middle school level. In either case, a systematic, planned program is required.

Direct Experience

The axiom that the best way to learn something is to do it probably holds true for the acquisition of information. Direct work experience clearly allows an individual to learn a great deal about a specific job and about the experience of work. Work experience is, therefore, a valuable strategy in career guidance. Many schools offer work experience programs and many job training programs provide on-the-job training. In schools, distributive education students are freed from academic courses for a half-day to work in retail establishments. This cooperation provides on-the-job training and the benefit of experiential learning. Increasing numbers of collegiate institutions are offering work-study programs. Part-time and summer jobs also provide exploratory opportunities that make the individual more occupationally aware. Again, however, these opportunities increase in value as participants have a chance for feedback to reinforce or stimulate career learnings.

Industrial "shadow" experiences are another form of acquiring experience of a sort. These visits to industry to observe and to experience work *in situ* are valuable for both counselors and students. For several years, the General Electric Company sponsored shadow experiences for counselors in order to give them a more realistic view of the work world. Counselees can also shadow workers for anywhere from a day to a week. Industry-education councils are also doing a great deal to provide valuable first hand observations and experience for counselors and for students.

Computers

Throughout this chapter, a recurrent theme has been that "traditional" methods of occupational information acquisition, storage, retrieval, and dissemination have not proved to be as effective as desired. There are many possible reasons for this relative failure. In some cases, programs have been spontaneously mounted with no thought of what came before or of what would come after; they have lacked adequate preparation and feedback opportunities. Whatever the reasons, we are not suggesting that counselors give up traditional approaches. They require little expenditure of money, no fantastic hardware, and no new educational system. It is equally clear, however, that a systematic approach to career guidance can utilize technology effectively.

Electronic data processing techniques were touted in the late 1960s and early 1970s as a potentially revolutionary mode for career guidance. Only now are they beginning to live up to the great promise. In the last 10 years scores of projects have attempted to use computer technology in career guidance. Some are merely information vehicles; others are more ambitious, attempting something closer to an interactive counseling approach. Although the promise has not yet been completely fulfilled, the great potential is still there. So, too, are the potential pitfalls and disadvantages, ranging from the failure to accommodate human factors to the vulnerability of confidentiality (Sampson, 1983). For these reasons and others, Sampson and Pyle (1983) urge that counselors mediate person-machine systems. Counselors can help to assuage problems of user anxiety that might impede effective use of a system: inadequately prepared users who are not at ease with the process of a system, inadequate follow-up after the counselee has accessed and experienced a system, out-of-date or inaccurate information in a system, and malfunctions or improper working of a system.

Unfortunately, the use of technology is not accomplished without concomitant problems. The financial outlay necessary for even simple turnkey computer usage can range from minimal to expensive, depending on the extent of hardware, software, and personnel (Maze, 1985). In fact, Krumboltz (1985) argues that, in many cases, there may well be less expensive ways to accomplish the same purposes. He further suggests additional presuppositions underlying computer use in counseling that are caveats to effective service delivery: programs may violate what we know about career development; computer use may lead to a lack of depth in career exploration; computer interventions may not take a lifelong focus; and certain programs may take decision making out of the hands of the client.

Preliminary designs of more comprehensive and theory-based computerized systems of career assistance address these concerns. For example, Crites (1985) reports on the development of a microcomputer system that combines occupational information and assessment in assisting individuals in mastering both the content and the process of career choice.

The use of technology opens other concerns. Counseling technology forces individuals to come to grips with their personal values and goals, which might otherwise remain unexamined. The result is frequently conflict. But this is true for much of career guidance. Invasion of privacy, or lack of safeguards for confidentiality, also can be troublesome. Faddism, intemperate usage, and depersonalization are further possible outcomes of the technology.

Counselors may be resistant to using computers because of a relatively unsophisticated mathematical orientation that makes counselors feel inadequate in relation to the computer's complexity, the computer's accuracy in contrast to the counselor's fallibility, the fear of a loss of autonomy, and the perceived deterministic character of the computer. Yet, with judicious planning and utilization, technology can provide a strong weapon among many in the counselor's arsenal.

Counselors have utilized computers in career guidance in three ways. In the first application, computers serve as data processing tools for counselors by storing counselee data and subsequently retrieving them in various ways. Second, computers are used as substitutes for some counselor functions that go beyond simple information processing. Here one may think in terms of reference systems that often permit the user and the computer to engage in a dialogue. Examples are the matching of students and colleges or the matching of workers and jobs (such as Employment Service job data banks). In a third application, the machine is viewed as a substitute counselor, at least for some counseling functions that involve systematic, consistent, and selective use of a limited number of simple skills (such as Student Interactive Guidance and Information System).

Computerized informational systems are typically based on one or another of the occupational classifications as described in Chapter 3 and one or another of the career development theories as described in Chapter 4. The DISCOVER II program, for example, incorporates Super's developmental stages and Tiedeman and O'Hara's decision-making model along with the data-people-things orientation of the DOT and the Holland categories and the World-of-Work Map.

Studies that report on the effectiveness of the use of the computer in career guidance are generally positive. A study by Pinder and Fitzgerald (1984) is typical of studies that evaluate the relative effectiveness of computer-mediated interventions compared with some other delivery mode. In this case, the evaluation was of a Canadian system, Computerized Heuristic Occupational Information and Exploration System (CHOICES). This system provides both information and guidance functions. It was utilized with 136 undergraduate and graduate students in Florida (64 control and 72 experimental). Pre- and post-measures were obtained on the Career Decision Scale (CDS). Assessment of Career Decision Making (ACDM), using the exploration section of CHOICES. The conclusion was that the use of CHOICES as a treatment does increase the career decision making of students in higher education as demonstrated in their pre- and post-scores on the ACDM and CDS.

In a comprehensive study of career planning among college students, Garis (1982) compared the effects of (1) the DISCOVER Career Guidance and Counselor Support system, (2) individual career counseling, and (3) combined DISCOVER/career counseling use. The 67 college student subjects were randomly assigned to treatments or control conditions and given a variety of pretest and posttest measures of progress in career planning. Selected results were as follows:

1. All treatments produced positive effects on subjects' self-rated progress in educational/career planning as compared to the control group.
2. The DISCOVER use contributed to greater subject use of the career library than the counseling-only condition.
3. The career counseling treatment was more effective than DISCOVER in stimulating subject contacts with career resource persons or services that could provide further assistance with educational/career planning.
4. Indications that the combined DISCOVER/counseling treatment produced stronger effects on career planning progress than either of its components used separately were inconclusive. Many criteria demonstrated no significant differences among treatment groups whereas one measure (Scale A Career Planning: Involvement in Thinking about the Future and Making Career Plans, College and University Form of the Career Development Inventory) indicated that the combined treatment produced the strongest effects on subject involvement in career planning.

Similar positive results have been reported by Glaize and Myrick (1984).

Sharf (1984a) conducted a study to determine if adding occupational information to a computerized interest inventory (Exploring Careers) would increase the instrument's validity and reliability. Although he found no evidence to that effect, he does suggest that counselors may find it useful to use an interest inventory either before or after a student has had an opportunity to explore occupational information.

M. J. Miller and Springer (1986) investigated whether paying for a computerized intervention was related to satisfaction. They used the self-information section (interests, abilities, and values) of DISCOVER with undergraduates and charged some students twenty dollars, others five dollars, and still others nothing. The criterion measure was a rating scale that measured satisfaction with a career exploration experience. They found that all students were satisfied with DISCOVER (for example, it was perceived as interesting, fun, easy to use, and accurate) regardless of financial cost. There were no differences among the three monetarily defined groups.

Although they used a sample of only 12 college students, Roselle and Hummel (1988) have produced some research that sheds light on the effects of DISCOVER in relation to a user's intellectual development. Specifically, students with higher levels of intellectual development "manipulate the system more effectively than do students with lower levels of development" (p. 248). This finding suggests that the common practice of indiscriminantly turning loose high school or college students to access and experience a program without assistance may not be a good idea. Kimball (1988), on the other hand, has once again proven that one can teach anything in some form to anybody. He has created a computerized system for functionally illiterate adults.

Another typical evaluation of the effects of a computer-based system is provided by Fukuyama, Probert, Neimeyer, Nevill, and Metzler, (1988). With 77 undergraduates, they used the Career Decision-Making Self-Efficacy Scale (CDMSES) and the Career Decision Scale (CDS) as outcome measures and the DISCOVER system as the intervention. Their conclusion was that DISCOVER "had a positive effect on career self-efficacy and career decision-making for undergraduate participants" (p. 61).

In a different type of evaluation, Sampson, Shahnasarian, and Reardon (1987) sought to gauge the national use of DISCOVER and SIGI. They determined that 54 percent of their sample used DISCOVER and 46 percent used SIGI. SIGI tended to be used primarily in community colleges, four-year colleges, and universities, while DISCOVER was much more heavily utilized in high schools. Neither system was used to any appreciable extent in vocational-technical schools. Most common for both systems (71 percent) was the availability of a single computer terminal or microcomputer for student use. These were located mainly in counseling centers, career planning and placement centers, career centers, and guidance offices. How do clients get to these systems? Usually, they are accessed through counseling referral, followed by walk-in, career course, and group counseling; in short, through existing career guidance interventions. Support resources (such as printed information, tests and inventories, audio and video tapes, and so on) are readily available in almost all sites. Usually, systems such as these evaluated their effectiveness simply by counting the number of clients who used the system and perhaps acquiring data on client satisfaction. This method, of course, does not allow for assessment of increases in self or occupational knowledge and/or changes in behavior.

Bloch and Kinnison (1989a) evaluated the contents and accuracy of five computer-based Career Informations Delivery Systems (CIDS) in general use in New York State. The results placed the five CIDS in rank order, although the first four achieved very similar scores. The ordering was as follows: (1) the National Career Information System (CIS) from the University of Oregon; (2) the Guidance Information System (GIS) from Houghton Mifflin; (3) CHOICES, from the Canada Systems Group (CSG); (4) DISCOVER from ACT; and (5) C-LECT from Chronicle Guidance Publications. At least by the criteria applied in this evaluation, any of the first four ranked CIDS would be acceptable for use.

Kuhlman (1988) describes a number of computer and video programs instituted at Brooklyn College, all of which allow students to retrieve appropriate information on their own (thus increasing services without increasing personnel). These range from employment and internship referral systems, calendars of recruiters and workshops with student sign-up capabilities, career video libraries, alumni mentor matching programs, and so on.

There are those who warn against the wholesale use of computerized career guidance and information systems on the grounds that they have not been subject to sufficient psychometric scrutiny (Johnston, Buescher, & Heppner, 1988). They cite four types of issues that need to be addressed: (1) *psychometric issues*, such as validity and reliability, sex fairness, fakeability, and so on; (2) *programming issues*, such as flexibility, accuracy of information, technical difficulties, readability, and so on; (3) *technical-service issues*, such as adequate service; and (4) *staffing issues*, such as who attends the computer, counselor's role, and staff attitudes.

One reason that so many computer effectiveness studies show positive results is that the validity of user ratings may be influenced by a novelty or halo effect. Another problem with the research thus far accomplished on computer-mediated career guidance effectiveness is that frequently the criterion measures used to indicate success or failure have little relationship to the stated objectives of the system. For example, career maturity is a frequent outcome measure, but the construct is so global that a single computer-mediated intervention could hardly be expected to achieve a significant increase. When and if it does, one is skeptical. Still another area for further research would be the effects of individualized prescriptions versus nondifferentiated group treatments. We also need more detailed descriptions of the individual characteristics of users and the moderating effects these may produce. Finally, we may require development of computer interventions with a guidance rather than a simple information focus to be used with adults in settings other than educational institutions. At the least, studies should be conducted to see if systems designed to be utilized in educational settings are equally effective in other environments. Nevertheless, these and other studies are instructive in that they point toward the effectiveness of computer-mediated techniques for the dissemination of occupational information. At the same time, they suggest that indiscriminate use of the computer may not be appropriate; some types of students benefit from computer-generated information more than do others. Finally, research into the use of computers in career guidance confirms once again that information acquisition is merely a first, albeit important, step in career planning. Individuals must be assisted through a variety of techniques to utilize data in a personally meaningful manner.

C. W. Ryan, Drummond, and Shannon (1980) evaluated the effects of the Guidance Information System (GIS) as used in both schools and human service agencies in Maine. They concluded that the primary influence of the system is in increasing users' career awareness and information-gathering activities. Most users enjoyed the process, but a few became confused when what they thought were clearly formed career goals before using the system turned out to be less clear after the fact. The investigators suggest immediate counselor access for such users. At the college level, third- and fourth-generation computer career guidance systems are beginning to emerge. For example, the CECIL program (Computerized Educational and Career Information Link) was developed at Virginia Polytechnic Institute and State University by incorporating the best features of CVIS (Computerized Vocational Information System) and DISCOVER. The resulting hybrid, CECIL, was found to be effective as an outreach adjunct to the university's counseling and career services (Schenk, Murphy, & Shelton, 1980).

Information-handling technology is indeed increasing at a rapid rate. Individuals now possess and use everything from handheld calculators and instructional devices to personal computers with intelligent videodisc systems. Computers are now ubiquitous, and the variety of career-oriented commercial products is growing. Our software, however, is frequently crude and untested. Snipes and McDaniels (1981) offer some sensible questions for those who would assess or evaluate these systems.

1. On what theory of career development is the system designed?
2. Are the implications of the theory consistently manifested throughout the design of the system?
3. Are the assessment instruments valid and reliable?
4. What analytical skills are assumed to be entering behaviors of users?
5. What skills are taught in the system?
6. Is the system designed to provide opportunities for users to attain the outcomes listed as objectives for the system? (p. 313)

The Association of Computer-Based Systems for Career Information has promulgated guidelines for the use of computer-based career information and guidance systems (Caulum & Lambert,1985). These are reproduced below in abbreviated form. The reader will note that most of these topics are covered in depth in this volume.

Theory and Practice

1.1. Each user site should adopt, adapt, or otherwise define its theory of career development.

1.2. Each user site should define a plan to facilitate the career-development process which will meet the needs of its students or clients.

1.3. The goals of the computer-based system should be compatible with the theory to which the user subscribes.

1.4. The process and content of the computer-based system should fit into the career development plan of the user site.

Process

2.1. Each user site should develop program goals for integrating use of the computer-based system into existing programs to meet student or client needs.

2.2. Each user site should develop objectives to implement each of the goals.

2.3. Each user site should develop a variety of activities to implement each objective.

2.4. The management team should recognize the importance of career planning in the context of the entire program and should monitor and evaluate its program.

2.5. Any student or client should be oriented to the system prior to usage and should be given follow-up assistance after use.

User Needs

3.1. Agencies should identify client populations.

3.2. The career-planning needs of each client population should be determined.

3.3. The career-planning needs of students or clients should be met by the counseling program by using the computer-based system as an integral tool.

System Site Management

4.1. All students or clients should have an opportunity to use the system.

4.2. The organization should make a long-term commitment to providing the system's service by including in the annual budget adequate funds to handle staff, system fees, hardware, and necessary supplies.

4.3. Site management should be involved in the evaluation of the system.

4.4. Site management should be involved with promotional activities at the site and in the local community.
4.5. The system should be regularly updated, based on releases from the system operator.
4.6. Management should insure that site coordinators receive periodic training from the system operator and that all staff receive "in-house" training in the use of the system each year.

Physical Environment

5.1. The facilities should have ample and accessible space.
5.2. The availability of computer equipment is essential to the use made of computer-based systems.

Personnel

6.1. Staff who are regularly involved with using the system should have thorough knowledge of its operation, theoretical process, and practical interpretation (a "facilitation" level of knowledge).
6.2. Each site should have at least one site coordinator. This person must have a special knowledge of the system through training offered by the system operator and needs to maintain liaison contact with the system operator.
6.3. Staff members should develop a process for identifying (and communicating or interacting with) related activities sponsored by other organizations (Examples: Career Days, College Fairs, College Representative Visitations).
6.4. Staff members should conduct in-house training and educational seminars for people needing "orientation" and "awareness" levels of knowledge, and for the end users of the system.
6.5. Incidental staff users need an "orientation" level of knowledge that can be obtained through annual updates.
6.6. Administrators, students, or clients, and others should have an "awareness" level of knowledge about the system that can be obtained through a yearly demonstration.

Evaluation

7.1. Objective measurement techniques should be used to provide quantitative data about use of the system. Such measurements may include number of users of various components of the system, number and types of users, percentage of target population reached, and time-of-day usage patterns.
7.2. Subjective indicators of usage should be obtained at least every other year by surveys of end users and staff members.
7.3. Evaluation information should be reported to site facilitators, administrators, the system operator, and other interested parties.*

K. Gray (1986) sees the computer as an assistant for the counselor. The computer assists in the sense that it performs routine work (such as case note records, lists of referrals, report writing, letters, automated scoring of tests and inventories). Ultimately, the computer may be more useful in individualizing its delivery so that users are able to take responsibility for their own information needs. It is clear that the best current way for clients to utilize available software programs is by means of the "prescription" system; that is, the client sees a counselor who prescribes that the client take all or, more likely, parts of a system as DISCOVER or SIGI that most meet the client's needs as discerned by both the counselor and the client.

*From *Guidelines for the Use of Computer-Based Career Information and Guidance Systems*, edited by D. Caulum and F. Lambert. Eugene, OR: Association of Computer-Based Systems for Career Information Clearinghouse, 1985. Reprinted by permission.

Katz (1988) describes the role of interventions involving information in the career decision-making process as "(a) to help students identify the information that is important to them for CDM; (b) to ensure that such information will be as accurate, comprehensive, and relevant as possible; (c) to make the information readily accessible; and (d) to help students use it in a reasonable way" (p. 515). In terms of SIGI and SIGI PLUS, Katz has set up the system to perform three major functions: (1) to help the user narrow or expand occupations to a comprehensive but manageable list of options for further consideration; (2) to help the user make distinctions between occupations on the basis of desirability and probability of successful entry; and (3) to help the user make plans and take actions designed to implement the choice. SIGI PLUS focuses on values, interests, and skills. Whether the values, interests, and skills included are all-encompassing is moot, and the theoretical bases on which they are chosen is also arguable. Nevertheless, the bases of construction are clear, if perhaps deficient.

Many of the standard tests, inventories, and decision-making systems traditionally available in paper-and-pencil form are accessible in computerized versions. Hence, a body of literature has evolved in the last decade or so that compares older delivery modes with the delivery medium of the computer. Loughead (1988) reviewed the computerized version of the Harrington-O'Shea Career Decision Making System (CDM) and concluded that although decision making per se is never addressed in the system and although the actual effects on the user are unknown,the CDM appears to have considerable face validity. McKee and Levinson (1990) reviewed the computerized version of Holland's Self-Directed Search (SDS-CV). Although the computerized SDS is over twice as expensive as the conventional SDS, the resulting report is thought to be so complete and clear that scoring and interpretation time are saved. Further, scoring errors (a persisting bugaboo of the conventional SDS) are eliminated in the computerized version. In all, at this stage of evaluation, it would appear that using such instruments as the CDM, SDS, and the Strong in the computerized version will do no harm and may have advantages. Cost is the primary deterrent to use at present.

Although the use of computers is increasing dramatically, the training of counselors to deal with this technology has lagged behind. C. S. Johnson and Sampson (1985) report that only about one-quarter of institutions are offering counselors preservice training in computer usage, and there is some question about the comprehensiveness of that preparation. At the very least, they advocate that counselors have competencies in the management and implementation of computer-assisted guidance, how to counsel effectively with a computer, how to select software and hardware, and how to integrate results in a group counseling setting. Gaushell (1984) defines computer literacy for counselors as the ability to (1) have a working knowledge of computer terminology, (2) be able to read and write simple programs, (3) understand the type of problems that are and are not open to computer solution, (4) know some of the history of computing, and (5) understand some of the moral and human impact issues of using computers.

Suggestions for effecting computer-assisted career guidance systems may be found in Sampson and Reardon (1990).

Finally, Herr (1985b) has delineated the role of professional organizations with regard to computer technology in career development. He lists four functions:

1. Clarifying the meaning of technology in career development
2. Identifying the counselor's role in technology
3. Encouraging appropriate preparation of counselors in the use of technology in career development, and

4. Stimulating attention to the ethical issues and problems generated by technology (p. 178)

In Table 15.5 we briefly describe only a few of the more commonly used computer-based systems.[2]

Career Centers

In the past decade, a career-center concept has surfaced. The terms *career resource center, educational information center,* or *career information center* are most often used. The idea of a career resource center is to enhance the use of career-related information by gathering together in a single place within an educational institution, an agency, or a workplace all educational, occupational, and financial aid information. The center also provides individuals with professional assistance in using the information and allows a physical space for clients to meet with representatives of educational and training institutions, potential employers, and community resource people. The emphasis is on facilitating easy accessibility for users.

Such a center, devoted to the acquisition, storage, retrieval, and dissemination of career-related information, may be a separate entity within an institution, such as the education information centers (EICs) established by PL 94-482 in higher education. EICs have also been created in the community for adults in such locations as shopping centers, libraries, and other easily accessed public places. They are to be found in residence halls, guidance and placement offices, and so on. Usually, they contain such components as microfilm and microfiche viewers, view-decks, books, pamphlets, occupational files, reference and resource volumes, catalogs, brochures, computers, video and audio tapes—virtually every kind of information media discussed in this chapter—and convenient spaces for clients to utilize the information. If in an educational setting, they may also serve as a dissemination center for other units within the educational enterprise (for example, adult and continuing education). At the elementary school level, it is sometimes called a guidance learning center. Outreach, consultation, and instruction are further activities often associated with centers. What few evaluations exist suggest the popularity and effectiveness of these types of centers. "How to" help with regard to the rudiments of setting up and evaluating a career center is available (Martin 1980; R. C. Reardon, Domkowski, & Jackson, 1980; S. T. Brown & D. Brown, 1990; Zunker, 1986a).

Career centers require planning and continual effort. They may require hiring a paraprofessional or training student or lay volunteer assistants. In any case, if career centers facilitate the acquisition, storage, retrieval, dissemination, and effective use of educational and occupational information, they are well worth the energy expenditure.

Networks

There are currently a number of national networking efforts directed toward producing better occupational information and disseminating it more effectively. Two of these are the National Occupational Information Coordinating Committee (NOICC) and the Occupational Data Analysis System (ODAS).

The National Occupational Information Coordinating Committee (NOICC).[3] The value of the National Occupational Information Coordinating Committee (NOICC) to counselors is in that it can provide a route to much of the most current, valid, localized, integrated, and comprehensive career informa-

[2]Gratitude is expressed to Scott Meier for his research into the extent of suitable software for career guidance.

[3]The authors thank Juliette Lester and her staff at NOICC for their contribution to the following description.

Table 15.5

Examples of Computer Systems and Software in Career Counseling

System	Publisher	Cost[1]	Description
Microskills	Eureka Corporation 5626 Sutter Ave. Richmond, CA 94804	$500	Personal skills assessment matched to 360 occupations
Job Search	Elliot & Fitzpatrick	400	Matches workers to jobs via DOT
Local Job Bank	P.O. Box 1945	125	Allows local data base of jobs
Vocreport	Athens, GA 30603	125	educational, vocational, and
Work Activity		200	personal information summary based on *Guide to Occupational Exploration*
Values Auction	Conover Company	150	Exploration of work values
Micro Art of Interpo Viewing	Box 155 Omro, WI 54963	150	Tips for job interviews
Values Auction		150	Exploration of work values
Work Activities Inventory		150	Interests and career clusters
Comprehensive Career Assessment and Planning		500	Career decision-making
Scholarships Today		65	Financial-aid information
C-LECT	Chronicle Guidance Moravia, NY 13118	1600	Interests, financial aids, educational and occupational information, values
SIGI + SIGI PLUS	ETS Princeton, NJ 08541	1200–2400	Financial aid, occupational information, values, interests
Interactive Career EXPLOR. Cluster	Precision People 3452 N. Ride Circle S.	300/Cluster	Vocational assessment and feedback
Integrated Career Profile Cluster	Jacksonville, FL 32217		Skill profiles, SDS, Myers-Briggs
Management DEVEL. Training Cluster			Stress analysis, work environment preference
Training Assistance Cluster			Work and learning styles (16PF, M-B)
GIS	Houghton-Mifflin Dept. 13, P.O. Box 683 Hanover, NH 03755	2500	Skill identification and educational and occupational information
Personal Habits for Job Success	Career Aids 8950 Lurline Ave. Dept. Q Chatsworth, CA 91311	65	Appropriate work behaviors
Career Scan IV/ College Scan IV	Educational Media Corp. Box 21311 Minneapolis, MN 55421	170–200	Explores careers (700) and colleges (1000+)
CASIE	SIU Career Planning Carbondale, IL 62901	150	Interests, values, majors and careers
Discover II	ACT 2210 N. Dodge St. P.O. Box 168 Iowa City, IA 52243	1750	Interests, skills, values, educational and occupational information, financial aid

Table 15.5 (Continued)

System	Publisher	Cost[1]	Description
Holland Occupations Finder	Psych Assessment Resources P.O. Box 98 Odessa, FL 33556	175	Holland codes and job titles
CHOICES	CSG CHOICES 277 S. Washington Suite 209 Alexandria, VA 22314	600–2000	Skills, interests, values, educational and occupational information
Values Search	Computer Concepts, Inc.	110	Job values
Job Hunter's Survival Kit	2909 Brandemere Dr. Tallahassee, FL 32312	300	Job-seeking behaviors (writes resumes)
Working	Queue, Inc. 562 Boston Ave Bridgeport, CT 06610	110	Job-seeking behaviors; work attitudes; world of work
Career Assessment and Planning Program	JIST Works, Inc. 720 North Park Ave. Indianapolis, IN 46202	485	Career assessment, selecting alternatives, career planning and job search, career exploration
Career Finder	Wintergreen Software P.O. Box 1229 Madison, WI 53701	287	Matching of student traits and 435 occupations
Career Information System	Nat'l Career Information System 1787 Agate Street U. of Oregon Eugene, OR 97403		Civilian and military occupations and school file. Financial aid
Computerized Educational Planning Program	Orchard House, Inc. 112 Balls Hill Rd. Concord, MA 01742		Primarily educational planning and interest assessment
Career Exploration and Planning Program	Meridian Educational Corp. 236 E. Front St. Bloomington, IL 61701		Appalachian Educational Laboratory materials (CDM) computerized
Career Point	Conceptual Systems, Inc. 1100 Wayne Ave. Silver Spring, MD 20910		Primarily for organizational career development

[1]Approximate costs may vary over time and depending on the number of units purchased. Most software designed to run on Apple II plus, IBM PC, TRS 80s, and clones.

tion available. It also supports counselors' use of career information through training and the development of resources to enhance the applicability of career information for a variety of student and client needs. It does so by encouraging coordination and collaboration among its federal and state member agencies.

The establishment of NOICC in 1976 was an initiative by Congress to improve the applicability of occupational and labor market information by promoting its development, dissemination, and use for two primary purposes: 1) planning education and training programs, and 2) assisting individuals needing labor market information for career planning and decision making. NOICC receives funding under authorization in both the Carl D. Perkins Vocational Education Act (PVEA) and the Job Training Partnership Act (JTPA). It is a Federal interagency committee of representatives from

10 agencies in the U.S. Departments of Labor, Education, Defense, Commerce, and Agriculture.

NOICC provides basic grants to a State Occupational Information Coordinating Committee (SOICC) in every state, the District of Columbia, and five U.S. territories. By law, SOICC members represent 1) state vocational education boards, 2) vocational rehabilitation agencies, 3) employment security agencies, 4) job training coordinating councils, and 5) economic development agencies. Many also invite representatives from higher education and other state agencies. SOICC directors, staff, committee members and others have formed the National Association of SOICC's (NASOICC), an affiliate of the American Vocational Association, to provide professional development opportunities for members and to strengthen the NOICC/SOICC network. NOICC/SOICC programs that are vitally important to career counselors include the National Career Development Guidelines, discussed in Chapter 1 and the Career Information Delivery Systems (CIDS), a descriptive and generic term for computer-based systems that provide information about occupations and education/training opportunities. CIDS, as we have previously observed, are an important resource in career and employment counseling, job placement, educational planning, and vocational and career education programs.

The CIDS contain information about hundreds of occupations and educational and job training programs. Each occupational description includes information on duties, employment outlook, earnings levels, working conditions and licensing, and educational requirements. The educational information includes descriptions of postsecondary and job training programs. Educational institutions are described in terms of admissions policies, services, financial aid, programs offered, and more. CIDS also help individuals relate and compare personal characteristics with occupational factors, often including scores from a variety of assessment instruments. CIDS offer menus of routines to search the information files in a structured way, as well as direct routes to information.

More than half of the CIDS users are in high schools; other prominent user groups include postsecondary students, adult learners, employment service and JTPA clients, vocational rehabilitation clients, elementary and middle/junior high school students, military separatees, corrections inmates, and library patrons. Counseling and career development program staff use CIDS as a tool in many of their activities with groups and individual students and clients. They can also be used interactively by individuals exploring career options and opportunities.

NOICC awarded grants to support development of about half of the statewide CIDS. Statewide CIDS are often adapted from available proprietary computer-assisted career guidance systems. These systems may have different search strategies and data files but consistently highlight state and local occupational and educational information. The NOICC/SOICC-sponsored CIDS are mandated to include that vital linkage with the Federal-state occupational and labor market statistics programs through the SOICC technical database known as the Occupational Information System (OIS). Considering those sources, the occupational information in the OIS-based CIDS is usually the most current and valid available.

The information in the CIDS is also typically available through other media, including microfiche, videos, and publications, such as career tabloids. The tabloids, published annually, contain charts of state occupational and training information, along with articles on sources of educational planning and job placement assistance and labor market trends.

Many CIDS, SOICCs, commercial system vendors, counselors, and others are members of the Association of Computer-based Systems of Career Information (ACSCI). The organization works to advance the use of career information, information technology, and user services through clearinghouse and public information efforts, professional development, and guidelines and standards for system operation.

The Audiovisual CIDS Enhancement (ACE) Consortium and Distribution Center is a group of SOICCs that has produced several supplementary career information and career development motivational videotape series. Most come with curriculum guides suitable for group or classroom use. The ACE Consortium has also developed prototype audiovisual interactive CIDS using both a computer/VCR interface and a computer/videodisc interface; at least one state is implementing a statewide audiovisual interactive CIDS using the ACE Consortium's technology. NOICC's fostering of the ACE Consortium's focus on leading-edge technology has also led to several recent collaborative counselor training efforts via satellite networks.

Most SOICCs offer Improve Career Decision Making (ICDM) training for counselors. ICDM workshops provide an orientation to the sources and uses of current national, state, and area labor market and career information that are based on the federal-state occupational and labor market statistics programs. NOICC develops the core curriculum package for the workshop, including the basic text *Using Labor Market Information in Career Exploration and Decision Making: A Resource Guide* that is scheduled for revision in 1991. ICDM training teams often include a counselor educator, a labor market analyst, a CIDS representative, and a SOICC staffer.

Counselors find that the emphasis on applications and uses of the resources with different types of settings, clients, and client needs is one of the strengths of the ICDM training provided by SOICCs. It also supports the Guidelines' counselor competencies related to career information resources and uses.

In support of both program planning and career information development and use, NOICC and the SOICCs have developed Occupational Information Systems (OISs). These are computerized databases that combine multiple-source occupational and educational data, integrating and formatting the data so that it can be analyzed in a variety of ways. To undergird the state OISs, NOICC maintains the NOICC Crosswalk Service Center to provide products and services based on the national Master Crosswalk. The Master Crosswalk enables cross-referencing and comparing of major occupational and educational coding structures, such as those used in the Census, *Dictionary of Occupational Titles*, and the *Classification of Instructional Programs*. The development and updating of the Master Crosswalk requires the support and cooperation of a number of agencies, particularly the U.S. Bureau of Labor Statistics. It also includes linkages between military and civilian occupational data that have been developed through NOICC's extensive work with the Department of Defense. The OISs support the SOICCs' publication of labor supply/demand and analysis reports for many states and areas. The OIS technical databases also may be used to support the more "user-friendly" CIDS.

SOICCs encourage the use of occupational information at the state and local levels in a variety of ways. Most SOICCs have implemented a state OIS and are now concentrating on enhancing the system. Some SOICCs publish occupational outlook reports, job hunter's guides, and career briefs. Some participate in job and career fairs and sponsor telephone hot-lines that provide career information. They provide training for counselors, counselor educators, and planners and administrators. Many SOICC directors welcome the opportunity to speak to conferences and classes about sources of career information available to counselors in their state.

Counselors who deal with career development issues need to know what is available from their State Occupational Information Coordinating Committee and how it can be helpful to them. The SOICC can often be viewed as a single point of contact with five or more state agencies involved in supporting programs that prepare citizens for productive participation in the workforce. SOICCs may be listed in state government directories, possibly in connection with one of the statutorily-designated agencies represented on the Committee. SOICCs also are listed in an appendix of the *Occupational Outlook Handbook*, and in NOICC's annual report, "Status of the NOICC/SOICC Network." For more information, write to the Executive Director, National Occupational Information Coordinating Committee, 2100 M Street, N.W., Suite 156, Washington, DC 20037.

The Occupational Data Analysis System (ODAS). A second example of networking is the Occupational Data Analysis System (ODAS), sponsored by the Vocational Technical Education Consortium of States (VTECS). ODAS is a computer-based system, originally developed by Michigan State University, and uses three sources of data: catalogs of performance objectives related to the DOT, keyword descriptors designed by the Job Service of the U.S. Department of Labor, and vocational preparation and occupations designed by NOICC. The system describes skill requirements of jobs and the level of education and training required, describes skills required in training programs, and identifies skills required by new and emerging occupations, among other functions. The system's primary use is in voc-tech schools, two-year colleges, adult education programs, high schools, vocational rehabilitation centers, and business and industry. Target populations include youth and adults in and out of school, unemployed, displaced, or dislocated workers, vocational rehabilitation clients, and reentry women. Applications are in curriculum development, assessment and training of displaced workers, placement and guidance, and so on. A terminal and a telephone modem is required, and training is provided.

What we have here in the NOICC and ODAS paradigms is basically an attempt at central planning and networking to reduce the potential chaos and overlap of existing government and private information systems and to extend in new directions occupational information gathering, storing, retrieving, and disseminating. Such objectives are appropriate to all systems of classifying information.

Summary

In this chapter we have discussed career guidance information in terms of criteria for "good" information and for the effective use of information. Various possibilities for the storage, retrieval, and dissemination of information have been explored. Examples of the types of materials available have been offered. We have described the NOICC and ODAS as useful models of multisystem approaches to the delivery of information at national, regional, state, and local levels. The underlying view in this chapter has been one of counselors helping individuals to integrate educational, occupational, and personal information in the decision-making process. The fostering of planfulness and career development involves not only helping counselees to acquire information but also assisting them to apply the knowledge to their personal characteristics.

CHAPTER 16

ASSESSMENT IN CAREER GUIDANCE AND COUNSELING

Key Concepts

- Assessment devices in career guidance and counseling provide vehicles to identify talent and to assist persons with self-understanding.
- The use of tests is extensive both for purposes of career development and for employment.
- Four major uses of tests are prediction, discrimination, monitoring, and evaluation.
- Prediction usually involves the use of either clinical or statistical processes.
- Computer-assisted testing is increasing in career guidance and counseling.
- Assessment is concerned with the content of choices to be made as well as with the readiness for choice of individuals doing the choosing.

We have been told so often that we are living in an age of extraordinary complexity, specialization, and growth that we frequently fail to realize the implications. We take for granted the vast proliferation of knowledge, the social mobility and flux of social roles, and the substantial changes in occupational structure and opportunity that characterize our time. Yet, this "progress" presents us with problems unparalleled in world history.

Two problems directly relevant to career guidance are the training and allocation of personnel in order to ensure maximum utilization of this most valuable of all resources. We need talent of diverse specializations; we require a means of identifying that talent. The chief method that has evolved is the standardized test.

In addition, we have come to accept the premise that assessment procedures help individuals to understand themselves not only in terms of their talents but also in terms of their interests, values, and personality characteristics. The greater the self-understanding an individual has, it is assumed, the more likely that person is to make realistic, satisfying educational and career choices. Although self-understanding does not guarantee good decision making, good decisions probably cannot be made without a realistic picture of one's abilities, interests, and other pertinent characteristics. Again, assessment devices provide a vehicle that contributes to the self-understanding and accurate appraisal of counselees.

Testing by private employers is not typically extensive, although larger companies (more than 25,000 employees) tend to test more than smaller companies. In the public sector, merit systems cover the great majority of employees, and about three-fourths of the systems use tests of some sort (Tenopyr, 1981). Tittle and Zytowski (1980) estimate that 3.5 million people take machine-scored interest inventories each year. Thus, the use of tests is substantial for both career exploration and employment purposes. Alternatives to testing, such as interviews, experience and educational factors, biodata instruments, and simulations, have been found to be less attractive than testing (Reilly & Chao, 1981). It behooves us, then, to use tests carefully in order to realize their full potential as an aid in career decision making, exploration, and employment selection.

Over the past decade several significant changes have occurred in the type and usage of tests employed in the service of providing guidance and counseling. Miller (1982), for example, points out that new types of instruments have been developed (such as career maturity inventories, large-scale assessment programs (such as the National Assessment of Education Progress) and multimatrix instruments, such as the ACT career assessment to be described in this chapter.) Further, we have witnessed the development of new techniques for adminstering, scoring, and reporting tests (such as computerized tests discussed in Chapter 15), and we have responded more adequately to the needs of special populations.

In this chapter we will consider four major uses of tests or assessment procedures. We will deal first with the *predictive* uses of tests, with standardized appraisal data that forecast success in educational and career behaviors. Second, we will discuss the use of tests and inventories for *discrimination*; that is, for permitting individuals to discover what occupational or educational groups they resemble. Together, predictive and discriminative uses of tests deal with information pertinent to the content of choices. Third, the *monitoring* function of assessment will be discussed. In a systematic approach to career guidance, it is important that those responsible for intervention be able to identify the vocationalization stage of any individual or group; monitoring provides this information. In essence, monitoring deals with the process of choice or readiness for choice. Further, monitoring indicates whether career behaviors are serving an adaptive or a maladaptive function, as in the measurement of job satisfaction, for example. Finally, we will summarize the use of assessment in *evaluating* how well goals are being achieved with the interventions provided. Thus, the four purposes of assessment in career guidance are prediction, discrimination, monitoring, and evaluation. A sampling of appropriate instruments for each function will be offered and related issues discussed.

PREDICTION

When the effectiveness of a test is evaluated in personnel selection and career guidance, the concern is how well test performance predicts some future performance (such as success in training, success on the job, and so forth). The test is called a predictor; the variable being predicted, a criterion. The entire procedure is one of establishing the predictive validity of a test. The higher the predictive validity of a test (as summarized in a correlation coefficient), the more adequately we can forecast group achievement and, to a lesser extent, individual achievement.

Clinical Versus Statistical Prediction

The actual process of making a prediction on the basis of assessment data can take one of two forms or can combine elements of both. The first is the clinical or case study. Here the counselor operates as a clinician, and on the basis of an individual's test data and other observations, the counselor formulates some hypotheses about the counselee's behavior. This approach is largely intuitive and is probably the prevalent modus operandi for most counselors.

The second form of prediction is actuarial or statistical. Here the counselee's test data are classified into a category representing his or her performance. The counselor then uses an actuarial table that provides statistical frequencies of behavior for other persons classified in the same way. The data are thus mechanically combined (for example, by means of a regression equation or expectancy table), and a probability figure results.

A continuing argument in career guidance focuses on the relative effectiveness of these two methods of making predictions from test data. Meehl's (1954) early work in this regard is instructive. He investigated 19 studies with unambiguous results that predicted success in some kind of training or schooling, recidivism, or recovery from a major psychosis, 10 of these studies failed to find a difference between the two methods; nine found differences in favor of the statistical method of prediction; none produced a difference in favor of the clinical approach. Meehl's pioneering work has been supported by later studies by J. S. Wiggins (1973).

The message that emerges from these studies is clear. In career guidance, the making of clinical predictions should be approached with extreme tentativeness. Further, whenever it is possible to collect the necessary data to make statistical predictions, this method is preferred. Therefore, it is mandatory that we know with what our tests correlate and precisely what we are predicting. Both test makers and counselors share responsibility for providing predictive validity data.

The Validity of Aptitude Tests for Career Guidance

It is safe to say that aptitude tests predict school performance and success in training better than they do performance in an occupation. This difference in favor of the training criterion is probably due to the narrower band of activity being predicted and to the fact that "success" in an occupation is difficult to assess. The use of typical tests of scholastic aptitude produces correlation coefficients between test performance and grade point average at the graduate school level ranging from 0.20 to 0.60 with a mean of 0.40 and at the baccalaureate level from 0.30 to 0.70 with a mean of 0.50. At the high school level, ability and grades are correlated at about 0.60. Personality factors add very little to predictive accuracy when they are combined with intellective factors, because they are largely discriminant variables rather than predictive variables.

The prediction of success in an occupation shows more modest results. One of the monumental and highly publicized studies in this regard was carried out by Thorndike and Hagen (1959). Their results represent a devastating condemnation of the validity of tests in predicting job performance. Approximately 10,000 men who had taken a one and one-half day battery of tests during World War II as applicants for aircrew training were followed up 12 years later in civilian life. The tests yielded 20 separate scores in the areas of verbal, numerical, spatial, perceptual, and motor abilities. The sample was sorted into 120 occupational groups, with each subject rated in terms of "success in the occupation." Within each occupational grouping, success indicators were correlated with each of the 20 test scores.

There were group differences in mean scores in sensible directions (for example, accountants scored better on numbers tests than on any other tests and also scored better than writers, for instance on the measure of numerical ability). However, there was wide variability in the total group of 10,000 (as an example, some accountants had numerical scores as low as the lowest truck driver's score). In general, the 12,000 correlations clustered around zero with as many in the negative direction as in the positive direction. The conclusion reached was that tests given at about age 20 cannot predict occupational success 12 years later.

Thorndike and Hagen offer some possible explanations for their findings. The most valid of these is probably the proposition that beyond survival in an occupation, "success" is a meaningless concept. Because of the institutionalization of rewards in many occupations (civil service, unions, and so on), in which pay scales, hours, and outputs are set by schedules or agreements, it is virtually impossible to secure a differential measure of success in an occupation. Yet, even granting this fact, the results of the research are most discouraging and point, at best, to the need for short-range rather than long-range career counseling.

A brighter picture of the validity of occupational aptitude tests is offered by Ghiselli (1966, 1973). He reviewed all the studies conducted before 1965 on the accuracy of tests in predicting training success and proficiency in occupations. For all occupations, the average of the validity coefficients is 0.30 for training criteria and 0.19 for proficiency criteria. This difference on the order of 0.10 in favor of training criteria holds for just about all occupational groups. Thus, predicting success in training for a job is more accurate than predicting success in the job itself.

Ghiselli's findings are confirmed in a follow-up of subjects in the well-known Project TALENT study. Eleven years after their high school graduation, Project TALENT participants were contacted to determine whether their occupational attainment was related to ability, interest, gender, and family socioeconomic status measures collected when they were in grade 10 (Austin & Hanisch, 1990). The results indicated that these types of data were indeed predictive of occupational categories over a protracted period of time, although the investigator's suggest that the use of interest data for prediction purposes should be lessened from its current heavy use. This caveat regarding the predictive uses of interest inventories is echoed by Holland, Gottfredson, and Baker (1990), who determined that an expressed preference or aspiration is even more predictive of occupation choice that is a formal interest inventory.

Until relatively recently, it had been thought that although certain types of test have significantly higher predictive power for training than for proficiency criteria, others do not. It seems that tests of intellectual, spatial, and mechanical abilities are more effective in predicting trainability than in predicting job proficiency. On the other hand, tests of perceptual accuracy and motor abilities predict trainability and job proficiency equally well.

Thus, the efficiency of aptitude tests in forecasting occupational success and trainability is moderate. For any given job, tests of one kind seem to give better predictions than others. The predictive power of a test must be determined for a specific job. When this is done, the maximal power of tests to predict success in training jumps to 0.47 and success on the job itself to approximately 0.35.

Newer research, however, casts doubt on the situation-specific superiority of tests in prediction (F. L. Schmidt & Hunter, 1981; Schmidt, Hunter, & Urry, 1976). According to this research, standard aptitude tests (verbal, quantitative, mechanical, spatial, inductive and deductive reasoning, and so on) are valid predictors of performance on the job and in training *for all jobs and in all settings*. It is argued that differences such as those reported by Ghiselli are due to statistical artifacts and, therefore, that validities are generalizable. In other words, it is claimed that all tests are valid at substantial levels for all jobs. Further, it is claimed that, based on large sample research, job performance is about as predictable as training (Pearlman, Schmidt, & Hunter, 1980).

Jensen (1984) agrees that the so-called *g* factor has predictive validity for job performance for practically all jobs, but argues that the value of *g* increases with job complexity. He reexamined available General Aptitude Test Battery (GATB) data and found the *g* factor about equally predictable for most jobs. Hence, he supported validity generalization in agreeing that most of the variation in validity coefficients across different studies, different jobs, and different situations is attributable to a number of statistical artifacts. Another voice is thus raised against the situational specificity of employment tests. Like Jensen, Thorndike (1985) reanalyzed extant data for the Differential Aptitude Tests (DATs), Army Classification Battery, and GATB. He concluded that 85 or 90 percent of predictable variance was accounted for by a single cognitive ability factor, *g*. The only exception appeared to be the psychomotor tests seem to be a nearly independent domain from the cognitive domain.

What these personnel selection studies analyses appear to indicate is that validity generalizes across situations within broad occupational clusters and that cognitive ability tests produce as high validity as any specific test. A challenge to these conclusions, however, comes from Schmitt, Gooding, Noe, and Kirsch (1984) who conducted a metanalysis of published studies from 1964 through 1982 and determined that sample size differences accounted for nowhere near the variance in validities reported by Hunter and Schmidt and that, contrary to the *g* hypothesis, "work samples, assessment centers, and supervisor/peer evaluations yield validities which are superior to those of general mental ability and special aptitude tests which are closest to those labeled ability measures . . . " (p. 420). Some differences in findings may be due to the use of published versus unpublished validity studies by investigators. Furthermore, L. R. James, Demaree, and Mulaik (1986) point out some of the methodological shortcomings in the analyses performed in validity generalization studies that may tend to overestimate the contributions of a *g* factor and minimize the contributions of situational specificity. Prediger (1989) also challenges the superiority of *g* in the prediction of job performance.

It is important to emphasize that in this volume we are primarily concerned with the use of tests to help individuals enhance their self-appraisal knowledge and to make decisions based on that information along with a host of other data. We are only peripherally concerned with the use of tests in employment selection. Nevertheless, we have included a brief discussion of aspects of employment testing, for the issue of "fairness" in employment testing remains a social concern (see, for example, Gottfredson & Sharf, 1988; Betz, 1986). Many individuals are convinced that tests have an adverse impact on the employment prospects of minorities. Some argue that this potential brings about quota systems (L. S. Gottfredson, 1990) and sleight-of-hand, performance-based score adjustments, while others maintain that racial differences are real and cannot be addressed simply by using these techniques to bring about equality.

The clearest recent example is the use of the General Aptitude Test Battery (GATB) described later in this chapter. Given validity generalization, the National Research Council (Hartigan & Wigdor, 1989) recommended a system for reinterpreting the ability test scores of African-Americans and Hispanics to make them competitive with those of whites (Holden, 1989). This system, in effect, recommended a continuation of the within-group scoring used with the GATB (that is, test results recomputed to reflect norms of an applicant's own group—African-American, Hispanic, and so on) on the grounds that the test was psychometrically sound and useful. As of this writing, the Justice Department has entered the fray and a moratorium has been declared on the practice of within-group scoring. A proposed policy of the Department of Labor (1990) would, in effect, cancel the use of the GATB for selection purposes and concentrate its use in counseling. Other instruments are also applying test results differentially, depending on the uses to which they are put. The

Armed Services Vocational Aptitude Battery (ASVAB), for example, employs some scores (mostly *g* loaded) for guidance purposes in career exploration and utilizes other, more specific scores for selection, classification, or assignment purposes.

The pendulum seems to swing historically between validity generalization and situational specificity, and it may be that newer statistical methodologies and/or better tests and criterion measures will cause additional swings in the future. Further, political considerations and implications are obvious. In any case, using tests for employment selection is quite a different matter from using them to help individuals in vocational self-exploration. Although aptitude tests clearly ought to correlate with criteria of vocational relevance, we can, using existing tests, help individuals to learn more about their possible differential abilities, no matter how much they are influenced by a *g* factor, in order to encourage differential exploration.

We have been speaking only of the predictive power of single tests. Combinations of tests yield greater validity. The evident conclusion is that tests can hold enough predictive power to be of practical value in the selection of personnel and of some value in counseling, depending on how they are used.

Appraisal and Career Guidance: Disillusionment

In recent years, several individuals have made derogatory and skeptical observations about the effectiveness of appraisal in career guidance. Career assessment procedures and their subsequent use have been variously termed "test 'em and tell 'em" activities and have been referred to as "three sessions and a cloud of dust." These are not the carpings of the ill-informed. In fact, some of the leading scholars in the field have expressed doubt about the usefulness of human assessment in enhancing career development and career choice (Crites, 1974; Goldman, 1982; Prediger 1974). These criticisms basically revolve around the fact that tests are still being used in the "square-peg, square-hole" trait-and-factor tradition and, usually, for purposes of informing immediate career choices rather than of enhancing general career development. Authorities generally agree, however, that if tests are not used in a mechanistic ritual, they can indeed be valuable for individuals.

Healy (1990) has identified four obstacles to the effective use of appraisal data in career counseling: "(1) casting clients as subordinates rather than collaborators; (2) discounting self-assessment by favoring counselor assessments; (3) de-emphasizing the influence of contexts in clients' development; and (4) focusing on a single choice rather than on strengthening client decision making and knowledge for follow-through" (p. 214). Consequently, he urges that clients be encouraged to develop self-assessment skills and to focus more on implementing their choice rather than simply looking for a fitting choice.

So long as appraisal data are used in career interventions in combination with everything else we know about an individual and so long as the client is helped to sort through the personal relevance and meaning of the data, vocational assessment is useful. The data are not useful if used in isolation, if they represent incomplete or partial information, if they are not personalized, or if they have no pertinence to career choice and decision making.

Computer-Assisted Testing

As we observed in Chapter 15, computer applications in testing have become very common and extend from administration through scoring to interpretation. Krug (1984), for example, estimated that there are approximately 200 computer test interpretation software products in use. Madsen (1986) speculated that perhaps only one-quarter or so of all tests given are computerized either in terms of administration, scoring, or interpretation. One-quarter of the massive number of tests given each year in America represents a substantial figure.

Computer-based test administration and interpretation, like every other tool available to a counselor, can be both a boon and a bane. On the positive side, they can be cost-effective and, in the case of microcomputers, provide test information virtually instantaneously. In general, clients seem to enjoy the experience and to achieve as much self-knowledge as when paper-and-pencil tests are utilized. Further, no violence seems to be visited upon the psychometric properties of accepted testing instruments that are computerized (that is, validity, reliability, and so on). The negatives of computer-based testing are more involved with the idiosyncratic aspects of a particular instrument, interpretive program, or hardware configuration than with the idea itself. Group administration is obviously difficult, if not impossible, because of the prohibitive cost of multiple stations; some programs are not user-friendly; some instruments are so new and rushed to market so quickly that they provide inadequate validity and normative data; and erroneous or overly generalized interpretations are possible. Further, there is as yet little research to determine individual differences in person-machine interactions. A final limitation is perhaps the most ominous: counselors may feel that because the machine is producing an impressive looking report, they need not have an in-depth knowledge of the test, its underlying constructs, its psychometric strengths and weaknesses, appropriate interpretations, and the need to integrate the results with everything else of relevant importance in the career development of the client.

As yet, few, if any, automated testing systems can match the comprehensiveness of the interpretation of a truly skilled clinician who has other data available to him. The MMPI is a case in point. In a frequently cited study, Eyde and Kowal (1984) ran the profile of a young adult male through three computerized interpretation systems and through a blind review by a skilled clinician. In addition, they conducted a clinical interview with the client. Results indicated that while all three computer programs described aspects of the client's difficulties, none identified several other potentially significant problems. Hence, reliance on computer interpretations by counselors who do not possess sophisticated training in assessment can lead to simpleminded and possibly harmful practices. On the other hand, most computer interpretation programs probably function more efficiently, accurately, and reliably than average and below-average clinicians.

The important variable, again as always, would appear to be not to use computer-based testing in isolation, but to be sure it is integrated with all other aspects of a comprehensive, systematic, articulated counseling program. The prescription approach described in Chapter 15 with regard to the use of computer-based information systems would seem to be equally appropriate with computer-based testing.

Meier and Geiger (1986) point out two other important concerns in the use of computer-assisted testing: counselor preparation and ethical concerns. In terms of preparation, most counselors received their pre-service education and training prior to the computer revolution. Their knowledge of computers has been gained largely through in-service preparation, formal and/or informal; consequently, it may be less complete than desirable. Newer counselors do not necessarily receive specialized training, although it is certainly becoming more common. In terms of ethics, we have the standard case of our hardware technology moving faster than our social and legislative technologies.

J. I. Hansen (1986) has summarized the current state of computer-assisted testing:

> Computers now have the capacity to give tests, compute scale scores, print results, and provide interpretive comments and diagnostic information for objective aptitude, ability, achievement, psychomotor, interest, and personality tests as well as for projective tests such as the Rorschach. The systems all have the potential to be self-contained. They require only a client who can read a video display and type or a clerk who can assist with the tasks. (p. 50)

The profession is scampering to catch up to the proliferation of computer-assisted testing issues. For instance, the American Psychological Association (1986) has produced guidelines for computer-based tests and interpretations. This document outlines how computer usage in mental health fits into the general ethical principles provided by APA (for example, *general principle*—"Psychologists shall limit their practice to their demonstrated areas of professional competence"; *specific computer application*—"Professionals will limit their use of computerized testing to techniques with which they are familiar and competent to use"). In addition, nine user responsibilities are offered (such as "Test performance should be monitored, and assistance to the test taker should be provided, as is needed and appropriate. If technically feasible, the proctor should be signaled automatically when irregularities occur.") Other sections detail the developers' responsibilities (such as "The validity of the computer version of a test should be established by those developing the test"). In addition to these guidelines, professional journals are increasingly and routinely reviewing software programs.

All in all, the potential advantages of computer-assisted testing seem clearly to outweigh the potential pitfalls. Abuses are certainly possible, however, and counselors should be alert both to their own deficits in knowledge and skill and to those of the providers as they both seek to serve the client's best interests.

Test Interpretation

Perhaps no other aspect of counselor functioning has received so little research attention as test interpretation. In fact, it is perhaps the most underresearched area in all of counseling. Although a plethora of articles appears in the professional literature in which individuals offer suggestions for the most effective interpretation of test scores and how they might best be integrated with the entire guidance and/or counseling process (for example, Mehrens & Lehmann, 1985; H. E. A. Tinsley & Bradley, 1986), few articles report the results of empirical research; fewer still are recent; and yet fewer are able to stand up to close scrutiny regarding research design and methodology. It is ironic, then, that one of the most continually debated areas of counselor functioning should be so ill-informed by research.

The effective use of tests in career guidance depends on the extent to which counselees understand and accept the results of test performance. Because we are considering the use of test results in a programmatic, systematic approach to career guidance, where everyone takes the same tests, our major concern is with group interpretation. Some research findings comparing various methods of group or individual interpretation are summarized as follows:

1. Whatever the method used, counselee attitudes toward the counselor or toward the value of the tests are much the same. However, recall of test results appears to be highest when the counselee has been dominant in an interpretation interview after a learning set for test interpretation has been established (J. Holmes, 1964).
2. Scholastic aptitude may be a significant variable in interpretation. Counselees with lower scholastic aptitude seem to recall scores more accurately with the use of audiovisual aids. There is also some evidence to suggest

that acceptance of test results is facilitated in individual sessions more than in group sessions (J. L. Walker, 1965).

3. Those who have the most accurate pictures of themselves before testing tend to learn most about themselves as a result of test interpretation, regardless of the interpretive technique utilized (Gustad & Tuma, 1957).

4. There is a good deal of evidence that counselors should be extremely careful about the manner in which they interpret test results for women (Tittle, 1973), visible minorities (Samuda, 1975), the handicapped (Banas & Nash, 1966), and the older worker (Fozard & Nuttall, 1972; Rimmer & Myers, 1982).

5. Mode of interpretation effectiveness studies are conflicting. Oliver (1977), for example, found individual interpretation superior to multiple interpretation or programmed interpretation. Sharf (1978), on the other hand, found no differences in effectiveness of interpretation when comparing a computer-based narrative report with standard profiles.

6. The client's previous vocationally related experience seems to have an effect on the interpretation of interest scores (Prediger & Swaney, 1986). People are more likely to have interest scores that correspond to their subsequent occupation when they have had experiences consonant with their predominant interests. Thus, when a client's major interests are without accompanying relevant experiences, test interpretation should be more cautious.

7. The type of language required in test interpretation should be related to the sophistication of the client. In the public eye, especially among younger individuals, concepts of intelligence and ability are distinguished from one another and mean different things (Nicholls, Patashnick, & Mettetal, 1986). In general, ability is thought of as more general than intelligence, thus having implications for the type of language required in test interpretation.

What these and other illustrative studies suggest is that no one method of test interpretation can be considered superior for all counselees. Given this finding, the following recommendations for test interpretation offered by Lister and McKenzie (1966) are extremely helpful:

> 1. The counselee must experience a need for the test information. Therefore, the counselor's role in motivation is most important. Counselees must be assisted to see that a knowledge of test performance will be beneficial to them.
>
> 2. Counselees' questions must be translated into operational terms that are acceptable to them. This means that the interpretation must be made in terms of some criterion of importance to the counselee.
>
> 3. The information must be clearly communicated to the counselee. Lister and McKenzie argue that the evaluation of the effectiveness of test interpretation must be based on more than simple accurate recall of test information, that recall must be accompanied by significant behavior change. Some type of action must be taken. A counselee who understands and accepts test results given in the form of a probability statement would play the odds. The counselee's behavior would be consistent with the test results and with other data, that is, he or she would pursue alternatives with a reasonable prognosis of success and would avoid alternatives for which chances of success are minimal. (p. 62–63)

Goodyear (1990), on the basis of his review of the literature in the area of test interpretation, suggests that the so-called "Barnum Effect" may be operative. The premise of this phenomenon is that test results do not have to be communicated accurately if they are communicated convincingly (for instance, subjects provided with fake interpretations accept them if they contain universal truths in the manner of psychics, graphology, astrology, and so on). Translated to the use of tests in counseling, the Barnum Effect would instruct counselors to provide interpretations that are positively rather than negatively worded.

Another guideline for interpretation is provided by N. J. Garfield and Prediger (1982), who discuss the testing competencies and responsibilities of vocational counselors. They suggest that counselors rate their own interpretation skills by using the following key:

1 = I do this routinely—as a regular practice.
2 = I have done this on occasion.
3 = I do not do this—but ought to consider doing this.
4 = Not applicable to the instrument(s) I am using.

Their list of interpretation responsibilities/competencies is as follows:

1. Study suggestions for interpretation provided by the test manual (and/or score report form) and determine which of them are supported by the psychometric data provided for the test.
2. Review, with the counselee, the purpose and nature of the test. Topics include the following:
   a. Why the test was given; what the test can and *cannot* do
   b. Who will receive the test results
   c. What the test results cover and how they will be used
3. Interpret test results in the context of the testing experience, the counselee's background, and other assessments (if any) of the same characteristics by doing the following:
   a. Encouraging a discussion of how the counselee felt about the testing experience, in general; his/her performance, in particular; and any difficulties or problems (such as nervousness, fatigue, or distractions) encountered
   b. Examining the possibility that the counselee's background (race, sex, handicap, age, and so on) may have influenced the test results
   c. Seeking additional information to explain any inconsistencies that become evident
4. Apply good counseling techniques to test interpretation by doing the following:
   a. Emphasizing "strengths" while objectively discussing "weaknesses"
   b. Allowing sufficient time for the counselee to assimilate information and respond
   c. Listening attentively to the counselee's responses (that is, attending to the counselee first and test results second)
   d. Checking the counselee's understanding of the test results from time to time; correcting misconceptions
5. Help the counselee begin (or continue) the career (educational and vocational) planning process by doing the following:
   a. Identifying, with the counselee, career options and steps for exploring each
   b. Providing assistance to the counselee through ongoing career guidance activities such as field trips, career conferences, filmstrips, library resources, and so on.
   c. Monitoring and encouraging career planning efforts through progress reports, follow-through counseling sessions, and so forth.

Anastasi (1985) offers some hints for interpreting results from multiscore batteries. She suggests offering score bands rather than single number scores in order to account for the reliability properties of the subtests in a battery, as expressed by the standard error of measurement. The same type of caution should be operative when a counselor interprets differences *between* scores or subscores or between gains in scores from one sitting to another. Intercorrelations among the subscores should not be higher than the size of the reliability coefficients of the subscores. Differential validity interpretations should be offered. Despite the *g* factor discussed earlier, Anastasi believes that "when specialized knowledge and skills are needed in a particular job, educational program, or other activity, these special requirements must also be assessed; such assessments represent essential supplements for the broader evaluation" (p. 64).

Types of Aptitude Tests

Assessment in the cognitive domain is usually achieved by administering a standardized battery of tests or individual tests measuring common aptitudes for which adequate criterion data are available. An aptitude may be defined as readiness for learning. An aptitude test is, therefore, one that predicts success in some occupation or training course. At present, the number of aptitudes for which psychologists have determined even minimally adequate validity data is limited. At best, it includes scholastic aptitude (verbal, numerical, and performance), perceptual speed and accuracy (clerical), manual dexterities, mechanical reasoning, spatial visualization, aesthetic judgment, artistic ability, and musical talent. Of these, the last three are highly specialized and have limited application. Thus, we are left with five basic aptitudes.

Various individual tests are capable of assessing aptitudes in each of these areas. However, for purposes of career guidance testing, the selection of individual tests poses problems. The main obstacle is that they have been standardized on different populations, and therefore norms are not consistent from test to test. Also, some individual tests fail to provide specific educational or occupational norms that would be useful in career guidance. Finally, choosing individual tests to assess multiple potentialities can typically run into large costs and present clerical problems in scoring.

Because of these deficiencies, psychologists have developed the test battery. Here a number of tests are employed together to predict various criteria. Individuals have several aptitudes, or patterns of strengths and weaknesses, that contribute to their total potential. The battery yields a multiscore summary of these differential patterns. Since all the tests in a battery are standardized on the same group, norms take on added meaning. It is becoming increasingly difficult to find an aptitude measure that does not have an accompanying interest inventory and, frequently, other career planning materials. Several of the most widely used instruments of this sort are briefly described below.

THE DIFFERENTIAL APTITUDE TESTS (DAT). Fifth Edition, Form C (1990). G. K. Bennett, H. G. Seashore, & A. G. Wesman. Grades 7–12 (one level for 7–9; another for 10–12; either level may be used with adults). Psychological Corporation. Requires approximately two and one-half hours working time.

Eight tests yielding 9 scores:

Verbal Reasoning
Numerical Reasoning
Abstract Reasoning
Perceptual Speed and Accuracy
Mechanical Reasoning
Space Relations
Spelling
Language Usage
Scholastic Ability (Verbal + Numerical)

Either hand or machine scored. Percentiles, stanines, and scaled scores separate for males and females (new norms). Career Interest Inventory also available. Both aptitude and interest data related to educational and occupational plans. Computerized Adaptive Edition available.

For personnel selection and classification in business, industry, government, and vocational education, the Differential Aptitude Tests for Personnel and Career Assessment are available.

Too new at time of writing for reviews. Review of previous edition may be found in Pennock-Roman (1988).

THE GENERAL APTITUDE TEST BATTERY (GATB) Forms A and B (1982); Forms C and D (1983). United States Employment Service. Requires two and one-half hours for administration.

Twelve tests measuring nine factors:

Intelligence (G)
Verbal Aptitude (V)
Numerical Aptitude (N)
Spatial Aptitude (S)
Form Perception (P)
Clerical Perception (Q)
Motor Coordination (K)
Finger Dexterity (F)
Manual Dexterity (M)

Standard Scores (Mean 100; standard deviation 20).

Cut-off scores for various occupational groups and job families according to DOT within group scoring.

Can be administered by those in non-USOE agencies if counselors take a short training course.

Now related to USES interest inventory.

Currently "on-hold" for use in personnel selection.

For review, see Koesling and Healy (1988).

ARMED SERVICES VOCATIONAL APTITUDE BATTERY (ASVAB). U.S. Department of Defense. High School level (juniors and seniors). ASVAB 19 (1991).

Nine tests:

Coding Speed
Word Knowledge
Arithmetic Reasoning
Tool Knowledge
Space Perception
Mechanical Comprehension
Shop Information
Automotive Information
Electronics Information

Yields three Academic Scales:

Academic Ability
Verbal
Mathematics

And four Occupational Scales:

Mechanical and Crafts
Business and Clerical
Electronics and Electrical
Health, Social, and Technological

Scores expressed in percentiles based on national norms.

Basically a recruitment device, but can yield valuable information at no cost

Scores related to military and civilian occupations via the *U.S. Army Career and Education Guide*

Student interactive workbook at no cost and SDS at no cost

For review, see Jensen (1988)

Excellent interpretive materials. Not just for students contemplating military careers.

CAREER PLANNING PROGRAM (CPP). Grades 8–11 (Houghton Mifflin). Grades 12–13 (ACT).

Components of CPP 8–11:

1. Interest Scales
   - Social Service
   - Business Contact
   - Business Detail
   - Technical
   - Science
   - Creative Arts
2. Experience Scales
   - Career-related activities and experiences
3. Ability Scales
   - Mechanical Reasoning

Space Relations
Clerical Skills
Numerical Skills
Reading Skills
Language Usage

Various other informal assessment components.

Related to *Exploring: You and Your Career* and *A Mini-Course in Career Planning*.

About two and one-half hours required for total program administration.

Abilities and interests reported in stanines.

Components of CPP 12–13:

1. Interest scales
   - Social Service
   - Business Contact
   - Business Detail
   - Trades, technical
   - Science
   - Arts
   - Health
2. Ability Scales
   - Space Relations
   - Reading Skills
   - Clerical Skills
   - Numerical Computation, Math Usage
   - Language Usage
   - Mecahnical Reasoning
   - Nonverbal Reasoning

Related to ACT Occupational Classification System and World-of-Work map for Job Families.

CPP 8–11 focus is primarily career exploration; CPP 12–13 emphasizes post-secondary planning.

Related to UNIACT Interest measure.

For a review, see Robertson (1988).

OCCUPATIONAL APTITUDE SURVEY AND INTEREST SCHEDULE (OASIS). (1983). PRO:ED. R. M. Parker. High school students. An aptitude survey based on the GATB consisting of six measures and requiring about 35 minutes. Aptitudes measured are: general ability, verbal aptitude, numerical aptitude, spatial aptitude, perceptual aptitude, and manual dexterity. Hand-scored. Results keyed to the DOT. Interest schedule measures USES twelve categories. Remer (1986; 1988) feels the survey has weak psychometric properties. Available in computerized version.

CAREER ABILITY PLACEMENT SURVEY (CAPS). (1976). Edits. The battery consists of eight 5-minute ability tests.

Results are reported in terms of stanines:

Mechanical Reasoning
Spatial Relations
Verbal Reasoning
Numerical Ability
Language Usage
Word Knowledge
Perceptual Speed and Accuracy
Manual Speed and Dexterity

May be used separately, but intended to accompany COPSystem interest and value measurement instruments and related to COPSystem career clusters (Service, Science, Technology, Outdoor, Business, Clerical, Communication, and Arts).

Machine- or self-scored. Norms for grades 8–12, community college, and selected occupational groups. Very short tests correlate moderately with longer tests (such as DAT, GATB). Contention is that when consideration of testing time is important, one can get as good prediction of high school grades with CAPS as with the GATB (L. Knapp, R. R. Strand, & Michael, 1978).

GRAFLEX VOCATIONAL EVALUATION SYSTEM. Singer Education and Training Products. Seven days to administer all tests.

Twenty-one "work stations":

Basic Tools
Bench Assembly

Drafting
Electrical Wiring
Plumbing and Pipe Fitting
Wood Working and Carpentry
Refrigeration, Air Conditioning, and Heating
Welding and Soldering
Clerk, Sales, and Office
Needle Trades
Masonry
Sheet Metal Working
Cooking and Baking
Small Engine Service
Medical Service
Cosmetology
Data Calculation and Recording
Soil Testing
Photo Lab Technician
Production Machine Operating

Unlike other tests, this is a work sample, hands-on determination of career aptitudes, interests, and work tolerances, used primarily for screening purposes in rehabilitation centers, vocational-technical schools, job centers, business and industry, and so on.

Systems such as these are usually housed in a "Work Evaluation Center."

Orientation and instruction for each work station followed by goal-directed work.

Very expensive to purchase.

Other work sample batteries are available and are equally good. See, for example: VOCATIONAL INTEREST, TEMPERAMENT, AND APTITUDE SCALE (VITAS) (Abrams, 1979); TOWER: Testing, Orientation, and Work Evaluation in Rehabilitation (Institute for the Crippled and Disabled, 1967). For a complete listing of these types of batteries, see Botterbusch (1987).

CAREER SURVEY. (1988). J. W. Wick, J. K. Smith, D. L. Beggs, & J. T. Mouw. American Testronics. Grades 7–12 and Adult. Approximately one and one-quarter hours.

Yields two ability scores: verbal and nonverbal, accompanied by 12 interest scales.

Grade-level percentile scores (also estimated ACT composite, SAT composite, and GATB-G score). Both same sex and combined sex norms.

Machine- or hand scored. Computer option available.

For a review, see Borman (1988).

DISCRIMINATION

It is generally conceded that at least two types of measurement are required for career guidance, where choice is the purpose: assessment of various capacities or aptitudes and assessment of interests. Each of these should be surveyed at various stages of an individual's development. The results should be communicated to the counselee in two ways: first, in terms of the groups in which the counselee may succeed, and second, in terms of the groups that the counselee most resembles with regard to interests, values, personality, and such. The "most like" description is achieved by means of a statistical technique called discriminant analysis. The former "goodness" probability statement emerges as a result of the regression analysis procedure discussed earlier. Hence, it is desirable to assess personal traits from both the cognitive (aptitudes) and noncognitive domains (interests) and to report results both in terms of the groups an individual is most like (discriminant analysis) and in terms of that individual's probability of success in given groups (regression analysis). In terms of the group an individual most resembles, for example, Laing, Lamb, and Prediger (1982) in a large-scale study have affirmed the use of basic interest scales in suggesting college majors to explore. Interest measurement is the most common application of discriminant analysis in career guidance. Although it is possible to use interest inventories for prediction, we do not view prediction as their primary value.

Interests

Super and Crites (1962) have observed that we may assess an individual's interests in four ways. We may look to *expressed* interests—what an individual expresses an interest in. Second, we may observe *manifest* interests—what an individual actually does as an indication of what one's interests are. Third, we may assess interests by *testing*—using an instrument like the Michigan Vocabulary Test, on the grounds that if an individual is really interested in something, that person will know the vocabulary involved in that area. Finally, we may examine *inventoried* interests—determining the pattern of an individual's interests from his or her responses to lists of occupations or activities.

This last technique is by far the most common means of assessing interests. Basically, two types of inventories have emerged. One is the so-called empirically keyed or criterion-keyed inventory, which results in interest scores related to specific occupations. The other is the ipsatively determined, or nonempirically keyed inventory, which yields score profiles in areas rather than in specific occupations and in relation to each other area rather than absolutely.

Research conducted by Reilly and Echternacht (1979) casts some doubts on the manner in which criterion-keying has been effected. Criterion-keying has been done without regard to the dimension of job satisfaction. There is now some evidence to suggest that job satisfaction within occupations should be considered in criterion-keyed interest scales (Assouline & Meir, 1987). Elements of both types of scoring may be combined in a given inventory.

The interpretation of interest inventories is no more informed by definitive research than is the interpretation of other tests as discussed earlier in this chapter. Sharf (1974) offers a thoughtful paradigm to serve as a structure for research into the question of differential effectiveness in test interpretation. His model would investigate the interaction of client variables, such as sex or age, with type of interpretation, such as programmed or computerized. Table 16.1 is a schematic of Sharf's model.

Of course some suggestions for interpretation are available in the manuals for the various inventories. Other suggestions are contained in the professional literature. Weinrach (1980) has resurrected an old technique that he calls "discrepancy identification." By this he means that clients simply predict their Kuder DD results and then compare them to actual outcomes. One often-used variation on this theme is to have parents predict the interest inventory results of their children. Their predictions rarely conform to actual profile results. The discrepancy serves as a stimulus for parent training.

Similar findings with congruence of work values of college students and their parents were reported by Vodanovich and Kramer (1989) who found the work values of both sons and daughters to be significantly different from both their parents' values.

Other researchers advocate a so-called integrative approach to test interpretation (Lange & Coffman, 1981). In this method, the counselor begins with the unique needs of the individual, compares these needs to those expressed by people in various occupations, and helps the individual to integrate this knowledge with an overview of the world of work. Several researchers urge the adoption of a systematic approach to the use and interpretation of tests; that is, specification of objectives, activities to achieve them, and careful evaluation of results. Obviously, we are in favor of such an approach.

Occasionally, studies have been carried out to try to determine if vocational preferences (as measured by interest inventories) are related to personality characteristics (as measured by personality inventories). The results have been inconsistent through the years. One study

Table 16.1

A Design Suggesting Future Directions in Research in Interest Inventory Interpretation

	Types of Interest Inventory Interpretation			
Client Variables	**Standard Profile Interpretation**	**Programmed Interpretation**	**Audio-video Interpretation**	**Computerized Interpretation**
Sex				
Age				
Education level				
Cultural group				
Personality type				
Type of vocational problem				

(Costa, McCrae, & Holland, 1984) compared scores on the Self-Directed Search (SDS) with scores on the NEO (Neuroticism-Extraversion-Openness) Inventory for 361 men and women aged 21 through 89. This study did, in fact, find strong relationships between personality dispositions and vocational interests, but the relationship may be simply a function of the two instruments used. Some relationships were in expected directions (such as extroversion with enterprising occupations). Others were intriguing (such as openness to new experience with investigative, artistic, and social occupations).

Kassera and Russo (1987) sought common factors in a personality measure (the Edwards Personal Preference Schedule—EPPS) and an interest inventory (Strong-Campbell—SCII). They confirmed the interaction of these two variables, identifying five factor-analytically derived types of college students. These were (1) the *Ardent-Involver* (an enthusiastic eager student who may be confronted and even at times overwhelmed with a myriad of choices); (2) the *Ascendent-Reacher* (an individual who is moving upward and tends to be purposive and externally directed as personal orientation and career interests interact); (3) the *Yielding-Controller* (someone who might readily submit to the external demands of a career context); (4) the *Compliant-Conformer* (represents a more passive orientation to work and learning. This seems to be someone who may feel compelled to act in accord with external criteria. Issues of organization and detail in personal orientation and vocational interests may prevail among this group); and (5) the *Concrete-Externalizer* (a more concrete, less sociable orientation toward work and personal relations) (pp. 64–65). In all, however, there are as yet insufficient data to make any definitive statement about the relationship of vocational interests to personality characteristics.

Card sorts are another assessment device sometimes used in career counseling. These are basically interest measurements or forced-choice devices that require the client to place cards, each, for example, containing an occupation or an activity, into a number of piles (the number varying with the particular card sort). These piles or categories might include such stimuli as: would not choose (or do), might choose (or do), and uncertain. The usual procedure is to take one pile and further refine it by forcing choice, until a rank-ordered, smaller number of options remain. The most well-known of these systems are the Occu-Sort (L. K. Jones, 1980a, 1980b) and Holland's Vocational Card Sort (VCS). This type of self-report mode is perhaps good for clients who are tactilely oriented and who might have difficulty with a more conventional instrument. In another example, Wellington (1986) reports on a card sort system for therapists of working women. She presents working women with 24 cards, each of which describes an issue, usually one related to interrole conflict. Clients sort them into one of three piles: apply to you directly, does not apply, doubtful. The chosen cards then serve as a basis for discussion.

One of the more interesting brouhahas in the use of appraisal data in career counseling (and counseling in general) concerns the Myers-Briggs Type Indicator (MBTI) (I. B. Myers & McCaulley, 1985). The MBTI was developed by a mother-daughter team who had no training in psychology but who were intrigued with Jung and his theory of psychological types. The instrument has been refined over half a century, and it elicits four preferences: (1) interests that represent *Extraversion* (the world of actions, objects, and persons) or *Introversion* (the inner world of concepts and ideas); (2) perception on the basis of *Sensing* (the immediate, real, practical facts of experience and life) or *Intuition* (the possibilities, relationships, and meanings of experiences); (3) judgment or decision making on the basis of *Thinking* (objectively, impersonally considering causes of events and where decision making may lead) or *Feeling* (subjectively and personally weighing values of choices and how they matter to others); and (4) preferences for living based on *Judgment* (in a planned, decisive, and orderly way aiming to regulate and control events) or *Perception* (in a spontaneous, flexible way, aiming to understand life and adapt to it). These four preferences may be combined into 16 types and described on the basis of the first letter of the descriptor (for instance, ISTJ means Introversion, Sensing, Thinking, and Judgment as the preferred interests, perceptions, decision making, and living modes of the individual). These four-letter code types are then all described in positive terms, leading some to maintain that the MBTI represents an example of the Barnum Effect previously discussed.

Advocates of the MBTI are a zealous group who have been known to put their four-letter code on personalized license plates. There is a journal devoted solely to the MBTI and Jungian types. Those who believe in the MBTI are almost religious in their fervor and are convinced of its usefulness and accuracy. Since presumably compatible occupations are suggested for each of the types, some practitioners use the MBTI in career counseling. One can find debates in the professional literature arguing the use of the MBTI (Carlson, 1989; Healy, 1989). For reviews, see Willis & Ham, (1988) and DeVito (1985).

Dillon and Weissman (1987) found many relationships between Holland and Jungian personality typologies when they administered both the MBTI and SCII to a group of college students. The best we can say at the present time is that there are extant instruments (described in this chapter) that offer measures of preferences, learning styles, and ways of viewing the world that have accumulated a great deal more validity data than has the MBTI. On the other hand, clients appear to enjoy their experience with the MBTI, and it probably does no harm. We would suggest that until further convincing data are available, counselors use the MBTI *only* in conjunction with other appraisal data and never as the sole self-information source.

Is an interest inventory in itself sufficient to meet the needs of clients or is additional counseling required? Pinkney (1987), for example, maintains that clients frequently oversimplify the role of assessment in career planning and assume that a test will tell them what to do. R. W. Johnson and Hoese (1988) attempted to answer this question with regard to 265 college students who took the Strong. The results of their study suggest that the Strong has limited use by itself with clients who manifest personal problems (in addition to career planning needs). In general, students had career needs that required attention even after a need for understanding their interests was satisfied, such as needs for self-understanding, career information, help with job placement, reassurance, and additional career options. In addition, many expressed a lack of interest in their major, a lack of job opportunities in their major, or unavailability of an appropriate major. The bottom line would seem to be that the administration and interpretation of an interest inventory in isolation—no matter how well done—is not likely to be sufficient to meet the career planning needs of most clients.

Whether vocational interests remain stable for long periods once they become crystallized in the late teens was investigated by J. L. Swanson and Hansen (1988). Students tested as college freshmen were retested at 4-, 8-, and 12-year intervals. Results indicated considerable group stability over each time period (in terms of rank-ordering) with interests being even more stable after college than during college, although there were obviously individual differences. Further, subjects themselves were apparently able to recognize whether their interests were stable or unstable over the 12 years.

Finally, readers should be aware that there is an Association for Interest Measurement (949 Peregrine Drive, Palatine, IL 60067) that offers a great deal of information about the construction and use of instruments involving interests.

Interest Inventories

Several of the most commonly used interest inventories are briefly described here:

OHIO VOCATIONAL INTEREST INVENTORY (OVIS) (2nd ed.). (1981) A. G. D'Costa, D. W. Winefordner, J. G. Odgers, and P. B. Koons, Jr., The Psychological Corporation, and others. Approximately one and one-half hours. Grades 7–13.

Twenty-three interest scales and a scale clarity score:

Agriculture and Life Sciences
Basic Services
Clerical
Communications
Crafts and Precise Operations
Customer Services
Education and Social Work
Engineering and Physical Sciences
Health Sciences
Legal Services
Machine Operation
Management
Manual Work
Marketing
Medical Services
Music
Numerical
Performing Arts
Quality Control
Regulations Enforcement
Skilled Personal Services
Sports and Recreation
Visual Arts

Scores expressed in percentiles.

Based on cubistic model (people, data, things) of DOT.

Includes a *Student Information Questionnaire* (six questions and one open-ended for a school to ask eight more questions of a locally pertinent nature).

Provides a *Student Report Folder*, and a *Guide to Career Exploration* to link interests to the world of work.

Machine- or hand-scored.

Reviewed positively by Harmon (1985) and Crites (1988)

Available in microcomputer version.

VOCATIONAL INTERESTS, EXPERIENCE, AND SKILL ASSESSMENT (VIESA).

Houghton Mifflin. Grades 8–12. Approximately 45 minutes.

Yields six job clusters (comparable to Holland's typology) and 25 job families that include 650 occupations. Self-scored.

Related to *Career Planning Program* described elsewhere in this chapter (i.e., the unisex form of the UNIACT).

Not a great deal of validity data yet accumulated regarding this instrument.

For a review, see Mehrens (1988).

STRONG INTEREST INVENTORY (formerly Strong-Campbell). E. K. Strong, Jo-Ida Hansen, and D. P. Campbell (1985). Stanford University Press, Consulting Psychologists Press. Grade 11–Adult. Approximately 30–45 minutes. 1985 Revised Norms. Yields 6 General Occupational Theme Scales (á la Holland) with 20 items in each scale.

These are related to 23 Basic Interest Scales:

- Realistic Theme
  - Agriculture
  - Nature
  - Adventure
  - Military Activities
  - Mechanical Activities
- Investigative Theme
  - Science
  - Mathematics
  - Medical Science
  - Medical Service
- Artistic Theme
  - Music/Dramatics
  - Art
  - Writing
- Social Theme
  - Teaching
  - Social Service
  - Athletics
  - Domestic Arts
  - Religious Activities
- Enterprising Theme
  - Public Speaking
  - Law/Politics
  - Merchandising
  - Sales
  - Business Management
- Conventional Theme
  - Office Practices

Also yields scores on 207 Occupational Scales, primarily professional level, although 17 vocational/technical occupations have been added.

Related to *Pathfinder* career decision-making system using interactive video.

Academic Comfort and Introversion-Extroversion Scales.

Broday and Braswell (1990) confirm that those who score higher on the Artistic and Investigative scales of the Strong tend to have higher Academic Comfort (AC) scores and that the AC scores of undergraduates are lower than those of graduate students.

Microcomputer version available.

The computer-based version of the SCII may have even better test-retest reliability than the paper-and-pencil version (Vansickle, Kimmel, & Kapes, 1989). For reviews of the SCII, see F. H. Borgen (1988) and V. L. Campbell (1987).

Campbell (1987) in her review of the SCII concludes that it "offers a breadth and depth in the measurement of occupational interests that is unmatched by any other single instrument" (p. 56). Similarly laudatory comments are offered by Borgen (1988) in his review.

OCCUPATIONAL PREFERENCE SURVEY (COPS). R. R. Knapp and others (1982). Educational and Industrial Testing Service. Grades 9–12. Approximately 40 minutes. Yields scores in 8 major groups according to 2 levels each (professional and skilled) á la Roe:

- Science
- Technology
- Business
- Linguistic
- Aesthetic
- Service

Outdoor
Clerical

Scores expressed in percentiles for males and females.

Machine- or hand-scored.

Computerized version available.

Kane (1989) offers a review of the COPS instrument in positive terms as a stimulus to career exploration, although he is less enthusiastic about its use in decision making involving immediate occupational choice because of incomplete psychometric data. Bauernfeind (1988) offers a similar evaluation in his review of the COPS.

CAREER KEY (CK) L. K. Jones. J. G. Ferguson. Produces a Holland code, listing of appropriate occupations, and references to the *Encyclopedia of Careers and Vocational Guidance*. Teaches the Holland theory. According to L. K. Jones (1989) and L. K. Jones, Gorman, and Schroeder (1990), the CK compares favorably with the SDS, at least in use with college students. A relatively new instrument.

CAREER ASSESSMENT INVENTORY (CAI). C. B. Johannson (1984 and 1986). National Computer Systems. Grade 8–Adult. Approximately 45 minutes. The Enhanced Version for careers requiring four years of college or less, or no postsecondary training. The Vocational Version for those entering careers immediately after high school or junior college.

Yields scores according to Holland's six types and 25 basic interests:

- Realistic
  - Mechanical/Fixing
  - Electronics
  - Carpentry
  - Manual/Skilled Trades
  - Agriculture
  - Nature/Outdoors
  - Animal Service
- Investigative
  - Science
  - Numbers
- Artistic
  - Writing
  - Performing/Entertaining
  - Arts/Crafts
- Social
  - Social Service
  - Teaching
  - Child Care
  - Medical Service
  - Religious Activities
- Enterprising
  - Business
  - Sales
- Conventional
  - Office Practices
  - Clerical/Clerking
  - Food Service

Also yields 91–111 specific occupational scores, 2 administrative indexes, and 4 nonoccupational scales.

Microcomputer form available.

Very similar to the Strong-Campbell.

For a review, see McCabe (1988).

KUDER OCCUPATIONAL INTEREST SURVEY (OIS) (Form DD). Science Research Associates (1985). Grades 9–12 and adults. Approximately 30 minutes.

Yields 119 occupational scales and 48 college major scales. Verification (V) scale and eight experimental scales.

Scores reported in terms of modified biserial correlations. Must be machine-scored.

For a review, see Jepsen (1988).

KUDER GENERAL INTEREST SURVEY (Form E). Science Research Associates (1975). Grades 7–12. Approximately 50 minutes.

Yields 10 interest scales plus verification (V) score:

Outdoor
Mechanical

Computational
Scientific
Persuasive
Artistic
Literary
Musical
Social Service
Clerical

Scores expressed in national percentiles.

Can be hand-scored or machine-scored.

Computer version available

For a review, see J. A. Williams and J. D. Williams (1988).

VOCATIONAL PREFERENCE INVENTORY (VPI). J. L. Holland. Consulting Psychologists Press. Grade 9–Adult. 1985 Revision. Approximately 30 minutes.

Yields 6 personality scales and 5 experimental scales:

Realistic
Investigative
Social
Conventional
Enterprising
Artistic
Self-Control
Masculinity-Femininity
Status
Infrequency
Acquiescence

Self-scored. Computerized version available.

Whether this instrument is a personality measure, an interest measure, or both, is still moot.

VOCATIONAL INTEREST INVENTORY (VII). P. W. Lunneborg (1981). Western Psychological Services. High school population. Intended for undecided students whose interests are not well differentiated. Approximately 20 minutes.

Forced choice format yields relative strength of interests in Roe's 8 areas:

Service
Business Contact
Organization
Technical
Outdoor
Science
General Cultural
Arts and Entertainment

Machine-scored. Scores reported in terms of percentiles and T scores for each scale.

Computer version available.

Controls for sex bias at item level and encourages exploration of nontraditional careers.

For less than positive review, see Krumboltz (1988b).

JACKSON VOCATIONAL INTEREST SURVEY. D. N. Jackson (1985). Research Psychologists Press. Grade 7–Adult. Approximately 40 minutes.

A Canadian-developed instrument that measures preferences in terms of vocational roles and vocational styles (activities and work environments).

Thirty-four basic interest scales arranged in 11 categories:

The Arts
Science and Mathematics
Practical, Outdoor Activities
Service Activities
Medicine and Health
Interpersonal and Job-Related Work Styles
Teaching and Social Welfare Activities
Business, Administrative, and Related Activities
Legal, Professional, Persuasive Work Roles
Literary, Academic
Work Styles Related to Job Activities

Hand- or machine-scored.

Computer version available.

Males and females measured equally.

Ten general occupational themes (expressive, logical, inquiring, practical, assertive, socialized, helping, conventional, enterprising, and communicative).

Academic orientation scale.

This inventory was carefully developed in terms of it psychometric qualities.

For a review, see Davidshofer (1988).

GEIST PICTURE INTEREST INVENTORY. H. Geist. Western Psychological Services. Grade 8–Adult. Some occupational norms. Intended for culture-limited and educationally deprived populations.

Requires minimum language competency.

Hand-scored.

Other non-verbal interest inventories are also available; for example, Reading-Free Vocational Interest Inventory-Revised (R-FVII-Revised) and the Picture Interest Exploration Survey (PIES).

JOB-O Career Interest Tests (Judgment of Occupational Behavior-Orientation). (1981) JIST.

Three Versions: JOB-O Elementary for grades 4–6; "classic" JOB-O for grades 7–10; and JOB-O Advanced for grade 10 through adult. 50 minutes.

Hand-scored.

Interests related to 120 occupations and college majors.

Nine scales: education, interest, inclusion, control, affection, physical activity, hands/tool/machinery, problem solving, and creating ideas.

MONITORING

It is useful to have some assessment of the stage of career development or career maturity of an individual or group. In one sense, monitoring can be thought of as an evaluation of an individual's career progress. Depending on the instrument used, it can tell us about individual readiness for choice rather than the content of choice. It tells us where individuals are vocationally and where they have to go. In another sense, monitoring informs us of such work-related factors as work values, job satisfaction, and a wide variety of other measurable variables pertinent to work life.

The career-related needs of individuals determine the goals to be achieved in a systematic approach; monitoring permits a continued check on these needs. There are diverse types of measures, both extant and in-process, that relate to this function. In development, for example, there are scales to determine degree of career "undecidedness" (see Chapter 14). Instruments exist to assess everything from work environment preference to career education needs assessment to job satisfaction and satisfactoriness. We are unable to cover all possible instruments.

A number of assessment devices, for use in career interventions, for example, are directed toward special populations. Halpern and his associates (1975), for instance, have developed the Social and Prevocational Information Battery (SPIB) for use with junior and senior high school educables with mental retardation. Of the nine domains appraised, two (job-related behaviors and job search skills) relate specifically to vocational aspects of development. Hegenauer and Brown (1990) and Daniels (1985) both view the SPIB as an instrument of considerable potential that requires further research. There are many similar devices available.

Other innovative techniques have been advocated. For example, Neimeyer (1989a) has suggested the use of the repertory grid technique (specifically, the Role Construct Repertory Test, or reptest) in vocational counseling. These types of tests are based on an individual's reaction to bipolar dimensions of constructs important in the world of work (for instance, nonphysical activity–physical labor; requires college–no college required). The client rates a number of these bipolar dimensions that were evolved by the client or by the counselor. Thus a grid is created. Valence ratings for each occupation are then obtained. What emerges is a profile that provides information about the client's levels of differentiation, integration, and conflict (see Chapter 15). In its current form, the technique seems unwieldy in practice, although the theory appears reasonable. Better (that is, simpler) implementation would be desirable.

What about "fringe" techniques? Can graphology, for example, predict occupational success? The evidence suggests that the analysis of handwriting by experts in graphology produces no better predictive efficiency than pure chance (Ben-Shakhar, Bar-Hillel, Bilu, Ben-Abba, & Flug, 1986). Although there are few, if any, studies in the literature regarding various psychics, phrenology, palmistry, and similar systems, it is probably safe to state that they too would not improve probabilities over a chance model.

One aspect of human behavior that is rarely assessed in terms of providing vocational self-knowledge to clients prior to their entering an occupation (with the exception of the developmentally disabled population) is that of competence in personal and social relationships. Although effective interaction at work is frequently assessed after the fact, there is seldom any a priori attempt to measure these social and personal dimensions as an aid to initial career decision making. Thus, the assessment of competence in relational contexts would appear to be an unmet need in career assessment. An introduction to the general field may be found in Spitzberg and Cupach (1989).

In any case, in the following section, we will consider some of the more prominent monitoring instruments in four distinct areas: career maturity, work values and personality, career planning, and job satisfaction.

Career Maturity

As discussed at length in Chapter 4, career maturity is a construct that naturally emerges from developmentally oriented career theories. If people do indeed go through a systematic series of stages in career development, then it ought to be possible to measure the rate and progress of that sequence and to compare where an individual is along that developmental line, both in terms of where one might reasonably be expected to be and in terms of where one's age peers are.

Depending on how far they depart from an expected norm, we may then classify them according to career maturity. Crites (1974a) has suggested that the measurement of career maturity has at least two types of utility: (1) a *research function* in that it enables us to "test" theoretical aspects of career development; and (2) a *practical function* in that it diagnoses the rate and progress of the career development of an individual and consequently suggests intervention strategies to enhance that development. In the latter sense, career maturity measurement can be used as both a type of needs analysis and as a criterion variable in the evaluation of the effectiveness of certain types of intervention strategies.

Generally, career maturity may be defined as the place reached on a continuum of career development from exploration to decline. Note that no current career maturity measure assesses any career-related maturational variables in the growth stage—that stage hypothesized to precede the exploratory stage. In broader terms, career maturity measures are an attempt to assess "the readiness of the individual to make decisions that are called for at a given decision point" (Super, 1974, p. 10).

A number of instruments designed to appraise career maturity from adolescence through adulthood have been devised.

Career Maturity Measures

CAREER DEVELOPMENT INVENTORY (CDI). D. E. Super, A. S. Thompson, R. H. Lindeman, J. P. Jordaan, and R. A. Myers

(1981). Consulting Psychologists Press. About one hour to complete. School form and college and university form.

Eight scales assessing knowledge and attitudes about career choice:

Career Planning (CP)—20 items
Career Exploration (CE)—20 items
Decision-Making (DM)—20 items
World-of-Work Information (WW)—20 items
Knowledge of Preferred Occupational Group (PO)—40 items
Career Development, Attitudes (CDA)—(CP & CE Combined)
Career Orientation Total (COT)—CP, CE, DM, & WW Combined

Generally acceptable discriminant validity (Kuhlman-Harrison & Neely, 1980).

Cautions for use are offered by Punch and Sheridan (1985) and J. I. Hansen (1985).

For an additional review, see Lacke (1988).

Machine-scored.

ADULT CAREER CONCERNS INVENTORY. D. E. Super and others (1985). Consulting Psychologists Press. Adult populations (few normative data as yet). 15-30 minutes. 12 substages to determine career planfulness in adults and their concerns with career development tasks at various life stages:

Exploration
1. Crystallization
2. Specification
3. Implementation

Establishment
4. Stabilization
5. Consolidation
6. Advancement

Maintenance
7. Holding
8. Updating
9. Innovating

Disengagement
10. Deceleration
11. Retirement planning
12. Retirement living

Subject rates self in relation to 61 concerns (for example, "using new methods and ideas on the job") on a 1–5 scale. Two separate scoring methods.

For a review, see Herr and Niles (1988).

CAREER MATURITY INVENTORY (Formerly called the Vocational Development Inventory). John O. Crites (1978). 50 attitude items. 100 competence items. Normative data for grades 6–13. 20–30 minutes for attitude test. Two to two and one-half hours for competency test.

Attitude Test
True-false format measuring five presumed attitude clusters with a total score:

1. Involvement in the choice process
2. Orientation toward work
3. Independence in decision making
4. Preference for choice factors
5. Conceptions of the choice process

Competency Test
Five multiple-choice tests: separate and total scores:

1. Problems: problem solving in career decision making
2. Planning: logical steps to career goals
3. Occupational Information: job duties and tasks, employment trends, and so on
4. Self-Appraisal: assessment of hypothetical person's assets and liabilities in relation to career success and satisfaction
5. Goal Selection: choosing the most realistic occupation for a fictitious individual

Attitude Test has been much more widely used than Competency Test up to this point.

Machine- or hand-scored.

For a review, see Frary (1988).

COGNITIVE VOCATIONAL MATURITY TEST (CVMT). B. W. Westbrook. 120 multiple choice items. 80–90 minutes. Normative data for grades 6–9.

Six subtests:

1. Fields of Work (20 items)
2. Job Selection (15 items)
3. Work Conditions (20 items)
4. Education Required (20 items)
5. Attributes Required (20 items)
6. Duties (25 items)

Reading level below grade 3.

Includes occupations in all Roe interests fields.

Subtests and total scores.

ADULT VOCATIONAL MATURITY INVENTORY (AVMI). D. I. Sheppard (1971). Male adults. Two forms: Form I, true-false; Form II, 5-point Likert scale. 40 items.

Five dimensions:

1. Involvement in the vocational choice process
2. Orientation toward work
3. Independence in decision making
4. Preference for vocational choice factors
5. Conceptions of the choice process

Small normative sample.

Westbrook (1974) has reviewed four of the inventories cited herein and two others that are less rigidly devised attempts to measure the construct. He has evolved a composite outline of the career behaviors that the tests are attempting to assess. In abbreviated form, the outline is:

I. Cognitive Domain (What the learner knows)
   - A. Individual attributes
   - B. Occupational information
   - C. Job selection
   - D. Course and curriculum selection
   - E. School and career planning
   - F. School and career problem solving

II. Psychomotor Domain (What the learner says he has done)
   - A. Involvement in career planning activities
   - B. Involvement in wide range of worker activities
   - C. Involvement in activities related to preferred occupation(s)

III. Affective Domain (Attitudes, preferences, and perceptions of learner)
   - A. Attitudes
   - B. Preferences
   - C. Perceptions

The six measures described above are clearly attempts to appraise the construct of career maturity. All are in the process of development; that is, they are being researched to determine their criterion-related validity and their construct validity and to discover what variables affect performance. Hundreds of studies have already been accomplished, and some useful data have emerged.

Unfortunately, career maturity scores from different instruments still do not correlate highly with each other. They do seem to be affected by scholastic aptitude, but not by sex or race (Westbrook, Sanford, & Donnelly, 1989).

Another disquieting aspect is that when career maturity is used as an outcome measure in very short-term and simple-minded career interventions, scores invariably increase. One would not think of being able to take someone who is generally determined to be "immature" in personality and to apply a two-session structured intervention, expecting to make the person "mature." Yet, this is essentially what we have been doing in the area of career maturity. Clearly, the construct's theoretical conceptions, operationalization, and measurement have to be developed further.

Work Values and Personality Instruments

A second type of monitoring instrument that is useful in both research and in career guidance is the work values measure. The values that one holds are clearly a determinant of career choice; therefore, an objective measure of the hierarchical structure of those values provides an individual with important input data for career decision making. Often these measures simply clarify what an individual already knows. Frequently, however, they open up hidden areas for exploration and consideration; they bring to the surface that which had remained dormant. Work values are sometimes confused with work interests. In fact, the two are distinctive domains, each measuring different variables. Work values appear to be related to job satisfaction (Rounds, Dawis, & Lofquist, 1987). A sampling of work values measures are described below.

THE VALUES SCALE. D. E. Super and D. D. Nevill. Research Edition. Consulting Psychologists Press. Measures intrinsic and extrinsic life-career values.

21 scales (106 items rated on a 4-point scale). 30–45 minutes:

Ability Utilization
Achievement
Advancement
Aesthetics
Altruism
Authority
Autonomy
Creativity
Economic Rewards
Lifestyle
Personal Development
Physical Activity
Prestige
Risk
Social Interaction
Social Relations
Variety
Working Conditions
Cultural Identity
Physical Prowess
Economic Security

Hand-scored or computer-scored.

For a review, see Harmon (1988).

L. V. Yates (1990) conducted research with the Value Scale that establishes some construct validity in that groups differ in their responses to the instrument according to age (for example, 18- to 25-year-olds place more emphasis on physical activity, advancement, and social interaction and less emphasis on autonomy and working conditions than 26- to 35-year-olds and 46- to 62-year-olds. In addition, the five occupational groups studied (by Holland code with artistic eliminated) differed in expected directions in their responses to the instrument.

WORK VALUES INVENTORY (WVI). D. E. Super. Houghton Mifflin. Grade 7-Adult. 15 minutes. 15 values relating to job success and satisfaction, combined into four factors: material, goodness of life, self-expression, and behavior control:

Intellectual Stimulation
Job Achievement
Way of Life
Economic Returns
Altruism
Creativity
Relationship with Associates
Job Security
Prestige
Management of Others
Variety
Aesthetics
Independence
Supervisory Relations
Physical Surroundings

Factor analysis of the WVI suggests 6 second-order dimensions (rather than the structural 4 into which the 15 values were organized): stimulating work, interpersonal satisfaction, economic security, responsible autonomy, comfortable existence, and esthetic concerns (Bolton, 1980).

SURVEY OF WORK VALUES (SWV). S. Wollack, J. G. Goodale, J. P. Wijting, and P. C. Smith. Late adolescent–Adult. Measures intrinsic (work-related values) and extrinsic (reward-related values) aspects of the Protestant work ethic.

54 items and 6 scales (9 items per scale):

Social Status of Job
Activity Preference
Upward Striving
Attitude Toward Earnings
Pride in Work
Job Involvement

CAREER ORIENTATION PLACEMENT AND EVALUATION SURVEY (COPES). R.R. Knapp & L.F. Knapp (1978). Edits. Junior high school to community college. May be used separately or as part of the more comprehensive Career Occupational Preference System (COP-System).

Offers 8 work-related value scales:

Investigative versus Accepting
Practical versus Carefree
Leadership versus Supportive
Orderliness versus Non-Compulsive
Recognition versus Privacy
Aesthetic versus Realistic
Social versus Self-Concern

Psychometric properties may be in need of strengthening (P. J. Mueller, 1985).

HALL OCCUPATIONAL ORIENTATION INVENTORY. Scholastic Testing Service. (1976)

Three levels: Grades 3-7; high school and college; handicapped adults. Based on Maslow's personality need theory and DOT.

Yields 22 scale scores:

Creativity, Independence
Risk
Information, Knowledge
Belongingness
Security
Aspiration
Esteem
Self-Actualization
Personal Satisfaction
Routine-Dependence
Data Orientation
Things Orientation
People Orientation
Location Concern
Aptitude Concern
Monetary Concern
Physical Abilities Concern
Environment Concern
Coworker Concern
Qualifications Concern
Time Concern
Defensiveness

OHIO WORK VALUES INVENTORY (OWVI). L. W. Hales and B. J. Fenner (1974). Publishers Test Service. Grades 4–12; 30 minutes to complete.

77 items yielding score on 11 work values:

Altruism
Object Orientation
Security
Control
Self-Realization
Independence
Money
Task Satisfaction
Solitude
Ideas/Data Orientation
Prestige

MINNESOTA IMPORTANCE QUESTIONNAIRE (MIQ). Vocational Psychology Research, University of Minnesota. Based on

Theory of Work Adjustment (R. V. Dawis & L. H. Lofquist,). Actually a measure of vocational needs rather than values. Most common form 1975 paired format with machine scoring. Fifth-grade reading level. 30–40 minutes. 20 statements representing 20 needs (for example, authority: I could tell people what to do) are paired with each other for a forced choice, then each of the 20 is rated absolutely.

Yield is scores on the 20 needs:

Ability Utilization
Achievement
Activity
Advancement
Authority
Company Policies and Practices
Compensation
Coworkers
Creativity
Independence
Moral Values
Recognition
Responsibility
Security
Social Service
Social Status
Supervision–Human Relations
Supervision–Technical
Variety
Working Conditions

Occupational Reinforcer Patterns (ORPs) are descriptions of reinforcer systems of selected occupations. (Scores also on 9 clusters of ORPs).

Machine-scored only.

For a review, see Benson (1988).

There are many other general values measures and many other work values instruments, but none of the latter have been more carefully devised and tested or have more direct applicability to careers than those we have listed. See, for example, Employment Readiness Scale, Study of Values, The Rokeach Value Survey, DF Opinion Survey, and so on.

Personality and Other Career Assessment Devices

Several other instruments have been devised to assess the knowledge or attitudes of individuals with regard to selected aspects of career development. These devices are intended to give both individuals and those responsible for career interventions a gauge of career-related awareness, knowledge, and attitudes. Some are criterion-referenced, and others are norm-referenced. Some are based on psychological constructs; some are not. They are, by and large, content measures. A sampling of some of these instruments follows.

It is possible to gain specific work-relevant information from extant instruments that are well-accepted measures of general personality. One example is the California Psychological Inventory (CPI) for which researchers (Gough, 1985) have developed a 40-item Wo scale to measure work orientation in the sense of self-discipline, dedication to obligations, and adherence to rule (that is, to the so-called Protestant work ethic). We have previously described the Myers-Briggs Type Indicator. Examples of a few other instruments follow.

EDWARDS PERSONAL PREFERENCE SCHEDULE (EPPS). A. L. Edwards (1959). The Psychological Corporation. Age 18–Adult. 45 minutes.

Provides relative ranking of 15 "normal" personality variables and can be related to career choice considerations. Based on Murray's Need System:

Achievement
Deference
Order
Exhibition
Autonomy
Affiliation

Intraception
Succorance
Dominance
Abasement
Nurturance
Change
Endurance
Heterosexuality
Aggression

Hand- or machine-scored.

TEMPERAMENT AND VALUES INVENTORY (TVI). C. B. Johannson & F. L. Weber (1977). NCS Professional Assessment Services. Grades 9–Adult. 30 minutes.

230-item instrument yielding scores on three scales:

- 7 temperament scales
  - Routine–Flexible
  - Quiet–Active
  - Attentive–Distractible
  - Serious–Cheerful
  - Consistent–Changeable
  - Reserved–Sociable
  - Reticent–Persuasive
- 7 reward value scales
  - Social Recognition
  - Managerial/Sales Benefits
  - Leadership
  - Social Service
  - Task Specificity
  - Philosophical Curiosity
  - Work Independence
- 4 administrative indices

Machine-scored only.

For a review, see K. G. Wheeler (1988).

SIXTEEN PF PERSONAL CAREER DEVELOPMENT PROFILE (PCDP). V. Walter (1986). Institute for Personality and Ability Testing. Age 16+. About 1 hour.

Career profile on the basis of responses to well-known personality assessment questionnaire.

Provides relevant information about individual strengths, behavioral attributes, and gratifications to accomplish personal career development objectives.

Offers scores of 16 personality dimensions arranged in dichotomous form:

Autonomous-Reserved—Participating-Warm
Concrete Thinking—Conceptual Thinking
Affected by Feelings—Calm-Unruffled
Considerate-Humble—Assertive-Competitive
Reflective-Serious—Talkative-Impulsive
Changeable-Expedient—Persistent-Conforming
Cautious-Shy—Socially Bold
Tough-Minded—Tender-Minded–Sensitive
Accepting-Trusting—Mistrusting-Oppositional
Conventional-Practical—Imaginative
Forthright-Unpretentious—Sophisticated-Shrewd
Confident–Self-Assured—Apprehensive-Concerned
Conservative-Traditional—Experimenting-Liberal
Group-Oriented—Self-Sufficient
Lax-Uncontrolled—Disciplined-Compulsive
Composed-Relaxed—Tense-Driven

Machine-scored only.

For a review, see Wholeben (1988).

The following instruments represent a sample of other career-related instruments.

Other Monitoring Instruments

WORLD OF WORK INVENTORY. J. W. Hudson and K. S. Hudson. World of Work, Inc. Grade 8–Adult.

3 sections

1. Career Interest Activities
2. Job Satisfaction Indicators
3. Vocational Training Potentials

Excellent interpretive manual.

COMPREHENSIVE CAREER ASSESSMENT SCALES (CCAS). S. L. Jackson and P. M. Goulding. Learning Concepts. Three scales: grades 3–7; grades 8–12+; teachers. Assesses familiarity with 75 occupations in the USOE clusters. Yields interest and familiarity profiles. Can be used for needs assessment, curriculum planning, and/or evaluation.

SELF-DIRECTED SEARCH (SDS) FORM E. J. L. Holland (1985). Consulting Psychologists Press. Self-administered and scored. Grade 4–Adult. 40 minutes.

Self-reports and estimates regarding:

1. Occupational daydreams
2. Preferences for activities
3. Competencies
4. Preferences for kinds of occupations
5. Abilities in various occupational areas

Yields summary codes according to Holland's scales and refers taker to *Jobs Finder.*

The Self-Directed Search has been combined with a Vocational Card Sort (VCS), an instructional booklet, and an action plan into the Vocational Exploration and Insight Kit (VEIK). In research on the VEIK, it is interesting to note that the VEIK failed to exceed the effect of its components (VCS and SDS) Takai & Holland, 1979).

The Self-Directed Search is illustrative of self-administered, self-scored, and essentially self-interpreted instruments. Although the approach is promising and certainly has been and is being subjected to research to establish its validity and effectiveness, there are several caveats to be noted. First, the SDS (and, we may infer, similar instruments) may yield inaccurate results in a substantial number of cases simply because of self-scoring errors and despite efforts to simplify the instrument. (R. W. Cummings & Maddux, 1987; T. R. Elliott & Byrd, 1985; and Tracey & Sedlacek; 1980). Holland has responded by producing Form E (for easy), which yields only a two-letter code, but there is no evidence to suggest that this instrument, as well as other self-administered, self-scored, and self-interpreted devices, is any less susceptible to error.

Second, the ability of individuals to estimate their own aptitudes is still a moot issue. Although some studies have suggested that counselees can accurately self-estimate aptitudes with which they have most familiarity (such as verbal and numerical), other studies have suggested that a significant proportion of individuals cannot accurately self-estimate either familiar or unfamiliar (for example, mechanical reasoning, clerical speed and accuracy, and such) aptitudes (C. D. Anderson, Warner, & Spencer, 1984; Hodgson & Cramer, 1977; J. L. Swanson & Lease, 1990).

Third, there appears to be some disagreement regarding how much, if any, counselor assistance is or should be required in relation to interpreting the SDS. In view of these three factors and others, perhaps the best advice that can be offered to counselors is that they proceed cautiously and accumulate their own data for evaluation.

Yet the SDS is widely used and will become more so as it is incorporated into the ASVAB testing program. The SDS is even recommended as a preferred assessment instrument for school psychologists who wish to include a vocational dimension in their psychoeducational assessments (E. M. Levinson, 1990).

For a review of the computer version of the Self-Directed Search (SDS: CV) see Urich (1990). N. J. Campbell's review (1988) is positive for *supervised* use.

It is especially troublesome to note that sometimes Holland codes derived from various instruments do not coincide to a degree that would give a counselor sufficient confidence. For example, Cappeto (1987) assessed agreement between SDS and SCII scores in terms of Holland high point codes and concluded that in about four out of 10 cases, high point codes of college students did not agree for those who took both instruments.

THE SALIENCE INVENTORY. D. E. Super and D. D. Nevill. Consulting Psychologists Press. Assesses relative importance of five major life roles: student, worker, homemaker, leisureite, and citizen. Evaluates client's orientation to life roles, readiness for career decisions, and exposure to work and occupations. Research edition (see Super & Nevill, 1984). For a review, see Zytowski (1988).

WPS CAREER PLANNING PROGRAM. J. N. Buck and others. Western Psychological Services. Amalgamates Assessment of Career Decision Making (ACDM) and The Vocational Interest Inventory (VII) with a student handbook containing 13 units of group activities and exercises. Helps clients understand their decision-making style, personal needs and values, and career interests. Assists in formulating career goals and planning for implementation of goals.

CAREER DECISION-MAKING SYSTEM. T. J. Harrington and A. J. O'Shea. American Guidance Service. Junior high–Adult. Either self-scored or computerized. Based on Holland's hexagonal theory of career development. Presumably systematic use of basic Holland-type data in decision making. Validity evidence from D. Brown, Ware, and S. T. Brown (1985). For a review see Droege (1988).

PLANNING CAREER GOALS (PCG). American Institutes for Research. Measures of interests, ability, career information, and a life and career plan inventory all in one package. This system is an outgrowth of Project Talent data.

THE VOCATIONAL ACTION PLAN. William Bloomfield and Associates, Inc. Independently functioning adults (special adolescent materials available). A combination assessment, counseling, and placement system, consisting of five stages:

1. Preassessment Interview
2. In-depth Assessment Interview
3. Development of Individual Action Plan
   a. Discovering Myself: Attitudes, Beliefs, and Ideas
   b. Options in Work, Jobs, and Careers
   c. The Job Search
4. Implementation of Patient Plan
5. Closure and Recommendations

MY VOCATIONAL SITUATION. J. L. Holland, D. C. Daiger, & P. G. Power. (1980). Consulting Psychologists Press. Grade 9+. 10 minutes.

Attempts to identify possible causes of vocational difficulties from among three possibilities: lack of vocational identity, lack of information or training. and/or environmental or personal barriers.

18 T–F statements and 2 multiple-part Y–N questions.

Hand-scored only.

For a review, see Westbrook (1988).

In Chapter 14, we discussed a number of measures of career indecision and undecidedness. A newer measure of career indecision is the Career Factors Inventory (Chartrand, Robbins, Morrill, & Boggs, 1990). This inventory consists of two information factors (need for career information and need for self-knowledge) and two personal-emotional factors (career choice anxiety and generalized indecisiveness). Prior to its use as a diagnostic tool, more validity and normative data will need to be gathered.

Job Satisfaction Measures

There are hundreds of measure of job satisfaction, worker attitudes, preference for work environments, and so on. A comprehensive annotation of these measures may be found in J.

D. Cook et al. (1981). Discussions of job satisfaction are contained in Chapters 2 and 13. We here present a sampling of some widely used instruments.

JOB SATISFACTION BLANK. R. Hoppock. Venerable overall measure of job satisfaction, containing only four basic questions. Respondents check alternatives that best tell how they feel about their jobs.

JOB DESCRIPTIVE INDEX. P. C. Smith, L. M. Kendall, and C. L. Hulin. A heavily used instrument. Five subscales (Type of Work—18 items; Promotion Opportunities—9 items; Supervision—18 items; Pay—9 items; and Coworkers—18 items). Each of the 72 items is an adjective or phrase and respondents indicate yes, uncertain, or no whether it describes the job aspect. Can also combine subscales for an overall score.

MICHIGAN ORGANIZATIONAL ASSESSMENT QUESTIONNAIRE. C. Cammann, M. Fichman, D. Jenkins, and J. Klesh. Contains measures of overall job satisfaction (3-item scale); intrinsic and extrinsic rewards; social rewards satisfaction; work attitudes and perceptions; job involvement; internal work motivation; task, job, and role characteristics; supervision; and work group functioning.

ORGANIZATIONAL COMMITMENT QUESTIONNAIRE. L. W. Porter and F. J. Smith. 15 items responded to on a 7-point scale. Organizational commitment is assumed to be more global and less transitory than job satisfaction. Measures how strongly an individual identifies with and is involved in a particular organization.

JOB-RELATED TENSION SCALE. R. L. Kahn, D. M. Wolfe, R. P. Quinn, J. D. Snoek, and R. Rosenthal. 15 items responded to on a 5-point scale. Respondents indicate how frequently they are bothered at work by each item (for example, "Feeling that you may not be liked and accepted by the people you work with").

WORK PREFERENCE QUESTIONNAIRE (WPQ) S. Fineman. Measures need for achievement in occupational settings. 24 forced-choice items yield scores on 9 aspects of an achievement (for example, responsibility, risk-taking, competitiveness).

ROLE AMBIGUITY AND ROLE CONFLICT SCALES. J. Rizzo, R. J. House, and S. I. Lirtzman. 6-item scale measuring role ambiguity ("predictability of outcomes of one's behavior and the existence of environmental guidelines to provide knowledge that one is behaving appropriately") and 8-item scale measuring role conflict (incompatibility of demands).

EVALUATION

Because a comprehensive discussion of evaluation in a systematic approach to career guidance was presented in Chapter 6, the following remarks are intended primarily as a summary. Built into any systematic approach is the process of evaluation. Evaluation is simply a series of activities designed to determine how well goals have been achieved. As such, evaluation implies valuing—saying what is desirable or good.

In a systematic approach, one looks for a relationship between career guidance processes (input) and counselee behavioral outcomes (output). In order to determine the strength of such a relationship, one must consider certain elements in the systematic model. These have been dealt with in earlier chapters; by way of review, selected aspects of the components of a systematic approach are presented as they have been classified by Wellman (1970):

1. *Needs*. The various developmental stages through which individuals pass determine

their needs at various developmental levels and, in turn, determine the goals of career guidance.

2. *Objectives.* Objectives or goals, which arise from counselee needs, are stated in both global and behaviorally specific terms.
3. *Process.* Process or treatment refers to specific activities carried out to achieve objectives. Treatments are dependent on and arise from the base built prior to their implementation and subsequently determine future process.
4. *Counselee variables.* Since certain career guidance processes are dependent on selected characteristics of the counselees who are exposed to those processes, it is frequently necessary in evaluation to conduct cross-breaks—that is, to determine differential effects of process on counselees because of differences in sex, socioeconomic level, culture, ability, and so on.
5. *Situational variables.* It is equally likely that career guidance processes may have differential effects in different situations. What works in a vocational school may not work in a comprehensive high school; what works in a liberal arts college may not work in a more technically oriented institution; what is effective in a rural area may not be effective in an urban area, and so on.
6. *Outcome variables.* Outcome variables are defined by objectives that are behaviorally specific and must, in some cases, present immediate, intermediate, and long-range goals.
7. *Feedback.* This concept refers to the need for continuous evaluation. Just as one continually uses monitoring procedures to keep aware of counselees' career needs, the counselor employs continual evaluation to determine how closely goals are being achieved. If goals are not being achieved, then processes must be changed for future groups.

For a detailed description of evaluation techniques that even the counselor who is unsophisticated in research procedures can accomplish, see S. H. Cramer, Herr, Morris, and Frantz (1970).

In summary, the procedures for evaluation within a systematic approach to career guidance are as follows:

1. Formulate the broad goals of the career guidance program.
2. Classify these goals so that an economy of thought and action can be achieved. Decide what developmental stages require which guidance processes for implementation.
3. Define objectives in behavioral terms.
4. Suggest situations in which the desired objectives and behaviors might be observed.
5. Develop or select appraisal techniques such as standardized tests, monitoring instruments, questionnaires, and so on.
6. Gather and interpret performance data and compare these data with the stated behavioral objectives.

This system of evaluation is, in a sense, an absolute system, since no comparisons are made between the career guidance program in a given institutional setting and the program in any other comparable setting. Those responsible for planning, implementing, and evaluating a systematic approach to career guidance may wish to make such comparisons to determine relative effectiveness.

Summary

In this chapter we have discussed the use of measurement and assessment procedures in four areas relating to career guidance: prediction, discrimination, monitoring, and evaluation. Selected aspects of each of these areas, with descriptions of a sampling of illustrative instruments, have been presented. Prediction and discrimination techniques provide data for individual decision making; monitoring and evaluation procedures enable counselors to plan more effectively in providing career guidance within a systematic framework. The use of any specific appraisal instrument, whether commercially standardized or locally developed, depends on the unique characteristics of a given population. Therefore, there is no such thing as *the* testing program in career guidance or *the* evaluation instruments. Institutions should be flexible and imaginative as they build their own appraisal programs.

An excellent resource for counselors who wish assistance in evaluating specific tests and inventories for use in career assessment is Kapes and Mastie (1988). A good source for assisting counselors in using specific types of career assessment instruments in career counseling is Zunker (1986b). For a specific discussion of the use of career assessment with adults, see Crites (1986).

CHAPTER 17

RESEARCH AND SOCIAL ISSUES IN CAREER GUIDANCE AND COUNSELING

Key Concepts

- Research studies have repeatedly demonstrated that career interventions do yield positive results and that their general utility is clear.
- Given the enormity of the possible questions that may be raised about the content and application of career interventions in different settings and with different populations, the quality and comprehensiveness of both the theory and research about career behavior and intervention in it are uneven.
- Since career behavior occurs within settings, life stages, and economic and political systems that are dynamic, new research questions are always forming.
- The fullest possible understanding of career development theory and of the effects of career interventions requires a wide range of research techniques and purposes: descriptive, correlational, case study, naturalistic, single subject, factorial, multivariate, subjective and qualitative, experimental, cross-sectional, ethnographic, longitudinal, and combinations of these.
- Although the typical statistical approaches to career behavior and treatment effects or interventions in career development have included discriminant analysis, analysis of variance, and correlational or regression approaches, additional and more sophisticated techniques are now emerging.

Research and speculation are abundant about the origins, structure, and persistence of career behavior and the forms of intervention that affect such behavior. Indeed, in the broadest sense, there is no longer a major question about the ability of career guidance or career counseling to improve or change career behavior. Meta-analyses and other research techniques have permitted researchers to summarize large numbers of studies and determine the collective effect of individual studies of a particular process on different forms of behavior. Such aggregate studies have shown that career education (Baker & Popowicz, 1983), career counseling (Holland, Magoon, & Spokane, 1981; Spokane and Oliver, 1983; Oliver & Spokane, 1988) and career guidance (Herr, 1986) do yield positive results and that the general efficacy of such interventions is no longer in question (Rounds & Tinsley, 1984).

If the results of career education, career guidance, or career counseling are as positive as stated in the above paragraph, why is this chapter needed? Is the chapter's content not redundant with what has been said throughout this book? These are important questions. Let us suggest first that the interpretation of the status of research in career education, guidance, and counseling was that "in its broadest sense" and in the aggregate the results are quite positive. Such a statement does not mean that every important question has been answered or that every study has yielded unequivocal results. Certainly, the quality and the comprehensiveness of both the speculation and the research about career behavior and interventions in it are uneven and less than comprehensive. Such unevenness and deficits in coverage arise from the scope of the field and the enormity of the issues and questions across populations, characteristics (such as age, gender, minority group, ethnicity, religion), settings (such as schools, work sites, community agencies), historical or developmental time (such as cohort effects, social and economic conditions) or intervention form (such as individual counseling, group counseling, classes, self-directed instruction, computer-directed processes). The vastness of the field of inquiry about career behavior and the interventions in it also derive from the multiple disciplinary lenses that can be applied to the understanding of such phenomena.

Since the terms *career counseling, career education*, *career guidance*, and *career intervention* are each used to describe a large inventory of processes and techniques applied to career behavior, it is logical to suggest that relevant research and theory can be found in many academic disciplines and at many levels of quality and sophistication. This same observation can be made about any realm of human behavior, but it nevertheless suggests the difficulty of being encyclopedic in analyzing the research base of the field as fully as some readers would desire.

An illustration of the complexity and the comprehensiveness of the problem of attempting to summarize research and social issues in career guidance and counseling is suggested by a review of the studies of vocational behavior published in only one year, 1989 (Morrow, Mullen, & McElroy, 1990). For that review 75 journals and some 521 articles were examined. Even so, other pertinent journals were not included, and some clusters of research on vocational behavior were not included because of space limitations. As one adds years of research the aggregate topics and results that are of interest to a researcher or practitioner grow exponentially.

As generally positive findings about the effects of career guidance, counseling, or education on career behavior have accumulated, the research questions have become more conscious of both the structure of career behavior and its change over time. Since the content of career counseling (for example, type of work activities, environments and options, freedom of opportunity, achievement images, systems of job information) is so dynamic and so intimately tied to changes in the occupational, political, social, and economic contexts of the nation, one could hardly expect that research on these matters would be static and totally encompassing. Individual behavior is a function of transactions with environmental expectations and opportunities intertwined with personal values, abilities, and skills. As any of these ingredients changes, so does the system within which individual behavior is triggered. In a sense, theory and research are virtually always running to catch up with such circumstances.

Much of the theory and research on career development to the present has assumed that individual action has been the predominant factor in how careers are forged and where intervention in such career behavior should be aimed. This is, of course, a view in which the lens is primarily psychological. However, as we discussed in Chapter 4, this view tends to underestimate the degree to which environments create and reinforce work roles and career opportunities; the degree to which persons are chosen rather than do the choosing. The latter views are predominantly sociological, anthropological, organizational, and economic. The influence of such perspectives on how individual career behavior is stimulated and shaped has not yet been as fully integrated into the conceptual and empirical bases of career guidance as is likely to emerge during the next decade (Bartol, 1981; Slaney & Russell, 1987).

The state of the conceptual and empirical bases of career guidance and career counseling is fundamental to the quality of services that practitioners offer in any setting. But these are not the only important questions to be raised. Also of concern are questions of social effects. As we have suggested, career guidance or career counseling does not occur in a political or social vacuum. Its content is largely derived from events in the larger society. Indeed, the types of questions that youths and adults bring to counselors are related to how they view current societal belief systems about personal choice, achievement, social interaction, self-initiative, marriage, prestige, occupational or educational status, role integration, and many other aspects of life. The resulting anxieties, deficits, or indecisiveness that persons experience as they compare themselves with what society's representatives (such as parents, employers, teachers, peers, spouses, the mass media) say they should believe or do is the content with which counselors deal. Societal filters also permit or discourage persons asking certain questions about themselves or their opportunities. And different societies, deliberately or inadvertently, support the use of some guidance and counseling techniques as ethical or appropriate and restrict or prohibit the use of other forms of intervention. In either case, as discussed in Chapter 1, career guidance and counseling in all societies tend to be sociopolitical processes.

From such a perspective, the question of social effects can be succinctly stated in this way: Because one can change behavior in certain ways, should one do so? If so, to what ends? The answers to such questions are not necessarily empirical; they are more likely to be philosophical and value oriented.

The terms *career education*, *counseling* and *guidance* represent deliberate instructional, counseling, and direct experiential interventions in the career development of youths and adults. Such different approaches stimulate hypotheses that ask if certain types of career guidance, counseling, or related processes (such as career education) are implemented, what specific student or client behaviors will result to benefit the individual or society? Many of the assumptions and much of the research upon which current models of career guidance and career counseling rest have already been referred to in this book. But not every observer accepts the assumptions stated, asks the same questions as those who advocate career counseling, career guidance, or career education, or believes that the existing research base is adequate to endorse expanding or even retaining present forms of career interventions. Questions continue to be raised and criticisms leveled at the effectiveness or the appropriateness of these processes in relation to the characteristics of the nation's economy, shifting values of the population, legitimate expectations of schooling, the potential social effects of the techniques used, and the status of research underlying these processes.

Savickas (1989) has suggested that although "we know that career interventions generally have positive effects. . . . Now we need to determine which interventions work with whom and under what circumstances" (p. 102). Consequently, researchers now and in the future must study how interventions achieve their effects and how to optimize these effects through a process which Gray and Braddy (1988) call "incremental staged innovation."

Although we hope that we have made a case for career education, guidance, and counseling in the preceding chapters, we continue to realize that many relevant research questions and social issues still need to be explored. Some are matters of substance; others, of methodology; still others, of philosophy. In this chapter we will briefly discuss some of the current views on these matters, identify some methodological issues, and inventory some research needs.

PERSPECTIVES ON RESEARCH AND THEORY

Depending on the training and interests of given observers, current perspectives on the state of the art of research in career guidance differ somewhat, although there are certain overarching views. For example, Healy (1982, pp. 586–588) has identified five research priorities pertinent to career development. In abridged form they include the following:

1. Counseling treatments must be specified in greater detail, ideally delineating factors such as key concepts and principles; the kinds of materials and exercises used in counseling and as homework; the quality of learning interaction; the total time for counseling and homework; the client's starting and closing mastery of concepts, principles, and skills; and the degree to which the client voluntarily selected and created the counseling program. . . .

2. Reports need to describe clients more comprehensively at the start and conclusion of counseling, using psychodiagnostic systems. . . . Demographics such as age, sex, grade and previous counseling are useful but insufficient. Replication and transportability require information about strengths and weaknesses of the clients and their environments and data about clients' aspirations and the urgency of their quest.

3. Counselors need to examine the modifications of traditional treatments, which may be necessary to serve atypical populations. . . . Relationships between client type and counseling method promise to be an important research concern.

4. Counselors need to test whether and how expansion of counseling to include strategies such as assigned reading, extra-counseling practice, mastery tests, and securing privileged access to resources for a client contribute to career advancement. . . .

5. Counselors need to improve their research designs. . . .

Healy's observations are helpful in defining some of the major problems associated with improving research in career guidance. A primary problem is methodological.

The Search for Acceptable Methodology

Gelso (1979) has suggested that in recent years counseling has experienced a polarization of views on what constitutes an acceptable methodology. He further suggests that it may well be the most prominent trend in the field and a healthy state of affairs "if it represents an expansion of what the field views as permissible bases for evidence, and if the strengths and limitations of each investigative style are recognized" (p. 9).

This chapter is not intended to be a research primer, but the maturing of theory development pertinent to career behavior and the understanding of the effects of career guidance "treatments" are likely to require all the research tools now available; for example, descriptive, correlational, case study, naturalistic, single subject, multivariate, factorial, subjective and qualitative, experimental, cross-sectional, longitudinal, ethnographic, and a combination of these. It is unlikely that single studies, however large in scale, can answer all of the important research questions that lie before us. Rather, we are likely to continue to rely on the aggregate effects of several studies, each true to the assumptions and design precautions appropriate to the specific questions being studied. It is out of such multiple observations that theory is tested and refined and new theory developed.

It is often true that the research techniques available are significantly ahead of practice in the field or that there are more powerful ways to study certain questions than are used. The study of "treatment effects" is one example. Gelso (1979) appropriately notes the effects of Kiesler's work (1971) in using factorial designs to study both main effects of treatment and organismic or individual differences variables. In such designs one can study two or more treatments in comparison to the outcomes associated with control groups as well as the effects of such treatments on different client populations defined by age, gender, experience, and so on, across time and as provided by counselors of different types. The study of interaction inherent in such factorial designs permits one to test several hypotheses simultaneously as one studies treatment effects against differences in client populations, counselor style, outcome measures, repeated observations, or other pertinent criteria. Factorial approaches typically involve analysis of variance or covariance or multivariate analysis of variance as the statistic of choice in addition to a post hoc significance test, although correlation or regression analysis is frequently the appropriate statistical approach.

As important as factorial designs are for comparative and experimental studies of "treatment effects" on different types of presenting problems, they are less useful for predicting patterns of longitudinal career development. For such purposes it is more likely that some type of regression analysis or discriminant function procedure will be used.

The Issue of Careers. In 1969 (Super 1969a; 1969b) Super discussed the state of methodology bearing on career issues. He began with the premise that vocational psychology from the beginning of this century until shortly after 1950 was a "psychology of occupations." Since that period we have also seen the emergence of a "psychology of careers." Methodological models in a psychology of occupations typically focus on the occupations as the subject and the persons in the occupations as the source of data about the occupation. According to Super (1969a) this model takes predictor data at an early stage of a career and uses regression methods to predict later success in one occupation or it uses discriminant analysis as a means of assessing the likelihood of being found—later—in each of several possible occupations. But such approaches tend to represent differential psychology, the study of individual differences, in a somewhat static sense. The psychology of careers requires more than differential diagnosis. It is more directly focused on the elements that underlie what Crites (1981) has called *dynamic diagnosis*, the concern with the etiology of career behavior, not just its classification.

Spokane (1990) has addressed the issues defined earlier by Super's analysis of the research implications of a psychology of occupations versus a psychology of careers. Spokane suggests that "most research in vocational psychology can be described by reference to two fundamental methodological viewpoints that have clearly stated assumptions and a large evidential and historical base underpinning their tenets. . . . These paradigms are (a) differential vocational psychology and (b) developmental vocational psychology" (p. 25). Spokane then emphasizes in his discussion the characteristics of the differential tradition.

He contends that two methodological thrusts undergird the differential approach: actuarial and experimental. The actuarial approach contains studies "that involve the construction and validation of various interest, ability, style, and, occasionally, personality measures related to choosing and adjusting to work for normal individuals. . . . these actuarial emphases also include studies that employ ANOVA, ANOCOVA, MANCOVA, factor analysis, multidimensional scaling analysis, or other multivariate techniques in an effort to test a theory, where control over the independent variable rather than the construction of a new instrument is the principal focus of the study" (p. 25). The experimental thrust, according to Spokane, tests "the effects of a variety of career interventions and treatments ranging from a single 20-minute session of reinforcement for exploratory behavior to semester-long-evaluations of the effectiveness of curricular/class interventions" (p. 25). Although the purposes of his discussion were not to focus on the characteristics of the developmental approach, he does contrast the two approaches as follows: "I would include under the *differential* rubric any studies evaluating interventions that were based on inventories or tests whose purpose was to distinguish one group of respondents from another, just as I would include under the *developmental* rubric any studies evaluating the effects of a career intervention that was based on developmental assumptions" (p. 34).

Careers are by definition developmental. Indeed, career development is itself a rubric for the complex interactions between the affective, cognitive, and psychomotor characteristics of persons potentially mediated by their values, family history, school climate, community reward system and many other possible variables that may or may not be affected by time. In a career model we are interested in predicting the sequence of positions that a person will occupy in pursuing a career (Super, 1969a). To achieve this understanding of careers, however, we need to understand not only the positions people occupy during their working life but also the interrelationship of factors that caused them to anticipate, plan, and implement one position rather than another at any given point in their life as well as the threads that link one choice to another or one position to the subsequent one. Our progress toward such goals has depended on the availability of statistical methods capable of handling the myriad of factors feeding into career development and on hardware (primarily computers) that allow a researcher to cope with sophisticated analyses of an enormous number of data points. Hardware problems are rapidly disappearing, but questions of statistical methodology continue to be formidable obstacles as we move forward with time series data.

Time series data, like any other research matter must rest upon a clear conceptualization of what one is attempting to study and of measurement strategies and instruments that capture the essence of the variables (constructs) of interest. Thus, since time series studies are frequently employed to study career development, it is first necessary to determine what is meant by development. The term *development* is not a singular term. It is a theoretical construct that has been defined in different ways by different theorists who have applied different sets of assumptions to the explanation of behavioral change: for example, mechanistic, organismic, developmental contextualism (Lerner, 1986). As Jepsen (1984a) has observed, "within counseling psychology, it is nearly a truism to say 'vocational choice is a developmental process' or 'vocational development is developmental.' No one has seriously challenged these points since they were first popularized in the 1950s. The result has been a somewhat haphazard use of the concept of development in vocational literature" (p. 178). Without addressing such conceptual caveats effectively, the collection of appropriate time series data is put at risk.

Schulenberg (1986) has contended that most of the existing research on the changes over time (or the differences across groups) in work values and career interests has focused at the quantitative level—changes in the magnitude or frequency of a construct—rather than the qualitative level—change in the underlying meaning of a construct. Thus, if the meaning of a construct to males or females or different racial groups actually changes over time (comes to be seen as carrying a different definition or content) then the utility of making purely quantitative comparisons becomes questionable. One proposed response to such quantitative/qualitative issues in time series data is the increased use of factor-analytic techniques to probe underlying meanings of constructs and their variance or invariance over time (Nesselroade & Baltes, 1984). As Schulenberg suggests, "for a developmentally meaningful construct, structural continuity across time or groups can be operationalized as the invariance of the factor loading patterns (i.e., factor invariances) while increased differentiations across time or groups can be represented by an increased number of factors and/or a decrease in the magnitude of the correlations among factors" (p. 20). While not the only method of conceiving time series data, the work of Schulenberg, Nesselroade, and Baltes, and, more recently, of Vondracek, Lerner, and Schulenberg (1986) have introduced many of the research techniques traditionally used in developmental psychology to vocational psychology.

Without getting into the extended discussion warranted by their proposed methodological agenda for the study of vocational behavior and career development, it is useful to acknowledge that Vondracek, Lerner, and Schulenberg (1986) and Vondracek (1990) have outlined the essential elements of developmental or time series studies of careers. In so doing, they have examined three interacting components of such designs: developmental, relational, and contextual. They have advanced important notions in the study of careers that advocate the use in longitudinal designs of several birth cohorts to look at the interaction of individual lives and historical times; and sequential designs to identify cohort effects, change-sensitive measures, multivariate measures, and multilevel research (psychological, biological, sociological, cultural, and historical).

Obviously, not all elements of career development require the same levels of sophistication or the same purpose as do time series questions. It is often necessary, for example, to conduct survey research by which the variables deserving systematic study in career development can be identified. Some questions that fall within this category are "What career behaviors develop as the individual matures? Are there group differences in the development of career behavior? What are the career behaviors essential to success in different work settings?"

Technique research is also necessary to career development. For example, the work of Crites on the Career Maturity Inventory, Holland on the Self-Directed Search and the Vocational Preference Inventory, Westbrook on the Cognitive Vocational Development Inventory, Super on the Values Inventory, the Salience Inventory, the Career Development Inventory, and the Adult Career Concerns Inventory are examples of efforts to create ways of collecting information that is pertinent to career development and quantifiable. Such research concerns the internal structure of available instruments as well as their relationship to external criteria determined largely by survey research to be important in career development.

Theoretical Research. Theoretical research has represented a stimulus to and an outcome of the survey and technique research cited. In the theoretical arena, hypothesis testing has attempted to evaluate the gross assumptions that career development is continuous and longitudinal, that it can be described as being composed of different developmental tasks at different life periods, that career development and personal development more broadly conceived are related, and that career development can be modified by certain forms of intervention or that specific variables are associated with the character of career development at some point in time. Much of this research is concerned with understanding the structure of career behavior as well as how it changes over time. Applied research, too, has been moving forward in testing various attempts to facilitate career development through the formal processes of schooling or other educative methods.

Statistical Methods. To reiterate to some degree what has already been said about methodology, the statistical methods used in these four research areas have included the following:

1. *Discriminant analysis* is a way of examining predictive validity in regard to group membership particularly where the criterion variables are nominal or ordinal, rather than continuously measured traits, or where the predictor variables are multidimensional as found in personality profiles. This approach has been important to our understanding of the personality variables by which career or curriculum groups are separated in measurement space—how individuals with particular traits resemble groups of persons engaging in an occupation or curriculum, for example.

2. *Analysis of variance* (factorial approaches), although important as a part of discriminant analysis strategy and frequently the statistic of choice for testing the null hypothesis, has often been used as a descriptive or classification method rather than in an experimental form. As such it has helped in the identification of shifts in means or variance on some dependent variable over time but has not advanced our understanding of the dynamics underlying such shifts as much as we would hope.

3. *Correlational or regression analysis* has also been widely used to determine the predictive power of certain individual traits or trait sets to different classes of career-related criterion variables—academic decisions, vocational aspirations, and vocational adjustment. Indeed, the various correlational modes, parametric and nonparametric, have been highly valuable, particularly in identifying associations between variables requiring further study. Certainly, multiple regression and partial correlation have been exceedingly valuable in our understanding of the ranking or weights of predictive variables in relation to each other. In some instances, canonical correlations have been helpful in analyzing the stability of the dispersion of scores over time (Gribbons & Lohnes, 1969, p. 32), determining the full extent of the interrelatedness of two sets of scores, and indexing the amount of common variance shared by the functions of two sets of measurement.

Essentially, the approaches that have just been identified are linear and represent an independent-variable-predicting-dependent-variables paradigm in which "the criterion variable is 'explained' by the pattern of its statistical dependency on a set of predictors. . . . Generally, the effort is to account for as much of the variance in the criterion as possible from the predictors' variance-covariance" (Gribbons & Lohnes, 1969, p. 185, 1982). Gribbons and Lohnes have attempted to move outside this perspective by using a stochastic model, in particular a Markov chain analysis, to examine the outcomes of a discrete measurement variable. Markov chains are probability models that can tell us how much of the variance in developmental outcomes can be explained by a theoretical model of the process itself without recourse to functional or statistical relations with outside variables (p. 186). Essentially, the model observes the paths taken by the subjects through the states of the variable over temporally separated stages to see if there is a probability law inherent in the "process" (the tree structure) of possible paths through the states over the stages.

Treating Career Data. Super (1969b) suggested in 1969 that four approaches might be useful to treating career data: lattice theory, Markov chains theory, path analysis, and the career tree. Although each of these approaches has been used in other disciplines, particularly sociology, over the nearly twenty years since Super's observations were made, these approaches have rarely been used in career development research.

Significant exceptions to the above generalization are the 20-year longitudinal study of Gribbons and Lohnes (1968, 1982) in which the use of Markov chains is a prominent feature, and the work of Cooley and others (for example, Flanagan & Cooley, 1966), which has applied the career tree approach to Project Talent data. Although there are some examples of the use of path analysis (O'Reilly, 1973; Enderlein, 1974; Watanabe, 1980) with career data, this methodology may be superceded by approaches to causal modeling (Jackson, 1983) or structural equation modeling (Fassinger, 1987).

Path analysis, causal modeling, and structural equation modeling are among the best methods we now know to handle longitudinal data, not simply cross-sectional data at different points in time. More important, perhaps, is the fact that most of the statistical techniques we have used deal with direct effects, *Y* on *X*, rather than indirect effects among variables. However, path analysis facilitates the examination of the cumulative indirect effects of a variable on some other variable.

Causal modeling techniques (structural equation modeling and covariance structure analysis) incorporate the functions of path analysis and increase the power to study alternative models of structural equations hypothesized to represent certain relationships occurring over a period of time (Bentler, 1980). It is also possible to examine the effects of several measured variables on one latent variable (unobserved) and therefore to increase the number of hypotheses that can be considered in relationship to how underlying structures affect career outcomes across time, whether the question concerns the direct and indirect effects of latent variables on each other or the composition of latent variables themselves.

In addition to analysis of causal patterns among unobserved variables by multiple measures, "It permits testing of causal hypotheses and theory, examination of psychometric adequacy, and enhancement of the explanatory power of correlational data that characterize counseling psychology research" (Fassinger, 1987, p. 425).

Although it is tempting to analyze each of these methods and the studies that have used them in some depth, that would be beyond the purpose of this chapter. Interested researchers are encouraged to read the references cited for elaboration of each of the techniques identified and particularly the special issue of the *Journal of Counseling Psychology* (October, 1987) which is devoted to quantitative foundations of counseling psychology research. The articles in this issue deal with most of the multivariate and factor-analytic techniques in addition to cluster analysis, log linear models, and scale construction.

Before leaving the treatment of career data, it is important to note other approaches that are relevant to but underused in examining the unfolding of career behavior. The first is P-technique factor analysis, which is a special case of single subject research involving intense, repeated measurement of an individual (Nesselroade & Ford, 1985; 1987). Such a technique allows one to study in depth the consistency or the variability of individual interests, values, preferences, or other characteristics to test whether such characteristics are truly stable (as frequently projected after mid-adolescence) or whether they are labile and dynamic. The second is ethnographic methodology (Wehrly & Watson-Gregeo, 1985) as applied to cross-cultural approaches to career development or cross-cultural career counseling. A qualitative rather than quantitative approach, ethnography studies naturalistic interaction and behavior, ways of living, expectations for behavior, specific cultural patterns, and rules for interpreting shared meaning among members of particular groups. Such an approach applied to the career development of various minority groups would likely bridge the understandings of career behavior from quantitative findings reported for majority groups to the subjective differences in meaning systems of culturally different groups as related to work salience, orientation to time, information-processing, and other cognitive or affective elements of significance to career behavior.

Methodologies useful to increasingly sophisticated study of career-related human behavior and the effects of interventions on this process are emerging rapidly. Even so, however, the complexity of the phenomena about which career guidance practitioners are concerned is vast enough to accommodate a wide range of research designs and statistical tools. In any case, there will continue to be an overarching need for what Goldman (1979) has called "disciplined creative search": "ideas and theories which come from the imagination and vision of people who look at and listen to career development issues and behaviors, counseling, career guidance, social trends with openness and an urge to understand and conceptualize" (p. 44). Such creativity and vision yield the theory, ideas, and hypotheses that then lead to the methodological issues cited here as they relate to the testing of such ideas.

Qualitative Approaches to the Treatment of Career Data

One of the methodological issues likely to become prominent in the 1990s is the use of qualitative or alternative approaches in the study of career behavior. Most of the research techniques described thus far in this chapter, with the exception of ethnographic methodology discussed in the previous section, derive from a positivist, quantitative, empirical tradition. However, growing concerns that such linear, quantitative, and hypothetico-deductive approaches are failing to adequately capture the richness and complexity of the interaction of individual and contextual factors; human action, consciousness, and agency; and the multiprobabilistic dynamics of career development has led to an emerging attention to qualitative approaches (for example, Polkinghorne, 1984; Manicas & Secord, 1983). As Young and Borgen (1990) suggest, "The argument in favor of alternative (qualitative) methodologies does not negate the contribution that can be made to knowledge through the use of the hypothetico-deductive method" (p. xiv). Instead, it seems fair to contend that quantitative/qualitative, deductive/inductive, and traditional/alternative approaches are different ways of knowing; that is, different ways of capturing and classifying human experience in the realm of careers.

The perspectives of Young and Borgen (that, in methodological terms, there are different ways of knowing) are consistent with the view that there are also different questions emerging about career development and how it can best be studied. Savickas (1989) has indicated that

> within the last 5 years career theorists and counselors have begun to explore how a new paradigm in developmental psychology, constructive-developmentalism, may inform their work. . . . The constructive-developmentalism perspective (Kegan, 1982) integrates constructivism (people constitute or construct reality) and developmentalism (people evolve through predictable eras) to conclude that what develops during the life-cycle is the activity of meaning-making or making sense of self and situation. Products of this new perspective appeared in . . . publications on career theory and practice written by counselors who used constructs from hermeneutics (the practice of interpreting texts or narratives), family systems, or life-narrative psychology to look (beyond matching the content of self-concepts to occupations) to the processes of self-conceiving and meaning making. Although these authors used different constructs, they all seemed to (a) view people as self-organizing systems, (b) believe that behavior is purposive, (c) attend to meaning and how people construct it, and (d) emphasize that people use their experiences to reconstruct meaning and move toward more completeness. . . . To date, most publications on meaning-making in career development and counseling have not been based on quantitative research. (p. 102)

In essence, such approaches have given renewed attention to qualitative or alternate methodologies.

There is a range of approaches that could be classified as qualitative or alternative approaches to the study of careers. For example, Bujold (1990) has described a biographical-hermeneutical approach based on a phenomenological perspective; Cochran (1990) uses narrative forms as one of his major paradigms for career research; Polkinghorne (1990) and Valach (1990) use action theory, a narrative attempt to describe the human capacity to choose freely from among alternatives in the context of other life choices and events. These approaches variously use autobiography, biography, life histories, psychobiography, life narratives, story or drama, ecological approaches, case studies, phenomenological approaches, self-confrontational interviews, and action analyses as career research methods.

The rationale for the use of such alternative career research methods takes several forms. Bujold (1990), for example, has observed that

> in every investigation, and particularly in those that focus on human beings, the level of understanding that we can reach is never equivalent to the level of complexity of the phenomena under study. A life history, including the history of a career, entails a certain amount of mystery, and it will no doubt always remain much more fascinating as such than all the theories, schemes, paradigms, or models that would claim to help us discover its thread or to identify satisfactorily the mechanisms underlying the development of a particular individual. (p. 57)
>
> [Biographical-hermeneutics becomes,] in the context of career development research, the method by which one attempts to draw out the meaning of human behavior. (p. 59)
>
> Biographies are seen in this context, as a link between research and practice, the role of the counseling being . . . to help people construct their own reality and to find the meaning of their life in the environment of which they are a part and to which they contribute. (p. 60)
>
> It is important to realize that looking at human lives from a biographical hermeneutical perspective puts the focus, at least in many cases, more on the processes than on the outcomes, and thus, the target of the study is much more dynamic than it is—or rather, than it appears to be—if traditional methods are put to use. (p. 67)

Cochran (1990) in discussing the use of narratives in career research states that

> research on career development is not of the same order as research on intellectual or physical development. The topic of career is not so much concerned with parts as with how parts are related and brought to a point in living. . . . In contrast to the spatial emphasis of physical science, narrative emphasizes time as lived. Lived time relates to human consciousness. (p. 71)
>
> In pursuing a career, we live meanings, and lived meanings make a career narratable, intelligible, and coherent. (p. 78)
>
> Case study is probably the preferred approach to narrative construction largely because an investigator can gather divergent sources of evidence and rich, compelling detail to support convergence into a narrative description. (p. 79)
>
> The great advantage of narrative research is that it offers the possibility of a greatly expanded scope for questions that are of direct significance to practice. . . . Having investigated many lives, one can investigate the plot of lives that are pervaded with meaning and those that are bereft of it. . . . One can examine common values, differences in decision making, the role of story telling to oneself, and so on. (p. 83)
>
> Hermeneutics, thick description, structural analysis, phenomenological reflection, and the like are powerful ways to enhance interpretation and they are certainly much more rigorous than the kind of interpretation found in most quantitative studies. (p. 82)

Obviously, the advocates for qualitative career research approaches have strong convictions about the importance of such approaches as methods to unearth how people interpret and make meaning from their career patterns. They believe that these approaches provide ways of knowing about career processes within individuals and across groups of individuals in ways that are not possible using traditional hypothetico-deductive designs. Among the questions that researchers will need to address in the future are the following: Are qualitative career research methods most effectively used preceding traditional quantitative, empirical designs as a basis to identify and classify possible hypotheses to be tested? What are the most effective models by which to integrate traditional and alternate, quantitative and qualitative methodologies? Are qualitative approaches preferred methodologies for selected career questions?

The Character of Career Development Theory

However important methodological issues are to understanding the state of the art of research in career counseling and career guidance, they are not the only matters of concern. The character of career development theory itself is important.

Theoretical Base. Chapters 4 and 6, in particular, have described the conceptual streams of thought that make up the current theoretical base in career development. Much of this material is still speculative—however perceptive and logical—and untested. There are also other characteristics worthy of note.

Many of the hypotheses and existing principles of career development have come originally from samples of white males. Such a condition has caused many critics of career development to assume that the major career theories are not applicable to women, minority groups, or lower-income persons. Emerging research is suggesting that such a view is not necessarily warranted. Many of the career development concepts embedded in the work of Super and Holland among others have utility across gender, racial groups, and socioeconomic status (Salomone & Slaney, 1978; Kidd, 1982). Indeed, some research indicates that more important than class or sex in career behavior is work salience—how important work is to the person as one of several major life roles (Super, 1984a; 1990). There is considerable need for major research efforts in these areas.

Even though there has been a virtual explosion of research on various aspects of women's career development in the past decade, there are as yet few comprehensive perspectives on the career development of women (Fitzgerald & Crites, 1980). Hackett (1985) has indicated that what is known about women's career development has not resulted in "a relevant theoretical conceptualization . . . which is capable of integrating existing knowledge and guiding future research and interventions" (p. 48).

Just as has been true with studies of men, there are emerging many segmental theories (such as self-efficacy, math anxiety) dealing with parts of women's career behavior. There has been relatively little systematic study pertinent to the career development of minority group members (Tinsley & Heesacker, 1984) whether classified racially, ethnically, or religiously. Much less attention has been given to the career development of the rural poor than to the urban poor. Likewise, systematic study of the effects of congenital versus adventitious, physical handicaps on career development is yet to be undertaken. Virtually no attention has been given to the career development of gay persons, the employment limitations they face, or appropriate career guidance strategies.

Much career development theory has evolved from descriptive research with samples restricted in size and in composition. As a result, many relationships and hypotheses about career behavior, the influences on them, or the effect of attempts to intervene in them remain to be tested. Indeed, interpretations of existing findings are often made without the benefit of validation or replication across samples that diverge in characteristics from those on whom the original findings were obtained.

In addition to any other criticisms of samples from which career development theory or research has come, many sample subjects have been students. In longitudinal samples, it makes sense to begin studying career development when individuals are in the early years of schooling and then watch their progression into and through adulthood. However, secondary school and university student samples have been the rule not only for longitudinal studies but for cross-sectional studies as well. Since most investigations of career development are conducted by persons in colleges and other educational settings, student samples are convenient, but they do not offer insight into the whole of career development, particularly its characteristics in adulthood and in persons with minimal educational experience.

In the few longitudinal studies now being conducted, the original student samples are maturing and proceeding through adulthood, but little has been published about them other than in terms of adolescent exploration and the early stages of young adulthood. As a result, we know less about the predictive validity of various patterns of early career development in relationship to the linearity of career development, midcareer change, or occupational dislocation than we need if we are to make career interventions more effective for persons beyond adolescence. (Niles & Herr, 1989) For example, we know comparatively little about the developmental progression of persons into retirement, although there is a growing demand for career guidance at this life stage. Thus, questions of when such career guidance should begin, what its emphases should be—use of leisure, volunteer possibilities, part-time work, economic planning—remain vague. Much the same could be said about the comprehensiveness of knowledge available about second careerists, midcareer dislocated, and other segments of the adult population, although recent findings about the relationships among unemployment, mental health, and stress-related diseases are yielding effective conceptual output.

Each of these observations is well known to researchers and theorists, and attempts to modify these voids, move away from restrictive samples, and improve the quality of theory and research in career development are proceeding apace. However, there is a new challenge that will likely affect the conceptualization of emerging programs of career development speculation and research. This challenge is found principally in life-span psychology.

Influence of Life-Span Psychology. Among other life-span psychologists, Vondracek and Lerner (1982), Vondracek, Lerner, and Schulenberg (1986), and Vondracek (1990) have been the most analytic in their view of the weaknesses of current views of career development as seen from the perspective of life-span psychology. They strongly suggest that many of the existing models of career development are personological and unidimensional rather than dynamic and interactional as would be useful. Citing the study of adolescents, in particular, they advocate the need for three key perspectives in the study of adolescent vocational role development: developmental, contextual, and relational. In a *developmental perspective*, "events prior to adolescence need to be considered as possible antecedents of vocational development; in turn, adolescent developments provide key antecedents of development in later life" (Vondracek & Lerner, 1982, p. 604). Longitudinal studies using Markov chains, path analysis, and causal modeling (mentioned in the previous section) would likely be of significant use in this area. A *contextual perspective* would emphasize the nature of the social (including political and economic), physical, and cultural milieu of adolescent vocational role development. "Thus the individual characteristics of the developing adolescent must be considered in relation to the particular features of the context within which the person is developing" (p. 604). A *relational perspective* would consider the goodness of fit between adolescent and contextual developments. It is further argued that although several important longitudinal studies of career development have been carried out (*The Career Pattern Study*, Super et al., 1957; *Project TALENT*, Flanagan, Shaycroft, Richards, & Claudy, 1971; *The Career Development Study*, Gribbons & Lohnes, 1969, 1982, and the *Youth in Transition Study*, Bachman, Kahn, Mednick, Davidson, & Johnston, 1970), none of these has employed a historical (for example, sequential) design suitable for appraising age- , cohort- , and time-related variance. Vondracek (1990) and several of his graduate students are now engaged in a longitudinal study of adolescent career development that is intended to vary age, sex, and cohort membership to incorporate developmental-contextual perspectives and thereby rectify some of the shortcomings perceived by Vondracek and colleagues to be present in other longitudinal studies of vocational behavior.

As Vondracek and Lerner (1982) assert,

> Although the current research literature on vocational development reflects a growing emphasis on a developmental perspective, there are still major shortcomings in the implementation of these orientations. These shortcomings involve problems of research design as well as problems of conceptualization—that is, a commitment to a life span developmental perspective cannot be best actualized in our view, through reliance on personological, organismic conceptions of vocational-role development. Instead, an appreciation of mutually adaptive interchanges between adolescents and their contexts must be attained. (p. 609)

From such a perspective, Vondracek and Lerner (1982) then contend, "Traditional interventions in vocational development need to be broadened to incorporate interventions targeted to the individual, the family, the community, and its institutions, and finally, social policy" (p. 612).

The challenge and observations posed by Vondracek and his colleagues are certainly not confined to thinking about the career development of adolescents. Rather, such views are equally pertinent to understanding the career development of adults and particularly the effects of context and fit with context. To some degree this matter was discussed in Chapter 2 with regard to the meaning of work and person-job relationships. It was also dealt with in Chapter 4 as situational approaches to career development were described. However, it remains a fertile field for research designed to test and refine existing theories of career development.

The Effects of Cultural and Economic Factors

As one might expect if the observations about a need for more attention to context are valid, less is known than is desirable about the effects of economic or cultural change on career behavior. Although most career development theorists have addressed the importance of situational variables to career development, they frequently have done so in abstract terms rather than researched the effects of such conditions on personal choice making and commitments. It is clear that the family history, home community, and socioeconomic status of the person all affect career development. The questions are, How much, when, under what conditions, and for whom? We often continue to treat persons described by a group characteristic—racial, ethnic, religious, age, sex—as though they are part of a homogeneous group. We tend not to take into account the extent of variance that operates in any group and examine its implications for given individuals.

Cross-Cultural Information

The same point can be made about cultures other than our own. We know little about the socialization of career behavior in developing nations, or indeed, in many of the contemporary developed or postindustrial societies. In some instances this situation occurs because pertinent research has not been done in other societies in which we might be interested; in other cases the research is not developmentally focused; in still others, useful research findings exist but have not been assimilated into the American view of career development. For example, many excellent publications on career development, occupational classification systems, and career interventions have been developed by the Occupational and Career Analysis and Development Branch of the Canadian Employment and Immigration Commission in Ottawa. Similarly, excellent material is available from the Federal Employment Institute of West Germany, the National Institute for Careers Education and Counselling in Cambridge, England, and the National Institute for Vocational and Employment Research (now the Japan Institute of Labour Research) in Tokyo. Additional examples of guidance interventions or career development theory could be identified in other nations. The point is, however, that even when such material is available it is not typically known and used in the United States.

Obviously, one way of testing the effects of cultural and economic factors in career development is to study the fit of current American views of career development in societies with different economic characteristics, belief systems regarding work values, or political assumptions about individual choice and development. One major example of such an effort began in September 1976 to test the validity of Super's theoretical concepts with a British population. Based at the National Institute for Careers Education and Counseling in Cambridge, this research is a longitudinal effort to replicate many of the American findings from Super's research with samples of British youth and adults. One of the early outcomes of this project was *Career Development in Britain* (Watts, Super, & Kidd, 1981). Among its many useful aspects, the book addresses the current state of the art in careers theory in Britain and introduces to the American reader the powerful influence that sociological perspectives play in such careers theory. From such a frame of reference, American theories of career development are contrasted with those of the British, and several concepts new to most American readers (such as low autonomy—high autonomy) are provided as ways of analyzing career history. In addition to *Career Development in Britain*, the work at the National Institute of Careers Education and Counselling has become part of a 14-nation Work Importance Study directed by Donald Super (1984b). More cross-cultural efforts to examine the effects of political, economic, and other social factors on career development should become increasingly evident in the American literature and as a fertile arena for international cooperation.

Cross-cultural studies of career development are principally seen as useful in macro terms. The emphasis tends to be on the comparisons of nations. At this level, frequent comparisons are made between the underdeveloped, developing, or developed nations, or between the nations of the Northern and the Southern Hemisphere or some other similar classification scheme. However useful such comparisons are across nations to study major cultural dimensions, it is also worth acknowledging the importance of such inquiry at a micro- or subnational level (Herr, 1985a). Many nations, particularly the United States and increasingly the countries of Western Europe, are becoming pluralistic in the population groupings they contain. Therefore, within nations there are groups of persons who could be considered underdeveloped, developing, and developed. Undoubtedly, the career development of each of the groups differs in ways that could be illuminated by applying paradigms similar to those useful in studies at national levels, and many of the cross-cultural constructs thought to be useful only to make national comparisons would also be helpful within multiethnic, multicultural populations.

Ultimately, as part of the analyses of the career development of different cultural groups, it will be necessary to identify those factors related to restricted socioeconomic status or other variables that limit people's ability to cope with skill mastery, attitude development, or achievement motivation, and design experiences that can systematically overcome such deficits. In essence, we must continue to determine whether our theories of career development are culture-bound or generally applicable and also whether our methods of intervening in career development are culture-bound.

Changing Sex Roles. A related issue is that of changing sex roles. As a cultural phenomenon, the elimination of sex-role stereotyping—"masculine" versus "feminine" occupations—tends to be proceeding rapidly. Sundal-Hansen (1985) has suggested that a "new" psychology of men and women is emerging and that researchers are studying men's and women's lives in a more integrative manner. However, more research needs to be directed to the career guidance processes most effective in facilitating this movement, when such interventions should occur, or how to most effectively help women or men reconsider their values in this area and consider nontraditional educational or occupational opportunities. That such work needs to and can be guided by theory has been well demonstrated by the recent work in self-efficacy and math anxiety as major constructs related to women's career development. Here again, it would be helpful to consider the experiences of other nations in dealing with such problems and how their career guidance responses might be adapted in this country. Sundal-Hansen (1985) has suggested the following topics as relevant to sex-role issues across cultures:

1. Sex-role stereotyping and socialization
2. Individual goals versus family and societal goals
3. Literacy and education as options
4. Sexual division of labors
5. Men's changing role in family
6. Degree of commitment to equality
7. The rate of societal change (p. 215)

Importance of Economic Factors. Not only does career development research need to include greater attention to cultural factors and to sociological insights, it also needs greater attention to economic factors. Free and Tiedeman (1980) have contended that both econometric and psychometric models need to be included in the foundational study of individual behavior and counseling. In their view, "Economics . . . focuses on interdependent choice and decision making in production, distribution and consumption as a control consideration just as counselors focus on these processes in the time choices and decision making that define personality" (p. 361). The study of economics extends the counselor's view of the individual in the environment and, indeed, of the ways the individual can construct desirable futures, both personal and societal. Free and Tiedeman contend, in fact, that the individual (client, counselee) "requires comprehension of the economic system itself to be an active participant in determining his or her economic future" (p. 362). As suggested in Chapter 2 the emerging global economy and the international economic competition at its core will affect the pool of occupational opportunities, the ways personal flexibility will be defined, and, in effect, will impose new economic dimensions on the psychology of career development.

A greater attention to economic factors in career development will need to include increased research concern for the implications for career guidance or career counseling of different forms of employment or unemployment. These terms are frequently treated as though, for example, all unemployment were caused by the same factors and affected every person in the society equally. However, depending on the definitions used, unemployment can be divided into at least four types: seasonal, frictional, cyclical, and structural. Each of these types of unemployment differs in its severity, its causes, and the groups most affected (Pierson, 1980). Determining which career guidance approaches are useful in reducing the severity or duration of these different forms of unemployment is an important research question that has rarely been asked. The question is likely to gain prominence in the next decade as the nation wrestles intensely with the wide-ranging effects of structural unemployment.

A few of the research concerns related to structural unemployment might be the following:

1. Developing career information that identifies which occupations are likely to be most vulnerable to shifts in technology and which links the occupational possibilities in the emerging global economy and the regional transnational markets
2. Assessing which worker skills are most elastic—able to be transferred across occupational boundaries with the least amount of retraining
3. Creating models of choice that help persons understand the knowledge bases and skills inherent in new occupational configurations
4. Examining changes in work organization and their effects on dual-career families, length of work life, retirement, the availability of overtime or leisure time
5. Understanding more fully which persons function best under conditions of low- or high-autonomy in the workplace; identifying how differences in supervisory style or the psychological conditions of the workplace affect individual productivity
6. Examining the direct relationships between education and work, training and retraining as work technologies rapidly change
7. Studying how affective work competencies or industrial discipline change as a result of changes in the workplace occasioned by automation, computerization, robotics
8. Studying what happens to those persons in the work force who are functionally illiterate, whose basic academic skills are inadequate to learning the skills necessary to new occupational technologies. Do we simply assume that under major occupation transitions some persons are destined to be unemployed and that one of the roles of career guidance is to assist such persons to prepare for unemployment just as one prepares for work?
9. Considering what advocacy roles career guidance has in assisting employers to recognize their employees as human capital resources to be developed and nurtured, just as they have historically emphasized the preventive maintenance of equipment; identifying what are the most effective models of career guidance in business and industry as shifts are made from personnel management to personnel development.

Such research areas are only the most superficial of possibilities as the implications of structural unemployment for career guidance are studied in the years ahead. Ways will need to be found to increase the understanding of career guidance practitioners of the dynamics of employment and unemployment. Although career guidance is likely to facilitate "employability" in persons, help them to plan for work more knowledgeably and purposefully, and assist them in their adjustment to work, it cannot create jobs or employment for them; the latter is a function of many complex factors such as population demographics, international competition, and fiscal policies, which cannot be decisively influenced by career guidance. Therefore, to argue that career guidance or career counseling will "reduce unemployment" is to misunderstand the dynamics of unemployment and to naively overpromise what career interventions cannot deliver.

From the standpoint of social effects as well as research concerns, it is useful to note that uninformed understandings of the factors initiating and maintaining unemployment cause some counselors, like lay citizens, to assume that after receiving career guidance or training, if one is still unemployed, one must want to be. That might be a reasonable assumption if the nation were providing full employment or if it were not in the middle of a major structural transition in work technology, but it is not providing full employment and it is engaged in a major structural transition. Therefore, we sometimes inadvertently blame the victims of unemployment for being victims and unintentionally intensify the feelings of frustration or helplessness they experience (Herr & Watts, 1981).

Another area of research concern still within the broad rubric of economic and cultural factors has to do with the characteristics of labor markets. Doeringer and Piore (1971) have described a dual labor market in the United States that has different "ports of entry" for workers depending on the industry involved; different levels of security, benefits, and training; and different possibilities for internal mobility. The primary and secondary labor markets, as they are known, require different job-search strategies, skills, and personal characteristics. The career ladders available, the commitments to and processes of on-the-job training and retraining, the sources of workers, and the hiring processes in the primary and secondary labor markets are each worthy of far more research attention than has been given to such matters to date. Without being aware of such distinctions in the labor force, career guidance practitioners and job seekers are likely to expend energies in efforts that are insufficiently tailored to the actual dynamics that occur in the various components of the structure. It is also likely that a person concentrating on seeking work in either the primary or secondary labor market underestimates the possibilities of self-employment (Gershuny & Pahl, 1979–1980). It seems likely that more work in the future than in the past will be subcontracted from large corporations to small entrepreneurs. In addition, consumers seem to be evidencing increased interest in handmade, quality goods available from individual or small groups of craftsmen as discretionary income continues to rise. However, again, self-employment (or entrepreneurial behavior), its availability, and the specific skills required in such informal labor markets has not typically been the subject of research in career guidance. Until it is, the employment potential in such areas will be less systematically sought and prepared for than would otherwise be appropriate.

Given the likely effects of the global economy on work organizations and organizational change over the next decade, London and Stumpf (1986) have suggested research topics of particular importance within workplaces. They suggest that career research should examine

> how workers effectively adjust to periods of transition and stability at different career stages. Research also needs to investigate ways to help individuals search for suitable alternatives and make career changes without feeling "locked in" by financial obligations. (p. 43)
>
> Career research is needed to help define general competency areas that guide people in making career transitions. (p. 44)

> Career research should examine how career resilience develops and changes over time. (p. 45)
>
> Career research needs to take a developmental perspective by examining how people and organizations change and affect each other over time. People go through many critical stages during their careers—at which time they are particularly susceptible to influence and need to adjust to major role transitions. Research needs to identify these stages and transitions and help organizations evaluate their efforts to provide support for employees at critical times. (p. 46)
>
> Research is needed to examine how career identity is changing overtime. . . . The impact of new career management systems on career and organizational commitment needs to be addressed in light of such changes. Therefore, evaluation research is needed on such management systems as alternative work schedules, flextime, childcare options, preretirement planning, and career and life counseling. (p. 47)

While there are many other research questions that are affected by economic factors, those cited here exemplify topical emphases that should guide research about individual-organizational change in the next decade.

Awareness of Cost-Benefit Effects

One of the major research arenas of the future must be the cost-benefit effects of career counseling, education, or guidance. Each of the research or evaluation studies that shows either positive or negative outcomes for such career services is important, in an empirical sense, for its value in testing some theoretical proposition or in evaluating the efficacy of a particular treatment in relation to some factor of age, gender, or population type.

The point of this section is, however, that research findings, particularly in the various career interventions, have meaning beyond the empirical. They are also important in cost-benefit terms: for example, private benefits that accrue directly to the individual as in greater job satisfaction and work productivity; external benefits that accrue to a third party, perhaps an employer, as in increased worker satisfactoriness or less absenteeism from work; social benefits that accrue to society as a whole as in reduced welfare payments or in increased contributions to taxes and charitable agencies. On the cost side are the expenditures for facilities, staff training, materials purchased, employee released time from work and the money, energy, or time required to produce some form(s) of benefit. The central questions of cost-benefit analyses are: How much does it cost to have a career counseling, education, or guidance program? How much will it cost not to have such a career counseling, education, or guidance program? What are the cost-benefit ratios and the economic tradeoffs or payoffs of having or not having such career services? Under the pressures for accountability and the wise management of scarce resources, such questions will be essential to the future availability of career programs in many settings.

Cost-benefit analyses of career services are not easy, and they typically require a somewhat different mentality than ordinarily characterizes the practitioners of the field. For example, cost-benefit analyses really require theorists, researchers, and practitioners to be willing to risk evaluating what they do, using as a criterion economic benefits that exceed economic costs. Within such a construct, if the economic benefits to individuals or to society exceed the cost of career guidance or career counseling one can argue that counselors are generators of resources, not simply consumers of them.

One might further argue that each of the positive effects of career education, counseling, or guidance cited throughout this book makes a direct or indirect contribution to the gross national product by increasing educational and occupational attainment or productivity, by decreasing losses associated with absence or vandalism, or by precluding the need for more expensive treatment in the future (Herr, 1982a, 1982b). The logic of such a perspective seems unassailable, but the connections between the empirically derived findings about career counseling or guidance effects and the economic health of individuals or the society at large have not typically been made. Although there are useful examples of such efforts within industry (Olbrisch, 1977; Alander & Campbell, 1975; Warren, 1978; Reardon, 1976), vocational rehabilitation (Worrall, 1978), and in health insurance plans (Cummings, 1977; Cumming, 1986; McGuire & Frisman, 1983) the systematic comparison of the economic benefit/cost ratios of career guidance to other systems of intervention is still in a primitive state. However, it has extraordinary promise.

Developing Measures of Career Development

Since much of our understanding of career development comes from observations of restricted samples, often not adequately representing women or minority persons, existing measures of career development can be considered susceptible to limited sensitivity in their observations of career behavior. When such instruments are applied to persons who might be different in their characteristics, they may miss, exclude, or overemphasize material relevant to the latter. Obviously, this criticism differs in its importance depending on whether the instrument is assessing values or unequivocal factual information or making judgments about the level of career maturity. The last is most problematic, although each must be viewed with caution depending on the procedures followed in developing and validating the instrument.

No specific instruments are mentioned here because the concerns expressed are well known to test developers and they are working diligently to correct imbalances in samples represented in the validation procedures. Nevertheless, because of the unevenness of coverage in current theories of career development of women and minority groups, the construction of instruments to assess career behavior across all population types will be difficult.

What also needs to be noted in the measurement of career development is that only some of the dimensions of current models of vocational or career maturity are well established or measured (Super, 1984a; Westbrook, Sanford, O'Neal, Horne, Fleenor, & Garren, 1985). Super and Hall (1978) observed in 1978 that the most highly developed instruments assess only one to six factors out of a total list of eighteen in the Crites model or nineteen in the Super model. Some of the other factors (such as realism) have been measured, but in unstandardized ways that make the comparison of results difficult. Furthermore, some factors (such as realism and consistency of preferences), appear to be meaningful theoretically and significant practically at some ages but not at others.

Certainly a major concern in measurement has to do with the outcomes to be expected from career education, career counseling, or career guidance. Are each of these categories of intervention intended to affect the same behaviors or are they to serve different purposes? What are the outcomes expected for each or for all? Crites (1981) indicates that for career counseling there are three broad outcomes: making a career choice, acquisition of decisional skills, and enhanced general adjustments. However, as has been identified elsewhere (Herr, 1979; Gottfredson, 1982; Slaney, 1988; Osipow, 1982) the outcomes expected to derive from career interventions are diverse and changing. Some are affective, others are cognitive, still others are behavioral. They frequently deal with a client's progress in decision making or the degree to which they experience indecision.

They vary with regard to whether they assess knowledge of self-characteristics, occupational or educational options, or the decision-making process. The foci of concern are often attitudes toward choice, independence in choice, or to adjustment. Sometimes the outcome measure focuses upon degree of anxiety, quality of job-search skills, achievement, persistence, work adjustment, academic performance, or other behavior. Jepsen (1984) has spoken of three career concept systems that tend to catalogue theoretical connections to practice. These, too, would be reflected at some level in attempts to measure them as outcomes of career guidance and counseling. They include the Work-Affect Concept System comprised of such concepts, attitudes, or preferences as career interests, career preferences, job satisfaction; the Cognitive-Activity Concept System made up of information about job titles, occupational images, occupational stereotypes, career choice, occupational scaling, occupational knowledge, job knowledge; and the Overt-Career-Behavior Concept System, which might involve job experiences, reality-testing experiences, career role-playing, career information-seeking behavior. Clearly, the dynamics of theoretical development are such that the complexity of assessment is compounded by both content and process issues related to predictive validity, diagnostic utility, and the matching of differential treatments to assessed outcomes. There is much to be done in such areas as theoretical concepts are translated into and evaluated as measurement dimensions.

Implicit in the development of career development measures are problems with the use of the language of careers. As has been suggested elsewhere (Herr, 1990),

> Perhaps the primary issue in the study of career is, what do we mean by career? Is it different from occupation or job? When we speak of career, are we concerned with the lifelong behavioral processes and the influences upon them that lead to individual work values, choice-making styles, work salience, role integration, self and career identity, pre- and post-work involvement, and related phenomena? On the other hand, are we principally concerned with the subset of individual career development, which might be defined in organizational terms as the stages that one undergoes in different work settings from induction to consolidation to retirement? Do we really mean that we are concerned with who enters particular occupations and why, the individual differences in interests and abilities found in particular groupings, and the overlap in these characteristics across occupational groupings, or are we really concerned with job satisfaction and work adjustment? (p. 3)

The point is that unless researchers are clear about what they perceive to be the boundaries of career versus occupations versus work choice or adjustment, it becomes difficult to know what the outcomes of research should be, how they should be addressed, or how research studies can be compared as to purpose and meaning. The language and constructs of career, then, need to be differentiated from the language of occupation, leisure, or general personal development in such a way that constructs and outcomes are clearly defined within such language systems.

Even if such clarity of outcomes is enhanced among researchers, there are likely to be complex decisions to be made about what to study or what one should expect of career interventions. For example, Fretz (1981) has suggested that the effects of a career development program could be classified into two groups: (a) client outcome and (b) program outcomes. He suggested that client outcomes might be classified in the following manner:

Career knowledge and skills

- Accuracy of self-knowledge
- Accuracy of occupational information
- Accuracy of job-seeking skills knowledge

- Planning and goal selection skills
- Appropriateness of choices (realism)
- Range of choices

Career behavior

- Career information seeking
- Relevant academic performance
- Seeking initial/new job
- Getting initial/new job
- Job ratings
- Being promoted
- Earnings

Sentiments

- Attitudes toward choices: certainty, satisfaction, commitment, career salience
- Job satisfaction
- Quality-of-life ratings
- Satisfaction with intervention
- Perceived effectiveness of intervention

Effective role functioning

- Self-concept adequacy
- Personal adjustment
- Relapses of career problems
- Contributions to community*

But, as useful as such perspectives about client outcomes are in general, they may not be appropriate for specific client populations. To be more precise, additional outcomes might be sought. For example, Tittle (1988) has proposed a life-pattern perspective that arises from gender research on plans for, attainment of, and satisfaction in adult roles. As a function of this model she has proposed outcome criteria for evaluating the validity of career interventions. Such criteria include (a) number of traditional and nontraditional occupations explored; (b) relation of fertility and educational plans to preferred occupations; (c) degree of commitment to career, marriage, and parenthood; (d) plans for the articulation of occupational and homemaking responsibilities; (e) plans for the integration of role cycles for husband and wife; (f) negotiation skills to implement preference for marriage, family, work, and homemaking activities; and (g) degree of gender-stereotyping of all adult roles.

The differential outcomes that career counseling or career guidance are intended to address require a variety of measurement forms. As work organizations change and the content of work undergoes modification, testing must also shift its emphases. As suggested in Chapter 2, the emerging concept of personal flexibility of workers to perform effectively within the change-filled environment of a global economy is likely to require new testing paradigms or processes to measure the ingredients of what individual nations or regional markets define as elements of personal flexibility. Among these emphases will likely be increased attention to testing in relation to the status of persons on various dimensions of the process of choice, in addition to testing about the content of choice. The "process of choice" is concerned with such behaviors as persons' independence from others in their choice making orientation or commitment to choice, assessment of barriers to choice, possession of information about choice options, and knowledge of and ability in decision making. Thus, the historical reasons for testing in vocational guidance for purposes of classifying, identifying, and creaming talent has shifted increasingly from assessing individual differences in performance or the matching of traits and factors making up the content of individual choices—aptitudes, interests, job requirements—however important they continue to be, to assessments primarily concerned with such questions as how ready is the in-

*From "Evaluating the Effectiveness of Career Interventions" by Bruce R. Fretz, *Journal of Counseling Psychology*, Vol. 28, No. 1, January 1981. Reprinted by permission.

dividual to choose, how planful, how knowledgeable about the choice process, how able is this person to define the choice problem immediately ahead, and to collect pertinent information and weigh its personal value. Pursuing such understanding, psychometricians and researchers have directed their attention to identifying the important influences that mediate how one's career behavior unfolds: undecidedness and indecisiveness, work salience, different decision-making styles, perception, self efficacy, the acquisition of academic and task approach skills, and the presence of irrational beliefs about work and personal capacity of career adaptability.

Historically, much of our routine testing has been concerned with content of choice issues, particularly the assessment of aptitudes, from which we can evaluate how competitive an individual can be in a particular job or career and the likely upper limits of their performance. However, in the future, as work organizations are likely to be less pyramidal or hierarchial in design, and less management driven, the assessment concerns of the global economy are likely to be less about how competitive the individual may be and more about the status of his or her skills in terms of "complementarity." For example, how is this person likely to function in a group, as a facilitator of the performance of others in the work place, as a leader of a problem-solving or participative decision-making group, as a conflict resolver? These are the skills of personal flexibility that are likely to be more and more prized in the work organizations that are emerging. Other assessments of growing importance to personal flexibility will be teachability, rigidity, and adaptability.

There are other changes in the need for assessments as well. One of them has to do with the quest for personal excellence. During the past decade, because of the rise in international competition and the increase in educational requirements stimulated by the pervasive adaptation of advanced technology, there has been much rhetoric in the U. S. about educational reform and the need for educational excellence. The pursuit of educational excellence is undoubtedly an appropriate national goal. However, educational excellence is shaped by and reciprocal with the willingness and the confidence of students or adults to pursue programs of action that challenge their abilities, provide access to earned opportunity, and that rest upon informed choice. Testing, then, must increasingly be seen as primarily to inform, enlighten, and stimulate the person tested to individual commitment to personal excellence at whatever level of achievement one can accomplish.

The need to use testing as a form of empowerment, self-efficacy, and information, as a way of helping workers or clients develop theories about what is important and how to choose it, will likely change the testing process itself. As Healy (1990) has persuasively described,

> If appraisals are to strengthen clients in their ongoing monitoring of their career . . . they need to improve clients self assessment skills. If appraisals intend to help clients create a career, rather than merely chart one leg of it, they need to assist clients in becoming aware of how influential their contexts are in shaping who they are, and they need to sensitize clients to how they can maneuver in their contexts to realize career ambitions. . . . Finally, leading the client through an expert's approach will strengthen a client in piloting a career only if the client clarifies how to incorporate aspects of the expert's process into his or her approach. (Healy, 1990, p. 22)

Embedded in these shifting perspectives on what measurement outcomes need to address, the forms of measurement that might be required in the future, and the paradigms of how the purposes of testing need to be modified are psychometric and social issues that require multidisciplinary forms of inquiry. Such needs are fertile areas for research and for new conceptual models.

Research and Career Guidance Interventions

As suggested in the observations of Healy (1982) cited earlier, research efforts too often have neglected to describe specifically enough for replication the type of career counseling or career guidance approach undertaken in regard to some criterion—occupational or self-exploration, development of planning skills, choice of vocational education, work adjustment. These limitations significantly reduce our knowledge of the specificity of effects among treatments or consumers' expectancies of action. As Holland, Magoon, and Spokane (1981) have observed, the forms of career assistance have grown rapidly if not explosively but the proliferation of materials and techniques has not been accompanied by a similar interest in evaluation. Therefore, the distribution of research about the many forms of career assistance is uneven.

Aside from the extensive work accumulating about the efficacy of behavioral approaches to information seeking and other exploratory behavior pertinent to decision making, little can be said about the likely effects of different types of career guidance or counseling techniques in relation to specific categories of individual problems or needs (Tinsley & Heesacker, 1984) or Attribute-by-Treatment Interactions that examine the notion that the outcomes of career intervention are a function of the interaction of client attributes with the treatments they receive (Fretz, 1981). More research is needed that links client goals to treatment using goal-attainment scaling (Cytrynbaum, Ginath, Birdwell, & Brandt, 1979) or diagnostic procedures (Jepsen & Prediger, 1981; Campbell & Cellini, 1981) to extend existing knowledge of client treatment interactions (Holland, Magoon, & Spokane, 1981). Equally important is a lack of information about the long-term effects of different career guidance interventions. Most of the data available about the comparative advantages of career guidance modes are based on the outcomes that can be assessed at the termination of contact with a student or client rather than over time.

Advances in Occupational Information in Relation to Career Decision Making

Considerable progress has been made during the last decade in developing both affective and cognitive information about various forms of work that is sensitive to sexual stereotyping and responsive to the types of questions and conceptual ability pertinent to persons at various developmental levels. However, more can be done.

Specifically, research needs to address such questions as, Do students or adults think in terms of careers or entry jobs, school subjects, and college majors or clusters of interests? How do such perspectives bear on achievement motivation, career motives, and occupational valuing as these bear upon planning or adjustment to work? How much information do persons need before they can make a commitment at a given choice point? What are the effects of the tentative goal-setting of preadolescent youth on later choice and how is available information related to such choice making? Are there differences among various population groups (defined by sex, race, ethnicity) in the types of occupational and career information preferred?

Another research issue concerning occupational or career information has to do with how to make it more localized. Most available information is national and, therefore, quite broad in its description of occupations and careers. Some research, however, has shown that local information, when it is available, is more important in decision making than is national information. But aside from Department of Labor regional labor surveys, the prototype computerized occupational information systems, job data bank information that is regionalized or localized in some areas in the country, or occasional community surveys taken by counselors, there is very little local occupational or career information useful for decision making. How such information can be effectively secured, what its characteristics are, and how valuable it is for different kinds of decisions are other important areas for research.

Major national studies conducted at the Educational Testing Service (Chapman & Katz, 1981, 1982a, 1982b) produced evidence that high school students use only a small portion of the career information available to them. This has led the researchers involved to assert that

> students lack a usable context in which to place and process the mountains of information contained in the resources. . . . The missing context for making these materials available to students is, first, knowledge of the learner—his or her values, aptitudes, or resources in the form of time, money, motivation, and stamina necessary for pursuit of occupational goals; and, second, an explicit decision-making strategy that helps students interpret and use information. (Chapman & Katz, 1982b, p. 11).

Such observations have led Chapman (1983) to propose a context for decision making in which the use of various forms of information are explicitly directed to assist persons in dealing with career decision-making behavior as a distinctive and subsequent aspect to that of career exploratory behavior (Jepsen, Dustin, & Miars, 1982).

The model proposed by Chapman (1983) to which various forms of information needs to be related includes the assumption that information is essential about both the individual decision maker and the occupation to be chosen. More specifically, the perspective is that the decision maker has values, aptitudes, and resources relevant to the decision. The occupation has the capacity to satisfy certain values (satisfactions), demands certain aptitudes for performance (requisites) and expenditures of resources for attainment (investments). Investments include occupational demands for training and education to get into them, as well as skill and luck in getting employed. The satisfactions or, more precisely, the opportunities for satisfactions that occupations offer are also seen as the potential rewards offered by an occupation; for example, earnings and respect. In such a perspective each decision maker exemplifies a unique combination of values, aptitudes, and resources; each occupation represents a unique combination of rewards, requisites, and investments. Information, then, is required by the decision maker in each of these areas of self-knowledge and of occupational knowledge if the decision maker is effectively to maximize the payoff (satisfy values) and minimize risk (select an option to which one can gain entry and succeed and in which the requisites and investments are congruent with the decision maker's aptitudes and resources).

Such a profile of information requirements for career decision making suggests that current information availability is uneven in its content and usefulness and in need of research about its connection to coherent models of decision making. One such connection relates to the cognitive structure of the chooser. For example, Neimeyer et al. (1985) have studied structural changes that occur in the cognitive schemata individuals use to process vocational information. Their results among college students indicate that vocational decision-making skills, career exploration, and career planning vary in relation to low and high integration of vocational structures among choosers. However, as the researchers suggest, there is a comprehensive need for research that examines the qualitative shifts and maps the relationships between vocational development and cognitive schemata across the life span, including how individuals may react differently to identical vocational interventions or to vocational information depending on their levels of differentiation and integration.

The Question of Work Values

A body of literature on worker alienation has emerged over the past several decades. Some speculate that its revelations about the tedium and limitations for personal fulfillment in work have turned many young people against a work ethic. Other speculation interspersed with some research suggests that young people want to work but primarily in occupations that are challenging, of service to mankind, and personally gratifying.

It is not now clear how or if such concepts have affected the thinking of most youth. For example, do vocational education and college preparatory students share similar perspectives on the meaning of work? Nor is it clear how youth view decision stress or the increasing burdens of psychological responsibility being portrayed by many writers as emerging social problems. Many research questions are pertinent to such emphases. Some examples follow.

Are youth experiencing indecisiveness as a general behavior pattern? Is it restricted to career choice? How widespread is indecisiveness among student populations of different socioeconomic or racial characteristics and at different educational levels? What characteristics and conditions differentiate those who are guided by security from those who are risk-takers in decision making? Are student values about work shifting dramatically? How? Are student values about education shifting? How? What forms of or emphases in career guidance do youth most value or desire? What career incentives do youth currently find most attractive (for example, contributions to others, service to society, high income, prestige) and what differences do these desires actually make at the point of choice? In a shifting employment picture, do youth find unemployment compensation, welfare, or other governmental subsidies attractive alternatives to work? Can youth or adults find personal significance outside of paid work if their physiological and security needs are met? Do the work values of youth and adults really differ or is this an intergenerational straw man?

Many of these questions might also be asked of various adult populations and the answers related to choices made. A fundamental question in either youth or adult populations is whether economic or psychological contingencies are really the more important at the point of choice for most persons in a highly industrialized society. A nagging concern among such questions is, What is the influence of the mass media in shaping personal aspirations and questions of psychological identity as compared with other mechanisms in the environment or the individual's intrinsic need structure?

The Question of Counselor Characteristics

Counselor role and function studies have a long and sometimes questionable history. Examples of recent position statements on counselor role in career guidance and in career education were cited in Chapter 1. For the most part, these position statements are based on speculation, not research about the most important functions of counselors in discharging their responsibilities in career guidance. Other research questions also remain.

What is the relationship of the counselor's socioeconomic background and work history to knowledge of careers or occupations, to attitudes toward decision making and exploratory behavior, to the place of career counseling, education, or guidance within a repertoire of counselor priorities? Some data suggest that counseling psychologists in training (Pinkney & Jacobs, 1985) and counselor educators who train such persons do not value the career aspects of their role as highly as those dealing with personal counseling, depression, and psychotherapy. Therefore, they have lost contact with the roots of their profession and have blurred their professional identity (for example, Nathan, 1977; Osipow, 1977; Fitzgerald & Osipow, 1986). The questions are: How widespread among counseling psychologists is such a perspective? Do they really not value career work?

Beyond such questions, what are the effects of counselor preparation in nonschool settings (for example, industrial internships, different amounts or types of paid employment, intern experiences in community and government agencies) on subsequent counselor effectiveness in career guidance? What are the relationships between the counselor's effectiveness in career counseling or guidance and previous occupational experience? How do career counseling or guidance skills and emphases differ among counselors working in a vocational education setting, a comprehensive educational setting, and a community agency? What do counselors in different settings actually know about vocational education? How do counselors rate their competencies on the various career guidance skills recommended in the position statements cited in Chapter 1? What do counselors know about employment and unemployment? About skill elasticities across occupations and settings? About the primary and secondary labor markets? What types of retraining or preservice models are most effective in preparing career counselors for the needs of the future?

RESEARCH FOR THE FUTURE: SOME MAJOR QUESTIONS

Throughout the previous sections, some of the major areas of necessary research have been suggested. In this section we will summarize some additional questions that warrant future attention and identify studies pertinent to them.

The Career Development of Females

- Are there differences in career salience between men and women? If so, what are the factors related to such differences? (Hardesty & Betz, 1980; Sekaran, 1982)
- What are the reciprocal effects of women's career and family attitudes and career behavior across the life span? (Faver, 1982)
- What are the predictors of preferences for traditional or egalitarian marriages on women? What are their implications for career choice and for dual-career families? (Kassner, 1981)
- How do women who choose nontraditional careers differ from women who choose traditional careers? (Wolfe & Betz, 1981)
- What social-psychological determinants relate to achievement (individualism) in high school girls and women? (Smith, 1980)
- How does the pressure of multiple role expectations, opportunities, and choices differentiate women who pursue homemaker, career, or homemaker-career orientations? (Tinsley & Faunce, 1980; Betz, 1982)
- Are background factors or characteristics of the present context and role expectations of others more effective in accounting for achievement motivation in high school girls? What are the resulting implications for career guidance interventions? (Farmer, 1980)
- What is the impact of technology on the traditional and nontraditional employment patterns of women? (Cianni & Weitz, 1986)

- What impact do birth order, parental influence, and the magnitude of role conflict have on women choosing traditional/nontraditional careers? (Wilson, Weikel, & Rose, 1982)
- Are females' career aspirations predictive of educational and career persistence? (Kerr, 1983)
- How do liberal sex-role attitudes and androgynous self-concept affect the career decision-making process? (Tinsley, Kass, Moreland, & Harren, 1983)
- What strategies are working mothers effectively using to manage their time and stress? (Anderson-Kulman & Paludi, 1986)
- Based upon the changing career interests of women, what trends in employment patterns can we anticipate? (Martinez, Sedlacek, & Bachhuber, 1985)
- Given the reality of the marketplace for women, would providing career services to recent alumni be more effective than to college students? (Martinez, Sedlacek, & Bachhuber, 1985)
- What are the effects of women's childrearing and employment plans on subsequent actions? (Granrose, 1985)
- What impact do counselor's conceptions of realism have on their female clients? (Brizze, 1986)
- What are some of the factors that enhance or impede success for women in nontraditional careers over time? (Cianni & Weitz, 1986)
- What are the dynamics of gender differences in work-family conflict within two-career couples? (Greenhaus, Parasuraman, Granrose, Rabinowitz, & Beutell, 1989)
- Do socialization or opportunities dominance, family factors, and choice rationales in career outcomes differ for males and females? (S. R. Jenkins, 1989)
- As opportunity conditions change, does the concept of traditional-nontraditional career choice continue to have viability or is the notion of career realism more appropriate? (Betz & Fitzgerald, 1987; Fitzpatrick & Silverman, 1989)
- To the degree that work status enhances women's self-esteem, under current social conditions do women who are not developing careers or job competencies have compromised self-esteem? (Stein, Newcomb, & Bentler, 1990)
- How do social and historical changes influence shifts in women's career aspirations? (Harmon, 1989)

Career Decision Making and Career Guidance Interventions

- What performance or non-test procedures should be used to supplement mental tests or measures of *g* to provide more efficient job selection systems and reduce adverse impact on culturally different individuals? (Gottfredson, 1988)
- What happens at the actual interface of school and work? How can this process best be conceptualized? (Lokan & Biggs, 1982).
- How can client personality types be most effectively matched to different career guidance approaches? (Kivligham, Hageseth, Tipton, & McGovern, 1981)
- How are career decision-making styles related to locus of control, social desirability, and passivity/activism? (Hesketh, 1982)
- What are the factors related to commitment to change? How can such information be used in the career exploration process? (Dixon & Claiborn, 1981)
- What types of career intervention are most effective with persons experiencing high levels of indecisiveness and poor vocational identity? (Fretz & Leong, 1982)
- In what ways are conceptual level of cognitive style related to career decision-making behavior? What are the implications for career guidance interventions? (Warner & Jepsen, 1979; Lokan & Biggs, 1982)

- How are differential counseling interventions most effectively related to stage and style of decision making? (Harren, Kass, Tinsley, & Morehead, 1978)
- What elements should be included in ideal career guidance programs for different settings? (Goodson, 1982)
- What are the effects of different counseling environments on client perceptions of those environments and on client behavior? (Kerr, 1982)
- How do career indecision subtypes differ? Should career counseling be conducted with different content or different processes to maximize the benefits to different subtypes? (Barak & Friedkes, 1982)
- What are the effects of peers, faculty, and other models in developing career decision-making skills? Are these the prime sources of social reinforcement in career choice? (Ware, 1980)
- Are models of career decision making most effectively conceptualized as idealized views of rationality toward which persons might strive? (Pitz & Harren, 1980)
- What factors (such as anxiety, organizational variables, work role salience) lead to employees' exploration as they proceed through various stages of career development?
- What are the major factors in occupational preference in relation to valence, instrumentality, cost-benefit perceptions? (Wheeler & Mahoney, 1981)
- How can career interventions be evaluated on cost-benefit terms as well as preferences of users? (Reardon, Bonnell, & Huddleston, 1982)
- Is increased occupational exploratory experience causally related to greater interest pattern development? (J. V. Miller, 1982b)
- Are increases in self-esteem and improved self-concept causally related to increases in information-seeking behavior? (M. F. Miller, 1982)
- Do exploratory experiences lead to improvements in self-esteem? (J. V. Miller, 1982a)
- "Would students who tend to avoid career-related problems benefit more from structured as opposed to unstructured intervention strategies? . . . would self-appraised effective problem-solvers who have more self-confidence and who approach problems have positive career planning outcomes with self-directed inventories or computer-interaction systems?" (Heppner, 1983, p. 247)
- How do the relationships between Holland codes and cognitive styles determine the effectiveness of various counseling modalities; for example, since investigative people are intellectual and rational, will they be more accepting of a cognitive approach? (York & Tinsley, 1986)
- What interventions are most effective at varying levels of career decidedness? (Slaney & Lewis, 1986)
- Can the difficulties of the decision-making process be decreased by increasing the number of dimensions along which information about the work environment is offered and personal assessment is conducted? (Salamone & Daughton, 1984)
- What variables determine career aspiration and success in nontraditional fields? (Haring-Hidore & Beyard-Tyler, 1984)
- What is the relationship between vocational maturity and vocational information-seeking behavior? (Sharf, 1984b)
- What variables other than state-trait anxiety, locus of control, and identity affect career indecision? (Hartman, Fuqua, & Blum, 1985)
- How does person-environment congruence interact with nonpsychological variables such as SES and cultural background in predicting stability? (Salamone & Sheehan, 1985)
- What, if any, relationship exists between Type A and B behavior and Hollands's occupational typology? (Matteson, Ivancevich, & Smith, 1984)

- What effects do age, education, experience, locus of control, and self-esteem have on self-assessments, and how are self-assessments related to the decision-making process? (Mihal & Graumenz, 1984)
- What impact does a vocational card sort have on client's perceptions of the decision-making process? What impact does a flat profile have on the counselor's motivation in working with the client?
- How effective are "focused interest" career courses in comparison with traditional courses composed of diverse interest groups? (Lent, Larkin, & Hasegawa, 1986)
- What impact do various types of interventions have on clients with varying levels of differentiation and integration? (Neimeyer et al., 1985)
- To what extent are experiences indicative of manifest interests, verified interests, or both? (Prediger & Swaney, 1986)
- What is the role of knowledge as an indicator of interest score validity? (Prediger & Swaney, 1986)
- How do socialization factors and work experience affect perceptions of value importance and likely attainment? (Sverko, 1989)
- Do interventions that bolster one's confidence with respect to decision-making tasks also foster exploratory activity? (Blustein, 1989; Lent & Hackett, 1987)
- To what degree and in what ways do organizational characteristics influence acceptability of job choices? (Osborn, 1990)
- Can variance in vocational identity among adolescents and college students be explained by conflictual family dynamics, anxiety, and academic adjustment difficulties? (Lopez, 1989)
- Is vocational undecidedness a multivariate phenomenon involving state and trait anxiety, self-esteem issues, locus of control differences, and variances in work, relationship or leisure orientation? (Lucas & Epperson, 1990)
- With what types or components of career indecision is anxiety related? (Fuqua, Newman, & Seaworth, 1990)

Job-Search Process, Work Adjustment, and Occupational Stress

- Do stressors, strains and coping mechanisms differ for males and females at different ranks and occupational settings? (Richard & Krieshok, 1989)
- How do labor market factors and individual characteristics interact to affect the job search process? What are the relationships between types of formal and informal job sources and subsequent work adjustment? (Allen & Keareny, 1980)
- How do value differences between workers and supervisors affect the work adjustment process? Do such factors and other demographic variables significantly moderate both communication behavior and employee performance? (Vecchiotti & Korn, 1980; Penley & Hawkins, 1980)
- What sources of hiring bias exist in relation to disabled interviewees? How can job search techniques be devised to reduce prejudicial employment practices and attitudes toward the disabled?
- Can differences in intraoccupational characteristics of specific job activities and organizational settings be identified in order to maximize the best match between an individual and job? (Erez & Shneorson, 1980)
- To what extent do occupational age stereotypes produce bias in the selection of job applicants? (Gordon & Arvey, 1986)
- How does age of a prospective employer predict the degree of age bias in employment settings? (Gordon & Arvey, 1986)
- In what ways do work values and nonwork values shift in the transition from school to career?
- How is the school-to-work transition affected by mastery of reading, math, science, prob-

lem solving, writing, and reasoning skills? (Junge, Daniels, & Karmos, 1984)

- Are different selection criteria employed over the course of the selection process? (Kinicki & Kammer, 1985)
- How do individuals identify themselves as incongruent; are they more likely to change themselves than their jobs; what effect does altering feelings of congruence have on clients' productivity? (Spokane, 1985)
- What are the roles of self-assessments of success and failure in performance motivation? (McIntire & Levine, 1984)
- As employees make the transition from outsiders to insiders, how does the relative importance of person-group and person-job fit change over time? (Ferris, Youngblood, & Yates, 1985)
- How does perceptual accuracy of recruiters affect the type of information offered in recruitment interviews, and is the information offered satisfying interviewees' needs? (Davis, Giles, & Field, 1985)
- Are career courses facilitative of career adjustment? (Lent, Larkin, & Hasegawa, 1986)
- What are the relationships among types of work stressors, perceived threat, coping behaviors, and work satisfaction and adjustment? (Manzi, 1986)
- How does adaptation to change underlie the career maintenance stage across occupations and organizations? (Williams & Savickas, 1990)

Implications of Midlife Career Changes and Retirement

- To what degree and in what ways does organizational plateauing of career promotability affect work productivity, commitment to the organization, and interinstitutional job changing? (Stout, Slocum, & Cron, 1988)
- How do the antecedents, experiences and outcomes differ for intra- and interinstitutional job changes? (West & Nicholson, 1989)
- How do organizationally dissatisfied and satisfied individuals engage in organizational withdrawal behaviors, including retirement? (Hanisch & Hulin, 1990)
- How do positive self-esteem, internal locus of control, and age influence job satisfaction across occupational levels and types following a period of unemployment? (Mallinckrodt, 1990)
- Do different kinds of career transitions require different kinds of support systems to be provided by work organizations? (Schlossberg & Leibowitz, 1980)
- What factors differentiate voluntary from involuntary career changers? How do their needs for career counseling differ? (Isaacson, 1981)
- Are decision-making styles interdependent throughout life or do they differ at various stages of life? (Phillips, 1982a)
- Can a typology of midlife career changes be established that includes blue-collar, professional, or management changes, personal desire for change versus external pressures to leave, radicalness of change, obstacles to change, and levels of satisfaction? (Thomas, 1980; Neopolitan, 1980)
- Are there motivators for retraining that can be identified and related to potential programs? (Schwarzwald & Shoham, 1981)
- How does an individual's definition of success change over time? (Slocum & Cron, 1985)
- How are organizations and managers dealing with increase in the number of managers who are unlikely to achieve future promotions (plateaued)? What coping mechanisms do plateaued managers use in dealing with stress? (Near, 1985)
- How does the ability to cope with occupational stressors develop through the life span? (Osipow, Doty, & Spokane, 1985)
- How can transition process and outcomes be accurately assessed? (Charner & Schlossberg, 1985)

- What types of coping strategies are individuals using in different types of life transitions? (Charner & Schlossberg, 1986)

Work and Leisure

- Do population groups differing in age, gender, and ethnicity differ in their understanding of the concepts of work, leisure, education, future, and self? What do these findings imply for the work-leisure relationship or for comprehensive career guidance approaches? (Rimmer & Kahnweiler, 1981)
- To what degree can occupation alone meet the psychological needs of the work force? How do occupations differ on this matter? What are the implications for a theory of leisure and of career guidance? (Bloland & Edwards, 1981)
- Are there relationships between personality and the selection of leisure activities? Does leisure have a compensatory effect for the vocationally dissatisfied? (Melamed & Meir, 1981)

Occupational/Career Information

- How can occupational information be most effectively clustered around transferability of skills? (Gottfredson, 1982)
- What are the effects of different types of occupational information on cognitive complexity/simplicity or different types of vocational undecidedness? (Cesari, Winer, Zychlinski, & Laird, 1982)
- What occupations may be categorized as traditional or nontraditional based upon the percentage of one gender of employees within them? (Haring-Hidore & Beyard-Tyler, 1984)
- What are the patterns of career development in nontraditional careers? (Haring-Hidore & Beyard-Tyler, 1984)
- What types of work settings are most satisfying for members who value intrinsic and extrinsic rewards? (Harpaz, 1985)
- What factors other than salary, benefits, and external working conditions are indicative of job satisfaction? (Wiggins, 1984)

Computer-Assisted Career Guidance

- How can we accurately assess the appropriateness of computer-assisted career guidance systems with individual clients? (Sampson, 1984)
- What counseling intervention strategies are effective in conjunction with computer-assisted career guidance systems? (Sampson, 1984)
- What impact do computer-assisted career guidance systems have on culturally distinct client groups? (Cairo, 1983b)
- Are there gender differences in computer aptitude and attitude in adult, nonstudent populations? (Dambrot, Watkins-Mallek, Silling, Marshall, & Garver, 1985)
- In using a computer-based career guidance system, are users more likely to use an expected utility model or sequential elimination model to consider the importance of information processed about occupations? Does the model used vary by age, purpose to be served, or other user attributes? (Gati & Tikotzki, 1990)

Special Populations

- In what ways are men's occupational options limited through sex-role stereotype? (Fitzgerald & Cherpas, 1985)
- Does career guidance with delinquent youth increase the likelihood of subsequent employment? (Pavlak & Kammer, 1985)
- How effective is persuasion skill training, or other strategies that improve expertness, attractiveness, and trustworthiness in preparing disabled or disadvantaged clients for job-seeking process? (Wild & Kerr, 1984)
- Are culturally defined occupations similar across cultures? How do interest inventories discriminate among those occupations that

are culturally defined? (Fouad, Hansen, & Arias-Galicia, 1986)

- How is self-efficacy related to black's career aspirations and expectations? (McNair & Brown, 1983)
- Because of employment barriers or prejudice against blacks, do they settle for jobs that do not match their vocational interests, thereby making their interest profiles less congruent, differentiated, or consistent than those of whites? (Greenlee, Damarin, & Walsh, 1988)

Summary Review of Research Needs

In the *Annual Review of Psychology*, the *Journal of Vocational Behavior*, and *The Counseling Psychologist*, as well as other pertinent journals, major summaries of the research literature and analyses of research needs in that literature are published. To conclude this chapter, selected highlights of reviews that go beyond what has been discussed earlier in this chapter will be summarized here.

For example, Bartol (1981) suggested,

> As greater emphasis is placed on the work life of individuals after initial occupational choices are made, researchers on vocational behavior and career development will increasingly find it necessary to synthesize research findings from the areas of industrial/organizational psychology, organizational sociology, and organizational behavior and theory. This factor may suggest greater collaboration among researchers across these fields in the future. In any event, the broadening base of relevant research, while challenging, also is an exciting development with rich potential for increased knowledge of vocational behavior. (p. 151)

Fretz and Leong (1982b) add to this perspective with their observations that more researchers are attending to environmental and organizational variables as major factors in career development:

> The affirmative results from this emphasis will have to be asserted repeatedly to counter the impact of several generations of intrapsychically oriented career counselors and researchers. Understanding both the unique and interactive contributions of environmental and organizational, as well as organismic, variables to the development and implementation of careers may well be a challenge we can meet in the 1980's. (p. 152)

The view of Fretz and Leong was placed into a somewhat different perspective in an annual review of vocational research by Slaney and Russell (1987), a counseling psychologist and an industrial psychologist. The authors believe that both of the perspectives they represent are centrally concerned with vocational behavior. Of particular importance in the development of their review was the fact that each of the authors found large quantities of research in their respective professional areas but a lack of overlap between them. While some of the research topics were the same—for example, sexual discrimination, sexual harassment, dual careers, burnout, and retirement—most were not, and neither literature tended to reference the other. Slaney and Russell argue the need for discussions on specific topics where collaboration would be most beneficial to both perspectives. For example, they ask

> Would it be productive for I/O (industrial/organization) psychologists to examine closely the research on career interventions in developing programs to aid the career development of employees? Conversely, would it make sense for counselors who deal with reentry women or retired persons to have a greater awareness of what provisions are made by employers for helping persons reenter the employment market, on the one hand, or depart successfully from paid employment, on the other? (p. 157)

That research on programs planned for career development in work settings is still limited is evident in the 1978 review of Super and Hall and 10 years later in the review of Phillips, Cairo, Blustein, and Myers (1988). In the view of the first authors most of the research available involved field studies of such matters as assignments to challenging jobs or various types of job enrichment. They contend that there is "a need for more research on how career identities develop and are shaped by work experiences, as well as studies of how people maintain or increase adaptability in the face of advancing age or technology" (p. 366). Just as is true in other settings, Super and Hall contend that there are needs for more experimental studies to evaluate career development interventions and comparative studies of the relative effectiveness of different interventions.

Super and Hall also express surprise that career theory has been used so little in trying to deal with career problems in the organizational context. In particular, they cite how the work of Schein (1968, 1971), Super (1974), and Holland (1973a) might be used to explore various career problems and to refine present theoretical conceptions in order to build stronger analytic tools. Finally, they suggest that perhaps the most troubling questions both in theoretical and practical terms are, What is development in the work career? in occupational success? in satisfaction? in growth and development of skills? in successful movement through life stages? (p. 367). Such questions, of course, return us to our earlier observation that many of our research concerns are not empirical, but rather philosophical or value-oriented.

Although Phillips, Cairo, Blustein, & Myers (1988) found a wider range of research approaches and questions than did Super and Hall a decade earlier, they continued to express concerns about voids in such areas. In particular they observed that

> there was relatively little attention during the present year to questions of adult career decision making, career development in organizational settings, and organizational induction, socialization and by extending some of the questions addressed in the choice and development domain to populations typically studied in the organization domain . . . many of the individual difference variables and measures employed by those who investigate pre-entry phenomena may account for some heretofore unexplained variance in organizational behavior. . . . Finally, we would underscore the encouraging use of theories and variables traditionally outside the domain of vocational behavior to provide a multidisciplinary perspective on career related concerns. (p. 167)

Finally, three representative sets of research needs are those suggested by Holland, Magoon, and Spokane (1981) in their comprehensive review of research and theory on career interventions, by Osipow, in his master lecture for the American Psychological Association in 1986, and by Gottfredson (1990) in his comprehensive analysis of where research on Holland's theory should go in the future and the status of research in career behavior more generally. Among the suggestions of Holland, Magoon, and Spokane are the following:

- More rigorous evaluations of all forms of vocational interventions are still required. The analysis of how interventions work needs to be continued and reexamined in the context of instructional technology, decision making, and information processing.
- More analytical evaluations in which client goals are linked to treatments are needed to acquire a comprehensive knowledge of client treatment interaction and related outcomes.
- More potent treatments should be developed by incorporating the influential characteristics of past treatments.
- The ordering effects of treatment chains should be investigated.
- The neglected but painfully relevant topics of job finding, placement strategies, and vocational adaptation require more attention.
- The classification research should be more completely exploited. (pp. 298–300)

Osipow (1986) suggested that there are several issues that should influence "the life span practice and research agenda for the near and middle-range future. Issues such as unemployment, underemployment, serial careers, the problems of part-time and temporary workers, disability and compensation, rehabilitation, labor force shifts, and working conditions have rarely been studied from a life-span perspective" (p. 164). In addition, however, he identified other topics that he also believed to be important and enduring concerns for research. They included, in adapted form, the following:

- The study of career stress and adjustment
- The effects of money and job security in career choices, adjustment, implementation, stress, and decision making
- Sexism and racism relative to assessment, equal worth of occupational activities, and discrimination and its effects in the work place
- Mid-career change and multiple careers
- The impact of the family context on career decision making and adjustment
- Leisure and retirement

Osipow concludes his analysis of research issues with a fascinating observation that embodies wisdom about demographics, development, and research. He states, "Much of this anticipated research agenda is stimulated by the aging population. The baby boom has been a prime factor in determining the research agenda on career development since the 1950s. When the 'boomers' were young, education and career entry; as they have aged, a variety of other services have been emphasized. The professional and research agenda will continue to be defined by this population bulge as it goes through the life span" (p. 166).

Finally, Gottfredson (1990), as a function of identifying areas of future applications and research using Holland's Theory of Careers, suggested four areas for cultivation and several admonitions for better designs with regard to areas for cultivation. His suggestions follow in adapted form:

- Self-efficacy Expectations in Career Behavior–"We need to learn how self-efficacy expectations develop, how people come to see themselves as competent and potentially successful in different areas" (p. 2).
- Effects Studies—Because counseling can be costly and difficult to provide to all who could benefit, the following research goals deserve renewed emphasis:
  (a) We need a range of practical treatments for people who need different levels and types of treatment.
  (b) We need more evidence about such basic items as the effects of providing different amounts and modes of information.
  (c) We need *experimental* tests of the implications of the [Holland] typology for the design of career interventions.
  (d) We should begin to link intervention research with social learning theory and attempt to develop interventions with dependable positive effects on self-efficacy expectations.
  (e) We need *experimental* tests of diagnostic ideas linking identity, barriers, and typological assessments to *levels* and *varieties* of assistance. (p. 4)
- Better Designs
  1. Use simple designs if they are appropriate.
  2. Conduct longitudinal research on the attention, selection, and retention or attrition of persons by environments.
  3. Conduct true experiments of the effects of vocational interventions. A few days spent resolving perceived obstacles to randomization is time better spent than time spent on non-experimental research.
  4. Attend to the population studies and the distribution of types of other variables in the population.
  5. Replicate excellent existing studies where few replications are available. . . . (p. 7)

Summary

In this chapter we have examined a broad spectrum of research issues and needs of relevance to the fuller understanding of both career behavior and potential interventions in such behavior. Research and statistical methods have been discussed in relation to how different statistical techniques are used to analyze particular types of questions. It has been suggested that quantitative and qualitative research methodologies are different ways of knowing. In particular, qualitative methods are emerging as ways of analyzing individual tendencies to "meaning-making" and to capture the richness of individual careers. We have discussed the importance to longitudinal career development studies of the challenges of life-span psychology and of such techniques as path analysis, causal modeling, and structural equation-modeling. We have also identified the areas in which research questions in career guidance or career development are present and inventories of such questions are provided. The range of such questions illustrates the complexity of career development processes and their dynamic quality. They also affirm that many of the major questions of concern to career guidance are not empirical, but rather matters of philosophy or values.

BIBLIOGRAPHY

Abbott, J., McClean, K., & Davidshofer, C. O. (1978). *Career development group: Leader's manual,* Fort Collins, CO: Colorado State University Counseling Center.

Abdel-Halim, A. A. (1981). Effects of role stress-job design-technology interact in employee work satisfaction. *Academy of Management Journal, 24*(2), 260–273.

Abdelnour, B. T., & Hall, D. T. (1980). Career development of established employees. *Career Development Bulletin, 2*(1), 5–8.

Abeles, R. P., Steel, L., & Wise, L. L. (1980). Patterns and implications of life-course organization: Studies from Project TALENT. In P. B. Baltes & O. G. Brim, Jr. (Eds.), *Life-span development and behavior* (pp. 308–339). New York: Academic Press.

Abrams, M. (1979). A new work sample battery for vocational assessment of the disadvantaged: VITAS. *Vocational Guidance Quarterly, 28*(1), 35–43.

ACES Position Paper. (1976). *Commission on counselor preparation for career development/career education.* Washington, DC: Association for Counselor Education and Supervision.

ACT. (1985). *Interim psychometric handbook for the 3rd edition ACT Career Planning Program (levels 1 and 2).* Iowa City, IA: The American College Testing Program.

Adams, A. V. & Magnum, G. (1978). *The lingering crisis of youth unemployment.* Kalamazoo, MI: Upjohn Institute for Employer Research.

Adams, A. V., Mangum, G., & Lenninger, S. F. (1978). The nature of youth unemployment. In A. Adams & G. L. Mangum (Eds.), *The lingering crisis of youth unemployment* (pp. 1–13). Kalamazoo, MI: Upjohn Institute for Employment Research.

Adler, A. (1927). *The practice and theory of individual psychology.* New York: Harcourt.

Adler, A. (1935). The fundamental views of individual psychology. *International Journal of Individual Psychology, 1,* 5–8.

Ainsworth, J., & Fifield, M. G. (1973, May). *Work simulation: An approach to vocational exploration (*Training paper*).* Logan, UT: Utah State University, Exceptional Child Center.

Alander, R., & Campbell, T. (1975). An evaluative study of an alcohol and drug recovery program: A case study of the Oldsmobile experience. *Human Resource Management, 14,* 14–18.

Allen, J. E., Jr. (1970, February). *Competence for all as the goal for secondary education.* Paper presented to the National Association of Secondary School Principals, Washington, DC.

Allen, L. R. (1980). Leisure and its relationship to work and career guidance. *Vocational Guidance Quarterly, 28*(3), 257–262.

Allen, R. E., & Kearny, T. J. (1980). The relative effectiveness of alternative job sources. *Journal of Vocational Behavior, 16,* 18–42.

Almquist, E. M. (1974). Sex stereotypes in occupational choice: The case for college women. *Journal of Vocational Behavior, 5,* 13–21.

Amatea, E., & Clark, J. (1984). A dual career workshop for college couples: Effects of an intervention program. *Journal of College Student Personnel, 25*(3), 271–272.

Amatea, E., Clark, J., & Cross, E. (1984). Life-styles: Evaluating a life role planning program for high school students. *Vocational Guidance Quarterly, 34,* 249–259.

Amatea, E., & Cross, E. G. (1986). Helping high school students clarify life role preferences: The life-styles unit. *The School Counselor, 33*(4), 306–313.

Amatea, E. S., & Cross, E. G. (1980). Going places: A career guidance program for high school students and their parents. *Vocational Guidance Quarterly, 28*(3), 274–282.

American Home Economics Association. (1988). *Survey of American Teens.* Washington, DC: Author.

American Institutes for Research. (1975). *Developing comprehensive career guidance programs.* Palo Alto, CA: AIR.

American Personnel and Guidance Association. (1975, March). *Career guidance: Role and functions of counseling and guidance practitioners in career education* (Position paper). Washington, DC: Author.

American Psychiatric Association. (1981). *Diagnostic and statistical manual of mental disorders* (3rd ed.). Washington, DC: Author.

American Psychological Association. (1974). *Standards for educational and psychological tests.* Washington, DC: Author.

American Psychological Association. (1979). Principles concerning the counseling and therapy of women. *The Counseling Psychologist, 8*(1), 21.

American Psychological Association. (1986). *Guidelines for computer-based tests and interpretations.* Washington, DC: Author.

American School Counselors Association. (1977a, August). *The unique role of the elementary school counselor* (Position paper adopted by ASCA Governing Board).

American School Counselors Association. (1977b, August). *The unique role of the middle/junior high school counselor* (Position paper adopted by ASCA Governing Board).

American School Counselors Association. (1981). The practice of guidance and counseling by school counselors. *The School Counselor, 29*(1), 7–12.

American School Counselors Association. (1985). The role of the school counselor in career guidance: Expectations and responsibilities. *The School Counselor, 32*(3), 164–168.

Americana Health Care Corporation (1980). *Aging in America: Trials and triumphs.* New York: Research and Forecast, Inc.

Anastasi, A. (1985). Interpreting scores from multiscore batteries. *Journal of Counseling and Development, 64,* 84–86.

Anderson, C. D., Warner, J. L., & Spencer, C. C. (1984). Inflation bias in self-assessment examinations: Implications for valid employee selection. *Journal of Applied Psychology, 69*(4), 574–580.

Anderson, K. L. (1980). Educational goals of male and female adolescents: The effects of parental characteristics and attitudes. *Youth and Society, 12,* 173–188.

Anderson-Kulman, R. E., & Paludi, M. A. (1986). Working mothers and the family context: Predicting positive coping. *Journal of Vocational Behavior, 28*(3), 241–253.

Aneshensel, C. S., & Stone, J. D. (1982). Stress and depression. *Archives of General Psychiatry, 39,* 1392–1396.

Aneshensel, C. W., & Rosen, B. C. (1980). Domestic roles and sex differences in occupational expectations. *Journal of Marriage and the Family, 42,* 121–131.

Angresano, J. (1980). Results of a survey of employer hiring practices. *Vocational Guidance Quarterly, 28*(4), 335–342.

Angrist, S. (1972). Changes in women's work aspirations during college. *International Journal of Sociology of the Family, 2,* 87–97.

Anh, N. T., & Healy, C. C. (1985). Factors affecting employment and job satisfaction of Vietnamese refugees. *Journal of Employment Counseling, 22,* 78–85.

Anthony, W. A. (1980). *The principles of psychiatric rehabilitation*. Baltimore: University Park Press.

Appel, V., Haak, R., & Witzke, D. (1970). Factors associated in the indecision about collegiate major and career choices. *Proceedings of the 78th Annual Convention of the American Psychological Association, 5,* 667–668.

Arbeiter, S., Aslanian, C. B., Schmerbeck, F. A., & Brickell, H. M. (1978). *40 million Americans in career transition: The need for information*. New York: College Entrance Examination Board.

Arbona, C. (1990). Career counseling research and Hispanics: A review of the literature. *The Counseling Psychologist, 18,* 300–323.

Arbuckle, D. S. (1963). Occupational information in the elementary school. *Vocational Guidance Quarterly, 12,* 77–84.

Argeropoulos, J. (1981). *Burnout, stress management, and wellness*. Moravia, NY: Chronicle Guidance.

Armstrong, J. C. (1981). Decision behavior and outcomes of midlife career changes. *Vocational Guidance Quarterly, 29*(3), 205–211.

Arnold, J. (1989). Career decidedness and psychological wellbeing: A two-cohort longitudinal study of undergraduate students and recent graduates. *Journal of Occupational Psychology, 62,* 163–176.

Arp, R. S., Holmberg, K. S., & Littrell, J. M. (1986). Launching adult students into the job market: A support group approach. *Journal of Counseling and Development, 65,* 166–167.

Arroba, T. (1977). Styles of decision-making and their use: An empirical study. *British Journal of Guidance and Counseling, 5*(2), 149–158.

Ash, K. S., & Mandelbaum, D. (1982). Using peer counselors in career development. *Journal of College Placement, 42*(3), 47–51.

Ashley, W. L., Cellini, J., Faddis, C., Pearsol, J., Wiant, A., & Wright, B. (1980). *Adaptation to work: An exploration of processes and outcomes*. Columbus, OH: National Center for Research in Vocational Education, Ohio State University.

Ashurst, P., & Hale, Z. (1989). *Understanding women in distress*. London: Tavistock/Routledge.

Aslanian, C. B., & Brickell, H. M. (1980). *Americans in transition: Life changes as reasons for adult learning*. New York: College Entrance Examination Board.

Association of Computer-Based Systems for Career Information. (1989). *Directory of state-based career information delivery systems, 1988–1989*. Eugene, OR: Author.

Association for Counselor Education and Supervision. (1976, April). *Position paper on counselor preparation for career development/career education*. Washington, DC: Author.

Assouline, M., & Meir, E. (1987). Meta-analysis of relationship between congruence and well-being measures. *Journal of Vocational Behavior, 31,* 319–332.

Astin, H. S. (1984). The meaning of work in women's lives: A sociopsychological model of career choice and work behavior. *The Counseling Psychologist, 12*(4), 117–126.

Atchley, R. C. (1979). Issues in retirement research. *The Gerontologist, 19*(1), 44–54.

Atkins, C. P., & Kent, R. L. (1988). What do recruiters consider important during the employment interview? *Journal of Employment Counseling, 25,* 98–103.

Atkinson, D. R., Morten, G., & Sue, D. W. (1983). *Counseling American minorities*. Dubuque, IA: William C. Brown.

Aubrey, R. G. (1977). *Career development needs of thirteen-year-olds: How to improve career development programs*. Washington, DC: National Advisory Council for Career Education.

Aubry, T., Tefft, B., & Kingsbury, N. (1990). Behavioral and psychological consequences of unemployment in blue-collar couples. *Journal of Community Psychology, 18,* 99–111.

Auster, C. J., & Auster, D. (1981). Factors influencing women's choice of nontraditional careers: The role of family, peers, and counselors. *Vocational Guidance Quarterly, 29,* 253–263.

Austin, J. T., & Hanisch, K. A. (1990). Occupational attainment as a function of abilities and interests: A longitudinal analysis using Project TALENT data. *Journal of Applied Psychology, 75,* 77–86.

Austin, W. M. (1986). The occupational outlook in brief. *Occupational Outlook Quarterly, Spring,* 3–29.

Axelrod, W. L., & Gavin, J. F. (1980). Stress and strain in blue-collar and white-collar management staff. *Journal of Vocational Behavior, 17,* 41–49.

Axelson, J. A. (1985). *Counseling and development in a multicultural society*. Pacific Grove, CA: Brooks/Cole Publishing Company.

Babcock, R. J., & Kaufman, M. A. (1976). Effectiveness of a career course. *Vocational Guidance Quarterly, 24*(3), 261–266.

Baca, P. M. (1980). Ex-P.O.: Exploring possible occupations. *The School Counselor, 28*(1), 54–58.

Bach, R. L. (1980). The new Cuban immigrants: Their background and prospects. *Monthly Labor Review, 103*(10), 39–46.

Bach, R. L., & Bach, J. B. (1980). Employment patterns of southeast Asian refugees. *Monthly Labor Review, 103*(10), 31–38.

Bachman, J. G., Kahn, R. L., Mednick, M., Davidson, T. N., & Johnston, L. D. (1970). *Youth in transition* (Vol. 2). Ann Arbor: University of Michigan, Institute for Social Research.

Backman, M. E., Lynch, J. J., & Loeding, D. J. (1979). Sex and ethnic differences in vocational aptitude patterns. *Measurement and Evaluation in Guidance, 12*(1), 35–43.

Baeher, M., & Orban, J. A. (1989). The role of intellectual abilities and personality characteristics in determining success in higher-level positions. *Journal of Vocational Behavior, 38,* 270–287.

Bailey, L. J., & Stadt, R. (1973). *Career education: New Approaches to human development*. Bloomington, IL: McKnight.

Baker, H. (1944). *Employee counseling*. Princeton, NJ: Princeton University Press.

Baker, S. B., & Popowicz, C. L. (1983). Meta-analysis as a strategy for evaluating effects of career education interventions. *Vocational Guidance Quarterly, 31,* 178–186.

Bamundo, P. J., & Kopelman, R. E. (1980). The moderating effects of occupation, age, and urbanization on the relationship between job satisfaction and life satisfaction. *Journal of Vocational Behavior, 17,* 106–123.

Banas, P., & Nash, A. (1966). Differential predictability: Selection of handicapped and nonhandicapped. *Personnel and Guidance Journal, 45,* 277–330.

Bandura, A. (1977). Self-efficacy: Toward a unifying theory of behavioral change. *Psychological Review, 84,* 191–215.

Bandura, A. (1982a). The psychology of chance encounters and life paths. *American Psychologist, 37*(7), 747–755.

Bandura, A. (1982b). Self-efficacy mechanism in human agency. *American Psychologist, 37,* 122–147.

Bandura, A., Adams, N. E., & Meyer, J. (1977). Cognitive processes mediating behavior change. *Journal of Personality and Social Psychology, 35,* 125–139.

Bank, I. M. (1969). Children explore careerland through vocational role models. *Vocational Guidance Quarterly, 17,* 284–289.

Barak, A., & Friedkes, R. (1982). The mediating effects of career indecision subtypes on career counseling effectiveness. *Journal of Vocational Behavior, 20,* 120–128.

Barak, A., & Rabbi Ben-Zion. (1982). Predicting persistence, stability, and achievement in college by major choice consistency: A test of Holland's consistency hypothesis. *Journal of Vocational Behavior, 20,* 235–243.

Barker, S. B., & Patten, G. L. (1989). Use of the Career Area Interest Checklist with Junior High School Students. *The School Counselor, 37,* 149–152.

Barling, J. (1986). Interrole conflict and marital functioning amongst employed fathers. *Journal of Occupational Behavior, 7,* 1–8.

Barling, J., & Rosenbaum, A. (1986). Work stressors and wife abuse. *Journal of Applied Psychology, 71*(2), 346–348.

Barnett, R. (1971). Personality correlates of vocational planning. *Genetic Psychology Monographs, 83,* 309–356.

Baron, R. A. (1983). Sweet smell of success? The impact of pleasant artificial scents on evaluations of job applicants. *Journal of Applied Psychology, 68,* 709–713.

Barrow, J., Cox, P., Sepich, R., & Spivak, R. (1989 January). Student needs assessment surveys: Do they predict student use of services? *Journal of College Student Development, 30,* 77–82.

Bartol, K. M. (1981). Vocational behavior and career development, 1980: A review. *Journal of Vocational Behavior, 19,* 123–162.

Baruch, G., Barnett, R., & Rivers, C. (1983). *Life prints: New patterns of love and work for today's women*. New York: New American Library.

Baruch, G. K., & Barnett, R. C. (1986). Father's participation in family work and children's sex-role attitudes. *Child Development, 57,* 1210–1223.

Baruch, G. K., Biener, L., & Barnett, R. C. (1987). Women and gender in research on work and family stress. *American Psychologist, 42,* 130–136.

Basow, S. A., & Howe, K. G. (1979). Model influences on career choices of college students. *Vocational Guidance Quarterly, 27*(3), 239–243.

Bauer, D., & Mott, D. (1990 May/June). Life themes and motivations of re-entry students. *Journal of Counseling and Development, 68,* 555–560.

Bauernfeind, R. H. (1988). Review of Career Occupational Preference System. In J. T. Kapes & M. M. Mastie (Eds.), *A counselor's guide to career assessment instruments* (pp. 81–85). Washington, DC: National Career Development Association.

Baumgardner, S. R. (1977). Vocational planning: The great swindle. *Personnel and Guidance Journal, 56,* 17–22.

Bayer, A. E. (1972). *The black college freshman: Characteristics and recent trends*. Washington, DC: American Council on Education.

Bayer, G. A., & Gerstein, L. H. (1990). EAP referrals and troubled employees: An analogue study of supervisors' decisions. *Journal of Vocational Behavior, 36,* 304–319.

Beane, A. L., & Zachmanoglou, M. A. (1979). Career education for the handicapped: A psychosocial impact. *Vocational Guidance Quarterly, 28*(1), 44–47.

Beck, A. T., Rush, A. J., Shaw, B. F., & Emery, G. (1979). *Cognitive therapy of depression*. New York: Guilford Press.

Beck, C. E. (1963). *Philosophical foundations of guidance*. Englewood Cliffs, NJ: Prentice-Hall.

Becker, B. E., & Krzystojiak, F. J. (1982). The influence of labor market discrimination on locus on control. *Journal of Vocational Behavior, 21,* 60–70.

Beehr, T. A., King, L. A., & King, D. W. (1990). Social support and occupational stress: Talking to supervisors. *Journal of Vocational Behavior, 36,* 61–81.

Beley, W., & Felker, S. (1981). Comprehensive training evaluation for clients with psychiatric impairments. *Rehabilitation Literature, 42,* 194–201.

Bell, A. P., Super, D. E., & Dunn, L. B. (1988). Understanding and implementing career theory: A case study approach. *Counseling and Human Development, 20*(8), 1–20.

Benight, C. C., & Kinicki, A. J. (1988). Interaction of Type A behavior and perceived controllability of stressors on stress outcomes. *Journal of Vocational Behavior, 33,* 50–62.

Benn, R. K. (1986). Factors promoting secure attachment relationships between employed mothers and their sons. *Child Development, 57,* 1224–1231.

Ben-Shakhar, G., Bar-Hillel, M., Bilu, Y., Ben-Abba, E., & Flug, A. (1986). Can graphology predict occupational success? Two empirical studies and some methodological ruminations. *Journal of Applied Psychology, 71,* 645–653.

Benson, P. G. (1988). Review of Minnesota Importance Questionnaire. In J. T. Kapes & M. M. Mastie (Eds.), *A counselor's guide to career assessment instruments* (pp. 144–149). Washington, DC: National Career Development Association.

Bentler, P. M. (1980). Multivariate analysis with latent variables: Causal modeling. In M. R. Rosenzweig & L. W. Porter (Eds.), *The Annual View of Psychology* (Vol. 31). Palo Alto: Annual Reviews.

Berg, I. (1975). *Education and jobs: The great training robbery.* Boston: Beacon Press.

Berg, I., & Hughes, M. (1979). Economic circumstances and the entangling web of pathologies: An esquisse. In L. A. Ferman & J. P. Gordus (Eds.), *Mental health and the economy* (Chap. 2). Kalamazoo, MI: The W. E. Upjohn Institute for Employment Research.

Bergland, B. W. (1974). Career planning: The use of sequential evaluated experience. In E. L. Herr (Ed.), *Vocational guidance and human development* (pp. 350–380). Boston: Houghton Mifflin.

Bergland, B. W., & Krumboltz, J. D. (1969). An optimal guide level for career exploration. *Vocational Guidance Quarterly, 18,* 29–33.

Berk, S. F. (1985). *The gender factory: The apportionment of work in American households*. New York: Plenum.

Berlin, G., & Sum, A. (1988). *Toward a more perfect union: Basic skills, poor families and our economic future* (Occasional Paper Number 3). New York: Ford Foundation.

Berman, E. (1980). *Re-entering*. New York: Crown.

Bernard, J. (1981). The good provider role: Its rise and fall. *American Psychologist, 6*(1), 1–12.

Berry, E. (1979). Guidance and counseling in the elementary school: Its theoretical base. *The Personnel and Guidance, 57*(10), 513–520.

Bertaux, D. (1982). The life course approach as a challenge to the social sciences. In T. K. Haraven & K. J. Adams (Eds.), *Aging and life course transitions: An interdisciplinary perspective* (pp. 127–150). New York: Guilford Press.

Betz, E. L. (1982). Need fulfillment in the career development of women. *Journal of Vocational Behavior, 20,* 53–66.

Betz, N. E., & Fitzgerald, L. F. (1987). *The career psychology of women*. Orlando, FL: Academic Press.

Betz, N. E., & Hackett, G. (1981). The relationship of career-related self-efficacy expectations to perceived career options in college women and men. *Journal of Counseling Psychology, 28,* 399–410.

Betz, N. E., & Hackett, G. (1983). The relationship of mathematics self-efficacy expectations to the selection of science-based college majors. *Journal of Vocational Behavior, 23,* 329–345.

Betz, N. E., & Hackett, G. (1986). Applications of self-efficacy theory to understanding career choice behavior. *Journal of Social and Clinical Psychology, 4,* 279–289.

Beutell, N. J., & Brenner, O. C. (1986). Sex differences in work values. *Journal of Vocational Behavior, 28,* 29–41.

Beutell, N. J., & Greenhaus, J. H. (1982). Interrole conflict among married women: The influence of husband and wife characteristics on conflict and coping behavior. *Journal of Vocational Behavior, 21,* 99–110.

Beyard-Tyler, K., & Haring, M. J. (1984). Navajo students respond to traditional occupations: Less information, less bias? *Journal of Counseling Psychology, 31*(2), 270–273.

Bhaerman, R. D. (1977). *Career education and basic academic achievement: A descriptive analysis of the research*. Washington, DC: U.S. Office of Education.

Bienstock, J. K. (1981). Reading and writing and the study of careers. *The College Board Review, 110,* 14–16.

Biggers, J. L. (1971). The use of information in vocational decision making. *Vocational Guidance Quarterly, 19*(3), 171–176.

Bigoness, W. J. (1978). Correlates of faculty attitudes toward collective bargaining. *Journal of Applied Psychology, 63*(2), 228–233.

Bird, C. (1975). *The case against college*. New York: David McKay.

Bird, G. W., Bird, G. A., & Scruggs, M. (1984). Determinants of family task sharing: A study of husbands and wives. *Journal of Marriage and the Family, 46*(2), 345–355.

Birk, J. A., & Blimline, C. A. (1984). Parents as career development facilitators: An untapped resource for the counselor. *The School Counselor, 31*(4), 310–317.

Bjorkquist, D. C. (1970). Technical education for the underemployed and unemployed. *Vocational Guidance Quarterly, 18,* 264–272.

Black, S. M. & Hill, C. E. (1984). The psychological well-being of women in their middle years. *Psychology of Women Quarterly, 8*(3), 282–292.

Blai, B. (1982). Programs for older persons: A compendium. *Journal of Employment Counseling 19*(3), 98–105.

Blau, P. M., Gustad, J. W., Jessor, R., Parnes, H. S., & Wilcock, R. C. (1956). Occupational choice: A conceptual framework. *Industrial Labor Relations* (rev. ed.), *9,* 531–543.

Bloch, D. P. (1989). From career information to career knowledge: Self, search, and synthesis. *Journal of Career Development, 16,* 119–128.

Bloch, D. P., & Kinnison, J. F. (1989a). A method for rating computer-based career information delivery systems. *Measurement and Evaluation in Counseling and Development, 21,* 177–187.

Bloch, D. P., & Kinnison, J. F. (1989b). Occupational and career information components: A validation study. *Journal of Studies in Technical Careers, 11,* 101–109.

Blocher, K., & Rogers, J. (1977). Career development for the majority. *Journal of College Placement, 37*(1), 69–72.

Block, H. H. (1983). Differential premises arising from different socialization of the sexes: Some conjectures. *Child Development, 54,* 1335–1354.

Bloland, P. A., & Edwards, P. B. (1981). Work and leisure: A counseling synthesis. *Vocational Guidance Quarterly, 30*(2), 101–108.

Blustein, D. L. (1988). A canonical analysis of career choice crystallization and vocational maturity. *Journal of Counseling Psychology, 35*(3), 294–297.

Blustein, D. L. (1989). The role of goal instability and career self-efficacy in the career exploration process. *Journal of Vocational Behavior, 35*(2), 194–203.

Blustein, D. L., Ellis, M. V., & Devenis, L. E. (1989). The development and validation of a two-dimensional model of the commitment to career choice process. *Journal of Vocational Behavior, 35,* 342–378.

Blustein, D. L., & Phillips, S. D. (1990). Relation between ego identity statuses and decision-making styles. *Journal of Counseling Psychology, 37,* 160–168.

Boese, R. R., & Cunningham, J. W. (1976). Systematically derived dimensions of human work. *JSAS Catalog of Selected Documents in Psychology, 6,* 57. (Ms. No. 1270)

Boll, A. S., & Briggs, J. I. (1979). Informational interviewing: Easing the student's entry into the working world. *Journal of College Placement, 39*(2), 53–55.

Bollendorf, M., Howrey, M., & Stephenson, G. (1990). Project Career REACH: Marketing strategies for effective guidance programs. *The School Counselor, 37*(3), 273–280.

Boocock, S. S. (1967). The life career game. *Personnel and Guidance Journal, 45,* 328–334.

Boocock, S. S. (1968). *Instructor's manual for life career.* New York: Bobbs-Merrill.

Bordin, E. S. (1946). Diagnosis in counseling and psychotherapy. *Education and Psychological Measurement, 6,* 169–184.

Bordin, E. S. (1955). *Psychological counseling*. New York: Appleton-Century-Crofts.

Bordin, E. S. (1984). Psychodynamic model of career choice and satisfaction. In D. Brown & L. Brooks (Eds.). *Career choice and development: Applying contemporary theories to practice* (Chap. 5). San Francisco: Jossey-Bass.

Bordin, E. S. (1990). Psychodynamic models of career choice and satisfaction. In D. Brown & L. Brooks (Eds.), *Career choice and development. Applying contemporary theories to practice* (2nd Ed., pp. 102–144). San Francisco: Jossey-Bass.

Bordin, E. S., & Kopplin, D. A. (1973). Motivational conflict and vocational development. *Journal of Counseling Psychology, 20*(2), 154–161.

Bordin, E. S., Nachmann, B., & Segal, S. J. (1963). An articulated framework for vocational development. *Journal of Counseling Psychology, 10,* 107–116.

Borgen, F. H. (1988). Review of Strong-Campbell Interest Inventory. In J. T. Kapes & M. M. Mastie (Eds.), *A counselor's guide to career assessment instruments* (pp. 121–126). Washington, DC: National Career Development Association.

Borgen, F. H., Layton, W. L., Veenhuizen, D. L., & Johnson, D. J. (1985). Vocational behavior and career development, 1984: A review. *Journal of Vocational Behavior, 27,* 218–269.

Borgen, F. H., Weiss, D. J., Tinsley, H. F. A., Dawis, R. V., & Lofquist, L. H. (1972). *Occupational reinforcer patterns: I.* Minneapolis, MI: Vocational Psychology Research, Department of Psychology.

Borgen, W., & Amundson, N. (1984). *The experience of unemployment, implications for counseling the unemployed*. Scarborough, Ontario: Nelson Canada.

Borgen, W. A., & Amundson, N. E. (1985). Counseling immigrants for employment. In R. Samuda & A. Wolfgang (Eds.), *Intercultural counseling: Global dimensions* (pp. 269–279). Toronto: C. J. Hografe.

Borgen, W. A., & Young, R. H. (1982). Career perceptions of children and adolescents. *Journal of Vocational Behavior, 21,* 37–49.

Borman, C. (1988). Review of Career Survey. In J. T. Kapes & M. M. Mastie (Eds.), *A counselor's guide to career assessment instruments* (pp. 203–207). Washington, DC: National Career Development Association.

Borman, G., & Colson, S. (1984). Mentoring—An effective career guidance technique. *Vocational Guidance Quarterly, 32*(3), 192–197.

Borman, K., Izzo, K. V., Penn, E. M., & Reisman, J. (1984). *The adolescent worker.* Columbus: Ohio State University, National Center for Research in Vocational Education.

Borow, H. (1961). Vocational development research: Some problems of logical and experimental form. *Personnel and Guidance Journal, 40,* 21–25.

Borow, H. (1970). Career development: A future for counseling. In W. Van Hoose & J. Pietrofesa (Eds.), *Counseling and guidance in the twentieth century* (pp. 30–46). Boston: Houghton Mifflin.

Borow, H. (1980). Career guidance uses of labor market information: Limitations and potentialities. In H. N. Drier & L. A. Pfister (Eds.), *Career and labor market information: Key to improved individual decision-making* (pp. 7–19). Columbus, OH: National Center for Research in Vocational Education.

Borow, H. (1984). Occupational socialization: Acquiring a sense of work. In N. C. Gysbers (Ed.), *Designing careers, counseling to enhance education, work and leisure* (Chap. 6). San Francisco: Jossey-Bass.

Borow, H. (1989). Youth in transition to work: Lingering problems. *Guidance and counseling, 4*(4), 7–14.

Bosse, R., Aldwin, C. M., Levenson, M. R., & Ekerdt, D. J. (1987). Mental health differences among retirees and workers: Findings from the normative aging study. *Psychology and Aging, 2*(4), 383–389.

Boston, B. (1980). Second-order dimensions of the Work Values Inventory (WVI). *Journal of Vocational Behavior, 17,* 33–40.

Boswell, J. (1981). The dual-career family: A model for egalitarian family politics. *Elementary School Guidance and Counseling, 15*(3), 262–269.

Botterbusch, K. F. (1987). *Vocational assessment and evaluation systems: A comparison.* Menomonie, WI: Materials Development Center, Stout Vocational Rehabilitation Institute.

Bottoms, J. R., & Matheney, K. (1969, March). *Occupational guidance, counseling, and job placement for junior high and secondary school youth.* Paper presented at the National Conference of Exemplary Programs and Projects Section of the Vocational Education Act, Amendment of 1968, Atlanta, GA.

Bowen, D. D. (1985). Were men meant to mentor women? *Training and Development Journal, February,* 30–34.

Bowen, D. E., & Greiner, L. E. (1986). Moving from production to service in human resources management. *Organizational Dynamics, Summer,* 35–53.

Bowlby, J. A. (1958). The nature of the child's tie to his mother. *International Journal of Psychoanalysis, 39,* 350–373.

Boy, A. V., & Pine, G. J. (1963). *Client-centered counseling in the secondary school.* Boston: Houghton Mifflin.

Bramel, D., & Friend, R. (1981). Hawthorne, the myth of the docile worker, and class bias in psychology. *The American Psychologist, 36*(8), 867–878.

Brammer, L. M., & Shostrom, L. L. (1960). *Therapeutic Psychology.* Englewood Cliffs, NJ: Prentice-Hall.

Brand, L. (1990). Occupational staffing patterns within industries through the year 2000. *Occupational Outlook Quarterly, 34*(3), 40–52.

Brass, D. J. (1981). Structural relationships, job characteristics, and worker satisfaction and performance. *Administrative Science Quarterly, 26*(3), 331–348.

Braude, L. (1975). *Work and workers: A sociological perspective.* New York: Praeger.

Braun, J. S., & Bayer, F. (1973). Social desirability of occupations revisited. *Vocational Guidance Quarterly, 21,* 202–205.

Brayfield, A. H., & Crites, J. O. (1964). Research on vocational guidance: Status and prospect. In H. Borow (Ed.), *Man in a world of work* (pp. 310–340). Boston: Houghton Mifflin.

Brenner, M. H. (1973). *Mental illness and the economy.* Cambridge: Harvard University Press.

Brenner, M. H. (1979). Health and the national economy: Commentary and general principles. In L. A. Ferman & J. P. Gordus (Eds.), *Mental health and the economy* (Chap. 3). Kalamazoo, MI: The W. E. Upjohn Institute for Employment Research.

Brenner, M. H. (1981). Importance of the economy to the nation's health. In L. Eisenberg & A. Kleinman (Eds.), *The relevance of social science for medicine* (pp. 371–396). Dordrecht, Holland: D. Reidel.

Brenner, M. H. (1987). Economic change, alcohol consumption and heart disease mortality in nine industrialized countries. *Social Science and Medicine, 25*(2), 119–132.

Brenner, M. H., & Swank, R. T. (1986). Homicide and economic change: Recent analysis of the Joint Economic Committee Report of 1984. *Journal of Quantitative Criminology, 2,* 81–103.

Bridges, J. S. (1988). Sex differences in occupational performance expectations. *Psychology of Women Quarterly, 12,* 75–90.

Brill, A. A. (1948). *Psychoanalytic psychiatry.* London: John Lehman.

Brim, O. G., & Kagan, J. (Eds.). (1980). *Constancy and change in human development.* Cambridge, MA: Harvard University Press.

Brizzi, J. S. (1986). The socialization of women's vocational realism. *Vocational Guidance Quarterly, 34*(3), 151–159.

Brockner, J. (1988). *Self-esteem at work: Research, theory, and practice.* Lexington, MA: Lexington Books.

Broday, S. F., & Braswell, L. C. (1990). The relationship between academic comfort and other Strong Campbell Interest Inventory scales. *Journal of College Student Development, 31,* 454–459.

Brolin, D. E., & Gysbers, N. C. (1979). Career education for persons with handicaps. *Personnel and Guidance Journal, 58*(4), 258–262.

Brolin, D. E., & Gysbers, N. C. (1989). Career education for students with disabilities. *Journal of Counseling and development, 68,* 155–159.

Bronfenbrenner, U. (1979). *The ecology of human development.* Cambridge, MA: Harvard University Press.

Brooks, L., & Betz, N. E. (1990). Utility of expectancy theory in predicting occupational choices in college students. *Journal of Counseling Psychology, 37*(1), 57–64.

Brooks, L., & Haigler, J. (1984). Contract career counseling: An option for some help seekers. *Vocational Guidance Quarterly, 33*(2), 178–182.

Brown, D. (1981). Emerging models of career development groups for persons at midlife. *Vocational Guidance Quarterly, 29*(4), 332–340.

Brown, D. (1984). Trait and factor theory. In D. Brown & L. Brooks (Eds.), *Career choice and development, applying contemporary theories to practice.* (Chap. 2). San Francisco: Jossey-Bass.

Brown, D. (1985). Career counseling: Before, after, or instead of personal counseling? *The Vocational Guidance Quarterly, 33*(3), 197–201.

Brown, D., & Brooks, L. (1991). *Career counseling techniques,* Boston: Allyn & Bacon.

Brown, D., & Feit, S. S. (1978). Making job placement work. *Vocational Guidance Quarterly, 27*(2), 176–183.

Brown, D., Ware, W. B., & Brown, S. T. (1985). A predictive validation of the career decision-making system. *Measurement and Evaluation in Counseling and Development, 17*(2), 81–85.

Brown, D. A. (1980). Life-planning workshop for high school students. *The School Counselor, 29*(1), 77-83.

Brown, G. S., & Strange, C. (1981). The relationship of academic major and career choice status to anxiety among college freshmen. *Journal of Vocational Behavior, 19*, 328–334.

Brown, J. H., & Brown, C. S. (1977). *Systematic counseling: A guide for the practitioner.* Champaign, IL: Research Press.

Brown, S. J. (1975). Career planning inventories: "Do-it-yourself" won't do. *Personnel and Guidance Journal, 53*, 512–517.

Brown, S. T., & Brown, D. (1990). *Designing and implementing a career information center.* Garrett Park, MD: Garrett Park Press.

Bruch, M. A., & Krieshok, T. S. (1981). Investigative versus realistic Holland types and adjustments in theoretical engineering majors. *Journal of Vocational Behavior, 18*, 162–173.

Brugnoli, G. A., Champion, J. E., & Basen, J. A. (1979). Racial bias in the use of work samples for personnel selection. *Journal of Applied Psychology, 64*(2), 119–123.

Bruhn, J. G. (1989). Job stress: An opportunity for professional growth. *Career development Quarterly, 37*, 306–315.

Bruner, J. (1973). Continuity of learning. *Saturday Review of Education, 1*(2), 21–24.

Buckingham, L., & Lee, A. M. (1973). *Placement and follow-up in career education.* Raleigh, NC: Center for Occupational Education, North Carolina State University.

Buehler, C. (1933). *Der menschliche lebenslauf als psychologisches problem.* Leipzig: Hirzel.

Buescher, K. L., Johnston, J. A., Lucas, E. B., & Hughey, K. F. (1989). Early intervention with undecided college students. *Journal of College Student Development, 30*, 375–376.

Bujold, C. (1990). Biographical-hermeneutical approaches to the study of career development. In R. A. Young and W. E. Borgen (Eds.), *Methodological approaches to the study of careers* (pp. 57–70). New York: Praeger.

Bunda, R., & Mezzano, J. (1968). A study of the effects of a work-experience program on performance of potential dropouts. *The School Counselor, 15*, 272–274.

Burack, E. H. (1977). Why all of the confusion about career planning? *Human Resources Management*, 21–23.

Burack, E. H., & Mathys, N. J. (1980). *Career management in organizations: A practical human resources planning approach.* Lake Forest, IL: Brace-Park Press.

Bureau of Labor Statistics. (1986). *Employment projection for 1995: Data and methods* (Bulletin 2253). Washington, DC: U.S. Government Printing Office.

Bureau of Labor Statistics. (1990). *Occupational Outlook Handbook.* (1990–1991, ed.) Washington, DC: U.S. Department of Labor.

Burke, R. J. (1986). Reemployment in a poorer job after a plant closing. *Psychological Reports, 58*, 559–570.

Burke, R. J. (1989). Toward a phase model of burnout. *Group and Organizational Studies, 14*, 23–32.

Burkhalter, B. B., Curtis, J. P., Toppins, A. D., & Mickler, M. L. (1983). An experiential career exploration program in science and technology. *Journal of Career Education, 10*(2), 129–133.

Burlew, L. (1989). The Life-Long Leisure Graph: A tool for Leisure Counseling. *Journal of Career Development, 15*(3), 164–172.

Burnett, F., & Burnett, S. (1988). *Working together: Entrepreneurial couples.* Berkeley: Ten Speed Press.

Burnstein, E. (1963). Fear of failure, achievement motivation, and aspiring to prestigeful occupations. *Journal of Abnormal and Social Psychology, 67*, 189–193.

Burr, P. L. (1980). Women: The emerging labor force. In C. S. Sheppard & D. C. Carroll (Eds.), *Working in the twenty-first century* (pp. 98–105). New York: Wiley.

Burris, V. (1983). The social and political consequences of overeducation. *American Sociological Review, 48*, 454–467.

Burtnett, F. E. (Ed.), (1980). *The school counselor's involvement in career education.* Falls Church, VA: APGA Press.

Business Advisory Commission, Education Commission of the States. (1985). *Reconnecting youth.* Denver, CO: Author.

Byham, W. C. (1982). Applying a systems approach to personnel activities. *Training and Development Journal, 36*, 70–75.

Byrne, D. G., & Reinhart, M. I. (1989). Work characteristics, occupational achievement and the Type A behavior pattern. *Journal of Occupational Psychology, 62*, 123–134.

Byrne, R. H. (1958). Proposed revisions of the Borden-Pepinsky Diagnostic Constructs. *Journal of Counseling Psychology, 5*, 184–187.

Cabral, A. C., & Salomone, P. R. (1990). Chance and careers: Normative versus contextual development. *Career Development Quarterly, 39*, 5–17.

Cahill, M., & Salomone, P. R. (1987). Career counseling for work life extension: Integrating the older worker into the labor force. *The Career Development Quarterly, 35*(3), 188–196.

Cairo, P. C. (1983a). Counseling in industry: A selected review of the literature. *Personnel Psychology, 36*, 1–18.

Cairo, P. C. (1983b). Evaluating the effects of computer-assisted counseling systems: A selective review. *The Counseling Psychologist, 11*(4), 55–59.

Cairo, P. C. (1985). Career planning and development in organizations. In Z. Leibowitz & D. Lea (Eds.), *Adult career development* (pp. 234–248). Washington, DC: National Career Development Association.

Calhoun, R. E. (1980). The new work ethic. *Training and Development Journal, 34*, 127–130.

California State Department of Education. (1972). *Identification of major occupational groups and entry level jobs in civilian public service.* Sacramento, CA: Author.

Campbell, D. P., & Holland, J. L. (1972). A merger in vocational interest research: Applying Holland's theory to Strong's data. *Journal of Vocational Behavior, 2*, 353–376.

Campbell, N. J. (1988). Review of Self-Directed Search. In J. T. Kapes & M. M. Mastie (Eds.), *A counselor's guide to career assessment instruments* (pp. 116–120). Washington, DC: National Career Development Association.

Campbell, N. K., & Hackett, G. (1986). The effects of mathematics task performances on math self-efficacy and task interest. *Journal of Vocational Behavior, 28*(2), 149–162.

Campbell, R. E. (1968). *Vocational guidance in secondary education: A national survey.* Columbus, OH: The Center for Vocational Education.

Campbell, R. E.,& Cellini, J. V. (1981). A diagnostic taxonomy of adult career problems. *Journal of Vocational Behavior, 19*(2), 175–190.

Campbell, R. E., Connel, J. B., Boyle, K. K., & Bhaerman, R. (1983). *Enhancing career development. Recommendations for action.* Columbus, OH: The National Center of Research in Vocational Education, The Ohio State University.

Campbell, R. E., & Parsons, J. L. (1972). Readiness for vocational planning in junior high school: A socioeconomic and geographic comparison. *Journal of Vocational Behavior, 2*, 401–417.

Campbell, R. E., Suzuki, W. N., & Gabria, M. J., Jr. (1972). A procedural model for upgrading career guidance programs. *American Vocational Journal, 47*(1), 101–103.

Campbell, V. L. (1987). Strong-Campbell Interest Inventory, Fourth Edition. *Journal of Counseling and Development, 66*, 53–56.

Caplan, N., Whitmore, J. K., & Choy, M. H. (1989). *The boat people and achievement in America: A study of family life, hard work, and cultural values*. Ann Arbor: University of Michigan Press.

Caplan, P. J., & Hall-McCorquodale, I. (1985a). Mother-blaming in major clinical journals. *American Journal of Orthopsychiatry, 55*(3), 345–353.

Caplan, P. J., & Hall-McCorquodale, I. (1985b). The scapegoating of mothers: A call for change. *American Journal of Orthopsychiatry, 55*(4), 610–613.

Caplow, T. (1954). *The sociology of work*. Minneapolis: University Of Minnesota Press.

Caplow, T. (1976). *Principles of organization*. New York: Harcourt, Brace Jovanovich.

Cappeto, M. A. (1977). Liberal arts versus business administration. *Journal of College Placement, 37*(1), 37–39.

Cappeto, M. A. (1987). Career interest test results: A paradox. *Journal of College Placement*, 69–71.

Card, J. J., Steel, L., & Abeles, R. P. (1980). Sex differences in realization of individual potential for achievement. *Journal of Vocational Behavior, 17*, 1–21.

Carden, A. D. (1990). Mentoring and adult career development: The evolution of a theory. *The Counseling Psychologist, 18*, 275–299.

Career Guidance, Counseling, and Placement Project. (1973). *Elements of an illustrative guide: Career guidance, counseling and placement for state department of education*. Columbia, MO: University of Missouri-Columbia.

Carey, M. L. (1980). Evaluating the 1975 projections of occupational employment. *Monthly Labor Review, 103*, 10–12.

Carey, M. L. (1981a). Three paths to the future: Occupational projections, 1980–90. *Occupational Outlook Quarterly, 25*(4), 3–11.

Carey, M. L. (1981b). Occupational employment growth through 1990. *Monthly Labor Review, 104*, 42–55.

Carkhuff, R. R. (1983), *The art of helping* (5th ed.). Amherst, MA: Human Resources Development Press.

Carlson, J. G. (1989). Affirmative: In support of researching the Myers-Briggs Type Indicator. *Journal of Counseling and Development, 67*, 484–486.

Carnevale, A. P., & Gainer, L. J. (1989). *The Learning Enterprise*. Washington, DC: U.S. Department of Labor, Employment and Training Administration/The American Society for Training and Development.

Carney, C. G., & Barak, A. (1976). A survey of student needs and student personnel services. *Journal of College Student Personnel, 17*, 280–284.

Carsten, J. M., & Spector, P. E. (1987). Unemployment, job satisfaction, and employee turnover: A meta-analytic test of the Muchinsky model. *Journal of Applied Psychology, 72*, 374–381.

Carter, D. J., & Wilson, R. (1989). *Eighth annual status report: Minorities in higher education*. Washington, DC: American Council on Education.

Carter, R. T., & Swanson, J. L. (1990). The validity of the Strong Interest Inventory with black Americans: A review of the literature. *Journal of Vocational Behavior, 36*, 195–209.

Carver, D. S., & Smart, D. W. (1985). The effects of a career and self-exploration course for undecided freshmen. *Journal of College Student Personnel, 26*(1), 37–42.

Cassel, R. N., & Mehail, T. (1973). The Milwaukee computerized vocational guidance system (VOCGUID). *Vocational Guidance Quarterly, 21*, 206–213.

Caston, H. L., & Watson, A. L. (1990). Vocational assessment and rehabilitation outcomes. *Rehabilitation Counseling Bulletin, 34*(1), 61–66.

Castricone, A. M., Finan, W. W., & Grumble, S. K. (1982). Focus on career search: A program for high school students and their parents. *The School Counselor, 29*(5), 411–413.

Caulum, D., & Lambert F., (Eds.). (1985). *Guidelines for the use of computer-based career information and guidance systems*. Eugene, OR: Association of Computer-Based Systems for Career Information Clearinghouse.

Cedoline, A. J. (1982). *Job burnout in public education: Symptoms, causes, and survival skills*. New York: Teachers College Press.

Cellarius, R., & Platt, J. (1972). Classification of crisis research studies by project areas. In R. Theobald (Ed.), *Futures conditional* (pp. 336–346). Indianapolis: Bobbs-Merrill.

Cesari, J. P. (1985). New women professionals in higher education: Counseling for intrapersonal mentoring. In D. Jones & S. S. Moore (Eds.), *Counseling adults: Life cycle perspectives*. Lawrence: University of Kansas.

Cesari, J. P., Winer, J. L., & Piper, K. R. (1984). Vocational decision status and the effect of four types of occupational information on cognitive complexity. *Journal of Vocational Behavior, 25*, 215–224.

Cesari, J. P., Winer J. L., Zychlinski, F., & Laird, I. O. (1982). Influence of occupational information giving on cognitive complexity in decided versus undecided students. *Journal of Vocational Behavior, 21*, 224–230.

Chansky, N. M. (1965). Race, aptitude and vocational interests. *Personnel and Guidance Journal, 43*, 783–784.

Chapman, W. (1983). *A context for career decision making* (Research report). Princeton, NJ: Educational Testing Service.

Chapman, W., & Katz, M. R. (1981). *Survey of career information systems in secondary schools: Final report of study*. Princeton, NJ: Educational Testing Service.

Chapman, W., & Katz, M. R. (1982a). *Career information system in secondary schools: Final report of study 2: Comparative effects of major types of resources*. Princeton, NJ: Educational Testing Service.

Chapman, W., & Katz, M. R. (1982b). *Summary of career information systems in secondary schools and assessment of alternative types*. Princeton, NJ: Educational Testing Service.

Chapman, W., & Katz, M. R. (1983). Career information systems in secondary schools: A survey and assessment. *Vocational Guidance Quarterly, 31*, 165–177.

Charner, I., & Schlossberg, N. K. (1986). Variations by theme: The life transitions of clerical workers. *Vocational Guidance Quarterly, 34*(4), 212–224.

Chartrand, J. M., Dohm, T. E., Dawis, R. V., & Lofquist, L. H. (1987). Estimating occupational prestige. *Journal of Vocational Behavior, 31*, 14–25.

Chartrand, J. M., Robbins, S. B., Morrill, W. H., & Boggs, K. (1990). Development and validation of the Career Factors Inventory. *Journal of Counseling Psychology, 37*, 491–501.

Chassin, L., Zeiss, A., Cooper, K., & Reaven, J. (1985). Role perceptions, self-role congruence and marital satisfaction in dual-worker couples with preschool children. *Social Psychology Quarterly, 48*(4), 301–311.

Cheatham, H. E. (1990). Africentricity and career development of African Americans. *The Career Development Quarterly, 38*, 334–346.

Cheloa, R. S., & Farr, J. L. (1980). Absenteeism, job involvement, and job satisfaction in an organizational setting. *Journal of Applied Psychology, 65*, 467–473.

Chelte, A. F., Wright, J., & Taosky, C. (1982). Did job satisfaction really drop during the 1970s? *Monthly Labor Review, 105*(11), 33–38.

Cherichello, F. J., & Gillian, C. (1980). An alumni panel: A component for National Career Guidance Week at Essex. *Journal of College Student Personnel, 21,* 170.

Cherniss, C. (1980a). *Staff burnout: Job stress in the human services.* Beverly Hills, CA: Sage Publications.

Cherniss, C. (1980b). *Professional burnout in human service organizations.* New York: Praeger.

Chervenik, E., Nord, D., & Aldridge, M. (1982). Putting career planning and placement together. *Journal of College Placement, 42*(2), 48–51.

Chiko, C. H., Tolsma, R. J., Kahn, S. E., & Marks, S. E. (1980). A model to systematize competencies in counselor education. *Counselor Education and Supervision, 19*(4), 283–292.

Choate, P. (1982). *Retooling the American force: Toward a training strategy.* Washington, DC: Northeast-Midwest Institute.

Christensen, K. C. Gelso, C. J., Williams, R. O., & Sedlacek, W. E. (1975). Variations in the administration of the self-directed search, scoring accuracy, and satisfaction with results. *Journal of Counseling Psychology, 22,* 12–16.

Christensen, K. C. (1988). *The new era of home-based work: Directions and policies.* Boulder: Westview Press.

Christy, P. T., & Horowitz, K. J. (1979). An evaluation of BLS projections of 1975 production and employment. *Monthly Labor Review, 102,* 8–19.

Chusid, H., & Cochran, L. (1989). Meaning of career change from the perspective of family roles and dramas. *Journal of Counseling Psychology, 36*(1), 34–41.

Chusmir, L. H. (1990). Men who make nontraditional career choices. *Journal of Counseling and Development, 69,* 11–16.

Cianni, M., & Weitz, A. D. (1986). The technological society: Implications for women in the workplace. *Journal of Counseling and Development, 64*(8), 501–503.

Ciardello, J. A., & Bingham, W. C. (1982). The career maturity of schizophrenic clients. *Rehabilitation Counseling Bulletin, 26*(2), 3–9.

Clack, R. J. (1968). Occupational prestige and vocational choice. *Vocational Guidance Quarterly, 16,* 282–286.

Clark, A. K. (1975). Career entry skills gap in the guidance chain. *Canadian Counselor, 9*(2), 126–131.

Clark, A. M., & Seals, J. M. (1975). Student perceptions of the social status of careers for college graduates. *Journal of College Student Personnel, 16*(4), 293–298.

Clark, B. R., & Trow, M. (1966). The organizational context. In T. M. Newcomb & E. K. Wilson (Eds.), *College peer groups.* Chicago: Aldine.

Clarke, K. M., & Greenberg, L. S. (1986). Differential effects of the Gestalt two-chair intervention and problem-solving in resolving decisional conflict. *Journal of Counseling Psychology, 33,* 11–15.

Clarke, R., Gelatt, H. B., & Levine, L. (1965). A decision-making paradigm for local guidance research. *Personnel and Guidance Journal, 44,* 40–51.

Clauson, J. G. (1980). Mentoring in managerial careers. In C. B. Derr (Ed.), *Work, family, and career* (pp. 131–145). New York: Praeger.

Clauson, J. G. (1985). Is mentoring necessary? *Training and Development Journal, 39*(4), 36–39.

Cobas, J. A. (1986). Paths to self-employment among immigrants: An analysis of four interpretations. *Sociological Perspectives, 29*(1), 101–120.

Cochran, D. J., Hetherington, C., & Strand, K. H. (1980). Career choice class: Caviar or caveat? *Journal of College Student personnel, 21,* 402–406.

Cochran, D., Hoffman, S., Strand, K., & Warren, P. (1977). Effects of client/computer interaction in career decision-making processes. *Journal of Counseling Psychology, 24,* 308–312.

Cochran, L. (1986). Harmonious values as a basis for occupational preference. *Journal of Vocational Behavior, 29,* 17–26.

Cochran, L. R. (1990). Narrative as a paradigm for career research. In K. A. Young and W. E. Borgen (Eds.), *Methodological approaches to the study of careers* (pp. 71–86). New York: Praeger.

Cochran, L., & Amundson, N. (1985). *Activity self-exploration workbook.* Richmond, British Columbia, Canada: Buchanan.

Cohn, R. M. (1979). Age and the satisfaction from work. *Journal of Gerontology, 34*(2), 264–272.

Coleman, J. S. (1974). *Youth: Transition to adulthood.* Chicago: University of Chicago Press.

College Board Commission on Precollege Guidance and Counseling. (1986, January). *Keeping the options open, an overview.* New York: Author.

Collins, J., Reardon, M., & Waters, L. K. (1980). Occupational interest and perceived personal success: Effects of gender, sex-role orientation, and the sexual composition of the occupation. *Psychological Reports, 47,* 1155–1159.

Colson, C., Borman, C., & Nash, W. R. (1978). A unique learning opportunity for high school students. *Phi Delta Kappan, 59,* 542–543.

Colwill, N., & Pollock, M. (1987). The mentor connection update. *Business Quarterly, 52,* 16–20.

Commission on Pre-College Guidance and Counseling. (1986). *Keeping the options open.* New York: The College Entrance Examination Board.

Commission on Workforce Quality and Labor Market Efficiency, U.S. Department of Labor. (1989). *Investing in people, a strategy to address America's workforce crisis.* Washington, DC: Author.

Committee on Definition, Division of Counseling Psychology, American Psychological Association. (1956). Counseling Psychology as a specialty. *American Psychologist, 11,* 282–285.

Conyne, R. K., & Cochran, D. J. (1973). Academia and career development: Toward integration. *Personnel and Guidance Journal, 52,* 217–223.

Cook, D. W. (1989). Systematic need assessment: A primer. *Journal of Counseling and Development. 67*(8), 462–464.

Cook, J. D., Hepworth, S. J., Wall, T., & Warr, P. B. (Eds.). (1981). *The experience of work.* New York: Academic Press.

Cook, H. E. (1968). Vocational guidance materials: A survey for teachers. *American Vocational Journal, 13,* 25–28.

Cooke, R. A., & Rousseau, D. M. (1984). Stress and strain from family roles and work-role expectations. *Journal of Applied Psychology, 69*(2), 252–260.

Cooker, P. G. (1973). Vocational values of children in grades four, five, and six. *Elementary School Guidance and Counseling, 8*(12), 112–118.

Cooper, C. L. (1986). Job distress: Recent research and the emerging role of the clinical occupational psychologist. *Bulletin of the British Psychological Society, 39,* 325–331.

Cooper, C. L., & Baglioni, A. J., Jr. (1988). A structural model approach toward the development of a theory of the link between stress and mental health. *British Journal of Medical Psychology, 61,* 87–102.

Cooper, C. L., & Marshall, J. (1980). *White collar and professional stress.* New York: Wiley.

Cooper, S. E. (1986). The effects of group and individual vocational counseling on career indecision and personal indecisiveness. *Journal of College Student Personnel, 27*(1), 39–42.

Cooper, S. E., & Robinson, D. A. G. (1989). Childhood play activities of women and men entering engineering and science careers. *The School Counselor, 36*(4), 338–347.

Corbishley, M. A., & Yost, E. B. (1989). Psychological aspects of career counseling. *Journal of Career Development, 16,* 43–51.

Corzine, J. B., Buntzman, G., & Busch, E. T. (1988). Machiavellianism and careers at plateau. *Psychological Reports, 63,* 243–246.

Costa, P. T., Jr., McCrae, R. R., & Holland, J. L. (1984). Personality and vocational interests in an adult sample. *Journal of Applied Psychology, 69*(3), 390–400.

Costello, T. W., & Zalkind, S. S. (Eds.). (1963). *Psychology in administration: A research orientation.* Englewood Cliffs, NJ: Prentice-Hall.

Counts, G. S. (1925). Social status of occupations. *School Review, 33,* 16–27.

Cox, T. (1987). Stress, coping, and problem-solving. *Work and Stress, 1,* 5–14.

Crabbs, M. A., Black, K. U., & Morton, S. P. (1986). Stress at work: A comparison of men and women. *Journal of Employment Counseling, 23*(1), 2–8.

Craft, J. A., Doctors, S. I., Shkop, Y. M., & Benecki, T. J. (1979). Simulated management perceptions, hiring decisions, and age. *Aging and Work, 2*(2), 95–102.

Cramer, J. C. (1980). Fertility and female employment: Problems of causal direction. *American Sociological Review, 45,* 167–190.

Cramer, S. H., Herr, E. L., Morris, C. N., & Frantz, T. T. (1970). *Research and the school counselor.* Boston: Houghton Mifflin.

Cramer, S. H., & Keitel, M. (1984). Family effects of dislocation, unemployment, and discouragement. In S. H. Cramer (Ed.), *Perspectives on work and the family* (pp. 81–93). Rockville, MD: Aspen Systems.

Cramer, S. H., Keitel, M., & Rossberg, R. H. (1986). The family and employed mothers. *International Journal of Family Psychiatry, 7*(1), 17–34.

Cramer, S. H., Wise, P. S., & Colburn, E. D. (1977). An evaluation of a treatment to expand the career perceptions of high school girls. *The School Counselor, 25,* 125–129.

Crawford, L. (1976). Imperatives regarding placement services in secondary schools. In T. H. Hohenshil (Ed.), *New dimensions in placement services* (pp. 16–28), Blacksburg, VA: VPI and State University.

Creason, F. & Schilson, D. L. (1970). Occupational concerns of sixth-grade children. *Vocational Guidance Quarterly, 18,* 219–224.

Cremin, L. A. (1961). *The transformation of the school.* New York: Alfred Knopf.

Crites, J. O. (1961). A model for the measurement of vocational maturity. *Journal of Counseling Psychology, 8,* 255–259.

Crites, J. O. (1965). Measurement of vocational maturity in adolescence: Attitude test of the vocational development inventory. *Psychological Monographs, 79*(1), Whole No. 595.

Crites, J. O. (1969). *Vocational psychology.* New York: McGraw-Hill.

Crites, J. O. (1973). *Career maturity inventory.* Monterey, CA: California Test Bureau/McGraw-Hill.

Crites, J. O. (1974a). Career development processes: A model for vocational maturity. In E. L. Herr (Ed.), *Vocational guidance and human development* (pp. 296–320). Boston: Houghton Mifflin.

Crites, J. O. (1974b). Methodological issues in the measurement of career maturity. *Measurement and Evaluation in Guidance, 6,* 200–209.

Crites, J. O. (1974c). Problems in the measurement of vocational maturity. *Journal of Vocational Behavior, 4,* 25–31.

Crites, J. O. (1974d). A reappraisal of vocational appraisal. *Vocational Guidance Quarterly, 22*(4), 272–279.

Crites, J. O. (1976). A comprehensive model of career development in early adulthood. *Journal of Vocational Behavior, 9,* 105–118.

Crites, J. O. (1978). *Theory and research handbook for the career maturity inventory.* Monterey, CA: CTB/McGraw-Hill.

Crites, J. O. (1981). *Career counseling: Models, methods, and materials.* New York: McGraw-Hill.

Crites, J. (1985, August). *A microcomputer system for educational/vocational assessment.* Paper presented at the American Psychological Association Convention.

Crites, J. O. (1986). Appraising adults' career capabilities: Ability, interest, and personality. In Z. Leibowitz & D. Lea (Eds.), *Adult career development: Concepts, issues, and practices* (pp. 63–83). Washington, DC: National Career Development Association.

Crites, J. O. (1988). Review of Ohio Vocational Interest Survey. In J. T. Kapes & M. M. Mastie (Eds.), *A counselor's guide to career assessment instruments* (pp. 110–115). Washington, DC: National Career Development Association.

Cronbach, L. J. (1979). The Armed Services Vocational Aptitude Battery—A test battery in transition. *Personnel and Guidance Journal, 57*(5), 232–237.

Crouse, R. H., & Weiss, S. A. (1984). A dual-career couples retreat for family housing residents. *Journal of College Student Personnel, 25*(4), 368–370.

Crowley, J. E. (1985). Longitudinal effects of retirement on men's psychological and physical well-being. In H. S. Parnes, et al. (Eds.), *Retirement among American men* (pp. 147–173). Lexington, MA: Lexington Books.

Cummings, N. A. (1977). The anatomy of psychotherapy under national health insurance. *American Psychologist, 32*(9), 711–718.

Cummings, N. A. (1986). The dismantling of our health system: Strategies for the survival of psychological practice. *American Psychologist, 41*(4), 426–431.

Cummings, R. W., & Maddux, C. D. (1987). Self-administration and scoring errors of learning disabled and non learning disabled students on two forms of the self-directed search. *Journal of Counseling Psychology, 34,* 83–85.

Cummings, S. (1980). White ethnics, racial prejudice, and labor market segmentation, *American Journal of Sociology. 86,* 938–950.

Cummins, R. (1989). Locus of control and social support: Clarifiers of the relationship between job stress and job satisfaction. *Journal of Applied Social Psychology, 19,* 772–788.

Curnow, T. C. (1989). Vocational development of persons with disability. *The Career Development Quarterly, 37,* 269–277.

Cytrynbaum, S., Ginath, Y., Birdwell, J., & Brandt, C. (1979). Goal attainment scaling. *Evaluation Quarterly, 3,* 5–40.

Czikszenthmihalyi M. (1975). *Beyond boredom and anxiety.* San Francisco: Jossey-Bass.

Daane, C. J. (1971). *Vocational exploration group* (3rd ed.). *Leader manual.* Tempe, AZ: Studies for Urban Man.

D'Alonzo, C. A., & Fleming, A. J. (1973). Occupational psychiatry through the medical periscope. In R. L. Noland (Ed.), *Industrial mental health and employee counseling* (pp. 160–167). New York: Behavioral Publications.

Dalton, G., Thompson, P., & Price, R. (1977). Career stages: A model of professional careers in organizations. *Organization Dynamics, 6,* 19–42.

Dambrot, F. H., Watkins-Malek, M. A., Silling, S. M., Marshall, R. S., & Garver, J. (1985). Correlates of sex differences in attitudes toward and involvement with computers. *Journal of Vocational Behavior, 27*(1), 71–86.

Daniels, M. H. (1982). The heuristic value of Harren's career decision-making model for practitioners. *Journal of College Student Personnel, 23*(1), 18–24.

Daniels, M. H. (1985). Review of Social and Prevocational Information Battery. In J. V. Mitchell (Ed.), *The ninth mental measurements yearbook* (pp. 1408–1409). NJ: Gryphon Press.

Danish, S. J. (1981). Life-span human development and intervention: A necessary link. *The Counseling Psychologist*, *9*(2), 40–43.

Danish, S. J., Galambos, N. L. & Laquatra, I. (1983). Life development intervention: Skill training for personal competence. In R. D. Felman, L. A. Jason, J. Mortisuqur, & S. S. Farber (Eds.), *Preventative psychology: Theory, research, and practice* (pp. 49–66). Elmsford, N.Y.: Pergammon Press.

D'Arcy, C., Syrotuik, J., & Siddique, C. M. (1984). Perceived job attributes, job satisfaction, and psychological distress: A comparison of working men and women. *Human Relations*, *57*(8), 603–611.

Darr, J. T. (1981). The role of the employment counselor as presented in the Journal of Employment Counseling. *Journal of Employment Counseling*, *18*(2), 87–96.

Davidshofer, C. O. (1988). Review of Jackson Vocational Interest Survey. In J. T. Kapes & M. M. Mastie (Eds.), *A counselor's guide to career assessment instruments* (pp. 95–99). Washington, DC: National Career Development Association.

Davis, K. R., Giles, W. F., & Field, H. S. (1985). Recruiter assessments of job applicants' preferences: How accurate are they? *Vocational Guidance Quarterly*, *33*(4), 315–323.

Davis, P. A., Hagen, N., & Strouf, J. (1962). Occupational choice of twelve-year-olds. *Personnel and Guidance Journal*, *40*, 628–629.

Davis, R. C., & Horne, A. M. (1986). The effect of small group counseling and a career course on career decidedness and maturity. *Vocational Guidance Quarterly*, *34*, 255–262.

Davis, S. J. (1990). The 1990–91 job outlook in brief. *Occupational Outlook Quarterly*, *34*(1), 18–45.

Dawis, R. V. (1984). Job satisfaction: workers aspirations, attitudes, and behavior. In N. C. Gysbers (Ed.), *Designing careers, counseling to enhance education, work and leisure* (Chap. 10). San Francisco: Jossey-Bass.

Dawis, R. V., & Lofquist, L. H. (1978). A note on the dynamics of work adjustment. *Journal of Vocational Behavior*, *12*, 76–79.

Dawis, R. V., Lofquist, L. H., Henly, G. A., & Rounds, J. B., Jr. (1979). *Minnesota Occupational Classification System II (MOCS II)*. Minneapolis: Vocational Psychology Research Work Adjustment Project.

Dayton, J. D., & Feldhusen, J. F. (1989). Characteristics and needs of vocational talented high school students. *The Career Development Quarterly, 37*(4), 355–364.

Dearman, N. B., & Plisko, V. W. (1981). *The condition of education* (1980 ed.). Washington, DC: National Center for Educational Statistics.

Deeg, M. E., & Paterson, D. G. (1947). Changes in social status of occupations. *Occupations, 25,* 205–208.

DeFrank, R. S., & Ivancevich, J. M. (1986). Job loss: An individual level review and model. *Journal of Vocational Behavior, 28,* 1–20.

DeFreitas, G. E. (1981). What is the occupational mobility of black immigrants? *Monthly Labor Review, 104,* 44–45.

Department of Labor. (1990, July 24). Proposed revised policy on use of validity generalization—General Aptitude Test Battery for selection and referral in employment and training programs; Notice and requests for comments. *Federal Register, 55*(142), 30162–30164.

Department chair. (1990). *1*(1), 8–9. Bolton, MA: Anker Publishing Company.

Deren, S., & Randell, J. (1990). The vocational rehabilitation of substance abusers. *Journal of Applied Rehabilitation Counseling*, *21*(2), 4–6.

Derr, C. B. (1980). More about career anchors. In C. B. Derr (Ed.), *Work, family, and the career* (166–187) New York: Praeger.

Derr, C. B. (1986). *Managing the new careerists*. San Francisco: Jossey-Bass.

DeVito, A. J. (1985). Review of Myers-Briggs Type Indicator. In J. V. Mitchell (Ed.), *The ninth mental measurements yearbook* (pp. 1030–1032). Lincoln: University of Nebraska.

Dewey, J. (1931). *Democracy and education*. New York: MacMillan.

Dewey, J. (1956). *School and society.* Chicago, IL: University of Chicago Press. (Originally published, 1900).

Diamond, E. (Ed.). (1975). *Issues of sex bias and sex fairness in career interest measurement*. Washington, DC: National Institute of Education.

Dickman, F., Challenger, B. R., Emener, W., & Hutchison, W. S., Jr. (1988). *Employee assistance programs: A basic text*. Springfield, IL: Charles C. Thomas, Publishers.

Dillard, J. M. (1976). Socioeconomic background and the career maturity of black youths. *Vocational Guidance Quarterly*, *25*(1), 65–70.

Dillard, J. M. (1980). Some unique career behavior characteristics of blacks: Career theories, counseling practice, and research. *Journal of Employment Counseling*, *17*(2), 288–298.

Dillard, J. M. (1982). Life satisfaction of nearly retired workers. *Journal of Employment Counseling*, *19*(3), 131–134.

Dillard, J. M. (1983). *Multicultural counseling*. Chicago: Nelson-Hall.

Dillard, J. M., & Campbell, N. J. (1981). Influences of Puerto Rican, black, and Anglo parents' career behavior in their adolescent children's career development. *Vocational Guidance Quarterly*, *30*(2), 129–148.

Dillon, M., & Weissman, S. (1987). Relationship between personality types on the Strong-Campbell and Myers-Briggs instruments. *Measure and Evaluation in Counseling and Development*, 68–79.

DiPrete, T. A. (1981). Unemployment over the life cycle: Racial differences and the effect of changing economic conditions. *American Journal of Sociology*, *87*(2), 286–307.

DiRusso, L., & Lucarino, V. (1989). Vocational education versus back to basics: A dilemma for counselors. *The School Counselor, 37*(2), 98–101.

District of Columbia Schools. (1976). *Career education in the inner city*. Interdisciplinary curriculum, grades 1–6. Washington, DC: Author.

Division 17. Education and Training Committee. (1982). Cross-cultural counseling competencies. *The Counseling Psychologist*, *10*(2), 45–52.

Dixon, D. N., & Claiborn, C. D. (1981). Effects of need and commitment on career exploration behaviors. *Journal of Counseling Psychology*, *28*(5), 411–415.

Doane, C. J. (1971). *Vocational exploration group* (3rd ed.). *Leader Manual*. Tempe, AZ: Studies for Urban Man.

Dobson, C., & Morrow, P. C. (1984). Effects of career orientation on retirement attitudes and retirement planning. *Journal of Vocational Behavior*, *24*(1), 73–83.

Doering, M. M., & Rhodes, S. R. (1989). Changing careers: A qualitative study. *The Career Development Quarterly*, *37*, 316–333.

Doering, P. B., & Piore, M. J. (1971). *Internal labor markets and manpower analysis*. Lexington, MA: Lexington Books.

Dohrenwend, B. P. (1975). Sociocultural and social psychological factors in the genesis of mental disorders. *Journal of Health and Social Behavior*, *16*, 365–392.

Dore, R. (1987). *Taking Japan Seriously: A Confucian perspective on leading economic issues*. Stanford, CA: Stanford University Press.

Dorfman, L. T., & Moffett, M. M. (1987). Retirement satisfaction in married and widowed rural women. *The Gerontologist, 27*, 215–221.

Dorn, F. J. (1986). Career development in business and industry. *Journal of Counseling and Development*, *64*, 653–654.

Doty, M., & Betz, N. E. (1979). Comparison of the concurrent validity of Holland's theory for men and women in an enterprising occupation. *Journal of Vocational Behavior*, *15*, 207–216.

Douce, L. A., & Hansen, J-I. C. (1990). Willingness to take risks and college women's career choice. *Journal of Vocational Behavior, 36*, 258–273.

Draguns, J. (1985). Psychological disorders across cultures. In P. Pederson (Ed.), *Handbook of cross-cultural counseling and therapy* (pp. 55–62). Westport, CT: Greenwood Press.

Dreher, G. F. (1980). Individual needs as correlates of satisfaction and involvement with a modified Scanlon Plan company. *Journal of Vocational Behavior*, *17*, 89–94.

Drier, H. N. (1971, June). *Implementing career development programs in high schools*. Paper presented at the Workshop on the Development of Guidelines for Planning Career Development Programs, K-12, Columbus, OH.

Drier, H. N. (1980) Career information for youth in transition: The need, system, and models. *Vocational Guidance Quarterly*, *29*(2), 135–143.

Droege, R. C., & Padgett, A. (1979). Development of an interest-oriented occupational classification system. *Vocational Guidance Quarterly*, *27*(4), 302–310.

Droege, R. C. (1988). Review of Harrington-O'Shea Career Decision-Making System. In J. T. Kapes & M. M. Mastie (Eds.), *A counselor's guide to career assessment instruments* (pp. 86–90). Wahingaton, DC: National Career Develpoment Association.

Drucker, P. F. (1982). *The changing world of the executive*. New York: Truman Talley.

Drucker, P. F. (1989). *The new realities. In government and politics/in economics and business/in society and the world view.* New York: Harper & Row.

Drucker, P. F. (1986). *Innovation and entrepreneurship. Practice and principles*. New York: Perennial Library.

Drummond, R. J., McIntire, W. G., & Skaggs, C. T. (1978). The relationship of work values to occupational level in young adult workers. *Journal of Employment Counseling*, *15*(3), 117–121.

Ducat, D. E. (1980). Cooperative education, career exploration, and occupational concepts for community college students. *Journal of Vocational Behavior*, *17*, 195–203.

Dudley, G. A., & Tiedeman, D. V. (1977). *Career development, exploration and commitment*. Muncie, IN: Accelerated Development.

Dunlop, K. H. (1981). Maternal employment and child care. *Professional Psychology*, *12*(1), 67–75.

Dunne, F., Elliott, R., & Carlsen, W. S. (1981). Sex differences in the educational and occupational aspirations of rural youth. *Journal of Vocational Behavior*, *18*, 56–66.

Dwight, A. H. (1979). Public relations design for college career counseling services. *Personnel and Guidance Journal*, *58*, 205–207.

Edelwich, J., & Brodsky, A. (1980). *Burnout: Stages of disillusionment in the helping professions*. New York: Human Sciences Press.

Eder, R. W., & Ferris, G. R. (Eds.). (1989). *The employment interview: Theory, research, and practice*. Newbury Park, CA: Sage Publications.

Edwards, P. B. (1980). *Leisure counseling techniques: Individual and group counseling step by step*. Los Angeles, CA: Constructive Leisure.

Eggeman, D. F., Campbell, R. E., & Garbin, A. P. (1969, December). *Problems in the transition from school to work as perceived by youth opportunity center counselors*. Columbus, OH: Center for Vocational and Technical Education, Ohio State University.

Ekerdt, D. J., Bosse, R., & Levkoff, S. (1985). An empirical test for phases of retirement: Findings from the normative aging study. *Journal of Gerontology*, *40*, 95–101.

Ekerdt, D. J., Bosse, R., & Mogery, J. M. (1980). Concurrent change in planned and preferred age for retirement. *Journal of Gerontology*, *35*(2), 232–240.

Elizur, D., & Shye, S. (1990). Quality of work life and its relation to quality of life. *Applied Psychology: An International Review*, *39*(3), 275–291.

Elksnin, L. K., & Elksnin, N. (1991). The school counselor as job search facilitator: Increasing employment of handicapped students through job clubs. *The School Counselor*, *38*(3), 215–220.

Ellermann, N. C., & Johnston, J. (1988). Perceived life roles and locus of control differences in women pursuing nontraditional and traditional academic majors. *Journal of College Student Development*, *29*, 142–146.

Elleson, V. J., & Onnink, A. G. (1976). Jobs Inc., In-school career education/experience. *Elementary School Guidance and Counseling*, *10*(4), 290–292.

Elliott, E. D. (1973). Effects of female role models on occupational aspiration levels of college freshman women. *Dissertation Abstracts International*, *34*, 1075a.

Elliott, T. R., & Byrd, E. K. (1985). Scoring accuracy of the self-directed search with ninth-grade students. *Vocational Guidance Quarterly*, *33*, 85–90.

Ellis, A. (1962). *Reason and emotion in psychotherapy*, Secaucus, NJ: Lyle Stuart.

Ellis, A., & Grieger, R. (1977). *Handbook of rational-emotive therapy*. New York: Springer.

Emener, W. G., & Rubin, S. E. (1980). Rehabilitation, counselor roles and functions and sources of role strain. *Journal of Applied Rehabilitation Counseling*, *11*(2), 57–69.

Employment and Training Administration, U. S. Department of Labor. (1980). *Self-directed job search: An introduction*. Washington, DC: Author.

Enderlein, T. E. (1974). *Causal relationships of student characteristics related to satisfaction in post high school employment*. Unpublished doctoral dissertation, Pennsylvania State University.

Endicott, F. S. (1965; 1975). *The Endicott Report*. Evanston, IL: Northwestern University.

England, G. W. (1990). The patterning of work meanings which are osterminous with outcome levels for individuals in Japan, Germany and the U.S.A. *Applied Psychology: An International Review*, *39*(1), 29–45.

Entine, A. D. (1984). Voluntary mid-life career change: Family effects. In S. H. Cramer (Ed.), *Perspectives on work and the family* (pp. 72–80). Rockville, MD: Aspen Systems.

Entrekin, L. V., & Everett, J. E. (1981). Age and midcareer crisis: An empirical study of academics. *Journal of Vocational Behavior*, *19*(1), 84–97.

Entwisle, D. R., & Greenberger, E. (1972). Adolescents views of women's work role. *American Journal of Orthopsychiatry*, *42*(4), 648–656.

Epperson, D., & Hammond, K. (1981). Use of interest inventories with Native Americans: A case for local norms. *Journal of Counseling Psychology*, *28*, 213–220.

Erdner, R. A., & Guy, R. F. (1990). Career identification and women's attitudes toward retirement. *International Journal of Aging and Human Development*, *30*, 129–139.

Erez, M., & Shneorson, Z. (1980). Personality types and motivational characteristics of academics versus professionals in industry in the same occupational disciplines. *Journal of Vocational Behavior*, *17*, 95–105.

ERIC/CAPS. (1982). *Conducting a needs assessment. Highlights . . . An ERIC/CAPS Fact Sheet*. Ann Arbor, MI: Author.

Erikson, E. H. (1950). *Childhood and society*, New York: Norton.

Erikson, E. H. (1963). *Childhood and society*, (2nd ed.). New York: Norton.

Erickson, R. J. (1980). The changing workplace and workforce. *Training and Development Journal*, *34*, 62–65.

Ermalinski, R., & Ruscelli, V. (1971). Incorporation of values by lower and middle socioeconomic class preschool boys. *Child Development*, *42*, 629–632.

Erwin, T. D. (1982). The predictive validity of Holland's construct of consistency. *Journal of Vocational Behavior*, *20*, 180–182.

Estroff, S. (1981). *Making it crazy*. Berkeley, CA: University of California Press.

Etaugh, C. (1974). Effects of maternal employment on children: A review of recent research. *Merrill-Palmer Quarterly of Behavior and Development*, *29*(2), 71–98.

Etaugh, C. (1980). Effects of nonmaternal care on children: Research evidence and popular views. *American Psychologist*, *35*(4), 309–319.

Etaugh, C. (1984). Effects of maternal employment on children: Implications for the family therapist. In S. H. Cramer (Ed.), *Perspectives on work and the family* (pp. 16–39). Rockville, MD: Aspen Systems.

Eulberg, J. R., Weekley, J. A., & Bhagat, R. S. (1988). Models of stress in organizational research: A metatheoretical perspective. *Human Relations*, *41*, 331–350.

Evanoski, P. O., & Tse, F. W. (1987). Career awareness program for Chinese and Korean American parents. *Journal of Counseling and Development*, *67*, 472–474.

Evans, R. N., & Herr, E. L. (1978). *Foundations of vocational education* (2nd ed.). Columbus, OH: Charles E. Merrill.

Eves, J. H., Jr. (1986). When a plant shuts down: Easing the pain. *Personnel*, *62* (2), 16–23.

Exum, H. A., & Lau, E. Y. (1988). Counseling style preference of Chinese college students. *Journal of multicultural Counseling and Development*, *16*, 84–92.

Eyde, L., & Kowal, D. (1984, August). *Ethical and professional concerns regarding computerized test interpretation services and users*. Paper presented at the American Psychological Association Convention.

Fain, T. S. (1980). Self-employed Americans: Their number has increased. *Monthly Labor Review*, *103*, 3–8.

Fallows, J. (1989). *More like us*. Boston: Houghton Mifflin.

Family Service America. (1984). *The state of families, 1984–85*. New York: Author.

Fanning, D. (1990, June 24). Weighing the fast track against family values. *The New York Times*, pp. D1.

Farber, B. A., & Heifetz, L. J. (1981). The satisfaction and stresses of psychotherapeutic work: A factor analytic study. *Professional Psychology*, *12*(5), 621–630.

Farmer, H. S. (1976). What inhibits achievement and career motivation in women? *The Counseling Psychologist*, *6*, 12–14.

Farmer, H. S. (1980). Environmental, background, and psychological variables related to optimizing achievement and career motivation for high school girls. *Journal of Vocational Behavior*, *17* 58–70.

Farmer, H. S. (1985). Model of career and achievement motivation for women and men. *Journal of Counseling Psychology*, *32*(3), 363–390.

Farrell, M. P., & Rosenberg, S. D. (1981). *Men at midlife*. Boston: Auburn House.

Fassinger, R. (1987). Use of structural equation modeling in counseling psychology research. *Journal of Counseling Psychology*, *34*(4), 425–436.

Fassinger, R. E. (1990). Causal models of career choice in two samples of college women. *Journal of Vocational Behavior*, *36*, 225–248.

Faver, C. A. (1982). Achievement orientation, attainment, values, and women's employment. *Journal of Vocational Behavior*, *20*, 67–80.

Faver, C. A. (1984). Women, achievement, and careers: Age variations in attitudes. *Psychology: A Quarterly Journal of Human Behavior*, *21*(1), 45–49.

Feather, N. T., & Davenport, P. R. (1981). Unemployment and depressive affect: A motivational and attributional analysis. *Journal of Personality and Social Psychology*, *41*(3), 422–436.

Feather, N. T., & O'Brien, G. E. (1986). A longitudinal study of the effects of employment and unemployment on school-leavers. *Journal of Occupational Psychology*, *59*, 121–144.

Feck, V. (1971). *What vocational education teachers and counselors should know about urban disadvantaged youth*. (Center for Vocational Technical Education, Information Series, No 46). Washington, DC: U. S. Government Printing Office.

Feingold, S. N., & Miller, N. R. (1983). *Emerging careers: New occupations for the year 2000 and beyond*. Garrett Park, MD: Garrett Park Press.

Fernandez, M. S. (1988). Issues in counseling Southeast Asian students. *Journal of Multicultural Counseling and Development*, *16*, 157–166.

Ferree, M. (1980). Working class feminism: A consideration of the consequences of employment. *The Sociological Quarterly*, *21*, 173–184.

Ferree, M. M. (1984). Class, housework, and happiness: Women's work and life satisfaction. *Sex Roles*, *11*(11/12), 1057–1074.

Ferrini, P., & Parker, L. S. (1978). *Career change, a handbook of exemplary programs in business and industrial firms, education institutions, government agencies, professional associations* (p. 64). Cambridge: Technical Education Research Centers.

Ferris, G. R., Youngblood, S. A., & Yates, V. L. (1985). Personality training, performance, and withdrawal: A test of the person-group fit hypothesis for organizational newcomers. *Journal of Vocational Behavior*, *27*(3), 377–388.

Festinger, L. A. (1957). *A theory of cognitive dissonance*. Stanford, CA: Stanford University Press.

Feuer, D. (1985). Retirement planning: A coming imperative. *Training*, 49–53.

Fielding, J. E. (1982). Effectiveness of employee health improvement programs. *Journal of Occupational Medicine*, *24*, 907–916.

Fifield, M. & Petersen, L. (1978). Job Simulation: A model of vocational exploration. *Vocational Guidance Quarterly*, *24*, 229–237.

Figler, H. E. (1973). PATH: Vocational exploration for liberal arts students. *Journal of College Placement*, *34*(1), 40–50.

Figler, H. E. (1978). Career counseling for the obscure, the meek, and the ugly. *Journal of College Placement*, *39*(1), 31–39.

Fine, M., & Asch, A. (1988). Disability beyond stigma: Social interactions, discrimination, and activism. *Journal of Social Issues*, *44*(1), 3–21.

Finn, J. D. (1989). Withdrawing from school. *Review of Educational Research*, *58*(2), 117–142.

Finnegan, R., Westefeld, J., & Elmore, R. (1981). A model for a midlife career decision-making workshop. *Vocational Guidance Quarterly*, *18*(3), 69–72.

Fiorentine, R. (1988). Increasing similarity in the values and life plans of male and female college students? Evidence and implications. *Sex Roles*, *18* (3/4), 143–157.

Firth, J. (1985). Personal meanings of occupational stress: Cases from the clinic. *Journal of Occupational Psychology*, *58*, 139–148.

Firth, J., & Shapiro, D. A. (1986). An evaluation of psychotherapy for job-related distress. *Journal of Occupational Psychology*, *59*, 111–119.

Fiske, M. (1980). Changing hierarchies of commitment in adulthood. In N. J. Smelser & E. H. Erikson (Eds.), *Themes of work and love in adulthood* (pp. 238–264). Cambridge, MA: Harvard University Press.

Fitz-enz, J. (1990). *Human Value Management. The Value-Adding Human Resource: Management Strategy for the 1990s*. San Francisco: Jossey-Bass.

Fitzgerald, L. F., & Betz, N. E. (1983). Issues in the vocational psychology of women. In W. B. Walsh & S. H. Osipow (Eds.), *The Handbook of Vocational Psychology* (pp. 83–159). Hillsdale, N.J.: Erlbaum.

Fitzgerald, L. F., & Betz, N. E. (1984). Astin's model in theory and practice: A technical and philosophical critique. *The Counseling Psychologist*, *12*(4), 135–138.

Fitzgerald, L. F., & Cherpas, C. C. (1985). On the reciprocal relationship between gender and occupation: Rethinking the assumptions concerning masculine career development. *Journal of Vocational Behavior*, *27*, 109–122.

Fitzgerald, L. F., & Crites, J. O. (1980). Toward a career psychology of women: What do we know? What do we need to know? *Journal of Counseling Psychology*, *27*, 44–62.

Fitzgerald, L. F., & Osipow, S. H. (1986). An occupational analysis of counseling psychology: How special is the specialty? *American Psychologist*, *41*(5), 535–544.

Fitzpatrick, E. W. (1979). Evaluating a new retirement planning program: Results with hourly workers. *Aging and work*, *2*(2), 87–94.

Fitzpatrick, E. W. (1980). An introduction to NCOA's Retirement Planning Program. *Aging and Work*, *3*(1), 20–26.

Fitzpatrick, J. L., & Silverman, T. (1989). Women's selection of careers in engineering: Do traditional-nontraditional differences still exist? *Journal of Vocational Behavior*, *34*(3), 266–278.

Flake, M. H., Roach, A. J., Jr., & Stenning, W. F. (1975). Effects of short-term counseling on career maturity of tenth-grade students. *Journal of Vocational Behavior*, *6*, 73–80.

Flanagan, J. C. (1978). *Perspectives on improving education: Project Talent's young adults look back*. New York: Praeger.

Flanagan, J. C., & Cooley, W. W. (1966). *Project Talent: One-year follow-up studies*. Pittsburgh, PA: University of Pittsburgh Press.

Flanagan, J. C., Shaycroft, J. F., Richards, J., Jr., & Claudy, J. G. (1971). *Project Talent: Five years after high school*. Pittsburgh, PA: American Institute for Research.

Flanders, R. B., & Baxter, N. (1981). The sweat of their brows: A look back over occupational information and career counseling. *Occupational Outlook Quarterly*, *25*(3), 9–11.

Fleishman, E. A. (1968). Attitudes versus skill factors in work group productivity. *Personnel Psychology*, *18*, 253–266.

Fleming, K. (1974). Reflections on manpower. *Vocational Guidance Quarterly*, *22*(3), 224–229.

Fletcher, B. J. (1976). Thoughts on parental involvement in the guidance program. Middle/junior high school counselor's corner. *Elementary School Guidance and Counseling*, *10*(3), 210–213.

Flores, T. R., & Olsen, L. C. (1967). Stability and realism of occupational aspiration in eighth and twelfth-grade males. *Vocational Guidance Quarterly*, *16*, 104–112.

Florida Department of Education. (1988). *Blueprint for Career Preparation*. Tallahassee, FL: Author.

Florida Department of Education. (1990). *Blueprint for Career Preparation. Special Edition*. Tallahassee, FL: Author.

Flynn, C., Vanderpool, N. M., & Brown, W. E. (1989). Reentry women's workshop: Program and evaluation. *Journal of College Student Development*, *30* (July), 377–378.

Fontana, A., & Frey, J. H. (1990). Postretirement workers in the labor force. *Work and Occupations*, *17*(3), 355–361.

Foote, B. (1980). Determined and undetermined students: How different are they? *Journal of College Student Personnel*, *21*(1), 29–34.

Forney, D. S., Wallace-Schutzman, F., & Wiggens, T. T. (1982). Burnout among career development professionals: Preliminary findings and implications. *Personnel and Guidance Journal*, *60*, 435–439.

Forrer, S. E., Leibowitz, Z., & Dickelman, G. J. (1989). *Career Point: A computer based career development system for organizations*. Silver Springs, MD: Conceptual Systems, Inc.

Fort, M. K., & Cordisco, J. H. (1981). Career development for women in industry. *Training and Development Journal*, *35*, 62–64.

Fortner, M. L. (1970). Vocational choices of high school girls: Can they be predicted? *Vocational Guidance Quarterly*, *18*, 203–206.

Foss, C. J., & Slaney, R. B. (1986). Increasing nontraditional career choices in women: Relation of attitudes toward women and responses to a career intervention. *Journal of Vocational Behavior*, *28*, 191–202.

Fottler, M. D., & Bain, T. (1980a). Managerial aspirations of high school seniors: A comparison of males and females. *Journal of Vocational Behavior*, *16*, 83–95.

Fottler, M. D., & Bain, T. (1980b). Sex differences in occupational aspirations. *Academy of Management Journal*, *23*(1), 144–149.

Fouad, N. A., Hansen, J. C., & Arias-Galicia, F. (1986). Multiple discriminant analyses of cross-cultural similarity of vocational interests of lawyers and engineers. *Journal of Vocational Behavior*, *28*(2), 85–96.

Fowler, E. M. (1990, February 20). Outplacement firms aiding the spouse. *The New York Times*, p. B40.

Fozard. J. L., & Nuttall, R. L. (1972). General aptitude test battery scores for men in different age and socio-economic groups. In G. M. Shatto (Ed.), *Employment of the middle aged*. Springfield, IL: Charles C. Thomas.

Frank, E. J. (1988). Business students' perceptions of women in management. *Sex Roles*, *19* (1/2), 107–118.

Frary, R. B. (1988). Review of Career Maturity Inventory. In J. T. Kapes & M. M. Mastie (Eds.), *A counselor's guide to career assessment instruments* (pp. 180–185). Washington, DC: National Career Development Association.

Fredrickson, R. H. (1986). Preparing gifted and talented students for the world of work. *Journal of Counseling and Development*, *64*, 556–557.

Free, C. G. & Tiedeman, D. V. (1980). Counseling and comprehension of the economics of change. *Personnel and Guidance Journal*, *58*(5), 358–367.

Frese, M., & Mohr, G. (1987). Prolonged unemployment and depression in older workers. *Social Science and Medicine*, *25*(2), 173–178.

Fretz, B. R. (1981). Evaluating the effectiveness of career interventions. *Journal of Counseling Psychology*, *28*(1), 77–90.

Fretz, B. R., Kluge, N. A., & Ossana, S. M. (1989). Intervention targets for reducing pre-retirement anxiety and depression. *Journal of Counseling Psychology, 36,* 301–307.

Fretz, B. R., & Leong, F. T. L. (1982a). Career development status as a predictor of career intervention outcomes. *Journal of Counseling Psychology*, *29*(4), 388–393.

Fretz, B. R., & Leong, F. T. L. (1982b). Vocational behavior and career development, 1981: A review. *Journal of Vocational Behavior*, *21*(2), 123–163.

Freudenberger, H. J. (1974). Staff burnout. *Journal of Social Issues*, *30*(1), 159–165.

Freudenberger, H. J., & Richelson, G. (1980). *Burnout: The high cost of high achievement*. Garden City, NY: Anchor Press.

Fried, Y., Rowland, K. M., & Ferris, G. R. (1984). The physiological measurement of work stress: A critique. *Personnel Psychology*, *37*, 583–615.

Friesen, J. (1986). The role of the family in vocational development. *International Journal for the Advancement of Counseling*, *9*(1), 5–10.

Froelich, C. P. (1949). *Evaluating guidance procedures*. Washington, DC: U. S. Office of Education.

Frone, M. R., & Rice, R. W. (1987). Work-family conflict: The effect of job and family involvement. *Journal of Occupational Behavior*, *8*, 45–53.

Fryer, D. (1922). Occupational-intelligence standard. *School and Society*, *16*, 273–277.

Fuchs, K. D. (1978). Intervention and life-span developmental psychology. *Human Development*, *21*, 370–373.

Fukuyama, M. A., Probert, B. S., Neimeyer, G. J., Nevill, D., & Metzler, A. E. (1988). Effects of DISCOVER on career self-efficacy and decision-making of undergraduates. *The Career Development Quarterly*, *37*, 56–62.

Fullerton, H. N., Jr. (1980). The 1995 labor force: A first look. *Monthly Labor Review*, *103*, 11–21.

Fuqua, D. R., Blum, C. R., & Hartman, B. W. (1988). Empirical support for the differential diagnosis of career indecision. *The Career Development Quarterly*, *36*, 364–373.

Fuqua, D. R., Newman, J. L., & Seaworth, T. B. (1990). Relation of state and trait anxiety to different components of career indecision. *Journal of Counseling Psychology*, *35*(2), 154–158.

Fuqua, D. R., Seaworth, T. B., & Newman, J. L. (1987). The relationship of career indecision and anxiety: A multivariate examination. *Journal of Vocational Behavior*, *30*, 175–186.

Fuqua, D. R., Seaworth, T. B., & Newman, J. L. (1988). Relation of state and trait anxiety to different components of career indecision. *Journal of Counseling Psychology*, *35*, 154–158.

Gade, E., Fuqua, D., & Hurlburt, G. (1984). Use of the Self-Directed-Search with Native American high school students. *Journal of Counseling Psychology*, *31*, 584–587.

Galassi, J. P., & Galassi, M. D. (1978). Preparing individuals for job interviews. Suggestions from more than 60 years of research. *Personnel and Guidance Journal*, *57*(4), 188–192.

Gallagher, R. P., & Scheuring, S. B. (1979). A more efficient way of planning outreach programming at a university counseling and placement service. *Journal of College Student Personnel*, *20*, 360.

Gallup, A. (1985). The Gallup Poll of teachers' attitudes toward the public schools, part 2. *Phi Delta Kappan*, *66*, 323–330.

Gallup Organization, Inc. (1987). *Career development survey*. Conducted for National Career Development Association. Princeton, N.J.: Author.

Gammuto, J. J. (1980). Technical training: A systematic approach. *Training and Development Journal*, *34*, 82–90.

Ganster, D. C., & Victor, B. (1988). The impact of social support on mental and physical health. *British Journal of Medical Psychology*, *61*, 17–36.

Garbin, A. P., Salomone, J. J., Jackson, D. P., & Ballweg, J. A. (1970). *Worker adjustment problems of youth in transition from high school to work*. Columbus, OH: Center for Vocational and Technical Education, Ohio State University.

Garden, A. M. (1989). Burnout: The effect of psychological type on research findings. *Journal of Occupational Psychology*, *62*, 223–234.

Gardner, E. R., & Hall, R. C. W. (1981). The professional stress syndrome. *Psychosomatics*, *22*, 672–680.

Garfield, C. (1986). *Peak performers*. NY: Avon Books.

Garfield, N. J., & Prediger, D. J. (1982). Testing competencies and responsibilities: A checklist for vocational counselors. In J. T. Kapes and M. M. Mastie (Eds.), *A counselor's guide to vocational guidance instruments* (pp. 21–28). Washington, DC: National Vocational Guidance Association.

Garis, J. W. (1982, August). *The integration of a computer-based system in a college counseling center: A comparison of the effects of DISCOVER and individual counseling upon career planning*. Unpublished doctoral dissertation, Pennsylvania State University.

Garis, J. W., & Hess, H. R. (1989). Career Navigator: Its use with college students beginning the job search process. *The Career Development Quarterly*, *38*, 65–74.

Garis, J. W., & Niles, S. G. (1990). The separate and combined effects of SIGI or DISCOVER and a career planning course on undecided university students. *The Career Development Quarterly*, *38*, 261–274.

Garland, H., & Smith, G. B. (1981). Occupational achievement motivation as a function of biological sex, sex-linked personality, and occupational stereotypes. *Psychology of Women Quarterly*, *5*(4), 568–585.

Garraty, S. A. (1978). *Unemployment in history, economic thought and public policy*. New York: Harper & Row.

Garrison, H. H. (1979). Gender differences in the career aspirations of recent cohorts of high school seniors. *Social Problems*, *27*(2), 170–185.

Gati, I. (1986). Making career decisions—A sequential elimination approach. *Journal of Counseling Psychology*, *33*(4), 408–417.

Gati, I. (1990). Why, when, and how to take into account the uncertainty involved in career decisions. *Journal of Counseling Psychology*, *37*, 277–280.

Gati, I., & Tikotzki, Y. (1990). Strategies for collection and processing of occupational information in making career decisions. *Journal of Counseling Psychology*, *36*(4), 430–439.

Gaushell, W. H. (1984). Microcomputers, the school and the counselor. *The School Counselor*, *31*(3), 229–233.

Gelatt, H. B. (1962). Decision-making. A conceptual frame of reference for counseling. *Journal of Counseling Psychology*, *9*, 240–245.

Gelatt, H. B. (1989). Positive uncertainty: A new decision-making framework for counseling. *Journal of Counseling Psychology*, *36*(2), 252–256.

Gelatt, H. B., Varenhorst, B., Carey, R. & Miller, G. P. (1973). *Decisions and outcomes*. New York: College Entrance Examination Board.

Gelso, C. J. (1979). Research in counseling: Methodological and professional issues. *The Counseling Psychologist*, *8*(3), 7–36.

Gelso, C. J., Collins, A. M., Williams, R. O., & Sedlacek, W. E. (1973). The accuracy of self-administration and scoring on Holland's self-directed search. *Journal of Vocational Behavior*, *3*, 375–382.

Gerhart, B. (1987). How important are dispositional factors as determinants of job satisfaction? Implications for job design and other personnel programs. *Journal of Applied Psychology*, *72*, 366–373.

Gerler, E. R., Jr. (1980). Mental imagery in multimodal career education. *Vocational Guidance Quarterly*, *28*(4), 312.

Gershuny, J. L. & Pahl, R. E. (1979–1980). Work outside employment: Some preliminary speculations. *New Universities Quarterly*, *34*(1), 120–135.

Gerstein, M. (1982). Vocational counseling for adults in varied settings: A comprehensive view. *Vocational Guidance Quarterly*, *30*(4), 315–321.

Gerstein, M. (1983). VIEW: Approaching 20 years of microfilm usage for career information. *Journal of Career Education*, *10*(2), 134–140.

Ghiselli, E. E. (1966). *The validity of occupational aptitude tests*. New York: Wiley.

Ghiselli, E. E. (1973). The validity of aptitude tests in personnel selection. *Personnel Psychology*, *26*, 461–477.

Gianakos, I., & Subich, L. M. (1986). The relationship of gender and sex-role orientation to vocational undecidedness. *Journal of Vocational Behavior*, *29*, 42–50.

Gianakos, I., & Subich, L. M. (1988). Student sex and sex role in relation to college major choice. *The Career Development Quarterly*, *36*, 259–268.

Gibson, J. J. (1979). *The ecological approach to visual perception*. Boston: Houghton Mifflin.

Gibson, R. C. (1987). Reconceptualizing retirement for Black Americans. *The Gerontologist*, *27*, 691–698.

Gibson, R. L. (1962). Pupil opinions of high school guidance programs. *Personnel and Guidance Journal*, *40*, 453–457.

Gibson, R. L. (1972). *Career development in the elementary school*. Columbus, OH: Charles Merrill.

Gifford, R., Ng, C. F., & Wilkinson, M. (1985). Nonverbal cues in the employment interview: Links between applicant qualities and interviewer judgment. *Journal of Applied Psychology*, *70*(4), 729–736.

Gilbert, H. G. (1966). *Children study American industry*. Dubuque, IA: William C. Brown.

Gilbert, L. A. (1985). *Men in dual-career families: Current realities and future prospects*. Hillsdale, NJ: Erlbaum.

Gilbert, L. A., Holahan, C. K., & Manning, L. (1981). Coping with conflict between professional and maternal roles. *Family Relations*, *30*(3), 419–426.

Gilbert, L. A., & Rachlin, V. (1987). Mental health and psychological functioning of dual-career families. *The Counseling Psychologist*, *15*, 7–49.

Giles, W. F., & Field, H. S. (1982). Accuracy of interviewers' perceptions of the importance of intrinsic and extrinsic job characteristics to male and female applicants. *Academy of Management Journal*, *25*(1), 148–157.

Gill, S. J., & Fruehling, J. A. (1979). Needs assessment and the design of service delivery systems. *Journal of College Student Personnel*, *20*, 322–328.

Gilligan, C. (1982a). *In a different voice*. Cambridge, MA: Harvard University Press.

Gilligan, C. (1982b, June). Why should a woman be more like a man? *Psychology Today*, pp. 68–77.

Gilligan, C. (1983, May). *Challenging existing theories: Conclusions*. Paper presented at Eighth Annual Conference for Helpers of Adults, University of Maryland, College Park.

Gilmore, D. C., Beehr, T. A., & Love, K. G. (1986). Effects of applicant sex, applicant physical attractiveness, type of rater, and type of job on interview decisions. *Journal of Occupational Psychology*, *59*, 103–109.

Gilmore, D. C., Beehr, T. A., & Richter, D. J. (1979). Effects of leader behaviors in subordinate performance and satisfaction: A laboratory experiment with student employees. *Journal of Applied Psychology*, *64*(2), 166–172.

Gingrich, D. E. (1982). The dual career couple dilemma. *Journal of College Placement*, *42*(2), 26–30.

Ginzberg, E. (1971). *Career guidance: Who needs it, who provides it, who can improve it*. New York: McGraw-Hill.

Ginzberg, E. (1972). Restatement of the theory of occupational choice. *Vocational Guidance Quarterly*, *20*(3), 169–176.

Ginzberg, E. (1975). *The manpower connection, education, and work*. Cambridge, MA: Harvard University Press.

Ginzberg, E. (1982, September). The mechanization of work. *Scientific American*, *247*(3), 66–75. Ginzberg, E. (1984). Career development. In D. Brown & L. Brooks (Eds.), *Career choice and development, applying contemporary theories to practice* (Chap. 7). San Francisco: Jossey-Bass.

Ginzberg, E., Ginsburg, S. W., Axelrad, S., & Herma, J. (1951). *Occupational choice: An approach to a general theory*. New York: Columbia University Press.

Glaberson, W. (1990, October 4). One in 4 young black men are in custody, study says. *The New York Times*, p. B4.

Gladwin, T. (1967). Social competence and clinical practice. *Journal for the Study of Interpersonal Processes*, *30*, 30–38.

Glaize, D. L., & Myrick, R. D. (1984). Interpersonal groups or computers? A study of career maturity and career decidedness. *Vocational Guidance Quarterly*, *32*, 168–176.

Glamser, F. D. (1981). The impact of preretirement programs in the retirement experience. *Journal of Gerontology*, *36*(2), 244–250.

Gmelch, W. H., Wilke, P. K., & Lovrich, N. P. (1986). Dimensions of stress among university faculty: Factor-analytic results from a national study. *Research in Higher Education*, *24*(3), 266–286.

Goeke, J. D., & Salomone, P. R. (1979). Job placement and the school counselor. *Vocational Guidance Quarterly*, *27*(3), 209–215.

Gold, D., & Andres, D. (1978). Developmental comparisons between adolescent children with employed and nonemployed mothers. *Merrill-Palmer Quarterly*, *24*, 243–254.

Gold, S. J. (1988). Refugees and small business: The case of Soviet Jews and Vietnamese. *Ethnic and Racial Studies*, *11*(4), 411–438.

Goldman, L. (1961). *Using tests in counseling*. New York: Appleton-Century-Crofts.

Goldman, L. (1962). Group guidance: Content and process. *Personnel and Guidance Journal*, *40*, 518–522.

Goldman, L. (1971). *Using tests in counseling* (2nd ed.). New York: Appleton-Century-Crofts.

Goldman, L. (1979). Research is more than technology. *The Counseling Psychologist*, *8*(3), 41–44.

Goldman, L. (1982). Assessment in counseling: A better way. *Measurement and Evaluation in Guidance*, *15*(1), 70–73.

Goldschmidt, M., Tipton, R. M., & Wiggins, R. C. (1981). Professional identity and counseling psychologists. *Journal of Counseling Psychology*, *28*, 158–167.

Goleman, D. (1990, July 10). Homophobia: Scientists find clues to its roots. *The New York Times*, pp. C1, C11.

Golembiewski, R. T. (1988). A note on Leiter's study: Highlighting two models of burnout. *Group and Organizational Studies*, *13*, 129–134.

Golembiewski, R. T., & Munzenrider, R. F. (1988). *The phase model of burnout*. New York: Praeger.

Goodman, H. H. (1981). Adult education and counseling: An emerging synthesis. *Personnel and Guidance Journal*, *59*(7), 465–469.

Goodman, P. S., & Friedman, A. (1971). An examination of Adams' theory of inequity. *Administrative Science Quarterly, 16*, 271–288.

Goodson, W. D. (1978). Which do college students choose first—Their major or their occupation? *Vocational Guidance Quarterly, 27*(2), 150–155.

Goodson, W. D. (1982). Status of career programs on colleges and university campuses. *Vocational Guidance Quarterly, 30*(3), 230–235.

Goodstein, L. D. (1972). Behavioral views of counseling. In B. Steffire & W. H. Grant (Eds.), *Theories of counseling* (pp. 243–286). New York: McGraw-Hill.

Goodyear, R. K. (1990). Research on the effects of test interpretation: A review. *The Counseling Psychologist, 18*, 240–257.

Gordon, M. (1974). *Higher education and the labor market*. New York: McGraw-Hill.

Gordon, M. (1979). Women and work: Priorities for the future. In C. Kerr, & J. M. Rosow (Eds.), *Work in America: The decade ahead* (pp. 111–137). New York: Van Nostrand.

Gordon, R. A., & Arvey, R. D. (1986). Perceived and actual ages of workers. *Journal of Vocational Behavior, 28*(1), 21–28.

Gordon, V. N. (1981). The undecided student: A developmental perspective. *Personnel and Guidance Journal, 49*(7), 433–439.

Gordon, V. N. (1983). Meeting the career needs of undecided honor students. *Journal of College Student Personnel, 24*, 82–83.

Gordon, V. N., Coscarelli, W. C., & Sears, S. J. (1986). Comparative assessments of individual differences in learning and career decision making. *Journal of College Student Personnel, 27*, 233–242.

Gordon, V. N., & Grites, T. J. (1984). Freshman seminar course: Helping students succeed. *Journal of College Student Personnel, 25*(4), 315–320.

Gottfredson, G. D. (1977). Career stability and redirection in adulthood. *Journal of Applied Psychology, 62*(4), 436–445.

Gottfredson, G. D. (1982). An assessment of a mobility-based occupational classification for placement and counseling. *Journal of Vocational Behavior, 21*, 71–98.

Gottfredson, G. D. (1990, August). *Applications and research using Holland's theory of careers: Where we would like to be and suggestions for getting there*. Paper prepared for a symposium, "Applications and Researching Using Holland's Theory of Careers: Some Evaluations," at the annual meeting of the American Psychological Association, Boston, MA.

Gottfredson, G. D., Holland, J. L., & Ogawa, D. K. (1982). *Dictionary of Holland Occupational Codes*. Palo Alto, CA: Consulting Psychologists Press.

Gottfredson, G. D., & Holland, J. L. (1990). A longitudinal test of the influence of congruence: Job satisfaction, competency utilization, and counterproductive behavior. *Journal of Counseling Psychology, 37*(4), 389–398.

Gottfredson, L. S. (1980). Construct validity of Holland's occupational typology in terms of prestige, census, Department of Labor, and other classification systems. *Journal of Applied Psychology, 65*(6), 697–714.

Gottfredson, L. S. (1981). Circumscription and compromise: A developmental theory of occupational aspirations. *Journal of Counseling Psychology, 28*(6), 545–579.

Gottfredson, L. S. (1982). Vocational research priorities. *The Counseling Psychologist, 10*(2), 69–84.

Gottfredson, L. S. (1986a). The g factor in employment. *Journal of Vocational Behavior, 29(3)*, 293–296.

Gottfredson, L. S. (1986b). Occupational Aptitude Patterns (OAP) Map: Development and implications for a theory of job aptitude requirements. *Journal of Vocational Behavior, 29*, 254–291.

Gottfredson, L. S. (1988). Reconsidering fairness: A matter of social and ethical priorities. *Journal of Vocational Behavior, 33*(3), 293–319.

Gottfredson, L. S. (1990, December 6). When job-testing "fairness" is nothing but a quota. *The Wall Street Journal*, p. 23.

Gottfredson, L. S., & Becker, H. J. (1981). A challenge to vocational psychology: How important are aspirations in determining male career development? *Journal of Vocational Behavior, 18*, 121.

Gottfredson, L. S., Finucci, J. M., & Childs, B. (1984). Explaining the adult careers of dyslexic boys: Variations in critical skills for high-level jobs. *Journal of Vocational Behavior, 24*, 355–373.

Gottfredson, L. S., & Sharf, J. C. (Eds.). (1988). Fairness in employment testing [Special issue]. *Journal of Vocational Behavior, 31*, 225–230.

Goudy, W. J. (1981). Changing work expectations: Findings from the retirement history study. *The Gerontologist, 21*(6), 644–649.

Gough, H. G. (1985). A work orientation scale for the California psychological inventory. *Journal of Applied Psychology, 70*(3), 505–513.

Gould, R. (1978). *Transformations: Growth and change in adult life*. New York: Simon and Schuster.

Gould, R. (1972). The phases of adult life: A study of developmental psychology. *American Journal of Psychiatry, 1929*(11), 33–43.

Gould, S. (1982). Correlates of career progression among Mexican-American college graduates. *Journal of Vocational Behavior, 20*, 93–110.

Goulet, L. R., & Baltes, P. B. (Eds). (1970). *Life-span developmental psychology*. New York: Academic Press.

Graef, M. I., Wells, D. L., Hyland, A. M., & Muchinsky, P. M. (1985). Life history antecedents of vocational indecision. *Journal of Vocational Behavior, 27*(3), 276–297.

Graney, J. J., & Cottam, D. M. (1981). Labor force nonparticipation of older people: United States, 1890–1970. *The Gerontologist, 21*(2), 138–141.

Graney, J. J., & Zimmerman, R. M. (1981). Causes and consequences of health self-report variations among older people. *International Journal of Aging and Human Development, 12*(4), 291–300.

Granrose, C. S. (1985). Plans for work career among college women who expect to have families. *Vocational Guidance Quarterly, 33*(4), 284–295.

Grant, C. A., & Sleeter, C. E. (1988). Race, class, and gender and abandoned dreams. *Teachers College Record, 90*(1), 19–40.

Graves, J. P., Dalton, G. W., & Thompson, P. H. (1980). Career stages in organizations. In C. B. Derr (Ed.), *Work, family, and the career* (pp. 18–37). New York: Praeger.

Gray, D. O., & Braddy, B. A. (1988). Experimental social innovation and client-centered job-seeking programs. *American Journal of Community Psychology, 16*, 325–343.

Gray, J. D. (1980). Counseling women who want both a profession and a family. *Personnel and Guidance Journal, 59*(1), 43–46.

Gray, K. (1986). Implications of microcomputers for counsellors. *British Journal of Guidance and Counseling, 14*(1), 12–20.

Gray, S., & Morse, D. (1980). Retirement and reengagement: Changing work options for older workers. *Aging and Work, 3*(2), 103–111.

Green, C. H. (1979). Managing career information: A librarian's perspective. *Vocational Guidance Quarterly, 28*(1), 83–91.

Green, L. B., & Parker, H. J. (1965). Parental influences upon adolescent's occupational choice: A test of an aspect of

Roe's theory. *Journal of Counseling Psychology, 12*, 379–383.

Greenfeld, S., Greiner, L., & Wood, M. M. (1980). The "feminine mystique" in male-dominated jobs: A comparison of attitudes and background factors of women in male-dominated versus female-dominated jobs. *Journal of Vocational Behavior, 17*, 291–309.

Greenhaus, J. H., Parasuraman, S., Granrose, C. S., Rabinowitz, S., & Beutell, N. J. (1988). Sources of work-family conflict among two-career couples. *Journal of Vocational Behavior, 34*(2), 133–153.

Greenhaus, J. H., & Sklarew, N. D. (1981). Some sources and consequences of career exploration. *Journal of Vocational Behavior, 18*, 1–12.

Greenlee, S. P., Damarin, F. L., & Walsh, W. B. (1988). Congruence and differentiation among Black and White males in two non-college-degreed operations. *Journal of Vocational Behavior, 32*(3), 298–306.

Gregg, C. H., & Dobson, K. (1980). Occupational sex role stereotyping and occupational interests in children. *Elementary School Guidance and Counseling, 15*(1), 66–75.

Gribbons, W. D., & Lohnes, P. R. (1968). *Emerging careers.* New York: Teachers College Press, Columbia University.

Gribbons, W. D., & Lohnes, P. R. (1969). *Career development from age 13 to 25* (Final Report, Project No. 6-2151). Washington, DC: U. S. Department of Health, Education, and Welfare.

Gribbons, W. D., & Lohnes, P. R. (1975). *Readiness for career planning* (revised). Buffalo, NY: State University of New York at Buffalo, Department of Educational Psychology.

Gribbons, W. D., & Lohnes, P. R. (1982). *Careers in theory and experience: A twenty-year longitudinal study.* Albany, NY: State University of New York Press.

Grieco, M. (1987). *Keeping it in the family: Social networks and employment chance.* London: Tavistock.

Griffith A. R. (1980a). Justification for a black career development. *Counselor Education and Supervision, 19*(4), 301–310.

Griffith, A. R. (1980b). A survey of career development in corporations. *Personnel and Guidance Journal, 58*(8), 537–543.

Griffith, A. R. (1981). A survey of career development in state and local government. *Journal of Employment Counseling, 18*(1), 12–23.

Grite, T. J. (1981). Being "undecided" might be the best decision they could make. *The School Counselor, 29*(1), 41–46.

Gronlund, N. E. (1970). *Stating behavioral objectives for classroom instruction.* New York: Macmillan.

Gross, E. (1975). Patterns of organizational and occupational socialization. *Vocational Guidance Quarterly, 24*(2), 140–149.

Gross, H. E. (1980). Dual-career couples who live apart: Two types. *Journal of Marriage and the Family, 42*(3), 567–576.

Grotevant, H. D., & Cooper, C. R. (1986). Exploration as a predictor of congruence in adolescents' career choices. *Journal of Vocational Behavior, 29*, 201–215.

Guidance information system guide: Edition 12. (1981). Hanover, NH: TSC, Houghton-Mifflin.

Gunnings, T. S. (1976). *A systemic approach to counseling.* East Lansing, MI: Michigan State University, Department of Psychiatry.

Gunter, B. G., & Gunter, N. (1980). Leisure styles: A conceptual framework for modern leisure. *The Sociological Quarterly, 21*, 361–374.

Gupta, N., & Jenkins, G. D., Jr. (1984). Substance use as an employee response to the work environment. *Journal of Vocational Behavior, 24*, 84–93.

Gustad, J. W., & Tuma, A. (1957). The effects of different methods of test introduction and interpretation on client learning in counseling. *Journal of Counseling Psychology, 4*, 313–317.

Guthrie, W. R., & Herman, A. (1982). Vocational maturity and its relationship to Holland's theory of vocational choice. *Journal of Vocational Behavior, 21*(2), 196–205.

Gutteridge, T. G. (1986). Organizational career development systems: The state of the practice. In D. T. Hall & Assoc. (Eds.), *Career development in oraganizations* (Chap. 2). San Francisco: Jossey-Bass.

Gutteridge, T. G., & Otte, F. (1983). Organizational career development: What's going on out there? *Training and Development Journal, 37*, 22–26.

Guttmann, D. (1978). Life events and decision making by older adults. *The Gerontologist, 18*(5), 462–467.

Gysbers, N. C. (1990). *Comprehensive guidance programs that work.* Ann Arbor: University of Michigan, ERIC/CAPS.

Gysbers, N. C., & Moore, E. J. (1971). Career development in the schools. In G. F. Law (Ed.), *Contemporary concepts in vocational education.* Washington, DC: American Vocational Association.

Gysbers, N. C., & Moore, E. J. (1981). *Improving guidance programs.* Englewood Cliffs, NJ: Prentice-Hall.

Gysbers, N. C., & Moore, E. J. (1986). *Career counseling, skills and techniques for practitioners.* Englewood Cliffs, NJ: Prentice-Hall.

Haase, R. F., Reed, C. F., Winer, J. L., & Bodden, J. L. (1979). Effect of positive, negative, and mixed occupational information on cognitive and affective complexity. *Journal of Vocational Behavior, 15*, 294–302.

Haber, S. (1980). Cognitive support for the career choices of college women. *Sex Roles, 6*(1), 129–138.

Haccoun, R. R., & Campbell, R. E. (1972). *Work entry problems of youth: A literature review.* Columbus: Ohio State University, Center for Vocational Technical Education.

Hackett, D. F. (1966). Industrial element for the elementary school. *School Shop, 25*, 58–62.

Hackett, G. (1985). The role of mathematics self-efficacy in the choice of math-related majors of college women and men: A path analysis. *Journal of Counseling Psychology, 32*, 47–56.

Hackett, G., & Betz, N. E. (1981). A self-efficacy approach to the career development of women. *Journal of Vocational Behavior, 18*, 326–339.

Hackett, G., Esposito, D., & O'Halloran, M. S. (1989). The relationship of role model influences to the career salience and educational and career plans of college women. *Journal of Vocational Behavior, 35*(2), 164–180.

Hackett, R. D. (1989). Work attitudes and employee absenteeism: A synthesis of the literature. *Journal of Occupational Psychology, 62*, 235–248.

Hackman, J. R., & Oldham, G. R. (1981). Work redesign: People and their work. In J. O'Toole, J. L. Scheiber, & L. C. Wood (Eds.), *Working, changes and choices* (pp. 173–182). New York: Human Sciences Press.

Hageman, M. B., & Gladding, S. T. (1983). The art of career exploration: occupational sex-role stereotyping among elementary school children. *Elementary School Guidance and Counseling, 17*, 280–287.

Hageseth, J. A. (1982). A modular approach to career programming at a university counseling center. *Journal of College Student Personnel, 23*, 154.

Hahn, W. A. (1980). The post-industrial boom in communications. In C. S. Sheappard, & D. C. Carroll (Eds), *Working in the twenty-first century* (pp. 30–38). New York: Wiley.

Hakel, M. D., Hollman, T. D., & Dunette, M. D. (1968). Stability and change in the social status of occupations over 21 and 42 year periods. *Personnel and Guidance Journal, 46*, 762–764.

Hale, L. L. (1974). A bold new blueprint for career planning and placement: Part L. *Journal of College Placement*, *35*(2), 34–40.

Hales, L. W., & Fenner, B. (1972). Work values of 5th, 8th, and 11th grade students. *Vocational Guidance Quarterly*, *20*(3), 199–203.

Hales, L. W., & Fenner, B. (1973). Sex and social class differences in work values. *Elementary School Guidance and Counseling*, *8*(1), 26–32.

Hall, C. S., & Lindzey, G. (1957). *Theories of personality*. New York: Wiley.

Hall, D. T. (1976). *Careers in organizations*. Pacific Palisades, CA: Goodyear.

Hall, D. T. (1985). Project work as an antidote to career plateauing in a declining engineering organization. *Human Resource Management*, *24*(3), 271–292.

Hall, D. T. (Ed.). (1986). *Career development in organizations*. San Francisco: Jossey-Bass.

Hall, D. T., & Schneider, B. (1973). *Organizational climates and careers: The work lives of priests*. New York: Seminar Press.

Halpern, A. S., Raffeld, P., Irvin, L. K., & Link, R. (1975). *Social and Prevocational Information Battery*. Monterey, CA: California Test Bureau/McGraw-Hill.

Halverson, P. M. (1970, January). *A rationale for a career development program in the elementary school*. Paper presented to the Program Development Committee of the Cobb County, Georgia, Schools.

Hamburg, D. A., & Takaniski, R. (1989). Preparing for life. The critical transition of adolescence. *American Psychologist*, *44*(5), 825–827.

Hamel, K., & Bracken, D. (1986). Factor structure of the Job Stress Questionnaire (JSQ) in three occupational groups. *Educational and Psychological Measurement*, *46*, 777–786.

Hamilton, J. A., & Jones, G. B. (1971). Individualizing Educational and vocational guidance: Developng a prototype program. *Vocational Guidance Quarterly*, *19*(4), 293–299.

Hamilton, R. F., & Wright, J. D. (1976). *College educated blue collar workers*. American Sociological Association meeting, New York.

Hammer-Higgens, P., & Atwood, V. A. (1989). The management game: An educational intervention for counseling women with nontraditional career goals. *The Career Development Quarterly*, *38*, 6–23.

Hamrin, R. D. (1981). The information economy. *The Futurist*, *15*(4), 25–30.

Handel, L. (1973). Three tips on career guidance activities. *Elementary School Guidance and Counseling*, *7*(4), 290–291.

Hanisch, K., & Hulin, C. L. (1990). Job attitudes and organizational withdrawal: An examination of retirement and other voluntary withdrawal behaviors. *Journal of Vocational Behavior*, *37*(1), 60–78.

Hannson, R. O., O'Connor, M. E., Jones, W. H., & Blocker, T. J. (1981). Maternal employment and adolescent sexual behavior. *Journal of Youth and Adolescence*, *10*(1), 55–60.

Hansen, D. A., & Johnson, V. (1989). Classroom lesson strategies and orientations toward work. In D. Stern and D. Eichorn (Eds.), *Adolescence and Work: Influences of social structure, labor markets, and culture* (pp. 75–100). Hillsdale, N.J.: Lawrence Erlbaum Associates.

Hansen, J. C., & Cramer, S. H. (Eds.). (1971). *Group guidance and counseling in the schools*. New York: Appleton-Century-Crofts.

Hansen, J.-I. (1985). Review of Career Development Inventory. *Measurement and Evaluation in Counseling and Development*, *17*(4), 220–224.

Hansen, J.-I. C. (1985). *Users guide for the SVIB-SII*. Palo Alto: Consulting Psychologists Press.

Hansen, J.-I. (1986). Computers and beyond in the career decision-making process. *Measurement and Evaluation in Counseling and Development*, *19*(1), 48–52.

Hansen, J.-I. C. (1987). Cross-cultural research on vocational interests. *Measurement and Evaluation in Counseling and Development*, *20*, 65–71.

Hansen, L. S. (1964–1965). The art of planmanship. *Chronicle guidance professional services*. Moravia, NY: Chronicle Guidance Publications.

Hansen, L. S. (1977). *An Examination of the Concepts and Definitions of Career Education*. Washington, D.C.: National Advisory Council for Career Education.

Hansen, L. S. (1981). New goals and strategies for vocational guidance and counseling. *International Journal for the Advancement of Counseling*, *4*(1), 21–34.

Hansen, L. S., & Keierleber, D. L. (1978). Born free: A collaborative consultation model for career development and sex-role stereotyping. *Personnel and Guidance Journal*, *56*(7), 395–399.

Hansen, L. S., & Minor, C. W. (1989). *Work, family, and career development: Implications for persons, policies, and practices*. Washington, D.C.: National Career Development Association.

Hansen, L. S., & Tenneyson, W. W. (1975, May). A career management model for counselor involvement. *Personnel and Guidance Journal*, *53*(9), 638–646.

Hansen, L. S., & Yost, M. (1989). Preparing youth for changing roles and tasks in society, work, and family. In R. Hanson (Ed.), *Career development: Preparing for the 21st century*. Knoxville: University of Tennessee, Department of Technological and Adult Education.

Hardesty, S. A., & Betz, N. E. (1980). The relationships of career salience, attitudes toward women, and demographic and family characteristics to marital adjustment in dual-career couples. *Journal of Vocational Behavior*, *17*(2), 242–250.

Haring, M. J., & Beyard-Tyler, K. C. (1984). Counseling with women: The challenge of nontraditional careers. *The School Counselor*, *31*(4), 301–309.

Haring-Hidore, M., & Beyard-Tyler, K. (1984). Counseling and research on nontraditional careers: A caveat. *Vocational Guidance Quarterly*, *33*(2), 113–119.

Harlow, H. F. (1953). Mice, monkeys, men, and motives. *Psychological Review*, *60*, 23–32.

Harmon, L. W. (1973). Sexual bias in interest measurement. *Measurement and Evaluation in Guidance*, *5*, 496–501.

Harmon, L. (1985). Review of the Ohio Vocational Interest Survey. *Measurement and Evaluation in Counseling and Development*, *17*(4), 224–226.

Harmon, L. W. (1988). Review of Values Scale. In J. T. Kapes & M. M. Mastie (Eds.), *A counselor's guide to vocational assessment instruments* (pp. 155–157). Washington, DC: National Career Development Association.

Harmon, L. W. (1989). Longitudinal changes in women's career aspirations: Developmental or historical? *Journal of Vocational Behavior*, *35*(1), 46–63.

Harootyan, R. A., & Feldman, N. S. (1990). Lifelong education, lifelong needs: Future roles in an aging society. *Educational Gerontology*, *16*, 347–358.

Harpaz, I. (1985). Meaning of working profiles of various occupational groups. *Journal of Vocational Behavior*, *26*(1), 25–40.

Harren, V. (1979). A model of career decision-making for college students. *Journal of Vocational Behavior*, *14*, 119–133.

Harren, V. A., Kass, R. A., Tinsley, H., & Morehead, J. R. (1978). Influence of sex role attitudes and cognitive styles on career decision-making. *Journal of Counseling Psychology, 25*(5), 390–398.

Harrington, C. C. (1975). A psychological anthropologist's view of ethnicity and schooling. *IRCD Bulletin, 10*(4).

Harris, J. S. (1968). The computerization of vocational information. *Vocational Guidance Quarterly, 17*, 20–21.

Harris, L. (1989). 2001: The world our students will enter. *College Board Review, 150*, (Winter), 20–24.

Harris, M. (1981). *America now: The anthropology of a changing culture*. New York: Simon & Schuster.

Harris, M. B., & Jones, L. (1981). Occu-Sort: A new career planning tool. *Journal of College Placement, 42*(1), 47–50.

Harris, T. L., & Wallin, J. S. (1978). Influencing career choices of seventh grade students. *Vocational Guidance Quarterly, 28*(1), 50–54.

Harrison, B. (1973). *Education, training, and the urban ghetto*. Baltimore: John Hopkins University Press.

Hart, D. H., Rayner, K., & Christensen, E. R. (1971). Planning, preparation and chance in occupational entry. *Journal of Vocational Behavior, 1*, 279–285.

Hartigan, J. A., & Wigdor, A. K. (Eds.). (1989). *Fairness in employment testing: Validity generalization, minority issues, and the General Aptitude Test Battery*. Washington, DC: National Academy Press.

Hartman, B., & Hartman, P. (1982). The concurrent and predictive validity of the career decision scale adapted for high school students. *Journal of Vocational Behavior, 20*, 244–252.

Hartman, B., Utz, P., & Farnum, S. (1979). Examining the reliability and validity of an adapted scale of educational-vocational undecidedness in a sample of graduate students. *Journal of Vocational Behavior, 15*, 224–230.

Hartman, B. W., Fuqua, D. R., & Blum, C. R. (1985). A path-analytic model of career indecision. *Vocational Guidance Quarterly, 33*(3), 231–240.

Hartman, B. W., Fuqua, D. R., & Jenkins, S. J. (1986a). The reliability/generalizability of the construct of career indecision. *Journal of Vocational Behavior, 28*, 142–148.

Hartman, S., Grigsby, D. W., Crino, M. D., & Chokar, J. S. (1986b). The measurement of job satisfaction by action tendencies. *Educational and Psychological Measurement, 46*, 317–329.

Hartman, S. J., Griffeth, R. W., Miller, L., & Kinicki, A. J. (1988). The impact of occupation, performance, and sex on sex role stereotyping. *The Journal of Social Psychology, 128*(4), 451–463.

Hatt, P. K. (1962). Occupation and social stratification. In S. Nosow & W. H. Form (Eds.), *Man, work, and society* (pp. 238–249). New York: Basic Books.

Havighurst, R. J. (1953). *Human development and education*. New York: Longmans, Green.

Havighurst, R. J. (1964) Human development and education. In H. Borow (Ed.), *Man in a world at work* (Chapter 10). Boston: Houghton Mifflin.

Havighurst, R. J. (1965). Counseling adolescent girls in the 1960's. *Vocational Guidance Quarterly, 13*, 153–160.

Haviland, M. G., & Hansen, J-I. C. (1987). Criterion validity of the Strong-Campbell Interest Inventory for American Indian college students. *Measurement and Evaluation in Counseling and Development, 20*, 196–201.

Haw, M. A. (1982). Women, work, and stress: A review and agenda for the future. *Journal of Health and Social Behavior, 23*, 132–144.

Hawley, P. (1980). *Sex-fair career counseling*. Washington, DC: National Vocational Guidance Association.

Hayes, D. G. (1982). Future shock and the counselor. In E. L. Herr & N. M. Pinson (Eds.), *Foundations for policy in guidance and counseling* (pp. 20–33). Washington, DC: American Personnel and Guidance Association.

Hayes, J., & Nutman, P. (1981). *Understanding the unemployed: The psychological effects of unemployment*. London: Tavistock.

Hayes, R. (1986). Gender nontraditional or sex atypical or gender dominant or . . . research: Are we measuring the same thing? *Journal of Vocational Behavior, 29*, 79–88.

Hayes, R. L. (1979). High school students' occupational interest as a function of projected sex ratios in male-dominated occupations. *Journal of Applied Psychology, 84*(3), 275–279.

Hayghe, H. (1981). Husbands and wives as earners: An analysis of family data. *Monthly Labor Review*, U. S. Department of Labor, Bureau of Labor Statistics, *104*(2), 47.

Hazler, R. J., & Latto, L. D. (1987). Employers' opinions in the attitudes and skills of high school graduates. *Journal of Employment Counseling, 24*(3), 130–136.

Hazler, R. J., & Roberts, G. (1984). Decision making in vocational theory: Evolution and implications. *Personnel and Guidance Journal, 62*(7), 408–410.

Healy, C. C. (1973). Toward a replicable method of group career counseling. *Vocational Guidance Quarterly, 21*, 214–221.

Healy, C. C. (1974). Evaluation of a replicable group career counseling procedure. *Vocational Guidance Quarterly, 22*, 34–40.

Healy, C. C. (1982). *Career development, counseling through the life stages*. Boston: Allyn & Bacon.

Healy, C. C. (1989). Negative: The MBTI: Not ready for routine use in counseling. *Journal of Counseling and Development, 67*, 487–488.

Healy, C. C. (1990). Reforming career appraisals to meet the needs of clients in the 1990s. *The Counseling Psychologist, 18*, 214–226.

Healy, C. C., & Reilly, K. C. (1989). Career needs of community college students: Implications for services and theory. *Journal of College Student Development, 30*(6), 541–545.

Heath, D. (1976). Adolescent and adult predictors of vocational adaptation. *Journal of Vocational Behavior, 9*, 1–19.

Hedstrom, J. E. (1978). Jobs for kids. *Elementary School Guidance and Counseling, 13*(2), 132–134.

Hegenauer, M., & Brown, S. (1990). A review of the Social and Prevocational Information Battery. *Journal of Counseling and Development, 68*, 338–340.

Heilbrun, A. B., Jr., & Renert, D. (1986). Type A behavior, cognitive defense, and stress. *Psychological Reports, 58*, 447–456.

Heilman, M. E. (1979). High school students occupational interest as a function of projected sex ratios in male-dominated occupations. *Journal of Applied Psychology, 84*(3), 275–279.

Heimlich, J. E., & Van Tilburg, E. V. (1988). RE:FIT: Assessing career potential for dislocated farmers. *The Career Development Quarterly, 37*, 87–90.

Heitzmann, D., Schmidt, A. K., & Hurley, F. W. (1986). Career encounters: Career decision-making through on-site visits. *Journal of Counseling and Development, 65*, 209–210.

Helliwell, T. (1981). Are you a potential burnout? *Training and Development Journal, 35*, 25–29.

Helman, C. (1985). Psyche, soma, and society: The social construction of psychosomatic disease. *Culture, Medicine and Psychiatry, 9*, 1–26.

Helms, S. T. (1973). Practical applications of the Holland occupational classification in counseling. *Communique, 2*, 69–71.

Helmstadter, G. C. (1964). *Principles of psychological measurement*. New York: Appleton-Century-Crofts.

Helpingstine, S. R., Head, T. C., & Sorensen, P. F. (1981). Job characteristics, job satisfaction, motivation and satisfaction with growth: A study of industrial engineers. *Psychological Reports, 49*, 381–382.

Henderson, K. A. (1990). The meaning of leisure for women: An integrative review of the research. *Journal of Leisure Research, 22*(3), 228–243.

Henley, B. (1986). The job interview: A workshop on self-esteem and dress for black students. *Journal of College Student Personnel, 27*(6), 564–566.

Hennig, M., & Jardin, A. (1977). *The managerial woman*. Garden City, NY: Anchor Press.

Henton, J. M., Russell, R., & Koval, J. E. (1983). Spousal perceptions of mid-life career change. *Personnel and Guidance Journal, 61*(5), 287–291.

Heppner, M. J., & Olson, S. K. (1982). Expanding college career centers to meet the needs of adults. *Journal of College Student Personnel, 23*, 123–127.

Heppner, P. P., & Krauskopf, C. J. (1987). An information-processing approach to personal problem solving. *The Counseling Psychologist, 15*, 371–447.

Heppner, P. P., & Krieshok, T. S. (1983). An applied investigation of problem-solving appraisal, vocational identity and career service requests, utilization and subsequent evaluations. *Vocational Guidance Quarterly, 31*(4), 240–249.

Herr, E. L. (1969, March). *Unifying an entire system of education around a career development theme*. Paper presented at the National Conference of Exemplary Programs and Projects Section of the 1968 Amendments to the Vocational Education Act, Atlanta, GA.

Herr, E. L. (1970). *Decision-making and vocational development*, Boston: Houghton Mifflin.

Herr, E. L. (1972). *Review and synthesis of foundations for career education*. Columbus, OH: Center for Vocational and Technical Education, Ohio State University.

Herr, E. L. (1974). The decade in prospect: Some implications for vocational guidance. In E. L. Herr (Ed.), *Vocational guidance and human development* (Chap. 22). Boston: Houghton Mifflin.

Herr, E. L. (1976a). Counseling accountability, reality, credibility. *Journal of Counseling Services, 1*,(1), 14–23.

Herr, E. L. (1976b). Introduction. *Career education in the elementary school*. Lewisburg, PA: Central Susquehanna Intermediate Unit, Career Development Field Guide Project.

Herr, E. L. (1976c). *Introduction to career education in the senior high school*. Lewisburg, PA: Central Susquehanna Intermediate Joint Career Development Field Guide Project.

Herr, E. L. (1976, April). *Does counseling work?* Speech presented to the Seventh International Roundtable for the Advancement of Counseling, University of Würzburg, Germany.

Herr, E. L. (1977a). The roots of career education. *College Board Review, 105*, 6–17, 32–33.

Herr, E. L. (1977b). *Career education: The state of research*. Columbus, OH: ERIC Clearinghouse for Career Education.

Herr, E. L. (1977c). Vocational planning: An alternate view. *Personnel and Guidance Journal, 56*, 25–27.

Herr, E. L. (1978a). Career development concepts and practices: Some international perspectives. *Counseling and Human Development, 11*(1), 1–11.

Herr, E. L. (1978b). *Research in career education: The state of the art*. Columbus, OH: ERIC Clearinghouse for Career Education.

Herr, E. L. (1979). The outcomes of career guidance. *Journal of Counseling Services, 3*(2), 6–15.

Herr, E. L. (1980). Recommendations for the improved use of labor market information in secondary schools. In H. N. Drier & L. A. Pfister (Eds.), *Career and labor market information: Key to improved individual decision-making* (pp. 43–60). Columbus: The National Center for Research in Vocational Education.

Herr, E. L. (1981). Policy in Guidance and Counseling: The U.S. Experience. *Educational and Vocational Guidance, 37*(1), 67–83.

Herr, E. L. (1982a). Career development and vocational guidance. In H. F. Silberman (Ed.), *Education and work* (Chap. 6). Chicago: University of Chicago Press.

Herr, E. L. (1982b). Perspectives on the philosophical, empirical, and cost-benefit effects of guidance and counseling. Implications for political action. *The Personnel and Guidance Journal, 60*(10), 594–597.

Herr, E. L. (1982c). Comprehensive career guidance: Future impact. *Vocational Guidance Quarterly, 30*(4), 367–376.

Herr, E. L. (1982d). The effects of guidance and counseling: Three domains. In E. L. Herr & N. M. Pinson (Eds.), *Foundations for policy in guidance and counseling*. Washington, DC: APGA Press.

Herr, E. L. (1982e, May). *Counselor education programs: Training for career development for exceptional people*. Paper presented at Johns Hopkins University, Baltimore.

Herr, E. L. (1984). Links among training, employability, and employment. In N. C. Gysbers (Ed.), *Designing careers. Counseling to enhance education, work, and leisure*. San Francisco: Jossey-Bass.

Herr, E. L. (1985a). International approaches to career counseling and guidance. In P. Pedersen (Ed.), *Handbook of cross-cultural counseling and therapy* (pp. 3–10). Westport, CT: Greenwood Press.

Herr, E. L. (1985b). The role of professional organizations in effecting the use of technology in career development. *Journal of Career Development 12*(2), 176–186.

Herr, E. L. (1986). *Why counseling?* (2nd ed.). Alexandria, VA: AACD Press.

Herr, E. L. (1989a). Career development and mental health. *Journal of Career Development, 16*(1), 5–18.

Herr, E. L. (1989b). *Counseling in a dynamic society. Opportunities and challenges*. Alexandria, VA: AACD Press.

Herr, E. L. (1990, August). *Counseling for personal flexibility in a global economy.* Plenary paper presented at the XIVth World Congress, Counseling in a Global Economy, of the International Association for Educational and Vocational Guidance, Montreal, Canada.

Herr, E. L., & Best, P. (1984). Computer technology and counseling: The role of the profession. *Journal of Counseling and Development, 63*(4), 192–195.

Herr, E. L., & Cramer, S. H. (1968). *Guidance of the college bound: Problems, practices, and perspectives*. New York: Appleton-Century-Crofts.

Herr, E. L., & Cramer, S. H. (1972). *Vocational guidance and career development in the schools: Toward a systems approach*. Boston: Houghton Mifflin.

Herr, E. L., & Cramer, S. (1987). *Controversies in the mental health professions*. Muncie, IN: Accelerated Development Press.

Herr, E. L., & Enderlein, T. (1976). Vocational maturity: The effects of school, grade, curriculum, and sex. *The Journal of Vocational Behavior, 8*, 227–238.

Herr, E. L., & Johnson, E. (1989). General employability skills for youths and adults: Goals for guidance and counseling programs. *Guidance & Counseling, 4*(4), 15–29.

Herr, E. L., & Lear, P. B. (1984). The family as an influence on career development. In S. H. Cramer (Ed.), *Perspectives on work and the family* (Chap. 1, pp. 1–15). Rockville, MD: Aspen Systems.

Herr, E. L., & Niles, S. G. (1988). Review of the Adult Career Concerns Inventory. In J. T. Kapes & M. M. Mastie (Eds.), *A counselor's guide to career assessment instruments* (pp. 160–164). Washington, DC: National Career Development Association.

Herr, E. L., & Watts, A. G. (1981). The implications of youth unemployment for career education and for counseling. *Journal of Career Education, 7*(3), 184–202.

Herr, E. L. & Watts, A. G. (1988). Work shadowing and work-related learning. *The Career Development Quarterly, 37*(1), 78–86.

Herr, E. L., Weitz, A., Good, R., & McCloskey, G. (1981). *Research on the effects of secondary school curricular and personal characteristics upon postsecondary educational and occupational patterns* (NIE-G-80-0027). University Park, PA: The Pennsylvania State University.

Herring, R. D. (1990). Attacking career myths among Native Americans: Implications for counseling. *The School Counselor, 38*, 13–18.

Hershenson, D. B. (1968). Life-state vocational development system. *Journal of Counseling Psychology, 15*, 23–30.

Hershenson, D. B. (1974). Vocational guidance and the handicapped. In E. L. Herr (Ed.), *Vocational guidance and human development* (pp. 478–501). Boston: Houghton Mifflin.

Hershenson, D. B., & Roth, R. M. (1966). A decisional process model of vocational development. *Journal of Counseling Psychology, 13*, 368–370.

Herzberg, F. (1968). One more time: How do you motivate employees? *Harvard Business Review, 46*(1), 53–62.

Herzberg, F., Mausner, B., & Snyderman, B. (1959). *The motivation to work.* New York: Wiley.

Hesketh, B. (1982). Decision-making style and career decision-making behaviors among school learners. *Journal of Vocational Behavior, 20*, 223–234.

Hesketh, B., Elmslie, S., & Kaldor, W. (1990). Career compromise: An alternative account to Gottfredson's theory. *Journal of Counseling Psychology, 37*(1), 49–56.

Hetherington, C., Hillerbrand, E., & Etringer, B. (1989). Career counseling with gay men: Issues and recommendations for research. *Journal of Counseling and Development, 67*, 452–454.

Hetherington, C., & Orzek, A. (1989). Career counseling and life planning with lesbian women. *Journal of Counseling and Development, 68*, 52–57.

Heyns, B., & Catsambis, S. (1986). Mother's employment and children's achievement: A critique. *Sociology of Education, 59*, 140–151.

Higgins, N. C. (1986). Occupational stress and working women: The effectiveness of two stress reduction programs. *Journal of Vocational Behavior, 29*, 66–78.

Hill, N. C. (1985). Career counseling: What employees should do and expect. *Personnel, 62*(8), 41.

Hill, R. E., & Miller, E. L. (1981). Job change and the middle seasons of a man's life. *Academy of Management Journal, 24*(1), 114–127.

Hiller, D. V., & Philliber, W. W. (1982). Predicting marital and career success among dual-worker couples. *Journal of Marriage and the Family, 44*(1), 53–62.

Hilton, T. J. (1962). Career decision-making. *Journal of Counseling Psychology, 9*, 291–298.

Hirschhorn, L. (1988). *The workplace within. Psychodynamics of organizational life.* Cambridge, MA: the MIT Press.

Hitchcock, A. A. (1980). Public policy and adult career occupational services. In R. E. Campbell & P. Shaltry (Eds.), *Perspectives on adult career development and guidance*. Columbus, OH: The National Center for Research in Vocational Education.

Hitchcock, A. A. (1984). Work, aging, and counseling. *Journal of Counseling and Development, 63*(4), 258–259.

Hock, E., Morgan, K., & Hock, M. D. (1985). Employment decisions made by mothers of infants. *Psychology of Women Quarterly, 9*(3), 383–402.

Hodge, R. W., Siegel, P. M., & Rossi, P. H. (1964). Occupational prestige in the United States: 1925–1963. *American Journal of Sociology, 70*, 286–302.

Hodgson, M., & Cramer, S. H. (1977). The relationship between selected self-estimated and measured abilities in adolescents. *Measurement and Evaluation in Guidance, 10*(2), 98–105.

Hoffman, D. (1973). Teaching self-understanding for productive living. *N.A.S.S.P. Bulletin, 57*, 74–79.

Hoffman, L. W. (1977). Changes in family roles, socialization and sex differences. *American Psychologist, 32*, 644–657.

Hoffman, L. W. (1979). Maternal employment: 1979. *American Psychologist, 34*(10), 859–865.

Hoffman, L. W. (1986). Work, family and the child. In M. S. Pallak and R. Perloff (Eds.), *Psychology and work: Productivity, change, and employment* (pp. 169–220). Washington, DC: American Psychological Association.

Hoffman, L. W. (1989). Effects of maternal employment in the two-parent family. *American Psychologist, 44*, 283–292.

Hoffreth, S. L., & Phillips, D. A. (1987). Child care in the United States; 1970 to 1985. *Journal of Marriage and the Family, 49*, 559–571.

Hogan, D. P., & Pazul, M. (1981). The career strategies of Black men. *Social Forces, 59*(4), 1217–1228.

Hogan, D. P., & Pazul, M. (1982). The occupational and earnings returns of education among black men in the North. *American Journal of Sociology, 87*(4), 905–920.

Hohenshil, T. H. (1980). The vocational education view of guidance and counseling. *Personnel and Guidance Journal, 58*(10), 668–669.

Holahan, C. K. (1981). Lifetime achievement patterns, retirement and life satisfaction of gifted aged women. *Journal of Gerontology, 36*(6), 741–749.

Holden, C. (1989). Academy panel joins the fray over job testing. *Science, 244*, 1036–1037.

Holland, J. L. (1963). Explanation of a theory of vocational choice: Vocational images and choices. *Vocational Guidance Quarterly, 11*, 232–239.

Holland, J. L. (1966). *The psychology of vocational choice*. Waltham, MA: Blaisdell.

Holland, J. L. (1970). *Self-directed search*. Palo Alto: CA: Consulting Psychologists Press.

Holland, J. L. (1972). The present status of a theory of vocational choice. In J. M. Whitely & A. Resnikoff (Eds.), *Perspectives on vocational development* (Chap. 3). Washington, DC: APGA Press.

Holland, J. L. (1973a). *Making vocational choices: A theory of careers*. Englewood Cliffs, NJ: Prentice-Hall.

Holland, J. L. (1973b). *Sexism, personal development, and the self-directed search*. Unpublished manuscript. Center for Social Organization of Schools, Johns Hopkins University.

Holland, J. L. (1982). *Some implications of career theory for adult development and aging*. Paper presented at the American Psychological Association, Washington, DC.

Holland, J. L. (1984). *A theory of careers: Some new developments and revisions*. Paper presented at the American Psychological Association Convention, Toronto, Canada.

Holland, J. L. (1985). *Making vocational choices. A theory of vocational personalities and work environments* (2nd ed.). Englewood cliffs, NJ: Prentice-Hall.

Holland, J. L., & Gottfredson, G. (1976). Using a typology of persons and environments to explain career: Some extensions and clarifications. *The Counseling Psychologist, 6*(3), 20–29.

Holland, J. L., & Gottfredson, G. D. (1990). *An Annotated Bibliography for Holland's theory of vocational personalities and work environments*. Baltimore, MD: Johns Hopkins University (July 19).

Holland, J. L., Gottfredson, G. D., & Baker, H. G. (1990). Validity of vocational aspirations and interest inventories: Extended, replicated, and reinterpreted. *Journal of Counseling Psychology, 37*, 337–342.

Holland, J. L., Gottfredson, G., & Nafziger, D. (1975). Testing the validity of some theoretical signs of vocational decision-making ability. *Journal of Counseling Psychology, 22*, 411–422.

Holland, J. L., Gottfredson, G., & Power, P. (1980). Some diagnostic scales for research in decision-making and personality: Identity, information, and barriers. *Journal of Personality and Social Psychology, 39*(6), 1191–1200.

Holland, J. L., & Holland, J. E. (1977). Distributions of personalities within occupations and fields of study. *Vocational Guidance Quarterly, 25*(3), 226–231.

Holland, J. L., Magoon, T. M., & Spokane, A. R. (1981). Counseling psychology: Career interventions, research, and theory. *Annual Review of Psychology, 32*, 279–300.

Holland, J. L., Viernstein, M. C., Kuo, H. M., Karweit, N. L., & Blum, S. D. (1970, November). A psychological classification of occupations (Report No. 90). Baltimore, MD: Johns Hopkins University, Center for the Study of Social Organization of Schools.

Holland, M. (1981). Relationships between vocational development and self-concept in sixth grade students. *Journal of Vocational Behavior, 18*, 228–236.

Hollander, M. A., & Parker, H. J. (1969). Occupational stereotypes and needs. Their relationship to vocational choice. *Vocational Guidance Quarterly, 18*, 91–98.

Hollander, M. A., & Parker, H. J. (1972). Occupational stereotypes and self-descriptions: Their relationship to vocational choice. *Journal of Vocational Behavior, 2*, 57–65.

Hollender, J. W. (1972). Differential parental influence on vocational interest development in adolescent males. *Journal of Vocational Behavior, 2*, 67–76.

Hollender, J. W. (1974). Development of vocational decisions during adolescence. *Journal of Counseling Psychology, 18*(3), 244–248.

Holmes, J. (1964). The presentation of test information to college freshmen. *Journal of Counseling Psychology, 11*, 54–58.

Holmes, T. H., & David, E. M. (Eds.). (1989). *Life change, life events, and illness: Selected papers*. New York: Praeger.

Holmes, T. H., & Rahe, R. H. (1967). The social readjustment rating scale. *Journal of psychosomatic research, 11*(2), 213–218.

Holms, V. L., & Esses, L. M. (1988). Factors influencing Canadian high school girls' career motivation. *Psychology of Women Quarterly, 12*, 313–328.

Holt, R. R. (1982). Occupational stress. In L. Goldberger & S. Breznitz (Eds.), *Handbook of stress: Theoretical and clinical aspects*. (pp. 419–444). New York: The Free Press.

Hopke, W. (1979). Work classification in ancient times. *Journal of Employment Counseling, 16*(1), 26–31.

Hoppock, R. (1935). *Job satisfaction*. New York: Harper.

Hoppock, R. (1950). Presidential address 1950. *Occupations, 28*, 497–499.

Hopson, B., & Scully, M. (1981). *Lifeskills teaching*. London: McGraw-Hill.

Hosford, R. E. (1970). Behavior counseling: A contemporary overview. *The Counseling Psychologist, 1*, 1–32.

Hotchkiss, L., & Borow, H. (1984). Sociological perspectives on career choice and attainment. In D. Brown & L. Brooks (Eds.), *Career choice and development: Applying contemporary theories to practice* (Chap. 6). San Francisco: Jossey-Bass.

Hotchkiss, L., & Borow, H. (1990). Sociological perspective on work and career development. In D. Brown and L. Brooks (Eds.), *Career choice and development. Applying contemporary theories to practice* (pp. 262–307). San Francisco: Jossey-Bass.

Hotelling, K., & Forrest, L. (1985). Gilligan's theory of sex-role development: A perspective for counseling. *Journal of Counseling and Development, 64*, 183–186.

House, E. A. (1986). Sex role orientation and marital satisfaction in dual- and one-provider couples. *Sex Roles, 14*(5/6), 245–259.

House, J. S. (1974). Effects of occupational stress on physical health. In J. O'Toole (Ed.), *Work and the quality of life*. Cambridge, MA: MIT Press.

Houseknecht, S. K., & Macke, A. S. (1981). Combining marriage and career: The marital adjustment of professional women. *Journal of Marriage and the Family, 43*(3), 651–661.

Houser, B. B., & Garvey, C. (1983). The impact of family, peers, and educational personnel upon career decision-making. *Journal of Vocational Behavior, 23*, 35–44.

Houser, R., Konstam, V., & Ham, M. A. (1990). Coping and marital satisfaction in dual career couples: Early stage dual career couples—wives as college students. *Journal of College Student Development, 31*, 325–329.

Howard, J. H., Rechnitzer, P. A., Cunningham, D. A., & Donner, A. P. (1986). Change in Type A behavior a year after retirement. *The Gerontologist, 26*(6), 643–649.

Hoyt, K. B. (1965). High school guidance and the specialty oriented student research program. *Vocational Guidance Quarterly, 13*, 229–236.

Hoyt, K. B. (1974). *An introduction to career education*. U.S. Office of Education Policy Paper. Washington, DC: U.S. Office of Education.

Hoyt, K. B. (1975). *Career education: Contributions to an evolving concept*. Salt Lake City: UT: Olympus.

Hoyt, K. B. (1978). Refining the concept of collaboration in career education. *Monographs on Career Education*. Washington, DC: U.S. Office of Education.

Hoyt, K. B. (1979). *A primer for career education*. Washington, DC: Office of Career Education.

Hoyt, K. B. (1980a). Contrasts between the guidance and the career education movements. In F. E. Burtnett (Ed.), *The school counselor's involvement in career education*. Falls Church, VA: American Personnel and Guidance Association.

Hoyt, K. B. (1980b). *Evaluation of K–12 career education: A status report*. Washington, DC: Office of Career Education.

Hoyt, K. B. (1982). Federal and state participation in career education: Past, present, and future. *Journal of Career Education, 9*(1), 5–15.

Hoyt, K. B. (1984). Career education and career guidance. *Journal of Career Education, 10*(3), 148–157.

Hoyt, K. B. (1985). Career guidance, educational reform, and career education. *Vocational Guidance Quarterly, 34*(1), 6–14.

Hoyt, K. B. (1988). The changing workforce: A review of projections—1986 to 2000. *The Career Development Quarterly, 37*, 31–39.

Hoyt, K. B., & Shylo, K. R. (1989). *Career education in transition: Trends and implications for the future*. Columbus, OH: The National Center for Research in Vocational Education.

Hudson Institute. (1987). *Workforce 2000: Work and workers for the 21st century*. Indianapolis, IN: Author.

Hudson, J., & Danish, S. J. (1980). The acquisition of information: An important life skill. *Personnel and Guidance Journal, 59*(3), 164–167.

Huffine, C. L., & Clausen, J. A. (1979). Madness and work: Short and long-term effects of mental illness on occupational careers. *Social forces. 57*(4), 1049–1062.

Hughes, C. M., Martinek, S. A., and Fitzgerald, L. F. (1985). Sex role attitudes and career choices: The role of children's self-esteem. *Elementary School Guidance and Counseling, 20*, 57–66.

Hulsart, R. (1983). *Employability skills study.* Denver, Colorado: Colorado Department of Education.

Humphrey, J. H. (1988). *Children and stress*. New York: AMS Press.

Hunt, E. E. (1970). *Career development K-6: A background paper or initial suggestions*. Paper presented to the Program Development Committee of the Cobb County Schools, GA.

Hunt, J. M. (1961). *Intelligence and experience*. New York: Ronald Press.

Hurk, W. M., & Kim, K. C. (1989). The "success" image of Asian Americans: Its validity and its practical and theoretical implications. *Ethnic and Racial Studies, 12*(4), 512–538.

Hurst, J. B., & Shepard, J. W. (1986). The dynamics of plant closings: An extended emotional rollercoaster ride. *Journal of Counseling and Development, 64*, 401–405.

Hutchinson, T., & Roe, A. (1968). Studies of occupational history: Part II. Attractiveness of occupational groups of the Roe system. *Journal of Counseling Psychology, 15*, 107–110.

Iaffaldano, M. T., & Muchinsky, P. M. (1985). Job satisfaction and job performance: A meta-analysis. *Psychological Bulletin, 97*(2), 251–273.

Ibrahim, F., & Herr, E. L. (1983). Attitude modification toward disability: Differential effects of two educational modes. *Rehabilitation Counseling Bulletin, 26*(8), 29–36.

Iglitzin, A. B. (1972). A child's-eye view of sex roles. *Today's Education, 61*, 23–25.

Illfelder, J. K. (1980). Fear of success, sex role attitudes, career salience, and anxiety level of college women. *Journal of Vocational Behavior, 16*, 7–17.

Institute for the Crippled and Disabled. (1967). *TOWER: Testing, orientation, and work evaluation in rehabilitation*. New York: Institute for the Crippled and Disabled.

International Labor Office. (1977a). *The ILO and the world of work*. Geneva, Switzerland: Author.

International Labor Office. (1977b). Why it's hard to cut youth unemployment. *ILO Information, 5*(1).

Ioracchini, E. V., & Aboud, R. R. (1981). A look at counselor education programs in light of Section 504 of the Rehabilitation Act of 1973. *Counselor Education and Supervision, 21*(2), 109–118.

Irvin, F. S. (1968). Personality characteristics and vocational identification. *Journal of Counseling Psychology, 15*, 329–333.

Isaacson, L. E. (1981). Counseling male midlife career changes. *Vocational Guidance Quarterly, 29*(4), 324–331.

Isaacson, L. E. (1985). *Basics of career counseling*. Boston, MA: Allyn and Bacon.

Jackson, A. W., & Hornbeck, D. W. (1989). Educating young adolescents. Why we must restructure middle schools. *American Psychologist, 44*(5), 831–836.

Jackson, D. N., & Williams, D. R. (1975). Occupational classification in terms of interest patterns. *Journal of Vocational Behavior, 6*, 269–280.

Jackson, E. L. (1988). Leisure constraints: A survey of past research. *Leisure Sciences, 10*, 203–215.

Jackson, G., Masnick, G., Bolton, R., Bartlett, S., & Pitkin, J. (1981). *Regional diversity: Growth in the United States, 1960–1990*. Boston: Auburn House.

Jackson, L. M. (1983). *Linear structural equation. Analysis of technical versus nontechnical career paths of engineers*. Unpublished doctoral dissertation, Pennsylvania State University.

Jacobs, R., & Solomon, T. (1977). Strategies for enhancing the prediction of job performance from job satisfaction. *Journal of Applied Psychology, 62*, 417–421.

James, F., III. (1963). Comment on Hilton's model of career decision making. *Journal of Counseling Psychology, 10*, 303–304.

James, L. R., Demaree, R. G., & Muliak, S. A. (1986). A note on validity generalization procedures. *Journal of Applied Psychology, 71*(3), 440–450.

Janis, I., & Mann, L. (1977). *Decision-making: A psychological analysis of conflict, choice, and commitment*. New York: The Free Press.

Janoff-Bulman, R., & Freise, I. (1983). A theoretical perspective for understanding reactions to victimization. *Journal of Social Issues, 39*, 1–17.

Jaramillo, P. T., Zapata, J. T., & MacPherson, R. (1982). Concerns of college-bound Mexican-American students. *The School Counselor, 29*(5), 375–380.

Jencks, C. (1972). *Inequality.* New York: Harper & Row.

Jenkins, L. E. (1989). The Black family and academic achievement. In G. L. Berry & J. K. Asamen (Eds.), *Black students: Psychosocial issues and academic achievement*. Newbury Park: Sage Publications.

Jenkins, S. R. (1989). Longitudinal prediction of women's careers: Psychological, behavioral, and social-structural influences, *Journal of Vocational Behavior, 34*(2), 204–235.

Jenner, J. R. (1986). A measure of chronic organizational stress. *Psychological Reports, 58*, 543–546.

Jensen, A. R. (1984). Test validity: *g* versus specificity doctrine. *Journal of Social Biological Structures, 7*, 93–118.

Jensen, A. R. (1988). Review of the Armed Services Vocational Aptitude Battery. In J. T. Kapes & M. M. Mastie (Eds.), *A counselor's guide to career assessment instruments* (pp. 58–62). Washington, DC: National Career Development Association.

Jepsen, D. A. (1974). Vocational decision-making strategy-types. An exploratory study. *Vocational Guidance Quarterly, 23*(2), 17–23.

Jepsen, D. A. (1984a). The developmental perspective on vocational behavior: A review of theory and research. In S. D. Brown & R. W. Lent (Eds.), *Handbook of counseling psychology* (pp. 178–215). New York: Wiley.

Jepsen, D. A. (1984b). Relationship between career development theory and practice. In N. C. Gysbers (Ed.), *Designing careers, counseling to enhance education, work and leisure* (Chap. 5). San Francisco: Jossey-Bass.

Jepsen, D. A. (1985). Review of Kuder Occupational Interest Inventory, Form DD. *Measurement and Evaluation in Counseling and Development, 17*(4), 217–219.

Jepsen, D. A. (1989). Adolescent career decision processes as coping responses for the social environment. In R. Hanson (Ed.), *Career development: Preparing for the 21st century* (Chapter 6). Knoxville, TN: The University of Tennessee, Department of Technological and Adult Education.

Jepson, D. A. & Dilley, J. S. (1974). Vocational decision-making models: A review and comparative analysis. *Review of Education Research, 44*(3), 331–349.

Jepsen, D. A., Dustin, R., & Miars, R. (1982). The effects of problem-solving training on adolescents' career exploration and career decision making. *The Personnel and Guidance Journal, 61*, 149–153.

Jepsen, D. A., & Prediger, D. J. (1981). Dimensions of adolescent career development: A multi-instrument analysis. *Journal of Vocational Behavior, 19*, 350–368.

Joelson, L., & Wahlquist, L. (1987). The psychological meaning of job insecurity and job loss. *Social Science and Medicine, 25*(2), 179–192.

Johnson, C. D., & Johnson, S. K. (1982). Competency based training of career development specialists or "Let's Get off the Calf Path." *Vocational Guidance Quarterly, 32*(4), 327–335.

Johnson, C. S., & Sampson, J. P., Jr. (1985). Training counselors to use computers. *Journal of Career Development, 12*(2), 118–128.

Johnson, G. J. (1990). Underemployment, underpayment, and self-esteem among Black men. *The Journal of Black Psychology, 16*(2), 23–44.

Johnson, M., Jr., Busacker, W. E., & Bowman, F. Q., Jr. (1961). *Junior high school guidance*. New York: Harper & Brothers.

Johnson, N. (1980). A free enterprise elementary career education project. *The School Counselor, 27*(4), 315–317.

Johnson, R. G. (1970). Simulation techniques in career development. *American Vocational Journal, 45*, 30–32.

Johnson, R. H. (1978). Individual styles of decision-making: A theoretical model for counseling. *Personnel and Guidance Journal, 56*, 530–536.

Johnson, R. H., & Myrick, R. D. (1971). MOLD: A new approach to career decision making. *Vocational Guidance Quarterly, 21*(1), 48–53.

Johnson, R. P., & Riker, H. C. (1981). Retirement maturity: A valuable concept for preretirement counselors. *Personnel and Guidance Journal 59*(5), 291–295.

Johnson, R. W., & Hoese, J. (1988). Career planning concerns of SCII clients. *The Career Development Quarterly, 36*, 251–258.

Johnston, J. A., Buescher, K. L., & Heppner, M. J. (1988). Computerized career information and guidance systems: Caveat emptor. *Journal of Counseling and Development, 67*, 39–41.

Joint Economic Committee, U.S. Congress. (1980, November). *Human resources and demographics: Characteristics of people and policy.* Washington, DC: Author.

Jolly, D. L., Grimm, J. W., & Wozniak, P. R. (1990). Patterns of sex desegregation in managerial and professional specialty fields, 1950–1980. *Work and Occupations, 17*, 30–54.

Jones, B., & Krumboltz, J. D. (1970). Stimulating vocational exploration through film-mediated problems. *Journal of Counseling Psychology, 17*, 107.

Jones, G., & Chenery, M. (1980). Multiple subtypes among vocationally undecided college students: A model and assessment instrument. *Journal of Counseling Psychology, 27*, 469–477.

Jones, G. B., Helliwell, C. B., & Ganschow, L. H. (1975). A planning model for career guidance: *Vocational Guidance Quarterly, 23*(3), 220–226.

Jones, L. K. (1977). *Occu-sort: A self-guided career exploration system*. Raleigh, NC: North Carolina State University, School of Education, Office of Publications.

Jones, L. K. (1979). Occu-sort: Development and evaluation of an occupational card sort system. *Vocational Guidance Quarterly, 28*(1), 56–62.

Jones, L. K. (1980a). Holland's typology and the new guide for occupational exploration. Bridging the gap. *Vocational Guidance Quarterly, 29*(1), 70–75.

Jones, L. K. (1980b). Issues in developing an occupational card sort. *Measurement and Evaluation in Guidance, 12*(4), 206–215.

Jones, L. K. (1981). *Occu-sort* (2nd ed.). Monterey, CA: Publishers Test Service, McGraw-Hill.

Jones, L. K. (1983). A comparison of two self-directed career guidance instruments: Occu-sort and Self-Directed Search. *The School Counselor, 30*, 204–211.

Jones, L. K. (1990). The Career Key: An investigation of the reliability and validity of its scales and its helpfulness to college students. *Measurement and Evaluation in Counseling and Development, 23*, 67–76.

Jones, L. K., & DeVault, R. M. (1979). Evaluation of a self-guided career exploration system: The Occu-sort. *The School Counselor, 26*(5), 334–341.

Jones, L. K., Gorman, S., & Schroeder, C. G. (1989). A comparison between the SDS and the Career Key among career undecided college students. *The Career Development Quarterly, 37*, 334–344.

Jones, L. M., & McBride, J. L. (1980). Sex role stereotyping in children as a function of maternal employment. *Journal of Social Psychology, 3*(2), 219–223.

Jordaan, J. P. (1963). Exploratory behavior: The formation of self and occupational concepts. In D. Super, R. Starishevsky, R. Matlin, & J. P. Jordaan (Eds.), *Career development: Self-concept theory*. New York: College Entrance Examination Board.

Jordaan, J. P., & Heyde, M. (1979). *Vocational maturity during the high school years*. New York: Teachers College Press.

Jung, C. G. (1933). *Psychological Types*. New York: Harcourt.

Jung, C. G. (1966). *Analytical Psychology.* New York: Moffat, Yard.

Junge, D. A., Daniels, M. H., & Karmos, J. S. (1984). Personnel managers' perceptions of requisite basic skills. *Vocational Guidance Quarterly, 33*(20), 138–146.

Jurgensen, C. E. (1978). Job preferences (What makes a job good or bad?) *Journal of Applied Psychology, 63*, 267–276.

Justice, B., Gold, R. S., & Klein, J. P. (1981). Life events and burnout. *Journal of Psychology, 108*, 219–226.

Kaback, G. R. (1960). Occupational information in elementary education. *Vocational Guidance Quarterly, 9*, 55–59.

Kaback, G. R. (1966). Occupational information for groups of elementary school children. *Vocational Guidance Quarterly, 14*, 163–168.

Kagan, N. (1977). Presidential address, division 17. *The Counseling Psychologist, 7*, 4–7.

Kahnweiler, J. B., & Kahnweiler, W. M. (1980). A dual-career family workshop for college undergraduates. *Vocational Guidance Quarterly, 28*(3), 225–230.

Kaiser, M. A., Peters, G. R., & Babchuk, N. (1982). When priests retire. *The Gerontologist, 22*(1), 89–94.

Kalder, D. R., & Zytowski, D. G. (1969). A maximizing model of occupational decision-making. *Personnel and Guidance Journal 47*, 781–788.

Kammer, P. P. (1985). Career and life-style expectations of rural eighth-grade students. *The School Counselor, 33*(1), 18–25.

Kamouri, A. L., & Cavanaugh, J. C. (1986). The impact of preretirement education programmes on worker's preretirement socialization. *Journal of Occupational Behavior, 7*, 245–256.

Kanchier, C., & Unruh, W. R. (1988). The career cycle meets the life cycle. *Career Development Quarterly, 37*(2), 127–137.

Kando, T. M., & Summers, W. C. (1971). The impact of work on leisure: Towards a paradigm and research strategy. *Pacific Sociological Review, 14*, 310–327.

Kane, S. T. (1989). A review of the COPS Interest Inventory. *Journal of Counseling and Development, 67*, 361–363.

Kantor, R. M. (1977a). *Men and women of the corporation*. New York: Basic Books.

Kantor, R. M. (1977b). *Work and family in the United States: A critical review and agenda for research and policy.* New York: Russell Sage.

Kanzaki, G. A. (1976). Fifty years of stability in the social status of occupations. *Vocational Guidance Quarterly, 25*, 101–105.

Kapes, J. T., & Mastie, M. M. (1982). *A counselor's guide to vocational guidance instruments*. Falls Church, VA: National Vocational Guidance Association.

Kapes, J. T., & Mastie, M. M. (Eds.) (1988). *A counselor's guide to career assessment instruments* (2nd Ed.). Alexandria, VA: The National Career Development Association.

Kapes, J. T., & Strickler, R. T. (1975). A longitudinal study of change in work values between ninth and twelfth grade as related to high school curriculums. *Journal of Vocational Behavior, 6*(1), 81–93.

Kaplan, S. P. (1984). Rehabilitation counseling students' perceptions of obese male and female clients. *Rehabilitation Counseling Bulletin, 27*(3), 172–181.

Kaplon, A. J., & Gordon, M. S. (1967). A critique of war and peace: A simulation game. *Social Education, 31*, 383–387.

Karayanni, M. (1981). Career maturity of emotionally maladjusted high school students. *Vocational Guidance Quarterly, 29*(3), 213–220.

Karpicke, S. (1980). Perceived and real sex differences in college students' career planning. *Journal of Counseling Psychology, 27*(3), 240–245.

Karre, I. (1976). Self-concept and sex role stereotype: An empirical study with children. *Dissertation Abstracts International, 36*, 4850–4851.

Kassera, W., & Russo, T. (1987). Factor analysis of personality preferences and vocational interests. *Psychological Reports, 60*, 63–66.

Kassner, M. (1981). Will both spouses have careers? Predictions of preferred traditional or egalitarian marriage among university students. *Journal of Vocational Behavior, 18*, 340–355.

Katchadourian, H. A., & Boli, J. (1985). *Careerism and intellectualism among college students: Patterns of academic and career choice in the undergraduate years*. San Francisco: Jossey-Bass.

Katz, M. (1958). *You: Today and tomorrow*. Princeton, NJ: Educational Testing Service.

Katz, M. (1963). *Decisions and values: A rationale for secondary school guidance*. New York: College Entrance Examination Board.

Katz, M. (1969). Can computers make guidance decisions for students? *College Board Review, 13*, 13–17.

Katz, M. (1973). The name and nature of vocational guidance. In H. Borow (Ed.), *Career guidance for a new page* (pp. 8233–134). Boston: Houghton Mifflin.

Katz, M. (1980). SIGI: An interactive aid to career decision-making. *Journal of College Student Personnel, 21*(1), 34–40.

Katz, M. (1986). Career and family values for males and females. *College Student Journal, 20*(1), 66–76.

Katz, M. R. (1988). Computerized guidance and the structure of occupational information. *Prospects, 18*, 515–525.

Katz, M., Norris, L., & Pears, L. (1978). Simulated occupational choice: A diagnostic measure of competencies in career decision-making. *Measurement and Evaluation in Guidance, 10*, 222–232.

Katz, R. L. (1974). Skills of an effective administrator. *Harvard Business Review, 52*, 90–102.

Katzell, R. A. (1964). Personal values, job satisfaction, and job behavior. In H. Borow (Ed.), *Man in a world at work*. Boston: Houghton Mifflin.

Katzell, R. A. (1979). Changing attitudes toward work. In C. Ken & J. M. Rosow (Eds.), *Work in America: The decade ahead*. New York: Van Nostrand.

Katzman, S. (1989). A response to the challenge of the year 2000. In R. Houson (Ed.), *Career development preparing for the 21st century* (Chapter 2). Knoxville: University of Tennessee, Department of Technological and Adult Education.

Kauffman, J., Schaefer, C., Lewis, M. V., Steven, D. W., & House, E. W. (1967). *The role of the secondary school in the preparation of youth for employment*. University Park, PA: Institute for Human Resources.

Kaufman, F. A., Harrel, G., Milam, C. P., Woolverton, N., & Miller, J. (1986). The nature, role, and influence of mentors in the lives of gifted adults. *Journal of Counseling and Development, 64*, 576–578.

Kaufman, G. M., & Beehr, T. A. (1986). Interactions between job stressors and social support: Some counterintuitive results. *Journal of Applied Psychology, 71*(3), 522–526.

Kaufman, R. L., & Spilerman, S. (1982). The age structure of occupations and jobs. *American Journal of Sociology, 87*, 827–851.

Kazanas, H. C. (1978). *Affective work competencies for vocational education*. Columbus, OH: National Center for Research in Vocational Education, Ohio State University.

Kegan, R. (1982). *The evolving self: Problems and process in human development*. Cambridge, MA: Harvard University Press.

Keith, P. M. (1981). Sex-role attitudes, family plans, and career orientations: Implications for counseling. *Vocational Guidance Quarterly, 29*(3), 244–252.

Keith, P. M., Goudy, W. J., & Powers, E. A. (1981). Employment characteristics and psychological well-being of men in two-job families. *Psychological Reports, 49*, 975–978.

Keith, P. M., & Schafer, R. B. (1980). Depression in one and two job families. *Psychological Reports, 47*(2), 669–670.

Keller, J. W., Piotrowski, C., & Rabold, F. L. (1990). Determinants of career selection in undergraduates. *Journal of College Student Development, 31*, 276–277.

Kelly, G. A. (1955). *The psychology of personal constructs*. New York: Norton.

Kelly, J. R. (1981). Leisure interaction and the social dialectic. *Social Forces, 60*(2), 304–322.

Kenzler, B. (1983). A model for paraprofessionals in career planning. *Journal of College Placement, 44*(1), 54–61.

Kerr, B. A. (1982). The setting of career counseling. *Vocational Guidance Quarterly, 30*(3), 210–218.

Kerr, B. A. (1983). Raising the career aspirations of gifted girls. *Vocational Guidance Quarterly, 32*(1), 37–43.

Kessler, R. C. & Clary, P. D. (1978). Social class and psychological distress. *American Sociological Review, 45*, 463–478.

Kessler, R. C., & McRae, J. A. (1982). The effects of wives' employment on the mental health of married men and women. *American Sociological Review, 47*, 216–227.

Khan, S. B., Alvi, S. A., Shaukat, N., Hussain, M. A., & Baig, T. (1990). A study of the validity of Holland's theory in a non-western culture. *Journal of Vocational Behavior, 36*, 132–146.

Kidd, J. M. (1982). Self and occupational concepts in occupational preferences and entry into work. Unpublished doctoral dissertation, National Institute of Careers Education and Counseling, Cambridge.

Kieffer, J. A. (1980). Counselors and the older worker: An overview. *Journal of Employment Counseling, 17*(1), 8–16.

Kiesler, D. J. (1971). Experimental designs in psychotherapy research. In A. E. Bergin & S. J. Garfield (Eds.), *Handbook of psychotherapy and behavior change*. New York: Wiley.

Kimball, J. C. (1988). Career interest search: A prototype computer-assisted occupational interest inventory for functionally illiterate adults. *Journal of Employment Counseling, 25*, 180–185.

Kimmel, D. C., & Weiner, I. B. (1985). *Adolescence: A developmental transition*. Hillsdale, N.J.: Lawrence Erlbaum.

King, S. (1989a). Sex differences in a causal model of career maturity. *Journal of Counseling and Development, 68*, 208–215.

King, S. (1989b). Unemployment and mental health in French Canada: *Journal of Counseling and Development, 67*, 358–360.

Kingson, E. R. (1981). Retirement circumstances of very early retirees: A life cycle perspective. *Aging and Work, 4*(3), 161–174.

Kinicki, A. J., & Griffeth, R. W. (1985). The impact of sex-role stereotypes on performance ratings and causal attributions of performance. *Journal of Vocational Behavior, 27*, 155–170.

Kinicki, A. J., & Latack, J. C. (1990). Explication of the construct of coping in the involuntary job loss. *Journal of Vocational Behavior, 36*, 339–360

Kinnick, B. C. (1968). Group discussion and group counseling applied to student problem solving. *The School Counselor, 15*, 350–356.

Kinicki, M. F., & Kammer, P. P. (1985). The effects of a career guidance program on the career maturity and self-concept of delinquent youth. *Journal of Vocational Behavior, 26*(2), 117–125.

Kinnier, R. T., Brigman, S. L., & Noble, F. C. (1990). Career indecision and family enmeshment. *Journal of Counseling and Development, 68*, 309–312.

Kinnier, R. T., & Krumboltz, J. D. (1984). Procedures for successful career counseling. In N. C. Gysbers (Ed.), *Designing careers* (pp. 307–335). San Francisco: Jossey-Bass.

Kirts, D. K., & Fisher, R. B. (1973). TRIPOD—A systems approach to career planning. *Journal of College Placement, 34*(4), 42–49.

Kitabachi, G., Murrell, P. H., & Crawford, R. L. (1979, December). Career/life planning for divorced women: An overview. *Vocational Guidance Quarterly, 27*(3), 137–145.

Kitano, H. H. L., & Matsushima, N. (1981). Counseling asian americans. In P. B. Pedersen, J. G. Draguns, W. J. Lonner, and J. E. Trimble (Eds.), *Counseling across cultures*. Honolulu: The University of Hawaii Press.

Kivligham, D. M., Jr., Hageseth, J. A., Tipton, R. M., & McGovern, T. V. (1981). Effects of matching treatment approaches and personality types in group vocational counseling. *Journal of Counseling Psychology, 28*(4), 315–320.

Kivligham, D. M., Jr., Johnson, B., & Fretz, B. (1987). Participant's perception of change mechanisms in career counseling groups: The role of emotional components in career problem solving. *Journal of Career Development, 14*(1), 35–44.

Kivligham, D. M., Jr., & Shapiro, R. M. (1987). Holland type as a predictor of benefit from self-help career counseling. *Journal of Counseling Psychology, 34*, 326–329.

Kjos, D. L. (1988). Job search activity patterns of successful and unsuccessful job seekers. *Journal of Employment Counseling, 25*, 4–6.

Klein, K. L., & Weiner, Y. (1977). Interest congruency as a moderator of the relationship between job tenure and job satisfaction and mental health. *Journal of Vocational Behavior, 10*, 91–98.

Kleinman, A. (1988). *Rethinking psychiatry. From cultural category to personal experience*. New York: The Free Press.

Kluth, L. J., & Muchinsky, P. M. (1984). Relative influence of sex composition on job desirability. *Journal of Vocational Behavior, 24*, 319–328.

Knapp, D. L., & Bedord, J. H. (1967). *The parent's role in career development*. Washington, DC: National Vocational Guidance Association.

Knapp, L., Knapp, R. R., Strand, L., & Michael, W. B. (1978). Comparative validity of the Career Ability Placement Survey (CAPS) and the General Aptitude Test Battery (GATB) for predicting high school course marks. *Educational and Psychological Measurement, 38*, 1053–1056.

Knapp, L., & Michael, W. B. (1980). Relationship of work values to corresponding academic success. *Educational and Psychological Measurement, 40*, 487–494.

Knapp, R. R., & Knapp, L. (1977). Interest changes and the classification of occupations. San Diego, CA: Edits.

Knefelkamp, L. L., & Slepitza, R. (1976). A cognitive developmental model of career development—an adaptation of the Perry scheme. *The Counseling Psychologist, 6*(3), 53–58.

Knickerbocker, B., & Chesney, M. (1975). *Life planning workshop* (Rev. ed.). University Counseling Center. Fort Collins, CO: Colorado State University.

Knieriam, K., & Stiffler, T. (1979). Peer outreach: Two viewpoints. *Journal of College Placement, 39*(2), 56–61.

Knowdell, R. L. (1982). Comprehensive Career programs in the workplace. *Vocational Guidance Quarterly, 30*(4), 323–326.

Knowdell, R. L. (1984). Career planning and development programs in the workplace. In N. C. Gysbers (Ed.), *Designing careers* (pp. 482–503). San Francisco: Jossey-Bass.

Knowles, M. (1977). The adult learner becomes less neglected. *Training, 14*(9), 16–18.

Koehn, S. (1978). Who's doing what? An update survey of career planning programs. *Journal of College Student Personnel, 18*, 523–526.

Koesling, J. W., & Healy, C. C. (1988). Review of USES General Aptitude Test Battery. In J. T. Kapes & M. M. Mastie (Eds.), *A counselor's guide to career assessment instruments* (pp. 69–74). Washington, DC: National Career Development Association.

Kohlan, R. G. (1968). Relationship between inventoried interests and inventoried needs. *Personnel and Guidance Journal, 46*, 592–598.

Kohlberg, L. (1968). The child as a moral philosopher. *Psychology Today, 2*(4), 24–30.

Kohn, M. L. (1977). *Class and conformity: A study in values* (2nd Ed.). Chicago: University of Chicago Press.

Koplik, E. K., & DeVito, A. J. (1986). Problems of freshmen: Comparison of classes of 1976 and 1986. *Journal of College Student Personnel, 27*(2), 124–131.

Koski, L. K., & Subich, L. M. (1985). Career and homemaking choices of college preparatory and vocational education students. *Vocational Guidance Quarterly, 34*(2), 116–123.

Kragie, E. R., Gerstein, M., & Lichtman, M. (1989). Do Americans plan for retirement? Some recent trends. *The Career Development Quarterly, 37*, 232–239.

Kram, K. E. (1984). *Mentoring at work: Developmental relationships in organizational life*. Glenview, IL: Scott, Foresman and Company.

Kram, K. E. (1985). Improving the mentoring process. *Training and Development Journal, 39*(4), 40–43.

Kramer, H. C., Berger, F., & Miller, G. (1974). Student concerns and sources of assistance. *Journal of College Student Personnel, 15*(5), 389–393.

Krasnow, B. S. (1968). Occupational information as a factor in the high school curriculum chosen by ninth-grade boys. *The School Counselor, 15*, 275–280.

Krau, E. (1981). Immigrants preparing for their second career: The behavioral strategies adopted. *Journal of Vocational Behavior, 18*, 289–303.

Krau, E. (1982). The vocational side of a new start in life: A career model of immigrants. *Journal of Vocational Behavior, 20*, 313–330.

Krau, E. (1984). Commitment to work in immigrants: Its functions and peculiarities. *Journal of Vocational Behavior, 24*, 329–339.

Krefting, L. A., & Berger, P. K. (1979). Masculinity-feminity perceptions of job requirements and their relationship to job-sex stereotypes. *Journal of Vocational Behavior, 15*, 164–174.

Kriedberg, B., Butcher, A. L., & White, K. M. (1978). Vocational role choice in second- and sixth-grade children. *Sex Roles, 4*, 145–181.

Krieshok, T. S., Arnold, J. J., Kuperman, B. D., & Schmitz, N. K. (1986). Articulation of career values: Comparison of three measures. *Journal of Counseling Psychology, 33*(4), 475–478.

Krug, S. E. (1984). *Psychware*. Kansas City, MO: Test Corporation of America.

Krumboltz, J. D. (1979). A social learning theory of career decision making. In A. M. Mitchell, G. G. Jame, & J. D. Krumboltz (Eds.), *Social learning and career decision making* (pp. 19–49). Cranston, RI: Carrole Press.

Krumboltz, J. D. (1983). *Private rules in career decision making*. Columbus, OH: The National Center for Research in Vocational Education.

Krumboltz, J. D. (1985). Presuppositions underlying computer use in career counseling. *Journal of Career Development, 12*(2), 165–170.

Krumboltz, J. D. (1988a). *Career Beliefs Inventory.* Palo Alto, CA: Consulting Psychologists Press.

Krumboltz, J. D. (1988b). Review of Vocational Interest Inventory. In J. T. Kapes & M. M. Mastie (Eds.), *A counselor's guide to career assessment instruments* (pp. 137–142). Washington, DC: National Career Development Association.

Krumboltz, J. D., Kinnier, R. T., Rude, S. S., Scherba, D. S., & Hamel, D. A. (1986). Teaching a rational approach to decision making: Who benefits most? *Journal of Vocational Behavior, 29*, 1–6.

Krumboltz, J. D., Mitchell, A., & Gellat, H. G. (1975). Applications of social learning theory of career selection. *Focus on Guidance, 8*(3), 1–16.

Krumboltz, J. D., & Schroeder, W. W. (1965). Promoting career planning through reinforcement and models. *Personnel and Guidance Journal, 44*, 19–26.

Krumboltz, J. D. & Thoresen, C. E. (1964). The effect of behavioral counseling in groups and individual settings on information-seeking behavior. *Journal of Counseling Psychology, 11*, 324–333.

Krumboltz, J. D. & Menetee, M. (1980). Counseling psychology of the future. *The Counseling Psychologist, 8*(4), 46–48.

Krumboltz, J. D., Mitchell, A. M., & Jones, G. B. (1976). A social learning theory of career selection. *The Counseling Psychologist, 6*, 71–81.

Krumboltz, J. D., Varenhorst, B., & Toresen, C. E. (1967). Non-verbal factors in effectiveness of models in counseling. *Journal of Counseling Psychology, 14*, 412–418.

Kryger, G. R., & Shikiar, T. (1978). Sexual discrimination in the use of letters of recommendation: A case of reverse discrimination. *Journal of Applied Psychology, 63*(3), 309–314.

Kubler-Ross, E. (1969). *On death and dying*. New York: Macmillan.

Kuhlman, G. A. (1988). Computer and video applications in career services programs. *The Career Development Quarterly, 37*, 177–182.

Kuhlman-Harrison, J., & Neely, M. A. (1980). Discriminant validity of career development inventory scales in grade 10 students. *Educational and Psychological Measurement, 40*, 475–478.

Kuhlmann, T. M. (1990). Coping with occupational stress among urban bus and tram drivers. *Journal of Occupational Psychology, 63*, 89–96.

Kuhn, T. S. (1962). *The structure of scientific revolutions*. Chicago: University of Chicago Press.

Kurolesky, W. P., Wright, D. E., & Juarez, R. Z. (1971). Status projections and ethnicity: A comparison of Mexican American, Negro, and Anglo youth. *Journal of Vocational Behavior, 1*, 137.

Kurpius, D., Burello, L., & Rozecki, T. (1990). Strategic planning in human service organizations. *Counseling and Human Development, 22*(9), 1–12.

Kurtz, N. R., Googins, B., & Howard, W. C. (1984). Measuring the success of occupational alcoholism programs. *Journal of Studies on Alcohol, 45*, 33–45.

Kurtz, R. R. (1974). Using a transactional analysis format in vocational group counseling. *Journal of College Students Personnel, 15*, 447–451.

Kutscher, R. E. (1989). Outlook 2000: Issues and implications. *Occupational Outlook Quarterly, 33*(3), 38–40.

LaFitte, P. C., & Phillips, B. (1980). Assertive job hunting: A lesson in integration. *Journal of College Student Personnel, 21*, 92–93.

LaGory, M., & Magnani, R. J. (1979). Structural correlates of black-white occupational differentiation: Will U. S. regional differences in status remain? *Social Problems, 27*(2), 157–168.

Laing, J., Lamb, R. R., & Prediger, D. J. (1982). An application of Strong's validity criteria to basic interest scales. *Journal of Vocational Behavior, 20*, 203–214.

Lamb, R. R., & Prediger, D. J. (1979). Criterion-related validity of sex-restrictive and unisex interest scales: A comparison. *Journal of Vocational Behavior, 15*, 231–246.

Lamb, S. H. (1980). Student interchange with business and industry. *Journal of College Student Personnel, 21*, 176–177.

Lance, L. M., Lourie, J., & Mayo, C. (1979). Needs of reentry university students. *Journal of College Student Personnel, 20*, 479–485.

Land, T. (1981). Global strategy: Confronting alcoholism at the workplace. *Alcoholism, 1*(6), 41–42.

Landau, J., Somers, P., & Amoss, L. M. (1984). Do career centers deliver? *Journal of Career Planning and Employment, 46*(4), 49–52.

Landy, F. J. (1989). *Psychology of work behavior* (4th ed.). Pacific Grove, CA: Brooks/Cole.

Lange, S., & Coffman, J. S. (1981). Integrative test interpretation. A career counselor tool. *Vocational Guidance Quarterly, 30*(1), 73–77.

Laramore, D. (1979). Career counseling for families (and other multi-age groups). *The Personnel and Guidance Journal, 57*(10), 555–556.

Laramore, D., & Thompson, J. (1970). Career experiences appropriate to elementary school grades. *The School Counselor, 17*, 262–263.

Larson, L. M., & Heppner, P. (1985). The relationship of problem-solving appraisal to career decision and indecision. *Journal of Vocational Behavior, 26*, 55–65.

Larson, L. M., Heppner, P. P., Ham, T., & Dugan, K. (1988). Investigating multiple subtypes of career indecision through cluster analysis. *Journal of Counseling Psychology, 35*, 439–446.

Lasker, H., Moore, J., & Simpson, E. L. (1980). *Adult development and approaches to learning*. Washington, DC: National Institute of Education.

Lassalle, A. D., & Spokane, A. R. (1987). Patterns of early labor force participation of American women. *The Career Development Quarterly, 36*(1), 55–65.

Lassiter, R. A. (1981, December). *Work evaluation and work adjustment for severely handicapped people. A counseling approach* (pp. 13–18). Paper presented at the International Roundtable for the Advancement of Counseling Consultation on Career Guidance and Higher Education, Cambridge, England.

Latack, J. C. (1986). Coping with job stress: Measures and future directions for scale development. *Journal of Applied Psychology, 71*(3), 377–385.

Lattanzi, M. E. (1981). Coping with work-related losses. *Personnel and Guidance Journal, 59*(6), 350–351.

Laudeman, K. A., & Griffith, P. (1978). Holland's theory of vocational choice and postulated value dimensions. *Educational and Psychological Measurement, 38*, 1165–1175.

LaVan, H., Mathys, N., & Drehmer, D. (1983). A look at the counseling practices of major U.S. corporations. *Personnel Administrator, 28*(6), 143–145.

Lawler, E. E. (1973). *Motivation in work organizations*. Monterey, CA: Brooks/Cole.

Lawler, E. E. (1982). Strategies for improving the quality of work life. *American Psychologist, 37*(5), 486–493.

Lazarus, A. A. (1976). *Multimodal behavior therapy*. New York: Springer.

Lazarus, R. S., & Folkman, S. (1984). *Stress, appraisal and coping*. New York: Behavioral Science Books.

Leclair, S. W. (1982). The dignity of leisure. *The School Counselor, 29*(4), 289–296.

Lee, C. C. (1984). Predicting the career choice attitudes of rural black, white, and native american high school students. *Vocational Guidance Quarterly, 32*(3), 177–184.

Lee, J. A., & Clemons, T. (1985). Factors affecting employment decisions about older workers. *Journal of Applied Psychology, 70*(4), 785–788.

Lee, R. (1982). The moderating effect of sex on the prediction of job satisfaction in the public sector. *Journal of Employment Counseling, 19*(1), 34–44.

Lee, R., Mueller, L., & Miller, K. J. (1981). Sex, wage-earner status, occupational level, and job satisfaction. *Journal of Vocational Behavior, 18*, 362–373.

Lee, S. S., & Rosen, E. A. (1984). Employee counseling services: Ethical dilemmas. *Personnel and Guidance Journal, 62*(5), 276–280.

Lefkowitz, J., & Brigando, L. (1980). The redundancy of work alienation and job satisfaction: Some evidence of convergent and discriminant validity. *Journal of Vocational Behavior, 16*, 115–131.

Lefstein, L. M., & Lipsitz, J. (1986). *3:00 to 6:00 p.m.: Program for young adolescents*. Chapel Hill, NC: Center for Early Adolescence, University of North Carolina at Chapel Hill.

Legislative Provisions for the Improvement of Guidance Programs and Personnel Development. (1979). *Various Modules*. Columbus, OH: National Center for Research in Vocational Education.

Leibowitz, Z. B., Farren, C., & Kaye, B. L. (1986). *Designing career development systems*. San Francisco: Jossey-Bass.

Leibowitz, Z. B., & Schlossberg, N. K. (1981). Training managers for their role in a career development system. *Training and Development Journal, 35*, 72–79.

Leigh, J. P. (1987). The effects of unemployment on the probability of suffering a disability. *Work and Occupations, 14*(3), 347–367.

Leiter, M. P. (1988). Burnout as a function of communication patterns. *Group and Organizational Studies, 13*, 111–128.

Leiter, M. P., & Meechan, K. A. (1986). Role structure and burnout in the field of human services. *The Journal of Applied Behavioral Science, 22*(1), 47–52.

Lemkau, J. P. (1979). Personality and background characteristics of women in male-dominated occupations: A review. *Psychology of Women Quarterly, 4*(2), 221–240.

Lemkau, J. P. (1984). Men in female-dominated occupations: Distinguishing personality and background features. *Journal of Vocational Behavior, 24*, 110–122.

Lent, R. W., & Hackett, G. (1987). Career self-efficacy: Empirical status and future directions. *Journal of Vocational Behavior, 30*, 347–382.

Lent, R. W., Larkin, K. C., & Hasegawa, C. S. (1986). Effects of a "focused interest" career course approach for college students. *Vocational Guidance Quarterly, 34*(3), 151–159.

Leonard, G. E. (1972). Career guidance in the elementary school. *Elementary School Guidance and Counseling, 6*, 283–286.

Leonard, G. E., & Brooks, L. P. (1980). Developmental career guidance for girls and young women. In E. Waters & J. Goodman (Eds.), *Resocializing sex roles: A guide for education*. Washington, DC: The National Vocational Guidance Association.

Leonards, J. T. (1981). Corporate psychology: An answer to occupational mental health. *Personnel and Guidance Journal. 30*(1), 47–51.

Leong, F. T. L., & Sedlacek, W. E. (1986). A comparison of international and U.S. students' preferences for help sources. *Journal of College Student Personnel, 27*, 426–430.

Lerner, R. M. (1986). *Concepts and Theories of Human Development* (2nd ed.). New York: Random House.

Lester, J. N., & Frugoli, P. (1989). Career and occupational information: current needs, future directions. In D. Broan & C. A. Minor (Eds.), *Working in America; A status report on planning and problems* (pp. 60–81). Alexandria, VA: National Career Development Association.

Leveson, I. (1980). Technology and society in the next thirty years: We have manageable choices. In C. S. Sheppart & D. C. Carroll (Eds), *Working in the twenty-first century* (pp. 39–48). New York: Wiley.

Levi, L. (1984). *Stress in industry*. Geneva, Switzerland: International Labor Office.

Levin, E. L. (1986). A support group for midlife students reentering college. *Journal of College Student Personnel, 27*(4), 371–372.

Levine, A. (1976). Educational and occupational choice: A synthesis of literature from sociology and psychology. *Journal of Consumer Research, 2*, 276–289.

Levine, H. Z. (1985). Consensus on career planning. *Personnel, 62*(11), 67–72.

Levine, M. L. (1988). *Age discrimination and the mandatory retirement controversy*. Baltimore: Johns Hopkins University Press.

Levine, S. V. (1979). The psychological and social effects of youth unemployment. *Children Today, 8*(6), 6–9, 40.

Levine, Z. L. (1985). Consensus on outplacement and severance pay practices. *Personnel, 62*(7), 13–21.

Levinson, D. J. (1977). The mid-life transition: A period in adult psychosocial development. *Psychiatry, 40*, 99–112.

Levinson, D. J. (1986). A conception of adult development, *American Psychologist, 41*, 3–13.

Levinson, D. J., Darrow, C. N., Klein, E. B., Levinson, M. H., & McKee, B. (1978). *The seasons of a man's life*. New York: Knopf.

Levinson, E. M. (1985). Vocational and career-oriented secondary school programs for the emotionally disturbed. *The School Counselor, 33*(2), 100–106.

Levinson, E. M. (1990). Vocational assessment involvement and use of the Self-Directed Search by school psychologists. *Psychology in the Schools, 27*, 217–228.

Levitan, S. A. (1987). Beyond "trendy" forecasts: The next 10 years for work. *The Futurist, 21*(6), 28–33.

Levitan, S., Johnson, W. & Taggart, R. (1974). Manpower programs and black progress. *Manpower, 6*(6), 2–10.

Leviton, L. C., & Whitely, S. E. (1981). Job seeking patterns of female and male Ph.D. recipients. *Psychology of Women Quarterly, 5*(5), 690–701.

Levy, D. A., Kaler, S. R., & Schall, M. (1988). An empirical investigation of role schemata: Occupations and personality characteristics. *Psychological Reports, 63*, 3–14.

Lewin-Epstein, N. (1989). Work characteristics and ill-health. Gender differences in Israel. *Work and occupations, 16*(1), 80–104.

Lewis, J. A., & Lewis, M. D. (1986). *Counseling programs for employees in the workplace*. Belmont, CA: Brooks/Cole.

Lewis, J. M., & Looney, J. G. (1988). *The long struggle: Well-functioning working-class Black families*. New York: Brunner/Mazel.

Ley, R. (1966). Labor turnover as a function of worker difference. *Journal of Applied Psychology, 50*(6), 497–500.

Lichter, D. (1988). Race, employment hardship and inequality in American non-metropolitan south. *American Sociological Review, 54*, 436–446.

Lieberman, L., & Lieberman, L. (1983). Second career concept. *Aging and Work, 6*(4), 277–289.

Liem, R., & Rayman, P. (1982). Health and social costs of unemployment. *American Psychologist, 37*(10), 1116–1123.

Lipman-Blumen, J., & Leavitt, H. S. (1977). Vicarious and direct achievement patterns in adulthood. In N. K. Schlossberg & A. D. Entine (Eds.), *Counseling adults*. Monterey, CA: Brooks/Cole.

Lipsett, L. (1962). Social factors in vocational development. *Personnel and Guidance Journal, 40*, 432–437.

Lipsett, L. (1980a). A career counselor in industry. *Vocational Guidance Quarterly, 28*(4), 269–273.

Lipsett, L. (1980b). Career path charts as counseling aids. *Vocational Guidance Quarterly, 30*(4), 360–368.

Liptak, J. (1990). Preretirement counseling: Integrating the leisure planning component. *The Career Development Quarterly, 38*, 360–367.

Lister, J. L., & McKenzie, D. H. (1966). A framework for the improvement of test interpretation in counseling. *Personnel and Guidance Journal, 45*, 61–66.

Livingston, J. S. (1970). The troubled transition: Why college and university graduates have difficulty developing careers in business. *Journal of College Placement, 30*, 34–41.

Lobodzinska, B. (1986). Post-war immigration in the United States and the state of Minnesota. *International Migration, 24*(2), 411–439.

LoBosco, M. (1985). Consensus on training programs. *Personnel, 62*(12), 55–59.

LoCascio, R. (1967). Continuity and discontinuity in vocational development theory. *Personnel and Guidance Journal, 46*, 32–36.

Locke, D. C. (1988). Review of Career Development Inventory. In J. T. Kapes & M. M. Mastie (Eds.), *A counselor's guide to career assessment instruments* (pp. 175–179). Washington, DC: National Career Development Association.

Locksley, A. (1980). On the effects of wives' employment on marital adjustment and companionship. *Journal of Marriage and the Family, 42*, 337–346.

Lockwood, O., Smith, D. B., & Trezise, R. (1966). Four worlds: An approach to vocational guidance. *Personnel and Guidance Journal, 45*, 641–643.

Loesch, L. C. (1980). Life-flow leisure counseling for older persons. *Journal of Employment Counseling, 17*(1), 49–56.

Loesch, L. C., & Sampson, J. P., Jr. (1978). Job knowledge and vocational preferences. *Vocational Guidance Quarterly, 27*(1), 55–60.

Loevinger, J. (1976). *Ego development: Conceptions and theories*. San Francisco: Jossey-Bass.

Lofquist, L. H., & Dawis, R. (1969). *Adjustment to work, a psychological view of man's problems in a work-oriented society.* New York: Appleton-Century-Crofts.

Lofquist, L. H., & Dawis, R. V. (1975). *Counseling and use of the Minnesota Importance Questionnaire*. Minneapolis: University of Minnesota Vocational Psychology Work Adjustment Project.

Lokan, J., & Biggs, J. (1982). Student characteristics and motivational and process factors in relation to styles of career development. *Journal of Vocational Behavior, 21*, 1–16.

Lombana, J. H. (1985). Guidance accountability: A new look at an old problem. *The School Counselor, 32*(5), 340–346.

Lombard, J. W. (1973). *Career guidance and the Kuder interest inventories*. Chicago: Science Research Associates.

London, M., & More, E. M. (1987). *Career management and survival in the workplace*. San Francisco, CA: Jossey-Basse.

London, M., & Stumpf, S. A. (1982). *Managing careers*. Reading, MA: Addison-Wesley.

London, M., & Stumpf, S. A. (1986). Individual and organizational career development in changing times. In D. T. Hall and Associates (Eds.), *Career Development in Organizaions* (pp. 21–49). San Francisco: Jossey-Bass.

Lopez, F. G. (1983). The victims of corporate failure: Some preliminary findings. *Personnel and Guidance Journal, 61*, 631–632.

Lopez, F. G. (1989). Current family dynamics, trait anxiety, and academic adjustment: Test of a family-based model of vocational identity. *Journal of Vocational Behavior, 35*(1), 76–87.

Lopez, F. G., & Andrews, S. (1987). Career indecision: A family systems perspective. *Journal of Counseling and Development, 65*(6), 304–307.

Loscocco, K. A. (1990). Reactions to blue-collar work: A comparison of men and women. *Work and Occupations, 17*(2), 152–177.

Loughead, T. A. (1988). The Harrington-O'Shea decision-making system, microcomputer edition, 1985: A review. *Measurement and Evaluation in Counseling and Development, 21*, 36–39.

Loughead, T. A. (1989). Career development curriculum (CDC) for the mentally ill. *Journal of Career Development, 16* (1), 53–61.

Lounsbury, J. W., & Hoopes, L. L. (1986). A vacation from work: Changes in work and nonwork outcomes. *Journal of Applied Psychology, 71*, 392–401.

Lowe, B. (1981). The relationship between vocational interest differentiation and career undecidedness. *Journal of Vocational Behavior, 19*, 346-349.

Lowenthal, M. F. (1977). Toward a sociopsychological theory of change in adulthood and old age. In J. E. Birren & K. W. Schaie (Eds.), *Handbook of the psychology of aging*. New York: Van Nostrand-Reinhold.

Lowenthal, M. F., & Pierce, R. (1975). The pretransitional stance. In M. F. Lowenthal, M. Thurnher, & D. Chiriboga (Eds.), *Four stages of life: A comparative study of men and women facing transitions* (pp. 201–222). San Francisco: Jossey-Bass.

Lowenthal, M. F., Thurnher, M., Chiroboga, D., and Associates. (1976). *Four stages of life*. San Francisco: Jossey-Bass.

Lucas, M. S., & Epperson, D. L. (1988). Personality types of vocationally undecided students. *Journal of College Student Development, 29*, 460–466.

Lucas, M. S., & Epperson, D. L. (1990). Types of vocational undecidedness: A relication and a refinement. *Journal of Counseling Psychology, 37*, 382–388.

Luchins, A. S. (1960). Influences of experiences with conflicting information and reactions to subsequent conflicting information. *Journal of Social Psychology, 5*, 367–385.

Lunneborg, C. E. (1982a). Role model influences of nontraditional professional women. *Journal of Vocational Behavior, 20*, 276–281.

Lunneborg, C. E. (1982b). Systematic biases in brief self-ratings of vocational qualifications. *Journal of Vocational Behavior, 20,* 255–275.

Lunneborg, P. (1976). Vocational indecision in college graduates. *Journal of Counseling Psychology*, 23(4), 402–404.

Lunneborg, P. (1980). Reducing sex bias in interest measurement at the item level. *Journal of Vocational Behavior, 16,* 226–234.

Lunneborg, P. W. (1990). *Women changing work*. Westport, CT: Greenwood Press.

Lunneborg, P. W., & Lunneborg, C. E. (1985). Nontraditional and traditional female college graduates: What separates them from the men? *Journal of College Student Personnel, 26*(1), 33–36.

Lynch, R. K., & Maki, D. R. (1981). Searching for structure: A trait-factor approach to vocational rehabilitation. *Vocational Guidance Quarterly, 30*(1), 61–68.

Lyson, T. A., & Brown, S. S. (1982). Sex-role attitudes, curriculum choice, and career ambition. A comparison between women in typical and atypical college majors. *Journal of Vocational Behavior, 20,* 366–375.

MacArthur, J. D. (1980). Career services for university international students. *Vocational Guidance Quarterly, 29,* 178–181.

Maccoby, M. (1976). *The gamesman*. New York: Simon and Schuster.

Maccoby, M. (1980). Work and human development. *Professional Psychology, 11,* 509-519.

Maccoby, M., & Terzi, K. (1981). What happened to the work ethic? In J. O'Toole, J. L. Scheiber, & L. C. Wood, (Eds.), *Working, changes and choices* (pp. 162-171). New York: Human Sciences Press.

Macdonald, S., & Dooley, S. (1990). Employee assistance programs: Emerging trends. *Canadian Journal of Community Mental Health, 9,* 97–105.

Mackay, W. R., & Miller, C. A. (1982). Relations of socioeconomic status and sex variables to the complexity of worker functions in the occupational choice of elementary school children. *Journal of Vocational Behavior, 20,* 31–39.

Macke, A. S., & Morgan, W. R. (1978). Maternal employment, race, and work orientation of high school girls. *Social Forces, 57*(1), 187–203.

Mackin, R. K., & Hansen, L. S. (1981). A theory-based career development course: A plant in the garden. *The School Counselor, 28*(5), 325–334.

MacKinnon, F. M. (1986). Career indecision in reentry and undergraduate women. *Journal of College Student Personnel, 27*(2), 114–119.

MacKota, C. (1980). Using work therapeutically. In H. Lamb (Ed.), *Community survival in long term patients*. San Francisco: Jossey-Bass.

MacMichael, D. C. (1974). Work ethics: Collision in the classroom. *Manpower, 6,* 15–20.

Maddox, G. L. (1972). Retirement as a social event in the United States. In B. L. Neugarten (Ed.), *Middle age and aging*. Chicago: University of Chicago Press.

Madsen, D. H. (1986). Computer-assisted testing and assessment in counseling. *Measurement and Evaluation in Counseling and Development, 19*(1), 6–14.

Mager, R. F. (1962). *Preparing instructional objectives*. Palo Alto, CA: Fearon.

Mahone, C. H. (1960). Fear of failure and unrealistic vocational aspiration. *Journal of Abnormal and Social Psychology, 60,* 253–261.

Mainiero, L. A., & Upham, P. J. (1987). Beating a stacked deck: Restructuring versus career development. *Personnel Journal, 66,* 126–129.

Mainquist, J., & Eichorn, D. (1989). Competence in work settings. Chapter 12 in *Adolescence and work, Influences of social structure, labor markets, and culture*. (pp. 327–361). Edited by David Stern and Dorothy Eichorn. Hillsdale, NJ: Lawrence Erlbaum Associates, Publishers.

Malcolm, S. M. (1990). Reclaiming our past. *The Journal of Negro Education, 59*(3), 246–259.

Mallinckrodt, B. (1990). Satisfaction with a new job after unemployment: Consequences of job loss for older professionals. *Journal of Counseling Psychology, 37*(2), 149–152.

Mallinckrodt, B., & Fretz, B. R. (1988). Social support and the impact of job loss on older professionals. *Journal of Counseling Psychology, 36,* 181–186.

Mangum, G. L. (1988). *Youth transition from adolescence to the world of work*. Paper prepared for Youth and America's Future: The William T. Grant Foundation Commission on Work, Family, and Citizenship. Washington, DC: The William T. Grant Foundation Commission.

Manicas, P. T., & Secord, P. F. (1983). Implications for psychology of the new philosophy of science. *American Psychologist, 38,* 399–413.

Mann, L., Beswick, G., Allouache, P., & Ivey, M. (1989). Decision workshops for the improvement of decision making skills and confidence. *Journal of Counseling and Development, 67,* 478–481.

Manneback, A. J., & Stillwell, W. E. (1974). Installing career education: A systems approach. *Vocational Guidance Quarterly, 22,* 180–188.

Manuele, C. A. (1984). Modifying vocational maturity in adults with delayed career development: A life skills approach. *Vocational Guidance Quarterly, 33*(2), 101–112.

Manzi, P. A. (1986). Cognitive appraisal, stress, and coping in teenage employment. *Vocational Guidance Quarterly, 34*(3), 160-170.

Maples, M. F. (1981). Dual career marriages: Elements for potential success. *Personnel and Guidance Journal, 60*(1), 19–23.

Marino, K. E., & White, S. E. (1985). Departmental structure, locus of control, and job stress: The effect of a moderator. *Journal of Applied Psychology, 70*(4), 782-784.

Marinoble, R. M. (1980). Community jobs for handicapped students: A career education technique. *Vocational Guidance Quarterly, 29*(2), 172–177.

Marland, S. P. (1972). Career education 300 days later. *American Vocational Journal, 47*(2),14–17.

Marland, S. P. (1974). *Career education: A proposal for reform*. New York: McGraw-Hill.

Marlowe, A. F. (1981). Passages: A program for career and life planning. *Vocational Guidance Quarterly, 29*(4), 355–361.

Marshall, A. E. (1979). Assisting college students to apply to graduate school: A career planning service. *Journal of College Student Personnel, 20,* 556–557.

Marshall, S. J., & Wijting, J. P. (1980). Relationships of achievement motivation and sex-role identity to college women's career orientation. *Journal of Vocational Behavior, 16,* 299–311.

Martin, G. M. (1979). Getting chosen: The job interview and before. *Occupational Outlook Quarterly, 23*(1), 2–9.

Martin, G. M. (1980). A guide to setting up a career resource information center. *Occupational Outlook Quarterly, 24*(3), 12–17.

Martinez, A. C., Sedlacek, W. E., & Bachhuber, T. D. (1985). Male and female college graduates—7 months later. *Vocational Guidance Quarterly, 34*(2), 77–84.

Martocchio, J. J., & O'Leary, A. M. (1989). Sex differences in occupational stress: A meta-analytic review. *Journal of Applied Psychology, 74,* 495–501.

Maslach, C. (1981). Burnout: A social psychological analysis. In J. W. Jones (Ed.), *The burnout syndrome: Current research, theory, interventions.* Park Ridge, IL: London House Press.

Maslach, C., & Jackson, J. E. (1981). The measurement of experienced burnout. *Journal of Occupational Behavior, 2,* 99–113.

Maslow, A. H. (1954). *Motivation and personality,* New York: Harper & Row.

Matheny, K. B., Aycock, D. W., Pugh, J. L., Curlette, W. L., & Cannella, K. (1986). Stress coping: A qualitative and quantitative synthesis with implications for treatment. *The Counseling Psychologist, 14,* 499–549.

Mathews, R. M., Damron, W. S., & Yuen, C. K. (1985). A seminar in job-finding skills. *Journal of Employment Counseling, 22*(4), 170–173.

Matteson, M. T., Ivancevich, J. M., & Smith, S. V. (1984). Relation of Type A behavior to performance and satisfaction among sales personnel. *Journal of Vocational Behavior, 25*(2), 203–214.

Matthay, E. R., & Linder, R. (1982). A team effort in planning for the academically disadvantaged. *The School Counselor, 29*(3), 226–231.

Matthews, D. B. (1990). A comparison of burnout in selected occupational fields. *The Career Development Quarterly, 38,* 230–239.

Maurer, J. G., Vrendenburgh, D. J., & Smith, R. L. (1981). An examination of the central life interest scale. *Academy of Management Journal, 24*(1), 174–182.

Maynard, M. (1979). The occupational, learning, and social support orientations of employees. *Journal of Employment Counseling, 16*(2), 94–109.

Maynard, P. E., & Hansen, J. C. (1970). Vocational maturity among inner city youths. *Journal of Counseling Psychology, 17* 400–404.

Maze, M. (1985). How much should a computerized guidance program cost? *Journal of Career Development, 12*(2), 157–164.

Mazen, A. A., & Lemkau, J. P. (1990). Personality profiles of women in traditional and nontraditional occupations. *Journal of Vocational Behavior, 37,* 46–59.

McBride, A. B. (1990). Mental health effects of women's multiple roles. *American Psychologist, 45,* 381–384.

McCabe, S. P. (1988). Review of Career Assessment Inventory—The enhanced version. In J. T. Kapes & M. M. Mastie (Eds.), *A counselor's guide to career assessment instruments* (pp. 76–80). Washington, DC: National Career Development Association.

McClellan, D. C. (1965). Toward a theory of motive acquisition. *American Psychologist, 20,* 321–333.

McCormac, M. E. (1989). Information sources and resources. *Journal of Career Development, 16,* 129–138.

McDaniel, J. W. (1963). Disability and vocational development. *Journal of Rehabilitation, 29*(4), 16–18.

McDaniels, C. (1968). Youth: Too young to choose. *Vocational Guidance Quarterly, 16,* 242–249.

McDaniels, C. (1978). The practice of career guidance and counseling. *INFORM, 7,* 1–2, 7–8.

McDaniels, C. (1980). Labor market information: How well equipped are counselors to assist students? In H. N. Drier & L. A. Pfister (Eds.), *Career and labor market information: Key to improved individual decision making* (pp. 27–39). Columbus, OH: The National Center for Research in Vocational Education.

McDaniels, C. (1982). Comprehensive career information systems for the 1980s. *Vocational Guidance Quarterly, 30*(4), 344–350.

McDaniels, C. (1984a). The work/leisure connection. *Vocational Guidance Quarterly, 33*(1), 35–44.

McDaniels, C. (1984b). Work and leisure in the career span. In *Designing careers, counseling to enhance education, work and leisure* (Chap. 21). San Francisco: Jossey-Bass.

McDaniels, C. (1989). *The changing workplace: Career counseling strategies for the 1990s and beyond.* San Francisco: Jossey-Bass.

McDowell, C. F. (1976). *Leisure counseling: Related lifestyle processed.* Eugene, OR: University of Oregon.

McGee, L., & Stillman, B. (1982). Interest measurement as a basis for elementary career awareness activities. *Elementary School Guidance and Counseling, 16*(3), 172–179.

McGraw, L. K. (1982). A selective review of programs and counseling interventions for the re-entry woman. *Personnel and Guidance Journal, 60,* 469–472.

McGuire, T. J., & Frisman, K. (1983). Reimbursement policy and cost-effective mental health care. *American Psychologist 38*(8), 939–940.

McIntire, S. A., & Levine, E. L. (1984). An empirical investigation of self-esteem as a composite construct. *Journal of Vocational Behavior, 25*(2), 290–303.

McKay, W. R., & Miller, C. A. (1982). Relations of socioeconomic status and sex variables to the complexity of worker functions in the occupational choices of elementary school children. *Journal of Vocational Behavior, 20,* 31–39.

McKee, L. M., & Levinson, E. M. (1990). A review of the computerized version of the Self-Directed Search. *The Career Development Quarterly, 38,* 325–333.

McLaughlin, S. D. (1978). Occupational sex identification and the assessment of male and female earnings inequality. *American Sociological Review, 43,* 909–921.

McLean, A. A. (1973). Occupational mental health: Review of an emerging art. In R. L. Noland (Ed.), *Industrial mental health and counseling* (Chap. 7). New York: Behavioral Publications.

McLean, A. A. (1985). One hundred years of occupational mental health. In P. A. Carone, S. N. Keiffer, S. F. Yolles, & L. W. Kvinsky (Eds.), *History of mental health and industry, the last hundred years,* Vol. 10 (Chap. 2). Problems of Industrial Psychiatric Medicine Series. New York: Human Sciences Press.

McMahon, G. G. (1970). Technical education: A problem of definition. *American Vocational Journal. 44,* 22–23.

McNair, D., & Brown, D. (1983). Predicting the occupational aspirations, occupational expectations, and career maturity of black and white male and female 10th graders. *Vocational Guidance Quarterly, 31,*(1), 29–36.

McRae, K. B. (1985). Career-management planning: A boon to managers and employees. *Personnel, 62*(5), 56–60.

Meckel, N. T. (1981). The manager as career counselor. *Training and Development Journal, 35,* 65–69.

Medvene, A. M. (1973). Early parent child interactions of educational, vocational, and emotional-social clients. *Journal of Counseling Psychology, 20,* 94–95.

Medvene, A. M., & Collins, A. (1974). Occupational prestige and its relationship to traditional and nontraditional views of women's roles. *Journal of Counseling Psychology, 21,* 139–143.

Meehl, P. E. (1954). *Clinical versus statistical prediction.* Minneapolis, MN: University of Minnesota Press.

Mehrens, W. A. (1988). Review of vocational interest, experience, and skill assessment. In J. T. Kapes & M. M. Mastie (Eds.), *A counselor's guide to career assessment instruments* (pp. 132–136). Washington, DC: National Career Development Association.

Mehrens, W. A., & Lehmann, I. J. (1985). Interpreting test scores to clients: What scores should one use? *Journal of Counseling and Development, 63,* 317–320.

Meichenbaum, D. (1977). *Cognitive-behavior modification*. New York: Plenum.

Meichenbaum, D., & Jaremko, M. E. (Eds.). (1983). *Stress reduction and prevention*. New York: Plenum.

Meier, S. T., & Geiger, S. M. (1986). Implications of computer-assisted testing and assessment for professional practice and training. *Measurement and Evaluation in Counseling and Development, 19*(1), 29–34.

Meir, E. I. (1978). A test of the independence of fields and levels in Roe's occupational classification. *Vocational Guidance Quarterly, 27*(2), 124–129.

Meir, E. I. (1988). The need for congruence between within-occupation interests and specialty in mid-career. *The Career Development Quarterly, 37*, 63–69.

Meir, E. I. (1989). Integrative elaboration of the congruence theory. *Journal of Vocational Behavior, 35*, 219–230.

Melamed, S., & Meir, E. (1981). The relationship between interests—job incongruity and selection of avocational activity. *Journal of Vocational Behavior, 18*, 310–325.

Mencke, R. A., & Cochran, D. J. (1974). Impact of a counseling outreach workshop on vocational development. *Journal of Counseling Psychology, 21*, 185–190.

Menning, A. (1981). How career services can assist undeclared majors. *Journal of College Placement, 41*(3), 44–47.

Menning, A. & Whittmayer, C. (1979). Administrative and program provisions for undecided students. *Vocational Guidance Quarterly, 28*(2), 175–181.

Mercado, P., & Atkinson, D. R. (1982). Effects of counselor sex, student sex, and student attractiveness in counselors' judgments. *Journal of Vocational Behavior, 20*, 304–312.

Merman, S. K., & McLaughlin, J. E. (1982, August). *Unleashing human potential: The role of the career counselor in industry*. Paper presented to the International Federation of Training and Development Organizations, Calgary, Alberta, Canada.

Mesa Public School. (1974). *Toward accountability*. A report on the Mesa approach to career guidance, counseling, and placement. Mesa, AZ: The Public Schools.

Meyer, J. B., Strowig, W., & Hosford, R. E. (1970). Behavioral-reinforcement counseling with rural high school youth. *Journal of Counseling Psychology, 17*, 127–132.

Meyers, C. E., Drinkard, K., & Zinner, E. G. (1975). *What I like to do*. Chicago: Science Research Associates.

Mihal, W. L., & Graumenz, J. L. (1984). An assessment of the accuracy of self-assessment for career decision-making. *Journal of Vocational Behavior 25*(2), 245–253.

Milburn, B. C. (1983). The career counselor as a community liaison. *The School Counselor, 30*, 381–386.

Miles, J. H. (1984). Serving the career guidance needs of the economically disadvantaged. In N. C. Gysbers (Ed.), *Designing careers: Counseling to enhance education, work, and leisure*, (pp. 384–402). San Francisco: Jossey-Bass.

Miller, A. J. (1972, April). *The emerging school based comprehensive education model*. Paper presented to the National Conference on Career Education for Deans of Colleges of Education, Columbus, OH.

Miller, A. L., & Tiedeman, D. V. (1972). Decision making for the 70's: The cubing of the Tiedeman paradigm and its application in career education. *Focus on Guidance, 5*(1) 1–15.

Miller, A. L., & Tiedeman, D. V. (1977). Structuring responsibility in adolescents actualizing "I" power through curriculum. In G. D. Miller (Ed.), *Developmental theory and its application in guidance programs: Systematic efforts to promote personal growth* (pp. 123–166). Minneapolis, MN: Minnesota Department of Education.

Miller, A. W. (1968). Learning theory and vocational decisions. *Personnel and Guidance Journal, 47*, 18–23.

Miller, C. (1973). Historical and recent perspectives on work and vocational guidance. In H. Borow (Ed.), *Career guidance for a new age*. Boston: Houghton Mifflin.

Miller, C. D., & Oetting, G. (1977). Barriers to employment and the disadvantaged. *Personnel and Guidance Journal, 56*(2), 89–93.

Miller, C. H. (1974). Career development theory in perspective. In E. L. Herr (Ed.), *Vocational guidance and human development*. Boston: Houghton Mifflin.

Miller, D. C., & Form, W. H. (1951). *Industrial sociology*. New York: Harper.

Miller, G. (1980). The interpretation of nonoccupational work in modern society: A preliminary discussion and typology. *Social Problems, 27*(4), 381–391.

Miller, J. (1977). *Career development needs of nine-year-olds: How to improve career development programs*. Washington, DC: National Advisory Council for Career Education.

Miller, J. (1980). Individual and occupational determinants of job satisfaction. *Sociology of Work and Occupations, 7*(3), 337–366.

Miller, J. V. (1982a). Lifelong career development for disadvantaged youth and adults. *Vocational Guidance Quarterly, 30*(4), 359–366.

Miller, J. V. (1982b), 1970's trends in assessing career counseling, guidance, and education. *Measurement and Evaluation in Guidance, 15*(2), 142–146.

Miller, M. F. (1974). Relationship of vocational maturity to work values. *Journal of Vocational Behavior 5*, 367–371.

Miller, M. F. (1978). Childhood experience antecedents of career maturity attitudes. *Vocational Guidance Quarterly, 27*(2), 137–143.

Miller, M. F. (1982). Interest pattern structure and personality characteristics of clients who seek career information. *Vocational Guidance Quarterly, 31*(1), 28–35.

Miller, M. J. (1989). Career counseling for the elementary school child: Grades K-5. *Journal of Employment Counseling*. *26*(4), 169–177.

Miller, M. J., & Springer, T. P. (1986). Perceived satisfaction of a computerized vocational counseling system as a function of monetary investment. *Journal of College Student Personnel, 27*, 142–145.

Miller, R. R. (1986). Reducing occupational circumscription. *Elementary School Guidance and Counseling, 20*, 250–253.

Milley, D. J., & Bee, R. H. (1982). A conditional logic model of collegiate major selection. *Journal of Vocational Behavior, 20*, 81–92.

Milliken, R. L. (1962). Realistic occupational appraisal by high school seniors. *Personnel and Guidance Journal, 40*, 541–544.

Milne, A. M., Myers, D. E., Rosenthal, A. S., & Ginsburg, A. (1986). Single parents, working mothers, and the educational achievement of school children. *Sociology of Education, 59*, 125–139.

Milsum, J. H. (1985). A model of the eustress system for health/illness. *Behavioral Science, 30*, 179.

Mitchel, J. O. (1982). Careers at the agency level. *Managers Magazine 53*(3), 28–35.

Mitchell, A. (1984). *The nine American lifestyles*. New York: Warner Books.

Mitchell, A. M. (1975). Emerging career guidance competencies. *Personnel and Guidance Journal, 53*(9), 700–705.

Mitchell, A. M. (1977). *Career development needs of seventeen year olds: How to improve career development programs*. Washington, DC: National Advisory Committee for Career Education.

Mitchell, L. K., & Krumboltz, J. D. (1984a). Research in human decision making: Implications for career decision making and counseling. In S. Brown & R. Lent (Eds.), *Handbook of counseling psychology,* (pp. 238–280). New York: Wiley.

Mitchell, L. K., & Krumboltz, J. D. (1984b). Social learning approach to career decision making: Krumboltz's theory. In D. Brown & L. Brooks (Eds.), *Career Choice and Development* (Chap. 9). San Francisco: Jossey-Bass.

Mitchell, L. K., & Krumboltz, J. D. (1987). Cognitive restructuring and decision-making training on career indecision. *Journal of Counseling and Development, 66,* 171–174.

Mitchell, L. K., & Krumboltz, J. D. (1990). Social learning approach to career decision making: Krumboltz's Theory. In D. Brown and L. Brooks (Eds.), *Career choice and development. Applying contemporary theories to practice* (pp. 145–196) (2nd Ed.). San Francisco: Jossey-Bass.

Moch, M. K. (1980). Racial differences in job satisfaction: Testing four common explanations. *Journal of Applied Psychology, 65,* 299–306.

Moen, P. (1989). *Working parents: Transformation in gender roles and public policy in Sweden.* Madison: University of Wisconsin Press.

Moen, P., Downey, G., & Bolger, N. (1990). Labor-force re-entry among U.S. homemakers in midlife: A life-course analysis. *Gender and Society, 4*(2), 230–243.

Mohney, C., & Anderson, W. (1988). The effect of life events and relationships on adult women's decisions to enroll in college. *Journal of Counseling and Development, 66,* 271–279.

Moir, E. (1981). Career resource centers in business and industry. *Training and Development Journal, 35*(2), 54–57.

Moore, G. D. (1961). A negative view toward therapeutic counseling in the schools. *Counselor Education and Supervision, 1,* 60–65.

Moore, K. (1976). Faculty advising: Panacea or placebo? *Journal of College Student Personnel, 17,* 371–375.

Moore, S. S. (1985). Introduction. In D. Jones & S. S. Moore (Eds.), *Counseling adults: Life cycle perspectives* (pp. vii–xii). Lawrence, KS: University of Kansas.

Moos, R. H., & Billings, A. G. (1982). Conceptualizing and measuring coping resources and processes. In E. Goldberger & S. Breznitz (Eds.), *Handbook of stress: Theoretical and clinical aspects* (pp. 212–230). New York: The Free Press.

Morgan, M. A. (1980). *Managing career development.* New York: Van Nostrand. Reinhold.

Morgan, P. I., Patton, J., & Baker, H. K. (1985). The organization's role in managing midlife crisis. *Training and Development Journal, 39,* 56–59.

Morrill, W. H., & Forrest, D. J. (1970). Dimensions of counseling for career development. *Personnel and Guidance Journal, 49,* 299–306.

Morris, J. L. (1966). Propensity for risk taking as determinant of vocational choice. *Journal of Personality and Social Psychology, 3,* 328–335.

Morris, R., & Bass, S. A. (Eds.). (1988). *Retirement reconsidered: Economic and social roles for older people.* New York: Springer.

Morrison, A. M., & VonGlinow, M. A. (1990). Women and minorities in management. *American Psychologist, 45*(2), 200–208.

Morrison, M. H. (1984). The aging of the U.S. population: Human resource implications. *Aging and Work, 7*(1), 79–83.

Morrow, P. C. (1981). Retirement planning programs: Assessing their attendance and efficacy. *Aging and Work, 4*(4), 244–252.

Morrow, P. C., & McElroy, J. C. (1984). The impact of physical attractiveness in evaluative contexts. *Basic and Applied Social Psychology, 5*(3), 171–182.

Morrow, P. C., Mullen, E. J., & McElroy, J. C. (1990). Vocational behavior 1989: The year in review. *Journal of Vocational Behavior, 37*(2), 121–195.

Morse, W. (1963). *Foreword to the vocational education act of 1963.* PL-88210. Washington, DC.

Mortimer, J. T., & Finch, M. D. (1986). The development of self-esteem in the early work career. *Work and occupations, 13*(2), 217–239.

Moser, H. P., Dubin, W., & Shelsky, I. (1956). A proposed modification of the Roe occupational classification. *Journal of Counseling Psychology, 3,* 27–31.

Moses, J. L., & Byham, W. C. (Eds.). (1977). *Applying the Assessment center method.* New York: Pergamon Press.

Motsch, P. (1980). Peer social modeling: A tool for assisting girls with career exploration. *Vocational Guidance Quarterly, 28*(3), 231–240.

Mottaz, C., & Potts, G. (1986). An empirical evaluation of models of work satisfaction. *Social Science Research, 15,* 153–173.

Mowbray, C. T., Lanir, S., & Hulce, M. (Eds.). *Women and mental health: New directions for change.* New York: The Haworth Press.

Muchinsky, P. M. (1978). Age and job facet satisfaction. A conceptual reconsideration. *Aging and Work, 1,*(3), 175–179.

Mueller, C. F. (1981). Migration of the unemployed: A relocation assistance program. *Monthly Labor Review, 104*(4), 62–64.

Mueller, D. J. (1985). Review of the Career Orientation Placement and Evaluation Survey. *Measurement and Evaluation in Counseling and Development, 17*(3), 132–134.

Murphy, G. (1974). *Personality: A biosocial approach to origins and structure,* New York: Harper & Row.

Murphy, L. R. (1984). Occupational stress management: A review and appraisal. *Journal of Occupational Psychology, 57,* 1–15.

Murray, H. (1938). *Explorations in personality.* New York: Oxford University Press.

Myers, I. B., & McCaulley, M. H. (1985). *Manual: A guide to the development and use of the Myers-Briggs Type Indicator.* Palo Alto, CA: Consulting Psychologists Press.

Myers, R. A., Linderman, R. H., Thompson, A. S., & Patrick, T. A. (1975). Effects of educational and career exploration systems on vocational maturity. *Journal of Vocational Behavior, 6,* 245–254.

Nafziger, D. H., Holland, J. L., Helms, S. T., & McPartland, J. M. (1974). Applying an occupational classification to the work histories of young men and women. *Journal of Vocational Behavior, 5,* 331–345.

Naisbitt, J. (1982). *Megatrends: Ten new directions transforming our lives.* New York: Warner Books.

Nathan, P. E. (1977). A clinical psychologist views counseling psychology. *The Counseling Psychologist, 7*(2), 36–37.

National Alliance of Business. (1984). *A nation at work: Education and the private sector.* Washington, DC: Author.

National Alliance of Business. (1986). *Employment policies: Looking to the year 2000.* Washington DC: Author.

National Association of Secondary School Principals. (1975). EBCF: A design for career education. *Curriculum Report, 4*(3), 1–11.

National Career Development Association. (1985). Consumer guidelines for selecting a career counselor. *Career Development, 1*(2), 1–2.

National Career Development Association. (1991, January 11). Position paper approved by the Board of Directors.

National Center for Educational Statistics. (1980). *Condition of education. 1980.* Washington, DC: Author.

National Center for Educational Statistics. (1981). *Digest of educational statistics, 1981*. Washington, DC: Author.

National Center for Research in Vocational Education. (1982). Factors relating to the job placement of former secondary vocational education students. *CENTERGRAM, 17*(3), 1–2.

National Commission for Employment Policy. (1981). *The federal role in vocational education*. Washington, DC: Author.

National Commission on Excellence in Education. (1983). *A nation at risk: The imperative for educational reform*. Washington, DC: Government Printing Office.

National Commission on Secondary Education for Hispanics. (1985). *Make something happen. Hispanics and urban school reform*, 2 vols. Washington, DC: Author.

National Commission on Secondary Vocational Education. (1985). *The unfinished agenda. The role of vocational education in the high school*. Columbus: Ohio State University, The National Center for Research in Vocational Education.

National Occupational Information Coordinating Committee. (1988). *The National Career Counseling and Development Guidelines-Postsecond-ary Institutions*. Washington, DC: Author.

National Occupational Information Coordinating Committee. (1990, January 11). Almost two-thirds of Americans would seek more information about career options if they had it to do over again, new survey finds. Press Release. Washington, DC: Author.

National Opinion Research Center. (1947). Jobs and occupations: A popular evaluation. *Opinion News, 9*, 3–13.

National Science Foundation. (1989). *Science and engineering indicators—1989*. Washington, DC: National Science Foundation.

National Student Aid Coalition. (1985). *Closing the information gap: Ways to improve student awareness of financial aid opportunities*. Washington DC: Author.

National Vocational Guidance Association. (1971). *Guidelines for the preparation and evaluation of career information media: Films, filmstrips, and printed materials*. Washington, DC: American Personnel and Guidance Association.

National Vocational Guidance Association. (1980). Guidelines for the preparation and evaluation of career information literature. *Vocational Guidance Quarterly, 28*(4), 291–296.

National Vocational Guidance Association. (1982, September). *Vocational/career counseling competencies approved by the board of directors*. Falls Church, VA: Author.

National Vocational Guidance Association/American Vocational Association. (1973). *The position paper on career development*. Washington, DC: Author.

Naughton, T. J. (1987). A conceptual view of workaholism and implications for career counseling and research. *Career Development Quarterly, 35*(3), 180–187.

Nealer, J. K., & Papalia, A. S. (1982). *So you want to get a job. A manual for the job seeker and vocational counselor.* Moravia, NY: Chronicle Guidance.

Neapolitan, J. (1980). Occupational change in mid-career: An exploratory investigation. *Journal of Vocational Behavior, 16*(2), 212–225.

Near, J. P. (1985). A discriminant analysis of plateaued versus non-plateaued managers. *Journal of Vocational Behavior, 26*(2), 177–188.

Near, J. P., Rice, R. W., & Hunt, R. G. (1980). The relationship between work and nonwork domains: A review of empirical research. *Academy of Management Review, 5*, 415–429.

Neely, M. A. (1980). Career maturity inventory interpretations for grade 9 boys and girls. *Vocational Guidance Quarterly, 29*(2), 113–124.

Neely, M. A., & Kosier, M. W. (1977). Physically impaired students and the vocational exploration group. *Vocational Guidance Quarterly, 26*(1), 37–44.

Neff, J. A. (1985). Race and vulnerability to stress: An examination of differential vulnerability. *Journal of Personality and Social Psychology, 49*, 481–491.

Neff, W. S. (1977). *Work and human behavior* (2nd ed.). Chicago: Aldine.

Neff, W. S. (1985). *Work and human behavior* (3rd ed.). New York: Aldine.

Neimeyer, G. J. (1988). Cognitive interaction and differentiation in vocational behavior. *The Counseling Psychologist, 16*, 440–475.

Neimeyer, G. J. (1989a). Applications of repertory grid technique to vocational assessment. *Journal of Counseling and Development, 67*, 585–589.

Neimeyer, G. J. (1989b). Personal construct systems in vocational development and information processing. *Journal of Career Development, 16*, 83–96.

Neimeyer, G. J., Brown, M. T., Metzler, A. E., Hagans, C., & Tanguy, M. (1989). The impact of sex, sex-role orientation, and construct type on vocational differentiation, integration, and conflict. *Journal of Vocational Behavior, 34*, 236–251.

Neimeyer, G. J., Metzler, A. E., & Bowman, R. (1988). Effects of sex, career orientation, and occupational type on vocational integration, differentiation, and conflict. *Journal of Counseling Psychology, 35*, 139–143.

Neimeyer, G. J., Nevill, D. D., Probert, B., & Fukuyama, M. (1985). Cognitive structures in vocational development. *Journal of Vocational Behavior, 27*, 191–201.

Nelson, A. G. (1956). Vocational maturity and client satisfaction. *Journal of Counseling Psychology, 3*, 254–256.

Nelson, G. (1990). Women's life strains, social support, coping, and positive and negative affect: Cross-sectional and longitudinal tests of the two-factor theory of emotional well-being. *Journal of Community Psychology, 18*, 239–256.

Nelson, R. C. (1963). Knowledge and interest concerning sixteen occupations among elementary and secondary students. *Educational and Psychological Measurement, 27*, 741–754.

Nelson, R. C. (1979). The CREST program: Helping children with their choices. *Elementary School Guidance and Counseling, 14*(4), 286–298.

Nelson, R. E. (1979). *Perceptions concerning occupational survival skills*. Springfield, IL: Department of Adult, Vocational and Technical Education, Illinois Office of Education.

Nesselroade, J. R., & Baltes, P. B. (1984). From traditional factor analysis to structural-causal modeling in developmental research. In V. Garris and A. Parducci (Eds.), *Perspectives in psychological experimentations: Toward the year 2000* (pp. 267–287). Hillsdale, NJ: Erlbaum.

Nesselroade, J. R., & Ford, D. H. (1985). P-technique comes of age: Multivariate, replicated, single-subject designs for studying older adults. *Research on Aging, 7*, 46–80.

Nesselroade, J. R. & Ford, D. H. (1987). Methodological considerations in modeling living systems. In M. E. Ford & D. H. Ford (Eds.), *Humans as self-constructing living systems: putting the framework to work* (pp. 47–79). Hillsdale, NJ: Erbaum.

Neugarten, B. L. (1982, August). *Successful ageing*. Paper presented to the annual meeting of the American Psychological Association.

Neugarten, B. L., Moore, J. C., & Lowe, J. C. (1965). Age nouns, age constraints and adult socialization. *American Journal of Sociology, 70*, 710–717.

Nevill, D. D., Neimeyer, G. J., Probert, B., & Fukuyama, M. (1986). Cognitive structures in vocational information processing and decision making. *Journal of Vocational Behavior, 28*(2), 110–122.

Nevill, D. D., & Schlecker, D. I. (1988). The relation of self-efficacy and assertiveness to willingness to engage in traditional/nontraditional career activities. *Psychology of Women Quarterly, 12,* 91–98.

Nevill, D. D., & Super, D. E. (1986). *The Values Scale: Theory, application, and research manual* (Research Edition). Palo Alto: Consulting Psychologists Press.

Nevo, O. (1987). Irrational expectations in career counseling and their confronting arguments. *The Career Development Quarterly, 35,* 239–250.

Nevo, O. (1990). Career counseling from the counselee perspective: Analysis of feedback questionnaires. *The Career Development Quarterly, 38,* 314–324.

New Jersey State Department of Education. (1973). Technology for children (T4C). *Elementary School Guidance and Counseling, 7*(3), 235.

Newton, T. J. (1989). Occupational stress and coping with stress: A critique. *Human Relations, 42,* 441–461.

New York State Education Department, Division of Occupational Education Programs. (1986). *Home and Career Skills. Grades 7 and 8*. Albany, NY: Author.

New York Times. (1989, November). Foreign students: Who are they? p. B11.

Nicholls, J. G., Patashnick, M., & Mettetal, G. (1986). Conceptions of ability and intelligence. *Child Development, 57,* 636–645.

Nieva, V. G., & Gutek, B. A. (1981). *Women and work.* New York: Praeger.

Niles, S. G., & Herr, E. L. (1989). Using secondary school behaviors to predict career behaviors in young adulthood: Does success breed success? *Career Development Quarterly, 37,* 345–354.

Niles, S. G., & Pate, R. H., Jr. (1989). Competency and training issues related to the integration of career counseling and mental health counseling. *Journal of Career Development, 16,* 63–71.

Noe, R. A., & Steffy, B. D. (1987). The influence of individual characteristics and assessment center evaluation on career exploration behavior and job involvement. *Journal of Vocational Behavior, 30,* 187–202.

Noeth, R. J., Engen, H. B., & Noeth, P. E. (1984). Making career decisions: A self-report of factors that help high school students. *Vocational Guidance Quarterly, 32*(4), 240–248.

Nolan, R. L. (Ed.), (1973). *Industrial mental health and employment counseling*. New York: Behavioral Objectives.

Norris, W. (1963). *Occupational information in the elementary school*. Chicago: Science Research Associates.

Norton, J. L. (1970). Current status of the measurement of vocational maturity. *Vocational Guidance Quarterly, 18,* 165–170.

Novaco, R. (1976). Treatment of chronic anger through cognitive and relaxation controls. *Journal of Consulting and Clinical Psychology, 44,* 681.

Nozik, S. (1986). *The relation of sex role self-concept and work values to traditionality of occupational choice among employed men*. Unpublished doctoral dissertation. State University of New York at Buffalo.

Oakland, J. A. (1969). Measurement of personality correlates of academic achievement in high school students. *Journal of Counseling Psychology, 16,* 452–457.

O'Connell, L., Betz, N., & Kurth, S. (1989). Plans for balancing work and family life: Do women pursuing traditional and nontraditional occupations differ? *Sex Roles, 20,* 35–45.

Offerman, L. R., & Gowing, M. K. (1990). Organizations of the future: Changes and challenges. *American Psychologist, 45,* 95–108.

O'Hara, R. P. (1966). Vocational self-concepts and high school achievement. *Vocational Guidance Quarterly, 15,* 106–112.

O'Hara, R. P. (1968). A theoretical foundation for the use of occupational information in guidance. *Personnel and Guidance Journal, 46,* 636–640.

O'Hare, M. M. (1987). Career decision-making models: Espoused theory versus theory-in-use. *Journal of Counseling and Development, 65*(6), 301–303.

O'Hare, M. M., & Tamburri, E. (1986). Coping as a moderator of the relationship between anxiety and career decision making. *Journal of Counseling Psychology, 33*(3), 255–264.

Oinonen, C. M. (1984). *Business and education survey: Employer and employee perceptions of school to work preparation*. Madison, WI: The Wisconsin Department of Public Instruction/The Parker Fund of the Janesville Foundation.

Okun, M. A. (1976). Adult age and cautiousness in decision-making. *Human Development, 19,* 220–233.

Olbrisch, M. E. (1977). Psychotherapeutic intervention in physical health: Effectiveness and economic efficiency. *American Psychologist. 32*(9), 761–777.

Oldham, G. R., & Fried, Y. (1987). Employee reactions to workspace characteristics. *Journal of Applied Psychology, 72,* 75–80.

Olive, H. (1973). Sex differences in adolescent vocational preferences. *Vocational Guidance Quarterly, 21*(3), 199–201.

Oliver, L. (1975). The relationship of parental attitudes and parent identification to career and home-making orientation in college women. *Journal of Vocational Behavior, 7,* 1–12.

Oliver, L. (1977). Evaluating career counseling outcome for three modes of test interpretation. *Measurement and Evaluation in Guidance, 10*(3) 153–161.

Oliver, L. W., & Spokane, A. R. (1988). Career-intervention outcome: What contributes to client gain? *Journal of Counseling Psychology, 35,* 447–462.

Olson, C., McWhirter, E., & Horan, J. J. (1989). A decision-making model applied to career counseling. *Journal of Career Development, 16,* 107–117.

Olson, S. K. (1981). Current status of corporate retirement preparation programs. *Aging and Work, 4*(3), 175–187.

O'Neil, J. M., & Heck, E. J. (1980). A sequential, self-help, job seeking training manual to help college students in the job-search process. *Journal of College Student Personnel, 21,* 170–171.

O'Neil, J. O., Price, G. E., & Tracy, T. J. (1979). The stimulus value, treatment effects, and sex differences when completing the Self-Directed Search and Strong-Campbell Interest Inventory, *Journal of Counseling Psychology, 26,* 45–50.

O'Neil, J. O., Ohlde, C., Tolefson, N., Barke, C., Piggott, T., & Watts, D. (1980). Factors, correlates, and problem areas affecting career decision-making of a cross-sectional sample of students. *Journal of Counseling Psychology, 27,* 571–580.

Oppong, J. R., Ironside, R. G., & Kennedy, L. W. (1988). Perceived quality of life in a centre-periphery framework. *Social Indicators Research, 20,* 605–620.

Oregon Occupational Information Coordinating Committee/ Oregon Career Information System. (1989). *Schoolwork, lifework. Integrating career information into high school career development programs*. Eugene, Oregon, Author.

O'Reilly, P. A. (1973). *Predicting the stability of expressed occupational choices of secondary students.* Unpublished doctoral dissertation, Pennsylvania State University.

Ornstein, S., & Isabella, L. (1990). Age vs. stage models of career attitudes of women: A partial replication and extension. *Journal of Vocational Behavior, 36,* 1–19.

O'Rourke, D. F., Houston, B. K., Harris, J. K., & Snyder, C. R. (1988). The Type A behavior pattern: Summary, conclusions, and implications. In B. K. Houston & C. R. Snyder (Eds.), *Type A behavior pattern: Research, theory, and intervention* (pp. 312–334). New York: John Wiley.

Osborn, D. P. (1990). A reexamination of the organizational choice process. *Journal of Vocational Behavior, 36*(1), 45–60.

Osipow, S. H. (1968). *Theories of career development,* New York: Appleton-Century-Crofts.

Osipow, S. H. (1977). Will the real counseling psychologist please stand up? *The Counseling Psychologist, 7*(2), 93–94.

Osipow, S. H. (1980). *Manual for the career decision scale.* Columbus, OH: Marathon Consulting and Press.

Osipow, S. H. (1982a). Counseling psychology: Applications in the world of work. *The Counseling Psychologist, 10*(3), 19–25.

Osipow, S. H. (1982b). Research in career counseling: An analysis of issues and problems. *The Counseling Psychologist, 10*(4), 27–34.

Osipow, S. H. (1983). *Theories of career development* (3rd ed.). Englewood Cliffs, NJ: Prentice-Hall.

Osipow, S. H. (1986). Career issues through the life span. In M. S. Pallak & R. Perloff (Eds.), *Psychology and work: Productivity, change and employment* (pp. 137–168). Washington, DC: American Psychological Association.

Osipow, S. H. (1990). Convergence in theories of career choice and development: Review and Prospect. *Journal of Vocational Behavior, 36,* 122–131.

Osipow, S. H., Ashby, J. D., & Wall, H. W. (1966). Personality types and vocational choice: A test of Holland's theory. *Personnel and Guidance Journal, 45,* 37–42.

Osipow, S. H., Carney, C., & Barak, A. (1976). A scale of educational-vocational undecidedness: A typological approach. *Journal of Vocational Behavior, 9,* 233–243.

Osipow, S. H., Carney, C. G., Winer, J. L., Yanico, B. J., & Koschir, M. (1976). *Career decision scale.* Columbus, OH: Marathon Press.

Osipow, S. H., Doty, R. E., & Spokane, A. R. (1985). Occupational stress, strain, and coping across the life span. *Journal of Vocational Behavior, 27*(1), 98–108.

Osipow, S. H., & Gold, J. A. (1967). Factors related to inconsistent career preference. *Personnel and Guidance Journal, 46,* 342–349.

Osipow, S. H., & Reed, R. (1985). Decision making style and career decision in college students. *Journal of Vocational Behavior, 27*(3), 368–373.

Osipow, S. H., & Spokane, A. R. (1984). Measuring occupational stress, strain, and coping. In S. Oskamp (Ed.), *Applied Social Psychology Annual,* Vol. 5 (pp. 67–86). New York: Sage

Osterman, P. (1980). *Getting started: The youth labor market.* Cambridge. MA: MIT Press.

Osterman, P. (1989). The Job Market for Adolescents. In D. Stern & D. Eichorn (Eds.), *Adolescence in work: Influences of social structure, labor markets, and culture.*(pp. 235–258) Hillsdale, NJ: Lawrence Erlbaum Associates.

O'Toole, J. (Ed.) (1973). *Work in America.* Cambridge, MA: MIT Press.

O'Toole, J. (1975). *The reserve army of the underemployed.* Monographs on Career Education. Washington, DC: U.S. Department of Health, Education, and Welfare.

O'Toole, J. (1981). Work in America. In J. O'Toole, J. L. Schiber, & L. C. Wood (Eds.). *Working: Changes and choices* (pp. 12–17). New York: Human Sciences Press.

O'Toole, J. (1982). How to forecast your own working future. *The Futurist, 16*(1), 5–11.

Ott, E. M. (1989). Effects of the male-female ratio at work. *Psychology of Women Quarterly, 13,* 41–57.

Otte, F. L., & Sharpe, D. L. (1979). The effects of career exploration on self-esteem, achievement motivation, and occupational knowledge. *Vocational Guidance Quarterly, 28*(1), 63–70.

Ottke, M. B., & Brogden, S. Y. (1990). The marketplace of skills: A different twist to career fairs. *Journal of College Student Development, 31,* 376–377.

Otto, L. B. (1984). Bringing parents back in. *Journal of Career Education, 10*(4), 255–265.

Otto, L. B., & Call, V. R. A. (1985). Parental influence on young people's career development. *Journal of Career Development, 12*(1), 65–69.

Ouchi, W. G. (1981). *Theory Z: How American business can meet the Japanese challenge.* Reading, MA: Addison-Wesley.

Palamore, E. (1969). Predicting longevity: A follow-up controlling for age. *Gerontologist, (9),* 247–250.

Palamore, E. B., Burchett, B. M., Fillenbaum, G. G., George, L. K., & Wallman, L. M. (1985). *Retirement: Causes and consequences.* New York: Springer.

Pallone, N. J. (1977). Counseling psychology: Toward an empirical definition. *The Counseling Psychologist, 7*(2), 29–32.

Palmer, S., & Cochran, L. (1988). Parents as agents of career development. *Journal of Counseling Psychology, 35,* 71–76.

Palmo, A. J., & DeVantier, J. (1976). An examination of the counseling needs of voc-tech students. *Vocational Guidance Quarterly, 25,* 170–176.

Paolitto, D. P. (1977). Group counseling in the junior high: Counselors and teachers as coleaders. *Focus on Guidance, 9*(2), 1–16.

Papalia, A. S., & Kaminski, W. (1981). Counseling and counseling skills in the industrial environment. *Vocational Guidance Quarterly, 30*(1), 37–42.

Parasuraman, S., & Alutto, J. A. (1981). An examination of the organizational antecedents of stress work. *Academy of Management Journal. 24*(1) 48–67.

Pardine, P., Higgins, R., Szeglin, A., Beres, J., Kravitz, R., & Fotis, J. (1981). Job-stress worker-strain relationship moderated off-the-job experience. *Psychological Reports, 48,* 963–970.

Parelius, A. P. (1975). Change and stability in college women's orientations toward education, family, and worker. *Social Problems, 22,* 420–432.

Parham, T. A. (1989). Cycles of psychological Nigrescence. *The Counseling Psychologist, 17*(2), 187–226.

Parker, D. A., Parker, E. S., Wolz, M. W., & Harford, T. C. (1980). Sex roles and alcohol consumption: A research note. *Journal of Health and Social Behavior, 21,* 43–48.

Parker, H. J. (1970). 29,000 seventh-graders have made occupational choices. *Vocational Guidance Quarterly, 18,* 219–224.

Parker, M., Peltier, S., & Wolleat, P. (1981). Understanding dual career couples. *Personnel and Guidance Journal, 60*(1), 14–18.

Parsons, F. (1909). *Choosing a vocation.* Boston: Houghton Mifflin.

Parsons, T. (1951). *The social system.* Glencoe, IL: The Free Press.

Partin, R. L., & Gargiolo, R. N. (1980). Burned out teachers have no class! Prescriptions for teacher burnout. *College Student Journal, 14*(4), 365–380.

Pate, R. H., Jr., Tulloch, J. B., & Dassance, C. R. (1981). A regional job and educational opportunities fair. *Personnel and Guidance Journal, 60*(3), 187–189.

Paterson, D. G. (1938, January). The genesis of modern guidance. *Educational Record, 19,* 36–46.

Patterson, J. (1985). Career development: Revolution, reform, and renaissance. *Journal of Career Development, 12*(2), 129–144.

Pavlak, M. F., & Kammer, P. P. (1985). The effects of a career guidance program on the career maturity and self-concept of delinquent youth. *Journal of Vocational Behavior, 26*(1), 41–54.

Peabody, D. (1985). *National characteristics.* New York: Cambridge University Press.

Peace, C. H. (1973). Pastoral counseling with the problem employee. In R. L. Noland (Ed.), *Industrial mental health and employee counseling* (Chap. 22). New York: Behavioral Publications.

Pearlin, L. I. (1982). Discontinuities in the study of aging. In T. K. Haraven & K. J. Adams (Eds.), *Aging and life course transitions: An interdisciplinary perspective* (pp. 55-74). New York: Guilford Press.

Pearlman, K. (1980). Job families: A review and discussion of their implications for personnel selection. *Psychological Bulletin, 87*(1), 1–28.

Pearlman, K., Schmidt, F. L., & Hunter, J. E. (1980). Validity generalization results for tests used to predict job proficiency and training success in clerical occupations. *Journal of Applied Psychology, 65,* 373–406.

Peatling, J. H., & Tiedeman, D. V. (1977). *Career development. Designing self.* Muncie, IN: Accelerated Development.

Pedersen, P. (1988). *A handbook for developing multicultural awareness.* Washington, DC: American Association for Counseling and Development.

Pedersen, P. (1990). The constructs of complexity and balance in multicultural counseling theory and practice. *Journal of Counseling and Development, 68,* 550–554.

Pedro, J. D. (1982). Career maturity in high school females. *Vocational Guidance Quarterly, 30*(3). 243–251.

Pedro, J. D., Wolleat, P., & Fennema, E. (1980). Sex differences in the relationship of career interests and mathematics plans. *Vocational Guidance Quarterly, 29*(1), 25–34.

Pelletier, D. M. (1981). The sales approach to the job hunt. *Journal of College Placement, 41*(4), 48–50.

Pendaris, E. D., Howley, A. & Howley, C. (1990). *The abilities of gifted children.* Englewood Cliffs, NJ: Prentice Hall.

Penley, L. P., & Hawkins, B. L. (1980). Organizational communication, performance, and job satisfaction as a function of ethnicity and sex. *Journal of Vocational Behavior, 16,* 368–384.

Pennock-Roman, M. (1988). Review of Differential Aptitude Tests. In J. T. Kapes & M. M. Mastie (Eds.), *A counselor's guide to career assessment instruments* (pp. 63–68). Washington, DC: National Career Development Association.

Pepinsky, H. B., Hill-Frederick, K., & Epperson, D. L. (1978). The journal of counseling psychology as a matter of policies. *The Journal of Counseling Psychology, 25*(6), 483–498.

Peregoy, J. J., & Schliebner, C. T. (1990). Long-term unemployment: Effects and counseling interventions. *International Journal for the Advancement of Counselling, 13,* 193–204.

Perosa, S. L., & Perosa, L. M. (1983). The mid-career crisis: A description of the psychodynamics of transition and adaptation. *Vocational Guidance Quarterly, 32,*(2), 69–77.

Perovich, G. M., & Mierzwa, J. A. (1980). Group facilitation of vocational maturity and self-esteem in college students. *Journal of College Student Personnel, 21,* 206–211.

Perrone, P. A. (1964). Factors influencing high school seniors' occupational preference. *Personnel and Guidance Journal, 42,* 976–979.

Perrone, P. A. (1973). A longitudinal study of occupational values in adolescents. *Vocational Guidance Quarterly, 22*(2), 116–123.

Perrone, P. A., Male, R. A., & Karshner, W. W. (1979). Career development needs of talented students: A perspective for counselors. *The School Counselor, 27*(1), 16–23.

Perry, L. (1982). Special populations: The demands of diversity. In E. L. Herr & N. M. Pinson (Eds.), *Foundations for policy in guidance and counseling.* Washington, DC: American Personnel and Guidance Association.

Perry, W. G. (1968). *Forms of intellectual and ethical development in the college years: A scheme.* New York: Holt, Rinehart & Winston.

Perry, W., Jr. (1970). *Intellectual and ethical development in the college years.* New York: Holt, Rinehart & Winston.

Petersen, M. L. (1974, July). *Simulated instructional systems SIS utilizing simulated occupational units in a career education program.* Paper presented at the meeting of the Utah Vocational Association, Salt Lake City.

Peterson, G. W., Sampson, J. P., & Reardon, R. C. (1991). *Career development and services: A cognitive approach.* Pacific Grove, CA: Brooks/Cole Publishing Company.

Peterson, K. L. (1985). Work commitment of college females. *College Student Journal, 19*(2), 213–216.

Peterson, R. R. (1989). *Women, work, and divorce.* Albany: State University of New York Press.

Phelps, L. A., & Lutz, R. J. (1977). *Career exploration in preparation for the special needs learner.* Boston: Allyn and Bacon.

Phillips, J. S., Barrett, G. V., & Rush, M. C. (1978). Job structure and age satisfaction. *Aging and Work, 1*(2), 109–119.

Phillips, A. S., & Bedeian, A. G. (1989). PMS and the workplace. *Social Behavior and Personality, 17*(2), 165–174.

Phillips, L., & Weiss, B. (1972). Career development for handicapped youth. *Elementary School Guidance and Counseling, 7*(2), 154–155.

Phillips, M. G. (1966). Learning materials and their implementation. *Review of Educational Research, 36*(3), 373–379.

Phillips, S. D. (1982a). Career exploration in adulthood. *Journal of Vocational Behavior, 20,* 129–140.

Phillips, S. D. (1982b). The development of career choices: The relationship between patterns of commitment and career outcomes in adulthood. *Journal of Vocational Behavior, 29,* 141–152.

Phillips, S. D., Cairo, P. C., Blustein, D. L., & Myers, R. A. (1988). Career development and vocational behavior, 1987: A review. *Journal of Vocational Behavior, 33*(2), 119–184.

Phillips, S. D., Friedlander, M. L., Kost, P. P., Specterman, R. V., & Robbins, E. S. (1988). Personal versus vocational focus in career counseling: A retrospective outcome study. *Journal of Counseling and Development, 67,* 287–292.

Phillips, S. D., Friedlander, M. L., Pazienza, N. J., & Kost, P. P. (1985). A factor analytic investigation of career decision-making styles. *Journal of Vocational Behavior, 26*(1), 106–115.

Phillips, S. D., Pazienza, N. J., & Walsh, D. J. (1984). Decision making styles and progress in occupational decision making. *Journal of Vocational Behavior, 25,* 96–105.

Phillips, S. D., & Strohmer, D. (1982). Decision-making style and vocational maturity. *Journal of Vocational Behavior, 20*(2), 215–222.

Phillips-Jones, L., Jones, G. B., & Drier, H. N. (1981). *Developing training competencies for career guidance personnel.* Falls Church, VA: National Vocational Guidance Association.

Piaget, J. (1929). *The child's conception of the world*. New York: Harcourt, Brace.

Pickering, J. W. (1986). A comparison of three methods of career planning for liberal arts majors. *The Career Development Quarterly*, *35*(2), 102–112.

Pickering, J. W., & Vacc, N. A. (1984). Effectiveness of career development interventions for college students. *Vocational Guidance Quarterly, 32,* 149.

Pierson, F. C. (1980). *The minimal level of unemployment and public policy.* Kalamazoo, MI: The W. E. Upjohn Institute for Employment and Research.

Pietrofesa, J. J., & Splete, H. (1975). *Career development: Theory and research*. New York: Grune and Stratton.

Pilot, M. (1980). Job outlook projections: Why do them? How are they made? How accurate are they? *Occupational Outlook Quarterly, 24,* 3–8.

Pinder, F. A., & Fitzgerald, P. (1984). The effectiveness of a computerized guidance system in promoting career decision-making. *Journal of Vocational Behavior, 24,* 123–131.

Pine, G. J. (1964–1965). Occupational and educational aspirations and delinquent behavior. *Vocational Guidance Quarterly, 13*, 107–111.

Pines, A., Aronson, E., & Kafry, D. (1981). *Burnout: From tedium to personal growth*. New York: The Free Press.

Pines, A., & Maslach, C. (1979). Burnout: The loss of human caring. In *Experiencing social psychology,* New York: Random House.

Pines, A., & Maslach, C. (1980). Combatting staff burnout in a day care center: A case study. *Child Care Quarterly, 9,* 5–16.

Pinkney, J. W. (1983). The Myers-Briggs Type Indicator as an alternative in career counseling. *Personnel and Guidance Journal, 62*(3), 173–177.

Pinkney, J. W. (1985). A card sort interpretive strategy for flat profiles on the Strong-Campbell Interest Inventory. *Vocational Guidance Quarterly*, *33*(4), 331–339.

Pinkney, J. W. (1987). Problem solving by career assessment: Some issues clients need to consider. *Journal of Career Development*, *14*, 45–51.

Pinkney, J. W., & Jacobs, D. (1985). New counselors and personal interest in the task of career counseling. *Journal of Counseling Psychology*, *32*(3), 454–457.

Pinson, N. M. (1980). School counselors as interpreters for and of the community: New roles in career education. In F. E. Burtnett (Ed.), *The school counselor's role in career education* (Chap. 3, pp. 123–149). Falls Church, VA: APGA Press.

Piost, M. (1974). Effect of sex and career models on occupational preferences of adolescents. *Audiovisual Communication Review, 22,* 41–50.

Pirnot, K., & Dustin, R. (1986). A new look at value priorities for homemakers and career women. *Journal of Counseling and Development, 64,* 432–436.

Pitz, G. F., & Harren, V. A. (1980). An analysis of career decision-making from the point of view of information-processing and decision theory. *Journal of Vocational Behavior, 16,* 320–346.

Plata, M. (1975). Stability and change in the prestige rankings of occupations over 49 years. *Journal of Vocational Behavior, 6,* 95–99.

Plata, M. (1981). Occupational aspirations of normal and emotionally disturbed adolescents: A comparative study. *Vocational Guidance Quarterly, 30*(2), 130–138.

Pleck, J. H., Staines, G. L., & Lang, L. (1980). Conflicts between work and family life. *Monthly Labor Review, 103*(3), 29–31.

Polkinghorne, D. E. (1984). Further extensions for methodological diversity for counseling psychology. *Journal of Counseling Psychology*, *31*, 416–429.

Polkinghorne, D. E. (1990). Action theory approaches to career research. In R. A. Young & W. E. Borgen (Eds.), *Methodological approaches to the study of careers* (pp. 87–106). New York: Praeger.

Poloma, M. M., & Garland, T. N. (1971). The married professional woman: A study in the tolerance of domestication. *Journal of Marriage and the Family, 33*(3), 531–540.

Pond, S. B. III, & Geyer, P. D. (1987). Employee age as a moderator of the relation between perceived work alternatives and job satisfaction. *Journal of Applied Psychology, 72,* 552–557.

Pope John Paul II. (1981, September #21). Laboreum exercens (on human work): Papal Encyclical. *The Catholic Register,* p. 7.

Porter, L. (1970). Adults have special counseling needs. *Adult leadership, 19*(9), 275–277.

Portes, A., & Stepick, A. (1985). Unwelcome immigrants: Experiences of 1980 (Mariel) Cuban and Haitian refugees in South Florida. *American Sociological Review, 50,* 493–514.

Portigal, A. H. (1976). *Towards the measurement of work satisfaction*. Paris: Organization for Economic Cooperation and Development.

Portwood, J. D., & Granrose, C. S. (1986). Organizational career management programs: What's available? What's effective? *Human Resources Planning, 9*(3), 107–119.

Post-Kammer, P. (1987). Intrinsic and extrinsic work values and career maturity of 9th and 11th grade boys and girls. *Journal of Counseling and Development, 65*(8), 420–423.

Post-Kammer, P., & Perrone, P. (1983). Career perceptions of talented individuals: A follow-up study. *Vocational Guidance Quarterly, 31*(3), 203–211.

Post-Kammer, P., & Smith, P. L. (1985). Sex differences in career self-efficacy, consideration, and interest of eighth and ninth graders. *Journal of Counseling Psychology, 32*(4), 551–559.

Potter, B. A. (1980). *Beating job burnout*. San Francisco: Harbor Publishing.

Pound, R. E. (1978). Using self-concept subscales in predicting career maturity for race and sex subgroups. *Vocational Guidance Quarterly, 27*(1), 61–70.

Powell, M., & Bloom, V. (1963). Development of and reasons for vocational choices of adolescents through the high school years. *Journal of Educational Research, 50*(3), 126–133.

Prager, K. J., & Freeman, A. (1979). Self-esteem, academic competence, educational aspiration and curriculum choice of urban community college students. *Journal of College Student Personnel, 20*(5), 392–397.

Pratzner, F. C., & Ashley, W. L. (1985). Occupational and adaptability and transferable skills: Preparing today's adults for tomorrow's careers. *Adults and the changing workplace*. Alexandria, VA: American Vocational Association.

Prediger, D. J. (1974). The role of assessment in career guidance: A reappraisal: *Impact, 3,* 3–4, 15–21.

Prediger, D. J. (1989). Ability differences across occupations: More than *g*. *Journal of Vocational Behavior, 34*(1), 1–27.

Prediger, D. J., Roth, J. D., & Noeth, R. J. (1973). *Nationwide study of student career development: Summary of results*. Iowa City, IA: The American College Testing Program.

Prediger, D. J., & Sawyer, R. L. (1985). Ten years of career development: A nationwide study of high school students. *Journal of Counseling and Development, 65*(1), 45–49.

Prediger, D. J., & Swaney, K. (1986). Role of counselee experiences in the interpretation of vocational interest scores. *Journal of Counseling and Development*, *64*, 440–444.

Pritchard, R. D. (1969). Equity theory: A review and critique. *Organizational Behavior and Human Performance, 4,* 176–211.

Punch, K. F., & Sheridan, B. E. (1985). Some measurement characteristics of the Career Development Inventory. *Measurement and Evaluation in Counseling and Development, 17*(4), 196–202.

Pursell, D. E., & Torrence, W. D. (1980). The older woman and her search for employment. *Aging and Work, 3*(2), 121–128.

Quinn, J. F. (1981). The extent and correlates of partial retirement. *The Gerontologist, 21*(6), 634–643.

Quinn, M. T. & Lewis, R. J. (1989). An attempt to measure a career-planning intervention in a traditional course. *Journal of College Student Development, 30*, 371–372.

Quinn, R. P., & Mandilovitch. M. S. B. (1980). Education and job satisfaction: 1962–1977. *Vocational Guidance Quarterly, 29*(2), 100–111.

Quinn, R. P., Staines, G. L., & McCullough, M. R. (1974). Job satisfaction: Is there a trend? *Manpower Research Monograph, 30*, Washington, DC: U.S. Department of Labor.

Rabinowitz, W., Falkenbach, K., Travers, J. R., Valentine, C. G., & Weener, P. (1983). Worker motivation: Unsolved problems or untapped resources? *California Management Review, 25*(2), 45–56.

Rachlin, H. (1989). *Judgment, decision, and choice: A cognitive/Behavioral synthesis*. New York: W. H. Freeman and Company.

Raelin, J. A. (1980). *Building a career. The effect of initial job experiences and related work attitudes on later employment.* Kalamazoo, MI: The W. E. Upjohn Institute for Employment Research.

Raelin, J. A. (1987). Two-track plans for one-track careers. *Personnel Journal, 66*, 96–101.

Ragheb, M. B., & Griffith, C. A. (1982). The contribution of leisure participation and leisure satisfaction to life satisfaction of older persons. *Journal of Leisure Research, 14*, 295–306.

Rantze, K. R., & Feller, R. W. (1985). Counseling career-plateaued workers during times of social change. *Journal of Employment Counseling, 22*(1), 23–28.

Rapoport, R., & Rapoport, R. N. (1971). *Dual-career families*. Middlesex, England: Penguin Books.

Rapoport, R., & Rapoport, R. N. (1976). *Dual-career families re-examined*. London: Martin Robertson & Co.

Raskin, A. H. (1980). Toward a more participative work force. In C. S. Sheppard & D. C. Carroll (Eds.), *Working in the twenty-first century* (pp. 90–97). New York: Wiley.

Rasmussen, K. G., Jr. (1984). Nonverbal behavior, verbal behavior, resume credentials, and selection interview outcomes. *Journal of Applied Psychology, 69*(4), 551–556.

Raths, L., Harmin, M., & Simon, S. (1966). *Values and teaching*. Columbus, OH: Charles E. Merrill.

Raup, J. L., & Myers, J. E. (1989). The empty-nest syndrome: Myth or reality? *Journal of Counseling and Development, 68*, 180–183.

Rayman, J. R., & Harris-Bowlsbey, J. A. (1977). DISCOVER: A model for a systematic career guidance program. *Vocational Guidance Quarterly, 26*(1), 4–12.

Raynor, J. O., & Entin, E. E. (1982). *Motivation, career striving, and aging*. New York: Hemisphere.

Reardon, R. C. (1984). Use of information in career counseling. In H. D. Burck & R. C. Reardon (Eds.), *Career development interventions* (pp. 53–68). Springfield, IL: Charles C. Thomas.

Reardon, R. C., Bonnell, R. O., & Huddleston, M. R. (1982). Self-directed career exploration. A comparison of choices and the self-directed search. *Journal of Vocational Behavior, 20*, 22–30.

Reardon, R. C., Domkowski, D., & Jackson, E. (1980). Career center evaluation methods: A case study. *Vocational Guidance Quarterly, 29*(2), 150–158.

Reardon, R. C., & Loughead, T. (1988). A comparison of paper-and-pencil and computer versions of the Self-Directed Search. *Journal of Counseling and Development, 67*, 249–252.

Reardon, R. C., Zunker, V., & Dyal, M. A. (1979). The status of career planning programs and career centers in colleges and universities. *Vocational Guidance Quarterly, 28*, 154–159.

Reardon, R. W. (1976). Help for the troubled worker in a small company. *Personnel, 53*(1), 50–54.

Redfering, D. L., & Cook, D. (1980). Relationships among vocational training, income, and job complexity of high school dropouts and high school graduates. *Journal of Vocational Behavior, 16*, 158–162.

Reeves, D. J., & Booth, R. F. (1979). Expressed vs. inventoried interests as predictors of paramedical effectiveness. *Journal of Vocational Behavior, 15*, 155–163.

Regehr, C. N., & Herman, A. (1981). Developing the skills of career decision making and self assessment in ninth grade students. *Vocational Guidance Quarterly, 28*(5), 335–342.

Reich, M. H. (1985). Executive views from both sides of mentoring. *Personnel, 62*(1), 42–46.

Reid, G. L. (1972). Job search and the effectiveness of job-finding methods. *Industrial and Labor Relations Review, 25*, 479–495.

Reilly, R. R., & Chao, G. T. (1981). *Validity and fairness of alternative employee selection procedures*. Unpublished manuscript, American Telephone and Telegraph Company, Morristown, NJ.

Reilly, R. R., & Echternacht, G. (1979). Some problems with the criterion-keying approach to occupational interest scale development. *Educational and Psychological Measurement, 39*, 85–94.

Remer, R. (1986). Review of Occupational Aptitude Survey and Interest Schedule (OASIS). *Journal of Counseling and Development, 64*, 467–468.

Remer, R. (1988). Review of Occupational Aptitude Survey and Interest Schedule. In J. T. Kapes & M. M. Mastie (Eds.), A counselor's guide to career assessment instruments (pp. 208–212). Washington DC: National Career Development Assocation.

Renwick, P. A. & Tosi, H. (1978). The effects of sex, marital status, and educational background on selection decisions. *Academy of Management Journal, 21*, 93–103.

Research and Forecasts, Inc. (1980). Retirement preparation: Growing corporate involvement. *Aging and Work, 3*(1), 1–13. New York: Author.

Research and Policy Committee, the Committee for Economic Development. (1985). *Investing in our children, business and public schools*. New York: The Committee.

Research Utilization Branch. (1986, September). *Youth in trouble: A vocational approach*. Research brief. Washington, DC: Division of Research Demonstration Grants, Social and Rehabilitation Services, Department of Health, Education, and Welfare.

Reubens, B. G. (1974). Vocational education. Performance and potential. *Manpower, 6*(7), 23–30.

Rhodes, S. R. (1983). Age-related differences in work attitudes and behavior: A review and conceptual analysis, *Psychological Bulletin, 93*(2), 328–367.

Rice, J. K. (1981). Career education comes of age. *Journal of Career Education, 7*(3), 212–219.

Rice, R. W., Near, J. P., & Hunt, R. G. (1980). The job satisfaction/life satisfaction relationship: A review of empirical research. *Basic and applied social psychology, 1*, 37–64.

Rich, N. S. (1979). Occupational knowledge: To what extent is rural youth handicapped? *Vocational Guidance Quarterly, 27*(4), 320–325.

Richard, G. V., & Krieshok, T. S. (1989). Occupational stress, strain, and coping in a university faculty. *Journal of Vocational Behavior*, *34*(1), 117–132.

Richardson, Bellows, Henry & Co., Inc. (1981). *Supervisory Profile Record*. Washington, DC: Author.

Richardson V., & Kilty, K. M. (1989). Retirement financial planning among black professionals. *The Gerontologist, 29,* 32–37.

Riddick, C. C. (1985). Life satisfaction for older female homemakers, retirees, and workers. *Research on Aging, 7,* 383–393.

Ridener, J. (1973). Careers of the month program. *Elementary School Guidance and Counseling, 7*(3), 235–236.

Riegle, D. W., Jr. (1982). Psychological and social effects of unemployment. *American Psychologist, 37*(10), 113–115.

Riley, M. W. (1982, April). Implications for the middle and later years. In P. W. Berman & E. R. Ramey (Eds.), *Women: A developmental perspective* (pp. 399–405) (NIH Publication No. 82-2298, 399–405). Washington, DC: U.S. Government Printing Office.

Riley, P. J. (1981). The influence of gender on occupational aspirations of kindergarten children. *Journal of Vocational Behavior, 19,* 244–250.

Rimmer, S. M. (1981). A systems approach model for counselor education program development and redefinition. *Counselor Education and Supervision, 21,* 7–15.

Rimmer, S. M., & Kahnweiler, W. M. (1981). The relationship among work, leisure, education, future, and self: An empirical investigation. *Vocational Guidance Quarterly, 30*(2), 109–116.

Rimmer, S. M., & Myers, J. W. (1982). Testing and older persons: A new challenge for counselors. *Measurement and Evaluation in Guidance, 15*(3), 182–193.

Ringle, P. M., & Savickas, M. L. Administrative leadership. Planning and time perspective. *Journal of Higher Education, 54*(6), 649–661.

Rizzo, J. R., House, R. J., & Lirtzman, S. L. (1970). Role conflict and ambiguity in complex organizations. *Administrative Science Quarterly, 15,* 155–163.

Robb, W. D. (1979). Counseling and placement: Must they be separate entities? *Journal of College Placement, 34*(4), 67–71.

Robbins, S. B., & Tucker, K. R., Jr. (1986). Relation of goal instability to self-directed and interactional career counseling workshops. *Journal of Counseling Psychology, 33*(4), 418–424.

Roberts, K. (1968). The entry into employment: An approach toward a general theory. *Sociological Review, 16,* 165–184.

Roberts, K. (1977). *From school to work, a study of the youth employment service*. Newton Abbott, England: David and Charles.

Robertson, A. G. (1988). Review of the ACT Career Planning Program. In J. T. Kapes & M. M. Mastie (Eds.), *A counselor's guide to career assessment instruments* (pp. 192–197). Washington, DC: National Career Development Association.

Robinson, F. P. (1963). Modern approaches to counseling diagnosis. *Journal of Counseling Psychology, 10,* 325–333.

Robison-Awana, P., Kehle, T. J., & Jenson, W. R. (1986). But what about smart girls? Adolescent self-esteem and sex role perceptions as a function of academic achievement. *Journal of Educational Psychology, 78*(3), 179–183.

Roche, G. R. (1979). Much ado about mentors. *Harvard Business Review, 57*(1), 14–28.

Rochelle, C. C., & Spellman, C. (1987). *Dreams betrayed: Working in the technological age*. Lexington, MA: Heath.

Rockwell, L. K., Hood, A. A., & Lee, V. F. (1980). APGA members in retirement and their advice to the rest of us. *Personal and Guidance Journal, 59*(3), 135–139.

Rockwell, T. (1987). The social construction of careers: Career development and career counseling viewed from a sociometric perspective. *Journal of Group Psychotherapy, Psychodrama and Sociometry,* Fall (1), 93–107.

Rodriguez, M., & Blocher, D. (1988). A comparison of two approaches to enhancing career maturity in Puerto Rican college women. *Journal of Counseling Psychology, 35,* 275–280.

Roe, A. (1953). A psychological study of eminent psychologists and anthropologists and a comparison with biological and physical scientists. *Psychological Monographs, 67*(2), 1–55.

Roe, A. (1954). A new classification of occupations. *Journal of Counseling Psychology, 1,* 215–220.

Roe, A. (1956). *The psychology of occupations*. New York: Wiley.

Roe, A., & Lunneborg, P. W. (1984). Personality development and career choice. In D. Brown & L. Brooks (Eds.), *Career choice and development, applying contemporary theories to practice* (Chap. 3). San Francisco: Jossey-Bass.

Roe, A., & Lunneborg, P. W. (1990). Personality Development and Career Choice. In D. Brown & L. Brooks (Eds.), *Career choice and development. Applying contemporary theories to practice* (pp. 68–101). San Francisco: Jossey-Bass.

Roe, A., & Siegelman, M. (1964). *The origin of interests*. Washington, DC: American Personnel and Guidance Association.

Roessler, R. T. (1987). Work, disability, and the future: Promoting employment for people with disabilities. *Journal of Counseling and Development, 66,* 188–190.

Roland, R. L. (1973). *Introduction to industrial mental health and employee counseling*. New York: Behavioral Publications.

Romero, G. J., & Garza, R. T. (1986). Attributions for the occupational success/failure of ethnic minority and nonminority women. *Sex Roles, 14*(7/8), 445–452.

Ronen, S. (1979). A cross-national study of employees' work goals. *International Review of Applied Psychology, 28,* 1–12.

Root, N. (1981). Injuries at work are fewer among older employees. *Monthly Labor Review, 104*(3), 30–34.

Roscow, J. M. (1983). Personnel policies for the 1980s. In J. S. Manuso (Ed.), *Occupational clinical psychology.* New York: Praeger.

Rose, H. A., & Elton, C. F. (1973). Sex and occupational choice. *Journal of Counseling Psychology, 18*(5), 456–461.

Rose, H. A., & Elton, C. F. (1982). The relation of congruence, differentiation and consistency to interest and aptitude scores in women with stable and unstable vocational choices. *Journal of Vocational Behavior, 20*(2), 162–174.

Rose, R., Hurst, M., & Herd, A. (1979). Cardiovascular and endocrine responses to work and the risk of psychiatric symptoms in air traffic controllers. In J. Barrett (Ed.). *Stress and mental disorder.* New York: Raven Press.

Rose, R. L., & Veiga, J. F. (1984). Assessing the sustained effects of a stress management intervention on anxiety and locus of control. *Academy of Management Journal, 27*(1), 190–198.

Roselle, B. E., & Hummel, T. J. (1988). Intellectual development and interaction effectiveness with DISCOVER. *The Career Development Quarterly, 36,* 241–249.

Rosen, S., Cochran, W., & Musser, L. M. (1990). Reactions to a match versus mismatch between an applicant's self-presentational style and work reputation. *Basic and Applied Social Psychology, 11,* 117-129.

Rosenbaum, J. E. (1979). Tournament mobility: Career patterns in a corporation. *Administrative Science Quarterly, 24,* 220–241.

Rosenberg, A. G., & Smith, S. S. (1985). Six strategies for career counseling. *Journal of College Placement, 45*(3), 42–46.

Rosenfeld, R. A. (1979). Women's occupational careers: Individual and structural explanations. *Sociology of Work and Occupations, 6*(3), 283–311.

Rosengarten, W. (1936). *Choosing your life work* (3rd ed.), New York: McGraw-Hill.

Rosenthal, D. A., & Chapman, D. C. (1980). Sex-role stereotypes: Children's perceptions of occupational competence. *Psychological Reports, 44,* 135–139.

Rosenthal, D., & Chapman, D. (1982). The lady spaceman: Children's perceptions of sex-stereotyped occupations. *Sex Roles, 8,* 959–965.

Rosove, B. (1982). Employability assessment: Its importance and one method of doing it. *Journal of Employment Counseling, 19*(3), 113–123.

Rotberg, H. L., Brown, D., & Ware, W. B. (1987). Career self-efficacy expectations and perceived range of career options in community college students. *Journal of Counseling Psychology, 34*(2), 164–170.

Roth, S., & Cohen, L. J. (1986). Approach, avoidance, and coping with stress. *American Psychologist, 41*(7), 813–819.

Rothstein, H. R., Schmidt, F. L., Erwin, F. W., Owens, W. A., & Sparks, C. P. (1990). Biographical data in employment selection: Can validities be made generalizable? *Journal of Applied Psychology, 75,* 175–184.

Rounds, J. B. (1990). The comparative and combined utility of work value and interest data in career counseling with adults. *Journal of Vocational Behavior, 37,* 32–45.

Rounds, J. B., Jr., Davison, M. L., & Davis, R. V. (1979). The fit between Strong-Campbell Interest Inventory general occupational themes and Holland's hexagonal model. *Journal of Vocational Behavior, 15,* 303–315.

Rounds, J. B., Jr., Dawis, R. V., & Lofquist, L. H. (1987). Measurement of person-environment fit and prediction of satisfaction in the theory of work adjustment. *Journal of Vocational Behavior, 31,* 297–318.

Rounds, J. B., Jr., Henly, G. A., Dawis, R. V., & Lofquist, L. H. (1981). *Manual for the Minnesota Importance Questionnaire: A measure of needs and values.* Minneapolis, MN: Vocational Psychology Research, University of Minnesota.

Rounds, J. B., Jr., Shubsachs, A. P. W., Dawis, R. V., & Lofquist, L. H. (1978). A test of Holland's formulations. *Journal of Applied Psychology, 63*(5), 609–616.

Rounds, J. B., Jr., & Tinsley, H. E. A. (1984). Diagnosis and treatment of vocational problems. In S. Brown & R. Lent (Eds.), *Handbook of Counseling Psychology* (pp. 137–177). New York: Wiley.

Rounds, J. B., Jr., & Tracey, T. J. (1990). From trait-and-factor to person-environment fit counseling: Theory and process. In W. B. Walsh & S. H. Osipow (Eds.), *Career counseling: Contemporary topics in vocational psychology* (pp. 1–44). Hillsdale, NJ: Lawrence Elbaum Associates.

Royston, W., Jr. (1970). Forsyth County Vocational High: An investment in youth. *American Vocational Journal, 45,* 58–61.

Rubinton, N. (1980). Instruction in career decision-making and decision-making styles. *Journal of Counseling Psychology, 27,* 581–588.

Rubinton, N. (1985). Career exploration for middle school youth: A university-school cooperative. *The Vocational Guidance Quarterly, 33*(3), 249–255.

Ruch, R. S. (1979). A path analytic study of the structure of employee job satisfaction: The critical role of top management. *Journal of Vocational Behavior, 15,* 277–293.

Rudnick, D. T., & Wallach, E. J. (1980). Women in technology: A program to increase career awareness. *Personnel and Guidance Journal, 58*(6), 445–448.

Rumberger, R. W. (1980). The economic decline of college graduates: Fact or fallacy? *Journal of Human Resources, 15,* 99–112.

Russel, J. H., & Sullivan, T. (1979). Student acquisition of career decision-making skills as a result of faculty advisor intervention. *Journal of College Student Personnel, 20,* 291–296.

Russo, N. F. (1990). Forging research priorities for women's mental health. *American Psychologist, 45,* 368–373.

Ryan, C. (1985). The mentor's place in an adult's life cycle. In D. Jones & S. S. Moore (Eds.), *Counseling adults: Life cycle perspectives.* Lawrence: University of Kansas.

Ryan, C. W., & Drummond, R. J. (1981). University based career education: A model for infusion. *Personnel and Guidance Journal, 60,* 89–92.

Ryan, C. W., Drummond, R. J., & Shannon, M. D. (1980). Guidance information systems: An analysis of impact on school counseling. *The School Counselor, 28*(2), 93–97.

Ryan, M. K. (1972). Middle school community program. *Elementary School Guidance and Counseling, 6*(4), 279–280.

Ryan, T. (1974). A systems approach to career education. *Vocational Guidance Quarterly, 22,* 172.

Ryan, T., & Krumboltz, J. D. (1964). Effect of planned reinforcement counseling on client decision-making behavior. *Journal of Counseling Psychology, 11,* 315–323.

Ryland, E. K., & Rosen, B. (1987). Personnel professionals' reactions to chronological and functional resume formats. *The Career Development Quarterly, 35,* 228–238.

Rynes, S., & Gerhart, B. (1990). Interviewer assessments of applicant "fit": An exploratory investigation. *Personnel Psychology, 43,* 13–35.

Ryscavage, P. M. (1979). BLS labor force projections: A review of methods and results. *Monthly Labor Review, 103,* 12–19.

Rytina, N. F. (1981). Occupational segregation and earnings differences by sex. *Monthly Labor Review, 104,* 49–53.

Sagal, K., & DeBlassie, R. (1981). The male midlife crisis and career change. *Journal of Employment Counseling, 18*(1), 34–42.

Salimi, L., & Hsi, M. L. (1977). Career counseling and the foreign student. *Journal of College Placement, 37*(1), 30–31.

Salomone, P. R. (1982). Difficult cases in career counseling: II. The indecisive client. *The Personnel and Guidance Journal, 60,* 496–500.

Salomone, P. R. (1989). Are "occupational" and "career" information synonymous *The Career Development Quarterly, 38,* 3–5.

Salomone, P. R., & Daughton, S. (1984). Assessing work environments for career counseling. *Vocational Guidance Quarterly, 33*(1), 45–54.

Salomone, P. R., & Sheehan, M. C. (1985). Vocational stability and congruence: An examination of Holland's proposition. *Vocational Guidance Quarterly, 34*(2), 91–98.

Salomone, P. R., & Slaney, R. B. (1978). The applicability of Holland's theory to nonprofessional workers. *Journal of Vocational Behavior, 13,* 63.

Salomone, P. R., & Slaney, R. B. (1981). The influence of chance and contingency factors on the vocational choice process of nonprofessional workers. *Journal of Vocational Behavior, 19,* 25–35.

Samby, G., & Healy, C. (1979). Developing a replicable career decision-making counseling procedure. *Journal of Counseling Psychology, 26,* 210–216.

Samler, J. (1968). Vocational counseling: A pattern and a projection. *Vocational Guidance Quarterly, 17,* 2–11.

Sampson, J. P. (1980). Using college alumni as resource persons for providing occupational information. *Journal of College Student Personnel, 21,* 172.

Sampson, J. P. (1983). Computer-assisted testing and assessment: Current status and implications for the future. *Measurement and Evaluation in Guidance, 15*(3), 293–299.

Sampson, J. P. (1984). Maximizing the effectiveness of computer applications in counseling and human development: The role of research and implementation strategies. *Journal of Counseling and Development, 63*(3), 187–191.

Sampson, J. P., & Loesch, L. C. (1981). Relationship among work values and job knowledge. *Vocational Guidance Quarterly, 29*(3), 229–235.

Sampson, J. P., Peterson, G. W., & Reardon, R. C. (1989). Counselor intervention strategies for computer-assisted career guidance: An information-processing approach. *Journal of Career Development, 16,* 139–154.

Sampson, J. P., & Pyle, K. R. (1983). Ethical issues involved with the use of computer-assisted counseling, testing, and guidance systems. *Personnel and Guidance Journal, 61*(3), 283–287.

Sampson, J. P., & Reardon, R. C. (Eds.). (1990). *Enhancing the design and use of computer-assisted career guidance systems.* Washington, DC: NCDA.

Sampson, J. P., & Reardon, R. C. (in press). Current development in computer-assisted career guidance in the USA. *British Journal of Guidance and Counseling.*

Sampson, J. P., Shahnasarian, M., & Reardon, R. C. (1987). Computer-assisted career guidance: A national perspective on the use of DISCOVER and SIGI. *Journal of Counseling and Development, 65,* 416–419.

Samuda, R. J. (1975). *Psychological testing of American minorities: Issues and consequences.* New York: Dodd, Mead.

Sander, D., Westerberg, W., & Hedstrom, J. E. (1978). Career education through children's literature. *Elementary School Guidance and Counseling, 13*(2), 129–132.

Sandmeyer, L. E. (1980). Choices and changes: A workshop for women. *Vocational Guidance Quarterly, 28*(4), 352–359.

Sarason, I. G., & Johnson, J. H. (1979). Life stress, organizational stress, and job satisfaction. *Psychological Reports, 44,* 75–79.

Sarason, S. B., Sarason, E., & Cowden, P. (1975). Aging and the nature of work. *American Psychologist, 30,* 584–592.

Sauter, D., Seidl, A., & Karbon, J. (1980). The effects of high school counseling experience and attitudes toward women's roles on traditional or nontraditional career choice. *Vocational Guidance Quarterly, 28*(3), 242–249.

Savickas, M. L., (1989). Annual review. Practice and research in career counseling and development, 1988. *The Career Development Quarterly, 38,* 100–134.

Savickas, M. L. (1990a). The career decision-making course: Description and field test. *The Career Development Quarterly, 38,* 275–284.

Savickas, M. L. (1990b January). Career interventions that create hope. Paper presented at the National Conference of the National Career Development Association, Scottsdale, AZ.

Savickas, M. L., Passen, A. J., & Jarjoura, D. G. (1988). Career concern and coping as indicators of adult career development. *Journal of Vocational Behavior, 33,* 82–98.

Savickas, M. L., Stilling, S. M., & Schwartz, S. (1984). Time perspective in vocational maturity and career decision making. *Journal of Vocational Behavior, 25,* 258–269.

Savicki, V., & Cooley, E. J. (1982). Implications of burnout research and theory for counselor educators. *Personnel and Guidance Journal, 60,* 415–419.

Savicki, V., & Cooley, E. (1987). The relationship of work environment and client contact to burnout in mental health professionals. *Journal of Counseling and Development, 65,* 249–252.

Scanlan, T. J. (1980). Toward an occupational classification for self-employed men; An investigation of entrepreneurship from the perspective of Holland's theory of career development. *Journal of Vocational Behavior, 16,* 163–172.

Scarr, S., Phillips, D., & McCartney, K. (1989). Working mothers and their families. *American Psychologist, 44,* 1402–1409.

Schaef, A. W., & Fassel, D. (1988). *The Addictive Organization.* San Francisco: Harper & Row.

Schaffer, K. (1976). Evaluating job satisfaction and success for emotionally maladjusted men. *Journal of Vocational Behavior, 9,* 329–335.

Schein, E. H. (1968). Organizational socialization and the process of management. *Industrial Management Review, 9,* 1–16.

Schein, E. H. (1971). The individual, the organization, and the career: A conceptual scheme. *Journal of Applied Behavioral Science, 7*(4), 415–416, 421–424.

Schein, E. H. (1978). *Career dynamics: Matching individual and organizational needs.* Reading, MA: Addison-Wesley.

Schenk, G. E., Murphy, P. P., & Shelton, R. L. (1980). Computerized career information systems on the college campus: A low-cost, do-it-yourself approach. *Personnel and Guidance Journal, 58*(8), 516–520.

Schill, W. J., McCarten, R., & Meyer, K. (1985). Youth employment: Its relationship to academic and family variables. *Journal of Vocational Behavior, 26*(2), 155–163.

Schlichter, K. J., & Horan, J. J. (1981). Effects of stress inoculation on the anger and aggression management skills of institutionalized juvenile delinquents. *Cognitive Therapy and Research, 5*(4), 359–365.

Schlossberg, N. K. (1978). Five propositions about adult development. *Journal of College Student Personnel, 19*(5), 418–423.

Schlossberg, N. K. (1981). A model for analyzing human adaptation to transition. *The Counseling Psychologist, 9*(2), 2–18.

Schlossberg, N. K. (1984). *Counseling adults in transition, linking practice with theory.* New York: Springer.

Schlossberg, N. K. (1986). Adult career development theories: Ways to illuminate the adult experience. In Z. Leibowitz & H. D. Lea (Eds.), *Adult Career Development, Concepts, Issues and Practices* (Chapter 1). Alexandria, VA: National Career Development Association.

Schlossberg, N. K., & Leibowitz, Z. (1980). Organizational support systems as buffers to job loss. *Journal of Vocational Behavior, 17,* 204–217.

Schlosstein, S. (1989). *The end of the American century.* New York: Congdon & Weed, Inc.

Schmidt, F. L., & Hunter, J. E. (1981). Employment testing: Old theories and new research findings. *American Psychologist, 36,* 1128–1137.

Schmidt, F. L., Hunter, J. E., & Urry, V. (1976). Statistical power in the criterion-related validity studies. *Journal of Applied Psychology, 61,* 473–485.

Schmidt, J. A. (1976). Self-concepts and career exploration. *Elementary School Guidance and Counseling, 11*(2), 145–153.

Schmitt, N., Gooding, R. Z., Noe, R. A., & Kirsch, M. (1984). Metanalysis of validity studies published between 1964 and 1982 and the investigation of study characteristics. *Personnel Psychology, 37,* 407–422.

Schmitt, N., & McCune, J. T. (1981). The relationship between job attitudes and the decision to retire. *Academy of Management Journal, 24*(4), 795–802.

Schmitt, N., & Mellon, P. M. (1980). Life and job satisfaction: Is the job central? *Journal of Vocational Behavior, 16,* 51–58.

Schoen, R., & Cohen, L. E. (1980). Ethnic endogamy among Mexican-American grooms: A reanalysis of generational and occupational effects. *American Journal of Sociology, 86*(2), 359–366.

Schonfeld, I. S. (1990). Coping with job-related stress: The case of teachers. *Journal of Occupational Psychology, 63,* 141–149.

Schontz, F. C. (1975). *The psychological aspects of physical illness and disability.* New York: Macmillan.

Schore, L. (1984). The Freemont experience: A counseling program for dislocated workers. *International Journal of Mental Health, 13,* 154–168.

Schrank, F. A. (1982). A faculty/counselor implemented career planning course. *Journal of College Student Personnel, 23,* 83–84.

Schriner, K. F., & Roessler, R. T. (1990). Employment concerns of college students with disabilities: Toward an agenda for policy and practice. *Journal of College Student Development, 31* (July), 307–312.

Schroer, A. C. P., & Dorn, F. J. (1986). Enhancing the career and personal development of gifted college students. *Journal of Counseling and Development, 64,* 567–571.

Schulenberg, J. E. (1986). *The factor structure of work values and career interests: Continuity and discontinuity during adolescence.* Unpublished doctoral dissertation, Pennsylvania State University.

Schulenberg, J. E., Vondracek, F. W., & Crouter, A. C. (1984). The influence of the family on vocational development. *Journal of Marriage and the Family, 46,* 129–143.

Schumacher, E. F. (1981). Good work. In J. O'Toole, J. L. Scheiber & L. C. Wood (Eds.), *Working, changes, and choices* (pp. 25–32). New York: Human Sciences Press.

Schwab, R. L. (1981). The relationship of role conflict, role ambiguity, teacher background variables and perceived burnout among teachers (Doctoral dissertation, University of Connecticut, 1980). *Dissertation Abstracts International, 41*(9), 3823-A.

Schwalbe, M. L. (1988). Sources of self-esteem in work. What's important for whom? *Work and Occupations, 15*(1), 24–35.

Schwartz, F. N. (1989). Management women and the new facts of life. *Harvard Business Review,* Jan/Feb, 65–76.

Schwartz, G. E. (1980). Stress management in occupational settings. *Public Health Reports, 95,* 99.

Schwartz, R. H., Andiappan, P., & Nelson, M. (1986). Reconsidering the support for Holland's congruence-achievement hypothesis. *Journal of Counseling Psychology, 33*(4), 425–428.

Schwarzwald, J., & Shoham, M. (1981). A trilevel approach to motivation for retraining. *Journal of Vocational Behavior, 18,* 265–276.

Scott, J., & Hatalla, J. (1990). The influence of chance and contingency factors on career patterns of college-educated women. *The Career Development Quarterly, 39,* 18–30.

Scott, M. L., Davis, G. N., & Difenderfer, R. (1984). Career development and assessment process model for coordinated vocational services. *Vocational Evaluation and Work Adjustment Bulletin,* Spring, 18–21.

Scott, T. B., & Anandon, M. (1980). A comparison of the vocational interest profiles of Native Americans and Caucasian college-bound students. *Measurement and Evaluation in Guidance, 13*(1), 35–42.

Search Institute. (1988). The risky business of growing up female. *Source, 4*(1), 1–4.

Sears, S. (1982). A definition of career guidance terms: A national vocational guidance association perspective. *Vocational Guidance Quarterly, 31*(2), 137–143.

Seccombe, K., & Lee, G. R. (1986). Gender differences in retirement satisfaction and its antecedents. *Research on Aging, 8,* 426–440.

Segall, M. H., Dasen, V. R., Berry, J. W., & Poortinga, V. H. (1990). *Human behavior in global perspective: An introduction to cross-cultural psychology.* New York: Pergamon Press.

Sehgal, E., & Vialet, J. (1980). Documenting the undocumented: Data, like aliens, are elusive. *Monthly Labor Review, 103,* 18–21.

Seidman, S. A., & Zager, J. (1987). The teacher burnout scale. *Educational Research Quarterly, 11,* 26–33.

Sekaran, U. (1982). An investigation of career salience for men and women in dual-career families. *Journal of Vocational Behavior, 20,* 111–119.

Sekaran, U. (1986a). *Dual-career families: Contemporary organizational and counseling issues.* San Francisco: Jossey--Bass.

Sekaran, U. (1986b). Self-esteem and sense of competence as moderators of the job satisfaction of professionals in dual-career families. *Journal of Occupational Behaviour, 7,* 341–344.

Seligman, L., Weinstock, L., & Owings, N. (1988, February). The role of family dynamics in career development of 5-year-olds. *Elementary School Guidance and Counseling,* 222–230.

Selye, H. (1975). *Stress without distress.* New York: Signet.

Selye, H. (1976). *The stress of life.* New York: McGraw-Hill.

Selz, N., Jones, J. S., & Ashley, W. L. (1980). *Functional competencies for adapting to the world of work.* Columbus, OH: National Center for Research in Vocational Education, Ohio State University.

Sepich, R. T. (1987). A review of the correlates and measurements of career indecision. *Journal of Career Development, 1*(1), 8–17.

Shamir, B. (1986a). Self-esteem and the psychological impact of unemployment. *Social Psychology Quarterly, 49*(1), 61–72.

Shamir, B. (1986b). Protestant work ethic, work involvement, and the psychological impact of unemployment. *Journal of Occupational Behavior, 7,* 25–38.

Shane, H. G. (1970). A curriculum continuum: Possible trends in the 70's. *Phi Delta Kappan, 51,* 389–392.

Sharf, R. S. (1974). Interest inventory interpretation: Implications for research and practice. *Measurement and Evaluation in Guidance, 7*(1), 16–23.

Sharf, R. S. (1978). Evaluation of a computer-based narrative interpretation of a test battery. *Measurement and Evaluation in Guidance, 11*(1), 50–53.

Sharf, R. S. (1984a). The effect of occupational information on a computerized vocational counseling system. *Vocational Guidance Quarterly, 33*(2), 130–137.

Sharf, R. S. (1984b). Vocational information-seeking behavior: Another view. *Vocational Guidance Quarterly, 33*(2), 120–129.

Shaw, M. C. (1968). The function of theory in guidance programs. *Guidance monograph series I: Organizations and administration.* Boston: Houghton Mifflin.

Sheehy, G. (1976). *Passages: Predictable crises of adult life.* New York: Dutton.

Sheehy, G. (1981). *Pathfinders.* New York: Bantam.

Shepard, J. M., Kim, D. I., & Houghland, J. G. (1979). Effects of Technology in industrialized and industrializing societies. *Sociology of Work and Occupations, 6*(4), 457–481.

Shepelak, N. J., Ogden, D., & Robin-Bennett, D. (1984). The influence of gender labels on the sex typing of imaginary occupations. *Sex Roles, 11,* 983–997.

Sheppard, D. I. (1971). The measurement of vocational maturity in adults. *Journal of Vocational Behavior, 1,* 399–406.

Sherry, P., & Staley, K. (1984). Career exploration groups: An outcome study. *Journal of College Student Personnel, 25*(2), 155–159.

Shontz, F. C. (1975). *The psychological aspects of physical illness and disability.* New York: Macmillan.

Shore, L. M., & Martin, H. J. (1989). Job satisfaction and organizational commitment in relation to work performance and turnover intentions. *Human Relations, 42,* 625–638.

Shostak, A. B. (1985). An overview of both the persisting and emerging problems. In P. A. Carone et al. (Eds.), *Mental health problems of workers and their families* (pp. 15–31). New York: Human Sciences Press.

Shultz, J. T. (1979). The private sector: A new frontier? *Vocational Guidance Quarterly, 27*(3), 276–280.

Siegel, C. L. F. (1973). Sex differences in the occupational choices of second graders. *Journal of Vocational Behavior, 3,* 15–19.

Siegfried, W. D., MacFarlane, I., Graham, D. G., Moore, N. A., & Young, P. L. (1981). A reexamination of sex differences in job preferences. *Journal of Vocational Behavior, 18,* 30–42.

Sievert, N. W. (1972). The role of the self-concept in determining an adolescent's occupational choice. *Journal of Industrial Teacher Education, 9*(3), 47–53.

Simmons, D. (1962). Children's ranking of occupational prestige. *Personnel and Guidance Journal, 41,* 332–336.

Simpson, E. J. (1972). The classification of educational objectives in the psychomotor domain. *The psychomotor domain: A resource book for media specialists* (pp. 43–56). The National Special Media Institutes. Washington, DC: Gryphon House.

Skinner, D. A. (1980). Dual-career family stress and coping: A literature review. *Family Relations, 29*(4), 473–481.

Skovholt, T. M., Morgan, J. I., & Negron-Cunningham, H. (1989). Mental imagery in career counseling and life planning: A review of research and intervention methods. *Journal of Counseling and Development, 67,* 287– 292.

Slakter, M. J., & Cramer, S. H. (1969). Risk-taking and vocational or curriculum choice. *Vocational Guidance Quarterly, 17*(2), 127–132.

Slaney, R. B., (1980a). Expressed vocational choice and vocational indecision. *Journal of Counseling Psychology, 27,* 122–129.

Slaney, R. B. (1980b). An investigation of racial differences in vocational values among college women, *Journal of Vocational Behavior, 16,* 197–207.

Slaney, R. B. (1988). The assessment of career decision making. In W. B. Walsh & S. H. Osipow (Eds.), *Career decision making* (pp. 33–76). Hillsdale: Erlbaum Associates.

Slaney, R. B., & Lewis, E. T. (1986). Effects of career exploration on career undecided reentry women: An intervention and follow-up study. *Journal of Vocational Behavior, 28,* 97–109.

Slaney, R. B., Palko-Nonemaker, D., & Alexander, R. (1981). An investigation of two measures of indecision. *Journal of Vocational Behavior, 18,* 92–103.

Slaney, R. B., & Russell, J. E. A. (1987). Perspectives on vocational behavior, 1986: A review. *Journal of Vocational Behavior, 31,* 111–173.

Slaney, R. B., Stafford, J. J., & Russell, J. E. A. (1981). Career indecision in adult women: A comparative and descriptive study. *Journal of Vocational Behavior, 19*(3), 335–345.

Slaughter, D. T., & Johnson, D. T. (Eds.). (1988). *Visible now: Blacks in private schools*. Westport, CT: Greenwood Press.

Slavenski, L. (1987). Career development: A systems approach. *Training and Development Journal,* 56–60.

Slocum, W. L., & Bowles, R. T. (1968). Attractiveness of occupations to high school students. *Personnel and Guidance Journal, 46,* 754–761.

Slocum, J. W., & Cron, W. L. (1985). Job attitudes and performance during three career stages. *Journal of Vocational Behavior, 26*(2), 126–145.

Smallwood, K. B. (1980). What do adult women college students really need? *Journal of College Student Personnel, 21,* 65–73.

Smart, J. C. (1986). College effects on occupational status attainment. *Research in Higher Education, 24*(1), 73–94.

Smart, J. C., Elton, C. F., & McLaughlin, G. W. (1986). Person-environment congruence and job satisfaction. *Journal of Vocational Behavior, 29,* 216–225.

Smith, A., & Chemers, M. M. (1981). Misperceptions of motivation of economically disadvantaged employees in work settings. *Journal of Employment Counseling, 18*(1), 24–33.

Smith, E. D. (1968). Innovative ideas in vocational guidance. *American Vocational Journal, 43,* 19–21.

Smith, E. D. (1977, September). Personal communication.

Smith, E. J. (1981). The working mother: A critique of the research. *Journal of Vocational Behavior, 18,* 191–211.

Smith, E. R. (Ed.). (1979a). *The subtle revolution*. Washington DC: The Urban Institute.

Smith, E. R. (1979b). *Women in the labor force in 1990*. Washington, DC: The Urban Institute.

Smith, E. R. (1980). Desiring and expecting to work among high school girls: Some determinants and consequences. *Journal of Vocational Behavior, 17*(2), 218–230.

Smith, H. L. (1986). Overeducation and underemployment: An agnostic review. *Sociology of Education, 59,* 85–99.

Smith, H. L., & Powell, B. (1990). Great expectations: Variations in income expectations among college seniors. *Sociology of Education, 63,* 194–207.

Smith, M. (1943). An empirical scale of prestige status occupations. *American Sociological Review, 8,* 185–192.

Smith, R. D., & Evans, J. R. (1973). Comparison of experimental group guidance and individual counseling as facilitators of vocational development. *Journal of Counseling Psychology, 20*(3), 202–208.

Smith, R. I., & Southern, C. (1980). Multimodal career counseling: An application of the "BASIC ID." *Vocational Guidance Quarterly, 29*(1), 56–64.

Smith, S. M., & Golden, B. J. (1982). Vocational services for older adults or "I want to work, but." *Journal of Employment Counseling, 19*(1), 29–33.

Sneegas, J. J. (1986). Components of life satisfaction in middle and later life adults: Perceived social competence, leisure participation and leisure satisfaction. *Journal of Leisure Research, 18*(4), 248–258.

Snipes, J. K., & McDaniels, C. (1981). Theoretical foundations for career information delivery systems. *Vocational Guidance Quarterly*, *29*(4), 307–314.

Snodgrass, G., & Healy, C. C. (1979). Developing a replicable career decision-making counseling procedure. *Journal of Counseling Psychology, 26,* 210–216.

Snyder, J. F., Hill, C. E., & Derksen, T. P. (1974). Why some students do not use university counseling services. *Journal of Counseling Psychology, 19*(4), 263–268.

Snyder, R. A., Williams, R. R., & Cashman, J. F. (1984). Age, tenure, and work perceptions as predictors of reaction to performance feedback. *Journal of Psychology, 116,* 11–21.

Sobol, M. G. (1978). Use of labor market forecasts by high school counselors. *The School Counselor, 26*(1), 57–61.

Solomon, B. A. (1985). Consensus on wellness programs. *Personnel, 62,* 67–72.

Sorokin, P. (1927). *Social mobility* (pp. 225 & 238). New York: Harper.

Sovilla, E. S. (1970). A plan for career planning. *Journal of College Placement, 21*(1), 50–58.

Spaeth, J. L. (1968). Occupation prestige expectations among male college graduates. *American Journal of Sociology, 73,* 548–558.

Spanard, J. M. A. (1990). Beyond intent: Reentering college to complete the degree. *Review of Educational Research, 60*(3), 309–344.

Spicuzza, F. J., & DeVoe, M. W. (1982). Burnout in the helping professions: Mutual aid as self-help. *Personnel and Guidance Journal, 61*(2), 95–99.

Spitzberg, B. H., & Cupach, W. R. (1989). *Handbook of interpersonal competence research.* New York: Springer-Verlag.

Spitze, G. D., & Huker, J. (1980). Changing attitudes toward women's nonfamily roles: 1938–1978. *Sociology of Work and Occupations, 7*(3), 317–335.

Spitze, G. D., & Waite, L. J. (1980). Labor force and work attitudes: Young women's early experiences. *Sociology of Work and Occupations, 7*(1), 3–32.

Spokane, A. (1985). A review of research on person-environment congruence in Holland's theory of careers. *Journal of Vocational Behavior*, *26,* 306–343.

Spokane, A. (1990). Supplementing differential research in vocational psychology using nontraditional methods. In R. A. Young and W. A. Borgen (Eds.), *Methodological approaches to the study of careers* (pp. 25–36) New York: Praeger.

Spokane, A. R. (1979). Validity of the Holland categories for college women and men. *Journal of College Student Personnel, 20*(4), 335–340.

Spokane, A. R. (1989). Are there psychological and mental health consequences of difficult career decisions? A reaction to Herr. *Journal of Career Counseling*, *16*, 19–24.

Spokane, A. R. (1991). *Career intervention.* Englewood Cliffs, NJ: Prentice-Hall.

Spokane, A. R. & Oliver, L. W. (1983). The outcomes of vocational intervention. In S. H. Osipow, & W. B. Walsh (Eds.), *Handbook of Vocational Psychology,* Vol. 2. Hillsdale, NJ: Erlbaum.

Spranger, E. (1928). *Types of men: The psychology and ethics of personality* (Paul J. W. Pigors, Trans.). Halle, Germany: Max Niemeyer Verlag.

Spreitzer, E., Snyder, E., & Larson, D. (1980). The relative effects of health and income in life satisfaction. *International Journal of Aging and Development, 10*(3), 283–288.

Sproles, E. K. (1988). Research indicates new approaches for counseling vocational education students. *The School Counselor, 36*(1), 18–23.

Spruell, G. (1987). Work fever. *Training and Development Journal, 41,* 41–45.

Staley, N. K., & Mangiesi, J. N. (1984). Using books to enhance career awareness. *Elementary School Guidance and Counseling, 18,* 200–208.

Stamm, M. L., & Nissman, B. S. (1973). The counselor's view of the middle school student. *The School Counselor, 21*(1), 34–38.

Standards and guidelines. (1985). Council for the Advancement of Standards for Student Services/Development Programs. Consortium of Professional Associations in Higher Education.

Staples, R. (1986). The political economy of black family life. *The Black Scholar, 17*(5), 2–11.

Steers, R. M., & Porter, L. W. (1975). *Motivation and work behavior.* New York: McGraw-Hill.

Stefflre, B. (1966). Vocational development: Ten propositions in search of a theory. *Personnel and Guidance Journal, 44,* 611–616.

Stein, J. A., Newcomb, M. D., & Bentler, P. M. (1990). The relative influence of vocational behavior and family involvement on self-esteem: Longitudinal analyses of young adult women and men. *Journal of Vocational Behavior, 36*(3), 320–338.

Stein, L. I., & Test, M. A. (1980). Alternative to mental hospital treatment: Conceptual model, treatment program, clinical evaluation. *Archives of General Psychiatry, 27*(4), 392–397.

Steiner, D. D., & Truxill, D. M. (1989). An improved test of the disaggregation hypothesis of job and life satisfaction. *Journal of Occupational Psychology, 62,* 33–39.

Steinweg, D. A. (1990). Implications of current research for counseling the unemployed. *Journal of Employment Counseling, 27,* 37–40.

Stephens, D. B., Watt, J. T., & Hobbs, W. S. (1979). Getting through the résumé preparation maze: Some empirically based guidelines for résumé format. *Vocational Guidance Quarterly, 28*(1), 25–34.

Stephens, W. R. (1970). *Social reform and the origins of vocational guidance*. Washington, DC: National Vocational Guidance Association.

Stern, B. E. (1977). *Toward a federal policy on education and work.* Washington, DC: U.S. Department of Health, Education, and Welfare.

Stern, D., & Nakata, Y. (1989). Characteristics of high school students' paid jobs, and employment experience after graduation. Chapter 8 in *Adolescence and work: Influences of social structure, labor markets, and culture* (pp. 189–234). Edited by David Stern and Dorothy Eichorn. Hillsdale, NJ: Lawrence Erlbaum Associates, Publishers.

Stevenson, W. (1978). The transition from school to work. In A. Adams and G. L. Mangum (Eds.), *The lingering crisis of youth unemployment* (pp. 65–90). Kalamazoo, MI: Upjohn Institute for Employment Research.

Stewart, A. J., & Healy, M. M., Jr. (1989). Linking individual development and social changes. *American Psychologist, 44*(1), 30–42.

Stewart, N. (1947). AGCT scores of army personnel grouped by occupations. *Occupations, 26,* 5–41.

Stewart, N. R., Winborn, B. B., Johnson, R. G., Burks, H. M., & Engelkes, J. R. (1978). *Systematic counseling*. Englewood Cliffs, NJ: Prentice-Hall.

Stockton, N., Berry, J., Shepson, J., & Utz, P. (1980). Sex role and innovative major choice among college students. *Journal of Vocational Behavior, 16,* 360–367.

Stone, C. I., & Sawatzki, B. (1980). Hiring bias and the disabled interviewee: Effects of manipulating work history and disability information of the disabled job applicant. *Journal of Vocational Behavior, 16,* 96–104.

Stone, D. L., & Stone, E. F. (1987). Effects of missing application-blank information on personnel selection decisions: Do privacy protection strategies bias the outcome? *Journal of Applied Psychology, 72,* 452–456.

Stonewater, B. B., Eveslage, S. A., & Dingerson, M. R. (1990). Gender differences in career development relationships. *Career Development Quarterly, 39,* 72–85.

Storey, W. D. (Ed.). (1978). *A guide for career development inquiry.* Madison, WI: American Society for Training and Development.

Stout, S. K., Slocum, J. W., & Cron, W. L. (1988). Dynamics of the career plateauing process. *Journal of Vocational Behavior, 34,* 102–114.

Stoyva, J., & Anderson, C. (1982). A coping-rest model of relaxation and stress management. In L. Goldberger, & S. Breznitz (Eds.), *Handbook of stress: Theoretical and clinical aspects* (pp. 745–763). New York: The Free Press.

Stryker, L. E., & Scorzelli, J. F. (1977). Work, counseling, and ex-offenders. *Offender Rehabilitation, 1*(3), 263–266.

Study finds 60% of 11 million who lost jobs got new ones. (1986, February 7). *New York Times,* pp. A1, A5.

Stumpf, S. A., Austin, E. J., & Hartman, K. (1984). The impact of career exploration and interview readiness on interview performance and outcomes. *Journal of Vocational Behavior, 24,* 221–235.

Stumpf, S. A., & Rabinowitz, S. (1981). Career stage as a moderator of performance relationships with facets of job satisfaction and role perceptions. *Journal of Vocational Behavior, 18,* 202–218.

Suchet, M., & Barling, J. (1985). Employed mothers: Interrole conflict, spouse support, and marital functioning. *Journal of Occupational Behaviour, 7,* 167–178.

Sue, D., & Padilla, A. (1986). Ethnic minority issues in the United States: Challenges for the educational system. In *Beyond language: Social and cultural factors in schooling language minority students* (pp. 34–72). Los Angeles: California State Department of Education.

Sue, S., & Abe, J. (1988). *Predictors of academic achievement among Asian American and white students* (Report No. 88-11). New York: College Entrance Examination Board.

Sue, S., & Okazaki, S. (1990). Asian-American educational achievements: A phenomenon in search of an explanation. *American Psychologist, 45,* (8), 913–920.

Sullivan, P. R. (1970). Counseling in the employment service or Sullivan's theories of employment counseling. *Journal of Employment Counseling, 7,* 127–128.

Sundal-Hansen, L. S. (1984). Interrelationship of gender and career. In N. C. Gysbers (Ed.), *Designing careers: Counseling to enhance education, work, and leisure.* San Francisco: Jossey-Bass.

Sundal-Hansen, L. S. (1985). Sex-role issues in counseling women and men. In P. Pedersen (Ed.), *Handbook of cross-cultural counseling and therapy* (pp. 213–222). Westport, CT: Greenwood Press.

Sundby, D. Y. (1980). The career quad: A psychological look at some divergent dual-career families. In C. B. Derr (Ed.), *Work, family, and the career: New frontiers in theory and research* (pp. 329–353). New York: Praeger.

Sundstrom, E., Burt, R. E., & Kamp, D. (1980). Privacy at work: Architectural correlates of job satisfaction and job performance. *Academy of Management Journal, 23,*(1), 101–117.

Super, D. E. (1951). Vocational adjustment: Implementing a self-concept. *Occupations, 30,* 88–92.

Super, D. E. (1953). A theory of vocational development. *American Psychologist, 8,* 185–190.

Super, D. E. (1954). Career patterns as a basis for vocational counseling. *Journal of Counseling Psychology, 1,* 12–20.

Super, D. E. (1955). Transition: From vocational guidance to counseling psychology. *Journal of Counseling Psychology, 2,* 3–9.

Super, D. E. (1957). *The psychology of careers.* New York: Harper & Row.

Super, D. E. (1962). The structure of work values in relation to status, achievement, interest, and adjustment. *Journal of Applied Psychology, 46,* 227–239.

Super, D. E. (1969a). Vocational development theory: Persons, positions, and processes. *The Counseling Psychologist, 1,* 2–9.

Super, D. E. (1969b). The natural history of a study of lives and of vocations. *Perspectives on Education, 2,* 13–22.

Super, D. E. (1974). The broader context of career development and vocational guidance: American trends in world perspective. In E. L. Herr (Ed.), *Vocational guidance and human development* (Chap. 3). Boston: Houghton Mifflin.

Super, D. E. (1976). *Career education and the meaning of work.* Monographs on career education. Washington, DC: The Office of Career Education, U.S. Office of Education.

Super, D. E. (1977). Vocational maturity in mid-career. *Vocational Guidance Quarterly, 25*(4), 294–302.

Super, D. E. (1980). A life-span, life space approach to career development. *Journal of Vocational Behavior, 16*(30), 282–298.

Super, D. E. (1981). Approaches to occupational choice and career development. In A. G. Watts, D. E. Super, & J. M. Kidd (Eds.), *Career development in Britain.* Cambridge, England: Hobsons Press.

Super, D. E. (1982). The relative importance of work: Models and measures for meaningful data. *The Counseling Psychologist, 10*(4), 95–104.

Super, D. E. (1983). Assessment in career guidance: Toward truly developmental counseling. *Personnel and Guidance Journal, 61*(9), 555–562.

Super, D. E. (1984a). Career and life development. In D. Brown, & L. Brooks (Eds.), *Career choice and development; applying contemporary approaches to practice.* San Francisco: Jossey-Bass.

Super, D. E. (1984b). Perspectives on the meaning and value of work. In N. C. Gysbers (Ed.), *Designing careers: Counseling to enhance education, work, and leisure* (Chap. 1). San Francisco: Jossey-Bass.

Super, D. E. (1985a). Career counseling across cultures. In P. Pedersen (Ed.), *Handbook of cross-cultural counseling and therapy* (pp. 11–20). Westport, CT: Greenwood Press.

Super, D. E. (1985b). *New dimensions in adult vocational and career counseling.* Occasional paper No. 106. Columbus, OH: The National Center for Research in Vocational Education.

Super, D. E. (1990). A life-span, life-space approach to career development. In D. Brown & L. Brooks (Eds.), *Career choice and development: Applying contemporary theories to practice* (pp. 197–261). San Francisco: Jossey-Bass.

Super, D. E., & Backrach, P. (1957). *Scientific careers and vocational development theory.* New York: Teachers College Press.

Super, D. E., Bohn, M. J., Forrest, D. J., Jordaan, J. P., Lindeman, R. H., & Thompson, A. A. (1971). *Career development inventory.* New York: Teachers College, Columbia University.

Super, D. E., Crites, J. O., Hummel, R. C., Moser, H. P., Overstreet, P. L., & Warnath, C. F. (1957). *Vocational development: A framework for research.* New York: Teachers College, Columbia University.

Super, D. E., and associates (1974). *Measuring vocational maturity for counseling and evaluation.* Washington, DC: National Vocational Guidance Association.

Super, D. E., & Forrest, D. J. (1972). *Preliminary manual: Career development inventory.* New York: Columbia University Teachers College.

Super, D. E., & Hall, D. T. (1978). Career development: Exploration and planning. *Annual Review of Psychology, 29,* 333–372.

Super, D. E., & Kidd, J. M. (1979). Vocational maturity in adulthood: Toward turning a model into a measure. *Journal of Vocational Behavior, 14*(3), 255–270.

Super, D. E., & Nevill, D. D. (1984). Work role salience as a determinant of career maturity in high school students. *Journal of Vocational Behavior, 25*, 30–44.

Super, D. E., & Overstreet, P. L. (1960). *The vocational maturity of ninth-grade boys*. New York: Teachers College, Columbia University.

Super, D. E., Starishevsky, R., Matlin, N., & Jordaan, J. P. (1963). *Career development: Self-concept theory*. New York: College Entrance Examination Board.

Sverko, B. (1989). Origin of individual differences in importance attached to work: A model and a contribution to its evaluation. *Journal of Vocational Behavior, 34*(1), 28–39.

Swanson, G. (1982). Vocational patterns in the United States. In H. F. Silverman (Ed.), *Education and work*. Eighty-first yearbook of the National Society for the Study of Education, Pt. 2. Chicago: University of Chicago Press.

Swanson, J. L., & Hansen, J-I. C. (1988). Stability of vocational interests over 4-year, 8-year, and 12-year intervals. *Journal of Vocational Behavior, 33*, 185–202.

Swanson, J. L., & Lease, S. H. (1990). Gender differences in self-ratings of abilities and skills. *The Career Development Quarterly, 38*, 347–359.

Swanson-Kauffman, K. M. (Ed.). (1987). *Women's work, families, and health*. New York: Hemisphere.

Swatko, M. K. (1981). What's in a title? Personality, job aspirations, and the nontraditional woman. *Journal of Vocational Behavior, 18*, 174–183.

Szilagyi, A. D., & Holland, W. E. (1980). Changes in social density: Relationships with functional interaction and perceptions of job characteristics, role stress, and work satisfaction. *Journal of Applied Psychology, 65*(1), 28–33.

Szinovacz, M. (1987). Preferred retirement timing and retirement satisfaction in women. *International Journal of Aging and Human Development, 24*, 301–315.

Taber, T. D., Cooke, R. A., & Walsh, J. T. (1990). A joint business-community approach to improve problem solving by workers displaced in a plant shutdown. *Journal of Community Psychology, 18*, 19–33.

Takai, R., & Holland, J. L. (1979). Comparison of the Vocational Card Sort, the SDS, and the Vocational Exploration and Insight Kit. *Vocational Guidance Quarterly, 27*(4), 312–318.

Taylor, A. (1986). Why women managers are bailing out. *Fortune, 114* (4), 16–23.

Taylor, D. E. (1981). Education, on-the-job training, and the black-white earnings gap. *Monthly Labor Review, 104*, 28–34.

Taylor, K. M., & Popma, J. (1990). An examination of the relationships among career decision-making self-efficacy, career salience, locus of control, and vocational indecision. *Journal of Vocational Behavior, 37*, 17–31.

Taylor, M. S. (1985). The roles of occupational knowledge and vocational self-concept crystallization in students' school-to-work transition. *Journal of Counseling Psychology, 32*(4), 539–550.

Taylor, N. B. (1985). How do career counselors counsel? *British Journal of Guidance and Counseling, 13*(2), 166–177.

Taylor, N. B., & Pryor, R. G. L. (1985). Exploring the process of compromise in career decision making. *Journal of Vocational Behavior, 27*, 171–190.

Taylor, R. L. (1990). Black youth: The endangered generation. *Youth and Society, 22*(1), 4–11.

Teglasi, H. (1981). Children's choices of and value judgments about sex-typed toys and occupations. *Journal of Vocational Behavior, 18*, 184–195.

Tennyson, W. W. (1967). The psychology of developing competent personnel. *American Vocational Journal, 42*, 27–29.

Tennyson, W. W., Hansen, L. S., Klaurens, M. K., & Antholz, M. B. (1975). *Educating for career development*. St. Paul, MN: Minnesota Department of Education (Revised 1980, National Vocational Guidance Association).

Tenopyr, M. L. (1981). The realities of employment testing. *American Psychologist, 36*, 1120–1127.

Tetrick, L. E., & LaRocco, J. M. (1987). Understanding, prediction, and control as moderators of the relationships between perceived stress, satisfaction, and psychological well-being. *Journal of Applied Psychology, 72*, 538–543.

Theobald, R. (1987). *The rapids of change*. Indianapolis, IN: Knowledge Systems Inc.

This, L. E. (1970). What is simulation? *American Vocational Journal, 45*, 20–22.

Thoits, P. A. (1982). Life stress, social support, and psychological vulnerability: Epidemiological considerations. *Journal of Community Psychology, 10*(4), 341–362.

Thomas, H. (1990). A likelihood-based model for validity generalization. *Journal of Applied Psychology, 75*, 13–20.

Thomas, H. B. (1974). The effects of social position, race, and sex on work values of ninth-grade students. *Journal of Vocational Behavior, 4*, 357–364.

Thomas, L. E. (1980). A typology of mid-life career changes. *Journal of Vocational Behavior, 16*(2), 173–182.

Thomas, R. G., & Bruning, C. R. (1984). Cognitive dissonance as a mechanism in vocational decision processes. *Journal of Vocational Behavior, 24*, 264–278.

Thomas, W. G. (1966). Placement's role in the university. *Journal of College Placement, 26*(4), 87–92.

Thompson, D. E., & Thompson, T. A. (1985). Task-based performance appraisal for blue-collar jobs: Evaluation of race and sex effects. *Journal of Applied Psychology, 70*(4), 747–753.

Thompson, J. W. (1980). Burnout in group home houseparents. *American Journal of Psychiatry, 137*(6), 710–714.

Thompson, P. H., Baker, R. Z., & Smallwood, N. (1986). Improving professional development by applying the four-stage career model. *Organizational Dynamics, 15*, 49–62.

Thoni, R. J., & Olsson, P. M. (1975). A systematic career development program in a liberal arts college. *Personnel and Guidance Journal, 53*, 672–675.

Thoresen, C. E., & Krumboltz, J. D. (1968). Similarity of social models and clients in behavioral counseling: Two experimental studies. *Journal of Counseling Psychology, 15*, 393–401.

Thoresen, C. E., Krumboltz, J. D., & Varenhorst, B. (1967). Sex of counselors and models: Effect on client career exploration. *Journal of Counseling Psychology, 14*, 503–508.

Thoresen, C. E., & Mehrens, W. A. (1967). Decision theory and vocational counseling: Important concepts and questions. *Personnel and Guidance Journal, 46*, 165–172.

Thorndike, R. L. (1985). The central role of general ability in prediction. *Multivariate Behavioral Research, 20*, 241–254.

Thorndike, R. L., & Hager, E. (1959). *10,000 careers*. New York: Wiley.

Thurow, L. C. (1977). Technological unemployment and occupational education. In T. Powers (Ed.), *Education for careers: Policy issues in a time of change*. University Park, PA: The Pennsylvania State University Press.

Tiedeman, D. V., (1961). Decision and vocational development: A paradigm and its implications. *Personnel and Guidance* Journal, *40*, 15–20.

Tiedeman, D. V., & Miller-Tiedeman, A. (1977). An "I" power primer: Part one: Structure and its involvements of intuition. *Focus on Guidance, 9*(7), 1–16.

Tiedeman, D. V., & Miller-Tiedeman, A. (1984). Career decision making: An individualistic perspective. In D. Brown & L. Brooks (Eds.), *Career choice and development; applying contemporary theories to practice*. (Chap. 10). San Francisco: Jossey-Bass.

Tiedeman, D. V., & O'Hara, R. P. (1963). *Career development: Choice and adjustment*. New York: College Entrance Examination Board.

Tillinghast, B. S., Jr. (1964). Choice orientations of guidance. *Vocational Guidance Quarterly, 13,* 18–20.

Tinsley, D. J., & Faunce, P. S. (1980). Enabling, facilitating, and precipitating factors associated with women's career orientation. *Journal of Vocational Behavior, 17,* 183–194.

Tinsley, H. E. A., & Bradley, R. W. (1986). Test interpretation. *Journal of Counseling and Development, 64,* 462–466.

Tinsley, H. E. A., & Heesacker, M. (1984). Vocational behavior and career development: A review. *Journal of Vocational Behavior, 25*(2), 139–190.

Tinsley, H. E. A., Kass, R. A., Moreland, J. R., & Harren, V. A. (1983). A longitudinal study of female college students' occupational decision-making. *Vocational Guidance Quarterly, 32*(2), 89–102.

Tinsley, H. E. A., & Tinsley, D. J. (1982). An analysis of leisure counseling models. *The Counseling Psychologist, 9,* 45–53.

Titley, R. W., & Titley, B. S. (1980). Initial choice of college major: Are only the "undecided" undecided? *Journal of College Student Personnel, 21,* 293–298.

Tittle, C. K. (1973). Sex bias in educational measurement: Fact or fiction? *Measurement and Evaluation in Guidance, 6,* 219–226.

Tittle, C. K. (1988). Validity, gender research, and studies of the effects of career development interventions. *Applied psychology: An international review, 37,* 121–131.

Tittle, C. K., & Zytowski, D. G. (Eds.). (1980). *Sex-fair interest measurement: Research and implications*. Washington, DC: National Institute of Education, U.S. Government Printing Office.

Toffler, A. (1980). *The third wave*. New York: Morrow.

Toomer, J. E. (1982). Counseling psychologists in business and industry. *The Counseling Psychologist, 10*(3), 9–18.

Townshend, A., & Gurin, P. (1981). Re-examining the frustrated homemaker hypothesis: Role fit, personal satisfaction, and collective discontent. *Sociology of Work and Occupations, 8*(4), 464–488.

Tracey, J. J., & Sedlacek, W. E. (1980). Comparison of error rates on the original Self-Directed Search and the 1977 version. *Journal of Counseling Psychology, 27,* 299–301.

Trantow, D. J. (1970). An introduction to evaluation: Program effectiveness and community needs. *Rehabilitation Literature, 31,* 2–10.

Trebilco, G. R. (1984). Career education and career maturity. *Journal of Vocational Behavior, 25,* 191–202.

Treiman, D. J. (1977). *Occupational prestige in comparative perspective*. New York: Academic Press.

Triandis, H. (1985). Some major dimensions of cultural variation in client populations. In P. Pedersen (Ed.), *Handbook of cross-cultural counseling and therapy* (pp. 21–28). Westport, CT: Greenwood Press.

Triandis, H. C., Feldman, J. M., Weldin, D. E., & Harvey, W. M. (1975). Ecosystem distrust in the hard-to-employ. *Journal of Applied Psychology, 60,* 44–56.

Trimble, J. E. (1981). Value differentials and their importance in counseling American Indians. In P. P. Pedersen, et al. (Eds.), *Counseling across cultures* (Rev. Ed., pp. 203–226). Honolulu: The University Press of Hawaii.

Troll, L. E., & Nowak, C. (1976). How old are you? The question of age bias in the counseling of adults. *The Counseling Psychologist, 6*(1), 41–44.

Troutt-Ervin, E. D., & Isberner, F. R. (1989). A job search course for technical students. *Journal of Studies in Technical Careers, XI,* 139–146.

Trower, P., Casey, A., & Dryden, W. (1988). *Cognitive-behavioral counseling in action*. Newbury Park, CA: Sage.

Tschirgi, H. D., & Huegli, J. M. (1979). Monitoring the employment interview. *Journal of College Placement, 39*(2), 37–39.

Tseng, M. S., & Carter, A. R. (1970). Achievement motivation and fear of failure as determinants of vocational choice, vocational aspiration, and perception of vocational prestige. *Journal of Counseling Psychology, 17,* 150–156.

Tucker, D. H. & Rowe, P. M. (1979). Relationship betweeen expectancy, causal attributions, and final hiring decisions in the employment interview. *Journal of Applied Psychology, 64*(4), 27–34.

Tung, R. L. (1980). Comparative analysis of the occupational stress profiles of male versus female administrators. *Journal of Vocational Behavior, 17,* 344–355.

Turner, S. A., Johnson, J. K., & Patterson, C. (1981). Career development of minorities. *Journal of College Placement, 41*(3), 38–42.

Tyler, L. E. (1961). *The work of the counselor* (3rd ed.). New York: Appleton-Century-Crofts.

Tyler, L. E. (Ed.). (1969). *Intelligence: Some recurring issues*. New York: Van Nostrand Reinhold.

Tyler, L. E., Sundberg, N. D., Rohila, P. K., & Greene, M. M. (1968). Patterns of choice in Dutch, American, and Indian adolescents. *Journal of Counseling Psychology, 15,* 522–529.

Tziner, A., & Latham, G. P. (1989). The effect of appraisal instrument, feedback and goal-setting on worker satisfaction and commitment. *Journal of Organizational Behavior, 10,* 145–153.

Ullrich, M. F. (1973). Several measures of expectancy of vocational counseling. *Psychological Reports, 33,* 299–304.

Underwood, J. W., & Hardy, R. E. (1985). The relationship of vocational adjustment to personal adjustment. *Psychology: A Quarterly Journal of Human Behavior, 22*(2), 24–30.

Urich, M. (1990). Software review of the Self-Directed Search: Computer version. *Measurement and Evaluation in Counseling and Development, 23,* 92–94.

Uris, A. (1988). *88 mistakes interviewers make and how to avoid them*. New York: AMACOM.

U.S. Bureau of the Census. (1982, March). *Provisional estimates of social, economic, and housing characteristics*. 1980 Census of population and housing. Supplementary Report. Washington, DC: U.S. Department of Commerce, 25–35.

U.S. Bureau of the Census. (1989). *Current population reports* (P-60, No. 162 & P-20, No. 431). Washington, DC: U.S. Bureau of Labor Statistics, Employment, and Earnings.

U.S. Department of Education. National Center for Educational Statistics. *Digest of Educational Statistics, 1988*. Washington, DC: U.S. Government Printing Office.

U.S. Department of Education & U.S. Department of Labor. (1988). *The bottom line: Basic skills in the workplace*. Washington, DC: U.S. Department of Labor.

U.S. Department of Health, Education, and Welfare. (1973). Special Task Force. *Work in America*. Cambridge, MA: MIT Press.

U.S. Department of Labor. (1974a). *Job satisfaction: Is there a trend?* (Manpower Research Monograph No. 30). Washington, DC: U.S. Government Printing Office.

U.S. Department of Labor. (1974b). *Manpower report of the president, 1974*. Washington, DC: U.S. Government Printing Office.

U.S. Department of Labor (1974c). *The United States economy in 1985*. Washington, DC: U.S. Government Printing Office.

U.S. Department of Labor. (1979). *International comparisons of unemployment*. Washington, DC: U.S. Government Printing Office.

U.S. Department of Labor. (1980a). *Occupational outlook handbook, 1980–1981 edition*. Washington, DC: U.S. Government Printing Office.

U.S. Department of Labor. (1980b). *Self-directed job search: An introduction*. Washington, DC: Employment and Training Administration.

U.S. Department of Labor. (1981). *Monthly Labor Review, 104*(2), Washington, DC: Bureau of Labor Statistics.

U.S. Department of Labor, Employment and Training Administration. (1989). *Work-based learning: Training America's workers*. Washington, DC: Author.

U.S. Office of Management and Budget. (1972). *Standard industrial classification manual*. Washington, DC: U.S. Government Printing Office.

Vacc, N. A., Wittmer, J., & DeVaney, S. B. (1988). *Experiencing and counseling multicultural and diverse populations*. Muncie IN: Accelerated Development press.

Vaillant, G. E. (1977). *Adaptation to life*. Boston: Little, Brown.

Vaizey, J., & Clark, C. F. O. (1976). *Education: The state of the debate in America, Britain, and Canada*. London: Duckworth.

Valach, L. (1990). A theory of goal-directed action in career analysis. In R. A. Young and W. E. Borgen (Eds.), *Methodological approaches to the study of careers* (pp. 107–126). New York: Praeger.

Vale, C. D. (1990). The Minnesota Clerical Assessment Battery: An application of computerized testing to business. *Measurement and Evaluation in Counseling and Development, 23*, 11–18.

Van der Embse, T. J., & Childs, J. M. (1979). Adults in transition: A profile of the older college student, *Journal of College Student Personnel, 20*, 475–479.

Vanderslice, V. J., Rice, R. W., & Julian, J. W. (1987). The effects of participation in decision-making on worker satisfaction and productivity: An organizational simulation. *Journal of Applied Social Psychology, 17*, 158–170.

Vansickle, T. R., Kimmel, C., & Kapes, J. T. (1989). Test retest equivalency of the computer-based and paper-pencil versions of the Strong Campbell Interest Inventory. *Measure ment and Evaluation in Counseling and Development, 22*, 88–93.

Varenhorst, B. B. (1969). Learning the consequences of life's decisions. In J. D. Krumboltz & C. E. Thoresen (Eds.), *Behavioral counseling: Cases and techniques* (pp. 306–319). New York: Holt, Rinehart and Winston.

Vecchio, R. P. (1980a). The function and meaning of work and the job. Morse and Weiss (1955) revisited. *Academy of Management Journal, 23*(2), 361–367.

Vecchio, R. P. (1980b). The test of moderator of the job satisfaction-job quality relationship: The case of religious affiliation. *Journal of Applied Psychology, 65*(2), 195–201.

Vecchio, R. P. (1980c). Worker alienation as a moderator of the job quality-job satisfaction relationship: The case of racial differences. *Academy of Management Journal, 23*(3), 479–486.

Vecchiotti, D. I., & Korn, J. H. (1980). Comparison of student and recruiter values. *Journal of Vocational Behavior, 16*, 43–50.

Veninga, R. L., & Spradley, J. P. (1981). *The work/stress connection: How to cope with job burnout*. Boston: Little, Brown.

Verlander, E. G. (1985). The system's the thing. *Training and Development Journal, 39*(4), 20–23.

Veroff, J., Kulka, R. A., & Douvan, E. (1981). *Mental health in America: Patterns of help-seeking from 1957 to 1976*. New York: Basic Books.

Vertiz, V. C., & Fortune, J. C. (1984). An ethnographic study of cultural barriers to employment among Indochinese immigrant youth. *College Student Journal, 18* (3), 229–235.

Vetter, B. M. (1989). *Professional women and minorities: A manpower data resource service* (8th Ed.). Washington, DC: Commission on Professionals in Science and Technology.

Vetter, E. W. (1985). Getting human resource planning on the dean's list. *Training and Development Journal, 39*(4), 16–18.

Vincenzi, H. (1977). Minimizing occupational stereotypes. *Vocational Guidance Quarterly, 25*(3), 265.

Vodanovich, S. J., & Kramer, T. J. (1989). An examination of the work values of parents and their children. *The Career Development Quarterly, 37*, 365–374.

Voight, N. L., Lawler, A., & Falkerson, K. F. (1980). Community-based guidance: A "Tupperware Party" approach to mid-life decision-making. *Personnel and Guidance Journal, 59*(2), 106–107.

Vondracek, F. (1990). A developmental-contextual approach to career development research. In R. A. Young and W. A. Borgen (Eds.), *Methodological approaches to the study of careers* (pp. 37–56). New York: Praeger.

Vondracek, F. W., Hostetler, M., Schulenberg, J. E., & Shimizu, K. (1990). Dimensions of career indecision. *Journal of Counseling Psychology, 37*, 98–106.

Vondracek, F. W., & Learner, R. M. (1982). Vocational role development in adolescence. In B. Wolman (Ed.), *Handbook of developmental psychology* (Chap. 33). Englewood Cliffs, NJ: Prentice-Hall.

Vondracek, F. W., Lerner, R. W., & Schulenberg, J. E. (1983). The concept of development in vocational theory and intervention. *The Journal of Vocational Behavior, 23*, 179–202.

Vondracek, F. W., Lerner, R. M., & Schulenberg, S. E. (1986). *Career development: A life-span developmental approach*. Hillsdale, NJ: Erlbaum.

Vondracek, F. W., & Schulenberg, J. E. (1986). Career development in adolescence: Some conceptual and intervention issues. *Vocational Guidance Quarterly, 34*(4), 247–254.

Vondracek, S. I., & Kirchner, E. P. (1974). Vocational development in early childhood: An examination of young children's expressions of vocational aspirations. *Journal of Vocational Behavior, 5*, 251–260.

Voss, J. H. (1980). Concepts of self, ideal self, and ideal woman held by college men and women: A comparison study. *Journal of College Student Personnel, 21*(1), 50–57.

Voss, J. H., & Skinner, D. A. (1975). Concepts of self and ideal woman held by college women: A replication. *Journal of College Student Personnel*, 210–213.

Voydanoff, P. (1980). Perceived job characteristics and job satisfaction among men and women. *Psychology of Women Quarterly, 5*(2), 177–185.

Vriend, J. (1968). *The vocational maturity of inner city boys*. Paper presented at the American Psychological Association Convention, San Francisco.

Vroom, V. H. (1964). *Work and motivation*. New York: Wiley.

Wagner, J. A., & Gooding, R. Z. (1987). Shared influence and organizational behavior: A meta-analysis of situational variables expected to modulate participation-outcome relationships. *Academy of Management Journal, 30*, 524–541.

Walker, J. E., Tansky, C., & Oliver, D. (1982). Men and women at work: Similarities and differences in work values within occupational groupings. *Journal of Vocational Behavior, 21*, 17–36.

Walker, J. L. (1965). Four methods of interpreting test scores compared. *Personnel and Guidance Journal, 44,* 402–404.

Walker, J. W., & Gutteridge, T. G. (1979). *Career planning practices: An AMA survey report.* American Management Association.

Walker, J. W., Kimmel, D. C., & Price, K. F. (1981). Retirement style and retirement satisfaction: Retirees aren't all alike. *International Journal of Aging and Human Development, 72,* 267–281.

Walker, L. S., & Walker, J. I. (1980). Trait anxiety in mothers: Differences associated with employment status, family size, and age of children. *Psychological Reports, 47*(1), 295–299.

Walls, R. T., & Gulkus, S. P. (1974). Reinforcers and vocational maturity in occupational aspiration, expectation, and goal deflection. *Journal of Vocational Behavior, 5,* 381–390.

Walsh, D. J. (1987). Individual variations within the vocational decision making process: A review and integration. *Journal of Career Development, 14,* 52–65.

Walsh, W. B., Bingham, R., Horton, J. A., & Spokane, A. (1979). Holland's theory and college degreed working black and white women. *Journal of Vocational Behavior, 15,* 217–223.

Walters, L., & Saddlemire, G. (1979). Career planning needs of college freshmen and their perceptions of career planning. *Journal of College Student Personnel, 20,* 224–229.

Walter-Samli, J. H., & Samli, A. C. (1979). A model of career counseling for international students. *Vocational Guidance Quarterly, 28*(1), 48–55.

Walz, G. R., & Benjamin, L. (1984). A systems approach to career guidance. *The Vocational Guidance Quarterly, 33*(1), 26–34.

Warchel, P., & Southern, S. (1986). Perceived importance of counseling needs among adult students. *Journal of College Student Personnel, 27*(1), 43–48.

Ward, C. M., & Walsh, W. B. (1981). Concurrent validity of Holland's theory for non-college degreed black women. *Journal of Vocational Behavior, 18,* 356–361.

Ware, M. E. (1980). Antecedents of educational/career preferences and choices. *Journal of Vocational Behavior, 16,* 312–319.

Warner, R. (1985). *Recovery from schizophrenia: Psychiatry and political economy.* New York: Routledge and Kegan Paul.

Warner, S. G., & Jepsen, D. L. (1979). Differential effects of conceptual level and group counseling format on adolescent career decision-making processes. *Journal of Counseling Psychology, 26*(6), 497–503.

Warren, J. M. (1978). Changing attitudes of supervisors. *Labor-Management Alcoholism Newsletter, 1,* 9.

Wasil, R. (1974). Job placement: Keynote of career development. *American Vocational Journal, 49,* 32.

Watanabe, A. (1980). *Developing a causal model for predicting college adjustment from pre-college characteristics.* Unpublished doctoral dissertations. Pennsylvania State University.

Watson, G. (1966). Resistance to change. In G. Watson (Ed.), *Concepts for social change.* Washington, DC: National Training Laboratories.

Watts, A. G. (1980). Educational and career guidance services for adults. *British Journal of Guidance and Counseling, 9*(1), 6–15.

Watts, A. G. (1986). *Work shadowing.* Report prepared for the School Curriculum Industry Partnership. York, England: Longman.

Watts, A. G., Dartois, C., & Plant, P. (1988a). *Educational and vocational guidance services for the 14–25 age group in the European Community.* Sittard, Netherlands: Commission of the European Communities.

Watts, A. G., Dartois, C., & Plant, P. (1988b). *Educational and vocational guidance services.* Education Policy Series 2. Sittard, Netherlands: Presses Interuniversitaires Europeans Maastricht.

Watts, A. G., & Herr, E. L. (1976). Career(s) education in Britain and the U.S.A.: Contrasts and common problems. *British Journal of Guidance and Counseling, 4*(2), 129–142.

Watts, A. G., Super, D. E., & Kidd, J. M. (1981). *Career development in Britain.* Cambridge, England: Hobson's Press.

Weagraff, P. J. (1974). The cluster concept: Development of curricular materials for the public service occupations cluster. *Journal of Research and Development in Education, 7*(3), 45–54.

Weaver, C. N. (1978). Black-White correlates for job satisfaction. *Journal of Applied Psychology, 63,* 255–258.

Weaver, C. N. (1980). Job satisfaction in the United States in the 1970's. *Journal of Applied Psychology, 65,* 364–367.

Wegmann, R., Chapman, R., & Johnson, M. (1989). *Work in the new economy: Careers and job seeking in the 21st century.* Indianapolis, IN: JIST Works.

Wehrly, B., & Watson-Gegeo, K. (1985). Ethnographic methodologies as applied to the study of cross-cultural counseling. In P. Pedersen (Ed.), *Handbook of cross-cultural counseling and therapy* (pp. 65–71). Westport, CT: Greenwood Press.

Weinrach, S. G. (1979). Trait and factor counseling: Yesterday and today. In S. G. Weinrach (Ed.), *Career counseling: Theoretical and practical perspectives.* New York: McGraw-Hill.

Weinrach, S. G. (1980). Discrepancy identification: A model for the interpretation of the Kuder DD and other interest inventories. *Vocational Guidance Quarterly, 29*(1), 42–55.

Weinrach, S. G. (1984). Determinants of vocational choice: Holland's theory. In D. Brown & L. Brooks (Eds.), *Career choice and development, Applying contemporary theories to practice* (Chap. 4). San Francisco: Jossey-Bass.

Weinrach, S. G., & Srebalus, D. J. (1990). Holland's theory of careers. In D. Brown & L. Brooks (Eds.), *Career choice and development: Applying contemporary theories to practice.* (2nd Ed., pp. 37–67). San Francisco: Jossey-Bass.

Weishaar, M. E., Green, B. J., & Craighead, L. W. (1981). Primary influences of initial vocational choices of college women. *Journal of Vocational Behavior, 18,* 67–78.

Weissberg, M., Berentsen, M., Cote, A., Cravey, B., & Heath, K. (1982). As assessment of the personal, career, and academic needs of undergraduate students. *Journal of College Student Personnel, 23,* 115–122.

Weissman, S., & Krebs, D. O. (1976). A decision-making model for career exploration. *Personnel and Guidance Journal, 54*(10), 517–518.

Welborn, A., & Moore, S. S. (1985). Counseling displaced homemakers. In D. Jones & S. S. Moore (Eds.), *Counseling adults: Life cycle perspectives* (pp. 103–107). Lawrence, KS: University of Kansas.

Wellington, J. (1986). A card sort system for therapists of working women. *Journal of Counseling and Development, 64,* 648–649.

Wellman, F. E. (1970, December). *Evaluation of vocational guidance: Local level.* Paper presented at the 64th annual Vocational Convention, New Orleans, LA.

Werts, C. E. (1968). Paternal influence on career choice. *Journal of Counseling Psychology, 15,* 48–52.

West, M. A., & Nicholson, N. (1989). The outcomes of job change. *Journal of Vocational Behavior, 34*(3), 335–349.

Westbrook, B. W. (1974). Content analysis of six career development tests. *Measurement and Evaluation in Guidance,* 7(3), 172–180.

Westbrook, B. W. (1979). *Career development needs of adults. How to improve career development programs.* Washington,

DC: National Vocational Guidance Association and the Association for Measurement and Evaluation in Guidance.

Westbrook, B. W. (1988). Review of My Vocational Situation. In J. T. Kapes & M. M. Mastie (Eds.), *A counselor's guide to career assessment instruments* (pp. 186–189). Washington, DC: National Career Development Association.

Westbrook, B. W., & Cunningham, J. W. (1970). The development and application of vocational maturity measures. *Vocational Guidance Quarterly, 18,* 171–175.

Westbrook, B. W., & Parry-Hill, J. W., Jr. (1973a). *The construction and validation of a measure of vocational maturity.* Raleigh, NC: Center for Occupational Education, North Carolina State University. (ERIC document #ED 101-145).

Westbrook, B. W., & Parry-Hill, J. W., Jr. (1973b). The measurement of cognitive vocational maturity. *Journal of Vocational Behavior, 3,* 239–252.

Westbrook, B. W., Sanford, E. E., & Donnelly, M. H. (1990). The relationship between Career Maturity 'Test' scores and appropriateness of career choices. A replication. *Journal of Vocational Behavior, 36,* 20–32.

Westbrook, B. W., Sanford, E. E., O'Neal, P., Horne, D. F., Fleenor, J., & Garren, R. (1985). Predictive and construct validity of six experimental measures of career maturity. *Journal of Vocational Behavior, 27,* 338–355.

Westbrook, B. W., Sanford, E. E., Merwin, G., Fleenor, J., & Gilleland, K. (1988). Career maturity in grade 9: Can students who make appropriate career choices for others also make appropriate career choices for themselves? *Measurement and Evaluation in Counseling and Development, 21,* 64–71.

Westcott, N. A. (1983). Application of the structured life-review technique in counseling elders. *Personnel and Guidance Journal, 62*(3), 180–181.

Wetzel, J. R. (1989). *American youth: A statistical snapshot.* Washington, DC. The William T. Grant Foundation, Commission on Work, Family and Citizenship.

Wheeler, C. L., & Carnes, E. F. (1968). Relationships among self-concepts, ideal self-concepts, and stereotypes of probably and ideal vocational choices. *Journal of Counseling Psychology, 15,* 530–535.

Wheeler, K. G. (1988). Review of Temperament and Values Inventory. In J. T. Kapes & M. M. Mastie (Eds.), *A counselor's guide to career assessment instruments* (pp. 243–247). Washington, DC: National Career Development Association.

Wheeler, K. G., & Mahoney, T. A. (1981). The expectancy model in the analysis of occupational preference and occupational choice. *Journal of Vocational Behavior, 19,* 113–122.

Whiston, S. C. (1990). Evaluation of the Adult Career Concerns Inventory. *Journal of Counseling and Development, 69,* 78–80.

White, L., & Brinkerhoff, D. B. (1981). The sexual division of labor: Evidence from childhood. *Social Forces, 60*(1), 170–181.

Wholeben, B. E. (1988). Review of Sixteen PF Personal Career Development Profile. In J. T. Kapes & M. M. Mastie (Eds.), *A counselor's guide to career assessment instruments* (pp. 238–242). Washington, DC: National Career Development Association.

Wiener, Y., Vardi, Y., & Muczyk, J. (1981). Antecedents of employees' mental health—The role of career and work satisfaction. *Journal of Vocational Behavior, 19,* 50–60.

Wiggins, J. D. (1984). Personality-environmental factors related to job satisfaction of school counselors. *Vocational Guidance Quarterly, 33*(2), 169–176.

Wiggins, J. S. (1973). *Personality and prediction: Principles of personality assessment.* Reading, MA: Addison-Wesley.

Wigington, J. H. (1982). Career maturity aspects of the Kuder Occupational Interest Survey. *Journal of Vocational Behavior, 20,* 175–179.

Wijting, J. P., Arnold, C. R., & Conrad, K. A. (1977). Relationships between work values, socioeducational and work experiences, and vocational aspirations of 6th, 9th, 10th, and 12th graders. *Journal of Vocational Behavior, 11*(1), 51–65.

Wilcox-Matthew, L., & Minor, C. W. (1989). The dual career couple: Concerns, benefits, and counseling implications. *Journal of Counseling and Development, 68,* 194–198.

Wild, B. K., & Kerr, B. A. (1984). Training adolescent job-seekers in persuasion skills. *Vocational Guidance Quarterly, 33*(1), 63–69.

Wiley, M. O., & Magoon, T. M. (1982). Holland high point social types: Is consistency related to persistence and achievement? *Journal of Vocational Behavior, 20,* 14–21.

Wilk, C. A. (1986). *Career women and childbearing: A psychological analysis of the decision process.* New York: Van Nostrand Reinhold.

Wilkie, J. R. (1981). The trend toward delayed parenthood. *Journal of Marriage and the Family, 43*(3), 583–591.

Willbur, J. (1987). Does mentoring breed success? *Training and Development Journal, 41,* 38–41.

William T. Grant Foundation Commission on work, family and citizenship. (1988). *The forgotten half: Non-college youth in America. An interim report on the school-to-work transition.* Washington, DC: Author.

Williams, C. L. (1989). *Gender differences at work: Women and men in nontraditional occupations.* Berkeley: University of California Press.

Williams, C. P., & Savickas, M. L. (1990). Developmental tasks of career maintenance. *Journal of Vocational Behavior, 36,* 166–175.

Williams, G. D., Lindsay, C. A., Burns, M. A., Wyckoff, J. H., & Wall, H. W. (1973). Urgency and types of adult counseling needs among continuing education students. *Journal of College Student Personnel, 14*(6), 501–506.

Williams, J., & Whitney, D. (1978). Vocational interests of minority disadvantaged students: Are they different? *National Association of Student Personnel Administrators Journal, 15*(4), 20–26.

Williams, J. A., & Williams, J. D. (1988). Review of Kuder Occupational Interest Inventory—Form DD. In J. T. Kapes & M. M. Mastie (Eds.), *A counselor's guide to career assessment instruments* (pp. 105–109). Washington, DC: National Career Development Association.

Williams, W. G. (1980). Civic education in a stressful society: A program of value clarity and tension reduction. In F. J. McGuigan, W. E. Sime, & J. M. Wallace (Eds.), *Stress and tension control* (pp. 17–35). New York: Plenum Press.

Williamson, E. G. (1939). *How to counsel students.* New York: McGraw-Hill.

Williamson, E. G. (1965). *Vocational counseling: Some historical, philosophical, and theoretical perspectives.* New York: McGraw-Hill.

Willingham, W. W. (1988). *Testing handicapped people.* Boston: Allyn and Bacon, Inc.

Willis, C. G. & Ham, T. L. (1988). Review of the Myers-Briggs Type Indicator. In J. T. Kapes & M. M. Mastie (Eds.), *A counselor's guide to career assessment instruments.* Washington, DC: National Career Development Association.

Wilson, J., & Daniel, R. (1981). The effects of a career-options workshop on social and vocational stereotypes. *Vocational Guidance Quarterly, 30*(4), 341–349.

Wilson, J., Weikel, W. J., & Rose, H. (1982). A comparison of nontraditional and traditional career women. *Vocational Guidance Quarterly, 31*(2), 109–117.

Wilson, P. J. (1986). *School counseling programs: A resource and planning guide*. Madison, WI: Wisconsin Department of Public Instruction.

Wilson, R. N. (1981). The courage to be leisured. *Social Forces, 60*(2), 282–302.

Winefield, A. H., & Tiggemann, M. (1989). Unemployment duration and affective well-being in the young. *Journal of Occupational Psychology, 62,* 327–336.

Winkles, E. J., & Johnson, R. H. (1973). A model for developing a career decision-making program. *Canadian Counselor, 7*(2), 139–143.

Winter, J., & Schmidt, J. S. (1974). A replicable career program for junior high. *Vocational Guidance Quarterly, 23*(2), 177–180.

Wircenski, J. L., Fales, J. G., & Wircenski, S. L. (1978). Career guidance in the elementary school. *Elementary School Guidance and Counseling, 12*(3), 212–215.

Wise, P. S. (1985). School psychologists' rankings of stressful events. *The Journal of School Psychology, 23,* 31–41.

Wise, R., Charner, I., & Randour, M. A. (1978). A conceptual framework for career awareness in career decision-making. In J. Whitely & A. Resnikoff (Eds.), *Career counseling* (pp. 216–231). Monterey, CA: Brooks/Cole.

Wish, P. A., & Hasazi, J. W. (1973). Motivational determinants of curricular choice in college males. *Journal of Counseling Psychology, 20,* 127–131.

Wittmer, J., Bostic, D., Phillips, T. D., & Waters, W. (1981). The personal, academic, and career problems of college student athletes: Some possible answers. *Personnel and Guidance Journal, 60*(1), 52–55.

Witwer, G., & Stewart, L. H. (1972). Personality correlates of preference for risk among occupation oriented junior college students. *Vocational Guidance Quarterly, 20*(4), 259–265.

Woal, S. T. (1974). Queries, influences, and vocational interests of junior high school students. *Journal of Career Education, 2,* 55–62.

Wolfe, L. K., & Betz, N. E. (1981). Traditionality of choice and sex-role identification as moderators of the congruence of occupational choice in college women. *Journal of Vocational Behavior, 18,* 43–55.

Wollack, S., Goodale, J. G., Wijting, J. P., & Smith, P. C. (1971). Development of the survey of work values. *Journals of Applied Psychology, 55,* 331–338.

Wolleat, P. L. (1989). Reconciling sex differences in information-processing and career outcomes. *Journal of Career Development, 16,* 97–106.

Women's Bureau. (1982). *20 facts on women workers*. Washington, DC: U.S. Department of Labor.

Wood, S. (1990). Initiating career plans with freshmen. *The School Counselor, 37,* 233–239.

Wool, S. T. (1974). Queries, influences, and vocational interests of junior high school students. *Journal of Career Education*, 2, 55–62.

Work in America Institute. (1980). *The future of older workers in America*. Scarsdale, NY: The Institute.

Worrell, J. (1978). A benefit-cost analysis of the vocational rehabilitation program. *The Journal of Human Resources, 13*(2), 285–298.

Worrell, J. (1980). New directions in counseling women. *Personnel and Guidance Journal, 58*(7), 477–484.

Wortley, D. B., & Amatea, E. S. (1982). Mapping adult life changes: A conceptual framework for organizing adult development theory. *Personnel and Guidance Journal, 60*(8), 477–482.

Wrenn, C. G. (1964). Human values and work in American life. In H. Borow (Ed.), *Man in a world of work*. Boston: Houghton Mifflin.

Wright, B. A. (1960). *Physical disability: A psychological approach*. New York: Harper Bros.

Wright, D., & Gutkin, T. B. (1981). School psychologists' job satisfaction and discrepancies between actual and desired work functions. *Psychological Reports, 49,* 735–738.

Wright, G. N. (1980). *Total rehabilitation*. Boston: Little, Brown.

Wright, J. D., & Hamilton, R. F. (1979). Education and job attitudes among blue-collar workers. *Sociology of Work and Occupations, 6*(1), 59–83.

Wright, P. M., Lichtenfels, P. A., & Pursell, E. D. (1989). The structured interview: Additional studies and a metaanalysis. *Journal of Occupational Psychology, 62,* 191–199.

Yabroff, W. (1969). Learning decision-making. In J. D. Krumboltz & C. E. Thoresen (Eds.), *Behavioral counseling: Cases and techniques* (pp. 329–343). New York: Holt, Rinehart and Winston.

Yanico, B. J. (1980). Students' self-reported amount of information about masculine and feminine occupations. *Vocational Guidance Quarterly, 28*(4), 244–350.

Yanico, B. J. (1981). Sex-role self concept and attitudes related to occupational daydreams and future fantasies of college women. *Journal of Vocational Behavior, 19,* 290–301.

Yanico, B. J. (1986). College students' self-estimated and actual knowledge of gender traditional and nontraditional occupations: A replication and extension. *Journal of Vocational Behavior, 28,* 229.

Yanico, B. J., & Hardin, S. I. (1981). Sex-role self-concept and persistence in a traditional versus nontraditional college major for women. *Journal of Vocational Behavior, 18,* 219–227.

Yankelovich, D. (1981). The meaning of work. In J. O'Toole, J. L. Scheiber, & L. C. Wood (Eds.), *Working: Changes and choices* (pp. 33–34). New York: Human Sciences Press.

Yankelovich, D., & Lefkowitz, B. (1982). Work and American expectations. *National Forum, 62*(2), 3–5.

Yates, J. F. (1990). *Judgment and decision making*. Englewood Cliffs, N.J.: Prentice Hall.

Yates, L. V. (1990). A note about values assessment of occupational and career stage age groups. *Measurement and Evaluation in Counseling and Development, 23,* 39–42.

Yogev, S. (1981). Do professional women have egalitarian marital relationships? *Journal of Marriage and the Family, 43*(4), 865–871.

Yogev, S., & Brett, J. (1985). Patterns of work and family involvement among single- and dual-earner couples. *Journal of Applied Psychology, 70*(4), 754–768.

Yolles, S. F., Krinsky, L. W., Kieffer, S. N., & Carone, P. A. (Eds.). (1984). *The aging employee*. New York: Human Sciences Press.

York, D. C., & Tinsley, H. E. A. (1986). The relationship between cognitive styles and Holland's personality types. *Journal of College Student Personnel, 27*(6), 535–541.

Yost, E. B., & Corbishley, M. A. (1987). *Career counseling: A psychological approach*. San Francisco: Jossey-Bass.

Young, A. M. (1980). Trends in educational attainment among workers in the 1970's. *Monthly Labor Review, 103,* 44–47.

Young, J. M. (1974). Community-oriented exploration program. *Elementary School Guidance and Counseling, 8*(3), 209–212.

Young, R. A., (1979). The effects of value confrontation and reinforcement counseling on the career planning attitudes and behavior of adolescent males. *Journal of Vocational Behavior, 15,* 1–11.

Young, R. A. (1988). Ordinary explanations and career theories. *Journal of Counseling and Development, 66,* 336–338.

Young, R. A., & Borgen, W. A. (Eds.). (1990). Introduction. *Methodological approaches to the study of careers*. New York: Praeger.

Yount, K. R. (1986). A theory of productive activity: The relationships among self-concept, gender, sex role stereotypes, and work-emergent traits. *Psychology of Women Quarterly, 10,* 63–88.

Zaccaria, J. S. (1965). Developmental tasks: Implications for the goals of guidance. *Personnel and Guidance Journal, 44,* 372–375.

Zaccaria, J. S. (1969). *Approaches to guidance in contemporary education*. Scranton, PA: International Textbook.

Zakay, D., & Barak, A. (1984). Meaning and career decision-making. *Journal of Vocational Behavior, 24,* 1–14.

Zaslow, M. J., & Pederson, F. A. (1981). Sex role conflicts and the experience of childbearing. *Professional Psychology, 12*(1), 47–55.

Zehring, J. W. (1976). Employing students as para-professional counselors. *Journal of College Placement, 36*(1), 43–47.

Zehring, J. W. (1979). Job sources for liberal arts graduates. *Journal of College Placement, 39*(2). 28–31.

Zenger, J. H. (1981). Career planning: Coming in from the cold. *Training and Development Journal, 35,* 47–52.

Ziller, R. C. (1957). Vocational choice and utility for risk. *Journal of Counseling Psychology, 4,* 61–64.

Zimmer, L. (1988). Tokenism and women in the workplace: The limits of gender-neutral theory. *Social Problems, 35,* 64–75.

Zunker, V. G. (1986a). *Career counseling: Applied concepts of life planning*. Monterey, CA: Brooks/Cole.

Zunker, V. G. (1986b). *Using assessment results in career counseling*. Monterey CA: Brooks/Cole.

Zytowski, D. G. (1969). Toward a theory of career development for women. *Personnel and Guidance Journal, 47,* 660–664.

Zytowski, D. G. (1988). Review of Salience Inventory. In J. T. Kapes & M. M. Mastie (Eds.), *A counselor's guide to career assessment instruments* (pp. 150–154). Washington, DC: National Career Development Association.

INDEXES

AUTHOR INDEX

SUBJECT INDEX